D1433142

THE PRACTICAL ASTROLOGER

THE PRACTICAL ASTROLOGER

Nicholas Campion

HAMLYN

Published 1987 by
Hamlyn Publishing
a division of The Hamlyn Publishing Group Limited
Bridge House, London Road
Twickenham, Middlesex, England

Created by Roxby General Books Limited
a division of Roxby Press Limited
98 Clapham Common North Side
London SW4 9SG

Contributor to Chapter 24: Philip Staniforth
Tables at the back of the book: Astro Computing Services
Editor: Rachel Grenfell
Art Direction: David Pearce
Design: Michelle Barnacle
Illustration: Gill Raphaeline
Natasha Ledwidge
Aziz Khan and John Woodcock
Typesetting: Tradespools Limited
Reproduction: F.E.Burman Limited
Printing and Binding: Tonsa, San Sebastian, Spain

ISBN 0 600 50304 6

CONTENTS

CHAPTER 1
INTRODUCTION

The positions of the stars and planets at birth provide a guide to a child's character and the general trends of its life.

There is no evidence that the planets literally determine a baby's personality or are the cause of events during its lifetime.

The cycles of life on Earth harmonize with the cycles of the heavens and the birth of the baby coincides with one significant moment. The celestial patterns at this moment provide an index of possibilities for all future developments in the child's life.

The astrologer is trained to interpret these possibilities and give advice on how their potential may be best fulfilled.

Astrology has two main purposes. First, it is used to gain understanding of present or past situations, and second, to predict the future – to help people adapt to the unexpected, and prepare them to make the best use of future opportunities.

The astrologer's ability to predict the future raises the problem of fate and free will. In many areas of human activity it is necessary to anticipate the outcome of events, and prediction is used not only in astrology but also in such studies as meteorology, sociology and economics. It is to the credit of astrology that it has confronted the awkward implications that predicting the future raises for human freedom of choice: if future events can be predicted does this mean that whatever is attempted, the outcome will be the same?

Astrologers argue that human beings are born with a potential for future development, and that this potential is revealed by the positions of the stars and planets at birth. Yet this is not absolutely fixed and the exact manner in which it is expressed can be altered by the exercise of free will. Astrology, by its ability to clarify the nature of this potential, and its likely development, enhances freedom of choice. Even when a predicted event is inevitable, astrology can help people to prepare for it.

BELIEFS AND USES

Astrology takes the changing patterns of the planets and stars and uses them to understand human life and events on Earth; everything that happens in the heavens above can be taken as a sign of changes on the Earth below.

Fundamental to this belief is an understanding that the entire universe is one gigantic whole in which all parts exist in a totally interdependent relationship with each other. Astrologers analyse the pattern of the planets and stars in relation to the Earth, from which they make detailed deductions about people's lives and sometimes about future events. The unity between Heaven and Earth is so all embracing that even astrologers are part of this larger order as they carry out their work. Most astrologers are aware of the remarkable coincidences which pervade their work and see these as signs of the great celestial pattern.

When astrologers talk of the planets causing events, affecting people's lives, and influencing affairs on Earth, they do not mean there is a clear physical connection between the movement of a planet and a subsequent event upon Earth. Neither do they believe that the planets cause events to take place on Earth in the accepted sense of the term, with the exception of such obvious examples as the physical effect of the Sun and Moon on climate and tides.

The planets and stars provide signs to indicate the nature of phenomena on Earth, and events in astrology can happen before the planetary configurations which cause them have taken place. As words such as 'cause' and 'effect', 'influence' and 'rule', have led to confusion over the nature of astrology, modern astrologers often prefer to say that planetary and other astrological configurations correlate with, or correspond to, events upon Earth. However, the old words are still very much part of astrological language.

Central to astrology is the curious nature of time. Astrology assumes that time is not just a matter of quantity (measuring hours, minutes and seconds) but of quality: certain times may be tense, while others may be relaxed. This is not such a startling notion and is derived from the basic human experience that time seems to pass at different speeds according to one's moods. For example, in periods of boredom time may seem to pass unbearably slowly while in those of excitement the passage is swift. This is 'subjective' time based upon experience, as opposed to 'objective' time of fixed hours, minutes and seconds.

Astrology provides many different scales for measuring time. Unlike objective time which provides but one uniform system of measurement, astrology draws on a different time scale for each of the 10 planets. In addition, there is an effectively unlimited series of permutations when the planets and other celestial bodies are connected in various combinations. On the one hand this provides a sophisticated system for understanding events, and on the other a reliable means to measure the ebb and flow of individual subjective time, each planet corresponding to a different psychological mood.

Astrology also extends the concept of the wholeness of the universe, from the complete simultaneous interconnection of space and time in the present to that of both past and future. This is a controversial belief central to the mystical traditions of both East and West, and one which is implied by some modern scientific opinion.

DIFFERENT APPROACHES TO ASTROLOGY

Many astrologers claim that astrology is a science because it is based on empirical evidence: experience, experiment and observation. The position is confused, however, by the use of the term 'occult science': such a description is anathema to most modern scientists, and a new breed of scientific researcher, who tests astrology using rigorous statistical methods, has evolved. Consequently, some astrologers claim that traditional astrology is a science, while others want to create a new scientific astrology separate from traditional practices. But it is unwise to take a dogmatic position. The truth is that sometimes astrology appears to be scientific while at others it is completely irrational. It may be compared to an art, but is not like the other arts. In the end each astrologer arrives at a personal understanding of astrology based entirely upon his or her own experiences. Presented with the same horoscope each astrologer will produce an interpretation that is, in the final analysis, individual and unique.

Several major psychological systems, such as that of Jung, have been connected to astrology, capable as it is of providing startlingly accurate personality descriptions. As this is very popular with the public, many astrologers have concentrated upon this aspect. Effectively astrology has become a brand of psychology for many astrologers.

Astrology may also be used for divination where intuition, rather than a scientific system, enables the astrologer to produce a correct interpretation.

Many modern astrologers find a personal spiritual motive behind their studies, although the ancient religious and mystical practices of astrology have been neglected. In the past each planet represented a different level of spiritual existence, forming a ladder which the astrologer climbed through meditation and ritual. After passing through the highest level of the stars he encountered the Divine. Such beliefs were common in the ancient world and in Renaissance Europe, often in combination with Christianity.

In Genesis it is written that the stars were placed in the sky as signs, and in ancient times the patterns of the sky were regarded as the signs of the times.

The three wise men, or magi, in the Gospel according to Matthew were astrologers who interpreted the Star of Bethlehem as a sign of the birth of the long-awaited Messiah.

Most astronomers believe that the star was a conjunction of Jupiter and Saturn in 4 BC, although there is a theory that it was Halley's Comet, which passed by the Earth in 12 BC.

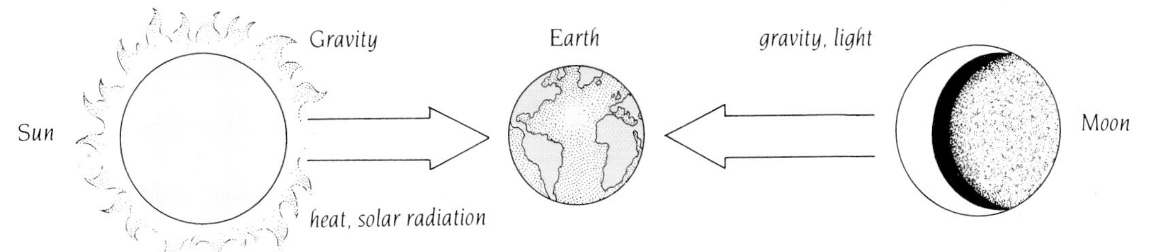

The Sun and the Moon exercise a strong physical effect on the Earth, but there is little evidence to suggest that any other planet exerts any direct influence. However, there is reason to believe that the general pattern of the planets is connected somehow to the intensity of solar radiation, which affects among other things, the weather on Earth. This is relevant to such matters as plant growth, but most astrology cannot be explained by physical effects.

4 + 4 = 8

DIVINATION

ASTRONOMY

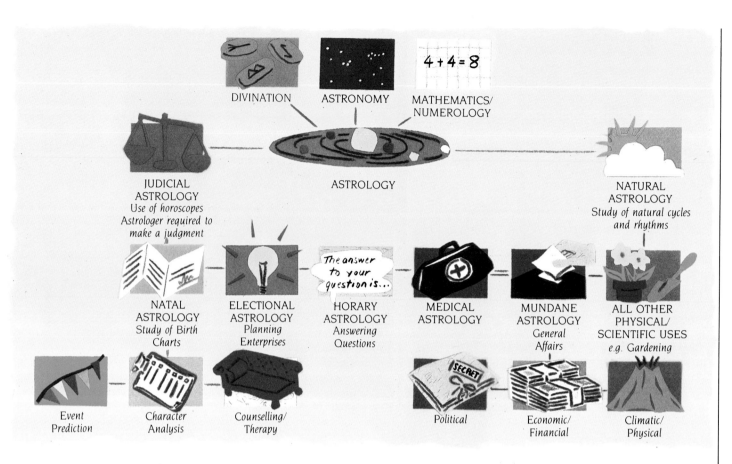

MATHEMATICS/
NUMEROLOGY

ASTROLOGY

JUDICIAL
ASTROLOGY
Use of horoscopes
Astrologer required to make a judgment

NATURAL
ASTROLOGY
Study of natural cycles and rhythms

The answer to your question is...

NATAL
ASTROLOGY
Study of Birth Charts

ELECTIONAL
ASTROLOGY
Planning Enterprises

HORARY
ASTROLOGY
Answering Questions

MEDICAL
ASTROLOGY

MUNDANE
ASTROLOGY
General Affairs

ALL OTHER
PHYSICAL/
SCIENTIFIC USES
e.g. Gardening

SECRET

Event Prediction

Character Analysis

Counselling/ Therapy

Political

Economic/ Financial

Climatic/ Physical

Most astrologers agree that astrology is a tremendously powerful symbolic language for the interpretation and understanding of life on Earth. The art of astrological interpretation is possible once the basics of this language have been learned. Unlike other languages astrology has very few symbols, but each one has a vast range of different meanings.

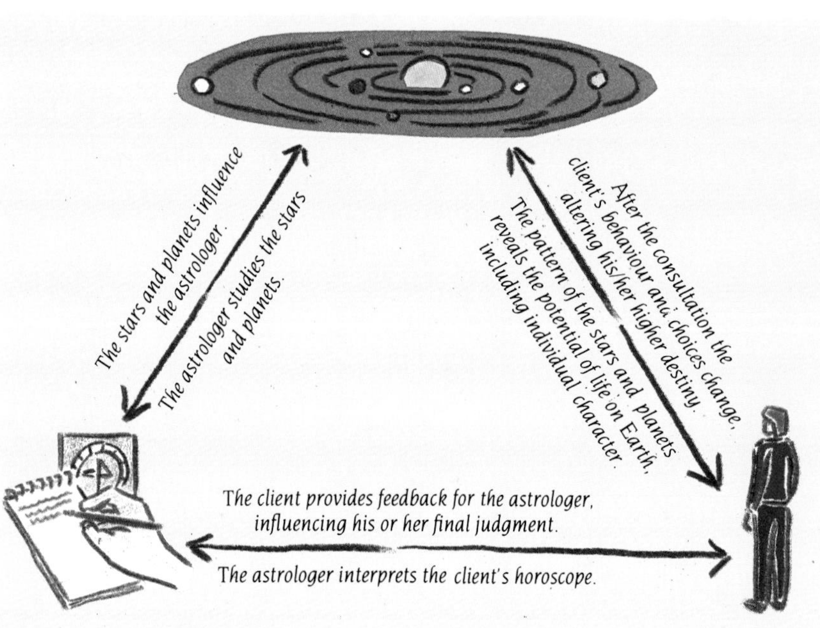

After the consultation the client's behaviour and choices change, altering his/her higher destiny.

The client provides feedback for the astrologer, influencing his or her final judgment.

THE DIFFERENT BRANCHES OF ASTROLOGY

Astrology is divided into two main branches: judicial and natural. Judicial astrology, as the name implies, is the more specific and requires the astrologer to make a judgment, perhaps a statement, about a person's character or life, or a prediction of a future event. Natural astrology is concerned more with general planetary influences. In practice these branches are not easy to separate, and they overlap in most areas.

NATAL ASTROLOGY concerns the lives of individuals and employs horoscopes drawn for the subject's time of birth or other important moments in life. This is the most popular and widely practised form of astrology, and within it, different areas of expertise may be distinguished:

Event-oriented astrology emphasizes the prediction of events such as marriage, career and children, and tends to be neglected by astrologers who move towards a psychological approach.

Basic psychological astrology is used to describe a person's character and psychological potential. The prediction of future events is replaced by an 'analysis of future trends', as it is assumed that an individual's psychological inclination at a future date will tend to produce certain types of behaviour. These then lead to a range of likely events, which are predicted only in general.

Astrological counselling combines psychological astrology with modern techniques of psychological analysis or therapy. The symbols in the horoscope are used to trigger the counselling process, the object being greater self-awareness and understanding. Prediction is ignored because the purpose is to enhance the subject's ability to alter his or her future by a change in behaviour. This is a highly practical and successful modification of psychological astrology. Counsellors often refer to their astrology as 'working with the chart'.

ELECTIONAL ASTROLOGY is concerned with the establishment of the most propitious time to begin an enterprise, such as a journey, a marriage, a business or a course of study.

HORARY ASTROLOGY provides precise answers to specific questions. A horoscope is cast for the time when a question is asked and the astrologer applies strict rules to arrive at the correct answer. Typical questions include 'will I get the job?', 'will I pass my exam?' or 'will I buy the house?' Horary astrology often provides more reliable predictions than other branches of astrology.

MUNDANE ASTROLOGY is a vast field which concerns all affairs involving groups of people and general world events. In the main it is concerned either with predictions or the analysis of events in retrospect. There are three principal areas:

Political astrology is not concerned just with politics in its narrow sense, but with all affairs involving groups of people and organizations. It overlaps other branches of astrology using the techniques of natal, electional and horary astrology to study the lives of politicians, plot events and inquire into the future.

Financial astrology is not separate from the other branches of astrology, but should be considered a speciality by virtue of the number of business people who seek such advice from astrologers specializing in financial affairs.

Geophysical astrology covers the examination of weather, climate, and all natural phenomena, especially disasters.

MEDICAL ASTROLOGY has its own traditions of diagnosis. In matters of treatment it is intimately connected with herbalism, homeopathy and other natural or holistic methods of healing.

There are few astrologers who practise all the different branches of astrology. Most of them start with the study of natal astrology in which they establish their own style, sometimes combining it with another branch.

Astrology has no inherent religion or morality of its own and may be adapted to suit the religious and ethical standards of the astrologer, whose beliefs may range from agnostic to deeply religious. Astrology is supremely flexible and there is no branch of human thought or belief with which it is incompatible.

The concept of synchronicity was devised by the psychologist C. G. Jung and is frequently used to explain modern astrology. Synchronicity abandons the belief that one event necessarily causes another and assumes that two events can be related because they happen at the same time. Such a connection is known as 'acausal'. As applied to astrology this means that an astrological event and an event on Earth are connected if they happen at the same time.

ASTROLOGICAL PATTERN TIME EVENT ON EARTH

The Solar System

As the sun hurtles through space it pulls the planets along with it. When extended in this way the circular orbits of the planets become a series of spirals. Astrological time has a basic spiral structure; the same general themes repeat themselves in cyclical patterns, yet the specifics are always different. The seasons follow each other in a strict order, yet each year has a different character.

Bottom right: The origins of astrology lie in the human desire to understand and measure the motions of the stars.

In early agricultural societies, religious worship centred on the solar and lunar divinities responsible for the cycle of the seasons, the rhythms of life.

The purpose of monuments such as Stonehenge, the first part of which was laid out around 2800 BC, was to predict the solstices and equinoxes that defined the seasons, and the eclipses which were a cause of much superstitious fear.

Stonehenge itself was a temple and observatory combined in one great edifice. Each year at the summer solstice the Sun rises over the 'Heel Stone', marking the longest day.

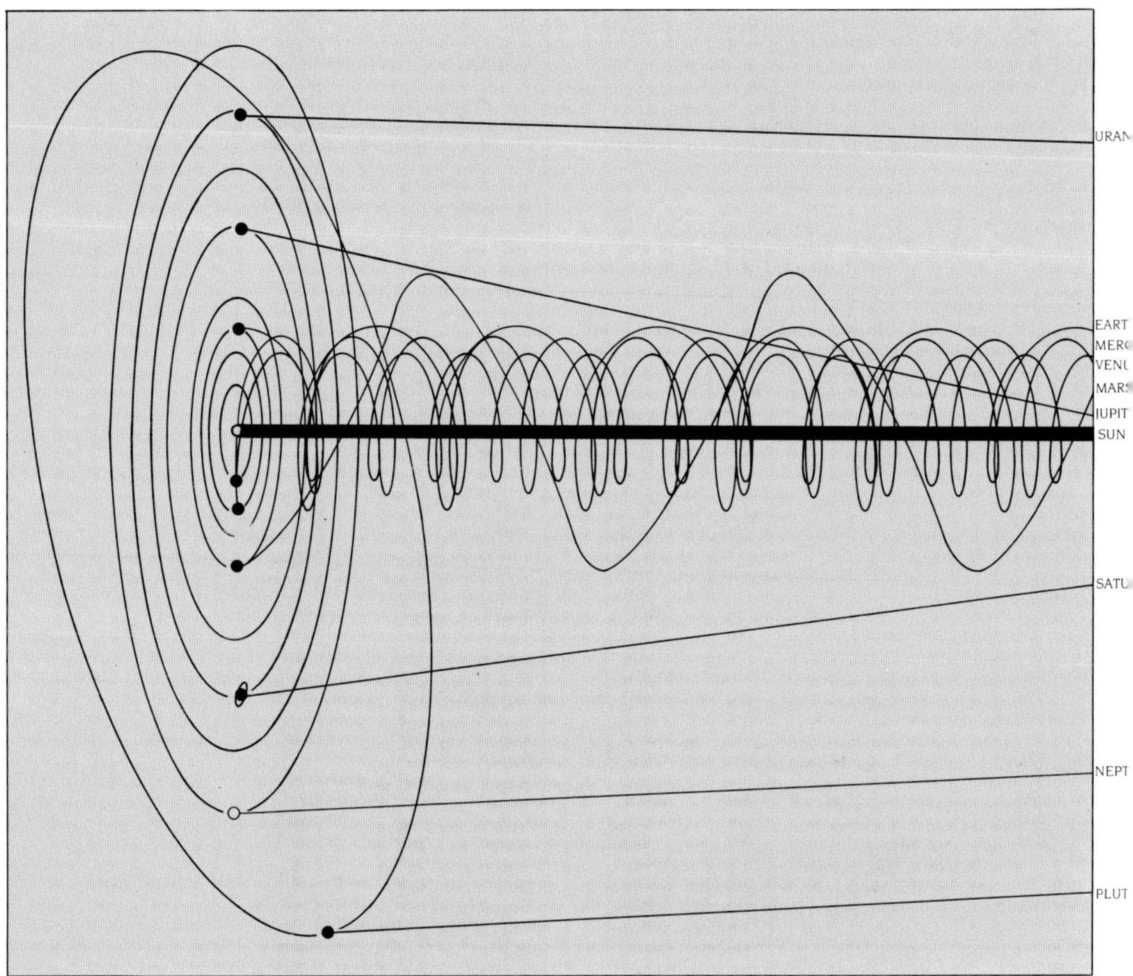

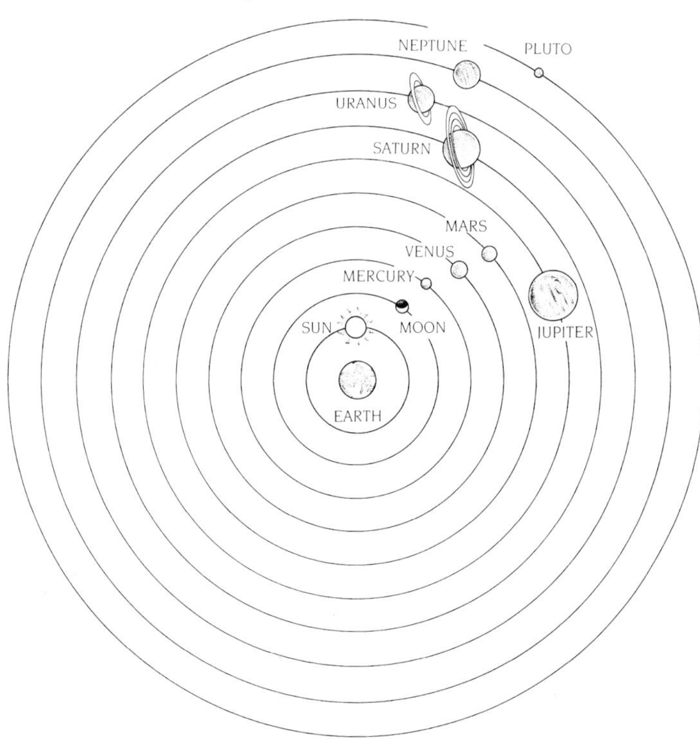

THE ASTROLOGICAL SOLAR SYSTEM

ASTROLOGY AND ASTRONOMY

Astrology and astronomy were once interchangeable terms used to describe the study of the stars. Since the scientific revolution of the seventeenth century they have been firmly separated and now have quite distinct meanings.

Astronomy is concerned solely with the physical study of the universe, while astrology gives a symbolic meaning to the patterns and phenomena of that universe. There is an overlap between the two disciplines because, at their most basic level, both concern the physical effects which the planets (especially the Sun and the Moon) have upon the Earth. In every other respect they are quite separate.

Astronomy shows that the Earth and the planets pursue a spiralling path through space, following the Sun as it hurtles around the galaxy. Astrology uses a more static and symbolic model in which the Earth remains motionless at the centre while the planets and Sun orbit around it. This is known as the Earth-centred or geocentric system as opposed to the Sun-centred or heliocentric system.

THE GEOCENTRIC FRAMEWORK

Astrologers use a system of great circles to define the structure and mathematical divisions of a **horoscope**. A **great circle** is any circle around the Earth's surface whose plane passes through the centre of the Earth. A detailed study of these circles is outside the scope of this book, and only the basic great circles need to be understood.

The equator is the imaginary line (a specific great circle) around the Earth which separates the northern from the southern hemisphere. It is known as the **terrestrial equator** in order to distinguish it from the **celestial equator**, its projection in space.

The **ecliptic** is the name for the Sun's path through the sky on its annual cycle. As a result of the tilt in the Earth's axis the ecliptic intersects with the celestial equator at an angle of nearly 23½°. This angle is known as the obliquity of the ecliptic, and is responsible for the changing cycle of the seasons.

Once a year the Sun reaches its maximum extension southwards, once a year its maximum extension northwards, and twice a year it is overhead at the equator. These four positions are known as the **cardinal points**. They define the four seasons and represent the keystones of the astrological year. They are of tremendous symbolic importance in the horoscope.

On 21 or 22 December each year the Sun reaches its maximum extension southwards. This marks the beginning of winter in the northern and of summer in the southern hemisphere and is known as the winter solstice. On 21 or 22 March each year the Sun is overhead at noon at the equator. This marks the beginning of spring in the northern hemisphere and autumn in the southern and is known as the spring or vernal equinox. On 21 or 22 June each year the Sun reaches its maximum extension northwards. This marks the beginning of summer in the northern hemisphere and winter in the southern and is known as the summer solstice. On 22 or 23 September each year the Sun is again overhead at the equator at noon. This marks the beginning of autumn in the northern hemisphere and spring in the southern and is known as the autumnal equinox.

The great circles and Cardinal points are the basis of the **horoscope** commonly known as the birth chart or natal chart. This is a diagram of the heavens set for a particular time, date and place. Using a system in which the sky is divided into 12 equal divisions known as the signs of the zodiac, the astrologer calculates the positions of the 10 planets in these signs.

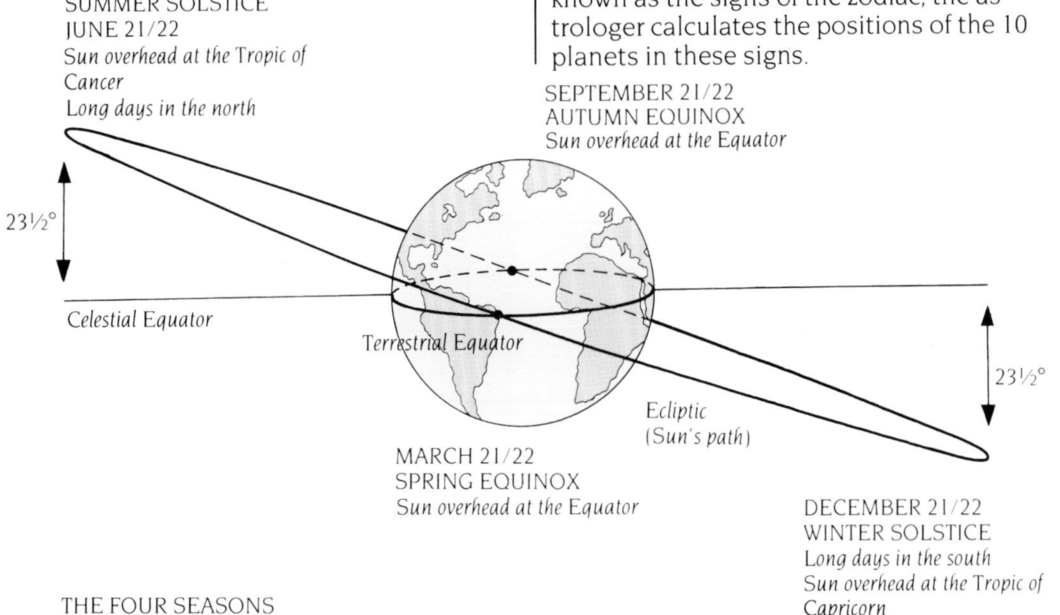

THE FOUR SEASONS

CHAPTER 2
THE PLANETS

In astrology the planets are the 10 major bodies in the solar system which appear to orbit the Earth: the Sun, the Moon, Mercury, Venus, Mars, Jupiter, Saturn, Uranus, Neptune and Pluto. These are extremely important and without them astrology as we know it would not exist.

Each planet represents a basic principle and it is the astrologer's task to work out how this principle will be manifested.

In natal astrology each planet indicates the type of circumstance which a person may encounter as well as the individual's basic psychological inclinations. In a dynamic sense the planets reveal the processes by which a person learns, grows and changes.

Planet	Glyph	Corresponding Sign	Sex	Metal	Colour
SUN	☉	♌ Leo	♀	Gold	Gold
MOON	☽	♋ Cancer	♀	Silver	Silver
MERCURY	☿	♊ ♍ Gemini Virgo	○	Mercury	Changeable
VENUS	♀	♉ ♎ Taurus Libra	♀	Copper	Blue/Green
MARS	♂	♈ ♏ Aries Scorpio	♀	Iron	Red
JUPITER	♃	♐ ♓ Sagittarius Pisces	♀	Tin	Royal purple
SATURN	♄	♑ ♒ Capricorn Aquarius	♀	Lead	Dull colours, grey, brown
URANUS	♅	♒ Aquarius (secondary ruler)		Uranium	Electric blue
NEPTUNE	♆	♓ Pisces (secondary ruler)		Neptunium	Gentle colours, blues, greens
PLUTO	♇	♏ Scorpio (secondary ruler)		Plutonium	Black/deep-red
CHIRON	⚷				
NORTH NODE	☊				
SOUTH NODE	☋				

The planets also rule physical objects and reveal the nature of events.

There are two orders employed to list the planets, one modern and one more traditional. The modern order starts with the Sun and the Moon as the most important, and then lists the others in their order of distance from the Sun: Mercury, Venus, Mars, Jupiter, Saturn, Uranus, Neptune and Pluto.

The second, but older system, is known as the Chaldean order. This lists the planets in the order of their velocity as seen from the Earth: the Moon, Mercury, Venus, the Sun, Mars, Jupiter and Saturn. Uranus, Neptune and Pluto are not included because the system was in use thousands of years before they were discovered. It is, however, still important to be aware of this order because it is the rationale behind some otherwise incomprehensible symbolic systems in astrology. For example, the planets' rulerships of the signs of the zodiac, days of the week and the hours of the day, are all calculated according to the Chaldean system.

PLANETARY CLASSIFICATIONS

The Sun and the Moon are known as the 'Lights', symbolizing their power as the sources of light and life. The Sun, Moon, Mercury, Venus and Mars are known as the Inner planets (for astronomical reasons – they are the innermost planets of the solar system) and the Personal planets. In a horoscope these planets are particularly responsible for providing people with individual characteristics.

Jupiter, Saturn, Uranus, Neptune and Pluto are known as the Outer planets because they are furthest from the Sun. Jupiter and Saturn are also known as the Impersonal planets because they connect us with other members of our own generation.

Uranus, Neptune and Pluto are also known as the Transpersonal planets because they manifest themselves in ways so profound as to go beyond the concerns of a generation.

The first seven planets from the Sun to Saturn are known as the Traditional planets because they have been used since astrology began. Uranus, Neptune and Pluto are known as the Modern planets because of their recent discovery.

Each planet may manifest itself in two main ways, negative or positive. For example, Mercury may either be intelligent and informed, or superficial and mendacious. Venus may be loving and artistic, or lazy and greedy. Mars may be courageous and bold, or violent and aggressive. In our society the former attributes, in each case, are considered more

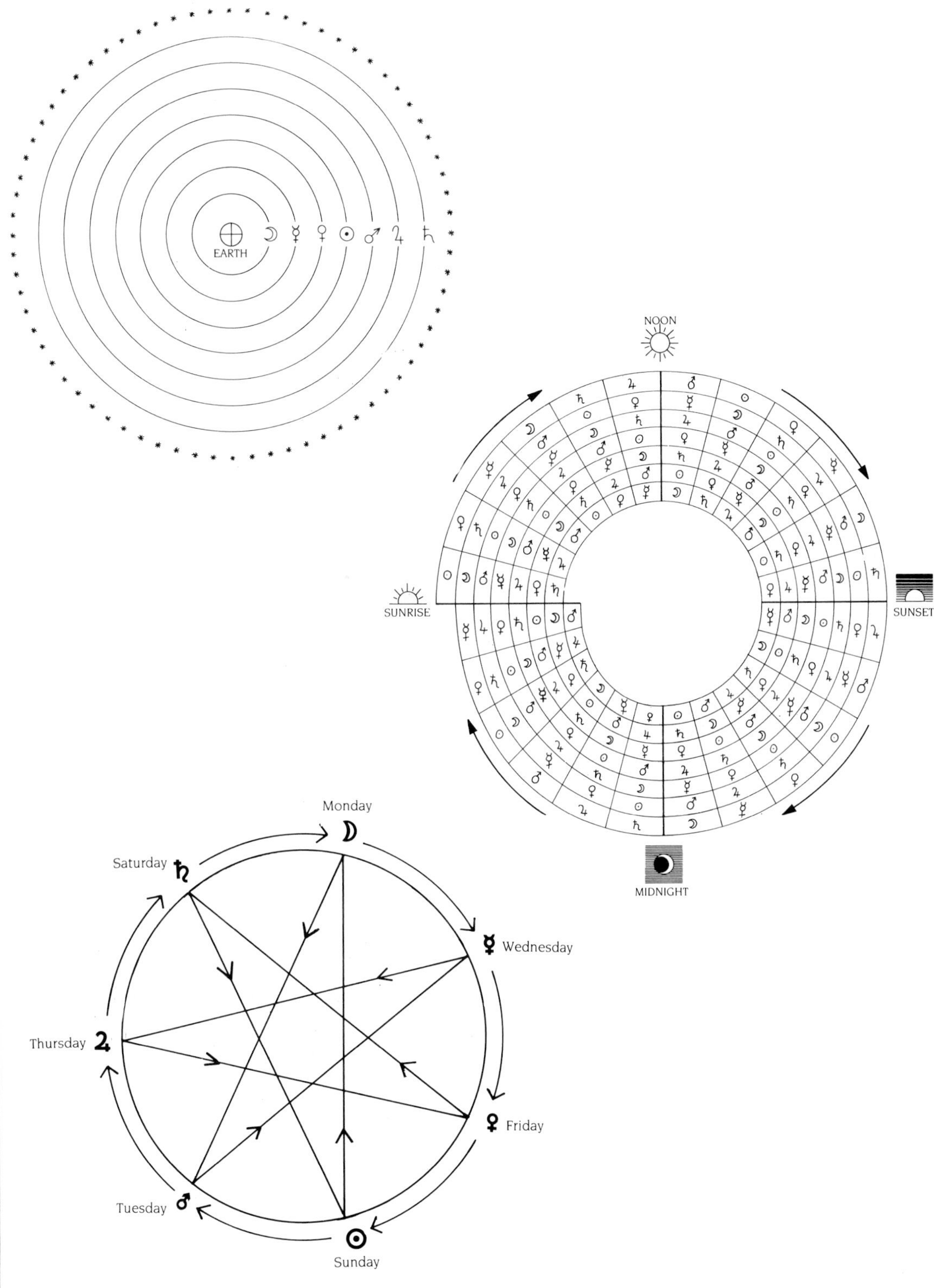

desirable (positive) than the latter (negative). To approach analysis of the planetary principles in this way is useful because it helps to highlight possibilities, but astrologers should never offer such simple moral judgments to clients.

Traditionally the planets are divided into malefic, benefic and neutral. In the astrological judgment of events the malefic planets introduce difficulties while the benefic planets bring rewards and good fortune. The neutral planets are open to influences from either malefic or benefic planets.

The malefic planets are Saturn ('the greater malefic') and Mars ('the lesser malefic'). The benefic planets are Jupiter ('the greater benefic'), Venus ('the lesser benefic') and the Moon. The Sun and Mercury are neutral. Uranus, Neptune and Pluto are not considered. A psychological approach to these

The Chaldean Order of the Planets

The planets and the days of the week
The planets are placed around the circle in the Chaldean order and a seven-sided star is drawn connecting each one. The pattern revealed is that of the seven days of the week. Sunday, Monday and Saturday are named after the Sun, Moon and Saturn. Tuesday (Mardi in French) is named after Tiu, the Saxon Mars, Wednesday (Mercredi in French) is named after Woden, the Saxon Mercury, Thursday (Jeudi in French) is named after Thor, the Saxon Jupiter, and Friday (Vendredi in French) is named after Freya, the Saxon Venus. Each day takes its character from its ruling planet.

The planetary hours
Each of the 24 hours of the day is ruled by one of the seven traditional planets, and ancient astrologers always took account of the hour for which a horoscope was cast. The character of each hour was taken from its planetary ruler; the best hour for travelling was the Mercury hour, the most auspicious for love was the Venus hour, and so on.

The planets are arranged in the Chaldean order as are the days of the week, but in a reverse sequence, beginning with Saturn and ending with the Moon. Unlike our modern hours the planetary hours are based on the varying lengths of day and night; a daytime hour is one-twelfth of the period from sunrise to sunset and a night-time hour is one-twelfth of that from sunset to sunrise.

The planet that rules the hour following dawn on each day is the ruler of the day itself; on Sunday the hour after dawn is ruled by the Sun, on Monday by the Moon, and so on. The following hours are then ruled by the planets in order.

The times of sunset and sunrise for every day are given in standard astronomical and nautical reference books, which should be available in any library. The length of the planetary hours can be worked out by taking the time between sunrise and sunset, (for the day hours) and between sunset and sunrise (for the night hours) and dividing these by 12.

categories reveals that the malefic planets cause pressing problems. They raise issues for the individual which must be tackled and cannot be ignored. On the other hand issues raised by Jupiter, Venus and the Moon may be less urgent and can be dealt with more easily.

The seven traditional planets are divided into sexes: the Sun, Mars, Jupiter and Saturn are male, the Moon and Venus female, and Mercury hermaphrodite.

These attributes can be useful in astrological interpretation if they are not confused with cultural stereotypes of male and female behaviour. Astrology stands for complete equality between the sexes by giving Mars the rulership of a female sign (Scorpio) and Venus the rulership of a male sign (Libra). There is thus an interchange of energy between male and female signs and planets; the difference between male and female characteristics is blurred. Every woman has male planets in her chart and every man female planets in his, and astrology has for thousands of years acknowledged

RETROGRADE PLANETS

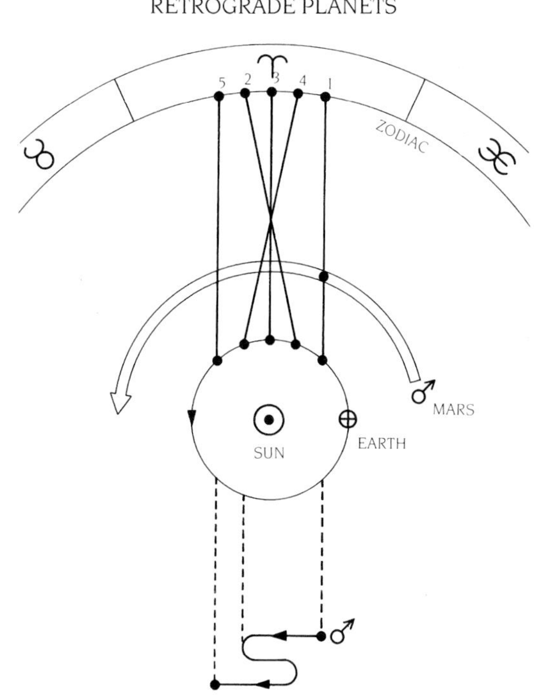

Retrograde Planets
In this example Mars appears to move backwards through the Zodiac as seen from the Earth.

Sun

Moon

Mercury Venus

Earth Mars

Jupiter Saturn

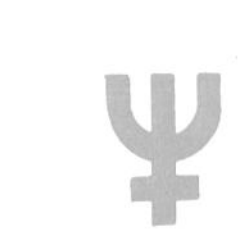
Uranus Neptune

Pluto

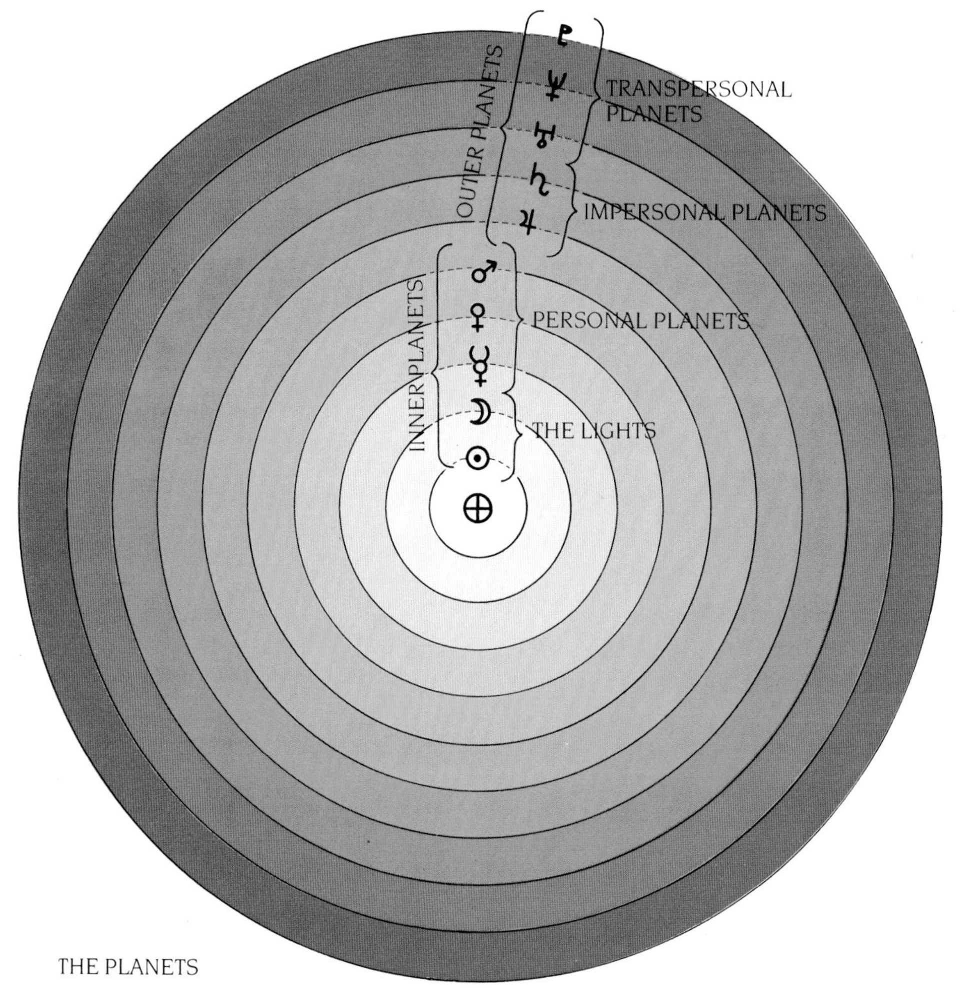

THE PLANETS

The planets may also be regarded as part of a single process in the life of an individual:
The Sun – the first stage of life in which the infant is only aware of the self.
The Moon – the infant becomes aware of the mother, the family, and begins to experiment with emotional demands.
Mercury – the child learns how to communicate, to crawl, to walk and to talk, becoming aware of the outside world.
Venus – the first friendships are formed as the child develops a relationship with the larger world.
Mars – the child becomes an adult, self-assertive, pushing individual interests.
Jupiter – the fruition of adulthood, career success, wealth, wisdom, home and family.
Saturn – old age, wisdom, status, death.
Shakespeare's "seven ages of man" in "As You Like It" are sometimes compared to the 7 planetary ages although he leaves out the Sun, beginning with the lunar phase and leaving the 7th age without a planetary ruler.

that all people contain female and male natures whatever their biological sex at birth.

RETROGRADE PLANETS

Retrograde planets appear to be travelling backwards through the zodiac. This is always marked by placing the capital letter 'R' next to the planetary glyph. The Sun and Moon are never retrograde. The five outer planets, Jupiter, Saturn, Uranus, Neptune and Pluto, are retrograde so often that this is not taken into account when interpreting a natal chart. However, being retrograde does affect the interpretation of Mercury, Venus and Mars in a natal chart, retrograde motion suggesting an inward looking character.

When Mercury is retrograde, the individual may be an introvert, lacking confidence in communicating and expressing ideas. When Venus is retrograde, the individual may be quiet socially, preferring a one-to-one relationship. When Mars is retrograde, the individual may find it difficult to galvanize his or her energies to get things done.

DEVELOPING PLANETARY MEANINGS

The aim of natal astrology is to enable people to gain control of their own planetary processes, allowing them to direct their own lives. If they fail to control the planetary processes, then fate may step in. For example, a person who fails to recognize his or her own aggressive Martian instincts may become the victim of violence. Someone who is unable to handle Saturnine responsibilities may find such responsibilities are imposed. An individual who is unable to let go of material security may find Uranus snatching it away.

The understanding of planetary principles as processes, rather than just fixed characteristics, may be difficult to grasp at first. It will become familiar with practice in chart interpretation. Natal astrology specializes in the psychological study of the individual; however, each person is in a continuous process of interaction with the environment, and the processes represented by the planets are both internal and external.

It helps to be able to see the planets as representing different functions of human behaviour. They may be seen as needs or, perhaps, as expectations. For example, Jupiter needs/expects success while Venus needs/expects affection. They may represent fears; for example, Saturn may expect/fear failure. They represent ways of doing things: for example, Mars does things in an assertive way, while Uranus does things in an unusual way.

There are as many ways of approaching the planets as there are modes of human behaviour, and by examining the planets in the light of different types of behaviour, the astrologer is able to increase the range of interpretation.

Some of the planets combine naturally in pairs which complement each other. For example, Jupiter and Mercury both rule mental processes, while Venus and Mars both rule emotional and sexual relationships. Some planets may easily be paired with more than one planet. For example, Venus may be connected to Neptune in its artistic capacity as well as to Mars in its social capacity. It is also useful to look at planets which are complete opposites, such as Jupiter and Saturn, to obtain an understanding of how they may be essential to one another. For example, Jupiter rules growth, but requires Saturn to give it a formal structure.

As students learn the planetary meanings they should not accept as absolute truth what is written down, but question it, and try to work out the patterns which connect the planets. This will enhance their understanding and lead to more interesting interpretations. Such understanding may not be learnt in books but will come naturally as experience in interpretation grows.

THE SUN

The Sun rules Leo.
The Sun is the most important of all the planets. In ancient astral religions it was invariably the focus of worship. The Greeks knew the Sun god as Apollo or Helios, the Egyptians as Ra, Horus or Aten. The worship of Aten is thought to have been the precursor of the Jewish belief in one supreme god.

The wearing of gold crowns by kings and queens, and the representation of saints with halos, originate from imitation of the Sun god.

'Sun-sign' popular astrology is often frowned upon by serious astrologers, but it is possible to produce a detailed character description of a person based solely upon a knowledge of his or her Sun sign (the sign containing the Sun at birth). The Sun is a symbol of power, energy and of life itself, and confers enormous importance on that section of the chart in which it is located. The sign containing the Sun will reveal dominant personality traits, and innate strengths and weaknesses. It will also show the fundamental processes by which individuals may change and grow as well as the type of experience encountered as they pass through life. The Sun is pre-eminently the planet of the great 'I'. Some call it the ego, others the self. It represents both the source of life and our innermost being.

THE MOON

The Moon rules Cancer.
This is normally considered the most important planet after the Sun, although it has claims to equality with it.

The speed with which the Moon moves is important in the assessment of the flow of events. For this reason it is often the most significant planet in medical, horary, electional and mundane astrology.

From the moon's place in the horoscope the astrologer is able to make deductions about the individual's mother and their relationship, and the individual's own maternal qualities. For obvious cultural reasons lunar qualities are most clearly expressed by women, but are no less important for men.

The Moon rules the home and family and the individual's relationship to his or her domestic environment. People born with the Moon strong in their horoscopes are often very domesticated, maternal, compassionate and drawn towards the 'caring' professions.

Traditionally, the Moon rules the metal silver and all silver colours. It also has an association with cool and moist weather.

Physically the Moon is responsible for the ebb and flow of the tides, and in astrology it is the main cause of fluctuating emotions. In a horoscope the Moon reveals a person's emotional state and the manner in which it is expressed. It also rules what psychologists call the persona, the mask or public face that people wear to conceal their true feelings and real sensitivity.

MERCURY

Mercury rules Gemini and Virgo.
In classical mythology Mercury was the messenger of the gods and goddesses on Mount Olympus. In astrology this planet rules all forms of communication, physical and mental, trivial and profound. For example, a short bus journey to see a friend is a Mercurial experience, as is also the deep process of psychoanalysis.

Mercury is the only planet which combines male and female qualities. As such it can be used to achieve the fundamental reconciliation between the opposing halves of our personalities. Although Mercury is apparently a superficial planet, its psychological purpose is to facilitate self-transformation by means of self-knowledge and understanding.

Mercury is necessary if we are to know the outside world. It rules short distance travel, all forms of learning and the acquisition of knowledge. It also rules the objects that we use to communicate with one another – telephones, books, trains, cars, newspapers, television, pencils and pens, and so on. In the modern world thinking machines – computers – are a Mercurial development.

In the birth chart Mercury reveals the manner in which the individual thinks and speaks, indicating intellectual interests and their manner of expression.

By examining Mercury in a birth chart the astrologer can advise on the best way to limit its weaknesses and enhance its strengths. People with Mercury highly developed in their charts should seek careers in the communications field – teaching, journalism, taxi driving, the travel business, secretarial work, for example.

VENUS

Venus rules Taurus and Libra.
Venus was the goddess of love in Roman times, but under other names – Ishtar, Astarte and Aphrodite – she was worshipped in all ancient cultures.

In astrology Venus rules the female half of the human psyche, showing feminine and female qualities in both men and women. In the main these qualities are soft, loving, diplomatic, artistic, creative and sensitive, but they also have a harder side. In politicial astrology Venus rules victory in war.

The major rulership of Venus is over all close partnerships and relationships, including marriage. In order to succeed in relationships most people develop the Venusian qualities of softness, sensitivity and diplomacy, but negatively the planet can become envious, jealous and aggressive. By examining the position of Venus in the birth chart the astrologer can deduce how it will affect partnerships, and whether these will be formed easily or not.

In a woman's horoscope Venus may show the image of female behaviour to which the individual aspires. In a man's chart Venus may reveal his expectations of women and the type of woman he finds attractive.

Venus rules all objects and behaviour which are pleasant, pleasurable, beautiful, graceful and attractive. Some people born with a strong presence of Venus in their birth charts become artists, while others are drawn towards self-indulgence and the pursuit of pleasure.

MARS

Mars rules Aries and Scorpio.
As the god of war in classical mythology, Mars rules energy, enterprise, dynamism, action and self-assertion. It also rules all objects connected with heat and violence; knives, guns, explosives, fires and so on.

In medical astrology it is linked to high temperatures, feverish complaints, accidents and all problems requiring surgery. By its placing in a birth chart Mars reveals a person's general energy level and overall behaviour pattern. It will show the manner in which the practical issues, affairs and problems of the world are approached and handled. Because it is partly concerned with action in the outside world, Mars reveals a lot about the way we express ourselves to others.

Mars has a specific function in relationships; if Venus is the force of attraction, then Mars reveals the active impulse which causes people to seek out each other. Venus and Mars together reveal all the possibilities in a complete emotional and sexual relationship.

Psychologically Mars rules the internal image we all have of the ideal man. In a man's chart it may show the role model he is obliged to live up to. In a woman's chart Mars will show how she manages with her own male half, as well as indicating her expectations of men and the type of man who attracts her.

The colours associated with Mars are red and bright yellow.

JUPITER

Jupiter rules Sagittarius and Pisces.
Jupiter in astrology shows two faces, both taken from classical mythology. On the one hand, Jupiter was the great king of the gods, dispensing justice with supreme wisdom, while on the other he was a licentious womanizer and glutton.

In astrology Jupiter is quite simply the planet of growth and expansion. These can take place in any realm – spiritual, emotional, mental or physical, depending on the location of Jupiter in the horoscope. Jupiter does everything on a grandiose and inflated scale. At best it is wise, generous, and bountiful but when it is completely uncontrolled it can become wasteful, extravagant and indulgent.

Jupiter has specific associations with religion, belief, philosophy and the law. It shares with Mercury hegemony over reason and the intellectual processes, but whereas Mercury rules knowledge and the communication of knowledge, Jupiter brings the wisdom and understanding that enables the utilization of knowledge.

Like Mercury, Jupiter rules travel, although its journeys are long voyages of exploration and adventure, whether physical, spiritual or intellectual. These are the means by which Jupiter accomplishes its principal aim – to grow.

Traditionally Jupiter has always been known as the planet which brings good fortune, rewards and opportunities. It is not, however, sufficient in itself, and to make Jupiterian good fortune permanent, Saturn is necessary.

SATURN

Saturn rules Capricorn and Aquarius.
In complete contrast to Jupiter, Saturn rules the principles of limitation and restriction. As Jupiter brings growth so Saturn provides the structures within which that growth must take place. In its positive form Saturn represents self-discipline and self-control while in its negative form it brings repression and inhibition. As a result, even though Saturn's astrological correlations are quite simple, its psychological manifestations can be complicated. The causes and results of inhibition and repression are many and varied.

Modern astrology has revived the ancient description of Saturn as the 'Dark Sun', giving this planet the role of the 'shadow', the part of the psyche in which all characteristics and behaviour are deposited when considered unacceptable. This material does not disappear, but finds its way into our lives in unwelcome ways.

Saturn often provokes difficult or challenging circumstances. Frequently these can be traced to individual behaviour and are self-induced, but sometimes they seem to be brought about by fate. These external circumstances force internal change. If the individual is ready for inner development, then in many cases the pressure of the environment will be alleviated. In general, Saturn causes delays, obstacles and material difficulties. It rules tradition, conservatism, established institutions, the authority of the state and religion, the police and social taboos. In its more positive form it is linked to self-discipline, hard work, organizational ability and loyalty.

URANUS

Uranus is the co-ruler of Aquarius.
If Saturn is the planet of order, stability and structure, then Uranus is the planet which tears down all established systems. Astrologers derive the symbolism of Uranus from its eccentric rotation (unlike the other planets Uranus turns on an east-west axis), and from the fact of its discovery at the end of the eighteenth century, which coincided with the political revolutions in America and France and the industrial revolution in England.

Uranus is revolutionary, radical, individualistic and independent. It tends to be progressive, but its main need is to be seen to be different; in a progressive atmosphere it may well be reactionary. Uranus is associated with humanitarianism and philanthropy, but also with chaos and terror. This planet is often antisocial and uncooperative; its function is to stir up all who have accepted conventional beliefs and behaviour. People with a strong Uranus presence in their chart are often motivated by a desire to separate themselves from what they see as the unthinking masses, and they are often unable to resist the temptation of trying to change society.

Uranus is a planet of personal transformation, which it accomplishes by bringing about sudden changes, and raising new possibilities, sometimes welcome, at others traumatic. In some cases the individual may be deprived of a life style which has been safe and secure, while in others radical changes may open up new vistas.

In the world of physical objects Uranus rules all new technology; for example, computers, electronics and nuclear power.

Sun

Moon

Mercury

Venus

Earth

Mars

Jupiter

Saturn

Uranus

Neptune

Pluto

NEPTUNE

Neptune is the co-ruler of Pisces.
Neptune in classical mythology ruled the oceans, and in astrology it is a planet of transformation, working like the sea eroding the land, steadily undermining life's physical certainties. Gradual change comes about as old attitudes, beliefs and life styles go out of fashion or are forgotten.

In politics Neptune is associated with socialism. In the world of economics it rules oil and is, therefore, of considerable importance in the modern world.

In its highest form Neptune rules mystical truth and the universal urge for union with the Divine, and in everyday life it influences the dreams and visions which are humanity's highest motivation. It encourages the charity, sensitivity and self-sacrifice often necessary to put these into effect. In its lower form Neptune brings greed, fraud and deception of self and others, its vision readily turning to disillusionment and cynicism.

Like the sea Neptune is difficult to pin down. Neptunian people are skilled at changing their disguise in order to adopt different faces. People who externalize this may become performers or gurus, while others may take refuge in fashion, religion, mysticism, or behind a smokescreen of drink and drugs.

PLUTO

Pluto is the co-ruler of Scorpio
Pluto is the planet at the furthest edge of the known solar system, although research indicates there may be other planets yet to be discovered. Astrologers combine the distance, mystery and darkness of Pluto with this god's classical rulership of the underworld to provide the planet's astrological attributes of deep, dark and unfathomable power.

Pluto is pre-eminently a planet of transformation. The changes it brings are often of the most profound kind, completely revolutionizing attitudes, beliefs and behaviour. It rules the deepest instincts of the unconscious mind which, when they become dominant, can lead to compulsive and obsessive behaviour. Pluto is also connected with underworld crime, communism and modern depth psychology.

Plutonic individuals often show a passionate interest in the mysteries of life. They tend to be dedicated, persistent and obstinate in following particular courses of action. Plutonic activities and interests include anything with an element of mystery. Some people take up magic, the occult, spiritual healing or mystical religion, while others pursue more orthodox scientific investigation and research. In whatever field they are involved Plutonic people make reform and renewal their highest priorities.

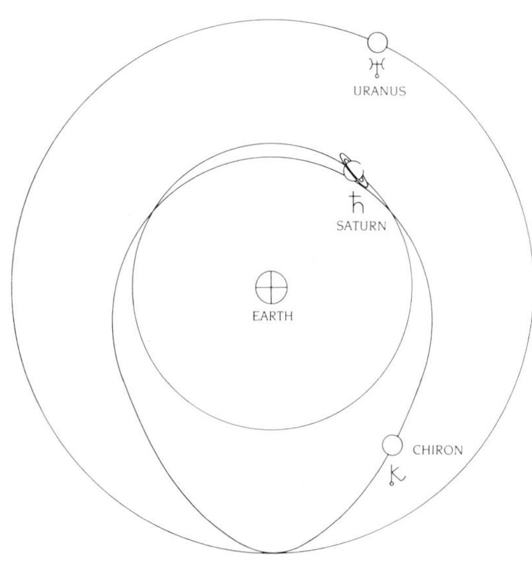

Chiron's orbit is so irregular that at its closest point to the Earth it is inside the orbit of Saturn and at its furthest it reaches that of Uranus. Astrologically it forms a bridge from the order, stability and limitation of Saturn to the anarchic individuality of Uranus. Its discovery in 1977 is associated with the rapid spread of psychological counselling and therapy. Chiron takes the way-out ideas of Uranus and, through Saturn, gives them a practical use.

CHIRON

In 1977 a new planet was discovered and named Chiron. Astronomers disagree whether Chiron belongs properly to our solar system, or whether it is a body from outer space captured by the Sun's gravity. Some call it a giant asteroid, others a planetoid. Astrologers include it as a planet in the zodiac and have begun to investigate its meaning. This is still at the experimental stage and some astrologers have not yet begun to use it. Starting with a study of its astronomical characteristics and an examination of the legend of Chiron who was a centaur (half horse, half human) in Greek mythology, astrologers have applied these clues to the role of Chiron in the horoscope.

Chiron was the wise centaur who taught the art of prophecy, among other subjects, to the Greek heroes. Because of this astrologers say the planet Chiron teaches lessons. These lessons may be unusual (maverick is one of this planet's keywords), startling or sudden. They may also be upsetting, but in the long run they assist a person who genuinely wishes to discover a deeper purpose in life. Chiron is a healer of emotional, spiritual and physical ills, the results of which may open doors to new realities and possibilities.

As this planet is so new there is no consensus concerning the sign it rules, or its function, when in the various houses and planets. Here is a chance for all astrologers to contribute to building the astrological picture of this new planet.

THE MOON'S NODES

The Moon has two nodes, the north and the south. These nodes are not planets but are the two points at which the Moon's monthly path crosses the Sun's annual path (ecliptic) around the Earth. These are abstract points, but astrology accords them the power and effective status of planets. The nodes are considered to be inseparable, each with an individual meaning but together forming a single principle. They are always exactly opposite each other, and the straight line connecting them across the horoscope is seen as the path of the soul through life.

The north node, also called the Dragon's Head, shows the direction in which the individual is heading. This may be difficult, for challenges must be met and new qualities developed.

The south node, also called the Dragon's Tail, shows where the individual is coming from; characteristics and behaviour taken for granted which should, perhaps, be left behind. In times of stress individuals may retreat for safety to the qualities of the south node but, unless they face up to the demands of the north node, there will be a failure to develop the birth potential to the full.

In practice, a great many astrologers have problems with the nodes, because it is difficult to give them psychological meanings as specific as those for the other planets.

Astrologers who believe in reincarnation claim that the north node represents the present life, while the south node reveals either past actions in the present life or the residue of past lives. This can be interesting, although peripheral to practical astrology.

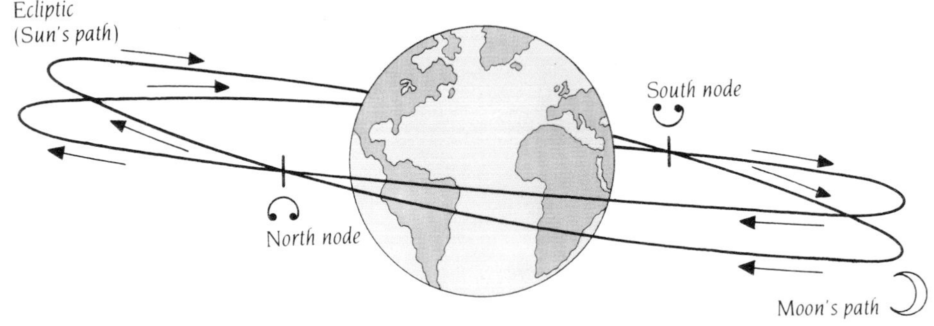

The Moon's Nodes
The nodes are the points at which a planet's path crosses that of the Sun. Usually only the Moon's nodes are used in astrology. The south node is the crossing point on the Moon's southward journey and the north node its crossing point on the northward journey.

CHAPTER 3
THE SIGNS

The zodiac is an imaginary band which encircles the Earth, and extends on either side of the ecliptic – the Sun's annual path. The 12 signs are equal divisions of the zodiac which together describe the entire cycle of human experience, analogous to that of the changing seasons. Individually each sign embodies a principle, has a distinct meaning and rules a range of psychological moods, types of behaviour and physical objects. These form the foundation of astrological interpretation.

The signs in order are Aries, Taurus, Gemini, Cancer, Leo, Virgo, Libra, Scorpio, Sagittarius, Capricorn, Aquarius and Pisces. Most people are familiar with them as the Sun signs or birth signs, the signs which contain the Sun at different times of year.

The signs of the zodiac and the seasons

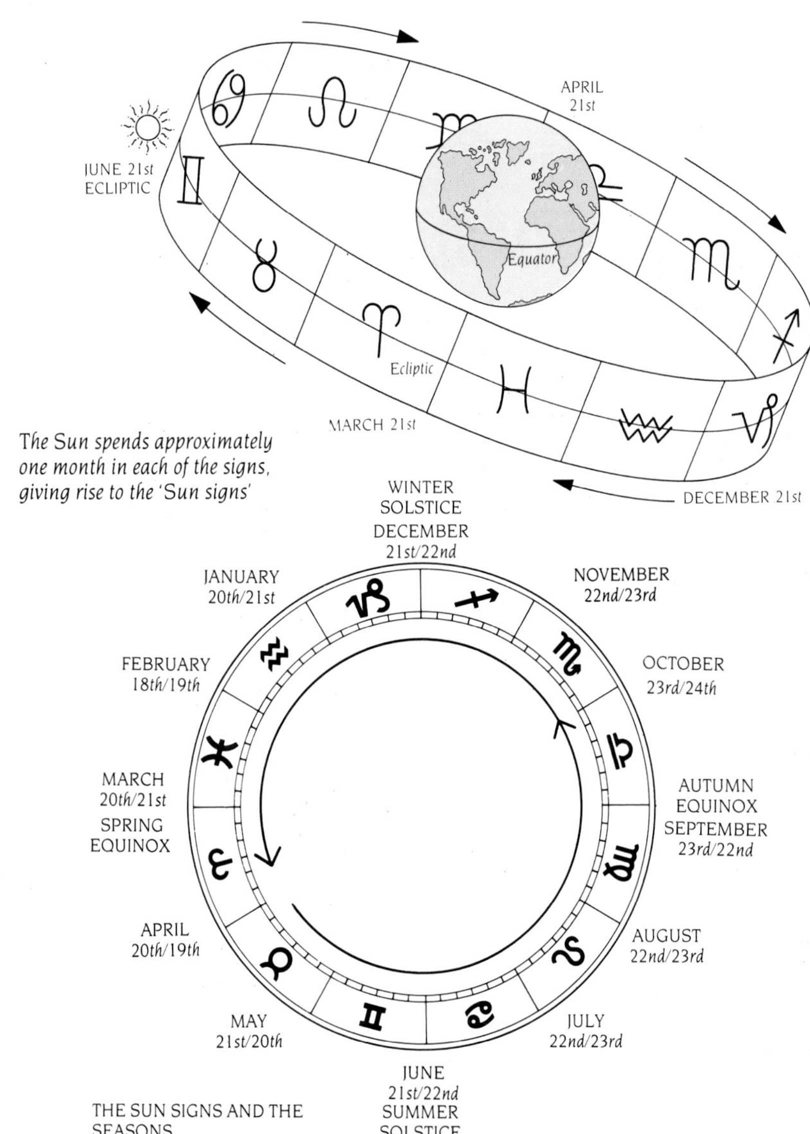

The Sun spends approximately one month in each of the signs, giving rise to the 'Sun signs'

THE SUN SIGNS AND THE SEASONS

Each horoscope, however, contains the entire zodiac and every single person lives out the potential of all 12 signs. No one is solely a product of their Sun sign, and most are combinations of three or four major signs with the other eight fulfilling lesser roles.

The interpretation of any one horoscope, therefore, requires a knowledge of the characteristics of every sign.

THE POLARITIES

The signs are divided into two types, male and female. These are sometimes known as positive and negative, although the Chinese philosophical terms yang (positive, bright and masculine) and yin (negative, dark and feminine) probably convey the meaning more accurately.

The sexes of the signs alternate: the male signs are Aries, Gemini, Leo, Libra, Sagittarius and Aquarius; the female signs are Taurus, Cancer, Virgo, Scorpio, Capricorn and Pisces.

The danger of calling signs male and female is that their natures may be equated literally with the cultural stereotypes of men and women. On the other hand, if this issue is dodged, and the signs are called positive and negative, then a rich source of imagery is lost. Essentially, the male signs may be seen as more active and extrovert, while the female signs are more sensitive, meditative and inward looking.

When these principles, combined with astrological interpretation, are seen through a cultural perspective, interesting interpretations become possible. For example, a boy born under Cancer may have a strong female nature; this may conflict with the male stereotyping he will receive from his education and environment. The astrologer will have to deduce the results on the basis of all the known facts. Similarly, a girl born with Aries strong in her horoscope may be unable to accept the secondary or submissive role which many cultures demand from women. The way in which she reacts to this conflict will depend on the totality of her horoscope and the opportunities provided by her culture.

In retaining the designation of signs as male and female the equality of the sexes is reinforced by astrology. Women have male characteristics just as men have female, and each may develop these.

THE QUALITIES

The qualities, or quadruplicities, are three categories of sign which influence the individual's relationship to the environment.

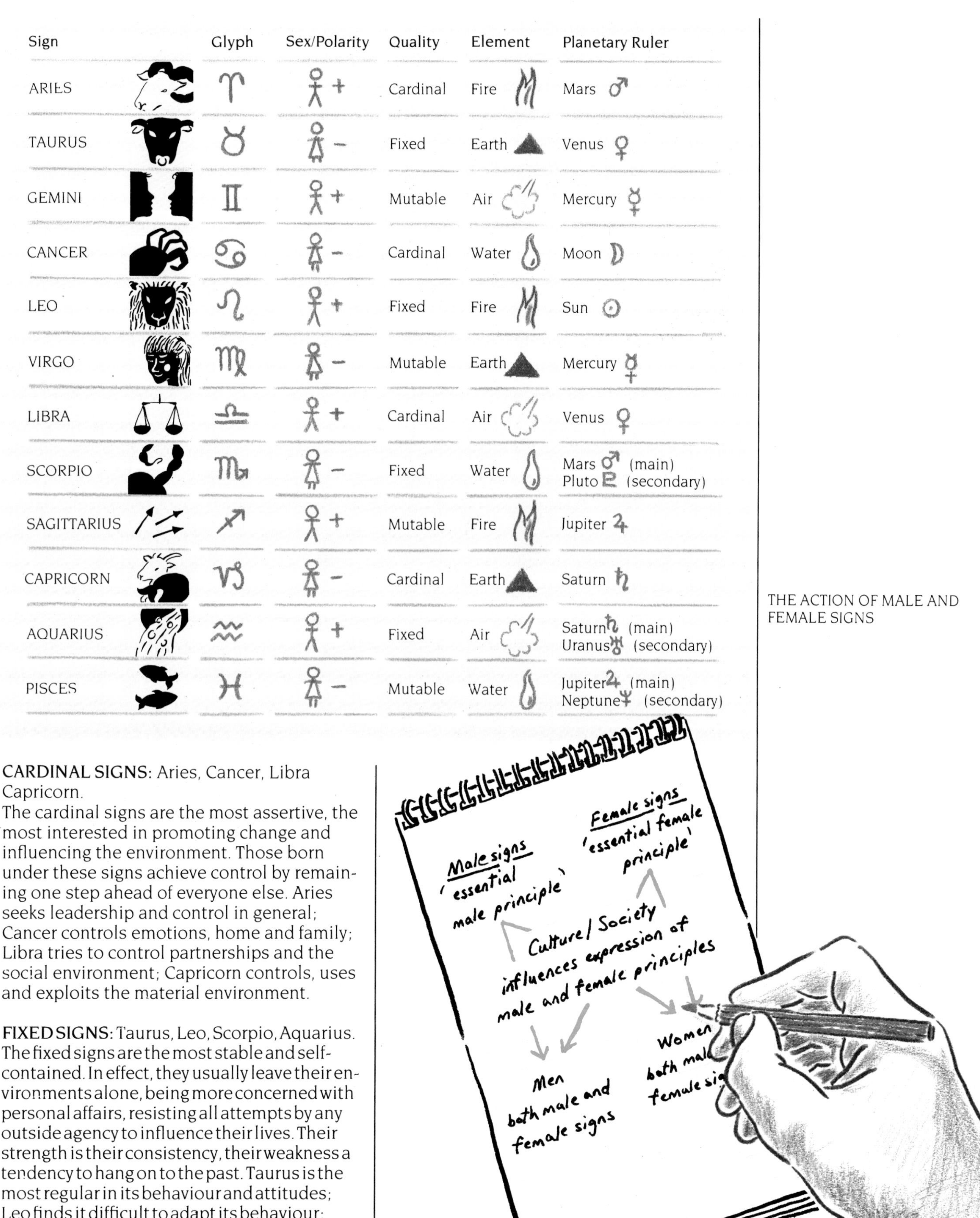

Sign	Glyph	Sex/Polarity	Quality	Element	Planetary Ruler
ARIES	♈	+	Cardinal	Fire	Mars ♂
TAURUS	♉	–	Fixed	Earth	Venus ♀
GEMINI	♊	+	Mutable	Air	Mercury ☿
CANCER	♋	–	Cardinal	Water	Moon ☽
LEO	♌	+	Fixed	Fire	Sun ☉
VIRGO	♍	–	Mutable	Earth	Mercury ☿
LIBRA	♎	+	Cardinal	Air	Venus ♀
SCORPIO	♏	–	Fixed	Water	Mars ♂ (main) Pluto ♇ (secondary)
SAGITTARIUS	♐	+	Mutable	Fire	Jupiter ♃
CAPRICORN	♑	–	Cardinal	Earth	Saturn ♄
AQUARIUS	♒	+	Fixed	Air	Saturn ♄ (main) Uranus ♅ (secondary)
PISCES	♓	–	Mutable	Water	Jupiter ♃ (main) Neptune ♆ (secondary)

THE ACTION OF MALE AND FEMALE SIGNS

CARDINAL SIGNS: Aries, Cancer, Libra Capricorn.
The cardinal signs are the most assertive, the most interested in promoting change and influencing the environment. Those born under these signs achieve control by remaining one step ahead of everyone else. Aries seeks leadership and control in general; Cancer controls emotions, home and family; Libra tries to control partnerships and the social environment; Capricorn controls, uses and exploits the material environment.

FIXED SIGNS: Taurus, Leo, Scorpio, Aquarius.
The fixed signs are the most stable and self-contained. In effect, they usually leave their environments alone, being more concerned with personal affairs, resisting all attempts by any outside agency to influence their lives. Their strength is their consistency, their weakness a tendency to hang on to the past. Taurus is the most regular in its behaviour and attitudes; Leo finds it difficult to adapt its behaviour; Scorpio gets stuck in emotional ruts; Aquarius can become trapped in a negative self-image.

MUTABLE SIGNS: Gemini, Virgo, Sagittarius, Pisces.
Mutable signs are the most unstable and the most open to influence by the environment. They find it naturally easy to let go, although they can react to their instability by a desire for security. Gemini tends to be changeable in its ideas; Virgo is dominated by its environment; Sagittarius has a continually changing view of life's possibilities; Pisces adapts itself superficially to the environment.

THE ELEMENTS

The elements, or triplicities, are four separate types of sign which provide rich sources of imagery for astrological interpretation.

FIRE SIGNS: Aries, Leo, Sagittarius.
Fiery types are energetic, explosive and volatile. They live by enthusiasm and faith in the future, they are adventurers, leaders and innovators. Their weakness is a tendency to burn themselves out and they should make sure their physical and emotional health is not neglected. They are impatient and react badly to obstacles and delays. They are also impractical, and rely on the earth signs to carry out their requirements.

EARTH SIGNS: Taurus, Virgo, Capricorn.
Earthy types are literally down to earth. They are practical, cautious and reliable. They lack imagination, but are vital for putting into effect the orders of fire signs, the ideas of air signs and the dreams of water signs.

AIR SIGNS: Gemini, Libra, Aquarius.
Air signs are responsible for intellectual activity, thought and communication. Without them no reasonable planning is possible, no one would be able to think, let alone communicate ideas to other people. There would be no speech, no memory, no knowledge and no ability to criticize the excesses of other elements. Like fire and water, air relies upon earth for practical support.

WATER SIGNS: Cancer, Scorpio, Pisces.
These are the emotional signs, those capable of exercising compassion, feeling love (and hate), and expressing affection. By their sensitivity they moderate the ideas of air, the unimaginative practicality of earth and the careless energy of fire. With their imagination and dreams they provide human life with its religious and mystical spirituality.

JUNG'S FOUR FUNCTIONS OF CONSCIOUSNESS

The psychologist C.G. Jung concluded that there are four basic functions of human consciousness, and these are widely connected by astrologers to the four elements.

INTUITION is responsible for seeking out new possibilities and discovering new potential in existing situations. Astrologically it corresponds to fire.

SENSATION makes for the awareness of the physical body, and corresponds to earth. Life is seen as a set of practical problems.

THINKING is the intellectual, critical function corresponding to air.

FEELING is the emotional function corresponding to water.

These functions shape behaviour and the perceptions of reality. For example, to a sensation type an apple may be merely something to eat, whereas to an intuitive type it may be a symbol of knowledge, the apple given by Eve to Adam. In another instance, when judging people, thinking types will interpret rules rigidly, whereas feeling types will be compassionate: a thinking type might sentence a man to be hanged for stealing a loaf of bread because the law must be obeyed, whereas a feeling type would exercise compassion, taking into account the desperate condition of the man's starving children.

COMBINING THE ELEMENTS

It is exceptionally rare to find individuals with planets in only one element of their birth chart. Most people have combinations of two or three elements. Combined elements offer different images:

FIRE-AIR. This combination is clearly volatile and explosive. Such people have sudden rushes of extraordinary energy which deplete their resources and leave them exhausted.

FIRE-EARTH. This combination has immense power, the energy of fire uniting with the stability of earth. However, if earth restricts fire too much, the result will be a volcanic eruption of energy which will shatter Earth's complacency.

FIRE-WATER. Fire-water types build up a head of steam, combining the intuition and imagination of these elements. This is easily dissipated, but if channelled by earth (or perhaps by a strong Saturn) the combination can be extremely powerful. They can be volatile because emotions tend to overheat.

AIR-EARTH. This is not an easy combination to interpret, since air and earth do not mix well. Astrologically, however, it is a useful combination as it allows thoughts to be given a solid, practical form.

AIR-WATER. The combination of air and water suggests mists or clouds. These people have their heads in the clouds, lacking the rootedness of the earth signs or the acquisitive ambition of fire. It is definitely a delicate and poetic combination.

EARTH-WATER. Earth and water combine to produce mud; not an inspiring image. Lacking the intellectual sparkle of the air signs, or the get-up-and-go spirit of the fire signs, these people may not be high achievers. However, this is a fertile combination, for it was in the primeval mud that life took form.

COMBINATIONS OF THREE OR MORE ELEMENTS. These are naturally complex, but can be worked out by linking the images of two-element combinations.

OPPOSITE SIGNS

It has been said that there are only six signs, each consisting of a pair of opposites. This is a useful way to think about the signs and to tease out further possibilities of interpretation. Each pair of opposites should be examined to check what they have in common, and how their manifestations vary. For example,
Aries emphasizes personal interests, Libra shared interests;
Taurus focuses on physical stability, Scorpio upon emotional stability;
Gemini emphasizes the search for knowledge, Sagittarius the quest for wisdom;
Cancer structures the emotions, Capricorn the physical world;
Leo believes in personal values, Aquarius promotes collective values;
Virgo practises physical self-sacrifice, Pisces emotional self-sacrifice.

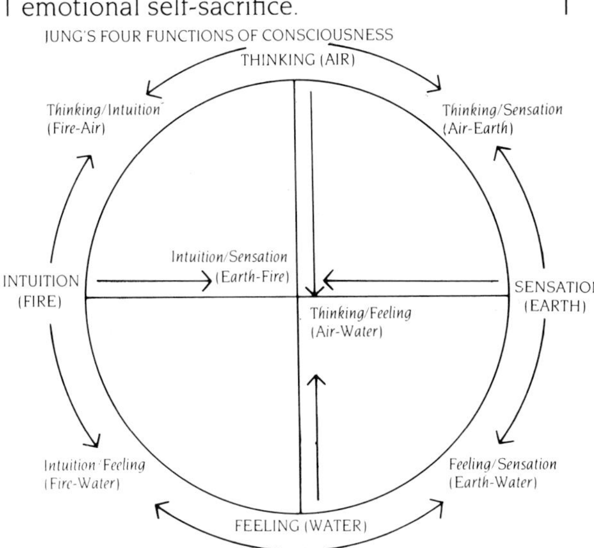

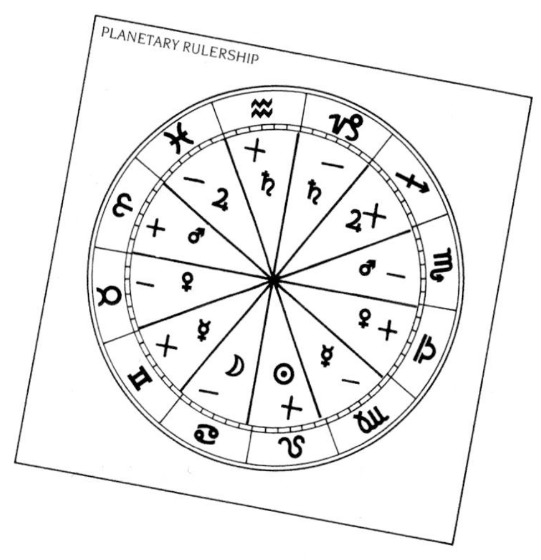

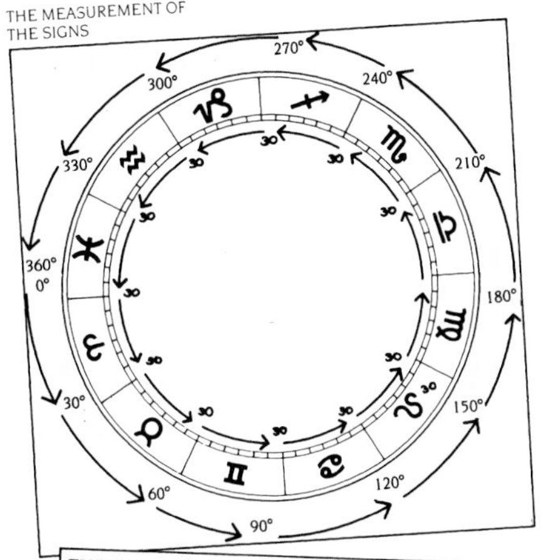

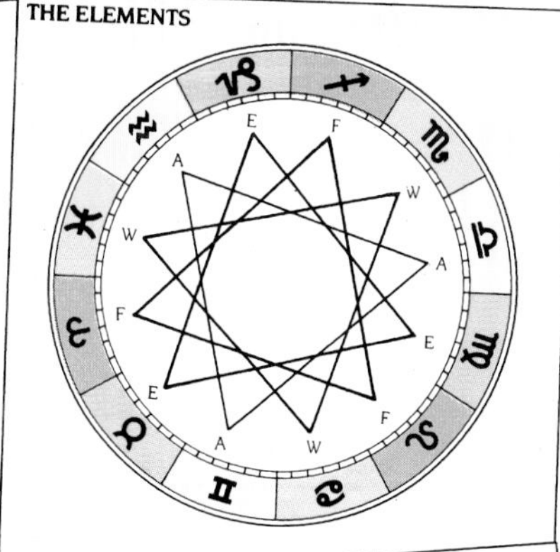

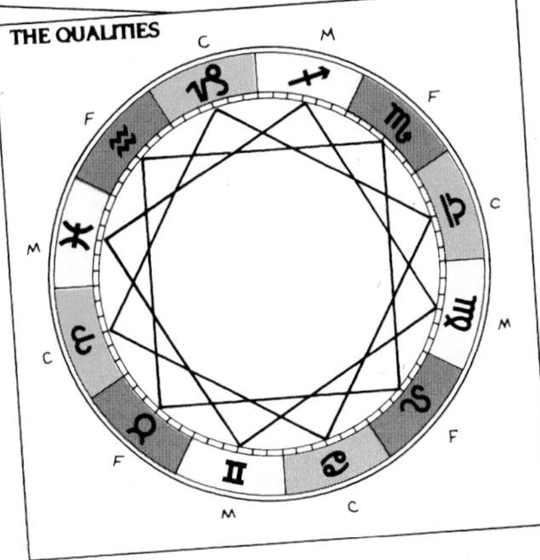

The Measurement of the Signs
Standard chart wheels are drawn to show the division of the full 360° of the zodiac into 12 signs of 30° each with subdivisions of 5° and 1°.

Measurement of the signs around the zodiac is known as ***celestial longitude****, usually expressed in terms of the signs of 30° each. However, sometimes it is necessary to use* ***absolute longitude****, measuring the zodiac in terms of the entire 360°, starting with 0° (Aries) and finishing with 360° (Pisces).*

The dividing line between two signs is known as the cusp.

Planetary Rulership of the Signs
The ancient system of planetary rulerships is based on the Chaldean order of the planets. The Sun and Moon rule one sign each and the other five traditional planets rule two signs each in order from Mercury to Saturn. Each of the five rules one female, negative, 'night-time' sign and one male, positive, 'day-time' sign. The Sun and the Moon are the 'Lights', ruling all the other planets – the Sun is the 'lord' of the day, and the Moon is the 'lady' of the night. Each, therefore, has two faces – Mercury has a purely intellectual face in Gemini but in Virgo is a practical worker and a healer; Venus in Taurus is sensual and concerned with personal pleasure but in Libra needs partners to share in these pleasures, Mars is direct, aggressive and assertive in Aries but deep and intense in Scorpio; Jupiter is the philosopher and traveller in Sagittarius, a mystic and recluse in Pisces; Saturn is materially ambitious in Capricorn but in Aquarius is devoted to the creation of intellectual order.

The three modern planets – Uranus, Neptune and Pluto – are 'secondary' rulers of Aquarius, Pisces and Scorpio, and are additional to the symmetry of the ancient system.

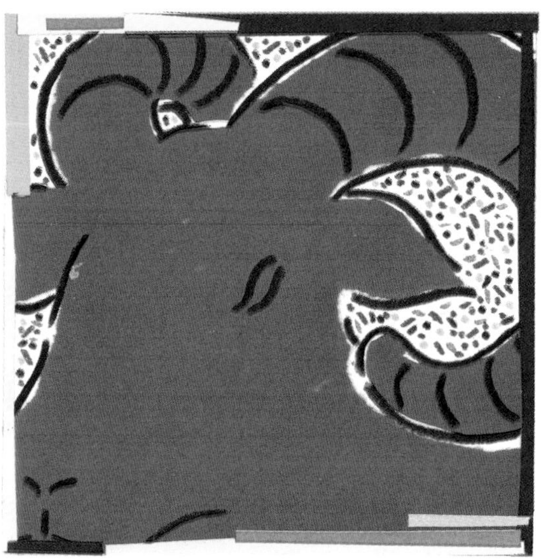

ARIES

Element : Fire — Quality : Cardinal
Ruling planet : Mars — Symbol : the Ram

Aries' reputation for egotism, action and self-assertion is not based solely upon its fiery, cardinal characteristics, but also upon its position as first sign of the zodiac. At the first degree of Aries the entire cycle of experience represented by the zodiac recommences. It represents the seed moment, the germ of all actions, the point at which movement commences. As such Ariens are entrepreneurs, leaders, adventurers, courageous, impulsive and highly motivated. Ariens spot future possibilities and develop them first, usually pushing their own interests.

Although Aries is the first and fastest of all the signs, it is by no means the noisiest; a great many Ariens are, in fact, quiet and unostentatious. In this respect Aries takes its character from Mars, a planet concerned solely with action, rather than glamour and the trappings of power.

The animal associated with Aries is the Ram, which is noted in astrology for being aggressive and headstrong. Aries is not a sign of subtlety, and when it meets an obstacle it will, like the ram, charge it. Ariens often bang their heads against walls.

Ariens have so much power and energy that they tend to burn themselves up. To avoid periods of collapse and exhaustion they should take care to replenish their resources.

In medical astrology, this sign rules the head, and headaches are a classic problem for the overworked Arien.

Aries is also the traditional ruler of England.

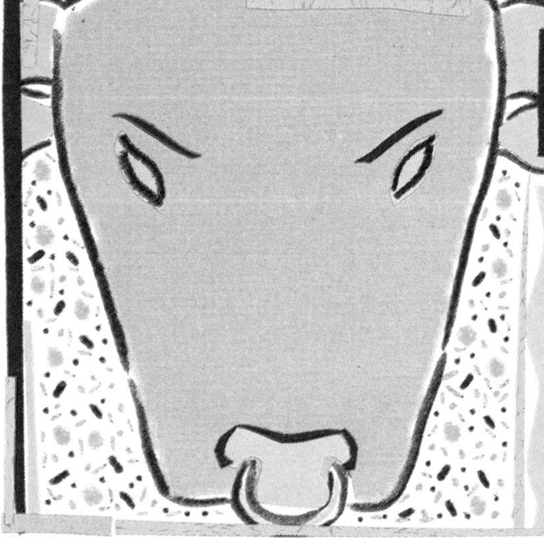

TAURUS

Element : Earth — Quality : Fixed
Ruling planet : Venus — Symbol : the Bull

In complete contrast with Aries, Taurus is stable, conservative and sensual, embodying all the characteristics of fixity and the earth element. This sign values a comfortable, safe and unchanging environment, and likes to hold on to the past. Taurus is down to earth and practical, and is also one of the most productive of signs. The bull is an ancient fertility symbol; Taureans like to be engaged in producing things which can be of use. A fine appreciation of beauty and form is combined with creative power; Taureans often have artistic skills. Typically they make good singers (Taurus rules the throat), but they may also be potters, sculptors, gardeners, or work with the earth in other ways.

Fidelity and consistency are this sign's virtues, obstinacy and a refusal to recognize the necessity for change are its weaknesses.

By temperament Taureans often reflect the nature of the bull. They appear to be passive and contented, but are easily angered when roused. Traditionally, they have a short, stocky stature, with strong shoulders and large necks. Being sensualists many Taureans are fond of smart clothes, jewellery and perfume. They are often attracted to a comfortable and leisured lifestyle.

Aries *Taurus*

Gemini *Cancer*

Leo *Virgo*

Libra *Scorpio*

Sagittarius *Capricorn*

Aquarius *Pisces*

GEMINI

Element : Air
Quality : Mutable
Ruling planet : Mercury
Symbol : the Twins

Gemini is an air sign ruled by Mercury, and it is pre-eminently the sign of rational and logical thought and the gathering of knowledge. The combination of air with the mutable quality renders this sign almost impossible to pin down; Geminian thought must have its freedom.

Geminians are often maddeningly inconsistent; they can argue one point of view one day and the completely opposite view on the next. It is the actual process of thinking and communicating that is important to Gemini, not the end result. A firm conclusion is not necessary so long as the mind is kept well exercised. Geminians often become writers, orators, journalists, teachers, secretaries, lawyers, computer programmers, or take up other activities in which their mental skills can be exercised.

Gemini's mental nervousness affects the body, and Geminians are obliged to work this off in physical exercise, running and walking being two common activities.

It has been said that the most natural animal for this sign would be the nervous chattering monkey with its permanently restless habits. As it is, the symbol of Gemini is the twins, embodying the essential split in this sign's nature; the divorce of the intellect from the emotions. Geminians find it difficult to express emotions as they often rationalize them first. They are subject to unexpected sudden changes of mood.

Geminians are versatile and can turn their hands to more than one thing at the same time – Jacks of all trades. However, if their talents are spread too thinly they may not achieve their aims.

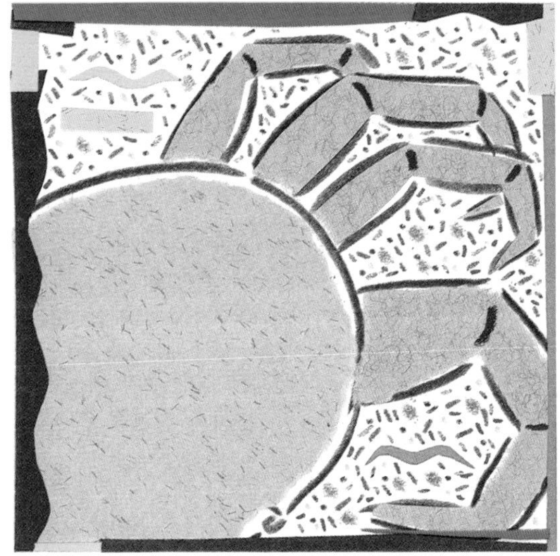

CANCER

Element : Water
Quality : Cardinal
Ruling planet : the Moon
Symbol : the Crab

The second of the cardinal signs, but the first of the water signs, Cancer combines the tough self-assertion of the former with the powerful emotions, softness and sensitivity of the latter. This contrast is embodied in Cancer's animal, the crab, with its soft and fleshy body covered by a hard and protective shell.

Cancer is a sign of compassion which embodies all that is best in the caring maternal instincts, but it often hides its emotions behind a mask which denies these inner feelings. Cancerians are vulnerable and easily hurt; the confident mask they wear in public serves as a defence against the rough and tumble of the world. When upset, Cancerians may withdraw further into their shell, but they also snap at people, imitating the crab's sharp pincers.

Cancerian emotions fluctuate, but they are tenacious, even ruthless, when it comes to defending their family and friends. Cancer people are renowned as homemakers and require domestic stability for happiness. As long as they have a firm base to which they can retreat to recuperate, they are able to venture into the world and make their cardinal presence felt.

In medical astrology, Cancer rules digestive difficulties and cold, shivery conditions.

Traditionally, it also rules all places which are near water.

LEO

Element : Fire Quality : Fixed
Ruling planet : the Sun Symbol : the Lion

A fire sign, ruled by the Sun and symbolized by the lion, the king of the jungle, this is the most egotistical, proud and ostentatious of all the signs. At their best creative, artistic, colourful, generous, honest, warm hearted and natural leaders, Leonians can easily cross the line into being excessively vain, flamboyant, extravagant and selfish. They require an audience and even quiet Leos contrive to make an impression – judging their own behaviour as reflected in the mirror of audience response. The myth of Leo is the myth of the king, but in all true kingship personal power is balanced by obligations and duties. Egocentric Leo must learn social responsibility. This may mean accepting the need for personal change, but for this obstinate sign change can be particularly difficult.

Leos can be difficult to love or to work with. They do not take kindly to limitation of any sort but thrive when given the maximum space and freedom. Their ideal career is acting and they are often found in work connected with the performing arts

Leo types are often recognized by their colourful dress, red and gold being their favourite colours. Traditionally, they are well built and have red hair.

In medical astrology, this sign is linked with back problems and complaints of the heart and circulation.

VIRGO

Element : Earth Quality : Mutable
Ruling planet : Mercury Symbol : the Virgin

The key to the understanding of Virgo lies in the symbol of the Virgin. This is not a passive, feeble virgin, but rather a form of the earth mother, the ancient fertility goddess. The virgin in this sense is pure, but also robust, fertile and potent. Virgo can be one of the most practical and productive of signs, and is prepared to sacrifice its own interests in order to complete its allotted tasks. It is above all a sign of service and self-sacrifice.

The rulership of Mercury brings to this solid sign the gift of analysis, which is crucial in achieving its practical objectives.

Virgoans are often too fussy, over concerned with cleanliness and order, and unable to deal with spontaneity and chaos. Their good-natured willingness to help out lays them open to exploitation by people who are too lazy to do things for themselves. Virgoans are natural bureaucrats. Socially they tend to be shy and lack confidence when expressing their feelings. They tend to resist anything which threatens to upset the boundaries of their expectations and established order. They have very high standards but, can be overcritical. If critical of others they can offend; if critical of themselves they can seriously erode their self-confidence.

They need to balance their perfectionism with a sense of the possible.

LIBRA

Element : Air Quality : Cardinal
Ruling planet : Venus Symbol : the Scales

Libra is best understood through its symbol, the scales or balance. The scales were originally those which the Egyptian gods used to weigh the souls of the dead, and Libra is a sign which spends its life weighing up different possibilities; few signs are so aware of different choices and possibilities as this one. Often Libran types are crippled by indecision, unable to make a firm choice and face the commitment that this involves. Some Librans resolve the dilemma by making a choice and, even though it may not be the best option, sticking to it through thick and thin for fear of having to make yet another decision.

Ideally Libra's function is to resolve opposing possibilities and to seek a third way. Being an air sign, Libra can use its mind to help with the resolution of all conflicts.

This sign is ruled by Venus and one of its major priorities is to establish harmonious and balanced partnerships. The importance of successful friendships is such that Librans will conceal those parts of their character that they imagine might offend other people, such as displays of anger.

Librans excel in groups of people. They are born diplomats, bringing enemies together to make them friends. Their charming artistic qualities enable them to create beautiful and pleasing environments.

This sign's paradox is that it aims to create a balance which can never really exist in a world undergoing constant change. Librans need to learn flexibility and to realize that their efforts to control their environment are unlikely to be successful in a world which contains the other 11 signs.

SCORPIO

Element : Water Quality : Fixed
Ruling planets : Mars with Pluto as co-ruler
Symbol : the Scorpion

Scorpio is the deepest of all the signs and takes its cue from the Scorpion, a creature which prefers to live in the dark and which is liable to react with a sharp sting when disturbed. The intense emotions of this sign are toughened by Mars, given an obsessive quality by Pluto and channelled into a rigid mould by the fixed quality. Scorpio types develop passionate interests and devotion to causes which they pursue with death defying dedication. Those under this sign have an instinctive sense of what is right and what is wrong, and though this may be in contradiction to accepted morality, it nevertheless provides a powerful personal motivation. Scorpio types fall deeply in love, but if hurt or rejected can spend hours plotting bitter revenge. They are usually interested in things deep, dark or hidden, which cover a range of activities. They may become psychologists, therapists, archaeologists, historians, healers, miners, pot-holers, astronomers, astrologers, detectives or members of mysterious religious cults or political groups.

The Scorpio solution to any problem is usually complete and total change. Its colours – red and black – are the colours of the anarchist flag.

This sign's great weakness is its inflexibility and reluctance to change, its strength is its powerful commitment.

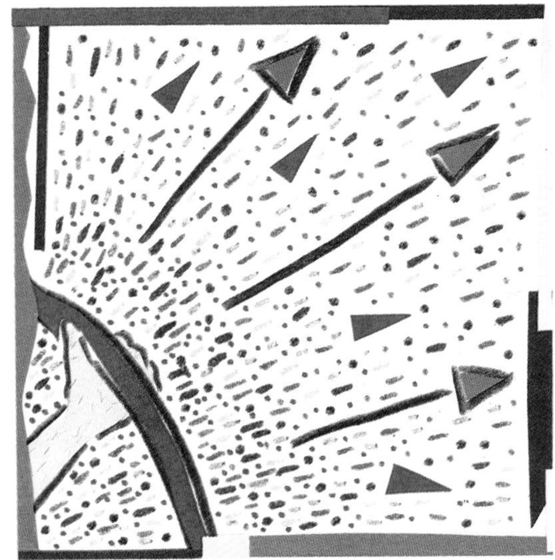

SAGITTARIUS

Element : Fire | Quality : Mutable
Ruling planet : Jupiter | Symbol : the Archer

The Sagittarian archer is a centaur, a creature with the rear quarters of a horse and the torso, head and arms of a human being. This suggests a complicated nature combining beast with human, instinct with reason, body with spirit: Sagittarius's deeper purpose is to reconcile these opposites. This paradox in the sign's nature is difficult to detect, only emerging in the form of sudden and changeable enthusiasms.

The combination of mutability with fire makes the sign unstable; its plans are often dropped before completion. In this characteristic Sagittarius takes its nature from the flying arrow; it is more important to travel than to arrive. This sign is marked by long journeys, whether of the mind, spirit or body. As it is the sign of Jupiter, the ruler of wisdom, Sagittarian journeys are often idealistic experiments in religion, philosophy, or the arts where the desire is to elevate the human spirit. Sometimes the journeys are physical; Sagittarians are often possessed by wanderlust. The purpose is the search for truth. The lesson to be learned by Sagittarians is that, like the arrow in motion, truth is difficult to pin down.

This sign's great strength lies in its optimism and enthusiasm, its weakness is its impracticality. If Sagittarians' faith is strong enough, lack of material success will prove to be no problem.

CAPRICORN

Element : Earth | Quality : Cardinal
Ruling planet : Saturn | Symbol : the Capricorn

The Capricorn is a mythical beast, with the head, front legs and torso of a goat, and the tail of a fish. Accordingly, this is a sign with two natures.

The most commonly known side of Capricorn is that described by the combination of the goat, Saturn and the earth element. This is dull, materialistic, practical, unimaginative, serious, and cautious. The Capricorn is the ideal industrialist or merchant, letting no humanitarian concerns interfere with the important business of making money. Of the goat, it is said there are two kinds: the first remains in domestic captivity, tethered to a post, the second is the wild mountain goat, leaping from peak to peak. The first will work hard to be rewarded with a position of minor responsibility, while the second becomes a captain of industry, the multimillionaire of western capitalism.

However, the tail of the Capricorn rests in the water, revealing quite another dimension to this sign. Capricorns harbour powerful emotions which, as this is an Earth sign, they may find difficult to express. Materialistic Capricorns need to understand and accept these feelings if they are not to be a problem. If these feelings are not acknowledged, they will nag until given adequate expression.

Together with these emotions Capricorns possess all the other qualities of the water element, positive and negative, healing power and great visions, but also the tendency to deception and the ability to manipulate.

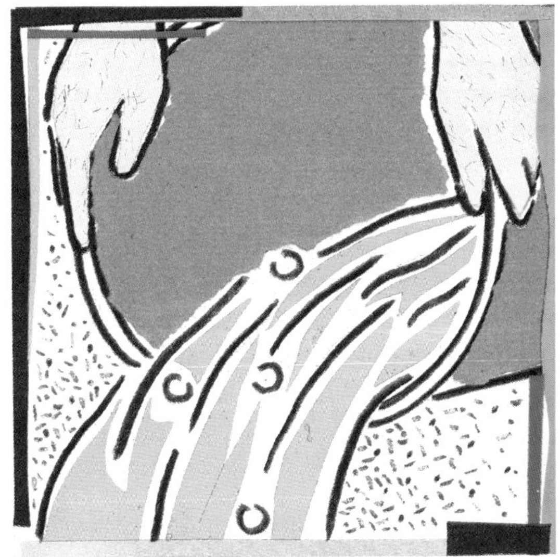

AQUARIUS

Element : Air Quality : Fixed
Ruling planets : Saturn with Uranus as co-ruler
Symbol : the Water Carrier

This is an enigmatic sign, ruled by two planets with totally incompatible natures, the one desiring order, the other tearing it down. There are many contradictions in this sign's character which make it one of the most interesting.

The water carrier is depicted pouring water out of a vast container, an image which symbolizes the ability of this sign to spread new ideas. Aquarius is concerned, sometimes to the point of obsession, with being new, radical and different. Often it is eccentric, frequently awkward, and always demanding complete personal freedom.

The Uranian face of Aquarius is an anarchist, yet the Saturn side believes in authority. The result of this paradox is that Aquarians often try to impose their own unusual ways on other people, against their will if necessary. It is up to them to establish order out of their own chaos, to take charge of their own unconventional instincts and to define and channel them.

Because Aquarius is a fixed sign, Aquarians often develop a life style, or a set of attitudes, which they find impossible to change. Here is another paradox; Aquarians establish themselves as different from everyone else but then they themselves remain unchanged.

Aquarians specialize in producing new ideas, but because these are impractical, they need the help of other signs to implement them.

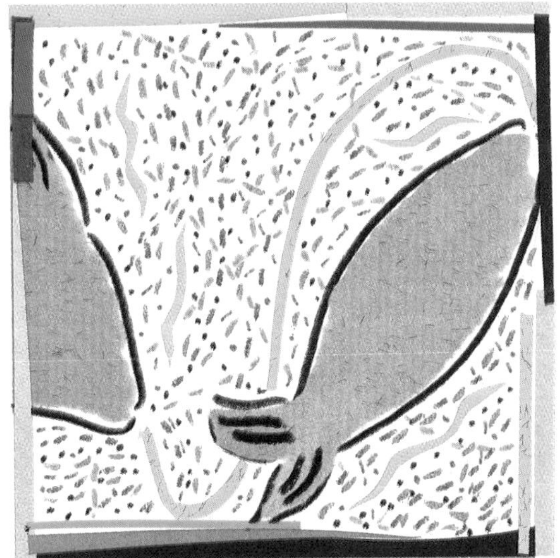

PISCES

Element : Water Quality : Mutable
Ruling planets : Jupiter with Neptune as co-ruler
Symbol : the Two Fishes

Pisces is the most unworldly of all the signs. Of its two planetary rulers, one rules religion, the other mysticism. This is hardly a combination to encourage success in worldly pursuits: Pisceans often withdraw from the world into a safe refuge.

Emotional, sensitive and vulnerable, Pisceans lack the hard shell of those under the influence of the other two water signs, Cancer and Scorpio. Their defence against the world is, therefore, to wear disguises, and these people are skilled in adapting to different situations, concealing their real feelings. They are like chameleons, changing their colour at will. They often appear to be a part of whatever is happening, when, in fact, they have drifted off into a private fantasy.

Pisceans are exceptionally imaginative and just as perceptive as Scorpios. If they develop practical skills, they are able to express their talents in a number of ways. They can be excellent artists, but they are also self-sacrificing, wanting to find a role which has a greater meaning. They are attracted to charitable work and are easily exploited.

This is a manipulative sign, and Pisceans succeed on the stage, in the church and in politics, where performance and ritual enable them to provide illusion and spectacle.

Piscean weakness in handling the real world can lead to chronic indecision. They tend to reject most worldly matters as unimportant, and they give the appearance of failing when, in fact, they have made no attempt to succeed.

CHAPTER 4
THE PLANETS IN THE SIGNS

In every horoscope the planets are distributed among the signs of the zodiac in a pattern which is unique, and the interpretation of the planets in the signs is fundamental to all astrological interpretation. There is a basic formula which is used to create the psychological interpretations of planets in signs and, once this is understood, the astrologer is able to interpret these without recourse to books. Such understanding comes with experience and the beginner has to rely on standard interpretations. The formula assumes that each planet represents a basic function and each sign a basic principle. The function represented by the planet then manifests itself according to the principle of the sign in which it is placed.

The interpretations given here are all general readings, combining the natures of sign and planet, but they by no means represent the last word on the subject. Astrologers create their own subtle differences in the act of reading a horoscope. Most learn by studying set interpretations such as those listed here, and then applying them to the horoscopes of friends and family. In each case, because of the total mix of factors, a slightly different emphasis will be given to each interpretation. The following list, therefore, represents a basic pattern to which the student will be able to add from personal experience.

THE BASIC PATTERN

Planets in Aries act assertively and powerfully.
Planets in Taurus become stable and practical.
Planets in Gemini become more unsettled and intellectual.
Planets in Cancer become more emotional and cautious.
Planets in Leo become bolder and more expressive.
Planets in Virgo become more practical and analytical.
Planets in Libra become more concerned with relationships and appearances.
Planets in Scorpio become more perceptive, determined and emotional.
Planets in Sagittarius become more unstable and concerned with personal freedom.
Planets in Capricorn become more practical and cautious.
Planets in Aquarius become more erratic and in need of freedom.
Planets in Pisces become more sensitive and emotional.

DIGNITY AND DETRIMENT EXALTATION AND FALL

Each of the planets is strong or weak when placed in certain signs. In Dignity and Exaltation the planets are strong and express

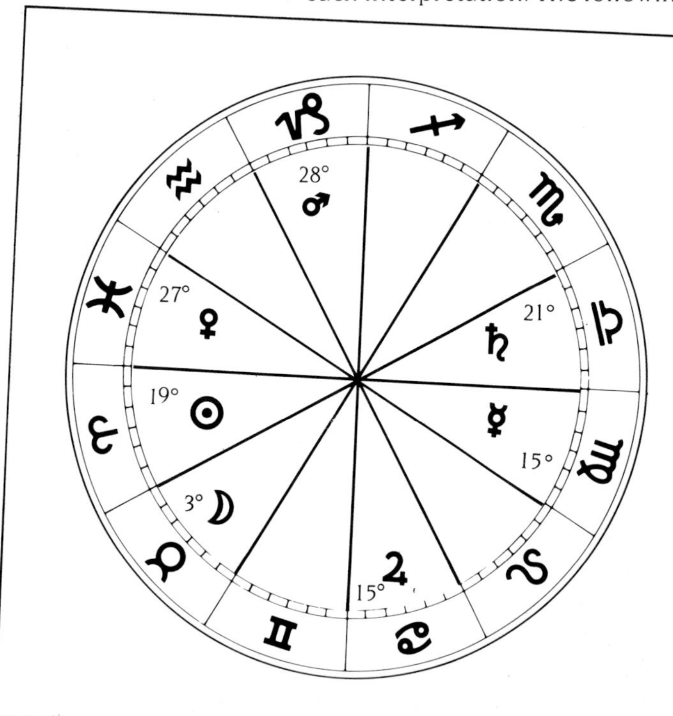

Left: The Exaltations of the Planets
Each planet is exalted in one sign and also has a degree of exaltation which is especially strong. Planets are in fall in exactly the opposite places.

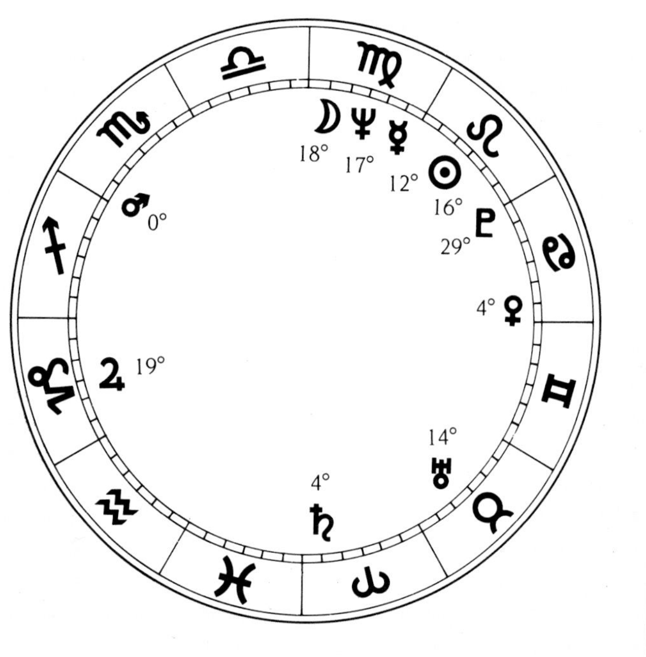

Right: Marking Planets on the Chart
Taking a blank chart wheel, mark each planet on the degree division shown for its particular place in its sign. The location of each planet is calculated for the time of the horoscope, according to the rules in Chapter 7.

In this example the Sun is in Leo, the Moon, Mercury and Neptune are in Virgo, Venus and Pluto are in Cancer, Mars is in Sagittarius, Jupiter is in Capricorn, Saturn is in Aries and Uranus is in Pluto.

themselves well, while in Detriment and Fall they are weak and face difficulties in their expression. Planets are in Dignity in those signs which they rule and in Detriment in the opposing signs. Only the seven traditional planets are included in the Exaltations and, in each case, they have both a sign of Exaltation and a single degree within that sign in which the Exaltation is strongest. Planets are in Fall when in the opposing positions to their Exaltation.

At the general level of psychological interpretation these considerations are already taken into account and need not be considered separately. However, their importance grows as the need for precision increases.

The Planets Acting Through the Signs

A planet expresses itself through the nature of the sign in which it is placed

Each planet has 12 basic manifestations through the signs. In this example Venus, the ruler of emotion, experiences the 12 different options through the different signs.

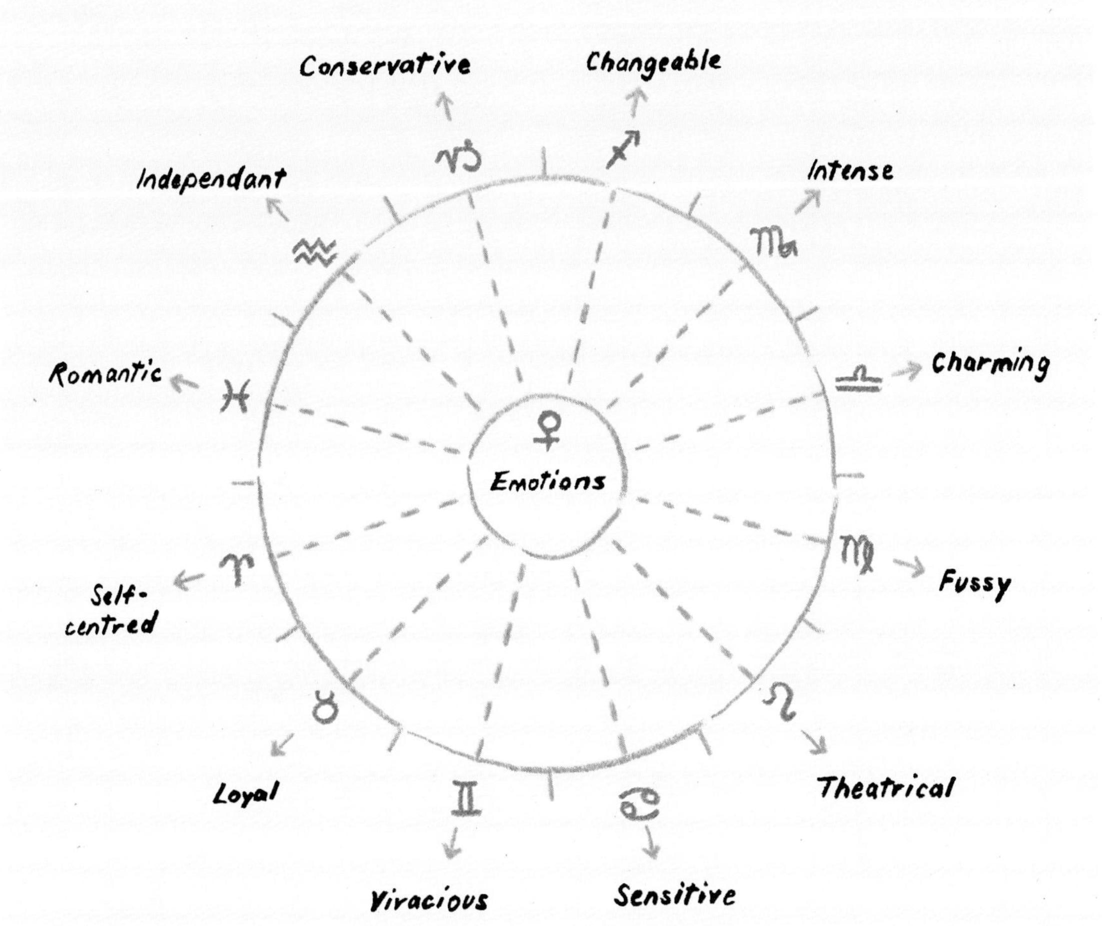

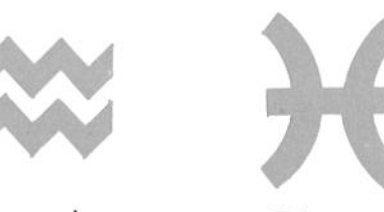

1 : *Sun in Aries*
2 : *Sun in Taurus*
3 : *Sun in Gemini*
4 : *Sun in Cancer*
5 : *Sun in Leo*

THE SUN

The sign which contains the Sun provides the basic key to the personality and life potential. It exposes the individual's major strengths and weaknesses, indicates the lessons to be learnt and skills to be tapped. It may also be equated with the male side of the personality as against the Moon's rulership of the female. There are few specifics to consider regarding the Sun, so the following descriptions are all brief. They are, however, most important.

SUN IN ARIES (Exaltation). These people are assertive and self-interested. They are leaders, initiating new ventures, but may rely on others to follow things through. They can make enemies by ignoring other people's welfare.

SUN IN TAURUS. Sun-Taurus types are essentially conservative, requiring stability. They hang on to the past, preserving what is best and refusing to let go what is worst. They are sensual and creative but unambitious, and slow to recognize an opportunity. Their natural fidelity is matched by their stubborn failure to change.

SUN IN GEMINI. Geminians are essentially intellectuals and require constant mental stimulation. Thinkers, talkers, readers and writers, these people need to be involved in acquiring and communicating knowledge. They can also be involved in travel and it is as natural for them to be cab drivers or postmen as teachers or journalists.

SUN IN CANCER. Sensitive Cancerians are marked by their powerful emotions, but they usually try to conceal these behind a public mask. A valuable clue to interpretation is that the sign containing the Moon (the planet ruling Cancer) gives the nature of the public face adopted by this sign. For example, people with Sun in Cancer but Moon in Aries give an appearance of great self-confidence, while with Moon in Gemini they may give the appearance of cool intellectual observers. Cancerians place great importance on security and do not like taking risks. Domestic and family security is the key to their happiness and, when they feel safe, they are free to express their caring and compassionate maternal qualities to the full. When deprived of security they can become sharp tongued, cynical and bitter.

SUN IN LEO (Dignity). Leos are creative in the broadest sense, and for them all the world's a stage. They are either proud, regal and generous, or vain, egotistical and wasteful. Even if they are unreliable as far as others are concerned, they are completely consistent in their own behaviour; unpunctuality may be a regular habit. They are instinctively faithful but easily distracted by flattery. Their resistance to change can be a major failing.

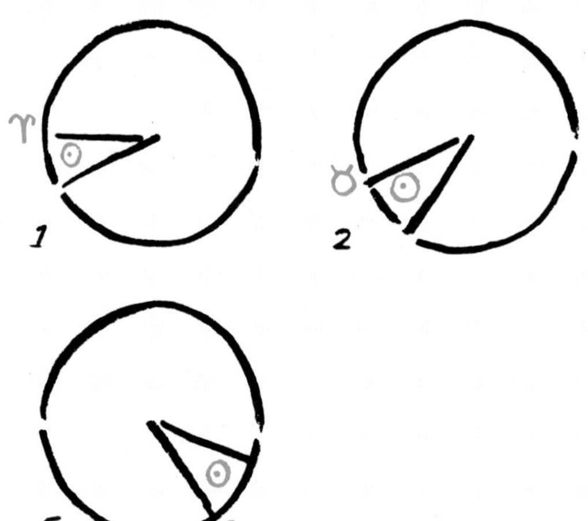

Sometimes they find that after holding the centre stage, the world moves on and leaves them stranded.

SUN IN VIRGO. Idealistic, perfectionist and practical, Virgos can be self-sacrificing, placing their own interests after those of a greater cause. They require a practical purpose in life and insist that this should show concrete results. High standards can make them excessively critical of others; self-criticism all too often lessens their self-confidence. They have organizational skills and an ability to cope with detail.

SUN IN LIBRA (Fall). Librans are dominated by an awareness of imbalance and motivated by the need to remedy it. They cannot tolerate a rough environment or uncouth behaviour, and often become skilled in creating beautiful and restful surroundings. Usually a sense of balance is achieved through relationships, and a need to succeed in these prompts typical pleasant manners and attractive appearance. Librans can be too dependent on other people's support and their approval.

SUN IN SCORPIO. Emotional, intense and perceptive, Sun-Scorpio types are driven by the instincts of the unconscious. At their best they have deep compassion and a powerful healing energy, but when hurt or rejected they can all too easily retreat to a black depression. Scorpios need to learn to accept, handle and express their own deep tempestuous and sometimes obsessive feelings.

SUN IN SAGITTARIUS. These people are adventurers and seekers after truth. Some are intellectuals who set off on philosophical or religious quests. Others seek experience and personal growth through foreign travel. They can help themselves by establishing a sense of inner security. They can inspire others with their enthusiasm, but can be tactless.

SUN IN CAPRICORN. Conservative and practical, Capricorns often lead very materialistic lives, judging people and opportunities by financial considerations, chasing status, prestige and possessions. However, they have very deep emotions which often go unrecognized or unacknowledged. It is worth their while to work at expressing their feelings more directly and openly.

SUN IN AQUARIUS (Detriment). Aquarians aspire to be different. They have a reputation for being progressive, radical and eccentric, and this is sometimes deserved. In a liberal atmosphere they may express their differentness by being authoritarian or conservative. They hate being tied down and treasure their independence. They often seem to be supremely self-confident but can suffer from a low opinion of their own talents. They need to be more at ease with their feelings and should learn to integrate their radical ideas with practical life.

SUN IN PISCES. Sensitive and emotional, Pisceans are imaginative dreamers. Often they prefer the safety of private fantasy to the fuss and bother of real life. They are impractical and avoid problems and conflicts by simply slipping away when these appear. Pisceans are impossible to pin down and hate committing themselves or taking decisions. If they discover a cause or a deep personal interest (perhaps artistic, philosophical, or charitable) they will follow it with unshakable dedication while remaining indifferent to everyday affairs. The symbol of two fishes swimming in opposite directions represents a need to reconcile contrasting possibilities.

1 : *Sun in Virgo*
2 : *Sun in Libra*
3 : *Sun in Scorpio*
4 : *Sun in Sagittarius*
5 : *Sun in Capricorn*
6 : *Sun in Aquarius*
7 : *Sun in Pisces*

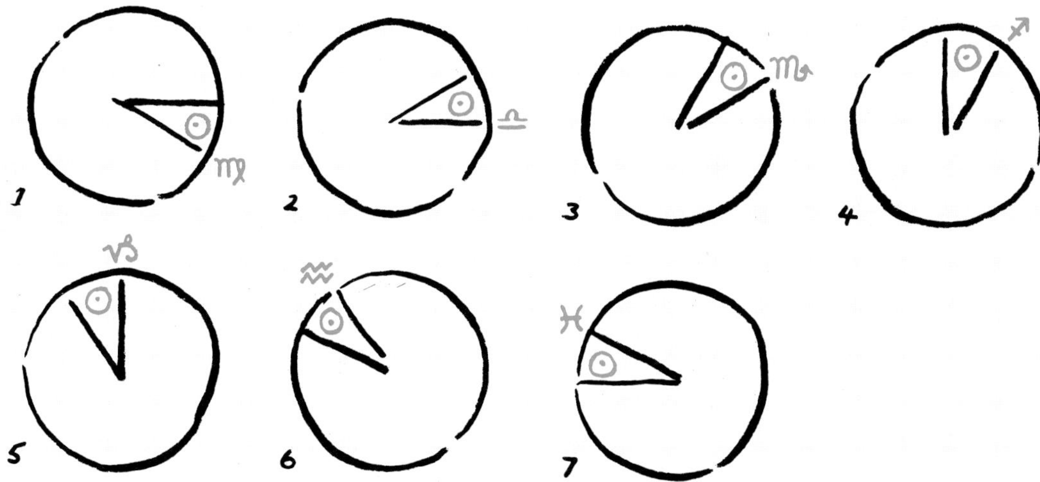

THE MOON

The sign containing the Moon provides clues for the astrologer concerning the person's general emotional state, the female half of the psyche, the mother, attitudes to the mother, maternal instincts, the home and family background and the general public face. There are a great many specific statements that can be made about this rich and varied planet, and the following sample interpretations provide a basic summary.

MOON IN ARIES. Generally assertive and emotionally powerful, these people need to control their domestic environments. They are generous in love but require a lot of affection in return. Women with this position are not prepared to take second place; men are likely to seek women with strong personalities. The result of these demands may be argument or friction.

MOON IN TAURUS (Exaltation). The female archetype embodied here is fertile, maternal and sexual, and these people can make excellent mothers. Overemphasized, these characteristics can be smothering. These people need domestic security and are practical and competent in running a home.

MOON IN GEMINI. These people rationalize all their emotional experience. As a result they can lose touch with their real feelings. Their nervous and animated dispositions can be reflected in changeable home conditions. Women with this position are likely to strive for intellectual achievement; men appreciate women with lively minds.

MOON IN CANCER (Dignity). Highly emotional, these people give a lot of affection, but must feel loved in return if they are to be happy and secure. A stable home life is extremely important as a safe haven for relaxation and privacy. This is one of the archetypal mother images and is strongly expressed in home-making and domestic skills. Men with this position can be very maternal, and may become strongly attached to a maternal woman.

MOON IN LEO. Self-expressive and extroverted, these people are social performers. Even their apparent emotional honesty can be part of the performance. Domestic life is often lively as the home becomes a stage. Women with this position are warm hearted, generous and unable to accept a subordinate place. Men may idealize strong and ambitious women, placing them on a pedestal.

MOON IN VIRGO. One of the classic images of the Moon in Virgo is that of the Virgin Mary, the embodiment of purity. Another is of Martha who faithfully waited on Christ. These people relish order and cleanliness, and abhor crude and uncouth behaviour. Dom-

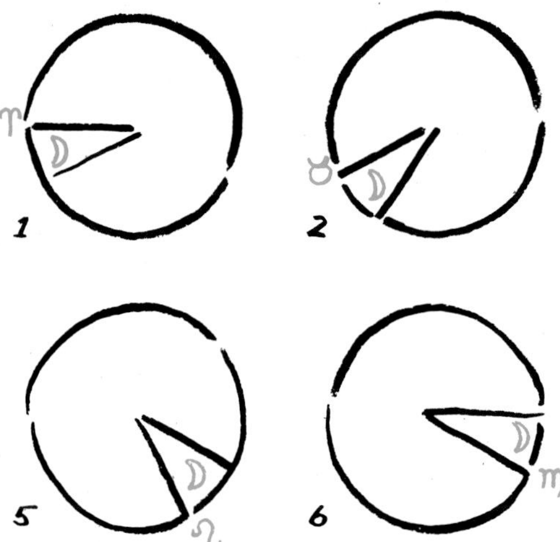

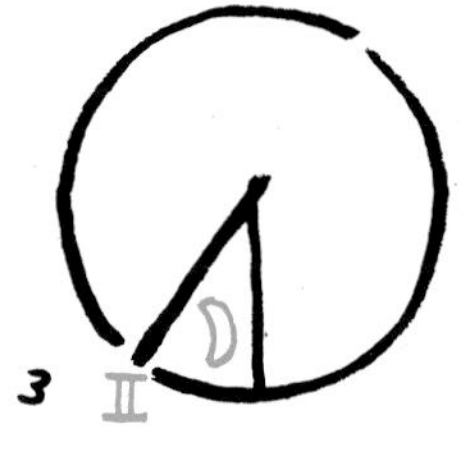

1 : *Moon in Aries*
2 : *Moon in Taurus*
3 : *Moon in Gemini*
4 : *Moon in Cancer*
5 : *Moon in Leo*
6 : *Moon in Virgo*

estic order is one of their priorities. They pick their friends carefully and are usually shy.

MOON IN LIBRA. These people need emotional calm. They cannot bear hostility and argument. They preserve the peace in relationships and at home through their diplomatic powers and efforts to create a pleasant environment. Their avoidance of confrontation can lead them to ignore their own feelings, especially their anger.

MOON IN SCORPIO (Fall). Secretive and intensely emotional, these people often exude an air of mystery. They need stable and secure conditions, which paradoxically are often affected by sudden disruption and confrontations. They are reserved socially, but can be passionate in close relationships.

MOON IN SAGITTARIUS. These people dislike constraints upon their behaviour and resist emotional and domestic ties. They need to be given as much freedom as possible. They often leave home to settle abroad. Men with this position are usually attracted to independent spirited women.

MOON IN CAPRICORN. (Detriment). Moon in Capricorn reveals conservatism in emotional and domestic matters. These people do not find it easy to show their feelings, and often form relationships for financial reasons, status or security. They apply their practical skills to maintaining their homes.

MOON IN AQUARIUS. Emotional independence is the key to this position. These people react very badly if they think they are being tied down emotionally or domestically. They resent obligations and responsibilities, and home conditions may be unusual and unsettled. The Moon in Aquarius is particularly connected to the women's liberation movement, although it is also connected to the traditional ways in which women assert themselves.

MOON IN PISCES. For these sensitive and shy people the home can provide a refuge from the hard knocks of the real world. They are compassionate and hospitable, but should try to develop a thicker skin without losing their natural kindness. Home life can be disorganized and relationships clouded by unrealistic desires. Men with this position have strong feminine natures.

MERCURY

Mercury in the various signs reveals the different ways in which people's minds work, their intellectual interests and aptitudes, and how they communicate.

MERCURY IN ARIES. Very self-willed and confident, these people know what they want. In arguments they are combative and convinced they are right. They are fast thinkers

Sun *Moon* *Mercury* *Venus* *Earth* *Mars* *Jupiter* *Saturn* *Uranus* *Neptune* *Pluto*

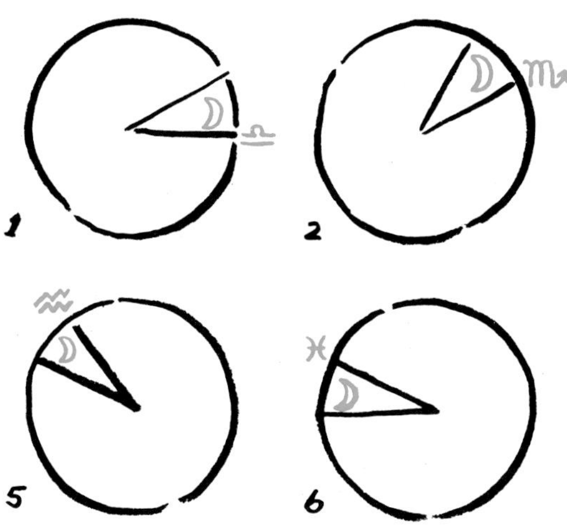
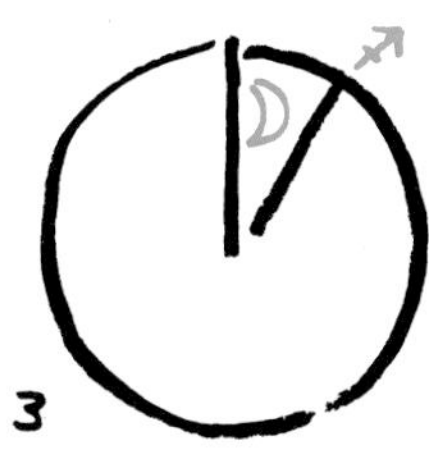
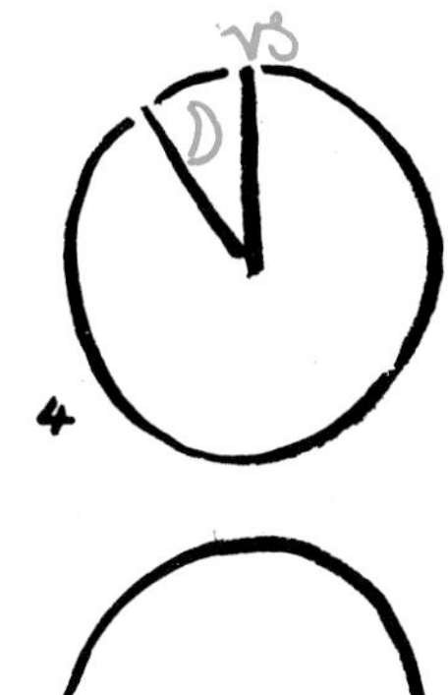
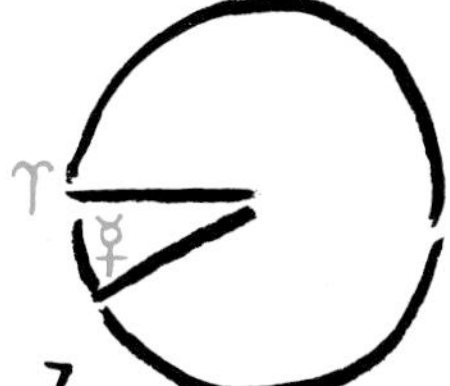

1 : *Moon in Libra*
2 : *Moon in Scorpio*
3 : *Moon in Sagittarius*
4 : *Moon in Capricorn*
5 : *Moon in Aquarius*
6 : *Moon in Pisces*
7 : *Mercury in Aries*

and have sharp tongues, and can be intellectually arrogant.

MERCURY IN TAURUS. Mental processes are turned to practical problems and abstract thought is usually considered a waste of time. Thought processes may be slow and attitudes conservative.

MERCURY IN GEMINI (Dignity). The collection and communication of knowledge is a major priority. These people have clear and logical minds and need mental stimulation. They love debate but their opinions are usually changeable. Physical exercise is necessary to work off nervous tension.

MERCURY IN CANCER. These people have retentive memories. Their thoughts are dominated by their feelings; their attitudes are naturally compassionate and poetic, and attempts to be scientific or objective will be superficial.

MERCURY IN LEO. With a high opinion of their own intellectual powers and plenty of mental energy, these people are quick to form opinions and often do not bother with facts. They like performing and they may be attracted to the theatre.

MERCURY IN VIRGO (Dignity and Exaltation). Pedantic, critical and analytical, these people have no time for frivolous ideas. The less interesting face of this position is to be found in the bureaucrat, the lover of intellectual order; the more interesting in those who use their minds for the practical good of the world.

MERCURY IN LIBRA. These people are born strategists, and use their powers of careful and balanced thought to reconcile opposing factions and forces. Their awareness of contrasting possibilities enables them to increase their choices in life, but can lead to indecision.

MERCURY IN SCORPIO. These people do not have ideas, they have instincts and beliefs, and often follow these with great dedication. They are deeply interested in all things dark, hidden or mysterious, including religion and political conspiracies, and in all forms of research.

MERCURY IN SAGITTARIUS (Detriment). These people are philosophers: ideas and opinions are more important to them than facts. They may be careless over detail, but often have an instinctive idea of the truth. They may develop a particular interest in foreign cultures and religion. They are often tactless.

MERCURY IN CAPRICORN. Practically minded and with down to earth interests, this is a classic position for engineers or mathematicians as well as people in business. The acquisition of wealth and status is often important.

MERCURY IN AQUARIUS. Independent minded, these people do not like being told what to think. They need the freedom to find their own intellectual interests and they frequently hold radical views. They like issues to be clear cut.

MERCURY IN PISCES (Detriment and Fall). Poetic and imaginative, these people have artistic minds and may have difficulty coping with practical and scientific studies. This is the most deceptive and gullible position for Mercury. Confusion can be avoided if attention is paid to detail.

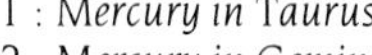

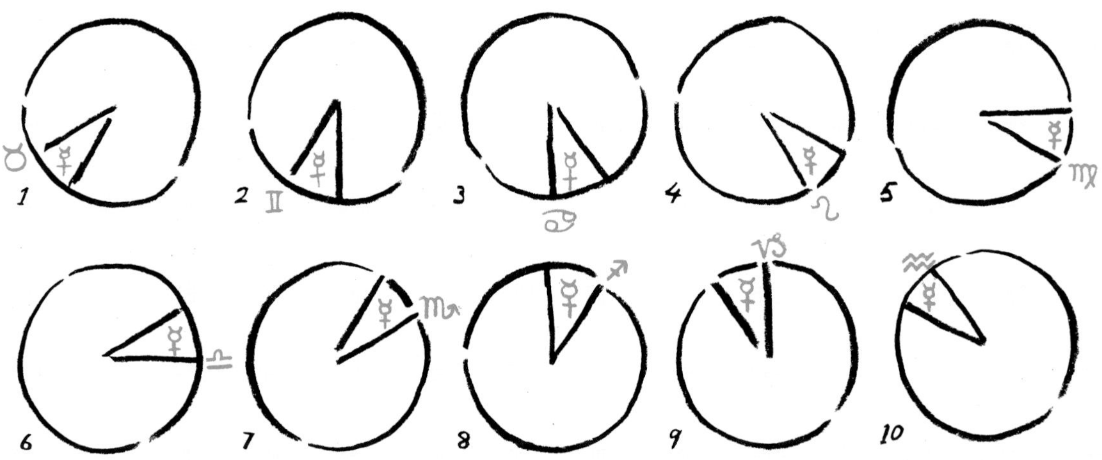

1 : *Mercury in Taurus*
2 : *Mercury in Gemini*
3 : *Mercury in Cancer*
4 : *Mercury in Leo*
5 : *Mercury in Virgo*
6 : *Mercury in Libra*
7 : *Mercury in Scorpio*
8 : *Mercury in Sagittarius*
9 : *Mercury in Capricorn*
10: *Mercury in Aquarius*

VENUS

The position of Venus in the signs provides clues concerning the individual's female nature, relationships, marriage and attitudes to pleasure and the arts.

VENUS IN ARIES (Detriment). These people have a pressing need for attention and affection. They can be passionate lovers, but may also be selfish. They are quick to assert their interests and are often argumentative. Men with this position will be attracted to bold, assertive women.

VENUS IN TAURUS (Dignity). Physical and emotional love are united by Venus in Taurus. These people are instinctively faithful, but can be too attracted to sensual experience to remain monogamous. Skill in the arts and crafts is likely.

VENUS IN GEMINI. These people distance themselves from emotional contacts by continually analysing their feelings. They may talk about these without actually facing the real issues. They find it easy to drift in and out of relationships.

VENUS IN CANCER. These people need emotional security. They are caring and sympathetic in emotional relationships, but can be possessive and need to be able to let go when a partnership has run its course. They are often reserved socially.

VENUS IN LEO. Colourful and vivacious, these people are drawn to the social whirl and relationships become a performance. Their egotism can be attractive, but relationships may run into difficulty if they ignore other people's feelings.

VENUS IN VIRGO (Fall). These people are often shy socially. They make few close friends because most people do not match up to their high standards. Their criticism of other people can be unjustified and result from their own lack of self-confidence. They should learn to trust their own feelings.

VENUS IN LIBRA (Dignity). Appearances are important and these people rely on making a good impression through pleasant behaviour and attractive clothes. They need to be liked and fear arguments and disagreements. Dependence on the latest fashions can result from a lack of emotional confidence. Their expectations of relationships can be too high.

VENUS IN SCORPIO (Detriment). The female archetype associated with this position is the dark temptress, a potent image throughout the ages. These people are passionate lovers, but sometimes make the mistake of falling in love with the wrong people. Love rejected can

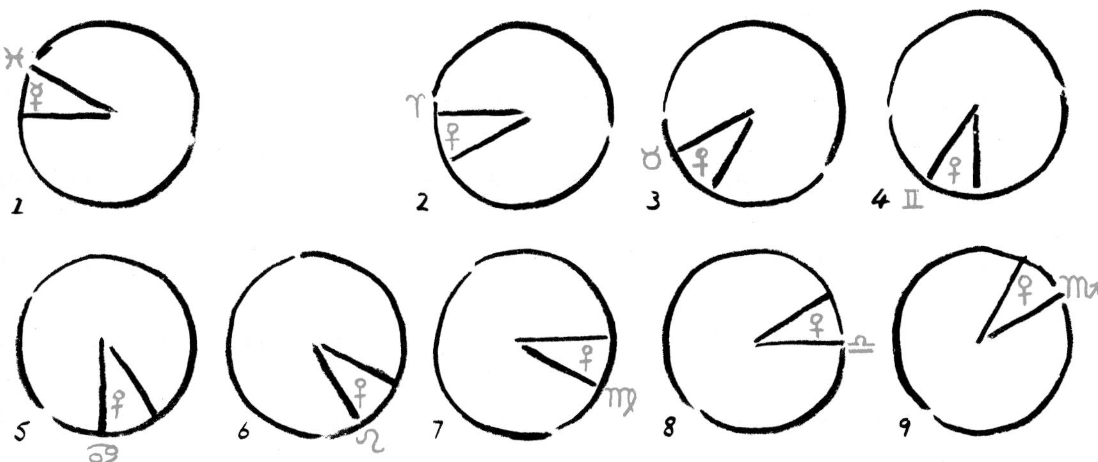

1 : *Mercury in Pisces*
2 : *Venus in Aries*
3 : *Venus in Taurus*
4 : *Venus in Gemini*
5 : *Venus in Cancer*
6 : *Venus in Leo*
7 : *Venus in Virgo*
8 : *Venus in Libra*
9 : *Venus in Scorpio*

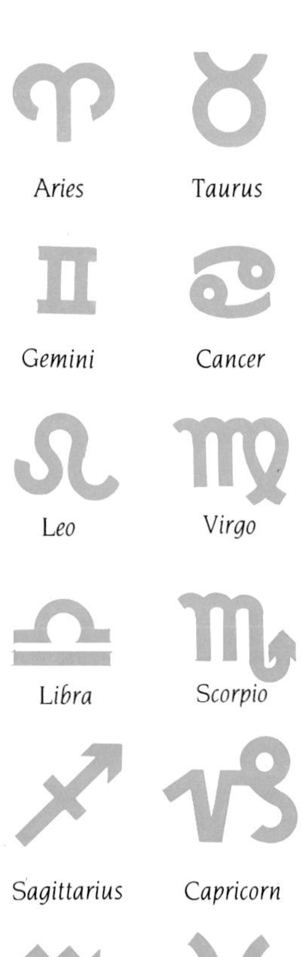

1 : Venus in Sagittarius
2 : Venus in Capricorn
3 : Venus in Aquarius
4 : Venus in Pisces
5 : Mars in Aries
6 : Mars in Taurus
7 : Mars in Gemini
8 : Mars in Cancer
9 : Mars in Leo

lead to bitterness and jealousy. They are often self-sacrificing, but also possessive and frequently relish emotional confrontation.

VENUS IN SAGITTARIUS. These people need emotional freedom. If successful relationships are to be formed they must be given the freedom to escape whenever they want to. They cannot tolerate emotional restriction.

VENUS IN CAPRICORN. Common sense is brought to bear on relationships, and personal feelings are pushed to one side. These people value tradition and seek status and security from emotional partnerships.

VENUS IN AQUARIUS. These people require interest, change and stimulation in their relationships. They resist social conventions and do not like to be tied down or forced into a role. The role they choose is often that of the rebel which can be used to bring partnerships to an end. They tend to have unrealistic intellectual expectations of relationships and can lose touch with their true feelings.

VENUS IN PISCES (Exaltation). The female image associated with Pisces is that of the ethereal pre-Raphaelite maiden. This is as unrealistic as the rest of this sign's romantic dreams. These people find all relationships a compromise between their fantasies and the reality of human life. They want to be self-sacrificing but are so concerned with their own feelings that they lose touch with their partners.

MARS

Mars in the signs shows the individual's general energy level, the way practical problems are handled, attitudes to men and expression of the male psyche.

MARS IN ARIES (Dignity). Energetic and assertive, these people are leaders in their field. They are impulsive, impatient and not good at coping with opposition. They exacerbate practical problems by carelessness.

MARS IN TAURUS (Detriment). Practical, capable and consistent, these people often get things done in the most sensible way. They are obstinate, however, and not good at adapting to new circumstances.

MARS IN GEMINI. These people often have sharp minds which they can apply to practical problems. They may take on too many tasks at the same time, and by spreading themselves too thinly may delay success.

MARS IN CANCER (Fall). Actions are dominated by emotional commitment and imagination rather than by practical considerations. They are sometimes prone to emotional outbursts.

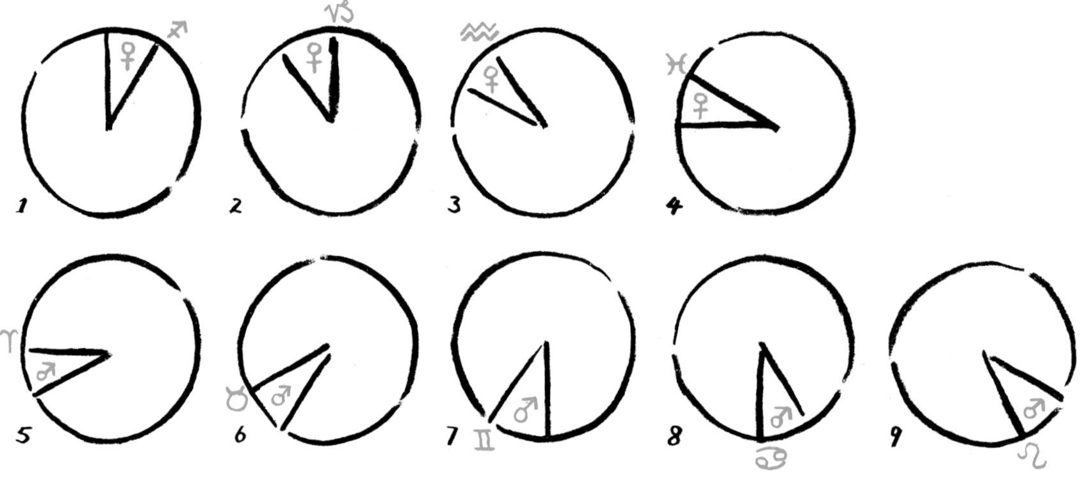

MARS IN LEO. Theatrical and dramatic, these people brook no opposition to their grand schemes. Often their actions are impressive and creative, but sometimes they are impractical and lack substance.

MARS IN VIRGO. This is an excellent combination for those involved in crafts or any precise practical activity. They have a flair for detail, thrive on routine, but lack imagination.

MARS IN LIBRA (Detriment). Energy is best used to restore harmony and balance, perhaps by developing artistic skills, or by reconciling people in conflict. Their awareness of opposing choices can lead to indecision or to an interesting range of experiences and skills in strategy.

MARS IN SCORPIO (Dignity). These people are invariably drawn to enigmatic and mysterious activities and bring emotional commitment to whatever they do. Their motivations are so strong that it is usually impossible to deflect them from a chosen course of action.

MARS IN SAGITTARIUS. It can take a lifetime for these people to achieve their far-flung ambitions. They set their sights on distant heights and leave others to sort out the details. They often become travellers.

MARS IN CAPRICORN (Exaltation). These people have a sound practical approach which makes them well fitted to be engineers and mechanics. They are best suited to living and working at a practical level.

MARS IN AQUARIUS. These people seek radical solutions to old problems. Too often these are fine in theory but chaotic in practice. They are idealistic but impractical.

MARS IN PISCES. This is the most impractical position for Mars. Although intuition and imagination helps these people to find the most attractive and, sometimes, the most sensible way of doing things, they usually lack the necessary skills.

JUPITER

Jupiter in each sign gives clues about the way people try to expand and grow. It takes an average of one year to pass through any one sign of the zodiac. Everybody born in a given 12-month period will have Jupiter in the same sign, and it gives false emphasis in a birth chart if too much importance is given to the sign containing Jupiter. Psychologically this planet should be seen as a general background influence, contributing to other tendencies in the chart.

JUPITER IN THE FIRE SIGNS. This reveals a personality with large-scale and personal ambitions, perhaps reaching the top of a career, excelling in a particular skill or merely striving to be the centre of attention. In Aries these tendencies may be most self-interested and their nature will be revealed by the other tendencies in the chart. In Leo ambitions are likely to be grandiose and accomplished with optimism and theatrical flair. In Sagittarius (Dignity) ambitions are more likely to be concerned with intellectual improvement or religious experience, and foreign travel.

JUPITER IN THE EARTH SIGNS. These people strive for self-development through practical work in order to achieve material results. In Virgo (Detriment) the purpose is likely to be idealistic but within an orderly structure; in Capricorn (Fall) material wealth may be a priority. Jupiter in Taurus may indicate a love of luxury and sensual experience.

1 : Mars in Virgo
2 : Mars in Libra
3 : Mars in Scorpio
4 : Mars in Sagittarius
5 : Mars in Capricorn
6 : Mars in Aquarius
7 : Mars in Pisces

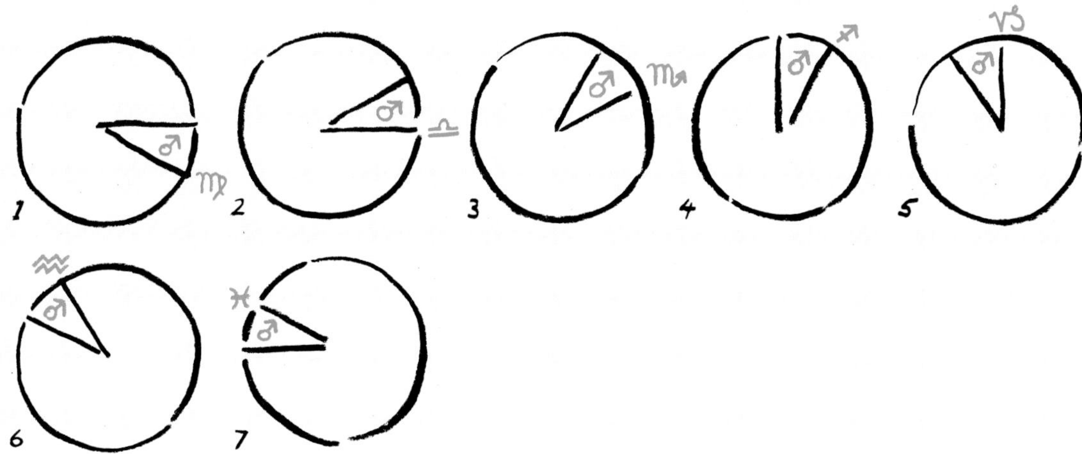

JUPITER IN THE AIR SIGNS. In the air signs Jupiter stresses personal growth through analysis and the use of the intellect. Some people may look inward and analyse themselves, examining their own motives, others may concentrate on sharing ideas. In Gemini (Detriment) the collection and communication of facts may be an end in itself. In Libra Jupiter may emphasize the use of knowledge for promoting peace and harmony, but requires a partnership to function properly. In Aquarius the emphasis may be on the creation and promotion of new ideas.

JUPITER IN THE WATER SIGNS. Jupiter in the water signs craves emotion. These people need love. While they aspire to the heights of romantic ecstasy, they can also be self-sacrificing and can wallow in self-pity and emotion. In Cancer (Exaltation) Jupiter emphasizes the virtues of helping other people through compassion, in Scorpio through healing and in Pisces (Dignity) through prayer and good intentions. Jupiter in Cancer may, on the other hand, lead to indulgence in domestic luxury, in Scorpio it may lead to licence in sex and other Scorpionic mysteries, and in Pisces there may be indulgence in escapist fantasies, dreams, religion or drugs.

SATURN

Saturn rules the principle of limitation. It shows the way in which people control themselves and are inhibited by their environment.

Saturn takes about 29½ years to travel around the zodiac, spending almost two and a half years in each sign. Its generational influence is even more pronounced than Jupiter's, and its meaning by sign has a far more general psychological influence in a horoscope than by house and aspect.

SATURN IN THE FIRE SIGNS. In the fire signs Saturn inhibits the overall energy level, restricts ambitions and reduces self-confidence. These people may constantly anticipate failure, avoid risks and reject opportunity, but the fear of failure can lead to concentrated hard work. Conservatism may influence creativity, artistic values and love affairs when Saturn is in Leo (Detriment); philosophy, beliefs and attitudes to foreign cultures when it is in Sagittarius; or attitudes to authority when it is in Aries (Fall).

SATURN IN THE EARTH SIGNS. These people may experience difficulties and challenges in physical and practical affairs. There

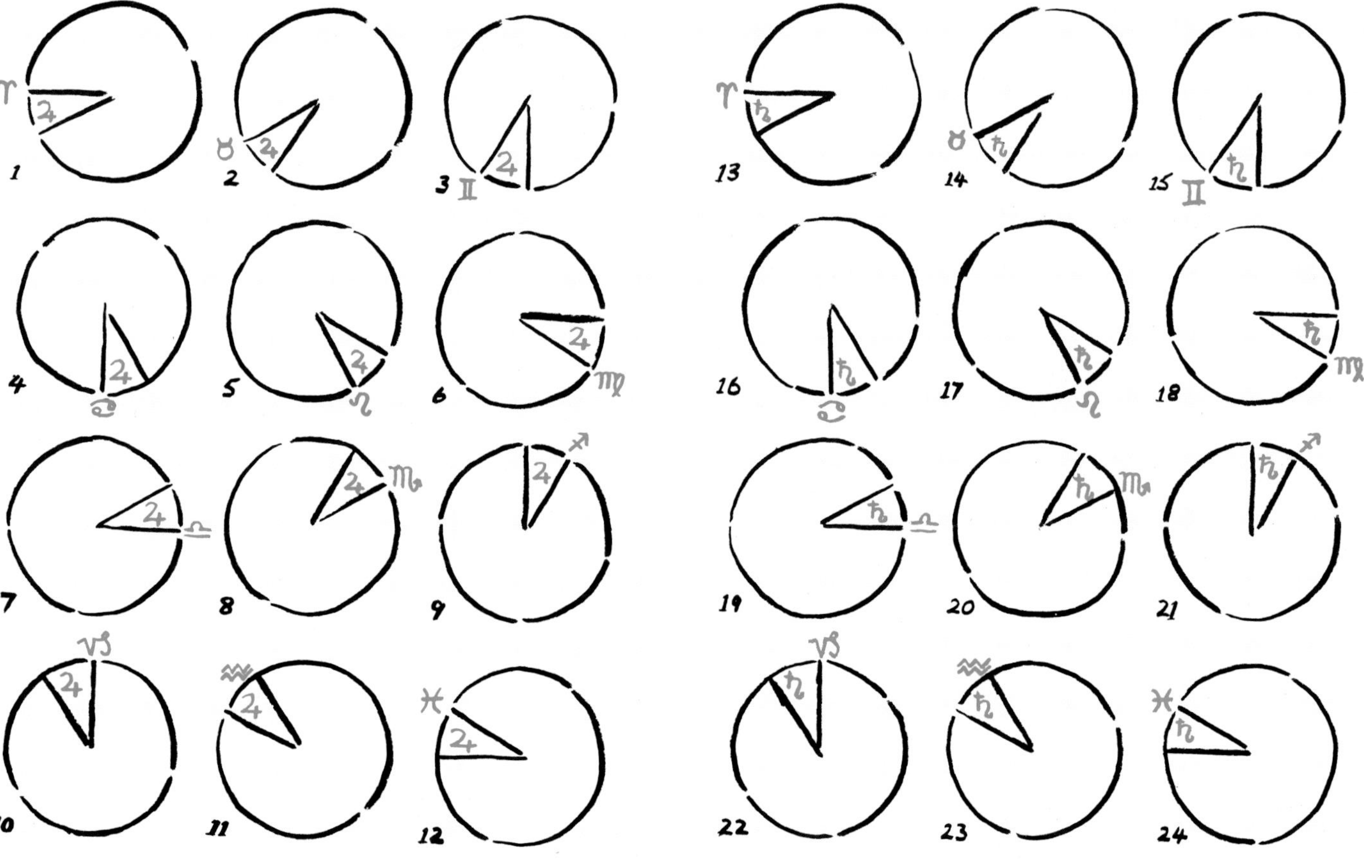

1 : *Jupiter in Aries*
2 : *Jupiter in Taurus*
3 : *Jupiter in Gemini*
4 : *Jupiter in Cancer*
5 : *Jupiter in Leo*
6 : *Jupiter in Virgo*
7 : *Jupiter in Libra*
8 : *Jupiter in Scorpio*
9 : *Jupiter in Sagittarius*
10 : *Jupiter in Capricorn*
11 : *Jupiter in Aquarius*
12 : *Jupiter in Pisces*
13 : *Saturn in Aries*
14 : *Saturn in Taurus*
15 : *Saturn in Gemini*
16 : *Saturn in Cancer*
17 : *Saturn in Leo*
18 : *Saturn in Virgo*
19 : *Saturn in Libra*
20 : *Saturn in Scorpio*
21 : *Saturn in Sagittarius*
22 : *Saturn in Capricorn*
23 : *Saturn in Aquarius*
24 : *Saturn in Pisces*

may be delays or obstacles to work, or financial difficulties. Saturn in Virgo is likely to weaken the self-confidence of this sign, but may increase its capacity for hard work. Saturn in its own sign of Capricorn (Dignity) brings out the individual's materialism and lack of emotion. In Taurus Saturn leads to increased conservatism and stubborness.

SATURN IN THE AIR SIGNS. Saturn in the air signs introduces either mental discipline or intellectual inhibition. There is likely to be conservatism in ideas and attitudes. In Gemini inability to communicate effectively may be balanced by a determined reliance on the facts. In Libra (Exaltation) there may be an emphasis upon stability in partnerships, and a balance of ideas. In Aquarius (Dignity), ideas and opinions tend to be authoritarian.

SATURN IN THE WATER SIGNS. Emotional inhibition is likely to result from Saturn placed in the water signs. There will certainly be an emphasis on emotional self-control. In Cancer (Detriment) this inclines towards a stable home, although the difficulties this sign has in expressing its feelings will be strengthened. In Scorpio emotions may become more obsessive but more easily hurt, while Pisces may be more vulnerable than usual.

CHIRON, URANUS, NEPTUNE AND PLUTO

Chiron takes between 49 and 51 years to complete one cycle of the zodiac. Uranus takes almost 84 years, Neptune almost 164 years and Pluto just over 245 years. Uranus spends about seven years in each sign, Neptune almost 14 years and Pluto an average of 21 years. Their meaning by sign in a birth chart is, therefore, so general as to provide only vague background information. To the psychological characteristics of the signs Uranus brings an unusual quality, Neptune a delicate sensitivity and inspiration and Pluto determination and power.

Psychologically these planets affect the character of generations, and their role in this respect will be discussed in Chapter 17 which deals with mundane and political astrology.

THE NODES

The importance attached to the nodes in the signs varies considerably. They are used to give general psychological interpretations.

The nodes should be taken together as a pair, the south node revealing the qualities being left behind, the north node those qualities being developed. There is an element of fate in the nodes due to their connection with the vast issues of reincarnation and karma (the law of cosmic cause and effect). Astrology argues that individuals can alter their fate by their actions, and the nodes show how this may be done. Hence the qualities of the south node may be seen as those which *should* be left behind while whose of the north node are those which *should* be developed.

NORTH NODE IN ARIES, SOUTH NODE IN LIBRA. These people should be more assertive and not rely on others too much.

NORTH NODE IN TAURUS, SOUTH NODE IN SCORPIO. These people should be more practical and less emotional.

NORTH NODE IN GEMINI, SOUTH NODE IN SAGITTARIUS. These people should be more clear headed, less idealistic.

NORTH NODE IN CANCER, SOUTH NODE IN CAPRICORN. These people should be more caring and compassionate, and less materialistic.

NORTH NODE IN LEO, SOUTH NODE IN AQUARIUS. These people should develop their personal authority and be less anarchic.

NORTH NODE IN VIRGO, SOUTH NODE IN PISCES. These people should be more down to earth, less dreamy and disorganized.

NORTH NODE IN LIBRA, SOUTH NODE IN ARIES. These people should be more considerate to others and less self-interested.

NORTH NODE IN SCORPIO, SOUTH NODE IN TAURUS. These people should give rein to their feelings and be less concerned with practical issues.

NORTH NODE IN SAGITTARIUS, SOUTH NODE IN GEMINI. These people should pay less attention to detail and develop a broader vision.

NORTH NODE IN CAPRICORN, SOUTH NODE IN CANCER. These people should be more practical and less sentimental.

NORTH NODE IN AQUARIUS, SOUTH NODE IN LEO. These people should be more ready to share and less egotistical.

NORTH NODE IN PISCES, SOUTH NODE IN VIRGO. These people should develop their sensitivity and emotions, and be less critical of themselves and others.

Sun

Moon

Mercury

Venus

Earth

Mars

Jupiter

Saturn

Uranus

Neptune

Pluto

CHAPTER 5 THE TWELVE HOUSES

Interpretation of the signs and planets enables the astrologer to describe character in general psychological terms, and to point to likely events in a person's life. However, until the houses are added to the interpretation, it remains necessarily vague. The 12 houses rule specific areas of life and they enable the astrologer to pinpoint the activities in which the potential of the signs and planets will be expressed.

Each house represents a basic principle, but has a range of manifestations, sometimes sharply different from one another. A prime example of this is the eighth house which can lead people either to a deep involvement in the occult, or a career in business, among other possibilities. The astrologer should be aware of these contrasts and try to arrive at the best interpretation, relying on astrological expertise and common sense.

The technical basis of the houses lies in the rotation of the ecliptic around the Earth (the apparent path around the Earth of the Sun on its annual cycle). The ecliptic is divided into 12 sections known as houses, connected in meaning to the 12 signs but, whereas the signs appear to rotate around the Earth once in every 24 hours, the position of the houses is effectively fixed. During a 24-hour period every possible combination of sign position relative to the houses occurs, and this greatly increases the range of astrological interpretation.

The Four Angles

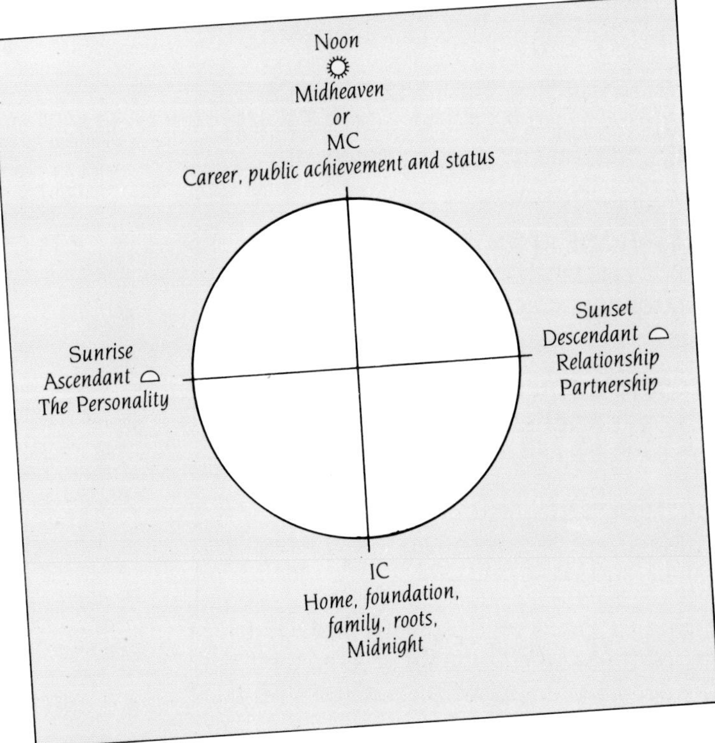

THE FOUR ANGLES

The framework upon which the house divisions are based are the four 'angles'. The **Ascendant** is the degree of the ecliptic which is rising over the eastern horizon. The **Descendant** is the exact opposite of the Ascendant, the degree of the ecliptic setting over the western horizon. The **Midheaven** is the degree of the zodiac which is at the highest point above the horizon, or culmination. The Latin translation of Midheaven is Medium Coeli (MC). **Imum Coeli** (IC) is the point directly opposite MC.

In the birth chart the Ascendant is as important as the Sun in determining the individual's personality and potential. The sign containing the Ascendant is known as the rising sign.

. The Descendant reveals the individual's attitude to partnerships, and what he or she seeks in a relationship.

The MC rules the need for public recognition, status in community and society, and the career.

The IC governs the home, the family background and the need for psychological roots and stability.

These **four angles** correspond to the meanings for the first house (the Ascendant), the fourth house (the IC), the seventh house (the Descendant) and the tenth house (the MC). These four houses, with their corresponding angles, have completely distinct meanings but may, nevertheless, be understood as part of a single process of human experience. The Ascendant symbolizes birth and infancy, the IC represents childhood and the discovery of an individual identity, the Descendant reveals the formation of adult relationships and the MC represents the culmination of public achievements.

The intermediate eight houses may be understood in the same manner, each having a distinct meaning but also forming part of a process of development through the horoscope, progressing from birth in the first house to dissolution in the twelfth. The beginner must learn the separate meanings of the houses, but an understanding of the process comes with experience.

THE HOUSES AND THE ELEMENTS

Strictly speaking the houses do not correspond directly to the elements, as these refer

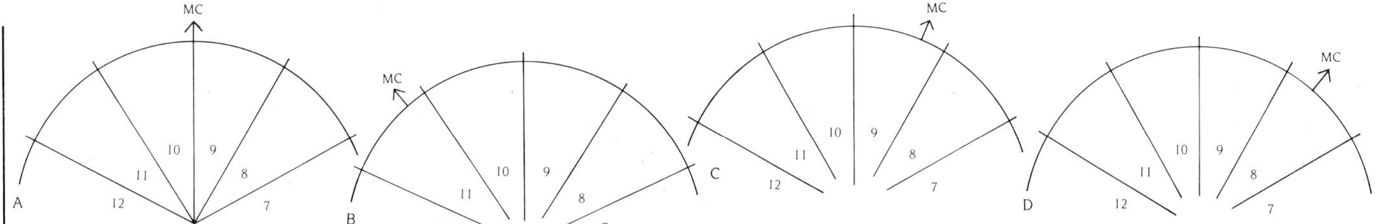

only to the signs. However, as the principles of the signs and houses overlap, it is possible to talk of the houses as being fiery (first, fifth and ninth), airy (third, seventh and eleventh), earthy (second, sixth and tenth) and watery (fourth, eighth and twelfth).

The difference between the two is that houses rule areas of life, whereas signs rule skills and talents. Therefore, when there are planets in the houses of an element, but not in the signs of that element, and vice versa, this opens up new possibilities for interpretation. For example, an individual may have planets in the water houses, but not in the water signs. This individual may be drawn to emotional experiences through the water houses, but lack the emotional capacity (provided by the water signs) needed to deal with them. In contrast, an individual may have planets in the practical earth signs but not in the earth houses. This individual may have plenty of practical energy (provided by the earth signs) but lack sufficient outlets to express this through the earth houses.

The same principle in interpretation may be applied to the other combinations of houses and signs, and can yield rich conclusions for the astrologer.

THE DIFFERENT HOUSE SYSTEMS

There is no astronomically perfect way of calculating the houses. Over the years astrologers have tried to devise ways of overcoming the weaknesses built into certain systems. The oldest system, dating back some two thousand years, is the Equal House system in which the Ascendant is always the cusp (beginning) of the first house, and the Descendant is always the cusp of the seventh house. The rest of the ecliptic is divided into 12 equal segments. The weakness of this system is that the MC and IC do not always fall in the same place as their equivalent house cusps (the tenth and the fourth).

All the other common systems place all four angles on their equivalent house cusps, and are known as the Quadrant systems. However, the mathematical and astronomical rationale of each one is different, and astrologers disagree as to which is the most appropriate. The Placidus, Topocentric and Koch houses are probably the most commonly used, although some astrologers prefer the Porphyry, Regiomontanus or Campanus systems.

Different arguments are put forward in support of particular house systems, and it is sometimes claimed that each system has a slightly different meaning. This is a genuine problem, for planets which fall in one house under one system may fall in another under a second. Each astrologer must pick the system and techniques which enable him or her to arrive at the most satisfactory interpretation. In this book the Equal House system is mainly used but for some charts the Placidus system is indicated.

A. Quadrant System

B. Continental System

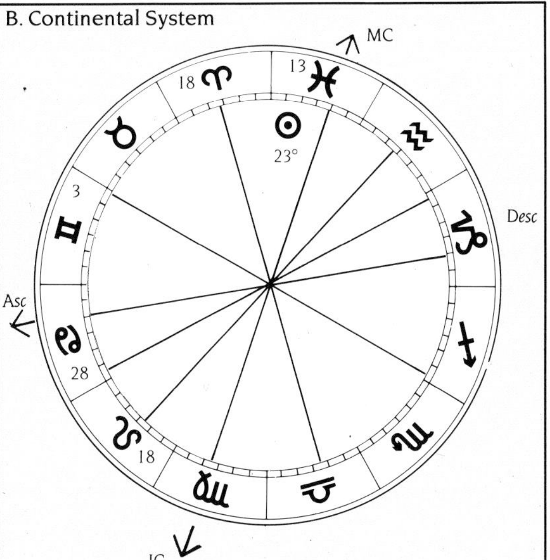

The MC in Equal House and Quadrant Systems.
In all quadrant house systems, including Placidus, Campanus, Regiomontanus, Koch and Topocentric, the Midheaven (MC) and the tenth house cusp always occupy exactly the same degree (Fig. A).
In the Equal House system the MC can fall in the eleventh, ninth, or even the eighth house (Figs. B, C, D).
In the first part of this book only the Equal House system is used, but in later chapters some horoscopes will be interpreted using other systems.

Placidus Houses.
The Placidus system is the most common system of quadrant house division in general use. Placidus houses may be drawn out in one of two styles. The more traditional is the simple system shown in Fig. A which, like the type of house division itself, is known as the quadrant style. Another popular option is the continental style Fig. B.
In the continental system the planets are drawn on to the chart in exactly the same way as in the Equal House system, each planet being marked on its exact degree. The quadrant style places the planets in their houses but only approximately according to sign position, and the sign containing the planet is always written alongside to avoid confusion.
Intercepted Signs. If a sign does not occupy any house cusps then it is intercepted. A planet in an intercepted sign can be weakened – if the house cusp is the anchor which holds the principle of a sign to real life circumstances, then in the absence of such a connection the sign, and the planets it contains, is cut adrift. In psychological terms this is a subtle interpretation which need not concern beginners.
In this example Taurus and Scorpio are intercepted signs and the Moon is intercepted in Scorpio.

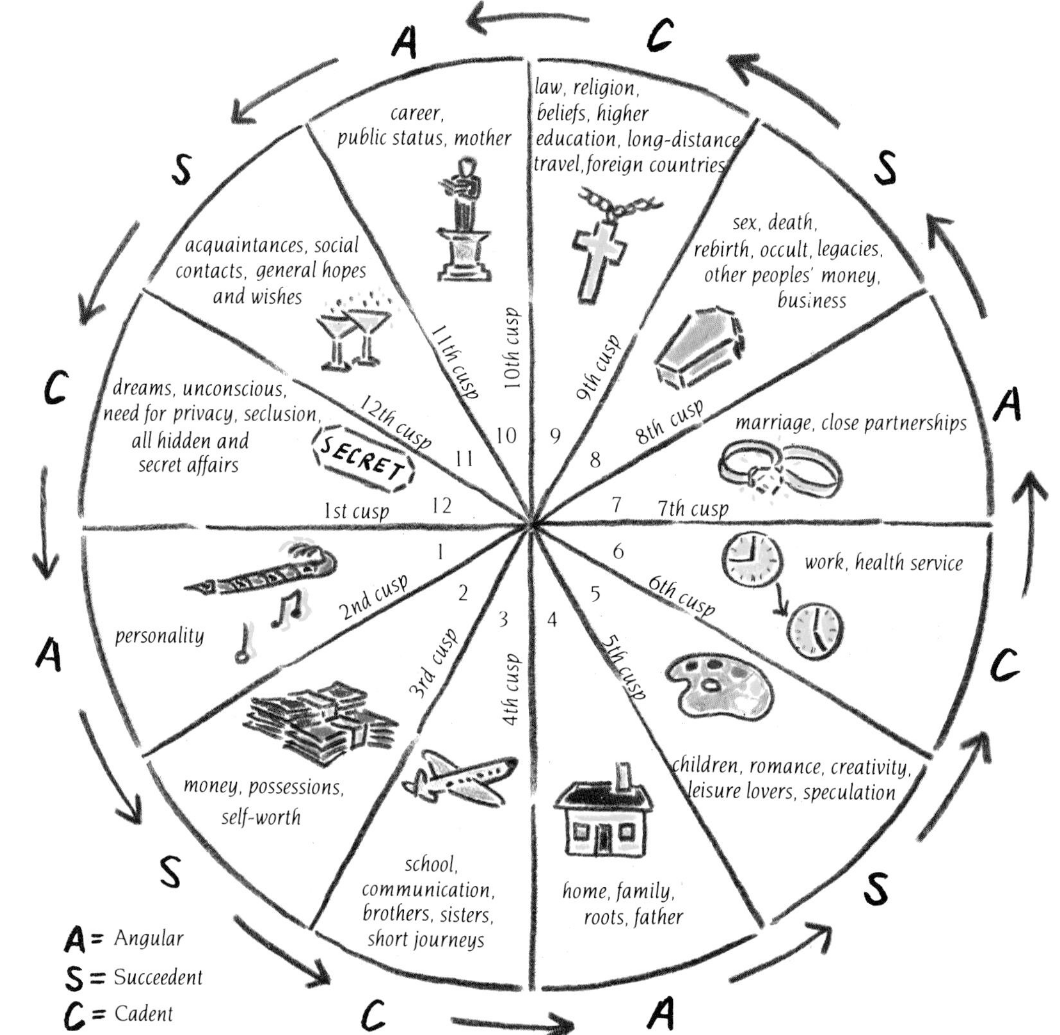

THE CLASSIFICATION OF THE HOUSES

Each house corresponds in meaning to one of the signs of the zodiac, as will be seen below. Each house is classified as Angular, Succedent or Cadent, corresponding to the Cardinal, Fixed and Mutable signs. Angular houses bring the initiation of new ideas, plans and projects. Succedent houses bring the stability necessary for their implementation. Cadent houses bring the completion of the process ready for a new beginning. Planets are more assertive in the Angular houses, most stable in the Succedent houses and unstable in the Cadent houses.

THE HOUSES AS PAIRS

Like the signs the houses may be grouped in pairs of opposites, each of which complements the other. Each house is in a sense incomplete without its opposite.

The first house shows personality and personal interests, while the seventh house indicates the ability and desire to share these and learn from others.

The second house represents the principle of 'holding on', building stability, while the eighth house represents 'letting go', taking risks and allowing change.

The third house rules the acquisition of facts and information, while the ninth house brings the wisdom which enables that information to be properly used.

The fourth house rules the building of personal foundations, while the tenth house rules the building of public foundations.

The fifth house rules personal creativity, while the eleventh house rules public cooperation and awareness.

The sixth house rules practical service and self-sacrifice, while the twelfth house rules spiritual service.

There are a range of similarities and differences between each of these pairs, and because they encourage the astrologer to consider the nature and characteristics of the signs they can stimulate imaginative interpretation.

THE FIRST HOUSE. Corresponds to Aries. The first house has a general rulership over the entire personality. In practical terms this means that the sign containing the Ascendant (the rising sign) is as important as the Sun sign, and any planet placed in the first house has enormous influence over the personality.

THE SECOND HOUSE. Corresponds to Taurus.
This house rules money and possessions, attitudes to them and how they are acquired and used. Psychologically, this house can show how much people value themselves.

THE THIRD HOUSE. Corresponds to Gemini. The third house reveals the nature of the mind, the style and manner of communication and the lower levels of education. It rules all the instruments of communication, and short journeys. It also rules brothers and sisters, although this is frequently ignored in psychological interpretation.

THE FOURTH HOUSE. Corresponds to Cancer. The fourth house rules the home, both the early environment and family background, and the home which the individual creates in later life. It reveals the needs which domestic life is called upon to satisfy, and the conditioning which caused them. Psychologically it rules the desire for strong roots and positive identity. This house also rules parents, especially the father.

THE FIFTH HOUSE. Corresponds to Leo. The fifth house rules the desire to create and all the ways in which creativity manifests itself. The psychological impulse is to leave a personal mark on the world. The specific areas ruled by this house are the arts, leisure, pleasure, romance, children, sport, speculation and gambling of all kinds.

THE SIXTH HOUSE. Corresponds to Virgo. The sixth house rules the principle of practical service, the desire to sacrifice the self to the community, or to a greater good. Specifically this house rules work and health.

THE SEVENTH HOUSE. Corresponds to Libra. This is the house which rules the desire for partnership, the attitudes towards it, and the needs and functions which relationships fulfil. Traditionally this is the house of marriage, although as the institution of marriage becomes less important in western countries its meaning has been broadened to include all close emotional relationships. This house also rules close working partnerships.

THE EIGHTH HOUSE. Corresponds to Scorpio.
The eighth house rules the entire process of life from birth to death. The first house is often considered a house of symbolic birth, being the beginning of the cycle, but the eighth house rules the actual processes of sex, conception and birth. There is a metaphysical side to this house – it rules reincarnation – and a psychological correlation with profund changes in life; 'born-again' Christians may be ruled by it. The eighth house also rules other people's money, legacies, investments and business affairs. Obviously this function overlaps with that of the second house. Its rulership of mystery extends to the occult and magic.

THE NINTH HOUSE. Corresponds to Sagittarius.
The ninth house represents the desire of the individual for union with something greater. This is the house of beliefs, religion and philosophy. It is also the house of foreign travel; the desire to leave one's own culture and inhabit another. It rules long journeys of the mind, spirit and body. Specifically this house rules higher education, the law, the church, publishing, foreign countries and overseas travel.

THE TENTH HOUSE. Corresponds to Capricorn.
The tenth house reveals the individual's desire to achieve an identity in the community. This is usually expressed through the career, although people without a career must direct their energies through other avenues. Together with the fourth house, this house rules parents, especially the mother.

THE ELEVENTH HOUSE. Corresponds to Aquarius.
The eleventh house rules the individual's desire to integrate with the community. Just as the fifth house rules creativity of a highly personal nature, this house reveals the individual being creative in a social setting. Specifically, it rules the wider social circle of acquaintances and groups, broader ambitions, general hopes and wishes, and political activity.

THE TWELFTH HOUSE. Corresponds to Pisces.
Like the sixth and ninth houses this house brings a desire for union with a greater reality, but in this case the impulse is far more mystical. The principle represented by this house is one of spiritual service and self-sacrifice. While this house has noble aspirations, it has a bad reputation for being disorganized and escapist. It is the house in which the cycle comes to an end prior to rebirth in the first house, and it embodies all the lessons learnt by the other 11 houses, including their accumulated mistakes. Specifically, it rules all forms of seclusion and privacy – prisons, hospitals, monasteries, dreams, the unconscious. It also rules hidden problems and secret opponents.

CHAPTER 6
THE PLANETS IN THE HOUSES

The interpretation of planets in houses at a basic level is relatively simple.

The area of life ruled by the house is that in which the planet or planets it contains will be expressed most strongly. By examining each planet in its house it is possible to make more specific judgments about a person's life than is the case with planets and signs alone.

The sample interpretations below are all designed to cover the most general eventualities. It is the astrologer's task to decide which of these is most appropriate to a particular person or horoscope.

MC
Desc
Asc
First cusp
Ascendant
Rising Sign
Chart ruler
Ascendant ruler
Ruling planet
IC

The Chart Ruler.

The Chart Ruler.
The chart ruler, sometimes known as the Ascendant ruler or ruling planet, is the planet that rules the Rising sign, and is always one of the most important planets in the chart. In this example the Rising sign is Capricorn, ruled by Saturn. Saturn is, therefore, the chart ruler, and its position in the sixth house emphasizes the importance of health and work issues.

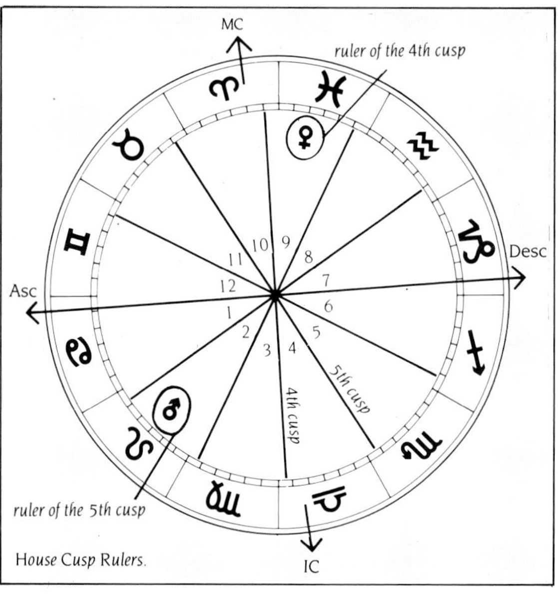

House Cusp Rulers.

Bottom: House Cusp Rulers.
The house ruler is the planet that rules the sign on the house cusp, and the sign and house containing this planet provide extra insights into the house it rules.
In this example the fourth cusp is in Libra, ruled by Venus. Venus is, therefore, the ruler of the fourth house and has a special importance in all fourth house affairs – the home and family. Venus itself is in the ninth house, ruler of foreign countries, so residence abroad would not be unexpected.
Mars, the ruler of the fifth cusp is in the second house. The fifth house rules the arts and the second house rules money, a combination which could lead to, for example, income earned through the arts, perhaps work as an art dealer.
If the house ruler is a male planet (the Sun, Mars, Jupiter or Saturn), then it is known as the lord of the house; if it is female (the Moon or Venus) then it is known as the lady of the house. Mercury strictly has no sex in astrology but was a classical god, so may be known as the lord of a house.

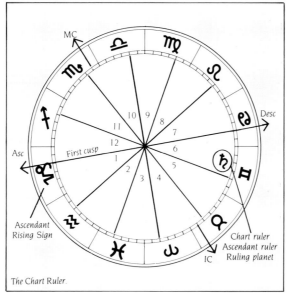

EMPTY HOUSES

The planets represent the functions which allow the houses to express themselves. When there is no planet in a house, there is no obvious way for the house to find expression. There are then two possibilities: either the person ignores the area of life represented by that house or makes a great effort to succeed in that area. For example, a person with no planets in the fifth house may have little obvious creative talent and leaves it at that, while another may make strenuous efforts to be more creative. However, even if a house contains no planets, it may contain other astrologically significant points. These may include the Moon's nodes or other factors yet to be considered. The full pattern of the chart should reveal whether an empty house is neglected or overdeveloped.

STELLIUM

When five or more planets are gathered in a single house then this is known as a satelletium, or stellium for short. Naturally, with so many planets in one house, this house becomes extremely important. The role that house plays in the life of the individual will also be quite complicated.

HOUSE CUSP RULERS

The sign on the house cusp is significant and modifies the manifestation of that house. The sign on the cusp of the first house is of great importance and this, the rising sign, is as important as the Sun sign. The signs on the cusps of the fourth, seventh and tenth houses are also important for these houses and rule home, marriage and career. Signs on the cusps of the remaining houses should also be taken into consideration.

The interpretation is quite straightforward once the principles have been grasped. For example, people with Taurus on the second cusp may be cautious (Taurus) with money (second house), Pisces on the fourth cusp may make for a disorganized (Pisces) home (fourth house), Aries on the seventh cusp may make people assertive and self-interested (Aries) in relationships (seventh house), and Capricorn on the tenth cusp may make them businesslike (Capricorn) in career (tenth house).

The possibilities can be increased by looking at the planet which rules the sign on the house cusp. This is most important for the planet that rules the rising sign (known as the chart-ruler or ruling planet): the house containing this planet is automatically increased in importance.

THE SUN

The house occupied by the Sun becomes very important in the chart.

THE SUN IN THE FIRST HOUSE. This denotes egotistical and strong willed people, good at pursuing their own interests and giving orders, but not much interested in cooperation. As it is likely that the Sun and Ascendant will be in the same sign, the influence of this sign is greatly increased.

THE SUN IN THE SECOND HOUSE. Material possessions and financial affairs are extremely important. Self-employment often suits these people as they like to be responsible for their own financial affairs. Some are motivated by a desire for more wealth, others by a fear of poverty, both of which can be manifestations of a deeper insecurity or lack of self-confidence.

THE SUN IN THE THIRD HOUSE. These people are communicators and fall into two types. On the one hand there are the intellectuals, writers, teachers, thinkers, researchers, and on the other postmen, cab and bus drivers, and so on. For some, such as those in the travel industry, the two may overlap.

THE SUN IN THE FOURTH HOUSE. Security is important and is found through putting down roots and establishing a stable home. These people need a safe base and like to be part of a large family. There may be a profound awareness of the past and the individual background.

THE SUN IN THE FIFTH HOUSE. These people retain childlike qualities, and spontaneity remains important throughout adult life. Their creative talents find outlets in the pursuit of love and pleasure as much as in artistic activity, but if the former is developed at the expense of the latter, they will become frustrated.

THE SUN IN THE SIXTH HOUSE. Self-sacrificing, hard working and in need of the security provided by routine, these people like to be of service to their families, communities and employers. Their interest in health inclines them towards medical or charitable work. They are often idealistic, but can be exploited.

THE SUN IN THE SEVENTH HOUSE. These people place enormous emphasis on partnerships. It is vital for them to have somebody to rely upon even though they like to have their own way. This applies to work as much as to marriage and emotional relationships. The partner becomes an intermediary between themselves and the world.

THE SUN IN THE EIGHTH HOUSE. These

Sun

Moon

Mercury

Venus

Earth

Mars

Jupiter

Saturn

Uranus

Neptune

Pluto

1 : Sun in the First House
2 : Sun in the Second House
3 : Sun in the Third House
4 : Sun in the Fourth House
5 : Sun in the Fifth House
6 : Sun in the Sixth House
7 : Sun in the Seventh House

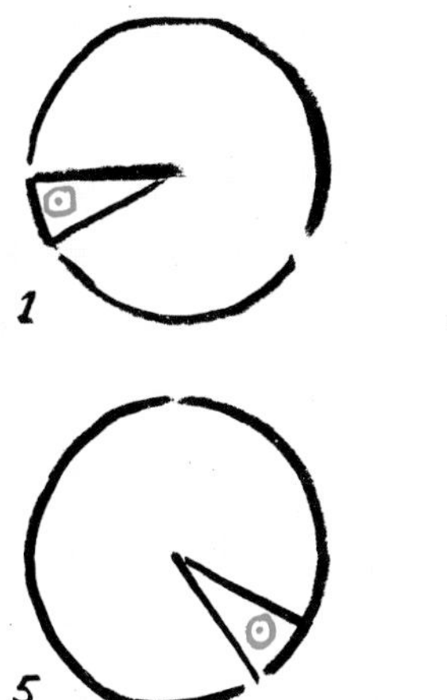

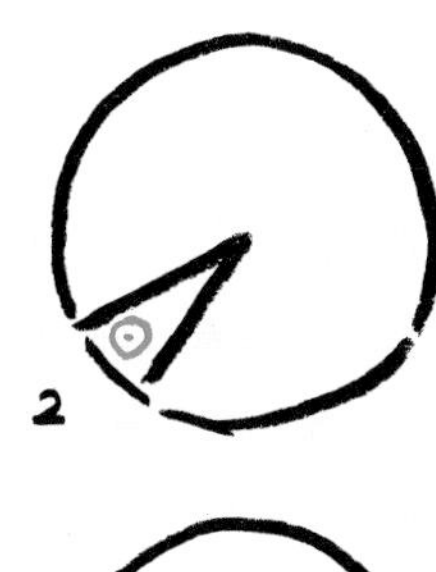

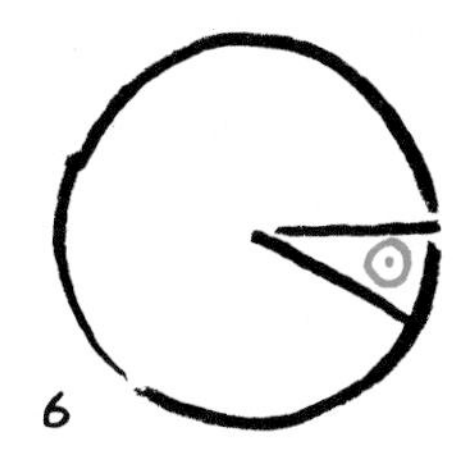

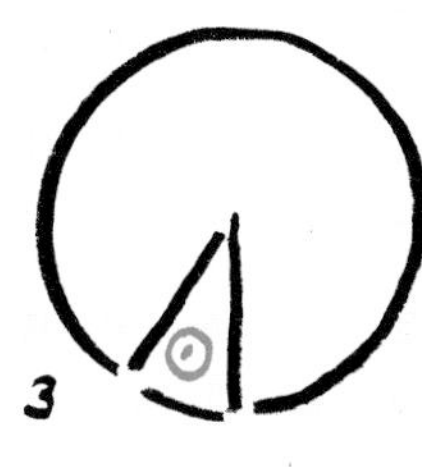

Aries Taurus

Gemini Cancer

Leo Virgo

Libra Scorpio

Sagittarius Capricorn

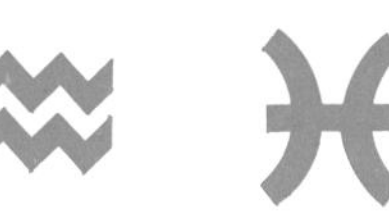

Aquarius Pisces

people are secretive. They are aware of all the deep and intense possibilities in life and are especially interested in the life cycle – from birth to death – of their fellow humans. There are a range of manifestations: some become mediums, occultists, therapists or healers; others enter the world of finance and business. All are interested in self-development, whether through inner exploration or the accumulation of wealth and power.

THE SUN IN THE NINTH HOUSE. This frequently indicates strong overseas connections, periods of travel or life abroad. These people often have strong beliefs which exercise a powerful influence over their actions, and a deep intellectual curiosity, which promotes success in higher education.

THE SUN IN THE TENTH HOUSE. These people require the prestige, status and recognition which a career brings. Those without a career need to find a substitute which allows them the same feelings of public identity. This house rules the mother and may show her character and influence.

THE SUN IN THE ELEVENTH HOUSE. These people like to mix in large groups, seeking social variety and stimulation, but avoiding the intimacy of close relationships. They join clubs and societies, and are often involved in political action, no matter how small scale.

THE SUN IN THE TWELFTH HOUSE. Secretive and sensitive, these people require privacy and seclusion, if only to recover from the stresses of the world. Their interests are esoteric and they sometimes study psychology or take up mystical practices.

THE MOON

The house occupied by the Moon becomes the focus for the expression of lunar qualities and aspirations: emotional needs and maternal qualities.

THE MOON IN THE FIRST HOUSE. These people have well developed maternal instincts and can be protective and caring but also possessive. An ability to provide security for others is complicated by a personal need for security. If the latter is satisfied then the former will operate well. They are particularly vulnerable to changeable emotions and moods.

THE MOON IN THE SECOND HOUSE. Security is found through money and material possessions. But occasionally these people reject materialism, and then a puritanical lifestyle and ideology are reassuring, providing their own certainties. Attitudes to money and changes in income are the result of emotional changes. Women may figure prominently in money matters.

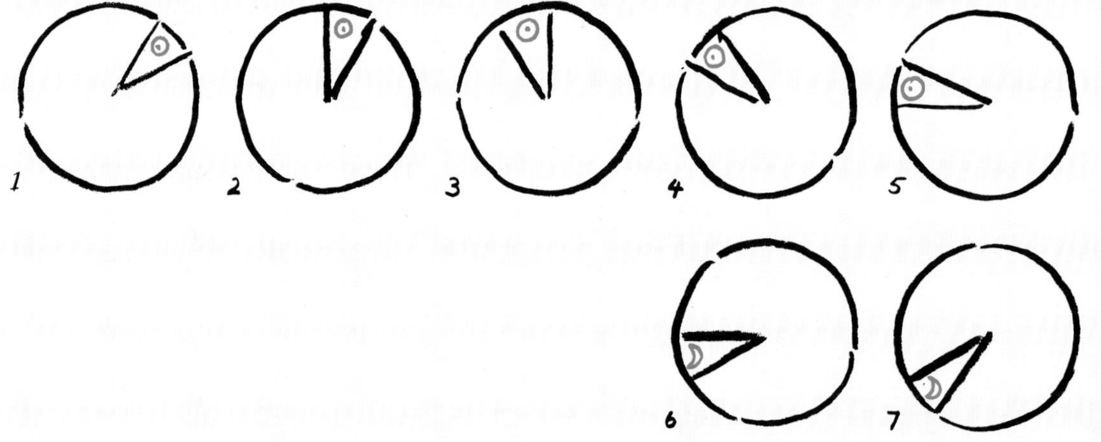

1 : *Sun in the Eighth House*
2 : *Sun in the Ninth House*
3 : *Sun in the Tenth House*
4 : *Sun in the Eleventh House*
5 : *Sun in the Twelfth House*
6 : *Moon in the First House*
7 : *Moon in the Second House*

THE MOON IN THE THIRD HOUSE. These are sensitive and poetic communicators and can make excellent teachers, especially of small children. They like to explore and talk about their own feelings. Their restless curiosity keeps them on the move.

THE MOON IN THE FOURTH HOUSE. Domestic security is vital. Even those who travel widely must have a sure sense of their own roots and identity. Most of them identify strongly with their family and place of origin. In the home they often play a maternal role.

THE MOON IN THE FIFTH HOUSE. Creative arts fulfil a vital emotional function. There is a strong need for a lively social life and romantic involvement. Pleasure may be gained from caring for children.

THE MOON IN THE SIXTH HOUSE. These people are good employees. They may be drawn to charitable work or the caring professions. They are ready to perform menial tasks at home and at work. Work and health are strongly affected by emotional changes.

THE MOON IN THE SEVENTH HOUSE. These people require close emotional relationships, and often fulfil a maternal role. They attract people who seek security, but they may come to resent this, for their own emotional needs change with the ebb and flow of lunar rhythms.

THE MOON IN THE EIGHTH HOUSE. These people have powerful emotional and sexual needs, but tend to be secretive about them. They have a good business sense, but can be too emotional to make correct decisions.

THE MOON IN THE NINTH HOUSE. Fascination with foreign cultures may bring emotional relationships with foreigners, marriage and even life abroad. Higher education and religion may attract these people ('mother' church or academic institutions may be a refuge from life's problems).

THE MOON IN THE TENTH HOUSE. The career should have significant 'female' qualities. It should be emotionally satisfying, involve helping other people and, perhaps, be in one of the caring professions. Career ambitions may be pursued at the expense of domestic interests.

THE MOON IN THE ELEVENTH HOUSE. These people socialize in large groups in which they often take a leading role. Political involvement is likely, especially in 'community politics'.

THE MOON IN THE TWELFTH HOUSE. Shy and sensitive, these people nevertheless put their compassion and imagination to work for the common good. Their good deeds will be unofficial and behind the scenes. The home is likely to be a place of seclusion and privacy.

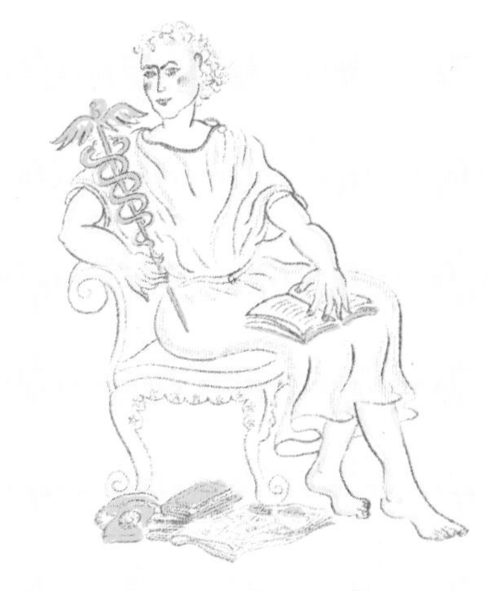

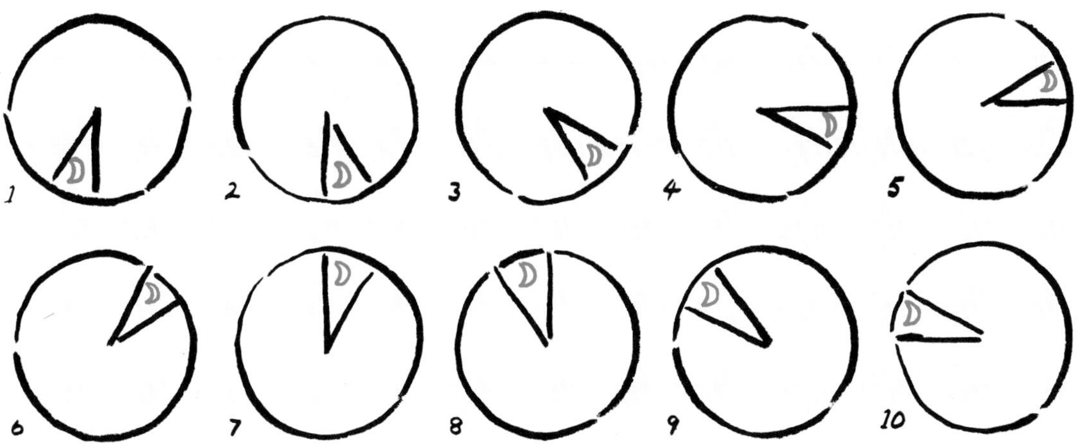

1 : *Moon in the Third House*
2 : *Moon in the Fourth House*
3 : *Moon in the Fifth House*
4 : *Moon in the Sixth House*
5 : *Moon in the Seventh House*
6 : *Moon in the Eighth House*
7 : *Moon in the Ninth House*
8 : *Moon in the Tenth House*
9 : *Moon in the Eleventh House*
10 : *Moon in the Twelfth House*

MERCURY

The house containing Mercury shows the area of life and the manner in which mental powers are expressed.

MERCURY IN THE FIRST HOUSE. These people have strong minds, are keen on learning and expressing their ideas. Some may be very talkative, while others prefer to write and think. They are physically restless and may have nervous habits.

MERCURY IN THE SECOND HOUSE. The mind focuses on wealth and material objects, and has plenty of ideas for spending as well as earning money. Self-employment is preferable, but work in any part of the communications or travel industry is appropriate.

MERCURY IN THE THIRD HOUSE. These people have active minds and are attracted to all Mercurial activities – studying, teaching, communicating, travelling. They are often restless and dislike staying too long in the same place.

MERCURY IN THE FOURTH HOUSE. These people often study at home. They develop interests in their own past, family history, environment and any subject which helps them to establish a sense of identity.

MERCURY IN THE FIFTH HOUSE. Intellectual aptitudes are combined with creative desires. These people may write, perhaps music or fiction, and have a talent for communication. The theatre is a likely medium for expression, and children appreciate their skill in telling stories.

MERCURY IN THE SIXTH HOUSE. If these people are mentally stimulated and allowed to express their own ideas at work, then they are methodical and precise employees. Employment in Mercurial fields is likely. They take a keen interest in health matters, but their own can be affected by nervous tension.

MERCURY IN THE SEVENTH HOUSE. Mental rapport in partnerships, including marriage, is essential. These people like to share interests, hobbies and attitudes with close friends. They are also interested in other people's problems, partly out of curiosity.

MERCURY IN THE EIGHTH HOUSE. These people have intense and secretive minds, and a fascination for all things arcane and mysterious. This may lead to serious study of psychology, sex, the occult and the roots of human behaviour. Their perception may also be the basis for a sound business sense.

MERCURY IN THE NINTH HOUSE. Fascinated by knowledge and with a desire for understanding, these people may reach academic heights. They often become perpetual students. Particular interest in religion, philosophy, the law and foreign cultures is likely.

MERCURY IN THE TENTH HOUSE. Careers must provide mental stimulation and utilize ideas and communicative skills. Job satisfaction is more important than monetary rewards. A career in teaching, journalism, secretarial work or travel is appropriate.

MERCURY IN THE ELEVENTH HOUSE. These people are very sociable. They use their friends and acquaintances as sounding boards for their ideas. They are often to be found in groups or societies which have a common interest, perhaps in local politics.

MERCURY IN THE TWELFTH HOUSE. These people are shy and secretive. This is reflected

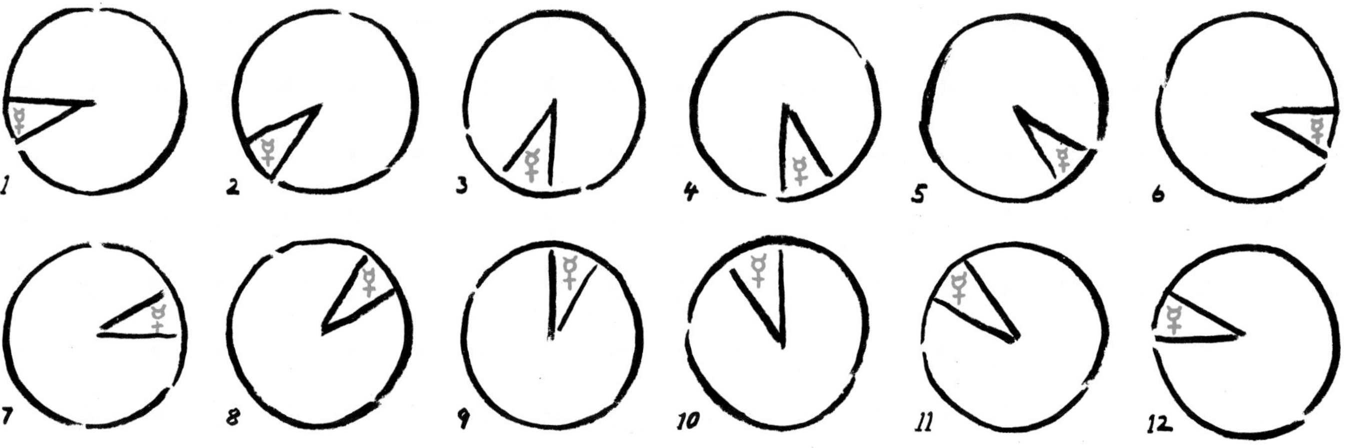

1 : Mercury in the First House
2 : Mercury in the Second House
3 : Mercury in the Third House
4 : Mercury in the Fourth House
5 : Mercury in the Fifth House
6 : Mercury in the Sixth House
7 : Mercury in the Seventh House
8 : Mercury in the Eighth House
9 : Mercury in the Ninth House
10 : Mercury in the Tenth House
11 : Mercury in the Eleventh House
12 : Mercury in the Twelfth House

in their interests which include psychology, mysticism and the occult. They need to develop greater confidence in expressing their ideas, as these are often carefully considered.

VENUS

The house containing Venus shows the area of life in which Venusian affairs will be expressed, especially artistic skills and the need for partnership.

VENUS IN THE FIRST HOUSE. Friendship is all important to these people. Their need to be liked is the main motivation behind their attractive image and charming manners. Many take an active interest in the arts and fashion.

VENUS IN THE SECOND HOUSE. Money can be earned through the arts and in partnerships, especially with women. It may be spent in the pursuit of social activities or in buying luxuries. Self-confidence is established through partnerships and material success.

VENUS IN THE THIRD HOUSE. These people have a persuasive charm and are good raconteurs. They make effective sales people. They are sociable and treat friends as part of their family. At school they do best in arts subjects.

VENUS IN THE FOURTH HOUSE. The home must be a peaceful and pleasant place as these people find if difficult to cope with domestic disorder or family quarrels. They are perfectionists at home, good at creating a friendly atmosphere and at defusing arguments.

VENUS IN THE FIFTH HOUSE. These people put a lot of energy into socializing and go to great lengths to be popular. They have creative talents and even their entertaining takes on a dramatic dimension. They form easy and affectionate relationships with children.

VENUS IN THE SIXTH HOUSE. Working conditions must be harmonious, preferably in a cooperative and sociable atmosphere. Competition or hostility at work is difficult to cope with. Venus indicates work with women, the arts, property, and in leisure activities.

VENUS IN THE SEVENTH HOUSE. Sociable, charming and diplomatic, these people are often popular and attractive. However, they may rely too much on other people for approval and make unrealistic emotional demands in partnerships.

VENUS IN THE EIGHTH HOUSE. Sexual experience is a vital part of emotional relationships; and sexual relationships require a deep and intense emotional commitment. These people can be possessive and jealous. Secrecy causes misunderstandings.

1 : Venus in the First House
2 : Venus in the Second House
3 : Venus in the Third House
4 : Venus in the Fourth House
5 : Venus in the Fifth House
6 : Venus in the Sixth House
7 : Venus in the Seventh House
8 : Venus in the Eighth House

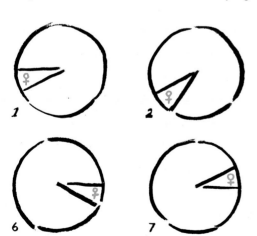

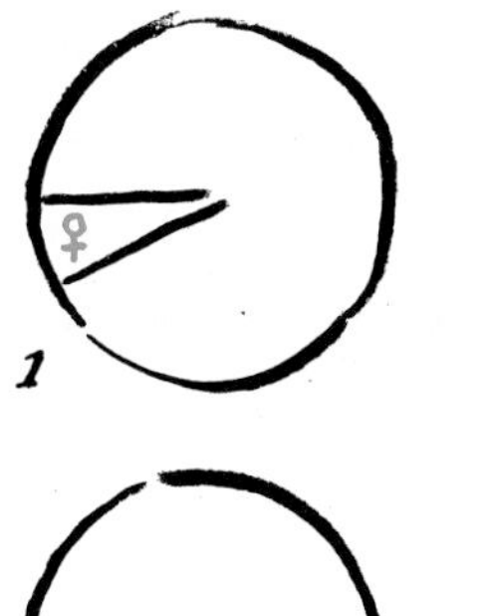
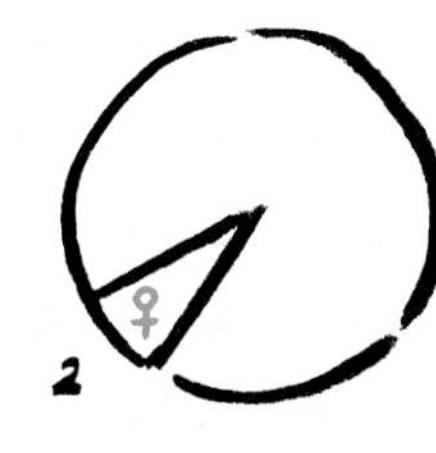
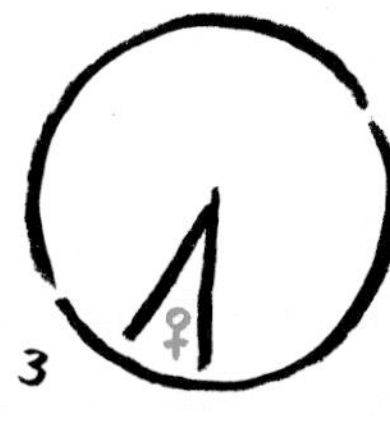

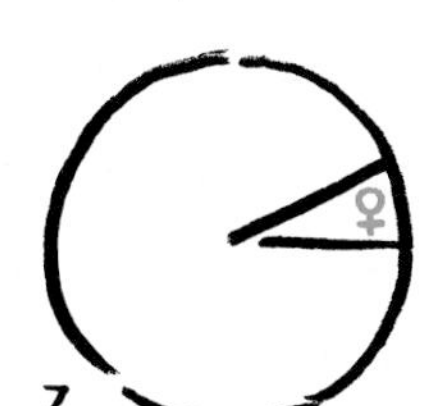

VENUS IN THE NINTH HOUSE. Emotional attraction to foreign cultures can lead to marriage or life abroad. Friends come from varied backgrounds. There is an affinity with religion and artistic interests will have religious and philosophical overtones.

VENUS IN THE TENTH HOUSE. Social skills prove an asset in a career connected with the arts, property or other Venusian areas. Work involving other people is appropriate. Social life may revolve around work.

VENUS IN THE ELEVENTH HOUSE. These people find social satisfaction in large groups and have a wide circle of acquaintances.

VENUS IN THE TWELFTH HOUSE. These people tend to be rather shy and have few close friends. They can benefit from being more confident and open in their feelings and emotional needs.

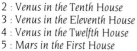

MARS

The house containing Mars reveals a major outlet for the energetic, active and assertive qualities of that planet.

MARS IN THE FIRST HOUSE. Assertive and energetic, these people usually put their own interests first. However, they apply equal vigour and flair when doing things for other people.

MARS IN THE SECOND HOUSE. A great deal of energy is put into earning and spending money. Self-employment is attractive to these people. They are competititive in business and inclined to take risks.

MARS IN THE THIRD HOUSE. These people are quick in mind and speech. They are forceful in putting their own ideas across, tactless and argumentative. They are restless and fond of travel. Their interests may lie in research work.

MARS IN THE FOURTH HOUSE. Domestic concerns occupy a good deal of energy, both in terms of practical jobs to be done and difficult relationships to be resolved. These people like to be in control in the home and do not take kindly to opposition.

MARS IN THE FIFTH HOUSE. This position brings energy and vigour to all creative, social and romantic activities. If too much time is spent entertaining, it will detract from artistic development. These people may put pressure on their children to succeed.

MARS IN THE SIXTH HOUSE. Hardworking, conscientious and competitive, these people are good employees as long as they have the chance to get on. They are impatient and do not find it easy to handle delays or obstacles.

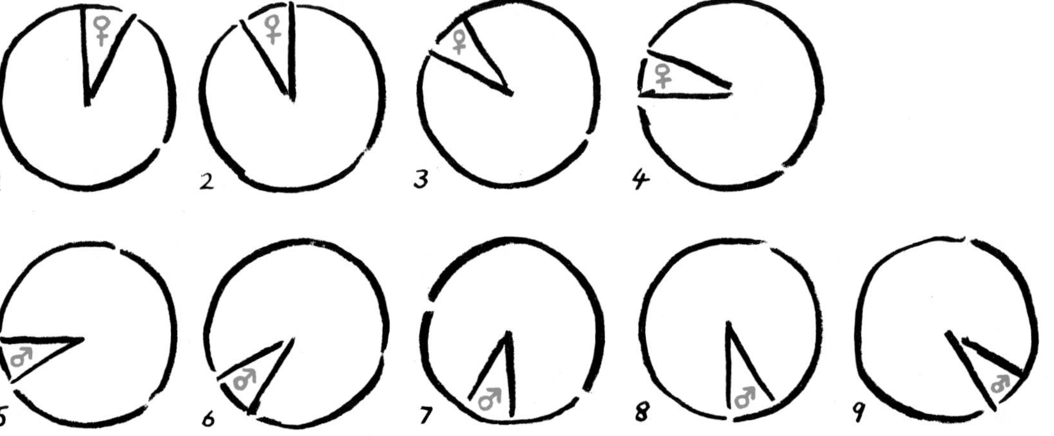

1 : Venus in the Ninth House
2 : Venus in the Tenth House
3 : Venus in the Eleventh House
4 : Venus in the Twelfth House
5 : Mars in the First House
6 : Mars in the Second House
7 : Mars in the Third House
8 : Mars in the Fourth House
9 : Mars in the Fifth House

They will clash with colleagues who stand in their way. Health may be affected by impatient and reckless behaviour.

MARS IN THE SEVENTH HOUSE. These people are sociable, outgoing and tend to organize other people's affairs. Their energy makes them popular, but they can offend by their forthright and outspoken ways. Emotional relationships may be formed and broken on impulse.

MARS IN THE EIGHTH HOUSE. These people have intense and deep motivations. Some develop an interest in the occult or mysticism, some form a series of sexual relationships, others become involved in business and high finance.

MARS IN THE NINTH HOUSE. Travel is vital for these people as it absorbs their surplus energy. They have strong beliefs and will promote them passionately.

MARS IN THE TENTH HOUSE. Ambitious and competitive, these people choose careers which give the best opportunities for personal advancement. They perform better as employers than employees, but can be too ruthless.

MARS IN THE ELEVENTH HOUSE. These people attract a vast number of casual acquaintances, all of whom are superficially close. They are attracted to political and organized groups but may antagonize them by their abrasive manners.

MARS IN THE TWELFTH HOUSE. Work behind the scenes, perhaps dedicated to a cause, is likely, but so is conspiracy and plotting. Unless a cause is found there is a lack of purpose and direction. Anger tends to be bottled up.

JUPITER

The house containing Jupiter shows the area of life in which growth, expansion and wisdom is sought, and which offers an opportunity for fulfilment.

JUPITER IN THE FIRST HOUSE. Outgoing and optimistic, these people have the enthusiasm to create fresh possibilities and opportunites wherever they go. They seek control over their lives and environment. Their weakness is overconfidence.

JUPITER IN THE SECOND HOUSE. These people divide into those who take an idealistic view of money and possessions, rejecting them in favour of 'higher' priorities, and those who work hard to acquire material wealth. Even if greedy, they are often generous and extravagant. Money is rarely a problem.

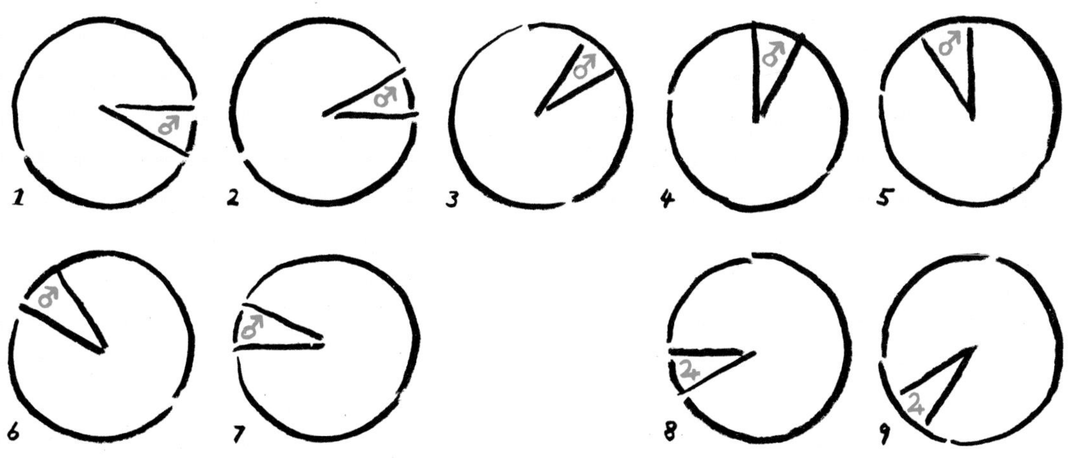

1 : *Mars in the Sixth House*
2 : *Mars in the Seventh House*
3 : *Mars in the Eighth House*
4 : *Mars in the Ninth House*
5 : *Mars in the Tenth House*
6 : *Mars in the Eleventh House*
7 : *Mars in the Twelfth House*
8 : *Jupiter in the First House*
9 : *Jupiter in the Second House*

JUPITER IN THE THIRD HOUSE. These people have grand ideas and a strong desire to inflict them on others. They may be skilled communicators and drawn to work in the media. They also enjoy travelling and may work in the travel industry.

JUPITER IN THE FOURTH HOUSE. There is usually a desire for a large or grandly decorated home. Periodic moves are likely, and may include living abroad. Pride in family and the immediate environment are important.

JUPITER IN THE FIFTH HOUSE. Self-confidence and idealism often carry these people to creative success. They are attracted to the performing arts, and their romantic and leisure activities are often theatrical in style.

JUPITER IN THE SIXTH HOUSE. These people are usually hard workers, especially if their work serves some larger cause. Job satisfaction is more important than money; in a job with no purpose they can be lazy. Health may be weakened by self-indulgence.

JUPITER IN THE SEVENTH HOUSE. Apparently friendly to all, these people often take the initiative in new relationships. They are generous, but also attracted to people who can be of benefit to them. They present a highly confident public image.

JUPITER IN THE EIGHTH HOUSE. The eighth house manifests itself in several distinct ways. Some of these people will concentrate on acquiring sexual experience, others are drawn to the occult, seeking esoteric knowledge, while others go into business, concentrating on acquiring wealth. If Jupiter is badly aspected (see Chapter 9), money can be lost.

JUPITER IN THE NINTH HOUSE. These people divide into two types: intellectuals and students of religion; or travellers seeking answers to their personal problems. Often they become dogmatic in their beliefs.

JUPITER IN THE TENTH HOUSE. These people are faced with a choice in their careers; to work in pursuit of their ideals and gain wisdom, or to work for status and power. Those denied respect and recognition will not give their best in work.

JUPITER IN THE ELEVENTH HOUSE. Gregarious and sociable, these people have a wide circle of acquaintances, few of whom will be real friends. They have broad ambitions and enlist their colleagues to assist them.

JUPITER IN THE TWELFTH HOUSE. Dissatisfied with the material world and attracted by mystical and religious solutions, these people are idealistic and may prefer the private world of the imagination to harsh reality.

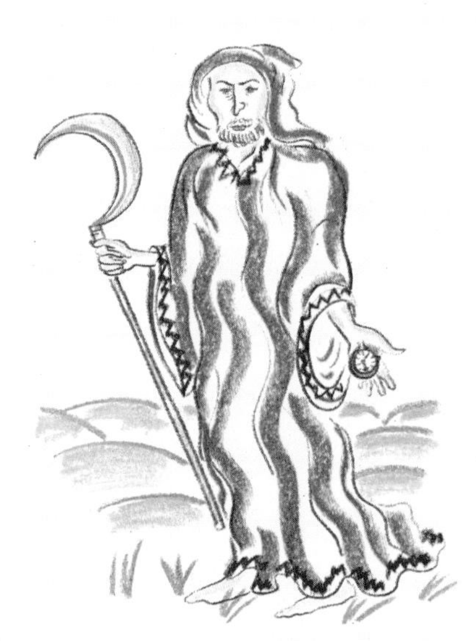

1 : *Jupiter in the Third House*
2 : *Jupiter in the Fourth House*
3 : *Jupiter in the Fifth House*
4 : *Jupiter in the Sixth House*
5 : *Jupiter in the Seventh House*
6 : *Jupiter in the Eighth House*
7 : *Jupiter in the Ninth House*
8 : *Jupiter in the Tenth House*
9 : *Jupiter in the Eleventh House*
10 : *Jupiter in the Twelfth House*

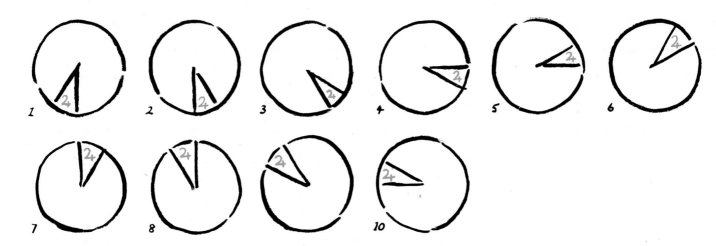

SATURN

The house containing Saturn shows the area of life in which Saturnine obstacles and difficulties are met and lessons learnt.

SATURN IN THE FIRST HOUSE. Instinctively conservative and sensitive to the restrictions of authority and their environment, these people often lose self-confidence. Some meet failure at every turn, while others achieve success by sheer hard work and dedication. To succeed they need to develop a sense of inner authority and self-discipline.

SATURN IN THE SECOND HOUSE. There may be a fear of poverty; as a result these people are careful with money. But excessive caution or meanness can lead to lost financial opportunities.

SATURN IN THE THIRD HOUSE. These people have structured and methodical minds well fitted to solving practical problems. Lack of confidence, however, may restrict full use of the imagination, and can hinder academic success.

SATURN IN THE FOURTH HOUSE. Domestic responsibilities or difficulties are likely. In childhood these may be the result of others' actions, but adults invariably attract these commitments. There is a need for domestic security – often provided by physical ties.

SATURN IN THE FIFTH HOUSE. These people lack confidence in their creative abilities and social skills. Artistic potential will only be developed if practical skills are acquired. There is a formality in social relationships and in dealings with children.

SATURN IN THE SIXTH HOUSE. Security may be found in hard work. These people have high expectations and meet challenges, delays and difficulties at work. Efforts are rewarded by slow advancement. They may worry unduly about their health.

SATURN IN THE SEVENTH HOUSE. There is a need for stability in partnerships, but there will usually be delays, sometimes caused by external obstacles such as parental opposition or financial difficulties, which can be used as excuses. These people have high expectations. They are often attracted to those who are older and more experienced, sometimes committed elsewhere. Few friends are allowed to get really close.

SATURN IN THE EIGHTH HOUSE. There is often a deep interest in occult mysteries. Attitudes to sex are serious and can be inhibited. These people are usually responsible with money, but need to take care of investments.

SATURN IN THE NINTH HOUSE. These people are influenced by the conservative religion and traditional values of their background. Even rebellion will change only the form and not the reality of their basic beliefs. Life or travel in foreign countries may be most successful if connected with work. Care should be taken to avoid difficulties in travel.

SATURN IN THE TENTH HOUSE. There may be delays in finding a career, but once the search is over these people will be stable and responsible workers, overcoming difficulties with effort and gaining gradual promotion. Work should be practical, and bring status and authority.

SATURN IN THE ELEVENTH HOUSE. These people either keep themselves to themselves or overcome their shyness by joining societies in which social life is centred around a

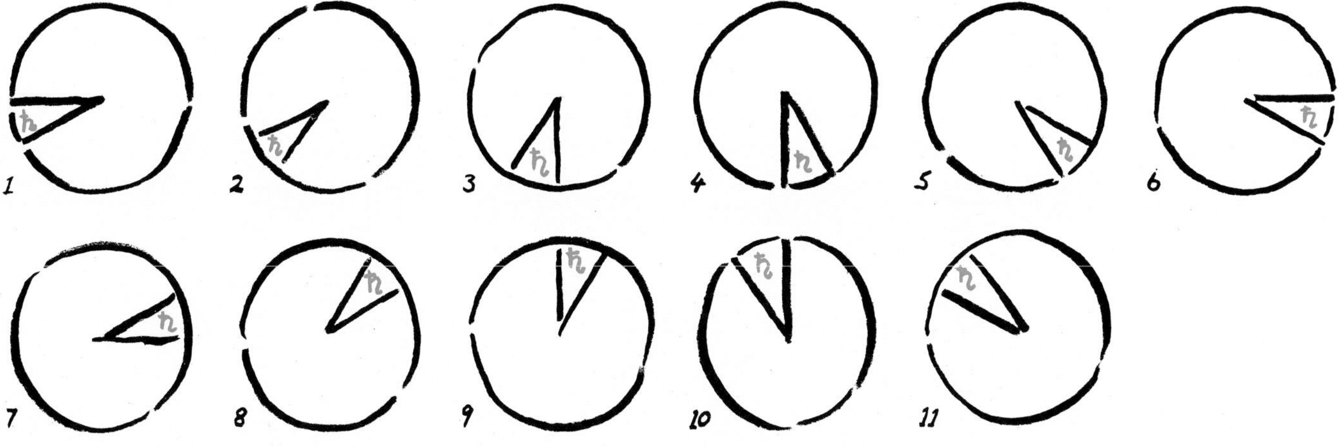

1 : *Saturn in the First House*
2 : *Saturn in the Second House*
3 : *Saturn in the Third House*
4 : *Saturn in the Fourth House*
5 : *Saturn in the Fifth House*
6 : *Saturn in the Sixth House*
7 : *Saturn in the Seventh House*
8 : *Saturn in the Eighth House*
9 : *Saturn in the Ninth House*
10 : *Saturn in the Tenth House*
11 : *Saturn in the Eleventh House*

purpose, sometimes political. Friends are often older and more experienced.

SATURN IN THE TWELFTH HOUSE. These people need a sense of inner purpose and make good behind-the-scenes organizers. They often suffer from an inexplicable fear of authority or concern about the future, and should find a way to develop self-confidence.

URANUS

The house containing Uranus shows the area of life in which the individual may experience sudden changes, or a pressing need for personal freedom.

URANUS IN THE FIRST HOUSE. These people hate to be tied down and resent limits on their personal freedom. They are individualists and are afraid of being submerged in the mass. They are innovators and inventors, better at competing than cooperating.

URANUS IN THE SECOND HOUSE. Financial affairs may be subject to unusual conditions, sudden gains or unexpected losses. Income may be earned in original or inventive work. These people may have strong ideas about how money should be used.

URANUS IN THE THIRD HOUSE. These people have original minds and may find it difficult to cope with the limitations of an orthodox educational system. They use their talents in idealistic ways such as teaching, in technology such as the communications industry, or in other inventive ways such as advertising.

URANUS IN THE FOURTH HOUSE. Domestic conditions may be out of the ordinary, unsettled or subject to unexpected changes. Chaos may be preferred to domestic routine, and family ties are not welcomed. There is a dislike of domestic responsibility.

URANUS IN THE FIFTH HOUSE. Creative flair may be expressed in art that extends the boundaries of the acceptable by using new techniques—abstract art, 'agitprop' or experimental theatre, electronic music and so on. Romantic attachments may be unorthodox. Their children may be unusual and stimulating.

URANUS IN THE SIXTH HOUSE. These people are attracted to work which is inventive, technical, unusual or idealistic. Stimulation at work is more important than financial gain, and frustration and friction result from dull working conditions. Health may be affected by nervous tension.

URANUS IN THE SEVENTH HOUSE. Friends and friendships are unusual and ideas about marriage unorthodox. These people are afraid of being tied down and losing their emotional independence; partners must give them

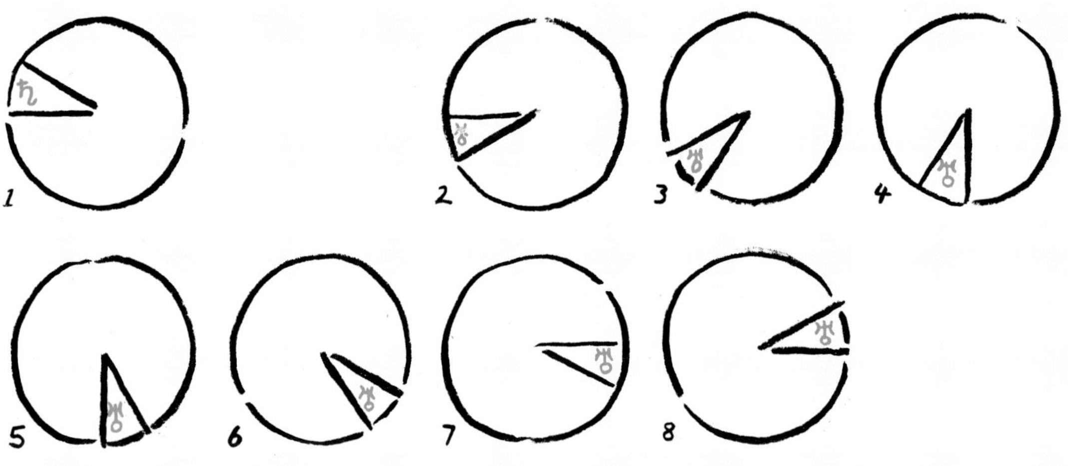

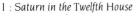

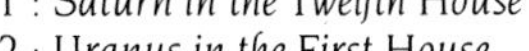
1 : *Saturn in the Twelfth House*
2 : *Uranus in the First House*
3 : *Uranus in the Second House*
4 : *Uranus in the Third House*
5 : *Uranus in the Fourth House*
6 : *Uranus in the Fifth House*
7 : *Uranus in the Sixth House*
8 : *Uranus in the Seventh House*

plenty of space. Partnerships can be made and unmade without warning.

URANUS IN THE EIGHTH HOUSE. There is a fascination for the occult and unusual answers to life's mysteries. These people need sexual variety. They have unconventional schemes for making money.

URANUS IN THE NINTH HOUSE. Beliefs may be unusual; these people are attracted to oriental religions and new cults. Foreign travel may be motivated by a search for unusual experiences.

URANUS IN THE TENTH HOUSE. These people may be reluctant to settle into a career unless it offers scope for their unusual talents or a challenge to their idealism. They need to be able to take personal decisions, and in an unsuitable career will be restless and likely to leave.

URANUS IN THE ELEVENTH HOUSE. Long-term ambitions are unusual and these people are often found in groups which have common inventive or ideological interests. There may be a large circle of acquaintances although these change frequently.

URANUS IN THE TWELFTH HOUSE. These people have strange and wonderful imaginations, and are often interested in subjects such as yoga, psychology, or mysticism and other ways of extending the consciousness.

NEPTUNE

The house containing Neptune shows where ideals are expressed, but also where confusion may arise.

NEPTUNE IN THE FIRST HOUSE. Sensitive and imaginative, these people are often in-

volved in the arts and fashion. They are gullible, but capable of deceiving others. They are idealistic, and attracted to philanthropic work and mystical beliefs.

NEPTUNE IN THE SECOND HOUSE. In financial matters these people can be confused, wasteful, deceptive, idealistic, generous or greedy. They either love money for the fantasies it can buy or despise it for being worldly. The best way of earning money is through putting the imagination to use, for example, in the arts.

NEPTUNE IN THE THIRD HOUSE. These people have poetic imaginations and are skilled in communicating fantasies and fiction. They make good journalists and teachers. They may find it difficult to express facts clearly, concentrating on images and theories.

Sun

Moon

Mercury

Venus

Earth

Mars

Jupiter

Saturn

Uranus

Neptune

Pluto

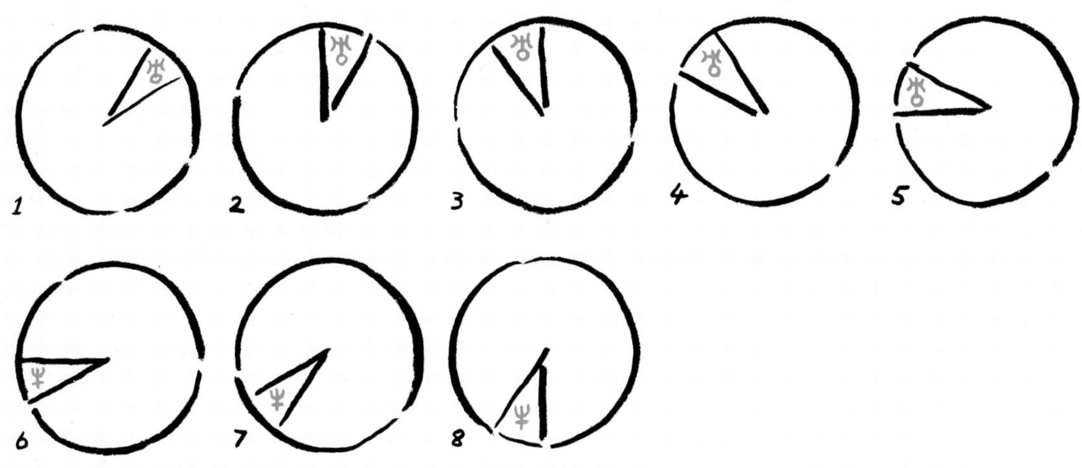

1 : *Uranus in the Eighth House*
2 : *Uranus in the Ninth House*
3 : *Uranus in the Tenth House*
4 : *Uranus in the Eleventh House*
5 : *Uranus in the Twelfth House*
6 : *Neptune in the First House*
7 : *Neptune in the Second House*
8 : *Neptune in the Third House*

NEPTUNE IN THE FOURTH HOUSE. The home background may have elements of mystery or confusion. These people have an image of their dream home, a haven of peace and quiet, and they prefer comfortable chaos to domestic routine.

NEPTUNE IN THE FIFTH HOUSE. Artistic talent is founded in a vivid imagination. There is a yearning for romance. Relations with children may be loving but confused.

NEPTUNE IN THE SIXTH HOUSE. Self-sacrificing instincts often attract these people to employment in which they are overworked and underpaid, perhaps charitable or medical work. Others find jobs in the arts or entertainment world. If in meaningless jobs, they will be lazy and disorganized. Their health may be undermined by a sensitivity to hard conditions.

NEPTUNE IN THE SEVENTH HOUSE. These people are idealistic in relationships, but their romantic expectations can be too high and result in disappointment. They are often attracted by superficial appearances misunderstanding the realities of a situation.

NEPTUNE IN THE EIGHTH HOUSE. Sexual relationships may be coloured by fantasies and unrealistic expectations. These people are fascinated by the mysteries of life and have an interest in magic and the occult. They have imaginative business ideas but may lack the practical expertise to carry them out.

NEPTUNE IN THE NINTH HOUSE. These people are attracted to mystical beliefs, and foreign cultures fascinate them, sometimes unrealistically. They are easily impressed by religious ritual and dogma. Legal matters should be approached with caution.

NEPTUNE IN THE TENTH HOUSE. In ordinary careers these people may have unrealistic aspirations and be disorganized. In careers where they can express their idealism or imagination – charitable and social work, films, fashion, advertising and the arts – great dedication is likely.

NEPTUNE IN THE ELEVENTH HOUSE. Long-term ambitions may be idealistic but difficult to define and easily influenced by the latest fashion. These people are shy in public.

NEPTUNE IN THE TWELFTH HOUSE. These people have sensitive dreams which may never be expressed in everyday life. There is often an interest in mysticism and psychology.

PLUTO

The house containing Pluto reveals an area of life that may be the subject of compulsive interest and activity, and in which profound changes are likely.

1 : Neptune in the Fourth House
2 : Neptune in the Fifth House
3 : Neptune in the Sixth House
4 : Neptune in the Seventh House
5 : Neptune in the Eighth House
6 : Neptune in the Ninth House
7 : Neptune in the Tenth House
8 : Neptune in the Eleventh House
9 : Neptune in the Twelfth House

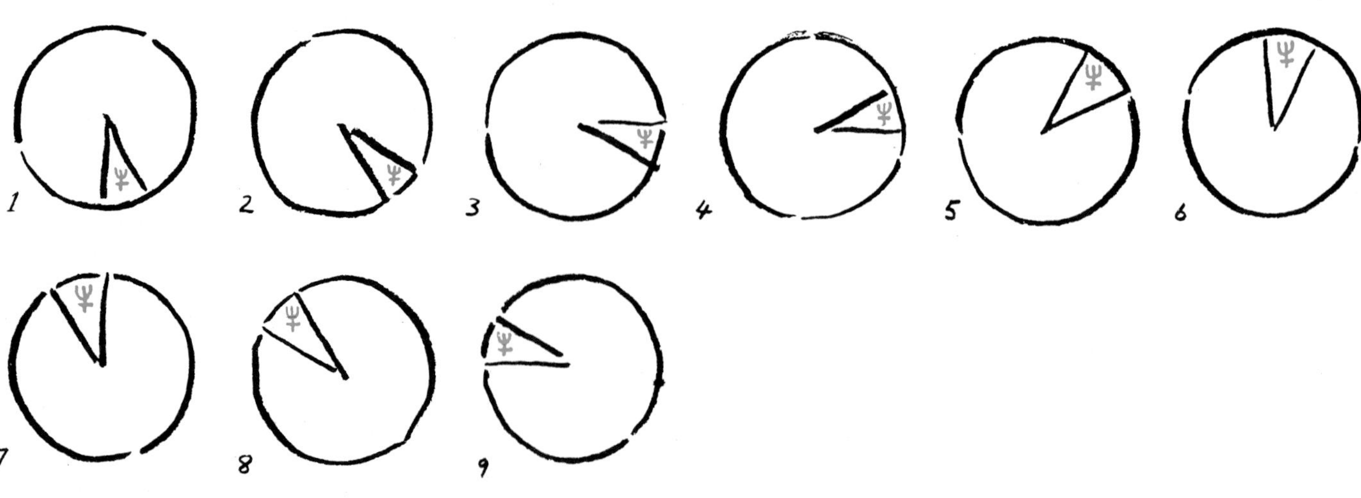

PLUTO IN THE FIRST HOUSE. These people are usually determined, intense and work hard to achieve their personal goals. They may often conceal their turbulent personalities, but may be subject to periodic revolutions in life style.

PLUTO IN THE SECOND HOUSE. Money and possessions are important to these people, not necessarily in themselves but as catalysts for personal transformation. Finances may be subject to sudden changes, and they may swing from rags to riches and back again, probably as a result of taking risks.

PLUTO IN THE THIRD HOUSE. The minds of these people harbour deep, dark and hidden interests. They are very perceptive and may be dissatisfied with an ordinary education.

PLUTO IN THE FOURTH HOUSE. Domestic upheavals are likely, partly provoked by the desire for change and partly by other people and circumstances. If domestic change is blocked, these people will boil up until an explosion occurs.

PLUTO IN THE FIFTH HOUSE. These people have a compulsive creative urge and may work hard to be accepted as artists. They may also direct their energies into frenetic social activity. Relations with children may be emotional but difficult

PLUTO IN THE SIXTH HOUSE. These people throw an enormous amount of energy into their work and will not tolerate inefficiency or obstruction from colleagues, nor obey unreasonable orders. If personally motivated, they are capable of bringing their healing energies to any situation. Emotional stress and strain may undermine their health.

PLUTO IN THE SEVENTH HOUSE. These people often expect partners to satisfy impossible emotional demands and will put them through gruelling tests to see if they are committed to the relationship. If their love is reciprocated they will respond with devotion and passion.

PLUTO IN THE EIGHTH HOUSE. Fascinated by the mysteries of the life force from birth to death, reincarnation and the occult, these people may develop a devotion to spiritual practices. Those who are more materially minded may become involved in sexual, business or financial adventures.

PLUTO IN THE NINTH HOUSE. These people hold deep beliefs which they will fight to defend. They may be morally self-righteous. Travel to distant countries is important to help in their search for other faiths.

PLUTO IN THE TENTH HOUSE. The career should be a vehicle for the expression and acquisition of personal power, sometimes matched paradoxically by a desire to serve the community. Suitable careers include medicine, psychology, religion, politics or detective work.

PLUTO IN THE ELEVENTH HOUSE. These people find personal power in group situations and are often attracted to politics. They become personally involved in political situations and expect politics to solve their individual problems.

PLUTO IN THE TWELFTH HOUSE. These people often develop an interest in psychology or the occult as a means of discovering their deeper natures. There may be a desire for union with the cosmos.

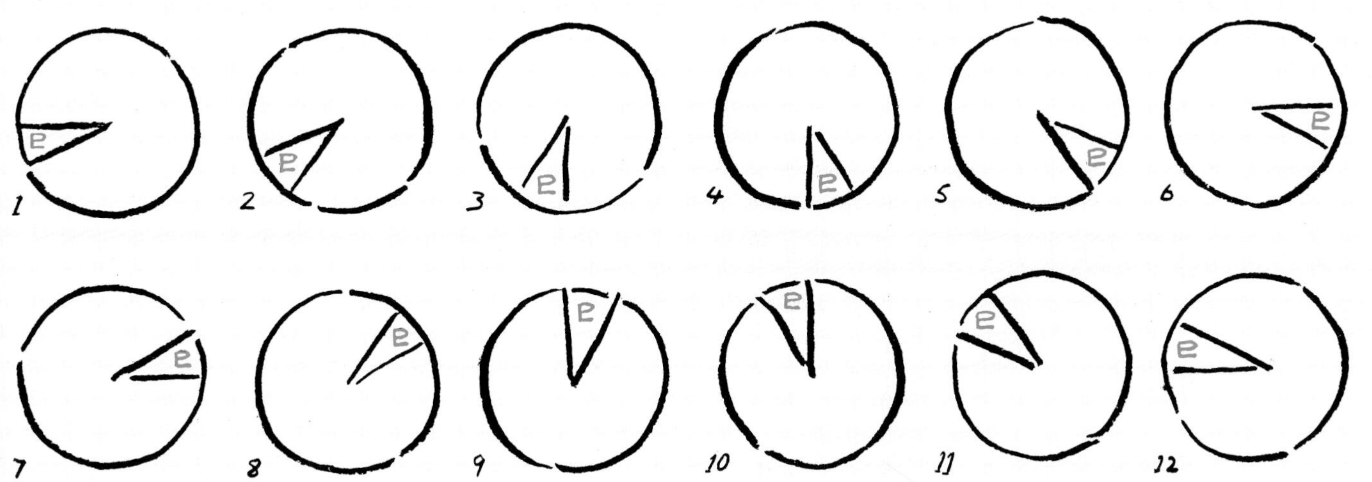

1 : *Pluto in the First House*
2 : *Pluto in the Second House*
3 : *Pluto in the Third House*
4 : *Pluto in the Fourth House*
5 : *Pluto in the Fifth House*
6 : *Pluto in the Sixth House*
7 : *Pluto in the Seventh House*
8 : *Pluto in the Eighth House*
9 : *Pluto in the Ninth House*
10 : *Pluto in the Tenth House*
11 : *Pluto in the Eleventh House*
12 : *Pluto in the Twelfth House*

CHAPTER 7 CALCULATION OF THE HOROSCOPE

There are two stages in casting a horoscope. First, calculation of the position of the planets in the signs of the zodiac; and second, calculation of the positions of the houses and rising sign. The first step, converting the time of birth into Greenwich Mean Time, is the same in each stage.

Unfamiliar technical jargon can make astrological calculation seem excessively complicated but, in fact, the calculations themselves are straightforward and, with the aid of calculators, have been made as easy as simple mathematics. Many astrologers have given up calculation altogether in favour of computers, although the astrologer who has no knowledge of calculation will be at a severe disadvantage when a computer is not available.

All astrologers can make mistakes in their calculations. Even computers produce erroneous charts when they are given the wrong information. The fact that errors can occur only reinforces the need for careful checking of data. Hours can be wasted if an interpretation of an inaccurate horoscope is prepared and it is always best to double check calculations before drawing up a horoscope.

The Horoscope – Data
The horoscope is based upon three items of data – the time, date and place of birth.

Place

Time/Clock

Calendar

EQUIPMENT

The astrologer must have access to certain items of equipment and reference tables before calculating a horoscope. A ruler and set of different coloured pens are the most obvious. Most astrologers also use printed chart wheels. Other necessary reference material is listed below:

The ephemeris (ephemerides in the plural) or planetary table lists the positions of the planets at regular intervals and gives other astronomical information. The level of detail supplied in different ephemerides varies and most astrologers have two versions, one a general edition containing basic information for a period of perhaps 50 years, and the other a detailed edition covering only one year. The ephemeris, at the back of this book, contains the planetary positions required for simple calculation.

The Tables of Houses list the house cusps including the Ascendant and Midheaven. There are different editions computed for the various house systems. The tables at the back of this book are designed for use with the Equal House system.

An atlas is necessary to look up the longitude and latitude for the place of birth or other locations for which the chart is to be cast.

Special astrological software is available for a variety of home computers, but these are not necessary for basic calculation. It is, however, very useful to have a calculator which uses degrees, minutes and seconds, and hours, minutes and seconds.

DATA

Since it is extremely important to obtain accurate data to guarantee correct interpretation, it is best if clients write down their own birth data as they are then responsible for any errors. If the astrologer is taking information over the telephone, it should be read back to the client for confirmation. It is especially important to check whether the time was morning (am) or afternoon and evening (pm).

The date of birth when written in figures can cause confusion, so it is best that the month should always be written down in full. For example, 7.4.1987 is the 4 July 1987 in the USA but the 7 April 1987 in Europe.

The place of birth should be as exact as possible. If the person was born in a large city such as London or Los Angeles, it is not strictly necessary to worry about the exact

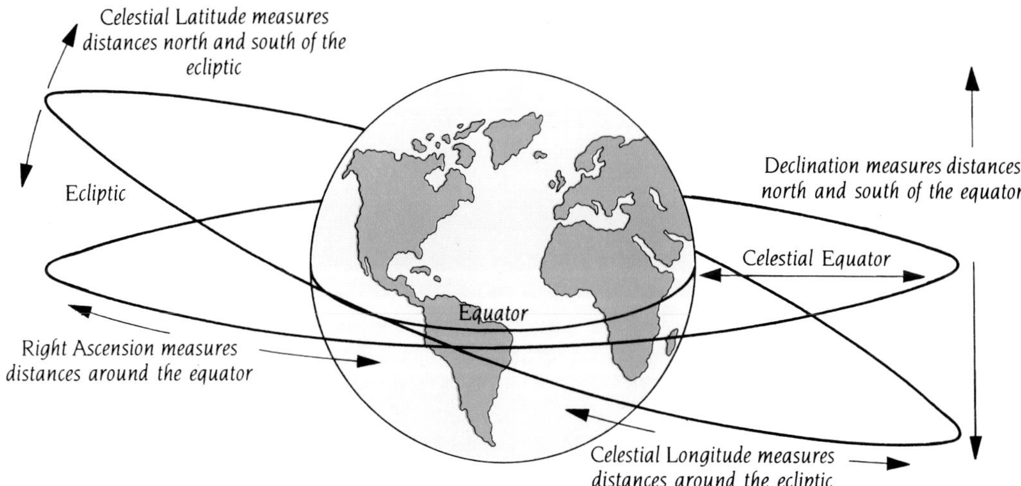
Celestial Latitude measures distances north and south of the ecliptic
Ecliptic
Declination measures distances north and south of the equator
Celestial Equator
Equator
Right Ascension measures distances around the equator
Celestial Longitude measures distances around the ecliptic

location of birth, even though there may be minute differences in the horoscope from one side of the city to the other. If a person was born in a small village then the distance from the nearest big town must be ascertained as the village itself might not be shown in any available atlas.

The time of birth needs to be known as precisely as possible, although most recorded birth times are technically inaccurate, and may differ by 15 or 30 minutes from the actual time of birth. Most people give their birth time as being on the quarter-hour, half-hour or hour, yet nature is never so regular. However, when a client does specify an exact time, the astrologer may assume it is accurate. When the time is stated only approximately, or not at all, the astrologer faces a dilemma.

If the subject reports that birth occurred 'between four and half-past', or 'between seven and eight', the astrologer should question this to see if the time can be pinpointed more accurately. If not the horoscope should be cast for the half-way point between the two times. It should be interpreted with an open mind, and if the subject disagrees sharply with any statements that are made, this may help to clarify the time of birth.

Some people give their birth time as 'in the early hours', 'before dawn', or 'around tea time'. The astrologer should question the client and then estimate the approximate time. For example, 'around tea-time' could indicate 5.00 pm. The resulting horoscope will be speculative but, by interpreting it, the astrologer may be able to work out a more accurate chart.

If no time of birth is given then the astrologer casts a 'solar' chart set either for midnight, dawn or noon, depending on the astrologer's preference. Most solar charts are cast for noon. Although the resulting chart is speculative it can still yield accurate interpretations.

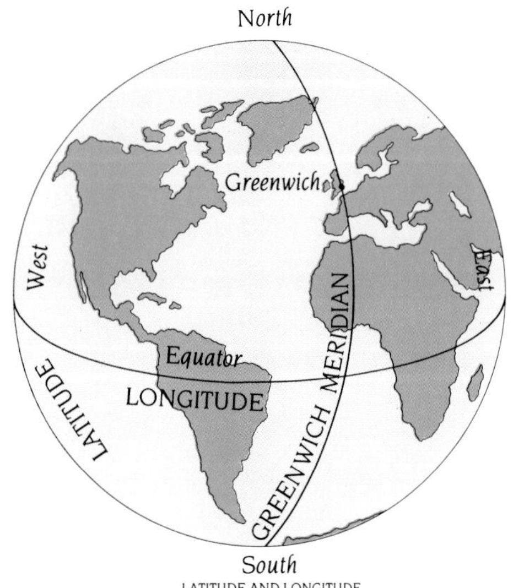
North
Greenwich
West
East
GREENWICH MERIDIAN
Equator
LONGITUDE
LATITUDE
South

LATITUDE AND LONGITUDE

Experienced astrologers are able to work out an accurate horoscope by comparing events in a person's life to the movement of the planets. This is known as rectifying the horoscope. Even though its practitioners claim it is scientific, no two astrologers will produce the same rectification for the same client. The results achieved are not necessarily better than those from the solar chart.

Measurement of Space
Four coordinates are used to fix a planet's location in space. Of these by far the most important is celestial longitude, which fixes a planet's place in relation to the ecliptic, the Sun's path through the sky. This measurement is expressed in terms of the signs of the zodiac, beginning at 0° Aries and finishing at 30° Pisces.

Centre: Lines of latitude run from east to west and measure distances north or south of the equator. Lines of longitude run from north to south and measure distances east or west of the Greenwich meridian.
The Sun passes through 1° of longitude in four minutes. The time that it takes the Sun to travel from Greenwich to a particular place is known as the Longitude Equivalent in Time (LET).

Bottom: Sidereal and Tropical Time
The tropical day on which ordinary time is based is divided into exactly 24 hours, one complete rotation of the Earth in relation to the Sun. The sidereal day is based on the rotation of the Earth in relation to the stars and is almost four minutes shorter than the tropical day.
If tropical and sidereal time are synchronized at the beginning of the day then by midnight tropical time, sidereal time will be 11.56.06 pm. After 17 days the difference between the two systems amounts to just over one hour. Tropical time is always converted into sidereal time during the calculation of the Ascendant and houses.

3 mins 54 secs

SIDEREAL TIME TROPICAL TIME

All recognized standard times are based on the Greenwich meridian, the line of longitude that runs through the Greenwich Observatory in London, and which divides east from west. Greenwich Mean Time (GMT) is the standard time for Britain. All time zones east of Greenwich are in advance of GMT and all zones west are behind GMT.

MEASUREMENT

SPACE. The circle of the zodiac is divided into 360 degrees, or 12 signs of 30 degrees each. Each degree consists of 60 minutes and each minute of 60 seconds. Seconds are rarely used. The symbol ° stands for degree; ′ for minute and ″ for second. If, for example, the Moon was at 1 degree, 16 minutes and 28 seconds in Gemini, this could be written in any of the following forms:
☽ is 1° 16′ 28″ ♊ or 1° 16′ ♊ or 1° ♊ 16′ or 1° ♊
Such measurement around the zodiac is based on the ecliptic and is known as **celestial longitude**. There are three other methods of defining a planet's location: **celestial latitude**, **declination** and **right ascension**.

***Standard Time Zones in the* USA**
The USA *is divided into four time zones. When the time is noon at Greenwich it is 7.00 am in the eastern* USA, *4.00 am in the west and 5.00 am and 6.00 am in the two central zones.*

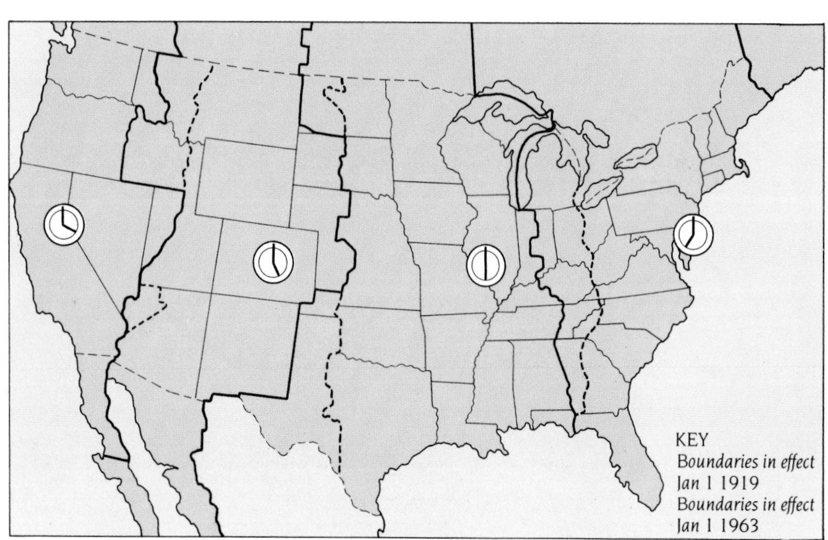

TIME. Astrological calculation uses two separate but interlocking systems of measuring time. The first is the familiar system of seconds, minutes, hours, days of 24 hours and years of 365 days (or 366 in a leap year). This is the normal system in which all events on Earth are measured. The year in this system is known as the **tropical year**.

The second system is that of **sidereal time**, based on the Earth's rotation in relation to the stars rather than to the Sun. The sidereal year is longer than the tropical year, being 365 days, 6 hours, 9 minutes and 9.5 seconds in duration. The sidereal day is shorter than the ordinary day, and is 23 hours, 56 minutes, 4.09 seconds long. Sidereal time is a vital part of the astrological calculation and must be worked out before the horoscope can be cast (see tables in the back of this book).

THE EARTH. The location of places on Earth is defined by **latitude** and **longitude**. Latitude measures distances north and south of the equator and longitude measures places east and west of the Greenwich meridian, both using degrees, minutes and seconds, although seconds are usually ignored. For example, the latitude of Los Angeles is 34° 03' N and its longitude is 118° 15' W. Melbourne, Australia, has a latitude of 37° 47' S and a longitude of 144° 58' E.

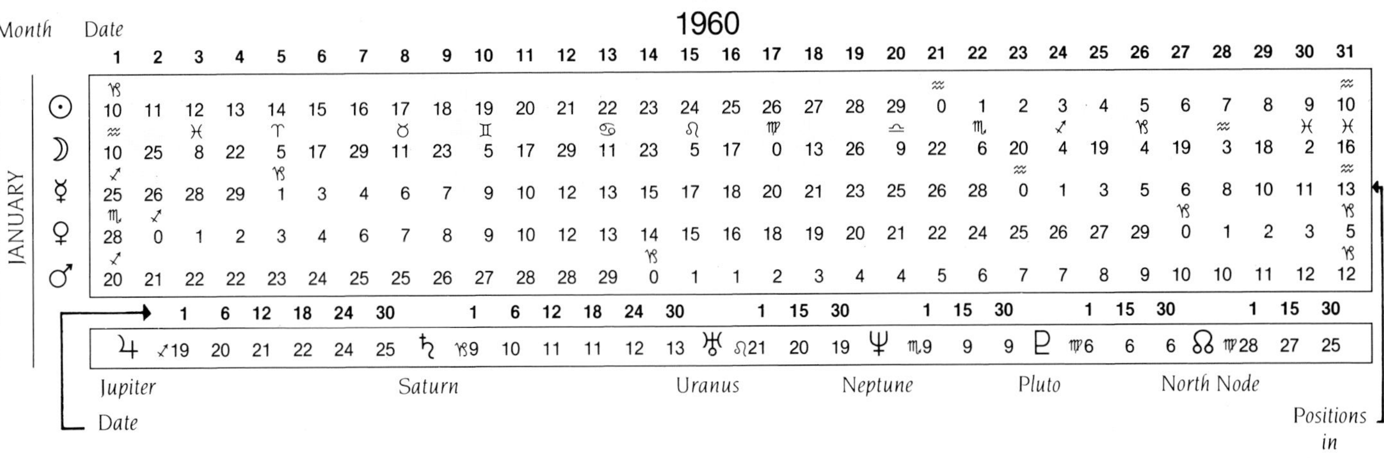

Year 1960 — JANUARY

Month / Date	1	2	3	4	5	6	7	8	9	10	11	12	13	14	15	16	17	18	19	20	21	22	23	24	25	26	27	28	29	30	31
☉	♑ 10	11	12	13	14	15	16	17	18	19	20	21	22	23	24	25	26	27	28	29	♒ 0	1	2	3	4	5	6	7	8	9	♒ 10
☽	♒ 10	25	♓ 8	22	♈ 5	17	29	♉ 11	23	♊ 5	17	29	♋ 11	23	♌ 5	17	♍ 0	13	26	♎ 9	22	♏ 6	20	♐ 4	19	♑ 4	19	♒ 3	18	♓ 2	♓ 16
☿	♐ 25	26	28	29	♑ 1	3	4	6	7	9	10	12	13	15	17	18	20	21	23	25	26	28	♒ 0	1	3	5	6	8	10	11	♒ 13
♀	♏ 28	♐ 0	1	2	3	4	6	7	8	9	10	12	13	14	15	16	18	19	20	21	22	24	25	26	27	29	♑ 0	1	2	3	♑ 5
♂	♐ 20	21	22	22	23	24	25	25	26	27	28	28	29	♑ 0	1	1	2	3	4	4	5	6	7	7	8	9	10	10	11	12	♑ 12

Planet	Date	Positions
♃ Jupiter	1, 6, 12, 18, 24, 30	♐19, 20, 21, 22, 24, 25
♄ Saturn	1, 6, 12, 18, 24, 30	♑9, 10, 11, 11, 12, 13
♅ Uranus	1, 15, 30	♌21, 20, 19
♆ Neptune	1, 15, 30	♏9, 9, 9
♇ Pluto	1, 15, 30	♍6, 6, 6
☊ North Node	1, 15, 30	♍28, 27, 25

Positions in degrees

CALCULATION 1: CONVERSION OF GIVEN TIME TO GREENWICH MEAN TIME

The given time is the time for which the horoscope must be cast. In the case of the birth chart this is the time of birth. It is essential that this is converted to **Greenwich Mean Time** (GMT), which is the standard time upon which all world time zones are based. It is also sometimes referred to as Universal Time (UT).

The world is divided into a series of **time zones** which run from north to south, and in most cases there is a one hour difference between adjacent zones. All zones east of Greenwich have times in advance of GMT and all zones west have times behind GMT. For example, New York (Eastern Standard Time) is five hours west of Greenwich while Berlin (Central European Time) is one hour east. When GMT is at noon, it is, therefore, 7.00 am in New York and 1.00 pm in Berlin.

In many countries the clocks are advanced by one hour during the summer months. This is known as **daylight saving time** although it is more commonly referred to as **summer time**. If two hours are added, then it is known as double summer time.

Local Mean Time (LMT) is local time fixed in relation to the Sun. In most countries it has now been replaced by zone standard time. It was abolished in Britain in 1880. Births early this century in Africa and Asia may, however, have been recorded in LMT and this should be checked by the astrologer.

CALCULATION

1. Make adjustment for zone standard time: if the zone is west of Greenwich, add zone standard to birth time; if east of Greenwich, subtract zone standard from birth time.
2. If daylight saving time (summer time) was in use, subtract one hour from birth time (see table in the back of this book).
3. If birth time is given in LMT, calculate the Longitude Equivalent in Time (LET), using the table in the back of this book. If place of birth is west of Greenwich then add LET to birth time. If place of birth is east of Greenwich then subtract LET from birth time.

Conversion of birth time to GMT can result in a **change of date**. In that case it is the new date, the GMT date, which is used to calculate the horoscope.

CALCULATION OF PLANET'S DAILY MOTION

Position at end of day	18° 13′
Position at beginning of day	– 16° 23′
Daily motion	1° 50′
Position at end of day	18°
Position at beginning of day	– 12°
Daily motion	6°

If the planet is retrograde, then the calculation must be reversed.

Position at beginning of day	12° 41′
Position at end of day	– 11° 43′
Daily motion	0° 58′

CONVERSION OF BIRTH TIME TO GREENWICH MEAN TIME (GMT)

	h	m	s
Birth date	21 Dec 1980		
Birth place	New York		
Birth time as given	11	0	0 pm
Zone standard (East –; West +)	+ 5	0	0
Summer time	–	–	–
GMT of birth	4	0	0 am
GMT date if different	22 Dec 1980		

CONVERSION OF BIRTH TIME TO GREENWICH MEAN TIME (GMT)

	h	m	s
Birth Date	20 Aug 1976		
Birth place	London		
Birth time as given	4	0	0 pm
Zone standard (East –; West +)	–	–	–
Summer time	– 1	0	0
GMT of birth	3	0	0 pm

Reading the Ephemeris

The ephemeris is a simple guide to planetary positions. The position of each planet is always given for midnight (zero hours) Greenwich Mean Time. The positions of the Sun, Moon, Mercury, Venus and Mars are given for each day, those of Jupiter and Saturn for every six days, and those for Uranus, Neptune, Pluto and the north node every 15 days. By following this table it is easy to see that at midnight on 1 January 1960 the Sun was at 10° Capricorn or that at midnight on 5 January the Moon was at 5° Aries.

The bottom line gives the positions of the five outer planets and the north node. On 1 January Jupiter was at 19° Sagittarius, Saturn was at 9° Capricorn and Uranus was at 21° Leo.

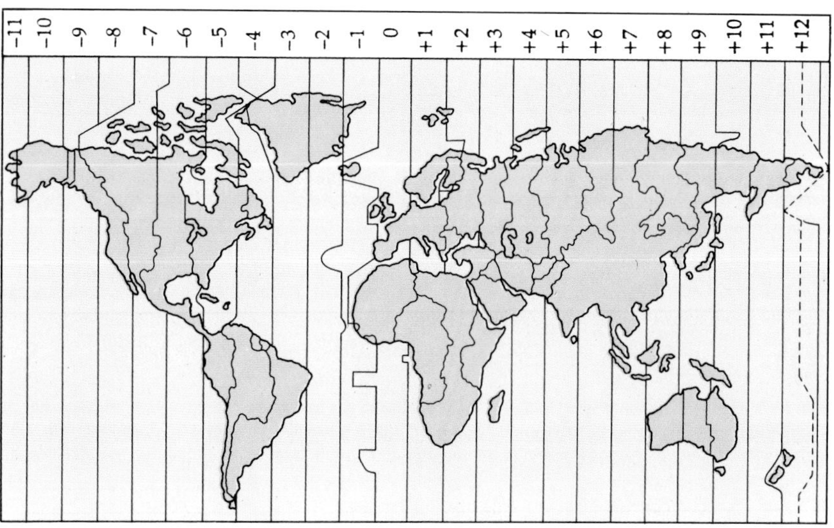

The Earth is divided into 24 time zones each of which corresponds to 15° of longitude. At the international date line, not only the hour but also the date changes.

CALCULATION 2: FINDING ZODIACAL LONGITUDE OF PLANETS

The position of planets is generally calculated to approximately the nearest degree and minute, and a variation of one or two minutes is acceptable. Using logarithms, calculators or computers, positions may be calculated to the nearest second, although this is unusual.

The planetary positions in the ephemeris are all given for midnight GMT and rounded to the nearest whole degree. This means that no calculation is required to find the approximate position for any of the planets except the Moon.

The Proportional Method can be used to calculate the position of the Moon to the nearest whole degree, and the position of any planet to the nearest minute in the following way:

1. Convert the given time of birth to GMT.
2. Calculate the interval, that is the time from midnight (00.00 hours) GMT to the time of birth. For example, if birth was at 7.00 am GMT the interval is seven hours. If birth was at 3.00 pm GMT, the interval is 15 hours.
3. Calculate the daily motion of the planet, that is the distance travelled by the planet during the day of birth; this can be worked out by subtracting the position at the beginning of the day from the position at the end of the day.
4. Divide the daily motion by 24 to find out how far the planet moved in one hour.
5. Multiply this result by the interval.
If a computer or calculator is not available, and unless absolute accuracy is required, it is permissible to simplify this calculation by rounding the interval to the nearest hour.
6. Add this result to the position of the planet at the beginning of the day. If the planet is retrograde, subtract the result from the planet's position at the beginning of the day.
7. The final result is the approximate position of the planet for the time of birth. The same method can be used to find the exact position of a planet to the nearest degree and minute, assuming an ephemeris is used which gives positions in degrees and minutes.

QUICK CALCULATION OF APPROXIMATE PLANETARY POSITION 1

Example set for 3.15 am GMT on 1 July 1986. The time is rounded down to 3.00 am for a simple calculation of the Moon's position.

Calculation using Proportional Method

	h m s
Interval of birth after midnight	3 0 0
Planet's position at end of day (☽)	13° 0′ 0″♉
Planet's position at beginning of day	− 1° 0′ 0″♉
Planet's daily motion	12° 0′ 0″
Planet's hourly motion (daily motion ÷ 24) {12° ÷ 24 = ½° = 0°30′}	0° 30′ 0″
Hourly motion × Interval (3 × 0°30′)	1° 30′ 0″
Planet's position at beginning of day	+ 1° 0′ 0″
Planet's position at time of birth	2° 30′ 0″♉

QUICK CALCULATION OF APPROXIMATE PLANETARY POSITION 2

In this example the Moon changes signs during the day. The calculation of the Moon's position is set for 9.00pm on 3 July 1986.

Calculation using Proportional Method

	h m s
Interval of birth after midnight	21 0 0
Planet's position at end of day	37° 0′ 0″ ♊
Planet's position at beginning of day	− 25° 0′ 0″ ♉
Planet's daily motion	12° 0′ 0″
Planet's hourly motion (daily motion ÷ 24)	0° 30′ 0″
Hourly motion × Interval (21 × 0°30′)	10° 30′ 0″
Planet's position at beginning of day	25° 0′ 0″ ♉
Planet's position at time of birth	5° 30′ 0″ ♊

CALCULATION 3: CALCULATING HOUSES AND ASCENDANT

Calculation of the houses takes into account the longitude and latitude of the place of birth and sidereal time. The key references are the Tables of Houses for Northern Latitudes. An adjustment is made in the final calculation to work out houses for the southern latitudes (see below). To make the calculation:

1. Convert birth time to GMT.
2. Look up longitude and latitude of place of birth, using any good atlas.
3. Look up the sidereal time for midnight (00.00) hours GMT for the date of birth, remembering to use the new date if an adjustment has been made to this for GMT (see tables in the back of this book).
4. Work out the interval from midnight (00.00 hours) to the GMT time of birth.
5. Add the interval to the sidereal time for midnight.
6. Work out the acceleration on the interval,

and add this to the previous figure (see table in the back of this book). The result is the sidereal time at Greenwich at birth.

7. Calculate the longitude equivalent in time or LET (see table in the back of this book). If longitude of birth place is east of Greenwich, then add the LET to the sidereal time at Greenwich at birth. If longitude of birth place is west of Greenwich then subtract the LET from the sidereal time at Greenwich at birth. The result is the local sidereal time at birth.

8. If the result is over 24 hours, subtract 24 hours.

9. Turn to the Tables of Houses for northern latitudes. Find the column for the latitude of the place of birth, look down the sidereal time column until you find the time which is closest to the local sidereal time at birth, and read off the Ascendant and the Midheaven.

FOR SOUTHERN LATITUDES:

1. Calculate the local sidereal time of birth as for northern latitudes.
2. Add 12 hours.
3. If the result is over 24 hours, subtract 24 hours.
4. Turn to the Table of Houses for equivalent northern latitude. For example, for 43° south look up tables for 43° north.
5. Look up the Ascendant and Midheaven.
6. Reverse the signs. For example, Aries becomes Libra and Scorpio becomes Taurus.

CALCULATION 4: ASCERTAINING THE EXACT ASCENDANT AND MIDHEAVEN

Having calculated the approximate Ascendant and Midheaven it is possible to draw up and interpret the chart, but it is customary to calculate the angles exactly. This is essential for certain predictive techniques.

To calculate the exact Ascendant and Midheaven:

1. Work out the local sidereal time at birth, then look in the Tables of Houses for the sidereal times immediately before and after this, and then the Ascendant and Midheaven for both these times.
2. Subtract the earlier sidereal time from the later sidereal time. Convert the result into seconds. For example, 3′ 10″ converts into 190″. Call this A.
3. Subtract the earlier sidereal time from the local sidereal time at birth. Convert the result into seconds and call this B.
4. Subtract the Midheaven at the earlier time from the Midheaven at the later time. Convert the result into minutes. For example 1° 0' converts into 60'. Call this C.
5. Subtract the Ascendant at the earlier time from the Ascendant at the later time. Convert the result into minutes and call this D.
6. Multiply B by D and divide the result by A. The result is in minutes and seconds. Using ordinary mathematics it is sufficient to get a result in minutes alone but with a pocket calculator the result will include seconds. Add this result to the earlier Ascendant to give the exact Ascendant at birth.
7. Multiply B by C and divide the result by A. As in calculating the Ascendant ordinary mathematics will give a result in minutes alone but if a calculator is used the result will be in minutes and seconds.

Add the result to the earlier Midheaven to give the exact Midheaven at birth.

DRAWING UP THE HOROSCOPE

There are various styles used to draw up horoscopes, depending on the preferences of individual astrologers and on the different house systems employed. Whatever style is used, neatness is an absolutely essential requirement.

Most astrologers use printed chart forms with a circle drawn out to show divisions for the signs and each degree, with spaces for writing information about the horoscope.

CALCULATION OF ASCENDANT AND MIDHEAVEN (AND EQUAL HOUSE CUSPS)

Birth date (GMT)	4 July 1986
	h m s
Birth time GMT	3 30 0 am
Birth place	Los Angeles
Latitude	34° 03′ 0″ N
Longitude	118° 15′ 0″ W
	h m s
Sidereal Time midnight (00.00 hrs) GMT	18 46 50
Interval of birth time after midnight	+ 3 30 0
Result	22 16 50
Acceleration on Interval	+ 0 0 34
Sidereal Time at Greenwich at birth	22 17 24
Longitude Equivalent in Time (East +; West −)	− 7 53
Local Sidereal Time at birth	14 24 24
Subtract 24 hours if necessary	
Result	14 24 24

From Table of Houses for Lat 34° N
Asc 19° ♑ approx
MC 8°♏ approx

QUICK CALCULATION OF EXACT PLANETARY POSITION 3

Using more detailed tables and a pocket calculator it is possible to calculate a planet's position to the nearest minute. This calculation of the Moon's position is set for 3.36 am GMT on the 4 July 1986.

Calculation using Proportional Method

	h m s
Interval of birth after midnight	3 46 0
Planet's position at end of day	18° 27′ 0″ ♊
Planet's position at beginning of day	− 6° 37′ 0″ ♊
Planet's daily motion	11° 50′ 0″
Planet's hourly motion (daily motion ÷ 24)	0° 9 ′35 ″
Hourly motion × Interval	1° 51′ 0″
Planet's position at beginning of day	+ 6° 37′ 0″
Planet's position at time of birth	8° 28′ 0″ ♊

A Complete Calculation

This example carries a calculation through from start to finish. The data is that of Wendy, a writer and dancer, who was born in Fulham, West London, at 10.25pm on 4 July 1950. Usually for any chart set for the Greater London area the latitude and longitude is taken for Greenwich with fairly accurate results. In this case the chart has been set for the exact location within London in order to achieve the greatest degree of accuracy. Detailed positions were used for the calculations of the planets and times were kept in hours and minutes and not rounded to the nearest hour as in the approximate calculations. A pocket calculator was used for the original calculations.
For reasons of space only the calculation of the Moon's position is shown in full. This horoscope is the basis for the sample interpretation in Chapter 10.

CALCULATION OF ASCENDANT AND MIDHEAVEN (AND EQUAL HOUSE CUSPS) FOR BIRTH IN THE SOUTHERN HEMISPHERE

Birth date (GMT)	5 Aug 1974		
	h	m	s
Birth time GMT	10	10	0 pm
Birth place	Melbourne		
Latitude	37°	47′	0″S
Longitude	144°	58′	0″E

	h	m	s
Sidereal Time midnight (00.00 hrs) GMT	20	52	40
Interval of birth time after midnight	+ 10	10	0
Result	31	02	40
Acceleration on Interval	+	1	40
Sidereal Time at Greenwich at birth	31	4	20
Longitude Equivalent in Time (East +; West −)	+ 9	39	52
Local Sidereal Time at birth	40	44	12
Subtract 24 hours if necessary	− 24	0	0
Result	16	44	12

From Table of Houses for Lat 37° N
Asc 1°♓
MC 13°♐

CALCULATION OF APPROXIMATE ASCENDANT AND MC

	h	m	s
Sidereal Time midnight (00.00 hrs) GMT	18	45	44
Interval of birth time after midnight	+ 21	25	0
Result	40	10	44
Acceleration on Interval	+ 0	3	31
Sidereal Time at Greenwich at birth	40	14	15
Longitude Equivalent in Time (East +; West −)	0	0	52
Local Sidereal Time at birth	40	13	23
Subtract 24 hours if necessary	− 24	0	0
Result	16	13	23

From Table of Houses for Lat 51° N
Asc 5°♒ approx
MC 5°♐ approx

ADJUSTMENT OF CALCULATION OF HOUSES FOR SOUTHERN LATITUDES

	h	m	s
Local Sidereal Time at birth	16	44	12
Add 12 hours	28	44	12
Subtract 24 hours if necessary	24	0	0
Result	4	44	12

From Table of Houses for Lat 37° N
Asc 14°♍ reverse sign = 14°♓
MC 12°♊ Reverse sign = 12°♐

CALCULATION OF EXACT ASCENDANT AND MIDHEADEN

	h	m	s
(1) Local Sidereal Time at birth	16	13	23
Sidereal Time before birth	16	12	13
Sidereal Time after birth	16	16	26
(2) Sidereal Time after birth	16	16	26
Sidereal Time before birth	− 16	12	13
Result	0	4	13
Convert into seconds	0°	0′	253″
Call this A			
(3) Local Sidereal Time at birth	16	13	23
Sidereal Time before birth	− 16	12	13
Result	0	1	10
Convert into seconds	0°	0′	70″
Call this B			
(4) MC for later Sidereal Time	6	0	0
MC for earlier time	− 5	0	0
Result	1	0	0
Convert into minutes	0°	60′	0″
Call this C			
(5) Asc for later time	6	32	0
Asc for earlier time	− 4	53	0
Result	1	39	0
Convert into minutes	0°	99′	0″
Call this D			
(6) B × D ÷ A	70 × 99 ÷ 253		
Result	0°	27′	23″
Asc for earlier time	+ 4°	53′	0″ ♒
Asc for time of birth	5°	20′	23″ ♒
(7) B × C ÷ A	70 × 60 ÷ 253		
Result	0	16	36
MC for earlier time	+ 5°	0′	0″ ♐
MC for time of birth	5°	16′	36″ ♐

CONVERSION OF BIRTH TIME TO GREENWICH MEAN TIME (GMT)

Birth date	4 July 1950		
Birth place	London		
Latitude	51°	28′	0″ N
Longitude	0°	13′	0″ W
	h	m	s
Birth time as given	10	25	0 pm
Zone standard (East −; West +)	−	−	−
Summer time	− 1	0	0
GMT of birth	9	25	0 pm

Calculation of Planetary Position using Proportional Method

	h	m	s
Interval of birth after midnight	21	25	0

Planet's position at end of day (☽)	18°	22′	0″ ♓
Planet's position at beginning of day	− 5°	33′	0″ ♓
Planet's daily motion	12°	49′	0″
Planet's hourly motion (daily motion ÷ 24)	0°	32′	0″
Hourly motion × Interval	11°	26′	0″
Planet's position at beginning of day	+ 5°	33′	0″
Planet's position at time of birth	16°	59′	0″ ♓

DRAWING OUT THE CHART 1. Most astrologers use printed chart wheels to save time, and help with neat presentation and easy reading of the horoscope. These are available commercially in different styles, although some astrologers prefer to design their own. Space around the chart wheel is given over to the inclusion of additional material and data.

Space is provided above the chart wheel for time, date and place of birth, the essential data for calculation.

Below the chart wheel are spaces for additional information including the house system used, the ruling planet and the numbers of planets in the different types of signs.

Space is provided to list planets that fall in the different types of house, angular, succeedent or cadent. These should not be considered when the Equal House system is used because the symbolic basis of the system is removed when the MC does not fall on the tenth house cusp.

Aspects and mutual reception will be explained in Chapter 8.

DRAWING OUT THE CHART 2. The first step is to place the signs in the 12 blank spaces around the outside of the wheel. Then mark the Ascendant, the MC and the house cusps on the chart. The 'horizon' of the chart, the first and seventh cusps, must be kept as horizontal as possible. Using a red pen mark the Ascendant in the left-hand space either above or below the 'horizon'. If the Ascendant is between 0° and 15° mark it in the lower space; if it is over 15° mark it in the higher. In our example the Ascendant is 5° ♒ so the lower of the two left-hand spaces is used.

Fill in the rest of the signs in their correct order anticlockwise around the chart, using a red pen for the sign containing the Midheaven (MC). Write in the degrees of the Ascendant and MC in their approximate places in the sign.

In this example Equal Houses are used which means that all the house cusps will be at 30° intervals. As the Ascendant is on the cusp of the first house, and is 5° 20′ ♒, all the house cusps will occupy 5° 20′ of their successive signs.

Drawing in the house cusps is then a simple matter of connecting 5° 20′ of each sign with 5° 20′ in the opposite sign by a straight line through the middle of the chart. The first and seventh house cusps, otherwise known as the Ascendant and Descendant, and the MC and IC are marked by a red arrow as shown, drawing attention to these as vital areas of the chart: notice that the MC falls almost exactly on the eleventh cusp.

Finally mark the number of each house close to the centre of the wheel so that you can see at a glance which house contains which planets.

DRAWING OUT THE CHART 3. Once the house cusps are drawn the planets can be placed in their positions. Locate each planet and mark it on the chart on the exact degree. On the inside of the mark draw the planetary glyph. Inside the glyph write in the degrees and the minutes (if used) of the planet's position. It is a good idea to write the minutes in smaller print than the degrees so that the two are clearly distinguished. If a planet is retrograde a small capital 'R' is placed on the inside of the minutes.

In this example Jupiter is the only retrograde planet and the 'R' is plainly marked alongside.

Notice that the Sun, which is placed at 12° ♋ is not exactly on its own degree: this is for reasons of space. When several planets are in a conjunction it becomes impossible to mark them in their exact positions, in which case place them as near as possible.

DRAWING OUT THE CHART 4. At this stage additional information can be entered around the chart wheel. Most of this is self-explanatory: Aquarius has two ruling planets, Saturn and Uranus. However, as Uranus is the modern secondary ruler both the planet and its house have been placed in brackets to indicate this.

The spaces for numbers of planets in angular, succeedent and cadent houses are left blank as these should not be used with Equal Houses. The space for mutual reception and the aspect grid are also left blank as these will be dealt with in Chapter 8.

The full completed chart form is given in Chapter 10.

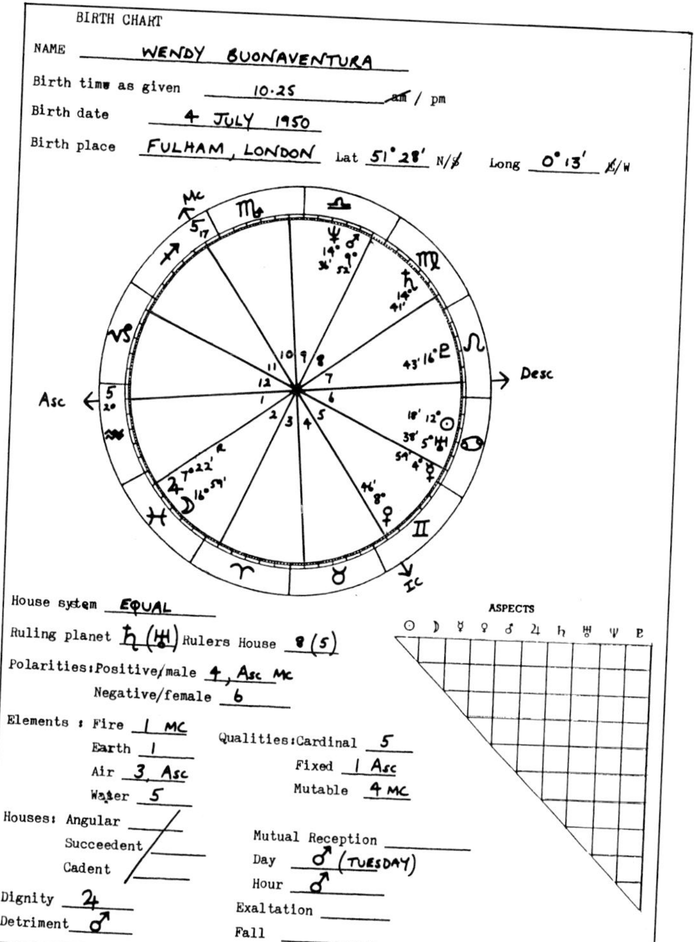

BIRTH CHART

NAME WENDY BUONAVENTURA

Birth time as given 10.25 ~~am~~ / pm

Birth date 4 JULY 1950

Birth place FULHAM, LONDON Lat 51°28′ N/~~S~~ Long 0°13′ ~~E~~/W

House system EQUAL

Ruling planet ♄ (♅) Rulers House 8 (5)

Polarities: Positive/male 4, Asc MC

Negative/female 6

Elements: Fire 1 MC

Earth 1

Air 3, Asc

Water 5

Qualities: Cardinal 5

Fixed 1 Asc

Mutable 4 MC

Houses: Angular

Succeedent

Cadent

Mutual Reception

Day ♂ (TUESDAY)

Hour ♂

Dignity ♃

Detriment ♂

Exaltation

Fall

ASPECTS

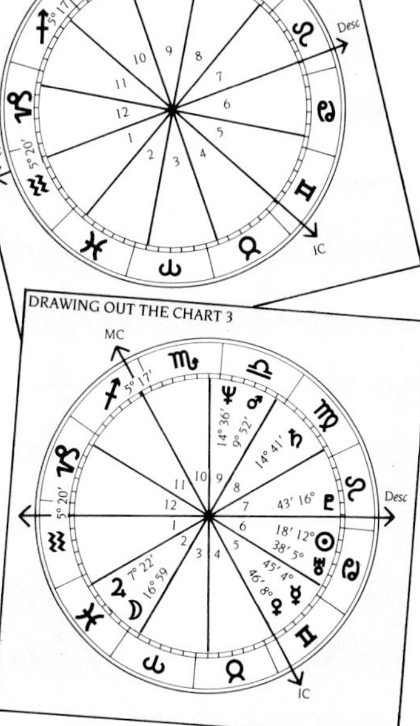

Drawing out the Charts:
Top – 4
Centre – 2
Bottom – 3

CHAPTER 8
THE ASPECTS

An aspect is the precise distance between any two points in a horoscope. Almost all aspects measure distances around the ecliptic. Usually aspects are formed between two planets, although aspects between any one planet and the angles (Ascendant, Descendant, MC and IC) are also considered.

The aspects are used to establish how the planets combine to stimulate and moderate each other's influence.

The aspects are divided into two categories, **major** or **minor**, and **harmonious** or **tense**. Generally, major aspects are much more powerful than the minor; but there are certain astrologers who place a greater than usual emphasis upon the minor aspects.

Aspects are formed by division of the circle of 360 degrees by certain numbers, and may be understood through the laws of numerology. Division of the circle by 3, 6 and 12 is harmonious and flowing, while division by 2, 4 and 8 is rigid, structured and difficult.

Harmonious aspects are also known as good, easy, positive, soft or benefic, and tense aspects are also known as bad, difficult, negative, hard or malefic.

The tense aspects cause friction between the planets involved. This friction brings difficulties and problems, which may be psychological, environmental or a combination of the two. In coping with these problems many people experience failure, but some will be driven to overcome their difficulties and in the process develop their astrological potential.

The harmonious aspects bring an easy relationship between the planets involved. They provide a helpful environment for innate abilities which the individual may take for granted, but fail to develop fully.

Each type of aspect, therefore, has two faces. The tense aspects bring difficulties which can result in great achievement, while the harmonious aspects bring easy conditions which can lead to wasted opportunities.

It is preferable to have a balance of tense and harmonious aspects. Individuals with only harmonious aspects may have plenty of potential but no drive to develop it, while those with only tense aspects may lack the faith and optimism to overcome difficulties.

There are nine aspects in common use: the five major aspects – conjunction, opposition, trine, square and sextile – and four minor aspects – the semi-sextile, semi-square, sesquiquadrate and quincunx. The quincunx is also known as the inconjunct.

Name	Glyph	Degrees Apart when Exact	Orb	Range of Operation	Strength	Nature	
Conjunction	☌	0° (360 ÷ 1)	8°	0°–8°	Major	Neutral	
Semi-Sextile	⚺	30° (360 ÷ 12)	2°	28°–32°	Minor	Harmonious	
Semi-square	∠	45° (360 ÷ 8)	2°	43°–47°	Minor	Tense	
Sextile	⚹	60° (360 ÷ 6)	4°	56°–64°	Major	Harmonious	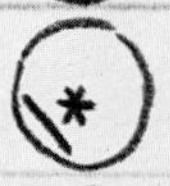
Square	□	90° (360 ÷ 4)	8°	82°–98°	Major	Tense	
Trine	△	120° (360 ÷ 3)	8°	112°–128°	Major	Harmonious	
Sesquiquadrate	⚼	135°	2°	133°–137°	Minor	Tense	
Quincunx or Inconjunct	⚻	150°	2°	148°–152°	Minor	Tense	
Opposition	☍	180° (360 ÷ 2)	8°	172°–188°	Major	Tense	

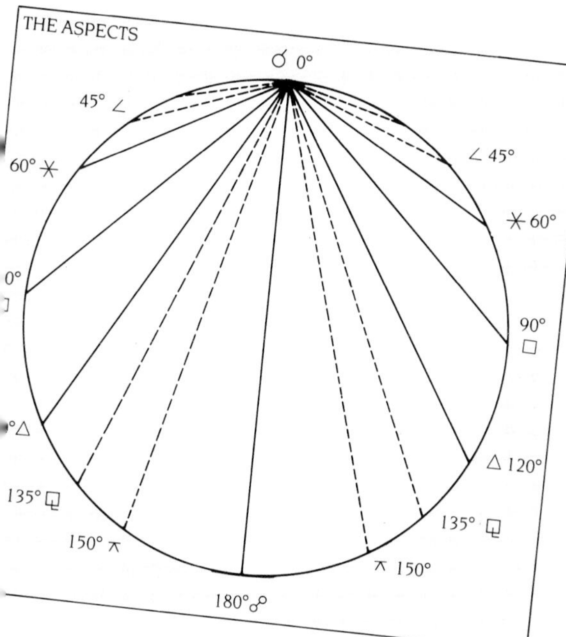

Conjunction is the most powerful aspect and combines two planets in a single force.

Opposition is extremely powerful and places the planets in conflict with each other, producing difficulties, but increasing the range of possibilities open to the individual.

Trine is the most powerful harmonious aspect, bringing the planets together in an easy combination.

Square is strong, but less powerful than opposition, and creates friction between planets.

Sextile is a strong harmonious aspect, but less powerful than the trine.

Semi-square, sesquiquadrate and quincunx are all minor tense aspects. Psychologically their effect may be seen as a very weak version of the square. Some astrologers give them additional importance in predicting events.

Semi-sextile is the only minor harmonious aspect, and psychologically is a weak version of the sextile.

APPLYING AND SEPARATING ASPECTS

When two planets are moving together to form an exact aspect they are applying. When they are moving apart from the exact aspect they are separating. Applying aspects are usually stronger psychologically than separating aspects. In event and horary horoscopes separating aspects refer to past events and applying aspects refer to future events.

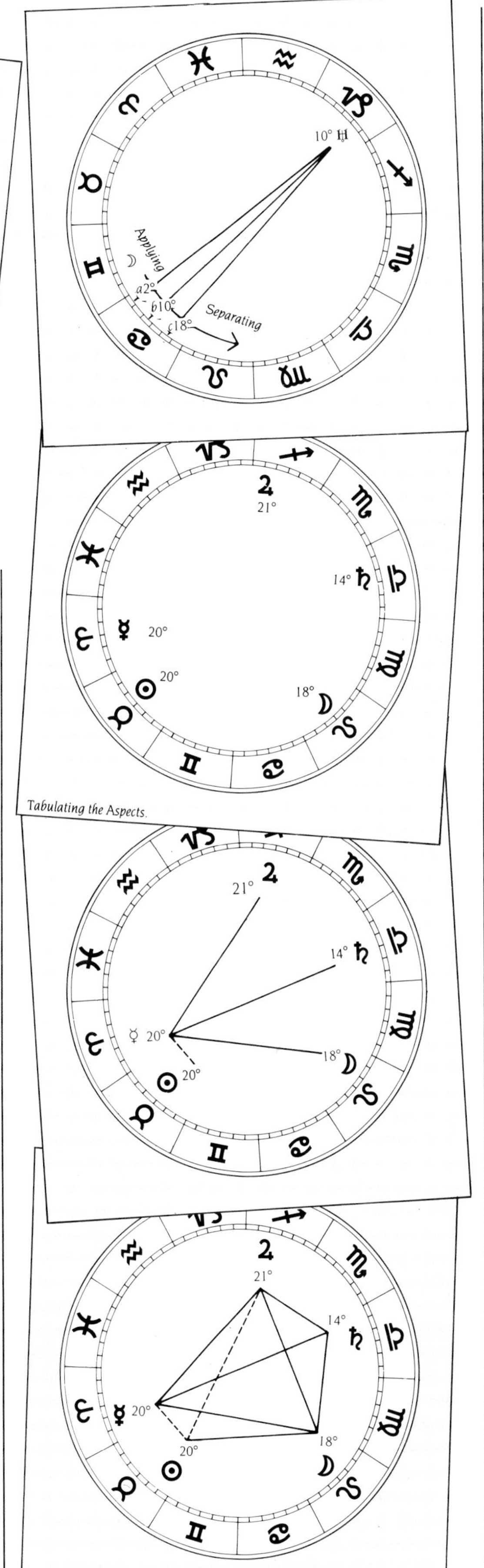

Tabulating the Aspects.

Applying and Separating Aspects

In this example the Moon, the fastest moving of all the planets, is shown passing through all phases of an opposition to Uranus.
At point a) the Moon at 2° Cancer enters the opposition to Uranus at 10° Capricorn, and from there until 10° Cancer the aspect is applying. At point b) the Moon reaches 10° Cancer and the aspect is exact. Thereafter it is separating until the Moon finally leaves the orb at 18° Cancer.

Tabulating the Aspects

When familiar with the layout of the horoscope then the aspects can be spotted at a glance. One sure guide is that two planets having similar degrees in their respective signs are almost certainly in aspect.
For the beginner working out the aspects is very much a question of taking each planet in turn and patiently counting the number of degrees separating it from the others. This process is simplified by the use of printed chart wheels in which the degrees are marked off in units of one, five and 30. When the distance between two planets corresponds to an aspect the aspect glyph is marked on the grid below the chart.

ASPECTS

	☽	☿	♀	♂	♃	♄	♅	♆	♇
☉		⊻			⊼				
☽		△			△	⚹			
☿					△	☍			
♀									
♂									
♃						⚹			
♄									
♅									
♆									
♇									

HARMONIOUS ASPECT

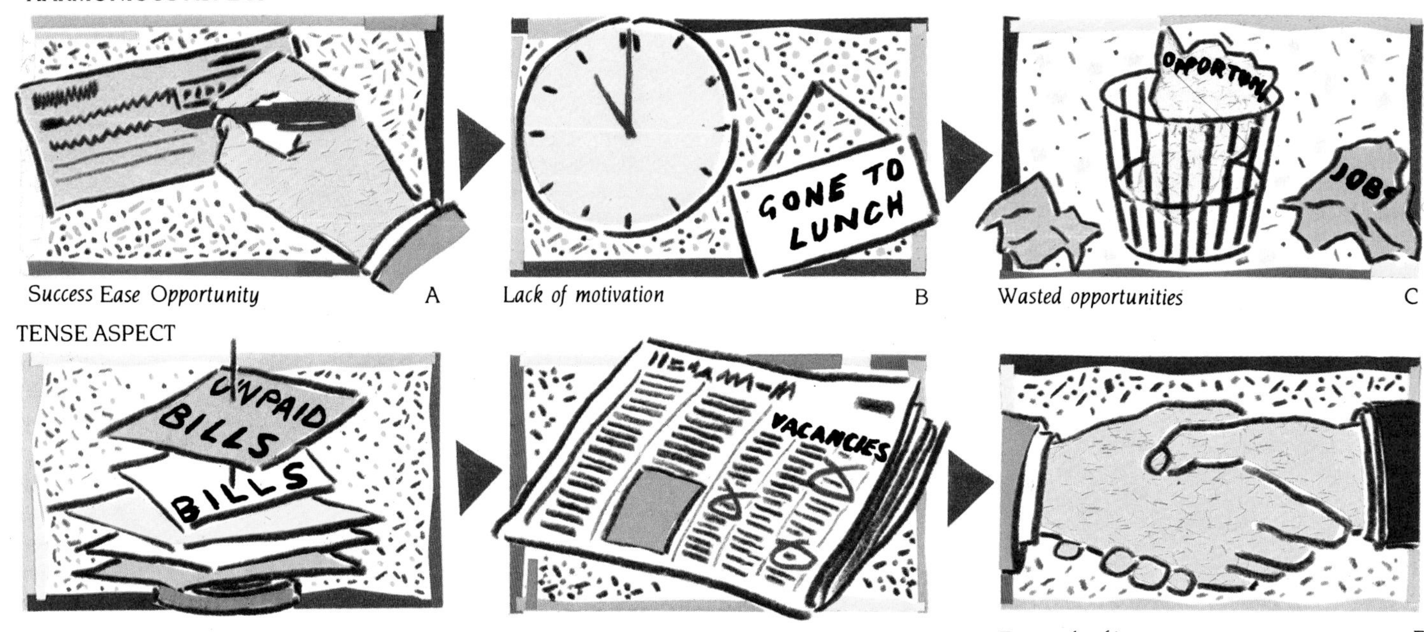

Success Ease Opportunity A

Lack of motivation B

Wasted opportunities C

TENSE ASPECT

Failure Tension Problems D

Motivation Energy E

Eventual achievement F

Dynamic Processes of the Aspects
Harmonious aspects bring benefits, skills and opportunities, but not necessarily final success, while tense aspects bring difficulties, tension and initial failure but often lead to eventual achievement. Seen from this perspective it is necessary to have a balance of tense and harmonious aspects and together these may be seen as a single process, phase C *leading to* D *and* F *to* A.
This example might be found with Mars-Saturn aspects, phase A *being a trine or sextile and* D *being a square or opposition.* A *person might be born with one Mars-Saturn configuration, but during a lifetime will experience all the different possibilities.*

ORBS

An orb is the distance by which a planet is allowed to deviate from the exact aspect. The deviation allowed is usually up to 8°. The more exact the aspect, the stronger the influence, the looser the aspect the weaker the influence. The more powerful aspects are allowed wider orbs than the less powerful ones.

ABUNDANCE OR SCARCITY OF ASPECTS

If there are sufficient major aspects to provide an interpretation in the required detail, then it is not necessary to interpret the minor ones. However, if explicit detail is required, or if there are only a few major aspects, more attention should be paid to the minor aspects.

UNASPECTED PLANETS

Opinions differ over the interpretation of unaspected planets. It is best to learn from experience, but the following guidelines are useful. First, the planet may be difficult to express. The principle it represents may be badly integrated with the rest of the personality and may even be neglected. In complete contrast, the lack of aspects may mean that the planet is unrestrained by other planets and therefore assumes an exaggerated importance.

Sun unaspected: these people may have a poor sense of self-identity, but may appear to be very egotistical.

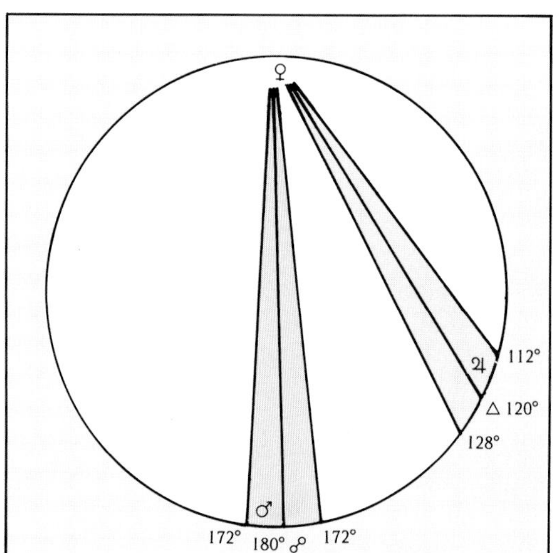

Above Right: Orbs
In this example Mars and Jupiter are not in exact aspect with Venus. They are, however, within orb, and Mars' opposition to Venus and Jupiter's trine to Venus are still valid.

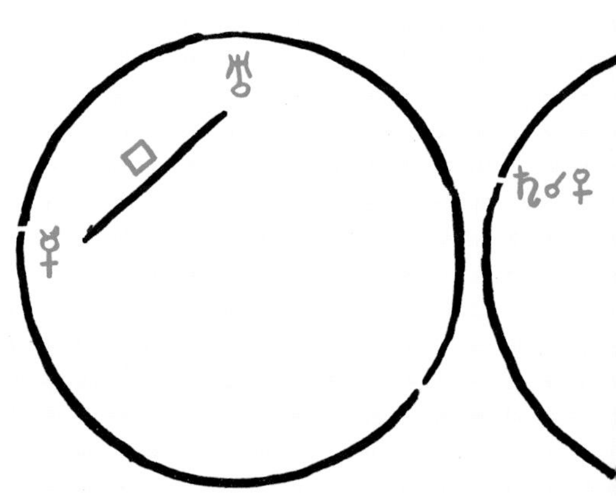

Moon unaspected: these people may feel out of touch with their home, family, emotions and roots, but make strenuous efforts to overcome the problem.

Mercury unaspected: these people may find it difficult to express their thoughts, may be quiet, but strive actively to develop intellectual skills.

Venus unaspected: these people may find it difficult to form close relationships, but may make great efforts to be sociable.

Mars unaspected: these people may find it difficult to motivate themselves but may have uncontrollable energy.

Jupiter unaspected: these people may have difficulty in creating opportunities, but spend a lot of energy looking for them.

Saturn unaspected: these people may find it difficult to recognize limitations and cope with difficulties, but may develop strong self-discipline.

Uranus unaspected: these people may have difficulty in expressing their personality, either neglecting or exaggerating it.

Neptune unaspected: these people may have difficulty in giving expression to their imagination and mystical aspirations, but become very dedicated to artistic work or religious activity.

Pluto unaspected: these people may find it difficult to harness emotional energy, and may seek emotional commitment and confrontation.

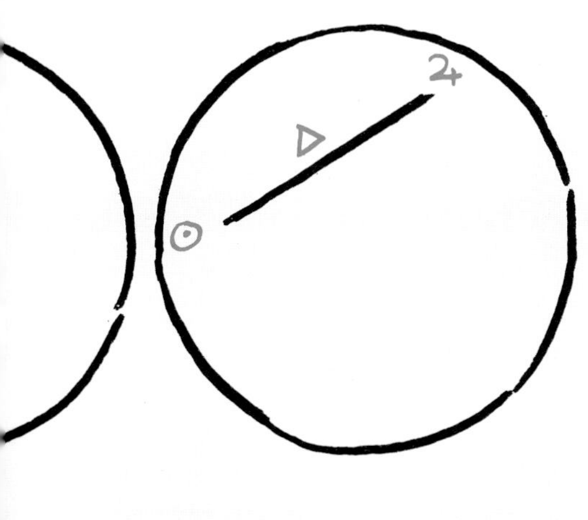

WORKING OUT THE INTERPRETATIONS

The process of interpretation becomes much easier if the astrologer is able to work from a knowledge of first principles. There are many possibilities inherent in each aspect; the sample interpretations below only cover the most likely, and do not extend to all the situations one is likely to encounter. The astrologer takes the two planets involved, considers the nature of the aspect – strong or weak, tense or harmonious – and tries to work out how this affects the natures of each and how they will combine.

It is useful to isolate the different levels at which the aspect (as with any astrological factor) may manifest itself.

1. Internal manifestation in a person's psychological processes.
2. Manifestation of these processes in their personal behaviour.
3. External circumstances and events; those created by the person and those by fate.

Three examples follow:

Saturn Conjunct Venus

The disciplining, delaying, structuring power of Saturn combines strongly with the emotion, affection and need for partnership of Venus.

1) Emotionally there will be a sense of limitation and restriction.
2) In partnerships behaviour will tend to be loyal, reserved and influenced by practical issues. There may be an attraction for older people.
3) Delays and obstacles may be experienced in all partnerships and emotional affairs.

Mercury Square Uranus

There is friction between the mental processes of Mercury and Uranus' need for freedom and independence.

1) There is a pressing need for independence in thought and speech.
2) There may be frequent arguments, an inability to see other people's point of view and the adoption of unusual interests and attitudes.
3) Sudden events and unexpected interruptions may interfere with travel and education.

Sun Trine Jupiter

The entire personality and life is harmonized with the expansive properties of Jupiter.

1) There is a desire for continual growth, expansion and improvement.
2) Behaviour will tend to be generous, proud, good natured and warm hearted.
3) May be born into comfortable circumstances. Through life will receive rewards and opportunities without any apparent effort.

Left: *Mercury square Uranus.*
Centre: *Saturn conjunct Venus.*
Right: *Sun trine Jupiter.*

Solution to the 'T' Square
A: via harmonious Aspects.
The tension of the 'T' Square can be released or positively expressed through the planet which makes the closest sextile or trine to any of the three planets in the 'T' Square. In this example the emotional tension of the Moon-Saturn-Uranus 'T' Square can be released through the sextile to Mars in Leo.
B. Development of Opposite Characteristics
The tension of the 'T' Square focuses on the planet at the apex, in this case Venus, and the part of the chart immediately opposite may also act as a focus for problems. By coping with them the whole situation can be eased and turned to advantage.
In this example Venus in the eighth house, squared to Uranus and Saturn, suggests business difficulties. This may bring second house problems – personal financial ones with an inability to handle money. By learning how to deal with these issues, the eighth house problems, and the whole 'T' Square, can be helped.

ASPECTS AND SIGNS

The nature of aspect interpretation will be modified by the character of the signs containing the planets. It is necessary to know which planet is stronger. For example, a Sun-Jupiter trine may bring either long distance travel if Jupiter is in Sagittarius, or religious interests if it is in Pisces.

ASPECTS IN DISSOCIATE SIGNS

The relationships between the major aspects are connected to those between the signs. Planets in conjunction are usually in the same sign, planets in sextile in the same polarity, planets in square in the same quality, planets in trine in the same element and planets in opposition in opposite signs. For example, a planet in Scorpio will usually make tense aspects to planets in the other fixed signs, squares to planets in Leo and Aquarius, oppositions to planets in Taurus and trines to planets in the other water signs, Pisces and Cancer. When this pattern is broken then the aspect is dissociate. This would occur if, for example, the planet in Scorpio was conjunct a planet in Libra or Sagittarius, trine a planet in Aquarius or in opposition to a planet in Gemini. If the planets in an aspect are in dissociate signs this makes the issues raised more varied and potentially complicated, but a true understanding of this can only be gained with experience in chart interpretation.

Much the same occurs when two planets are in a conjunction but in adjacent houses rather than in the same house.

A

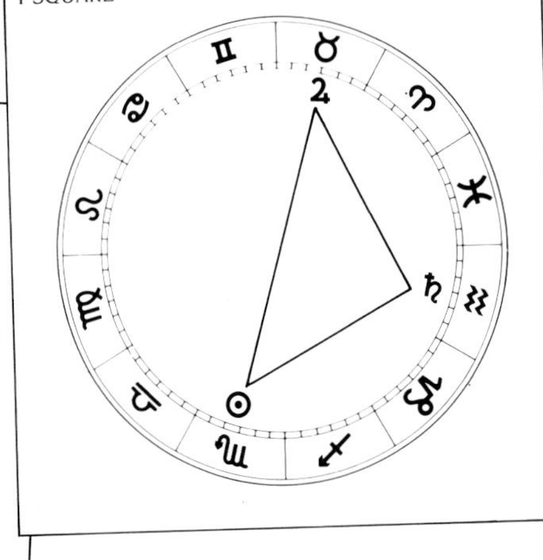
T SQUARE

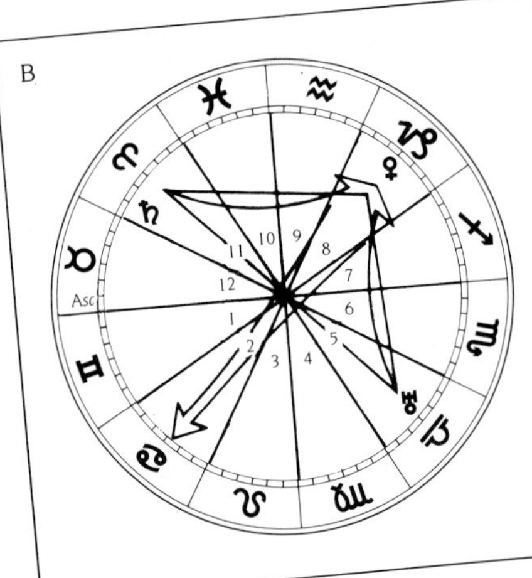
B

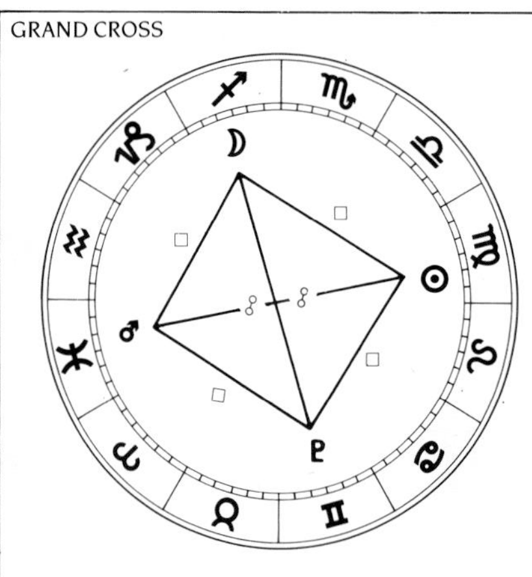
GRAND CROSS

ASPECTS AND HOUSES

Any aspect will have a general influence over the personality, and be specifically relevant to the areas of life ruled by the houses containing the planets. For example, a Saturn-Venus conjunction in the tenth house will have a special influence over the career, while a Mercury-Saturn opposition from the fifth to eleventh houses will involve personal creative desires (fifth house) and public activities (eleventh house.)

ASPECT PATTERNS

When three or more planets are connected to each other by aspect, they form a pattern with a meaning of its own.

'T' SQUARE:
Two planets in opposition are both in square to a third planet. This brings tension and sharp, pressing problems, the result of which may be great energy and consequently a better than average chance of success throughout life.

When interpreting a 'T' Square all the factors involved – planets, signs and houses – must be taken separately and then built up into a picture of the choices, difficulties and solutions which each planet suggests.

When the 'T' Square is in:
Cardinal Signs, there is exceptional dynamism and energy;
Fixed Signs, people may be excessively stubborn, fighting personal battles to the bitter end.
Mutable Signs, they may try to solve, or even avoid, the problems associated with the 'T' Square by being flexible and adaptable.

GRAND CROSS:
The Grand Cross consists of four planets connected by four squares and two oppositions. In effect this consists of four 'T' Squares and, although the process of interpretation is essentially the same as that for a 'T' Square, the complexity and pos-

sibilities are considerably more varied. This pattern is not necessarily more dynamic than the 'T' Square.

When the Grand Cross is in:

Cardinal Signs, problems and difficulties are more likely to result in energetic and assertive behaviour.

Fixed Signs, people may hang on to their problems and be exceptionally stubborn and resistant to change.

Mutable Signs, they may be very adaptable but may also exacerbate their problems by evading them.

GRAND TRINE:

Three planets are connected by three trines to form a triangle, the Grand Trine, around which planetary influences circulate with ease. This brings a wealth of natural talent indicated by the signs and houses containing the planets, but may require tense aspects to provide the motivation for its expression.

When the Grand Trine is in:

Fire Signs, talents lie in enthusiasm, and the search for new possibilities.

Earth Signs, talents lie in practical work and experience.

Air Signs, talents lie in intellectual work and the communication of ideas.

Water Signs, talents are rooted in sympathy, compassion and intuition.

YOD:

Also known as the Finger of Fate or the Finger of God, Yod is the name given to two planets in opposition connected to two other planets, one by semi-sextiles and the other by quincunxes. There is a consensus that this pattern is important, but few astrologers make much use of it. The two additional planets provide a choice of paths for the individual to express or discharge the tension of the opposition.

MYSTIC RECTANGLE:

This consists of four planets connected in a rectangle of two squares and two trines, together with two oppositions connecting the opposite planets. Despite the name there is nothing mystical about this pattern. The combination of tense and harmonious aspects produces the best possible potential for the constructive use of natural talents.

KITE:

The person with a kite pattern may be a 'high flyer'. All three planets in a grand trine are connected to a fourth planet, one by an opposition and the other two by sextiles. This is a useful combination of tense and harmonious aspects in which the two planets connected by trines and sextiles provide outlets for the tension of the opposition.

MUTUAL RECEPTION

When two planets are each located in signs ruled by the other they are in mutual reception. For example, Venus in Scorpio is in mutual reception with Mars in Libra, while Saturn in Pisces is in mutual reception with Jupiter in Capricorn. The effect is to bring the planets together as in a conjunction.

There are variations on this rule which can be applied to planets in each other's exaltations. For example, Jupiter in Libra is in mutual reception with Saturn in Cancer. It is also possible to apply mutual reception when dignity and exaltation are involved. For example, the Moon in Pisces, the sign of Venus' exaltation, could be in mutual reception with Venus in Cancer the sign of the Moon's dignity.

The use of exaltation in mutual reception is usually only applied in horary astrology, and should only be used in natal astrology if it enables the astrologer to make a more detailed examination of a particular configuration in the chart.

Mutual Reception
The Sun in Pisces, ruled by Jupiter, is in mutual reception with Jupiter in Leo, ruled by the Sun.
The Moon in Aquarius, ruled by Saturn, is in mutual reception with Saturn in Cancer, ruled by the Moon.

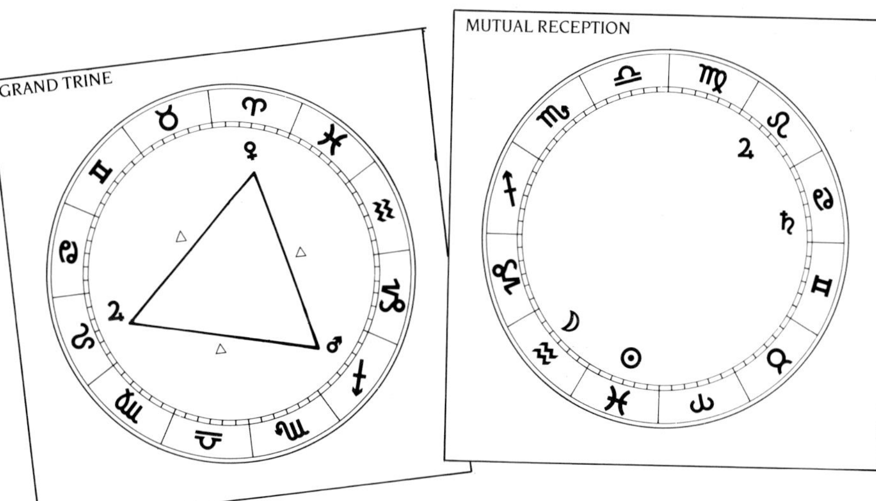

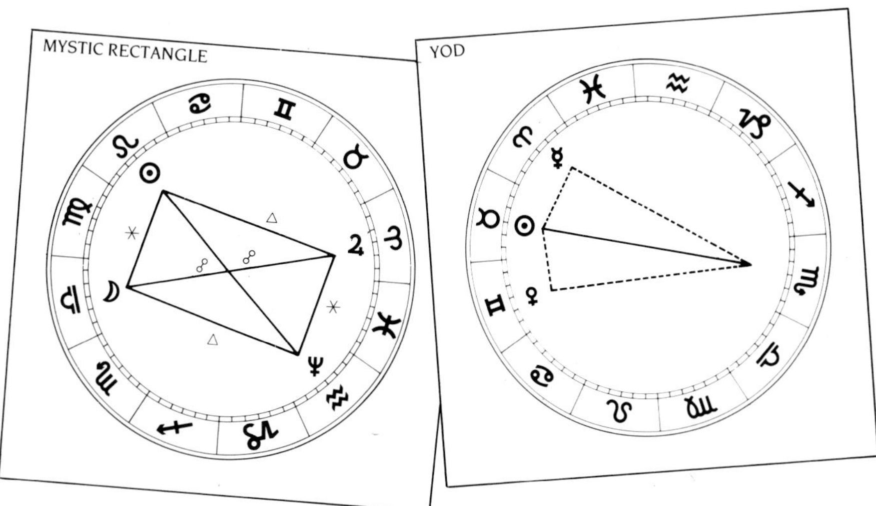

CHAPTER 9
INTERPRETING THE ASPECTS

The planetary aspects are the connecting threads that knit together all the apparently separate interpretations of the planets in their signs and houses, welding them into a whole. Understanding of the aspects is vital to the work of the astrologer, but beginners usually start by using standard interpretations such as those given below.

The interpretations are summarized under three headings which refer specifically to the major aspects: harmonious aspects (trine and sextile), conjunction, and tense aspects (opposition and square). In fact, there is usually an overlap of meaning and it is useful to read all three in order to gain a full understanding of the ways in which any two planets combine. For the semi-sextile use the interpretations for harmonious aspects, and for the semi-square, sesquiquadrate and quincunx use those given for the tense aspects. But it should be understood that in the case of these minor aspects the interpretations will often have only a slight significance.

To understand how a planet operates in an aspect it is worthwhile examining its aspects with a variety of planets. For example, by studying the aspects of Uranus with Venus and the Moon, a more complete picture will be gained of the effect Uranus has on the emotions than if only Uranus-Venus aspects were checked.

Each aspect has a personality which may be described in human terms; for example, the astrologer may remark that Mercury opposed to Jupiter is extremist or that Moon trine Venus is pleasant.

In most cases the language used is very general because this allows as many manifestations as possible to be encompassed. It is then the astrologer's task to make the generalizations more specific in the light of commonsense, knowledge of the person and astrological experience. For example, Mercury in opposition to Mars is very impatient. The astrologer may conclude that this raises the risk of hasty, wrong-headed decisions and physical accidents, problems which can be avoided by the cultivation of care, patience and attention to detail. Any of the sample interpretations may be extended like this, and the astrologer should look for ways to bring out the positive potential of the tense aspects and guard against the negative potential of the harmonious aspects.

Each sign and planet has both positive and negative, easy and difficult, manifestations. Difficult aspects to a planet may stimulate the negative qualities whereas harmonious aspects may stimulate the positive qualities of the planet and the house or sign in which it is placed. For example, Mercury in Pisces can be either intuitive or confused. A harmonious aspect to Mercury may enhance intuition, while a tense aspect may stimulate confusion. Jupiter in the fourth house may lead to either pride or selfishness at home. Harmonious aspects to Jupiter may enhance pride and generosity, while tense aspects stimulate selfishness.

ASPECTS BETWEEN THE OUTER PLANETS

Aspects between the outer planets – Jupiter, Saturn, Uranus, Neptune and Pluto – are far less specific from an individual point of view

ASPECT

MOON CONJUNCT PLUTO

NEED

EMOTIONAL COMMITMENT FROM FAMILY

CIRCUMSTANCES

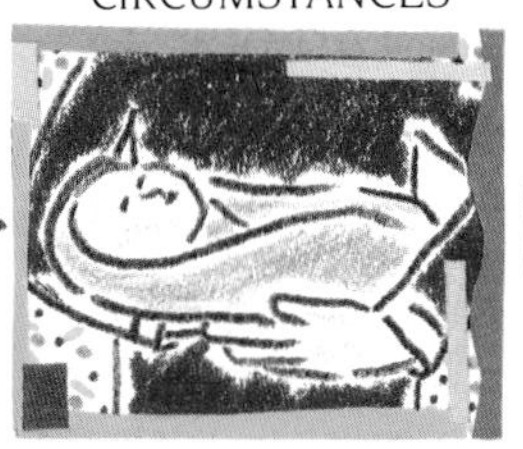

WARM, LOVING ENVIRONMENT

BEHAVIOUR

HAPPY, STABLE, RESPONSIBLE

COLD, UNCARING ENVIRONMENT

ANGRY, DISRUPTIVE, IRRESPONSIBLE

Needs and Circumstances
Although harmonious and tense aspects tend to produce easy and awkward behaviour respectively, each contains a little of the other, and the final manifestation is often based on a person's circumstances. This is clearest in conjunctions.
The key is often found in a consideration of the needs that each aspect brings. For example, an emotionally volatile aspect such as the Moon conjunct Pluto needs emotional commitment from family members. If this is forthcoming, then the person is happy, and the occasional domestic upheavals that Pluto brings will be welcomed. If there is no emotional support, then the result will be angry confrontation and disruption.

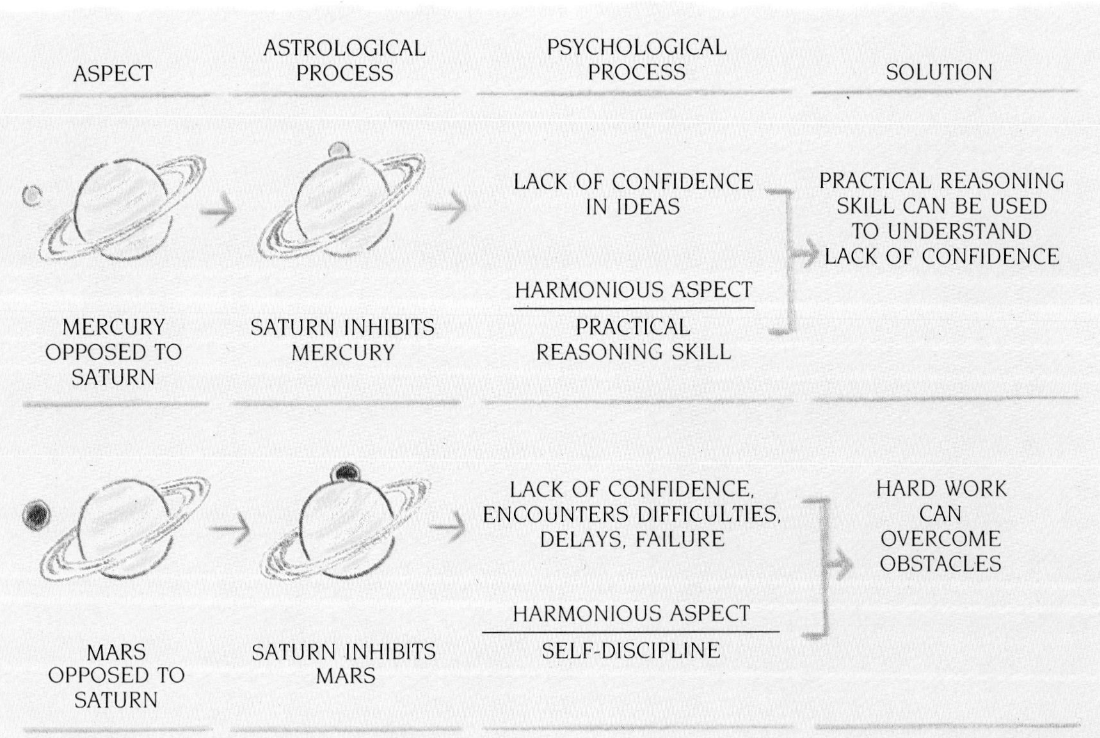

ASPECT
ASTROLOGICAL PROCESS
PSYCHOLOGICAL PROCESS
SOLUTION
LACK OF CONFIDENCE IN IDEAS
PRACTICAL REASONING SKILL CAN BE USED TO UNDERSTAND LACK OF CONFIDENCE
HARMONIOUS ASPECT
MERCURY OPPOSED TO SATURN
SATURN INHIBITS MERCURY
PRACTICAL REASONING SKILL
LACK OF CONFIDENCE, ENCOUNTERS DIFFICULTIES, DELAYS, FAILURE
HARD WORK CAN OVERCOME OBSTACLES
HARMONIOUS ASPECT
MARS OPPOSED TO SATURN
SATURN INHIBITS MARS
SELF-DISCIPLINE

Problems and Solutions
Tense aspects bring problems, the solution to which is often provided by the harmonious aspects between the same planets. For example, a Mercury-Saturn opposition can bring a serious lack of confidence which can encourage failure at school. Yet a way round this can be provided by developing the clear and logical skills of the Mercury-Saturn trine. A Mars-Saturn opposition often brings failure through a lack of nerve and jobs are abandoned before they are completed. People who behave in this way can help themselves by developing the self-discipline of the Mars-Saturn trine.

than are aspects that involve the inner planets. Their interpretations in natal astrology tend to be vague because their major influence is over historical events and the gradual change in the character of generations.

It is up to the astrologer to decide whether these aspects will have a noticeable psychological effect in the natal chart. Aspects with tighter orbs are more likely to be influential than those with looser orbs, and applying aspects should be more significant than those that are separating.

However, it is the aspects to inner planets that give these impersonal outer planet aspects personal relevance. For example, millions of people may be born with a Neptune-Pluto conjunction, but for many this will have no individual psychological significance. Yet those people who have these two planets in conjunction with the Sun, the Moon, the Ascendant or MC, may feel profound effects upon their lives.

PLANETS IN ASPECT TO ANGLES

Aspects between planets and the four angles are significant for the general character, home, family, partnerships and career. The most important aspect is the conjunction, and this is always vital to interpretation of the birth chart. Sample interpretations are not listed here, but the examples given in Chapter 6 for planets in houses may be used. For planets conjunct the Ascendant look up the interpretations for planets in the first house, for conjunctions with the I.C., those for planets in the fourth house, for conjunctions with the Descendant those for planets in the seventh house, and for conjunctions with the M.C. those for planets in the tenth house.

Planets in square to the angles bring tension and those in trines or sextiles signify harmony.

THE PLANETARY ASPECTS

SUN – MOON

Harmonious aspects: these contribute towards a balanced, peaceful, settled nature and increase the general chances of satisfaction and success in life. Relations with home and family and with the opposite sex should be good.

Conjunction: these people may be individualistic and encounter problems in dealing with changing circumstances. Relations with the home and family may be so strong that it is difficult to escape from their influence.

Tense aspects: these will be reflected in a fundamental conflict, perhaps between parents, parents and children, career or public affairs and domestic or private interests. Emotions may be strong and difficult to control.

SUN – MERCURY . These two planets are never more than 28° apart so the only major aspect that occurs is the conjunction: these people are subjective and creative, good at expressing opinions and working in the arts, but poor at handling logic, detail and technical studies. There is often intellectual

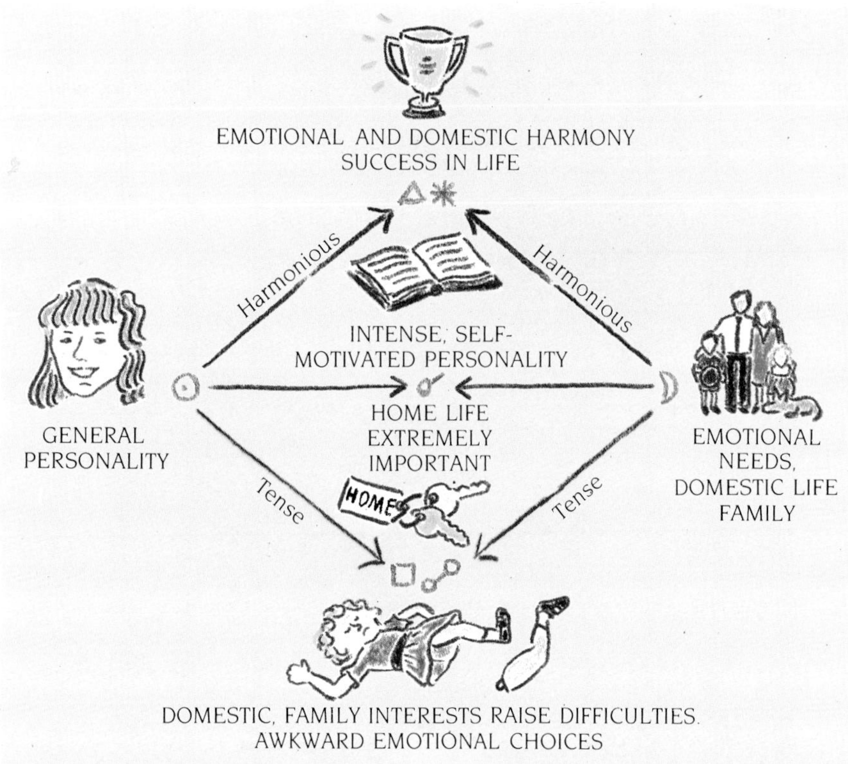

Sun-Moon Aspects
All combinations of planets have three main results, one through the harmonious aspects, one through the conjunction and one through the tense aspects. When the Sun and the Moon combine this has a general influence over the personality and a specific effect on domestic and emotional affairs.

arrogance and prejudice. This is an excellent aspect for performers.

SUN – VENUS. These planets are never more than 48° apart so the only major aspect that occurs is the conjunction.

Conjunction: this strengthens the female nature in both men and women, and is excellent for all creative and artistic activities. There is a love of refined pursuits and sensual pleasures, a need for partnership, a flair for fashion and style, and charming manners. Vanity and self-centred behaviour are failings.

SUN – MARS
Harmonious aspects: the personality is self-motivated, adventurous, energetic and competitive, decisive and impatient. These people may become investigators, researchers and seekers after hidden truths.

Conjunction: this is the aspect of the explorer and the warrior. These people have a vast amount of energy although sometimes they push themselves to the point of exhaustion.

Tense aspects: these increase the tendency to overwork, to take risks and put up with personal discomfort. These people are good-natured and warm-hearted, but they are also impulsive, excitable, reckless and egotistical.

SUN – JUPITER
Harmonious aspects: these give a generally sensible, optimistic and good humoured personality. These people divide into those who receive their inspiration from travel and adventure, and those who seek inner inspiration from religion or intellectual studies. Their idealism and optimism attracts opportunity.

Conjunction: this confers both intellectual wisdom and material benefit. These people are often proud and worldly, and even those who follow an ascetic or religious path tend to be self-important.

Tense aspects: there is strong idealism and these people join causes, often impractical or unpopular, and pursue them to the point of self-sacrifice. They have a strong faith in their own destiny, a deep need for personal freedom, dislike order and routine, and often become travellers.

SUN – SATURN
Harmonious aspects: these people are conscientious workers, fulfilling obligations and observing responsibilities. There may be some self-inhibition.

Conjunction: there is plenty of self-discipline and fondness for a routine life with a sense of order. These people often face difficult material circumstances, conflict with authority, or obstacles and delays. Difficulties erode their self-confidence, but this can be restored by hard work.

Tense aspects: these people fall into two types. There are those who give in to the failure and frustration and those who react to this by such disciplined hard work that they achieve great things. They put up with difficult circumstances, if necessary.

SUN – URANUS
Harmonious aspects: these people are independent and unconventional. They are idealistic, and associate themselves with causes and movements. They often become leaders because other people admire their unusual way of doing things.

Conjunction: these people are inventive, independent,radical and unconventional. By their refusal to accept established beliefs and behaviour they force other people to reconsider their ways.

Tense aspects: the personality is individualist, egotistical, eccentric and unconventional. Independence is prized above all else. Often these people are reckless and disorganized in their behaviour. Nervous exhaustion and carelessness are possible.

SUN – NEPTUNE
Harmonious aspects: the personality is sentimental, kindly and inclined to charitable work. There is a good creative imagination, an attraction to the arts and mysticism and a preference for a pleasant life.

Conjunction : intuition, imagination, sensitivity, self-sacrifice, compassion and impracticality are the main qualities. There are two types; those who find their purpose in asceticism, mysticism and selfless charitable work, and those who are drawn to the world of fashion, glamour, art and style.

Tense aspects: too much compassion and selflessness lay these people open to exploitation and deception. Sometimes they sacrifice their own interests. Religion, fashion, or the use of drink and drugs, is often attractive as a means of shutting out the real world.

SUN – PLUTO
Harmonious aspects: these add emotional power and determination to the personality. These people can be obstinate, secretive and interested in the deeper and darker mysteries of life.

Conjunction: this is an intense, emotional and volcanic aspect; life is often disrupted by profound upheavals. Different means are chosen to help this personal revolution; some may choose psychoanalysis or therapy, others religion, or magic or politics.

Tense aspects: these people thrive on emotional confrontation. They are obstinate, determined and dedicated and, challenge other people to change their ways.

MOON – MERCURY
Harmonious aspects: a good memory, a poetic mind and common sense are the main qualities. These people make fine journalists or teachers. They are interested in their background and environment.

Conjunction: the poetic and common sense qualities of the harmonious aspects are strengthened. Clear thought and analysis may be the best ways to resolve emotional problems. There is a love of gossip, and contacts with family members are often close.

Tense aspects: there may be nervous tension, domestic misunderstandings and a tendency to jump to hasty conclusions. These people have a sharp perception of the truth.

MOON – VENUS
Harmonious aspects: the temperament is even, manners graceful and appearance often attractive. These people cultivate social success. Their artistic talents are frequently turned to the creation of a pleasant domestic environment.

Conjunction: success in life is achieved more through natural charm than through work or skill. There is a taste for the finer things in life and a love of luxury. These people need a pleasant and balanced environment, especially in the home and family, and use all their diplomatic skills to create it.

Tense aspects: there is often confusion about true feelings and emotional needs. There may be difficult domestic choices, and external obstacles such as rivals in love.

MOON – MARS
Harmonious aspects: the personality is generally constructive and practical. There is usually a good understanding of domestic problems, and a positive will to resolve them. There is honesty in the expression of feelings and a warm, hospitable manner.

Conjunction: emotional, courageous, daring and adventurous, these people take personal risks. In the family and home they know just what they want and are unprepared to take second place. They are often entrepreneurs, explorers and travellers.

Tense aspects: these aspects bring emotional tension, impulsive and reckless behaviour, a readiness to face personal danger and confrontation within the family. Domestically there are three types: the compulsive home maker, always putting things up and taking

Psychological Processes
Each aspect represents a psychological process which can be worked out by considering the nature of each planet and the way in which they combine, whether harmonious or tense. If the aspects are analysed in this way, then it becomes easier for the astrologer to offer advice. For example, if the difficulty lies in a Sun-Uranus opposition, then life may be constantly disrupted by sudden losses which seem to be outside personal control. Yet the astrologer can often explain that these problems may be partly of the individual's own making, and that personal disruptive behaviour is caused by a deep desire for independence, itself the product of some deep fear. If the underlying situation is understood, it can often be turned to personal advantage.

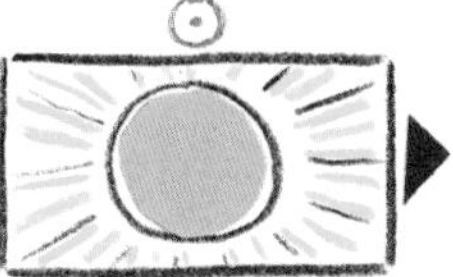

THE RULER OF THE PERSONALITY AND LIFE IN GENERAL

IS OPPOSED TO

THE RULER OF SUDDEN, DRAMATIC CHANGE AND UNCONTROLLABLE UNCONSCIOUS FORCES

LEADING TO A CONSCIOUS AWARENESS OF THE THREAT OF PERSONAL CHAOS

AND, IN ORDER TO AVOID THE CHAOS CREATED BY OTHERS, A STRONG URGE FOR PERSONAL INDEPENDENCE

THE NET RESULT IS A LACK OF COOPERATION AND THAT VERY CHAOS THAT WAS SO FEARED

them down; the emotional fighter who seeks confrontation; and the wanderer who is too restless to create a home.

MOON – JUPITER
Harmonious aspects: sympathetic, generous, helpful and optimistic, these people attract good fortune by their very openness. They are idealistic, but appreciate a pleasant and comfortable home. Like all harmonious aspects to Jupiter, this assists in legal affairs and higher education.

Conjunction: there are two sides to this aspect: on the one hand it is very generous, spontaneous, warm and hospitable, but on the other it can be very demanding, requiring affection, love, large families, luxurious homes, foreign travel and, for the more introverted, religious experience and intellectual study. There can be selfishness in achieving these ambitions. Life abroad is likely.

Tense aspects: there is a continual desire for 'more'; more emotion, affection, luxury or, for the introverted type, more religion. Emotional needs may be temporarily satisfied by material consumption, religious obsessions or extreme beliefs. These people need to find personal motivation in order to alleviate their dependence upon external stimuli.

MOON – SATURN
Harmonious aspects: these people regulate their emotional and family lives by doing what they consider to be right, being faithful, practical and punctual.

Conjunction: faithful, reliable and loyal, even in times of difficulty, these people lack confidence in their feelings. They may avoid emotional entanglement by being cold, or burying themselves in work and domestic cares; men will be attracted to older women. Emotional relationships may be delayed, but once formed are very stable.

Tense aspects: there is usually difficulty in expressing emotion, and feelings are often concealed behind a mask. There is a need for a stable and secure home, but often domestic responsibilities are allowed to dominate family life.

MOON – URANUS
Harmonious aspects: emotional and domestic independence is important to these people. They resent social pressures, and conditions in the home are often unusual.

Conjunction: the need for emotional and domestic freedom is so strong that all ties will be resisted and cooperation with partners and family members becomes difficult. These people need variety. Expression of the emotions may be superficially open,but feelings are often ignored, only to explode later.

Tense aspects: uncooperative attitudes may bring about unexpected domestic upheavals. Domestic chaos is preferred to routine. These people are attracted to 'alternative' life styles, such as communal living, but their individualism works against such ventures.

MOON – NEPTUNE
Harmonious aspects: these aspects bring a kindly and compassionate personality and the home is often a pleasant and hospitable place, if a little disorganized. The home and family may be romanticized.

Conjunction: there is often a deep yearning for something greater than the self, and this may be found through mystical religion, in romantic love, or by attachment to the family. There are often self-sacrificing tendencies and other people may take advantage. There is an attraction for art and fashion. The home may be exotic and mysterious, if rather disorganized.

Tense aspects: the qualities of the tense aspects are similar to those of the conjunction but heighten the tendencies to confusion, especially in the home. Unrealistic fantasies tend to obscure daily reality. There is a vivid artistic imagination, and a feeling for fashion and style.

MOON – PLUTO
Harmonious aspects: there is emotional intensity and a desire for change and improvement in the home. These people bring their emotional problems to the surface even if this causes domestic confrontation.

Conjunction: these people are very obstinate, especially over domestic issues; their refusal to compromise often guarantees conflict. They try to bottle up their feelings, but the more they do this, the more likely are they to explode. Such explosions may be the catalyst for complete revolution in home and life style. These people have the choice of using their emotional energy for destructive or constructive purposes.

Tense aspects: the emotions are deep, relationships and domestic affairs can be complicated. Domestic upheavals may be caused by events apparently outside personal control. Their interests are deep and often include psychology, the occult, revolutionary life styles, and healing.

MERCURY–VENUS Mercury and Venus make two major aspects–conjunction and sextile.

Sextile: this brings balance, commonsense and pleasant charming manners. All social, emotional and educational affairs benefit, and communication is straightforward.

Conjunction: this aspect brings eloquence, social charm, teaching skill, persuasive powers, and balanced opinions. These people are able to understand their emotions, but if too rational they may deny their true feelings.

MERCURY – MARS
Harmonious aspects: these aspects strengthen the mind, which is energetic and perceptive. There is a liking for practical research and investigation, which will be tackled with commonsense and precision.

Conjunction: the mind is sharp, perceptive and witty, with a feel for sarcasm and satire. These people love argument. They are strongly drawn to research in practical subjects, but often exhaust themselves mentally through overwork. Their weakness is impatience.

Tense aspects: these people have strong and energetic minds, but can be too argumentative and impatient. Sometimes they attach themselves to causes, becoming determined reformers, attacking abuses in society; investigative journalists come under these aspects.

MERCURY – JUPITER
Harmonious aspects: these people are optimistic, philosophical, good natured and open to new ideas. Intellectual interests are often pursued at the expense of worldly considerations. There is a restlessness and love of travel.

Conjunction: this brings a love of ideas and a thirst for knowledge, which may be expressed in a variety of ways. Some people will be collectors of facts, others study philosophy or religion, while still others travel the world. There is a belief in freedom of speech and dislike of orthodox education, which may limit academic success.

Tense aspects: these people are extremists, swinging between scepticism and belief. They find it difficult to reconcile facts with theory, or to think clearly. There is great restlessness and curiosity, and they frequently travel or reside in foreign countries. As with all tense Jupiter aspects there may be difficulties with the law.

MERCURY – SATURN
Harmonious aspects: these people deal well with routine, tend towards conservative opinions, think clearly and are attracted to practical subjects. An ability to work hard and consistently, enhances academic success.

Conjunction: the mind is serious, attitudes conservative and practical. These people lack confidence in their ideas and imagination, and find security in detail and precision. They work hard academically, but difficulty with expressing ideas can limit their success.

Tense aspects: these bring the same conservatism and preference for practical studies as the conjunction, but emphasize a lack of confidence in personal ideas and imagination. These people, however, are often hard-headed, materialist and business-like, and in their struggle to overcome the prospect of educational failure, they achieve undreamed of success.

MERCURY – URANUS
Harmonious aspects: Uranus brings its electric qualities to the mind and these aspects are quick-witted, inventive and skilled in finding new solutions to old problems. Such solutions may lie in high technology – or in new possibilities in human thought and awareness. These people thrive on debate and argument.

Conjunction: these people are independently minded. Their main interest is to challenge accepted values and they easily become eccentric reactionaries or flag-waving anarchists. Those with more practical interests are usually drawn towards new technology. Nervous tension is common.

Tense aspects: these people can be extremist in their opinions, vain and arrogant in their beliefs and ideas, which are often highly unusual and completely impractical. They become members of odd religious cults or fringe political groups. They are often in the intellectual vanguard, for today's fringe idea is tomorrow's accepted belief.

MERCURY – NEPTUNE
Harmonious aspects: these people are imaginative, idealistic, refined and artistic, but are not good with detail. They may be at home with such diverse interests as photography, fashion and mysticism. They may be gullible.

Conjunction: this brings intuition, imagination, mysticism, intellectual sensitivity and breadth of vision. These are expressed best through the arts or idealistic work, but there may be an inability to handle practical studies. These people may be unwilling to face difficult choices and often retreat into a dream world.

Sun

Moon

Mercury

Venus

Earth

Mars

Jupiter

Saturn

Uranus

Neptune

Pluto

Aries Taurus Gemini Cancer Leo Virgo Libra Scorpio Sagittarius Capricorn Aquarius Pisces

Tense aspects: as artists or mystics these people are very highly motivated. Their opinions are flexible, although deep beliefs may be held with sincere conviction. Too often they resort to deceiving themselves, or others, as an easy way out of a complicated situation.

MERCURY – PLUTO
Harmonious aspects: these people are obstinate, perceptive and interested in research into deep and mysterious subjects such as psychology, magic, criminology and sub-atomic physics. They like argument and debate.

Conjunction: unconscious and conscious minds merge, beliefs and ideas become as one, with the result that these people are obstinate, opinionated and argumentative. Some study subjects such as astronomy or physics, while others become involved in the occult, psychotherapy or healing.

Tense aspects: the mind is dominated by beliefs and instincts; these people often have many prejudices. They study in short intense bursts followed by exhaustion. There is a relentless search for truth, and practical considerations are usually ignored.

VENUS – MARS
Harmonious aspects: passionate with lovers, warm and friendly with strangers, these people have a fondness for the pleasures of the flesh and leisure activities. They are energetic, with a relaxed and easy attitude towards work.

Conjunction: these people have warm and powerful emotions with a continual need for social, physical and sexual experience. They are energetic, assertive, self-interested and often popular. Quick to anger, they do not bear grudges and find it easy to make amends.

Tense aspects: these aspects are as vigorous as the conjunction, but these people are more ready to take offence, friendly one moment and hostile the next. They are impatient and impulsive, placing unrealistic emotional demands on partners. They are likely to have sudden enthusiasms which they drop without warning.

VENUS – JUPITER
Harmonious aspects: the personality is affectionate and manners graceful. These people sense the prevailing social mood and fit in with the latest fashion. They are usually hospitable and generous. This aspect benefits all legal and financial matters.

Conjunction: these people are exceptionally generous and loving, but require a great deal of affection and social stimulation in return. There is often an expectation that partners will provide material support. Social confidence and optimism are the keys to their success.

Tense aspects: these people are spontaneous and vivacious, but emotionally demanding. Friendships are often disrupted by Jupiterian activities: for example, religion, travel or devotion to idealistic causes. They possess artistic ambitions, but not necessarily any talent. These people do best in independent enterprises where conflicts with others will not arise.

VENUS – SATURN
Harmonious aspects: these people are quiet, responsible and faithful in all social and emotional affairs. Conventional behaviour and stable relationships provide security and counteract fears of rejection and lack of confidence. Often these people are attracted to friends who are older than themselves. They are usually careful with money and resources.

Conjunction: the conjunction repeats the qualities of the harmonious aspects, but is much stronger. There may be delays in forming relationships, but once formed these will be stable. Fidelity is taken to such lengths that a marriage may be maintained when there is no love left. These people need to develop confidence in their own feelings.

Tense aspects: similar to the other aspects, but more likely to encounter delays and obstacles – from parents, lack of money or work. Loyal and faithful, they usually subordinate their own feelings to practical considerations; they may marry for security. Like the other aspects they need to develop confidence in their own emotional needs. These people sometimes suffer from a fear of poverty, and take care of resources.

VENUS – URANUS
Harmonious aspects: there is a need for change and interest in all friendships. These people preserve their emotional independence even in marriage, and reduce ties to a minimum. Their original and unusual behaviour is a source of social popularity.

Conjunction: emotional independence is vital; these people resent obligations and expectations. They are superficially direct and open with their emotions, but keep their true feelings to themselves. If they feel their independence is threatened they may become cold and distant, or leave without warning, but given their freedom are devoted and loyal. Artistic talents are original and may be combined with an interest in technology.

Tense aspects: the need for emotional independence is so great that any commitment is seen as a threat. The emotions fluctuate and these people may experience many partnerships in their search for the ideal. Their expectations are high; they prefer emotional conflict to remaining in an unsatisfactory relationship. In the arts they are eccentric and original. There are likely to be sudden monetary gains and losses.

VENUS–NEPTUNE
Harmonious aspects: these bring romance, compassion and intuition to all relationships. These people have inventive imaginations which is advantageous in artistic activities, and are conscious of style, image and fashion.

Conjunction: in relationships these people are highly sensitive, romantic and idealistic, consequently often confused, and muddled. They are shy and sometimes prefer fantasy to a real relationship. Once the ideal partner is found they are self-sacrificing and devoted. Artistic imagination is vivid and there may be a fascination with film, photography and fashion. Financial affairs may suffer from confusion.

Tense aspects: these people are extremely romantic, with the result that confusion and misunderstanding are more common. Fantasy may be preferred to the reality of relationships. Sometimes they divert their energies into mysticism or the arts. They need to develop a clear head and a thick skin.

VENUS – PLUTO
Harmonious aspects: these people tend to be serious and committed in relationships. They have high expectations of partners and are prepared to risk confrontation when these are not satisfied.

Conjunction: the emotions are deep, intense and inflexible, and there is a need for passionate emotional and sexual commitment. These people are fiercely jealous and do not take kindly to rejection. They are secretive and bottle up their feelings.

Tense aspects: these people may love and hate with equal intensity. They are secretive and conceal their true passions. There is a deep brooding imagination often expressed through the arts. Their pursuit of emotional power may be channelled into business activities and the quest for money.

MARS – JUPITER
Harmonious aspects: these people are active and energetic. They are always looking for ways to improve themselves through sport and physical fitness, travel, or education.

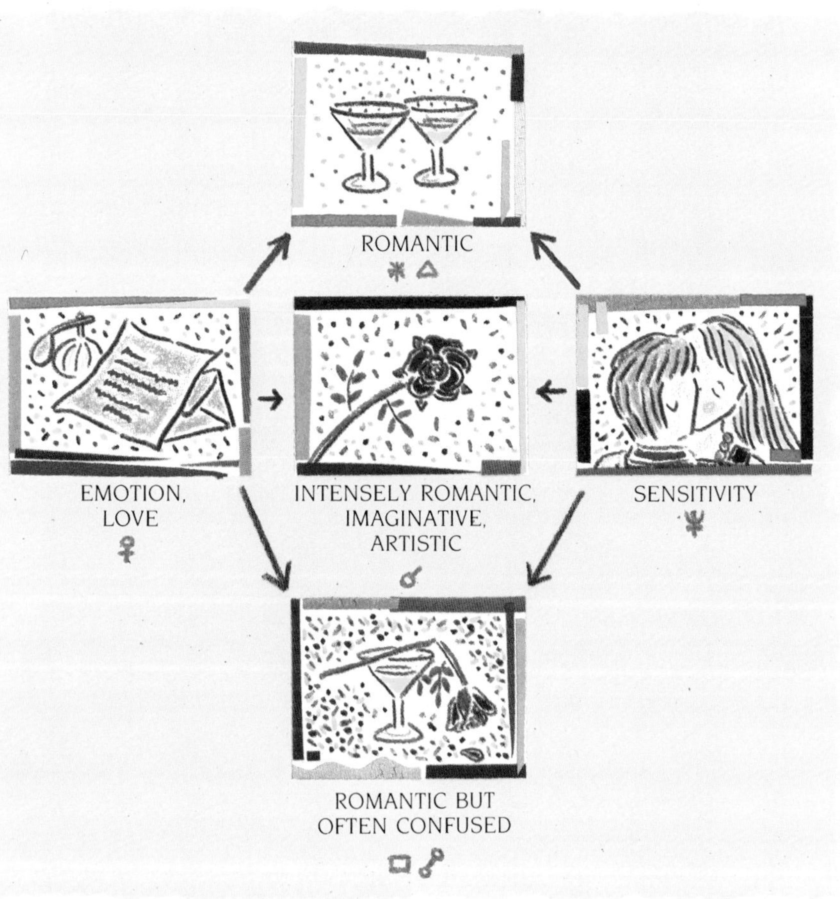

Venus-Neptune Aspects
Venus-Neptune aspects are those of the true romantic and often bring artistic talents.

Conjunction: these people are crusaders opening up opportunities for themselves and others. They sometimes become athletes, adventurers or explorers. Their weaknesses are self-importance and pursuit of personal power and wealth.

Tense aspects: restless and reckless, these people tend towards extremes. There are some who are greedy for possessions, power and money, and others who renounce their personal interests for an idealistic cause. There is a love of adventure and travel.

MARS – SATURN
Harmonious aspects: these people are hard workers. They make good entrepreneurs for, although cautious, they can withstand personal hardship and danger. They lack imagination, an advantage for those with dangerous tasks to perform.

Conjunction: these people are hard workers, practical organizers, careful with resources and good at dealing with the obstacles and delays they often encounter. They value security and stability, and do not take risks.

Tense aspects: these people develop sudden enthusiasms for practical projects, but often give them up, either as a result of some external obstacle – lack of money, opposition from authority – or a failure of will, confidence or energy. They need to be more consistent.

MARS – URANUS

Harmonious aspects: these people are strong individualists and their activities tend to be unusual. They may participate in fringe political and reformist movements, or apply their inventive skills to technology and engineering.

Conjunction: independent and individualist, in and inventive, these people find it difficult to follow a routine or cooperate at work. They must take responsibility for their own actions.

Tense aspects: eccentric and individualistic, these people sometimes join fringe religious or political groups, but are too restless to be committed. Only by developing practical skills can they turn their plans into action.

MARS – NEPTUNE

Harmonious aspects: these aspects are impractical; they do well in work which requires imagination, artistic skill, or idealism.

Conjunction: there is need for a greater purpose in life and, if this is satisfied, these people will put their dreams into practice. Otherwise they will be impractical and confused. Imaginative and idealistic work is often found in the arts, in fashion or films.

Jupiter-Uranus Aspects
Under aspects of Jupiter and Uranus people reach for the stars. The first manned landing on the moon in 1969 took place under an exact Jupiter-Uranus conjunction.

Tense aspects: these aspects increase feeling for music, the arts, fantasy and mysticism, but are impractical. Some become revolutionaries or mystics, attacking materialist society. These people sacrifice their lives to their imagination.

MARS – PLUTO

Harmonious aspects: these aspects bring dedication, persistence, and emotional commitment to all work and activities. These people are obstinate and difficult to divert from a chosen course of action.

Conjunction: these people are self-willed, and determined, and listen to no advice. If they are attracted to religious or political causes they become strong leaders.

Tense aspects: major confrontations and revolutions in life style are to be expected. These people are determined, persistent, obstinate and perceptive, with an unrealistic belief in absolute truth and their own destiny.

JUPITER – SATURN

Harmonious aspects: these are extremely beneficial and constructive aspects which provide a firm base from which to develop the potential of the whole chart.

Conjunction: these people are faced with a choice between restricting Saturn and expansive Jupiter. If a balance is reached then considerable achievement is possible.

Tense aspects: these people are faced with conflicting possibilities. The dilemma is whether to change or remain the same, to take a risk or refuse an opportunity. If this is reconciled much may be achieved.

JUPITER – URANUS

Harmonious aspects: the personality is idealistic, thoughtful and independent.

Conjunction: optimistic, expansive and adventurous, this brings grand ambitions and desires which may be difficult to control or implement. These people have great faith in their own originality and a belief in the future.

Tense aspects: there is a reckless and all-consuming need for experience, variety and independence. Sometimes this results in originality and inventiveness, but dogmatic beliefs.

JUPITER – NEPTUNE

Harmonious aspects: these aspects bring compassion, reforming ideals, artistic inclinations, a wandering spirit and sometimes a religious vision. These tendencies, are subtle and easily overwhelmed by more forceful ones.

Conjunction: this aspect is excessively sensitive. Often there is exceptional idealism and a love of religion. There may be a fascination for travel, the arts and fashion.

Tense aspects: these aspects are confused and oversensitive. They lead people to sacrifice themselves to great causes, escape into private fantasies or lives of rootless wandering.

JUPITER – PLUTO
Harmonious aspects: these indicate tenacity, determination and the desire for self-improvement.

Conjunction: these people fight for the truth, but also seek personal power. The combination of the two planets is very deep and inclines to interests in art, religion, politics, psychology and endless foreign travel.

Tense aspects: there is a need for personal exploration through travel, revolution or religion, often accompanied by a self-interested, obstinate and militant attitude.

SATURN – URANUS
Harmonious aspects: these aspects combine sound practical skills with innovative and original abilities which form an extremely useful foundation for developing the birth potential.

Conjunction: determination and hard work combine with originality to offer new solutions to old problems. These people have democratic ideals, but are authoritarian in practice.

Tense aspects: these aspects lead to erratic behaviour, ranging between an authoritarian need for order and a belief in total anarchy.

SATURN – NEPTUNE
Harmonious aspects: dreams, imagination and inspiration become the basis for practical action. Beliefs tend to be conservative.

Conjunction: if these people can reconcile the opposing principles of the two planets, their imagination will be disciplined and their dreams realized. If this equation is not resolved confusion may upset practical ambitions. Attitudes to religion are conservative.

Tense aspects: these aspects tend to block the satisfactory expression of the imagination and create muddle in practical affairs. Beliefs and opinions are inclined to be reactionary.

SATURN – PLUTO
Harmonious aspects: these bring a sense of purpose, a desire for self-improvement and an emotional commitment to ambition.

Conjunction: this brings a profound desire for personal change and development. These people are often very stubborn and ambitious. They tend to be self-controlled.

Tense aspects: there may be a desire to revolutionize personal life or reform society, but aspirations are confused.

URANUS – NEPTUNE
Harmonious aspects: these increase the imagination and desire for meaning in life, but the influence is subtle.

Conjunction: this aspect brings a profound desire for change, extending beyond the individual into political and mystical revolution. Only those people who are in the vanguard of their generation will truly manifest this aspect. For most it will be experienced in terms of the unsettling events through which they live.

Tense aspects: these indicate a potential for chaos and upheaval, a willingness to tear down the old and welcome the new. For many people these aspects will be experienced in terms of external events which affect their lives.

URANUS – PLUTO
Harmonious aspects: these aspects reinforce the emotional commitment to change and a desire for personal transformation. Most people experience these aspects through external events.

Conjunction: these people will experience profound revolutionary change in their lives. This conjunction is very infrequent and coincides with periods of historic upheaval.

Tense aspects: these aspects are similar in effect to the conjunction. Psychologically they indicate tension and need for change.

NEPTUNE – PLUTO
Harmonious aspects: the two planets are in sextile continuously from 1945 to 1995, an aspect associated with the massive changes in the world since the Second World War.

Conjunction: this brings historic upheaval – the people born under this aspect in the 1890s were the generation that lived through the First World War. If especially prominent in a natal chart, it signifies emotional intensity, mysticism and a need for personal revolution.

Tense aspects: signifies a period of historical change partly prompted by intellectual or religious crisis. When prominent in a birth chart there may be extremism mixed with uncertainty in personal beliefs.

Sun

Moon

Mercury

Venus

Earth

Mars

Jupiter

Saturn

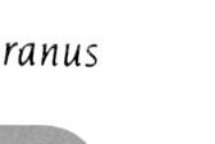

Uranus

Neptune

Pluto

CHAPTER 10 INTERPRETING THE HOROSCOPE: FIRST STEPS

Astrology revolves around the interpretation of the horoscope, a process which often seems mysterious to the uninitiated but is second nature to the experienced. Experience is gained by endless practice for which there is no substitute.

Only by making copious notes on a chart and producing detailed written interpretations, is it possible to become familiar with the meanings of the astrological significators – the signs, planets, houses and aspects. As one becomes more familiar with the meanings of these symbols, it gradually becomes unnecessary to write notes and increasingly easy to interpret horoscopes spontaneously.

The first stage of a written interpretation is **analysis**. Each of the major significators is taken in order of priority and a brief interpretation is written alongside, copied or summarized from one of the sample interpretations in Chapters 4 to 9.

The second stage is **integration**. The different general themes and areas of life to be considered must all be gathered together under common headings.

The third stage is **synthesis** in which all the different sections of the second stage are incorporated into a single report.

ANALYSIS

The significators should be taken in the following order:

1. Factors indicating major tendencies:
   (a) balance of elements – is there an emphasis on one or two elements?
   (b) balance of qualities – is there an emphasis on one or two of these?
   (c) strong aspect patterns – is there a 'T' Square, Grand Cross, Grand Trine or other significant pattern?
2. The Ascendant and the Rising sign; position by sign and house of the Ascendant ruler (the planet ruling the Rising sign, aspects made by the Ascendant and Ascendant ruler. The Ascendant ruler is also known as the chart ruler or ruling planet.
3. The Sun sign, and house and aspects.
4. The Sun ruler (the planet ruling the sign containing the Sun), its sign, house and aspects.
5. The Moon sign, and house and aspects made by the Moon.
6. The remaining planets in order from Mercury to Pluto, their houses, signs and aspects.
7. The nodes and any other factors to be considered.

It is helpful to read through the notes on the chart analysis and insert next to each interpretation the subheading under which it should be considered. Most of the interpretations will fall naturally under one subheading, but some may have to be considered under two or even three.

When looking at a house consider the planets in the house first, then the sign on the cusp and then the house ruler (the planet ruling the sign on the cusp). Consideration of the house ruler should be left to the last because although it provides more information it can be confusing for the beginner. Interpretation of the house ruler becomes more important when there are no planets in a house.

The following subheadings are useful as a rough guide for a thorough interpretation, although these may be combined or added to as necessary. For example, emotions and relationships may be considered either together or separately.

1. **General character:** the Ascendant; planets in the first house; the Sun and Moon; major patterns and outstanding features such as element emphasis; Ascendant ruler; any other general features.

2. **Family:** planets in the fourth house; fourth house ruler (planet ruling the sign on the cusp of the fourth house); fifth house (children); third house (brothers and sisters); tenth house and the tenth house ruler, if relevant; Moon (Mother); fourth house with Sun and Saturn (father), if relevant.

3. **Emotions:** the Moon, Venus, planets in water signs.

4. **Relationships:** the Descendant; planets in the seventh house and the seventh house ruler (close partnerships and marriage); planets in the fifth house and the fifth house ruler (romance); planets in the eleventh house and the eleventh house ruler (groups, acquaintances); planets in Libra (partnerships); Mars (social energy); Moon, Venus and planets in water signs, if relevant.

5. **Mind, intellect and education:** Mercury; planets in the third house and the third house ruler (ability to communicate, school education, general interests and mental skills); Jupiter; planets in the ninth house and the ninth house ruler (higher education,

philosophical outlook); eighth and twelfth houses (indications of intuitive skills); Neptune (imagination); planets in Gemini and Virgo, if relevant.

6. **Artistic and creative ability:** planets in the fifth house and the fifth house ruler; Mercury, Venus, Mars and Neptune, if relevant; planets in earth signs (practical skill).

7. **Career, work:** MC; planets in the tenth house and the tenth house ruler (career); planets in the sixth house and the sixth house ruler (working conditions, nature of job); Mars (practical energy); Saturn (self-organization and discipline).

8. **Money:** planets in the second house and the second house ruler; planets in the eighth house and the eighth house ruler.

9. **Travel:** planets in the third house (short journeys); planets in the ninth house (long journeys).

10. **Health:** planets in the sixth house and the sixth house ruler; general indications from other significators.

Should any other information be required, turn to the relevant house in the horoscope and examine the planets it contains, the sign on its cusp and the planet ruling this sign, and the general planetary ruler. For example, for the law turn first to the ninth house (which rules the law), the planets it contains and the planet which rules its cusp, and then to Jupiter, the general ruler of the law. For leisure activities examine Venus, the fifth house and general factors such as the Sun sign.

The beginner will find it very useful to rewrite the notes of the analysis under these separate headings, but with a little experience this stage can be shortened or dropped to the point where all that is needed is a note of the relevant subheading next to each interpretation in the analysis.

EXAMPLE CHART FOR WENDY

Wendy was born at 10.25 pm British Summer Time (9.25 pm GMT) on 4 July 1950 in Fulham, London.

DOMINANCE OF WATER: generally emotional, sensitive, imaginative.

DOMINANCE OF CARDINAL/MUTABLE: changeable restless, unstable.

'T' SQUARE IN MUTABLE: tension, energy directed into search for change, new circumstances.

Asc♒ **ASCENDANT – AQUARIUS:** requires independence and freedom, needs to be different, intellectual, idealistic, impractical, resents restrictions.

♄♍ **ASCENDANT RULER – SATURN IN VIRGO:** need for physical order.

♄8 **SATURN IN THE EIGHTH HOUSE:** needs to work very hard in business; possibility of losses, delays in business.

♄⚹☉ **SATURN SEXTILE SUN:** self-discipline, good sense of order, ability to cope with responsibilities and routine.

♄☍☽ **SATURN OPPOSITION MOON:** emotionally reserved; difficulty in expressing feelings; needs emotional stability; material difficulties in the home, eg. lack of money, disagreements between parents, opposition from family members.

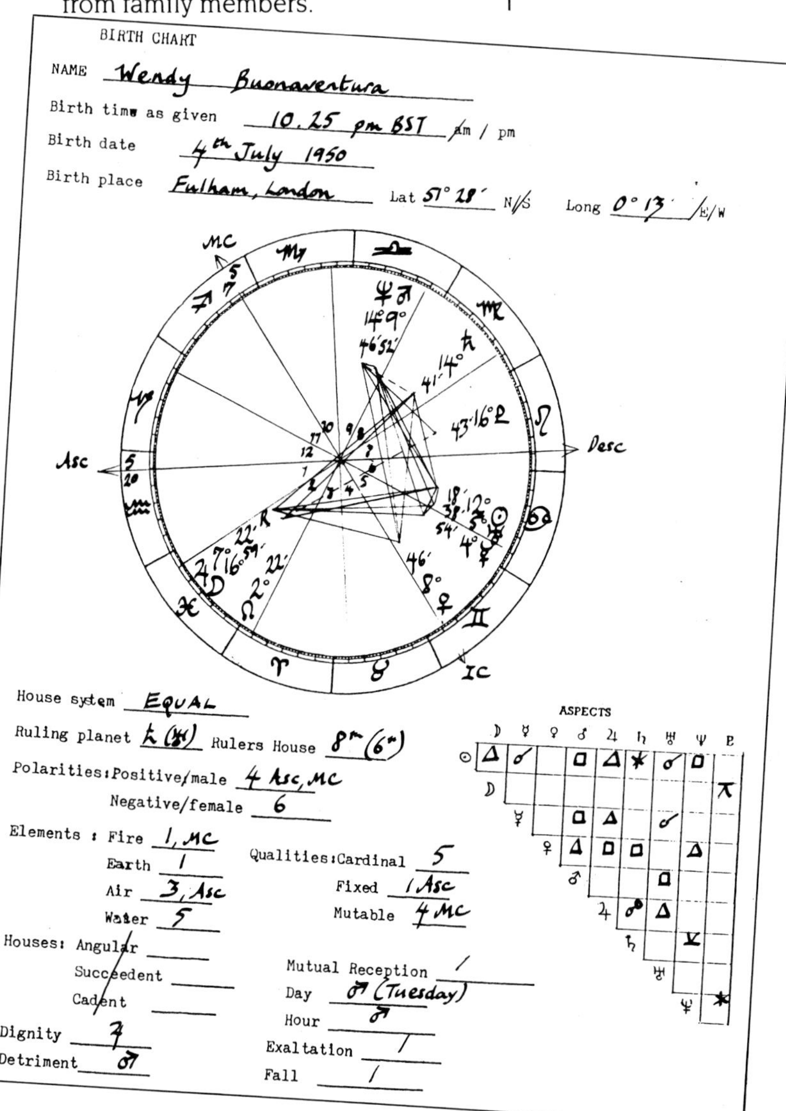

♄□♀ **SATURN SQUARE VENUS:** difficulties and delays in forming relationships; shy in expressing feelings; needs emotional security; faithful in relationships; conservative in artistic attitudes; possibility of financial restrictions.

♄☍♃ **SATURN OPPOSITION JUPITER:** the basic need for order and restriction is in conflict with the desire for expansion and growth – there may be continual difficulties posed by the demand for change on the one hand and for stability on the other.

♄⚺♆ **SATURN SEMI-SEXTILE NEPTUNE:** ability to express the imagination through practical skills.

♅♋ **ASCENDANT CO-RULER URANUS IN CANCER:** seeks emotional independence, domestic change. In most cases the position of Uranus by sign has only a general psychological meaning, but this is heightened by the conjunction of Uranus with the Sun.

♅5 **URANUS IN THE FIFTH HOUSE:** requires independence in leisure activities and romance; artistically original; relations with children unusual; the children themselves will be independent.

♅☌6th cusp **URANUS ON THE SIXTH CUSP:** technically Uranus is in the fifth house, but it is in an exact conjunction with the sixth cusp so it may be considered to have a role in sixth house matters. Work will be highly original; there will be a need to work independently and a dislike of routine. Health may be affected by nervous tension.

♅☌☉ **URANUS CONJUNCT SUN:** the orb is wide and the aspect is separating, but it is important because of the Sun's general significance. There is an exceptionally strong need for independence and a desire to follow an original and unusual life style; resists commitments and routine.

♅☌☿ **URANUS CONJUNCT MERCURY:** an orb of less than 1° makes this a very strong aspect. Strong, unusual, original, independent ideas; needs mental stimulation; likes debate and argument.

♅□♂ **URANUS SQUARE MARS:** individualistic behaviour; prefers acting alone to obeying orders; impatient with established routine; needs to innovate.

♅△♃ **URANUS TRINE JUPITER:** beliefs tend to be independent, unusual.

♅⚻ Asc **URANUS QUINCUNX ASCENDANT:** independent spirit.

♅⚻ MC **URANUS QUINCUNX MC:** requires independence and change in career.

☉♋ **SUN IN CANCER:** Sun-sign characteristics are exceptionally important. Emotional, sensitive, compassionate, maternal; needs secure home and stable family life; moods fluctuate.

☉6 **SUN IN THE SIXTH HOUSE:** conscientious worker; likes to look after people; worries about health (Cancer types are worriers); physical health subject to emotional moods.

☉△☽ **SUN TRINE MOON:** well balanced; home and family life harmonious; generally well-integrated personality.

☉☌☿ **SUN CONJUNCT MERCURY:** the orb for this aspect is very wide but it is applying and therefore given added importance. Strong minded, strong willed; the mind is subjective and the ideas are personal; impatient with clear or logical thought.

☉□♂ **SUN SQUARE MARS:** adventurous; fights battles, with little thought of personal welfare; likes a challenge; can be reckless and impatient.

☉△♃ **SUN TRINE JUPITER:** optimistic, expansive and self-confident.

☉□♆ **SUN SQUARE NEPTUNE:** vivid imagination but tendency to confusion and dismissal of practical considerations.

☽♓ **MOON IN PISCES**
extreme sensitivity, deep imagination, changeable, dreamy, impractical; home and family life needs to be calm, peaceful and relaxed, but may be disorganized with an element of mystery.

☽2 **MOON IN THE SECOND HOUSE:** financial affairs fluctuate; money earned through women; attitudes to money and possessions based on emotions, not practical needs.

☽⚻♇ **MOON QUINCUNX PLUTO:** need for

INSECURITY v INDEPENDENCE RESOLUTION

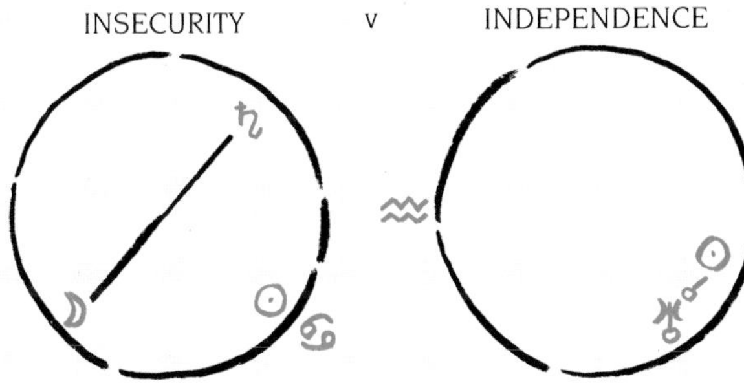

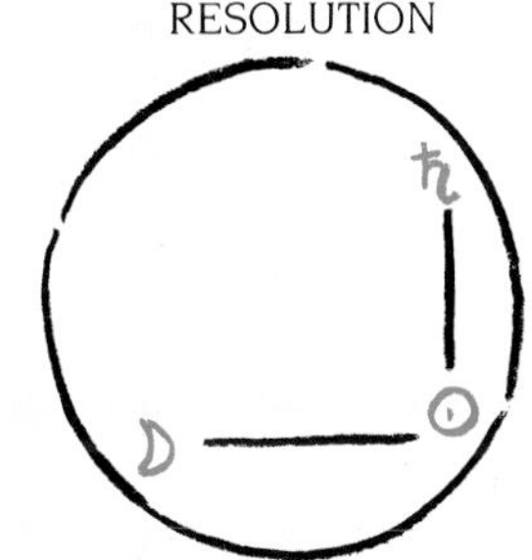

Contradictions

Contradictory factors can be a help in interpretation because they show the difficult choices that often bring people to consult an astrologer.

Wendy faces a major choice between the need for security indicated by her Sun in Cancer and Moon-Saturn opposition and the desire for independence of her Sun-Uranus conjunction and Aquarian Ascendant. Trines from the Sun to the Moon and a sextile to Saturn show her ability to reach a balance, and the Sun in the sixth house shows that this is achieved largely through her work.

emotional and domestic change and renewal.

☿♋ **MERCURY IN CANCER:** the mind, ideas and ideals are dominated by the emotions; better at intuitive than rational thought; good memory.

☿5 **MERCURY IN THE FIFTH HOUSE:** intellect and skills need to be used creatively in communication.

☿☌6 cusp **MERCURY ON THE SIXTH CUSP:** Like Uranus, Mercury is in an exact conjunction with the sixth cusp and so may be considered to have a sixth house function. Needs mental stimulation in work; must utilize communicative skills.

☿□♂ **MERCURY SQUARE MARS:** impatient, fond of argument and debate; seeks truth; sharp tongued; must have intellectual stimulation; restless; fond of travel; may suffer from nervous tension.

☿△♃ **MERCURY TRINE JUPITER:** good commonsense; beliefs and ideas harmonize.

☿⚻ Asc **MERCURY QUINCUNX ASCENDANT:** mental tension increases need for intellectual achievement.

☿⚻ MC **MERCURY QUINCUNX MC:** mental tension leads to need for intellectual stimulation in career.

♀♊ **VENUS IN GEMINI:** socially lively and vivacious; rationalizes emotions; likes to talk about feelings; intellectual approach to the arts.

♀5 **VENUS IN THE FIFTH HOUSE:** emotional energy is directed into artistic activity; likes entertaining; needs mental rapport with friends; relations with children lively and affectionate.

♀△♂ **VENUS TRINE MARS:** warm, hospitable, sociable; well balanced emotionally and socially; charm assists in achievement of aims and ambitions; financial affairs balanced.

♀□♃ **VENUS SQUARE JUPITER:** strong need for affection; love of luxury and comfort; high artistic ambitions; perfectionist.

♀△♆ **VENUS TRINE NEPTUNE:** very romantic; idealistic and imaginative in the arts.

♀△ Asc **VENUS TRINE ASCENDANT:** sense of beauty; social charm and grace.

♀☍ MC **VENUS OPPOSITION MC:** likelihood of disagreements with colleagues at work; emotional need for a beautiful and pleasant home.

♂♎ **MARS IN LIBRA:** indecision in practical affairs; energy best expressed through the arts, creation of a pleasant environment; diplomatic and social skills.

♂9 **MARS IN THE NINTH HOUSE:** strong beliefs; will fight for what is right; need to travel and work abroad.

♂☌♆ **MARS CONJUNCT NEPTUNE:** confusion in practical affairs; does best in work requiring inspiration, imagination, artistic skill, eg. theatre, films; lofty ambitions.

♂△ Asc **MARS TRINE ASCENDANT:** good practical energy.

♂⚹ MC **MARS SEXTILE MC:** sound practical attitude to career.

♃♓ **JUPITER IN PISCES:** sense of justice, wisdom, sensitivity.

♃2 **JUPITER IN THE SECOND HOUSE:** extravagant; idealistic; possessions not valued highly; prefers beautiful to practical objects; possibility of unexpected financial windfalls.

♃□ MC **JUPITER SQUARE MC:** desire for status, success and recognition in the career; high ambitions.

♆/♎ **NEPTUNE IN LIBRA:** belief in justice, fairness, idealistic in partnerships. Unless it is especially emphasized the sign position of Neptune has little psychological significance. In this case Neptune is the co-ruler of Pisces, the Moon sign, but is not itself of special importance.

♆/9 **NEPTUNE IN THE NINTH HOUSE:** beliefs are mystical and idealistic; deep inspiration is gained from foreign travel and cultures.

♆/⚹♇ **NEPTUNE SEXTILE PLUTO:** desire for a sense of personal purpose and meaning. This aspect is in orb for about 60 years, from 1942 until the turn of the century, and except in rare cases has little individual psychological significance.

♇♌ **PLUTO IN LEO:** Pluto was in Leo from 1939 to 1957. This has no individual psychological significance unless it is heavily emphasized in a chart.

♇7 **PLUTO IN THE SEVENTH HOUSE:** relationships are dominated by deep expectations influenced by the past; strong personal needs, perfectionism and personal commitment.

INTEGRATION

Integrating the analysis of the horoscope is not solely a matter of rearranging all the individual interpretations under their separate headings. It is necessary to make connections between different factors in the chart, combining interpretations which go well together and attempting to reconcile the contradictions between those that do not. It is through examining the contradictions contained in any chart that the true complexity of an individual character may be understood.

Wendy's chart contains several basic contradictions which arise in her life in terms of difficult choices and conflicts of interest. The most obvious of these is between the need for security represented by the Sun in Cancer and the Moon-Saturn opposition and the desire for independence and change revealed in the Aquarian Ascendant and the Sun-Uranus conjunction. Supporting factors may be found for each possibility, not least of which is Saturn's dual role as bringer of security and ruler of Aquarian independence. The astrologer can see the tension that these opposites bring to the character and by looking at the entire chart, build up a comprehensive picture of their effect. As Cancer and the Moon both rule the home the pressure is felt most keenly in the conflicting desires for a stable home life and Uranian-Aquarian change and upheaval. A resolution is offered astrologically through the harmonious trine of the Moon to Uranus and sextile of the Sun to Saturn. In practical terms the best compromise is a secure home base combined with plenty of personal freedom.

Venus is another focus for contradictions. On the one hand it is in Gemini and squared Jupiter, a combination which is lively, talkative and prepared to discuss emotions. On the other it is square Saturn indicating reserve and shyness, a characteristic backed up by the Sun in Cancer (naturally reserved) and the Moon in opposition to Saturn. Indications of reserve are the stronger, so while Wendy can be socially vivacious she is usually rather quiet and shy.

It is also necessary to draw links between planets, signs, houses and aspects that are not spelt out in the analysis. For example, the Sun in the sixth house indicates a conscientious worker, but the Sun in Cancer seeks personal emotional fulfilment. The result is that Wendy is a conscientious worker so long as she is emotionally committed to her work.

Similarly with the Saturn-Jupiter opposition: this reflects a general conflict which reinforces the need for security versus the need for change symbolized by the Sun in Cancer and the Aquarian Ascendant. However, when it is seen that Jupiter is in the second house and Saturn in the eighth then the aspect can be interpreted particularly in terms of Wendy's financial affairs. These may be subject to sharp fluctuation as the two planets alternate in dominance, and the desire to spend symbolized by Jupiter is held in check by restricted business possibilities symbolized by Saturn. In Wendy's life this relates particularly to the difficulties involved in making a living as an artist.

In this interpretation house cusp rulers have been used only sparingly to provide additional information. The main example concerns the eleventh house, ruler of acquaintances and the larger social circle. In Wendy's chart Sagittarius is on the cusp of the eleventh house, and this sign is ruled by Jupiter. By examining Jupiter's location and aspects further information can be gathered about Wendy's social life. The indications are contradictory, as Jupiter's opposition to Saturn shows reserve but its square to Venus is vivacious. The astrologer adds this information to what is already known to build up a more comprehensive interpretation.

From Wendy's chart we can deduce:

GENERAL CHARACTER. ☉♋6th aspects, ☽♓2nd + aspects, ascendant ♒ + aspects, general condition of chart rulers, ♄ and ♅ (as there are two rulers, Saturn, the traditional, should be taken as more important), water-cardinal-mutable emphasis.

This person is obviously highly emotional (☉♋□♆, ☽♓) and requires complete personal independence (☉☌♅, Asc♒). There will be many difficult choices to make between the desire for change and travel (☉☌♅, ☉□♂9th) and the need for security and stability (☉♋, ☽☍♄, ♃☍♄). She is naturally hard working (☉6th⚹♄) but requires emotional commitment to any practical activity (☉♋6th, ☽♓). She tends to be impractical (☉□♆, ♂☌♆) and her practical energies fluctuate with her emotions (☉♋□♂).

The tension between her opposing needs for change and stability (♃☍♄) are channelled into artistic work (♀5th at apex of 'T' Sq.). In spite of her sensitivity she is remarkably tough (Cardinal Emphasis) and can adapt to change ('T' Square Mutable).

FAMILY. ☽♓+aspects, fourth house and ♀, ruler of the fourth cusp, fifth house and ☿, ruler of the fifth cusp. The ☽ stands out as by far the strongest significator of domestic conditions, so much so that in this case the others may be virtually ignored unless specific questions arise.

There is a strong need for a pleasant, peaceful and imaginative home environment (☽♓) although there are strong indications of domestic problems, lack of money and difficulties either between or with parents (☽☍♄), particularly conflict with the father (Wendy, symbolized by the ☽ ruler of women, is opposed to ♄, ruler of the father). However, there are excellent signs that such difficulties will be overcome and domestic harmony restored (☽△☉). The home will probably be quite stable (4th cusp in ♉) although there is a restless desire for change (♀, ruler of 4th, in ♊). A desire for a large family (♀5th□♃) is balanced by a reluctance to take on responsibility (♀5th□♄). The astrologer must work out which planet is stronger, ♃ or ♄. Each has a claim: ♃ is strong in its own sign, ♓, but ♄ exerts a powerfully restrictive opposition on the ☽.

EMOTIONS AND RELATIONSHIPS. Planets in water signs, ♀ and ♂, planets in ♎, the seventh and eleventh houses. This person is clearly exceptionally emotional and sensitive (☉♋□♆, ☽♓) and comes to terms quite well with her strong feelings (☉△☽). She needs security and stability but she must also have independence, freedom, variety and stimulation (Asc ♒, ☉☌♅, ♀♊). She is extremely romantic (☉♋□♆, ☽♓) but her moods can change without warning (☉□♂, ☉□♆), though she tends to be discreet in public (☉☍♄, ☉♋).

Socially she can be talkative and vivacious (♃, ruler of 11th □♀5th, △☉ ruler of 7th cusp) although she is quite shy and reserved most of the time (☽☍♄, ☉♋). She tends to be most reserved in larger groups (♃ ruler of 11th ☍♄). She requires emotional commitment in partnerships, is very faithful (☽☍♄, ♇7th, ☉♋) but does not like formal ties (☉☌♅, Asc ♒).

MIND, INTELLECT, EDUCATION. The mind is completely dominated by the emotions and imagination (☿♋☌☉) and is unusual, independent and inventive (☿☌♅). Ideas are strongly held and there is a reluctance to compromise (☿☌☉, ☿□♂). Behind the emotional front she is commonsensical and fair minded (☿△♃).

Beliefs are strong and balanced (♂ ruler of 3rd in ♎, 9th). There are strong indications of a creative imagination which will be expressed through artistic activity (♀ ruler of 9th cusp in 5th) probably writing (♀♊5th△♂ ruler of 3rd), signifying creative energy. Attitudes to the arts will be quite conservative (♀5th□♄), original (♅☌☿, ruler of 5th) and extremely enthusiastic (♀5th□♃). There is a strong ambition to succeed (♀5th□♃,♃□MC).

In view of the artistic skills and intuitive mind, Wendy will always do better in the arts than in the sciences.

CAREER, WORK. Wendy is a conscientious worker (☉6th⚹♄) and drawn towards work which is personally satisfying and can help others (☉♋6, ruler of 6th in ♓). Her attitude to work is basically idealistic and imaginative but unworldly (☉6th□♆, ☽ ruler of 6th in ♓). She will work hard to get things right, often sacrificing her own interests (☉6th□♆) sometimes to the point of physical exhaustion (☉6th□♂). Her work involves her intellectual and communicative talents although the nervous tension this creates may affect her health (☿☌♅ on the sixth cusp of work and health). Her career may involve foreign countries and travel (♂ ruler of MC in 9th), the arts or public relations (♂ ruler of MC in ♎△♀).

MONEY. Money will be earned through women (☽ general significator of women in

Sun

Moon

Mercury

Venus

Earth

Mars

Jupiter

Saturn

Uranus

Neptune

Pluto

the second house), the arts or imagination (☽2nd♓). There may be a fear of poverty, and loss in business alternating with times of plenty (☽2nd☌♃, ☍♄). Extravagance is tempered by caution (♃2nd☍♄8th), but she can be hard headed in business (♄8th).

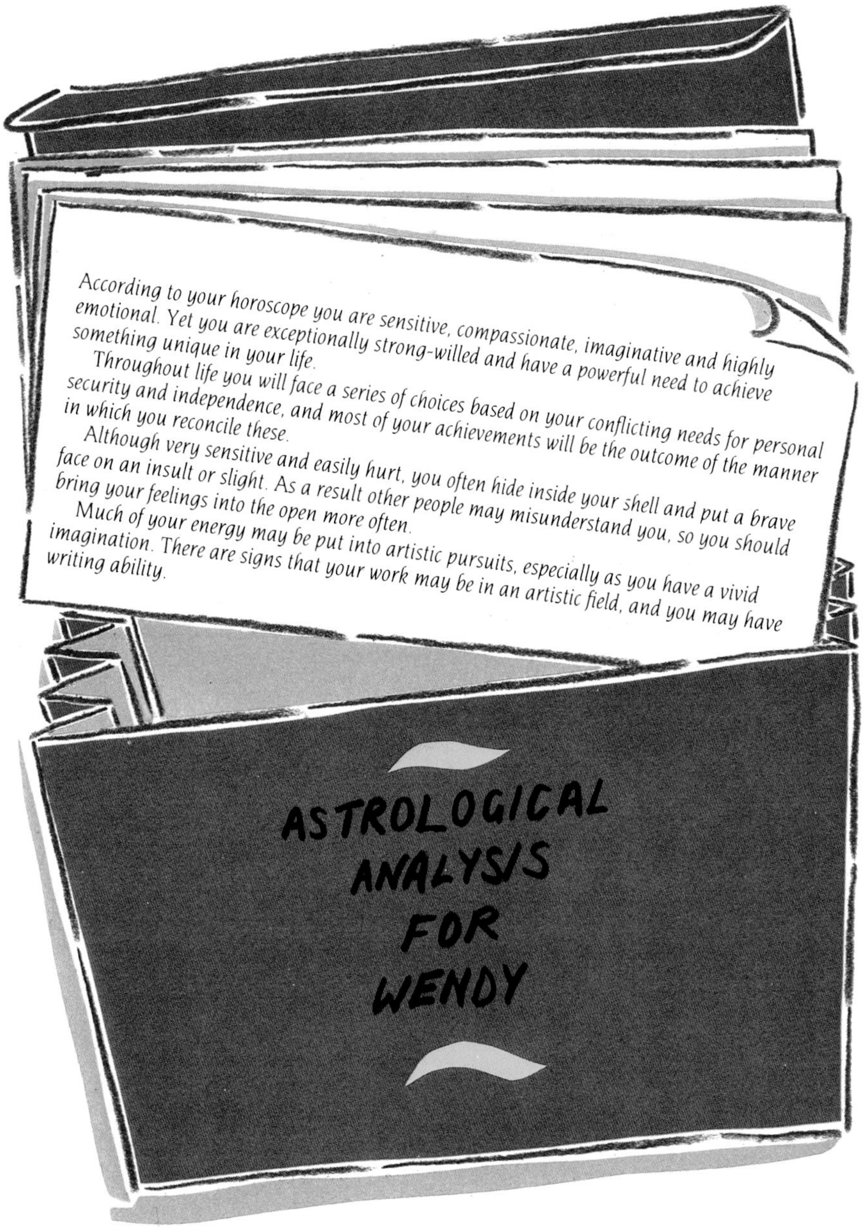

According to your horoscope you are sensitive, compassionate, imaginative and highly emotional. Yet you are exceptionally strong-willed and have a powerful need to achieve something unique in your life.

Throughout life you will face a series of choices based on your conflicting needs for personal security and independence, and most of your achievements will be the outcome of the manner in which you reconcile these.

Although very sensitive and easily hurt, you often hide inside your shell and put a brave face on an insult or slight. As a result other people may misunderstand you, so you should bring your feelings into the open more often.

Much of your energy may be put into artistic pursuits, especially as you have a vivid imagination. There are signs that your work may be in an artistic field, and you may have writing ability.

ASTROLOGICAL ANALYSIS FOR WENDY

The Final Report
Most astrologers prepare a final report on the horoscope. Often this is written, but sometimes recorded on tape. Astrological jargon is left out and all the different factors are synthesized into one final interpretation.

HEALTH. Health problems are likely to arise from nervous tension (☿☌♅ on the sixth cusp) and worry (Cancers are great worriers) and are subject to emotional changes and sensitivity (☽ ruler of the sixth house in ♓).

SYNTHESIS

The astrologer may now proceed to the third stage, that of synthesis, in which the whole interpretation is written out in a form which is easy for the subject to read and understand.

Most professional astrologers give only verbal consultations which, since the advent of modern recording equipment, are taped for the client.

The reason for this is that full written reports are laborious to complete and do not take into account any dialogue between astrologer and client. Nevertheless, the written report has its advantages, especially as the client can refer far more easily to a sentence on a page than to a passage on a tape. For the student the preparation of written reports is the best way to learn the meanings of astrological symbols, become familiar with the process of interpretation and develop confidence as an astrologer.

In the final interpretation it is open to the astrologer to use examples, figures of speech and metaphors in order to make the interpretation more colourful and to emphasize certain points. Astrological jargon should be left out of the final draft as this is usually meaningless to the client, although the technical information such as the positions of the planets, should be listed separately. Psychological jargon should also be avoided as this often serves only to obscure the real issues.

In the case of the subject of our horoscope, Wendy is a writer and dancer. The chart clearly indicates an interest in writing, through Venus in Gemini in the fifth house, and by the trine to Mars in Libra (ruled by Venus) in the ninth house of higher education (Wendy studied literature at university). Her published work has been well received. Success is also shown by the trine to Mars in Libra in the ninth house, this house being the ruler of publishers. Less obvious from the chart is Wendy's skill as a dancer. However, to the astrologer versed in symbolism, dancing is represented by Pisces, the sign which rules the feet. The Moon in Pisces emphasizes the sign and also rules Cancer, the sign on the cusp of the sixth house of work. The astrologer may, therefore, make a connection between her work and a flair for dance.

There is a clear contradiction in the chart between conservatism and originality in the field of art. Feedback from the subject shows how these have been reconciled. Wendy spécializes in the traditional solo dances of the Middle East, dances which are thousands of years old. She has pioneered their acceptance in Britain, thus introducing an unusual dance form to Western society. In this she has expressed her own conjunction of Uranus with the Sun (natural ruler of the fifth house of creativity) and Mercury (ruler of the fifth cusp in the birth chart). The fact that she is the exponent of an ancient art form is reflected in the conservative square of Saturn to Venus in the fifth house. Mars, ruler of the MC (career) in the ninth house (foreign countries) indicates both the foreign inspiration of Wendy's dances and the frequency with which she works abroad.

Wendy's income – like that of most artists – tends to fluctuate and, as the chart suggests, times of plenty alternate with periods when funds are low. Remarkably, with the Moon in the second house, she does indeed earn her money through women, for her dances are traditional female dances, and only women attend her classes.

Wendy works independently with great dedication and energy, frequently sacrificing material interests to the cause of perfecting her art, all of which tendencies are clearly shown in the conjunction of the Sun with Uranus and its squares to Neptune and Mars. In fact, she works to exhaustion (Sun square Mars), and the strain of self-employment is a factor which can affect her health (Mercury conjunct Uranus indicates nervous tension). She has in the past collaborated with other dancers, but these partnerships have tended to be short-lived (Mars square Sun, ruler of the seventh cusp of partnerships outweighs the harmonious effect of the Mars-Venus trine).

It is interesting to see how one theme in Wendy's life, her dancing, draws together so many significators in the horoscope, including the second, fifth, sixth, seventh, eighth, ninth and tenth houses.

Before becoming a dancer Wendy worked in public relations (Mars in Libra) for a community arts cooperative, which she left because she was too independent minded for the organization. By checking back with the chart the astrologer is able to see that Jupiter, ruler of the eleventh house of the community, is in a difficult square to Venus, ruling public relations in Gemini, sign of ideas, in the fifth house of the arts. It is doubtful if any astrologer could have achieved such an exact interpretation from this configuration; but by getting feedback from the client the astrologer will be able to make more fruitful use of the chart.

The astrological conclusions concerning Wendy's emotions, home and family also prove correct. She is highly romantic, but dislikes formal ties, partly a reflection of her need to feel independent. A major influence on her life has been the straitened financial circumstances of her childhood (Moon opposition Saturn),and while her attitude to money is basically idealistic (Jupiter in the second house) she nonetheless needs material comforts for her peace of mind.

A consistent and difficult choice which Wendy has had to face reflects the larger issue in her life: whether to seek stability or change. The need for a stable home (fourth cusp in Taurus, Sun in Cancer, Moon opposed Saturn) has been contradicted by a desire to live and travel abroad (Sun conjunct Uranus, square Mars in the ninth house). Possibly due to the strength of the Moon-Saturn opposition she has established a settled home in England, but one with few responsibilities, making possible the frequent journeys attendant on her work.

At this stage of the consultation no predictions were necessary, but the simple character delineation itself was extremely useful. Clarification of the major issues in the horoscope, especially the sharp conflict between the opposing needs for change and stability, enabled Wendy to understand her life with greater confidence and certainty.

Once the horoscope had been studied and an interpretation prepared, the final consultation took the form of a dialogue between Wendy and the astrologer. The astrologer provided the basic interpretation, Wendy reacted to this, and he was then able to clarify and elaborate the interpretation, playing down certain factors while highlighting others. The final interpretation was, therefore, the result of a collaboration between the astrologer and the client, a process which is more fruitful for both than if the horoscope is prepared in a vacuum.

To sum up, astrologers should not play at being God. They do not have access to some absolute truth, even if astrology is capable of providing answers that other disciplines cannot. Astrologers should always listen to the client. In some cases they may accept the client's criticism of the interpretation and modify it accordingly. In others they may feel that the client is refusing to face up to some awkward implication and they must try to find another way of explaining it.

Above all, the qualities demanded of an astrologer are sensitivity, tact, humility and consideration for the problems and circumstances of the client. People go to astrologers with a great deal of trust and it is up to the astrologer to respect this confidence.

Aries *Taurus*

Gemini *Cancer*

Leo *Virgo*

Libra *Scorpio*

Sagittarius *Capricorn*

Aquarius *Pisces*

CHAPTER 11 PREDICTION: THE TRANSITS

New Moons And Full Moons – The Sun-Moon Cycle

The phases of the Moon are extremely important, even forming the basis of the 12-month calendar. There are 12 complete Sun-Moon cycles in a year, each one reaching two peaks – the new Moon in conjunction with the Sun and the full Moon in opposition to the Sun.

The new Moon represents a seed moment at which energy is revitalized, increasing during the waxing phase and reaching fruition at the full Moon. Thereafter energy declines in the waning phase until the new Moon.

Close major aspects from new and full Moons to birth planets are always important and, if strong enough, point to the major events of the year.

If either Sun or Moon is eclipsed then the effect is much stronger. There are usually between three and six eclipses every year.

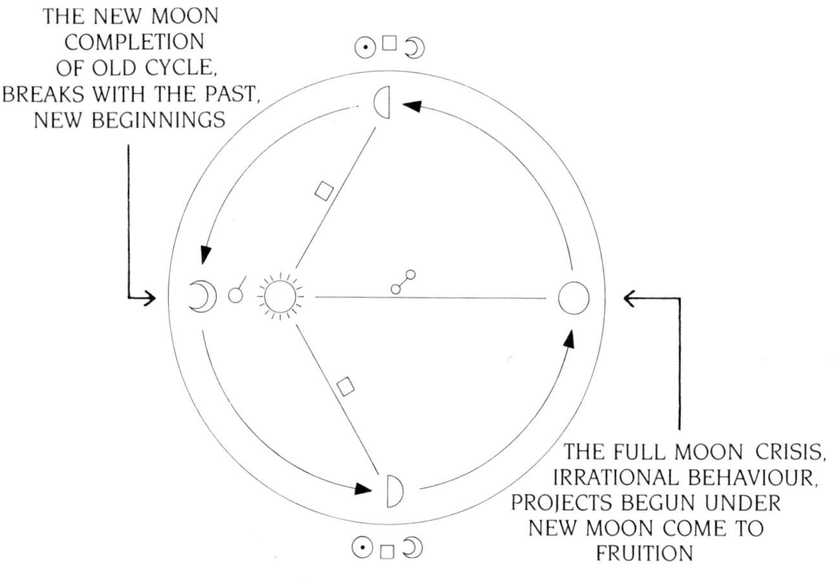

Forecasting the future was the original aim of the ancient astrologers, but now with the growth of psychological astrology prediction has lost some of its importance. However, no astrological consultation is complete without prediction for the simple reason that the astrologer must know what the client is experiencing in the present and near future.

The first step in prediction is the analysis of the patterns of the birth chart. The analysis is then brought up to the present and projected into the future so that the astrologer can give practical and relevant advice. It is best to start by looking at changing psychological moods, predicting, for example, periods of optimism or pessimism, of intense emotions or of level-headed practical effort. The astrologer also looks in general at the person's changing circumstances, anticipating periods of restriction or of opportunity, of change or stability. Such general prediction is commonly known as the 'analysis of future trends'.

Major events may also be predicted. It is usually a fairly simple matter to pinpoint career or major partnership changes, and domestic moves together with the approximate date, or dates, when these are likely to occur. In a given year there may be three or four dates when a build up of astrological factors indicates such a major change. But it is extremely difficult to make exact predictions concerning the time, place and exact nature of an event using the birth chart. Usually such accuracy is only possible if a fair measure of intuition or clairvoyance is also involved.

Caution, commonsense and tact are essential in prediction as people are often afraid of what the future holds. It is all too easy for the clumsy astrologer to alarm, dismay and depress by predicting disaster, usually wrongly. The astrologer's task is to offer encouragement and support enabling people to make choices and helping them to deal with the present and prepare for the future.

Most people who ask to have horoscopes cast have a question or problem they wish the astrologer to answer or solve. In many cases they are not able to define what is troubling them. Using the transits the astrologer is able to clarify the nature of the question or problem, predict the outcome and suggest ways in which the client might deal with the situation.

The transits are the most common source for predictions and have the added advantage of requiring almost no calculation. A transit is the actual movement of a planet through the zodiac from day to day, week to week and year to year. The transits are marked around the outside of the birth chart, each one falling in one of the natal houses, making aspects to the natal planets. To look up the transits for any one day it is necessary only to turn to the ephemeris for that day and read off the planetary positions. The Moon is the only planet for which calculation may be necessary, and in most cases this need only be approximate. The method of calculation is exactly the same as that for the natal Moon. Transiting planets are always signified by the letter T. For example, transiting Sun is written T☉.

TRANSITS AND THE BIRTH CHART.

The transits 'release' or 'trigger' the potential of the birth chart. They are the signposts that show the way forward into the future, but can only be read in relation to the birth chart. Therefore, the interpretation of a transit by sign, house or aspect must take into account the natal sign, house and aspect of that planet. For example, a person may have Mars in Pisces in the fifth house which gives him or her imagination and creative energy, and whatever house or sign Mars subsequently transits, the essential natal character will be retained. If Mars transits the sixth house in Aries indicating extra effort at work, the intuition of Pisces and the creativity of the fifth house will still be of paramount importance.

The same principle applies to aspects. For example, if Mercury is opposed to Mars in the natal chart a person may take hurried decisions without thinking the issues through properly. However, at a particular time he or she may experience a trine from transiting

THE NEW MOON COMPLETION OF OLD CYCLE, BREAKS WITH THE PAST, NEW BEGINNINGS

THE FULL MOON CRISIS, IRRATIONAL BEHAVIOUR, PROJECTS BEGUN UNDER NEW MOON COME TO FRUITION

Mercury to natal Mars, an aspect which indicates firm and positive decisions. In spite of this harmonious transiting aspect, there will still be a marked tendency to the impatience and recklessness of the natal aspect.

To get around this problem astrologers couch their predictions in general terms, forecasting tendencies rather than specific events except when the indications are especially strong.

The astrologer must also take into account the general disposition of the birth chart as this shows how people will react to future events. For example, two people may have transiting Uranus in opposition to the natal Sun, an aspect which can bring shattering changes. One of these people may be a Capricorn who hates change while the other a Piscean who thrives on uncertainty. The Capricorn will have a miserable time, experiencing the collapse of a structured existence, while the Piscean will have the time of his life relishing the new possibilities that Uranus brings.

It often happens that a planet turns retrograde and returns to aspect a natal planet over which it has recently passed. The same planet will then change direction and aspect the natal planet for a third time. The effective duration of a transiting aspect is then substantially increased and is exact on three occasions. Each time the aspect will be experienced in a different way in line with the person's changing circumstances. It is often said that on the first occasion the issues or problems associated with the aspect are raised. On the second occasion the person learns how to deal with them and on the third, all being well, a solution is successfully implemented, and life moves forward to a new phase.

Transits not only bring changing moods and circumstances, they bring lessons to learn, and it can be useful if a planet does indeed turn retrograde. In learning such lessons individuals mature and gain in experience and wisdom, and astrology becomes less a means to mere prediction and more a guide to self-development.

TIMING

As all the planets move at different speeds the transits last for different periods of time. A transit of Pluto, for example, can last for 18 months, but a transit of the Moon can be over in an hour. The more exact the aspect from a transiting planet to a natal planet, the more intense is the psychological experience and the more likely that significant events will occur. Frequently one finds that a number of transiting planets make aspects to the same part of the birth chart with the result that major changes become more likely. For example, a square from transiting Pluto to the natal Moon may be joined by a trine from transiting Saturn and a conjunction from transiting Mars. Such a build up of aspects would almost certainly indicate a move of home (the Moon ruling the home), while a single aspect might bring only minor changes.

The transits of the three outermost planets, Uranus, Neptune and Pluto, indicate periods of between six and 18 months in which profound change takes place bringing events which can alter the direction of life. Transits of Saturn may last between one and nine months, bringing difficulties and restriction, while transits of Jupiter may last between one week and nine months and bring opportunity. Transits of Mercury, Venus and Mars may last for any period from one day to several weeks, depending on the speed of motion, and are psychologically far more superficial. The events they cause may be trivial, but they can also act as catalysts for creating the life-shattering events symbolized by the slow-moving outer planets. Transits of the Sun last for two days and, if combined with other planetary transits, often indicate the days on which major events occur.

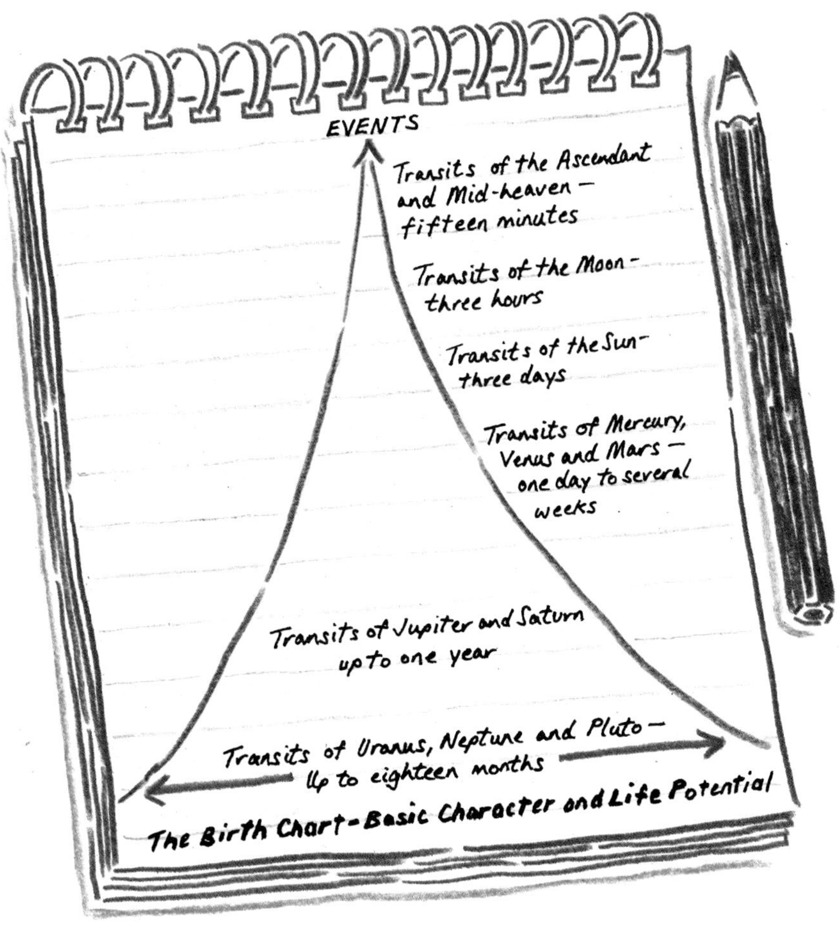

Time Scales, Character and Events
The slower a planet moves the deeper are its psychological changes and the more long-lasting the events it signifies. Faster moving planets have a less profound significance. However, major events happen when slow and fast moving transits are simultaneously strong.

Transits Through The Houses
The house of the birth chart occupied by a planet will always show the area of life in which that planet is most important, but as it transits the other houses its effects unfold like a kaleidoscope. For example, suppose that a man is born with Mars in the second house and tends to argue about money, the passage of Mars through the other houses may show the changing causes of these arguments.

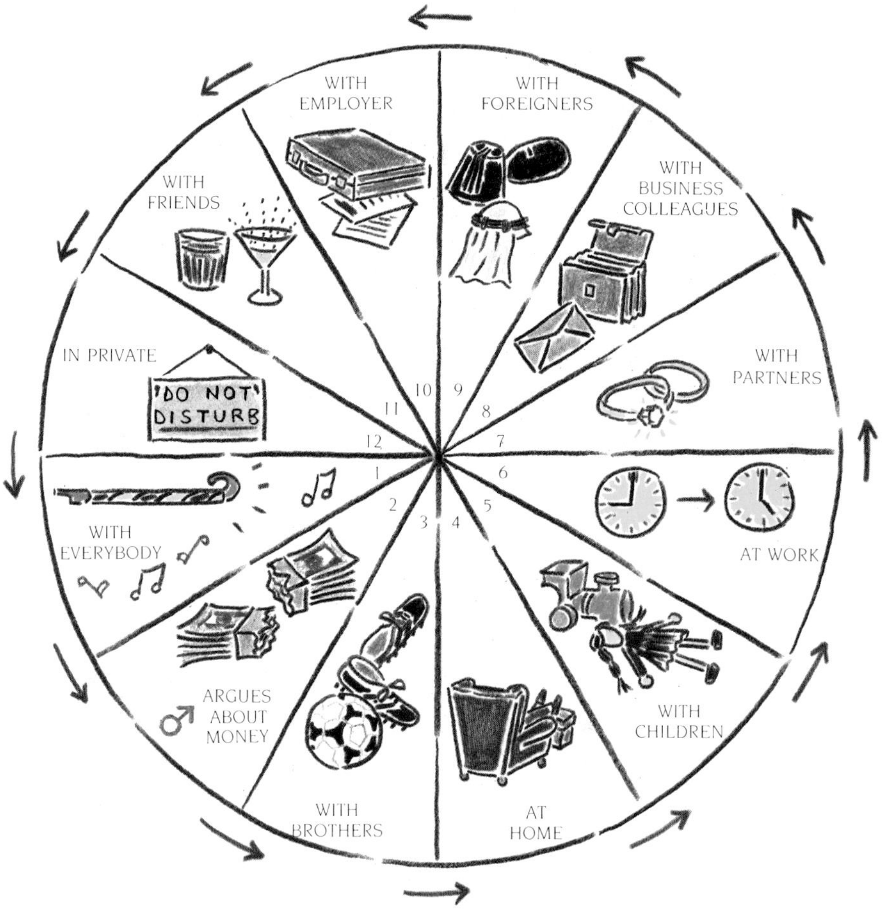

Planetary Cycles
With the exception of Uranus, Neptune and Pluto, whatever aspect two planets make at birth, or even if they are not in aspect, they will make every variety of aspect by transit during the course of one lifetime.

A person born under a Mars-Saturn square will have the characteristics of this aspect, but during the next two and a half years will experience every possible combination of aspects from transiting Mars to natal Saturn. By the age of 29 transiting Saturn will have made every possible aspect to natal Mars.

Although the natal position remains the foundation, every person has the chance to experience and use the complete range of planetary combinations. We can picture this as a wave motion with the sequence of aspects describing the rhythms of life. Analysis of the transits can show how this rhythm should best be followed.

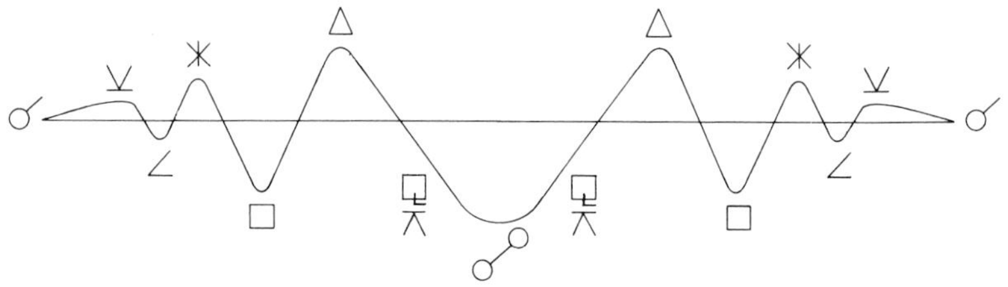

Transits of the Moon last for one or two hours and often indicate the time at which an event takes place. New Moons and full Moons are always important and when a new or full Moon makes powerful aspects to a birth chart this indicates that major events are likely to occur within a few days.

New Moons represent the birth of a new cycle and full Moons show the culmination of an old cycle. The period between the new Moon and the full Moon – the waxing Moon – is considered a period of increasing energy and the period from the full Moon to the new Moon – the waning Moon – is considered a period of declining energy.

Eclipses strengthen the significance of a new or full Moon. There are several eclipses each year and these often bring crises which have been building up for some time.

It is also possible to use the transiting Ascendant and MC, which can be calculated for any particular time. Aspects from the transiting Ascendant and MC to the birth chart often indicate the exact time at which an event takes place, but few astrologers go into such detail when making predictions.

TRANSITS THROUGH HOUSES AND SIGNS The principles of interpretation for transiting planets are the same as those for natal planets, bearing in mind that the passage of a planet through a sign or house represents only a phase in one's life. To interpret the transits through houses and signs refer to the standard interpretations for natal planets in houses and signs in Chapters 4 and 6. Generally, little attention is paid to transits through signs as these only slightly modify the overwhelming strength of the natal positions. However, transits through houses are extremely important as these show changing circumstances.

INTERPRETING THE ASPECTS. Brief interpretations are listed in this chapter for all the main combinations of aspects from transiting planets to natal planets. Detail can be added by referring to the more thorough interpretations for natal aspects in Chapter 9.

It is extremely important to draw distinctions between aspects from transiting outer planets to natal inner planets on the one hand, and transiting inner planets to natal outer planets on the other. The effect of the former will be profound and long lasting, while that of the latter will be over quite quickly and often cause only trivial events.

This must be borne in mind when using the sample interpretations. For example, the sun conjunct Pluto brings psychological and emotional intensity and the prospect of major changes. If the transiting Sun is making a conjunction to natal Pluto, as it does once a year, then the psychological mood will pass in two days and the event may be significant but not revolutionary. However, if transiting Pluto is making a conjunction to the natal Sun, the person may enter a period of up to 18 months when his or her mood is obsessive, deep and intense and an entire way of life may be turned upside down.

In general it is best to use only major aspects in transits – the conjunction, sextile, square, trine and opposition. Minor aspects may be added later if more detail is required.

Orbs should be kept as tight as possible; the standard orb is 1°.

PREDICTING EVENTS. The standard interpretations are all worked out for general situations and, therefore, tend to be vague and psychological. Events can only be predicted by looking at a combination of transits, and when several transits point to the same conclusion then it is a fair bet that the event will take place. Events occur as much under tense aspects as under harmonious ones, although it is, of course, necessary to understand the precise nature of the planets involved.

Harmonious aspects bring benefits, but do not guarantee success; tense aspects bring difficulties, but do not guarantee failure. To predict a particular event look for the time when there are a number of relevant transits occurring at the same time.

General changes: transits to the natal Ascendant, Sun and Moon.

Moves of home: transits to the natal Moon and IC and through the fourth house.

Marriage: the same as for moves of home combined with transits to natal Venus, Descendant and planets in the seventh house.

Career: transits to natal MC and through the natal tenth house.

Money: transits through the natal second and eighth houses and to natal planets in these houses.

Health: transits through the natal sixth house and to planets in the sixth house.

Education: transits to natal Mercury and the third house (school), to natal Jupiter and the ninth house (higher education).

Signing contracts: transits to natal Mercury and the natal third house.

Travel: transits to natal Mercury and the natal third house (short journeys) to natal Jupiter and the natal ninth house (long journeys).

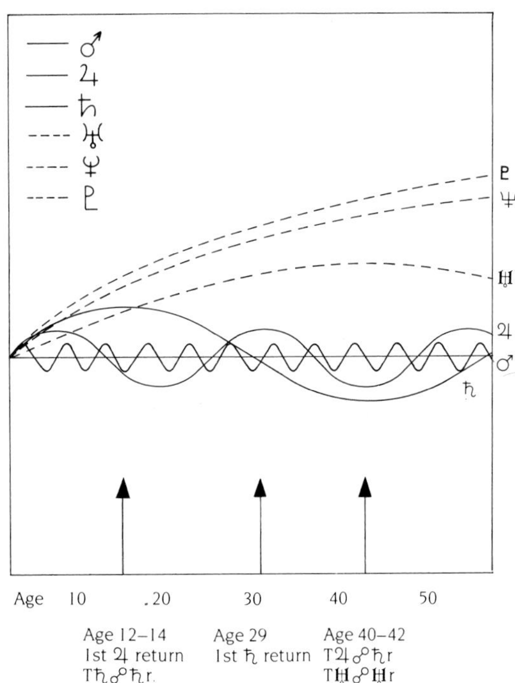

Planetary Life Cycles

The aspects made by transits of the slower moving planets to their places in the birth chart indicate major phases of life and show how people mature.

Adolescence is the first such point and coincides approximately with Jupiter's return to its position at birth and the opposition of transiting Saturn to natal Saturn. Jupiter's need for growth and new experience and Saturn's for carefully structured conflict account for some of the difficulties of this age.

Change often occurs at age 29 when, in the Saturn return, this planet arrives back at its birth position. This frequently brings profound dissatisfaction with life's achievements, and is a time of crisis for many people. The end-result of this upheaval is usually a greater sense of stability and maturity.

The 'mid-life crisis' around the age of 40 coincides with an impressive series of aspects and, under pressure to develop their individual potential, many people rebel against the home life and career that they have spent so long creating.

Retrograde Planets

If a transiting planet turns retrograde, it frequently aspects a natal planet three times over the same period. If this happens, the effect is intensified; the problems may be greater, but the chances of doing something about them are enhanced.

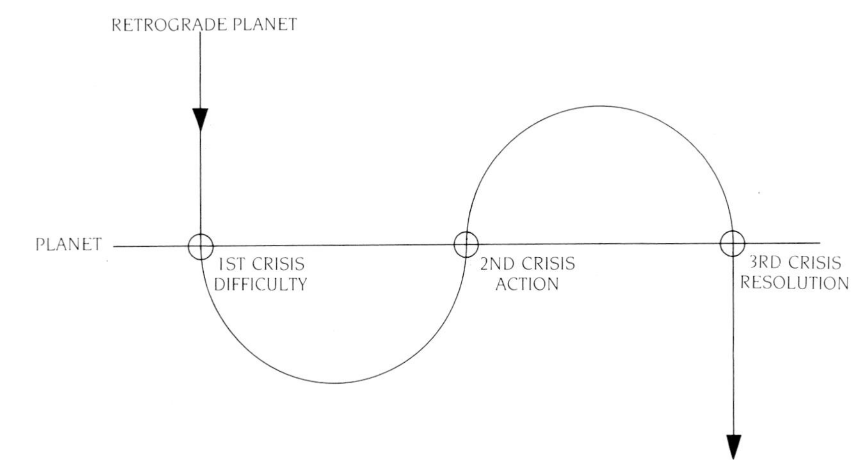

TRANSITS OF THE SUN

T☉ – ☉r

⚹ △ Generally beneficial – brings success.

□ ☍ Likelihood of slight tension or difficulty.

☌ This is the birthday, known to astrologers as the solar return. It is a significant point for which an entirely new chart may be drawn.

T☉ – ☽r

⚹ △ Generally beneficial; excellent for beginning new enterprises; benefits emotional, domestic affairs.

□ ☍ General tension and difficulty, especially in family and home. The opposition is the full Moon, often a point of crisis.

☌ This is the new Moon, a time of renewal of energy and new beginnings.

T☉ – ☿r

⚹ △ Beneficial for all communication, decision making, short journeys.

□ ☍ Difficulties in communication, mental tension.

☌ Self-will, intellectual confidence.

T☉ – ♀r

⚹ △ Good humour; beneficial for socializing, partnerships, the arts.

□ ☍ Emotional tension can bring friction in partnerships.

☌ Emotional and social energy at a peak.

T☉ – ♂r

⚹ △ Harmonious energy, benefits all general activities.

□ ☍ Likelihood of tension, impatience, difficulties, accidents.

☌ Strong dynamic energy.

T☉ – ♃r

⚹ △ Generally beneficial especially for travel, higher education and legal affairs; brings optimism and opportunity.

□ ☍ Need for personal freedom and adventure; possibility of reckless behaviour; difficult for legal affairs, education, travel.

☌ Vital energy, desire for personal freedom, possibility of opportunity and reward for past work; long journeys likely.

T☉ – ♄r

⚹ △ Good, constructive energy, self-discipline, likelihood of welcome new responsibilities.

□ ☍ Obstacles, delays, material difficulties, feelings of personal restriction, responsibilities may be burdensome, hard work likely.

☌ Seriousness, responsibility, hard work, restriction, need to cope with authority, need to learn self-discipline and organization.

T☉ – ♅r

⚹ △ Probability of interesting changes, new openings, alternative possibilities.

□ ☍ Restlessness, dramatic changes, need for personal freedom, sudden upheavals, rebellious behaviour, dislike of routine, impatience with established life, desire for radical change.

☌ Dramatic change; need for personal independence; individualist; unreliable; new possibilities.

T☉ – ♆r

⚹ △ Benefits imagination, increases sensitivity, brings subtle changes.

□ ☍ Unworldly ambitions, desire to transcend physical limitations, artistic imagination at a peak, impractical, confused.

☌ Sensitivity, compassion, idealism impracticality, unworldliness, subtle but sometimes profound changes in life style.

T☉-♇r

⚹△ Emotional strength, commitment to personal development and renewal.

□☍ Strong need for personal commitment and self-development; likelihood of conflict, confrontation; changes can be deep and traumatic.

☌ Commitment, intensity, personal revolution, need to discover personal ability and power; changes likely to be deep and long lasting.

T☉–Asc, Desc r

⚹△ Generally beneficial.

□ Likelihood of friction, especially with partners.

☌Asc, ☍Desc Self-interest strong; difficulty in partnerships.

☍Asc, ☌Desc Benefits all social affairs.

T☉–MC, ICr

⚹△ Beneficial for career and home.

□ Friction in career and home.

☌MC, ☍IC Energy in career, friction at home.

☍MC, ☌IC Benefits domestic affairs, brings friction to career.

TRANSITS OF THE MOON

T☽–☽r

⚹△ Generally beneficial, especially regarding home and family.

☍□ Emotional tension may disrupt domestic, family affairs.

☌ Emotional renewal.

T☽–☿r

⚹△ Excellent for decision making, commonsense, communication and short journeys, especially if connected to home or family.

☍□ Nervous tension; possible emotional

and domestic misunderstandings.
☌ Probable need to make choices or take decisions concerning domestic and emotional matters.

T☽–♀r
⚹△ Balanced emotions; excellent for all social and domestic affairs.
☌ All emotional and social affairs strongly emphasized.
□☍ Emotional, domestic and social friction.

T☽–♂r
⚹△ Balanced energies beneficial to social life, work and home.
☍□ Emotional tension, anger, arguments especially with family members, impulsive behaviour, accidents.
☌ Passionate emotions, self-will, especially in domestic and emotional affairs.

T☽–♃r
⚹△ Hope, optimism, opportunity, expansion and change in domestic situations, overseas contacts likely.
☍□ Need for change, especially in domestic affairs; restlessness, recklessness, waste of opportunities; long journeys likely; not good for legal affairs.
☌ Optimism, opportunities, growth and change in all emotional and domestic activities. Long distance or foreign travel likely.

T☽–♄r
⚹△ Sense of determination, self-discipline, desire for order, especially in emotional and domestic affairs.
□☍ Deep need for stability in emotional and domestic affairs, but obstacles, delays and material difficulties likely.
☌ Need for emotional security, domestic stability; unsociable, emotionally inhibited; a time to lay foundations for the future.

T☽–♅r
⚹△ Home, family and emotional affairs are livened by interesting and unusual changes.
□☍ Unexpected events disrupt domestic and emotional affairs; deep personal need for emotional freedom; changes can be sudden and dramatic.
☌ Emotional and domestic instability, sudden changes, the end of old conditions and the birth of a new and sometimes radical life style.

T☽–♆r
⚹△ Heightened intuition, sensitivity, imagination, unrealistic desire for domestic change.
□☍ Deeply romantic, highly sensitive, confused, impractical especially in home and emotional affairs.
☌ Emotional and domestic dreams may be put into practice; romantic, confused, idealistic, compassionate, impractical.

T☽–♇r
⚹△ Strong emotions, desire for change and renewal in home and family.
□☍ Intense emotions, likelihood of domestic confrontation, breaks in the status quo resulting in a complete change of circumstances.
☌ Emotional tension, desire for domestic transformation, confrontation, conflict, determination and personal revolution.

T☽–Asc, Desc r
⚹△ Beneficial conditions especially in home and family.
□ Emotional tension likely.
☌Asc, ☍Desc Strong emotions, possible disagreements with partners.
☍Asc, ☌Desc Excellent for partnerships, especially family relationships.

T☽–MC–IC
⚹△ Beneficial for career and partnerships.
□ Friction in career and partnerships.
☌MC, ☍IC Career interests dominated by emotional moods; tension at home.
☍MC, ☌IC Emotional moods benefit home but disrupt career.

TRANSITS OF MERCURY

T☿–☿r
⚹△ Good for education, communication, decision making and short journeys.
□☍ Nervous tension; not good for communication, taking decisions, short journeys.
☌ High mental energy, new ideas, strong will.

T☿–♀r
⚹△ Beneficial for all social affairs, partnerships, decision making, communication and short journeys.
□☍ Emotional and mental tension can lead to wrong decisions, misunderstandings.
☌ Strong mental and emotional energy benefits social and partnership affairs; communication good.

T☿–♂r
⚹△ Strong mental energy helps with all practical activities.
□☍ Strong will but impatience, arguments, accidents, wrong decisions, sudden changes of opinion.
☌ Strong ideas, sharp mind, determination, impatience, decisions and choices are made quickly; arguments likely.

T☿–♃r
⚹△ Beneficial for education, communication, decision making, travel and legal affairs.

☉ Sun
☽ Moon
☿ Mercury
♀ Venus
⊕ Earth
♂ Mars
♃ Jupiter
♄ Saturn
♅ Uranus
♆ Neptune
♇ Pluto

□☍ Mental confusion; decisions may be hasty and muddled; misunderstandings likely; idealistic.

☌ Idealistic, strong-willed; new interests, new courses of study likely; restlessness; travel likely.

T☿–♄r

⚹△ Ideas, decisions and communication will be serious, considered and constructive; respect gained through study.

□☍ Mental energy low; delays and obstacles affect courses of study, decision making, communication and short journeys.

☌ Seriousness, slow and considered thought; decisions may be deferred but when taken lay practical foundations for later life.

T☿–♅r

⚹△ Unusual interests, original ideas, new attitudes.

□☍ Nervous tension; need to develop original and individual interests; disagreements likely; sudden changes in attitude; idealism; short journeys disrupted.

☌ Strong will; dramatic changes in attitude; original ideas; sudden changes in plan; unconventional courses of study; unusual short journeys.

T☿–♆r

⚹△ Ideas and decisions strongly influenced by dreams and imagination.

□☍ Mind strongly affected by imagination and romantic dreams; idealism, but ideas changeable and impractical; liable to deception.

☌ Mind dominated by imagination, intuition, idealism, artistic talent, but may be confused and impractical. Journeys may be undertaken in search of romance.

T☿–♇

⚹△ Ideas, curiosity, strong desire for knowledge. Self-discipline in study.

□☍ Desire for truth, quest for knowledge, strong will, difficult decisions, conflict and arguments.

☌ Self-will, strong ideas, emotional opinions, change of opinions, dedication in study, deep and serious interests.

T☿–Asc, Desc r

⚹△ Beneficial for all communication, thought and decision making.

□ Friction in all communication, thought and decision making.

☌Asc, ☍Desc Strongly held ideas but likely disagreements with partners.

☍Asc, ☌Desc Benefits all communication.

T☿–MC, IC r

⚹△ Beneficial for all communications and decisions involving home or career.

□ Misunderstandings likely regarding home and career.

☌MC, ☍IC Mental stimulation in work; decisions and choices likely to affect career; disagreements at home.

☍MC, ☌IC Domestic affairs may require decisions and choices.

TRANSITS OF VENUS

T♀–♀r

⚹△ Benefits all social, emotional, artistic and financial affairs.

□☍ Emotional tension; friction in partnerships; not good for financial affairs.

☌ Emotional energy strong; romantic encounters likely.

T♀–♂r

⚹△ Benefits all social, emotional and practical affairs.

□☍ Dynamic physical and emotional energy; likelihood of arguments, fights and passionate encounters.

☌ Emotional and physical energy at a peak.

T♀–♃r

⚹△ Balanced moods; benefits all social, emotional, artistic, financial, legal and travel affairs.

□☍ Powerful need for emotional freedom and satisfaction; can be selfish; misunderstandings likely; not good for travel, legal affairs; waste of resources.

T♀-♄r

☌ Emotional energy, optimism, enthusiasm; new partnerships good for travel.

⚹△ Stability and seriousness in emotional and social affairs; benefits financial affairs.

□☍ Emotional and social restriction; stability and possibility of formal ties in partnerships; delays likely.

☌ Emotional stability; foundations laid for future partnerships; old friendships reassessed.

T♀–♅

⚹△ Need for variety and change in emotional and social life; new friendships.

□☍ Old emotional ties broken, new friendships formed, emotions change dramatically, financial affairs fluctuate.

☌ Emotional tension; sudden changes in partnerships; dramatic financial change.

T♀–♆

⚹△ Romance in partnerships, imagination in all creative activities.

□☍ Extreme sensitivity, romantic idealism, artistic inspiration, practical confusion.

☌ Romantic, inspired, dreamy, idealistic, open to deception, impractical;

changes in attitudes to friends subtle but long lasting.

T♀–♇
⚹△ Intense feelings likely to lead to a different style in partnerships.
□☍ Emotional conflicts likely; changes in partnerships.
☌ Profound emotional changes likely; confrontation possible; old partnerships come to an end, new ones born.

T♀–Asc, Desc r
⚹△ Generally beneficial.
□ Emotional tension.
☌Asc, ☍Desc Benefits emotional and social affairs, but can be selfish.
☍Asc, ☌ Desc Pleasurable partnerships.

T♀–MC, IC r
⚹△ Benefits all career and domestic affairs.
□ Partners may clash with domestic and career interests.
☌MC, ☍IC Beneficial career partnerships.
☍MC, ☌IC Pleasurable conditions in the home.

TRANSITS OF MARS

T♂–♂r
⚹△ Balanced and constructive exertion benefits all practical enterprises.
□☍ Strong, dynamic energy but this may be directed into conflict, anger, strife.
☌ Forcefulness; fast work in all practical affairs; risk of confrontation.

T♂–♃ r
⚹△ Enthusiasm, optimism, adventurousness.
□☍ Recklessness, impatience, crusading spirit, conflicts, accidents, difficulty in travel, legal battles.
☌ Optimism, idealism, new enterprises, long journeys, adventures.

T♂–♄ r
⚹△ Self-discipline, organization, hard work, caution, practicality.
□☍ Practical affairs afflicted by material difficulties, delays and obstacles; likelihood of hard work.
☌ Practical affairs at crossroads; new foundations must be laid; strong desire for order and stability; hard work necessary but energy may be low.

T♂–♅r
⚹△ Unusual behaviour, new activities.
□☍ Powerful need for personal freedom disrupts practical affairs; carelessness, impatience, likelihood of accidents.
☌ Self-will, individuality, erratic and unusual behaviour, unconventional activities, practical necessity sacrificed to personal independence.

T♂–♆r
⚹△ Practical affairs aided by intuition and imagination.
□☍ All practical activities suffer from unworldly ambitions and confusion.
☌ Excellent for artistic affairs but otherwise highly impractical.

T♂–♇
⚹△ Persistence, dedication, obstinacy, desire for self-improvement.
□☍ Conflict, confrontation, personal revolution, upheaval, accidents.
☌ Volatile behaviour, personal transformation, need for self-improvement.

T♂–Asc, Desc r
⚹△ Good balanced energies.
□ General friction.
☌Asc, ☍Desc Self-interest strong, conflicts likely.
☍Asc, ☌Desc Energy put into partnership and social affairs.

T♂–MC,IC r
⚹△ Benefits career and domestic activities.
□ Tension in career and home life.
☌Asc, ☍Desc Energy in career, friction at home.
☍Asc, ☌Desc Friction in career, energy at home.

TRANSITS OF JUPITER

T♃–♃r
⚹△ Optimism, opportunities and rewards of lasting benefit.
□☍ Desire for change, dissatisfaction with life, restlessness, waste of opportunity.
☌ This is the Jupiter return, when the planet returns to the place it occupied at birth. This occurs every 12 years and coincides with a desire for personal growth, need for freedom and acquisitiveness. The first Jupiter return corresponds roughly with the beginning of puberty and adolescence. The second occurs around 24 years of age, symbolizing the development of the adult. Subsequent returns are less marked, but always bring growth, optimism and opportunity.

T♃–♄r
⚹△ Perseverance and self discipline bring social recognition and opportunities.
□–☍ Substantial changes are likely in practical affairs; material difficulties likely.
☌ Major changes, shift in life style, new practical foundations are laid, old ones crumble.

T♃–♅r
⚹△ Beneficial changes; presents new horizons; development of individual abilities.
□☍ Sudden, sometimes dramatic

changes in life style; unusual opportunities may be offered but wasted.

☌ Optimism, growth, expansion, dramatic opportunities, new possibilities opened up, old attitudes discarded.

T♃–♆r

⚹△ Strengthens intuition, imagination, spiritual aspirations.

□☍ Longing for the intangible and the transcendant that is difficult to satisfy; possibility of confusion, deception.

☌ Dreams come true; artistic imagination reaches a peak; disorganized.

T♃-♇r

⚹△ Brings need for a sense of significance and a desire for spiritual and emotional renewal and regeneration.

□☍ Powerful need to transform existing conditions, to place life on a sounder spiritual footing.

☌ Substantial changes in life style; the old is thrown out, the new is welcomed; changes can be traumatic.

T♃–Asc,Desc r

⚹△ Generally beneficial.

□☍ High ambitions but wasted opportunities.

☌ Brings opportunities, rewards, benefits, personal growth and development; benefits all partnerships; opportunities from friends.

T♃-MC, IC r

⚹△ Opportunities for career and in domestic affairs.

□ Domestic and career opportunities may be wasted.

☌MC, ☍IC Career opportunities; possible change to a better career, or advance within present career; domestic interests neglected.

☍MC, ☌IC Change, opportunity and expansion in the home and family.

TRANSITS OF SATURN

T♄-♄

⚹△ Constructive change; opportunities result from past experience and hard work.

□☍ Difficulty, stress, hard work, responsibilities, material loss, general restriction; if such problems are dealt with well then the result is greater maturity.

☌ The Saturn returns are a major point of change. The first return, which occurs between the ages of 28 and 29, usually coincides with a period of introspection, personal reassessment, dissatisfaction; those who learn Saturn's difficult lessons become stronger individuals.

T♄–♅ r

⚹△ Excellent for making positive use of unexpected opportunities and opening new possibilities through personal effort.

□☍ Difficult changes, erratic behaviour, contradictory actions, conflict between the desire for stability and the need to adapt to new circumstances.

☌ A period of personal reassessment and change; upheaval in life style; radical change must be reconciled with need for stability.

T♄–♆r

⚹△ Imagination and intuition confer benefits on practical affairs.

□☍ Practical changes are motivated by romantic imagination but undermined by impracticality and confusion.

☌ Imagination and intuition combine well with practical ambition and self-discipline to lay foundations for a new phase of life.

T♄-♇r

⚹△ Brings commitment to change and self-improvement.

□☍ Conflict, confrontation, major change in life style, material difficulties.

☌ Upheavals, profound changes in life style, confrontation; the search for a new direction in life.

T♄–Asc, Desc r

⚹△ Positive and constructive energy.

□ Difficulties, delays, obstacles.

☌Asc, ☍Desc A period of critical self-assessment, material restriction, social withdrawal, hard work; can result in enhanced prestige, self-respect and greater maturity.

☍Asc, ☌Desc. Partnerships benefit from formal ties; new responsibilities; need for serious and stable friendships.

T♄–MC, IC r

⚹△ Stability in career and home.

□ Difficulties and delays in career and home life.

☌MC, ☍IC Possibility of delays and difficulties in the career, but hard work is rewarded with greater prestige and authority.

☍MC, ☌IC Difficulties and new responsibilities in the home; increased domestic security and stability.

TRANSITS OF URANUS

T♅–♅r

⚹△ New possibilities are raised, horizons are broadened.

□☍ A period of rebellion and the assertion of individuality and independence. The square occurs first around the age of 14, during the transformation from childhood to adulthood. The opposition occurs at about 42, and is associated with the 'mid-life crisis', a period of dissatisfaction with the ties and responsibilities of adulthood; some people at this time experience a 'second adolescence'.

☌ The Uranus return occurs at about 84 and it is said that at this time people learn to face up to the prospect of death.

T♅–♇r

⚹△ Gradual change, the opening up of the imagination and a desire for a sense of personal meaning.

□☍ There is a need for personal re-birth or renewal but this may be impractical and unrealistic.

☌ Unworldly, inspired, imaginative; ambitions are unrealistically high; changes may result from the undermining of practical life.

T♅–♇r

⚹△ Changes result from the search for a sense of purpose.

□☍ Profound change; major crises likely; the life style may be replaced by a totally different one; ambitions show a disregard for practical necessity.

☌ Changes likely to be profound; some may discover a new sense of direction, others will completely transform their lives.

T♅-Asc,Desc r

⚹△ Optimism, readiness for change, open to new possibilities.

□☍ Change can be dramatic, sudden opportunities, unexpected events, breaks and new beginnings in partnerships.

☌Asc, ☍Desc Dramatic changes and events, sometimes traumatic; new and unexpected possibilities open up.

☍Asc, ☌Desc Sudden changes in partnerships; old friendships broken and new friendships made.

T♅Mc, IC r

⚹△ New possibilities open up in career and home life.

□ Difficulties in career and home life; moves and changes likely.

☌MC, ☍IC Dramatic changes in career likely; dissatisfaction with existing work.

☍MC, ☌IC Move of home or other dramatic domestic change likely.

TRANSITS OF NEPTUNE

T♆–♅r

⚹△ The sextile occurs around the age of 27 and the trine around 55, and both are associated with the need for a deeper spiritual purpose and an awakening of the imagination.

□☍ The square occurs at about 41 and is associated with the frustration and desire for a new direction during the 'mid-life crisis'. The square occurs at about 82.

☌ This does not occur until 164 years after birth.

T♆–♇r

⚹△ Desire for a sense of meaning and a new direction.

□☍ Otherworldly ambitions; dissatisfaction with material life.

☌ Profound upheaval; deep seated changes in needs, attitudes and behaviour.

T♆–Asc,Desc r

⚹△ Enhances imagination; romantic desires help shape change.

□ Impractical ambitions, unworldly dreams.

☌Asc, ☍Desc A period of transformation, awakening imagination and inspiration although impractical and unrealistic.

☍Asc, ☌Desc Romance and idealism but probable confusion in relationships.

T♆–MC, IC r

⚹△ Changes in home and career stimulated by imagination and dreams.

□ Confusion in home and career.

☌MC, ☍IC Change and confusion in career; benefits artistic and 'caring' work.

☍MC, ☌IC Domestic uncertainty; possible move of home.

TRANSITS OF PLUTO

T♇–♇r

⚹△ The sextile occurs around the age of 41 and is associated with the rebellious phase of the 'mid-life crisis'. The trine occurs at about 82 and contributes to a greater spiritual awareness.

□☍ The square occurs around 61 and is associated with retirement and the onset of old age. The opposition does not occur until 123 years after birth.

☌ This does not occur until 245 years after birth.

T♇–Asc, Desc r

⚹△ Period of determination and personal improvement.

□ Brings tension, difficulty, conflict, profound changes.

☌Asc, ☍Desc Profound and sometimes traumatic upheavals in life style.

☍Asc, ☌Desc Deep changes in partnerships; conflict, confrontation, passionate attachments.

T♇–MC,IC r.

⚹△ Need for renewal and improvement in career, home and family relations.

□ Confrontation and deep change likely in home, family and career.

☌MC, ☍IC Conflicts and change of career likely; increased authority possible.

☍MC, ☌IC Conflicts at home; move of home likely.

CHAPTER 12
PREDICTION: THE PROGRESSIONS

Progressions, which are also sometimes known as directions, are based on the symbolical movements of the planets, unlike transits which are based on the actual movements. Behind the principle of progression lies the ancient belief that any complete unit of time shares the same essential quality as every other complete unit, even those of a different duration. Thus one day, one week, one month and one year all represent in their own ways the same basic cycle of experience; the day moves on its endless cycle symbolizing a phase in the life of the Sun; the seven days of the week symbolize one complete journey through the seven traditional planets; the month is based on the vital passage of the Moon from new to full and back again, and the year moves through the cycle of the seasons.

SECONDARY PROGRESSIONS. There are about 20 different types of progression although only a few are in common use. The most used are the secondary progressions, popularly known as 'Day for a Year' progressions. If the type of progression used is not specified, then it is always assumed that the Day for a Year method is used. In the Day for a Year system each day of life is regarded as equivalent to one year of life. The planetary positions for each day are used to make predictions for the equivalent year; those for the first day are used to make predictions for the first year, those for the second day for the second year, and so on. If a child experiences a major astrological configuration 10 days after birth then there will be significant developments around 10 years of age. The infant who has a dramatic astrological pattern on the fiftieth day after birth will experience great upheavals in the fiftieth year of life. Day for a Year progressions are simple to calculate and require no expertise in interpretation beyond that needed for transits.

Cyclical Time
All complete units of time have the same symbolic cyclical quality and, therefore, any two units may be used as the basis of a system of progression. Astrologers use day for a week, day for a lunar month, day for a calendar month progressions as well as the standard Day for a Year system.

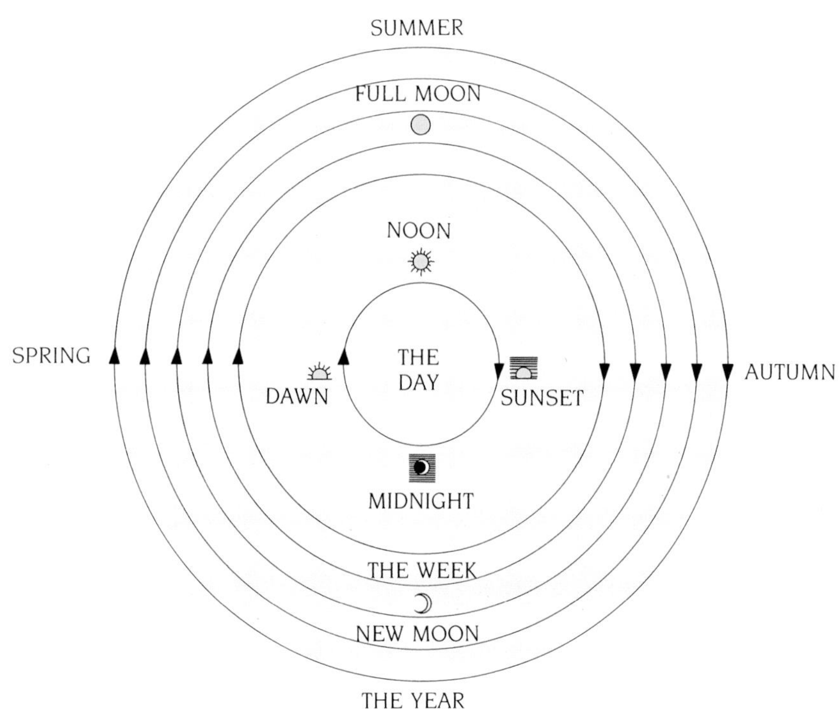

CALCULATIONS OF DAY FOR A YEAR PROGRESSIONS. The first stage is to work out the day for which the progressed planets must be calculated. If the subject's date of birth is 4 March 1953, to work out progressions for age 17, just add that number to 4: 4 + 17 = 21. Planetary positions on 21 March 1953 are then equivalent to progressed planets for 1970 at age 17.

Frequently the progressed date will be in the month following the month of birth, or even the month after that. This problem can be solved by adding the relevant age to the date of birth, then subtracting the number of days in the months preceding that in which the progressed date falls.

To work out progressions for age 30 (born on 4 March 1953): 4 + 30 = 34 − 31 (because there are 31 days in March) = 3. Planetary positions on 3 April (the month following March) 1953 correspond to the progressed planets in 1983 at age 30. The planets are then looked up in the ephemeris in the usual way; the planets for one day referring to the whole of the equivalent year. For all planets except the Moon this is sufficient, but it is also possible to work out the exact positions of the progressed planets for any day.

The progressed planets and angles (Ascendant and Midheaven) should be calculated for the birthday each year. Follow the normal procedure for casting a horoscope using the GMT time of birth, the place of birth and the sidereal time and planetary positions for the progressed day.

By working out the progressed horoscope for two successive birthdays (ie. two successive days in the ephemeris) it is possible to work out how far a planet or angle progresses in one year. Division of the annual motion by 12 gives the monthly motion, from which it is

If Wendy was born	at 9.25 pm GMT on 4 July 1950		
then planetary positions	at 9.25 pm GMT on 5 July 1950	correspond to progressed positions for	4 July 1951, age 1
,,	9.50 pm GMT on 6 July 1950	,,	4 July 1952, age 2
,,	9.25 pm GMT on 7 July 1950	,,	4 July 1953, age 3
,,	9.25 pm GMT on 7 Aug. 1950	,,	4 July 1984, age 34
,,	9.25 pm GMT on 8 Aug. 1950	,,	4 July 1985, age 35

Calculation of Wendy's Progressions
If progressions are calculated for the GMT birth time, this means that they are exact for the birthday every year.

possible to work out the exact progressed positions for any day of the year.

To work out the progressed day corresponding to 1984 for the example birth chart interpreted in Chapter 10, follow the sequence above.

INTERPRETATION OF THE PROGRESSIONS. The principles of interpretation are exactly the same as for transits. Usually only the first five planets – Sun, Moon, Mercury, Venus and Mars – are used, together with the Ascendant and MC. The outer five planets progress so slowly that they sometimes scarcely move.

The progressed planets make aspects to the natal planets which should be interpreted exactly like transiting aspects to natal planets, with the qualification that they last much longer and are, therefore, more profound; for example, an aspect from the progressed Sun to the birth chart lasts two years. The orb for aspects should be 1°, the same as for transiting aspects; minor aspects should also be used.

Aspects between the progressed MC and Ascendant always indicate significant points in life and take their character from the nature of the planet which is aspected in exactly the same way as aspects between natal MC and Ascendant and transiting planets.

The movement of a progressed planet into a new house or sign of the birth chart always marks a significant development bringing a change in character or a new focus of attention.

Interpretations for all the progressions can be based on the standard interpretations for natal positions and transits given in previous chapters. For example, an interpretation of progressed Mercury conjunct natal Sun will be essentially the same as natal Mercury conjunct natal Sun or transiting Mercury conjunct natal Sun, given that the duration of effect is different in each case. The aspect from natal Mercury to the Sun indicates the basic life-long character, progressed Mercury a phase of mental development over one or two years and transiting Mercury a lively and interesting day.

ADDITIONAL TECHNIQUES

SOLAR ARC PROGRESSIONS. These are in common use and are simple to work out. All the planets and angles progress at the same rate as the progressed Sun, which means that only the position of the Sun needs to be calculated. As the Sun usually moves 0° 59′ per day this means that all points in the horoscope progress by about 0° 59′ per year.

CONVERSE PROGRESSIONS. Strange as it may seem the astrologer can look backwards in the ephemeris from the birth date in order to make predictions. For example, using converse Day for a Year progressions the astrologer looks at the tenth day before birth to discover what will happen on the tenth day of the child's life. Sceptics find it difficult to accept such a proposition, but practice shows the technique to be effective. Any type of progression can be used in this way although most astrologers use converse progressions only for their own interest, rather than as a part of professional work.

PRIMARY DIRECTIONS. These are based on the rotation of the Earth but are scarcely ever used as the calculations are extremely complicated. It is likely, however, that they will become increasingly important as computers become more common.

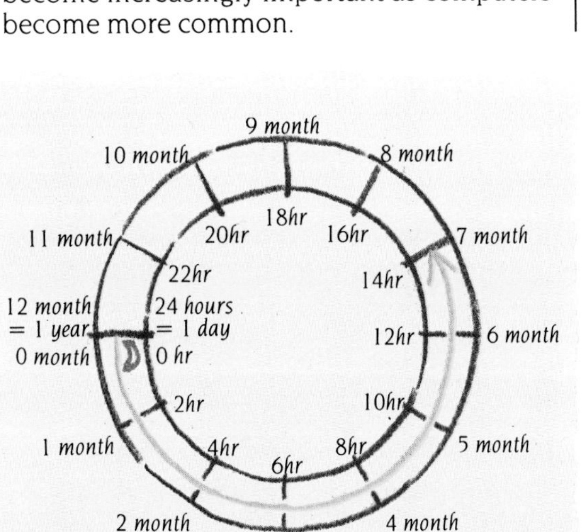

Day for a Year Progressions
The time scales of the day and the year are matched so that two hours of ordinary time correspond to one month of progressed time and one day of ordinary time is equivalent to one year of progressed time. The movement of a planet over, say, 14 hours of ordinary time is the basis for its progression over seven months.

CHAPTER 13 COMBINING PROGRESSIONS AND TRANSITS

Opposite: Wendy's progressions calculated for 4 July 1984 (calculations for 7 August 1950) and 4 July 1985 (calculations for 8 August 1950).

In normal practice only the monthly positions of the Moon are calculated while the progressions of Jupiter, Saturn, Uranus, Neptune and Pluto are so slight that they are usually ignored.

Two systems are better than one, and progressions are used together with transits to provide more reliable predictions. If both systems point to the same conclusions then the astrologer can speak with greater confidence. The combination results in the inclusion of 30 planets in the horoscope, each planet having its natal, progressed and transiting position. But the situation can be simplified by reducing the number of planets to be considered: progressions of Uranus, Neptune and Pluto are so slow that they are always ignored, while progressions of Jupiter and Saturn are only considered rarely.

Transits of the five inner planets, the Sun, Moon, Mercury, Venus and Mars, are so fast that they are only considered if they combine with natal and progressed planets in a particularly significant pattern such as a strong conjunction or 'T' Square. Unless an exceptionally detailed synopsis is required for an exact date or event, it is usual in the first instance to consider only the conjunctions and oppositions these planets make to the progressed and natal planets.

The transiting Moon makes so many aspects that normally the astrologer pays attention only to the new and full Moons and the aspects these make to the birth chart. Conjunctions and oppositions from these to natal planets often bring changes.

There is no inherent difference between the nature of a progressed planet and a transiting planet: the purpose of using the two systems together is to provide the astrologer with greater freedom and variety in

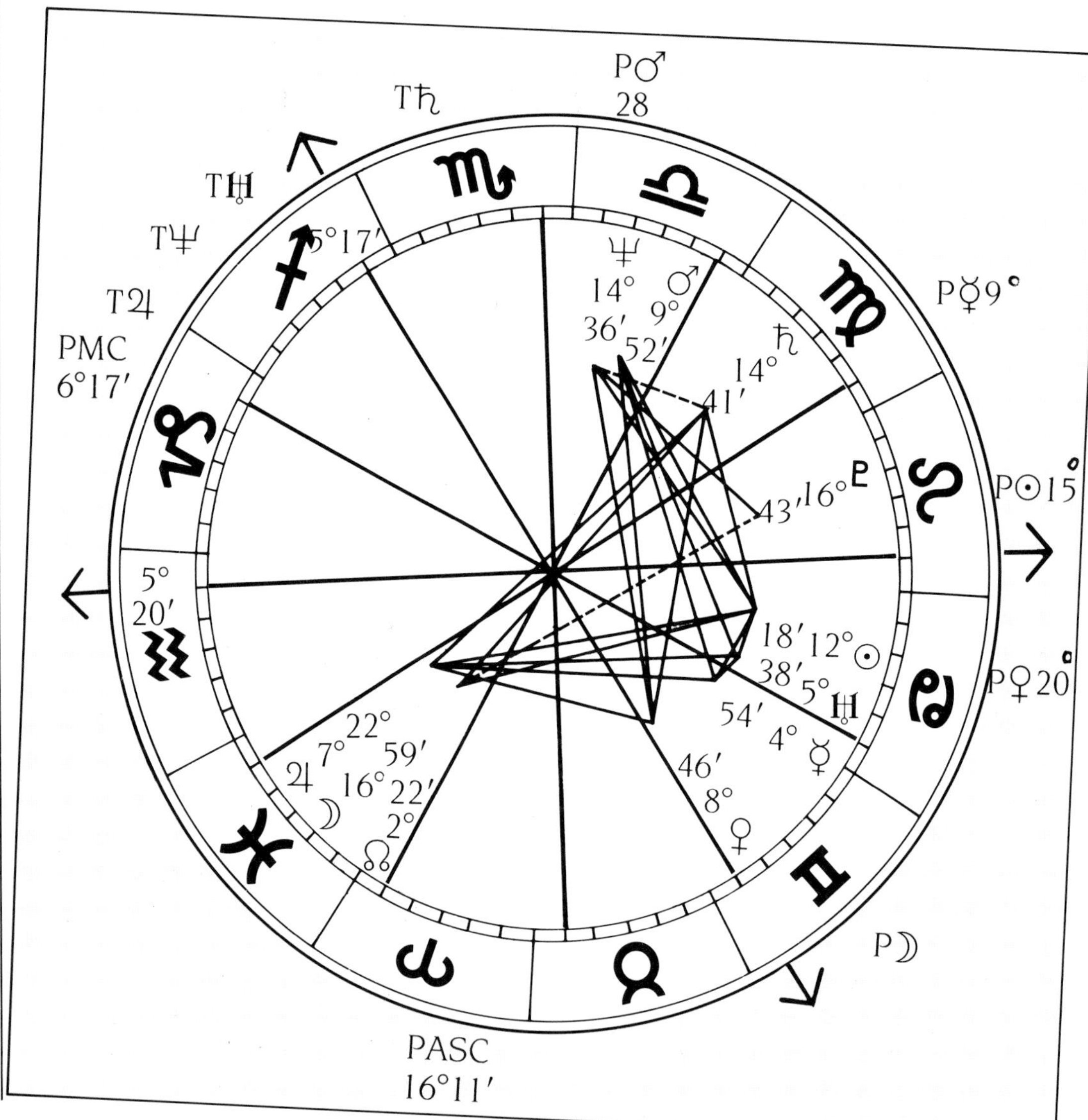

Wendy's Chart With Progressions And Transits For 1984
Rather than draw the complete progressed horoscope the progressed positions are usually pencilled in around the edge of the birth chart in their approximate positions. Progressed positions (for Ascendant, MC and inner planets) are shown by the letter P and transiting positions (for outer planets) by the letter T.

	Asc	mc	☉	☽	☿	♀	♂	♃	♄	♅	♆	
4 July 1984	16°12′	6°18′	14°47′	7°18′	8°44′	19°26′	28°19°	4°48′	17°57′	7°33′	15°3′	17°44°
	♈	♑	♌	♊	♍	♋	♎	♓ r	♍	♋	♎	♌
4 July 1985	18°27′	7°12′	15°45′	19°20′	10°9°	20°39′	28°55′	4°42′	18°4′	7°36′	15°4′	17°45′
	♈	♑	♌	♊	♍	♋	♎	♓ r	♍	♋	♎	♌
Annual motion	2°15′	0°54′	0°58	12°2′	1°25′	1°13′	0°36′	0°6′	0°7′	0°3′	0°1′	0°1′
Monthly motion	0°11′	0°5′	0°5′	1°0′	0°7′	0°6′	0°3′					

interpretation. Most astrologers use only one type of progression, usually Day for a Year to avoid cluttering up the chart with so much information that interpretation becomes impossible.

In addition to noting aspects between progressions and natal planets, and between transits and natal planets, mutual aspects between progressed planets are used. These are rare, however, except for aspects involving the progressed Moon. Aspects between progressions and transits are also important, although they should be treated as less significant.

Aspects between two transiting planets are not of personal importance but have an overall significance. It is these aspects which form the basis of daily newspaper Sun-sign columns in which millions of people are given the same predictions. However, a strong build up of transiting planets will be significant for the individual if there are strong aspects to the birth chart.

When composing general predictions it is best only to assess monthly trends for the year ahead and thereafter produce an annual summary for up to five years.

Many astrologers use a grid to tabulate the relevant aspects for each month. This makes it simpler to assess the monthly prospects for different areas of life and generally changing circumstances.

If the subject requires advice on a specific question, then the astrologer must focus on this, but in most cases a general view of the future is required and this should be laid out as a month by month report. It is up to subject and astrologer to agree on the amount of detail required. Sometimes the astrologer will, in the first instance, give only a general outline and then respond to more detailed questions.

The following example is a six-month survey of future trends laid out in the usual style, starting, for the sake of convenience, on

FUTURE TRENDS FOR WENDY
JULY – DECEMBER 1984

THE YEAR AHEAD

You are emerging from a period of great advance in your career and the major focus of	T♃☌T♅☌MCr 1983.
change in your life over the coming months is likely to be domestic.	☽P 4th.
These changes have been building up over the spring and especially since last May.	T♅, T♃☍♀, ruler of 4th cusp, from Nov. 1983; ☽p ☌IC.
They are most likely to come to a head in October when a move of home is possible.	P☽☍T♅, ☍P♀; T♄△☽r, □☉p; T♃☌MCP, ☍☿r.

JULY

Hopes are high, you are impatient and ambitious in your work and a new venture seems likely.	P☽□♃r; T♃☌MCP, ☍☿r, ☍♅r (☿, ♀ r on 6th cusp).
Your energy is well-balanced and success seems likely.	T♂△☉r, △☽r.
However, your vitality and enthusiasm may be undermined by a lack of consistency and organization.	Lack of ♄ aspects – T♄⊻♂r only aspect.
Health problems may arise from a tendency to work too hard without rest.	T♃☍☿♅6.
Partnership affairs may be stormy, especially around the 16th. Disagreements are likely around the 28th.	T♂□♇r; T☿☌♇7th; T♀☌♇7th; N☽☌ Desc. □T♄.

AUGUST

A key month for domestic change – you are feeling very restless and there could be a split in your home or with a friend or partner.	P☽☌♀, ruler of IC, ♊.
Difficult decisions have to be taken around the 4th but are unlikely to be finalized before the 24th.	T☿☌☿P, P☽□☿r.
Disagreements with partners are likely, especially around the second week of the month. You will be expecting maximum support from friends both socially and at work.	T☉☌☉p, ☌♇r, in 7th; F☽☍☉p, ♇r; T♀☌☿p.
Be prepared for extra expenditure around the 26th, perhaps to pay for previous domestic responsibilities. Extra career commitments are likely at the end of the month.	N☽ on 8th cusp ☍♃r on 2nd cusp; T♂☍IC r; T♀☌♄r; T♀☍☽r. T♂☌MCr.

SEPTEMBER

P☽☍T♂; P☽△♂ r, T☉☍☽ r; T♂□☽ r, □♄ r; (♄ r□☽ r).

Home affairs are again high on the agenda. These consume much of your energy and are likely to provoke conflicts, especially around the 3rd, 9th, 12th and 15th.

N☽☌☽♓ r in 2nd.

The new Moon on the 10th is likely to bring a break with the past as far as your emotions are concerned and will make you face up to the financial implications of your current domestic plans. You may be asked to pay out money and do so against your better judgment.

T☿☌♄ r, ☍☽ r from 21st-24th.

Important news concerning home and financial conditions is likely around the 22nd.

T♄△☉ r; P☽△♂ r; T♄✶♄ P; T♂△Asc p.

In general, your energy for the month is balanced, positive and constructive.

OCTOBER

T♄□☉ p, □♇ r; T♃☍☿ r, ☍♅ r; P☽☍T♅.

This looks like a month of stress and strain, of structural changes in your life, in which new foundations will be laid and current domestic and partnership problems settled, at least in the short term.

T♃, T♂☌MC P.

There will be considerable pressure in your career around the middle of the month and you will be in peak condition, searching for new opportunities and ready to innovate.

T♃, T♂☍IC P, ☍☿♅ r in 6th.

However you will be distracted by domestic upheavals and confusion, and your working environment will be disorganized.

T♃☍☿ r, ☍♅ r, ☌MC P; T♂☍☿ r, ☍♅ r☌MC P; T☉☌♂ P.

There is a conflict of interest between career and home affairs especially on the 1st, 9th, 12th, 13th, 14th, 16th and 22nd.

NOVEMBER

November brings few astrological changes and should be a month of consolidation. You will settle down after the strains of October.

T☿☌MC r, ☍♀ r, ☍☽ p, T♀☍☿ p, ☍♅ p, ☌MC P☍☉ r, ☍♀ p. Solar eclipse ☌ MC.

The continuing conflict of interest between career and home will be unresolved and may necessitate a difficult choice between the 10th and 14th.

This problem is, however, likely to remain until the end of the month.

Eclipse□♇ r, ☉P.

Partnerships will drain a lot of energy and disagreements are likely around the 8th.

DECEMBER

☽p⊻☉ r; T♃△♄ r✶☽ r.

The indications for the month are helpful and home conditions may at last feel more settled.

T♅△☉ p.

You will be in the mood for new opportunities and this will colour your activities, although you will be quite patient.

T☉☍☿ r, ☍♅ r, ☌MC P.

The 26th to 28th brings renewed initiative in your career and there is a need for quiet thought and hard work. It may be useful to pay attention to your health.

the birthday, 4 July 1984. Astrological significators are marked in the margin for the astrologer's convenience, but these would normally not be included unless specifically requested.

Feedback from Wendy showed that domestic concerns did indeed dominate much of this period: In May 1984, when the progressed Moon was exactly in conjunction with her natal IC, she decided to move away from London, where she had lived for most of her life, to Bristol in the west of England. In August, when the progressed Moon was in conjunction with the natal Venus, she found accommodation in Bristol and on 22 October she moved to her new home.

The opposition from progressed Moon to transiting Uranus in October to November never became exact in 1984. In fact, the exact opposition was not reached until April to May 1985, coinciding with a decision to move home again.

The conjunction of transiting Jupiter and Uranus with the natal MC in 1983, had coincided with a dramatic advance in our subject's career – the publication of a book and national publicity – and the conjunction of transiting Jupiter with the progressed MC during July 1984 coincided with a successful theatre production. The transit over the natal MC was somewhat more dramatic than that over the progressed MC, partly perhaps because the natal MC was in Sagittarius and the progressed MC in the more stable sign of Capricorn.

ASPECT GRID FOR WENDY JULY-DECEMBER 1984

If all the aspects are listed month by month on a grid then the qualities of different times can be clearly seen. The amount of detail required is up to each astrologer. This example shows:

1) The monthly position of the progressed Moon, all its aspects to natal and progressed planets and oppositions and conjunctions to transiting planets.
2) All aspects from Uranus, Neptune and Pluto to natal and progressed planets.
3) Major aspects from Mars, Jupiter and Saturn to progressed and natal planets. One aspect to another transit is noted: the conjunction of Mars with Jupiter in October 1984 was enhanced by its conjunction with the progressed MC and its opposition to the powerful natal Mercury-Uranus conjunction.
4) Conjunctions and oppositions from the Sun, Mercury and Venus to natal and progressed planets. The date of the exact aspect is also shown.
5) Dates of new and full Moons with a note if

this is an eclipse. Positions and aspects are only shown if strong major aspects are made to the birth chart.

The letter w shows that an aspect is weak and not exact, r stands for radical or natal planet, p stands for progressed and T for transit.

The general pattern of the grid shows that October was the month with the most aspects, including some strong configurations; on 22 October, transiting Sun was conjunct progressed Mars and transiting Mars was opposed to natal Sun. This, as it turned out, was the day of Wendy's move.

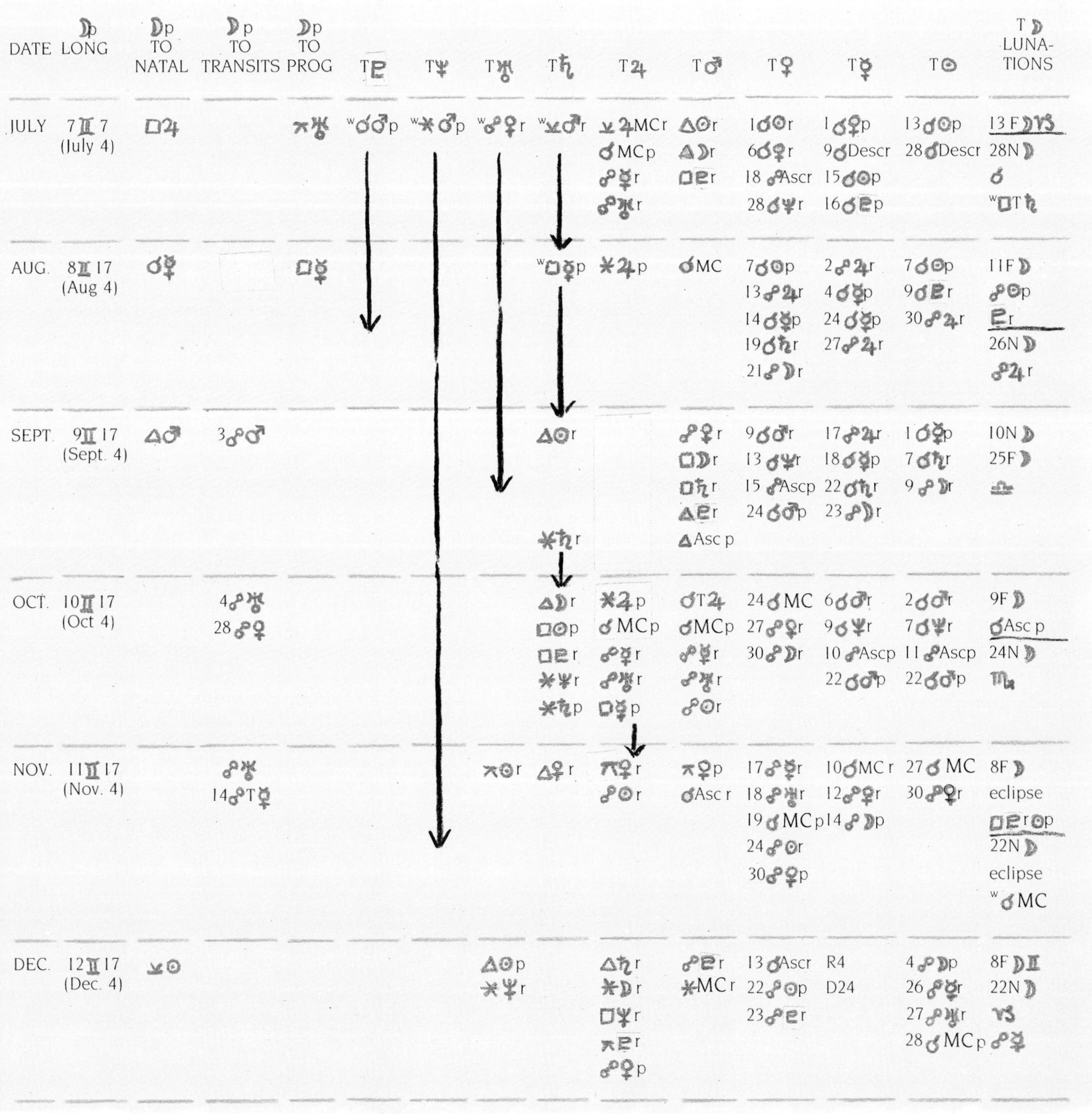

DATE	☽p LONG	☽p TO NATAL	☽p TO TRANSITS	☽p TO PROG	T♇	T♆	T♅	T♄	T♃	T♂	T♀	T☿	T☉	T☽ LUNATIONS
JULY	7♊7 (July 4)	□♃		⚻♅	w☌♂p	w✶♂p	w☍♀r	w⚺♂r	⚺♃MCr ☌MCp ☍☿r ☍♅r	△☉r △☽r □♇r	1☌☉r 6☌♀r 18☍Ascr 28☌♆r	1☌♀p 9☌Descr 15☌☉p 16☌♇p	13☌☉p 28☌Descr	13F☽♑ 28N☽ ☌ w□T♄
AUG.	8♊17 (Aug 4)	☌☿		□☿				w□☿p	✶♃p	☌MC	7☌☉p 13☍♃r 14☌☿p 19☌♄r 21☍☽r	2☍♃r 4☌☿p 24☌☿p 27☍♃r	7☌☉p 9☌♇r 30☍♃r	11F☽ ☍☉p ♇r 26N☽ ☍♃r
SEPT.	9♊17 (Sept. 4)	△♂	3☍♂					△☉r ✶♄r		☍♀r □☽r □♄r △♇r △Asc p	9☌♂r 13☌♆r 15☍Ascp 24☌♂p	17☍♃r 18☌☿p 22☌♄r 23☍☽r	1☌☿p 7☌♄r 9☍☽r	10N☽ 25F☽ ♎
OCT.	10♊17 (Oct 4)		4☍♅ 28☍♀					△☽r □☉p □♇r ✶♆r ✶♄p	✶♃p ☌MCp ☍☿r ☍♅r □☿p	☌T♃ ☌MCp ☍☿r ☍♅r ☍☉r	24☌MC 27☍♀r 30☍☽r	6☌♂r 9☌♆r 10☍Ascp 22☌♂p	2☌♂r 7☌♆r 11☍Ascp 22☌♂p	9F☽ ☌Asc p 24N☽ ♏
NOV.	11♊17 (Nov. 4)		☍♅ 14☍T☿				⚻☉r	△♀r	⚻♀r ☍☉r	⚻♀p ☌Asc r	17☍☿r 18☍♅r 19☌MCp 24☍☉r 30☍♀p	10☌MC r 12☍♀r 14☍☽p	27☌MC 30☍♀r	8F☽ eclipse □♇r☉p 22N☽ eclipse w☌MC
DEC.	12♊17 (Dec. 4)	⚺☉					△☉p ✶♆r		△♄r ✶☽r □♆r ⚻♇r ☍♀p	☍♇r ✶MC r	13☌Ascr 22☍☉p 23☍♇r	R4 D24	4☍☽p 26☍☿r 27☍♅r 28☌MCp	8F☽♊ 22N☽ ♑ ☍☿

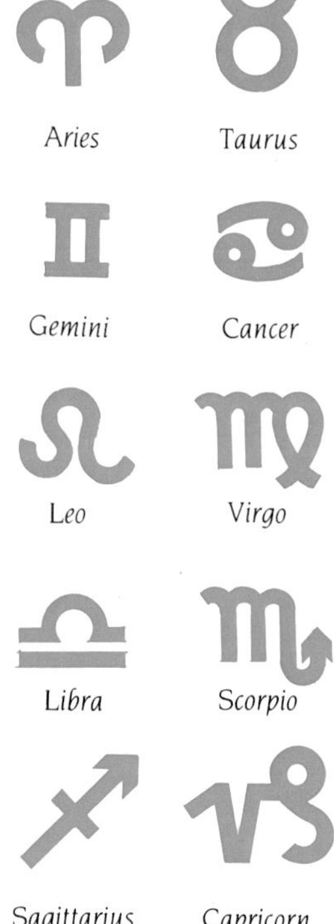

CHAPTER 14 RELATIONSHIPS AND THE COMPARISON OF CHARTS

The general nature and circumstances of one person's relationships can be worked out quite simply from the birth chart, mainly by studying the seventh house, Venus and all associated factors. There are also special techniques for examining individual relationships that a person may form, whether with husband or wife, parents or childen, brothers or sisters, employers or employees or anybody else with whom he or she might come into contact.

Horoscopes are compared with each other in a process known technically as synastry. At its simplest level synastry works through the comparison of Sun signs, a process which offers remarkably deep insights into the mysterious sources of attraction between two people. There are certain classic combinations of Sun sign that often produce close relationships. The commonest of these are relationships between signs of the same element, and between opposite signs, although people born under adjacent Sun signs also often experience a deep attraction. Every combination of sign produces difficulties as well as benefits and the easiest way to understand these is by looking at the combination of elements.

Fire–Fire. These people share their enthusiasm, energy and adventurous spirits, but a distaste for compromise and an inability to cooperate can lead to disagreement.

Fire–Earth. This is an interesting combination as, ironically, the attraction between these signs rests in their profound differences. The energetic fire person is able to give full vent to that element's adventurous instincts in the full knowledge that the earth partner will provide security, continuity and stability. Meanwhile the earth partner can remain as stodgy as desired, relying on the fire partner to work for change and create opportunities. But there can be sharp differences, the earth partner resenting fire's impulsive need for change, and fire becoming impossibly irritated with earth's lack of ambition.

Fire–Air. This relationship is often extremely lively as air's intellect and fire's enthusiasm spark off interesting ideas and a willingness to change. Differences are often settled quickly. However, difficulty in expressing feelings and a tendency to ignore practical necessities can produce long-term problems.

Fire–Water. These elements share powerful emotions, but their feelings are of very different kinds and misunderstanding is more common than understanding. Water is dismayed by fire's complete lack of sensitivity and fire is completely baffled by water's quiet introverted secrecy and apparent lack of worldly ambition. Casual friendships work better than close relationships as the latter often suffer from deep emotional conflict.

Earth–Earth. Two people both with Suns in earth signs share a common outlook on life, and a joint fondness for stability and routine can lead to long-lasting relationships. However, there can be a lack of stimulation, emotional depth and ambition, and even when these relationships last for a long time there can be an absence of real feeling.

Earth–Air. These elements can be brought together by self-interest. Earth benefits from air's ideas and air gains from earth's practical skills. The result is a relationship founded on commonsense, but together these elements lack emotional depth and wordly ambition.

Earth–Water. Earth and water often form deep and lasting friendships. They are comfortable with each other and water admires earth's practical skills as much as earth is fascinated by water's emotional depth and sensitivity. But if the relationship is too close then long-term irritation can set in; earth loses patience with water's muddled impracticality and water becomes bored by earth's love of order and routine.

Air–Air. People with Suns in air signs share a lively and curious approach to life and can find each other immensely stimulating. There is usually a great deal of communication but deeper feelings are all too easily ignored with the result that long-term problems can arise. The relationship tends to be impractical although this is not necessarily a problem.

Air–Water. This can be a highly stimulating combination; air's clarity of thought and water's intuition and sensitivity produce an interesting and imaginative relationship. In closer relationships misunderstandings may arise which add to the difficulties in dealing with practical issues.

Water–Water. Mutual understanding is often deep and a shared longing for romantic love can take these people into a world of dreams and fantasy. When things go wrong, however, they tend to wallow in their troubles. They may find it impossible to plan for the future.

In general, the presence of Suns in the same sign is not an indication of a long-term relationship because as both partners have the same basic strengths and weaknesses, they fail to provide either mutual stimulation or balance. People with Suns in adjacent signs (such as Aries–Taurus or Capricorn–Sagittarius) and opposite signs (such as Taurus–Scorpio or Aries–Libra) are often very close, as each provides something that the other needs, bringing a welcome balance, but serious differences can lead to deep arguments. Suns in signs that are in a sextile to each other (such as Pisces–Taurus or Aquarius–Aries) can produce good friendships, but the differences between them, may work against long-term relationships. Suns in signs that are in a square to each other (such as Pisces–Gemini or Aries–Capricorn) are often extremely stimulating, but the very differences that make for a lively friendship may place obstacles in the way of closer relationships. Most favoured of all are relationships produced by Suns in signs that are in trine to each other (such as Pisces–Scorpio or Libra–Gemini) as these have enough similarities to provide deep understanding but sufficient differences to create interest and stimulation.

Sun in	Harmonious	Difficult	
Same sign	*Usually an immediate close rapport and understanding; often mutual admiration.*	*Lack of stimulation; weaknesses and negative habits are emphasized.*	
Adjacent signs	*Profound differences in personality and life style can produce mutual fascination. The strengths of one compensate for the weaknesses of the other.*	*Complete antipathy; there is nothing in common.*	
Alternate signs	*Sufficient similarities to create an easy, friendly relationship. Sufficient differences to create stimulation and interest.*	*Few difficulties; disagreements tend to be mild, but there is a lack of commitment to the long-term.*	
Signs in same Quality Cardinal, Fixed or Mutable)	*Sufficient differences to provide strong mutual fascination. Good for deep friendship.*	*Fundamentally different attitudes to life bring disagreement in close partnerships.*	
Signs in same Element (Fire, Air, Earth, Water)	*The best combination for compatibility in friendships and close partnerships of all kinds.*	*Joint weaknesses may be emphasized.*	
Signs in Quincunx	*Similar to adjacent signs*	*Similar to adjacent signs.*	
Opposite signs	*Often produces a deep, attraction. Each partner exactly balances the other, compensates for their weaknesses and provides an extra dimension that is otherwise lacking.*	*In close long-term relationships deep attraction often gives way to irritation and disagreement as differences of attitude and behaviour become more marked.*	

The Astrological Relationship Between Signs
This table shows the relationships between the different signs. It is a useful guide for assessing compatibility between people of different Sun signs.

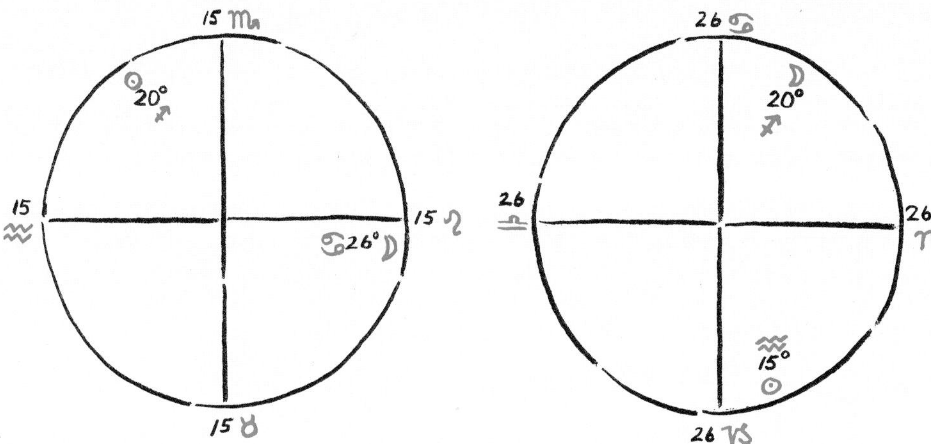

Inter-Chart Aspects
An emphasis on compatibility of Sun signs often conceals the full picture as most lasting partnerships and friendships are based on a variety of inter-chart aspects. In this case the aspect between the Sun in Sagittarius in one chart and the Sun in Aquarius in the other, is not usually considered a basis for a strong relationship. Yet the close conjunctions between the Sun, Moon and angles in each chart provide a firm foundation for the relationship.
A Sun-Moon conjunction is perhaps the strongest aspect between any two charts, especially between the Moon in a woman's chart and the Sun in a man's chart.

COMPARISON OF CHARTS. Comparison of two horoscopes is based mainly on the aspects made between the planets in one chart and those in the other. The aspects between any two charts can be divided into five categories.

1 Aspects between the Sun, Moon and angles (Ascendant and Midheaven) of one chart and those of the other are exceptionally important. Conjunctions between one person's Moon and the other's Sun reveal a deep attraction, and the conjunction of one person's Sun or Moon with the other's Ascendant or Descendant often indicates a long-lasting relationship.

2 Aspects between one person's Sun, Moon and angles and the other's Mercury, Venus or Mars do not in themselves lead to a close relationship but to compatibility in certain areas and activities.

3 Aspects between Mercury, Venus and Mars in both charts can be important indicators of compatibility. These are most significant when the aspect involves the same planet in each chart. For example, aspects between two Mercurys indicate intellectual compatibility or incompatibility, aspects between two Venuses indicate mutual affection or antipathy, and aspects between two Mars reveal either harmony in joint activities or strong antagonism.

4 Aspects between inner planets of one chart and outer planets of the other usually seem to be less significant and often contribute little to an understanding of the relationship. These aspects occur most importantly between contemporaries. For example, the child with Sun squared Pluto will also have his Sun squared to the Plutos of all other children of the same age. All the child's relationships will be coloured by this aspect and it will, therefore, be less significant for judging particular partnerships. Such aspects are also often found between parents and children in which case they should be given slightly more significance.

5 Aspects between the outer planets of two charts have still less significance in individual chart comparison. They usually occur between the horoscopes of people of different generations. For example, people born at 29-year intervals have their Saturns in a conjunction. All children born in 1966 have Pluto squared to the Plutos of people born in 1900, and those born in 1982 have Saturn in conjunction with the Plutos of those born in 1979. These aspects show how people relate to each other en masse, and their use in the comparison of two charts must always take this into account.

Unless it is necessary to take an in depth look at one particular factor in a chart, only the major aspects should be used. This cuts down the amount of information the astrologer has to consider and allows only the most important features to stand out.

As a general rule the greater the number of strong aspects between significant planets and angles in two charts, the greater is the prospect of a close relationship. It often happens that a planet in one chart aspects a strong configuration – such as a 'T' Square – in another. The prospects of a close relationship are then dramatically emphasized.

THE USE OF ORBS. There is no consensus concerning the width of orbs to be used for aspects between planets in one chart and those in another. However, a general rule is that wider orbs should be given to aspects between the most significant planets and that more attention should be given to the stronger aspects – a conjunction is always far more significant than a sextile. The table opposite gives a list of orbs which allows the astrologer to focus on the most significant aspects, although these may be adapted to individual experience.

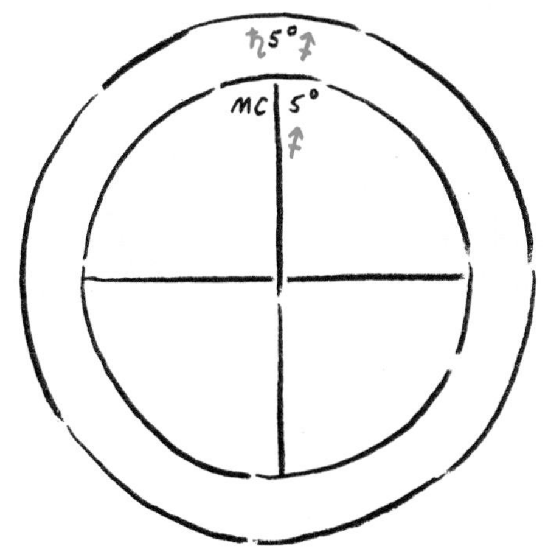

	☉ ☽	☿ ♀ ♂	♃ ♄	♅ ♆ ♇	Asc. MC	☊
☉,☽	8	6	4	2	8	8
☿,♀,♂		4	2	2	8	8
♃,♄			2	2	4	4
♅,♆,♇				2	4	4
Asc, MC					8	8
☊						8

CONSIDERATIONS BEFORE INTERPRETATION. The astrologer should always take into account commonsense and human factors. Two horoscopes may indicate attraction, but only one person may actually have the necessary feelings. The other may be happily involved elsewhere and not interested in a new relationship, or just not feel the same emotions. The astrologer can search for astrological significators for such circumstances, by going back to each person's horoscope and analysing their individual needs and expectations in relationships. Sometimes it is possible to deduce from inter-chart aspects which partner will respond in which way, but ultimately it is impossible to be sure. For example, one person may have Saturn conjunct another's MC, bringing the principle of limitation and discipline to the career. The possibilities in interpretation are not clear. It may be expected that the Saturn person blocks the other's career. A more beneficial alternative is that the Saturn person helps the other to organize his or her career. Perhaps, on the other hand, the Saturn person will be completely unconscious of the fact that the other is learning the virtues of self-discipline and organization. The person with the MC might in turn provide career opportunities for the Saturn person. In short, there is a two-way flow and the astrologer can only point out the general areas of contact, not the specific details of the relationship.

It is also well nigh impossible for the astrologer to work out whether two people will actually like each other. It is well known that some people thrive on antagonistic relationships and are inexorably drawn together only to spend their lives locked in combat. The astrologer can deduce the strength and general nature of attraction, but not whether two people like or dislike each other.

THE NODES. An additional astrological factor to consider is the Moon's north node which often reveals strong attraction between people. The astrological reason is clear. In the birth chart, the north node represents the direction in which a person is travelling through life, the challenges he or she must face and the lessons that must be learnt in order to change. People with the Sun, Moon or Ascendant in conjunction to another's north node become those in whom the challenges are met and from whom the lessons can be learnt. For example, a person with the north node in Aquarius may need to become more independent, and will learn self-reliance from encounters with those with the Sun, Moon or Ascendant in Aquarius.

THE HOUSES. In depth comparison of charts goes a step beyond the analysis of aspects and also examines house positions. The planets from one chart are superimposed on to the houses of the other enabling the astrologer to see in which area of life each partner will experience the relationship most intensely. For example, if partner A's planets fall in partner B's second house then B may be concerned with joint security and finances, while if B's planets fall in A's fifth house then this relationship may add zest and sparkle to A's life. One classic contact in the charts of married couples is the location of one partner's Sun in the other's seventh house. This often explains compatibility between couples whose Suns and Moons make no aspects to each other.

THE SIGNS. The signs may also be brought into use in detailed examination of a particular aspect, but as with the use of houses, the possibilities are both complex and subtle and it is not feasible to go into every variation. An understanding of houses and signs in synastry can only be gradually acquired by building on the experience of ordinary chart interpretation.

Above Left: Saturn Aspects
Long-term partnerships often show a close major aspect from Saturn in one chart to the Sun, Moon or one of the angles in the other – a common one is a conjunction between Saturn and the MC. Like other Saturn aspects this is a very powerful stabilizing factor, but each partner needs to be aware of Saturn's inhibiting powers. If these are allowed to get out of control then one partner may easily feel repressed by the other. A good balance to Saturn aspects is provided by Uranus aspects, which introduce spontaneity into a relationship and prevent boredom.

Above Right: Orbs for Inter-Chart Aspects
There is no consensus on the size of orbs to be used for inter-chart aspects. When every aspect between charts is to be taken into consideration wider orbs should be given to those between the Sun, Moon, Ascendants and Midheavens, and the narrowest to aspects between outer planets. The table above provides a guide to the size of orb used, although in some circumstances they may be wider.

Sun
Moon
Mercury
Venus
Earth
Mars
Jupiter
Saturn
Uranus
Neptune
Pluto

INTER-CHART ASPECTS

☉–☉

- ☌ Immediate close rapport, but relationship can be unstimulating.
- ⚹△ Good, easy relationship.
- □☍ Disagreements, but can be stimulating.

☉–☽

- ☌ Very close emotional relationship. This is a classic indicator of marriage, especially when the Moon in a woman's chart is conjunct to the Sun in a man's chart.
- ⚹△ Deep understanding, strong attraction; sound basis for a good friendship.
- □☍ Brings different approaches to life but can be stimulating.

☉–Asc. Desc.

- ☌ Close, strong, friendships likely.
- ⚹△ Brings harmony to a relationship.
- □ Can bring mild disagreements.

☉–MC IC

- ☌MC Close relationship, may have career implications.
- ☌IC Deep understandings likely; strengthens domestic relationships.
- ⚹△ Brings harmony.
- □ Can cause dissension.

☉–☿

- ☌ Relationship may centre around shared interests.
- ⚹△ Brings mutual understanding.
- □☍ Contributes to disagreements.

☉–♀

- ☌ Emotional attraction likely.
- ⚹△ Contributes to harmonious relationships.
- □☍ Can lead to emotional misunderstandings.

☉–♂

- ☌ Strong active relationship, but arguments likely.
- ⚹△ Brings harmony to shared activities.
- □☍ Arguments arise in shared activities.

☉–♃

- ☌ The relationship is likely to be profitable for one or for both partners.
- ⚹△ Brings harmony.
- □☍ Can bring impatience, recklessness.

☉♄

- ☌ There is an element of discipline and control; one partner may either repress the other or provide welcome stability and support.
- ⚹△ Generally helpful; provides stability.
- □☍ Can bring a feeling of limitation or repression.

☉–♅

- ☌ Unusual conditions; one partner stirs the other up.
- ⚹△ Interest and variety.
- □☍ Can be disruptive.

☉–♆

- ☌ Romantic attraction likely.
- ⚹△ Imagination and harmony.
- □☍ Can cause confusion.

☉–♇

- ☌ Relationship may be volatile, explosive.
- ⚹△ Brings helpful commitment.
- □☍ Disruptive.

☽–☽

- ☌ Often brings close emotional relationship.
- ⚹△ Helpful, harmonious; a strong basis for a lasting friendship.
- □☍ Emotional, domestic differences likely.

☽–Asc. Desc.

- ☌ Close, lasting emotional relationships likely.
- ⚹△ Emotional harmony.
- □ Emotional differences likely.

☽–MC, IC

- ☌MC Often signifies a close, lasting relationship. One partner assumes a maternal role. This sometimes occurs in business partnerships.
- ☌IC Firm foundation for a close emotional relationship.
- ⚹△ Emotional harmony.
- □ Contributes to emotional differences.

☽–☿

- ☌ Good emotional understanding.
- ⚹△ Contributes to general agreement.
- □☍ Emotional misunderstandings likely.

☽–♀

- ☌ Affectionate relationship likely.
- ⚹△ Brings affection.
- □☍ Contributes to emotional conflict.

☽–♂

- ☌ Strong attraction likely; helps with shared activities.
- ⚹△ Brings harmony to shared activities.
- □☍ Can bring physical attraction, but also disagreements over shared activities.

☽–♃

- ☌ Relationship likely to be profitable,

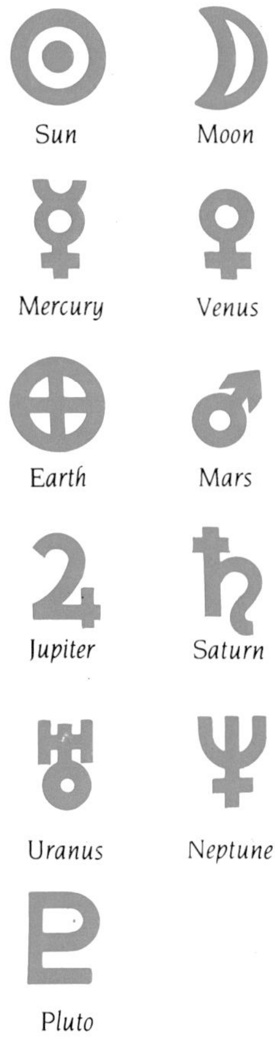

especially in domestic affairs; may lead to life abroad.

⚹△ Contributes to a friendly, optimistic relationship.

□☍ Can lead to carelessness, recklessness, especially in domestic affairs.

☽–♄

☌ Emotional stability but one partner may feel restricted by the other.

⚹△ Enhances emotional stability.

□☍ Can bring emotional restriction for one or both partners.

☽–♅

☌ Indicates lively emotional relationship; sudden changes likely.

⚹△ Interest and changing circumstances.

□☍ Can be disruptive.

☽–♆

☌ Romantic attraction.

⚹△ Contributes to general harmony.

□☍ Can cause confusion.

☽–♇

☌ Powerful attraction, can be explosive.

⚹△ Contributes to sense of commitment.

□☍ Disrupts emotional and domestic relationships.

☿–☿

☌ Brings similar attitudes and good chance of agreement.

⚹△ Contributes to agreement and mutual understanding.

□☍ Causes disagreements, but exchange of ideas can be stimulating.

☿–Asc. Desc.

☌ Provides close mental rapport.

⚹△ Contributes to mutual understanding.

□ Contributes to disagreements.

☿–MC, IC

☌MC Contributes to mutual understanding; useful in career partnerships.

☌IC Helps with domestic understanding and agreement.

⚹△ Contributes to general harmony.

□ Contributes to disagreements.

☿–♀

☌ Provides sound basis for mutual attraction and understanding.

⚹△ Contributes to general agreement.

□☍ Can cause disagreements.

☿–♂

☌ Can be productive – one partner's ideas contribute to the other's activities and vice versa.

⚹△ Brings agreement to shared activities.

□☍ Brings disagreement but can be stimulating.

☿–♃

☌ Contributes to intellectual compatibility; likelihood of travel.

⚹△ General agreement.

□☍ Contributes to disagreement.

☿–♄

☌ Useful partnership involves shared interests; one partner can help discipline the ideas of the other.

⚹△ Contributes to long-lasting agreement.

□☍ Can lead to a feeling that ideas and interests are being restricted.

☿–♅

☌ Stimulates lively exchange of ideas.

⚹△ Contributes to interest and new ideas.

□☍ Disagreements likely, but differences of opinion can be stimulating.

☿–♆

☌ The imagination of one partner and the ideas of the other can prove a fruitful combination.

⚹△ General agreement likely.

□☍ Can lead to confusion, misunderstanding.

☿–♇

☌ The exchange of ideas can lead to profound insights for both partners.

⚹△ Contributes to commitment over long-term interests.

□☍ Explosive disagreements likely, but arguments can be brief.

♀–♀

☌ Often indicates strong emotional attraction.

⚹△ Agreement and harmony.

□☍ Can lead to emotional differences.

♀–Asc. Desc.

☌ Good basis for affectionate relationships.

⚹△ Benefits all partnerships.

□ Contributes to emotional differences.

♀–MC, IC

☌MC Excellent indications for business partnerships.

☌IC Brings benefits to all domestic relationships.

⚹△ Encourages general harmony.

□ Contributes to emotional differences.

♀–♂

☌ Strong emotional or physical attraction.

⚹△ Contributes to a lively friendship.
□☍ Physical and emotional attraction can be deep, but arguments are likely to be strong.

♀–♃
☌ Brings mutual emotional encouragement and optimism.
⚹△ Contributes to a beneficial long-term relationship.
□☍ Emotional needs may be out of step.

♀–♄
☌ Contributes to emotional stability and security.
⚹△ Good foundation for long-term partnership.
□☍ One partner may feel emotionally restricted by the other.

♀–♅
☌ Emotional change, social variety.
⚹△ Contributes to a lively, interesting friendship.
□☍ Can be disruptive.

♀–♆
☌ Deep romantic attachment likely.
⚹△ Brings harmony.
□☍ Emotional confusion, deception likely.

♀–♇
☌ Powerful emotional attraction, but very volatile.
⚹△ Contributes to long-term commitment.
□☍ Can be explosive, disruptive.

♂–♂
☌ Similarity in activities and behaviour, not necessarily good for cooperation.
⚹△ Contributes to constructive friendship.
□☍ Fundamental differences of approach can bring arguments but also stimulation.

♂–Asc. Desc.
☌ Strong active relationship; prospects for agreement or disagreement will be indicated by other factors.
⚹△ Contributes to harmony in joint activities.
□ Differences of approach can be stimulating but cause arguments.

♂–MC, IC
☌MC Good for active working partnerships if other factors indicate agreement.
☌IC Joint domestic activities.
⚹△ Contributes to constructive, active friendship.
□ Differences arise over joint activities.

♂–♃
☌ Benefits joint activities.
⚹△ Good basis for working partnerships. Constructive possibilities.
□☍ Contributes to carelessness in joint activities.

♂–♄
☌ Contributes to stability and organization in joint activities.
⚹△ Benefits working partnerships and joint activities.
□☍ May obstruct or cause delays in joint activities.

♂–♅
☌ Unusual joint activities, possible sharp differences.
⚹△ Contributes to a lively partnership.
□☍ Can bring disruptive arguments.

♂–♆
☌ Can bring physical attraction.
⚹△ General harmony.
□☍ Possible deception, confusion.

♂–♇
☌ Explosive, volatile partnership.
⚹△ Commitment to long-term joint activities.
□☍ Contributes to arguments, disagreements.

♃–♃
☌ Partnership is likely to be profitable for both parties.
⚹△ Generally beneficial influences.
□☍ Care should be taken to avoid waste in joint enterprises.

♃–Asc. Desc.
☌ Both partners are likely to gain from this relationship.
⚹△ General harmony of purpose.
□ Can bring waste in joint activities.

♃–MC, IC
☌MC Profitable, especially in working partnerships.
☌IC Likely to bring domestic benefits.
⚹△ Generally beneficial.
□ Can result in wasted opportunities.

♃–♄
☌ Can signify an important relationship; useful for working partnerships.
⚹△ A positive, constructive influence.
□☍ Can indicate a fundamental difference in long-term objectives.

♃–♅
☌ A force for change in any relationship.
⚹△ Introduces unexpected possibilities.

□☍ Disruptive.

♃–♆
☌ Can bring a deep and intuitive mutual understanding.
⚹△ Contributes to romantic attraction.
□☍ Can contribute to misunderstandings.

♃–♇
☌ Contributes to passion and commitment in close relationships, but can also exacerbate difficulties.
⚹△ Can be generally productive and positive.
□☍ Deep conflict likely, perhaps focusing on different ideologies and beliefs.

THE OUTER PLANETS AND THE ANGLES

Aspects between Saturn, Uranus, Neptune and Pluto indicate connections between people from one generation to another and need not be considered in ordinary chart comparison. Aspects from these planets to the angles may, however, be significant.

♄–Asc. Desc.
☌ Brings stability; one partner can restrict the other; Useful in working partnerships.
⚹△ Contributes stability and consistence to any relationship.
□ Often contributes to a feeling of restriction in one or both partners; delays are possible in joint activities.

♄–MC, IC
☌MC Stability and possibly restriction; useful in working relationships.
☌IC Can bring domestic responsibilities.
⚹△ Stability.
□☍ Can bring delays, material problems, restriction.

♅–Asc. Desc.
☌ Contributes to an interesting relationship but does not encourage emotional closeness; can lead to instant attraction or dislike.
⚹△ Often brings unusual circumstances.
□☍ Can be disruptive.

♅–MC, IC
☌MC Unusual circumstances, especially in career partnerships.
☌IC Unsettling domestic circumstances.
⚹△ Adds interest and sparkle, especially to career and home.
□ Disruptive especially to working and domestic relationships.

♆–Asc. Desc.
☌ Can bring mysterious, romantic attraction.
⚹△ General harmony.
□ Can bring confusion, deception.

♆–MC, IC
☌MC Can bring romantic attraction; may be a hindrance in career partnerships.
☌IC Romantic attraction, but mysterious or confused circumstances in domestic relationships.
⚹△ General harmony.
□ Can bring confusion, deception.

♇–Asc. Desc.
☌ Can signify deep and compulsive attraction but also strong arguments.
⚹△ Contributes to deep long-term commitment.
□ Can bring disagreements, arguments.

♇–MC, IC
☌MC Deep emotional connection, but can lead equally to attraction or dislike.
☌IC Volatile conditions, especially in domestic relationships.
⚹△ Contributes depth to long-term relationships.
□ Disagreements.

ASPECTS BETWEEN THE OUTER PLANETS

Aspects between the outer planets show how members of different generations get on with each other, and the changes in fashion, behaviour and attitudes that often occur. These aspects relate to the great changes wrought by the long-term cycles of the outer planets (see Chapter 17).

♄–♄
☌ This aspect often connects the horoscopes of parents and their children; in people of different generations it can show working relationships or people who exercise joint authority or responsibility.
⚹△ Supports solid practical relationships.
□☍ can introduce practical difficulties in partnerships and conflicts over authority.

♄–♅
☌ Brings together two fundamentally different approaches to life; often disruptive but can be stimulating.
⚹△ Generally beneficial.
□☍ Clash of behaviour and attitudes.

♈ Aries ♉ Taurus
♊ Gemini ♋ Cancer
♌ Leo ♍ Virgo
♎ Libra ♏ Scorpio
♐ Sagittarius ♑ Capricorn
♒ Aquarius ♓ Pisces

☉ Sun ☽ Moon
☿ Mercury ♀ Venus
⊕ Earth ♂ Mars
♃ Jupiter ♄ Saturn
♅ Uranus ♆ Neptune
♇ Pluto

♄–♆

☌ Reconciles fundamentally different approaches to life; can be productive in working partnerships.

⚹△ Generally beneficial.

□☍ Brings a clash of authority between generations; between individuals can cause deception.

♄–♇

☌ A strong, potent, volatile connection; one generation may challenge the authority of its predecessor; couples may experience crises.

⚹△ Commitment and a common identity of interest.

□☍ Head on confrontations are likely between generations; friction is increased between individuals.

♅–♅

☌ This aspect only occurs between people of the same age, or those born at 84 year intervals.

⚹△ Brings a general harmony of interests.

□☍ Brings conflict – this is a classic indicator of the 'generation gap'.

♅–♆

☌ Can bring together two different sets of beliefs and ideas.

⚹△ Fashions, styles and beliefs harmonize.

□☍ Brings differences of belief between two generations.

♅–♇

☌ Potentially explosive; conflicts of authority between generations.

⚹△ Generally harmonious.

□☍ Conflicts of authority between generations.

♆–♆

☌ This aspect only occurs between people of the same age.

⚹△ General sympathy between generations.

□☍ Differences in style, fashion and belief between the generations.

♆–♇

☌ Deep connections, associated with beliefs and religious sympathies.

⚹△ Generally beneficial; reconciles the beliefs of different generations.

□☍ Differences of belief.

♇–♇

☌ Only occurs between people of the same age.

⚹△ Generally beneficial.

□ Fundamental differences in standards of behaviour.

COMPOSITE CHARTS

The composite chart is a single horoscope which can prove remarkably effective in demonstrating the salient points in a relationship. Whereas chart comparison complicates matters because two horoscopes create so many interpretative possibilities, the composite chart provides stunningly simple insights into any partnership.

There are two types of composite chart. One known as the Relationship chart, is based on the exact point in time halfway between the births of the two people, and the exact halfway point between their birth places, both in latitude and longitude. As this is very complicated to calculate without a computer, most astrologers use the second type.

The second type of chart is worked out by adding up the position of each pair of planets – Ascendants, Midheavens, Suns, Moons, and so on – in turn and then dividing the result by two. The position of each planet is converted into absolute longitude – its position in terms of the whole zodiac of 360° – and then added to its equivalent planet. Division of the result by two gives the composite position. If the Equal House system is used, only the composite Ascendant and MC need be calculated – all the other house cusps will follow the usual order at 30° intervals after the Ascendant.

Composite horoscopes can be interpreted in exactly the same way as any natal chart, except of course that the readings are being applied to a relationship, not a person. Aspects, sign and house position can all be used to build up a picture of the relationship, its strengths, weaknesses and what each partner has to gain from it. Transits over the composite chart indicate major stages in the relationship and most composite charts are affected by very strong transits at the time when the two people meet.

In another variation on this theme the composite chart is based on the partners' progressed charts for the same time. For example, a progressed composite chart for the time of a marriage would be based on each person's progressions for the marriage. However, in practice few astrologers go into this detail.

PRINCE CHARLES AND PRINCESS DIANA. The first step in analysing the relationship between Prince Charles and Princess Diana is to assess the needs of each employing ordinary methods of birth-chart interpretation. The second is to compare their charts, looking mainly at the aspects formed between the planets in both charts. The third is to cast the composite chart which may then be interpreted in the same way as a natal chart.

The most striking pattern in their composite chart is the conjunction of Mars and Neptune and the sextile this makes to Pluto, the square to Uranus and the quincunx to the Moon. Each of these aspects may be interpreted separately, but the total effect is to create a relationship based on mutual stimulation, activity, diversity, change and unusual interests. The combination of an Ascendant in Libra and the Moon in Pisces brings a willingness to compromise and a love of peace and quiet. The trine from the Sun to Jupiter is very beneficial, especially as Jupiter is in a conjunction with the IC, the ruler of the home.

Transits over composite charts often indicate key stages in a relationship. Around the outside of Charles' and Diana's composite chart are marked some of the transits for the day of their wedding in 1981. Very noticeable is Uranus, aspecting five composite planets.

Aspects from composite to natal charts reveal the role of each partner and the benefits they gain from the relationship. The opposition from Diana's Saturn to composite Uranus shows her ability to anchor (Saturn) the exciting potential (Uranus) in the marriage, as well as the ability of the partnership to change (Uranus) her previous way of life (Saturn).

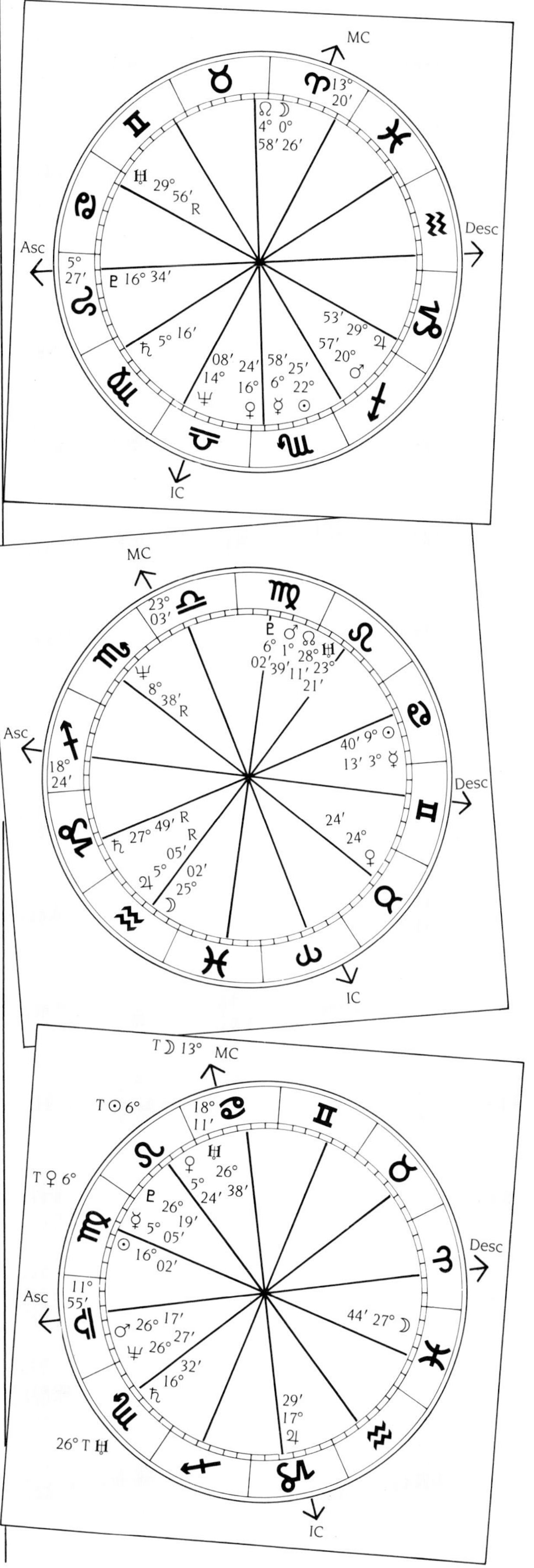

Top: Prince Charles
Chart set for 9.14 pm GMT, 14 November 1948, London

Centre: Princess Diana
Chart set for 6.45 pm GMT, 1 July 1961, Sandringham, England

Bottom: Composite chart for Prince Charles and Princess Diana

Calculation of Composite Positions

Charles's Sun
22° 25′ Scorpio = 232° 25′ absolute longitude

Diana's Sun
9° 40′ Cancer = 99° 40′ absolute longitude

332° 05′

332° 05′ ÷ 2 = 166° 02′ absolute longitude = 16° 02′ Virgo Composite Sun = 16° 02′ Virgo.
Note: If the sum of absolute longitude is over 360°, then subtract 360°

CHAPTER 15
EXPANDING THE CHART: ADVANCED INTERPRETATION

ADDITIONAL TECHNIQUES

There are dozens of techniques in use which do not form part of basic natal astrology but which, used sparingly, expand the possibilities of interpretation. Some of these are of ancient origin while others are recent innovations and each has its own validity if applied with care and thought.

Inevitably astrologers are fascinated by some techniques but are not interested in others, which tends to lead to arguments over the competing claims of different practices. However, such disputes are more a matter of opinion than of scientific evidence. In the final analysis all that matters is that the techniques applied produce the appropriate interpretation.

This chapter covers only the major possibilities in an area of unlimited experimentation. It is crucial that too many methods of technical analysis should not be applied to the same chart, otherwise there will be no clear interpretation. Selectivity is the order of the day.

ADDITIONAL ASPECTS

During the seventeenth century astrologers, including the great Johannes Kepler, invented a series of minor aspects. Of these only four – the semi-sextile, semi-square, sesquiquadrate and quincunx – became part of mainstream astrology, leaving the others as extras which are sometimes included but usually left out. The result of this expansion of the zodiacal aspects was that other aspects, some of which are not even based on the zodiac, have been unjustly neglected. The value of these aspects lies in their ability to show relationships between planets that the mainstream aspects may conceal. The major non-zodiacal aspects are the parallels.

CHART SHAPING

The general location of planets in the chart has long been an important consideration, but it was only in this century that certain patterns were formally identified and labelled, initially by the American astrologer Marc Edmund Jones. Examination of the chart shape forms a very useful part of any basic reading of the horoscope.

Parallels
There are two types of parallel. The parallel of declination is made by planets exactly the same distance away from the equator, and the parallel of latitude is made by planets exactly the same distance from the ecliptic. The symbol for a parallel is either P or ||, so Sun parallel Mercury would be written as ⊙P☿ or ⊙||☿. The orb allowed is 1°

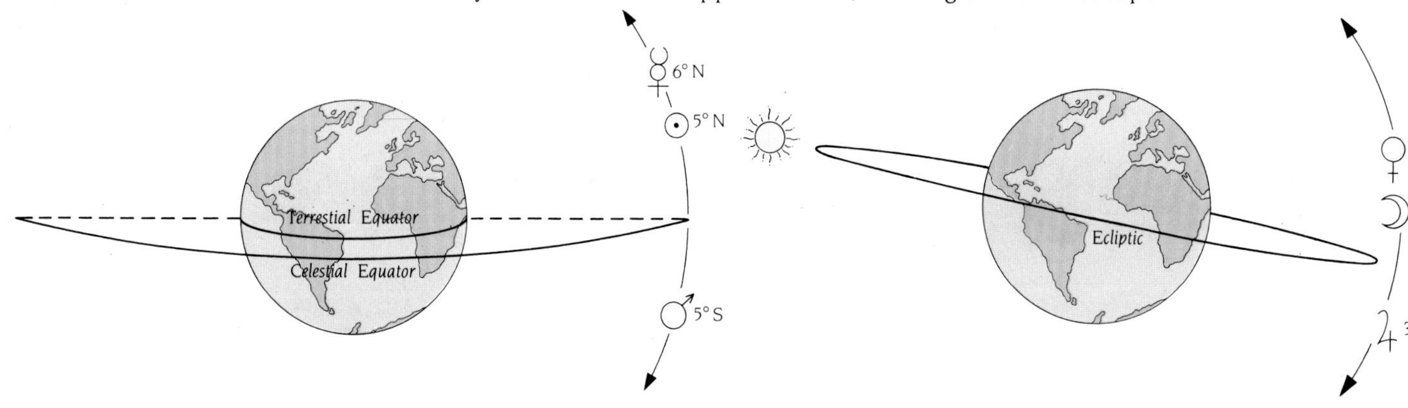

Left: Parallel of Declination
The Sun is parallel with both Mercury and Mars. The parallel with Mercury is equivalent to a conjunction because they are both on the same side of the equator, and the parallel with Mars is equivalent to an opposition because they are on opposite sides. Mercury and Mars are also in a parallel.

Right: Parallel of Latitude
The Moon is parallel with Jupiter and Venus. The parallel with Venus is equivalent to a conjunction because both are on the same side of the ecliptic. The parallel with Jupiter is equivalent to an opposition because Jupiter is south of the ecliptic while the Moon is north.

Aspect	Symbol	Distance apart	Orb	Meaning	Comments
Biquintile	BQ	144°	2°	Creativity	The only two of nine aspects, which are in common use Originated by modern astrologers
Quintile	Q	72°	2°	Creativity	
Parallel of Declination	P or ||	0°	1°	As ☌	Planets on same side of celestial equator
		Variable	1°	As ☍	Planets on opposite sides of celestial equator
Parallel of Latitude	P or ||	0°	1°	As ☌	Planets on same side of ecliptic
		Variable	1°	As ☍	Planets on opposite sides of ecliptic
Mundane Aspects	As ordinary aspects	—	–	As ordinary aspects	Aspects between planets on house cusps

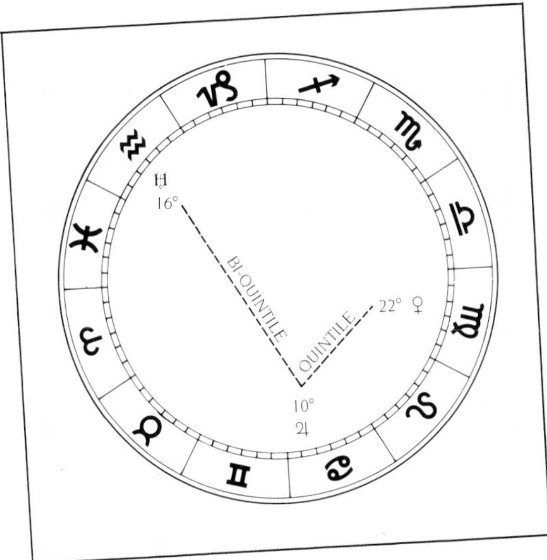

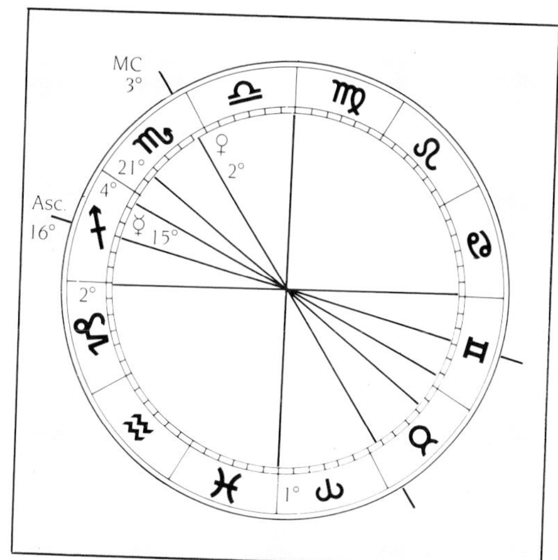

Top Left: The quintile and bi-quintile are two additional minor aspects. They are derived from a division of the zodiac by five and relate to creativity. Planets in quintile are 72° apart and in bi-quintile are 144° apart. The orb allowed is 2°. Other minor aspects have been invented but none is in every day use.

Top Right: The most important of the mundane aspects is the mundane square, also known as the paran, made between two planets each exactly conjunct an angle – Ascendant, Descendant, MC or IC. The meaning is essentially the same as that for ordinary squares, but relates particularly to difficult circumstances.
In this example of a chart drawn using the Placidus method, Venus conjunct the MC is in a paran with Mercury on the Ascendant.

MIDPOINTS. The use of midpoints provides an unlimited extension of the principle of aspects so that any two planets always have a relationship. This relationship exists only in potential unless a third planet, or angle, falls exactly on the midpoint, whether in the birth chart or by transit or progression. The interpretation of a midpoint is, therefore, rather subtle but can be understood once aspect patterns such as 'T' Squares, which involve three planets, has been understood.

The most significant midpoints are those between the Sun, Moon, Ascendant and Midheaven and these refer not only to their specific areas (home, family, career, etc) but to life in general. Other midpoints have more specific applications. The Moon-Venus midpoint obviously refers to the 'female' nature, all artistic activities, home and family affairs, sensitivity and emotion, while the Mars-Saturn midpoint refers to the need for struggle, hard work, and material accomplishment. The Sun-Mars midpoint is archetypal 'male' – assertive, impulsive, aggressive – while the Mercury-Jupiter midpoint is typically intellectual, concerned with the meeting of knowledge and wisdom. Each midpoint is probably best understood by looking at the meaning of the conjunction between two planets, while a third planet, which activates the midpoint, is in conjunction with both.

Each pair of planets has two midpoints, one close and one further away; the closer one is always used. A midpoint is symbolized by an oblique, so that the Mars-Jupiter midpoint is written ♂/♃ and the Moon-Midheaven midpoint is written ☽/MC.

There are three ways in which midpoints

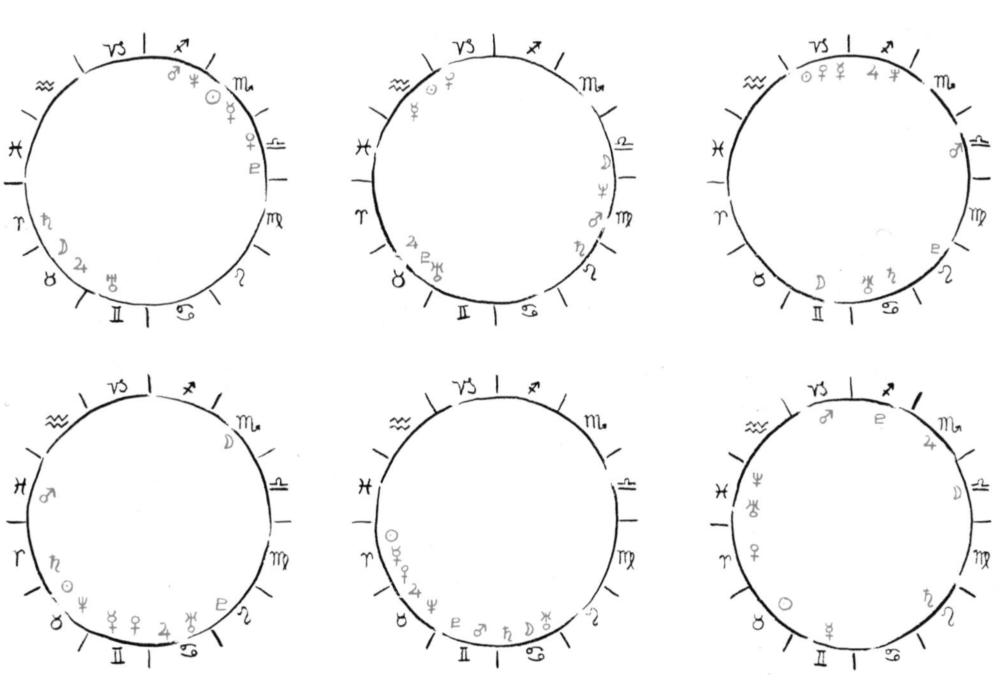

Top Left: See-Saw
The planets are gathered in two opposing groups. This suggests a person who may be pulled in two completely different directions. There may be an awareness of opposing possibilities and an ability to manipulate these.

Top Centre: Splay
The planets are grouped in tight bunches emphasizing a few houses and signs. This suggests a person who may be highly motivated in several completely different directions.

Top Right: Locomotive
All the planets are gathered within 240°. The unoccupied sector of the chart tends to remain unexpressed.

Bottom Left: Bucket
All the planets are contained in one half of the chart except for one 'singleton' in the opposite half. This planet is the 'handle' of the bucket and assumes extra importance.

Bottom Centre: Bundle
All the planets are contained within 120°. The individual tends to focus on one part of life's potential and ignores the rest. This pattern is especially strong if all the planets are on one side of either the Ascendant-Descendant axis or the MC-IC axis.

Bottom Right: Splash
The planets are evenly dispersed around the zodiac. The individual has a wide range of abilities and experiences but may fail to concentrate sufficiently on any one goal.

become significant. The first is if a third planet or point occupies the midpoint within an orb of 1°: it is written as follows –

Natal Jupiter on the Mars-Saturn midpoint ♃ = ♂/♄

Transiting Pluto on the Sun-Moon midpoint T♇ = ☉/☽

Progressed Moon on the Sun-Pluto midpoint ☽P = ☉/♇

The second is if two midpoints coincide, a rare occurrence which produces complex possibilities: it is written as follows –

Moon-Jupiter midpoint on the Mercury-Mars midpoint ☽/♃ = ☿/♂

The third way for a midpoint to activate is through a tense aspect from a third planet. The aspects used are the square, semi-square and sesquiquadrate, and the orb should be 1°, although some astrologers use as much as 2° or as little as ½°. If a planet is opposed to a midpoint then it is actually conjunct the far midpoint, so should be considered as conjunct the midpoint: it is written as follows –

Jupiter squared the Sun-Uranus midpoint ♃□☉/♅

However, no distinction is usually made between the different tense aspects, and if Jupiter is conjunct, semi-square, square, or opposed to the Sun-Uranus midpoint, these may all be written as ♃ = ☉/♅.

The interpretation of midpoints is influenced by reliance on the tense aspects which characteristically strengthen the personality and bring events to life. Midpoints are, therefore, associated with important achievements or work as well as with whatever happens to people.

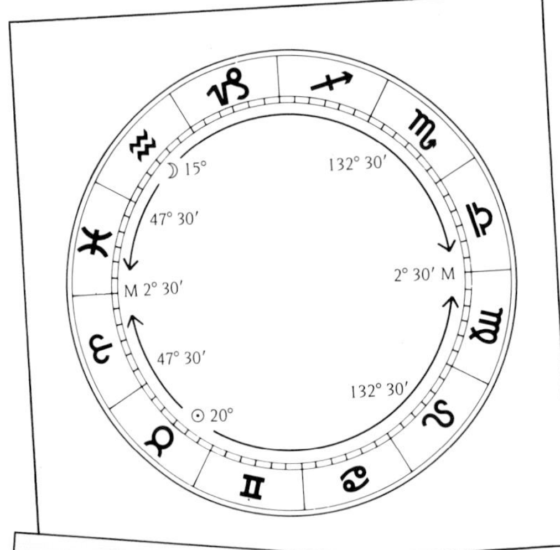

Sun = 20° Taurus = 50° absolute longitude
Moon = 15° Aquarius = 315° absolute longitude
= 365°
365° ÷ 2 = 182° 30′ absolute longitude
Therefore the Sun-Moon midpoint is 2° 30′ Libra or the opposite point, 2° 30′ Aries.

Midpoints
Each pair of planets has two midpoints, one nearer and one exactly opposite further way: in practice there is no difference between the two.

The midpoint is worked out by converting the position of the two planets (or the Ascendant and MC if these are used) into absolute longitude, adding these together and then halving the result.

HARMONIC CHARTS. It is possible to divide the signs, and the zodiac itself, by any number. One can divide the zodiac and signs into 10 subdivisions, or 15 or even 25. This is a practice which has ancient roots in Western astrology but has only caught on in recent years, largely inspired by a strange combination of traditional Indian astrology and modern statistical research.

In India these sub-horoscopes are known as *shodasa vargas*, in the West they have been christened harmonic charts. A division of the zodiac by two creates the second harmonic, division by three gives rise to the third harmonic, and so on. These charts form an essential part of basic astrology in India, each having its own precise meaning and being interpreted in accordance with the standard Indian rules.

The meaning of each harmonic corresponds approximately to the meaning of the equivalent house so that the second harmonic rules wealth, the third harmonic brothers and sisters, and so on. The ninth harmonic is accorded much greater importance than all the others: it is known as the *navamsa* chart, and specifically reveals the marriage partner, but it has a deeper meaning as the ruler of one's greater destiny. Indian astrologers cast the *navamsa* chart as a matter of course together with the birth chart.

There are, however, subtle differences between the Indian and Western systems of house rulership – in India the fifth house rules education whereas in the West this is divided between the third and ninth houses.

In the West astrologers are unsure and have not developed a coordinated approach: in other words the use of harmonic charts is still very much at an experimental stage. One approach, which has proved effective, is to forget for the present certain anomalies between the meanings of houses and harmonics, and cast the second to twelfth harmonic charts to gain deeper insight into the affairs signified by each house. For example, supposing somebody is having trouble expressing his or her creative aspirations and the birth chart fails to shed sufficient light on this problem, the fifth harmonic might show a fixed grand cross indicating the need for patient hard work and the dedicated acquisition of skill (that is, working with the stable qualities of fixity and through the tensions of the grand cross).

The Equal House system should be used throughout. Some Western astrologers do not mark houses on harmonic charts but experience shows that these are important for a full interpretation. For example, in the fourth harmonic chart, signifying home and family, the second house may indicate the family's resources and finances.

To calculate harmonic charts:

1. Convert the position of the planet, Ascendant and Midheaven, into absolute longitude. This is the planet's position in terms of the whole circle so that 0° Taurus corresponds to 30°, 0° Gemini corresponds to 60° etc.
2. Multiply this by the number of the harmonic. For the fifth harmonic multiply by five, for the seventh harmonic multiply by seven.
3. The result will usually be over 360°, sometimes as much as several thousand. It is therefore necessary to subtract units of 360° until the figure is below 360°.
4. Convert the absolute longitude into ordinary sign position. For example, if the result is 340° this converts to 10° Aquarius.

Example: Calculation of ninth harmonic.
Sun natal position 24° 28′ ♑
Absolute longitude 294° 28′ (24° 28′ + 270°)
9 × 294° 28′ = 2,650° 12′
Subtract 360° seven times = 130° 12′ absolute longitude
Sun ninth harmonic position = 10° 12′ Leo

THE FIXED STARS. In ancient times the planets were known as the 'wandering' stars on account of their strange movements across the sky. The mass of stars which constantly retained exactly the same relationship with each other were known as the fixed stars, and some of these were thought to exercise a critical influence on the Earth. All in all, there are several hundred stars which have astrological significance, but only about 10 are in common usage, mainly in mundane, horary and electional astrology. The stars tend to have fixed meanings – good or bad – which explains why they are often ignored in psychological astrology. However, they seem to have a strange impact on destiny and often signify events over which there is very little control.

The meaning of each star is often expressed in terms of corresponding planets. For example, a star which is compared to Venus or Jupiter is likely to bring success and one compared to Mars or Saturn suggests difficulty or conflict.

The fixed stars should only be used if they make conjunctions to planets or angles in the horoscope, and orbs should be kept tight – 1° is the standard allowed. Stars are not marked on the horoscope although a note of their position may be made on the chart if they do prove to be significant.

Although fixed in relation to each other the stars move through the zodiac by 1° every 72 years, so over long periods their positions change significantly. Their positions are given below for 1986, after which they move forward by 50 seconds every year.

	1st harmonic (natal chart)	*2nd harmonic*	*3rd harmonic*	*4th harmonic*	*5th harmonic*
☉	2° ♉	4° ♊	6° ♋	8° ♌	10° ♍
☽	28° ♊	26° ♍	24° ♐	22° ♓	20° ♊
☿	17° ♈	4° ♉	21° ♉	8° ♊	25° ♊

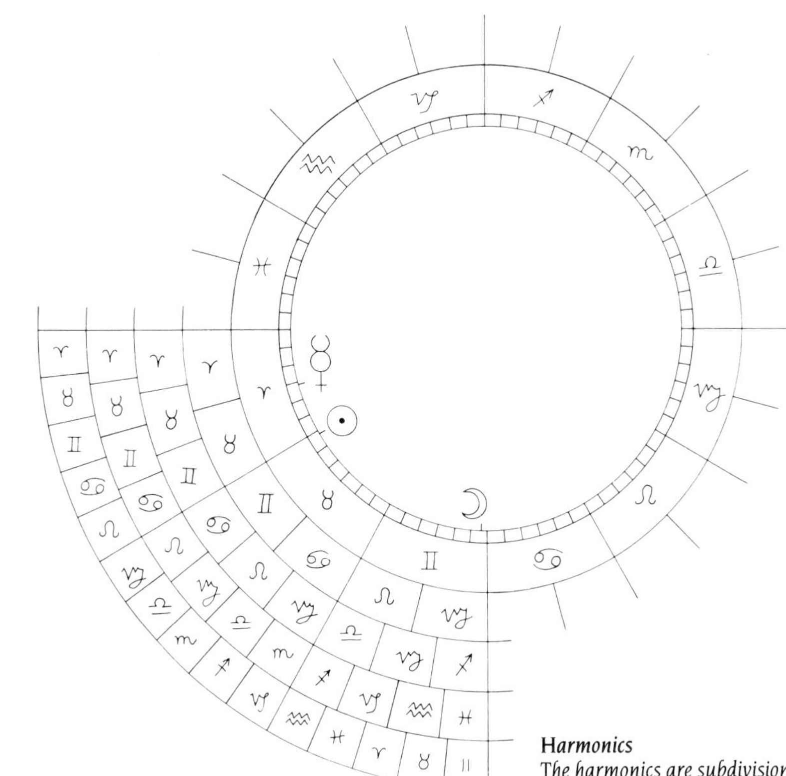

Harmonics
The harmonics are subdivisions of the signs. The second harmonic is a division by two, the third harmonic a division by three, and so on. The third and thirteenth harmonics were in use in ancient Greece, but the other harmonics have only been recently introduced into the West from India.
In this example the Sun, Moon and Mercury change signs as their positions are converted into the different harmonics. In the fifth harmonic (creativity), the Moon and Mercury make a conjunction, forming a relationship that is not apparent in the birth chart. This suggests skill and sensitivity in communication and creative matters. In plain English this indicates poetic ability.

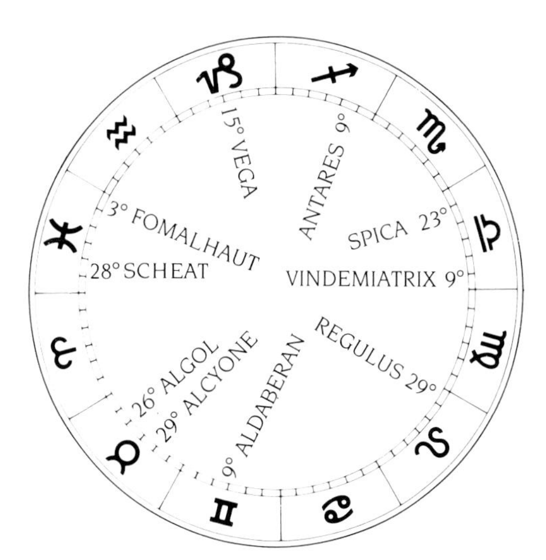

Bottom: The Major Fixed Stars
Fomalhaut, Antares, Regulus and Aldaberan form a loose Grand Cross, and were once known as the Rulers of the Year.

	Position	Corresponding Planets	Horary, Mundane, Electional Charts	Birth Charts
Algol	26° 06′ ♉	♂♄	*Severe difficulties, failure*	*Problems caused through carelessness: astrologer should advise caution*
Alcyone	29° 51′ ♉	☽♂	*Compassion, emotion, failure, disappointment*	*Emotion, self-pity: astrologer should advise clarity of mind*
Aldaberan	9° 35′ ♊	♂	*Violence, victory and heroism in war*	*Confidence, energy, leadership qualities*
Regulus	29° 37′ ♌	☉	*Signifies royalty, good fortune, success*	*Pride, good fortune, success*
Vindemiatrix	9° 46′ ♎	♄☿	*War, misfortune*	*Self-denial, martyrdom, perhaps for mystical motives*
Spica	23° 38′ ♎	♀♂	*Success, prosperity, great good fortune*	*Enhances prospects for success, prosperity*
Antares	9° 38′ ♐	♂♃	*War, conflict, violence*	*Self-confidence, self-assertion*
Vega	15° 07′ ♑	♀☿	*Success in political and financial affairs*	*Good fortune in worldly ambitions*
Fomalhaut	3° 29′ ♓	☿♀	*Variable, brings success or failure depending on its aspects*	*Can be beneficial if aspected to Sun, Venus, Jupiter*
Scheat	28° 58′ ♓	♂☿	*Difficulty, failure, especially associated with accidents at sea*	*Can be difficult*

THE PART OF FORTUNE

The Part of Fortune, or Fortuna, is a point in the horoscope the same distance from the Moon as the Sun is from the Ascendant. It is calculated by adding up the combined positions of the Moon and Ascendant in absolute longitude, and subtracting that of the Sun.

Moon = 20° Pisces = 350° absolute longitude
\+ Ascendant = 10° Gemini = 70° absolute longitude
420°
− Sun = 15° Cancer = 105° absolute longitude

Part of Fortune = 315° absolute longitude = 15° Aquarius

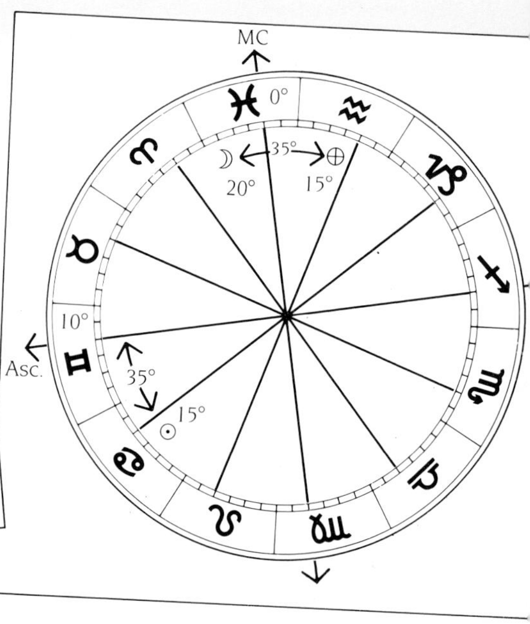

THE PART OF FORTUNE. The Part of Fortune, also sometimes known as Fortuna, is the only 'Arabic Part' in common use. It is one of about a hundred such 'parts' which are calculated by adding together two points in a horoscope and subtracting a third. Many of the 'parts' have specific meanings relating to career, commerce, marriage and other human concerns.

The Part of Fortune, whose glyph is ⊕, is a beneficial point indicating where one's fortune lies. This may be interpreted literally as meaning success and prosperity, or in a more general sense as good fortune. In a deeper sense it may have something to do with destiny and the activities through which this is discovered. For example, Fortuna in the third house might indicate a person whose destiny is discovered through writing or teaching, while with Fortuna in the seventh house destiny may be discovered or worked out through other people and relationships. Fortuna is emphasized in a chart through its aspects. Obviously these are strongest in the case of conjunctions, while squares and oppositions may bring difficulties in its expression, and trines and sextiles bring ease. Planets in trine and sextile to Fortuna themselves benefit in an almost Jupiterian manner – receiving reward and opportunity without apparent effort. Sun or Moon trine Fortuna are the most promising aspects. In the long run, however, the difficult aspects can be the most productive in cases where the problems they bring drive people to higher achievement.

FINDING THE BIRTH TIME – CHART RECTIFICATION. The problem of the uncertain birth time has bedevilled astrology for the past two thousand years. When a birth time is unknown the astrologer may cast a solar chart, either for midnight, dawn, or noon, depending on personal preference. However, many astrologers attempt to work out an exact birth time by a process known as rectification. There is no uniformly accepted procedure but the standard practice is to take major events from the individual's life and correlate these with the expected transits over the Ascendant and Midheaven. This is relatively simple if the approximate birth time is known and if all that is required is to establish the degree of the Ascendant. However, if there is no record of an approximate birth time, the astrologer has to cope with many different possibilities.

A guess at a likely rising sign might be made in the light of the individual's known behaviour and by looking at characteristics that are not accounted for by the Sun and Moon signs. Some astrologers take notice of the physical appearance as this is often partly signified by the Ascendant. For example, if a person has red hair this may indicate an Ascendant in one of the fire signs – Aries, Leo or Sagittarius – while dark intense eyes are often a sign of a Scorpio Ascendant. Once a possible Ascendant has been established the other houses can be filled in and the distribution of planets in houses correlated with the person's interests and circumstances.

The first events the astrologer considers are those that happen in early childhood, especially serious illnesses, accidents or other traumatic events which should be shown by major transits over the Ascendant or perhaps by major aspects from the progressed Ascendant. For example, if the astrologer has decided on a Virgo Ascendant and finds that at the age of three, when Mars and Uranus were conjunct at 10° Virgo, the child had a near fatal accident, this would be taken as evidence in favour of an Ascendant of 10° Virgo.

Events in later life, such as marriage, can also be used to indicate the Ascendant and birth time. Princess Diana's engagement to Prince Charles gives us a suitable example. Her accepted birth time gives an Ascendant of 18° Sagittarius and a Midheaven of 23° Libra, but at the time of her engagement progressed Venus (indicating love) was at 16° Gemini approaching an opposition to her natal Ascendant, and transiting Pluto (indicating transformation in life style) was at 21° Libra, approaching a conjunction with her Midheaven. An astrologer rectifying her chart might decide that at her engagement progressed Venus and transiting Pluto must have been in exact aspect with her birth chart, giving her an Ascendant of 16° Sagittarius and a Midheaven of 21° Libra, and a birth time eight minutes prior to the recorded time.

Rectification, however, is a subtle job which depends totally on the impressions of the astrologer. There is nothing scientific in it and to imagine that a rectified time is the objectively 'correct' birth time is nonsense. There is always evidence to suggest a different birth time. For example, in Princess Diana's case, transiting Neptune at her engagement was at 22° Sagittarius, suggesting an Ascendant of 22° Sagittarius and a birth time 16 minutes later than her recorded time.

TRAVELLING – RELOCATION CHARTS AND ASTRO-CARTOGRAPHY. The birth chart shows the entire potential for the whole of a person's life, yet is cast only for the place of birth. During the course of a lifetime many people travel widely, migrate and sometimes settle in foreign countries. Often people feel

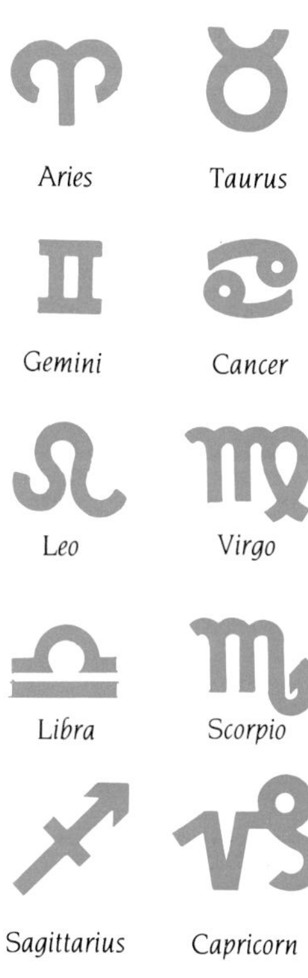

drawn to a particular place and repelled by another, they experience good fortune in one yet difficulties elsewhere. Such occurrences are inexplicable in ordinary terms yet astrology has found a way to explain and understand them through the relocation chart.

The horoscope is cast for the date and GMT time of birth as usual, but for a location other than the place of birth. A person born in Los Angeles may wish to have a relocation chart cast for Cairo and a person from New York may want a relocation chart for Bombay. In each case the new chart will contain exactly the same configuration of planets in signs (ruling basic character) but all the house positions (ruling circumstances) will have changed. It is difficult to think of a more practical use for astrology than to move to the areas in which certain houses are strengthened: to make money move to where the second house is strongest; to move home to where the fourth house is best aspected; and to succeed in career move to the place where the tenth house is best.

Obviously it is not practical for most people to move around the world in this way, and in some cases it may be absurd even to consider it. The ambitious businessman may find that his second house is strongest in the middle of the Atlantic Ocean. However, connections with other places often arise in unexpected ways, and it is not always necessary to move.

Drawing on the principle that angular planets – those conjunct the Ascendant, Descendant, Midheaven or IC – are especially strong, an additional concept has been developed known as astro-cartography. This is based on the theory that at the time of birth every planet is on one of the four angles

Birth Chart and Astro-Cartography for Jimmy Carter

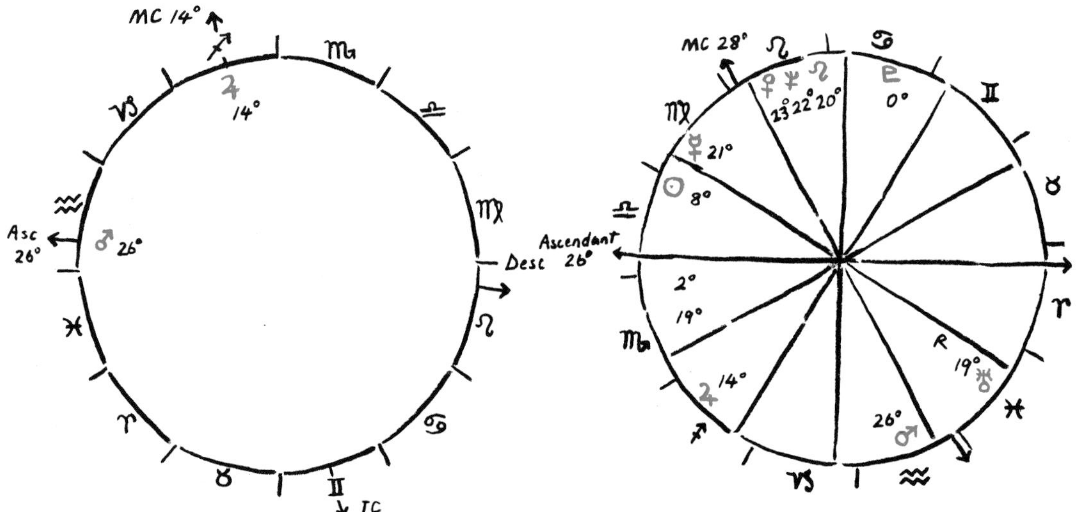

Right: Jimmy Carter's birth chart cast for Plains, Georgia, gives little indication of the difficulties he would face from Iran. When his relocation chart is cast for the exact time of his birth, but set for Tehran, Jupiter falls exactly on the MC and Mars on the Ascendant, forming a tense challenging mundane square, or paran.

Left: Jimmy Carter's relocation chart for Tehran showing the paran between Mars and Jupiter.

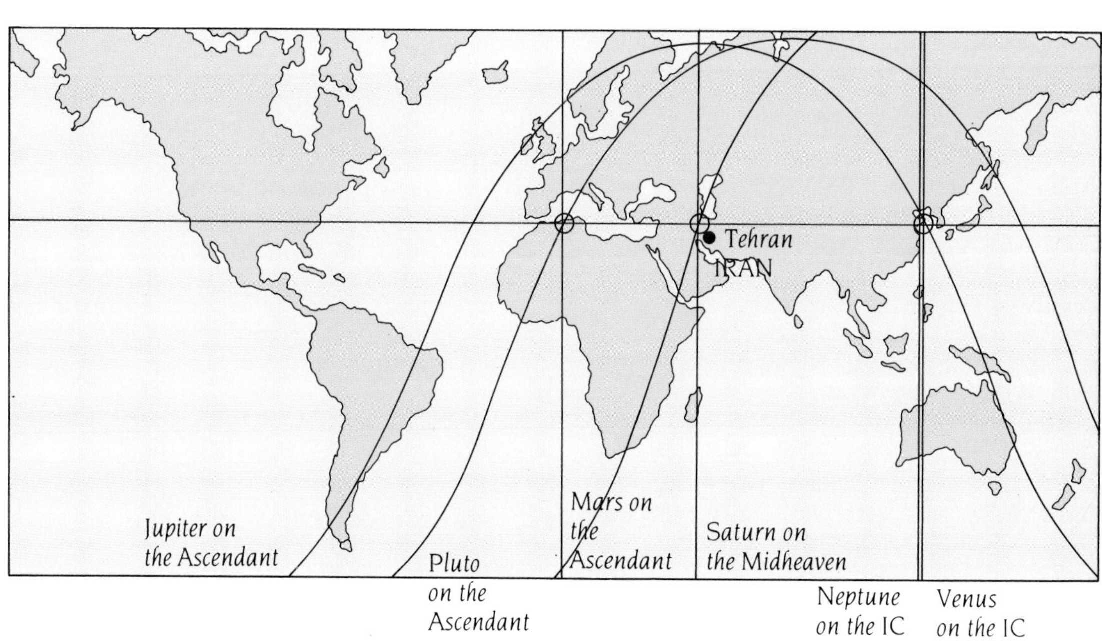

Jimmy Carter, former President of the USA, was born at 1.00 pm GMT on the 1 October 1924 in the town of Plains, Georgia. At the moment of his birth Jupiter was exactly on the MC and Mars was on the Ascendant at Teheran, capital of Iran. When one planet is on the MC and another on the Ascendant they form an aspect known as a mundane square, or paran. The interpretation is the same as for an ordinary square, but is more likely to affect circumstances than character. The great British astrologer, Charles Carter, wrote that this aspect brings 'extremist tendencies in politics'. So it was that the extremist politics of the Islamic fundamentalists in Iran resulted in the taking of American hostages and the destruction of Carter's presidency.

somewhere in the world. In fact, it is found that each planet occupies all four angles simultaneously, although in different places. Uranus may be on the Midheaven in Tokyo, on the Ascendant in Iran, on the IC in the middle of the Atlantic and on the Descendant in Hawaii. When projected on to a map of the world all the places on which one planet is on a particular angle connect up to form a line which goes right round the globe. The Midheaven and IC lines run directly north to south while the Ascendant and Descendant lines curve, running generally in a north-westerly or south-easterly direction. Everywhere under a particular line comes under the influence of that line so that everywhere on the Jupiter-Midheaven line tends to be beneficial for the career, while everywhere on the Uranus-Descendant line may bring lively partnerships with unusual people.

A strange feature noticed on astro-cartography maps, which the ordinary horoscope completely fails to show, is that certain latitudes become important. These latitudes are those at which two planetary lines cross, which means that each planet is exactly conjunct one of the angles. When several crossing points occur at the same latitude, then the entire latitude becomes charged with the potential for life-changing events, even if the person never sets foot in the place itself. When President Jimmy Carter's astro-cartography map was drawn up, it was found that his Jupiter-Midheaven and Mars-Ascendant lines crossed almost exactly over Teheran. On the same latitude were the crossing points of the Saturn-Midheaven and Pluto-Descendant lines, and the Jupiter Ascendant with the Neptune-IC and Venus IC lines. This is a powerful combination of planets suggesting overconfidence, conflict, deception and crisis, and even though Carter never went to Teheran, it was the taking of the American hostages by the Iranian revolutionary guards in 1979 which eventually destroyed his presidency.

Astro-cartography shows up the fate of another American president with equal force. At his birth John Kennedy's Pluto was within a few degrees of the Midheaven at Dallas, with the result that his Pluto-Midheaven line runs exactly through that city. In addition, there were four crossings on exactly the same latitude as Dallas: Mars-Midheaven and Uranus-Descendant, Uranus-IC and Mars-Descendant, Mars-Ascendant and Neptune-IC, Uranus-Ascendant and Sun-IC. This is a striking combination whose negative potential warns of the threat of violent accidents (Mars and Uranus) with deception (Neptune). It was where the latitude of these four points crossed the Pluto line that President Kennedy was murdered.

Using transits and progressions, the principle of astro-cartography can be applied to horoscopes other than birth charts, for example, for the founding of new states. Astro-cartography maps are also often drawn for new moons, full moons and eclipses to discover where their effect will be strongest. The only trouble is that they are almost impossible to calculate without a computer, if only because the calculations take so long. Thirty years ago enthusiasts worked out their astro-cartography maps with great patience and skill, but these days most people rely on the computer services of Californian astrologer Jim Lewis who has specialized in promoting this fascinating branch of astrology.

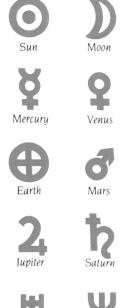

Sun

Moon

Mercury

Venus

Earth

Mars

Jupiter

Saturn

Uranus

Neptune

Pluto

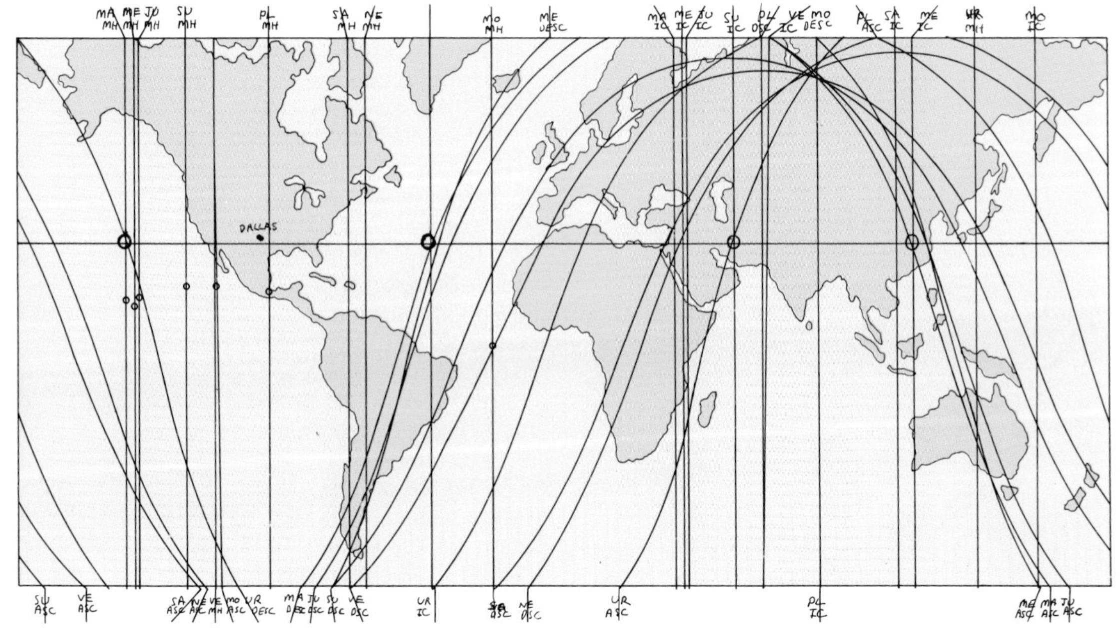

Astro-Cartography Map for John Kennedy

*President Kennedy's Astro-cartography map cast for his birth time of 8.00 pm GMT on 29 May 1917, shows Pluto on the MC at Dallas, the scene of his assassination in 1963. Four other 'crossing points' occur on exactly the same latitude, three of them involving Mars. This map is produced by permission of Astro*Carto*Graphy. Astro*Carto*Graphy is the registered trademark used by Californian astrologer Jim Lewis*

The Astrological Journey
The belief that it is possible to embark on a spiritual journey through the planets or the signs of the zodiac occurs in a number of different traditions.
In ancient Rome, the adept began the journey on Earth and, using religious discipline and ritual, progressed through the planets finally arriving at Saturn. As this is the most distant of the planets it was believed that it was closest to the stars, and to heaven.
Medieval alchemists reversed the direction. In their practice they attempted to transmute base metal into gold using mercury. Astrologically this equates to a journey commencing at Saturn, the ruler of lead and culminating at the Sun, the ruler of gold, on the way passing through Mercury, the teacher of wisdom. This represents the desire to attain enlightenment and transcend the bondage of physical life.
Earlier traditions sought no final destination, believing that the spiritual journey was endless. Myths described the circular passage of the Sun through the 12 signs or, in some cases, the 13 lunar months.
Modern astrologers have replaced the spiritual dimension with a belief in the psychological process. In each case the spur is the human desire for a more fulfilling experience and greater wisdom.

ASTROLOGY, PSYCHOLOGY AND MYTHOLOGY

For the beginner interpretation is very much a question of coping with the routine analysis of the chart but, with experience, reading the horoscope becomes second nature. Once astrologers reach this level they bring their own preferences and personalities to their work. Some become traditionalists, looking to ancient astrology for their inspiration, others experiment with the latest techniques, but an increasing number are looking to mythology and psychology to provide depth and colour in the horoscope.

Advanced psychological astrology has reached an impressive level of sophistication in recent years with consideration of such processes as compensation and projection. When compensation occurs there is an unconscious need to develop qualities opposite to those in the birth chart – the intuitive Piscean, for example, trying to become an intellectual Gemini or a practical Virgo, or the diplomatic Libran struggling to become a fiery Arien. Projection assumes that the qualities of the birth chart are transferred to other people. This might occur in the case of a man who finds his feminine and maternal Moon in Cancer difficult to accept and spends his life under the domination of maternal Moon-Cancer women.

The astrologer's job in these cases is to enable the individual to understand these processes and achieve some measure of conscious control over them. To help in this work an increasing number of astrologers are turning to psychotherapy, using techniques such as Jungian analysis, gestalt and psychosynthesis together with regular astrological analysis, although special aptitude and training are required.

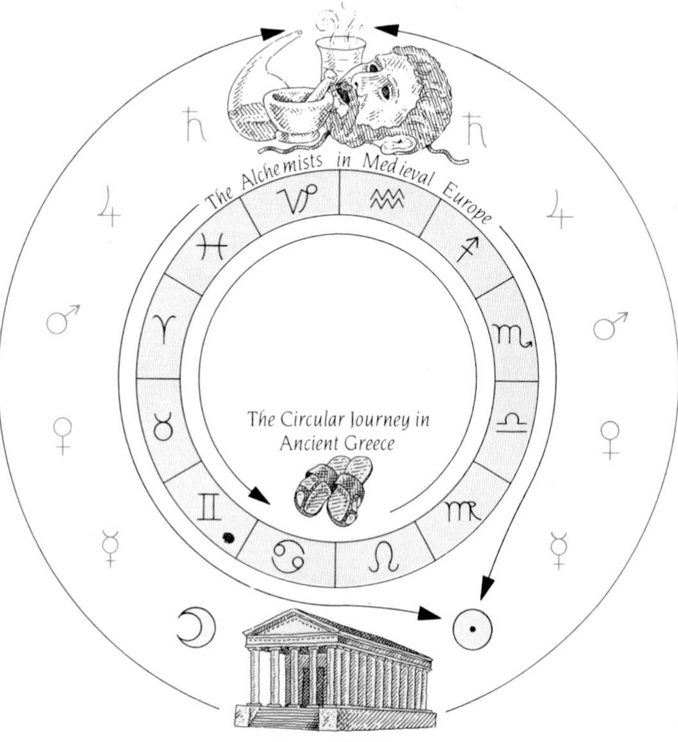

Above all the astrologer must continually ask questions – how does a sign respond under certain conditions? how do the signs deal with anger or frustration? what are their ideals? how do they cope with success or failure? Such questions may seem obvious, but the astrologer who ceases to question stagnates.

Underlying the belief in astrology as a set of psychological processes are the ancient myths which describe metaphorically the purpose of life as a journey through the stars. Sometimes these myths were based on the journey of the Sun through the signs of the zodiac, or in even earlier times through the 13 lunar months. The labours of Hercules constitute one such myth. Each labour represents for Hercules a great challenge and the way in which he overcomes it contains an astrological meaning. The essence of this meaning lies in a discovery of the 'greater purpose' of each zodiacal sign. This mythical attitude turns the normal conception of the Sun sign on its head. In everyday practice the Sun sign is treated as the simple foundation from which more complex interpretations are constructed using the other planets, aspects and so on; many astrologers are contemptuous of the simplicity of popular Sun sign astrology. However, this particular mythical approach implies a far deeper role for the Sun sign: the individual's ultimate task is the discovery and development of his or her Sun sign's 'greater purpose' and all the other factors in the horoscope are subordinated to this end. The discovery of the Sun sign may be portrayed as the culmination of a journey around the horoscope. A complete voyage around the zodiac itself necessitates the discovery of all 12 signs, a complete cycle of psychological or spiritual experience.

Other myths relate to the spiritual journey through the planets which are climbed like a ladder. Beginning on Earth the ladder takes the seeker to the Moon, Mercury, Venus, the Sun and Jupiter and culminates at Saturn, the keeper of time, the lord of wisdom, and known as the Sun of the night. If the initiate passes the tests set by Saturn, he will find enlightenment and salvation.

ASTROLOGICAL MODELS OF THE PSYCHE. Among the many models of the human psyche devised to explain human behaviour a number have been correlated with astrological symbolism. There are no scientifically measurable analogies because both psychology and astrology are human studies which depend very largely on personal interpretation. It is possible to establish correlations between astrology and recorded events and between psychology and human behaviour, but to compare astrology with psychology is to compare two different systems of judgment. It is fascinating, however, that they seem to work so well together, and their interaction has added a new dimension to modern natal astrology.

One of the most effective psychological systems was devised by C. G. Jung — so much so that Jungian astrology is now recognized as a separate development within mainstream astrology. As there is no standard correlation between Jung's system and the traditional planetary meanings, individual astrologers are able to devise the connections which work best for them. The following correlation between the two systems is based on the work of Liz Greene, an astrologer and Jungian analyst who has done much work in this field.

If the human psyche is pictured as a circle, a shape appropriate for astrology, then the centre is occupied by the Self. This is the very core of human existence, which is not contained in any one of the astrological symbols, and which spiritually corresponds to the soul.

The top half of the circle is occupied by the conscious mind. The Sun is the Ego, the essential recognizable personality. The Moon is the Persona, the socially acceptable mask that people wear in public. Venus is the anima, the female psyche in men, and Mars is the animus, the male psyche in women. Mercury can be related to different archetypes but in general should be regarded as the force which facilitates communication between all the other planets. Its vital role is well illustrated in medieval alchemy: Mercury was the metal which, it was hoped, would accomplish the transmutation of lead into gold, mythologically the conversion of the dark Sun of the night into the brilliant Sun of the day.

Across the middle of the circle, from left to right, runs the realm of the personal unconscious, occupied by Jupiter and Saturn. Usually these planets are referred to as the impersonal planets, and describe the characteristics of generations, but in this Jungian model their definition is slightly altered. Saturn has a special function as the 'Shadow', which Jung saw as the accumulation of all those characteristics, which for personal or social reasons, are suppressed. Such a role for Saturn, firmly rooted in the Greek conception of the 'Sun of the night', provides an appropriate psychological cause for the difficulties it signifies astrologically.

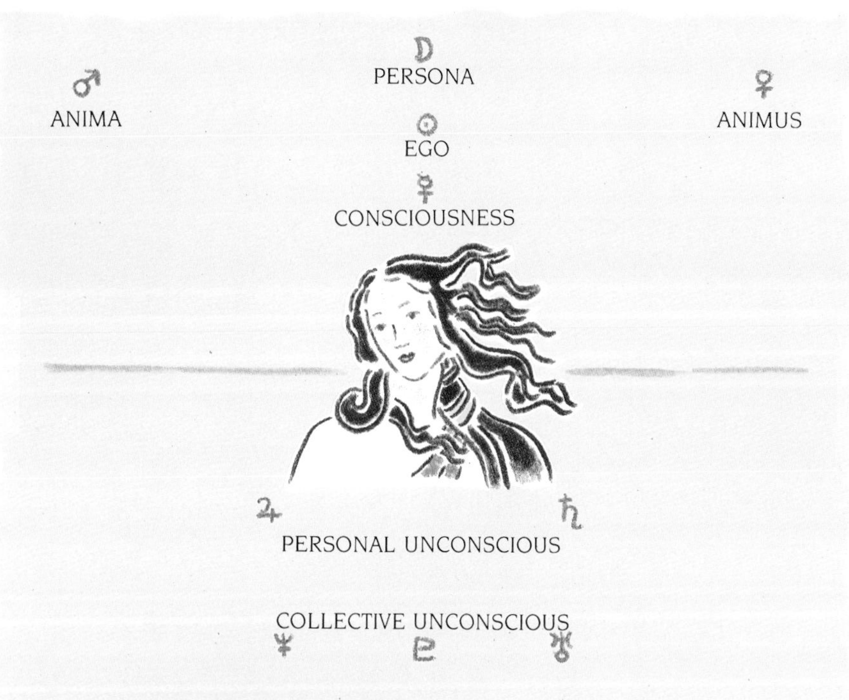

An Astrological Model of the Psyche Comparing the Planets to the Theories of C. G. Jung

The bottom part of the circle is the realm of the collective unconscious, the deep layer of existence which unites all members of the human race. In this deepest level live the three transpersonal planets, Uranus, Neptune and Pluto, the symbols of upheaval in society and transformation in human beings.

In practical interpretation the Jungian system is used to point out the unconscious pressures of which people are unaware, these being shown most clearly by aspects between conscious and unconscious planets. For example, a Saturn-Venus opposition ordinarily brings difficulties in love and marriage, and the traditional astrologer would make this statement and leave it at that. However, the Jungian astrologer can see the pressures of the unresolved Shadow (Saturn) causing difficulties (opposition) in the person's expression of his or her desires and feelings (Venus) and conclude that deep psychological conflicts may result in an unsatisfactory relationship. Using the techniques of counselling and therapy the skilled astrologer can then get to the psychological root of the problem and help the person give up the negative behaviour pattern. The individual may then be able to develop the positive facets of the Venus-Saturn relationship: loyalty, fidelity, responsibility and stability.

When the transpersonal planets are emphasized, perhaps by aspect to the personal planets, this indicates people who are at the forefront of change in their generation, driven by historical pressure to create new ideas, new fashions and new life styles.

CHAPTER 16 ASKING QUESTIONS: HORARY ASTROLOGY

In former times, when births were often not recorded, astrologers relied heavily on horoscopes cast for the asking of questions. People who had no idea of their birth time could, therefore, receive advice as detailed as those with an accurate natal chart.

Horoscopes cast to answer questions are known as horary charts, and the branch of astrology used to interpret the charts is known as horary astrology.

Horary charts are useful either on their own or used with natal astrology. Often the horary chart can provide a prediction of a future event when the natal chart can only give a rough indication of future trends.

Prediction is not the only purpose of horary astrology. Answers to questions posed about the future are often used as a guide to the best course of action, showing the consequences of contrasting options. Questions may also be asked about past events, about the identity of unknown people, or even about philosophical problems.

Horary astrology requires a greater degree of precision and clarity than the practice of psychological astrology. Once it is properly understood, horary methods may be applied to the study of birth charts and the other branches of astrology.

Locating Significance
Horary astrology places central importance on the house cusp rulers. A planet which rules the sign on the house cusp is the significator of the area of life ruled by that house. The astrologer works only with those significators which are relevant to the question.

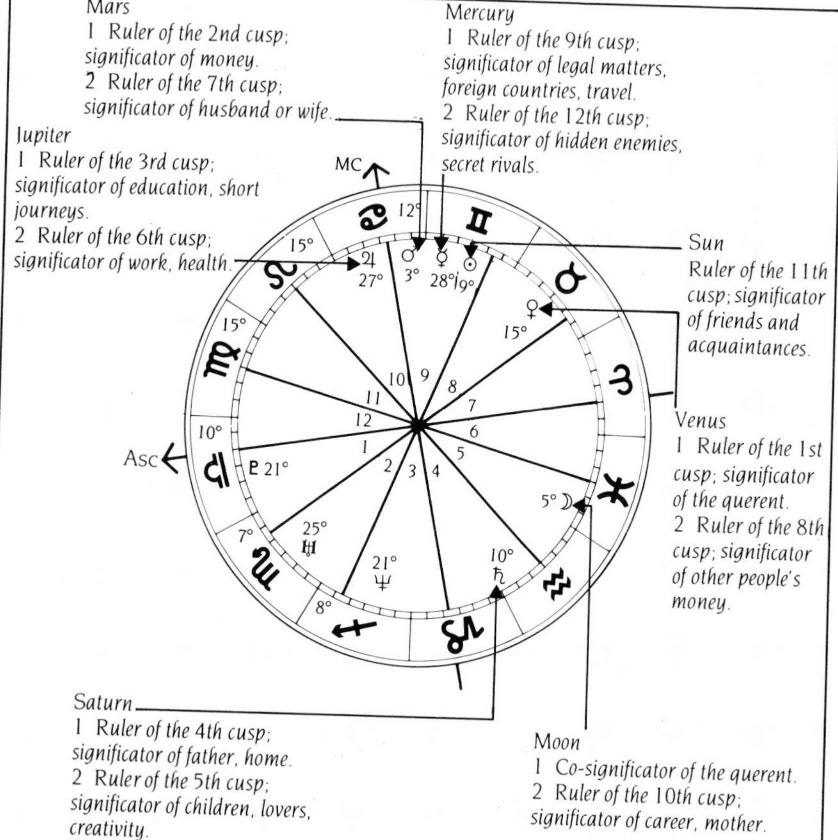

Mars
1 Ruler of the 2nd cusp; significator of money.
2 Ruler of the 7th cusp; significator of husband or wife.
Mercury
1 Ruler of the 9th cusp; significator of legal matters, foreign countries, travel.
2 Ruler of the 12th cusp; significator of hidden enemies, secret rivals.
Jupiter
1 Ruler of the 3rd cusp; significator of education, short journeys.
2 Ruler of the 6th cusp; significator of work, health.
Sun
Ruler of the 11th cusp; significator of friends and acquaintances.
Venus
1 Ruler of the 1st cusp; significator of the querent.
2 Ruler of the 8th cusp; significator of other people's money.
Saturn
1 Ruler of the 4th cusp; significator of father, home.
2 Ruler of the 5th cusp; significator of children, lovers, creativity.
Moon
1 Co-significator of the querent.
2 Ruler of the 10th cusp; significator of career, mother.
MC
Asc
12°
15°
27°
3°
28°
19°
15°
15°
10°
21°
25°
7°
21°
10°
5°
8°
1
2
3
4
5
6
7
8
9
10
11
12

CALCULATION. The calculation of the horoscope follows exactly the same method as for the birth chart. The place is always the location of the astrologer and the time is always that at which the astrologer becomes aware of the question; if the question is asked in a letter written in London and sent to an astrologer in Los Angeles then the chart is set for Los Angeles at the moment the astrologer reads the letter.

LOCATING SIGNIFICANCE. Unlike natal astrology, horary astrology uses only those parts of the horoscope which are directly relevant to the question. When complex issues are involved the entire chart may be called into play. In some cases as few as two planets and two houses may be sufficient.

The first stage of interpretation is to relate the question to the horoscope. This is known as locating significance and is always accomplished in the first instance by assigning querent and quesited to their relevant houses and planets.

The querent – the person asking the question – is always ruled by the first house. The planet ruling the sign on the first cusp – the Ascendant – is the **significator of the querent**. The Moon is always the **co-significator of the querent** and often reveals the outcome of a situation when the querent's own significator does not.

The quesited – the subject of the question – is always ruled by the appropriate house. For example, finance is ruled by the second house, health by the sixth and career by the tenth. The planet ruling the sign on the cusp of the house is the **significator of the quesited**. Beginners should use only the seven traditional planets as significators.

THE PLANETS

Rulerships of house cusps provide planets with specific roles in the horary chart. Additional background information is provided by their ordinary rulerships. For example, if the sixth house cusp (ruling health) is in Aries, then Mars the ruler of Aries is the significator of health.

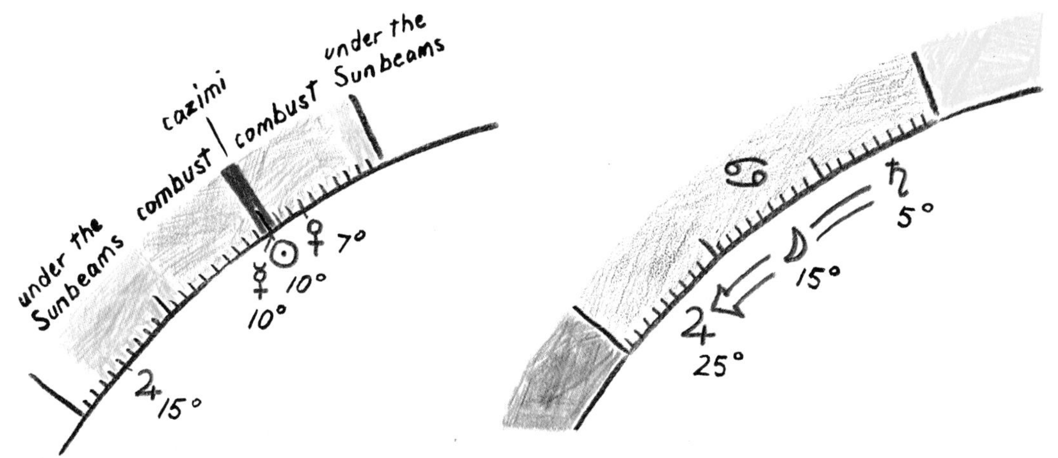

Left: Solar Aspects
These three aspects with the Sun, Cazimi, Combust and Under the Sunbeams, only apply to planets in the same sign as the Sun. In this example Mercury is Cazimi (greatly strengthened), Venus is Combust (greatly weakened) and Jupiter is Under the Sunbeams (mildly weakened).

Right: Applying and Separating Aspects
Separating aspects represent past circumstances and applying aspects indicate future circumstances. In this example the Moon is separating from a conjunction with Saturn and applying to a conjunction with Jupiter. In a horary chart a basic interpretation of this pattern sees the querent (the Moon) leaving behind restrictive conditions (Saturn) and approaching a period of opportunity (Jupiter).

Beneficity and Maleficity. Central to horary astrology are the old strict designations of malefic and benefic planets. Jupiter (the greater benefic) and Venus (the lesser benefic) are in general the most helpful planets, bringing fortunate circumstances; Saturn (the greater malefic) and Mars (the lesser malefic) are the most difficult planets, bringing delay, obstruction or conflict. However, the benefic and malefic labels are dropped if the planet concerned is a significator of either the querent or the quesited. For example, if Capricorn is rising then the significator of the querent is Saturn, the ruler of Capricorn. This implies that the person asking the question may be of a 'saturnine' disposition, cautious and perhaps concerned with responsibility, but there are no malefic connotations. The degree of maleficity or beneficity is also varied by the planet's house position and whether it is dignified or debilitated. For example, if Saturn is retrograde (which always weakens planets in horary charts) and in Cancer, the sign of its Detriment, then its obstructive power is considerably lessened.

The Sun, Moon and Mercury are all neutral. The Sun, however, can behave either as a benefic or malefic depending on three additional aspects (see below). The three modern planets Uranus, Neptune and Pluto, have not been definitely assigned as either benefic or malefic although they are generally regarded as malefic. Caution and reliance on personal experience is the best course with these planets.

In addition to the planets other bodies have malefic and benefic properties. The Part of Fortune and the North Node are benefic and the South Node is malefic. The major fixed stars are also important. Spica and Regulus are strongly benefic and Algol, Vindemiatrix and Scheat are powerful malefics.

Aspects between significators – querent or quesited – and benefics indicate positive answers, and those between significators and malefics incline towards negative solutions.

Dignities and Debilities. Exaltation and Fall, Dignity and Detriment are vital to the horary chart. If a significator is in its Exaltation or Dignity then it is greatly strengthened and a positive outcome is suggested. Significators in Fall or Detriment are weakened and the chances of a negative outcome are increased.

THE ASPECTS. Whereas in natal astrology the use of additional and minor aspects can help focus on a particular situation in detail, in horary astrology they confuse the issues. Therefore, of the common aspects, only the five major ones are used – the conjunction, sextile, square, trine and opposition.

There are, however, three additional aspects which must be used, all of which are varieties of conjunctions with the Sun:

Under the Sunbeams occurs when a planet is in the same sign as the Sun and within 17°. The planet is moderately weakened.
Combust occurs when a planet is in a regular conjunction with the Sun within an orb of 8° (some astrologers use smaller orbs). It is said to be 'burnt up' by the heat of the Sun and is seriously weakened.
Cazimi describes the greatly strengthened state of a planet when it is within 0° 17′ of the Sun.

Considering the Sun's normal role as the giver of life the destructive power of Under the Sunbeams and Combust needs explaining. In the hot dry countries where astrology originated the Sun is not necessarily a benevolent planet for it can bring drought, famine and death. These two aspects, therefore, embody a very ancient tradition concerning the Sun which has been lost in the temperate countries of Europe where the Sun is regarded as benevolent. In Cazimi the Sun returns to its usual function as the lord of life.

Separation and Application. Applying aspects indicate future events, developments and circumstances and separating aspects indicate those in the past. This is a very important distinction which enables the changing flow of circumstances to be properly plotted. If a question is asked about a past event it is the separating aspects that provide the answer, if about the future, the applying aspects.

When checking the condition of an aspect it is necessary to look ahead to make sure that the separating aspect does not turn retrograde and return to an exact aspect for a second and, perhaps, a third time.

When two planets form an exact aspect this signifies the occurrence of an event, the nature of the event being described by the planets.

An ephemeris such as *Raphael's Ephemeris*, which gives the exact times at which every planetary aspect occurs, should be used.

The Moon's Aspects. The Moon is the fastest moving planet and its aspects have an overall importance in describing past and future circumstances. The only aspects that should be taken into account are those which are exact during the Moon's transit of the sign it occupies at the time the question is asked. The Moon's final exact major aspect before it leaves the sign reveals the final outcome. The best results are generally indicated by sextiles or trines to the benefic planets (Venus and Jupiter) and the best possible outcome is found in a trine to the Sun. Difficult aspects to Mars or Saturn generally indicate negative consequences.

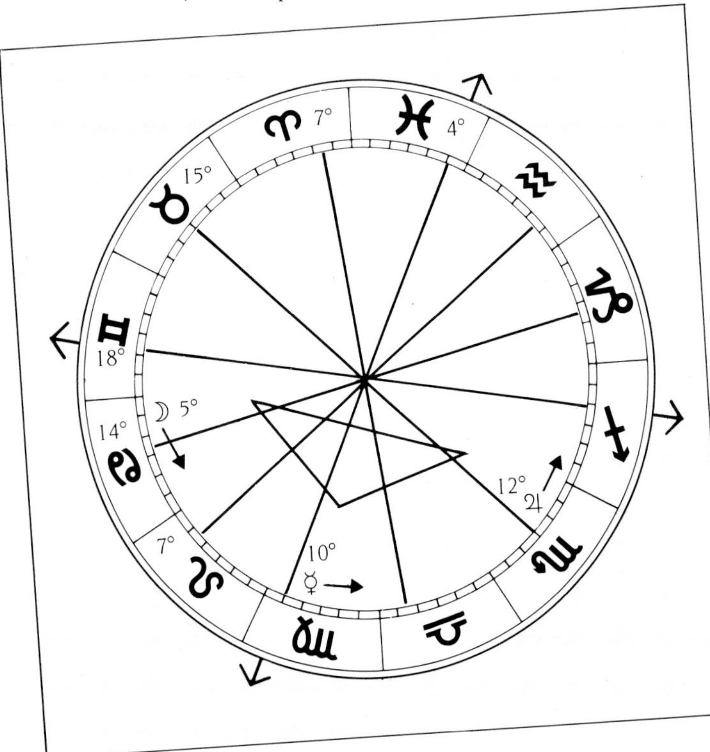

Positive answers: Applying Aspects A sure indication of a positive outcome for any question asked about a future event is found when the significators are in applying aspects. In this chart, set for a question concerning marriage, the querent is shown by Mercury, ruler of the first cusp, and the Moon; marriage is shown by Jupiter, the ruler of the seventh cusp. All three planets are in applying harmonious aspects, indicating that the answer to the question, 'Will I get married?' is yes.

Benefic and Malefic. Harmonious and tense aspects are known in horary astrology by their traditional descriptions benefic and malefic. The benefic aspects (sextile and trine) facilitate the smooth passage of events and the malefic aspects (square and opposition) bring difficult conditions which obstruct the smooth flow of events. The conjunction is neutral.

Astrology deals with a cosmic frame of reality which extends beyond human desires, and it is quite possible for a harmonious aspect to indicate a bad outcome in human terms. For example, if a question concerns the launch of a ship but the chart indicates that the ship might sink, then benefic aspects indicate that the ship might sink easily.

Fixed Stars. The only aspect used with Fixed Stars is the conjunction and a maximum orb of 1° is permitted.

THE HOUSES. It is important to be clear about the different house meanings in order to be sure that the right house has been chosen to represent the question.

Turning the Chart. The practice of turning the chart has slipped out of use among natal astrologers in this century, but it is absolutely central to the answering of a horary question. The principle is that each of the 12 houses can take on any of the meanings of any of the other houses. This is much simpler than it sounds.

A frequent example occurs in questions concerning partners, wives and husbands. The partner is ruled by the seventh house. This house then becomes the first house of the partner. The eighth house of the chart becomes the second house of the partner, the ninth house becomes the third, and so on. Therefore, the eighth house of the chart (the second of the partner) rules the partner's money and possessions. The ninth house of the chart (the third of the partner) rules the partner's brothers and sisters.

If the question concerns the father, ruled by the fourth house of the chart, then the fifth house becomes the father's second house and rules his money.

Turning the chart increases the versatility of a horoscope to a greater extent than any other technique, except perhaps harmonics, which are not used in horary astrology.

House systems. The Equal House system should not be used for horary charts. Any of the other house systems may be used. Placidus is the most common although Campanus, Regiomontanus and Topocentric are also popular. The calculation of these house

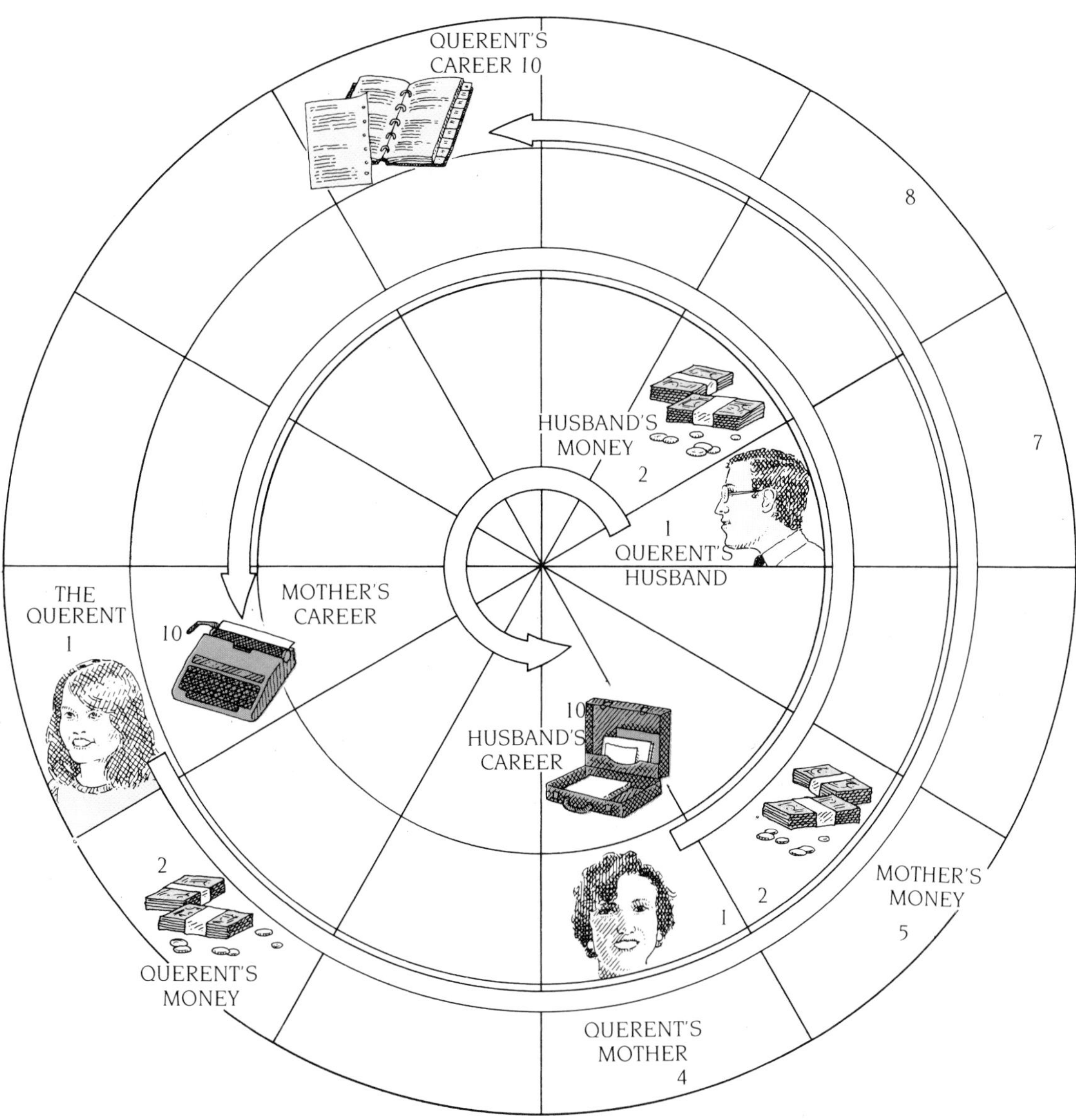

systems is exactly the same as for Equal Houses, but an additional table of houses must be acquired. These are available, or can be ordered, from most bookshops.

CONSIDERATIONS BEFORE JUDGMENT

Traditionally astrologers have believed that certain horoscopes could not be interpreted; and that if they were, the judgment might be faulty. The rules used to assess whether a chart may be interpreted are known as the **considerations before judgment**, and if a horoscope is passed under these rules then it is known as **radical**.

STRICTURES AGAINST JUDGMENT. The strictures against judgment do not necessarily forbid interpretation of the chart. In some circumstances they may warn that the astrologer's judgment may be faulty or that discretion is necessary and no public answer should be given. There is no commonly agreed set of strictures and most of them allow for certain exceptions.

The major exception occurs when the Moon is void of course.

A planet is void of course when it leaves the sign it is in without making any more exact major aspects. It can still be in orb of aspect with another planet so long as it is separating from the exact aspect. Strictly speaking when the Moon is void of course, the chart should not be read. However, some astrologers consider that the Moon void of course brings a standard answer that 'nothing will come of the matter asked about', in effect a negative answer. So, if the question is 'will I buy the house?', the answer is 'no', and if the question is 'will I fail my exam?' the answer is

Turning the Chart
In this example, set for a question involving a woman (the querent), her mother and husband, and the incomes and careers of each, seven houses altogether are involved. If the fourth house represents the mother, then the fifth (the mother's second) is the mother's money and the first (the mother's tenth) is her career. The seventh house rules the querent's husband, the eighth (the husband's second) his money and the fourth (the husband's tenth) his career.

Negative Answers

1) Two significators applying to an exact aspect indicate success, but if either of them first makes an aspect with a third planet, it can interfere with the chances of a positive outcome and even change the answer to a negative one.

In this case the two significators, Mercury and Jupiter, are in an applying conjunction. However, before Mercury reaches Jupiter, it makes a conjunction with Saturn. Saturn represents a powerful restriction, symbolically blocking Mercury and bringing a negative answer.

2) If the significators are separating from an aspect, or not in aspect at all, then the immediate indications are negative.

3) If one significator turns retrograde before an exact aspect is completed then the answer is negative. In this case Mercury applies to a conjunction with Venus, indicating success, but turns retrograde before making the exact aspect.

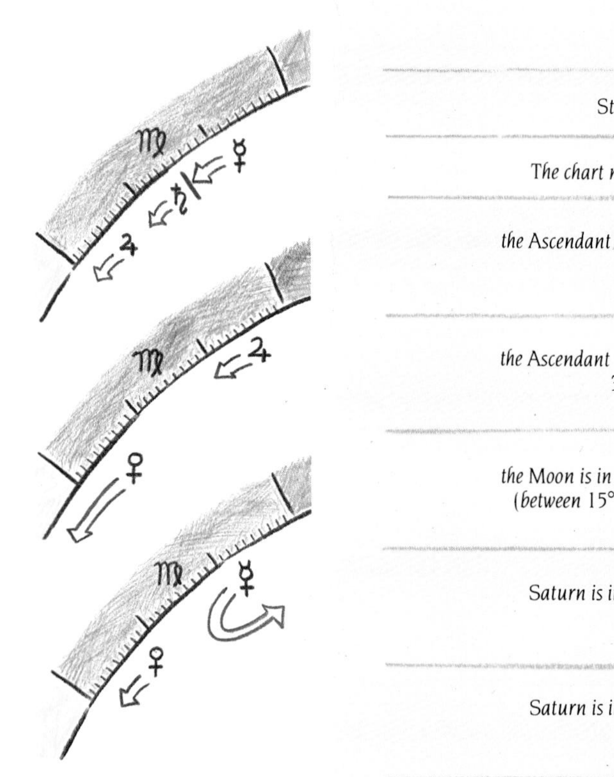

also 'no'. In most cases this answer is satisfactory, although bearing in mind the fact that the void of course Moon is a stricture, the astrologer should exercise caution when dealing with clients on such a basis.

The other strictures, and their exceptions, are given in the table on this page.

ANSWERING THE QUESTION. The basic rules of interpretation are relatively simple, yet unless the chart itself is clear, considerable skill and subtlety is required. Often the horoscope gives contradictory indications from which the astrologer must derive the correct answer.

Positive Answers – Perfection. A positive answer can be given when either of the significators of the querent applies to an exact major aspect with the significator of the quesited before either planet changes sign. The conjunction gives the best sign of success and trines and sextiles also indicate a favourable outcome. Squares and oppositions indicate a positive answer if the significators are otherwise strong by sign, house and aspect. If, however, the significators are weak then success may be eluded or only gained after much difficulty, or in spite of adverse circumstances.

When the significators are not in aspect they can still be brought together through either Translation of Light or Collection of Light. In Translation of Light a faster moving planet applies from a major aspect with one significator to a major aspect with the other before any of the three changes signs. Collection of Light occurs when two significators apply to a major aspect with a third slower moving planet before any of them changes signs. Both suggest a positive answer.

A positive answer is also likely if the significator of the quesited is in the first house. This implies that the querent controls the situation and that the outcome is assured.

The prospect of a positive answer is increased if the significators are in Dignity or Exaltation or well aspected to other bodies such as the Part of Fortune or benefic fixed stars.

Negative Answers – Denial of Perfection: If perfection depends on two significators reaching an exact aspect and if either first makes an exact aspect to a third planet, perfection may be denied. If, however, the relevant aspect is a benefic aspect to a benefic planet, such as a trine to Jupiter or a sextile to Venus, this suggests that although

STRICTURES AGAINST JUDGMENT

Stricture	*Exception*
The chart may not read if:	*The stricture does not apply if:*
the Ascendant is between 0° and 3°	*the querent's Ascendant is between 0° and 3°*
the Ascendant is between 27° and 30°	*the querent's Ascendant is between 27° and 30°*
the Moon is in the Via Combusta (between 15° ♎ and 15° ♏)	*the querent's Moon is in the Via Combusta*
Saturn is in the 7th house	*the question was asked by the astrologer*
Saturn is in the 1st house	*the question was not asked by the astrologer*

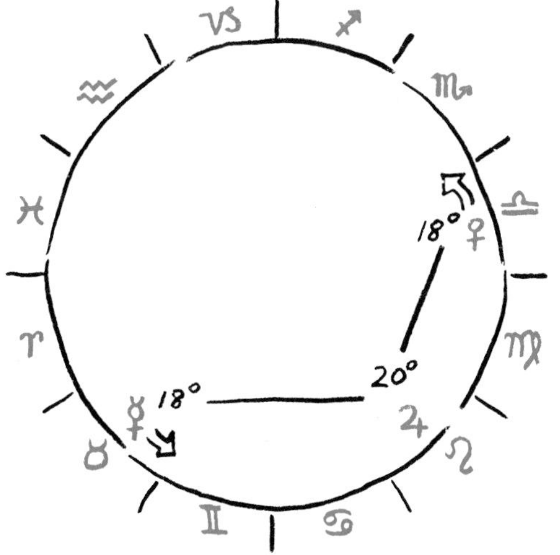

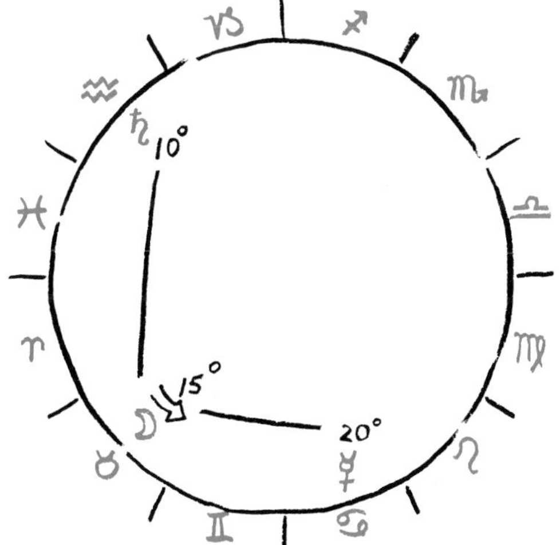

Left: Collection of Light
In this example the two significators, Venus and Mercury, are not in aspect. By itself this suggests a negative answer. However, Jupiter is collecting the light which means that Mercury is applying to a square and Venus to a sextile. The two significators are brought together by Jupiter and the result is a positive outcome.

Right: Translation of Light
In this example the two significators, Mercury and Saturn, are not in aspect. Normally this would indicate a negative answer. However, the Moon is translating the light from Saturn to Mercury which means that it is separating from a square to Saturn and applying to a sextile to Mercury. Given that there were no other difficulties in the chart, this would bring the two significators together resulting in a positive answer.

circumstances may change the answer will be positive. Malefic aspects to benefic planets and benefic aspects to malefic planets suggest difficulties which may be overcome. Malefic aspects to malefic planets, of which the worst are oppositions to Saturn, invariably bring negative answers.

The chances of a negative answer are enhanced if the significators are weakened in any other way, for example, by being in Detriment or Fall, retrograde or conjunct a malefic fixed star.

ruler of the 1st cusp (the ...), is receiving applying ... from Mercury, ruler of the ...sp (marriage), and the co-significator of the ...t. This assures a positive

MC
19°
10°
20°
15°
4°
ASC
10°
18°
26°
26°

The Moon, the co-significator of the querent, is applying to an opposition with Saturn. This shows an approaching difficulty.

MC
10°
18°
8°
16°
0°
ASC
20°
25°
18°
26°
5°

Mercury, ruler of the 7th cusp (marriage), is separating from a trine to Jupiter, ruler of the 1st cusp (the querent).

Below left: Questions about marriage are ruled by the seventh house. In this chart, cast for the question 'Should I get married?' the querent is signified by Jupiter, the ruler of the first cusp. The querent is in a strong position, Jupiter being in its own sign, Sagittarius. The proposed marriage partner is signified by Mercury, the ruler of the seventh cusp. Mercury is in the querent's house (showing a very close contact) and is applying to a square with Jupiter: as the significators meet the marriage should go ahead. In addition, the Moon, the co-significator of the querent, is in Libra (the sign of partnership), the seventh house (the house of marriage), and is applying to aspects with both significators. The answer is a resounding yes.

Below right: This chart is also set for the question 'Should I get married?' But in this case the answer is a firm no. The querent is signified by Jupiter, ruler of the first cusp, and the proposed partner by Mercury, ruler of the seventh cusp. The two planets are in a trine, showing a close relationship, but as Mercury is faster moving it is separating from the aspect. The chances of a marriage are, therefore, receding. The negative answer is confirmed by the approach of the Moon, the querent's co-significator, to an opposition with Saturn, showing that progress will be blocked.

CHAPTER 17 POLITICS AND WORLD AFFAIRS: MUNDANE ASTROLOGY

Mundane astrology is the astrology of world affairs. It takes as its subject the entire sweep of world history, the rise and fall of nations and even of religions. Its scope extends from human affairs – politics, economics, fashion, the arts, war and revolution – to the physical environment in all its forms, from plant growth to the weather, and disturbance such as volcanic eruptions and earthquakes.

The Planets in Mundane Astrology

The Sun	*The centre of authority, monarch, leader or other figurehead; power, authority and government in general.*
The Moon	*The general public, the 'masses', democracy and public opinion; women, family life, sense of community; agriculture.*
Mercury	*Education, literature, propaganda, the media, communication.*
Venus	*The arts, fashion, music, theatre, pleasures, leisure activities; victory in war.*
Mars	*Agression, violence, war, soldiers.*
Jupiter	*Religion, philosophy, priests; prosperity, bankers, expansion; charities; the aristocracy and upper classes; publishers.*
Saturn	*Order, authority, limitation, taboos, conservatism, stability, tradition; the police and administration of law.*
Uranus	*Innovation, sudden change, revolution, anarchy, autocracy, radicalism, new ideologies; advanced technology (including nuclear energy).*
Neptune	*Idealism, reform, philanthropy; fashion, style, the arts (overlaps with Venus).*
Pluto	*Disruption, violence, crime, national decline and regeneration.*

In practice the subject is so broad that it is best to recognize different areas of interest and expertise so that political astrology can be distinguished from financial astrology and these in turn can be separated from the study of the physical environment.

Mundane horoscopes are cast both for events and for groups of people: for battles and wars, the launching of ships and space craft, the independence of nations, general elections and the coronation of kings and queens, for organizations such as trades unions and political parties. The simplest form of mundane horoscope is the composite chart which is drawn for the relationship between two people, and which overlaps with natal astrology. At the other end of the scale the horoscope for communist China represents hundreds of millions of people and the chart for the foundation of the United Nations organisation signifies a common venture uniting almost the entire population of the earth.

Mundane astrology differs from the other branches of the art in that horoscopes are drawn not only for human affairs but also for astronomical events which are then used to indicate the general trends for the coming weeks, months or years. The principal charts are those for the **ingresses** – the times of the entry of planets into new signs – and the fortnightly new Moons and full Moons.

The political astrologer also uses the techniques of the other branches of astrology, studying the natal charts of politicians and public figures, or asking horary questions to gain insights into specific situations. It is necessary to understand and study all the other forms of astrology and to have a grasp of current affairs.

HISTORY AND MYTHOLOGY

Just as the historian looks at history and gives significance to certain events so the astrologer looks at the horoscope and distributes significance amongst the various factors. Historical evidence is often extremely vague and open to differing interpretations, and even accepted facts may support completely different theories of historical change. Differing interpretations are deeply connected with myths and fashions current at a particular time.

There are two lessons for the mundane astrologer. First, caution and commonsense are necessary when equating historical events with astrological configurations. Second, handled with respect, astrology provides a mythic structure through which the apparently incomprehensible flow of history falls into place. Mundane astrology both

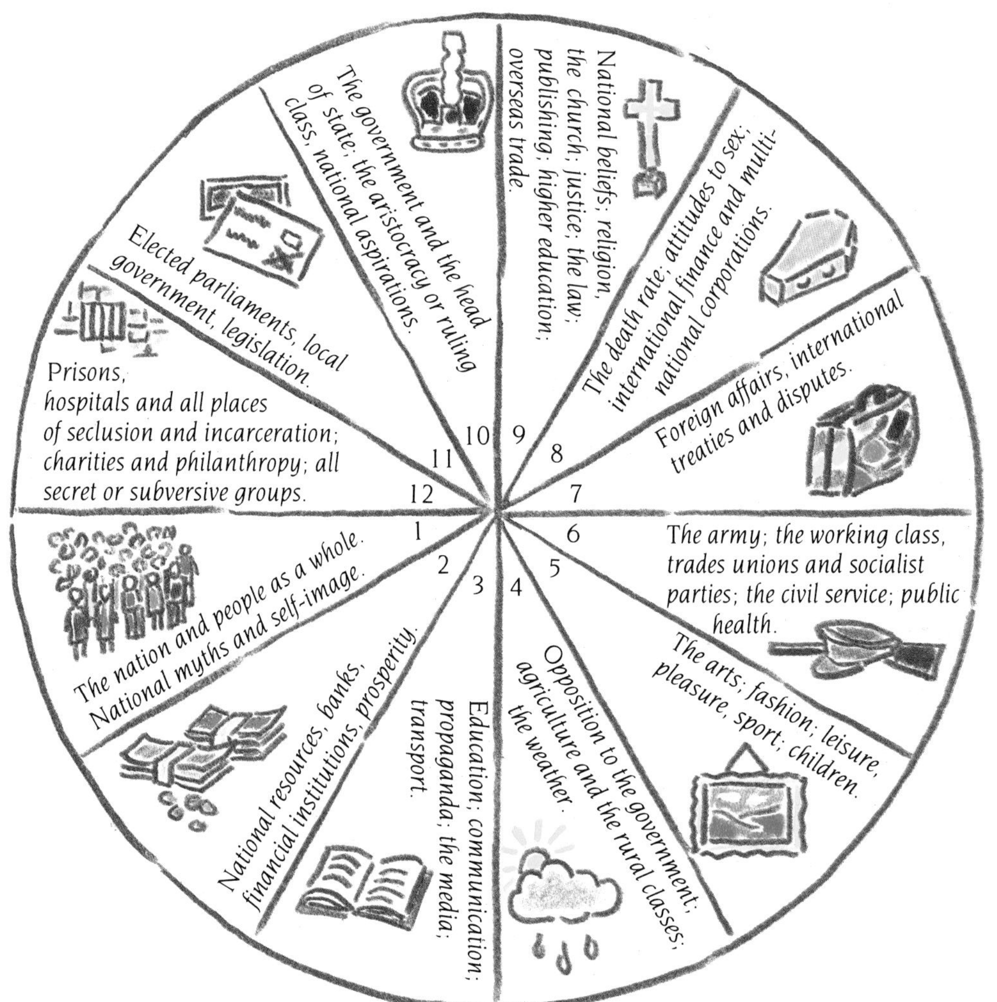

1
The nation and people as a whole. National myths and self-image.
2
National resources, banks, financial institutions, prosperity.
3
Education; communication; propaganda; the media; transport.
4
Opposition to the government; agriculture and the rural classes; the weather.
5
The arts; fashion; leisure, pleasure, sport; children.
6
The army; the working class, trades unions and socialist parties; the civil service; public health.
7
Foreign affairs, international treaties and disputes.
8
The death rate; attitudes to sex; international finance and multi-national corporations.
9
National beliefs; religion, the church; justice; the law; publishing; higher education; overseas trade.
10
The government and the head of state; the aristocracy or ruling class, national aspirations.
11
Elected parliaments, local government, legislation.
12
Prisons, hospitals and all places of seclusion and incarceration; charities and philanthropy; all secret or subversive groups.

The Houses in Mundane Astrology
The essential meanings of the houses are exactly the same as in natal astrology, but the interpretations are adapted to the circumstances of political life.

Aries

Taurus

Gemini

Cancer

Leo

Virgo

Libra

Scorpio

Sagittarius

Capricorn

Aquarius

Pisces

casts new light on recorded events and reveals the myths, beliefs and images which help bind society together into a homogeneous whole.

THE PLANETS IN THE SIGNS. The signs of the zodiac have exactly the same meanings as in natal astrology and the principles of interpreting planets in signs are as outlined in Chapter 4. These can be applied to mundane astrology at whatever level required. For example, Venus in Capricorn in natal astrology reveals an individual who is shy, conservative and practical in matters of love. In the horoscope of Nazi Germany, Venus was in Capricorn, a correlation with the subordination of all human relationships to the interests of the state: marriages between Germans and Jews were forbidden, and amongst Germans themselves individuals were selected to provide children on purely functional grounds – the creation of a 'master race'. A signature of Venus in Capricorn is found in the Nazi slogan 'Joy through Work', joy being Venus and work being Capricorn. Psychologically this corresponds to the suppression (Capricorn) of the feminine principle (Venus) in the German psyche, thus making possible the barbarity of war and genocide.

The interpretation of planets in signs in mundane astrology may be approached at different levels, exactly as in the natal chart, and is straightforward once natal principles have been understood. The interpretation of the outer planets through the signs is dealt with below.

THE TRANSPERSONAL PLANETS. Uranus, Neptune and Pluto symbolize the changes that take place from one generation to the next. Their movements are relevant to natal astrology as they continually make and unmake aspects to the personal planets. For example, while Uranus was in Cancer an entire generation of Sun-Cancers was born who differred from those that came before and after in that they found it difficult to accept Cancer's home-making qualities: Uranus upset them by continually demanding independence from domestic routine. Naturally this was strongest for all those with a close Sun-Uranus conjunction.

During the passage of Pluto through Leo an entire generation of Sun-Leos was born whose emotional intensity often lead to their being mistaken for Scorpios. Obviously this was strongest for those with the Sun in close conjunction with Pluto, but those with their Ascendants and Moons in Leo also bear the mark of Pluto.

URANUS THROUGH THE SIGNS
Aries (1927–35): creation of new forms of authority – the rise of fascism.

Taurus (1934–42): revolution in physical environment, trade and business.

Gemini (1941–49): new humanitarian ideals; crises in thought and ideology.

Cancer (1948–56): revolution in domestic and family life.

Leo (1955–62): rebellion against authority; rejection of tradition; artistic revolution.

Virgo (1962–69): technological revolution at work; antimaterialism.

Libra (1969–75): experimentation in human relationships and communication.

Scorpio (1974–81): quest for new answers to emotional problems, for solutions to age-old mysteries.

Sagittarius (1897–1904, 1981–89): expansiveness, innovation, exploration; challenge to religious conventions.

Capricorn (1904–12, 1988–96): crisis in all traditional and established structures.

Aquarius (1912–19, 1995–2003): revolution in ideas, radicalism; new forms of communication.

Pisces (1919–28): a quest for meaning, for new forms of mysticism.

NEPTUNE THROUGH THE SIGNS
Aries : belief in the values of the individual; religion of aggression.

Taurus : belief in material values, artistic beauty and the pursuit of great wealth and luxury.

Gemini (1887–1902): exploration in human thought; search for new forms of communication.

Cancer (1901–15): romance, nostalgia, belief in the past and tradition.

Leo (1914–29): belief in individuality, creative self-expression.

Virgo (1928–43): materialism in belief; conservatism in fashion.

Libra (1942–56): belief in peace and harmony; beauty in fashion; idealism in relationships.

Scorpio (1955–70): confrontation in fashion; emotional intensity in belief.

Sagittarius (1970–84): optimism expansiveness and mysticism in religion and fashion.

Capricorn (1984–98): conservative fashions; materialistic beliefs.

Aquarius (1998–2012): humanitarian ideals; thought and mysticism merge.

Pisces : romanticism; profound mysticism.

PLUTO THROUGH THE SIGNS
Aries : international conflict; the cult of the hero and man of action.

Taurus : economic revolution, transformation of material values.

Gemini (1882–1914): revolution in ideas.

Cancer (1914–39): revolution in home and family life.

Leo (1938–58): challenge to established structures; authoritarianism and individualism clash.

Virgo (1957–72): crisis in the environment; revolution in work.

Libra (1971–84): upheaval in the pattern of human relationships.

Scorpio (1984–95): sexual revolution; emotional confrontation; the need to investigate and experience life's mysteries.

Sagittarius : (1995–2008): revolution in air and space travel; emotional intensity in philosophy and religion.

Capricorn : material revolution; profound conservatism.

Aquarius : emotional commitment to humanitarian ideals; intellectual revolution; intolerance.

Pisces : mystical beliefs and fashion focus on need for emotional experience and confrontation.

Planetary Cycles
The outer planets combine to create the long-term cycles which indicate the ebb and flow of human ideals and behaviour. Each combination of planets has its own meaning and the length of the cycles – from one conjunction to the next – varies from 12 to almost 500 years.

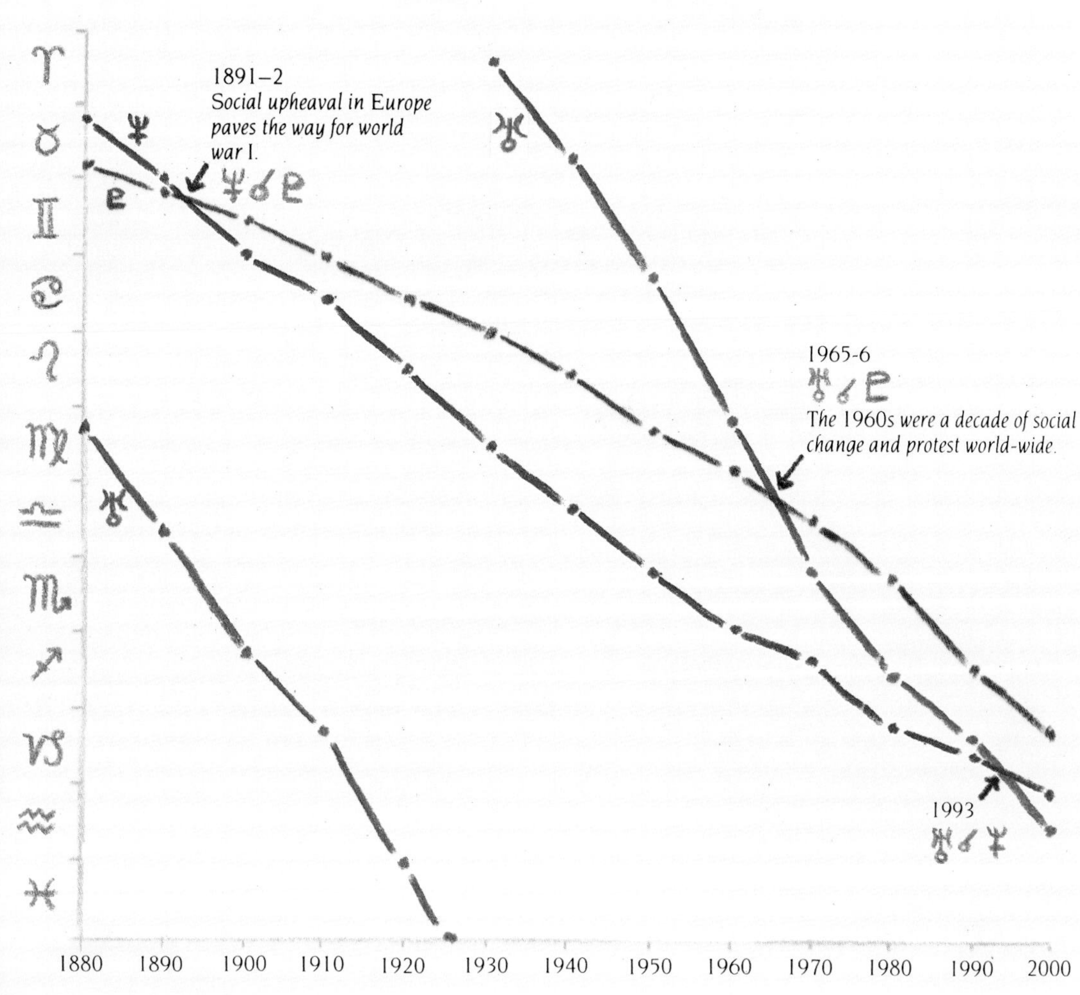
1891–2
Social upheaval in Europe paves the way for world war I.
1965-6
The 1960s were a decade of social change and protest world-wide.
1993
1880
1890
1900
1910
1920
1930
1940
1950
1960
1970
1980
1990
2000

Cycle	Average	Meanings
Jupiter-Saturn	20 years	Varies depending on the sign, but this is the basic cycle of historical change.
Jupiter-Uranus	14 years	Enterprise, innovation, expansion, discovery, exploration.
Jupiter-Neptune	13 years	Religion, mysticism, speculation, inflation.
Jupiter-Pluto	12 years	Power struggles, violent conflicts.
Saturn-Uranus	45 years	Right wing and authoritarian politics, material innovation.
Saturn-Neptune	36 years	Democracy and socialism.
Saturn-Pluto	33 years	Political restructuring, conflict.
Uranus-Neptune	172 years	Revolution in human beliefs.
Uranus-Pluto	127 years	Social upheaval, revolution.
Neptune-Pluto	492 years	Major historical change

1848 and 1968 stand out as years of revolution, when many countries witnessed rebellion and social change. The historian can find no connection between these two dates but the astrologer knows that both upheavals occurred under a Uranus-Pluto conjunction, within two years of the aspect being exact in each case.

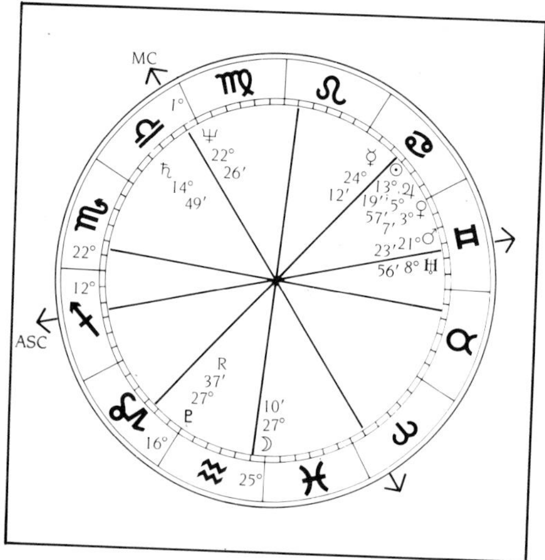

The United States of America
The subject of the USA's birth chart is a source of endless controversy amongst astrologers. The chart is set for the signing of the Declaration of Independence in the late afternoon on 4 July 1776 in Philadelphia. However, no exact time was recorded. The chart given here has the best pedigree as it was first published in 1787. The time given was 5.10 pm.

The Moon (the people as a whole) in Aquarius (idealism) in the third house (communication) is a fitting description of the signing of the Declaration, with its ringing tone of high minded aspirations to freedom. Sagittarius rising is an appropriate sign of the spirit of individual liberty and enterprise which lies at the heart of the 'American dream'. It is interesting that the Sun is in Cancer, for this puts it exactly opposite England's national Sun: the two countries were then enemies.

THE SOLAR CYCLE: INGRESS CHARTS. Among all the ingress charts – the horoscopes for entry of planets into new signs – the solar ingresses are the most important. Of these it is the four cardinal ingresses that carry the secrets of the year.

The charts are cast for the exact time when the Sun enters the sign in question and for the place for which the interpretation is to be made. When the chart is set for a country, then the capital city is always used. The horoscopes are calculated and interpreted in the normal manner and any of the techniques of natal astrology, as well as the traditional techniques preserved by horary astrology, may be applied.

The Capricorn ingress chart reveals the trends for the coming year, but does not specify exactly when these will occur. However, the transits over the year may give the astrologer a good idea of critical dates.

THE SUN-MOON CYCLE: LUNATION CHARTS. The exact progress of events throughout the year is illustrated by the charts for the new Moons (lunations) and full Moons, cast for the exact time that the Moon reaches its conjunction (new Moon) or opposition (full Moon) with the Sun, and for the place for which the interpretation is to be set. As with ingress charts the horoscope is set for the capital city if the entire country is concerned. It is difficult to make exact predictions with these charts but they show in outline the type of event and occurrence which can be expected.

Ordinary new and full Moon charts are relevant only to the subsequent fortnight, but eclipses can be valid for months and even years. A general rule is that eclipses in fixed signs will have the most long-term effects, those in mutable signs will also last a long time but be less consistent, and those in cardinal signs have the shortest duration. In effect, eclipses often coincide with irrational events, sometimes violent outbursts. At other times there will be no immediate correlation, but a subsequent transit over the eclipse degree may trigger the effect. For example, if the eclipse brings violent potential, this may be triggered later by a transit of Mars. There is no standard rule for timing such phenomena and in each case the astrologer must apply experience and knowledge as if working without precedent.

NATIONAL CHARTS. National horoscopes are cast for the time, date and place of major historical events such as the Declaration of Independence, the proclamation of a regime or coronation of a monarch. These charts both describe 'national character' and predict major events with remarkable accuracy.

In many cases there is more than one contender for the title of national chart. Great Britain has five main national horoscopes, each with its own validity. The potential for confusion is considerable, but does not arise in practice because most astrologers work with only one or two charts.

In the United States the situation is similar. There are many different versions of the horoscope for the Declaration of Independence, each with its own champion. Most of these are based on vague astrological speculation rather than historical evidence; the Sagittarius rising chart has the best historical claim.

THE BIRTH CHART IN MUNDANE ASTROLOGY. Natal and mundane astrology often seem to be pointing in different directions, natal astrology inspires people to develop their potential and mundane astrology deals with events over which they have very little control. In fact, there is no contradiction, for

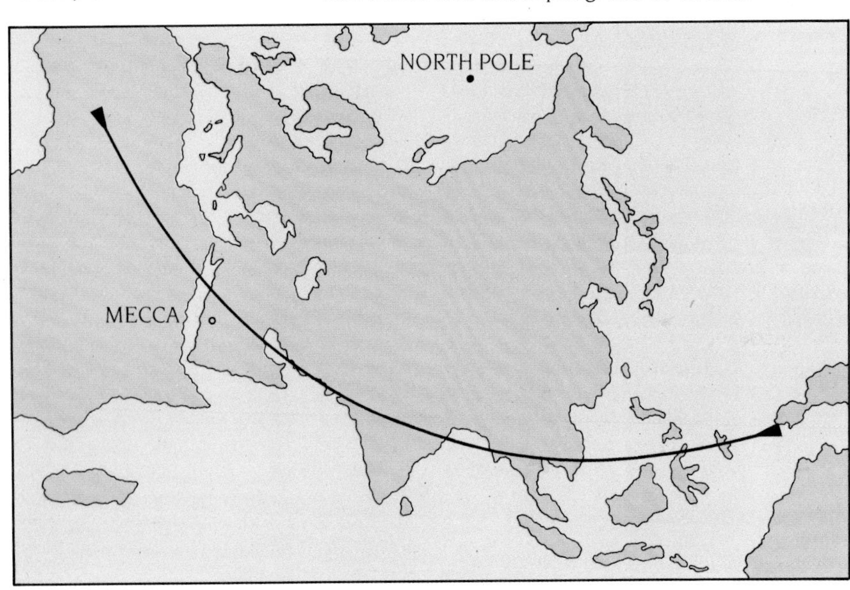

Eclipse Paths
A solar eclipse may be of sufficiently long duration to affect a considerable part of the Earth's surface. The areas over which it passes are those where its influence will be greatest. This map shows the eclipse path for 1 August 566 associated with the birth of Mohammed by the American astrologer Charles Emmerson. The path covers the approximate area over which Islam, the religion founded by Mohammed, has spread, from West Africa to Indonesia.

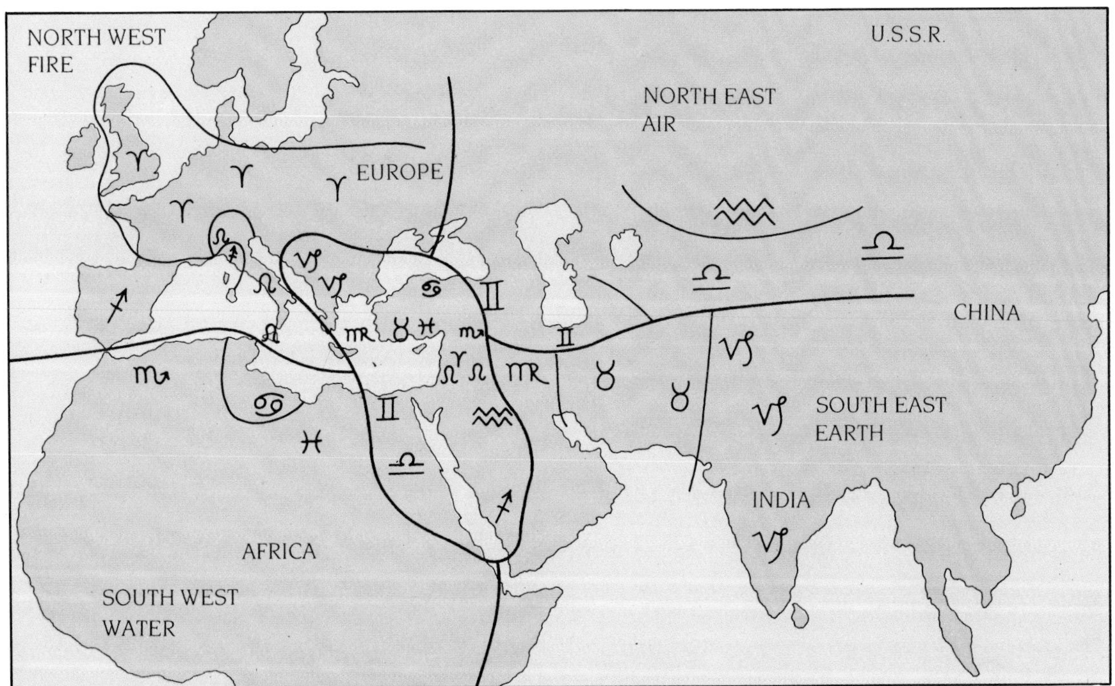

Earth Zodiacs
Two thousand years ago the Greek mathematician and astronomer Ptolemy divided the world into quarters, each of which was ruled by one of the elements. Within each quarter were smaller areas ruled by the signs, and in the centre of the plan was an area of overlapping influences. Remarkably, this scheme is still in use although many modern astrologers prefer the greater precision provided by national charts.

the belief in personal freedom must take account of material circumstances and human dependence on the environment.

Mundane astrology deals with the environment, the overall framework within which individuals live out their own unique birth potential. The comparison of natal charts with national and other mundane horoscopes often reveals why success may be found in one place but failure in another. At a simple level all natal astrologers take mundane astrology into account through the study of the transits, and the new and full Moons. Projected on to a natal chart these reveal the unique twists to which every life is subject, yet the postions of the transiting planets are exactly the same for everyone.

EVENT HOROSCOPES. Horoscopes may be cast for events both in advance and in retrospect. Often these can be useful for advising on possible courses of action or, if cast for incidents long past, in developing an understanding of astrological techniques and symbolism.

Such horoscopes naturally relate to the charts of the countries in which the incidents take place, and to the birth charts of the principal characters. The techniques of chart comparison may be used to clarify links between the charts. Often, however, event horoscopes make more sense if they are read without too much emphasis on comparison with other charts. The general disposition of the planets often shows the overall nature of the event, but as the astrologer is basically asking a question about the outcome and the significance of the event, it makes sense to work through the chart quite carefully, using the traditional techniques of horary astrology. Read according to the traditional rules, the chart for the sinking of the *Titanic* shows quite clearly the threat of disaster. However, as the chart for the overwhelmingly successful 'Live Aid' concert shows, astrologers should not rush to make gloomy predictions.

HISTORICAL CYCLES: THE AGE OF AQUARIUS. The dawning of the Age of Aquarius became one of the astrological catchphrases of the 1960s. Many people who know little of astrology are familiar with the concept of the 'New age' or millenarianism. The conviction that the world is about to enter a new and glorious age is an ancient one. The belief in the coming of the Age of

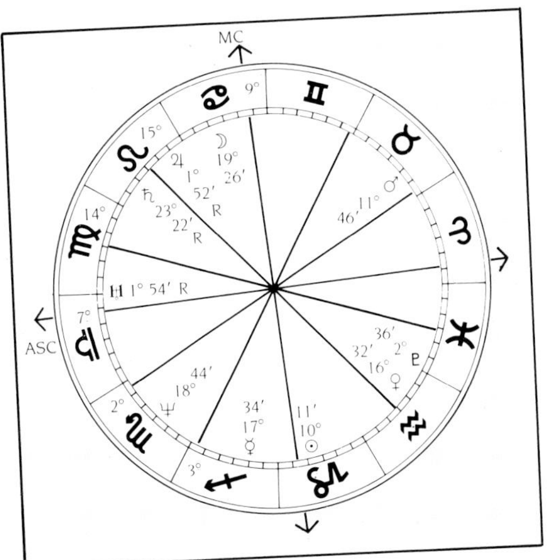

The National Horoscope of the United Kingdom
This is the horoscope for the official foundation of the United Kingdom of Great Britain and Ireland at midnight on 1 January 1801.

Transits over this chart have been found to accord very well with major stages in British history since 1801. The Sun in Capricorn sums up the conservatism of the British and their well-known reserve. The Moon rules the general public, and in the tenth house (government) symbolizes the institution of parliamentary democracy which, in its present form, was largely evolved in Britain. The Libran Ascendant is a good description of the national self-image (deserved or otherwise) of fair play and justice.

Aquarius is the contemporary astrological form of this myth.

The Age of Aquarius is one of a sequence of 12 'Great Months' (one for each sign of the zodiac) each lasting about 2,160 years. The duration of each Great Month is based on the movement of the stars in relation to the zodiac by 1° every 72 years. Twelve Great Months add up to one Great Year of about 25,900 years, and the Great Years follow each other in an endless cycle. In the West the zodiac, known as the tropical zodiac, is based on the seasons, but in the East an alternative zodiac is in use, known as the sidereal zodiac and fixed to the positions of the stars (see Chapter 15). As the stars move so the entire sidereal zodiac moves against the tropical zodiac and gradually Eastern and Western systems diverge.

Each month is ruled by the sign that the Sun occupies at the spring equinox. In the Western system the Sun always enters Aries at the exact moment of the spring equinox, but in the Eastern system after 2,160 years this falls in a new sign. Currently the equinox occurs in Pisces but within a few hundred years it will take place in Aquarius. When this happens then the present Age of Pisces will come to an end and the Age of Aquarius will begin. Exactly when the change will occur is not known, for there is no agreement on the beginning and end of the sidereal signs. Some astrologers ignore the astronomical definition altogether and take the symbolism of historical events as their guide. The earliest starting date given is 1762 and the latest around 3000, although the consensus is approximately 2360–70, so the Age of Pisces still has some way to run.

Literal comparisons of the Ages to human history tend to be misleading. For example, some astrologers claim that the Age of Taurus (approximately 4000 to 2000 BC) was an age of massive monuments, such as the pyramids in Egypt, and the worship of the bull; and that the Age of Aries (approximately 2000 BC to 0 AD) witnessed the rise of great empires. But they fail to explain why other animals were also worshipped in the Age of Taurus, and why great empires and monuments were also built in later Ages.

However, taken as myths of the times, the Ages can provide a framework for some inspired thought. A notable connection links

The Great Ages
Astrology treats historical time as a spiral progressing through endless sequences of Great Ages. In each age the same basic pattern is repeated, yet the circumstances differ.

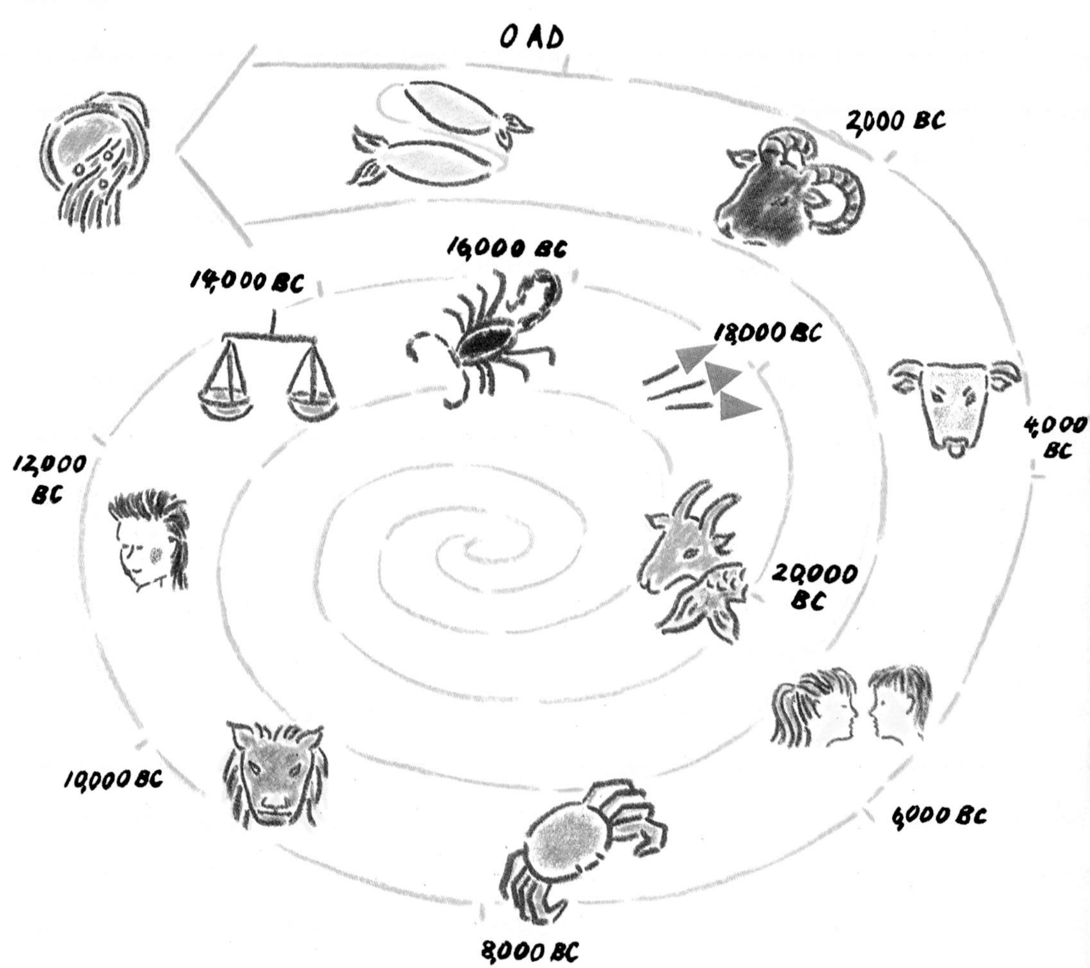

the beginning of the Age of Pisces (about two thousand years ago) with the use of the fish as a symbol of Christ by the early Christians.

The myths surrounding the Age of Aquarius suggest the coming of an age of peace and equality and, however unrealistic this may seem, the myth will have fulfilled its purpose if it inspires people to work for such a goal.

NATURAL CYCLES: COSMOBIOLOGY. The evidence connecting the movements of the solar system with events on Earth through any natural mechanism is tenuous yet this area of research continually promises a substantial breakthrough. At present the picture resembles a jigsaw in which half the pieces are missing, and yet reveals a tantalizing glimpse of what might be. Such an approach to astrology takes the field of expertise away from divination, the reading of symbols and the concept of astrology as a language, and into a new area of natural science that has been labelled cosmobiology.

The most obvious celestial cycle is that of the Moon, whose physical effect on the Earth is pronounced and was understood in ancient times. Ironically, when astrology went out of fashion in the seventeenth century many people began to doubt the effect of the Moon on the tides. What is taken for granted by modern scientists is, in fact, an ancient relic of astrological learning.

It is well known that the lunar cycle correlates with the female fertility cycle, but the connections between lunar rhythms and human behaviour may be much more extensive. The belief that the full Moon causes 'lunatic' behaviour finds its mythical form in the legend of the werewolf, but the fiction is not necessarily stranger than the fact. In 1961 the American Institute of Medical Climatology found evidence to back up the folklore.

It reported that the Philadelphia police department found that erratic and apparently motiveless crimes reached a peak around the full moon. This comes as no surprise to astrologers who have long noted the connection of physical violence with the full Moon. The question is whether there is a natural connection which may work on a different level to that of ordinary astrological symbolism.

A major occurrence associated with the Sun is the sunspot cycle. Sunspots are little understood either in terms of their cause or effect. They are dark cool patches on the Sun's surface and possess a strong magnetic field. Their frequency varies according to an astonishingly regular cycle, reaching a peak every 11 years. They are probably produced by some internal mechanism in the Sun, and there is some evidence connecting them with a general pattern of the planets. The fact that they bombard the Earth with solar radiation would suggest powerful consequences on terrestrial affairs, yet in terms of human behaviour it is difficult to find connections.

However, earlier in the century, Soviet scientist Professor A.L. Tchijevsky produced an analysis of the history of warfare which found an 11-year cycle in 'human excitability'. Typically it is found that a sunspot peak coincides with an increase in rebellion, riot, revolution and war as political crises come to a head.

The last peak was in 1979, a year which saw revolutions in Iran and Nicaragua, the Soviet invasion of Afghanistan and the election of Ronald Reagan as President of the United States and brought East-West tensions to their most critical point since the Cuban Missile crisis.

Tchijevsky's research has never been seriously checked, and the fact that he based his conclusions on the ancient and medieval periods, for which records are very scarce, must call them into question. The case for connections between sunspot cycles and mass behaviour is in principle strong, yet evidence is required. The problem at present is that such evidence is either not available or extremely elusive.

Precession of the Equinoxes
At the present time the spring equinox takes place at 0° Aries in the Tropical zodiac but at 5° Pisces in the constantly shifting Sidereal Zodiac. When the Equinox takes place at 0° Aquarius in the Sidereal zodiac, which will occur in between three and four hundred years time, then the Age of Aquarius will begin.

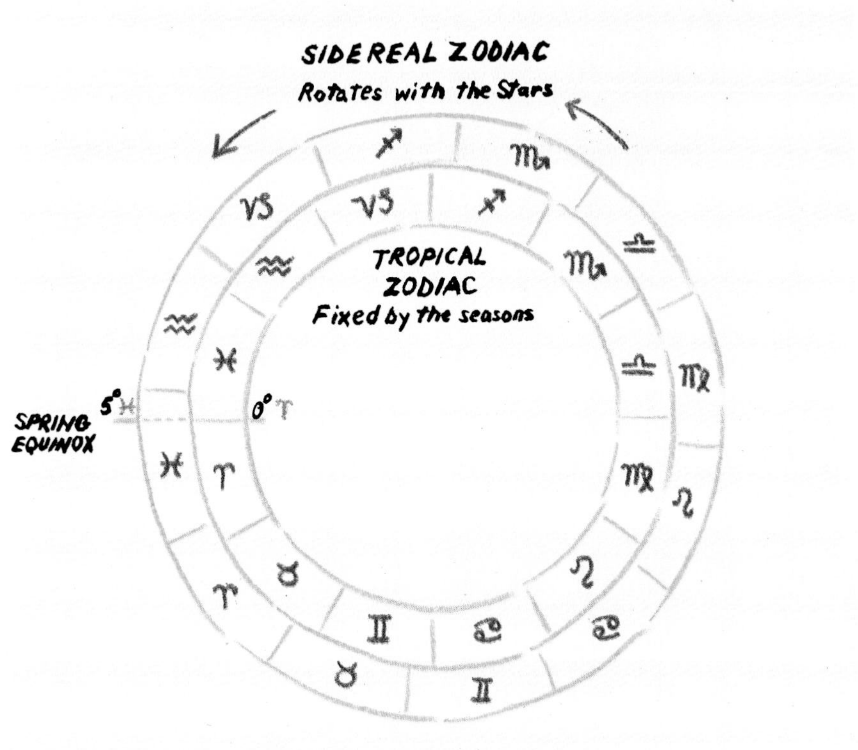

CHAPTER 18 ASTRO-ECONOMICS: FINANCIAL ASTROLOGY

Financial astrology, sometimes known by the grand title astro-economics, is technically included under the umbrella of mundane astrology, although many natal astrologers are approached for business advice. The risks are great, for on the astrologer's advice, large sums of money can be made or lost. Some brokers and businessmen use astrology themselves and there is no doubt that profits are made on astrological principles. However, there is no simple method – if there were, astrologers would all be millionaires. The situation is analagous to that of the gambler who discovers a system that 'works' for him but not for anybody else. Each successful financial astrologer must evolve a method that suits his or her own particular experience and expertise.

GENERAL PRINCIPLES

Astrological advisors on economic matters face difficulties similar to those encountered by the natal astrologer when giving psychological advice, or the mundane astrologer when commenting on historical events. All these disciplines are far from scientific, all are vague and dependent on the opinions of the people who study them. In economics it is the researcher who selects the area of economic activity, devises the means to measure it and interprets the results. As the saying goes, 'there are three kinds of lies: lies, damned lies and statistics'. John Maynard Keynes, one of the greatest economists of the twentieth century, was more elegant when he described economics as a 'branch of theology'.

The difficulty inherent in relating economics to astrology is complicated by the fact that what is bad for one person may be good for another; a decline in one sector of the economy may coincide with a boom elsewhere. Given this confusion, financial astrology is most accurate in the simple comparison of planetary movements with the fluctuations of stock markets and commodity prices.

Although it is possible to use astrology to make money it should always be borne in mind that the real purpose of financial astrology lies not in helping people to store up private wealth but in revealing the higher levels within which economic activity takes place. If it is ever possible to construct a global economic system which is run for the benefit of all, then astro-economics would have a major role to play.

PLANETARY CYCLES. Much modern economic analysis is rooted in the concept of cycles in which it is assumed that all business activity follows repetitive patterns of alternating growth and recession. Cycles of different lengths are identified, and while some determinants are economic it is also believed that psychological factors are vital.

The basis of the comparison of astrology with business cycles lies in the daily motions of the transiting planets. Studies of planetary cycles generally ignore sign or house position

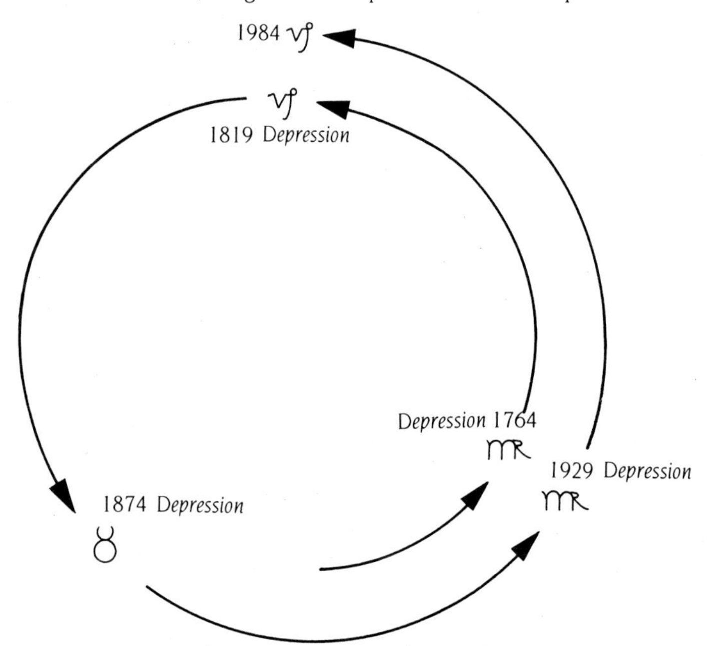

Bottom Left: Neptune and Economic Cycles
The passage of planets through the signs has an economic significance. Evidence suggests that the entry of Neptune, normally associated with inflation, into the stable earth signs correlates with periodic market crashes. The market crashes themselves are recognized by economists as forming part of the Kondratief cycle, a cycle of growth, boom, crash and recession which lasts an average of 54 years. The last four such recessions have occurred within three years of Neptune's entry into one of the Earth signs. The precise circumstances of each instance are varied by Neptune's aspects and other planetary cycles.

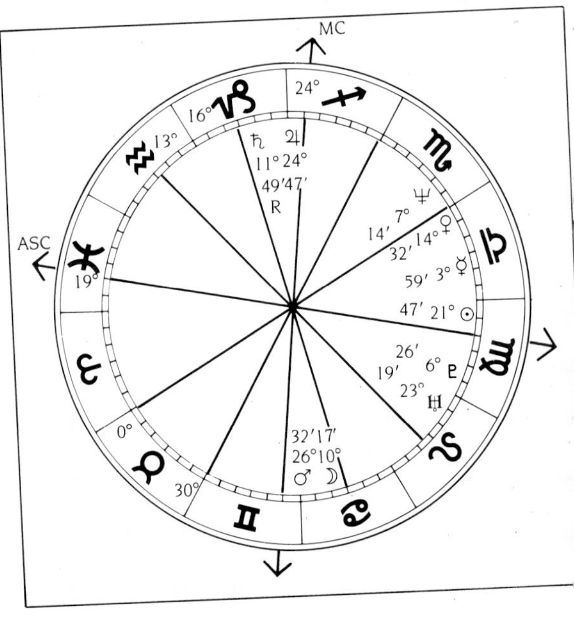

Bottom Right: OPEC
This is the horoscope for the announcement of the formation of the Organization of Petroleum-Exporting Countries at 3.00 pm GMT on 14 September 1960 in Baghdad.

Jupiter conjunct the MC in its own sign, Sagittarius, is an excellent symbol for success and prosperity. However, Jupiter's square to the Sun and opposition to Mars indicates rash actions.

and concentrate exclusively on those factors which describe planetary relationships. Aspects are the main factors but midpoints and harmonics are relevant to deeper studies.

Given that it is the total configuration which is important, the astrologer needs to understand the potential of each planetary combination. Aspects between inner planets are so common and of such brief duration that they are usually considered only of minor importance. Aspects between Uranus, Neptune and Pluto on the other hand may be of such a duration as to show long-term economic changes, but too long to reveal daily market fluctuations. The crucial planets are Jupiter and Saturn, for their movements are slow enough to indicate major changes but fast enough to have their effects confined to a day or a week. Aspects between inner planets and either other inner planets or the outer planets have a generally reinforcing effect in building up a general pattern for a whole day.

The general planetary principles are adapted from natal astrology. Saturn is more likely to indicate pessimism, recession, falling prices or stability, and Jupiter optimism, growth, inflation and rising prices. Neptune is associated with unrealistic and inflated hopes and Uranus with unexpected shocks.

The major aspects mark the critical turning points. Conjunctions and oppositions are strongest, but sextiles, squares and trines all have a role to play. Tense aspects indicate the times when the market hits a low and begins to rise and harmonious aspects mark the high points that often immediately precede a fall. Obviously the situation is complicated when contradictory cycles coincide. For example, a Jupiter aspect to Neptune may indicate inflation at the same time as a Jupiter aspect to Saturn promises deflation. The situation must be carefully balanced and a cautious judgment reached.

The Jupiter-Uranus cycle, being the supreme significator of individual enterprise, is regarded as the ruler of 'free-market' capitalism. In 1983, when these planets were in a conjunction, the Western world, led by the United States, shook itself out of the recession that had gripped it since 1979. Under the pressure of high interest rates market prices reached their highest ever levels. On 8 January 1986 the two planets reached the next phase of their cycle, the sextile. Although they later recovered, stock prices on this day experienced their biggest fall since the Wall Street crash of 1929.

The correlation of business and planetary cycles is one of the most sophisticated areas of astrology. The astrologer has to be correct as wrong interpretations hit where, it is often said, it hurts most – in the pocket.

HOROSCOPES. The general equation of business with planetary cycles is brought down to specifics by the use of horoscopes. These are read using the same range of techniques found in natal, mundane and horary astrology although the interpretations are given an economic perspective. Charts are cast for the foundation or inauguration of banks, stock exchanges, businesses and currency systems. Mundane charts – for countries, governments, ingresses and lunations – can be used to provide a general perspective. Birth charts for people involved in business are also important, especially if the whole operation revolves around one person. When specific questions arise – such as whether to buy or sell property – then horary charts often give the clearest answer.

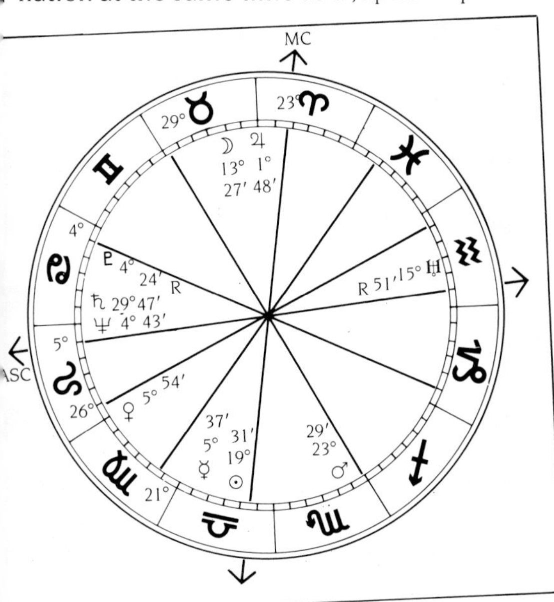

Bottom Left: General Motors
The American company General Motors is one of the largest multinational corporations in the world. This horoscope is set for the company's inauguration on 13 October 1916 in Delaware. As the time is unknown a solar chart has been cast for midnight.

There are a number of astrological 'signatures' in this chart to describe General Motors' main occupation — the manufacture of motor cars. A mutual reception between Mercury and Venus from the second house (money) to the third (communication) describes a business based on transport. The Mars-Saturn trine indicates engineering and the Moon square Uranus indicates the unsettling and even revolutionary effects of the increasing number of cars on people's way of life.

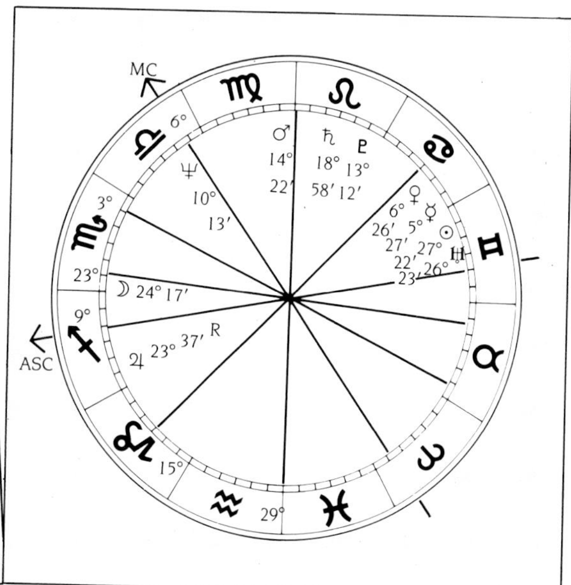

Bottom Right: The Deutsche Mark
Horoscopes for currencies can be effective if the date of their foundation is known. This is the chart for the currency reform in West Germany when the Deutsche Mark was launched. This occurred at 8.00 pm on 18 June 1948 and the chart is set for Frankfurt.

Note the opposition from Jupiter to Uranus. The Jupiter-Uranus cycle is associated with the entrepreneurial spirit of the free market, and West Germany has been a model of capitalist success. Jupiter is important in this chart because it is the ruler of the Ascendant, is in its Dignity in Sagittarius and is in the first house.

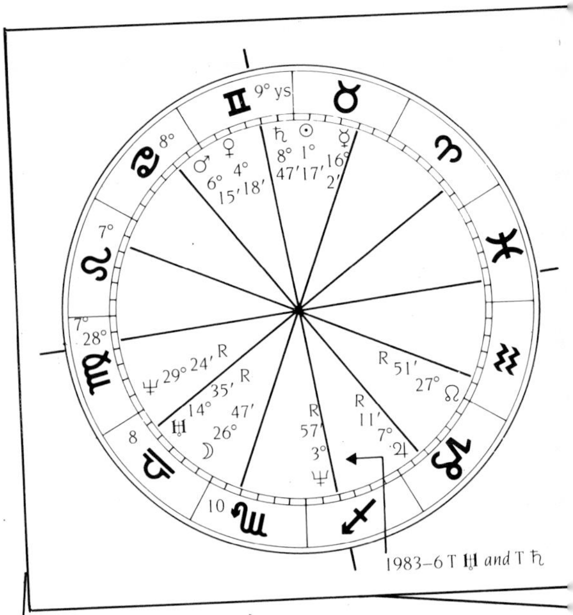

Top: Political Charts
In most Asian countries astrology is regularly used to time major political events. This is the horoscope for the proclamation of the Republic of Sri Lanka (formerly Ceylon) with great ceremony at 12.34 pm on 22 May 1972. Every moment during the day's celebrations was pre-arranged by the government's astrologers. The chart is drawn out in the western style although eastern astrologers use a different zodiac and a square format.

This chart is evidence that elected charts have considerable power. When transiting Saturn and Uranus were conjunct the IC from 1983 to 1986 simmering racial trouble erupted into a full scale civil war.

India, Burma, Thailand and Nepal also have horoscopes chosen by astrologers.

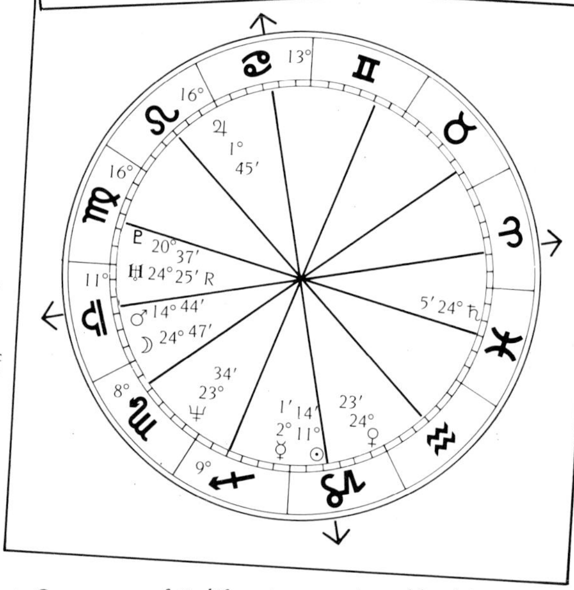

Bottom: Ronald Reagan Becomes Governor of California
When Ronald Reagan was inaugurated as Governor of California at 00.16 on 1 January 1967 in Sacramento, all the major American newspapers were perplexed by the choice of such a strange time. Most gubernatorial inaugurations take place around midday. Reagan's known interest in astrology gave rise to the belief that the time had been 'elected'. An interesting feature of this chart is the close aspects between the Moon, Venus, Saturn, Neptune and Uranus. The Moon is just past an exact conjunction with Spica.

CHAPTER 19 PLANNING THE FUTURE: ELECTIONAL ASTROLOGY

Electional astrology has nothing to do with political elections, but is the fourth traditional division of judicial astrology – the others being natal, horary and mundane. When the astrologer calculates the most auspicious hour for an event to begin it is said that he elects the time – hence electional astrology.

If the one purpose of astrology is to develop freedom of choice, electional astrology sees that purpose fulfilled. If astrology is the study of the changing quality of time and of human submission to it, then electional astrology sees the astrologer becoming an active participant in this process.

The aim of electional astrology is to harmonize with the universe, not to control it. Its purpose is to assess the best moment to begin any undertaking, using the shifting nature of time much as a bird uses currents of air to facilitate flight.

It must be understood, however, that there is a level of existence that transcends even that signified by astrology itself, and the best elected chart in the world will not guarantee success in a project that is fundamentally flawed. On the other hand even a difficult chart can be improved by dedication, hard work and a will to succeed.

PRACTICAL CONSIDERATIONS

Often astrologers must begin work with a consideration of the circumstances rather than of the planetary positions. The reason is obvious; day and night, public and religious holidays and just plain common sense all determine whether an event is possible or not. For example, it is unlikely that a public meeting will be held at the dead of night; or a book launched before it is printed. In most matters such considerations limit the number of possibilities open to the astrologer. Nevertheless, in many cases astrology is the paramount consideration: in the Southeast Asian state of Burma, astrologers insisted that independence from the British be granted at 4.20 am. In the United States it is said that Ronald Reagan's inauguration as Governor of California was timed by his astrologers for the unusual hour of 16 minutes past midnight.

LOCATING SIGNIFICANCE

THE HOUSES. Depending on the nature of the proposed venture, the first step must be to decide which houses are important. For example, the second and eighth houses rule business affairs, the third rules short journeys, the seventh marriage, the ninth higher education and legal affairs, the tenth career, and so on. It is important that the significant houses contain helpful planets such as Venus and Jupiter, and that their rulers are well placed. Being well placed means being in Exaltation or Dignity, and making harmonious rather than tense aspects. A trine to Jupiter is always far preferable to an opposition to Saturn. Applying aspects are always more important than separating aspects.

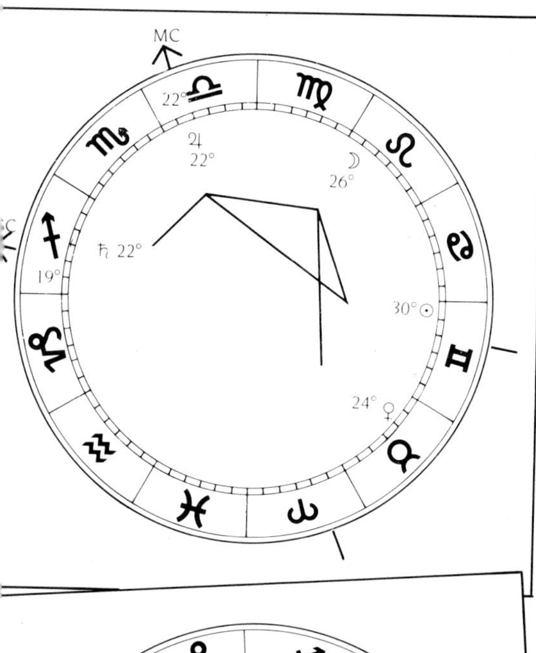

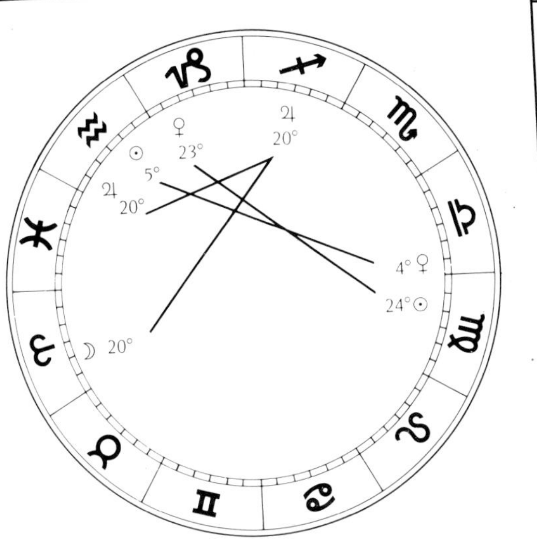

THE MOON. The speed and phases of the Moon are very influential. According to tradition no new enterprise should ever be started under a new Moon, a belief that goes back to the days when dark nights before the crescent Moon reappeared were equated with death. The full Moon should also be avoided, and the waxing phase (from new to full) is considered more helpful than the waning phase (from full to new). The Moon is best placed from three days after the new Moon until three days before the full Moon. The Moon will bring success more quickly if it is moving faster than average.

The Moon assumes a similar importance in electional as in horary astrology because of the number and variety of aspects it makes. It is essential to pay close attention to the rapid passage of the Moon.

THE ASCENDANT and its ruler should be well aspected.

THE PLANETS IN GENERAL. Jupiter and Venus should be as strong as possible by aspect, house and sign. Unless the matter being planned is specifically ruled by Mars (such as a battle) or Saturn (such as a new responsibility) these two planets should be as weak as possible. At all costs they should not be in applying squares or oppositions to any of the significant planets – Ascendant ruler, the Sun, Moon or the rulers of the significant houses. Uranus, Neptune and Pluto, whose influence can be unpredictable, should be insignificant, unless they rule the matter in hand.

RETROGRADE PLANETS should be avoided. The outer planets are retrograde so often that this is not always possible, but Mercury retrograde is a difficult influence in general.

THE BIRTH CHART. The relevant natal charts should always be taken into consideration. This may be difficult for the launching of a ship in which a lot of people are involved (although one may take the chart of the owner or the captain), but is straightforward if the election concerns one person. In electing the time for a marriage the astrologer may take the chart for each person or a composite chart drawn for them both.

Ideally the transits for the election should be as well aspected as possible to the natal planets, if possible by trines and sextiles, to indicate a smooth passage.

DIFFICULT INDICATIONS. No elected chart will ever be perfect and even a chart with one ideal pattern may contain another that promises difficulties. The best the astrologer can do is achieve a sensible balance so that difficult and easy factors work together, the former bringing the testing circumstances that are necessary for personal growth and the latter bringing the optimism and opportunity to win through in the end.

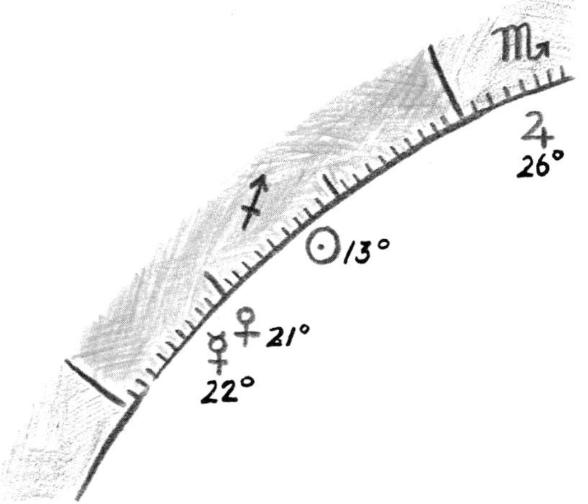

Top: The Astrological Association

When British astrologers set up their Astrological Association at 7.22 pm GMT on 21 June 1958 in London, the time had been elected in advance. Five planets form part of a critical pattern. The significance of the day is twofold. There is an exact sextile between Jupiter, planet of expansion, and Saturn, planet of structure, a very beneficial aspect for a public organization. The Sun is also about to enter Cancer, marking the summer solstice.

Jupiter and Saturn are on the Ascendant and MC. In addition, the beneficial star Spica is on the MC. The Moon is separating from a square to Venus, ruler of the MC, and applying to a sextile to the Sun, in accordance with the rules of electional charts.

One important rule is broken – Saturn is on the Ascendant. However, Saturn here is part of a beneficial pattern, being in both a sextile and mutual reception with Jupiter.

Bottom: The Coronation of Elizabeth I

One of the most successful elected horoscopes of all time was for the coronation of Elizabeth I, arguably England's greatest monarch. The time was chosen by her astrologer, John Dee.

The coronation horoscope was arranged so that Venus and Jupiter (the benefics) and the Sun and the Moon (the lights) made harmonious aspects to the Sun, Venus and Jupiter in Elizabeth's birth chart.

Planets in the left half of the circle are those for the coronation, those in the right are her natal planets.

Business Astrology

Astrologers are often asked to elect horoscopes for businesses. This is an extract from the horoscope for the Bombay Brasserie, a popular restaurant in London. The time chosen was 11.00 am on 5 December 1982. An important consideration was that for the first time in eight weeks Mercury, Venus and Jupiter were all visible in the sky. The astrologer was Indian and working from a traditional perspective: when planets are invisible they are combust the Sun and, therefore, weakened.

CHAPTER 20
GAMES, CONTESTS AND COMPETITIONS

Sporting competitions offer a heaven sent opportunity for astrologers to relax and experiment with their art without the pressures to solve peoples' problems.

Horoscopes may be set for any competition or contest from a chess championship to a boxing match or a football game.

There are no foolproof methods and, although it is often possible to predict the winner, forecasts often come unstuck, and the astrologer who places a bet on the basis of a horoscope must have a sense of humour.

The rules applied to contests are the same as those applied in other areas of astrology, but draw heavily on the traditional principles of horary astrology, the reason being that precision is necessary if a definite answer is required. It is no use giving a psychological interpretation of a contest chart if the aim is to discover the winner. Contest charts may be considered under the general umbrella of mundane astrology, and the principles of contest interpretation can be applied to events in the political sphere such as general elections, invasions and the beginnings of wars.

CONTEST CHARTS

When there is a clear contest between two teams or individuals then the chart is set for the exact time and location of the beginning of the contest. In most cases one side or contestant will be the reigning champion, the title holder or the home team and the other will be the challenger or away team. The champion, title holder or home team is always ruled by the first house and the Ascendant. The team's significator is the ruler of the Ascendant. The challenger or away team is always ruled by the seventh house and the Descendant, and its significator is the ruler of the Descendant.

HOUSES. In contest charts the tenth house rules the reputation and status of the champion or home side. The fifth house, the ruler of leisure, pleasure and speculation, is extremely important and indicates the champion's/home team's chances of winning.

For the challenger/away team the houses are 'turned' as in horary astrology so that the seventh house becomes the first, and the eleventh house becomes the fifth. The eleventh house of the chart, the challenger's/away team's fifth, therefore, indicates their chances of victory. The house is examined in the normal way, with great attention paid to the strength of its ruling planet. If the ruler of the Ascendant applies by a conjunction, trine or sextile to the ruler of the fifth, then this favours a win by the champion/home team, but if the ruler of the Descendant applies by conjunction, trine or sextile to the ruler of the eleventh house, then this favours a win by the challenger/away team. Inevitably the chart is rarely so clear and often many more factors have to be considered.

THE MOON. The Moon's applying aspects are very important. Applying conjunctions, trines and sextiles to the rulers of the Ascendant and the fifth house favour the champion/

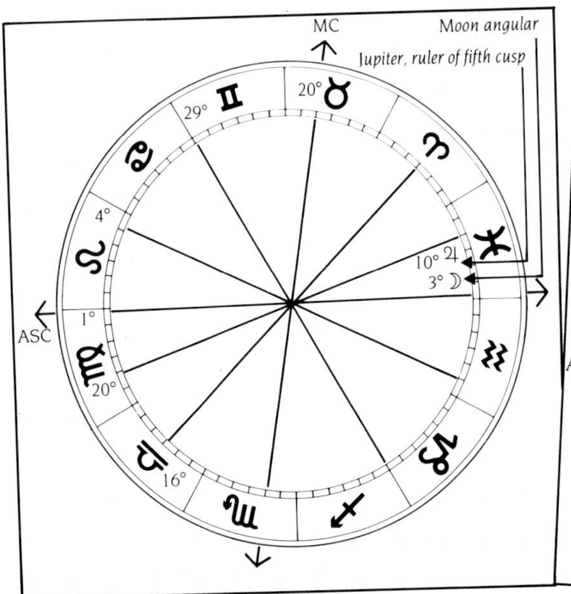

Bottom Left: Horse Racing
The Grand National is an important race in the English sporting calendar. This chart, for the Grand National on 5 April 1986, illustrates the importance of the fifth cusp in confirming a winner. The chart is set for the beginning of the race at 2.28 pm at Aintree. The winner is signified by the Moon in Pisces on the Descendant, the most angular planet. This opinion was confirmed by the application of the Moon to a conjunction with Jupiter, ruler of the cusp of the fifth house and significator of games, contests and sport.

Before the race most astrologers were attracted towards horses whose names had Piscean connotations, such as Grease Paint, suggesting the arts, disguises, masks and illusions. In fact, the winner was called West Tip, signified by the Descendant, the angle of the western horizon. The jockey's colours were Piscean pale blue.

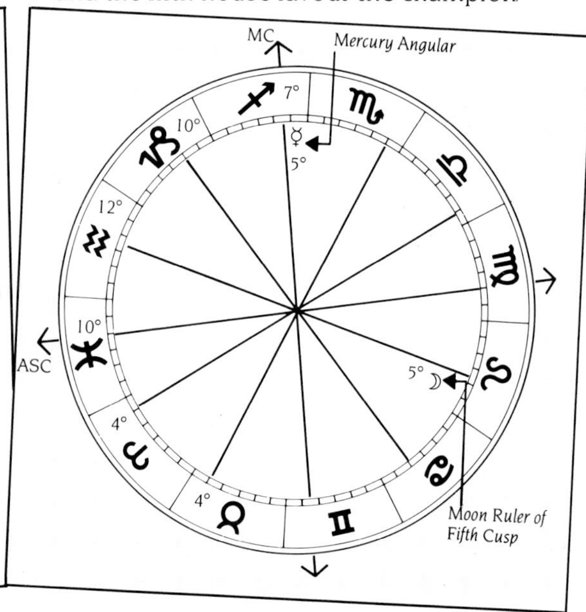

Bottom Right:
This is the horoscope for the 1985 Melbourne Cup, the main race in the Australian calendar.

The winner, What a Nuisance, was picked astrologically because Mercury was the most angular planet. Mercury, the ruler of confidence tricksters, liars and pickpockets, is the significator of exactly the type of irritation that the name 'What a Nuisance' suggests. Mercury's power was confirmed by its exact trine to the Moon, the ruler of the fifth cusp.

home team, but the same aspects applying to the rulers of the Descendant and the eleventh favour a victory by the challenger/away team.

GENERAL DIGNITIES AND DEBILITIES. If there is difficulty in working out which planet, the ruler of the Ascendant or Descendant, is stronger, then the Dignities and Debilities of the planets should be used as in horary astrology. These include Dignity, Detriment, Exaltation and Fall, and aspects to other planets and stars. For example, a planet is strengthened by applying trines to Jupiter and weakened by applying oppositions to Saturn.

HORSE RACING

Horoscopes for horse races are always cast for the exact time and location of the start of the race. Because of the number of contestants interpretation can be more complicated than in ordinary contest charts.

ANGULAR PLANETS. Unless it is making strong difficult aspects or is seriously debilitated, the planet in the closest conjunction with one of the four angles will represent the winner. It will indicate the name of the winner, once the list of contestants is known, in addition to other supplementary information concerning the jockey and the colours worn. For example, Neptune on an angle might indicate a name connected with alcohol, film fantasy or mysticism and a pale blue colour, Mars a name connected with energy, aggression, leadership or war and a red colour. A planet conjunct the Ascendant or MC is normally more powerful than a planet conjunct the Descendant or IC. The angular planet is the significator of the winner. If there is no angular planet then the most powerful other feature in the chart must be used. Obviously judgment is then less certain.

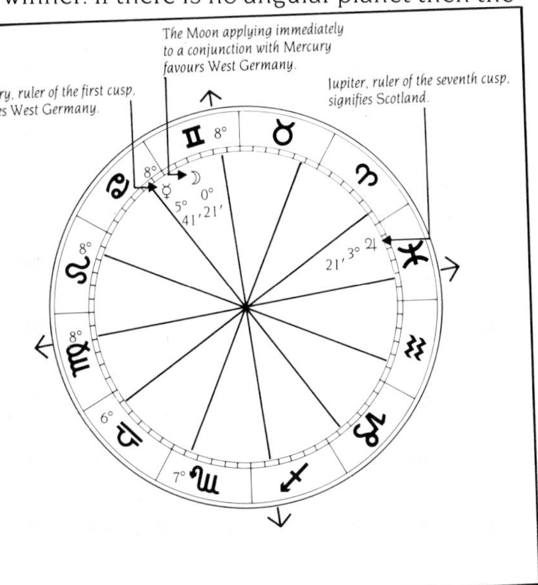
The Moon applying immediately to a conjunction with Mercury favours West Germany.
Jupiter, ruler of the seventh cusp, signifies Scotland.

***Left:* Football Matches**
This soccer game showed a clear winner. This is the horoscope for the World Cup match between West Germany and Scotland played at Querétaro in Mexico on 8 June 1986. In this case the significators are assigned according to the betting odds. West Germany, the favourites, were signified by the first cusp. Scotland were signified by the seventh cusp. West Germany were, therefore, signified by Mercury, the ruler of Virgo and Scotland by Jupiter, the ruler of Pisces. The Moon was applying to aspects to both planets, but its conjunction wth Mercury was prior to its trine to Jupiter. On this basis a win by the favourites – West Germany – was forecast. West Germany beat Scotland by two goals to one. Unfortunately contest charts are rarely this simple.

THE ODDS. Under one rule the Sun, Jupiter and Venus angular favour favourites and horses under shorter odds, Saturn, Mars, Uranus, Neptune and Pluto favour outsiders and longer odds, and the Moon may favour either top favourites or outsiders. According to another rule a planet conjunct the MC or IC favours horses which are placed in the middle, and are, therefore, neither favourites nor outsiders.

THE HOROSCOPES OF HORSE AND JOCKEY. Some astrologers go to great lengths to research the horoscopes of horses and jockeys, although experience has shown that this is not necessary. When analysing these horoscopes the skill and experience of each must be taken into account; a champion jockey is more likely to win than a novice even if the novice's chart is better for the day.

GAMBLING

A main consideration in placing a bet is not just whether the contest chart gives a clear indication of the winner but whether the natal chart for the day shows the likelihood of a win. Gambling is ruled by the fifth house and helpful transits to this are encouraging. Attention should also be paid to the second house (one's own money) and the eighth house (other peoples' money) for signs of success in gambling. Precise rules have been published for success in gambling, but while they may 'work' for their inventors, other astrologers usually have to find their own methods.

Experience shows that sometimes a clear winner can be picked but at others the results can be unusual. In 1983, a race in England began with the Moon void of course. The astrologers realized that it was possible that 'nothing would come of the matter', and that the race would not be run; but seeing a horse in the lists called 'My Last Chance', they thought this such a good description of a void of course Moon that a bet was placed. In fact, shortly before the race was due to begin, with Jupiter and Uranus, the significators of sudden storms, on the IC ('the final outcome'), much of England was hit by a torrential hail storm. The race was cancelled!

Fortunately bets on cancelled races are repaid and the astrologers were able to reclaim their money. If there is a moral in this story, it is never to take astrology for granted, for there is always the chance of an unexpected twist of fate.

Sun
Moon
Mercury
Venus
Earth
Mars
Jupiter
Saturn
Uranus
Neptune
Pluto

CHAPTER 21 HEALING THE BODY: MEDICAL ASTROLOGY

The application of astrology to healing the physical body has a long and distinguished history, and its principles are today frequently combined with the techniques of 'complementary' medicine such as homeopathy and acupuncture.

The underlying theory of astrological medicine is that of 'as above, so below', the Earth being an exact mirror of heaven with each human body reflecting the astrological cosmos of planet, signs and houses – an 'internal' zodiac to match the one in the sky. The horoscope throws light on the state of health of both body and mind; and in the past a training in medicine was considered an essential part of the astrologer's work.

True health occurs when the individual is in a state of harmony with nature, which may be described as being in a state of 'ease'. Dis-ease occurs when the state of harmony is destroyed, and it is the task of the astrological physician to help maintain a state of ease, or perfect health. This is an impossible goal for astrology itself assumes that the cosmos is in a state of perpetual change. Human beings are, therefore, engaged in a search for perfect health, a goal as elusive as a mirage in the desert. In the astrological scheme of things the pursuit of health is a continual process, not something to take up when a mild state of dis-ease gives way to an acute or chronic condition.

Orthodox medical practice treats parts of the body in isolation whereas, like the other complementary therapies, astrological medicine is 'holistic', treating the entire person.

Even when physical symptoms are apparently dominant the astrologer considers that emotional and mental symptoms, normally lumped together as 'psychological', are of vital importance. For example, two people may each have a serious accident but one will panic while the other bears his injuries stoically. Another two people will have pneumonia, one of whom is afraid of dying and needs sympathy, while the other wants to be left alone. In each case the orthodox practitioner tends to treat only the physical symptoms while the astrologer also considers the emotional and mental conditions.

Astrology also has a controversial attitude towards germs and viruses, one which is finding some support amongst orthodox doctors. If causes and symptoms can be attributed to anything other than physical (ie spiritual, mental or emotional) sources, it must follow that germs and viruses are not wholly to blame for many illnesses. Most healthy bodies contain or come into contact with microbes and bacteria which are potentially harmful, yet suffer no ill effects. The astrological assumption is that these only become harmful when the body, already weakened through its state of 'dis-ease', allows them to.

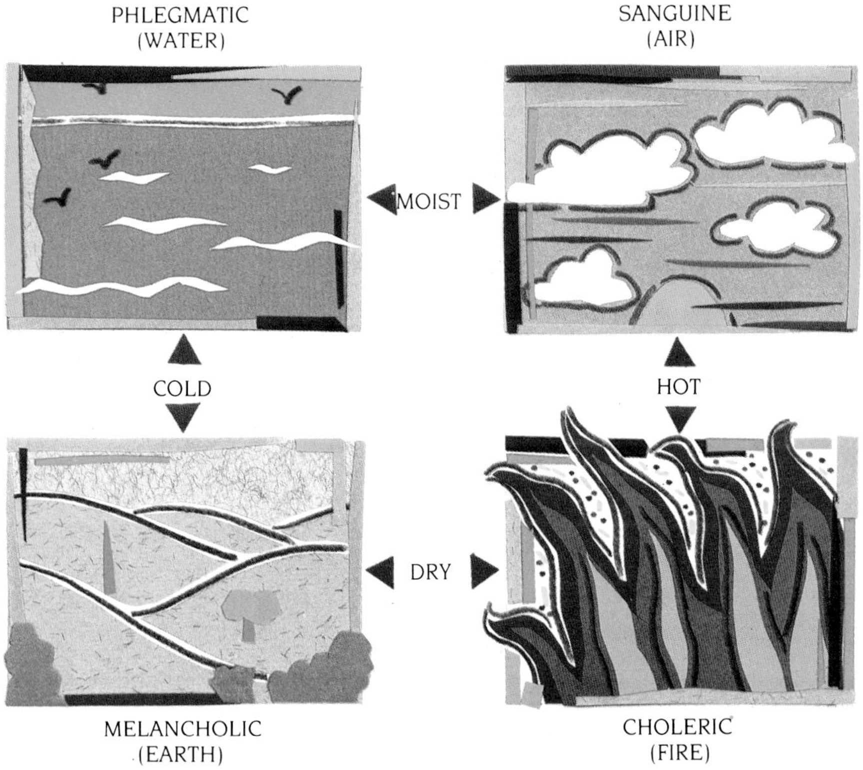

THE FOUR HUMOURS

Each of the four elements corresponds to one of the four physical types, or humours. These form the basis for diagnosis, for the physician must ascertain the humour of the patient and then, using the appropriate remedies, harmonize these. The four basic physical qualities are hot, cold, dry and moist. Fire, which corresponds to the choleric humour, is hot and dry; air, which corresponds to the sanguine humour is hot and moist; water, which corresponds to the phlegmatic humour, is cold and moist; and earth, which corresponds to the melancholic humour, is cold and dry.

The psychological characteristics of the humours are the same as those of the elements, but include physical properties as well. As a rough guide, choleric and melancholic (fire and earth) bodies tend to be

The Four Qualities, Humours and Elements
Each element is a combination of two qualities, hot, cold, moist or dry. The humours are extensions of the psychological properties of the elements into physical characteristics.

slender, and sanguine and phlegmatic (air and water) bodies tend to be plump. The logic is quite simple; choleric and melancholic are dry humours so their bodies contain less water than the fleshy bodies of the sanguine and phlegmatic types.

Even at this basic level astrology gives rise to a definition and diagnosis of disease that combines simplicity with subtlety. For example, a hot dry fever, a choleric disturbance, is an entirely different problem to a hot sweaty fever, a sanguine disturbance. A combination of cold shivers and sweat is phlegmatic, but a cold condition is melancholic.

The traditional planets also have physical qualities which are used in diagnosis. The Sun and Mars are hot and dry, Jupiter is hot and moist, Mercury and Saturn are cold and dry and the Moon and Venus are cold and moist. Such an approach to medicine may seem oddly antiquated, yet remains the basis of homeopathy and, in its Chinese form, acupuncture, both of which can be highly effective methods of treatment.

THE PLANETS

THE SUN is connected with the vital force which maintains life in the body, and is associated with growth and well being. It is specifically associated with ailments of the heart and hot, feverish complaints. The part of the body ruled by the sign in which the Sun is found will be emphasized and often weak; Taureans may be prone to sore throats, Leos may have weak backs, while Capricorns often have trouble with their knees.

THE MOON is connected with the regulation of fluids and water in the body, and the physical problems which occur when these are in excess or insufficient. The Moon is always linked to changing emotional moods, which suggests a relationship between excess (or perhaps lack) of water in the body and difficulty in expressing emotions.

MERCURY is ruler of the nervous system. It is associated with nervous disorders and problems arising from too much mental stimulation – exhaustion, headaches, loss of memory.

VENUS is associated with venereal diseases, and all problems caused by self-indulgence. This is an emotional planet with a cool and watery nature, and may be related to problems of water retention. It is certainly connected to kidney disorders.

MARS, always a planet associated with heat and aggression, rules hot, feverish and angry complaints, inflammation, haemorrhages, high blood pressure, deep burning pains, violent contagious and eruptive diseases, and all treatment by surgery. Superficial problems ruled by Mars include insect stings and bites, burns and scalds, and accidents caused by hasty or impulsive action. It is clear that at both the chronic and acute levels Martian problems may be self-inflicted due to aggressive and unthinking or uncoordinated behaviour, or overwork.

The Zodiacal Rulerships
Each sign rules an area of the body, within which it also governs individual organs, bones and tissues, although these also may have their own subrulers.

Aries
Rules the head; a classic Aries complaint is the headache caused by strain and overwork.

Taurus
Rules the throat.

Gemini
Rules the lungs, nerves, shoulders, arms, hands and fingers. Geminian types may suffer from nervous complaints.

Cancer
Rules the breast, chest area and stomach; being a sign which worries about the future, Cancerian complaints often emerge in digestive difficulties.

Leo
Rules the heart and the spine.

Virgo
Rules the intestines: as with Cancer, the worrying to which this sign is prone often results in digestive troubles.

Libra
Rules the loins and kidneys, the perfectionism of this sign being reflected in the cleansing function of the organ.

Scorpio
Rules the reproductive and excretory organs.

Sagittarius
Rules the thighs.

Capricorn
Rules the knees.

Aquarius
Rules the ankles.

Pisces
Rules the feet.

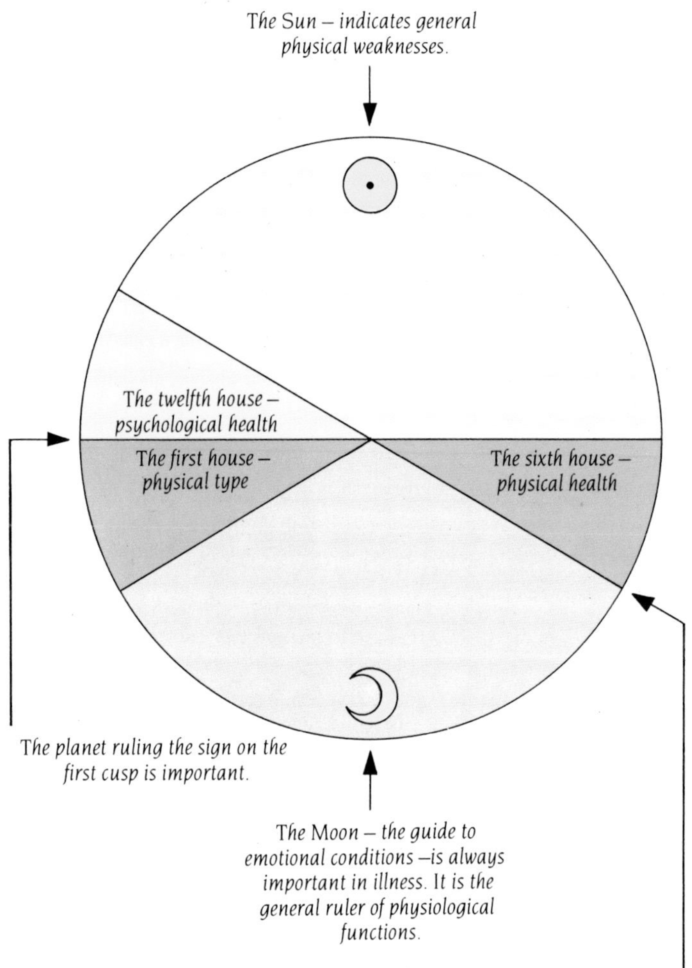
The Sun – indicates general physical weaknesses.
The twelfth house – psychological health
The first house – physical type
The sixth house – physical health
The planet ruling the sign on the first cusp is important.
The Moon – the guide to emotional conditions – is always important in illness. It is the general ruler of physiological functions.
The planet ruling the sixth house cusp is important.

Health in the Birth Chart
Physical health, just like personality, can only be properly judged by examining the entire horoscope. However, major indications can always be found by examining the Sun, Ascendant and sixth house. The Moon and twelfth house are important for adding an emotional and psychological dimension.

JUPITER rules the liver. Its general effect on the body is to speed things up, encourage growth, and increase the circulation. It rules tumours and other growths, whether malignant or benign, and it is also associated with problems arising from overweight or excessive consumption of food, drugs or alcohol.

SATURN rules the skin, and the entire bone structure, and is the essential principle which holds the body together. This planet slows everything down, producing blockages and underfunction, poor growth and poorly functioning organs.

URANUS connects with all dramatic or sudden events, perhaps a violent rupture or haemorrhage, or an unexpected cure. It is also associated with accidents, nervous problems and fast or erratic functions.

NEPTUNE rules the gradual erosion of physical powers and can be associated with lethargy or wasting diseases. A strong Neptunian type will also easily suffer the negative effects of alcohol or drug (prescribed or otherwise) consumption.

PLUTO is associated with complaints of the reproductive or excretory system and with deep changes, either sudden or long-term, in the physical condition.

THE BIRTH CHART. The birth chart should be read with specific reference to physical disposition, but also with a view to understanding the psychological patterns which underlie many chronic ailments. In many cases a physical ailment can be alleviated by a change of habit and attitude.

General Pattern. The general pattern of the chart shows the basic predisposition to physical problems and any factor may be read in terms of its implications for health. For example, a 'T' Square shows a tendency to physical tension, trines and sextiles an ability to relax, the stubborn fixed signs may hang on to their ailments, cardinal signs exhaust themselves and mutable signs are the best at getting out of stressful situations.

Sun Sign and Ascendant. The Ascendant, being the part of the horoscope that signifies physical birth, rules the body as a whole and often this reflects the characteristic of the rising sign – Libra rising gives a graceful body, Scorpio rising a dark and intense appearance, Leo rising gingerish-reddish colouring, and so on. In fact, the entire chart describes the physical type and the Ascendant is, along with the Sun sign, one of the main significators of appearance. The Sun sign invariably marks a part of the body that is weakened, an interesting manifestation of the Sun in its 'malefic' role.

The Sixth House. The sixth house is the ruler of physical health and the sign on the cusp, its ruler, and the planets it contains are all used to gauge the possibilities of health or sickness. The sign on the cusp often indicates the part of the body at risk and the ruler of this sign, its position by sign, house and aspect all provide further clues in exactly the same way as in any other chart. For example, a tight square from the sixth house ruler to Mars might indicate the possibility of accidents, perhaps the result of carelessness. Planets in the sixth house often indicate the source of physical problems: Mercury represents nervous tension, Jupiter self-indulgence, and Saturn a generally pessimistic character – illnesses associated with guilt, loneliness and depression.

Aspects. Combinations of planets provide examples of extreme characters. Mars-Saturn is the classic aspect of physical accidents through these planets' joint rulership of headstrong impatience and sudden obstacles, although Uranus also features strongly in accident horoscopes. Jupiter-Venus is the typical combination of overindulgence and all diseases caused by too much food, drink or sex, and too little exercise. Saturn the pessimist and Neptune the fantasizer combine as the typical rulers of hypochondria, chronic anxiety about the state of one's health. Mercury-Mars and Mercury-Uranus are the classic indications of nervous tension, an inability to relax and all diseases that result from this.

The Decumbiture Chart. If the time of the onset of an illness is known then a special horoscope may be cast, known as a decumbiture chart. This is then applied together with the birth chart, or even by itself, as a basis for diagnosis and treatment. The motion of the Moon and its aspects in this chart are used to work out the most auspicious times for treatment.

FORMS OF TREATMENT. The astrologer's task is to restore balance once the essential problem has been diagnosed. There are two approaches to treatment. The simplest is the prescription of a remedy which has opposite qualities to those of the symptoms, so that, for example, if the basic problem is Venusian then a Martian remedy should be applied. More complicated is the principle of treatment through sympathy. In this case a Venusian remedy would be applied to a Venusian problem. The more confused the symptoms and obscure the causes the greater the difficulty in settling on an appropriate remedy.

Change of life style. Sometimes the remedy lies in a change of life style rather than in medical treatment. For example, the lazy Venus-Jupiter person might benefit from developing the qualities of Mars and taking regular exercise. On the other hand the tense and nervous Mars-Mercury individual might benefit from some Venus-Jupiter self-indulgence. Marsilio Ficino, the Italian Renaissance philosopher, thought that the best remedy for reclusive intellectual saturnine types (of whom he was one) was to develop the properties of Venus-Jupiter by getting drunk and chasing the opposite sex.

Talismans. In former times it was the custom to make planetary talismans to correct an imbalance in astrological make-up. These were small objects cast in the planetary metal, made on the hour and day of the planet (see pages 12–13). For example, if the symptoms were Martian – such as hot fevers or headaches or excessive bleeding – these would be countered by a Venusian talisman, made out of copper during the hour of Venus, on a Friday (Venus' day) and with Venus strong in the chart. Such talismans may be compared to that of faith healing, but are rarely used in twentieth century Western society.

Herbs. Herbal remedies lie at the very core of traditional astrological medicine and every herb and plant is ruled by one of the seven

Bottom Left: Decumbitures
Decumbiture charts are cast for the moment that an illness develops, if a time can be taken. This example is from the collection of Nicholas Culpeper, the great seventeenth century English herbalist. It is set for 8.00 pm on 12 January 1641 in Paris. Note that only the seven traditional planets are used as Uranus, Neptune and Pluto had not been discovered.

The main symptoms shown are a fever with a dry cough, and Culpeper's diagnosis is of a choleric, or fiery, problem: Mercury, ruler of the Ascendant is in a fire sign, Sagittarius, and combust the Sun. Both planets are separating from a trine to Mars in Aries, another fire sign. The origin of the problem was exhaustion: the Moon on the sixth cusp, ruling physical health, is applying to a conjunction with Saturn, ruler of exhaustion. It is also in Aquarius, Saturn's sign.

Culpeper does not tell us what the treatment might have been but plenty of rest (to cope with Saturn) and cool Venusian herbs (to balance the fire) might be expected.

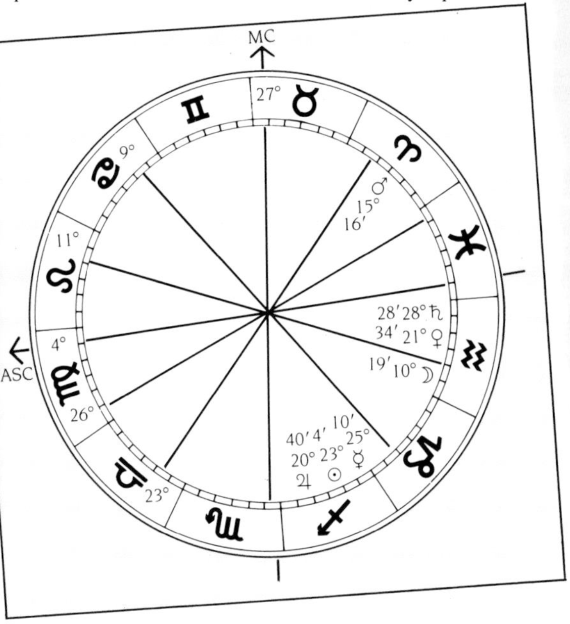

The Signs of the Zodiac and the Homeopathic Cell Salts

	Sign	Cell Salt
♈	Aries	Kali Phos.
♉	Taurus	Nat. Sulph.
♊	Gemini	Kali Mur.
♋	Cancer	Calc. Chlor.
♌	Leo	Mag. Phos.
♍	Virgo	Kali Sulph.
♎	Libra	Nat. Phos.
♏	Scorpio	Calc. Sulph.
♐	Sagittarius	Silica
♑	Capricorn	Calc. Phos.
♒	Aquarius	Nat. Mur.
♓	Pisces	Ferrum Phos.

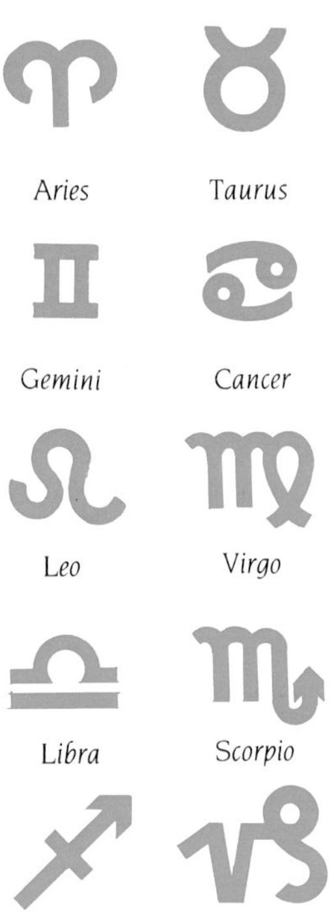

traditional planets. In basic treatment a herb is prescribed which counteracts the physical symptoms so that a herb under the rulership of cold-moist Venus may be given to alleviate the problems caused by hot-dry Mars . One of the classic remedies for migraine, a typical Mars complaint, is the Venusian herb feverfew, which, interestingly, has been used by orthodox doctors who have been unable to find any other cure for this problem.

Homeopathy. Homeopathic diagnosis and treatment is usually practised separately from astrology, although the two systems have very close affinities and are often used together with excellent results. Homeopathy uses the principle of healing by sympathy: a remedy similar to the symptoms is administered. For example, coffee, which induces a state of high nervousness, is ruled by Mars (perhaps with Mercury), yet in its homeopathic form coffee is also a remedy for such a condition. In the case of broken bones, ruled by Saturn, the remedy is symphitum, made from the herb comfrey, known as 'knitbone' and also ruled by Saturn. In other words a Saturn herb comes to the aid of a Saturn problem. In spite of its apparent simplicity, considerable expertise in homeopathy is required before such treatments can be effectively applied.

There is no systematic correlation of homeopathic remedies with astrological conditions, and with two such subtle disciplines a fixed system would probably create problems. However, many of those trained in the two practices are well aware of the close correspondences. It is interesting to note that there are 12 homeopathic remedies (Cell Salts) which correspond to the 12 signs and which are routinely taken as a tonic. Generally that salt is used which corresponds to the Ascendant, Sun or Moon sign, depending on which is most appropriate.

In diagnosis many homeopaths use a system in which each of the four elements corresponds to one of the four levels of human existence. Fire corresponds to the spirit, air to the mind, water to the emotions and earth to the body. These are arranged in a hierarchy with fire at the top, and air, water and earth in order below. Most homeopaths spend up to an hour questioning their patients to establish the cause of their disease. Spiritual causes are invariably impossible to discern. Physical causes are relevant only when first-aid is required, so great effort is put into establishing whether the origin of the disease is primarily mental (air) or emotional (water).

Bach Flower Remedies. Edward Bach invented the flower remedies which are based on the principle of homeopathy. Each remedy equates to a certain emotional and mental type – one may be full of anger, one cold and distant, another full of fear – and is prescribed for those whose psychological state equates with the remedy's 'symptom picture'. As with homeopathy, there is no standard correlation with astrology; the astrologer analyses the overall disposition of the chart and selects the most appropriate remedy. For example, a remedy associated with fear might be prescribed for a very Saturnine person.

One remedy which is of general use is Olive flower, prescribed for complete mental exhaustion. The remedy is equated with Virgo, and as the olive tree itself is ruled by Jupiter, it has been successfully prescribed for conditions of physical and mental collapse which overtake the overworked Piscean. The connections are subtle and flexible, but effective.

Acupuncture. Traditional acupuncture, which is gaining increasing popularity in the West, is intimately connected with Chinese astrology, the acupuncturist taking into account the individual's natal disposition, the season, the weather and other relevant information. As an oriental system, acupuncture does not correspond exactly to Western astrology but work is in progress to enable the two systems to be used together.

THE COSMIC FRAMEWORK

Lunar Cycles. Folklore is steeped in traditions and customs that vary according to the phases of the Moon. One saying has it that hair will grow thick if cut when the Moon is waxing and 'C' shaped, and long if cut under a Moon which is waning and 'D' shaped. In fact such customs may have more truth in them than meets the eye. It is known that a wide range of living creatures harmonize with the daily motion of the Moon, their metabolic rates reaching a trough when it is on the IC and a peak when it is on the MC. Recent evidence has suggested that bleeding ulcers and heart pains are more frequent around full Moon, reinforcing the age-old belief that people bleed more easily at this time. Deaths from tuberculosis also appear to follow the monthly cycle, perhaps, it is suggested because the blood is affected by variations in magnetism.

Evidence from hospitals suggests that the number of attempted suicides also increases around full moon.

Solar Cycles. Initial research has demonstrated the possibility that year and month of birth are connected to the incidence of several major diseases, including polio and cancer. Such evidence may be of immense potential in enabling researchers to direct their resources towards those most at risk, and yet is completely ignored by the medical establishment.

The sunspot cycle itself has been related to major epidemics as well as to diseases of the heart and industrial accidents, the last being the result of the effect of atmospheric disturbance on the nervous system. Even the Sun's daily cycle corresponds to changes in the human body, and it has been found that the constitution of the blood changes sharply immediately before dawn.

Comets. Comets are generally ignored by modern astrologers, although in classical and medieval times there were complicated rules for interpretation based on their appearance. They have traditionally been portents of doom, bringing death and disaster, although the ancient Romans and Greeks also believed that a comet was the soul of a dead hero on its way to take its place as a star in the Milky Way. In view of comets' traditional association with disease one modern theory is particularly interesting. Two eminent professors of astronomy, Chandra Wickramsinghe and Fred Hoyle, have argued that comets carry micro-organisms which are picked up by the Earth when it passes through the trail left in the comet's wake. These micro-organisms bring epidemics, particularly new strains of influenza. One comet that seems to be particularly involved is Enke's comet, which is associated with a four-yearly periodicity in 'flu epidemics. It has been suggested that comets were not only responsible for the great plague in Athens in 429 BC, and the 'flu epidemic of 1918–19 which killed 30 million people, but also the arrival of the AIDS virus.

FERTILITY, CONCEPTION AND BIRTH. In 1968 a remarkable experiment took place in Czechoslovakia in which a new system of birth control devised by Dr Eugen Jonas was used by 1,252 women for a year. At the end of the experiment the method had proved 98 percent effective and only 28 women had become pregnant.

Jonas had found that the exact distance between the Sun and Moon at birth seemed to be the critical factor and that the most fertile part of the female cycle occurred in the 24 hours before the Sun and Moon returned to this exact aspect (which takes place about 13 times a year). Jonas considered that 85 percent of all pregnancies occurred at this time and advised women to abstain from intercourse for a four-day period on either side of their exact Sun-Moon aspect.

Jonas also believed that, if conception took place at new Moon or full Moon, it could indicate a problem pregnancy, although this and his other conclusions are regarded with scepticism in some quarters. There has been no conclusive testing of his work in the West and women who have used his astrological birth control method would advise taking some additional precautions.

Astrology has long assumed that positions of planets at birth are connected to those at conception; and the conception chart has been in use for almost as long as the birth chart. Conception charts have never caught on for the obvious reason that the time of conception is impossible to fix. However, one tradition, known as the Trutine of Hermes, claims that the position of the Moon at birth was that of the Ascendant at conception and the position of the Ascendant at birth was that of the Moon at conception. This principle has been elaborated by modern astrologers into a chart known as the 'pre-natal epoch', which is not the actual conception chart, but a symbolic equivalent set for about nine months before birth.

Whatever the difficulties involved in setting up the conception chart, the astrological connections between conception and birth are suggested by those between parents and children. The birth of a child always takes place when the parent is having significant transits, and it would be against all astrological experience if conception did not also take place under strong transits. One may therefore assume strong connections between the child's birth chart and the conception chart, whenever this may be.

The connections between the charts of parents and children formed the basis of some interesting research by French scientist Michel Gauquelin. Gauquelin found that parents born with certain planets angular (conjunct the Ascendant or Descendant) – the Moon, Venus, Mars, Jupiter and Saturn – tended to have children with those same planets angular. That there is a cycle in the frequency of births is strongly suggested by evidence showing that more children are born at the end of the night and early in the day – with the Sun rising – or with the Moon close to the MC. Gauquelin went further and suggested that baby, parent and planets are connected to a rhythm timed by a 'cosmic clock', and that birth occurs when all three are synchronized.

Unfortunately Gauquelin found that his statistical results broke down when faced with induced births and caesarian operations, with consequences that may not be clear for some time.

CHAPTER 22
PLANTING BY THE STARS: ASTROLOGICAL GARDENING

The entire universe pulsates to an intricate series of beats and rhythms, and scientists are aware of only the simplest. The potential of even these is ignored, and yet the evidence suggests that, if they were taken into account, the world's whole system of agriculture could be organized on a more rational basis. Out of all the uses of astrology, the regulation of gardening and agriculture according to cosmic cycles, has the greatest practical potential.

THE TRADITION. Astrology lays down very exact rules for obtaining the greatest benefit from planting, growing and harvesting plants, in which the crucial stages of each plant's life must occur during certain favourable times. These are based on the belief that every type of plant is ruled by a planet whose nature it shares. For example ginger, a typically hot spice ruled by Mars, should if possible be planted with Mars in Dignity by sign (in Aries or Scorpio), or in its Exaltation (in Capricorn), in the sixth house (in which it is said to 'rejoice'), and in good aspects such as applying trines to the Moon, Jupiter and Venus. If such perfect conditions never arise then the astrologer must find the best that he can! Similarly Sun-ruled plants need to be sown under a strong Sun, Moon-ruled plants under a strong Moon, and so on.

Astrological gardening of this precision takes on a ritual quality and its function is indicated by the recent evidence suggesting connections between the health of plants and their environment. It is no longer considered unusual that plants are more robust after being talked to or being exposed to sensitive music. In strict astrological gardening the effect is much the same. By taking a ritualistic approach the gardener adopts a certain attitude with the result that, care and cultivation of the plant is enhanced.

Whatever their specific rulerships all plants come under the general sway of the Moon. The principal lunar cycle is the full Moon–new Moon cycle, but traditions differ as to whether plants should be sown around new Moon (the beginning of the waxing phase) or at full Moon (the beginning of the waning phase). Generally, the new Moon is favoured. Some say that only root crops should be planted during the waning Moon.

The rules are based on the proposition that just before new Moon energy reaches a trough, after which growth accelerates, reaching a peak at full Moon. At the new Moon moisture absorption is at its lowest and at full Moon at its highest. For this reason crops should be harvested for storage at the new Moon, when they are driest, and for immediate consumption at full Moon, when they are at their most succulent. In France from 1669 until the Revolution it was the law that timber could only be felled at new Moon.

THE EVIDENCE. Crop yield and planet behaviour is fairly easy to measure and this is one area where the tools of science are qualified to measure the claims of astrology. Results obtained by recent research show that plants respond to changes in the Earth's magnetic field caused by the cycles of the Sun and the Moon; plant growth speeds up around full Moon, sap rises faster and up to 35 percent more water is absorbed than at new Moon. The metabolic rate of even the humble potato is up to 15 percent greater at full Moon than at new Moon.

Some cycles peak at both new and full Moons – the electrical potential of trees and the amount of oxygen absorbed by seeds both seem to maximize at these times. Other cycles vary depending on the needs of the plant at different phases – at new Moon more

Gardening by the Lunar Calendar

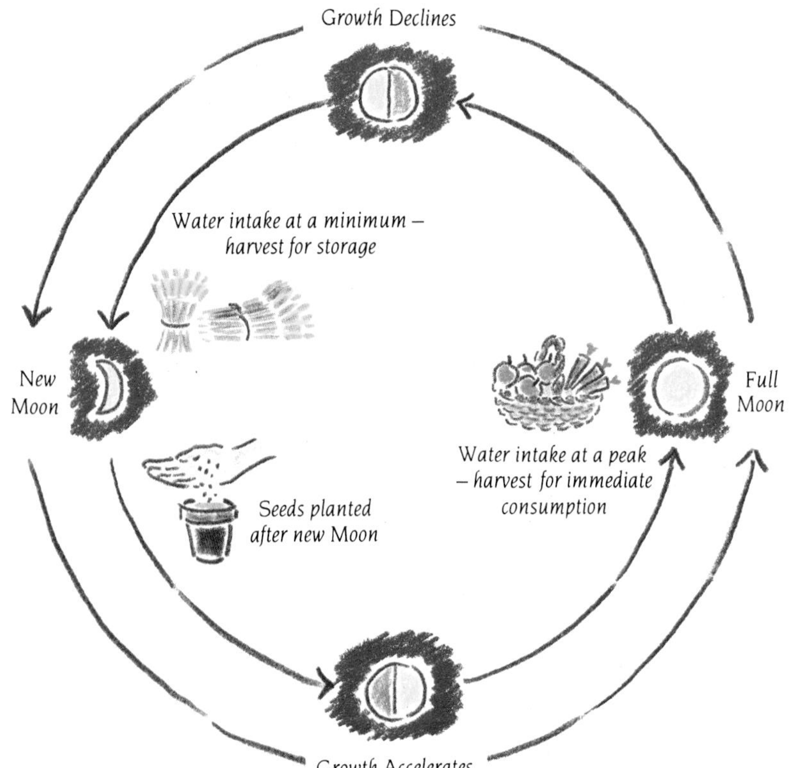

potassium is absorbed and at full Moon phosphorus intake is maximized, a fact which should be taken into account if chemical fertilizers are used.

One project revealed that the medicinal effect of certain herbs decreases sharply at both the new and full Moons, supporting the traditional practices of medical astrologers in preparing their remedies at specified times.

Eclipses are important, and can actually inhibit or even prevent germination even at otherwise favourable times. The Moon's distance from the Earth also seems to be influential, and if it is too close this may lead to stress and rapid unbalanced growth.

The sunspot cycle, with its general effect on the weather, is a critical long-term cycle, and there is little doubt that root-crop yields reach a maximum when sunspots are at their most frequent.

BIODYNAMIC GARDENING. It was not until the 1950s that a comprehensive system of lunar gardening was worked out by Maria Thun, a follower of the mystic Rudolf Steiner.

Thun's main innovation was to relate plant structure to the four elements. Previously tradition had regarded the three water signs as ideal for the sowing and germinating of seeds, the earth signs, especially Taurus and Capricorn, as suitable for root crops (though not as beneficial as water signs), the air signs as indifferent, and the hot-dry Fire signs as harmful and likely to lead to famine.

Thun divided plants into four sections – the root, related to earth, the leaf related to water, the flower related to air and the fruit or seed related to fire. Next she classified different crops under these categories so that, for example, potato equates to root/earth and cabbage to leaf/water.

The basic practice is quite simple – crops should be sown or planted when the Moon is in the relevant element. However, there is one major drawback: Thun used the sidereal zodiac of Indian astrology not the standard tropical zodiac of the West because the sidereal zodiac produced the required results. Unfortunately the ordinary ephemeris shows only the tropical signs and converting these into sidereal is simple but laborious. Luckily, two British experts, Simon Best and Nick Kollerstrom, have solved this problem by publishing a yearly calendar containing gardening instructions.

Tests have shown that when this system is applied crop yields increase by as much as 54 percent, but that the use of chemical fertilizers destroys the effect. The Biodynamic system is thus both a powerful argument in favour of the use of organic farming methods and a pointer to the most positive help which astrology can offer.

It is often said that astrology is a luxury for those with time to dwell on their own problems. Yet if astrology can help to feed the starving there can be no greater reason for the spread of its study and use.

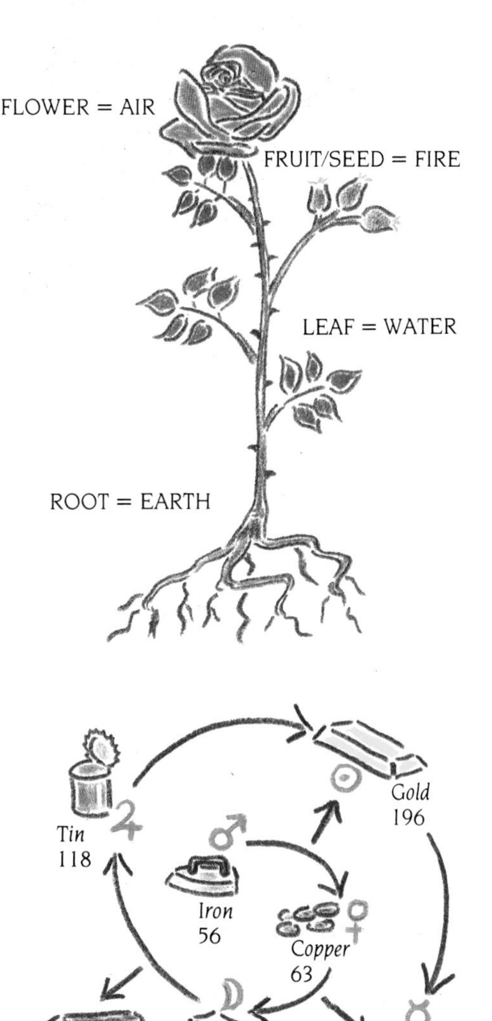

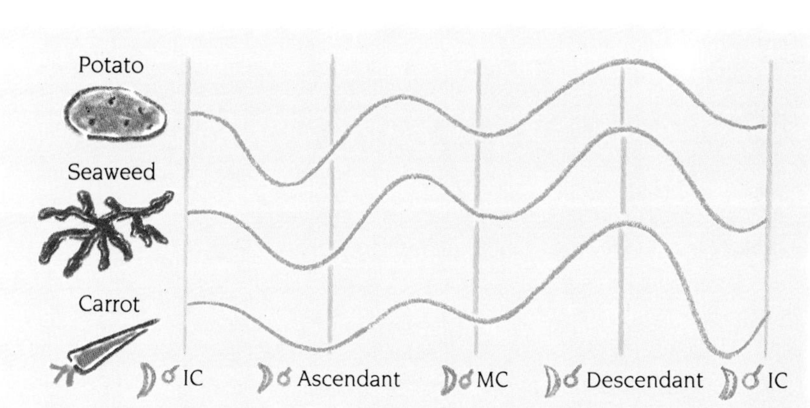

***Top:* The Four Divisions of Plants and the Four Elements**
Evidence shows that different categories of plant are most productive if sown when the Moon is in the appropriate element in the sidereal zodiac.

***Centre:* Chemical Reactions**
The connection of plant growth to cosmic cycles brings astrology down to the level of basic physical existence. Increased crop yields may be associated with the increased rate of chemical reactions which occurs at sunspot peaks. However, at the centre of such phenomena lies a magical view of the universe that takes us straight back to ancient astrology.

If the planets are arranged in their Chaldean order, and alternate planets (the Sun, Mercury and Saturn) are displaced to form a spiral, then an interesting fact emerges. The order of the planets in the spiral, beginning with Mars follows the sequence of planetary metals when arranged in order of increasing weight.

In astrology modern physical science meets ancient mystical wisdom. The displaced planets – the Sun, Mercury and Saturn – were those crucial to medieval alchemy (see Chapter 15).

***Bottom:* Lunar Rhythms**
The metabolism, measured by oxygen consumption, of a range of plants varies with the position of the Moon. A sharp increase in oxygen intake takes place shortly before the Moon rises, a trough is reached when it is on the MC and a second peak when it is on the Descendant. Biodynamic gardeners tend to plant seeds when the Moon is in the tenth, eleventh or twelfth houses. For further information see The Cosmic Clocks *by Michel Gauquelin.*

CHAPTER 23 PREDICTING THE WEATHER: ASTRO-METEOROLOGY

The four seasons occupy a critical role for on the one hand they regulate all human life and on the other they are the foundation of the signs of the tropical zodiac. It is through the seasons that the great cycles of stars and of climate interact.

As might be expected, the most obvious correlation between weather and cosmic cycles is provided by the Moon, whose phases have been shown to connect with rainfall patterns. On a grander scale the 18-year 'saros' cycle, which measures eclipses, seems to correlate with an 18–20 year drought cycle in North America. The Dust Bowl of the mid-1930s was the result of one such drought and if the theory is correct, the next one is due in 1991–2. As the United States depends for its global influence partly on its role as a world grain supplier, this may not be without its political consequences.

The sunspot cycle also correlates with rainfall, periods of greatest rain coinciding with the sunspot peak. All these cycles interact and it is quite possible for the anticipated sunspot peak of 1991–2 to balance the influence of the drought expected then.

There are also a number of longer-term cycles which ranges from the 180-year cycle corresponding to a major rhythm in the sunspot cycle, to a 25,000 year cycle which relates to the same phenomenon that produces the shift of the stars and the astrological Great Ages.

Weather prediction on a day-to-day basis is a very different matter to the measurement of long-term climatic fluctuations, and depends very largely on a reading of the traditional planetary aspects. The signs are accorded little importance and the houses none at all.

Astrological weather prediction is always qualified by location: it is most appropriate to temperate climates which experience a complete range of possible types of weather from flood to drought and from occasional tropical heat to periodic freezing conditions.

Climatic Cycles
One of the clearest medium term climatic cycles is an 11 year rhythm that corresponds to the sunspot cycle. Mean temperatures, shown here for London, increase to coincide with sunspot peaks.

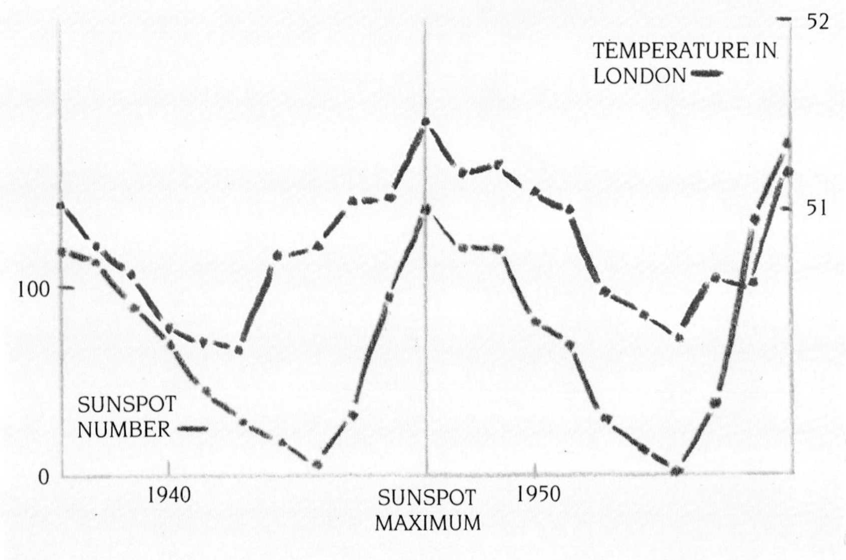

THE PLANETS

THE SUN. Traditionally hot and dry but its main effect is to emphasize the planets with which it is in contact. So, for example, a Sun-Jupiter conjunction will bring warm weather but a Sun-Saturn conjunction brings cooler conditions.

THE MOON. Its traditional nature is cold and moist but, like the Sun, its main effect is through aspects to other planets. For example, a trine to Mars produces warm dry weather and a trine to Venus cool wet weather. The Moon's many aspects are responsible for rapid changes in weather, but are less important than those of the Sun.

MERCURY. A cold dry planet, Mercury's main responsibility is in bringing winds and hence changeable weather.

VENUS. Traditionally cold and moist, Venus signifies rainfall but tends towards mild conditions.

MARS. Signifies rapid rises in temperature, hot weather and dry conditions.

JUPITER. Traditionally a hot moist planet, Jupiter denotes warm weather.

SATURN. Signifies cold weather, often with damp conditions.

URANUS. Brings erratic weather and extremes; it often signifies a drop in temperature and sudden winds.

NEPTUNE. Its character is mild and moist and it signifies damp and temperate conditions.

PLUTO. Role uncertain, but Pluto may be associated with violent conditions and powerful storms.

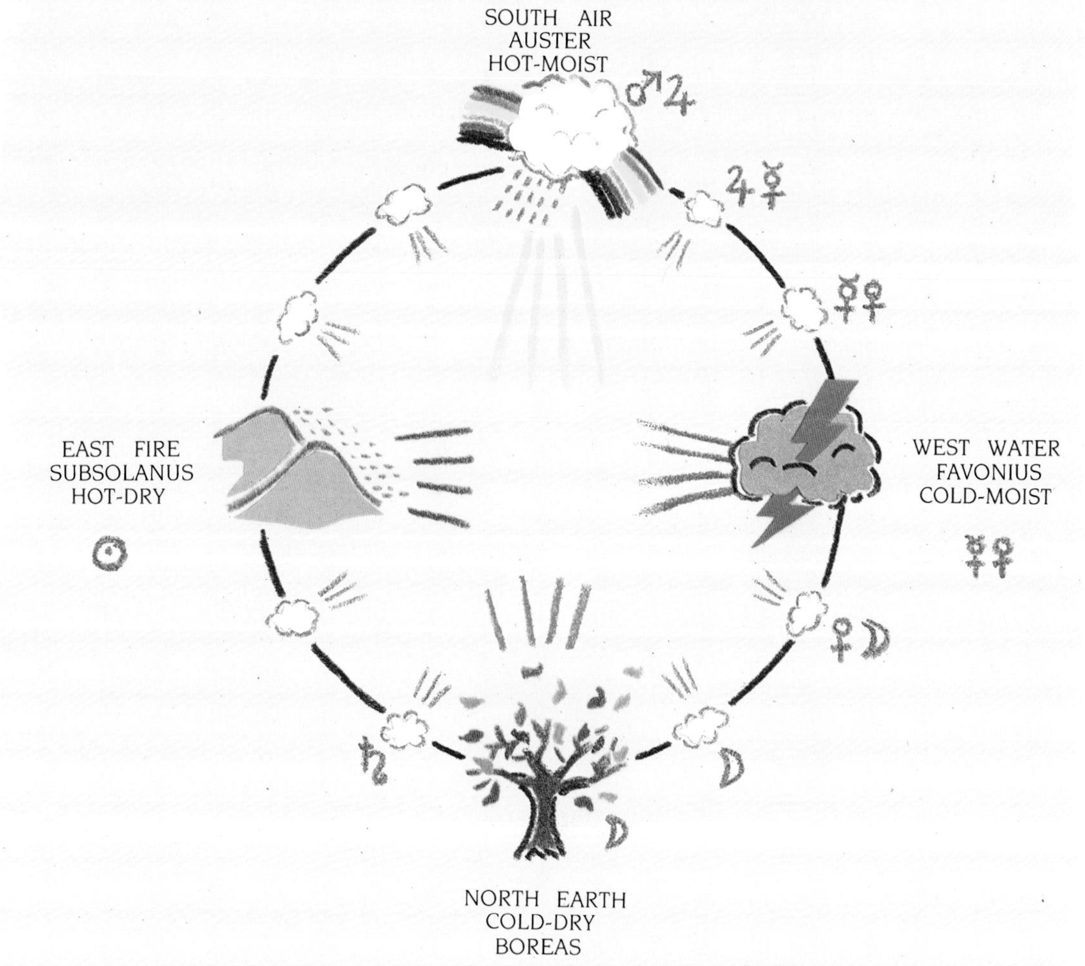

SOUTH AIR
AUSTER
HOT-MOIST

EAST FIRE
SUBSOLANUS
HOT-DRY

WEST WATER
FAVONIUS
COLD-MOIST

NORTH EARTH
COLD-DRY
BOREAS

Sun Moon

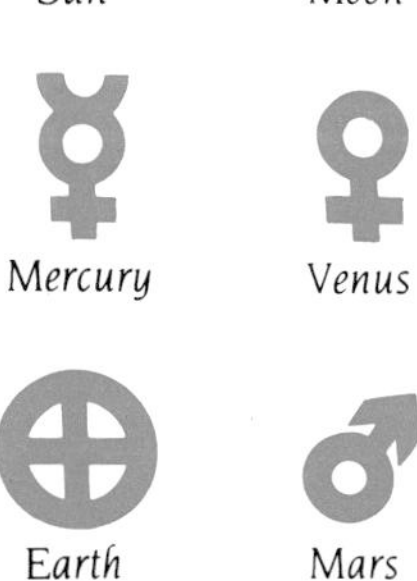

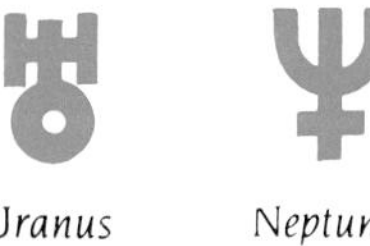

Pluto

The Four Winds
It was a traditional belief that there were four major winds responsible for climatic changes. These corresponded to the four elements: the east wind, Subsolanus, to fire; the south wind, Auster, to air; the west wind, Favonius, to water; and the north wind, Boreas, to Earth. The quality of the wind – hot, cold, dry or moist – was derived from its corresponding element. In addition there were eight minor winds making a total of 12. There was no clear correspondence with the signs of the zodiac, but some correspondences with planets were recognized.

ASPECTS

As a general rule only the major aspects should be used. Aspects to the Sun should be regarded as the most powerful, those between other planets less powerful and those to the Moon least powerful. If two strong aspects contradict each other – for example, if one promises hot dry weather and the other cold and wet – then the strongest aspect will be that which has most supporting features in the chart. These should first be found in other aspects which denote the same type of weather condition, but if there is doubt then the key may lie in each planet's exact disposition in the signs, its Dignity and so on.

Essentially this use of astrology is experimental, for the same conditions never arise twice and the astrologer is always faced with an immediate test of his predictions. As weather conditions cannot be put in a laboratory and replicated there is little hope of a science of astro-meteorology at the level of specific prediction. The meanings of the planets when connected by aspect are quite clear: Mercury-Venus brings mild weather, some wind and rain; Mercury-Saturn brings cold rain and so on. The combination of Mars and Saturn is the most contradictory, but if this contradiction of hot and cold is projected on to the weather system, the result is violent disturbance in the atmosphere and winds of considerable strength.

THE SIGNS

The signs should have a background effect in terms of their qualities, cold, dry, hot or moist, but it is best to concentrate on the planets and aspects initially to gain some expertise.

HOROSCOPES

In general there is no need to use horoscopes, but only to keep abreast of daily transits. However, the solar ingress and new and full Moon charts can be used to indicate weather patterns for the coming season and fortnight, respectively. National horoscopes may also indicate unusual conditions such as severe drought or flood.

CHAPTER 24 COMPUTERS IN ASTROLOGY

The rapid spread of computers represents a revolution in human communication to rival the invention of printing. In astrology even those who do not yet have their own machine use ephemerides and tables of houses which have been calculated by computer.

Choosing a computer is very much a question of economics. It is quite possible to purchase a computer and some basic programmes (software) for under £100 ($150). All that is needed to complete the system is an ordinary televison set and a small cassette recorder. On the other hand the most sophisticated equipment and the most elaborate programmes may cost £2,000 ($3,000).

The pace of change is so rapid that just as the scope of astrology programmes expands so the price of both software and hardware is reduced. Any authoritative listing of what is available becomes out of date within months!

Computer Horoscopes
The quality of printed computerized horoscopes varies. The best is made by Astro Computing Services of San Diego, who include options for additional material to be included with the chart wheel (see opposite).

When home computers first appeared in the late 1970s there were few astrology programmes available and these were usually designed for specific models. However, most programmes are now available for any machine providing, of course, there is sufficient capacity.

A computer's capacity is known as its memory, and the memory needed for a basic chart calculation programme is about 8k. As even the smallest modern computer has a memory of 32k there is no danger of buying a machine that is too small for the simple astrological requirements.

The value of a new computer drops drastically as soon as it is purchased, so second-hand models often come on the market for less than half the original price. However, it is usually better to buy a new machine with a guarantee.

Before buying a computer it is useful to assess its additional functions. The availability of programmes for word processing, business accounts, games or educational purposes is an important consideration.

It is also useful to buy a programme which is part of a series. If there is a choice between two basic interpretation programmes then it is obviously much more profitable to buy the one which may have other programmes added for, say, transits, progressions or chart comparison.

One essential piece of equipment is a printer on to which charts can be 'dumped'. Most of the more expensive programmes can now draw horoscopes out in a standard circular style, although the cheaper versions tend to produce square charts. Computers are obviously of most use in calculation. Much of what the computer does in this area is simple but laborious. It is not difficult to calculate a birth chart, with transits, progressions, harmonics, midpoints, solar and lunar returns and so on, but it is time consuming. If the astrologer is relieved of this task then there is more time available to develop the art of interpretation. However, computers take away from the astrologer tasks that are not only laborious but also complex. There are programmes available to work out primary directions, converse progressions, relationship charts and other variants that would otherwise fall into disuse. For those who wish to experiment with different houses some programmes will actually work out 10 different systems for one horoscope.

Also available are chart interpretation packages which print out ready made interpretations. These start with the basic routine of planets in houses and signs and aspects, and can be expanded to include chart comparison, transits and progressions.

However, these are really only of use for commercially minded astrologers keen to tap the market for computer interpretations. The cheapest chart interpretation package costs only £24 ($36). The most expensive versions in the USA cost up to £700 ($1,000) for a complete system and are ideally suited to the IBM computers.

The third type of programme is that devised for research. For example, it may be possible to ask the computer for all the horoscopes on file with Mars in the first house, or Venus in sesquiquadrate with Uranus. Some programmes will carry out statistical analyses of all the charts on file. Fascinating as such work can be beginners should not be seduced into research until they have really understood both the nature of astrology and the difficulties of the science-astrology relationship, otherwise they will be unable to reach any valid conclusions.

The cream of astrological software is produced by Matrix, a company based in Illinois, USA. Matrix produce two remarkable programmes, the Blue Star 64 costing about £100 ($150) for the complete package and the M65A which costs about £200 ($300). The M65A can handle just about every technique ever devised by astrologers and can cope with 40 jobs at once. The astrologer feeds in 40 sets of data with instructions and the computer provides results that could otherwise take weeks to calculate.

The M65A will work on any main computer including Apple, IBM and Commodore models. Matrix also publish a magazine called Astrotalk which contains the latest information about new developments in computer astrology.

In the UK the widest range of programmes is available from Astrocalc who are fast catching up with the high standards set by Matrix in the USA. Like Matrix their programmes are adaptable for most models.

For the do-it-yourself programmer there is a manual written by Michael Erlewine, the founder of Matrix. Most programmers prefer to work out their own software to their own specifications, but Erlewine's book is an excellent starting point.

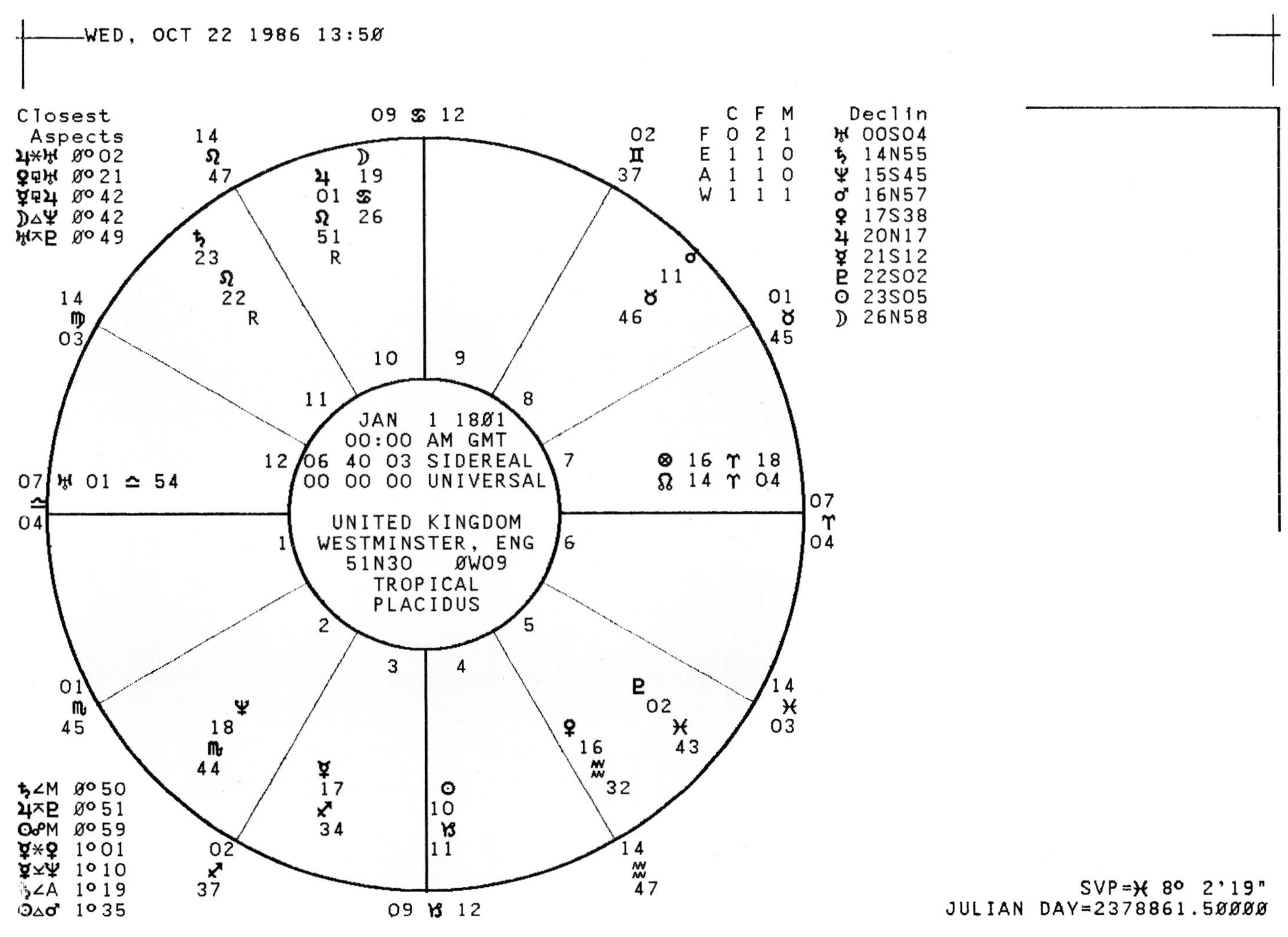

1930

JANUARY

	1	2	3	4	5	6	7	8	9	10	11	12	13	14	15	16	17	18	19	20	21	22	23	24	25	26	27	28	29	30	31
☉	♑10	11	12	13	14	15	16	17	18	19	20	21	22	23	24	25	26	27	28	29	♒0	1	2	3	4	5	6	7	8	9	♒10
☽	♑21	♒3	15	26	♓8	21	♈3	15	28	♉12	26	♊10	25	♋10	25	♌10	26	♍11	25	♎9	22	♏5	18	♐0	12	24	♑6	18	♒0	12	♒24
☿	♑28	29	♒1	2	3	4	5	6	7	7	8	8	8	8	8	7	7	6	5	4	3	1	0	♑29	28	26	25	25	24	23	♑23
♀	♑1	2	4	5	6	7	9	10	11	12	14	15	16	17	19	20	21	22	24	25	26	27	29	♒0	1	2	4	5	6	8	♒9
♂	♑2	3	3	4	5	6	6	7	8	9	9	10	11	12	13	13	14	15	16	16	17	18	19	19	20	21	22	22	23	24	♑25

	1	6	12	18	24	30
♃	♊8	7	7	7	6	6
♄	♑4	4	5	6	6	7

	1	15	30
♅	♈8	8	8
♆	♍3	3	3
♇	♋19	18	18
☊	♉10	9	7

FEBRUARY

	1	2	3	4	5	6	7	8	9	10	11	12	13	14	15	16	17	18	19	20	21	22	23	24	25	26	27	28
☉	♒11	12	13	14	15	16	17	19	20	21	22	23	24	25	26	27	28	29	♓0	1	2	3	4	5	6	7	8	♓9
☽	♓6	18	♈0	12	25	♉8	21	♊5	19	♋3	18	♌3	18	♍4	19	♎3	17	♏1	14	26	♐9	21	♑3	15	27	♒8	20	♓2
☿	♑22	22	22	22	23	23	23	24	24	25	26	27	27	28	29	♒0	1	3	4	5	6	7	9	10	11	12	14	♒15
♀	♒10	11	13	14	15	16	18	19	20	21	23	24	25	26	28	29	♓0	1	3	4	5	6	8	9	10	11	13	♓14
♂	♑26	26	27	28	29	29	♒0	1	2	3	3	4	5	6	6	7	8	9	9	10	11	12	13	13	14	15	16	♒17

	1	6	12	18	24	28
♃	♊6	6	7	7	7	8
♄	♑7	8	8	9	9	10

	1	15	28
♅	♈8	9	10
♆	♍3	2	2
♇	♋18	18	18
☊	♉7	5	4

MARCH

	1	2	3	4	5	6	7	8	9	10	11	12	13	14	15	16	17	18	19	20	21	22	23	24	25	26	27	28	29	30	31
☉	♓10	11	12	13	14	15	16	17	18	19	20	21	22	23	24	25	26	27	28	29	♈0	1	2	3	4	5	6	7	8	9	♈10
☽	♓15	27	♈9	22	♉5	18	♊1	15	28	♋13	27	♌12	27	♍12	27	♎11	25	♏9	22	♐5	17	29	♑11	23	♒5	17	29	♓11	23	♈6	♈18
☿	♒17	18	19	21	22	24	25	27	29	♓0	2	3	5	7	8	10	12	13	15	17	19	21	22	24	26	28	♈0	2	4	6	♈8
♀	♓15	16	18	19	20	21	23	24	25	26	28	29	♈0	1	3	4	5	6	8	9	10	11	13	14	15	16	17	19	20	21	♈22
♂	♒17	18	19	20	20	21	22	23	24	24	25	26	27	27	28	29	♓0	1	1	2	3	4	5	5	6	7	8	8	9	10	♓11

	1	6	12	18	24	30
♃	♊8	8	9	10	10	11
♄	♑10	10	11	11	11	11

	1	15	30
♅	♈10	10	11
♆	♍2	2	1
♇	♋18	17	17
☊	♉4	3	3

APRIL

	1	2	3	4	5	6	7	8	9	10	11	12	13	14	15	16	17	18	19	20	21	22	23	24	25	26	27	28	29	30
☉	♈11	12	13	13	14	15	16	17	18	19	20	21	22	23	24	25	26	27	28	29	♉0	1	2	3	4	5	6	7	8	♉9
☽	♉1	15	28	♊11	25	♋9	23	♌8	22	♍7	21	♎5	19	♏3	16	♐0	12	25	♑7	19	♒1	13	25	♓7	19	♈1	14	27	♉10	♉24
☿	♈10	12	14	16	18	20	22	24	26	29	♉1	3	5	7	8	10	12	14	15	17	19	20	22	23	24	25	26	27	28	♉29
♀	♈24	25	26	27	29	♉0	1	2	4	5	6	7	8	10	11	12	13	15	16	17	18	20	21	22	23	24	26	27	28	♉29
♂	♓12	12	13	14	15	15	16	17	18	19	19	20	21	22	22	23	24	25	26	26	27	28	29	29	♈0	1	2	3	3	♈4

	1	6	12	18	24	30
♃	♊12	13	14	15	16	17
♄	♑12	12	12	12	12	12

	1	15	30
♅	♈11	12	13
♆	♍1	1	1
♇	♋17	17	18
☊	♉3	3	3

MAY

	1	2	3	4	5	6	7	8	9	10	11	12	13	14	15	16	17	18	19	20	21	22	23	24	25	26	27	28	29	30	31
☉	♉10	11	12	13	14	15	16	17	18	19	20	21	22	22	23	24	25	26	27	28	29	♊0	1	2	3	4	5	6	7	8	♊9
☽	♊8	22	♋6	20	♌4	19	♍3	17	♎1	15	28	♏12	25	♐8	20	♑3	15	27	♒9	21	♓3	15	27	♈9	22	♉5	19	♊3	17	♋2	♋16
☿	♊0	0	1	2	2	2	2	3	3	3	2	2	2	2	1	1	0	0	♉29	29	28	27	27	26	26	25	25	25	24	24	♉24
♀	♊1	2	3	4	5	7	8	9	10	12	13	14	15	16	18	19	20	21	23	24	25	26	27	29	♋0	1	2	3	5	6	♋7
♂	♈5	6	6	7	8	9	9	10	11	12	13	13	14	15	16	16	17	18	19	19	20	21	22	22	23	24	25	25	26	27	♈28

	1	6	12	18	24	30
♃	♊17	18	20	21	22	24
♄	♑12	12	12	11	11	11

	1	15	30
♅	♈13	14	14
♆	♍1	1	1
♇	♋18	18	18
☊	♉3	3	2

JUNE

	1	2	3	4	5	6	7	8	9	10	11	12	13	14	15	16	17	18	19	20	21	22	23	24	25	26	27	28	29	30
☉	♊10	11	12	13	14	15	16	16	17	18	19	20	21	22	23	24	25	26	27	28	29	♋0	1	2	3	4	5	6	7	♋7
☽	♌1	15	♍0	14	28	♎11	25	♏8	21	♐4	16	29	♑11	23	♒5	17	29	♓11	23	♈5	17	♉0	13	27	♊11	26	♋11	26	♌11	♌25
☿	♉24	24	24	24	24	24	25	25	26	26	27	28	28	29	♊0	1	2	3	4	6	7	8	10	11	12	14	16	17	19	♊21
♀	♋8	9	11	12	13	14	15	17	18	19	20	21	23	24	25	26	27	29	♌0	1	2	3	5	6	7	8	9	10	12	♌13
♂	♈28	29	♉0	1	1	2	3	4	4	5	6	7	7	8	9	10	10	11	12	12	13	14	15	15	16	17	18	18	19	♉20

	1	6	12	18	24	30
♃	♊24	25	27	28	29	♋1
♄	♑11	10	10	10	9	9

	1	15	30
♅	♈14	15	15
♆	♍1	1	1
♇	♋18	18	19
☊	♉2	1	0

JULY

	1	2	3	4	5	6	7	8	9	10	11	12	13	14	15	16	17	18	19	20	21	22	23	24	25	26	27	28	29	30	31
☉	♋8	9	10	11	12	13	14	15	16	17	18	19	20	21	22	23	24	25	26	27	28	28	29	♌0	1	2	3	4	5	6	♌7
☽	♍10	24	♎8	22	♏5	18	♐1	13	25	♑8	20	♒2	14	26	♓7	19	♈1	13	26	♉9	22	♊5	19	♋4	19	♌4	20	♍5	20	♎4	♎18
☿	♊22	24	26	28	♋0	2	4	6	8	11	13	15	17	19	21	23	26	28	♌0	2	4	6	8	10	12	14	16	18	19	21	♌23
♀	♌14	15	16	18	19	20	21	22	23	25	26	27	28	29	♍0	2	3	4	5	6	7	8	10	11	12	13	14	15	16	18	♍19
♂	♉20	21	22	23	23	24	25	25	26	27	28	28	29	♊0	0	1	2	2	3	4	4	5	6	7	7	8	9	9	10	11	♊11

	1	6	12	18	24	30
♃	♋1	2	3	5	6	7
♄	♑9	8	8	7	7	7

	1	15	30
♅	♈15	15	15
♆	♍1	2	2
♇	♋19	19	20
☊	♉0	♈0	27

AUGUST

	1	2	3	4	5	6	7	8	9	10	11	12	13	14	15	16	17	18	19	20	21	22	23	24	25	26	27	28	29	30	31
☉	♌8	9	10	11	12	13	14	15	16	17	18	19	20	20	21	22	23	24	25	26	27	28	29	♍0	1	2	3	4	5	6	♍7
☽	♏2	15	28	♐10	23	♑5	17	29	♒11	23	♓4	16	28	♈10	22	♉5	18	♊1	14	28	♋13	28	♌13	28	♍13	28	♎13	27	♏11	24	♐7
☿	♌25	26	28	♍0	1	3	5	6	8	9	11	12	14	15	16	18	19	20	22	23	24	25	26	27	28	29	♎0	1	2	3	♎3
♀	♍20	21	22	23	24	25	27	28	29	♎0	1	2	3	4	5	7	8	9	10	11	12	13	14	15	16	17	18	19	21	22	♎23
♂	♊12	13	13	14	15	15	16	17	17	18	19	19	20	21	21	22	23	23	24	25	25	26	27	27	28	28	29	♋0	0	1	♋2

	1	6	12	18	24	30
♃	♋8	9	10	11	12	13
♄	♑6	6	6	6	5	5

	1	15	30
♅	♈15	15	15
♆	♍2	3	3
♇	♋20	20	20
☊	♈27	26	25

SEPTEMBER

	1	2	3	4	5	6	7	8	9	10	11	12	13	14	15	16	17	18	19	20	21	22	23	24	25	26	27	28	29	30
☉	♍8	9	10	11	12	13	14	15	16	17	18	19	19	20	21	22	23	24	25	26	27	28	29	♎0	1	2	3	4	5	♎6
☽	♐19	♑2	14	26	♒8	20	♓1	13	25	♈7	20	♉2	14	27	♊10	24	♋8	22	♌7	21	♍6	21	♎6	21	♏5	19	♐2	15	28	♑10
☿	♎4	5	5	6	6	6	7	7	7	7	7	6	6	5	5	4	3	2	1	0	♍29	28	27	26	25	24	23	23	22	♍22
♀	♎24	25	26	27	28	29	♏0	1	2	3	4	5	6	7	8	9	10	11	11	12	13	14	15	16	17	18	19	19	20	♏21
♂	♋2	3	3	4	5	5	6	7	7	8	8	9	10	10	11	11	12	12	13	14	14	15	15	16	17	17	18	18	19	♋19

	1	6	12	18	24	30
♃	♋14	15	16	17	17	18
♄	♑5	5	5	5	5	6

	1	15	30
♅	♈15	14	14
♆	♍3	4	5
♇	♋20	21	21
☊	♈25	24	24

OCTOBER

	1	2	3	4	5	6	7	8	9	10	11	12	13	14	15	16	17	18	19	20	21	22	23	24	25	26	27	28	29	30	31
☉	♎7	8	9	10	11	12	13	14	15	16	17	18	19	20	21	22	23	24	25	26	27	28	29	♏0	1	2	3	4	5	6	♏7
☽	♑22	♒4	16	28	♓10	22	♈4	16	29	♉11	24	♊7	21	♋4	18	♌2	16	♍1	16	♎0	15	29	♏13	27	♐10	23	♑6	18	♒1	13	♒24
☿	♍22	22	22	23	23	24	25	26	27	28	♎0	1	3	4	6	7	9	10	12	14	15	17	19	21	22	24	26	27	29	♏1	♏2
♀	♏22	23	24	24	25	26	27	27	28	29	29	♐0	1	1	2	2	3	3	4	4	5	5	5	6	6	6	7	7	7	7	♐7
♂	♋20	20	21	22	22	23	23	24	24	25	25	26	26	27	27	28	28	29	29	♌0	0	1	1	2	2	3	3	3	4	4	♌5

	1	6	12	18	24	30
♃	♋18	19	19	20	20	20
♄	♑6	6	6	6	7	7

	1	15	30
♅	♈14	13	13
♆	♍5	5	5
♇	♋21	21	21
☊	♈24	24	24

NOVEMBER

	1	2	3	4	5	6	7	8	9	10	11	12	13	14	15	16	17	18	19	20	21	22	23	24	25	26	27	28	29	30
☉	♏8	9	10	11	12	13	14	15	16	17	18	19	20	21	22	23	24	25	26	27	28	29	♐0	1	2	3	4	5	6	♐7
☽	♓6	18	♈0	12	25	♉8	21	♊4	17	♋1	15	29	♌13	27	♍11	26	♎10	24	♏8	22	♐5	18	♑1	14	26	♒8	20	♓2	14	♓26
☿	♏4	6	7	9	11	12	14	15	17	19	20	22	23	25	27	28	♐0	1	3	4	6	7	9	10	12	14	15	17	18	♐20
♀	♐7	7	7	7	7	7	7	7	6	6	6	5	5	5	4	4	3	3	2	1	1	0	0	♏29	28	28	27	27	26	♏26
♂	♌5	6	6	6	7	7	8	8	8	9	9	9	10	10	11	11	11	12	12	12	12	13	13	13	14	14	14	14	15	♌15

	1	6	12	18	24	30
♃	♋20	21	20	20	20	20
♄	♑7	8	8	9	9	10

	1	15	30
♅	♈12	12	12
♆	♍5	6	6
♇	♋21	21	21
☊	♈24	23	23

DECEMBER

	1	2	3	4	5	6	7	8	9	10	11	12	13	14	15	16	17	18	19	20	21	22	23	24	25	26	27	28	29	30	31
☉	♐8	9	10	11	12	13	14	15	16	17	18	19	20	21	22	23	24	25	26	27	28	29	♑0	1	2	3	5	6	7	8	♑9
☽	♈8	20	♉3	16	29	♊13	27	♋11	25	♌10	24	♍8	22	♎6	20	♏4	17	♐1	14	27	♑9	22	♒4	16	28	♓10	22	♈4	16	28	♉11
☿	♐21	23	24	26	27	29	♑0	2	3	5	6	7	9	10	12	13	14	15	16	17	19	19	20	21	21	22	22	22	22	22	♑21
♀	♏25	25	24	24	23	23	23	23	22	22	22	22	22	22	22	22	22	22	23	23	23	24	24	24	25	25	26	26	27	27	♏28
♂	♌15	15	15	15	16	16	16	16	16	16	16	17	17	17	17	17	17	17	17	17	17	17	17	17	17	16	16	16	16	16	♌16

	1	6	12	18	24	30
♃	♋20	19	19	18	17	17
♄	♑10	11	11	12	13	13

	1	15	30
♅	♈12	11	11
♆	♍6	6	6
♇	♋21	20	20
☊	♈23	22	20

1931

JANUARY

	1	2	3	4	5	6	7	8	9	10	11	12	13	14	15	16	17	18	19	20	21	22	23	24	25	26	27	28	29	30	31
☉	♑10	11	12	13	14	15	16	17	18	19	20	21	22	23	24	25	26	27	28	29	♒0	1	2	3	4	5	6	7	8	9	♒10
☽	♉24	♊7	21	♋5	20	♌5	19	♍4	19	♎3	17	♏1	14	27	♐10	23	♑6	18	♒0	13	25	♓6	18	♈0	12	24	♉6	19	♊1	15	♊29
☿	♑21	20	19	18	16	15	14	12	11	10	9	8	7	7	6	6	6	6	6	7	7	8	8	9	10	10	11	12	13	14	♑15
♀	♏28	29	29	♐0	1	1	2	3	4	4	5	6	7	8	8	9	10	11	12	13	14	15	16	17	18	18	19	20	21	22	♐23
♂	♌16	15	15	15	15	15	14	14	14	13	13	13	12	12	12	11	11	11	10	10	10	9	9	8	8	8	7	7	6	6	♌6

	1	6	12	18	24	30		1	6	12	18	24	30		1	15	30		1	15	30		1	15	30		1	15	30
♃	♋16	16	15	14	13	13	♄	♑14	14	15	16	16	17	♅	♈11	12	12	♆	♍6	5	5	♇	♋20	20	19	☊	♈20	19	17

FEBRUARY

	1	2	3	4	5	6	7	8	9	10	11	12	13	14	15	16	17	18	19	20	21	22	23	24	25	26	27	28
☉	♒11	12	13	14	15	16	17	18	19	20	21	22	23	24	25	26	27	28	29	♓0	1	2	3	4	5	6	7	♓8
☽	♋13	28	♌13	28	♍13	28	♎13	27	♏11	24	♐7	20	♑3	15	27	♒9	21	♓3	15	27	♈9	21	♉3	15	27	♊10	23	♋7
☿	♑16	18	19	20	21	23	24	25	27	28	29	♒1	2	4	5	6	8	9	11	13	14	16	17	19	20	22	24	♒25
♀	♐24	25	26	27	28	29	♑1	2	3	4	5	6	7	8	9	10	11	12	13	14	16	17	18	19	20	21	22	♑23
♂	♌5	5	4	4	4	3	3	3	2	2	2	1	1	1	0	0	0	0	♋29	29	29	29	29	28	28	28	28	♋28

	1	6	12	18	24	28		1	6	12	18	24	28		1	15	28		1	15	28		1	15	28		1	15	28
♃	♋12	12	11	11	11	11	♄	♑17	18	19	19	20	20	♅	♈12	13	13	♆	♍5	5	4	♇	♋19	19	19	☊	♈17	16	15

MARCH

	1	2	3	4	5	6	7	8	9	10	11	12	13	14	15	16	17	18	19	20	21	22	23	24	25	26	27	28	29	30	31
☉	♓9	10	11	12	13	14	15	16	17	18	19	20	21	22	23	24	25	26	27	28	29	♈0	1	2	3	4	5	6	7	8	♈9
☽	♋21	♌6	21	♍6	21	♎7	21	♏6	20	♐4	17	♑0	12	24	♒6	18	♓0	12	24	♈6	18	♉0	12	24	♊7	20	♋3	16	♌0	15	♌29
☿	♒27	29	♓0	2	4	6	8	9	11	13	15	17	19	21	22	24	26	28	♈0	2	4	6	8	10	12	14	16	18	20	22	♈24
♀	♑24	26	27	28	29	♒0	1	2	4	5	6	7	8	9	10	12	13	14	15	16	17	19	20	21	22	23	24	26	27	28	♒29
♂	♋28	28	28	28	28	27	27	27	27	27	27	28	28	28	28	28	28	28	28	28	28	28	29	29	29	29	29	♌0	0	0	♌0

	1	6	12	18	24	30		1	6	12	18	24	30		1	15	30		1	15	30		1	15	30		1	15	30
♃	♋11	10	10	11	11	11	♄	♑20	21	21	22	22	22	♅	♈13	14	15	♆	♍4	4	4	♇	♋19	19	19	☊	♈15	15	14

APRIL

	1	2	3	4	5	6	7	8	9	10	11	12	13	14	15	16	17	18	19	20	21	22	23	24	25	26	27	28	29	30
☉	♈10	11	12	13	14	15	16	17	18	19	20	21	22	23	24	25	26	27	28	29	♉0	1	2	3	4	5	6	7	8	♉9
☽	♍14	29	♎15	29	♏14	28	♐12	25	♑8	21	♒3	15	27	♓9	21	♈3	14	27	♉9	21	♊4	17	♋0	13	27	♌10	25	♍9	24	♎8
☿	♈26	27	29	♉1	2	4	5	6	7	8	9	10	11	12	12	13	13	13	13	13	13	13	13	13	12	12	11	11	10	♉9
♀	♓0	1	3	4	5	6	7	8	10	11	12	13	14	16	17	18	19	20	22	23	24	25	26	28	29	♈0	1	2	3	♈5
♂	♌0	1	1	1	1	2	2	2	3	3	3	3	4	4	4	5	5	6	6	6	7	7	7	8	8	8	9	9	10	♌10

	1	6	12	18	24	30		1	6	12	18	24	30		1	15	30		1	15	30		1	15	30		1	15	30
♃	♋11	12	12	13	14	15	♄	♑22	23	23	23	23	23	♅	♈15	16	17	♆	♍3	3	3	♇	♋19	19	19	☊	♈14	14	14

MAY

	1	2	3	4	5	6	7	8	9	10	11	12	13	14	15	16	17	18	19	20	21	22	23	24	25	26	27	28	29	30	31
☉	♉10	11	12	13	14	15	15	16	17	18	19	20	21	22	23	24	25	26	27	28	29	♊0	1	2	3	4	5	6	7	8	♊9
☽	♎23	♏8	22	♐6	20	♑4	17	29	♒11	24	♓5	17	29	♈11	23	♉5	18	♊0	13	26	♋10	23	♌7	21	♍5	19	♎4	18	♏2	17	♐1
☿	♉9	8	7	7	6	6	5	5	4	4	4	4	4	4	4	4	4	4	5	5	6	6	7	8	8	9	10	11	12	13	♉14
♀	♈6	7	8	9	11	12	13	14	15	17	18	19	20	21	23	24	25	26	27	29	♉0	1	2	3	5	6	7	8	10	11	♉12
♂	♌11	11	11	12	12	13	13	13	14	14	15	15	16	16	17	17	18	18	19	19	20	20	20	21	21	22	22	23	23	24	♌24

	1	6	12	18	24	30		1	6	12	18	24	30		1	15	30		1	15	30		1	15	30		1	15	30
♃	♋15	16	17	18	19	20	♄	♑23	23	23	23	23	23	♅	♈17	17	18	♆	♍3	3	3	♇	♋19	19	19	☊	♈14	14	13

JUNE

	1	2	3	4	5	6	7	8	9	10	11	12	13	14	15	16	17	18	19	20	21	22	23	24	25	26	27	28	29	30
☉	♊10	11	11	12	13	14	15	16	17	18	19	20	21	22	23	24	25	26	27	28	29	♋0	1	2	2	3	4	5	6	♋7
☽	♐15	28	♑12	25	♒7	19	♓1	13	25	♈7	19	♉1	13	26	♊9	22	♋6	20	♌4	18	♍2	16	♎0	14	28	♏12	26	♐10	24	♑7
☿	♉15	17	18	19	20	22	23	25	26	28	29	♊1	3	5	6	8	10	12	14	16	18	20	22	24	27	29	♋1	3	5	♋7
♀	♉13	14	16	17	18	19	20	22	23	24	25	26	28	29	♊0	1	2	4	5	6	7	9	10	11	12	13	15	16	17	♊18
♂	♌25	25	26	27	27	28	28	29	29	♍0	0	1	1	2	2	3	3	4	5	5	6	6	7	7	8	8	9	10	10	♍11

	1	6	12	18	24	30		1	6	12	18	24	30		1	15	30		1	15	30		1	15	30		1	15	30
♃	♋20	21	22	24	25	26	♄	♑23	22	22	22	21	21	♅	♈18	19	19	♆	♍3	3	4	♇	♋19	20	20	☊	♈13	12	10

JULY

	1	2	3	4	5	6	7	8	9	10	11	12	13	14	15	16	17	18	19	20	21	22	23	24	25	26	27	28	29	30	31
☉	♋8	9	10	11	12	13	14	15	16	17	18	19	20	21	22	23	23	24	25	26	27	28	29	♌0	1	2	3	4	5	6	♌7
☽	♑20	♒3	15	27	♓9	21	♈3	15	27	♉9	21	♊4	17	♋1	15	29	♌13	28	♍12	27	♎11	25	♏9	23	♐7	20	♑3	16	29	♒11	♒24
☿	♋10	12	14	16	18	20	22	24	26	28	♌0	2	4	6	8	10	11	13	15	16	18	20	21	23	24	26	27	29	♍0	1	♍3
♀	♊19	21	22	23	24	26	27	28	29	♋0	2	3	4	5	7	8	9	10	11	13	14	15	16	18	19	20	21	22	24	25	♋26
♂	♍11	12	12	13	14	14	15	15	16	16	17	18	18	19	19	20	21	21	22	22	23	24	24	25	25	26	27	27	28	28	♍29

	1	6	12	18	24	30		1	6	12	18	24	30		1	15	30		1	15	30		1	15	30		1	15	30
♃	♋26	28	29	♌0	1	3	♄	♑21	21	20	20	19	19	♅	♈19	19	19	♆	♍4	4	4	♇	♋20	20	21	☊	♈10	9	7

AUGUST

	1	2	3	4	5	6	7	8	9	10	11	12	13	14	15	16	17	18	19	20	21	22	23	24	25	26	27	28	29	30	31
☉	♌8	9	10	11	12	13	14	14	15	16	17	18	19	20	21	22	23	24	25	26	27	28	29	♍0	1	2	3	4	5	6	♍7
☽	♓6	18	29	♈11	23	♉5	17	29	♊12	25	♋9	23	♌8	22	♍7	22	♎7	22	♏6	20	♐4	17	♑0	13	26	♒8	20	♓2	14	26	♈8
☿	♍4	5	6	8	9	10	11	12	13	14	15	15	16	17	17	18	18	19	19	19	20	20	20	20	19	19	19	18	18	17	♍16
♀	♋27	29	♌0	1	2	4	5	6	7	8	10	11	12	13	15	16	17	18	20	21	22	23	24	26	27	28	29	♍1	2	3	♍4
♂	♎0	0	1	1	2	3	3	4	5	5	6	6	7	8	8	9	10	10	11	11	12	13	13	14	15	15	16	17	17	18	♎19

	1	6	12	18	24	30		1	6	12	18	24	30		1	15	30		1	15	30		1	15	30		1	15	30
♃	♌3	4	6	7	8	10	♄	♑19	18	18	18	17	17	♅	♈19	19	19	♆	♍4	5	6	♇	♋21	21	22	☊	♈7	6	6

SEPTEMBER

	1	2	3	4	5	6	7	8	9	10	11	12	13	14	15	16	17	18	19	20	21	22	23	24	25	26	27	28	29	30
☉	♍8	9	10	11	11	12	13	14	15	16	17	18	19	20	21	22	23	24	25	26	27	28	29	♎0	1	2	3	4	5	♎6
☽	♈20	♉1	13	26	♊8	21	♋4	17	♌1	16	♍1	16	♎1	16	♏1	15	♐0	13	27	♑10	23	♒5	17	29	♓11	23	♈5	17	28	♉10
☿	♍15	14	13	12	11	11	10	9	8	7	7	6	6	6	6	6	6	7	8	8	9	10	11	13	14	15	17	18	20	♍22
♀	♍6	7	8	9	11	12	13	14	16	17	18	19	21	22	23	24	26	27	28	29	♎1	2	3	4	5	7	8	9	10	♎12
♂	♎19	20	20	21	22	22	23	24	24	25	26	26	27	28	28	29	♏0	0	1	2	2	3	4	4	5	6	7	7	8	♏9

	1	6	12	18	24	30		1	6	12	18	24	30		1	15	30		1	15	30		1	15	30		1	15	30
♃	♌10	11	12	13	15	16	♄	♑17	17	17	17	17	17	♅	♈19	18	18	♆	♍6	6	7	♇	♋22	22	22	☊	♈6	5	5

OCTOBER

	1	2	3	4	5	6	7	8	9	10	11	12	13	14	15	16	17	18	19	20	21	22	23	24	25	26	27	28	29	30	31
☉	♎7	8	9	10	11	12	13	14	15	16	17	18	19	20	21	22	23	24	25	26	27	28	29	♏0	1	2	3	4	5	6	♏7
☽	♉22	♊5	17	♋0	13	26	♌10	24	♍9	24	♎9	24	♏9	24	♐8	22	♑6	19	♒2	14	26	♓8	20	♈2	14	25	♉7	19	♊2	14	♊27
☿	♍23	25	27	29	♎0	2	4	6	8	9	11	13	15	16	18	20	21	23	25	27	28	♏0	1	3	5	6	8	10	11	13	♏14
♀	♎13	14	15	17	18	19	20	22	23	24	25	27	28	29	♏0	2	3	4	5	7	8	9	10	12	13	14	15	17	18	19	♏20
♂	♏9	10	11	11	12	13	13	14	15	15	16	17	18	18	19	20	20	21	22	22	23	24	25	25	26	27	27	28	29	♐0	♐0

	1	6	12	18	24	30		1	6	12	18	24	30		1	15	30		1	15	30		1	15	30		1	15	30
♃	♌16	17	18	19	19	20	♄	♑17	17	17	17	17	18	♅	♈18	17	17	♆	♍7	7	7	♇	♋22	22	22	☊	♈5	5	5

NOVEMBER

	1	2	3	4	5	6	7	8	9	10	11	12	13	14	15	16	17	18	19	20	21	22	23	24	25	26	27	28	29	30
☉	♏8	9	10	11	12	13	14	15	16	17	18	19	20	21	22	23	24	25	26	27	28	29	♐0	1	2	3	4	5	6	♐7
☽	♋9	22	♌6	19	♍3	18	♎2	17	♏2	17	♐2	17	♑1	14	27	♒10	23	♓5	17	28	♈10	22	♉4	16	28	♊11	23	♋6	19	♌3
☿	♏16	17	19	21	22	24	25	27	28	♐0	1	3	4	6	7	9	10	12	13	14	16	17	19	20	21	23	24	25	27	♐28
♀	♏22	23	24	25	27	28	29	♐0	2	3	4	5	7	8	9	10	12	13	14	15	17	18	19	20	22	23	24	25	27	♐28
♂	♐1	2	2	3	4	5	5	6	7	8	8	9	10	11	11	12	13	13	14	15	16	16	17	18	19	19	20	21	22	♐22

	1	6	12	18	24	30		1	6	12	18	24	30		1	15	30		1	15	30		1	15	30		1	15	30
♃	♌20	21	21	22	22	22	♄	♑18	18	19	19	20	20	♅	♈17	16	16	♆	♍8	8	8	♇	♋22	22	22	☊	♈5	4	3

DECEMBER

	1	2	3	4	5	6	7	8	9	10	11	12	13	14	15	16	17	18	19	20	21	22	23	24	25	26	27	28	29	30	31
☉	♐8	9	10	11	12	13	14	15	16	17	18	19	20	21	22	23	24	25	26	27	28	29	♑0	1	2	3	4	5	6	7	♑8
☽	♌16	♍0	14	28	♎12	27	♏11	26	♐10	25	♑9	22	♒5	18	♓1	13	25	♈6	18	♉0	12	24	♊7	20	♋3	16	29	♌13	27	♍11	♍25
☿	♐29	♑0	1	2	3	4	5	5	6	6	6	6	6	6	6	5	4	3	2	0	♐29	28	26	25	24	23	22	21	21	20	♐20
♀	♐29	♑0	2	3	4	5	7	8	9	10	12	13	14	15	17	18	19	20	22	23	24	25	26	28	29	♒0	1	3	4	5	♒6
♂	♐23	24	25	25	26	27	28	28	29	♑0	1	1	2	3	4	4	5	6	7	8	8	9	10	11	11	12	13	14	14	15	♑16

	1	6	12	18	24	30		1	6	12	18	24	30		1	15	30		1	15	30		1	15	30		1	15	30
♃	♌23	23	23	23	22	22	♄	♑20	21	22	22	23	24	♅	♈16	15	15	♆	♍8	8	8	♇	♋22	22	21	☊	♈3	2	0

1932

JANUARY

	1	2	3	4	5	6	7	8	9	10	11	12	13	14	15	16	17	18	19	20	21	22	23	24	25	26	27	28	29	30	31
☉	♑9	10	11	12	13	14	15	16	18	19	20	21	22	23	24	25	26	27	28	29	♒0	1	2	3	4	5	6	7	8	9	♒10
☽	♎9	23	♏7	21	♐5	19	♑3	17	♒0	13	26	♓8	20	♈2	14	26	♉8	20	♊2	15	28	♋11	24	♌8	22	♍7	21	♎5	20	♏4	♏18
☿	♐20	20	20	21	21	22	23	23	24	25	26	27	28	29	♑1	2	3	4	5	7	8	9	11	12	14	15	16	18	19	21	♑22
♀	♒8	9	10	11	13	14	15	16	18	19	20	21	23	24	25	26	27	29	♓0	1	2	4	5	6	7	8	10	11	12	13	♓15
♂	♑17	18	18	19	20	21	21	22	23	24	25	25	26	27	28	28	29	♒0	1	2	2	3	4	5	5	6	7	8	9	9	♒10

	1	6	12	18	24	30
♃	♌22	21	21	20	20	19
♄	♑24	24	25	26	26	27

	1	15	30
♅	♈15	16	16
♆	♍8	8	7
♇	♋21	21	21
☊	♈0 ♓29	27	

FEBRUARY

	1	2	3	4	5	6	7	8	9	10	11	12	13	14	15	16	17	18	19	20	21	22	23	24	25	26	27	28	29
☉	♒11	12	13	14	15	16	17	18	19	20	21	22	23	24	25	26	27	28	29	♓0	1	2	3	4	5	6	7	8	♓9
☽	♐2	15	29	♑13	26	♒9	22	♓4	16	28	♈10	22	♉4	16	28	♊10	23	♋5	19	♌2	17	♍1	16	♎0	15	♏0	14	28	♐12
☿	♑24	25	27	28	♒0	1	3	5	6	8	9	11	13	14	16	18	19	21	23	25	26	28	♓0	2	4	5	7	9	♓11
♀	♓16	17	18	19	21	22	23	24	26	27	28	29	♈0	2	3	4	5	6	8	9	10	11	12	13	15	16	17	18	♈19
♂	♒11	12	13	13	14	15	16	16	17	18	19	20	20	21	22	23	24	24	25	26	27	28	28	29	♓0	1	1	2	♓3

	1	6	12	18	24	29
♃	♌19	18	17	16	16	15
♄	♑27	28	29	29	♒0	1

	1	15	29
♅	♈16	17	17
♆	♍7	7	7
♇	♋21	20	20
☊	♓27	27	26

MARCH

	1	2	3	4	5	6	7	8	9	10	11	12	13	14	15	16	17	18	19	20	21	22	23	24	25	26	27	28	29	30	31
☉	♓10	11	12	13	14	15	16	17	18	19	20	21	22	23	24	25	26	27	28	29	♈0	1	2	3	4	5	6	7	8	9	♈10
☽	♐26	♑9	22	♒5	18	♓0	13	25	♈7	19	♉0	12	24	♊6	18	♋1	13	27	♌10	24	♍9	24	♎9	24	♏9	24	♐8	22	♑6	19	♒2
☿	♓13	15	17	19	21	23	25	26	28	♈0	2	4	6	8	9	11	13	14	16	17	18	20	21	22	22	23	24	24	25	25	♈25
♀	♈21	22	23	24	25	26	28	29	♉0	1	2	3	5	6	7	8	9	10	11	12	14	15	16	17	18	19	20	21	22	24	♉25
♂	♓4	5	5	6	7	8	9	9	10	11	12	13	13	14	15	16	16	17	18	19	20	20	21	22	23	24	24	25	26	27	♓27

	1	6	12	18	24	30
♃	♌15	14	14	13	13	13
♄	♒1	1	2	2	3	3

	1	15	30
♅	♈17	18	19
♆	♍7	6	6
♇	♋20	20	20
☊	♓26	26	26

APRIL

	1	2	3	4	5	6	7	8	9	10	11	12	13	14	15	16	17	18	19	20	21	22	23	24	25	26	27	28	29	30
☉	♈11	12	13	14	15	16	17	18	19	20	21	22	23	24	25	26	27	28	29	♉0	1	2	3	4	5	6	7	7	8	♉9
☽	♒15	27	♓10	22	♈4	15	27	♉9	21	♊3	15	27	♋9	22	♌5	19	♍3	17	♎2	17	♏2	17	♐3	17	♑2	15	29	♒12	24	♓7
☿	♈25	25	25	24	24	23	23	22	21	21	20	19	18	18	17	16	16	15	15	14	14	14	14	14	14	14	14	14	15	♈15
♀	♉26	27	28	29	♊0	1	2	3	4	5	6	7	8	9	10	11	12	13	14	15	16	17	18	19	20	21	22	23	24	♊25
♂	♓28	29	♈0	1	1	2	3	4	4	5	6	7	8	8	9	10	11	11	12	13	14	14	15	16	17	18	18	19	20	♈21

	1	6	12	18	24	30
♃	♌13	13	13	13	13	13
♄	♒3	4	4	4	4	5

	1	15	30
♅	♈19	20	20
♆	♍6	5	5
♇	♋20	20	20
☊	♓26	26	25

MAY

	1	2	3	4	5	6	7	8	9	10	11	12	13	14	15	16	17	18	19	20	21	22	23	24	25	26	27	28	29	30	31
☉	♉10	11	12	13	14	15	16	17	18	19	20	21	22	23	24	25	26	27	28	29	♊0	1	2	3	4	5	5	6	7	8	♊9
☽	♓19	♈1	12	24	♉6	18	♊0	12	24	♋6	19	♌2	15	28	♍12	26	♎11	25	♏11	26	♐11	26	♑10	24	♒8	21	♓3	15	27	♈9	♈21
☿	♈16	16	17	18	18	19	20	21	22	23	24	25	26	28	29	♉0	1	3	4	6	7	9	10	12	14	15	17	19	21	22	♉24
♀	♊25	26	27	28	29	♋0	1	1	2	3	4	4	5	6	6	7	8	8	9	10	10	11	11	12	12	13	13	13	14	14	♋14
♂	♈21	22	23	24	24	25	26	27	27	28	29	♉0	0	1	2	3	3	4	5	6	6	7	8	9	9	10	11	12	12	13	♉14

	1	6	12	18	24	30
♃	♌13	14	14	15	16	16
♄	♒5	5	5	5	5	5

	1	15	30
♅	♈21	21	22
♆	♍5	5	5
♇	♋20	20	21
☊	♓25	24	23

JUNE

	1	2	3	4	5	6	7	8	9	10	11	12	13	14	15	16	17	18	19	20	21	22	23	24	25	26	27	28	29	30
☉	♊10	11	12	13	14	15	16	17	18	19	20	21	22	23	24	25	26	27	27	28	29	♋0	1	2	3	4	5	6	7	♋8
☽	♉3	15	27	♊9	21	♋3	16	29	♌12	25	♍8	22	♎6	20	♏5	20	♐4	19	♑4	18	♒2	16	29	♓11	24	♈6	18	29	♉11	♉23
☿	♉26	28	♊0	2	4	6	8	10	13	15	17	19	21	24	26	28	♋0	2	4	7	9	11	13	15	17	19	20	22	24	♋26
♀	♋15	15	15	15	15	15	15	15	15	15	15	15	15	15	14	14	14	13	13	12	12	11	11	10	10	9	9	8	7	♋7
♂	♉15	15	16	17	17	18	19	20	20	21	22	23	23	24	25	25	26	27	28	28	29	♊0	0	1	2	3	3	4	5	♊5

	1	6	12	18	24	30
♃	♌17	17	18	19	20	21
♄	♒5	4	4	4	4	3

	1	15	30
♅	♈22	23	23
♆	♍5	5	6
♇	♋21	21	21
☊	♓23	22	20

JULY

	1	2	3	4	5	6	7	8	9	10	11	12	13	14	15	16	17	18	19	20	21	22	23	24	25	26	27	28	29	30	31
☉	♋9	10	11	12	13	14	15	16	17	18	18	19	20	21	22	23	24	25	26	27	28	29	♌0	1	2	3	4	5	6	7	♌8
☽	♊5	17	♋0	13	25	♌9	22	♍5	19	♎3	17	♏1	15	♐0	14	28	♑13	27	♒10	24	♓7	19	♈2	14	26	♉7	19	♊1	13	26	♋8
☿	♋28	29	♌1	3	4	6	7	9	10	12	13	15	16	17	18	20	21	22	23	24	25	26	27	27	28	29	♍0	0	1	1	♍1
♀	♋6	5	5	4	4	3	3	2	2	1	1	0	0	0	0	♊29	29	29	29	29	29	29	29	29	29	29	♋0	0	0	0	♋1
♂	♊6	7	8	8	9	10	10	11	12	12	13	14	14	15	16	17	17	18	19	19	20	21	21	22	23	23	24	25	25	26	♊27

	1	6	12	18	24	30
♃	♌22	23	24	25	26	27
♄	♒3	3	2	2	1	1

	1	15	30
♅	♈23	23	23
♆	♍6	6	7
♇	♋21	22	22
☊	♓20	19	18

AUGUST

	1	2	3	4	5	6	7	8	9	10	11	12	13	14	15	16	17	18	19	20	21	22	23	24	25	26	27	28	29	30	31
☉	♌9	9	10	11	12	13	14	15	16	17	18	19	20	21	22	23	24	25	26	27	28	29	♍0	1	2	3	3	4	5	6	♍7
☽	♋21	♌4	18	♍2	15	29	♎14	28	♏12	26	♐10	24	♑8	22	♒6	19	♓2	15	27	♈10	22	♉4	15	27	♊9	21	♋4	16	29	♌13	♌27
☿	♍2	2	2	2	2	2	1	1	1	0	0	♌29	28	27	27	26	25	24	23	22	22	21	20	20	20	19	19	19	19	20	♌20
♀	♋1	2	2	2	3	3	4	4	5	6	6	7	7	8	9	10	10	11	12	12	13	14	15	16	17	17	18	19	20	21	♋22
♂	♊27	28	29	29	♋0	1	1	2	3	3	4	5	5	6	7	7	8	9	9	10	11	11	12	13	13	14	15	15	16	16	♋17

	1	6	12	18	24	30
♃	♌28	29	♍0	1	3	4
♄	♒1	1	0	0 ♑29	29	

	1	15	30
♅	♈23	23	23
♆	♍7	7	8
♇	♋22	23	23
☊	♓18	17	17

SEPTEMBER

	1	2	3	4	5	6	7	8	9	10	11	12	13	14	15	16	17	18	19	20	21	22	23	24	25	26	27	28	29	30
☉	♍8	9	10	11	12	13	14	15	16	17	18	19	20	21	22	23	24	25	26	27	28	29	♎0	1	2	3	4	5	6	♎7
☽	♍11	25	♎9	24	♏8	23	♐7	21	♑5	19	♒2	15	28	♓11	23	♈6	18	♉0	12	23	♊5	17	29	♋12	24	♌7	21	♍5	19	♎3
☿	♌21	21	22	23	24	25	27	28	♍0	1	3	4	6	8	10	11	13	15	17	19	21	23	24	26	28	♎0	2	4	5	♎7
♀	♋23	24	24	25	26	27	28	29	♌0	1	2	3	4	5	6	7	8	9	10	11	12	13	14	16	17	18	19	20	21	♌22
♂	♋18	18	19	20	20	21	21	22	23	23	24	25	25	26	26	27	28	28	29	♌0	0	1	1	2	3	3	4	4	5	♌6

	1	6	12	18	24	30
♃	♍4	6	7	8	9	11
♄	♑29	29	28	28	28	28

	1	15	30
♅	♈23	23	22
♆	♍8	8	9
♇	♋23	23	23
☊	♓17	17	17

OCTOBER

	1	2	3	4	5	6	7	8	9	10	11	12	13	14	15	16	17	18	19	20	21	22	23	24	25	26	27	28	29	30	31
☉	♎8	9	10	11	12	13	14	14	15	16	17	18	19	20	21	22	23	24	25	26	27	28	29	♏0	1	2	3	4	5	6	♏7
☽	♎18	♏3	18	♐3	18	♑2	16	29	♒12	25	♓8	20	♈2	14	26	♉8	20	♊2	14	26	♋8	20	♌3	16	29	♍13	27	♎11	27	♏12	♏27
☿	♎9	11	12	14	16	17	19	21	22	24	26	27	29	♏1	2	4	5	7	8	10	11	13	14	16	17	19	20	22	23	25	♏26
♀	♌23	24	25	26	28	29	♍0	1	2	3	4	5	7	8	9	10	11	12	13	15	16	17	18	19	20	22	23	24	25	26	♍27
♂	♌6	7	7	8	8	9	10	10	11	11	12	12	13	14	14	15	15	16	16	17	18	18	19	19	20	20	21	21	22	22	♌23

	1	6	12	18	24	30
♃	♍11	12	13	14	15	16
♄	♑28	28	28	28	28	29

	1	15	30
♅	♈22	21	21
♆	♍9	9	10
♇	♋23	23	23
☊	♓17	17	16

NOVEMBER

	1	2	3	4	5	6	7	8	9	10	11	12	13	14	15	16	17	18	19	20	21	22	23	24	25	26	27	28	29	30
☉	♏8	9	10	11	12	13	14	15	16	17	18	19	20	21	22	23	24	25	26	27	28	29	♐0	2	3	4	5	6	7	♐8
☽	♐12	27	♑11	25	♒9	22	♓5	17	29	♈11	23	♉5	17	29	♊11	23	♋5	17	29	♌12	24	♍8	21	♎5	20	♏5	20	♐5	20	♑5
☿	♏27	29	♐0	2	3	4	6	7	8	9	10	12	13	14	15	16	17	18	18	19	20	20	20	21	21	20	20	20	19	♐18
♀	♍29	♎0	1	2	3	5	6	7	8	9	11	12	13	14	15	17	18	19	20	21	23	24	25	26	28	29	♏0	1	2	♏4
♂	♌23	24	25	25	26	26	27	27	28	28	29	29	♍0	0	1	1	1	2	2	3	3	4	4	5	5	6	6	7	7	♍7

	1	6	12	18	24	30
♃	♍17	18	19	19	20	21
♄	♑29	29	29	♒0	0	1

	1	15	30
♅	♈21	20	20
♆	♍10	10	10
♇	♋23	23	23
☊	♓16	14	13

DECEMBER

	1	2	3	4	5	6	7	8	9	10	11	12	13	14	15	16	17	18	19	20	21	22	23	24	25	26	27	28	29	30	31
☉	♐9	10	11	12	13	14	15	16	17	18	19	20	21	22	23	24	25	26	27	28	29	♑0	1	2	3	4	5	6	7	8	♑9
☽	♑20	♒4	18	♓1	14	26	♈8	20	♉2	14	26	♊8	20	♋2	14	26	♌9	21	♍4	17	♎1	15	29	♏13	28	♐13	28	♑13	28	♒12	♒26
☿	♐17	16	15	13	12	11	9	8	7	6	5	5	5	4	4	5	5	5	6	7	7	8	9	10	11	12	13	15	16	17	♐18
♀	♏5	6	7	9	10	11	12	14	15	16	17	18	20	21	22	23	25	26	27	28	♐0	1	2	3	5	6	7	8	10	11	♐12
♂	♍8	8	9	9	9	10	10	11	11	11	12	12	12	13	13	14	14	14	14	15	15	15	16	16	16	17	17	17	17	18	♍18

	1	6	12	18	24	30
♃	♍21	22	22	23	23	23
♄	♒1	1	2	3	3	4

	1	15	30
♅	♈20	20	19
♆	♍10	10	10
♇	♋23	23	23
☊	♓13	11	10

1933

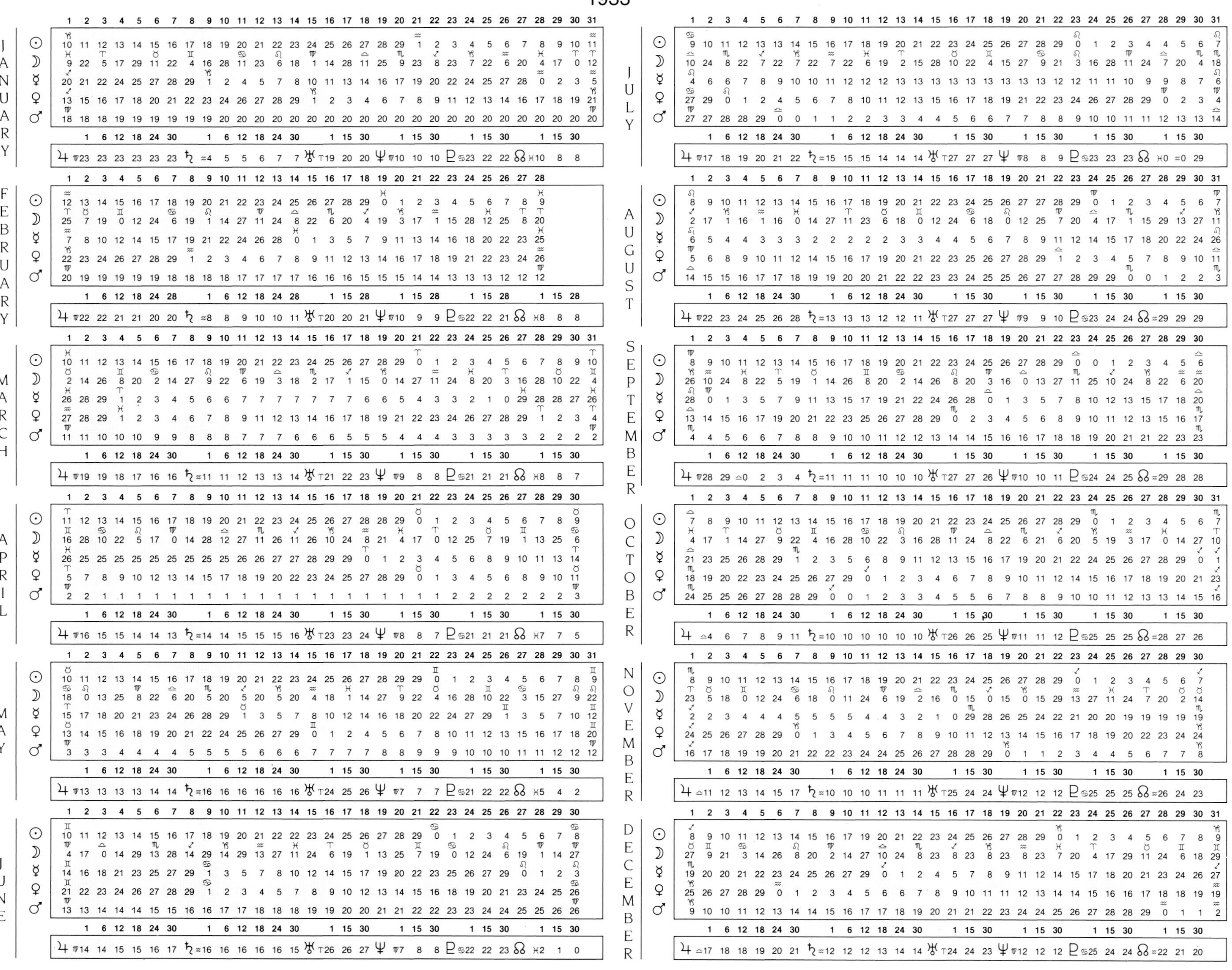

JANUARY

	1	2	3	4	5	6	7	8	9	10	11	12	13	14	15	16	17	18	19	20	21	22	23	24	25	26	27	28	29	30	31
☉	♑10	11	12	13	14	15	16	17	18	19	20	21	22	23	24	25	26	27	28	29	♒1	2	3	4	5	6	7	8	9	10	♒11
☽	♓9	22	♈5	17	29	♉11	22	♊4	16	28	♋11	23	♌6	18	♍1	14	28	♎11	25	♏9	23	♐8	23	♑7	22	♒6	20	♓4	17	♈0	♈12
☿	♐20	21	22	24	25	27	28	29	♑1	2	4	5	7	8	10	11	13	14	16	17	19	20	22	24	25	27	28	♒0	2	3	♒5
♀	♐13	15	16	17	18	20	21	22	23	24	26	27	28	29	♑1	2	3	4	6	7	8	9	11	12	13	14	16	17	18	19	♑21
♂	♍18	18	18	19	19	19	19	19	19	20	20	20	20	20	20	20	20	20	20	20	20	20	20	20	20	20	20	20	20	20	♍20

	1	6	12	18	24	30		1	6	12	18	24	30		1	15	30		1	15	30		1	15	30		1	15	30
♃	♍23	23	23	23	23	23	♄	♒4	5	5	6	7	7	♅	♈19	20	20	♆	♍10	10	10	♇	♋23	22	22	☊	♓10	8	8

FEBRUARY

	1	2	3	4	5	6	7	8	9	10	11	12	13	14	15	16	17	18	19	20	21	22	23	24	25	26	27	28
☉	♒12	13	14	15	16	17	18	19	20	21	22	23	24	25	26	27	28	29	♓0	1	2	3	4	5	6	7	8	♓9
☽	♈25	♉7	19	♊0	12	24	♋6	19	♌1	14	27	♍11	24	♎8	22	♏6	20	♐4	19	♑3	17	♒1	15	28	♓12	25	♈8	♈20
☿	♒7	8	10	12	14	15	17	19	21	22	24	26	28	♓0	1	3	5	7	9	11	13	14	16	18	20	22	23	♓25
♀	♑22	23	24	26	27	28	29	♒1	2	3	4	6	7	8	9	11	12	13	14	16	17	18	19	21	22	23	24	♒26
♂	♍20	19	19	19	19	19	18	18	18	18	17	17	17	17	16	16	16	15	15	15	14	14	13	13	13	12	12	♍12

	1	6	12	18	24	28		1	6	12	18	24	28		1	15	28		1	15	28		1	15	28		1	15	28
♃	♍22	22	21	21	20	20	♄	♒8	8	9	10	10	11	♅	♈20	20	21	♆	♍10	9	9	♇	♋22	22	21	☊	♓8	8	8

MARCH

	1	2	3	4	5	6	7	8	9	10	11	12	13	14	15	16	17	18	19	20	21	22	23	24	25	26	27	28	29	30	31
☉	♓10	11	12	13	14	15	16	17	18	19	20	21	22	23	24	25	26	27	28	29	♈0	1	2	3	4	5	6	7	8	9	♈10
☽	♉2	14	26	♊8	20	♋2	14	27	♌9	22	♍6	19	♎3	18	♏2	17	♐1	15	♑0	14	27	♒11	24	♓8	20	♈3	16	28	♉10	22	♊4
☿	♓26	28	29	♈1	2	3	4	5	6	6	7	7	7	7	7	7	7	6	6	5	4	3	3	2	1	0	♓29	28	28	27	♓26
♀	♒27	28	29	♓1	2	3	4	6	7	8	9	11	12	13	14	16	17	18	19	21	22	23	24	26	27	28	29	♈1	2	3	♈4
♂	♍11	11	10	10	10	9	9	8	8	8	7	7	7	6	6	6	5	5	5	4	4	4	3	3	3	3	3	2	2	2	♍2

	1	6	12	18	24	30		1	6	12	18	24	30		1	15	30		1	15	30		1	15	30		1	15	30
♃	♍19	19	18	17	16	16	♄	♒11	11	12	13	13	14	♅	♈21	22	23	♆	♍9	8	8	♇	♋21	21	21	☊	♓8	8	7

APRIL

	1	2	3	4	5	6	7	8	9	10	11	12	13	14	15	16	17	18	19	20	21	22	23	24	25	26	27	28	29	30
☉	♈11	12	13	14	15	16	17	18	19	20	21	22	23	24	25	26	27	28	28	29	♉0	1	2	3	4	5	6	7	8	♉9
☽	♊16	28	♋10	22	♌5	17	♍0	14	28	♎12	27	♏11	26	♐11	26	♑10	24	♒8	21	♓4	17	♈0	12	25	♉7	19	♊1	13	25	♋6
☿	♓26	25	25	25	25	25	25	25	25	25	26	26	27	27	28	29	29	♈0	1	2	3	4	5	6	8	9	10	11	13	♈14
♀	♈5	7	8	9	10	12	13	14	15	17	18	19	20	22	23	24	25	27	28	29	♉0	1	3	4	5	6	8	9	10	♉11
♂	♍2	2	1	1	1	1	1	1	1	1	1	1	1	1	1	1	1	1	1	1	1	1	2	2	2	2	2	2	2	♍3

	1	6	12	18	24	30		1	6	12	18	24	30		1	15	30		1	15	30		1	15	30		1	15	30
♃	♍16	15	15	14	14	13	♄	♒14	14	15	15	15	16	♅	♈23	23	24	♆	♍8	8	7	♇	♋21	21	21	☊	♓7	7	5

MAY

	1	2	3	4	5	6	7	8	9	10	11	12	13	14	15	16	17	18	19	20	21	22	23	24	25	26	27	28	29	30	31
☉	♉10	11	12	13	14	15	16	17	18	19	20	21	22	23	24	25	26	27	28	29	29	♊0	1	2	3	4	5	6	7	8	♊9
☽	♋18	♌0	13	25	♍8	22	♎6	20	♏5	20	♐5	20	♑5	20	♒4	18	♓1	14	27	♈9	22	♉4	16	28	♊10	22	♋3	15	27	♌9	♌22
☿	♈15	17	18	20	21	23	24	26	28	29	♉1	3	5	7	8	10	12	14	16	18	20	22	24	27	29	♊1	3	5	7	10	♊12
♀	♉13	14	15	16	18	19	20	21	22	24	25	26	27	29	♊0	1	2	4	5	6	7	8	10	11	12	13	15	16	17	18	♊20
♂	♍3	3	3	4	4	4	4	5	5	5	5	6	6	6	7	7	7	7	8	8	9	9	9	10	10	10	11	11	12	12	♍12

	1	6	12	18	24	30		1	6	12	18	24	30		1	15	30		1	15	30		1	15	30		1	15	30
♃	♍13	13	13	13	14	14	♄	♒16	16	16	16	16	16	♅	♈24	25	26	♆	♍7	7	7	♇	♋21	22	22	☊	♓5	4	2

JUNE

	1	2	3	4	5	6	7	8	9	10	11	12	13	14	15	16	17	18	19	20	21	22	23	24	25	26	27	28	29	30
☉	♊10	11	12	13	14	15	16	17	18	19	20	21	22	22	23	24	25	26	27	28	29	♋0	1	2	3	4	5	6	7	♋8
☽	♍4	17	♎0	14	29	♏13	28	♐14	29	♑14	29	♒13	27	♓11	24	♈6	19	♉1	13	25	♊7	19	♋0	12	24	♌6	19	♍1	14	♍27
☿	♊14	16	18	21	23	25	27	29	♋1	3	5	7	8	10	12	14	15	17	19	20	22	23	25	26	27	29	♌0	1	2	♌3
♀	♊21	22	23	24	26	27	28	29	♋1	2	3	4	5	7	8	9	10	12	13	14	15	16	18	19	20	21	23	24	25	♋26
♂	♍13	13	14	14	14	15	15	16	16	17	17	18	18	18	19	19	20	20	21	21	22	22	23	23	24	24	25	25	26	♍26

	1	6	12	18	24	30		1	6	12	18	24	30		1	15	30		1	15	30		1	15	30		1	15	30
♃	♍14	14	15	15	16	17	♄	♒16	16	16	16	16	15	♅	♈26	26	27	♆	♍7	8	8	♇	♋22	22	23	☊	♓2	1	0

JULY

	1	2	3	4	5	6	7	8	9	10	11	12	13	14	15	16	17	18	19	20	21	22	23	24	25	26	27	28	29	30	31
☉	♋9	10	11	12	13	13	14	15	16	17	18	19	20	21	22	23	24	25	26	27	28	29	♌0	1	2	3	4	4	5	6	♌7
☽	♎10	24	♏8	22	♐7	22	♑7	22	♒7	22	♓6	19	♈2	15	28	♉10	22	♊4	15	27	♋9	21	♌3	16	28	♍11	24	♎7	20	♏4	♏18
☿	♌4	6	6	7	8	9	10	10	11	12	12	12	13	13	13	13	13	13	13	13	13	12	12	11	11	10	9	9	8	7	♌6
♀	♋27	29	♌0	1	2	4	5	6	7	8	10	11	12	13	15	16	17	18	19	21	22	23	24	26	27	28	29	♍0	2	3	♍4
♂	♍27	27	28	28	29	♎0	0	1	1	2	2	3	3	4	4	5	6	6	7	7	8	8	9	10	10	11	11	12	13	13	♎14

	1	6	12	18	24	30		1	6	12	18	24	30		1	15	30		1	15	30		1	15	30		1	15	30
♃	♍17	18	19	20	21	22	♄	♒15	15	15	14	14	14	♅	♈27	27	27	♆	♍8	8	9	♇	♋23	23	23	☊	♓0	♒0	29

AUGUST

	1	2	3	4	5	6	7	8	9	10	11	12	13	14	15	16	17	18	19	20	21	22	23	24	25	26	27	28	29	30	31
☉	♌8	9	10	11	12	13	14	15	16	17	18	19	20	21	22	23	24	25	26	27	27	28	29	♍0	1	2	3	4	5	6	♍7
☽	♐2	17	♑1	16	♒1	16	♓0	14	27	♈11	23	♉6	18	♊0	12	24	♋6	18	♌0	12	25	♍7	20	♎4	17	♏1	15	29	♐13	27	♑11
☿	♌6	5	4	4	3	3	3	2	2	2	2	2	3	3	4	4	5	6	7	8	9	11	12	14	15	17	18	20	22	24	♌26
♀	♍5	6	8	9	10	11	12	14	15	16	17	19	20	21	22	23	25	26	27	28	29	♎1	2	3	4	5	7	8	9	10	♎11
♂	♎14	15	15	16	17	17	18	19	19	20	20	21	22	22	23	23	24	25	25	26	27	27	28	29	29	♏0	0	1	2	2	♏3

	1	6	12	18	24	30		1	6	12	18	24	30		1	15	30		1	15	30		1	15	30		1	15	30
♃	♍22	23	24	25	26	28	♄	♒13	13	13	12	12	11	♅	♈27	27	27	♆	♍9	9	10	♇	♋23	24	24	☊	♒29	29	29

SEPTEMBER

	1	2	3	4	5	6	7	8	9	10	11	12	13	14	15	16	17	18	19	20	21	22	23	24	25	26	27	28	29	30
☉	♍8	9	10	11	12	13	14	15	16	17	18	19	20	21	22	23	24	25	26	27	28	29	♎0	0	1	2	3	4	5	♎6
☽	♑26	♒10	24	♓8	22	♈5	19	♉1	14	26	♊8	20	♋2	14	26	♌8	20	♍3	16	♎0	13	27	♏11	25	♐10	24	♑8	22	♒6	♒20
☿	♌28	♍0	1	3	5	7	9	11	13	15	17	19	21	22	24	26	28	♎0	1	3	5	7	8	10	12	13	15	17	18	♎20
♀	♎13	14	15	16	17	19	20	21	22	23	25	26	27	28	29	♏0	2	3	4	5	6	8	9	10	11	12	13	15	16	♏17
♂	♏4	4	5	6	6	7	8	8	9	10	10	11	12	12	13	14	14	15	16	16	17	18	18	19	20	21	21	22	23	♏23

	1	6	12	18	24	30		1	6	12	18	24	30		1	15	30		1	15	30		1	15	30		1	15	30
♃	♍28	29	♎0	2	3	4	♄	♒11	11	11	10	10	10	♅	♈27	27	26	♆	♍10	10	11	♇	♋24	24	25	☊	♒29	28	28

OCTOBER

	1	2	3	4	5	6	7	8	9	10	11	12	13	14	15	16	17	18	19	20	21	22	23	24	25	26	27	28	29	30	31
☉	♎7	8	9	10	11	12	13	14	15	16	17	18	19	20	21	22	23	24	25	26	27	28	29	♏0	1	2	3	4	5	6	♏7
☽	♓4	17	♈1	14	27	♉9	22	♊4	16	28	♋10	22	♌3	16	28	♍11	24	♎8	22	♏6	21	♐6	20	♑5	19	♒3	17	♓0	14	27	♈10
☿	♎21	23	25	26	28	29	♏1	2	3	5	6	8	9	11	12	13	15	16	17	19	20	21	22	24	25	26	27	28	29	♐0	♐1
♀	♏18	19	20	22	23	24	25	26	27	29	♐0	1	2	3	4	6	7	8	9	10	11	12	14	15	16	17	18	19	20	21	♐23
♂	♏24	25	25	26	27	28	28	29	♐0	0	1	2	3	3	4	5	5	6	7	8	8	9	10	10	11	12	13	13	14	15	♐16

	1	6	12	18	24	30		1	6	12	18	24	30		1	15	30		1	15	30		1	15	30		1	15	30
♃	♎4	6	7	8	9	11	♄	♒10	10	10	10	10	10	♅	♈26	26	25	♆	♍11	11	12	♇	♋25	25	25	☊	♒28	27	26

NOVEMBER

	1	2	3	4	5	6	7	8	9	10	11	12	13	14	15	16	17	18	19	20	21	22	23	24	25	26	27	28	29	30
☉	♏8	9	10	11	12	13	14	15	16	17	18	19	20	21	22	23	24	25	26	27	28	29	♐0	1	2	3	4	5	6	♐7
☽	♈23	♉5	18	♊0	12	24	♋6	18	♌0	11	24	♍6	19	♎2	16	♏0	15	♐0	15	♑0	15	29	♒13	27	♓11	24	♈7	20	♉2	♉14
☿	♐2	2	3	4	4	4	5	5	5	5	4	4	3	2	1	0	♏29	28	26	25	24	22	21	20	20	19	19	19	19	♏19
♀	♐24	25	26	27	28	29	♑0	1	3	4	5	6	7	8	9	10	11	12	13	14	15	16	17	18	19	20	22	23	24	♑24
♂	♐16	17	18	19	19	20	21	22	22	23	24	24	25	26	27	28	28	29	♑0	1	1	2	3	4	4	5	6	7	7	♑8

	1	6	12	18	24	30		1	6	12	18	24	30		1	15	30		1	15	30		1	15	30		1	15	30
♃	♎11	12	13	14	15	17	♄	♒10	10	10	11	11	11	♅	♈25	24	24	♆	♍12	12	12	♇	♋25	25	25	☊	♒26	24	23

DECEMBER

	1	2	3	4	5	6	7	8	9	10	11	12	13	14	15	16	17	18	19	20	21	22	23	24	25	26	27	28	29	30	31
☉	♐8	9	10	11	12	13	14	15	16	17	19	20	21	22	23	24	25	26	27	28	29	♑0	1	2	3	4	5	6	7	8	♑9
☽	♉27	♊9	21	♋3	14	26	♌8	20	♍2	14	27	♎10	24	♏8	23	♐8	23	♑8	23	♒8	23	♓7	20	♈4	17	29	♉11	24	♊6	18	♊29
☿	♏19	20	20	21	22	23	24	25	26	27	29	♐0	1	2	4	5	7	8	9	11	12	14	15	17	18	20	21	23	24	26	♐27
♀	♑25	26	27	28	29	♒0	1	2	3	4	5	6	6	7	8	9	10	11	11	12	13	14	14	15	16	16	17	18	18	19	♒19
♂	♑9	10	10	11	12	13	14	14	15	16	17	17	18	19	20	21	21	22	23	24	24	25	26	27	28	28	29	♒0	1	1	♒2

	1	6	12	18	24	30		1	6	12	18	24	30		1	15	30		1	15	30		1	15	30		1	15	30
♃	♎17	18	18	19	20	21	♄	♒12	12	12	13	14	14	♅	♈24	24	23	♆	♍12	12	12	♇	♋25	24	24	☊	♒22	21	20

1934

JANUARY

	1	2	3	4	5	6	7	8	9	10	11	12	13	14	15	16	17	18	19	20	21	22	23	24	25	26	27	28	29	30	31
☉	♑10	11	12	13	14	15	16	17	18	19	20	21	22	23	24	25	26	27	28	29	♒0	1	2	3	4	5	6	7	8	9	♒10
☽	♋11	23	♌5	17	29	♍11	24	♎6	19	♏3	17	♐1	16	♑1	16	♒1	16	♓1	15	29	♈13	26	♉8	20	♊3	14	26	♋8	20	♌2	♌14
☿	♐29	♑0	2	3	5	7	8	10	11	13	14	16	18	19	21	23	24	26	28	29	♒1	3	4	6	8	9	11	13	15	16	♒18
♀	♒20	20	21	21	22	22	22	23	23	23	23	23	24	24	24	24	24	24	23	23	23	23	22	22	22	21	21	20	20	19	♒19
♂	♒3	4	5	5	6	7	8	9	9	10	11	12	12	13	14	15	16	16	17	18	19	20	20	21	22	23	24	24	25	26	♒27

1	6	12	18	24	30	1	6	12	18	24	30	1	15	30	1	15	30	1	15	30	1	15	30
♃ ♎21	22	22	23	23	23	♄ ♒14	15	16	16	17	18	♅ ♈23	24	24	♆ ♍12	12	12	♇ ♋24	24	23	☊ ♒20	19	19

FEBRUARY

	1	2	3	4	5	6	7	8	9	10	11	12	13	14	15	16	17	18	19	20	21	22	23	24	25	26	27	28
☉	♒11	12	13	14	16	17	18	19	20	21	22	23	24	25	26	27	28	29	♓0	1	2	3	4	5	6	7	8	♓9
☽	♌26	♍8	21	♎3	16	29	♏13	26	♐10	25	♑10	24	♒9	24	♓9	23	♈7	21	♉4	16	29	♊11	23	♋5	17	28	♌10	♌22
☿	♒20	22	23	25	27	29	♓0	2	4	6	7	9	10	12	13	14	16	17	18	19	19	20	20	20	20	20	20	♓20
♀	♒18	18	17	16	16	15	15	14	13	13	12	12	11	11	10	10	9	9	9	9	8	8	8	8	8	8	8	♒8
♂	♒27	28	29	♓0	1	1	2	3	4	5	5	6	7	8	9	9	10	11	12	12	13	14	15	16	16	17	18	♓19

1	6	12	18	24	28	1	6	12	18	24	28	1	15	28	1	15	28	1	15	28	1	15	28
♃ ♎23	23	23	23	23	23	♄ ♒18	19	19	20	21	21	♅ ♈24	24	25	♆ ♍12	11	11	♇ ♋23	23	23	☊ ♒19	19	19

MARCH

	1	2	3	4	5	6	7	8	9	10	11	12	13	14	15	16	17	18	19	20	21	22	23	24	25	26	27	28	29	30	31
☉	♓10	11	12	13	14	15	16	17	18	19	20	21	22	23	24	25	26	27	28	29	♈0	1	2	3	4	5	6	7	8	9	♈10
☽	♍5	17	♎0	13	26	♏10	23	♐7	21	♑5	19	♒4	18	♓3	17	♈1	15	28	♉12	24	♊7	19	♋1	13	25	♌6	18	♍1	13	26	♎9
☿	♓19	18	18	17	16	15	14	13	12	11	10	9	8	8	7	7	7	6	6	6	6	7	7	7	8	8	9	10	10	11	♓12
♀	♒8	8	8	9	9	9	10	10	10	11	11	12	12	13	13	14	14	15	16	16	17	18	18	19	20	20	21	22	23	24	♒24
♂	♓20	20	21	22	23	23	24	25	26	27	27	28	29	♈0	0	1	2	3	4	4	5	6	7	7	8	9	10	11	11	12	♈13

1	6	12	18	24	30	1	6	12	18	24	30	1	15	30	1	15	30	1	15	30	1	15	30
♃ ♎22	22	22	21	20	20	♄ ♒21	22	23	23	24	24	♅ ♈25	25	26	♆ ♍11	11	10	♇ ♋23	23	23	☊ ♒19	19	18

APRIL

	1	2	3	4	5	6	7	8	9	10	11	12	13	14	15	16	17	18	19	20	21	22	23	24	25	26	27	28	29	30
☉	♈11	12	13	14	15	16	16	17	18	19	20	21	22	23	24	25	26	27	28	29	♉0	1	2	3	4	5	6	7	8	♉9
☽	♎22	♏6	20	♐4	18	♑2	16	♒0	14	28	♓12	26	♈10	23	♉7	20	♊2	15	27	♋9	21	♌2	14	26	♍9	21	♎4	17	♏1	♏15
☿	♓13	14	15	16	17	18	19	20	22	23	24	26	27	28	♈0	1	3	4	6	7	9	11	12	14	16	17	19	21	23	♈25
♀	♒25	26	27	28	29	♓0	1	1	2	3	4	5	6	7	8	9	10	11	12	13	14	15	16	17	18	19	20	21	22	♓23
♂	♈14	14	15	16	17	17	18	19	20	20	21	22	23	23	24	25	26	27	27	28	29	♉0	0	1	2	3	3	4	5	♉5

1	6	12	18	24	30	1	6	12	18	24	30	1	15	30	1	15	30	1	15	30	1	15	30
♃ ♎19	19	18	17	16	16	♄ ♒25	25	26	26	27	27	♅ ♈26	27	28	♆ ♍10	10	10	♇ ♋23	23	23	☊ ♒18	17	15

MAY

	1	2	3	4	5	6	7	8	9	10	11	12	13	14	15	16	17	18	19	20	21	22	23	24	25	26	27	28	29	30	31
☉	♉10	11	12	13	14	15	16	17	18	19	20	21	22	23	23	24	25	26	27	28	29	♊0	1	2	3	4	5	6	7	8	♊9
☽	♏29	♐14	28	♑13	27	♒11	25	♓9	23	♈6	19	♉2	15	28	♊11	23	♋5	17	29	♌10	22	♍4	16	29	♎12	25	♏9	24	♐8	23	♑8
☿	♈27	28	♉0	2	4	6	9	11	13	15	17	19	21	23	26	28	♊0	2	4	6	9	11	13	15	17	19	21	22	24	26	♊28
♀	♓24	25	26	27	29	♈0	1	2	3	4	5	6	7	8	9	10	12	13	14	15	16	17	18	19	20	22	23	24	25	26	♈27
♂	♉6	7	8	8	9	10	11	11	12	13	14	14	15	16	17	17	18	19	19	20	21	22	22	23	24	24	25	26	27	27	♉28

1	6	12	18	24	30	1	6	12	18	24	30	1	15	30	1	15	30	1	15	30	1	15	30
♃ ♎16	15	15	14	14	13	♄ ♒27	27	28	28	28	28	♅ ♈28	29	♉29	♆ ♍10	10	10	♇ ♋23	23	23	☊ ♒15	14	12

JUNE

	1	2	3	4	5	6	7	8	9	10	11	12	13	14	15	16	17	18	19	20	21	22	23	24	25	26	27	28	29	30
☉	♊10	11	12	13	14	15	16	17	17	18	19	20	21	22	23	24	25	26	27	28	29	♋0	1	2	3	4	5	6	7	♋8
☽	♑23	♒7	22	♓6	20	♈3	16	29	♉12	25	♊7	19	♋1	13	25	♌7	19	♍1	13	25	♎7	20	♏4	18	♐2	17	♑2	17	♒2	♒17
☿	♊29	♋1	3	4	6	7	8	10	11	12	13	15	16	17	18	19	19	20	21	21	22	23	23	23	24	24	24	24	24	♋24
♀	♈28	♉0	1	2	3	4	5	6	8	9	10	11	12	13	14	16	17	18	19	20	21	23	24	25	26	27	28	♊0	1	♊2
♂	♉29	♊0	0	1	2	2	3	4	4	5	6	7	7	8	9	9	10	11	12	12	13	14	14	15	16	16	17	18	18	♊19

1	6	12	18	24	30	1	6	12	18	24	30	1	15	30	1	15	30	1	15	30	1	15	30
♃ ♎13	13	13	13	14	14	♄ ♒28	28	28	28	28	28	♅ ♉0	0	1	♆ ♍10	10	10	♇ ♋23	23	24	☊ ♒12	11	11

JULY

	1	2	3	4	5	6	7	8	9	10	11	12	13	14	15	16	17	18	19	20	21	22	23	24	25	26	27	28	29	30	31
☉	♋8	9	10	11	12	13	14	15	16	17	18	19	20	21	22	23	24	25	26	27	28	29	29	♌0	1	2	3	4	5	6	♌7
☽	♓1	16	♈0	13	26	♉9	22	♊4	16	28	♋10	22	♌4	16	27	♍9	21	♎4	16	29	♏12	26	♐10	25	♑10	25	♒10	25	♓10	25	♈9
☿	♋24	23	23	23	22	22	21	21	20	19	19	18	18	17	16	16	15	15	15	14	14	14	14	14	14	15	15	16	16	17	♋18
♀	♊3	4	5	7	8	9	10	11	12	14	15	16	17	18	20	21	22	23	24	26	27	28	29	♋0	1	3	4	5	6	7	♋9
♂	♊20	21	21	22	23	23	24	25	25	26	27	27	28	29	29	♋0	1	1	2	3	3	4	5	5	6	7	7	8	9	9	♋10

1	6	12	18	24	30	1	6	12	18	24	30	1	15	30	1	15	30	1	15	30	1	15	30
♃ ♎14	14	15	15	16	17	♄ ♒28	28	27	27	27	26	♅ ♉1	1	1	♆ ♍10	10	11	♇ ♋24	24	25	☊ ♒11	10	10

AUGUST

	1	2	3	4	5	6	7	8	9	10	11	12	13	14	15	16	17	18	19	20	21	22	23	24	25	26	27	28	29	30	31
☉	♌8	9	10	11	12	13	14	15	16	17	18	19	20	21	21	22	23	24	25	26	27	28	29	♍0	1	2	3	4	5	6	♍7
☽	♈23	♉6	19	♊1	13	25	♋7	19	♌1	13	25	♍6	19	♎1	13	26	♏9	22	♐6	20	♑4	19	♒4	19	♓4	19	♈3	17	♉1	15	♉27
☿	♋19	20	21	22	23	25	26	27	29	♌1	2	4	6	8	10	12	14	16	18	20	22	24	26	28	♍0	2	4	6	8	10	♍11
♀	♋10	11	12	13	15	16	17	18	20	21	22	23	24	26	27	28	29	♌0	2	3	4	5	7	8	9	10	11	13	14	15	♌16
♂	♋11	11	12	13	13	14	15	15	16	17	17	18	19	19	20	21	21	22	23	23	24	24	25	26	26	27	28	28	29	♌0	♌0

1	6	12	18	24	30	1	6	12	18	24	30	1	15	30	1	15	30	1	15	30	1	15	30
♃ ♎17	18	19	19	20	22	♄ ♒26	26	25	25	24	24	♅ ♉1	1	1	♆ ♍11	11	12	♇ ♋25	25	25	☊ ♒10	10	10

SEPTEMBER

	1	2	3	4	5	6	7	8	9	10	11	12	13	14	15	16	17	18	19	20	21	22	23	24	25	26	27	28	29	30
☉	♍8	9	10	11	12	13	14	15	16	17	18	19	20	20	21	22	23	24	25	26	27	28	29	♎0	1	2	3	4	5	♎6
☽	♊10	22	♋4	16	28	♌10	21	♍3	15	28	♎10	23	♏6	19	♐2	16	♑0	14	28	♒13	27	♓12	27	♈11	25	♉9	23	♊6	18	♋0
☿	♍13	15	17	19	21	22	24	26	28	29	♎1	3	4	6	7	9	11	12	14	15	17	18	20	21	22	24	25	27	28	♎29
♀	♌18	19	20	21	22	24	25	26	27	29	♍0	1	2	4	5	6	7	8	10	11	12	13	15	16	17	18	20	21	22	♍23
♂	♌1	2	2	3	3	4	5	5	6	7	7	8	8	9	10	10	11	12	12	13	13	14	15	15	16	17	17	18	18	♌19

1	6	12	18	24	30	1	6	12	18	24	30	1	15	30	1	15	30	1	15	30	1	15	30
♃ ♎22	23	24	25	26	28	♄ ♒24	23	23	23	22	22	♅ ♉1	1	0	♆ ♍12	12	13	♇ ♋25	26	26	☊ ♒10	9	8

OCTOBER

	1	2	3	4	5	6	7	8	9	10	11	12	13	14	15	16	17	18	19	20	21	22	23	24	25	26	27	28	29	30	31
☉	♎7	8	9	10	11	12	13	14	15	16	17	18	19	20	21	22	23	24	25	26	27	28	29	♏0	1	2	3	4	5	6	♏7
☽	♋12	24	♌6	18	♍0	12	24	♎7	19	♏2	16	29	♐13	26	♑10	24	♒9	23	♓7	21	♈6	20	♉4	17	♊1	13	26	♋8	20	♌2	♌14
☿	♏0	2	3	4	5	7	8	9	10	11	12	13	14	15	16	16	17	18	18	18	19	19	19	19	19	18	18	17	16	15	♏14
♀	♍25	26	27	28	♎0	1	2	3	5	6	7	8	10	11	12	13	15	16	17	18	20	21	22	23	25	26	27	28	♏0	1	♏2
♂	♌20	20	21	21	22	23	23	24	24	25	26	26	27	27	28	29	29	♍0	0	1	2	2	3	3	4	5	5	6	6	7	♍7

1	6	12	18	24	30	1	6	12	18	24	30	1	15	30	1	15	30	1	15	30	1	15	30
♃ ♎28	29	♏0	1	3	4	♄ ♒22	22	22	22	22	22	♅ ♉0	0	♈0	♆ ♍13	14	14	♇ ♋26	26	26	☊ ♒8	7	6

NOVEMBER

	1	2	3	4	5	6	7	8	9	10	11	12	13	14	15	16	17	18	19	20	21	22	23	24	25	26	27	28	29	30
☉	♏8	9	10	11	12	13	14	15	16	17	18	19	20	21	22	23	24	25	26	27	28	29	♐0	1	2	3	4	5	6	♐7
☽	♌26	♍8	20	♎2	15	28	♏11	25	♐9	23	♑7	21	♒5	19	♓4	18	♈1	15	29	♉12	26	♊9	21	♋4	16	28	♌10	22	♍4	♍15
☿	♏13	12	10	9	8	7	6	5	4	3	3	3	3	3	4	4	5	6	7	8	9	10	11	12	14	15	16	18	19	♏21
♀	♏3	5	6	7	8	10	11	12	13	15	16	17	18	20	21	22	23	25	26	27	28	♐0	1	2	4	5	6	7	9	♐10
♂	♍8	9	9	10	10	11	11	12	13	13	14	14	15	15	16	17	17	18	18	19	19	20	20	21	21	22	23	23	24	♍24

1	6	12	18	24	30	1	6	12	18	24	30	1	15	30	1	15	30	1	15	30	1	15	30
♃ ♏5	6	7	8	9	11	♄ ♒22	22	22	22	22	22	♅ ♈29	29	28	♆ ♍14	14	14	♇ ♋26	26	26	☊ ♒6	4	3

DECEMBER

	1	2	3	4	5	6	7	8	9	10	11	12	13	14	15	16	17	18	19	20	21	22	23	24	25	26	27	28	29	30	31
☉	♐8	9	10	11	12	13	14	15	16	17	18	19	20	21	22	23	24	25	26	27	28	29	♑0	1	3	4	5	6	7	8	♑9
☽	♍28	♎10	23	♏6	20	♐4	18	♑2	17	♒1	16	♓0	14	28	♈12	26	♉9	22	♊5	17	♋0	12	24	♌6	18	♍0	12	23	♎6	18	♏1
☿	♏22	24	25	27	28	♐0	1	3	4	6	7	9	10	12	13	15	17	18	20	21	23	24	26	27	29	♑1	2	4	5	7	♑9
♀	♐11	12	14	15	16	17	19	20	21	22	24	25	26	27	29	♑0	1	2	4	5	6	7	9	10	11	12	14	15	16	18	♑19
♂	♍25	25	26	26	27	27	28	28	29	29	♎0	0	1	1	2	2	3	3	4	4	5	5	6	6	7	7	7	8	8	9	♎9

1	6	12	18	24	30	1	6	12	18	24	30	1	15	30	1	15	30	1	15	30	1	15	30
♃ ♏11	12	13	14	15	17	♄ ♒23	23	23	24	24	25	♅ ♈28	28	28	♆ ♍15	15	15	♇ ♋26	26	25	☊ ♒3	2	1

1935

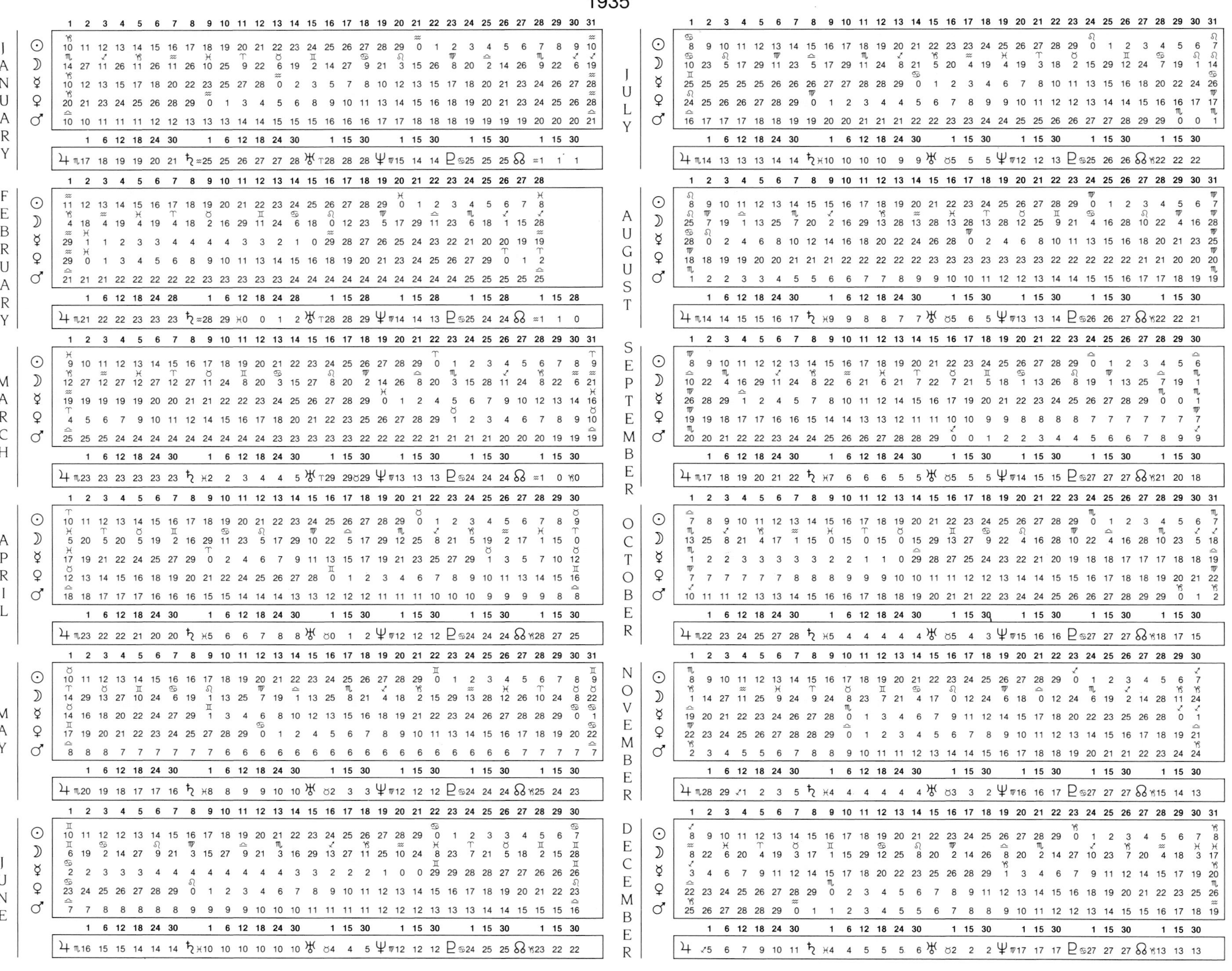

JANUARY

	1	2	3	4	5	6	7	8	9	10	11	12	13	14	15	16	17	18	19	20	21	22	23	24	25	26	27	28	29	30	31
☉	♑10	11	12	13	14	15	16	17	18	19	20	21	22	23	24	25	26	27	28	29	♒0	1	2	3	4	5	6	7	8	9	♒10
☽	♏14	27	♐11	26	♑11	26	♒11	26	♓10	25	♈9	22	♉6	19	♊2	14	27	♋9	21	♌3	15	26	♍8	20	♎2	14	26	♏9	22	♐6	♐19
☿	♑10	12	13	15	17	18	20	22	23	25	27	28	♒0	2	3	5	7	8	10	12	13	15	17	18	20	21	23	24	26	27	♒28
♀	♑20	21	23	24	25	26	28	29	♒0	1	3	4	5	6	8	9	10	11	13	14	15	16	18	19	20	21	23	24	25	26	♒28
♂	♎10	10	11	11	11	12	12	13	13	13	14	14	15	15	15	16	16	16	17	17	18	18	18	19	19	19	19	20	20	20	♎21

1	6	12	18	24	30	1	6	12	18	24	30	1	15	30	1	15	30	1	15	30	1	15	30
♃ ♏17	18	19	19	20	21	♄ ♒25	25	26	27	27	28	♅ ♈28	28	28	♆ ♍15	14	14	♇ ♋25	25	25	☊ ♒1	1	1

FEBRUARY

	1	2	3	4	5	6	7	8	9	10	11	12	13	14	15	16	17	18	19	20	21	22	23	24	25	26	27	28
☉	♒11	12	13	14	15	16	17	18	19	20	21	22	23	24	25	26	27	28	29	♓0	1	2	3	4	5	6	7	♓8
☽	♑4	18	♒4	19	♓4	19	♈4	18	♉2	16	29	♊11	24	♋6	18	♌0	12	23	♍5	17	29	♎11	23	♏6	18	♐1	15	♐28
☿	♒29	♓1	1	2	3	3	4	4	4	4	3	3	2	1	0	♒29	28	27	26	25	24	23	22	21	20	20	19	♒19
♀	♒29	♓0	1	3	4	5	6	8	9	10	11	13	14	15	16	18	19	20	21	23	24	25	26	27	29	♈0	1	♈2
♂	♎21	21	21	22	22	22	22	22	23	23	23	23	23	24	24	24	24	24	24	24	24	24	24	25	25	25	25	♎25

1	6	12	18	24	28	1	6	12	18	24	28	1	15	28	1	15	28	1	15	28	1	15	28
♃ ♏21	22	22	23	23	23	♄ ♒28	29	♓0	0	1	2	♅ ♈28	28	29	♆ ♍14	14	13	♇ ♋25	24	24	☊ ♒1	1	0

MARCH

	1	2	3	4	5	6	7	8	9	10	11	12	13	14	15	16	17	18	19	20	21	22	23	24	25	26	27	28	29	30	31
☉	♓9	10	11	12	13	14	15	16	17	18	19	20	21	22	23	24	25	26	27	28	29	♈0	1	2	3	4	5	6	7	8	♈9
☽	♑12	27	♒12	27	♓12	27	♈12	27	♉11	24	♊8	20	♋3	15	27	♌8	20	♍2	14	26	♎8	20	♏3	15	28	♐11	24	♑8	22	♒6	♒21
☿	♒19	19	19	19	19	20	20	21	21	22	22	23	24	25	26	27	28	29	♓0	1	2	4	5	6	7	9	10	12	13	14	♓16
♀	♈4	5	6	7	9	10	11	12	14	15	16	17	18	20	21	22	23	25	26	27	28	29	♉1	2	3	4	6	7	8	9	♉10
♂	♎25	25	25	24	24	24	24	24	24	24	24	24	23	23	23	23	23	22	22	22	22	21	21	21	21	20	20	20	19	19	♎19

1	6	12	18	24	30	1	6	12	18	24	30	1	15	30	1	15	30	1	15	30	1	15	30
♃ ♏23	23	23	23	23	23	♄ ♓2	2	3	4	4	5	♅ ♈29	29	♉29	♆ ♍13	13	13	♇ ♋24	24	24	☊ ♒1	0	♑0

APRIL

	1	2	3	4	5	6	7	8	9	10	11	12	13	14	15	16	17	18	19	20	21	22	23	24	25	26	27	28	29	30
☉	♈10	11	12	13	14	15	16	17	18	19	20	21	22	23	24	25	26	27	28	29	♉0	1	2	3	4	5	6	7	8	♉9
☽	♓5	20	♈5	20	♉5	19	♊2	16	29	♋11	23	♌5	17	29	♍10	22	♎5	17	29	♏12	25	♐8	21	♑5	19	♒2	17	♓1	15	♈0
☿	♓17	19	21	22	24	25	27	29	♈0	2	4	6	7	9	11	13	15	17	19	21	23	25	27	29	♉1	3	5	7	10	♉12
♀	♉12	13	14	15	16	18	19	20	21	22	24	25	26	27	28	♊0	1	2	3	4	6	7	8	9	10	11	13	14	15	♊16
♂	♎18	18	17	17	17	16	16	16	15	15	14	14	14	13	13	12	12	12	11	11	11	10	10	10	9	9	9	9	8	♎8

1	6	12	18	24	30	1	6	12	18	24	30	1	15	30	1	15	30	1	15	30	1	15	30
♃ ♏23	22	22	21	20	20	♄ ♓5	6	6	7	8	8	♅ ♉0	1	2	♆ ♍12	12	12	♇ ♋24	24	24	☊ ♑28	27	25

MAY

	1	2	3	4	5	6	7	8	9	10	11	12	13	14	15	16	17	18	19	20	21	22	23	24	25	26	27	28	29	30	31
☉	♉10	11	12	13	14	15	16	16	17	18	19	20	21	22	23	24	25	26	27	28	29	♊0	1	2	3	4	5	6	7	8	♊9
☽	♈14	29	♉13	27	♊10	24	♋6	19	♌1	13	25	♍7	19	♎1	13	25	♏8	21	♐4	18	♑2	15	29	♒13	28	♓12	26	♈10	24	♉8	♉22
☿	♉14	16	18	20	22	24	27	29	♊1	3	4	6	8	10	12	13	15	16	18	19	21	22	23	24	26	27	28	28	29	♋0	♋1
♀	♊17	19	20	21	22	23	24	25	27	28	29	♋0	1	2	4	5	6	7	8	9	10	11	13	14	15	16	17	18	19	20	♋22
♂	♎8	8	8	7	7	7	7	7	7	6	6	6	6	6	6	6	6	6	6	6	6	6	6	6	6	6	7	7	7	7	♎7

1	6	12	18	24	30	1	6	12	18	24	30	1	15	30	1	15	30	1	15	30	1	15	30
♃ ♏20	19	18	17	17	16	♄ ♓8	8	9	9	10	10	♅ ♉2	3	3	♆ ♍12	12	12	♇ ♋24	24	24	☊ ♑25	24	23

JUNE

	1	2	3	4	5	6	7	8	9	10	11	12	13	14	15	16	17	18	19	20	21	22	23	24	25	26	27	28	29	30
☉	♊10	11	12	12	13	14	15	16	17	18	19	20	21	22	23	24	25	26	27	28	29	♋0	1	2	3	3	4	5	6	♋7
☽	♊6	19	♋2	14	27	♌9	21	♍3	15	27	♎9	21	♏3	16	29	♐13	27	♑11	25	♒10	24	♓8	23	♈7	21	♉5	18	♊2	15	♊28
☿	♋2	2	3	3	3	4	4	4	4	4	4	4	4	3	3	2	2	2	1	0	0	♊29	29	28	28	27	27	26	26	♊26
♀	♋23	24	25	26	27	28	29	♌0	1	2	3	4	6	7	8	9	10	11	12	13	14	15	16	17	18	19	20	21	22	♌23
♂	♎7	7	8	8	8	8	8	9	9	9	9	10	10	10	11	11	11	11	12	12	12	13	13	13	14	14	15	15	15	♎16

1	6	12	18	24	30	1	6	12	18	24	30	1	15	30	1	15	30	1	15	30	1	15	30
♃ ♏16	15	15	14	14	14	♄ ♓10	10	10	10	10	10	♅ ♉4	4	5	♆ ♍12	12	12	♇ ♋24	25	25	☊ ♑23	22	22

JULY

	1	2	3	4	5	6	7	8	9	10	11	12	13	14	15	16	17	18	19	20	21	22	23	24	25	26	27	28	29	30	31
☉	♋8	9	10	11	12	13	14	15	16	17	18	19	20	21	22	23	23	24	25	26	27	28	29	♌0	1	2	3	4	5	6	♌7
☽	♋10	23	♌5	17	29	♍11	23	♎5	17	29	♏11	24	♐8	21	♑5	20	♒4	19	♓4	19	♈3	18	♉2	15	29	♊12	24	♋7	19	♌1	♌14
☿	♊25	25	25	25	25	26	26	26	27	27	28	28	29	♋0	1	2	3	4	6	7	8	10	11	13	15	16	18	20	22	24	♋26
♀	♌24	25	26	26	27	28	29	♍0	1	2	3	4	4	5	6	7	8	9	9	10	11	12	12	13	14	14	15	16	16	17	♍17
♂	♎16	17	17	17	18	18	19	19	20	20	21	21	21	22	22	23	23	24	24	25	25	26	26	27	27	28	29	29	♏0	0	♏1

1	6	12	18	24	30	1	6	12	18	24	30	1	15	30	1	15	30	1	15	30	1	15	30
♃ ♏14	13	13	13	14	14	♄ ♓10	10	10	10	9	9	♅ ♉5	5	5	♆ ♍12	12	13	♇ ♋25	26	26	☊ ♑22	22	22

AUGUST

	1	2	3	4	5	6	7	8	9	10	11	12	13	14	15	16	17	18	19	20	21	22	23	24	25	26	27	28	29	30	31
☉	♌8	9	10	11	12	13	14	15	15	16	17	18	19	20	21	22	23	24	25	26	27	28	29	♍0	1	2	3	4	5	6	♍7
☽	♌25	♍7	19	♎1	13	25	♏7	20	♐2	16	29	♑13	28	♒13	28	♓13	28	♈13	28	♉12	25	♊9	21	♋4	16	28	♌10	22	♍4	16	♍28
☿	♋28	♌0	2	4	6	8	10	12	14	16	18	20	22	24	26	28	♍0	2	4	6	8	10	11	13	15	16	18	20	21	23	♍25
♀	♍18	18	19	19	20	20	21	21	21	22	22	22	22	22	23	23	23	23	23	23	23	22	22	22	22	22	21	21	20	20	♍20
♂	♏1	2	2	3	3	4	5	5	6	6	7	7	8	9	9	10	10	11	12	12	13	14	14	15	15	16	17	17	18	19	♏19

1	6	12	18	24	30	1	6	12	18	24	30	1	15	30	1	15	30	1	15	30	1	15	30
♃ ♏14	14	15	15	16	17	♄ ♓9	9	8	8	7	7	♅ ♉5	6	5	♆ ♍13	13	14	♇ ♋26	26	27	☊ ♑22	22	21

SEPTEMBER

	1	2	3	4	5	6	7	8	9	10	11	12	13	14	15	16	17	18	19	20	21	22	23	24	25	26	27	28	29	30
☉	♍8	9	10	11	12	12	13	14	15	16	17	18	19	20	21	22	23	24	25	26	27	28	29	♎0	1	2	3	4	5	♎6
☽	♎10	22	♏4	16	29	♐11	24	♑8	22	♒6	21	♓6	21	♈7	22	♉7	21	♊5	18	♋1	13	26	♌8	19	♍1	13	25	♎7	19	♏1
☿	♍26	28	29	♎1	2	4	5	7	8	10	11	12	14	15	16	17	19	20	21	22	23	24	25	26	27	28	29	♏0	0	♏1
♀	♍19	19	18	17	17	16	16	15	14	14	13	13	12	11	11	10	10	9	9	8	8	8	8	7	7	7	7	7	7	♍7
♂	♏20	20	21	22	22	23	24	24	25	26	26	27	28	28	29	♐0	0	1	2	2	3	4	4	5	6	6	7	8	9	♐9

1	6	12	18	24	30	1	6	12	18	24	30	1	15	30	1	15	30	1	15	30	1	15	30
♃ ♏17	18	19	20	21	22	♄ ♓7	6	6	6	5	5	♅ ♉5	5	5	♆ ♍14	15	15	♇ ♋27	27	27	☊ ♑21	20	18

OCTOBER

	1	2	3	4	5	6	7	8	9	10	11	12	13	14	15	16	17	18	19	20	21	22	23	24	25	26	27	28	29	30	31
☉	♎7	8	9	10	11	12	13	14	15	16	17	18	19	20	21	22	23	24	25	26	27	28	29	♏0	1	2	3	4	5	6	♏7
☽	♏13	25	♐8	21	♑4	17	♒1	15	♓0	15	♈0	15	♉0	15	29	♊13	27	♋9	22	♌4	16	28	♍10	22	♎4	16	28	♏10	23	♐5	♐18
☿	♏1	2	2	3	3	3	3	3	2	2	1	1	0	♎29	28	27	25	24	23	22	21	20	19	18	18	17	17	17	18	18	♎19
♀	♍7	7	7	7	7	7	8	8	8	9	9	9	10	10	11	11	12	12	13	14	14	15	15	16	17	18	18	19	20	21	♍22
♂	♐10	11	11	12	13	13	14	15	16	16	17	18	18	19	20	21	21	22	23	24	24	25	26	26	27	28	29	29	♑0	1	♑2

1	6	12	18	24	30	1	6	12	18	24	30	1	15	30	1	15	30	1	15	30	1	15	30
♃ ♏22	23	24	25	27	28	♄ ♓5	4	4	4	4	4	♅ ♉5	4	3	♆ ♍15	16	16	♇ ♋27	27	27	☊ ♑18	17	15

NOVEMBER

	1	2	3	4	5	6	7	8	9	10	11	12	13	14	15	16	17	18	19	20	21	22	23	24	25	26	27	28	29	30
☉	♏8	9	10	11	12	13	14	15	16	17	18	19	20	21	22	23	24	25	26	27	28	29	♐0	1	2	3	4	5	6	♐7
☽	♑1	14	27	♒11	25	♓9	24	♈9	24	♉8	23	♊7	21	♋4	17	♌0	12	24	♍6	18	♎0	12	24	♏6	19	♐2	14	28	♑11	♑24
☿	♎19	20	21	22	23	24	26	27	28	♏0	1	3	4	6	7	9	11	12	14	15	17	18	20	22	23	25	26	28	♐0	♐1
♀	♍22	23	24	25	26	27	28	28	29	♎0	1	2	3	4	5	6	7	8	9	10	11	12	13	14	15	16	17	18	19	♎21
♂	♑2	3	4	5	5	6	7	8	8	9	10	11	11	12	13	14	14	15	16	17	18	18	19	20	21	21	22	23	24	♑24

1	6	12	18	24	30	1	6	12	18	24	30	1	15	30	1	15	30	1	15	30	1	15	30
♃ ♏28	29	♐1	2	3	5	♄ ♓4	4	4	4	4	4	♅ ♉3	3	2	♆ ♍16	16	17	♇ ♋27	27	27	☊ ♑15	14	13

DECEMBER

	1	2	3	4	5	6	7	8	9	10	11	12	13	14	15	16	17	18	19	20	21	22	23	24	25	26	27	28	29	30	31
☉	♐8	9	10	11	12	13	14	15	16	17	18	19	20	21	22	23	24	25	26	27	28	29	♑0	1	2	3	4	5	6	7	♑8
☽	♒8	22	♓6	20	♈4	19	♉3	17	♊1	15	29	♋12	25	♌8	20	♍2	14	26	♎8	20	♏2	14	27	♐10	23	♑7	20	♒4	18	♓3	♓17
☿	♐3	4	6	7	9	11	12	14	15	17	18	20	22	23	25	26	28	29	♑1	3	4	6	7	9	11	12	14	15	17	19	♑20
♀	♎22	23	24	25	26	27	28	29	♏0	2	3	4	5	6	7	8	9	11	12	13	14	15	16	18	19	20	21	22	23	25	♏26
♂	♑25	26	27	28	28	29	♒0	1	1	2	3	4	5	5	6	7	8	8	9	10	11	12	12	13	14	15	15	16	17	18	♒19

1	6	12	18	24	30	1	6	12	18	24	30	1	15	30	1	15	30	1	15	30	1	15	30
♃ ♐5	6	7	9	10	11	♄ ♓4	4	5	5	5	6	♅ ♉2	2	2	♆ ♍17	17	17	♇ ♋27	27	27	☊ ♑13	13	13

1936

JANUARY

	1	2	3	4	5	6	7	8	9	10	11	12	13	14	15	16	17	18	19	20	21	22	23	24	25	26	27	28	29	30	31
☉	♑9	10	11	12	13	14	16	17	18	19	20	21	22	23	24	25	26	27	28	29	♒0	1	2	3	4	5	6	7	8	9	♒10
☽	♈1	15	29	♉13	27	♊11	24	♋7	20	♌3	16	28	♍10	22	♎4	16	28	♏10	22	♐5	18	♑1	15	29	♒13	28	♓13	27	♈12	26	♉10
☿	♑22	23	25	27	28	♒0	1	3	4	6	7	9	10	11	12	14	15	15	16	17	17	18	18	18	17	17	16	15	14	13	♒12
♀	♏27	28	29	♐0	2	3	4	5	6	8	9	10	11	12	14	15	16	17	18	20	21	22	23	24	26	27	28	29	♑1	2	♑3
♂	♒19	20	21	22	22	23	24	25	26	26	27	28	29	♓0	0	1	2	3	3	4	5	6	7	7	8	9	10	10	11	12	♓13

	1	6	12	18	24	30		1	6	12	18	24	30		1	15	30		1	15	30		1	15	30		1	15	30
♃	♐12	13	14	15	16	17	♄	♓6	6	7	8	8	9	♅	♉2	2	2	♆	♍17	17	16	♇	♋27	26	26	☊	♑13	13	12

FEBRUARY

	1	2	3	4	5	6	7	8	9	10	11	12	13	14	15	16	17	18	19	20	21	22	23	24	25	26	27	28	29
☉	♒11	12	13	14	15	16	17	18	19	20	21	22	23	24	25	26	27	28	29	♓0	1	2	3	4	5	6	7	8	♓9
☽	♉24	♊7	21	♋4	17	29	♌12	24	♍6	18	♎0	12	24	♏6	18	♐0	13	25	♑9	22	♒7	21	♓6	21	♈7	22	♉6	20	♊4
☿	♒11	10	8	7	6	5	4	4	3	2	2	2	2	2	2	2	3	3	4	4	5	6	7	7	8	9	10	11	♒13
♀	♑4	5	7	8	9	10	11	13	14	15	16	18	19	20	21	22	24	25	26	27	29	♒0	1	2	3	5	6	7	♒8
♂	♓14	14	15	16	17	17	18	19	20	21	21	22	23	24	24	25	26	27	28	28	29	♈0	1	1	2	3	4	4	♈5

	1	6	12	18	24	29		1	6	12	18	24	29		1	15	29		1	15	29		1	15	29		1	15	29
♃	♐18	19	20	20	21	22	♄	♓9	10	10	11	12	12	♅	♉2	2	3	♆	♍16	16	16	♇	♋26	26	25	☊	♑12	12	11

MARCH

	1	2	3	4	5	6	7	8	9	10	11	12	13	14	15	16	17	18	19	20	21	22	23	24	25	26	27	28	29	30	31
☉	♓10	11	12	13	14	15	16	17	18	19	20	21	22	23	24	25	26	27	28	29	♈0	1	2	3	4	5	6	7	8	9	♈10
☽	♊18	♋1	14	26	♌9	21	♍3	15	27	♎9	21	♏2	14	26	♐9	21	♑4	17	♒1	15	29	♓14	♈0	15	♉0	15	♊0	14	27	♋10	♋23
☿	♒14	15	16	17	19	20	21	23	24	25	27	28	♓0	1	3	4	6	7	9	10	12	14	15	17	19	21	22	24	26	28	♈0
♀	♒10	11	12	13	14	16	17	18	19	21	22	23	24	26	27	28	29	♓0	2	3	4	5	7	8	9	10	12	13	14	15	♓16
♂	♈6	7	8	8	9	10	11	11	12	13	14	14	15	16	17	17	18	19	20	20	21	22	23	23	24	25	26	26	27	28	♈29

	1	6	12	18	24	30		1	6	12	18	24	30		1	15	30		1	15	30		1	15	30		1	15	30
♃	♐22	23	23	24	24	24	♄	♓13	13	14	15	15	16	♅	♉3	3	4	♆	♍16	15	15	♇	♋25	25	25	☊	♑11	9	8

APRIL

	1	2	3	4	5	6	7	8	9	10	11	12	13	14	15	16	17	18	19	20	21	22	23	24	25	26	27	28	29	30
☉	♈11	12	13	14	15	16	17	18	19	20	21	22	23	24	25	26	27	28	29	♉0	1	2	3	4	5	6	7	8	8	♉9
☽	♌6	18	♍0	12	24	♎6	18	29	♏11	23	♐6	18	♑0	13	26	♒10	24	♓8	23	♈8	23	♉8	23	♊8	22	♋6	19	♌2	15	♌27
☿	♈1	3	5	7	9	11	13	15	17	19	21	24	26	28	♉0	2	4	6	8	10	12	14	16	18	20	22	24	25	27	♉28
♀	♓18	19	20	21	23	24	25	26	28	29	♈0	1	2	4	5	6	7	9	10	11	12	13	15	16	17	18	20	21	22	♈23
♂	♈29	♉0	1	2	2	3	4	5	5	6	7	7	8	9	10	10	11	12	13	13	14	15	15	16	17	18	18	19	20	♉20

	1	6	12	18	24	30		1	6	12	18	24	30		1	15	30		1	15	30		1	15	30		1	15	30
♃	♐24	24	24	24	24	24	♄	♓16	17	17	18	19	19	♅	♉4	5	6	♆	♍15	14	14	♇	♋25	25	25	☊	♑8	6	5

MAY

	1	2	3	4	5	6	7	8	9	10	11	12	13	14	15	16	17	18	19	20	21	22	23	24	25	26	27	28	29	30	31
☉	♉10	11	12	13	14	15	16	17	18	19	20	21	22	23	24	25	26	27	28	29	♊0	1	2	3	4	5	6	6	7	8	♊9
☽	♍9	21	♎3	14	26	♏8	20	♐3	15	27	♑10	23	♒6	20	♓4	18	♈2	17	♉2	17	♊2	16	♋0	14	27	♌10	23	♍5	17	29	♎11
☿	♊0	1	3	4	5	6	7	8	9	10	11	12	12	13	13	13	14	14	14	14	14	14	14	13	13	13	12	12	11	11	♊10
♀	♈25	26	27	28	29	♉1	2	3	4	6	7	8	9	10	12	13	14	15	17	18	19	20	22	23	24	25	26	28	29	♊0	♊1
♂	♉21	22	23	23	24	25	25	26	27	28	28	29	♊0	0	1	2	3	3	4	5	5	6	7	7	8	9	10	10	11	12	♊12

	1	6	12	18	24	30		1	6	12	18	24	30		1	15	30		1	15	30		1	15	30		1	15	30
♃	♐24	23	23	22	22	21	♄	♓19	20	20	21	21	22	♅	♉6	7	7	♆	♍14	14	14	♇	♋25	25	26	☊	♑5	4	4

JUNE

	1	2	3	4	5	6	7	8	9	10	11	12	13	14	15	16	17	18	19	20	21	22	23	24	25	26	27	28	29	30
☉	♊10	11	12	13	14	15	16	17	18	19	20	21	22	23	24	25	26	27	28	28	29	♋0	1	2	3	4	5	6	7	♋8
☽	♎23	♏5	17	29	♐12	24	♑7	20	♒3	17	♓0	14	28	♈13	27	♉12	26	♊10	25	♋9	22	♌5	18	♍1	13	25	♎7	19	♏1	♏13
☿	♊10	9	8	8	7	7	7	6	6	6	6	6	5	6	6	6	6	7	7	8	8	9	10	10	11	12	13	14	15	♊17
♀	♊3	4	5	6	7	9	10	11	12	14	15	16	17	19	20	21	22	23	25	26	27	28	♋0	1	2	3	4	6	7	♋8
♂	♊13	14	14	15	16	16	17	18	19	19	20	21	21	22	23	23	24	25	25	26	27	27	28	29	29	♋0	1	1	2	♋3

	1	6	12	18	24	30		1	6	12	18	24	30		1	15	30		1	15	30		1	15	30		1	15	30
♃	♐21	20	19	19	18	17	♄	♓22	22	22	22	22	23	♅	♉7	8	9	♆	♍14	14	14	♇	♋26	26	26	☊	♑4	4	3

JULY

	1	2	3	4	5	6	7	8	9	10	11	12	13	14	15	16	17	18	19	20	21	22	23	24	25	26	27	28	29	30	31
☉	♋9	10	11	12	13	14	15	16	17	18	18	19	20	21	22	23	24	25	26	27	28	29	♌0	1	2	3	4	5	6	7	♌8
☽	♏25	♐8	20	♑3	16	29	♒13	27	♓11	25	♈9	24	♉8	22	♊6	20	♋4	17	♌1	14	26	♍9	21	♎3	15	27	♏9	21	♐3	15	♐28
☿	♊18	19	21	22	24	25	27	28	♋0	2	4	6	8	10	12	14	16	18	20	22	24	26	29	♌1	3	5	7	9	11	13	♌15
♀	♋9	11	12	13	14	16	17	18	19	20	22	23	24	25	27	28	29	♌0	2	3	4	5	6	8	9	10	11	13	14	15	♌16
♂	♋3	4	5	5	6	7	7	8	9	9	10	11	11	12	13	13	14	15	15	16	17	17	18	19	19	20	21	21	22	23	♋23

	1	6	12	18	24	30		1	6	12	18	24	30		1	15	30		1	15	30		1	15	30		1	15	30
♃	♐17	17	16	16	15	15	♄	♓23	23	22	22	22	22	♅	♉9	9	9	♆	♍14	15	15	♇	♋26	27	27	☊	♑3	3	3

AUGUST

	1	2	3	4	5	6	7	8	9	10	11	12	13	14	15	16	17	18	19	20	21	22	23	24	25	26	27	28	29	30	31
☉	♌9	10	10	11	12	13	14	15	16	17	18	19	20	21	22	23	24	25	26	27	28	29	♍0	1	2	3	4	4	5	6	♍7
☽	♑11	25	♒8	22	♓7	21	♈6	20	♉5	19	♊3	17	♋0	13	27	♌10	22	♍5	17	29	♎11	23	♏5	17	29	♐11	23	♑6	19	♒3	♒17
☿	♌17	19	21	23	25	26	28	♍0	2	4	5	7	9	10	12	13	15	16	18	19	21	22	24	25	26	28	29	♎0	2	3	♎4
♀	♌18	19	20	21	22	24	25	26	27	29	♍0	1	2	4	5	6	7	9	10	11	12	13	15	16	17	18	20	21	22	23	♍25
♂	♋24	25	25	26	26	27	28	28	29	♌0	0	1	2	2	3	4	4	5	6	6	7	7	8	9	9	10	11	11	12	13	♌13

	1	6	12	18	24	30		1	6	12	18	24	30		1	15	30		1	15	30		1	15	30		1	15	30
♃	♐15	15	15	15	15	15	♄	♓22	22	21	21	21	20	♅	♉10	10	10	♆	♍15	16	16	♇	♋27	28	28	☊	♑3	3	1

SEPTEMBER

	1	2	3	4	5	6	7	8	9	10	11	12	13	14	15	16	17	18	19	20	21	22	23	24	25	26	27	28	29	30
☉	♍8	9	10	11	12	13	14	15	16	17	18	19	20	21	22	23	24	25	26	27	28	29	♎0	1	2	3	4	5	6	♎7
☽	♓1	16	♈1	16	♉1	15	29	♊13	27	♋10	23	♌6	19	♍1	14	26	♎8	20	♏2	14	25	♐7	19	♑2	14	27	♒11	25	♓9	♓24
☿	♎5	6	7	8	9	10	11	12	13	13	14	15	15	16	16	16	16	16	16	16	16	16	15	15	14	13	12	11	10	♎9
♀	♍26	27	28	29	♎1	2	3	4	6	7	8	9	11	12	13	14	16	17	18	19	20	22	23	24	25	27	28	29	♏0	♏2
♂	♌14	14	15	16	16	17	18	18	19	20	20	21	21	22	23	23	24	25	25	26	26	27	28	28	29	♍0	0	1	1	♍2

	1	6	12	18	24	30		1	6	12	18	24	30		1	15	30		1	15	30		1	15	30		1	15	30
♃	♐15	16	16	17	17	18	♄	♓20	20	19	19	18	18	♅	♉9	9	9	♆	♍16	17	17	♇	♋28	28	29	☊	♑1	0	♐0

OCTOBER

	1	2	3	4	5	6	7	8	9	10	11	12	13	14	15	16	17	18	19	20	21	22	23	24	25	26	27	28	29	30	31
☉	♎8	9	10	11	12	13	14	15	16	17	17	18	19	20	21	22	23	24	25	26	27	28	29	♏0	1	2	3	4	5	6	♏7
☽	♈9	25	♉10	25	♊9	23	♋7	20	♌3	16	28	♍11	23	♎5	17	29	♏10	22	♐4	16	28	♑10	23	♒6	19	♓3	18	♈2	18	♉3	♉18
☿	♎8	7	5	4	4	3	2	2	1	1	1	2	2	3	3	4	5	6	8	9	10	12	13	15	16	18	19	21	23	24	♎26
♀	♏3	4	5	6	8	9	10	11	13	14	15	16	17	19	20	21	22	24	25	26	27	29	♐0	1	2	3	5	6	7	8	♐10
♂	♍3	3	4	5	5	6	6	7	8	8	9	10	10	11	11	12	13	13	14	14	15	16	16	17	18	18	19	19	20	21	♍21

	1	6	12	18	24	30		1	6	12	18	24	30		1	15	30		1	15	30		1	15	30		1	15	30
♃	♐18	19	20	21	22	23	♄	♓18	17	17	17	16	16	♅	♉9	8	8	♆	♍17	18	18	♇	♋29	29	29	☊	♐28	27	25

NOVEMBER

	1	2	3	4	5	6	7	8	9	10	11	12	13	14	15	16	17	18	19	20	21	22	23	24	25	26	27	28	29	30
☉	♏8	9	10	11	12	13	14	15	16	17	18	19	20	21	22	23	24	25	26	27	29	♐0	1	2	3	4	5	6	7	♐8
☽	♊3	18	♋2	16	♌0	13	25	♍8	20	♎2	14	26	♏7	19	♐1	13	25	♑7	20	♒3	16	29	♓13	27	♈11	26	♉11	26	♊11	♊26
☿	♎28	29	♏1	3	4	6	7	9	11	12	14	16	17	19	20	22	24	25	27	28	♐0	2	3	5	6	8	9	11	12	♐14
♀	♐11	12	13	14	16	17	18	19	21	22	23	24	25	27	28	29	♑0	1	3	4	5	6	8	9	10	11	12	14	15	♑16
♂	♍22	22	23	24	24	25	25	26	27	27	28	28	29	♎0	0	1	1	2	3	3	4	4	5	6	6	7	7	8	9	♎9

	1	6	12	18	24	30		1	6	12	18	24	30		1	15	30		1	15	30		1	15	30		1	15	30
♃	♐23	24	26	27	28	29	♄	♓16	16	16	16	16	16	♅	♉8	7	6	♆	♍18	19	19	♇	♋29	29	29	☊	♐25	24	24

DECEMBER

	1	2	3	4	5	6	7	8	9	10	11	12	13	14	15	16	17	18	19	20	21	22	23	24	25	26	27	28	29	30	31
☉	♐9	10	11	12	13	14	15	16	17	18	19	20	21	22	23	24	25	26	27	28	29	♑0	1	2	3	4	5	6	7	8	♑9
☽	♋10	24	♌8	21	♍4	16	29	♎11	22	♏4	16	28	♐10	22	♑4	17	♒0	13	26	♓9	23	♈7	21	♉5	20	♊5	19	♋4	18	♌2	♌16
☿	♐16	17	19	20	22	23	25	26	28	♑0	1	3	4	6	7	9	10	12	13	15	16	18	19	20	22	23	24	26	27	28	♑29
♀	♑17	18	20	21	22	23	24	26	27	28	29	♒0	2	3	4	5	6	8	9	10	11	12	14	15	16	17	18	19	21	22	♒23
♂	♎10	10	11	11	12	13	13	14	14	15	16	16	17	17	18	18	19	20	20	21	21	22	22	23	23	24	25	25	26	26	♎27

	1	6	12	18	24	30		1	6	12	18	24	30		1	15	30		1	15	30		1	15	30		1	15	30
♃	♑0	1	2	4	5	6	♄	♓16	16	16	17	17	17	♅	♉6	6	6	♆	♍19	19	19	♇	♋29	28	28	☊	♐24	24	24

1937

JANUARY

	1	2	3	4	5	6	7	8	9	10	11	12	13	14	15	16	17	18	19	20	21	22	23	24	25	26	27	28	29	30	31
☉	♑10	11	12	13	14	15	16	17	18	19	20	21	22	23	24	25	26	27	29	♒0	1	2	3	4	5	6	7	8	9	10	♒11
☽	♌29	♍12	24	♎7	19	♏1	12	24	♐6	18	♑1	13	26	♒9	22	♓6	20	♈4	18	♉2	16	♊0	14	28	♋13	26	♌10	24	♍7	20	♎2
☿	♑29	♒0	1	1	1	2	1	1	1	0	♑29	28	27	26	24	23	22	20	19	18	17	17	16	16	16	15	15	16	16	16	♑17
♀	♒24	25	26	28	29	♓0	1	2	3	4	6	7	8	9	10	11	12	13	15	16	17	18	19	20	21	22	23	24	25	26	♓27
♂	♎27	28	28	29	♏0	0	1	1	2	2	3	3	4	4	5	5	6	6	7	7	8	9	9	10	10	11	11	12	12	13	♏13

	1	6	12	18	24	30		1	6	12	18	24	30		1	15	30		1	15	30		1	15	30		1	15	30
♃	♑7	8	9	11	12	13	♄	♓17	18	18	19	19	20	♅	♉6	6	6	♆	♍19	19	19	♇	♋28	28	27	☊	♐24	24	23

FEBRUARY

	1	2	3	4	5	6	7	8	9	10	11	12	13	14	15	16	17	18	19	20	21	22	23	24	25	26	27	28
☉	♒12	13	14	15	16	17	18	19	20	21	22	23	24	25	26	27	28	29	♓0	1	2	3	4	5	6	7	8	♓9
☽	♎14	26	♏8	20	♐2	14	26	♑9	21	♒4	18	♓2	16	♈0	14	28	♉13	27	♊11	25	♋9	22	♌6	19	♍2	15	28	♎10
☿	♑17	18	19	19	20	21	22	23	24	25	26	28	29	♒0	1	3	4	5	6	8	9	11	12	14	15	16	18	♒20
♀	♓29	♈0	1	2	3	4	5	6	7	8	9	10	10	11	12	13	14	15	16	17	18	19	19	20	21	22	23	♈23
♂	♏14	14	14	15	15	16	16	17	17	18	18	19	19	20	20	20	21	21	22	22	23	23	23	24	24	25	25	♏25

	1	6	12	18	24	28		1	6	12	18	24	28		1	15	28		1	15	28		1	15	28		1	15	28
♃	♑14	15	16	17	18	19	♄	♓20	21	21	22	23	23	♅	♉6	6	6	♆	♍19	18	18	♇	♋27	27	27	☊	♐23	22	21

MARCH

	1	2	3	4	5	6	7	8	9	10	11	12	13	14	15	16	17	18	19	20	21	22	23	24	25	26	27	28	29	30	31
☉	♓10	11	12	13	14	15	16	17	18	19	20	21	22	23	24	25	26	27	28	29	♈0	1	2	3	4	5	6	7	8	9	♈10
☽	♎22	♏4	16	28	♐10	22	♑4	16	29	♒12	26	♓10	25	♈9	24	♉9	23	♊8	22	♋5	19	♌2	16	29	♍11	24	♎6	19	♏1	12	♏24
☿	♒21	23	24	26	27	29	♓1	2	4	6	7	9	11	13	15	16	18	20	22	24	26	28	♈0	2	4	6	8	10	12	14	♈16
♀	♈24	25	26	26	27	28	28	29	♉0	0	1	1	2	2	3	3	4	4	4	5	5	5	5	6	6	6	6	6	6	6	♉6
♂	♏26	26	27	27	27	28	28	28	29	29	29	♐0	0	0	1	1	1	1	2	2	2	2	3	3	3	3	4	4	4	4	♐4

	1	6	12	18	24	30		1	6	12	18	24	30		1	15	30		1	15	30		1	15	30		1	15	30
♃	♑19	20	21	22	23	24	♄	♓23	24	25	25	26	27	♅	♉7	7	8	♆	♍18	17	17	♇	♋27	27	27	☊	♐20	19	17

APRIL

	1	2	3	4	5	6	7	8	9	10	11	12	13	14	15	16	17	18	19	20	21	22	23	24	25	26	27	28	29	30
☉	♈11	12	13	14	15	16	17	18	19	20	21	22	23	24	25	26	27	28	29	29	♉0	1	2	3	4	5	6	7	8	♉9
☽	♐6	18	♑0	12	24	♒7	20	♓4	18	♈3	18	♉3	18	♊3	17	♋2	16	29	♌13	26	♍8	21	♎3	15	27	♏9	21	♐3	15	♐27
☿	♈18	20	22	24	26	28	♉0	2	4	5	7	9	10	12	13	15	16	17	18	19	20	21	22	23	23	24	24	24	24	♉24
♀	♉5	5	5	5	4	4	4	3	3	2	2	1	1	0	0	♈29	28	28	27	26	26	25	25	24	23	23	22	22	22	♈21
♂	♐4	5	5	5	5	5	5	5	5	5	5	5	6	6	6	6	5	5	5	5	5	5	5	5	5	5	5	4	4	♐4

	1	6	12	18	24	30		1	6	12	18	24	30		1	15	30		1	15	30		1	15	30		1	15	30
♃	♑24	25	26	26	27	27	♄	♓27	28	28	29	♈0	1	♅	♉8	9	10	♆	♍17	17	16	♇	♋27	27	27	☊	♐17	16	15

MAY

	1	2	3	4	5	6	7	8	9	10	11	12	13	14	15	16	17	18	19	20	21	22	23	24	25	26	27	28	29	30	31
☉	♉10	11	12	13	14	15	16	17	18	19	20	21	22	23	24	25	26	27	28	29	♊0	0	1	2	3	4	5	6	7	8	♊9
☽	♑9	21	♒3	16	29	♓12	27	♈11	26	♉11	26	♊11	26	♋11	25	♌9	22	♍5	18	♎0	12	24	♏6	18	♐0	12	24	♑6	18	♒0	♒12
☿	♉24	24	24	24	24	23	23	22	22	21	21	20	19	19	18	18	17	17	16	16	16	15	15	15	15	15	16	16	16	17	♉17
♀	♈21	20	20	20	20	20	20	19	19	19	19	20	20	20	20	20	21	21	21	22	22	22	23	23	24	24	25	25	26	27	♈27
♂	♐4	4	3	3	3	3	2	2	2	2	1	1	1	0	0	0	♏29	29	29	28	28	28	27	27	27	26	26	25	25	25	♏24

	1	6	12	18	24	30		1	6	12	18	24	30		1	15	30		1	15	30		1	15	30		1	15	30
♃	♑27	27	27	27	27	27	♄	♈1	1	2	2	3	3	♅	♉10	10	11	♆	♍16	16	16	♇	♋27	27	27	☊	♐15	15	15

JUNE

	1	2	3	4	5	6	7	8	9	10	11	12	13	14	15	16	17	18	19	20	21	22	23	24	25	26	27	28	29	30
☉	♊10	11	12	13	14	15	16	17	18	19	20	21	22	23	23	24	25	26	27	28	29	♋0	1	2	3	4	5	6	7	♋8
☽	♒25	♓8	22	♈6	20	♉5	19	♊5	20	♋5	19	♌4	18	♍1	14	27	♎9	21	♏3	15	27	♐9	21	♑3	15	27	♒9	22	♓5	♓18
☿	♉18	18	19	20	20	21	22	23	24	25	26	28	29	♊0	1	3	4	6	7	9	11	12	14	16	18	20	22	24	26	♊28
♀	♈28	28	29	♉0	1	1	2	3	4	4	5	6	7	8	8	9	10	11	12	13	14	15	15	16	17	18	19	20	21	♉22
♂	♏24	24	24	23	23	23	22	22	22	22	21	21	21	21	21	20	20	20	20	20	20	20	20	20	20	20	20	20	20	♏20

	1	6	12	18	24	30		1	6	12	18	24	30		1	15	30		1	15	30		1	15	30		1	15	30
♃	♑27	27	26	26	25	24	♄	♈3	4	4	4	5	5	♅	♉11	12	13	♆	♍16	16	16	♇	♋27	27	28	☊	♐15	15	15

JULY

	1	2	3	4	5	6	7	8	9	10	11	12	13	14	15	16	17	18	19	20	21	22	23	24	25	26	27	28	29	30	31
☉	♋9	10	11	12	13	13	14	15	16	17	18	19	20	21	22	23	24	25	26	27	28	29	♌0	1	2	3	4	4	5	6	♌7
☽	♈2	16	♉0	14	29	♊13	28	♋13	28	♌12	26	♍9	22	♎5	18	♏0	12	23	♐5	17	29	♑11	24	♒6	19	♓2	15	29	♈12	26	♉10
☿	♋0	2	4	6	8	11	13	15	17	19	21	23	26	28	♌0	2	4	6	8	9	11	13	15	17	19	20	22	24	25	27	♌29
♀	♉23	24	25	26	27	28	29	♊0	1	2	3	4	5	6	7	8	9	11	12	13	14	15	16	17	18	19	20	21	22	24	♊25
♂	♏20	20	20	20	20	20	20	20	20	21	21	21	21	21	22	22	22	22	23	23	23	23	24	24	24	25	25	25	26	26	♏26

	1	6	12	18	24	30		1	6	12	18	24	30		1	15	30		1	15	30		1	15	30		1	15	30
♃	♑24	24	23	22	21	21	♄	♈5	5	5	5	5	5	♅	♉13	13	14	♆	♍16	17	17	♇	♋28	28	29	☊	♐15	14	14

AUGUST

	1	2	3	4	5	6	7	8	9	10	11	12	13	14	15	16	17	18	19	20	21	22	23	24	25	26	27	28	29	30	31
☉	♌8	9	10	11	12	13	14	15	16	17	18	19	20	21	22	23	24	25	26	27	28	28	29	♍0	1	2	3	4	5	6	♍7
☽	♉24	♊9	23	♋7	22	♌6	20	♍4	17	♎1	13	26	♏8	20	♐1	13	25	♑7	20	♒2	15	28	♓12	25	♈9	23	♉7	21	♊5	19	♋3
☿	♍0	2	3	5	6	8	9	10	12	13	14	15	17	18	19	20	21	22	23	24	25	25	26	27	28	28	29	29	29	29	♎0
♀	♊26	27	28	29	♋0	1	2	4	5	6	7	8	9	10	11	13	14	15	16	17	18	20	21	22	23	24	25	26	28	29	♌0
♂	♏27	27	28	28	28	29	29	♐0	0	0	1	1	2	2	3	3	4	4	5	5	6	6	7	7	8	8	9	10	10	11	♐11

	1	6	12	18	24	30		1	6	12	18	24	30		1	15	30		1	15	30		1	15	30		1	15	30
♃	♑20	20	19	19	18	18	♄	♈5	5	5	4	4	4	♅	♉14	14	14	♆	♍17	18	18	♇	♋29	29	29	☊	♐14	13	11

SEPTEMBER

	1	2	3	4	5	6	7	8	9	10	11	12	13	14	15	16	17	18	19	20	21	22	23	24	25	26	27	28	29	30
☉	♍8	9	10	11	12	13	14	15	16	17	18	19	20	21	22	23	24	25	26	27	28	29	♎0	1	2	2	3	4	5	♎6
☽	♋18	♌2	15	29	♍13	26	♎9	21	♏4	16	28	♐9	21	♑3	15	27	♒10	23	♓7	20	♈4	19	♉3	18	♊2	16	♋0	14	28	♌12
☿	♎0	0	♍29	29	29	28	28	27	26	26	25	24	23	22	21	20	19	18	17	16	16	16	15	15	15	16	16	17	18	♍19
♀	♌1	2	4	5	6	7	8	9	11	12	13	14	15	17	18	19	20	21	23	24	25	26	27	29	♍0	1	2	3	5	♍6
♂	♐12	12	13	13	14	15	15	16	16	17	18	18	19	19	20	21	21	22	23	23	24	25	25	26	26	27	28	28	29	♑0

	1	6	12	18	24	30		1	6	12	18	24	30		1	15	30		1	15	30		1	15	30		1	15	30
♃	♑18	18	17	18	18	18	♄	♈3	3	3	2	2	1	♅	♉14	13	13	♆	♍18	19	19	♇	♋29	♌29	0	☊	♐11	10	8

OCTOBER

	1	2	3	4	5	6	7	8	9	10	11	12	13	14	15	16	17	18	19	20	21	22	23	24	25	26	27	28	29	30	31
☉	♎7	8	9	10	11	12	13	14	15	16	17	18	19	20	21	22	23	24	25	26	27	28	29	♏0	1	2	3	4	5	6	♏7
☽	♌25	♍9	22	♎5	17	♏0	12	24	♐6	17	29	♑11	23	♒5	18	♓1	15	28	♈13	27	♉12	27	♊12	27	♋11	25	♌9	22	♍5	18	♎1
☿	♍20	21	22	23	25	26	28	29	♎1	3	4	6	8	9	11	13	15	16	18	20	21	23	25	27	28	♏0	2	3	5	7	♏8
♀	♍7	8	10	11	12	13	14	16	17	18	19	21	22	23	24	25	27	28	29	♎0	2	3	4	5	7	8	9	10	12	13	♎14
♂	♑0	1	2	2	3	4	4	5	6	7	7	8	9	9	10	11	11	12	13	14	14	15	16	16	17	18	19	19	20	21	♑21

	1	6	12	18	24	30		1	6	12	18	24	30		1	15	30		1	15	30		1	15	30		1	15	30
♃	♑18	18	19	19	20	21	♄	♈1	1	0	0	0	♓29	♅	♉13	13	12	♆	♍19	20	20	♇	♌0	0	0	☊	♐8	7	6

NOVEMBER

	1	2	3	4	5	6	7	8	9	10	11	12	13	14	15	16	17	18	19	20	21	22	23	24	25	26	27	28	29	30
☉	♏8	9	10	11	12	13	14	15	16	17	18	19	20	21	22	23	24	25	26	27	28	29	♐0	1	2	3	4	5	6	♐7
☽	♎14	26	♏8	20	♐2	14	26	♑7	19	♒1	14	26	♓9	23	♈6	21	♉5	20	♊6	21	♋6	20	♌5	19	♍2	15	28	♎11	23	♏5
☿	♏10	11	13	15	16	18	19	21	23	24	26	27	29	♐0	2	3	5	6	8	9	11	12	14	15	17	18	20	21	23	♐24
♀	♎15	17	18	19	20	21	23	24	25	26	28	29	♏0	1	3	4	5	6	8	9	10	11	13	14	15	16	18	19	20	♏22
♂	♑22	23	24	24	25	26	26	27	28	29	29	♒0	1	2	2	3	4	5	5	6	7	8	8	9	10	11	11	12	13	♒14

	1	6	12	18	24	30		1	6	12	18	24	30		1	15	30		1	15	30		1	15	30		1	15	30
♃	♑21	22	23	24	25	26	♄	♓29	29	29	29	28	28	♅	♉12	11	11	♆	♍20	21	21	♇	♌0	0	0	☊	♐6	6	6

DECEMBER

	1	2	3	4	5	6	7	8	9	10	11	12	13	14	15	16	17	18	19	20	21	22	23	24	25	26	27	28	29	30	31
☉	♐8	9	10	11	12	13	14	15	17	18	19	20	21	22	23	24	25	26	27	28	29	♑0	1	2	3	4	5	6	7	8	♑9
☽	♏17	29	♐11	23	♑4	16	28	♒10	23	♓5	18	♈1	15	29	♉13	28	♊13	29	♋14	29	♌14	28	♍11	25	♎7	20	♏2	14	26	♐8	♐20
☿	♐26	27	29	♑0	1	3	4	5	7	8	9	10	11	12	13	14	14	15	15	16	16	15	15	15	14	13	12	11	10	8	♑7
♀	♏23	24	25	27	28	29	♐0	2	3	4	5	7	8	9	10	12	13	14	15	17	18	19	20	22	23	24	25	27	28	29	♑0
♂	♒14	15	16	17	17	18	19	20	20	21	22	23	23	24	25	26	26	27	28	29	29	♓0	1	2	2	3	4	5	5	6	♓7

	1	6	12	18	24	30		1	6	12	18	24	30		1	15	30		1	15	30		1	15	30		1	15	30
♃	♑26	27	28	♒0	1	2	♄	♓28	28	28	29	29	29	♅	♉11	10	10	♆	♍21	21	21	♇	♌0	0	♋0	☊	♐6	6	6

1938

JANUARY

	1	2	3	4	5	6	7	8	9	10	11	12	13	14	15	16	17	18	19	20	21	22	23	24	25	26	27	28	29	30	31
☉	♑10	11	12	13	14	15	16	17	18	19	20	21	22	23	24	25	26	27	28	29	♒0	1	2	3	4	5	6	7	8	9	♒10
☽	♑1	13	25	♒7	20	♓2	15	28	♈11	24	♉8	22	♊7	22	♋7	22	♌7	21	♍6	20	♎3	16	29	♏11	23	♐4	16	28	♑10	22	♒4
☿	♑5	4	3	2	1	0	0	0	♐29	29	29	♑0	0	0	1	2	2	3	4	5	6	7	8	9	10	12	13	14	15	17	♑18
♀	♑2	3	4	6	7	8	9	11	12	13	14	16	17	18	19	21	22	23	24	26	27	28	29	♒1	2	3	4	6	7	8	♒9
♂	♓8	9	9	10	11	12	12	13	14	15	15	16	17	18	18	19	20	21	21	22	23	24	24	25	26	27	27	28	29	♈0	♈0

	1	6	12	18	24	30		1	6	12	18	24	30		1	15	30		1	15	30		1	15	30		1	15	30
♃	♒3	4	5	7	8	9	♄	♓29	29	♈0	0	1	1	♅	♉10	10	10	♆	♍21	21	21	♇	♋29	29	29	☊	♐6	5	4

FEBRUARY

	1	2	3	4	5	6	7	8	9	10	11	12	13	14	15	16	17	18	19	20	21	22	23	24	25	26	27	28
☉	♒11	12	14	15	16	17	18	19	20	21	22	23	24	25	26	27	28	29	♓0	1	2	3	4	5	6	7	8	♓9
☽	♒16	29	♓12	25	♈8	21	♉5	18	♊2	16	♋1	16	♌0	15	29	♍14	27	♎11	24	♏6	19	♐1	13	24	♑6	18	♒0	♒13
☿	♑19	21	22	23	25	26	28	29	♒1	2	4	5	7	8	10	11	13	15	16	18	20	21	23	25	26	28	♓0	♓2
♀	♒11	12	13	14	16	17	18	20	21	22	23	25	26	27	28	♓0	1	2	3	5	6	7	8	10	11	12	13	♓15
♂	♈1	2	3	3	4	5	6	6	7	8	9	9	10	11	11	12	13	14	14	15	16	17	17	18	19	20	20	♈21

	1	6	12	18	24	28		1	6	12	18	24	28		1	15	28		1	15	28		1	15	28		1	15	28
♃	♒10	11	13	14	15	16	♄	♈1	2	3	3	4	4	♅	♉10	10	10	♆	♍21	20	20	♇	♋29	28	28	☊	♐4	2	1

MARCH

	1	2	3	4	5	6	7	8	9	10	11	12	13	14	15	16	17	18	19	20	21	22	23	24	25	26	27	28	29	30	31
☉	♓10	11	12	13	14	15	16	17	18	19	20	21	22	23	24	25	26	27	28	29	♈0	1	2	3	4	5	6	7	8	9	♈10
☽	♒25	♓8	21	♈4	18	♉1	15	29	♊13	27	♋11	26	♌10	24	♍8	22	♎6	19	♏2	14	26	♐8	20	♑2	14	26	♒8	21	♓3	16	♈0
☿	♓3	5	7	9	11	13	14	16	18	20	22	24	26	28	♈0	2	4	6	8	10	12	14	16	17	19	21	22	24	25	27	♈28
♀	♓16	17	18	20	21	22	23	25	26	27	28	♈0	1	2	3	4	6	7	8	9	11	12	13	14	16	17	18	19	21	22	♈23
♂	♈22	23	23	24	25	25	26	27	28	28	29	♉0	0	1	2	3	3	4	5	6	6	7	8	8	9	10	11	11	12	13	♉13

	1	6	12	18	24	30		1	6	12	18	24	30		1	15	30		1	15	30		1	15	30		1	15	30
♃	♒16	18	19	20	21	23	♄	♈4	5	6	7	7	8	♅	♉10	11	12	♆	♍20	20	19	♇	♋28	28	28	☊	♐1	♏0	28

APRIL

	1	2	3	4	5	6	7	8	9	10	11	12	13	14	15	16	17	18	19	20	21	22	23	24	25	26	27	28	29	30
☉	♈11	12	13	14	15	16	17	18	18	19	20	21	22	23	24	25	26	27	28	29	♉0	1	2	3	4	5	6	7	8	♉9
☽	♈13	27	♉11	26	♊10	24	♋8	22	♌6	20	♍4	18	♎1	14	27	♏10	22	♐4	16	28	♑10	22	♒4	16	28	♓11	24	♈8	22	♉6
☿	♈29	♉0	1	2	3	4	4	5	5	5	6	6	6	5	5	5	4	4	3	2	2	1	0	0	♈29	28	28	27	27	♈26
♀	♈24	26	27	28	29	♉1	2	3	4	5	7	8	9	10	12	13	14	15	17	18	19	20	21	23	24	25	26	28	29	♊0
♂	♉14	15	15	16	17	18	18	19	20	20	21	22	23	23	24	25	25	26	27	27	28	29	29	♊0	1	2	2	3	4	♊4

	1	6	12	18	24	30		1	6	12	18	24	30		1	15	30		1	15	30		1	15	30		1	15	30
♃	♒23	24	25	26	27	28	♄	♈8	9	10	10	11	12	♅	♉12	13	13	♆	♍19	19	19	♇	♋28	28	28	☊	♏28	27	27

MAY

	1	2	3	4	5	6	7	8	9	10	11	12	13	14	15	16	17	18	19	20	21	22	23	24	25	26	27	28	29	30	31
☉	♉10	11	12	13	14	15	16	17	18	19	20	21	22	23	24	24	25	26	27	28	29	♊0	1	2	3	4	5	6	7	8	♊9
☽	♉20	♊5	20	♋4	19	♌3	17	♍1	14	28	♎11	24	♏6	18	♐1	13	25	♑6	18	♒0	12	24	♓7	19	♈2	16	♉0	14	29	♊14	♊29
☿	♈26	26	25	25	25	25	25	25	26	26	26	27	27	28	29	29	♉0	1	2	3	4	5	6	7	8	10	11	12	14	15	♉17
♀	♊1	2	4	5	6	7	9	10	11	12	13	15	16	17	18	20	21	22	23	24	26	27	28	29	♋0	2	3	4	5	6	♋8
♂	♊5	6	6	7	8	8	9	10	10	11	12	12	13	14	15	15	16	17	17	18	19	19	20	21	21	22	23	23	24	25	♊25

	1	6	12	18	24	30		1	6	12	18	24	30		1	15	30		1	15	30		1	15	30		1	15	30
♃	♒28	29	♓0	0	1	1	♄	♈12	13	13	14	14	15	♅	♉13	14	15	♆	♍19	18	18	♇	♋28	28	28	☊	♏27	27	27

JUNE

	1	2	3	4	5	6	7	8	9	10	11	12	13	14	15	16	17	18	19	20	21	22	23	24	25	26	27	28	29	30
☉	♊10	11	12	13	14	15	16	17	18	18	19	20	21	22	23	24	25	26	27	28	29	♋0	1	2	3	4	5	6	7	♋8
☽	♋14	29	♌13	27	♍11	25	♎8	21	♏3	15	28	♐10	21	♑3	15	27	♒9	21	♓3	15	28	♈11	24	♉8	22	♊7	22	♋7	23	♌8
☿	♉18	20	21	23	25	26	28	♊0	2	4	6	8	10	12	14	16	18	20	22	24	27	29	♋1	3	5	8	10	12	14	♋16
♀	♋9	10	11	12	14	15	16	17	18	20	21	22	23	24	26	27	28	29	♌0	2	3	4	5	6	7	9	10	11	12	♌13
♂	♊26	27	27	28	29	29	♋0	1	1	2	3	3	4	5	5	6	7	7	8	9	9	10	11	11	12	12	13	14	14	♋15

	1	6	12	18	24	30		1	6	12	18	24	30		1	15	30		1	15	30		1	15	30		1	15	30
♃	♓2	2	2	2	2	2	♄	♈15	16	16	17	17	17	♅	♉15	16	17	♆	♍18	18	19	♇	♋28	29	29	☊	♏27	27	26

JULY

	1	2	3	4	5	6	7	8	9	10	11	12	13	14	15	16	17	18	19	20	21	22	23	24	25	26	27	28	29	30	31
☉	♋9	9	10	11	12	13	14	15	16	17	18	19	20	21	22	23	24	25	26	27	28	29	29	♌0	1	2	3	4	5	6	♌7
☽	♌22	♍7	21	♎4	17	♏0	12	25	♐7	18	♑0	12	24	♒6	18	♓0	12	25	♈7	20	♉4	17	♊1	16	♋1	16	♌1	16	♍1	16	♎0
☿	♋18	20	22	24	26	28	♌0	2	3	5	7	9	10	12	13	15	17	18	20	21	22	24	25	26	28	29	♍0	1	2	3	♍4
♀	♌15	16	17	18	19	20	22	23	24	25	26	27	29	♍0	1	2	3	4	5	7	8	9	10	11	12	14	15	16	17	18	♍19
♂	♋16	16	17	18	18	19	20	20	21	22	22	23	24	24	25	26	26	27	27	28	29	29	♌0	1	1	2	3	3	4	5	♌5

	1	6	12	18	24	30		1	6	12	18	24	30		1	15	30		1	15	30		1	15	30		1	15	30
♃	♓2	2	2	1	1	0	♄	♈17	18	18	18	18	18	♅	♉17	17	18	♆	♍19	19	19	♇	♋29	29	♌29	☊	♏26	25	24

AUGUST

	1	2	3	4	5	6	7	8	9	10	11	12	13	14	15	16	17	18	19	20	21	22	23	24	25	26	27	28	29	30	31
☉	♌8	9	10	11	12	13	14	15	16	17	18	19	20	21	22	22	23	24	25	26	27	28	29	♍0	1	2	3	4	5	6	♍7
☽	♎13	26	♏9	21	♐3	15	27	♑9	21	♒3	15	27	♓9	22	♈4	17	♉0	14	27	♊11	25	♋10	25	♌10	25	♍9	24	♎8	21	♏5	♏17
☿	♍5	6	7	8	9	9	10	11	11	11	12	12	12	12	12	12	12	12	11	11	10	10	9	8	7	7	6	5	4	3	♍2
♀	♍20	21	23	24	25	26	27	28	29	♎0	1	3	4	5	6	7	8	9	10	11	12	13	14	16	17	18	19	20	21	22	♎23
♂	♌6	6	7	8	8	9	10	10	11	12	12	13	14	14	15	15	16	17	17	18	19	19	20	21	21	22	22	23	24	24	♌25

	1	6	12	18	24	30		1	6	12	18	24	30		1	15	30		1	15	30		1	15	30		1	15	30
♃	♓0	♒29	28	28	27	26	♄	♈18	18	18	18	18	17	♅	♉18	18	18	♆	♍19	20	20	♇	♌0	0	1	☊	♏24	22	21

SEPTEMBER

	1	2	3	4	5	6	7	8	9	10	11	12	13	14	15	16	17	18	19	20	21	22	23	24	25	26	27	28	29	30
☉	♍8	9	10	11	12	13	14	15	16	17	18	19	20	21	21	22	23	24	25	26	27	28	29	♎0	1	2	3	4	5	♎6
☽	♐0	12	24	♑6	18	29	♒11	24	♓6	19	♈1	14	27	♉11	24	♊8	22	♋6	20	♌5	19	♍4	18	♎2	16	29	♏13	25	♐8	♐20
☿	♍1	1	0	0	♌29	29	29	29	29	♍0	0	1	2	3	4	5	6	7	9	10	12	14	15	17	19	21	22	24	26	♍28
♀	♎24	25	26	27	28	29	♏0	1	2	3	4	5	6	7	8	9	10	10	11	12	13	14	15	16	17	17	18	19	20	♏21
♂	♌26	26	27	28	28	29	29	♍0	1	1	2	3	3	4	5	5	6	6	7	8	8	9	10	10	11	12	12	13	13	♍14

	1	6	12	18	24	30		1	6	12	18	24	30		1	15	30		1	15	30		1	15	30		1	15	30
♃	♒26	25	25	24	23	23	♄	♈17	17	17	16	16	15	♅	♉18	18	17	♆	♍20	21	21	♇	♌1	1	1	☊	♏21	19	19

OCTOBER

	1	2	3	4	5	6	7	8	9	10	11	12	13	14	15	16	17	18	19	20	21	22	23	24	25	26	27	28	29	30	31
☉	♎7	8	9	10	11	12	13	14	15	16	17	18	19	20	21	22	23	24	25	26	27	28	29	♏0	1	2	3	4	5	6	♏7
☽	♑2	14	26	♒7	20	♓2	14	27	♈10	23	♉7	21	♊5	19	♋3	17	♌1	15	29	♍13	27	♎11	24	♏8	21	♐3	16	28	♑10	22	♒3
☿	♎0	1	3	5	7	9	10	12	14	16	17	19	21	22	24	26	27	29	♏1	2	4	6	7	9	10	12	13	15	17	18	♏20
♀	♏22	22	23	24	24	25	26	27	27	28	28	29	♐0	0	1	1	2	2	2	3	3	4	4	4	4	5	5	5	5	5	♐5
♂	♍15	15	16	17	17	18	18	19	20	20	21	22	22	23	24	24	25	25	26	27	27	28	29	29	♎0	0	1	2	2	3	♎4

	1	6	12	18	24	30		1	6	12	18	24	30		1	15	30		1	15	30		1	15	30		1	15	30
♃	♒23	23	22	22	22	23	♄	♈15	15	14	14	13	13	♅	♉17	17	16	♆	♍21	22	22	♇	♌1	1	2	☊	♏19	18	18

NOVEMBER

	1	2	3	4	5	6	7	8	9	10	11	12	13	14	15	16	17	18	19	20	21	22	23	24	25	26	27	28	29	30
☉	♏8	9	10	11	12	13	14	15	16	17	18	19	20	21	22	23	24	25	26	27	28	29	♐0	1	2	3	4	5	6	♐7
☽	♒15	27	♓10	22	♈5	18	♉2	16	♊0	14	29	♋13	28	♌12	26	♍10	24	♎7	21	♏4	16	29	♐11	24	♑6	18	♒0	11	23	♓5
☿	♏21	23	24	26	27	29	♐0	1	3	4	6	7	9	10	11	13	14	15	17	18	19	20	22	23	24	25	26	27	27	♐28
♀	♐5	5	5	5	4	4	4	4	3	3	2	2	1	1	0	0	♏29	29	28	27	27	26	26	25	24	24	23	23	22	♏22
♂	♎4	5	6	6	7	7	8	9	9	10	11	11	12	12	13	14	14	15	16	16	17	17	18	19	19	20	21	21	22	♎22

	1	6	12	18	24	30		1	6	12	18	24	30		1	15	30		1	15	30		1	15	30		1	15	30
♃	♒23	23	23	24	24	25	♄	♈13	13	12	12	12	11	♅	♉16	16	15	♆	♍23	23	23	♇	♌2	1	1	☊	♏18	18	18

DECEMBER

	1	2	3	4	5	6	7	8	9	10	11	12	13	14	15	16	17	18	19	20	21	22	23	24	25	26	27	28	29	30	31
☉	♐8	9	10	11	12	13	14	15	16	17	18	19	20	21	22	23	24	25	26	27	28	29	♑0	2	3	4	5	6	7	8	♑9
☽	♓17	♈0	13	26	♉10	24	♊8	23	♋8	23	♌8	22	♍7	21	♎4	17	♏0	13	26	♐8	20	♑2	14	26	♒8	20	♓2	14	26	♈8	♈21
☿	♐29	29	♑0	0	0	0	♐29	29	28	27	26	25	24	22	21	20	18	17	16	15	14	14	14	13	13	14	14	14	15	16	♐16
♀	♏22	21	21	21	20	20	20	20	20	20	20	20	20	20	20	20	20	21	21	21	22	22	22	23	23	24	24	25	25	26	♏27
♂	♎23	24	24	25	26	26	27	28	28	29	29	♏0	1	1	2	3	3	4	4	5	6	6	7	8	8	9	9	10	11	11	♏12

	1	6	12	18	24	30		1	6	12	18	24	30		1	15	30		1	15	30		1	15	30		1	15	30
♃	♒25	26	27	28	29	♓0	♄	♈11	11	11	11	11	11	♅	♉15	14	14	♆	♍23	23	23	♇	♌1	1	1	☊	♏18	17	16

1939

JANUARY

	1	2	3	4	5	6	7	8	9	10	11	12	13	14	15	16	17	18	19	20	21	22	23	24	25	26	27	28	29	30	31
☉	♑10	11	12	13	14	15	16	17	18	19	20	21	22	23	24	25	26	27	28	29	♒0	1	2	3	4	5	6	7	8	9	♒10
☽	♉4	18	♊2	16	♋1	16	♌2	17	♍2	16	♎0	14	27	♏10	23	♐5	17	29	♑11	23	♒5	17	29	♓11	23	♈5	17	♉0	13	26	♊10
☿	♐17	18	19	20	21	22	23	25	26	27	28	♑0	1	2	4	5	6	8	9	11	12	14	15	17	18	20	21	23	24	26	♑27
♀	♏27	28	29	29	♐0	1	2	2	3	4	5	6	6	7	8	9	10	11	12	13	14	15	15	16	17	18	19	20	21	22	♐23
♂	♏12	13	14	14	15	16	16	17	17	18	19	19	20	21	21	22	22	23	24	24	25	25	26	27	27	28	29	29	♐0	0	♐1

	1	6	12	18	24	30
♃	♓0	1	3	4	5	7
♄	♈11	12	12	12	13	13

	1	15	30
♅	♉14	14	14
♆	♍23	23	23
♇	♌1	1	0
☊	♏16	15	14

FEBRUARY

	1	2	3	4	5	6	7	8	9	10	11	12	13	14	15	16	17	18	19	20	21	22	23	24	25	26	27	28
☉	♒11	12	13	14	15	16	17	18	19	20	21	22	23	24	25	26	27	28	29	♓0	1	2	3	4	5	6	8	♓9
☽	♊24	♋9	24	♌10	25	♍10	25	♎9	23	♏6	19	♐2	14	26	♑8	20	♒2	14	26	♓8	20	♈2	14	27	♉9	22	♊6	♊19
☿	♑29	♒0	2	4	5	7	9	10	12	14	15	17	19	20	22	24	26	28	29	♓1	3	5	7	9	11	12	14	♓16
♀	♐24	25	26	28	29	♑0	1	2	3	4	5	6	7	8	9	10	11	13	14	15	16	17	18	19	20	21	23	♑24
♂	♐2	2	3	3	4	5	5	6	6	7	8	8	9	9	10	11	11	12	12	13	14	14	15	15	16	17	17	♐18

	1	6	12	18	24	28
♃	♓7	8	10	11	12	13
♄	♈13	14	14	15	15	16

	1	15	28
♅	♉14	14	14
♆	♍23	23	22
♇	♌0	0	0
☊	♏13	12	11

MARCH

	1	2	3	4	5	6	7	8	9	10	11	12	13	14	15	16	17	18	19	20	21	22	23	24	25	26	27	28	29	30	31
☉	♓10	11	12	13	14	15	16	17	18	19	20	21	22	23	24	25	26	27	27	28	29	♈0	1	2	3	4	5	6	7	8	♈9
☽	♋3	18	♌3	18	♍3	18	♎3	17	♏1	15	28	♐10	23	♑5	17	29	♒10	22	♓4	16	29	♈11	24	♉6	19	♊3	16	♋0	14	28	♌13
☿	♓18	20	22	24	26	28	29	♈1	3	4	6	8	9	10	12	13	14	15	16	16	17	17	17	18	18	17	17	17	16	16	♈15
♀	♑25	26	27	28	29	♒1	2	3	4	5	6	7	9	10	11	12	13	14	16	17	18	19	20	21	23	24	25	26	27	28	♓0
♂	♐18	19	20	20	21	21	22	22	23	24	24	25	25	26	26	27	28	28	29	29	♑0	0	1	1	2	3	3	4	4	5	♑5

	1	6	12	18	24	30
♃	♓14	15	16	18	19	21
♄	♈16	17	17	18	19	19

	1	15	30
♅	♉14	15	16
♆	♍22	22	22
♇	♌0	♋0	29
☊	♏10	10	9

APRIL

	1	2	3	4	5	6	7	8	9	10	11	12	13	14	15	16	17	18	19	20	21	22	23	24	25	26	27	28	29	30
☉	♈10	11	12	13	14	15	16	17	18	19	20	21	22	23	24	25	26	27	28	29	♉0	1	2	3	4	5	6	7	8	♉9
☽	♌27	♍12	26	♎11	25	♏9	22	♐6	18	♑1	13	25	♒7	19	♓0	13	25	♈7	20	♉3	16	29	♊13	27	♋11	25	♌9	23	♍7	♍22
☿	♈15	14	13	12	11	11	10	9	8	8	7	7	6	6	6	6	6	6	6	6	6	7	7	8	8	9	10	10	11	♈12
♀	♓1	2	3	4	5	7	8	9	10	11	13	14	15	16	17	19	20	21	22	23	25	26	27	28	29	♈0	2	3	4	♈5
♂	♑6	6	7	7	8	9	9	10	10	11	11	12	12	13	13	14	14	15	15	16	16	17	17	18	18	19	19	19	20	♑20

	1	6	12	18	24	30
♃	♓21	22	24	25	26	28
♄	♈20	20	21	22	23	23

	1	15	30
♅	♉16	16	17
♆	♍21	21	21
♇	♋29	29	29
☊	♏9	8	8

MAY

	1	2	3	4	5	6	7	8	9	10	11	12	13	14	15	16	17	18	19	20	21	22	23	24	25	26	27	28	29	30	31
☉	♉10	11	12	13	14	15	16	17	17	18	19	20	21	22	23	24	25	26	27	28	29	♊0	1	2	3	4	5	6	7	8	♊9
☽	♎6	20	♏4	17	♐0	13	26	♑8	21	♒3	15	26	♓8	20	♈3	15	28	♉11	25	♊9	23	♋7	21	♌6	20	♍4	18	♎2	16	♏0	♏13
☿	♈13	14	15	16	17	18	20	21	22	23	25	26	28	29	♉1	2	4	5	7	9	11	12	14	16	18	20	22	24	26	28	♊0
♀	♈6	8	9	10	11	12	14	15	16	17	18	20	21	22	23	24	26	27	28	29	♉0	2	3	4	5	7	8	9	10	11	♉13
♂	♑21	21	22	22	23	23	23	24	24	25	25	25	26	26	27	27	27	28	28	28	29	29	29	♒0	0	0	1	1	1	1	♒2

	1	6	12	18	24	30
♃	♓28	29	♈0	1	2	3
♄	♈23	24	25	25	26	27

	1	15	30
♅	♉17	18	19
♆	♍21	21	21
♇	♋29	29	♌29
☊	♏8	8	8

JUNE

	1	2	3	4	5	6	7	8	9	10	11	12	13	14	15	16	17	18	19	20	21	22	23	24	25	26	27	28	29	30
☉	♊10	11	12	12	13	14	15	16	17	18	19	20	21	22	23	24	25	26	27	28	29	♋0	1	2	3	4	4	5	6	♋7
☽	♏26	♐9	22	♑4	17	29	♒11	23	♓4	16	28	♈11	23	♉6	19	♊3	17	♋2	16	♌1	16	♍1	15	29	♎13	26	♏10	23	♐5	♐18
☿	♊2	4	6	8	10	13	15	17	19	21	24	26	28	♋0	2	4	6	8	10	12	14	16	18	20	21	23	25	26	28	♌0
♀	♉14	15	16	17	19	20	21	22	23	25	26	27	28	29	♊1	2	3	4	6	7	8	9	10	12	13	14	15	16	18	♊19
♂	♒2	2	2	3	3	3	3	3	4	4	4	4	4	4	4	4	4	5	5	5	5	5	5	5	5	5	5	5	4	♒4

	1	6	12	18	24	30
♃	♈4	4	5	6	7	7
♄	♈27	27	28	29	29	♉0

	1	15	30
♅	♉19	20	21
♆	♍21	21	21
♇	♌0	0	0
☊	♏8	8	7

JULY

	1	2	3	4	5	6	7	8	9	10	11	12	13	14	15	16	17	18	19	20	21	22	23	24	25	26	27	28	29	30	31
☉	♋8	9	10	11	12	13	14	15	16	17	18	19	20	21	22	23	24	24	25	26	27	28	29	♌0	1	2	3	4	5	6	♌7
☽	♑1	13	25	♒7	19	♓1	13	25	♈7	19	♉1	14	28	♊11	26	♋10	25	♌10	26	♍10	25	♎9	23	♏7	20	♐3	15	28	♑10	22	♒4
☿	♌1	3	4	5	7	8	9	11	12	13	14	15	16	17	18	19	20	21	21	22	22	23	23	24	24	24	24	24	24	24	♌24
♀	♊20	21	23	24	25	26	27	29	♋0	1	2	4	5	6	7	8	10	11	12	13	15	16	17	18	19	21	22	23	24	26	♋27
♂	♒4	4	4	4	4	4	3	3	3	3	3	2	2	2	2	2	1	1	1	0	0	0	0	♑29	29	29	29	28	28	28	♑27

	1	6	12	18	24	30
♃	♈7	8	8	9	9	9
♄	♉0	0	0	1	1	1

	1	15	30
♅	♉21	21	22
♆	♍21	21	21
♇	♌0	1	1
☊	♏7	5	4

AUGUST

	1	2	3	4	5	6	7	8	9	10	11	12	13	14	15	16	17	18	19	20	21	22	23	24	25	26	27	28	29	30	31
☉	♌8	9	10	11	12	13	14	15	16	16	17	18	19	20	21	22	23	24	25	26	27	28	29	♍0	1	2	3	4	5	6	♍7
☽	♒16	28	♓10	21	♈3	15	28	♉10	23	♊6	20	♋4	19	♌4	19	♍4	19	♎4	19	♏3	16	29	♐12	25	♑7	19	♒1	13	25	♓7	♓18
☿	♌23	23	23	22	21	21	20	19	18	18	17	16	15	15	14	13	13	13	12	12	12	12	12	13	13	14	15	16	17	18	♌19
♀	♋28	29	♌1	2	3	4	5	7	8	9	10	12	13	14	15	17	18	19	20	21	23	24	25	26	28	29	♍0	1	3	4	♍5
♂	♑27	27	27	26	26	26	26	26	25	25	25	25	25	25	24	24	24	24	24	24	24	24	24	24	24	24	24	24	24	24	♑24

	1	6	12	18	24	30
♃	♈9	9	9	8	8	7
♄	♉1	1	1	1	1	1

	1	15	30
♅	♉22	22	22
♆	♍21	22	22
♇	♌1	2	2
☊	♏3	2	1

SEPTEMBER

	1	2	3	4	5	6	7	8	9	10	11	12	13	14	15	16	17	18	19	20	21	22	23	24	25	26	27	28	29	30
☉	♍8	9	10	11	12	13	13	14	15	16	17	18	19	20	21	22	23	24	25	26	27	28	29	♎0	1	2	3	4	5	♎6
☽	♈0	12	24	♉7	19	♊2	15	29	♋13	27	♌12	27	♍13	28	♎13	27	♏11	25	♐8	21	♑4	16	28	♒10	22	♓3	15	27	♈9	♈22
☿	♌20	22	23	25	26	28	♍0	1	3	5	7	9	11	13	15	16	18	20	22	24	26	28	29	♎1	3	5	7	8	10	♎12
♀	♍6	8	9	10	11	13	14	15	16	18	19	20	21	22	24	25	26	27	29	♎0	1	2	4	5	6	7	9	10	11	♎12
♂	♑24	24	25	25	25	25	25	25	26	26	26	26	27	27	27	27	28	28	28	29	29	29	♒0	0	0	1	1	2	2	♒2

	1	6	12	18	24	30
♃	♈7	7	6	5	4	3
♄	♉1	1	1	0	0	♈29

	1	15	30
♅	♉22	22	22
♆	♍22	23	24
♇	♌2	2	3
☊	♏0	0	♎0

OCTOBER

	1	2	3	4	5	6	7	8	9	10	11	12	13	14	15	16	17	18	19	20	21	22	23	24	25	26	27	28	29	30	31
☉	♎7	8	9	10	11	12	13	14	15	16	17	18	19	20	21	22	23	24	25	26	27	28	29	♏0	1	2	3	4	5	6	♏7
☽	♉4	16	29	♊12	25	♋9	23	♌7	22	♍6	21	♎6	21	♏5	19	♐3	16	29	♑12	24	♒6	18	♓0	12	24	♈6	18	♉0	13	26	♊9
☿	♎13	15	17	18	20	22	23	25	27	28	♏0	1	3	4	6	7	9	10	12	13	15	16	18	19	20	22	23	24	26	27	♏28
♀	♎14	15	16	17	19	20	21	22	24	25	26	27	29	♏0	1	2	4	5	6	7	9	10	11	12	14	15	16	17	19	20	♏21
♂	♒3	3	4	4	4	5	5	6	6	7	7	8	8	9	9	10	10	11	11	12	12	13	14	14	15	15	16	16	17	17	♒18

	1	6	12	18	24	30
♃	♈3	3	2	1	1	0
♄	♈29	29	29	28	28	27

	1	15	30
♅	♉22	21	21
♆	♍24	24	25
♇	♌3	3	3
☊	♎29	29	29

NOVEMBER

	1	2	3	4	5	6	7	8	9	10	11	12	13	14	15	16	17	18	19	20	21	22	23	24	25	26	27	28	29	30
☉	♏8	9	10	11	12	13	14	15	16	17	18	19	20	21	22	23	24	25	26	27	28	29	♐0	1	2	3	4	5	6	♐7
☽	♊22	♋6	20	♌3	18	♍2	16	♎1	15	29	♏13	27	♐11	24	♑7	20	♒2	14	26	♓8	20	♈2	14	26	♉9	22	♊5	18	♋2	♋16
☿	♐0	1	2	3	4	6	7	8	9	10	10	11	12	13	13	14	14	14	14	14	13	13	12	11	10	9	8	7	5	♐4
♀	♏22	24	25	26	27	29	♐0	1	2	4	5	6	7	9	10	11	12	14	15	16	17	19	20	21	22	24	25	26	27	♐29
♂	♒19	19	20	20	21	22	22	23	23	24	25	25	26	26	27	28	28	29	♓0	0	1	1	2	3	3	4	5	5	6	♓7

	1	6	12	18	24	30
♃	♈0♓29	29	29	29	29	
♄	♈27	27	26	26	25	25

	1	15	30
♅	♉20	20	19
♆	♍25	25	25
♇	♌3	3	3
☊	♎29	29	29

DECEMBER

	1	2	3	4	5	6	7	8	9	10	11	12	13	14	15	16	17	18	19	20	21	22	23	24	25	26	27	28	29	30	31
☉	♐8	9	10	11	12	13	14	15	16	17	18	19	20	21	22	23	24	25	26	27	28	29	♑0	1	2	3	4	5	6	7	♑8
☽	♌0	14	29	♍13	27	♎11	25	♏9	22	♐6	19	♑2	15	28	♒10	22	♓4	16	28	♈9	22	♉4	17	♊0	13	27	♋11	26	♌10	25	♍9
☿	♐3	1	0	♏29	29	28	28	28	28	28	28	29	29	♐0	1	2	3	4	5	6	7	9	10	11	12	14	15	16	18	19	♐21
♀	♑0	1	2	3	5	6	7	8	10	11	12	13	15	16	17	18	20	21	22	23	25	26	27	28	♒0	1	2	3	5	6	♒7
♂	♓7	8	9	9	10	11	11	12	13	13	14	15	15	16	17	17	18	19	19	20	21	21	22	23	23	24	25	25	26	27	♓27

	1	6	12	18	24	30
♃	♓29	29	29	♈0	0	1
♄	♈25	25	25	25	24	24

	1	15	30
♅	♉19	19	18
♆	♍25	25	26
♇	♌3	3	2
☊	♎29	28	26

1940

JANUARY

	1	2	3	4	5	6	7	8	9	10	11	12	13	14	15	16	17	18	19	20	21	22	23	24	25	26	27	28	29	30	31
☉	♑9	10	11	12	13	15	16	17	18	19	20	21	22	23	24	25	26	27	28	29	♒0	1	2	3	4	5	6	7	8	9	♒10
☽	♍24	♎8	22	♏5	19	♐2	15	28	♑11	23	♒6	18	♓0	12	24	♈5	17	29	♉12	24	♊7	21	♋5	19	♌4	19	♍4	19	♎4	18	♏2
☿	♐22	24	25	27	28	♑0	1	3	4	6	7	9	10	12	13	15	16	18	20	21	23	24	26	28	29	♒1	3	4	6	8	♒9
♀	♒8	10	11	12	13	14	16	17	18	19	21	22	23	24	26	27	28	29	♓1	2	3	4	5	7	8	9	10	12	13	14	♓15
♂	♓28	29	29	♈0	1	1	2	3	3	4	5	5	6	7	7	8	9	10	10	11	12	12	13	14	14	15	16	16	17	18	♈18

1	6	12	18	24	30	1	6	12	18	24	30	1	15	30	1	15	30	1	15	30	1	15	30
♃ ♈1	2	3	4	5	6	♄ ♈24	24	25	25	25	25	♅ ♉18	18	18	♆ ♍26	25	25	♇ ♌2	2	2	☊ ♎26	24	23

FEBRUARY

	1	2	3	4	5	6	7	8	9	10	11	12	13	14	15	16	17	18	19	20	21	22	23	24	25	26	27	28	29
☉	♒11	12	13	14	15	16	17	18	19	20	21	22	23	24	25	26	27	28	29	♓0	1	2	3	4	5	6	7	8	♓9
☽	♏16	29	♐12	25	♑8	20	♒2	15	27	♓8	20	♈2	14	26	♉8	20	♊3	16	29	♋13	27	♌12	27	♍13	28	♎13	27	♏12	♏26
☿	♒11	13	15	16	18	20	22	24	25	27	29	♓1	3	4	6	8	10	12	13	15	17	18	20	21	23	24	25	26	♓27
♀	♓16	18	19	20	21	22	24	25	26	27	29	♈0	1	2	3	5	6	7	8	9	10	12	13	14	15	16	18	19	♈20
♂	♈19	20	20	21	22	22	23	24	25	25	26	27	27	28	29	29	♉0	1	1	2	3	3	4	5	5	6	7	7	♉8

1	6	12	18	24	29	1	6	12	18	24	29	1	15	29	1	15	29	1	15	29	1	15	29
♃ ♈6	7	8	9	11	12	♄ ♈26	26	26	27	27	28	♅ ♉18	18	18	♆ ♍25	25	25	♇ ♌2	1	1	☊ ♎23	22	21

MARCH

	1	2	3	4	5	6	7	8	9	10	11	12	13	14	15	16	17	18	19	20	21	22	23	24	25	26	27	28	29	30	31
☉	♓10	11	12	13	14	15	16	17	18	19	20	21	22	23	24	25	26	27	28	29	♈0	1	2	3	4	5	6	7	8	9	♈10
☽	♐9	22	♑5	17	29	♒12	23	♓5	17	29	♈11	23	♉5	17	29	♊12	25	♋8	22	♌6	20	♍5	21	♎6	21	♏6	20	♐4	18	♑1	♑14
☿	♓28	29	29	♈0	0	0	0	0	0	♓29	29	28	27	26	25	24	24	23	22	21	20	19	19	18	18	17	17	17	17	17	♓17
♀	♈21	22	23	25	26	27	28	29	♉0	2	3	4	5	6	7	8	9	11	12	13	14	15	16	17	18	20	21	22	23	24	♉25
♂	♉9	9	10	11	11	12	13	13	14	15	15	16	17	17	18	19	19	20	21	21	22	23	23	24	25	25	26	27	27	28	♉29

1	6	12	18	24	30	1	6	12	18	24	30	1	15	30	1	15	30	1	15	30	1	15	30
♃ ♈12	13	14	16	17	19	♄ ♈28	28	29	♉0	0	1	♅ ♉18	19	20	♆ ♍25	24	24	♇ ♌1	1	1	☊ ♎21	20	20

APRIL

	1	2	3	4	5	6	7	8	9	10	11	12	13	14	15	16	17	18	19	20	21	22	23	24	25	26	27	28	29	30
☉	♈11	12	13	14	15	16	17	18	19	20	21	22	23	24	25	26	27	28	29	♉0	1	2	3	4	5	6	7	8	9	♉9
☽	♑26	♒8	20	♓2	14	26	♈8	20	♉2	14	26	♊9	21	♋4	18	♌1	15	♍0	14	29	♎14	29	♏14	28	♐12	26	♑9	22	♒5	♒17
☿	♓17	18	18	18	19	19	20	21	22	23	23	24	25	26	27	29	♈0	1	2	3	5	6	8	9	10	12	13	15	17	♈18
♀	♉26	27	28	29	♊0	1	2	3	4	5	6	7	8	9	10	11	12	13	14	15	16	17	18	19	20	21	22	23	24	♊24
♂	♉29	♊0	1	1	2	3	3	4	5	5	6	7	7	8	9	9	10	11	11	12	13	13	14	15	15	16	17	17	18	♊19

1	6	12	18	24	30	1	6	12	18	24	30	1	15	30	1	15	30	1	15	30	1	15	30
♃ ♈19	20	22	23	25	26	♄ ♉1	2	3	4	4	5	♅ ♉20	20	21	♆ ♍24	23	23	♇ ♌1	1	1	☊ ♎20	20	20

MAY

	1	2	3	4	5	6	7	8	9	10	11	12	13	14	15	16	17	18	19	20	21	22	23	24	25	26	27	28	29	30	31
☉	♉10	11	12	13	14	15	16	17	18	19	20	21	22	23	24	25	26	27	28	29	♊0	1	2	3	4	5	6	7	7	8	♊9
☽	♒29	♓11	23	♈4	16	28	♉11	23	♊5	18	♋1	15	28	♌12	26	♍10	24	♎9	23	♏8	22	♐7	21	♑4	17	♒0	13	25	♓7	19	♈1
☿	♈20	21	23	25	27	28	♉0	2	4	6	8	10	12	14	16	18	20	22	24	27	29	♊1	3	5	7	10	12	14	16	18	♊20
♀	♊25	26	27	28	29	29	♋0	1	2	2	3	4	4	5	6	6	7	8	8	9	9	10	10	11	11	11	12	12	12	13	♋13
♂	♊19	20	21	21	22	22	23	24	24	25	26	26	27	28	28	29	♋0	0	1	2	2	3	3	4	5	5	6	7	7	8	♋9

1	6	12	18	24	30	1	6	12	18	24	30	1	15	30	1	15	30	1	15	30	1	15	30
♃ ♈26	28	29	♉0	2	3	♄ ♉5	6	7	7	8	9	♅ ♉21	22	23	♆ ♍23	23	23	♇ ♌1	1	1	☊ ♎20	20	19

JUNE

	1	2	3	4	5	6	7	8	9	10	11	12	13	14	15	16	17	18	19	20	21	22	23	24	25	26	27	28	29	30
☉	♊10	11	12	13	14	15	16	17	18	19	20	21	22	23	24	25	26	27	28	29	29	♋0	1	2	3	4	5	6	7	♋8
☽	♈13	25	♉7	19	♊2	15	28	♋11	25	♌9	23	♍7	21	♎5	19	♏3	17	♐1	15	29	♑12	26	♒8	21	♓3	15	27	♈9	21	♉3
☿	♊22	24	26	28	♋0	2	4	6	7	9	11	12	14	15	17	18	19	21	22	23	24	26	27	28	29	29	♌0	1	2	♌3
♀	♋13	13	13	13	13	13	13	13	13	13	13	12	12	12	11	11	11	10	10	9	9	8	7	7	6	6	5	4	4	♋3
♂	♋9	10	11	11	12	12	13	14	14	15	16	16	17	18	18	19	20	20	21	21	22	23	23	24	25	25	26	27	27	♋28

1	6	12	18	24	30	1	6	12	18	24	30	1	15	30	1	15	30	1	15	30	1	15	30
♃ ♉3	5	6	7	8	9	♄ ♉9	10	10	11	11	12	♅ ♉23	24	25	♆ ♍23	23	23	♇ ♌1	1	2	☊ ♎19	18	16

JULY

	1	2	3	4	5	6	7	8	9	10	11	12	13	14	15	16	17	18	19	20	21	22	23	24	25	26	27	28	29	30	31
☉	♋9	10	11	12	13	14	15	16	17	18	19	19	20	21	22	23	24	25	26	27	28	29	♌0	1	2	3	4	5	6	7	♌8
☽	♉15	27	♊10	23	♋7	21	♌5	19	♍3	17	♎2	16	♏0	14	28	♐11	25	♑8	21	♒4	17	29	♓11	23	♈5	17	29	♉11	23	♊5	♊18
☿	♌3	4	4	4	5	5	5	5	5	5	5	5	5	4	4	3	3	2	1	1	0	♋29	29	28	27	27	26	26	25	25	♋25
♀	♋3	2	1	1	0	0	♊29	29	29	28	28	28	27	27	27	27	27	27	27	27	27	27	27	27	28	28	28	28	29	29	♋0
♂	♋28	29	♌0	0	1	2	2	3	4	4	5	5	6	7	7	8	9	9	10	11	11	12	12	13	14	14	15	16	16	17	♌18

1	6	12	18	24	30	1	6	12	18	24	30	1	15	30	1	15	30	1	15	30	1	15	30
♃ ♉9	10	11	12	13	14	♄ ♉12	13	13	13	14	14	♅ ♉25	25	26	♆ ♍23	23	24	♇ ♌2	2	3	☊ ♎16	15	14

AUGUST

	1	2	3	4	5	6	7	8	9	10	11	12	13	14	15	16	17	18	19	20	21	22	23	24	25	26	27	28	29	30	31
☉	♌9	10	10	11	12	13	14	15	16	17	18	19	20	21	22	23	24	25	26	27	28	29	♍0	1	2	3	4	5	5	6	♍7
☽	♋1	15	29	♌14	28	♍13	28	♎12	27	♏11	25	♐8	22	♑5	18	♒0	13	25	♓7	19	♈1	13	25	♉7	19	♊1	13	26	♋10	23	♌7
☿	♋25	25	25	25	25	26	26	27	27	28	29	♌0	1	3	4	5	7	9	10	12	14	16	17	19	21	23	25	27	29	♍1	♍3
♀	♋0	0	1	1	2	2	3	4	4	5	6	6	7	8	8	9	10	11	11	12	13	14	15	15	16	17	18	19	20	21	♋22
♂	♌18	19	19	20	21	21	22	23	23	24	24	25	26	26	27	28	28	29	♍0	0	1	1	2	3	3	4	5	5	6	7	♍7

1	6	12	18	24	30	1	6	12	18	24	30	1	15	30	1	15	30	1	15	30	1	15	30
♃ ♉14	14	15	15	15	16	♄ ♉14	14	15	15	15	15	♅ ♉26	26	26	♆ ♍24	24	25	♇ ♌3	3	3	☊ ♎13	12	12

SEPTEMBER

	1	2	3	4	5	6	7	8	9	10	11	12	13	14	15	16	17	18	19	20	21	22	23	24	25	26	27	28	29	30
☉	♍8	9	10	11	12	13	14	15	16	17	18	19	20	21	22	23	24	25	26	27	28	29	♎0	1	2	3	4	5	6	♎7
☽	♌22	♍7	22	♎7	22	♏7	21	♐5	18	♑2	15	27	♒10	22	♓4	16	28	♈10	22	♉4	15	27	♊10	22	♋5	18	♌2	16	♍0	♍15
☿	♍5	7	9	11	13	15	17	18	20	22	24	26	27	29	♎1	3	4	6	8	9	11	13	14	16	17	19	20	22	23	♎25
♀	♋23	24	24	25	26	27	28	29	♌0	1	2	3	4	5	6	7	8	9	11	12	13	14	15	16	17	18	19	20	21	♌22
♂	♍8	8	9	10	10	11	12	12	13	14	14	15	16	16	17	17	18	19	19	20	21	21	22	23	23	24	24	25	26	♍26

1	6	12	18	24	30	1	6	12	18	24	30	1	15	30	1	15	30	1	15	30	1	15	30
♃ ♉16	16	16	15	15	15	♄ ♉15	15	15	14	14	14	♅ ♉26	26	26	♆ ♍25	25	26	♇ ♌3	4	4	☊ ♎11	11	11

OCTOBER

	1	2	3	4	5	6	7	8	9	10	11	12	13	14	15	16	17	18	19	20	21	22	23	24	25	26	27	28	29	30	31
☉	♎8	9	10	11	12	13	14	15	16	17	18	19	20	20	21	22	23	24	25	26	27	28	29	♏0	1	2	3	4	5	6	♏7
☽	♎0	15	♏0	15	♐0	14	28	♑11	24	♒7	19	♓1	13	25	♈7	19	♉1	12	24	♊7	19	♋1	14	27	♌11	25	♍9	23	♎8	23	♏9
☿	♎26	28	29	♏1	2	4	5	6	8	9	10	12	13	14	15	16	18	19	20	21	22	23	24	24	25	26	27	27	28	28	♏28
♀	♌23	25	26	27	28	29	♍0	1	2	4	5	6	7	8	9	10	12	13	14	15	16	17	19	20	21	22	23	24	26	27	♍28
♂	♍27	28	28	29	♎0	0	1	2	2	3	3	4	5	5	6	7	7	8	9	9	10	11	11	12	13	13	14	14	15	16	♎16

1	6	12	18	24	30	1	6	12	18	24	30	1	15	30	1	15	30	1	15	30	1	15	30
♃ ♉15	14	13	13	12	11	♄ ♉14	13	13	13	12	12	♅ ♉26	25	25	♆ ♍26	26	27	♇ ♌4	4	4	☊ ♎11	11	11

NOVEMBER

	1	2	3	4	5	6	7	8	9	10	11	12	13	14	15	16	17	18	19	20	21	22	23	24	25	26	27	28	29	30
☉	♏8	9	10	11	12	13	14	15	16	17	18	19	20	21	22	23	24	26	27	28	29	♐0	1	2	3	4	5	6	7	♐8
☽	♏24	♐8	23	♑7	20	♒3	16	28	♓10	22	♈4	16	27	♉9	21	♊4	16	28	♋11	24	♌7	21	♍4	18	♎3	17	♏2	17	♐2	♐16
☿	♏28	28	28	27	27	26	25	24	23	22	21	19	18	17	16	15	14	13	12	12	12	12	12	13	13	14	15	16	17	♏18
♀	♍29	♎0	2	3	4	5	6	8	9	10	11	12	14	15	16	17	18	20	21	22	23	24	26	27	28	29	♏1	2	3	♏4
♂	♎17	18	18	19	20	20	21	22	22	23	24	24	25	26	26	27	28	28	29	♏0	0	1	2	2	3	3	4	5	5	♏6

1	6	12	18	24	30	1	6	12	18	24	30	1	15	30	1	15	30	1	15	30	1	15	30
♃ ♉11	10	9	9	8	7	♄ ♉12	11	11	10	10	9	♅ ♉25	24	24	♆ ♍27	27	27	♇ ♌4	4	4	☊ ♎11	10	9

DECEMBER

	1	2	3	4	5	6	7	8	9	10	11	12	13	14	15	16	17	18	19	20	21	22	23	24	25	26	27	28	29	30	31
☉	♐9	10	11	12	13	14	15	16	17	18	19	20	21	22	23	24	25	26	27	28	29	♑0	1	2	3	4	5	6	7	8	♑9
☽	♑1	15	28	♒11	24	♓6	18	♈0	12	24	♉6	18	♊0	12	25	♋8	21	♌4	18	♍1	15	29	♎13	27	♏12	26	♐10	25	♑9	23	♒6
☿	♏19	20	21	22	24	25	26	28	29	♐1	2	4	5	7	8	9	11	12	14	16	17	19	20	22	23	25	26	28	29	♑1	♑3
♀	♏5	7	8	9	10	12	13	14	15	17	18	19	20	22	23	24	25	27	28	29	♐0	1	3	4	5	6	8	9	10	11	♐13
♂	♏7	7	8	9	9	10	11	11	12	13	13	14	15	15	16	17	17	18	19	19	20	21	21	22	23	23	24	25	25	26	♏27

1	6	12	18	24	30	1	6	12	18	24	30	1	15	30	1	15	30	1	15	30	1	15	30
♃ ♉7	7	6	6	6	6	♄ ♉9	9	9	8	8	8	♅ ♉24	23	23	♆ ♍27	28	28	♇ ♌4	4	4	☊ ♎9	8	6

1941

JANUARY

	1	2	3	4	5	6	7	8	9	10	11	12	13	14	15	16	17	18	19	20	21	22	23	24	25	26	27	28	29	30	31
☉	♑10	11	12	13	14	15	16	17	18	19	20	21	22	23	24	25	26	28	29	♒0	1	2	3	4	5	6	7	8	9	10	♒11
☽	♒19	♓2	14	26	♈8	20	♉2	14	26	♊8	21	♋3	17	♌0	14	28	♍12	26	♎10	24	♏8	22	♐6	20	♑4	18	♒1	14	27	♓10	♓22
☿	♑4	6	7	9	10	12	14	15	17	18	20	22	23	25	27	28	♒0	2	3	5	7	9	10	12	14	16	17	19	21	22	♒24
♀	♐14	15	16	18	19	20	21	23	24	25	26	28	29	♑0	1	3	4	5	6	8	9	10	11	13	14	15	16	18	19	20	♑21
♂	♏27	28	29	29	♐0	1	1	2	3	3	4	5	6	6	7	8	8	9	10	10	11	12	12	13	14	14	15	16	16	17	♐18

	1	6	12	18	24	30
♃	♉6	6	6	6	7	7
♄	♉8	8	8	8	8	8

	1	15	30
♅	♉23	22	22
♆	♍28	28	27
♇	♌4	3	3
☊	♎6	4	3

FEBRUARY

	1	2	3	4	5	6	7	8	9	10	11	12	13	14	15	16	17	18	19	20	21	22	23	24	25	26	27	28
☉	♒12	13	14	15	16	17	18	19	20	21	22	23	24	25	26	27	28	29	♓0	1	2	3	4	5	6	7	8	♓9
☽	♈4	16	28	♉10	21	♊3	16	28	♋11	25	♌9	23	♍7	21	♎6	20	♏5	19	♐3	17	♑1	14	27	♒10	23	♓6	18	♈0
☿	♒26	27	29	♓1	2	4	5	7	8	9	10	11	12	12	13	13	13	13	13	13	12	12	11	10	9	8	7	♓6
♀	♑23	24	25	26	28	29	♒0	1	3	4	5	6	8	9	10	11	13	14	15	16	18	19	20	21	23	24	25	♒26
♂	♐18	19	20	20	21	22	22	23	24	25	25	26	27	27	28	29	29	♑0	1	1	2	3	3	4	5	6	6	♑7

	1	6	12	18	24	28
♃	♉7	8	9	10	10	11
♄	♉8	9	9	9	10	10

	1	15	28
♅	♉22	22	23
♆	♍27	27	27
♇	♌3	3	2
☊	♎3	2	2

MARCH

	1	2	3	4	5	6	7	8	9	10	11	12	13	14	15	16	17	18	19	20	21	22	23	24	25	26	27	28	29	30	31
☉	♓10	11	12	13	14	15	16	17	18	19	20	21	22	23	24	25	26	27	28	29	♈0	1	2	3	4	5	6	7	8	9	♈10
☽	♈12	24	♉6	18	29	♊11	24	♋6	19	♌3	16	♍1	15	♎0	15	♏0	15	29	♐14	27	♑11	24	♒7	20	♓2	15	27	♈9	21	♉2	♉14
☿	♓5	4	3	2	1	1	0	0	♒29	29	29	29	29	29	29	♓0	0	1	1	2	3	4	4	5	6	7	8	9	10	12	♓13
♀	♒28	29	♓0	1	3	4	5	6	8	9	10	11	13	14	15	16	18	19	20	21	22	24	25	26	27	29	♈0	1	2	4	♈5
♂	♑8	8	9	10	10	11	12	12	13	14	14	15	16	17	17	18	19	19	20	21	21	22	23	23	24	25	26	26	27	28	♑28

	1	6	12	18	24	30
♃	♉11	12	13	14	16	17
♄	♉10	11	11	12	12	13

	1	15	30
♅	♉23	23	24
♆	♍27	26	26
♇	♌2	2	2
☊	♎2	2	2

APRIL

	1	2	3	4	5	6	7	8	9	10	11	12	13	14	15	16	17	18	19	20	21	22	23	24	25	26	27	28	29	30
☉	♈11	12	13	14	15	16	17	18	19	20	21	22	23	24	25	26	27	28	29	♉0	0	1	2	3	4	5	6	7	8	♉9
☽	♉26	♊8	20	♋2	15	28	♌11	25	♍9	23	♎8	23	♏9	24	♐9	23	♑7	21	♒4	17	29	♓12	24	♈6	18	29	♉11	23	♊5	♊17
☿	♓14	15	17	18	19	21	22	23	25	26	28	♈0	1	3	4	6	8	9	11	13	15	17	18	20	22	24	26	28	♉0	♉2
♀	♈6	7	9	10	11	12	14	15	16	17	19	20	21	22	24	25	26	27	28	♉0	1	2	3	5	6	7	8	10	11	♉12
♂	♑29	♒0	0	1	2	2	3	4	4	5	6	7	7	8	9	9	10	11	11	12	13	13	14	15	16	16	17	18	18	♒19

	1	6	12	18	24	30
♃	♉17	18	20	21	22	24
♄	♉13	14	15	15	16	17

	1	15	30
♅	♉24	24	25
♆	♍26	26	25
♇	♌2	2	2
☊	♎2	2	1

MAY

	1	2	3	4	5	6	7	8	9	10	11	12	13	14	15	16	17	18	19	20	21	22	23	24	25	26	27	28	29	30	31
☉	♉10	11	12	13	14	15	16	17	18	19	20	21	22	23	24	25	26	27	28	29	♊0	1	1	2	3	4	5	6	7	8	♊9
☽	♊29	♋11	24	♌7	20	♍3	17	♎2	16	♏2	17	♐2	17	♑2	16	♒0	13	26	♓9	21	♈3	15	26	♉8	20	♊2	14	26	♋8	21	♌4
☿	♉4	6	8	10	13	15	17	19	21	23	26	28	♊0	2	4	6	8	10	12	14	16	18	19	21	23	24	26	28	29	♋0	♋2
♀	♉13	15	16	17	18	19	21	22	23	24	26	27	28	29	♊1	2	3	4	5	7	8	9	10	12	13	14	15	17	18	19	♊20
♂	♒20	20	21	22	22	23	24	24	25	26	26	27	28	29	29	♓0	1	1	2	3	3	4	5	5	6	7	7	8	9	9	♓10

	1	6	12	18	24	30
♃	♉24	25	27	28	29	♊1
♄	♉17	18	18	19	20	21

	1	15	30
♅	♉25	26	27
♆	♍25	25	25
♇	♌2	2	2
☊	♎1	0	♍1

JUNE

	1	2	3	4	5	6	7	8	9	10	11	12	13	14	15	16	17	18	19	20	21	22	23	24	25	26	27	28	29	30
☉	♊10	11	12	13	14	15	16	17	18	19	20	21	22	23	23	24	25	26	27	28	29	♋0	1	2	3	4	5	6	7	♋8
☽	♌16	♍0	13	27	♎11	26	♏10	25	♐10	25	♑10	24	♒8	22	♓4	17	29	♈11	23	♉5	17	29	♊11	23	♋5	18	♌1	14	27	♍10
☿	♋3	4	5	7	8	9	10	10	11	12	13	13	14	14	15	15	15	16	16	16	16	16	15	15	15	14	14	13	13	♋12
♀	♊21	23	24	25	26	28	29	♋0	1	2	4	5	6	7	9	10	11	12	13	15	16	17	18	20	21	22	23	24	26	♋27
♂	♓11	11	12	12	13	14	14	15	16	16	17	18	18	19	20	20	21	21	22	23	23	24	25	25	26	26	27	28	28	♓29

	1	6	12	18	24	30
♃	♊1	2	4	5	7	8
♄	♉21	22	22	23	24	24

	1	15	30
♅	♉27	28	29
♆	♍25	25	25
♇	♌2	3	3
☊	♍29	28	26

JULY

	1	2	3	4	5	6	7	8	9	10	11	12	13	14	15	16	17	18	19	20	21	22	23	24	25	26	27	28	29	30	31
☉	♋9	10	11	12	13	14	14	15	16	17	18	19	20	21	22	23	24	25	26	27	28	29	♌0	1	2	3	4	5	5	6	♌7
☽	♍24	♎7	21	♏6	20	♐5	19	♑4	18	♒3	16	♓0	13	25	♈7	19	♉1	13	25	♊7	19	♋1	14	27	♌10	23	♍7	20	♎4	18	♏2
☿	♋12	11	10	10	9	9	8	8	7	7	7	6	6	6	6	6	7	7	7	8	8	9	10	11	12	13	14	15	16	18	♋19
♀	♋28	29	♌1	2	3	4	5	7	8	9	10	12	13	14	15	16	18	19	20	21	23	24	25	26	27	29	♍0	1	2	3	♍5
♂	♓29	♈0	0	1	2	2	3	3	4	4	5	5	6	7	7	8	8	9	9	10	10	11	11	12	12	13	13	13	14	14	♈15

	1	6	12	18	24	30
♃	♊8	9	10	12	13	14
♄	♉24	25	25	26	27	27

	1	15	30
♅	♉29	29	♊29
♆	♍25	25	26
♇	♌3	4	4
☊	♍26	25	24

AUGUST

	1	2	3	4	5	6	7	8	9	10	11	12	13	14	15	16	17	18	19	20	21	22	23	24	25	26	27	28	29	30	31
☉	♌8	9	10	11	12	13	14	15	16	17	18	19	20	21	22	23	24	25	26	27	28	29	29	♍0	1	2	3	4	5	6	♍7
☽	♏16	♐1	15	29	♑13	27	♒11	25	♓8	20	♈3	15	27	♉9	21	♊3	15	27	♋10	22	♌5	19	♍2	16	♎0	15	29	♏13	27	♐12	♐26
☿	♋21	22	24	26	28	♌0	1	3	5	7	9	11	13	15	17	20	22	24	26	28	♍0	2	3	5	7	9	11	13	15	16	♍18
♀	♍6	7	8	9	11	12	13	14	16	17	18	19	20	22	23	24	25	26	28	29	♎0	1	2	4	5	6	7	8	10	11	♎12
♂	♈15	16	16	16	17	17	18	18	18	19	19	19	20	20	20	21	21	21	21	22	22	22	22	22	23	23	23	23	23	23	♈23

	1	6	12	18	24	30
♃	♊14	15	16	17	18	19
♄	♉27	27	28	28	28	28

	1	15	30
♅	♊0	0	0
♆	♍26	26	27
♇	♌4	4	5
☊	♍24	23	23

SEPTEMBER

	1	2	3	4	5	6	7	8	9	10	11	12	13	14	15	16	17	18	19	20	21	22	23	24	25	26	27	28	29	30
☉	♍8	9	10	11	12	13	14	15	16	17	18	19	20	21	22	23	24	25	26	27	28	29	♎0	1	2	3	3	4	5	♎6
☽	♑10	23	♒7	20	♓3	16	29	♈11	23	♉5	17	29	♊11	23	♋5	17	♌0	13	27	♍11	25	♎10	24	♏9	24	♐8	23	♑7	20	♒4
☿	♍20	22	23	25	27	28	♎0	2	3	5	6	8	9	11	12	14	15	17	18	19	21	22	23	25	26	27	28	♏0	1	♏2
♀	♎13	14	16	17	18	19	20	21	23	24	25	26	27	29	♏0	1	2	3	5	6	7	8	9	10	12	13	14	15	16	♏17
♂	♈23	24	24	24	24	24	24	24	24	24	24	24	23	23	23	23	23	23	23	22	22	22	22	22	21	21	21	21	20	♈20

	1	6	12	18	24	30
♃	♊19	20	20	21	21	21
♄	♉28	29	29	29	28	28

	1	15	30
♅	♊0	0	0
♆	♍27	27	28
♇	♌5	5	5
☊	♍23	23	23

OCTOBER

	1	2	3	4	5	6	7	8	9	10	11	12	13	14	15	16	17	18	19	20	21	22	23	24	25	26	27	28	29	30	31
☉	♎7	8	9	10	11	12	13	14	15	16	17	18	19	20	21	22	23	24	25	26	27	28	29	♏0	1	2	3	4	5	6	♏7
☽	♒17	♓0	13	25	♈7	20	♉2	13	25	♊7	19	♋1	13	26	♌8	21	♍5	19	♎3	18	♏3	18	♐3	18	♑3	17	♒1	14	27	♓10	♓22
☿	♏3	4	5	6	7	8	8	9	10	11	11	11	12	12	12	12	12	12	11	11	10	9	8	7	6	5	3	2	1	0	♎29
♀	♏19	20	21	22	23	24	26	27	28	29	♐0	1	3	4	5	6	7	8	9	11	12	13	14	15	16	17	18	20	21	22	♐23
♂	♈20	19	19	19	19	18	18	18	17	17	17	16	16	16	15	15	15	15	14	14	14	14	13	13	13	13	12	12	12	12	♈12

	1	6	12	18	24	30
♃	♊21	21	21	21	21	21
♄	♉28	28	28	27	27	27

	1	15	30
♅	♊0	0	♉0
♆	♍28	28	29
♇	♌5	6	6
☊	♍23	22	22

NOVEMBER

	1	2	3	4	5	6	7	8	9	10	11	12	13	14	15	16	17	18	19	20	21	22	23	24	25	26	27	28	29	30
☉	♏8	9	10	11	12	13	14	15	16	17	18	19	20	21	22	23	24	25	26	27	28	29	♐0	1	2	3	4	5	6	♐7
☽	♈4	16	28	♉10	22	♊4	16	28	♋10	22	♌4	17	♍0	13	27	♎11	26	♏11	26	♐12	27	♑12	26	♒10	23	♓6	19	♈1	13	♈25
☿	♎28	27	27	26	26	26	27	27	28	28	29	♏0	1	2	4	5	6	7	9	10	12	13	15	16	18	19	21	22	24	♏25
♀	♐24	25	26	27	28	♑0	1	2	3	4	5	6	7	8	9	10	11	12	13	14	15	16	17	19	20	21	21	22	23	♑24
♂	♈12	12	11	11	11	11	11	11	11	11	11	11	11	11	11	11	11	11	12	12	12	12	12	12	12	13	13	13	13	♈13

	1	6	12	18	24	30
♃	♊21	20	20	19	18	18
♄	♉26	26	26	25	25	24

	1	15	30
♅	♉29	29	28
♆	♍29	29	♎29
♇	♌6	6	6
☊	♍22	21	20

DECEMBER

	1	2	3	4	5	6	7	8	9	10	11	12	13	14	15	16	17	18	19	20	21	22	23	24	25	26	27	28	29	30	31
☉	♐8	9	10	11	12	13	14	16	17	18	19	20	21	22	23	24	25	26	27	28	29	♑0	1	2	3	4	5	6	7	8	♑9
☽	♉7	19	♊1	13	25	♋7	19	♌1	14	26	♍9	22	♎6	20	♏4	19	♐4	20	♑5	20	♒4	18	♓2	15	28	♈10	22	♉4	16	28	♊10
☿	♏27	28	♐0	2	3	5	6	8	9	11	12	14	16	17	19	20	22	23	25	27	28	♑0	1	3	5	6	8	9	11	13	♑14
♀	♑25	26	27	28	29	♒0	1	2	3	4	4	5	6	7	8	9	9	10	11	11	12	13	14	14	15	15	16	17	17	18	♒18
♂	♈14	14	14	14	15	15	15	16	16	16	17	17	17	18	18	18	19	19	19	20	20	21	21	21	22	22	23	23	24	24	♈24

	1	6	12	18	24	30
♃	♊17	17	16	15	14	14
♄	♉24	24	23	23	22	22

	1	15	30
♅	♉28	27	27
♆	♎0	0	0
♇	♌6	5	5
☊	♍19	18	16

1942

JANUARY

	1	2	3	4	5	6	7	8	9	10	11	12	13	14	15	16	17	18	19	20	21	22	23	24	25	26	27	28	29	30	31
☉	♑10	11	12	13	14	15	16	17	18	19	20	21	22	23	24	25	26	27	28	29	♒0	1	2	3	4	5	6	7	8	9	♒10
☽	♊22	♋4	16	28	♌11	23	♍6	19	♎2	16	♏0	14	28	♐13	28	♑13	28	♒12	26	♓10	23	♈6	18	♉0	12	24	♊6	18	♋0	12	♋24
☿	♑16	17	19	21	22	24	26	27	29	♒1	2	4	6	7	9	10	12	13	15	16	18	19	21	22	23	24	25	26	26	27	♒27
♀	♒18	19	19	20	20	20	20	21	21	21	21	21	21	21	21	21	21	21	20	20	20	20	19	19	18	18	17	17	16	16	♒15
♂	♈25	25	26	26	27	27	28	28	29	29	♉0	0	1	1	2	2	3	3	4	4	5	5	6	6	7	7	8	8	9	9	♉10

1	6	12	18	24	30	1	6	12	18	24	30	1	15	30	1	15	30	1	15	30	1	15	30
♃ ♊13	13	12	12	12	11	♄ ♉22	22	22	22	22	22	♅ ♉27	27	26	♆ ♎0	0	0	♇ ♌5	5	5	☊ ♍16	15	14

FEBRUARY

	1	2	3	4	5	6	7	8	9	10	11	12	13	14	15	16	17	18	19	20	21	22	23	24	25	26	27	28
☉	♒12	13	14	15	16	17	18	19	20	21	22	23	24	25	26	27	28	29	♓0	1	2	3	4	5	6	7	8	♓9
☽	♌7	20	♍3	16	29	♎13	27	♏11	25	♐9	23	♑8	22	♒6	20	♓4	18	♈1	13	26	♉8	20	♊2	14	26	♋8	20	♌3
☿	♒27	27	27	26	26	25	24	23	22	21	19	18	17	16	15	14	13	13	12	12	12	12	12	12	12	12	13	♒13
♀	♒14	14	13	12	12	11	11	10	10	9	9	8	8	7	7	7	6	6	6	6	6	6	6	6	6	6	6	♒6
♂	♉10	11	12	12	13	13	14	14	15	15	16	17	17	18	18	19	19	20	21	21	22	22	23	23	24	25	25	♉26

1	6	12	18	24	28	1	6	12	18	24	28	1	15	28	1	15	28	1	15	28	1	15	28
♃ ♊11	11	11	12	12	12	♄ ♉22	22	22	22	23	23	♅ ♉26	26	27	♆ ♎0	♍0	29	♇ ♌4	4	4	☊ ♍14	13	13

MARCH

	1	2	3	4	5	6	7	8	9	10	11	12	13	14	15	16	17	18	19	20	21	22	23	24	25	26	27	28	29	30	31
☉	♓10	11	12	13	14	15	16	17	18	19	20	21	22	23	24	25	26	27	28	29	♈0	1	2	3	4	5	6	7	8	9	♈10
☽	♌15	28	♍12	25	♎9	23	♏7	21	♐6	20	♑4	18	♒2	16	29	♓13	26	♈9	21	♉4	16	28	♊10	22	♋4	16	28	♌10	23	♍6	♍20
☿	♒14	14	15	16	17	18	18	19	20	22	23	24	25	26	27	29	♓0	1	3	4	5	7	8	10	11	13	14	16	18	19	♓21
♀	♒6	6	7	7	7	8	8	8	9	9	10	10	11	12	12	13	13	14	15	15	16	17	18	18	19	20	21	22	22	23	♒24
♂	♉26	27	27	28	29	29	♊0	0	1	2	2	3	3	4	5	5	6	6	7	8	8	9	9	10	10	11	12	12	13	13	♊14

1	6	12	18	24	30	1	6	12	18	24	30	1	15	30	1	15	30	1	15	30	1	15	30
♃ ♊12	13	13	14	15	16	♄ ♉23	23	24	24	25	25	♅ ♉27	27	28	♆ ♍29	29	28	♇ ♌4	4	4	☊ ♍13	13	13

APRIL

	1	2	3	4	5	6	7	8	9	10	11	12	13	14	15	16	17	18	19	20	21	22	23	24	25	26	27	28	29	30
☉	♈11	12	13	14	15	16	17	18	19	19	20	21	22	23	24	25	26	27	28	29	♉0	1	2	3	4	5	6	7	8	♉9
☽	♎4	18	♏2	17	♐2	16	♑1	15	29	♒13	26	♓9	22	♈5	17	♉0	12	24	♊6	18	♋0	12	24	♌6	18	♍1	14	28	♎12	♎26
☿	♓23	24	26	28	29	♈1	3	5	7	9	11	13	14	16	18	20	23	25	27	29	♉1	3	5	7	9	12	14	16	18	♉20
♀	♒25	26	27	28	29	29	♓0	1	2	3	4	5	6	7	8	9	10	11	12	13	14	15	16	17	18	19	20	21	22	♓23
♂	♊15	15	16	16	17	18	18	19	20	20	21	21	22	23	23	24	24	25	26	26	27	27	28	29	29	♋0	0	1	2	♋2

1	6	12	18	24	30	1	6	12	18	24	30	1	15	30	1	15	30	1	15	30	1	15	30
♃ ♊16	17	18	19	20	21	♄ ♉26	26	27	27	28	29	♅ ♉28	28	29	♆ ♍28	28	27	♇ ♌4	3	4	☊ ♍13	13	12

MAY

	1	2	3	4	5	6	7	8	9	10	11	12	13	14	15	16	17	18	19	20	21	22	23	24	25	26	27	28	29	30	31
☉	♉10	11	12	13	14	15	16	17	18	19	20	21	22	23	24	24	25	26	27	28	29	♊0	1	2	3	4	5	6	7	8	♊9
☽	♏11	26	♐11	26	♑11	25	♒9	23	♓6	19	♈2	14	27	♉9	21	♊3	15	27	♋8	20	♌2	14	27	♍9	23	♎6	20	♏5	19	♐5	♐20
☿	♉22	24	26	28	♊0	1	3	5	7	8	10	11	12	14	15	16	17	18	19	20	21	22	23	23	24	24	25	25	25	26	♊26
♀	♓25	26	27	28	29	♈0	1	2	3	4	5	6	8	9	10	11	12	13	14	15	16	18	19	20	21	22	23	24	25	27	♈28
♂	♋3	3	4	5	5	6	7	7	8	8	9	10	10	11	11	12	13	13	14	15	15	16	16	17	18	18	19	19	20	21	♋21

1	6	12	18	24	30	1	6	12	18	24	30	1	15	30	1	15	30	1	15	30	1	15	30
♃ ♊21	22	24	25	26	27	♄ ♉29	♊0	0	1	2	3	♅ ♉29	♊29	1	♆ ♍27	27	27	♇ ♌4	4	4	☊ ♍12	11	9

JUNE

	1	2	3	4	5	6	7	8	9	10	11	12	13	14	15	16	17	18	19	20	21	22	23	24	25	26	27	28	29	30
☉	♊10	11	12	13	14	15	16	17	18	18	19	20	21	22	23	24	25	26	27	28	29	♋0	1	2	3	4	5	6	7	♋8
☽	♑5	20	♒5	19	♓3	16	29	♈11	24	♉6	18	♊0	12	24	♋6	17	29	♌11	24	♍6	19	♎2	15	29	♏13	28	♐13	28	♑14	♑29
☿	♊26	26	25	25	25	25	24	24	23	23	22	22	21	21	20	20	19	19	18	18	18	17	17	17	17	17	17	17	18	♊18
♀	♈29	♉0	1	2	3	5	6	7	8	9	10	11	13	14	15	16	17	18	20	21	22	23	24	25	27	28	29	♊0	1	♊2
♂	♋22	23	23	24	24	25	26	26	27	27	28	29	29	♌0	1	1	2	2	3	4	4	5	5	6	7	7	8	9	9	♌10

1	6	12	18	24	30	1	6	12	18	24	30	1	15	30	1	15	30	1	15	30	1	15	30
♃ ♊28	29	♋0	2	3	4	♄ ♊3	4	4	5	6	7	♅ ♊1	2	3	♆ ♍27	27	27	♇ ♌4	4	5	☊ ♍9	7	6

JULY

	1	2	3	4	5	6	7	8	9	10	11	12	13	14	15	16	17	18	19	20	21	22	23	24	25	26	27	28	29	30	31
☉	♋9	9	10	11	12	13	14	15	16	17	18	19	20	21	22	23	24	25	26	27	28	29	♌0	0	1	2	3	4	5	6	♌7
☽	♒13	28	♓12	25	♈8	21	♉3	15	27	♊9	21	♋3	14	26	♌8	21	♍3	16	28	♎11	25	♏9	23	♐7	22	♑7	22	♒7	22	♓6	♓20
☿	♊19	19	20	20	21	22	23	24	25	26	28	29	♋0	2	3	5	6	8	10	12	13	15	17	19	21	23	25	28	♌0	2	♌4
♀	♊4	5	6	7	8	9	11	12	13	14	15	17	18	19	20	21	23	24	25	26	27	28	♋0	1	2	3	4	6	7	8	♋9
♂	♌10	11	12	12	13	14	14	15	15	16	17	17	18	19	19	20	20	21	22	22	23	24	24	25	25	26	27	27	28	29	♌29

1	6	12	18	24	30	1	6	12	18	24	30	1	15	30	1	15	30	1	15	30	1	15	30
♃ ♋5	6	7	9	10	11	♄ ♊7	7	8	9	9	10	♅ ♊3	3	4	♆ ♍27	27	28	♇ ♌5	5	5	☊ ♍6	5	4

AUGUST

	1	2	3	4	5	6	7	8	9	10	11	12	13	14	15	16	17	18	19	20	21	22	23	24	25	26	27	28	29	30	31
☉	♌8	9	10	11	12	13	14	15	16	17	18	19	20	21	22	23	23	24	25	26	27	28	29	♍0	1	2	3	4	5	6	♍7
☽	♈3	16	29	♉11	24	♊6	17	29	♋11	23	♌5	17	♍0	13	25	♎8	22	♏5	19	♐3	17	♑2	17	♒1	16	♓0	14	28	♈11	24	♉7
☿	♌6	8	10	12	14	16	18	20	22	24	26	28	♍0	2	4	5	7	9	11	12	14	16	17	19	20	22	24	25	27	28	♍29
♀	♋10	12	13	14	15	17	18	19	20	21	23	24	25	26	27	29	♌0	1	2	3	5	6	7	8	10	11	12	13	14	16	♌17
♂	♍0	0	1	2	2	3	4	4	5	5	6	7	7	8	9	9	10	11	11	12	12	13	14	14	15	16	16	17	18	18	♍19

1	6	12	18	24	30	1	6	12	18	24	30	1	15	30	1	15	30	1	15	30	1	15	30
♃ ♋12	13	14	15	16	17	♄ ♊10	10	11	11	12	12	♅ ♊4	4	5	♆ ♍28	28	29	♇ ♌5	6	6	☊ ♍4	4	4

SEPTEMBER

	1	2	3	4	5	6	7	8	9	10	11	12	13	14	15	16	17	18	19	20	21	22	23	24	25	26	27	28	29	30
☉	♍8	9	10	11	12	13	14	15	16	17	18	19	20	21	22	22	23	24	25	26	27	28	29	♎0	1	2	3	4	5	♎6
☽	♉20	♊2	14	26	♋7	19	♌1	14	26	♍9	22	♎5	18	♏2	16	♐0	14	28	♑13	27	♒11	25	♓9	23	♈6	19	♉2	15	27	♊10
☿	♎1	2	4	5	6	8	9	10	11	13	14	15	16	17	18	19	20	21	22	22	23	24	24	25	25	26	26	26	26	♎26
♀	♌18	19	21	22	23	24	26	27	28	29	♍0	2	3	4	5	7	8	9	10	12	13	14	15	17	18	19	20	22	23	♍24
♂	♍19	20	21	21	22	23	23	24	25	25	26	26	27	28	28	29	♎0	0	1	2	2	3	4	4	5	6	6	7	8	♎8

1	6	12	18	24	30	1	6	12	18	24	30	1	15	30	1	15	30	1	15	30	1	15	30
♃ ♋18	19	20	21	22	22	♄ ♊12	12	12	12	13	13	♅ ♊5	5	4	♆ ♍29	29	♎29	♇ ♌6	7	7	☊ ♍4	4	4

OCTOBER

	1	2	3	4	5	6	7	8	9	10	11	12	13	14	15	16	17	18	19	20	21	22	23	24	25	26	27	28	29	30	31
☉	♎7	8	9	10	11	12	13	14	15	16	17	18	19	20	21	22	23	24	25	26	27	28	29	♏0	1	2	3	4	5	6	♏7
☽	♊22	♋3	15	27	♌9	22	♍4	17	♎0	14	28	♏12	26	♐11	25	♑9	24	♒8	21	♓5	19	♈2	15	28	♉11	23	♊5	18	♋0	11	♋23
☿	♎26	25	25	24	24	23	22	21	20	18	17	16	15	14	13	12	11	11	11	11	11	11	11	12	13	14	15	16	17	18	♎19
♀	♍25	27	28	29	♎0	2	3	4	5	7	8	9	10	11	13	14	15	17	18	19	20	22	23	24	25	27	28	29	♏0	2	♏3
♂	♎9	9	10	11	11	12	13	13	14	15	15	16	17	17	18	19	19	20	21	21	22	23	23	24	25	25	26	27	27	28	♎29

1	6	12	18	24	30	1	6	12	18	24	30	1	15	30	1	15	30	1	15	30	1	15	30
♃ ♋22	23	24	24	25	25	♄ ♊12	12	12	12	12	11	♅ ♊4	4	4	♆ ♎0	0	1	♇ ♌7	7	7	☊ ♍4	3	2

NOVEMBER

	1	2	3	4	5	6	7	8	9	10	11	12	13	14	15	16	17	18	19	20	21	22	23	24	25	26	27	28	29	30
☉	♏8	9	10	11	12	13	14	15	16	17	18	19	20	21	22	23	24	25	26	27	28	29	♐0	1	2	3	4	5	6	♐7
☽	♌5	17	29	♍12	25	♎8	22	♏6	21	♐6	21	♑5	20	♒4	18	♓2	15	29	♈12	24	♉7	19	♊2	14	26	♋8	20	♌1	13	♌25
☿	♎21	22	24	25	27	28	♏0	1	3	5	6	8	9	11	13	14	16	18	19	21	22	24	25	27	29	♐0	2	3	5	♐7
♀	♏4	5	7	8	9	10	12	13	14	15	17	18	19	20	22	23	24	25	27	28	29	♐0	2	3	4	5	7	8	9	♐10
♂	♎29	♏0	1	1	2	3	3	4	5	5	6	7	7	8	9	10	10	11	12	12	13	14	14	15	16	16	17	18	18	♏19

1	6	12	18	24	30	1	6	12	18	24	30	1	15	30	1	15	30	1	15	30	1	15	30
♃ ♋25	25	25	25	25	25	♄ ♊11	11	11	10	10	9	♅ ♊4	3	2	♆ ♎1	1	2	♇ ♌7	7	7	☊ ♍2	0	♌1

DECEMBER

	1	2	3	4	5	6	7	8	9	10	11	12	13	14	15	16	17	18	19	20	21	22	23	24	25	26	27	28	29	30	31
☉	♐8	9	10	11	12	13	14	15	16	17	18	19	20	21	22	23	24	25	26	27	28	♑0	1	2	3	4	5	6	7	8	♑9
☽	♍7	20	♎3	16	♏0	14	29	♐14	29	♑14	29	♒14	28	♓12	26	♈9	21	♉4	16	29	♊11	23	♋5	16	28	♌10	22	♍4	16	29	♎11
☿	♐8	10	11	13	14	16	18	19	21	22	24	25	27	29	♑0	2	3	5	6	8	10	11	13	14	16	17	19	21	22	24	♑25
♀	♐12	13	14	15	17	18	19	21	22	23	24	26	27	28	29	♑1	2	3	4	6	7	8	9	11	12	13	14	16	17	18	♑19
♂	♏20	20	21	22	23	23	24	25	25	26	27	27	28	29	♐0	0	1	2	2	3	4	4	5	6	7	7	8	9	9	10	♐11

1	6	12	18	24	30	1	6	12	18	24	30	1	15	30	1	15	30	1	15	30	1	15	30
♃ ♋25	24	24	23	23	22	♄ ♊9	9	8	8	7	7	♅ ♊2	2	1	♆ ♎2	2	2	♇ ♌7	7	7	☊ ♌29	27	26

1943

January

	1	2	3	4	5	6	7	8	9	10	11	12	13	14	15	16	17	18	19	20	21	22	23	24	25	26	27	28	29	30	31
☉	♑10	11	12	13	14	15	16	17	18	19	20	21	22	23	24	25	26	27	28	29	♒0	1	2	3	4	5	6	7	8	9	♒10
☽	♎25	♏8	22	♐7	22	♑7	23	♒8	23	♓7	21	♈5	18	♉1	13	26	♊8	20	♋2	13	25	♌7	19	♍1	13	25	♎8	21	♏4	17	♐1
☿	♑27	28	♒0	1	2	4	5	6	7	8	9	10	10	11	11	11	11	10	10	9	8	7	6	5	4	2	1	0	♑29	28	♑27
♀	♑21	22	23	24	26	27	28	29	♒1	2	3	4	6	7	8	10	11	12	13	15	16	17	18	20	21	22	23	25	26	27	♒28
♂	♐11	12	13	14	14	15	16	16	17	18	19	19	20	21	21	22	23	24	24	25	26	27	27	28	29	29	♑0	1	2	2	♑3

	1	6	12	18	24	30
♃	♋22	21	20	19	19	18
♄	♊7	6	6	6	6	6

	1	15	30
♅	♊1	1	1
♆	♎2	2	2
♇	♌7	6	6
☊	♌26	25	25

February

	1	2	3	4	5	6	7	8	9	10	11	12	13	14	15	16	17	18	19	20	21	22	23	24	25	26	27	28
☉	♒11	12	13	14	15	16	17	18	19	20	21	22	23	24	25	26	27	28	29	♓0	1	2	3	5	6	7	8	♓9
☽	♐16	♑0	15	♒1	16	♓1	15	29	♈13	27	♉10	22	♊4	16	28	♋10	22	♌4	16	28	♍10	22	♎5	18	♏1	14	28	♐12
☿	♑26	26	25	25	25	25	25	25	26	26	27	27	28	29	29	♒0	1	2	3	4	5	6	8	9	10	11	12	♒14
♀	♓0	1	2	3	5	6	7	8	10	11	12	13	14	16	17	18	19	21	22	23	24	26	27	28	29	♈1	2	♈3
♂	♑4	5	5	6	7	7	8	9	10	10	11	12	13	13	14	15	16	16	17	18	18	19	20	21	21	22	23	♑24

	1	6	12	18	24	28
♃	♋18	17	16	16	16	15
♄	♊6	6	6	6	6	6

	1	15	28
♅	♊1	1	1
♆	♎2	2	1
♇	♌6	6	5
☊	♌25	25	25

March

	1	2	3	4	5	6	7	8	9	10	11	12	13	14	15	16	17	18	19	20	21	22	23	24	25	26	27	28	29	30	31
☉	♓10	11	12	13	14	15	16	17	18	19	20	21	22	23	24	25	26	27	28	29	♈0	0	1	2	3	4	5	6	7	8	♈9
☽	♐26	♑10	25	♒9	24	♓9	23	♈7	21	♉4	18	♊0	13	25	♋7	18	♌0	12	24	♍6	19	♎1	14	28	♏11	25	♐8	22	♑6	21	♒5
☿	♒15	16	18	19	21	22	24	25	27	28	♓0	1	3	4	6	8	9	11	13	15	16	18	20	22	23	25	27	29	♈1	3	♈5
♀	♈4	6	7	8	9	10	12	13	14	15	17	18	19	20	22	23	24	25	26	28	29	♉0	1	3	4	5	6	7	9	10	♉11
♂	♑24	25	26	27	27	28	29	♒0	0	1	2	3	3	4	5	6	6	7	8	9	9	10	11	12	12	13	14	15	15	16	♒17

	1	6	12	18	24	30
♃	♋15	15	15	15	15	16
♄	♊6	6	7	7	7	8

	1	15	30
♅	♊1	1	2
♆	♎1	1	0
♇	♌5	5	5
☊	♌25	25	24

April

	1	2	3	4	5	6	7	8	9	10	11	12	13	14	15	16	17	18	19	20	21	22	23	24	25	26	27	28	29	30
☉	♈10	11	12	13	14	15	16	17	18	19	20	21	22	23	24	25	26	27	28	29	♉0	1	2	3	4	5	6	7	8	♉9
☽	♒19	♓3	17	♈2	15	29	♉12	25	♊8	20	♋2	14	26	♌8	20	♍2	14	27	♎10	23	♏7	21	♐5	19	♑3	17	♒2	16	♓0	♓14
☿	♈7	9	11	13	15	17	19	21	23	25	28	♉0	2	4	6	8	10	11	13	15	17	19	20	22	23	25	26	27	28	♉29
♀	♉12	13	15	16	17	18	19	21	22	23	24	25	27	28	29	♊0	1	3	4	5	6	7	8	10	11	12	13	14	16	♊17
♂	♒18	18	19	20	21	21	22	23	24	24	25	26	27	27	28	29	♓0	0	1	2	3	3	4	5	6	6	7	8	9	♓9

	1	6	12	18	24	30
♃	♋16	16	17	17	18	19
♄	♊8	9	9	10	10	11

	1	15	30
♅	♊2	2	3
♆	♎0	0	0
♇	♌5	5	5
☊	♌24	23	22

May

	1	2	3	4	5	6	7	8	9	10	11	12	13	14	15	16	17	18	19	20	21	22	23	24	25	26	27	28	29	30	31
☉	♉10	11	12	13	14	15	16	17	18	18	19	20	21	22	23	24	25	26	27	28	29	♊0	1	2	3	4	5	6	7	8	♊9
☽	♓27	♈11	24	♉8	21	♊4	16	28	♋10	22	♌4	16	28	♍10	22	♎5	18	♏2	15	♐0	14	29	♑13	28	♒12	27	♓10	24	♈8	21	♉4
☿	♊0	1	2	3	3	4	5	5	5	6	6	6	6	6	5	5	5	4	4	4	3	2	2	1	1	0	0	♉29	29	28	♉28
♀	♊18	19	20	21	23	24	25	26	27	28	29	♋1	2	3	4	5	6	7	9	10	11	12	13	14	15	16	17	19	20	21	♋22
♂	♓10	11	12	12	13	14	15	16	16	17	18	19	19	20	21	22	22	23	24	24	25	26	27	27	28	29	♈0	0	1	2	♈3

	1	6	12	18	24	30
♃	♋19	20	20	21	22	24
♄	♊11	12	13	13	14	15

	1	15	30
♅	♊3	4	5
♆	♎0	♍0	29
♇	♌5	5	5
☊	♌22	20	19

June

	1	2	3	4	5	6	7	8	9	10	11	12	13	14	15	16	17	18	19	20	21	22	23	24	25	26	27	28	29	30
☉	♊10	11	12	13	13	14	15	16	17	18	19	20	21	22	23	24	25	26	27	28	29	♋0	1	2	3	4	4	5	6	♋7
☽	♉17	♊0	12	25	♋7	19	♌0	12	24	♍6	18	♎0	13	26	♏10	24	♐8	23	♑8	23	♒8	22	♓7	21	♈5	18	♉1	14	27	♊9
☿	♉28	27	27	27	27	27	27	27	28	28	28	29	29	♊0	1	1	2	3	4	5	6	7	9	10	11	12	14	15	17	♊19
♀	♋23	24	25	26	27	28	29	♌1	2	3	4	5	6	7	8	9	10	11	12	13	14	15	16	17	18	19	20	21	22	♌23
♂	♈3	4	5	6	6	7	8	9	9	10	11	11	12	13	14	14	15	16	17	17	18	19	19	20	21	22	22	23	24	♈24

	1	6	12	18	24	30
♃	♋24	25	26	27	29	♌0
♄	♊15	16	17	17	18	19

	1	15	30
♅	♊5	6	7
♆	♍29	29	29
♇	♌5	6	6
☊	♌19	17	17

July

	1	2	3	4	5	6	7	8	9	10	11	12	13	14	15	16	17	18	19	20	21	22	23	24	25	26	27	28	29	30	31
☉	♋8	9	10	11	12	13	14	15	16	17	18	19	20	21	22	23	24	25	25	26	27	28	29	♌0	1	2	3	4	5	6	♌7
☽	♊21	♋3	15	27	♌9	21	♍3	14	27	♎9	22	♏5	18	♐2	16	♑1	16	♒1	17	♓2	16	♈1	14	28	♉11	24	♊6	18	♋0	12	♋24
☿	♊20	22	24	25	27	29	♋1	3	5	7	9	11	14	16	18	20	22	24	26	29	♌1	3	5	7	9	11	13	15	17	19	♌20
♀	♌24	25	26	26	27	28	29	♍0	1	2	3	3	4	5	6	7	7	8	9	10	10	11	12	12	13	14	14	15	15	16	♍16
♂	♈25	26	27	27	28	29	29	♉0	1	1	2	3	3	4	5	6	6	7	8	8	9	10	10	11	12	12	13	14	14	15	♉15

	1	6	12	18	24	30
♃	♌0	1	2	4	5	6
♄	♊19	20	20	21	22	22

	1	15	30
♅	♊7	7	8
♆	♍29	♎29	0
♇	♌6	6	7
☊	♌16	16	16

August

	1	2	3	4	5	6	7	8	9	10	11	12	13	14	15	16	17	18	19	20	21	22	23	24	25	26	27	28	29	30	31
☉	♌8	9	10	11	12	13	14	15	16	17	17	18	19	20	21	22	23	24	25	26	27	28	29	♍0	1	2	3	4	5	6	♍7
☽	♌6	18	♍0	12	24	♎6	18	♏1	14	27	♐11	25	♑10	25	♒10	25	♓10	25	♈9	23	♉7	20	♊3	15	27	♋9	21	♌3	15	27	♍9
☿	♌22	24	26	28	29	♍1	3	4	6	7	9	11	12	13	15	16	18	19	20	22	23	24	25	27	28	29	♎0	1	2	3	♎4
♀	♍17	17	18	18	18	19	19	19	20	20	20	20	20	20	21	21	21	20	20	20	20	20	20	19	19	18	18	18	17	17	♍16
♂	♉16	17	17	18	19	19	20	21	21	22	22	23	24	24	25	25	26	27	27	28	28	29	29	♊0	1	1	2	2	3	3	♊4

	1	6	12	18	24	30
♃	♌7	8	9	11	12	13
♄	♊23	23	24	24	25	25

	1	15	30
♅	♊8	8	9
♆	♎0	0	1
♇	♌7	7	8
☊	♌16	16	16

September

	1	2	3	4	5	6	7	8	9	10	11	12	13	14	15	16	17	18	19	20	21	22	23	24	25	26	27	28	29	30
☉	♍8	9	10	11	12	13	14	14	15	16	17	18	19	20	21	22	23	24	25	26	27	28	29	♎0	1	2	3	4	5	♎6
☽	♍21	♎3	15	28	♏10	24	♐7	21	♑5	19	♒3	18	♓3	18	♈3	17	♉2	15	29	♊11	24	♋6	18	♌0	11	23	♍5	17	♎0	♎12
☿	♎5	5	6	7	7	8	8	9	9	9	9	9	9	9	9	8	8	7	7	6	5	4	3	2	0	♍29	28	27	27	♍26
♀	♍16	15	14	14	13	13	12	11	11	10	10	9	8	8	7	7	7	6	6	5	5	5	5	5	4	4	4	4	4	♍4
♂	♊4	5	5	6	6	7	7	8	8	9	9	10	10	11	11	12	12	13	13	13	14	14	15	15	15	16	16	16	17	♊17

	1	6	12	18	24	30
♃	♌14	15	16	17	18	19
♄	♊25	26	26	26	26	27

	1	15	30
♅	♊9	9	9
♆	♎1	1	2
♇	♌8	8	8
☊	♌16	16	15

October

	1	2	3	4	5	6	7	8	9	10	11	12	13	14	15	16	17	18	19	20	21	22	23	24	25	26	27	28	29	30	31
☉	♎7	8	9	10	11	12	13	14	15	16	17	18	19	20	21	22	23	24	25	26	27	28	29	♏0	1	2	3	4	5	6	♏7
☽	♎25	♏7	21	♐4	17	♑1	15	29	♒13	28	♓12	27	♈11	26	♉10	23	♊7	19	♋2	14	26	♌8	20	♍1	13	26	♎8	21	♏4	17	♐0
☿	♍25	25	25	25	25	25	26	26	27	28	29	♎0	1	3	4	5	7	8	10	12	13	15	17	18	20	22	23	25	27	28	♏0
♀	♍5	5	5	5	5	6	6	6	7	7	8	8	9	9	10	10	11	11	12	13	13	14	15	16	16	17	18	19	20	20	♍21
♂	♊17	18	18	18	19	19	19	20	20	20	20	20	21	21	21	21	21	21	22	22	22	22	22	22	22	22	22	22	22	22	♊22

	1	6	12	18	24	30
♃	♌19	20	21	22	23	24
♄	♊27	27	27	27	26	26

	1	15	30
♅	♊9	8	8
♆	♎2	3	3
♇	♌8	9	9
☊	♌15	13	12

November

	1	2	3	4	5	6	7	8	9	10	11	12	13	14	15	16	17	18	19	20	21	22	23	24	25	26	27	28	29	30
☉	♏8	9	10	11	12	13	14	15	16	17	18	19	20	21	22	23	24	25	26	27	28	29	♐0	1	2	3	4	5	6	♐7
☽	♐14	28	♑12	26	♒10	24	♓8	22	♈6	20	♉4	18	♊1	14	27	♋10	22	♌4	16	27	♍9	21	♎3	16	29	♏12	26	♐10	24	♑8
☿	♏2	3	5	7	8	10	12	13	15	16	18	20	21	23	24	26	28	29	♐1	2	4	5	7	8	10	12	13	15	16	♐18
♀	♍22	23	24	25	26	26	27	28	29	♎0	1	2	3	4	5	6	7	8	9	10	11	12	13	14	15	16	18	19	20	♎21
♂	♊22	22	22	22	22	22	22	21	21	21	21	21	20	20	20	20	19	19	19	19	18	18	18	17	17	16	16	16	15	♊15

	1	6	12	18	24	30
♃	♌24	25	25	26	26	27
♄	♊26	26	26	25	25	24

	1	15	30
♅	♊8	7	7
♆	♎3	3	4
♇	♌9	9	9
☊	♌12	10	9

December

	1	2	3	4	5	6	7	8	9	10	11	12	13	14	15	16	17	18	19	20	21	22	23	24	25	26	27	28	29	30	31
☉	♐8	9	10	11	12	13	14	15	16	17	18	19	20	21	22	23	24	25	26	27	28	29	♑0	1	2	3	4	5	6	7	♑8
☽	♑22	♒7	21	♓5	19	♈3	17	♉0	14	27	♊10	23	♋5	18	♌0	12	23	♍5	17	29	♎11	24	♏7	20	♐4	18	♑2	17	♒2	16	♓1
☿	♐19	21	22	24	25	27	28	♑0	1	3	4	6	7	9	10	12	13	14	16	17	18	19	20	21	22	23	24	24	25	25	♑25
♀	♎22	23	24	25	26	27	29	♏0	1	2	3	4	5	6	8	9	10	11	12	13	14	16	17	18	19	20	21	23	24	25	♏26
♂	♊15	14	14	13	13	13	12	12	12	11	11	10	10	10	9	9	9	8	8	8	8	7	7	7	7	6	6	6	6	6	♊6

	1	6	12	18	24	30
♃	♌27	27	27	27	27	27
♄	♊24	24	23	23	22	22

	1	15	30
♅	♊7	6	6
♆	♎4	4	4
♇	♌9	8	8
☊	♌9	7	7

1944

JANUARY

	1	2	3	4	5	6	7	8	9	10	11	12	13	14	15	16	17	18	19	20	21	22	23	24	25	26	27	28	29	30	31
☉	♑9	10	11	13	14	15	16	17	18	19	20	21	22	23	24	25	26	27	28	29	♒0	1	2	3	4	5	6	7	8	9	♒10
☽	♓15	♈0	14	27	♉11	24	♊7	19	♋2	14	26	♌8	20	♍2	13	25	♎7	19	♏2	15	28	♐11	26	♑10	25	♒10	25	♓10	25	♈9	♈24
☿	♑25	24	24	23	22	21	20	19	17	16	15	13	12	11	11	10	9	9	9	9	9	9	9	10	10	11	11	12	13	14	♑15
♀	♏27	29	♐0	1	2	3	5	6	7	8	9	11	12	13	14	15	17	18	19	20	21	23	24	25	26	27	29	♑0	1	2	♑3
♂	♊5	5	5	5	5	5	5	5	5	5	5	5	5	5	5	5	5	5	5	5	6	6	6	6	6	6	7	7	7	7	♊7

	1	6	12	18	24	30		1	6	12	18	24	30		1	15	30		1	15	30		1	15	30		1	15	30
♃	♌27	26	26	25	24	24	♄	♊22	21	21	21	20	20	♅	♊6	5	5	♆	♎4	4	4	♇	♌8	8	8	☊	♌7	7	7

FEBRUARY

	1	2	3	4	5	6	7	8	9	10	11	12	13	14	15	16	17	18	19	20	21	22	23	24	25	26	27	28	29
☉	♒11	12	13	14	15	16	17	18	19	20	21	22	23	24	25	26	27	28	29	♓0	1	2	3	4	5	6	7	8	♓9
☽	♉7	21	♊4	16	29	♋11	23	♌5	17	28	♍10	22	♎4	16	28	♏11	23	♐6	20	♑4	18	♒3	18	♓3	18	♈3	18	♉3	♉17
☿	♑16	17	18	19	20	21	23	24	25	27	28	29	♒1	2	3	5	6	8	9	11	12	14	15	17	18	20	22	23	♒25
♀	♑5	6	7	8	10	11	12	13	14	16	17	18	19	21	22	23	24	25	27	28	29	♒0	2	3	4	5	7	8	♒9
♂	♊8	8	8	8	9	9	9	9	10	10	10	11	11	11	12	12	12	13	13	13	14	14	15	15	15	16	16	17	♊17

	1	6	12	18	24	29		1	6	12	18	24	29		1	15	29		1	15	29		1	15	29		1	15	29
♃	♌24	23	22	21	21	20	♄	♊20	20	20	20	20	20	♅	♊5	5	5	♆	♎4	4	4	♇	♌8	7	7	☊	♌7	7	6

MARCH

	1	2	3	4	5	6	7	8	9	10	11	12	13	14	15	16	17	18	19	20	21	22	23	24	25	26	27	28	29	30	31
☉	♓10	11	12	13	14	15	16	17	18	19	20	21	22	23	24	25	26	27	28	29	♈0	1	2	3	4	5	6	7	8	9	♈10
☽	♊0	13	26	♋8	20	♌2	14	25	♍7	19	♎1	13	25	♏8	20	♐3	16	29	♑13	27	♒12	26	♓11	26	♈11	26	♉11	25	♊8	22	♋4
☿	♒26	28	♓0	2	3	5	7	9	10	12	14	16	18	20	22	23	25	27	29	♈1	3	5	7	9	11	13	15	17	19	21	♈23
♀	♒10	11	13	14	15	16	18	19	20	21	22	24	25	26	27	29	♓0	1	2	4	5	6	7	8	10	11	12	13	15	16	♓17
♂	♊17	18	18	19	19	19	20	20	21	21	22	22	23	23	24	24	24	25	25	26	26	27	27	28	28	29	29	♋0	0	1	♋1

	1	6	12	18	24	30		1	6	12	18	24	30		1	15	30		1	15	30		1	15	30		1	15	30
♃	♌20	19	19	18	18	17	♄	♊20	20	20	20	21	21	♅	♊5	5	6	♆	♎3	3	3	♇	♌7	7	6	☊	♌6	5	4

APRIL

	1	2	3	4	5	6	7	8	9	10	11	12	13	14	15	16	17	18	19	20	21	22	23	24	25	26	27	28	29	30
☉	♈11	12	13	14	15	16	17	18	19	20	21	22	23	24	25	26	27	28	29	♉0	1	2	3	4	5	6	7	8	9	♉10
☽	♋16	29	♌10	22	♍4	16	28	♎10	22	♏5	17	♐0	13	26	♑10	23	♒7	21	♓6	20	♈5	20	♉5	19	♊3	16	♋0	12	25	♌7
☿	♈25	27	29	♉0	2	4	5	7	8	9	10	11	12	13	14	15	15	16	16	16	16	16	16	16	16	16	15	15	14	♉14
♀	♓18	20	21	22	23	24	26	27	28	29	♈1	2	3	4	6	7	8	9	10	12	13	14	15	17	18	19	20	22	23	♈24
♂	♋2	2	3	3	4	4	5	5	6	6	7	8	8	9	9	10	10	11	11	12	12	13	13	14	14	15	16	16	17	♋17

	1	6	12	18	24	30		1	6	12	18	24	30		1	15	30		1	15	30		1	15	30		1	15	30
♃	♌17	17	17	17	17	17	♄	♊21	22	22	23	23	24	♅	♊6	6	7	♆	♎3	2	2	♇	♌6	6	6	☊	♌4	3	1

MAY

	1	2	3	4	5	6	7	8	9	10	11	12	13	14	15	16	17	18	19	20	21	22	23	24	25	26	27	28	29	30	31
☉	♉10	11	12	13	14	15	16	17	18	19	20	21	22	23	24	25	26	27	28	29	♊0	1	2	3	4	5	6	7	7	8	♊9
☽	♌19	♍0	12	24	♎6	18	♏1	14	26	♐10	23	♑6	20	♒4	18	♓2	16	♈1	15	29	♉13	27	♊11	25	♋8	20	♌3	15	27	♍8	♍20
☿	♉13	13	12	11	11	10	10	9	8	8	8	7	7	7	7	7	7	7	7	7	8	8	9	9	10	11	11	12	13	14	♉15
♀	♈25	26	28	29	♉0	1	3	4	5	6	7	9	10	11	12	14	15	16	17	19	20	21	22	23	25	26	27	28	♊0	1	♊2
♂	♋18	18	19	19	20	21	21	22	22	23	23	24	25	25	26	26	27	27	28	29	29	♌0	0	1	1	2	3	3	4	4	♌5

	1	6	12	18	24	30		1	6	12	18	24	30		1	15	30		1	15	30		1	15	30		1	15	30
♃	♌18	18	18	19	19	20	♄	♊24	24	25	26	27	27	♅	♊7	8	9	♆	♎2	2	2	♇	♌6	7	7	☊	♌1	0	♋0

JUNE

	1	2	3	4	5	6	7	8	9	10	11	12	13	14	15	16	17	18	19	20	21	22	23	24	25	26	27	28	29	30
☉	♊10	11	12	13	14	15	16	17	18	19	20	21	22	23	24	25	26	27	28	29	29	♋0	1	2	3	4	5	6	7	♋8
☽	♎2	14	27	♏9	22	♐5	19	♑2	16	♒0	15	29	♓13	27	♈11	25	♉9	23	♊7	20	♋3	16	28	♌10	23	♍4	16	28	♎10	♎22
☿	♉16	17	18	19	21	22	23	25	26	28	29	♊1	2	4	6	8	9	11	13	15	17	19	21	23	25	28	♋0	2	4	♋6
♀	♊3	4	6	7	8	9	11	12	13	14	16	17	18	19	20	22	23	24	25	27	28	29	♋0	1	3	4	5	6	8	♋9
♂	♌5	6	7	7	8	8	9	10	10	11	11	12	12	13	14	14	15	15	16	17	17	18	18	19	20	20	21	21	22	♌23

	1	6	12	18	24	30		1	6	12	18	24	30		1	15	30		1	15	30		1	15	30		1	15	30
♃	♌20	21	22	23	24	25	♄	♊28	28	29	♋0	0	1	♅	♊9	10	11	♆	♎1	1	2	♇	♌7	7	7	☊	♋29	28	28

JULY

	1	2	3	4	5	6	7	8	9	10	11	12	13	14	15	16	17	18	19	20	21	22	23	24	25	26	27	28	29	30	31
☉	♋9	10	11	12	13	14	15	16	17	18	19	20	20	21	22	23	24	25	26	27	28	29	♌0	1	2	3	4	5	6	7	♌8
☽	♏5	17	♐0	14	27	♑11	26	♒10	25	♓9	24	♈8	22	♉6	20	♊3	16	29	♋12	24	♌7	19	♍1	13	25	♎6	18	♏0	13	25	♐8
☿	♋8	11	13	15	17	19	21	23	25	27	29	♌1	3	5	7	9	11	12	14	16	18	19	21	23	24	26	27	29	♍0	1	♍3
♀	♋10	11	13	14	15	16	17	19	20	21	22	24	25	26	27	29	♌0	1	2	3	5	6	7	8	10	11	12	13	15	16	♌17
♂	♌23	24	24	25	26	26	27	27	28	29	29	♍0	1	1	2	2	3	4	4	5	5	6	7	7	8	9	9	10	10	11	♍12

	1	6	12	18	24	30		1	6	12	18	24	30		1	15	30		1	15	30		1	15	30		1	15	30
♃	♌25	26	27	28	♍0	1	♄	♋1	2	3	4	4	5	♅	♊11	11	12	♆	♎2	2	2	♇	♌7	8	8	☊	♋28	28	28

AUGUST

	1	2	3	4	5	6	7	8	9	10	11	12	13	14	15	16	17	18	19	20	21	22	23	24	25	26	27	28	29	30	31
☉	♌9	10	11	11	12	13	14	15	16	17	18	19	20	21	22	23	24	25	26	27	28	29	♍0	1	2	3	4	5	6	6	♍7
☽	♐22	♑5	20	♒4	19	♓4	19	♈4	18	♉3	17	♊0	13	26	♋9	21	♌3	16	28	♍9	21	♎3	15	27	♏9	21	♐4	17	♑0	14	♑28
☿	♍4	5	7	8	9	10	11	13	14	15	16	16	17	18	19	20	20	21	21	22	22	22	22	22	22	22	22	22	21	21	♍20
♀	♌18	19	21	22	23	24	26	27	28	29	♍1	2	3	4	5	7	8	9	10	12	13	14	15	17	18	19	20	22	23	24	♍25
♂	♍12	13	14	14	15	15	16	17	17	18	19	19	20	20	21	22	22	23	24	24	25	26	26	27	27	28	29	29	♎0	1	♎1

	1	6	12	18	24	30		1	6	12	18	24	30		1	15	30		1	15	30		1	15	30		1	15	30
♃	♍1	2	4	5	6	7	♄	♋5	6	6	7	8	8	♅	♊12	13	13	♆	♎2	2	3	♇	♌8	9	9	☊	♋28	28	27

SEPTEMBER

	1	2	3	4	5	6	7	8	9	10	11	12	13	14	15	16	17	18	19	20	21	22	23	24	25	26	27	28	29	30
☉	♍8	9	10	11	12	13	14	15	16	17	18	19	20	21	22	23	24	25	26	27	28	29	♎0	1	2	3	4	5	6	♎7
☽	♒12	27	♓13	28	♈13	28	♉12	26	♊10	23	♋6	18	♌1	13	25	♍6	18	♎0	12	24	♏6	18	♐0	13	26	♑9	22	♒6	21	♓6
☿	♍20	19	18	17	16	15	14	13	12	11	11	10	9	9	9	9	9	9	9	10	10	11	12	13	14	15	17	18	20	♍21
♀	♍26	28	29	♎0	1	3	4	5	6	8	9	10	11	12	14	15	16	17	19	20	21	22	24	25	26	27	28	♏0	1	♏2
♂	♎2	3	3	4	5	5	6	6	7	8	8	9	10	10	11	12	12	13	14	14	15	16	16	17	18	18	19	20	20	♎21

	1	6	12	18	24	30		1	6	12	18	24	30		1	15	30		1	15	30		1	15	30		1	15	30
♃	♍8	9	10	12	13	14	♄	♋8	9	9	10	10	10	♅	♊13	13	13	♆	♎3	4	4	♇	♌9	10	10	☊	♋27	26	25

OCTOBER

	1	2	3	4	5	6	7	8	9	10	11	12	13	14	15	16	17	18	19	20	21	22	23	24	25	26	27	28	29	30	31
☉	♎8	9	10	11	12	13	14	15	16	17	18	19	20	21	22	23	23	24	25	26	27	28	29	♏0	1	2	3	4	5	6	♏7
☽	♓21	♈6	21	♉6	21	♊5	19	♋2	15	27	♌10	22	♍3	15	27	♎9	21	♏3	15	27	♐10	23	♑5	19	♒2	16	♓0	15	29	♈14	♉0
☿	♍23	25	26	28	♎0	2	3	5	7	9	10	12	14	16	17	19	21	22	24	26	28	29	♏1	3	4	6	7	9	11	12	♏14
♀	♏3	5	6	7	8	10	11	12	13	14	16	17	18	19	21	22	23	24	25	27	28	29	♐0	2	3	4	5	6	8	9	♐10
♂	♎22	22	23	24	24	25	26	26	27	28	28	29	♏0	0	1	2	2	3	4	4	5	6	6	7	8	9	9	10	11	11	♏12

	1	6	12	18	24	30		1	6	12	18	24	30		1	15	30		1	15	30		1	15	30		1	15	30
♃	♍14	15	17	18	19	20	♄	♋10	11	11	11	11	11	♅	♊13	13	12	♆	♎4	5	5	♇	♌10	10	10	☊	♋25	23	22

NOVEMBER

	1	2	3	4	5	6	7	8	9	10	11	12	13	14	15	16	17	18	19	20	21	22	23	24	25	26	27	28	29	30
☉	♏8	9	10	11	12	13	14	15	16	17	18	19	20	21	23	24	25	26	27	28	29	♐0	1	2	3	4	5	6	7	♐8
☽	♉14	29	♊13	27	♋10	23	♌6	18	♍0	12	24	♎6	18	♏0	12	24	♐7	20	♑3	16	29	♒13	26	♓10	25	♈9	24	♉8	23	♊7
☿	♏15	17	19	20	22	23	25	26	28	29	♐1	2	4	5	7	8	10	11	13	14	16	17	18	20	21	23	24	25	27	♐28
♀	♐11	13	14	15	16	17	19	20	21	22	24	25	26	27	28	♑0	1	2	3	4	6	7	8	9	11	12	13	14	15	♑17
♂	♏13	13	14	15	15	16	17	18	18	19	20	20	21	22	22	23	24	25	25	26	27	27	28	29	♐0	0	1	2	2	♐3

	1	6	12	18	24	30		1	6	12	18	24	30		1	15	30		1	15	30		1	15	30		1	15	30
♃	♍20	21	22	23	24	25	♄	♋11	11	10	10	10	10	♅	♊12	12	11	♆	♎5	6	6	♇	♌10	10	10	☊	♋21	20	19

DECEMBER

	1	2	3	4	5	6	7	8	9	10	11	12	13	14	15	16	17	18	19	20	21	22	23	24	25	26	27	28	29	30	31
☉	♐9	10	11	12	13	14	15	16	17	18	19	20	21	22	23	24	25	26	27	28	29	♑0	1	2	3	4	5	6	7	8	♑9
☽	♊21	♋5	18	♌1	14	26	♍8	20	♎2	14	26	♏8	20	♐3	16	29	♑12	26	♒9	23	♓7	21	♈5	20	♉4	18	♊2	16	♋0	13	♋26
☿	♐29	♑0	2	3	4	5	6	7	7	8	8	9	9	9	9	8	8	7	6	5	4	3	1	0	♐29	27	26	25	24	24	♐23
♀	♑18	19	20	21	23	24	25	26	27	29	♒0	1	2	3	5	6	7	8	9	10	12	13	14	15	16	18	19	20	21	22	♒23
♂	♐4	5	5	6	7	7	8	9	10	10	11	12	12	13	14	15	15	16	17	18	18	19	20	21	21	22	23	23	24	25	♐26

	1	6	12	18	24	30		1	6	12	18	24	30		1	15	30		1	15	30		1	15	30		1	15	30
♃	♍25	25	26	27	27	27	♄	♋9	9	9	8	8	7	♅	♊11	11	10	♆	♎6	6	6	♇	♌10	10	10	☊	♋19	19	18

1945

JANUARY

	1	2	3	4	5	6	7	8	9	10	11	12	13	14	15	16	17	18	19	20	21	22	23	24	25	26	27	28	29	30	31
☉	♑10	11	12	13	14	15	16	17	18	19	20	21	22	23	24	26	27	28	29	♒0	1	2	3	4	5	6	7	8	9	10	♒11
☽	♌9	21	♍4	16	28	♎10	21	♏3	16	28	♐11	24	♑7	21	♒5	19	♓3	18	♈2	17	♉1	15	29	♊12	26	♋9	22	♌4	17	29	♍12
☿	♐23	23	23	23	23	23	24	25	25	26	27	28	29	♑0	1	2	3	4	6	7	8	9	11	12	13	15	16	18	19	20	♑22
♀	♒24	26	27	28	29	♓0	1	3	4	5	6	7	8	9	10	11	13	14	15	16	17	18	19	20	21	22	23	24	26	27	♓28
♂	♐26	27	28	29	29	♑0	1	2	2	3	4	5	5	6	7	8	8	9	10	11	11	12	13	14	14	15	16	17	17	18	♑19

	1	6	12	18	24	30
♃	♍27	27	27	27	27	27
♄	♋7	7	6	6	5	5

	1	15	30
♅	♊10	10	9
♆	♎6	6	6
♇	♌10	9	9
☊	♋18	18	18

FEBRUARY

	1	2	3	4	5	6	7	8	9	10	11	12	13	14	15	16	17	18	19	20	21	22	23	24	25	26	27	28
☉	♒12	13	14	15	16	17	18	19	20	21	22	23	24	25	26	27	28	29	♓0	1	2	3	4	5	6	7	8	♓9
☽	♍24	♎6	17	29	♏11	23	♐6	18	♑1	15	29	♒13	28	♓12	27	♈12	27	♉11	25	♊9	22	♋6	18	♌1	14	26	♍8	♍20
☿	♑23	25	26	28	29	♒1	2	4	6	7	9	10	12	14	15	17	19	20	22	24	26	27	29	♓1	3	5	6	♓8
♀	♓29	♈0	1	2	3	4	5	6	7	8	9	9	10	11	12	13	14	15	16	17	17	18	19	20	21	21	22	♈23
♂	♑20	20	21	22	23	24	24	25	26	27	27	28	29	♒0	0	1	2	3	4	4	5	6	7	7	8	9	10	♒10

	1	6	12	18	24	28
♃	♍27	27	26	25	25	24
♄	♋5	5	4	4	4	4

	1	15	28
♅	♊9	9	9
♆	♎6	6	6
♇	♌9	9	8
☊	♋18	18	17

MARCH

	1	2	3	4	5	6	7	8	9	10	11	12	13	14	15	16	17	18	19	20	21	22	23	24	25	26	27	28	29	30	31
☉	♓10	11	12	13	14	15	16	17	18	19	20	21	22	23	24	25	26	27	28	29	♈0	1	2	3	4	5	6	7	8	9	♈10
☽	♎2	14	26	♏8	20	♐2	14	26	♑9	23	♒7	21	♓6	21	♈6	21	♉6	21	♊5	19	♋2	15	28	♌11	23	♍5	17	29	♎11	23	♏5
☿	♓10	12	14	16	18	20	22	24	26	28	29	♈1	3	5	7	9	11	12	14	16	17	19	20	21	23	24	25	25	26	27	♈27
♀	♈24	24	25	26	26	27	28	28	29	29	♉0	0	1	1	2	2	2	3	3	3	3	3	3	4	4	4	4	3	3	3	♉3
♂	♒11	12	13	14	14	15	16	17	17	18	19	20	21	21	22	23	24	24	25	26	27	28	28	29	♓0	1	1	2	3	4	♓5

	1	6	12	18	24	30
♃	♍24	24	23	22	21	20
♄	♋4	4	4	4	4	4

	1	15	30
♅	♊9	9	10
♆	♎6	5	5
♇	♌8	8	8
☊	♋17	16	14

APRIL

	1	2	3	4	5	6	7	8	9	10	11	12	13	14	15	16	17	18	19	20	21	22	23	24	25	26	27	28	29	30
☉	♈11	12	13	14	15	16	17	18	19	20	21	22	23	24	25	26	27	28	29	♉0	1	1	2	3	4	5	6	7	8	♉9
☽	♏16	28	♐11	23	♑5	18	♒1	15	29	♓14	29	♈14	♉0	15	♊0	14	28	♋12	25	♌7	20	♍2	14	26	♎8	20	♏2	13	26	♐8
☿	♈28	28	28	28	28	28	27	27	26	26	25	24	24	23	22	22	21	20	19	19	18	18	18	17	17	17	17	17	17	♈17
♀	♉3	2	2	2	1	1	0	0	♈29	29	28	28	27	26	26	25	25	24	23	23	22	22	21	20	20	20	19	19	18	♈18
♂	♓5	6	7	8	8	9	10	11	12	12	13	14	15	15	16	17	18	19	19	20	21	22	22	23	24	25	25	26	27	♓28

	1	6	12	18	24	30
♃	♍20	20	19	19	18	18
♄	♋4	5	5	5	6	6

	1	15	30
♅	♊10	11	11
♆	♎5	5	4
♇	♌8	8	8
☊	♋14	12	11

MAY

	1	2	3	4	5	6	7	8	9	10	11	12	13	14	15	16	17	18	19	20	21	22	23	24	25	26	27	28	29	30	31
☉	♉10	11	12	13	14	15	16	17	18	19	20	21	22	23	24	25	26	27	28	29	♊0	1	1	2	3	4	5	6	7	8	♊9
☽	♐20	♑2	15	28	♒11	25	♓9	23	♈8	23	♉8	23	♊8	22	♋6	20	♌3	16	28	♍11	23	♎5	16	28	♏10	22	♐4	17	29	♑12	♑25
☿	♈17	18	18	19	19	20	21	21	22	23	24	25	26	27	28	29	♉0	2	3	4	6	7	9	10	12	13	15	16	18	20	♉22
♀	♈18	18	17	17	17	17	17	17	17	17	18	18	18	18	18	19	19	19	20	20	21	21	22	22	23	23	24	25	25	26	♈26
♂	♓29	29	♈0	1	2	2	3	4	5	5	6	7	8	9	9	10	11	12	12	13	14	15	15	16	17	18	18	19	20	21	♈21

	1	6	12	18	24	30
♃	♍18	18	18	18	18	18
♄	♋7	7	8	8	9	10

	1	15	30
♅	♊11	12	13
♆	♎4	4	4
♇	♌8	8	8
☊	♋11	10	9

JUNE

	1	2	3	4	5	6	7	8	9	10	11	12	13	14	15	16	17	18	19	20	21	22	23	24	25	26	27	28	29	30
☉	♊10	11	12	13	14	15	16	17	18	19	20	21	22	23	24	24	25	26	27	28	29	♋0	1	2	3	4	5	6	7	♋8
☽	♒8	21	♓5	19	♈3	18	♉2	17	♊2	16	♋1	15	28	♌11	24	♍7	19	♎1	13	25	♏7	19	♐1	13	26	♑8	21	♒5	18	♓2
☿	♉23	25	27	29	♊1	3	5	7	9	11	14	16	18	20	22	24	27	29	♋1	3	5	7	10	12	14	16	18	20	22	♋23
♀	♈27	28	29	29	♉0	1	2	2	3	4	5	6	6	7	8	9	10	11	12	13	14	15	15	16	17	18	19	20	21	♉22
♂	♈22	23	24	24	25	26	27	27	28	29	♉0	0	1	2	3	3	4	5	6	6	7	8	8	9	10	11	11	12	13	♉14

	1	6	12	18	24	30
♃	♍18	18	19	19	20	21
♄	♋10	10	11	12	13	13

	1	15	30
♅	♊13	14	15
♆	♎4	4	4
♇	♌8	9	9
☊	♋9	9	9

JULY

	1	2	3	4	5	6	7	8	9	10	11	12	13	14	15	16	17	18	19	20	21	22	23	24	25	26	27	28	29	30	31
☉	♋9	10	11	12	13	14	15	15	16	17	18	19	20	21	22	23	24	25	26	27	28	29	♌0	1	2	3	4	5	6	6	♌7
☽	♓16	♈0	14	28	♉12	27	♊11	25	♋9	23	♌6	19	♍2	15	27	♎9	21	♏3	15	27	♐9	21	♑4	17	♒0	14	28	♓12	26	♈11	♈25
☿	♋25	27	29	♌1	2	4	6	7	9	10	12	13	15	16	17	19	20	21	22	24	25	26	27	28	29	29	♍0	1	2	2	♍3
♀	♉23	24	25	26	27	28	29	♊0	1	2	3	4	6	7	8	9	10	11	12	13	14	15	16	17	18	20	21	22	23	24	♊25
♂	♉14	15	16	16	17	18	19	19	20	21	21	22	23	23	24	25	26	26	27	28	28	29	♊0	0	1	2	2	3	4	5	♊5

	1	6	12	18	24	30
♃	♍21	21	22	23	24	25
♄	♋14	14	15	16	17	17

	1	15	30
♅	♊15	16	16
♆	♎4	4	4
♇	♌9	9	10
☊	♋9	9	9

AUGUST

	1	2	3	4	5	6	7	8	9	10	11	12	13	14	15	16	17	18	19	20	21	22	23	24	25	26	27	28	29	30	31
☉	♌8	9	10	11	12	13	14	15	16	17	18	19	20	21	22	23	24	25	26	27	28	29	29	♍0	1	2	3	4	5	6	♍7
☽	♉9	23	♊7	21	♋5	18	♌2	15	28	♍10	23	♎5	17	29	♏11	23	♐5	17	29	♑12	25	♒9	23	♓7	22	♈6	21	♉6	20	♊4	♊18
☿	♍3	4	4	4	5	5	5	5	5	4	4	4	3	2	2	1	0	♌29	29	28	27	26	25	24	24	23	23	22	22	22	♌22
♀	♊26	27	28	29	♋1	2	3	4	5	6	7	9	10	11	12	13	14	15	17	18	19	20	21	22	24	25	26	27	28	29	♌1
♂	♊6	7	7	8	9	9	10	11	11	12	13	13	14	14	15	16	16	17	18	18	19	20	20	21	22	22	23	23	24	25	♊25

	1	6	12	18	24	30
♃	♍25	26	27	29	♎0	1
♄	♋18	18	19	20	20	21

	1	15	30
♅	♊16	17	17
♆	♎4	5	5
♇	♌10	10	11
☊	♋9	8	7

SEPTEMBER

	1	2	3	4	5	6	7	8	9	10	11	12	13	14	15	16	17	18	19	20	21	22	23	24	25	26	27	28	29	30
☉	♍8	9	10	11	12	13	14	15	16	17	18	19	20	21	22	23	24	25	26	27	28	29	♎0	1	2	3	4	4	5	♎6
☽	♋2	15	28	♌11	24	♍6	19	♎1	13	25	♏7	19	♐1	13	25	♑7	20	♒3	17	♓1	16	♈1	16	♉1	16	♊0	15	28	♋12	♋25
☿	♌22	22	23	23	24	25	26	27	28	♍0	1	2	4	6	7	9	11	13	14	16	18	20	22	24	25	27	29	♎1	3	♎5
♀	♌2	3	4	5	6	8	9	10	11	12	14	15	16	17	18	20	21	22	23	24	26	27	28	29	♍0	2	3	4	5	♍6
♂	♊26	26	27	28	28	29	29	♋0	1	1	2	2	3	4	4	5	5	6	6	7	8	8	9	9	10	10	11	11	12	♋12

	1	6	12	18	24	30
♃	♎1	2	4	5	6	8
♄	♋21	22	22	23	23	24

	1	15	30
♅	♊17	17	17
♆	♎5	6	6
♇	♌11	11	11
☊	♋7	6	5

OCTOBER

	1	2	3	4	5	6	7	8	9	10	11	12	13	14	15	16	17	18	19	20	21	22	23	24	25	26	27	28	29	30	31
☉	♎7	8	9	10	11	12	13	14	15	16	17	18	19	20	21	22	23	24	25	26	27	28	29	♏0	1	2	3	4	5	6	♏7
☽	♌8	21	♍3	16	28	♎10	22	♏4	16	27	♐9	21	♑3	16	28	♒11	25	♓9	24	♈9	24	♉9	24	♊9	24	♋8	22	♌5	18	♍0	♍13
☿	♎6	8	10	12	13	15	17	18	20	22	23	25	27	28	♏0	2	3	5	6	8	9	11	12	14	16	17	18	20	21	23	♏24
♀	♍8	9	10	11	13	14	15	16	17	19	20	21	22	24	25	26	27	29	♎0	1	2	3	5	6	7	8	10	11	12	13	♎15
♂	♋13	13	14	14	15	15	16	16	17	17	18	18	19	19	20	20	21	21	22	22	22	23	23	24	24	24	25	25	26	26	♋26

	1	6	12	18	24	30
♃	♎8	9	10	11	13	14
♄	♋24	24	24	25	25	25

	1	15	30
♅	♊17	17	17
♆	♎6	7	7
♇	♌11	12	12
☊	♋5	3	2

NOVEMBER

	1	2	3	4	5	6	7	8	9	10	11	12	13	14	15	16	17	18	19	20	21	22	23	24	25	26	27	28	29	30
☉	♏8	9	10	11	12	13	14	15	16	17	18	19	20	21	22	23	24	25	26	27	28	29	♐0	1	2	3	4	5	6	♐7
☽	♍25	♎7	19	♏1	13	24	♐6	18	♑0	12	25	♒7	20	♓4	18	♈2	17	♉2	17	♊3	18	♋2	17	♌0	14	27	♍9	22	♎4	♎16
☿	♏26	27	29	♐0	1	3	4	6	7	8	9	11	12	13	14	15	17	18	19	19	20	21	22	22	23	23	23	23	23	♐23
♀	♎16	17	18	20	21	22	23	25	26	27	28	♏0	1	2	3	5	6	7	8	10	11	12	13	15	16	17	18	20	21	♏22
♂	♋27	27	27	28	28	28	29	29	29	29	♌0	0	0	1	1	1	1	1	2	2	2	2	2	2	3	3	3	3	3	♌3

	1	6	12	18	24	30
♃	♎14	15	17	18	19	20
♄	♋25	25	25	25	25	24

	1	15	30
♅	♊17	16	16
♆	♎7	8	8
♇	♌12	12	12
☊	♋2	1	0

DECEMBER

	1	2	3	4	5	6	7	8	9	10	11	12	13	14	15	16	17	18	19	20	21	22	23	24	25	26	27	28	29	30	31
☉	♐8	9	10	11	12	14	15	16	17	18	19	20	21	22	23	24	25	26	27	28	29	♑0	1	2	3	4	5	6	7	8	♑9
☽	♎28	♏9	21	♐3	15	27	♑9	22	♒4	17	♓0	14	28	♈12	26	♉11	26	♊11	25	♋10	24	♌8	22	♍5	18	♎0	12	24	♏6	18	♐0
☿	♐22	21	20	19	18	17	16	14	13	12	10	9	8	8	7	7	7	7	7	7	8	8	9	10	11	12	13	14	15	16	♐17
♀	♏23	25	26	27	28	♐0	1	2	3	5	6	7	9	10	11	12	14	15	16	17	19	20	21	22	24	25	26	27	29	♑0	♑1
♂	♌3	3	3	3	3	3	3	3	3	3	3	3	3	3	3	2	2	2	2	2	1	1	1	1	0	0	0	0	♋29	29	♋29

	1	6	12	18	24	30
♃	♎20	21	22	23	24	25
♄	♋24	24	24	23	23	23

	1	15	30
♅	♊16	15	15
♆	♎8	8	9
♇	♌12	12	11
☊	♋0	0	0

1946

JANUARY

	1	2	3	4	5	6	7	8	9	10	11	12	13	14	15	16	17	18	19	20	21	22	23	24	25	26	27	28	29	30	31
☉	♑10	11	12	13	14	15	16	17	18	19	20	21	22	23	24	25	26	27	28	29	♒0	1	2	3	4	5	6	7	8	9	♒11
☽	♐12	24	♑6	19	♒1	14	27	♓11	24	♈8	22	♉6	21	♊5	19	♋4	18	♌2	16	♍0	13	26	♎8	20	♏2	14	26	♐8	20	♑2	♑14
☿	♐18	20	21	22	24	25	26	28	29	♑1	2	3	5	6	8	9	11	12	14	15	17	18	20	22	23	25	26	28	♒0	1	♒3
♀	♑2	4	5	6	7	9	10	11	12	14	15	16	18	19	20	21	23	24	25	26	28	29	♒0	1	3	4	5	6	8	9	♒10
♂	♋28	28	28	27	27	26	26	26	25	25	24	24	24	23	23	22	22	22	21	21	21	20	20	19	19	19	18	18	18	18	♋17

	1	6	12	18	24	30
♃	♎25	25	26	26	27	27
♄	♋22	22	21	21	20	20

	1	15	30
♅	♊14	14	14
♆	♎9	9	9
♇	♌11	11	11
☊	♋0	0	♊0

FEBRUARY

	1	2	3	4	5	6	7	8	9	10	11	12	13	14	15	16	17	18	19	20	21	22	23	24	25	26	27	28
☉	♒12	13	14	15	16	17	18	19	20	21	22	23	24	25	26	27	28	29	♓0	1	2	3	4	5	6	7	8	♓9
☽	♑27	♒10	23	♓7	21	♈5	19	♉3	17	♊1	15	29	♋13	27	♌11	24	♍8	21	♎3	16	28	♏10	22	♐4	15	27	♑10	♑22
☿	♒4	6	8	9	11	13	15	16	18	20	22	23	25	27	29	♓1	2	4	6	8	10	12	14	16	17	19	21	♓23
♀	♒11	13	14	15	16	18	19	20	21	23	24	25	26	28	29	♓0	1	3	4	5	6	8	9	10	11	13	14	♓15
♂	♋17	17	16	16	16	16	16	15	15	15	15	15	15	15	14	14	14	14	14	14	14	14	14	14	14	14	14	♋14

	1	6	12	18	24	28
♃	♎27	27	27	27	27	27
♄	♋20	20	19	19	18	18

	1	15	28
♅	♊14	13	13
♆	♎8	8	8
♇	♌11	10	10
☊	♊29	•29	27

MARCH

	1	2	3	4	5	6	7	8	9	10	11	12	13	14	15	16	17	18	19	20	21	22	23	24	25	26	27	28	29	30	31
☉	♓10	11	12	13	14	15	16	17	18	19	20	21	22	23	24	25	26	27	28	29	♈0	1	2	3	4	5	6	7	8	9	♈10
☽	♒5	18	♓2	16	♈0	15	29	♉14	28	♊12	26	♋10	24	♌7	20	♍4	16	29	♎12	24	♏6	18	♐0	12	23	♑5	18	♒0	13	26	♓10
☿	♓25	26	28	29	♈1	2	4	5	6	7	8	9	9	10	10	10	10	10	10	10	9	8	8	7	6	5	5	4	3	2	♈1
♀	♓16	18	19	20	21	23	24	25	26	28	29	♈0	1	3	4	5	6	8	9	10	11	13	14	15	16	18	19	20	21	23	♈24
♂	♋14	15	15	15	15	15	15	15	15	16	16	16	16	16	17	17	17	17	18	18	18	18	19	19	19	19	20	20	20	21	♋21

	1	6	12	18	24	30
♃	♎27	27	26	26	25	24
♄	♋18	18	18	18	18	18

	1	15	30
♅	♊13	14	14
♆	♎8	8	7
♇	♌10	10	10
☊	♊27	26	24

APRIL

	1	2	3	4	5	6	7	8	9	10	11	12	13	14	15	16	17	18	19	20	21	22	23	24	25	26	27	28	29	30
☉	♈11	12	13	14	15	16	17	18	19	20	21	21	22	23	24	25	26	27	28	29	♉0	1	2	3	4	5	6	7	8	♉9
☽	♓24	♈9	24	♉9	24	♊8	23	♋7	21	♌4	17	♍0	13	26	♎8	20	♏2	14	26	♐8	20	♑2	14	26	♒8	21	♓5	18	♈3	♈17
☿	♈1	0	♓29	29	28	28	28	28	28	28	28	28	28	29	29	♈0	0	1	2	2	3	4	5	6	7	8	9	10	12	♈13
♀	♈25	26	27	29	♉0	1	2	4	5	6	7	9	10	11	12	14	15	16	17	18	20	21	22	23	25	26	27	28	29	♊1
♂	♋21	22	22	22	23	23	24	24	24	25	25	25	26	26	27	27	28	28	28	29	29	♌0	0	1	1	1	2	2	3	♌3

	1	6	12	18	24	30
♃	♎24	23	23	22	21	20
♄	♋18	18	18	19	19	19

	1	15	30
♅	♊14	15	15
♆	♎7	7	6
♇	♌10	9	9
☊	♊24	22	22

MAY

	1	2	3	4	5	6	7	8	9	10	11	12	13	14	15	16	17	18	19	20	21	22	23	24	25	26	27	28	29	30	31
☉	♉10	11	12	13	14	15	16	17	18	19	20	21	22	23	24	25	25	26	27	28	29	♊0	1	2	3	4	5	6	7	8	♊9
☽	♉2	17	♊2	17	♋2	17	♌1	14	27	♍10	23	♎5	17	29	♏11	23	♐5	17	29	♑11	23	♒5	17	♓0	13	27	♈11	26	♉11	26	♊11
☿	♈14	16	17	18	20	21	23	24	26	27	29	♉1	2	4	6	8	10	11	13	15	17	19	21	23	25	27	♊0	2	4	6	♊8
♀	♊2	3	4	6	7	8	9	10	12	13	14	15	16	18	19	20	21	23	24	25	26	27	29	♋0	1	2	3	5	6	7	♋8
♂	♌4	4	5	5	6	6	7	7	8	8	8	9	9	10	10	11	11	12	13	13	14	14	15	15	16	16	17	17	18	18	♌19

	1	6	12	18	24	30
♃	♎20	20	19	19	18	18
♄	♋19	20	20	21	21	22

	1	15	30
♅	♊15	16	17
♆	♎6	6	6
♇	♌9	10	10
☊	♊21	21	21

JUNE

	1	2	3	4	5	6	7	8	9	10	11	12	13	14	15	16	17	18	19	20	21	22	23	24	25	26	27	28	29	30
☉	♊10	11	12	13	14	15	16	17	18	19	19	20	21	22	23	24	25	26	27	28	29	♋0	1	2	3	4	5	6	7	♋8
☽	♊26	♋11	25	♌10	23	♍7	20	♎2	14	26	♏8	20	♐2	14	26	♑8	20	♒2	14	27	♓10	23	♈7	21	♉5	19	♊4	19	♋4	♋19
☿	♊11	13	15	17	19	21	24	26	28	♋0	2	4	6	8	10	11	13	15	17	18	20	22	23	25	26	28	29	♌0	2	♌3
♀	♋9	11	12	13	14	15	17	18	19	20	21	23	24	25	26	27	29	♌0	1	2	3	4	6	7	8	9	10	12	13	♌14
♂	♌19	20	20	21	21	22	23	23	24	24	25	25	26	26	27	28	28	29	29	♍0	0	1	2	2	3	3	4	4	5	♍6

	1	6	12	18	24	30
♃	♎18	18	17	17	18	18
♄	♋22	23	24	24	25	26

	1	15	30
♅	♊17	18	19
♆	♎6	6	6
♇	♌10	10	10
☊	♊21	21	21

JULY

	1	2	3	4	5	6	7	8	9	10	11	12	13	14	15	16	17	18	19	20	21	22	23	24	25	26	27	28	29	30	31
☉	♋9	10	10	11	12	13	14	15	16	17	18	19	20	21	22	23	24	25	26	27	28	29	♌0	0	1	2	3	4	5	6	♌7
☽	♌4	18	♍2	15	28	♎11	23	♏5	17	29	♐11	22	♑4	17	29	♒11	24	♓7	20	♈3	17	♉1	15	29	♊14	28	♋13	28	♌12	26	♍10
☿	♌4	5	6	7	8	9	10	11	12	13	13	14	15	15	15	16	16	16	16	16	16	16	16	16	15	15	14	14	13	12	♌12
♀	♌15	16	17	19	20	21	22	23	24	26	27	28	29	♍0	1	3	4	5	6	7	8	9	11	12	13	14	15	16	17	18	♍20
♂	♍6	7	7	8	8	9	10	10	11	11	12	13	13	14	14	15	16	16	17	17	18	19	19	20	20	21	22	22	23	23	♍24

	1	6	12	18	24	30
♃	♎18	18	19	19	20	20
♄	♋26	26	27	28	29	♌0

	1	15	30
♅	♊19	20	20
♆	♎6	6	6
♇	♌10	11	11
☊	♊21	21	20

AUGUST

	1	2	3	4	5	6	7	8	9	10	11	12	13	14	15	16	17	18	19	20	21	22	23	24	25	26	27	28	29	30	31
☉	♌8	9	10	11	12	13	14	15	16	17	18	19	20	21	22	23	23	24	25	26	27	28	29	♍0	1	2	3	4	5	6	♍7
☽	♍23	♎6	19	♏1	13	25	♐7	19	♑1	13	25	♒8	20	♓3	17	♈0	14	28	♉12	26	♊10	24	♋8	23	♌7	21	♍5	18	♎1	14	♎27
☿	♌11	10	9	9	8	7	7	6	6	5	5	5	5	5	5	5	6	6	7	8	9	10	11	12	14	15	16	18	20	21	♌23
♀	♍21	22	23	24	25	26	27	29	♎0	1	2	3	4	5	6	7	8	9	10	12	13	14	15	16	17	18	19	20	21	22	♎23
♂	♍25	25	26	27	27	28	28	29	♎0	0	1	2	2	3	3	4	5	5	6	7	7	8	9	9	10	10	11	12	12	13	♎14

	1	6	12	18	24	30
♃	♎21	21	22	23	24	25
♄	♌0	0	1	2	3	3

	1	15	30
♅	♊20	21	21
♆	♎6	7	7
♇	♌11	12	12
☊	♊20	19	17

SEPTEMBER

	1	2	3	4	5	6	7	8	9	10	11	12	13	14	15	16	17	18	19	20	21	22	23	24	25	26	27	28	29	30
☉	♍8	9	10	11	12	13	14	15	16	17	18	19	20	21	22	23	23	24	25	26	27	28	29	♎0	1	2	3	4	5	♎6
☽	♏9	21	♐3	15	27	♑9	21	♒3	16	29	♓12	26	♈10	24	♉8	22	♊7	21	♋5	19	♌3	17	♍0	14	27	♎10	23	♏5	17	♏29
☿	♌25	27	29	♍1	3	4	6	8	10	12	14	16	18	20	22	23	25	27	29	♎1	2	4	6	8	9	11	13	14	16	♎18
♀	♎24	25	26	27	28	29	♏0	1	2	3	4	5	6	7	8	8	9	10	11	12	13	14	15	15	16	17	18	19	19	♏20
♂	♎14	15	16	16	17	18	18	19	20	20	21	22	22	23	24	24	25	26	26	27	28	28	29	♏0	0	1	2	2	3	♏4

	1	6	12	18	24	30
♃	♎25	26	27	29	♏0	1
♄	♌4	4	5	5	6	7

	1	15	30
♅	♊21	22	22
♆	♎7	8	8
♇	♌12	13	13
☊	♊17	16	14

OCTOBER

	1	2	3	4	5	6	7	8	9	10	11	12	13	14	15	16	17	18	19	20	21	22	23	24	25	26	27	28	29	30	31
☉	♎7	8	9	10	11	12	13	14	15	16	17	18	19	20	21	22	23	24	25	26	27	28	29	♏0	1	2	3	4	5	6	♏7
☽	♐11	23	♑5	17	29	♒11	24	♓7	21	♈5	19	♉3	18	♊3	17	♋2	16	♌0	13	27	♍10	23	♎6	19	♏1	13	25	♐7	19	♑1	♑13
☿	♎19	21	22	24	26	27	29	♏0	2	3	5	6	8	9	10	12	13	15	16	17	19	20	21	22	24	25	26	27	28	♐0	♐1
♀	♏21	22	22	23	24	24	25	26	26	27	27	28	28	29	29	♐0	0	1	1	1	2	2	2	2	2	2	2	2	2	2	♐2
♂	♏4	5	6	6	7	8	8	9	10	10	11	12	13	13	14	15	15	16	17	17	18	19	20	20	21	22	22	23	24	24	♏25

	1	6	12	18	24	30
♃	♏1	2	3	5	6	7
♄	♌7	7	7	8	8	8

	1	15	30
♅	♊22	22	21
♆	♎8	9	9
♇	♌13	13	13
☊	♊14	13	12

NOVEMBER

	1	2	3	4	5	6	7	8	9	10	11	12	13	14	15	16	17	18	19	20	21	22	23	24	25	26	27	28	29	30
☉	♏8	9	10	11	12	13	14	15	16	17	18	19	20	21	22	23	24	25	26	27	28	29	♐0	1	2	3	4	5	6	♐7
☽	♑25	♒7	19	♓2	15	29	♈13	27	♉12	27	♊12	27	♋11	26	♌10	24	♍7	20	♎3	16	28	♏10	22	♐4	16	28	♑9	21	♒3	♒15
☿	♐2	2	3	4	5	6	6	7	7	7	7	7	7	7	6	5	5	4	2	1	0	♏28	27	26	25	24	23	22	22	♏21
♀	♐2	2	2	2	1	1	1	0	0	♏29	29	28	28	27	27	26	25	25	24	24	23	22	22	21	21	20	20	19	19	♏19
♂	♏26	27	27	28	29	29	♐0	1	2	2	3	4	4	5	6	7	7	8	9	10	10	11	12	13	13	14	15	15	16	♐17

	1	6	12	18	24	30
♃	♏8	9	10	12	13	14
♄	♌9	9	9	9	9	9

	1	15	30
♅	♊21	21	20
♆	♎9	10	10
♇	♌13	13	13
☊	♊12	12	12

DECEMBER

	1	2	3	4	5	6	7	8	9	10	11	12	13	14	15	16	17	18	19	20	21	22	23	24	25	26	27	28	29	30	31
☉	♐8	9	10	11	12	13	14	15	16	17	18	19	20	21	22	23	24	25	26	27	29	♑0	1	2	3	4	5	6	7	8	♑9
☽	♒28	♓10	23	♈7	21	♉5	20	♊5	20	♋5	20	♌5	19	♍3	17	♎0	13	25	♏7	19	♐1	13	25	♑6	18	♒0	12	24	♓7	20	♈2
☿	♏21	21	21	22	22	23	24	25	26	27	28	29	♐0	1	2	4	5	6	8	9	11	12	14	15	16	18	19	21	22	24	♐25
♀	♏18	18	18	18	17	17	17	17	17	17	17	17	18	18	18	18	19	19	19	20	20	21	21	22	22	23	23	24	24	25	♏26
♂	♐18	18	19	20	21	21	22	23	24	24	25	26	27	27	28	29	♑0	0	1	2	3	3	4	5	6	6	7	8	9	10	♑10

	1	6	12	18	24	30
♃	♏14	15	17	18	19	20
♄	♌9	9	8	8	8	8

	1	15	30
♅	♊20	20	19
♆	♎10	11	11
♇	♌13	13	13
☊	♊12	12	11

1947

JANUARY

	1	2	3	4	5	6	7	8	9	10	11	12	13	14	15	16	17	18	19	20	21	22	23	24	25	26	27	28	29	30	31
☉	♑10	11	12	13	14	15	16	17	18	19	20	21	22	23	24	25	26	27	28	29	♒0	1	2	3	4	5	6	7	8	9	♒10
☽	♈16	29	♉13	28	♊13	28	♋13	28	♌13	28	♍12	26	♎9	22	♏4	16	28	♐10	22	♑3	15	27	♒9	22	♓4	17	29	♈12	26	♉9	♉23
☿	♐27	28	♑0	1	3	4	6	8	9	11	12	14	15	17	19	20	22	24	25	27	29	♒0	2	4	5	7	9	10	12	14	♒16
♀	♏27	27	28	29	29	♐0	1	2	3	4	4	5	6	7	8	9	10	11	12	13	13	14	15	16	17	18	19	20	21	22	♐23
♂	♑11	12	13	13	14	15	16	16	17	18	19	20	20	21	22	23	23	24	25	26	27	27	28	29	♒0	0	1	2	3	4	♒4

	1	6	12	18	24	30
♃	♏20	21	22	23	24	25
♄	♌7	7	7	6	6	5

	1	15	30
♅	♊19	18	18
♆	♎11	11	11
♇	♌13	13	12
☊	♊11	11	10

FEBRUARY

	1	2	3	4	5	6	7	8	9	10	11	12	13	14	15	16	17	18	19	20	21	22	23	24	25	26	27	28
☉	♒11	12	13	14	15	16	17	18	19	20	21	22	23	24	25	26	27	28	♓0	1	2	3	4	5	6	7	8	♓9
☽	♊7	22	♋6	21	♌6	21	♍6	20	♎4	17	♏0	12	24	♐6	18	♑0	12	24	♒6	18	♓1	13	26	♈9	23	♉6	20	♊4
☿	♒17	19	21	23	25	26	28	♓0	2	3	5	7	8	10	12	13	15	16	17	19	20	21	21	22	23	23	23	♓23
♀	♐24	26	27	28	29	♑0	1	2	3	4	5	6	7	8	9	11	12	13	14	15	16	17	18	20	21	22	23	♑24
♂	♒5	6	7	7	8	9	10	11	11	12	13	14	14	15	16	17	18	18	19	20	21	22	22	23	24	25	26	♒26

	1	6	12	18	24	28
♃	♏25	26	26	27	27	27
♄	♌5	5	4	4	3	3

	1	15	28
♅	♊18	18	18
♆	♎11	11	10
♇	♌12	12	12
☊	♊10	9	7

MARCH

	1	2	3	4	5	6	7	8	9	10	11	12	13	14	15	16	17	18	19	20	21	22	23	24	25	26	27	28	29	30	31
☉	♓10	11	12	13	14	15	16	17	18	19	20	21	22	23	24	25	26	27	28	29	♈0	1	2	3	4	4	5	6	7	8	♈9
☽	♊18	♋2	16	♌1	15	♍0	14	28	♎11	25	♏8	20	♐2	14	26	♑8	20	♒2	14	26	♓9	22	♈5	19	♉3	16	♊0	14	29	♋13	♋27
☿	♓23	23	22	22	21	20	19	18	17	16	15	14	14	13	12	11	11	10	10	9	9	9	9	9	10	10	10	11	11	12	♓12
♀	♑25	26	27	29	♒0	1	2	3	4	6	7	8	9	10	11	12	14	15	16	17	18	19	21	22	23	24	25	27	28	29	♓0
♂	♒27	28	29	29	♓0	1	2	3	3	4	5	6	7	7	8	9	10	10	11	12	13	14	14	15	16	17	18	18	19	20	♓21

	1	6	12	18	24	30
♃	♏27	27	28	28	27	27
♄	♌3	3	2	2	2	2

	1	15	30
♅	♊18	18	18
♆	♎10	10	9
♇	♌12	11	11
☊	♊7	5	4

APRIL

	1	2	3	4	5	6	7	8	9	10	11	12	13	14	15	16	17	18	19	20	21	22	23	24	25	26	27	28	29	30
☉	♈10	11	12	13	14	15	16	17	18	19	20	21	22	23	24	25	26	27	28	29	♉0	1	2	3	4	5	6	7	8	♉9
☽	♌11	25	♍9	23	♎6	20	♏3	15	28	♐10	22	♑4	16	28	♒10	22	♓4	17	♈0	14	28	♉12	26	♊11	25	♋9	24	♌8	22	♍6
☿	♓13	14	15	16	17	18	19	20	21	22	23	24	26	27	28	♈0	1	3	4	6	7	9	10	12	13	15	17	19	20	♈22
♀	♓1	2	4	5	6	7	8	10	11	12	13	14	16	17	18	19	20	21	23	24	25	26	27	29	♈0	1	2	3	5	♈6
♂	♓21	22	23	24	25	25	26	27	28	28	29	♈0	1	2	2	3	4	5	5	6	7	8	9	9	10	11	12	12	13	♈14

	1	6	12	18	24	30
♃	♏27	27	26	26	25	24
♄	♌2	2	2	2	2	3

	1	15	30
♅	♊18	19	19
♆	♎9	9	9
♇	♌11	11	11
☊	♊4	3	3

MAY

	1	2	3	4	5	6	7	8	9	10	11	12	13	14	15	16	17	18	19	20	21	22	23	24	25	26	27	28	29	30	31
☉	♉10	11	12	13	14	15	16	17	18	19	19	20	21	22	23	24	25	26	27	28	29	♊0	1	2	3	4	5	6	7	8	♊9
☽	♍19	♎3	16	29	♏11	24	♐6	18	♑0	12	24	♒6	18	♓0	12	25	♈8	22	♉6	20	♊5	20	♋5	19	♌4	18	♍2	16	♎0	13	♎25
☿	♈24	26	28	♉0	1	3	5	7	9	12	14	16	18	20	22	24	27	29	♊1	3	5	7	10	12	14	16	18	20	22	24	♊25
♀	♈7	8	9	11	12	13	14	15	17	18	19	20	21	23	24	25	26	27	29	♉0	1	2	4	5	6	7	8	10	11	12	♉13
♂	♈15	15	16	17	18	19	19	20	21	22	22	23	24	25	25	26	27	28	28	29	♉0	1	1	2	3	4	4	5	6	7	♉7

	1	6	12	18	24	30
♃	♏24	24	23	22	21	21
♄	♌3	3	3	4	4	5

	1	15	30
♅	♊19	20	21
♆	♎9	8	8
♇	♌11	11	11
☊	♊3	3	3

JUNE

	1	2	3	4	5	6	7	8	9	10	11	12	13	14	15	16	17	18	19	20	21	22	23	24	25	26	27	28	29	30
☉	♊10	11	12	13	14	14	15	16	17	18	19	20	21	22	23	24	25	26	27	28	29	♋0	1	2	3	4	5	5	6	♋7
☽	♏8	20	♐3	15	27	♑8	20	♒2	14	26	♓8	21	♈3	17	♉0	14	29	♊13	28	♋14	29	♌14	28	♍12	26	♎9	22	♏5	17	♐0
☿	♊27	29	♋1	2	4	6	7	9	10	11	13	14	15	16	18	19	20	21	21	22	23	24	24	25	26	26	26	27	27	♋27
♀	♉14	16	17	18	19	20	22	23	24	25	26	28	29	♊0	1	3	4	5	6	7	9	10	11	12	13	15	16	17	18	♊20
♂	♉8	9	10	10	11	12	13	13	14	15	15	16	17	18	18	19	20	21	21	22	23	23	24	25	26	26	27	28	28	♉29

	1	6	12	18	24	30
♃	♏21	20	19	19	18	18
♄	♌5	5	6	7	7	8

	1	15	30
♅	♊21	22	23
♆	♎8	8	8
♇	♌11	12	12
☊	♊3	2	2

JULY

	1	2	3	4	5	6	7	8	9	10	11	12	13	14	15	16	17	18	19	20	21	22	23	24	25	26	27	28	29	30	31
☉	♋8	9	10	11	12	13	14	15	16	17	18	19	20	21	22	23	24	25	25	26	27	28	29	♌0	1	2	3	4	5	6	♌7
☽	♐12	24	♑5	17	29	♒11	23	♓5	17	♈0	12	25	♉9	23	♊7	22	♋7	22	♌7	22	♍7	22	♎5	19	♏2	14	27	♐9	21	♑2	♑14
☿	♋27	27	27	27	27	26	26	26	25	24	24	23	23	22	21	21	20	19	19	18	18	18	17	17	17	17	17	17	18	18	♋18
♀	♊21	22	23	24	26	27	28	29	♋1	2	3	4	5	7	8	9	10	12	13	14	15	16	18	19	20	21	23	24	25	26	♋27
♂	♊0	1	1	2	3	3	4	5	6	6	7	8	8	9	10	10	11	12	13	13	14	15	15	16	17	17	18	19	19	20	♊21

	1	6	12	18	24	30
♃	♏18	18	18	18	18	18
♄	♌8	9	9	10	11	12

	1	15	30
♅	♊23	24	24
♆	♎8	8	8
♇	♌12	12	13
☊	♊2	1	1

AUGUST

	1	2	3	4	5	6	7	8	9	10	11	12	13	14	15	16	17	18	19	20	21	22	23	24	25	26	27	28	29	30	31
☉	♌8	9	10	11	12	13	14	15	16	17	17	18	19	20	21	22	23	24	25	26	27	28	29	♍0	1	2	3	4	5	6	♍7
☽	♑26	♒8	20	♓2	14	27	♈9	22	♉5	18	♊2	16	♋1	16	♌1	16	♍1	16	♎0	14	27	♏10	23	♐5	17	29	♑11	23	♒5	17	♒29
☿	♋19	20	21	21	22	24	25	26	27	29	♌0	2	4	5	7	9	11	13	15	17	19	21	23	25	27	29	♍1	3	5	7	♍9
♀	♋29	♌0	1	2	4	5	6	7	9	10	11	12	13	15	16	17	18	20	21	22	23	25	26	27	28	♍0	1	2	3	5	♍6
♂	♊21	22	23	23	24	25	25	26	27	27	28	29	29	♋0	1	1	2	3	3	4	5	5	6	7	7	8	9	9	10	10	♋11

	1	6	12	18	24	30
♃	♏18	18	19	19	20	21
♄	♌12	12	13	14	15	16

	1	15	30
♅	♊25	25	26
♆	♎8	9	9
♇	♌13	13	14
☊	♊0	♉29	27

SEPTEMBER

	1	2	3	4	5	6	7	8	9	10	11	12	13	14	15	16	17	18	19	20	21	22	23	24	25	26	27	28	29	30
☉	♍8	9	10	11	12	13	14	14	15	16	17	18	19	20	21	22	23	24	25	26	27	28	29	♎0	1	2	3	4	5	♎6
☽	♓11	24	♈6	19	♉2	15	29	♊12	26	♋11	25	♌10	25	♍9	24	♎8	22	♏5	18	♐1	13	26	♑7	19	♒1	13	25	♓7	20	♈3
☿	♍10	12	14	16	18	20	22	23	25	27	29	♎0	2	4	5	7	8	10	12	13	15	16	18	19	21	22	24	25	26	♎28
♀	♍7	8	9	11	12	13	14	16	17	18	19	21	22	23	24	26	27	28	29	♎1	2	3	4	6	7	8	9	11	12	♎13
♂	♋12	12	13	14	14	15	15	16	17	17	18	19	19	20	20	21	22	22	23	23	24	25	25	26	26	27	28	28	29	♋29

	1	6	12	18	24	30
♃	♏21	21	22	23	24	25
♄	♌16	16	17	18	18	19

	1	15	30
♅	♊26	26	26
♆	♎9	10	10
♇	♌14	14	14
☊	♉27	26	24

OCTOBER

	1	2	3	4	5	6	7	8	9	10	11	12	13	14	15	16	17	18	19	20	21	22	23	24	25	26	27	28	29	30	31
☉	♎7	8	9	10	11	12	13	14	15	16	17	18	19	20	21	22	23	24	25	26	27	28	29	♏0	1	2	3	4	5	6	♏7
☽	♈16	29	♉12	26	♊9	23	♋7	21	♌6	20	♍4	18	♎3	17	♏0	13	26	♐9	21	♑3	15	27	♒9	21	♓3	16	28	♈11	24	♉8	♉22
☿	♎29	♏0	2	3	4	6	7	8	9	10	12	13	14	15	16	17	17	18	19	20	20	21	21	21	21	21	21	21	21	20	♏19
♀	♎14	16	17	18	19	21	22	23	24	26	27	28	29	♏1	2	3	4	6	7	8	9	11	12	13	14	15	17	18	19	20	♏22
♂	♌0	1	1	2	2	3	3	4	5	5	6	6	7	7	8	8	9	9	10	11	11	12	12	13	13	14	14	15	15	16	♌16

	1	6	12	18	24	30
♃	♏25	26	28	29	♐0	1
♄	♌19	20	20	21	21	22

	1	15	30
♅	♊26	26	26
♆	♎10	11	11
♇	♌14	15	15
☊	♉24	24	23

NOVEMBER

	1	2	3	4	5	6	7	8	9	10	11	12	13	14	15	16	17	18	19	20	21	22	23	24	25	26	27	28	29	30
☉	♏8	9	10	11	12	13	14	15	16	17	18	19	20	21	22	23	24	25	26	27	28	29	♐0	1	2	3	4	5	6	♐7
☽	♊5	20	♋4	18	♌2	17	♍1	15	28	♎12	26	♏9	22	♐4	17	29	♑11	23	♒5	17	29	♓11	23	♈6	19	♉2	16	♊0	14	♊29
☿	♏19	18	16	15	14	13	11	10	9	8	7	6	6	6	5	6	6	6	7	8	8	9	10	11	13	14	15	16	18	♏19
♀	♏23	24	25	27	28	29	♐0	2	3	4	5	7	8	9	10	12	13	14	15	17	18	19	20	22	23	24	25	27	28	♐29
♂	♌17	17	18	18	19	19	20	20	21	21	22	22	22	23	23	24	24	25	25	26	26	26	27	27	28	28	28	29	29	♌29

	1	6	12	18	24	30
♃	♐2	3	4	5	7	8
♄	♌22	22	22	22	23	23

	1	15	30
♅	♊26	25	25
♆	♎12	12	12
♇	♌15	15	15
☊	♉23	23	23

DECEMBER

	1	2	3	4	5	6	7	8	9	10	11	12	13	14	15	16	17	18	19	20	21	22	23	24	25	26	27	28	29	30	31
☉	♐8	9	10	11	12	13	14	15	16	17	18	19	20	21	22	23	24	25	26	27	28	29	♑0	1	2	3	4	5	6	7	♑8
☽	♋14	28	♌13	27	♍11	25	♎9	22	♏5	18	♐1	13	25	♑7	19	♒1	13	25	♓7	19	♈1	14	27	♉10	24	♊8	23	♋7	23	♌8	♌23
☿	♏20	22	23	25	26	28	29	♐1	2	4	5	7	8	10	11	13	14	16	18	19	21	22	24	25	27	28	♑0	2	3	5	♑6
♀	♑0	2	3	4	5	7	8	9	10	12	13	14	15	17	18	19	20	22	23	24	25	27	28	29	♒0	1	3	4	5	6	♒8
♂	♍0	0	1	1	1	2	2	2	2	3	3	3	4	4	4	4	5	5	5	5	6	6	6	6	6	7	7	7	7	7	♍7

	1	6	12	18	24	30
♃	♐8	9	11	12	13	15
♄	♌23	23	23	23	22	22

	1	15	30
♅	♊25	24	24
♆	♎12	13	13
♇	♌15	15	15
☊	♉23	23	23

1948

JANUARY

	1	2	3	4	5	6	7	8	9	10	11	12	13	14	15	16	17	18	19	20	21	22	23	24	25	26	27	28	29	30	31
☉	♑9	10	12	13	14	15	16	17	18	19	20	21	22	23	24	25	26	27	28	29	♒0	1	2	3	4	5	6	7	8	9	♒10
☽	♍7	22	♎6	19	♏2	15	28	♐10	22	♑4	16	28	♒10	22	♓4	16	28	♈10	22	♉5	18	♊2	16	♋0	15	♌1	16	♍1	16	♎1	♎15
☿	♑8	10	11	13	14	16	18	19	21	23	24	26	28	29	♒1	3	4	6	8	9	11	13	15	16	18	20	21	23	24	26	♒27
♀	♒9	10	11	13	14	15	16	18	19	20	21	23	24	25	26	27	29	♓0	1	2	4	5	6	7	8	10	11	12	13	15	♓16
♂	♍7	7	7	7	8	8	8	8	8	8	8	8	7	7	7	7	7	7	7	7	7	6	6	6	6	6	5	5	5	5	♍4

	1	6	12	18	24	30
♃	♐15	16	17	19	20	21
♄	♌22	22	21	21	21	20

	1	15	30
♅	♊24	23	23
♆	♎13	13	13
♇	♌15	14	14
☊	♉22	21	20

FEBRUARY

	1	2	3	4	5	6	7	8	9	10	11	12	13	14	15	16	17	18	19	20	21	22	23	24	25	26	27	28	29
☉	♒11	12	13	14	15	16	17	18	19	20	21	22	23	24	25	26	27	28	29	♓0	1	2	3	4	5	6	7	8	♓9
☽	♎29	♏12	25	♐7	19	♑1	13	25	♒7	19	♓1	13	25	♈7	19	♉1	14	27	♊11	25	♋9	24	♌9	24	♍9	24	♎9	23	♏7
☿	♒29	♓0	1	2	3	4	5	6	6	6	7	6	6	6	5	4	4	3	2	1	♒29	28	27	26	25	24	24	23	♒22
♀	♓17	18	19	21	22	23	24	25	27	28	29	♈0	1	3	4	5	6	7	9	10	11	12	13	15	16	17	18	19	♈20
♂	♍4	4	3	3	3	2	2	2	1	1	1	0	0	♌29	29	29	28	28	27	27	27	26	26	25	25	25	24	24	♌24

	1	6	12	18	24	29
♃	♐21	22	23	24	25	26
♄	♌20	19	19	19	18	18

	1	15	29
♅	♊22	22	22
♆	♎13	13	12
♇	♌14	14	13
☊	♉20	18	16

MARCH

	1	2	3	4	5	6	7	8	9	10	11	12	13	14	15	16	17	18	19	20	21	22	23	24	25	26	27	28	29	30	31
☉	♓10	11	12	13	14	15	16	17	18	19	20	21	22	23	24	25	26	27	28	29	♈0	1	2	3	4	5	6	7	8	9	♈10
☽	♏20	♐3	16	28	♑10	22	♒4	16	28	♓10	22	♈4	16	29	♉11	24	♊7	21	♋4	19	♌3	18	♍3	18	♎2	17	♏1	15	28	♐11	♐24
☿	♒22	22	22	22	22	22	22	22	23	23	24	25	25	26	27	28	29	♓0	1	2	3	4	5	6	8	9	10	12	13	14	♓16
♀	♈22	23	24	25	26	27	29	♉0	1	2	3	4	5	7	8	9	10	11	12	13	14	15	17	18	19	20	21	22	23	24	♉25
♂	♌23	23	23	22	22	22	21	21	21	21	20	20	20	20	19	19	19	19	19	19	19	18	18	18	18	18	18	18	18	18	♌18

	1	6	12	18	24	30
♃	♐26	27	27	28	28	29
♄	♌18	17	17	17	16	16

	1	15	30
♅	♊22	22	22
♆	♎12	12	12
♇	♌13	13	13
☊	♉16	15	15

APRIL

	1	2	3	4	5	6	7	8	9	10	11	12	13	14	15	16	17	18	19	20	21	22	23	24	25	26	27	28	29	30
☉	♈11	12	13	14	15	16	17	18	19	20	21	22	23	24	25	26	27	28	29	♉0	1	2	3	4	5	6	7	8	9	♉10
☽	♑6	18	♒0	12	24	♓6	18	♈0	13	25	♉8	21	♊4	18	♋1	15	29	♌13	28	♍12	27	♎11	25	♏9	23	♐6	19	♑2	14	♑26
☿	♓17	19	20	22	23	25	27	28	♈0	2	3	5	7	9	10	12	14	16	18	20	22	24	26	28	♉0	2	4	6	8	♉10
♀	♉26	27	28	29	♊0	2	3	4	5	6	7	8	9	10	11	12	13	13	14	15	16	17	18	19	20	21	22	23	23	♊24
♂	♌18	18	18	18	18	18	19	19	19	19	19	19	19	19	20	20	20	20	20	21	21	21	21	22	22	22	22	23	23	♌23

	1	6	12	18	24	30
♃	♐29	29	29	29	29	29
♄	♌16	16	16	16	16	16

	1	15	30
♅	♊23	23	24
♆	♎12	11	11
♇	♌13	13	13
☊	♉15	14	14

MAY

	1	2	3	4	5	6	7	8	9	10	11	12	13	14	15	16	17	18	19	20	21	22	23	24	25	26	27	28	29	30	31
☉	♉11	11	12	13	14	15	16	17	18	19	20	21	22	23	24	25	26	27	28	29	♊0	1	2	3	4	5	6	7	8	8	♊9
☽	♒8	20	♓2	14	26	♈8	21	♉4	17	♊0	14	28	♋12	26	♌10	25	♍9	23	♎7	21	♏5	18	♐1	15	27	♑10	22	♒4	16	28	♓10
☿	♉13	15	17	19	21	23	25	28	♊0	2	4	6	7	9	11	13	15	16	18	19	21	22	24	25	26	27	28	♋0	1	1	♋2
♀	♊25	26	27	27	28	29	♋0	0	1	2	3	3	4	4	5	6	6	7	7	8	8	9	9	9	10	10	10	10	11	11	♋11
♂	♌24	24	24	25	25	25	26	26	26	27	27	27	28	28	28	29	29	♍0	0	0	1	1	2	2	3	3	3	4	4	5	♍5

	1	6	12	18	24	30
♃	♐29	28	28	27	27	26
♄	♌16	16	16	17	17	17

	1	15	30
♅	♊24	24	25
♆	♎11	11	10
♇	♌13	13	13
☊	♉14	14	14

JUNE

	1	2	3	4	5	6	7	8	9	10	11	12	13	14	15	16	17	18	19	20	21	22	23	24	25	26	27	28	29	30
☉	♊10	11	12	13	14	15	16	17	18	19	20	21	22	23	24	25	26	27	28	29	♋0	0	1	2	3	4	5	6	7	♋8
☽	♓22	♈4	16	29	♉12	25	♊9	23	♋7	22	♌7	21	♍5	20	♎4	18	♏1	14	28	♐11	23	♑6	18	♒0	12	24	♓6	18	♈0	♈12
☿	♋3	4	5	5	6	6	7	7	7	7	7	7	7	7	7	7	6	6	5	5	4	4	3	3	2	1	1	0	0	♊29
♀	♋11	11	11	11	11	11	11	11	10	10	10	10	9	9	8	8	7	7	6	6	5	5	4	3	3	2	1	1	0	♋0
♂	♍6	6	7	7	8	8	9	9	9	10	10	11	11	12	12	13	13	14	14	15	16	16	17	17	18	18	19	19	20	♍20

	1	6	12	18	24	30
♃	♐26	25	24	24	23	22
♄	♌17	18	18	19	19	20

	1	15	30
♅	♊25	26	27
♆	♎10	10	10
♇	♌13	13	13
☊	♉14	13	12

JULY

	1	2	3	4	5	6	7	8	9	10	11	12	13	14	15	16	17	18	19	20	21	22	23	24	25	26	27	28	29	30	31
☉	♋9	10	11	12	13	14	15	16	17	18	19	20	20	21	22	23	24	25	26	27	28	29	♌0	1	2	3	4	5	6	7	♌8
☽	♈24	♉7	20	♊4	17	♋2	16	♌1	16	♍1	16	♎0	14	28	♏11	25	♐7	20	♑2	15	27	♒9	21	♓3	15	27	♈8	21	♉3	15	♉28
☿	♊29	29	29	28	28	28	28	29	29	29	♋0	0	1	1	2	3	4	5	6	7	8	10	11	13	14	16	18	19	21	23	♋25
♀	♊29	29	28	28	27	27	26	26	26	25	25	25	25	25	25	25	25	25	25	25	25	25	25	26	26	26	27	27	28	28	♊28
♂	♍21	21	22	23	23	24	24	25	25	26	26	27	28	28	29	29	♎0	0	1	2	2	3	3	4	5	5	6	6	7	8	♎8

	1	6	12	18	24	30
♃	♐22	22	21	20	20	20
♄	♌20	21	21	22	23	24

	1	15	30
♅	♊27	28	29
♆	♎10	10	11
♇	♌14	14	14
☊	♉12	11	10

AUGUST

	1	2	3	4	5	6	7	8	9	10	11	12	13	14	15	16	17	18	19	20	21	22	23	24	25	26	27	28	29	30	31
☉	♌9	10	11	12	12	13	14	15	16	17	18	19	20	21	22	23	24	25	26	27	28	29	♍0	1	2	3	4	5	6	7	♍7
☽	♊12	26	♋10	25	♌10	25	♍10	25	♎10	24	♏8	21	♐4	17	♑0	12	24	♒6	18	♓0	12	24	♈5	17	29	♉12	24	♊7	21	♋4	♋19
☿	♋27	29	♌1	3	5	7	9	11	13	15	17	19	21	23	25	27	29	♍1	3	5	7	9	11	12	14	16	18	19	21	23	♍24
♀	♊29	29	♋0	1	1	2	2	3	4	4	5	6	6	7	8	9	9	10	11	12	13	14	14	15	16	17	18	19	20	21	♋22
♂	♎9	9	10	11	11	12	12	13	14	14	15	16	16	17	17	18	19	19	20	21	21	22	22	23	24	24	25	26	26	27	♎28

	1	6	12	18	24	30
♃	♐19	19	19	19	19	19
♄	♌24	24	25	26	27	28

	1	15	30
♅	♊29	29	♋29
♆	♎11	11	11
♇	♌14	15	15
☊	♉10	9	7

SEPTEMBER

	1	2	3	4	5	6	7	8	9	10	11	12	13	14	15	16	17	18	19	20	21	22	23	24	25	26	27	28	29	30
☉	♍8	9	10	11	12	13	14	15	16	17	18	19	20	21	22	23	24	25	26	27	28	29	♎0	1	2	3	4	5	6	♎7
☽	♌3	18	♍4	19	♎4	19	♏3	17	♐1	14	26	♑9	21	♒3	15	27	♓9	21	♈2	14	27	♉9	21	♊4	17	♋0	14	28	♌12	♌27
☿	♍26	27	29	♎1	2	4	5	7	8	9	11	12	14	15	16	18	19	20	21	22	24	25	26	27	28	29	♏0	1	1	♏2
♀	♋23	24	25	25	26	27	28	29	♌0	1	2	3	4	6	7	8	9	10	11	12	13	14	15	16	17	18	19	20	22	♌23
♂	♎28	29	♏0	0	1	2	2	3	4	4	5	6	6	7	8	8	9	10	10	11	12	12	13	14	14	15	16	16	17	♏18

	1	6	12	18	24	30
♃	♐19	20	20	21	21	22
♄	♌28	28	29	♍0	1	1

	1	15	30
♅	♋0	0	1
♆	♎11	12	13
♇	♌15	16	16
☊	♉7	6	5

OCTOBER

	1	2	3	4	5	6	7	8	9	10	11	12	13	14	15	16	17	18	19	20	21	22	23	24	25	26	27	28	29	30	31
☉	♎8	9	10	11	12	13	14	15	16	17	18	19	20	21	22	23	24	25	26	27	27	28	29	♏0	1	2	3	4	5	6	♏7
☽	♍12	27	♎12	27	♏11	25	♐9	22	♑5	17	♒0	12	24	♓5	17	29	♈11	23	♉6	18	♊1	14	27	♋10	24	♌8	22	♍7	21	♎6	♎21
☿	♏3	3	4	5	5	5	5	5	5	5	5	4	4	3	2	1	0	♎29	28	27	25	24	23	22	21	21	20	20	20	20	♎20
♀	♌24	25	26	27	28	29	♍1	2	3	4	5	6	7	9	10	11	12	13	14	15	17	18	19	20	21	23	24	25	26	27	♍28
♂	♏19	19	20	21	21	22	23	23	24	25	26	26	27	28	28	29	♐0	1	1	2	3	3	4	5	6	6	7	8	8	9	♐10

	1	6	12	18	24	30
♃	♐22	23	24	25	26	27
♄	♍1	2	3	3	4	4

	1	15	30
♅	♋1	1	0
♆	♎13	13	14
♇	♌16	16	16
☊	♉5	5	5

NOVEMBER

	1	2	3	4	5	6	7	8	9	10	11	12	13	14	15	16	17	18	19	20	21	22	23	24	25	26	27	28	29	30
☉	♏8	9	10	11	12	13	14	15	17	18	19	20	21	22	23	24	25	26	27	28	29	♐0	1	2	3	4	5	6	7	♐8
☽	♏5	19	♐3	17	♑0	13	26	♒8	20	♓2	14	25	♈7	20	♉2	14	27	♊10	24	♋7	21	♌5	19	♍3	17	♎1	16	♏0	14	♏28
☿	♎21	21	22	23	24	25	26	27	29	♏0	1	3	4	6	7	9	10	12	13	15	16	18	20	21	23	24	26	27	29	♐1
♀	♎0	1	2	3	4	6	7	8	9	10	12	13	14	15	17	18	19	20	21	23	24	25	26	28	29	♏0	1	2	4	♏5
♂	♐11	11	12	13	14	14	15	16	17	17	18	19	20	20	21	22	23	23	24	25	26	26	27	28	29	29	♑0	1	2	♑2

	1	6	12	18	24	30
♃	♐27	28	29	♑1	2	3
♄	♍4	5	5	5	6	6

	1	15	30
♅	♋0	0	♊0
♆	♎14	14	15
♇	♌16	17	17
☊	♉5	5	5

DECEMBER

	1	2	3	4	5	6	7	8	9	10	11	12	13	14	15	16	17	18	19	20	21	22	23	24	25	26	27	28	29	30	31
☉	♐9	10	11	12	13	14	15	16	17	18	19	20	21	22	23	24	25	26	27	28	29	♑0	1	2	3	4	5	6	7	8	♑9
☽	♐11	25	♑8	21	♒3	16	28	♓10	21	♈3	15	27	♉10	23	♊6	19	♋3	17	♌1	15	♍0	14	28	♎12	26	♏10	24	♐7	20	♑3	♑16
☿	♐2	4	5	7	8	10	12	13	15	16	18	19	21	23	24	26	27	29	♑0	2	4	5	7	8	10	12	13	15	17	18	♑20
♀	♏6	7	9	10	11	12	14	15	16	17	18	20	21	22	23	25	26	27	28	♐0	1	2	3	5	6	7	8	10	11	12	♐13
♂	♑3	4	5	5	6	7	8	8	9	10	11	12	12	13	14	15	15	16	17	18	18	19	20	21	22	22	23	24	25	26	♑26

	1	6	12	18	24	30
♃	♑3	4	6	7	9	10
♄	♍6	6	6	6	6	6

	1	15	30
♅	♊29	29	28
♆	♎15	15	15
♇	♌17	16	16
☊	♉5	4	3

1949

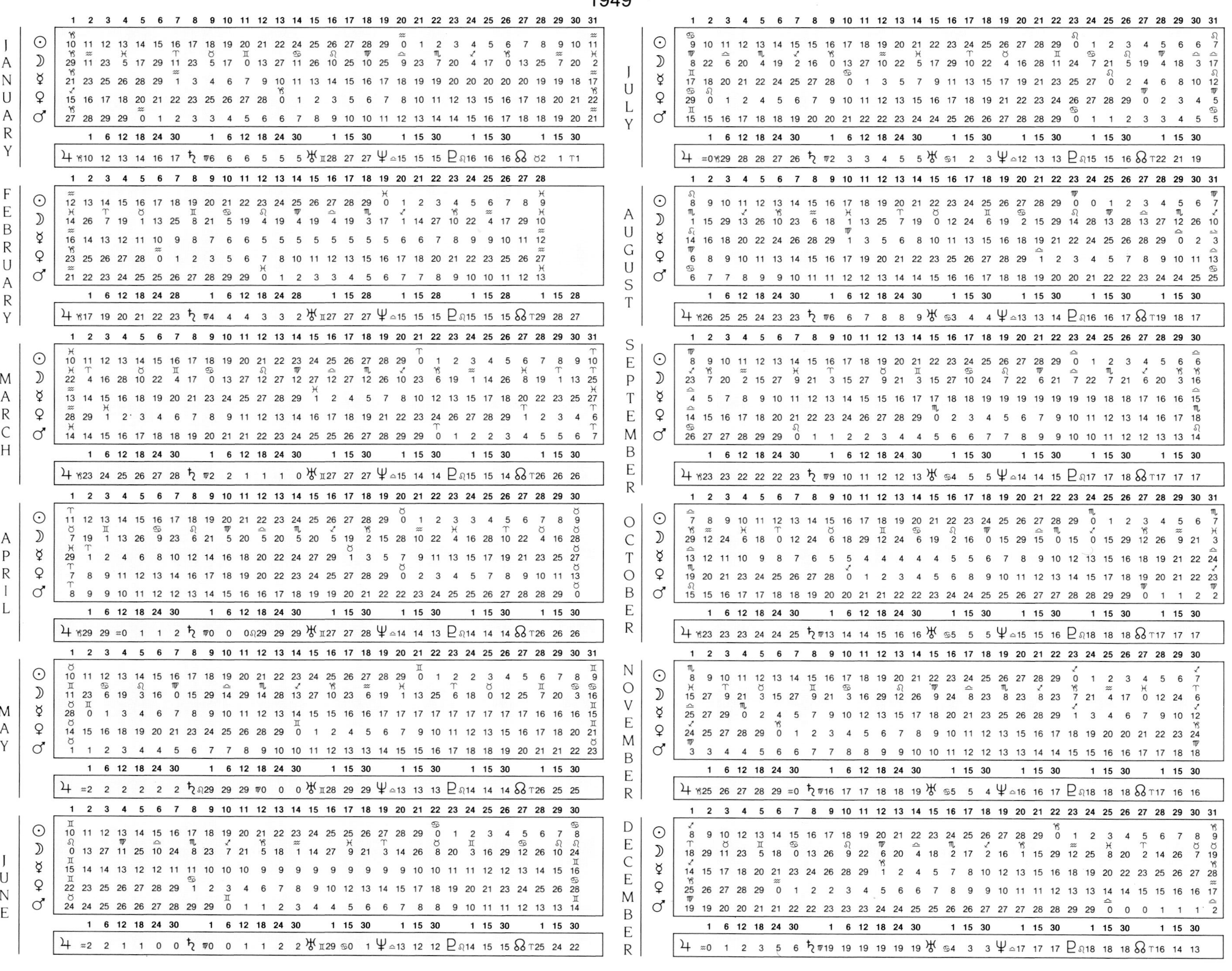

1950

JANUARY

	1	2	3	4	5	6	7	8	9	10	11	12	13	14	15	16	17	18	19	20	21	22	23	24	25	26	27	28	29	30	31
☉	♑10	11	12	13	14	15	16	17	18	19	20	21	22	23	24	25	26	27	28	29	♒0	1	2	3	4	5	6	8	9	10	♒11
☽	♊1	14	26	♋9	22	♌6	19	♍3	17	♎0	14	29	♏13	27	♐11	25	♑9	23	♒7	20	♓3	15	28	♈10	22	♉3	15	27	♊9	22	♋4
☿	♑29	♒0	1	2	3	3	4	4	4	4	4	3	2	1	0	♑29	28	27	25	24	23	22	21	20	19	19	18	18	18	18	♑18
♀	♒17	17	18	18	18	18	18	19	19	19	19	19	19	18	18	18	18	18	17	17	17	16	16	15	15	14	13	13	12	12	♒11
♂	♎2	3	3	3	4	4	4	5	5	5	6	6	6	6	7	7	7	8	8	8	8	9	9	9	9	9	10	10	10	10	♎10

	1	6	12	18	24	30
♃	♒7	8	9	10	12	13
♄	♍19	19	19	19	19	19

	1	15	30
♅	♋3	2	2
♆	♎17	17	17
♇	♌18	18	17
☊	♈13	11	9

FEBRUARY

	1	2	3	4	5	6	7	8	9	10	11	12	13	14	15	16	17	18	19	20	21	22	23	24	25	26	27	28
☉	♒12	13	14	15	16	17	18	19	20	21	22	23	24	25	26	27	28	29	♓0	1	2	3	4	5	6	7	8	♓9
☽	♋17	♌1	15	28	♍13	27	♎11	25	♏10	24	♐8	22	♑5	19	♒2	15	28	♓11	23	♈6	18	29	♉11	23	♊5	17	29	♋12
☿	♑19	19	19	20	21	21	22	23	24	25	26	27	28	29	♒0	1	3	4	5	6	8	9	11	12	13	15	16	♒18
♀	♒10	10	9	9	8	7	7	6	6	5	5	5	4	4	4	4	3	3	3	3	3	3	3	3	3	4	4	♒4
♂	♎10	10	11	11	11	11	11	11	11	11	11	11	11	11	11	11	11	11	11	11	11	10	10	10	10	10	10	♎9

	1	6	12	18	24	28
♃	♒14	15	16	18	19	20
♄	♍18	18	18	17	17	17

	1	15	28
♅	♋2	1	1
♆	♎17	17	17
♇	♌17	17	16
☊	♈9	8	8

MARCH

	1	2	3	4	5	6	7	8	9	10	11	12	13	14	15	16	17	18	19	20	21	22	23	24	25	26	27	28	29	30	31
☉	♓10	11	12	13	14	15	16	17	18	19	20	21	22	23	24	25	26	27	28	29	♈0	1	2	3	4	5	6	7	8	9	♈10
☽	♋25	♌9	23	♍7	21	♎6	21	♏6	20	♐4	18	♑2	16	29	♒12	25	♓7	20	♈2	14	26	♉8	19	♊1	13	25	♋8	20	♌3	17	♍1
☿	♒19	21	22	24	25	27	29	♓0	2	3	5	7	9	10	12	14	16	17	19	21	23	25	27	29	♈1	3	5	7	9	11	♈13
♀	♒4	5	5	5	6	6	7	7	8	8	9	9	10	11	11	12	13	13	14	15	16	16	17	18	19	20	20	21	22	23	♒24
♂	♎9	9	9	9	8	8	8	7	7	7	7	6	6	6	5	5	4	4	4	3	3	3	2	2	1	1	1	0	0	♍29	♍29

	1	6	12	18	24	30
♃	♒20	22	23	24	26	27
♄	♍17	16	16	15	15	14

	1	15	30
♅	♋1	1	1
♆	♎17	17	16
♇	♌16	16	16
☊	♈8	7	7

APRIL

	1	2	3	4	5	6	7	8	9	10	11	12	13	14	15	16	17	18	19	20	21	22	23	24	25	26	27	28	29	30
☉	♈11	12	13	14	15	16	17	18	19	20	21	22	22	23	24	25	26	27	28	29	♉0	1	2	3	4	5	6	7	8	♉9
☽	♍15	♎0	15	♏0	15	♐0	14	29	♑12	26	♒9	22	♓4	17	29	♈11	23	♉4	16	28	♊10	22	♋4	16	29	♌12	25	♍9	23	♎8
☿	♈15	17	19	21	23	25	27	29	♉1	3	5	7	8	10	12	13	15	16	18	19	20	21	22	23	24	25	25	26	27	♉27
♀	♒25	26	27	28	28	29	♓0	1	2	3	4	5	6	7	8	9	10	11	12	13	14	15	16	17	18	19	21	22	23	♓24
♂	♍29	28	28	28	27	27	27	26	26	26	25	25	25	25	24	24	24	24	23	23	23	23	23	23	22	22	22	22	22	♍22

	1	6	12	18	24	30
♃	♒27	28	29	♓0	2	3
♄	♍14	14	14	13	13	13

	1	15	30
♅	♋1	2	2
♆	♎16	16	15
♇	♌16	16	16
☊	♈7	7	7

MAY

	1	2	3	4	5	6	7	8	9	10	11	12	13	14	15	16	17	18	19	20	21	22	23	24	25	26	27	28	29	30	31
☉	♉10	11	12	13	14	15	16	17	18	19	20	21	22	23	24	25	26	26	27	28	29	♊0	1	2	3	4	5	6	7	8	♊9
☽	♎23	♏8	23	♐8	23	♑8	22	♒5	19	♓1	14	26	♈8	20	♉1	13	25	♊7	19	♋1	13	26	♌8	21	♍5	18	♎2	16	♏1	16	♐1
☿	♉27	27	28	28	27	27	27	27	26	26	25	25	24	24	23	23	22	21	21	20	20	20	19	19	19	19	19	19	19	19	♉19
♀	♓25	26	27	28	29	♈0	1	2	3	5	6	7	8	9	10	11	12	13	15	16	17	18	19	20	21	22	24	25	26	27	♈28
♂	♍22	22	22	22	22	22	22	22	22	22	22	22	23	23	23	23	23	23	23	24	24	24	24	24	25	25	25	25	26	26	♍26

	1	6	12	18	24	30
♃	♓3	3	4	5	6	6
♄	♍13	13	13	13	13	13

	1	15	30
♅	♋2	3	4
♆	♎15	15	15
♇	♌16	16	16
☊	♈7	7	6

JUNE

	1	2	3	4	5	6	7	8	9	10	11	12	13	14	15	16	17	18	19	20	21	22	23	24	25	26	27	28	29	30
☉	♊10	11	12	13	14	15	16	17	18	19	20	20	21	22	23	24	25	26	27	28	29	♋0	1	2	3	4	5	6	7	♋8
☽	♐17	♑2	16	♒0	14	27	♓10	23	♈5	17	28	♉10	22	♊4	16	28	♋10	23	♌5	18	♍1	15	28	♎12	26	♏11	25	♐10	25	♑10
☿	♉19	20	20	21	21	22	23	23	24	25	26	27	28	29	♊0	2	3	4	6	7	9	10	12	14	15	17	19	21	23	♊25
♀	♈29	♉0	2	3	4	5	6	7	9	10	11	12	13	14	15	17	18	19	20	21	22	24	25	26	27	28	29	♊1	2	♊3
♂	♍26	27	27	27	28	28	28	29	29	29	♎0	0	0	1	1	2	2	2	3	3	4	4	4	5	5	6	6	7	7	♎8

	1	6	12	18	24	30
♃	♓6	7	7	7	7	7
♄	♍13	13	13	14	14	14

	1	15	30
♅	♋4	4	5
♆	♎15	15	15
♇	♌16	16	17
☊	♈5	4	2

JULY

	1	2	3	4	5	6	7	8	9	10	11	12	13	14	15	16	17	18	19	20	21	22	23	24	25	26	27	28	29	30	31
☉	♋9	10	11	11	12	13	14	15	16	17	18	19	20	21	22	23	24	25	26	27	28	29	♌0	1	1	2	3	4	5	6	♌7
☽	♑24	♒9	22	♓6	18	♈1	13	25	♉7	19	♊0	12	25	♋7	19	♌2	15	28	♍12	25	♎9	23	♏7	21	♐5	20	♑4	19	♒3	17	♓0
☿	♊27	29	♋1	3	5	7	9	11	14	16	18	20	22	24	26	29	♌1	3	5	7	9	11	12	14	16	18	20	21	23	25	♌27
♀	♊4	5	7	8	9	10	11	12	14	15	16	17	18	20	21	22	23	24	26	27	28	29	♋0	2	3	4	5	6	8	9	♋10
♂	♎8	8	9	9	10	10	11	11	12	12	13	13	14	14	15	15	16	17	17	18	18	19	19	20	20	21	21	22	23	23	♎24

	1	6	12	18	24	30
♃	♓7	7	7	7	6	6
♄	♍14	15	15	16	16	17

	1	15	30
♅	♋5	6	7
♆	♎15	15	15
♇	♌17	17	17
☊	♈2	1	0

AUGUST

	1	2	3	4	5	6	7	8	9	10	11	12	13	14	15	16	17	18	19	20	21	22	23	24	25	26	27	28	29	30	31
☉	♌8	9	10	11	12	13	14	15	16	17	18	19	20	21	22	23	24	24	25	26	27	28	29	♍0	1	2	3	4	5	6	♍7
☽	♓14	26	♈9	21	♉3	15	27	♊9	21	♋3	15	28	♌11	24	♍8	22	♎6	20	♏4	18	♐2	16	♑0	14	28	♒12	26	♓9	22	♈4	♈17
☿	♌28	♍0	1	3	4	6	7	9	10	12	13	14	16	17	18	19	20	22	23	24	25	26	27	27	28	29	♎0	0	1	1	♎2
♀	♋11	12	14	15	16	17	18	20	21	22	23	24	26	27	28	29	♌0	2	3	4	5	7	8	9	10	11	13	14	15	16	♌18
♂	♎24	25	25	26	27	27	28	28	29	♏0	0	1	1	2	3	3	4	4	5	6	6	7	8	8	9	9	10	11	11	12	♏13

	1	6	12	18	24	30
♃	♓6	5	4	4	3	2
♄	♍17	18	18	19	20	21

	1	15	30
♅	♋7	8	9
♆	♎15	15	16
♇	♌18	18	18
☊	♓29	29	28

SEPTEMBER

	1	2	3	4	5	6	7	8	9	10	11	12	13	14	15	16	17	18	19	20	21	22	23	24	25	26	27	28	29	30
☉	♍8	9	10	11	12	13	14	15	16	17	18	19	20	21	22	23	24	25	25	26	27	28	29	♎0	1	2	3	4	5	♎6
☽	♈29	♉11	23	♊5	16	29	♋11	23	♌6	19	♍3	17	♎1	15	♏0	14	29	♐13	27	♑11	25	♒8	22	♓5	18	♈0	13	25	♉7	♉19
☿	♎2	2	2	2	2	2	2	2	1	1	0	♍29	28	27	26	25	24	23	22	21	20	20	19	18	18	18	18	18	18	♍19
♀	♌19	20	21	23	24	25	26	27	29	♍0	1	2	4	5	6	7	9	10	11	12	14	15	16	17	18	20	21	22	23	♍25
♂	♏13	14	15	15	16	17	17	18	19	19	20	21	21	22	23	23	24	25	25	26	27	27	28	29	29	♐0	1	2	2	♐3

	1	6	12	18	24	30
♃	♓2	1	0	0	♒29	29
♄	♍21	21	22	23	24	24

	1	15	30
♅	♋9	9	9
♆	♎16	16	17
♇	♌18	19	19
☊	♓28	28	28

OCTOBER

	1	2	3	4	5	6	7	8	9	10	11	12	13	14	15	16	17	18	19	20	21	22	23	24	25	26	27	28	29	30	31
☉	♎7	8	9	10	11	12	13	14	15	16	17	18	19	20	21	22	23	24	25	26	27	28	29	♏0	1	2	3	4	5	6	♏7
☽	♊1	13	25	♋7	19	♌1	14	27	♍11	25	♎9	24	♏9	24	♐9	23	♑8	22	♒5	19	♓2	14	27	♈9	21	♉3	15	27	♊9	21	♋3
☿	♍20	20	21	22	24	25	26	28	29	♎1	2	4	5	7	9	11	12	14	16	17	19	21	22	24	26	28	29	♏1	3	4	♏6
♀	♍26	27	28	♎0	1	2	3	5	6	7	8	10	11	12	13	15	16	17	18	20	21	22	23	25	26	27	28	♏0	1	2	♏3
♂	♐4	4	5	6	6	7	8	9	9	10	11	11	12	13	14	14	15	16	16	17	18	19	19	20	21	22	22	23	24	25	♐25

	1	6	12	18	24	30
♃	♒28	28	28	28	28	28
♄	♍25	25	26	27	27	28

	1	15	30
♅	♋9	9	9
♆	♎17	17	18
♇	♌19	20	20
☊	♓28	28	28

NOVEMBER

	1	2	3	4	5	6	7	8	9	10	11	12	13	14	15	16	17	18	19	20	21	22	23	24	25	26	27	28	29	30
☉	♏8	9	10	11	12	13	14	15	16	17	18	19	20	21	22	23	24	25	26	27	28	29	♐0	1	2	3	4	5	6	♐7
☽	♋15	27	♌10	22	♍5	19	♎3	17	♏2	17	♐3	18	♑3	17	♒2	15	29	♓11	24	♈6	18	♉0	12	24	♊6	18	♋0	12	24	♌6
☿	♏8	9	11	12	14	16	17	19	20	22	24	25	27	28	♐0	1	3	4	6	7	9	11	12	14	15	17	18	20	21	♐23
♀	♏5	6	7	8	10	11	12	14	15	16	17	19	20	21	22	24	25	26	27	29	♐0	1	2	4	5	6	7	9	10	♐11
♂	♐26	27	28	28	29	♑0	1	1	2	3	4	4	5	6	7	7	8	9	10	10	11	12	13	13	14	15	16	17	17	♑18

	1	6	12	18	24	30
♃	♒28	28	28	29	29	♓0
♄	♍28	29	29	♎0	0	1

	1	15	30
♅	♋9	9	9
♆	♎18	18	19
♇	♌20	20	20
☊	♓27	27	25

DECEMBER

	1	2	3	4	5	6	7	8	9	10	11	12	13	14	15	16	17	18	19	20	21	22	23	24	25	26	27	28	29	30	31
☉	♐8	9	10	11	12	13	14	15	16	17	18	19	20	21	22	23	24	25	27	28	29	♑0	1	2	3	4	5	6	7	8	♑9
☽	♌18	♍1	14	27	♎11	26	♏10	25	♐11	26	♑11	26	♒10	24	♓8	21	♈3	15	27	♉9	21	♊3	15	27	♋9	21	♌3	16	28	♍11	♍24
☿	♐24	26	27	28	♑0	1	3	4	5	7	8	9	11	12	13	14	15	16	16	17	18	18	18	18	18	18	17	16	15	14	♑13
♀	♐12	14	15	16	17	19	20	21	22	24	25	26	27	29	♑0	1	3	4	5	6	8	9	10	11	13	14	15	16	18	19	♑20
♂	♑19	20	20	21	22	23	23	24	25	26	27	27	28	29	♒0	0	1	2	3	4	4	5	6	7	8	8	9	10	11	11	♒12

	1	6	12	18	24	30
♃	♓0	1	1	2	3	4
♄	♎1	1	1	2	2	2

	1	15	30
♅	♋9	8	7
♆	♎19	19	19
♇	♌20	20	20
☊	♓25	24	22

1951

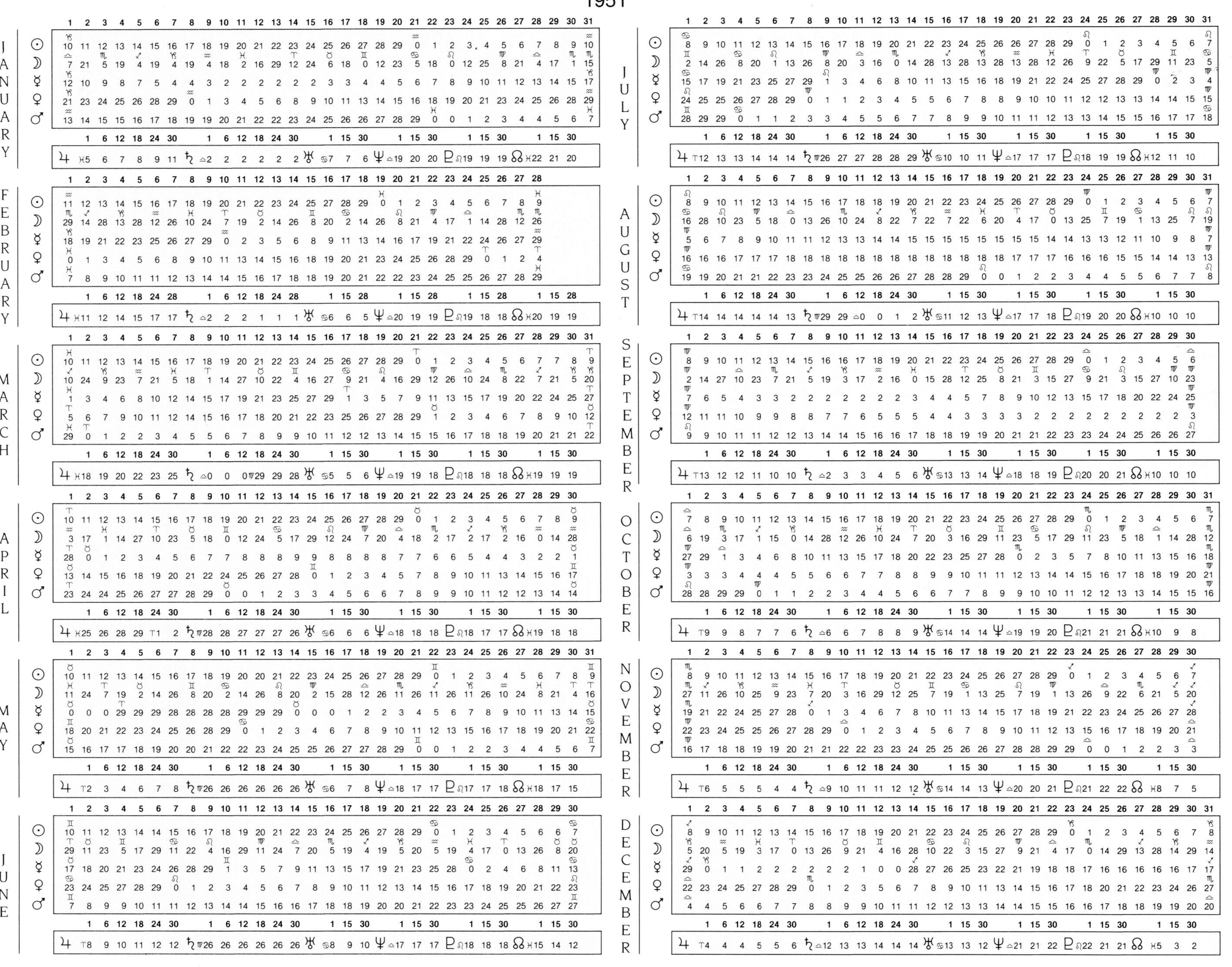

JANUARY

	1	2	3	4	5	6	7	8	9	10	11	12	13	14	15	16	17	18	19	20	21	22	23	24	25	26	27	28	29	30	31
☉	♑10	11	12	13	14	15	16	17	18	19	20	21	22	23	24	25	26	27	28	29	♒0	1	2	3,	4	5	6	7	8	9	♒10
☽	♎7	21	♏5	19	♐4	19	♑4	19	♒4	18	♓2	16	29	♈12	24	♉6	18	♊0	12	23	♋5	18	♌0	12	25	♍8	21	♎4	17	♏1	♏15
☿	♑12	10	9	8	7	5	4	4	3	2	2	2	2	2	2	3	3	4	4	5	6	7	8	9	10	11	12	13	14	15	♑17
♀	♑21	23	24	25	26	28	29	♒0	1	3	4	5	6	8	9	10	11	13	14	15	16	18	19	20	21	23	24	25	26	28	♒29
♂	♒13	14	15	15	16	17	18	19	19	20	21	22	22	23	24	25	26	26	27	28	29	♓0	0	1	2	3	4	4	5	6	♓7

	1	6	12	18	24	30		1	6	12	18	24	30		1	15	30		1	15	30		1	15	30		1	15	30
♃	♓5	6	7	8	9	11	♄	♎2	2	2	2	2	2	♅	♋7	7	6	♆	♎19	20	20	♇	♌19	19	19	☊	♓22	21	20

FEBRUARY

	1	2	3	4	5	6	7	8	9	10	11	12	13	14	15	16	17	18	19	20	21	22	23	24	25	26	27	28
☉	♒11	12	13	14	15	16	17	18	19	20	21	22	23	24	25	27	28	29	♓0	1	2	3	4	5	6	7	8	♓9
☽	♏29	♐14	28	♑13	28	♒12	26	♓10	24	♈7	19	♉2	14	26	♊8	20	♋2	14	26	♌8	21	♍4	17	♎1	14	28	♏12	♏26
☿	♑18	19	21	22	23	25	26	27	29	♒0	2	3	5	6	8	9	11	13	14	16	17	19	21	22	24	26	27	♒29
♀	♓0	1	3	4	5	6	8	9	10	11	13	14	15	16	18	19	20	21	23	24	25	26	28	29	♈0	1	2	♈4
♂	♓7	8	9	10	11	11	12	13	14	14	15	16	17	18	18	19	20	21	22	22	23	24	25	25	26	27	28	♓29

	1	6	12	18	24	28		1	6	12	18	24	28		1	15	28		1	15	28		1	15	28		1	15	28
♃	♓11	12	14	15	17	17	♄	♎2	2	2	1	1	1	♅	♋6	6	5	♆	♎20	19	19	♇	♌19	18	18	☊	♓20	19	19

MARCH

	1	2	3	4	5	6	7	8	9	10	11	12	13	14	15	16	17	18	19	20	21	22	23	24	25	26	27	28	29	30	31
☉	♓10	11	12	13	14	15	16	17	18	19	20	21	22	23	24	25	26	27	28	29	♈0	1	2	3	4	5	6	7	7	8	♈9
☽	♐10	24	♑9	23	♒7	21	♓5	18	♈1	14	27	♉10	22	♊4	16	27	♋9	21	♌4	16	29	♍12	26	♎10	24	♏8	22	♐7	21	♑5	♑20
☿	♓1	3	4	6	8	10	12	14	15	17	19	21	23	25	27	29	♈1	3	5	7	9	11	13	15	17	19	20	22	24	25	♈27
♀	♈5	6	7	9	10	11	12	14	15	16	17	18	20	21	22	23	25	26	27	28	29	♉1	2	3	4	6	7	8	9	10	♉12
♂	♓29	♈0	1	2	2	3	4	5	5	6	7	8	9	9	10	11	12	12	13	14	15	15	16	17	18	18	19	20	21	21	♈22

	1	6	12	18	24	30		1	6	12	18	24	30		1	15	30		1	15	30		1	15	30		1	15	30
♃	♓18	19	20	22	23	25	♄	♎0	0	0	♍29	29	28	♅	♋5	5	6	♆	♎19	19	18	♇	♌18	18	18	☊	♓19	19	19

APRIL

	1	2	3	4	5	6	7	8	9	10	11	12	13	14	15	16	17	18	19	20	21	22	23	24	25	26	27	28	29	30
☉	♈10	11	12	13	14	15	16	17	18	19	20	21	22	23	24	25	26	27	28	29	♉0	1	2	3	4	5	6	7	8	♉9
☽	♒3	17	♓1	14	27	♈10	23	♉5	18	♊0	12	24	♋5	17	29	♌12	24	♍7	20	♎4	18	♏2	17	♐2	17	♑2	16	♒0	14	♒28
☿	♈28	♉0	1	2	3	4	5	6	7	7	8	8	8	9	9	8	8	8	8	7	7	6	6	5	4	4	3	2	2	♉1
♀	♉13	14	15	16	18	19	20	21	22	24	25	26	27	28	♊0	1	2	3	4	5	7	8	9	10	11	13	14	15	16	♊17
♂	♈23	24	24	25	26	27	27	28	29	♉0	0	1	2	3	3	4	5	6	6	7	8	9	9	10	11	12	12	13	14	♉14

	1	6	12	18	24	30		1	6	12	18	24	30		1	15	30		1	15	30		1	15	30		1	15	30
♃	♓25	26	28	29	♈1	2	♄	♍28	28	27	27	27	26	♅	♋6	6	6	♆	♎18	18	18	♇	♌18	17	17	☊	♓19	18	18

MAY

	1	2	3	4	5	6	7	8	9	10	11	12	13	14	15	16	17	18	19	20	21	22	23	24	25	26	27	28	29	30	31
☉	♉10	11	12	13	14	15	16	17	18	19	20	20	21	22	23	24	25	26	27	28	29	♊0	1	2	3	4	5	6	7	8	♊9
☽	♓11	24	♈7	19	♉2	14	26	♊8	20	♋2	14	26	♌8	20	♍2	15	28	♎12	26	♏11	26	♐11	26	♑11	26	♒10	24	♓8	21	♈4	♈16
☿	♉0	0	0	♈29	29	29	28	28	28	28	29	29	29	♉0	0	0	1	2	2	3	4	5	6	7	8	9	10	11	13	14	♉15
♀	♊18	20	21	22	23	24	25	26	28	29	♋0	1	2	3	4	6	7	8	9	10	11	12	13	15	16	17	18	19	20	21	♋22
♂	♉15	16	17	17	18	19	20	20	21	22	22	23	24	25	25	26	27	27	28	29	♊0	0	1	2	2	3	4	4	5	6	♊7

	1	6	12	18	24	30		1	6	12	18	24	30		1	15	30		1	15	30		1	15	30		1	15	30
♃	♈2	3	4	6	7	8	♄	♍26	26	26	26	26	26	♅	♋6	7	8	♆	♎18	17	17	♇	♌17	17	18	☊	♓18	17	15

JUNE

	1	2	3	4	5	6	7	8	9	10	11	12	13	14	15	16	17	18	19	20	21	22	23	24	25	26	27	28	29	30
☉	♊10	11	12	13	14	14	15	16	17	18	19	20	21	22	23	24	25	26	27	28	29	♋0	1	2	3	4	5	6	6	♋7
☽	♈29	♉11	23	♊5	17	29	♋11	22	♌4	16	29	♍11	24	♎7	20	♏5	19	♐4	19	♑5	20	♒5	19	♓4	17	♈0	13	26	♉8	♉20
☿	♉17	18	20	21	23	24	26	28	29	♊1	3	5	7	9	11	13	15	17	19	21	23	25	28	♋0	2	4	6	8	11	♋13
♀	♋23	24	25	27	28	29	♌0	1	2	3	4	5	6	7	8	9	10	11	12	13	14	15	16	17	18	19	20	21	22	♌23
♂	♊7	8	9	9	10	11	11	12	13	14	14	15	16	16	17	18	18	19	20	20	21	22	23	23	24	25	25	26	27	♊27

	1	6	12	18	24	30		1	6	12	18	24	30		1	15	30		1	15	30		1	15	30		1	15	30
♃	♈8	9	10	11	12	12	♄	♍26	26	26	26	26	26	♅	♋8	9	10	♆	♎17	17	17	♇	♌18	18	18	☊	♓15	14	12

JULY

	1	2	3	4	5	6	7	8	9	10	11	12	13	14	15	16	17	18	19	20	21	22	23	24	25	26	27	28	29	30	31
☉	♋8	9	10	11	12	13	14	15	16	17	18	19	20	21	22	23	24	25	26	26	27	28	29	♌0	1	2	3	4	5	6	♌7
☽	♊2	14	26	♋8	20	♌1	13	26	♍8	20	♎3	16	♏0	14	28	♐13	28	♑13	28	♒13	28	♓12	26	♈9	22	♉5	17	29	♊11	23	♋5
☿	♋15	17	19	21	23	25	27	29	♌1	3	4	6	8	10	11	13	15	16	18	19	21	22	24	25	27	28	29	♍0	2	3	♍4
♀	♌24	25	25	26	27	28	29	♍0	1	1	2	3	4	5	5	6	7	8	8	9	10	10	11	12	12	13	13	14	14	15	♍15
♂	♊28	29	29	♋0	1	1	2	3	3	4	5	5	6	7	7	8	9	9	10	11	11	12	13	13	14	15	15	16	17	17	♋18

	1	6	12	18	24	30		1	6	12	18	24	30		1	15	30		1	15	30		1	15	30		1	15	30
♃	♈12	13	13	14	14	14	♄	♍26	27	27	28	28	29	♅	♋10	10	11	♆	♎17	17	17	♇	♌18	19	19	☊	♓12	11	10

AUGUST

	1	2	3	4	5	6	7	8	9	10	11	12	13	14	15	16	17	18	19	20	21	22	23	24	25	26	27	28	29	30	31
☉	♌8	9	10	11	12	13	14	15	16	17	18	18	19	20	21	22	23	24	25	26	27	28	29	♍0	1	2	3	4	5	6	♍7
☽	♋16	28	♌10	23	♍5	18	♎0	13	26	♏10	24	♐8	22	♑7	22	♒7	22	♓6	20	♈4	17	♉0	13	25	♊7	19	♋1	13	25	♌7	♌19
☿	♍5	6	7	8	9	10	11	11	12	13	13	14	14	15	15	15	15	15	15	15	15	14	14	13	13	12	11	10	9	8	♍7
♀	♍16	16	16	17	17	17	18	18	18	18	18	18	18	18	18	18	18	18	18	17	17	17	16	16	16	15	15	14	14	13	♍13
♂	♋19	19	20	21	21	22	23	23	24	25	25	26	26	27	28	28	29	♌0	0	1	2	2	3	4	4	5	5	6	7	7	♌8

	1	6	12	18	24	30		1	6	12	18	24	30		1	15	30		1	15	30		1	15	30		1	15	30
♃	♈14	14	14	14	14	13	♄	♍29	29	♎0	0	1	2	♅	♋11	12	13	♆	♎17	17	18	♇	♌19	20	20	☊	♓10	10	10

SEPTEMBER

	1	2	3	4	5	6	7	8	9	10	11	12	13	14	15	16	17	18	19	20	21	22	23	24	25	26	27	28	29	30
☉	♍8	9	10	11	12	13	14	15	16	16	17	18	19	20	21	22	23	24	25	26	27	28	29	♎0	1	2	3	4	5	♎6
☽	♍2	14	27	♎10	23	♏7	21	♐5	19	♑3	17	♒2	16	♓0	15	28	♈12	25	♉8	21	♊3	15	27	♋9	21	♌3	15	27	♍10	♍23
☿	♍7	6	5	4	3	3	2	2	2	2	2	2	2	3	4	4	5	7	8	9	10	12	13	15	17	18	20	22	24	♍25
♀	♍12	11	11	10	9	9	8	8	7	7	6	5	5	5	4	4	3	3	3	3	2	2	2	2	2	2	2	2	2	♍3
♂	♌9	9	10	11	11	12	12	13	14	14	15	16	16	17	18	18	19	19	20	21	21	22	23	23	24	24	25	26	26	♌27

	1	6	12	18	24	30		1	6	12	18	24	30		1	15	30		1	15	30		1	15	30		1	15	30
♃	♈13	12	12	11	10	10	♄	♎2	3	3	4	5	6	♅	♋13	13	14	♆	♎18	18	19	♇	♌20	20	21	☊	♓10	10	10

OCTOBER

	1	2	3	4	5	6	7	8	9	10	11	12	13	14	15	16	17	18	19	20	21	22	23	24	25	26	27	28	29	30	31
☉	♎7	8	9	10	11	12	13	14	15	16	17	18	19	20	21	22	23	24	25	26	27	28	29	♏0	1	2	3	4	5	6	♏7
☽	♎6	19	♏3	17	♐1	15	♑0	14	28	♒12	26	♓10	24	♈7	20	♉3	16	29	♊11	23	♋5	17	29	♌11	23	♍5	18	♎1	14	28	♏12
☿	♍27	29	♎1	3	4	6	8	10	11	13	15	17	18	20	22	23	25	27	28	♏0	2	3	5	7	8	10	11	13	15	16	♏18
♀	♍3	3	3	4	4	4	5	5	6	6	7	7	8	8	9	9	10	11	11	12	13	14	14	15	16	17	18	18	19	20	♍21
♂	♌28	28	29	29	♍0	1	1	2	2	3	4	4	5	6	6	7	7	8	9	9	10	10	11	12	12	13	13	14	15	15	♍16

	1	6	12	18	24	30		1	6	12	18	24	30		1	15	30		1	15	30		1	15	30		1	15	30
♃	♈9	9	8	7	7	6	♄	♎6	6	7	8	8	9	♅	♋14	14	14	♆	♎19	19	20	♇	♌21	21	21	☊	♓10	9	8

NOVEMBER

	1	2	3	4	5	6	7	8	9	10	11	12	13	14	15	16	17	18	19	20	21	22	23	24	25	26	27	28	29	30
☉	♏8	9	10	11	12	13	14	15	16	17	18	19	20	21	22	23	24	25	26	27	28	29	♐0	1	2	3	4	5	6	♐7
☽	♏27	♐11	26	♑10	25	♒9	23	♓7	20	♈3	16	29	♉12	25	♊7	19	♋1	13	25	♌7	19	♍1	13	26	♎9	22	♏6	21	♐5	♐20
☿	♏19	21	22	24	25	27	28	♐0	1	3	4	6	7	8	10	11	13	14	15	17	18	19	21	22	23	24	25	26	27	♐28
♀	♍22	23	24	25	25	26	27	28	29	♎0	1	2	3	4	5	6	7	8	9	10	11	12	13	15	16	17	18	19	20	♎21
♂	♍16	17	18	18	19	19	20	21	21	22	22	23	23	24	25	25	26	26	27	28	28	29	29	♎0	0	1	2	2	3	♎3

	1	6	12	18	24	30		1	6	12	18	24	30		1	15	30		1	15	30		1	15	30		1	15	30
♃	♈6	5	5	5	4	4	♄	♎9	10	11	11	12	12	♅	♋14	14	13	♆	♎20	20	21	♇	♌21	22	22	☊	♓8	7	5

DECEMBER

	1	2	3	4	5	6	7	8	9	10	11	12	13	14	15	16	17	18	19	20	21	22	23	24	25	26	27	28	29	30	31
☉	♐8	9	10	11	12	13	14	15	16	17	18	19	20	21	22	23	24	25	26	27	28	29	♑0	1	2	3	4	5	6	7	♑8
☽	♑5	20	♒5	19	♓3	17	♈0	13	26	♉9	21	♊4	16	28	♋10	22	♌3	15	27	♍9	21	♎4	17	♏0	14	29	♐13	28	♑14	29	♒14
☿	♐29	♑0	1	1	2	2	2	2	2	2	1	0	0	♐28	27	26	25	23	22	21	19	18	18	17	16	16	16	16	16	17	♐17
♀	♎22	23	24	25	27	28	29	♏0	1	2	3	5	6	7	8	9	10	11	13	14	15	16	17	18	20	21	22	23	24	26	♏27
♂	♎4	4	5	6	6	7	7	8	8	9	9	10	11	11	12	12	13	13	14	14	15	15	16	16	17	18	18	19	19	20	♎20

	1	6	12	18	24	30		1	6	12	18	24	30		1	15	30		1	15	30		1	15	30		1	15	30
♃	♈4	4	4	5	5	6	♄	♎12	13	13	14	14	14	♅	♋13	13	12	♆	♎21	21	22	♇	♌22	21	21	☊	♓5	3	2

1952

JANUARY

	1	2	3	4	5	6	7	8	9	10	11	12	13	14	15	16	17	18	19	20	21	22	23	24	25	26	27	28	29	30	31
☉	♑10	11	12	13	14	15	16	17	18	19	20	21	22	23	24	25	26	27	28	29	♒0	1	2	3	4	5	6	7	8	9	♒10
☽	♒29	♓13	27	♈10	23	♉6	18	♊1	13	25	♋7	19	♌0	12	24	♍6	18	♎0	13	26	♏9	23	♐7	22	♑6	22	♒7	22	♓7	21	♈5
☿	♐18	18	19	20	21	22	23	24	25	26	27	28	♑0	1	2	4	5	6	8	9	10	12	13	15	16	18	19	21	22	24	♑25
♀	♏28	29	♐0	1	3	4	5	6	7	9	10	11	12	13	15	16	17	18	19	21	22	23	24	26	27	28	29	♑0	2	3	♑4
♂	♎21	21	22	22	23	23	24	24	25	25	26	26	27	27	28	28	29	29	♏0	0	0	1	1	2	2	3	3	4	4	4	♏5

	1	6	12	18	24	30
♃	♈6	6	7	8	9	10
♄	♎14	15	15	15	15	15

	1	15	30
♅	♋12	11	11
♆	♎22	22	22
♇	♌21	21	21
☊	♓2	1	1

FEBRUARY

	1	2	3	4	5	6	7	8	9	10	11	12	13	14	15	16	17	18	19	20	21	22	23	24	25	26	27	28	29
☉	♒11	12	13	14	15	16	17	18	19	20	21	22	23	24	25	26	27	28	29	♓0	1	2	3	4	5	6	7	8	♓9
☽	♈19	♉2	15	27	♊10	22	♋4	15	27	♌9	21	♍3	15	27	♎10	23	♏6	19	♐2	16	♑1	15	♒0	15	♓0	15	29	♈13	♈27
☿	♑27	28	♒0	1	3	5	6	8	10	11	13	15	16	18	20	21	23	25	27	29	♓0	2	4	6	8	10	12	13	♓15
♀	♑5	7	8	9	10	11	13	14	15	16	17	19	20	21	22	24	25	26	27	29	♒0	1	2	3	5	6	7	8	♒10
♂	♏5	6	6	7	7	7	8	8	8	9	9	10	10	10	11	11	11	12	12	12	13	13	13	14	14	14	14	15	♏15

	1	6	12	18	24	29
♃	♈10	11	12	14	15	16
♄	♎15	15	15	14	14	14

	1	15	29
♅	♋11	10	10
♆	♎22	22	21
♇	♌21	20	20
☊	♓1	1	1

MARCH

	1	2	3	4	5	6	7	8	9	10	11	12	13	14	15	16	17	18	19	20	21	22	23	24	25	26	27	28	29	30	31
☉	♓10	11	12	13	14	15	16	17	18	19	20	21	22	23	24	25	26	27	28	29	♈0	1	2	3	4	5	6	7	8	9	♈10
☽	♉10	23	♊6	18	♋0	12	24	♌6	18	♍0	12	24	♎7	20	♏3	16	29	♐13	27	♑11	25	♒10	24	♓9	23	♈7	21	♉5	18	♊1	♊14
☿	♓17	19	21	23	25	27	29	♈1	2	4	6	7	9	11	12	13	15	16	17	18	18	19	20	20	20	20	20	20	20	20	♈19
♀	♒11	12	13	15	16	17	18	19	21	22	23	24	26	27	28	29	♓0	2	3	4	5	7	8	9	10	12	13	14	15	17	♓18
♂	♏15	15	16	16	16	16	17	17	17	17	17	17	18	18	18	18	18	18	18	18	18	18	18	18	18	18	18	18	18	18	♏18

	1	6	12	18	24	30
♃	♈16	17	19	20	21	23
♄	♎14	14	13	13	12	12

	1	15	30
♅	♋10	10	10
♆	♎21	21	21
♇	♌20	20	19
☊	♓1	0	0

APRIL

	1	2	3	4	5	6	7	8	9	10	11	12	13	14	15	16	17	18	19	20	21	22	23	24	25	26	27	28	29	30
☉	♈11	12	13	14	15	16	17	18	19	20	21	22	23	24	25	26	27	28	29	♉0	1	2	3	4	5	6	7	8	9	♉10
☽	♊26	♋8	20	♌2	14	26	♍8	20	♎3	16	29	♏12	26	♐10	24	♑8	22	♒6	20	♓4	18	♈2	16	♉0	13	26	♊9	22	♋4	♋16
☿	♈19	18	17	17	16	15	14	14	13	12	11	11	10	10	9	9	9	9	9	9	9	9	9	10	10	11	11	12	13	♈13
♀	♓19	20	21	23	24	25	26	28	29	♈0	1	2	4	5	6	7	9	10	11	12	14	15	16	17	18	20	21	22	23	♈25
♂	♏18	18	18	18	18	18	17	17	17	17	17	17	16	16	16	16	15	15	15	14	14	14	13	13	13	12	12	12	11	♏11

	1	6	12	18	24	30
♃	♈23	25	26	27	29	♉0
♄	♎12	11	11	10	10	10

	1	15	30
♅	♋10	10	11
♆	♎21	20	20
♇	♌19	19	19
☊	♓0	♒0	28

MAY

	1	2	3	4	5	6	7	8	9	10	11	12	13	14	15	16	17	18	19	20	21	22	23	24	25	26	27	28	29	30	31
☉	♉11	12	13	13	14	15	16	17	18	19	20	21	22	23	24	25	26	27	28	29	♊0	1	2	3	4	5	6	7	8	9	♊9
☽	♋28	♌10	22	♍4	16	28	♎11	24	♏7	21	♐5	20	♑4	19	♒3	17	♓1	15	29	♈12	26	♉9	22	♊5	18	♋0	12	24	♌6	18	♍0
☿	♈14	15	16	17	18	19	20	21	22	24	25	26	28	29	♉1	2	4	5	7	8	10	12	13	15	17	19	21	23	25	27	♉29
♀	♈26	27	28	♉0	1	2	3	4	6	7	8	9	11	12	13	14	16	17	18	19	20	22	23	24	25	27	28	29	♊0	1	♊3
♂	♏11	10	10	10	9	9	8	8	8	7	7	7	6	6	6	5	5	5	4	4	4	4	3	3	3	3	3	2	2	2	♏2

	1	6	12	18	24	30
♃	♉1	2	3	5	6	7
♄	♎10	9	9	9	8	8

	1	15	30
♅	♋11	11	12
♆	♎20	19	19
♇	♌19	19	19
☊	♒27	26	25

JUNE

	1	2	3	4	5	6	7	8	9	10	11	12	13	14	15	16	17	18	19	20	21	22	23	24	25	26	27	28	29	30
☉	♊10	11	12	13	14	15	16	17	18	19	20	21	22	23	24	25	26	27	28	29	♋0	1	1	2	3	4	5	6	7	♋8
☽	♍11	24	♎6	19	♏2	16	♐0	14	29	♑14	28	♒13	28	♓12	26	♈9	23	♉6	19	♊2	14	26	♋9	21	♌2	14	26	♍8	20	♎2
☿	♊1	3	5	7	9	11	14	16	18	20	22	25	27	29	♋1	3	5	7	9	11	13	15	17	19	21	23	24	26	28	♋29
♀	♊4	5	6	8	9	10	11	13	14	15	16	17	19	20	21	22	24	25	26	27	28	♋0	1	2	3	5	6	7	8	♋10
♂	♏2	2	2	1	1	1	1	1	1	1	1	1	1	1	1	1	1	2	2	2	2	2	2	2	3	3	3	3	3	♏4

	1	6	12	18	24	30
♃	♉8	9	10	11	12	14
♄	♎8	8	8	8	8	9

	1	15	30
♅	♋12	13	14
♆	♎19	19	19
♇	♌19	20	20
☊	♒25	23	22

JULY

	1	2	3	4	5	6	7	8	9	10	11	12	13	14	15	16	17	18	19	20	21	22	23	24	25	26	27	28	29	30	31
☉	♋9	10	11	12	13	14	15	16	17	18	19	20	21	21	22	23	24	25	26	27	28	29	♌0	1	2	3	4	5	6	7	♌8
☽	♎14	27	♏10	24	♐8	23	♑7	23	♒8	23	♓7	22	♈6	20	♉3	16	29	♊11	23	♋5	17	29	♌11	23	♍5	17	29	♎11	23	♏6	♏19
☿	♌1	2	4	5	7	8	10	11	12	14	15	16	17	18	19	20	21	22	23	23	24	25	25	26	26	27	27	27	27	27	♌27
♀	♋11	12	13	14	16	17	18	19	21	22	23	24	26	27	28	29	♌0	2	3	4	5	7	8	9	10	12	13	14	15	16	♌18
♂	♏4	4	4	5	5	5	6	6	6	6	7	7	7	8	8	9	9	9	10	10	11	11	11	12	12	13	13	14	14	15	♏15

	1	6	12	18	24	30
♃	♉14	15	16	17	17	18
♄	♎9	9	9	9	10	10

	1	15	30
♅	♋14	15	16
♆	♎19	19	19
♇	♌20	20	21
☊	♒22	22	22

AUGUST

	1	2	3	4	5	6	7	8	9	10	11	12	13	14	15	16	17	18	19	20	21	22	23	24	25	26	27	28	29	30	31
☉	♌9	10	11	12	13	13	14	15	16	17	18	19	20	21	22	23	24	25	26	27	28	29	♍0	1	2	3	4	5	6	7	♍8
☽	♐3	17	♑1	16	♒1	16	♓1	16	♈1	15	29	♉12	25	♊8	20	♋3	15	26	♌8	20	♍2	14	26	♎8	20	♏3	15	28	♐12	26	♑10
☿	♌27	27	26	26	26	25	24	24	23	22	21	21	20	19	18	17	17	16	16	15	15	15	15	15	15	16	16	17	17	18	♌19
♀	♌19	20	21	23	24	25	26	28	29	♍0	1	2	4	5	6	7	9	10	11	12	14	15	16	17	18	20	21	22	23	25	♍26
♂	♏15	16	16	17	17	18	18	19	19	20	21	21	22	22	23	23	24	24	25	25	26	27	27	28	28	29	♐0	0	1	1	♐2

	1	6	12	18	24	30
♃	♉19	19	20	20	21	21
♄	♎10	11	11	12	12	13

	1	15	30
♅	♋16	16	17
♆	♎19	19	20
♇	♌21	21	22
☊	♒22	22	21

SEPTEMBER

	1	2	3	4	5	6	7	8	9	10	11	12	13	14	15	16	17	18	19	20	21	22	23	24	25	26	27	28	29	30
☉	♍8	9	10	11	12	13	14	15	16	17	18	19	20	21	22	23	24	25	26	27	28	29	♎0	1	2	3	4	5	6	♎7
☽	♑24	♒9	24	♓9	24	♈9	24	♉8	21	♊4	17	29	♋11	23	♌5	17	29	♍11	23	♎5	17	♏0	12	25	♐9	22	♑6	20	♒4	♒18
☿	♌20	22	23	24	26	28	29	♍1	3	4	6	8	10	12	14	16	17	19	21	23	25	27	29	♎0	2	4	6	8	9	♎11
♀	♍27	28	♎0	1	2	3	4	6	7	8	9	11	12	13	14	16	17	18	19	20	22	23	24	25	27	28	29	♏0	2	♏3
♂	♐3	3	4	4	5	6	6	7	8	8	9	9	10	11	11	12	13	13	14	15	15	16	17	17	18	19	19	20	21	♐21

	1	6	12	18	24	30
♃	♉21	21	21	21	21	20
♄	♎13	14	14	15	16	17

	1	15	30
♅	♋17	18	18
♆	♎20	20	21
♇	♌22	22	23
☊	♒21	21	21

OCTOBER

	1	2	3	4	5	6	7	8	9	10	11	12	13	14	15	16	17	18	19	20	21	22	23	24	25	26	27	28	29	30	31
☉	♎8	9	10	11	12	13	14	15	16	17	18	19	20	21	22	23	24	25	26	27	28	29	♏0	1	2	3	4	5	6	7	♏8
☽	♓3	18	♈3	17	♉2	16	29	♊12	25	♋8	20	♌2	13	25	♍7	19	♎1	14	26	♏9	22	♐5	19	♑3	16	♒0	14	29	♓13	27	♈12
☿	♎13	14	16	18	19	21	23	24	26	28	29	♏1	2	4	5	7	8	10	11	13	14	16	17	19	20	22	23	24	26	27	♏28
♀	♏4	5	6	8	9	10	11	13	14	15	16	18	19	20	21	22	24	25	26	27	29	♐0	1	2	3	5	6	7	8	10	♐11
♂	♐22	23	24	24	25	26	26	27	28	28	29	♑0	1	1	2	3	3	4	5	6	6	7	8	9	9	10	11	11	12	13	♑14

	1	6	12	18	24	30
♃	♉20	20	19	19	18	17
♄	♎17	17	18	19	19	20

	1	15	30
♅	♋18	18	19
♆	♎21	21	22
♇	♌23	23	23
☊	♒21	20	18

NOVEMBER

	1	2	3	4	5	6	7	8	9	10	11	12	13	14	15	16	17	18	19	20	21	22	23	24	25	26	27	28	29	30
☉	♏9	10	11	12	13	14	15	16	17	18	19	20	21	22	23	24	25	26	27	28	29	♐0	1	2	3	4	5	6	7	♐8
☽	♈26	♉10	24	♊7	20	♋3	15	28	♌9	21	♍3	15	27	♎9	22	♏5	18	♐1	15	29	♑13	27	♒11	25	♓9	23	♈7	21	♉5	♉19
☿	♐0	1	2	4	5	6	7	8	9	10	11	12	13	14	15	15	16	16	16	17	16	16	16	15	15	14	13	11	10	♐9
♀	♐12	13	14	16	17	18	19	20	22	23	24	25	27	28	29	♑0	1	3	4	5	6	7	9	10	11	12	14	15	16	♑17
♂	♑14	15	16	17	17	18	19	20	20	21	22	23	23	24	25	26	26	27	28	29	29	♒0	1	2	2	3	4	5	5	♒6

	1	6	12	18	24	30
♃	♉17	16	15	15	14	13
♄	♎20	21	22	22	23	24

	1	15	30
♅	♋19	18	18
♆	♎22	23	23
♇	♌23	23	23
☊	♒18	17	15

DECEMBER

	1	2	3	4	5	6	7	8	9	10	11	12	13	14	15	16	17	18	19	20	21	22	23	24	25	26	27	28	29	30	31
☉	♐9	10	11	12	13	14	15	16	17	18	19	20	21	22	23	24	25	26	27	28	29	♑0	1	2	3	4	5	6	7	8	♑9
☽	♊2	15	28	♋11	23	♌5	17	29	♍11	23	♎5	17	♏0	13	26	♐10	24	♑8	23	♒7	22	♓6	20	♈4	18	♉2	15	28	♊11	24	♋7
☿	♐7	6	5	4	3	2	1	1	0	0	0	1	1	1	2	3	4	5	6	7	8	9	10	11	12	14	15	16	18	19	♐21
♀	♑18	20	21	22	23	24	26	27	28	29	♒0	1	3	4	5	6	7	9	10	11	12	13	14	16	17	18	19	20	21	23	♒24
♂	♒7	8	9	9	10	11	12	12	13	14	15	15	16	17	18	19	19	20	21	22	22	23	24	25	25	26	27	28	29	29	♓0

	1	6	12	18	24	30
♃	♉13	13	12	12	11	11
♄	♎24	24	25	25	26	26

	1	15	30
♅	♋18	17	17
♆	♎23	23	24
♇	♌23	23	23
☊	♒15	14	13

1953

JANUARY

	1	2	3	4	5	6	7	8	9	10	11	12	13	14	15	16	17	18	19	20	21	22	23	24	25	26	27	28	29	30	31
☉	♑10	11	12	13	14	15	16	17	18	19	20	21	23	24	25	26	27	28	29	♒0	1	2	3	4	5	6	7	8	9	10	♒11
☽	♋19	♌1	13	25	♍7	19	♎1	13	25	♏8	20	♐4	18	♑2	16	♒1	16	♓1	16	♈1	15	29	♉12	25	♊8	21	♋4	16	28	♌10	♌22
☿	♐22	23	25	26	28	29	♑1	2	4	5	7	8	10	11	13	14	16	17	19	21	22	24	25	27	29	♒0	2	4	5	7	♒9
♀	♒25	26	27	28	29	♓1	2	3	4	5	6	7	8	10	11	12	13	14	15	16	17	18	19	20	22	23	24	25	26	27	♓28
♂	♓1	2	2	3	4	5	5	6	7	8	9	9	10	11	12	12	13	14	15	15	16	17	18	19	19	20	21	22	22	23	♓24

	1	6	12	18	24	30		1	6	12	18	24	30		1	15	30		1	15	30		1	15	30		1	15	30
♃	♉11	11	11	11	12	12	♄	♎26	27	27	27	27	27	♅	♋17	16	16	♆	♎24	24	24	♇	♌23	23	22	☊	♒13	12	12

FEBRUARY

	1	2	3	4	5	6	7	8	9	10	11	12	13	14	15	16	17	18	19	20	21	22	23	24	25	26	27	28
☉	♒12	13	14	15	16	17	18	19	20	21	22	23	24	25	26	27	28	29	♓0	1	2	3	4	5	6	7	8	♓9
☽	♍4	15	27	♎9	21	♏3	16	29	♐12	26	♑10	24	♒9	24	♓10	25	♈10	24	♉8	22	♊5	18	♋1	13	25	♌7	19	♍1
☿	♒10	12	14	16	17	19	21	23	25	26	28	♓0	2	4	5	7	9	11	13	15	16	18	20	21	23	24	26	♓27
♀	♓29	♈0	1	2	3	4	5	6	7	8	8	9	10	11	12	13	14	15	16	16	17	18	19	19	20	21	22	♈22
♂	♓25	25	26	27	28	28	29	♈0	1	1	2	3	4	5	5	6	7	8	8	9	10	11	11	12	13	14	14	♈15

	1	6	12	18	24	28		1	6	12	18	24	28		1	15	28		1	15	28		1	15	28		1	15	28
♃	♉12	13	13	14	15	16	♄	♎27	27	27	27	27	27	♅	♋15	15	15	♆	♎24	24	24	♇	♌22	22	22	☊	♒12	12	12

MARCH

	1	2	3	4	5	6	7	8	9	10	11	12	13	14	15	16	17	18	19	20	21	22	23	24	25	26	27	28	29	30	31
☉	♓10	11	12	13	14	15	16	17	18	19	20	21	22	23	24	25	26	27	28	29	♈0	1	2	3	4	5	6	7	8	9	♈10
☽	♍12	24	♎6	18	♏0	13	25	♐8	21	♑4	18	♒3	17	♓2	18	♈3	18	♉3	17	♊1	14	27	♋10	22	♌4	16	28	♍9	21	♎3	♎15
☿	♓28	29	♈0	1	2	2	3	3	3	3	3	2	2	1	1	0	♓29	28	27	26	25	25	24	23	22	22	21	21	20	20	♓20
♀	♈23	24	24	25	26	26	27	27	28	28	29	29	29	♉0	0	0	1	1	1	1	1	1	1	1	1	1	1	1	1	0	♉0
♂	♈16	17	17	18	19	19	20	21	22	22	23	24	25	25	26	27	28	28	29	♉0	1	1	2	3	3	4	5	6	6	7	♉8

	1	6	12	18	24	30		1	6	12	18	24	30		1	15	30		1	15	30		1	15	30		1	15	30
♃	♉16	16	18	19	20	21	♄	♎27	27	26	26	26	25	♅	♋15	14	14	♆	♎24	23	23	♇	♌22	21	21	☊	♒12	12	11

APRIL

	1	2	3	4	5	6	7	8	9	10	11	12	13	14	15	16	17	18	19	20	21	22	23	24	25	26	27	28	29	30
☉	♈11	12	13	14	15	16	17	18	19	20	21	22	23	24	25	26	27	28	29	♉0	1	2	3	4	4	5	6	7	8	♉9
☽	♎27	♏10	22	♐5	18	♑1	14	28	♒12	26	♓11	26	♈11	26	♉11	25	♊9	22	♋5	18	♌0	12	24	♍6	18	♎0	12	24	♏6	♏19
☿	♓20	20	20	20	20	21	21	22	22	23	24	25	25	26	27	28	29	♈0	1	3	4	5	6	8	9	10	12	13	15	♈16
♀	♉0	♈29	29	28	28	27	27	26	26	25	25	24	23	23	22	21	21	20	20	19	19	18	18	17	17	16	16	16	16	♈15
♂	♉9	9	10	11	11	12	13	14	14	15	16	16	17	18	19	19	20	21	21	22	23	24	24	25	26	26	27	28	28	♉29

	1	6	12	18	24	30		1	6	12	18	24	30		1	15	30		1	15	30		1	15	30		1	15	30
♃	♉21	22	24	25	26	28	♄	♎25	25	24	24	23	23	♅	♋14	15	15	♆	♎23	22	22	♇	♌21	21	21	☊	♒10	9	7

MAY

	1	2	3	4	5	6	7	8	9	10	11	12	13	14	15	16	17	18	19	20	21	22	23	24	25	26	27	28	29	30	31
☉	♉10	11	12	13	14	15	16	17	18	19	20	21	22	23	24	25	26	27	28	29	♊0	1	2	3	3	4	5	6	7	8	♊9
☽	♐2	15	28	♑11	25	♒8	22	♓7	21	♈6	20	♉5	19	♊3	17	♋0	13	26	♌8	20	♍2	14	26	♎8	20	♏2	15	28	♐11	24	♑8
☿	♈18	19	21	23	24	26	28	♉0	1	3	5	7	9	11	13	15	17	19	21	23	25	27	♊0	2	4	6	8	11	13	15	♊17
♀	♈15	15	15	15	15	15	15	15	15	16	16	16	16	17	17	17	18	18	19	19	20	20	21	21	22	23	23	24	24	25	♈26
♂	♊0	1	1	2	3	3	4	5	5	6	7	7	8	9	10	10	11	12	12	13	14	14	15	16	16	17	18	18	19	20	♊20

	1	6	12	18	24	30		1	6	12	18	24	30		1	15	30		1	15	30		1	15	30		1	15	30
♃	♉28	29	♊1	2	3	5	♄	♎23	22	22	22	21	21	♅	♋15	16	16	♆	♎22	22	21	♇	♌21	21	21	☊	♒7	6	5

JUNE

	1	2	3	4	5	6	7	8	9	10	11	12	13	14	15	16	17	18	19	20	21	22	23	24	25	26	27	28	29	30
☉	♊10	11	12	13	14	15	16	17	18	19	20	21	22	23	24	25	26	26	27	28	29	♋0	1	2	3	4	5	6	7	♋8
☽	♑21	♒5	19	♓3	18	♈2	16	♉0	14	28	♊12	25	♋9	21	♌4	16	28	♍10	22	♎4	16	28	♏10	23	♐6	19	♑3	17	♒1	♒16
☿	♊19	21	23	25	27	29	♋1	3	5	7	9	10	12	14	15	17	18	20	21	22	24	25	26	27	28	♌0	1	2	2	♌3
♀	♈27	27	28	29	♉0	0	1	2	3	4	5	5	6	7	8	9	10	11	12	13	14	15	16	17	17	18	19	20	21	♉22
♂	♊21	22	22	23	24	25	25	26	27	27	28	29	29	♋0	1	1	2	3	3	4	5	5	6	7	7	8	9	9	10	♋11

	1	6	12	18	24	30		1	6	12	18	24	30		1	15	30		1	15	30		1	15	30		1	15	30
♃	♊5	6	8	9	11	12	♄	♎21	21	21	21	21	21	♅	♋16	17	18	♆	♎21	21	21	♇	♌21	21	22	☊	♒4	4	3

JULY

	1	2	3	4	5	6	7	8	9	10	11	12	13	14	15	16	17	18	19	20	21	22	23	24	25	26	27	28	29	30	31
☉	♋9	10	11	12	13	14	15	16	16	17	18	19	20	21	22	23	24	25	26	27	28	29	♌0	1	2	3	4	5	6	7	♌7
☽	♓0	14	29	♈13	27	♉11	25	♊8	21	♋4	17	♌0	12	24	♍6	18	♎0	12	24	♏6	18	♐1	14	28	♑12	26	♒10	25	♓10	25	♈9
☿	♌4	5	5	6	7	7	8	8	8	8	8	8	8	8	8	8	7	7	6	6	5	5	4	3	2	2	1	0	0	♋29	♋29
♀	♉23	24	25	26	27	29	♊0	1	2	3	4	5	6	7	8	9	10	11	12	13	14	16	17	18	19	20	21	22	23	24	♊25
♂	♋11	12	13	13	14	14	15	16	16	17	18	18	19	20	20	21	22	22	23	24	24	25	26	26	27	28	28	29	29	♌0	♌1

	1	6	12	18	24	30		1	6	12	18	24	30		1	15	30		1	15	30		1	15	30		1	15	30
♃	♊12	13	14	16	17	18	♄	♎21	21	21	21	21	22	♅	♋18	19	20	♆	♎21	21	21	♇	♌22	22	22	☊	♒3	3	3

AUGUST

	1	2	3	4	5	6	7	8	9	10	11	12	13	14	15	16	17	18	19	20	21	22	23	24	25	26	27	28	29	30	31
☉	♌8	9	10	11	12	13	14	15	16	17	18	19	20	21	22	23	24	25	26	27	28	29	♍0	1	1	2	3	4	5	6	♍7
☽	♈24	♉8	21	♊5	18	♋1	14	26	♌9	21	♍3	15	26	♎8	20	♏2	14	27	♐9	22	♑6	20	♒4	19	♓4	19	♈4	19	♉4	18	♊2
☿	♋28	28	28	28	28	28	28	28	28	29	♌0	0	1	2	3	4	6	7	8	10	12	13	15	17	19	20	22	24	26	28	♍0
♀	♊27	28	29	♋0	1	2	3	4	6	7	8	9	10	11	12	14	15	16	17	18	19	21	22	23	24	25	26	28	29	♌0	♌1
♂	♌1	2	3	3	4	5	5	6	7	7	8	9	9	10	10	11	12	12	13	14	14	15	16	16	17	17	18	19	19	20	♌21

	1	6	12	18	24	30		1	6	12	18	24	30		1	15	30		1	15	30		1	15	30		1	15	30
♃	♊18	19	20	21	22	23	♄	♎22	22	22	23	23	24	♅	♋20	21	22	♆	♎21	22	22	♇	♌22	23	23	☊	♒3	3	3

SEPTEMBER

	1	2	3	4	5	6	7	8	9	10	11	12	13	14	15	16	17	18	19	20	21	22	23	24	25	26	27	28	29	30
☉	♍8	9	10	11	12	13	14	15	16	17	18	19	20	21	22	23	24	25	26	27	28	29	♎0	1	2	3	4	5	6	♎7
☽	♊15	28	♋11	23	♌6	18	♍0	12	23	♎5	17	29	♏11	23	♐5	18	♑1	14	28	♒12	27	♓12	27	♈12	28	♉13	27	♊11	25	♋8
☿	♍2	4	6	8	10	12	14	16	17	19	21	23	25	27	28	♎0	2	4	5	7	9	10	12	14	15	17	18	20	21	♎23
♀	♌2	3	5	6	7	8	9	11	12	13	14	15	17	18	19	20	21	23	24	25	26	27	29	♍0	1	2	3	5	6	♍7
♂	♌21	22	23	23	24	24	25	26	26	27	28	28	29	♍0	0	1	1	2	3	3	4	5	5	6	6	7	8	8	9	♍10

	1	6	12	18	24	30		1	6	12	18	24	30		1	15	30		1	15	30		1	15	30		1	15	30
♃	♊23	24	25	25	26	26	♄	♎24	25	25	26	27	27	♅	♋22	22	23	♆	♎22	22	23	♇	♌23	24	24	☊	♒3	2	1

OCTOBER

	1	2	3	4	5	6	7	8	9	10	11	12	13	14	15	16	17	18	19	20	21	22	23	24	25	26	27	28	29	30	31
☉	♎8	9	9	10	11	12	13	14	15	16	17	18	19	20	21	22	23	24	25	26	27	28	29	♏0	1	2	3	4	5	6	♏7
☽	♋20	♌3	15	27	♍9	20	♎2	14	26	♏8	20	♐2	15	27	♑10	23	♒7	21	♓6	20	♈5	21	♉6	21	♊5	20	♋3	16	29	♌11	♌23
☿	♎25	26	28	29	♏0	2	3	5	6	8	9	10	12	13	14	15	17	18	19	20	21	22	23	24	25	26	27	28	29	29	♐0
♀	♍8	10	11	12	13	14	16	17	18	19	21	22	23	24	26	27	28	29	♎0	2	3	4	5	7	8	9	10	12	13	14	♎15
♂	♍10	11	12	12	13	13	14	15	15	16	17	17	18	18	19	20	20	21	22	22	23	23	24	25	25	26	27	27	28	28	♍29

	1	6	12	18	24	30		1	6	12	18	24	30		1	15	30		1	15	30		1	15	30		1	15	30
♃	♊26	26	26	26	26	26	♄	♎27	28	29	29	♏0	1	♅	♋23	23	23	♆	♎23	24	24	♇	♌24	25	25	☊	♒1	♑1	28

NOVEMBER

	1	2	3	4	5	6	7	8	9	10	11	12	13	14	15	16	17	18	19	20	21	22	23	24	25	26	27	28	29	30
☉	♏8	9	10	11	12	13	14	15	16	17	18	19	20	21	22	23	24	25	26	27	28	29	♐0	1	2	3	4	5	6	♐7
☽	♍5	17	29	♎11	23	♏5	17	29	♐12	25	♑7	20	♒4	17	♓1	15	♈0	14	29	♉14	29	♊13	27	♋11	24	♌7	19	♍2	14	♍26
☿	♐0	0	1	1	1	0	0	♏29	29	28	27	26	24	23	22	20	19	18	17	16	15	15	15	15	15	15	15	16	17	♏17
♀	♎17	18	19	20	22	23	24	25	27	28	29	♏0	2	3	4	5	7	8	9	10	12	13	14	15	17	18	19	20	22	♏23
♂	♎0	0	1	1	2	3	3	4	5	5	6	6	7	8	8	9	10	10	11	11	12	13	13	14	14	15	16	16	17	♎18

	1	6	12	18	24	30		1	6	12	18	24	30		1	15	30		1	15	30		1	15	30		1	15	30
♃	♊26	26	25	25	24	23	♄	♏1	2	2	3	4	4	♅	♋23	23	23	♆	♎24	25	25	♇	♌25	25	25	☊	♑28	26	25

DECEMBER

	1	2	3	4	5	6	7	8	9	10	11	12	13	14	15	16	17	18	19	20	21	22	23	24	25	26	27	28	29	30	31
☉	♐9	10	11	12	13	14	15	16	17	18	19	20	21	22	23	24	25	26	27	28	29	♑0	1	2	3	4	5	6	7	8	♑9
☽	♎7	19	♏1	13	26	♐8	21	♑4	17	♒1	14	28	♓12	26	♈10	24	♉9	23	♊7	22	♋5	19	♌2	15	27	♍9	21	♎3	15	27	♏9
☿	♏18	19	20	21	23	24	25	26	28	29	♐1	2	3	5	6	8	9	11	12	14	15	17	18	20	21	23	24	26	27	29	♑0
♀	♏24	25	27	28	29	♐0	2	3	4	5	7	8	9	10	12	13	14	15	17	18	19	21	22	23	24	26	27	28	29	♑1	♑2
♂	♎18	19	19	20	21	21	22	22	23	24	24	25	25	26	27	27	28	29	29	♏0	0	1	2	2	3	3	4	5	5	6	♏6

	1	6	12	18	24	30		1	6	12	18	24	30		1	15	30		1	15	30		1	15	30		1	15	30
♃	♊23	22	22	21	20	19	♄	♏5	5	6	6	7	7	♅	♋23	22	22	♆	♎25	26	26	♇	♌25	25	25	☊	♑25	24	24

1954

JANUARY

	1	2	3	4	5	6	7	8	9	10	11	12	13	14	15	16	17	18	19	20	21	22	23	24	25	26	27	28	29	30	31
☉	♑10	11	12	13	14	15	16	17	18	19	20	21	22	23	24	25	26	27	28	29	♒0	1	2	3	4	5	7	8	9	10	♒11
☽	♏21	♐4	17	♑0	13	26	♒10	24	♓8	23	♈7	21	♉5	19	♊3	17	♋1	14	27	♌10	23	♍5	17	29	♎11	23	♏5	17	29	♐12	♐24
☿	♑2	4	5	7	8	10	11	13	15	16	18	20	21	23	24	26	28	29	♒1	3	5	6	8	10	11	13	15	17	18	20	♒22
♀	♑3	4	6	7	8	9	11	12	13	14	16	17	18	19	21	22	23	24	26	27	28	♒0	1	2	3	5	6	7	8	10	♒11
♂	♏7	8	8	9	9	10	10	11	12	12	13	13	14	15	15	16	16	17	18	18	19	19	20	20	21	22	22	23	23	24	♏24

	1	6	12	18	24	30		1	6	12	18	24	30		1	15	30		1	15	30		1	15	30		1	15	30
♃	♊19	18	18	17	17	17	♄	♏7	8	8	9	9	9	♅	♋22	21	20	♆	♎26	26	26	♇	♌25	24	24	☊	♑24	24	24

FEBRUARY

	1	2	3	4	5	6	7	8	9	10	11	12	13	14	15	16	17	18	19	20	21	22	23	24	25	26	27	28
☉	♒12	13	14	15	16	17	18	19	20	21	22	23	24	25	26	27	28	29	♓0	1	2	3	4	5	6	7	8	♓9
☽	♑7	21	♒5	19	♓4	18	♈3	17	♉2	16	♊0	14	27	♋10	23	♌6	19	♍1	13	25	♎7	19	♏1	13	25	♐7	19	♑2
☿	♒24	25	27	29	♓0	2	4	5	7	8	9	11	12	13	14	15	15	16	16	16	16	16	16	15	14	14	13	♓12
♀	♒12	13	15	16	17	18	20	21	22	23	25	26	27	28	♓0	1	2	3	5	6	7	8	10	11	12	13	15	♓16
♂	♏25	26	26	27	27	28	28	29	♐0	0	1	1	2	2	3	3	4	5	5	6	6	7	7	8	8	9	9	♐10

	1	6	12	18	24	28		1	6	12	18	24	28		1	15	28		1	15	28		1	15	28		1	15	28
♃	♊17	16	16	17	17	17	♄	♏9	9	9	9	9	9	♅	♋20	20	19	♆	♎26	26	26	♇	♌24	24	23	☊	♑24	24	23

MARCH

	1	2	3	4	5	6	7	8	9	10	11	12	13	14	15	16	17	18	19	20	21	22	23	24	25	26	27	28	29	30	31
☉	♓10	11	12	13	14	15	16	17	18	19	20	21	22	23	24	25	26	27	28	29	♈0	1	2	3	4	5	6	7	8	9	♈10
☽	♑15	29	♒13	27	♓12	27	♈12	27	♉12	26	♊10	24	♋7	20	♌3	15	28	♍10	22	♎4	16	28	♏10	22	♐4	16	28	♑11	24	♒7	♒21
☿	♓11	10	9	8	7	6	5	4	3	3	2	2	2	2	2	2	2	2	3	3	4	4	5	6	6	7	8	9	10	11	♓12
♀	♓17	18	20	21	22	23	25	26	27	28	♈0	1	2	3	5	6	7	8	10	11	12	13	15	16	17	18	19	21	22	23	♈24
♂	♐10	11	11	12	12	13	14	14	15	15	16	16	17	17	17	18	18	19	19	20	20	21	21	22	22	23	23	24	24	24	♐25

	1	6	12	18	24	30		1	6	12	18	24	30		1	15	30		1	15	30		1	15	30		1	15	30
♃	♊17	17	18	18	19	20	♄	♏9	9	9	9	8	8	♅	♋19	19	19	♆	♎26	26	25	♇	♌23	23	23	☊	♑23	22	21

APRIL

	1	2	3	4	5	6	7	8	9	10	11	12	13	14	15	16	17	18	19	20	21	22	23	24	25	26	27	28	29	30
☉	♈11	12	13	14	15	16	17	18	19	20	21	22	23	24	24	25	26	27	28	29	♉0	1	2	3	4	5	6	7	8	♉9
☽	♓5	20	♈5	21	♉6	21	♊6	20	♋4	17	♌0	13	25	♍7	19	♎1	13	25	♏7	19	♐1	13	25	♑7	20	♒3	16	♓0	14	♓29
☿	♓13	14	16	17	18	19	21	22	23	25	26	28	29	♈1	2	4	6	7	9	11	12	14	16	18	19	21	23	25	27	♈29
♀	♈26	27	28	29	♉1	2	3	4	6	7	8	9	10	12	13	14	15	17	18	19	20	22	23	24	25	26	28	29	♊0	♊1
♂	♐25	26	26	27	27	27	28	28	29	29	29	♑0	0	0	1	1	2	2	2	3	3	3	3	4	4	4	5	5	5	♑5

	1	6	12	18	24	30		1	6	12	18	24	30		1	15	30		1	15	30		1	15	30		1	15	30
♃	♊20	21	22	23	24	25	♄	♏8	8	7	7	6	6	♅	♋19	19	19	♆	♎25	25	24	♇	♌23	23	23	☊	♑20	19	17

MAY

	1	2	3	4	5	6	7	8	9	10	11	12	13	14	15	16	17	18	19	20	21	22	23	24	25	26	27	28	29	30	31
☉	♉10	11	12	13	14	15	16	17	18	19	20	21	22	23	24	25	26	27	27	28	29	♊0	1	2	3	4	5	6	7	8	♊9
☽	♈14	29	♉14	29	♊14	29	♋12	26	♌9	22	♍4	16	28	♎10	22	♏4	16	28	♐10	22	♑4	17	♒0	13	26	♓10	24	♈8	23	♉8	♉23
☿	♉1	3	5	7	9	11	14	16	18	20	22	24	27	29	♊1	3	5	7	9	11	13	15	17	19	21	22	24	26	27	29	♋0
♀	♊3	4	5	6	7	9	10	11	12	14	15	16	17	18	20	21	22	23	24	26	27	28	29	♋0	2	3	4	5	6	8	♋9
♂	♑6	6	6	6	7	7	7	7	7	7	8	8	8	8	8	8	8	8	8	8	8	9	9	9	9	8	8	8	8	8	♑8

	1	6	12	18	24	30		1	6	12	18	24	30		1	15	30		1	15	30		1	15	30		1	15	30
♃	♊25	26	27	29	♋0	1	♄	♏6	5	5	4	4	4	♅	♋20	20	21	♆	♎24	24	24	♇	♌23	23	23	☊	♑17	16	15

JUNE

	1	2	3	4	5	6	7	8	9	10	11	12	13	14	15	16	17	18	19	20	21	22	23	24	25	26	27	28	29	30
☉	♊10	11	12	13	14	15	16	17	18	19	20	20	21	22	23	24	25	26	27	28	29	♋0	1	2	3	4	5	6	7	♋8
☽	♊8	22	♋7	21	♌4	17	♍0	12	24	♎6	18	♏0	12	24	♐6	19	♑1	14	27	♒10	23	♓6	20	♈4	19	♉3	17	♊2	16	♋1
☿	♋2	3	5	6	7	8	10	11	12	13	13	14	15	16	16	17	17	18	18	18	19	19	19	19	19	19	18	18	18	♋17
♀	♋10	11	12	14	15	16	17	18	20	21	22	23	24	26	27	28	29	♌0	2	3	4	5	6	7	9	10	11	12	13	♌14
♂	♑8	8	8	8	8	7	7	7	7	7	6	6	6	6	5	5	5	5	4	4	4	3	3	3	3	2	2	2	1	♑1

	1	6	12	18	24	30		1	6	12	18	24	30		1	15	30		1	15	30		1	15	30		1	15	30
♃	♋2	3	4	5	7	8	♄	♏4	3	3	3	3	3	♅	♋21	21	22	♆	♎24	23	23	♇	♌23	23	23	☊	♑15	15	15

JULY

	1	2	3	4	5	6	7	8	9	10	11	12	13	14	15	16	17	18	19	20	21	22	23	24	25	26	27	28	29	30	31
☉	♋9	10	11	11	12	13	14	15	16	17	18	19	20	21	22	23	24	25	26	27	28	29	♌0	1	2	2	3	4	5	6	♌7
☽	♋15	29	♌12	25	♍8	20	♎3	15	26	♏8	20	♐2	15	27	♑10	23	♒6	19	♓3	17	♈1	15	29	♉14	28	♊12	26	♋10	24	♌7	♌20
☿	♋17	16	16	15	14	14	13	12	12	11	11	10	10	10	10	9	9	9	9	10	10	10	11	11	12	13	14	15	16	17	♋18
♀	♌16	17	18	19	20	21	23	24	25	26	27	28	♍0	1	2	3	4	5	6	8	9	10	11	12	13	14	16	17	18	19	♍20
♂	♑1	0	0	0	0	♐29	29	29	28	28	28	28	27	27	27	27	27	27	26	26	26	26	26	26	26	26	26	26	26	26	♐26

	1	6	12	18	24	30		1	6	12	18	24	30		1	15	30		1	15	30		1	15	30		1	15	30
♃	♋8	10	11	12	14	15	♄	♏3	3	3	3	3	3	♅	♋22	23	24	♆	♎23	23	23	♇	♌23	24	24	☊	♑15	15	15

AUGUST

	1	2	3	4	5	6	7	8	9	10	11	12	13	14	15	16	17	18	19	20	21	22	23	24	25	26	27	28	29	30	31
☉	♌8	9	10	11	12	13	14	15	16	17	18	19	20	21	22	23	24	25	25	26	27	28	29	♍0	1	2	3	4	5	6	♍7
☽	♍3	16	28	♎11	23	♏4	16	28	♐10	23	♑5	18	♒1	15	29	♓13	27	♈12	26	♉11	25	♊9	23	♋6	20	♌3	16	29	♍12	24	♎7
☿	♋19	21	22	24	25	27	29	♌1	3	4	6	8	10	12	14	16	18	20	23	25	27	29	♍1	2	4	6	8	10	12	14	♍16
♀	♍21	22	23	24	26	27	28	29	♎0	1	2	3	4	5	6	8	9	10	11	12	13	14	15	16	17	18	19	20	21	22	♎23
♂	♐26	26	26	26	26	26	26	26	26	26	27	27	27	27	27	28	28	28	28	29	29	29	♑0	0	0	0	1	1	2	2	♑2

	1	6	12	18	24	30		1	6	12	18	24	30		1	15	30		1	15	30		1	15	30		1	15	30
♃	♋15	16	18	19	20	21	♄	♏3	3	4	4	4	5	♅	♋24	25	26	♆	♎23	24	24	♇	♌24	25	25	☊	♑15	14	13

SEPTEMBER

	1	2	3	4	5	6	7	8	9	10	11	12	13	14	15	16	17	18	19	20	21	22	23	24	25	26	27	28	29	30
☉	♍8	9	10	11	12	13	14	15	16	17	18	19	20	21	22	23	24	25	26	26	27	28	29	♎0	1	2	3	4	5	♎6
☽	♎19	♏1	12	24	♐6	18	♑0	13	26	♒9	23	♓7	22	♈7	21	♉6	21	♊5	20	♋3	17	♌0	13	26	♍8	21	♎3	15	27	♏9
☿	♍17	19	21	23	24	26	28	29	♎1	3	4	6	7	9	10	12	13	15	16	18	19	21	22	23	25	26	27	29	♏0	♏1
♀	♎24	25	26	27	28	29	♏0	1	2	3	4	5	6	7	7	8	9	10	11	12	13	13	14	15	16	17	17	18	19	♏20
♂	♑3	3	3	4	4	5	5	6	6	6	7	7	8	8	9	9	10	10	11	11	12	12	13	14	14	15	15	16	16	♑17

	1	6	12	18	24	30		1	6	12	18	24	30		1	15	30		1	15	30		1	15	30		1	15	30
♃	♋22	23	24	25	26	26	♄	♏5	6	6	7	7	8	♅	♋26	27	27	♆	♎24	25	25	♇	♌25	26	26	☊	♑13	12	10

OCTOBER

	1	2	3	4	5	6	7	8	9	10	11	12	13	14	15	16	17	18	19	20	21	22	23	24	25	26	27	28	29	30	31
☉	♎7	8	9	10	11	12	13	14	15	16	17	18	19	20	21	22	23	24	25	26	27	28	29	♏0	1	2	3	4	5	6	♏7
☽	♏21	♐3	14	26	♑9	21	♒4	17	♓1	15	♈0	15	♉0	15	♊1	15	♋0	13	27	♌10	23	♍5	18	♎0	12	24	♏6	18	♐0	11	♐23
☿	♏2	3	4	6	7	8	9	9	10	11	12	13	13	14	14	14	15	15	15	15	14	14	13	13	12	11	10	8	7	6	♏5
♀	♏20	21	22	22	23	24	24	25	25	26	26	27	27	28	28	28	29	29	29	29	♐0	0	0	0	0	0	0	0	0	0	♏29
♂	♑17	18	19	19	20	20	21	22	22	23	23	24	25	25	26	26	27	28	28	29	♒0	0	1	2	2	3	4	4	5	6	♒6

	1	6	12	18	24	30		1	6	12	18	24	30		1	15	30		1	15	30		1	15	30		1	15	30
♃	♋27	27	28	29	29	29	♄	♏8	9	9	10	11	11	♅	♋27	28	28	♆	♎25	26	26	♇	♌26	26	27	☊	♑10	9	7

NOVEMBER

	1	2	3	4	5	6	7	8	9	10	11	12	13	14	15	16	17	18	19	20	21	22	23	24	25	26	27	28	29	30
☉	♏8	9	10	11	12	13	14	15	16	17	18	19	20	21	22	23	24	25	26	27	28	29	♐0	1	2	3	4	5	6	♐7
☽	♑5	17	♒0	13	26	♓9	24	♈8	23	♉8	24	♊9	24	♋8	23	♌6	19	♍2	15	27	♎9	21	♏3	15	27	♐8	20	♑2	14	♑27
☿	♏3	2	1	0	0	♎29	29	29	29	29	♏0	0	1	2	3	4	5	6	8	9	10	12	13	14	16	17	19	20	22	♏23
♀	♏29	29	29	28	28	28	27	27	26	26	25	24	24	23	23	22	21	21	20	20	19	19	18	18	17	17	16	16	16	♏15
♂	♒7	8	8	9	10	10	11	12	12	13	14	14	15	16	16	17	18	19	19	20	21	21	22	23	23	24	25	26	26	♒27

	1	6	12	18	24	30		1	6	12	18	24	30		1	15	30		1	15	30		1	15	30		1	15	30
♃	♌0	0	0	0	0	0	♄	♏12	12	13	14	14	15	♅	♋28	28	27	♆	♎26	27	27	♇	♌27	27	27	☊	♑7	6	6

DECEMBER

	1	2	3	4	5	6	7	8	9	10	11	12	13	14	15	16	17	18	19	20	21	22	23	24	25	26	27	28	29	30	31
☉	♐8	9	10	11	12	13	14	15	16	17	18	19	20	21	22	23	25	26	27	28	29	♑0	1	2	3	4	5	6	7	8	♑9
☽	♒9	22	♓5	19	♈3	17	♉2	17	♊2	17	♋2	16	♌1	15	28	♍11	23	♎6	18	♏0	11	23	♐5	17	29	♑11	24	♒6	19	♓2	♓15
☿	♏25	26	28	♐0	1	3	4	6	7	9	10	12	14	15	17	18	20	21	23	24	26	28	29	♑1	2	4	6	7	9	10	♑12
♀	♏15	15	15	15	15	15	15	15	15	15	15	15	16	16	16	17	17	17	18	18	19	19	20	20	21	22	22	23	24	24	♏25
♂	♒28	28	29	♓0	0	1	2	3	3	4	5	5	6	7	8	8	9	10	10	11	12	13	13	14	15	15	16	17	18	18	♓19

	1	6	12	18	24	30		1	6	12	18	24	30		1	15	30		1	15	30		1	15	30		1	15	30
♃	♌0 ♋29	29	28	28	27		♄	♏15	16	16	17	18	18	♅	♋27	27	26	♆	♎27	28	28	♇	♌27	27	27	☊	♑6	6	6

1955

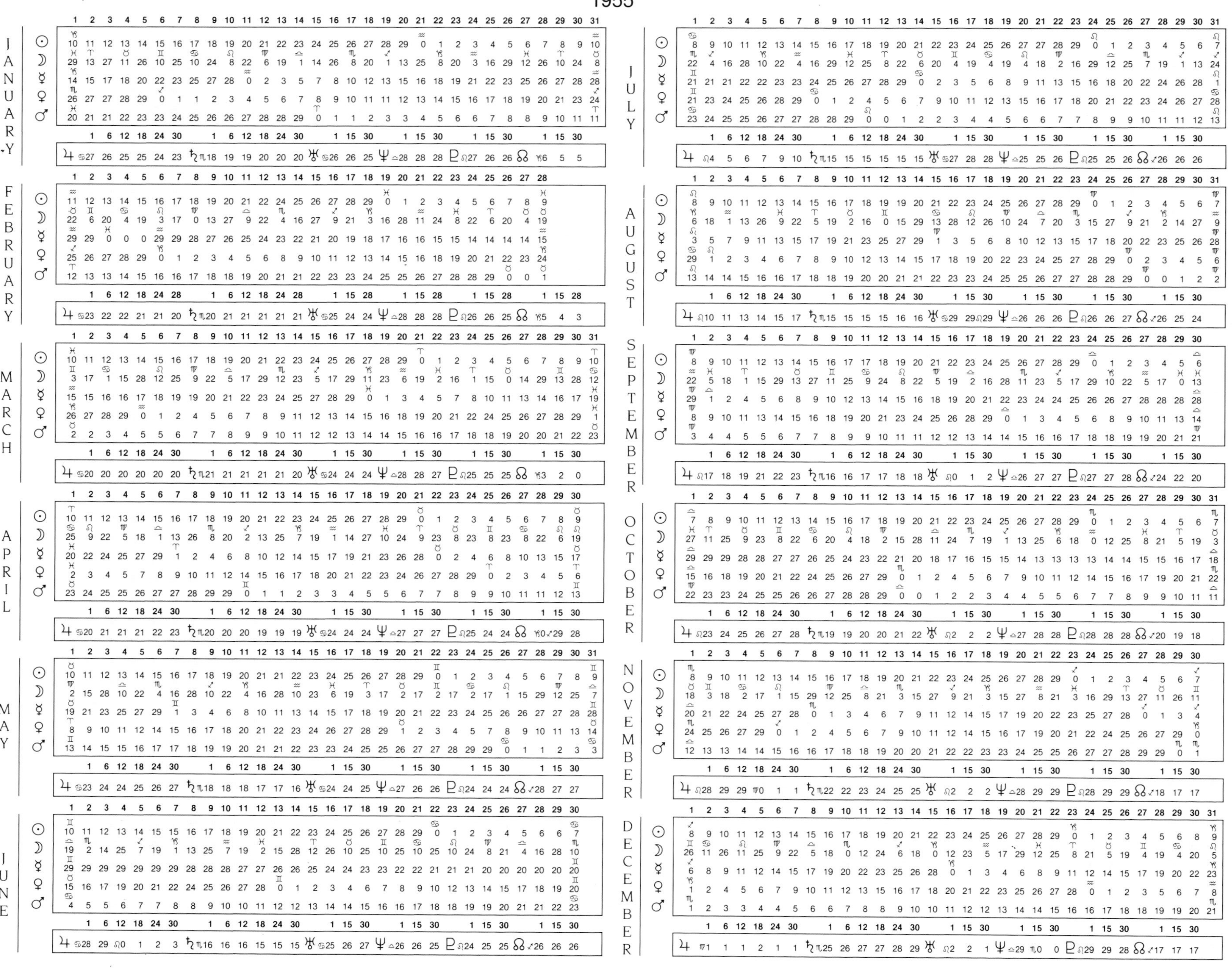

JANUARY

	1	2	3	4	5	6	7	8	9	10	11	12	13	14	15	16	17	18	19	20	21	22	23	24	25	26	27	28	29	30	31
☉	♑10	11	12	13	14	15	16	17	18	19	20	21	22	23	24	25	26	27	28	29	♒0	1	2	3	4	5	6	7	8	9	♒10
☽	♓29	♈13	27	♉11	26	♊10	25	♋10	24	♌8	22	♍6	19	♎1	14	26	♏8	20	♐1	13	25	♑8	20	♒3	16	29	♓12	26	♈10	24	♉8
☿	♑14	15	17	18	20	22	23	25	27	28	♒0	2	3	5	7	8	10	12	13	15	16	18	19	21	22	23	25	26	27	28	♒28
♀	♏26	27	27	28	29	♐0	1	1	2	3	4	5	6	7	8	9	10	11	11	12	13	14	15	16	17	18	19	20	21	23	♐24
♂	♓20	21	21	22	23	23	24	25	26	26	27	28	28	29	♈0	1	1	2	3	3	4	5	6	6	7	8	8	9	10	11	♈11

♃ 1	6	12	18	24	30	♄ 1	6	12	18	24	30	♅ 1	15	30	♆ 1	15	30	♇ 1	15	30	☊ 1	15	30
♋27	26	25	25	24	23	♏18	19	19	20	20	20	♋26	26	25	♎28	28	28	♌27	26	26	♑6	5	5

FEBRUARY

	1	2	3	4	5	6	7	8	9	10	11	12	13	14	15	16	17	18	19	20	21	22	23	24	25	26	27	28
☉	♒11	12	13	14	15	16	17	18	19	20	21	22	24	25	26	27	28	29	♓0	1	2	3	4	5	6	7	8	♓9
☽	♉22	♊6	20	♋4	19	♌3	17	♍0	13	27	♎9	22	♏4	16	27	♐9	21	♑3	16	28	♒11	24	♓8	22	♈6	20	♉4	♉19
☿	♒29	29	♓0	0	0	♒29	29	28	27	26	25	24	23	22	21	20	19	18	17	16	16	15	15	14	14	14	14	♒15
♀	♐25	26	27	28	29	♑0	1	2	3	4	5	6	8	9	10	11	12	13	14	15	16	18	19	20	21	22	23	♑24
♂	♈12	13	13	14	15	16	16	17	18	18	19	20	21	21	22	23	23	24	25	25	26	27	28	28	29	♉0	0	♉1

♃ 1	6	12	18	24	28	♄ 1	6	12	18	24	28	♅ 1	15	28	♆ 1	15	28	♇ 1	15	28	☊ 1	15	28
♋23	22	22	21	21	20	♏20	21	21	21	21	21	♋25	24	24	♎28	28	28	♌26	26	25	♑5	4	3

MARCH

	1	2	3	4	5	6	7	8	9	10	11	12	13	14	15	16	17	18	19	20	21	22	23	24	25	26	27	28	29	30	31
☉	♓10	11	12	13	14	15	16	17	18	19	20	21	22	23	24	25	26	27	28	29	♈0	1	2	3	4	5	6	7	8	9	♈10
☽	♊3	17	♋1	15	28	♌12	25	♍9	22	♎5	17	29	♏12	23	♐5	17	29	♑11	23	♒6	19	♓2	16	♈1	15	♉0	14	29	♊13	28	♋12
☿	♒15	15	16	16	17	18	19	19	20	21	22	23	24	25	27	28	29	♓0	1	3	4	5	7	8	10	11	13	14	16	17	♓19
♀	♑26	27	28	29	♒0	1	2	4	5	6	7	8	9	11	12	13	14	15	16	18	19	20	21	22	24	25	26	27	28	29	♓1
♂	♉2	2	3	4	5	5	6	7	7	8	9	9	10	11	12	12	13	14	14	15	16	16	17	18	18	19	20	20	21	22	♉23

♃ 1	6	12	18	24	30	♄ 1	6	12	18	24	30	♅ 1	15	30	♆ 1	15	30	♇ 1	15	30	☊ 1	15	30
♋20	20	20	20	20	20	♏21	21	21	21	21	20	♋24	24	24	♎28	28	27	♌25	25	25	♑3	2	0

APRIL

	1	2	3	4	5	6	7	8	9	10	11	12	13	14	15	16	17	18	19	20	21	22	23	24	25	26	27	28	29	30
☉	♈10	11	12	13	14	15	16	17	18	19	20	21	22	23	24	25	26	27	28	29	♉0	1	2	3	4	5	6	7	8	♉9
☽	♋25	♌9	22	♍5	18	♎1	13	26	♏8	20	♐2	13	25	♑7	19	♒1	14	27	♓10	24	♈9	23	♉8	23	♊8	23	♋8	22	♌6	♌19
☿	♓20	22	24	25	27	29	♈1	2	4	6	8	10	12	14	15	17	19	21	23	26	28	♉0	2	4	6	8	10	13	15	♉17
♀	♓2	3	4	5	7	8	9	10	11	12	14	15	16	17	18	20	21	22	23	24	26	27	28	29	♈0	2	3	4	5	♈6
♂	♉23	24	25	25	26	27	27	28	29	29	♊0	1	1	2	3	3	4	5	5	6	7	7	8	9	9	10	11	11	12	♊13

♃ 1	6	12	18	24	30	♄ 1	6	12	18	24	30	♅ 1	15	30	♆ 1	15	30	♇ 1	15	30	☊ 1	15	30
♋20	21	21	21	22	23	♏20	20	20	19	19	19	♋24	24	24	♎27	27	27	♌25	24	24	♑0	♐29	28

MAY

	1	2	3	4	5	6	7	8	9	10	11	12	13	14	15	16	17	18	19	20	21	22	23	24	25	26	27	28	29	30	31
☉	♉10	11	12	13	14	15	16	17	18	19	20	21	21	22	23	24	25	26	27	28	29	♊0	1	2	3	4	5	6	7	8	♊9
☽	♍2	15	28	♎10	22	♏4	16	28	♐10	22	♑4	16	28	♒10	23	♓6	19	♈3	17	♉2	17	♊2	17	♋2	17	♌1	15	29	♍12	25	♎7
☿	♉19	21	23	25	27	29	♊1	3	4	6	8	10	11	13	14	15	17	18	19	20	21	22	23	24	25	26	26	27	27	28	♊28
♀	♈8	9	10	11	12	14	15	16	17	18	20	21	22	23	24	26	27	28	29	♉1	2	3	4	5	7	8	9	10	11	13	♉14
♂	♊13	14	15	15	16	17	17	18	19	19	20	21	21	22	23	23	24	25	25	26	27	27	28	29	29	♋0	1	1	2	3	♋3

♃ 1	6	12	18	24	30	♄ 1	6	12	18	24	30	♅ 1	15	30	♆ 1	15	30	♇ 1	15	30	☊ 1	15	30
♋23	24	24	25	26	27	♏18	18	18	17	17	16	♋24	24	25	♎27	26	26	♌24	24	24	♐28	27	27

JUNE

	1	2	3	4	5	6	7	8	9	10	11	12	13	14	15	16	17	18	19	20	21	22	23	24	25	26	27	28	29	30
☉	♊10	11	12	13	14	15	15	16	17	18	19	20	21	22	23	24	25	26	27	28	29	♋0	1	2	3	4	5	6	6	♋7
☽	♎19	♏2	14	25	♐7	19	♑1	13	25	♒7	19	♓2	15	28	♈12	26	♉10	25	♊10	25	♋10	25	♌10	24	♍8	21	♎4	16	28	♏10
☿	♊29	29	29	29	29	29	29	28	28	28	27	27	26	26	25	24	24	23	23	22	22	21	21	21	20	20	20	20	20	♊20
♀	♉15	16	17	19	20	21	22	24	25	26	27	28	♊0	1	2	3	4	6	7	8	9	10	12	13	14	15	17	18	19	♊20
♂	♋4	5	5	6	7	7	8	8	9	10	10	11	12	12	13	14	14	15	16	16	17	18	18	19	19	20	21	21	22	♋23

♃ 1	6	12	18	24	30	♄ 1	6	12	18	24	30	♅ 1	15	30	♆ 1	15	30	♇ 1	15	30	☊ 1	15	30
♋28	29	♌0	1	2	3	♏16	16	16	15	15	15	♋25	26	27	♎26	26	25	♌24	25	25	♐26	26	26

JULY

	1	2	3	4	5	6	7	8	9	10	11	12	13	14	15	16	17	18	19	20	21	22	23	24	25	26	27	28	29	30	31
☉	♋8	9	10	11	12	13	14	15	16	17	18	19	20	21	22	23	24	25	26	27	27	28	29	♌0	1	2	3	4	5	6	♌7
☽	♏22	♐4	16	28	♑10	22	♒4	16	29	♓12	25	♈8	22	♉6	20	♊4	19	♋4	19	♌4	18	♍2	16	29	♎12	25	♏7	19	♐1	13	♐24
☿	♊21	21	21	22	22	23	23	24	25	26	27	28	29	♋0	2	3	5	6	8	9	11	13	15	16	18	20	22	24	26	28	♌1
♀	♊21	23	24	25	26	28	29	♋0	1	2	4	5	6	7	9	10	11	12	13	15	16	17	18	20	21	22	23	24	26	27	♋28
♂	♋23	24	25	25	26	27	27	28	28	29	♌0	0	1	2	2	3	4	4	5	6	6	7	7	8	9	9	10	11	11	12	♌13

♃ 1	6	12	18	24	30	♄ 1	6	12	18	24	30	♅ 1	15	30	♆ 1	15	30	♇ 1	15	30	☊ 1	15	30
♌4	5	6	7	9	10	♏15	15	15	15	15	15	♋27	28	28	♎25	25	26	♌25	25	26	♐26	26	26

AUGUST

	1	2	3	4	5	6	7	8	9	10	11	12	13	14	15	16	17	18	19	20	21	22	23	24	25	26	27	28	29	30	31
☉	♌8	9	10	11	12	13	14	15	16	17	18	19	19	20	21	22	23	24	25	26	27	28	29	♍0	1	2	3	4	5	6	♍7
☽	♑6	18	♒1	13	26	♓9	22	♈5	19	♉2	16	♊0	15	29	♋13	28	♌12	26	♍10	24	♎7	20	♏3	15	27	♐9	21	♑2	14	27	♒9
☿	♌3	5	7	9	11	13	15	17	19	21	23	25	27	29	♍1	3	5	6	8	10	12	13	15	17	18	20	22	23	25	26	♍28
♀	♋29	♌1	2	3	4	6	7	8	9	10	12	13	14	15	17	18	19	20	22	23	24	25	27	28	29	♍0	2	3	4	5	♍6
♂	♌13	14	14	15	16	16	17	18	18	19	20	20	21	21	22	23	23	24	25	25	26	27	27	28	28	29	♍0	0	1	2	♍2

♃ 1	6	12	18	24	30	♄ 1	6	12	18	24	30	♅ 1	15	30	♆ 1	15	30	♇ 1	15	30	☊ 1	15	30
♌10	11	13	14	15	17	♏15	15	15	15	16	16	♋29	29	♌29	♎26	26	26	♌26	26	27	♐26	25	24

SEPTEMBER

	1	2	3	4	5	6	7	8	9	10	11	12	13	14	15	16	17	18	19	20	21	22	23	24	25	26	27	28	29	30
☉	♍8	9	10	11	12	13	14	15	16	17	17	18	19	20	21	22	23	24	25	26	27	28	29	♎0	1	2	3	4	5	♎6
☽	♒22	♓5	18	♈1	15	29	♉13	27	♊11	25	♋9	24	♌8	22	♍5	19	♎2	16	28	♏11	23	♐5	17	29	♑10	22	♒5	17	♓0	♓13
☿	♍29	♎1	2	4	5	6	8	9	10	12	13	14	15	16	18	19	20	21	22	23	24	24	25	26	26	27	28	28	28	♎28
♀	♍8	9	10	11	13	14	15	16	18	19	20	21	23	24	25	26	28	29	♎0	1	3	4	5	6	8	9	10	11	13	♎14
♂	♍3	4	4	5	5	6	7	7	8	9	9	10	11	11	12	12	13	14	14	15	16	16	17	18	18	19	19	20	21	♍21

♃ 1	6	12	18	24	30	♄ 1	6	12	18	24	30	♅ 1	15	30	♆ 1	15	30	♇ 1	15	30	☊ 1	15	30
♌17	18	19	21	22	23	♏16	16	17	17	18	18	♌0	1	2	♎26	27	27	♌27	27	28	♐24	22	20

OCTOBER

	1	2	3	4	5	6	7	8	9	10	11	12	13	14	15	16	17	18	19	20	21	22	23	24	25	26	27	28	29	30	31
☉	♎7	8	9	10	11	12	13	14	15	16	17	18	19	20	21	22	23	24	25	26	27	28	29	♏0	1	2	3	4	5	6	♏7
☽	♓27	♈11	25	♉9	23	♊8	22	♋6	20	♌4	18	♍2	15	28	♎11	24	♏7	19	♐1	13	25	♑6	18	♒0	12	25	♓8	21	♈5	19	♉3
☿	♎29	29	29	28	28	27	27	26	25	24	23	22	21	20	18	17	16	15	15	14	13	13	13	13	14	14	15	15	16	17	♎18
♀	♎15	16	18	19	20	21	22	24	25	26	27	29	♏0	1	2	4	5	6	7	9	10	11	12	14	15	16	17	19	20	21	♏22
♂	♍22	23	23	24	25	25	26	26	27	28	28	29	♎0	0	1	2	2	3	4	4	5	5	6	7	7	8	9	9	10	11	♎11

♃ 1	6	12	18	24	30	♄ 1	6	12	18	24	30	♅ 1	15	30	♆ 1	15	30	♇ 1	15	30	☊ 1	15	30
♌23	24	25	26	27	28	♏19	19	20	20	21	22	♌2	2	2	♎27	28	28	♌28	28	28	♐20	19	18

NOVEMBER

	1	2	3	4	5	6	7	8	9	10	11	12	13	14	15	16	17	18	19	20	21	22	23	24	25	26	27	28	29	30
☉	♏8	9	10	11	12	13	14	15	16	17	18	19	20	21	22	23	24	25	26	27	28	29	♐0	1	2	3	4	5	6	♐7
☽	♉18	♊3	18	♋2	17	♌1	15	29	♍12	25	♎8	21	♏3	15	27	♐9	21	♑3	15	27	♒8	21	♓3	16	29	♈13	27	♉11	26	♊11
☿	♎20	21	22	24	25	27	28	♏0	1	3	4	6	7	9	11	12	14	15	17	19	20	22	23	25	27	28	♐0	1	3	♐4
♀	♏24	25	26	27	29	♐0	1	2	4	5	6	7	9	10	11	12	14	15	16	17	19	20	21	22	24	25	26	27	29	♑0
♂	♎12	13	13	14	14	15	16	16	17	18	18	19	20	20	21	22	22	23	23	24	25	25	26	27	27	28	29	29	♏0	♏1

♃ 1	6	12	18	24	30	♄ 1	6	12	18	24	30	♅ 1	15	30	♆ 1	15	30	♇ 1	15	30	☊ 1	15	30
♌28	29	29	♍0	1	1	♏22	22	23	24	25	25	♌2	2	2	♎28	29	29	♌28	29	29	♐18	17	17

DECEMBER

	1	2	3	4	5	6	7	8	9	10	11	12	13	14	15	16	17	18	19	20	21	22	23	24	25	26	27	28	29	30	31
☉	♐8	9	10	11	12	13	14	15	16	17	18	19	20	21	22	23	24	25	26	27	28	29	♑0	1	2	3	4	5	6	8	♑9
☽	♊26	♋11	26	♌11	25	♍9	22	♎5	18	♏0	12	24	♐6	18	♑0	12	23	♒5	17	29	♓12	25	♈8	21	♉5	19	♊4	19	♋4	20	♌5
☿	♐6	8	9	11	12	14	15	17	19	20	22	23	25	26	28	♑0	1	3	4	6	8	9	11	12	14	15	17	19	20	22	♑23
♀	♑1	2	4	5	6	7	9	10	11	12	13	15	16	17	18	20	21	22	23	25	26	27	28	♒0	1	2	3	5	6	7	♒8
♂	♏1	2	3	3	4	4	5	6	6	7	8	8	9	10	10	11	12	12	13	14	14	15	16	16	17	18	18	19	19	20	♏21

♃ 1	6	12	18	24	30	♄ 1	6	12	18	24	30	♅ 1	15	30	♆ 1	15	30	♇ 1	15	30	☊ 1	15	30
♍1	1	1	2	1	1	♏25	26	27	27	28	29	♌2	2	1	♎29	♏0	0	♌29	29	28	♐17	17	17

1956

JANUARY

	1	2	3	4	5	6	7	8	9	10	11	12	13	14	15	16	17	18	19	20	21	22	23	24	25	26	27	28	29	30	31
☉	♑10	11	12	13	14	15	16	17	18	19	20	21	22	23	24	25	26	27	28	29	♒0	1	2	3	4	5	6	7	8	9	♒10
☽	♌19	♍4	18	♎1	14	27	♏9	21	♐3	15	27	♑9	20	♒2	14	27	♓9	21	♈4	17	♉0	14	28	♊13	27	♋12	27	♌12	27	♍12	♍26
☿	♑25	26	28	29	♒1	2	4	5	6	8	9	10	11	12	12	13	13	13	13	13	13	12	12	11	10	9	7	6	5	4	♒2
♀	♒10	11	12	13	14	16	17	18	19	21	22	23	24	26	27	28	29	♓0	2	3	4	5	7	8	9	10	11	13	14	15	♓16
♂	♏21	22	23	23	24	25	25	26	27	27	28	29	29	♐0	1	1	2	3	3	4	5	5	6	6	7	8	8	9	10	10	♐11

	1	6	12	18	24	30
♃	♍1	1	1	0	♌29	29
♄	♏29	29	♐0	0	1	1

	1	15	30
♅	♌1	1	0
♆	♏0	0	0
♇	♌28	28	28
☊	♐17	17	16

FEBRUARY

	1	2	3	4	5	6	7	8	9	10	11	12	13	14	15	16	17	18	19	20	21	22	23	24	25	26	27	28	29
☉	♒11	12	13	14	15	16	17	18	19	20	21	22	23	24	25	26	27	28	29	♓0	1	2	3	4	5	6	7	8	♓9
☽	♎10	23	♏5	18	♐0	12	24	♑5	17	29	♒11	23	♓6	18	♈1	14	27	♉11	24	♊8	22	♋7	21	♌6	21	♍5	20	♎4	♎17
☿	♒1	0	0	♑29	28	28	28	28	28	28	28	28	29	29	♒0	0	1	2	3	4	5	6	7	8	9	10	11	13	♒14
♀	♓18	19	20	21	22	24	25	26	27	28	♈0	1	2	3	4	6	7	8	9	10	12	13	14	15	16	17	19	20	♈21
♂	♐12	12	13	14	14	15	16	16	17	18	18	19	20	20	21	22	22	23	24	24	25	26	26	27	27	28	29	29	♑0

	1	6	12	18	24	29
♃	♌28	28	27	26	26	25
♄	♐1	2	2	2	3	3

	1	15	29
♅	♌0	♋0	29
♆	♏0	0	0
♇	♌28	27	27
☊	♐16	14	13

MARCH

	1	2	3	4	5	6	7	8	9	10	11	12	13	14	15	16	17	18	19	20	21	22	23	24	25	26	27	28	29	30	31
☉	♓10	11	12	13	14	15	16	17	18	19	20	21	22	23	24	25	26	27	28	29	♈0	1	2	3	4	5	6	7	8	9	♈10
☽	♏1	13	26	♐8	20	♑2	13	25	♒7	20	♓2	15	28	♈11	24	♉8	21	♊5	19	♋3	17	♌1	16	♍0	14	28	♎12	25	♏9	21	♐4
☿	♒15	16	18	19	21	22	23	25	26	28	29	♓1	2	4	6	7	9	10	12	14	16	17	19	21	23	24	26	28	♈0	2	♈4
♀	♈22	23	24	26	27	28	29	♉0	1	2	4	5	6	7	8	9	10	11	13	14	15	16	17	18	19	20	21	22	23	24	♉26
♂	♑1	1	2	3	3	4	5	5	6	7	7	8	9	9	10	11	11	12	13	13	14	14	15	16	16	17	18	18	19	20	♑20

	1	6	12	18	24	30
♃	♌25	24	23	23	22	22
♄	♐3	3	3	3	3	3

	1	15	30
♅	♋29	28	28
♆	♏0	0	0
♇	♌27	27	26
☊	♐13	11	10

APRIL

	1	2	3	4	5	6	7	8	9	10	11	12	13	14	15	16	17	18	19	20	21	22	23	24	25	26	27	28	29	30
☉	♈11	12	13	14	15	16	17	18	19	20	21	22	23	24	25	26	27	28	29	♉0	1	2	3	4	5	6	7	8	9	♉10
☽	♐16	28	♑10	21	♒3	15	28	♓10	23	♈6	20	♉3	17	♊1	16	♋0	14	28	♌12	26	♍10	24	♎8	21	♏4	17	29	♐12	24	♑6
☿	♈6	8	10	12	14	16	18	20	22	24	26	29	♉1	3	5	7	9	11	13	15	16	18	20	22	23	25	26	28	29	♊0
♀	♉27	28	29	♊0	1	2	3	4	5	6	7	8	9	10	11	12	13	14	14	15	16	17	18	19	20	21	22	22	23	♊24
♂	♑21	22	22	23	24	24	25	26	26	27	27	28	29	29	♒0	1	1	2	3	3	4	4	5	6	6	7	8	8	9	♒10

	1	6	12	18	24	30
♃	♌22	22	22	21	22	22
♄	♐2	2	2	2	1	1

	1	15	30
♅	♋28	28	28
♆	♏0	♎29	29
♇	♌26	26	26
☊	♐10	9	8

MAY

	1	2	3	4	5	6	7	8	9	10	11	12	13	14	15	16	17	18	19	20	21	22	23	24	25	26	27	28	29	30	31
☉	♉11	12	13	13	14	15	16	17	18	19	20	21	22	23	24	25	26	27	28	29	♊0	1	2	3	4	5	6	7	8	9	♊10
☽	♑17	29	♒11	23	♓6	18	♈1	14	28	♉12	26	♊11	26	♋10	25	♌9	23	♍7	21	♎4	17	♏0	13	25	♐8	20	♑2	14	26	♒7	♒19
☿	♊1	2	3	4	5	6	7	7	8	8	8	9	9	9	9	9	9	8	8	8	7	7	6	6	5	5	4	4	3	3	♊2
♀	♊25	26	26	27	28	29	29	♋0	1	1	2	2	3	4	4	5	5	6	6	7	7	7	8	8	8	8	9	9	9	9	♋9
♂	♒10	11	11	12	13	13	14	14	15	16	16	17	18	18	19	19	20	21	21	22	22	23	24	24	25	25	26	26	27	28	♒28

	1	6	12	18	24	30
♃	♌22	22	22	23	23	24
♄	♐1	1	0	0	♏29	29

	1	15	30
♅	♋29	29	29
♆	♎29	28	28
♇	♌26	26	26
☊	♐8	8	8

JUNE

	1	2	3	4	5	6	7	8	9	10	11	12	13	14	15	16	17	18	19	20	21	22	23	24	25	26	27	28	29	30
☉	♊10	11	12	13	14	15	16	17	18	19	20	21	22	23	24	25	26	27	28	29	♋0	1	1	2	3	4	5	6	7	♋8
☽	♓1	14	26	♈9	22	♉6	20	♊5	20	♋5	20	♌4	19	♍4	18	♎1	14	27	♏10	22	♐5	17	29	♑11	22	♒4	16	28	♓10	♓22
☿	♊2	1	1	1	0	0	0	0	0	0	1	1	1	2	2	3	4	4	5	6	7	8	9	10	11	13	14	15	17	♊18
♀	♋9	9	9	9	9	8	8	8	8	7	7	7	6	6	5	5	4	3	3	2	2	1	0	0	♊29	28	28	27	27	♊26
♂	♒29	29	♓0	0	1	1	2	3	3	4	4	5	5	6	6	7	7	8	8	9	9	10	10	11	11	12	12	13	13	♓13

	1	6	12	18	24	30
♃	♌24	25	26	27	28	29
♄	♏29	28	28	28	27	27

	1	15	30
♅	♌0	0	1
♆	♎28	28	28
♇	♌26	26	27
☊	♐8	8	8

JULY

	1	2	3	4	5	6	7	8	9	10	11	12	13	14	15	16	17	18	19	20	21	22	23	24	25	26	27	28	29	30	31
☉	♋9	10	11	12	13	14	15	16	17	18	19	20	21	22	22	23	24	25	26	27	28	29	♌0	1	2	3	4	5	6	7	♌8
☽	♈5	18	♉1	14	29	♊13	28	♋13	28	♌13	28	♍13	27	♎11	24	♏7	19	♐2	14	26	♑8	19	♒1	13	25	♓7	19	♈2	14	27	♉10
☿	♊20	22	23	25	27	29	♋0	2	4	6	8	10	12	15	17	19	21	23	25	27	♌0	2	4	6	8	10	12	14	16	18	♌20
♀	♊26	25	25	24	24	24	23	23	23	23	23	23	23	23	23	23	23	23	23	23	23	24	24	24	25	25	26	26	26	27	♊27
♂	♓14	14	15	15	16	16	16	17	17	17	18	18	18	19	19	19	20	20	20	21	21	21	21	22	22	22	22	22	23	23	♓23

	1	6	12	18	24	30
♃	♌29	♍0	1	2	3	4
♄	♏27	27	26	26	26	26

	1	15	30
♅	♌1	2	3
♆	♎28	28	28
♇	♌27	27	28
☊	♐8	7	6

AUGUST

	1	2	3	4	5	6	7	8	9	10	11	12	13	14	15	16	17	18	19	20	21	22	23	24	25	26	27	28	29	30	31
☉	♌9	10	11	12	13	13	14	15	16	17	18	19	20	21	22	23	24	25	26	27	28	29	♍0	1	2	3	4	5	6	7	♍8
☽	♉24	♊7	22	♋6	21	♌7	22	♍7	22	♎6	20	♏3	16	28	♐11	23	♑5	16	28	♒10	22	♓4	16	29	♈11	24	♉7	20	♊3	17	♋1
☿	♌21	23	25	27	29	♍0	2	4	5	7	9	10	12	13	15	16	18	19	20	22	23	24	26	27	28	29	♎0	2	3	4	♎5
♀	♊28	29	29	♋0	0	1	2	2	3	4	5	5	6	7	8	8	9	10	11	12	13	13	14	15	16	17	18	19	20	21	♋22
♂	♓23	23	23	23	23	24	24	24	24	24	24	24	24	24	24	23	23	23	23	23	23	23	23	22	22	22	22	22	22	21	♓21

	1	6	12	18	24	30
♃	♍5	6	7	8	10	11
♄	♏26	26	26	26	27	27

	1	15	30
♅	♌3	4	5
♆	♎28	28	28
♇	♌28	28	29
☊	♐6	5	3

SEPTEMBER

	1	2	3	4	5	6	7	8	9	10	11	12	13	14	15	16	17	18	19	20	21	22	23	24	25	26	27	28	29	30
☉	♍9	9	10	11	12	13	14	15	16	17	18	19	20	21	22	23	24	25	26	27	28	29	♎0	1	2	3	4	5	6	♎7
☽	♋16	♌0	15	♍0	15	♎0	14	28	♏11	24	♐7	19	♑1	13	25	♒7	19	♓1	13	25	♈8	21	♉4	17	♊0	14	28	♋12	26	♌10
☿	♎6	7	7	8	9	10	10	11	11	12	12	12	12	12	12	12	12	11	11	10	9	8	7	6	5	4	3	2	1	♎0
♀	♋23	24	25	26	27	28	29	♌0	1	2	3	4	5	6	7	8	9	10	11	12	13	14	15	16	18	19	20	21	22	♌23
♂	♓21	21	20	20	20	19	19	19	19	18	18	18	18	17	17	17	17	16	16	16	16	15	15	15	15	15	14	14	14	♓14

	1	6	12	18	24	30
♃	♍11	12	14	15	16	18
♄	♏27	27	28	28	29	29

	1	15	30
♅	♌5	6	6
♆	♎28	29	29
♇	♌29	29	♍29
☊	♐3	2	1

OCTOBER

	1	2	3	4	5	6	7	8	9	10	11	12	13	14	15	16	17	18	19	20	21	22	23	24	25	26	27	28	29	30	31
☉	♎8	9	10	11	12	13	14	15	16	17	18	19	20	21	22	23	24	25	26	27	28	29	♏0	1	2	3	4	5	6	7	♏8
☽	♌25	♍9	24	♎8	22	♏6	19	♐2	15	27	♑9	21	♒3	15	27	♓9	21	♈4	17	♉0	13	27	♊11	25	♋9	23	♌7	21	♍5	19	♎3
☿	♍29	28	28	28	27	27	27	28	28	29	♎0	1	2	3	4	5	7	8	10	11	13	14	16	18	19	21	23	24	26	28	♎29
♀	♌24	25	26	28	29	♍0	1	2	3	4	6	7	8	9	10	11	12	14	15	16	17	18	20	21	22	23	24	25	27	28	♍29
♂	♓14	14	14	13	13	13	13	13	13	13	13	13	13	13	13	13	13	14	14	14	14	14	14	14	15	15	15	15	15	16	♓16

	1	6	12	18	24	30
♃	♍18	19	20	21	22	23
♄	♏29	♐0	0	1	1	2

	1	15	30
♅	♌6	7	7
♆	♎29	♏0	0
♇	♍0	0	0
☊	♐0	0	♏0

NOVEMBER

	1	2	3	4	5	6	7	8	9	10	11	12	13	14	15	16	17	18	19	20	21	22	23	24	25	26	27	28	29	30
☉	♏9	10	11	12	13	14	15	16	17	18	19	20	21	22	23	24	25	26	27	28	29	♐0	1	2	3	4	5	6	7	♐8
☽	♎17	♏1	14	27	♐10	23	♑5	17	29	♒11	23	♓5	17	29	♈12	25	♉8	22	♊6	20	♋5	19	♌3	18	♍2	16	♎0	14	27	♏10
☿	♏1	3	4	6	8	9	11	13	14	16	17	19	21	22	24	25	27	29	♐0	2	3	5	6	8	10	11	13	14	16	♐17
♀	♎0	1	3	4	5	6	7	9	10	11	12	13	15	16	17	18	20	21	22	23	24	26	27	28	29	♏1	2	3	4	♏5
♂	♓16	16	17	17	17	17	18	18	18	19	19	19	20	20	21	21	21	22	22	23	23	23	24	24	25	25	26	26	26	♓27

	1	6	12	18	24	30
♃	♍24	25	26	27	28	28
♄	♐2	3	4	4	5	6

	1	15	30
♅	♌7	7	7
♆	♏0	1	1
♇	♍0	0	0
☊	♏29	29	29

DECEMBER

	1	2	3	4	5	6	7	8	9	10	11	12	13	14	15	16	17	18	19	20	21	22	23	24	25	26	27	28	29	30	31
☉	♐9	10	11	12	13	14	15	16	17	18	19	20	21	22	23	24	25	26	27	28	29	♑0	1	2	3	4	5	6	7	8	♑9
☽	♏23	♐6	18	♑1	13	25	♒7	19	♓1	12	25	♈7	20	♉3	16	♊0	14	29	♋14	29	♌14	28	♍13	27	♎10	24	♏7	20	♐2	15	♐27
☿	♐19	20	22	23	25	26	28	♑0	1	3	4	6	7	9	10	11	13	14	16	17	18	20	21	22	23	24	25	26	26	27	♑27
♀	♏7	8	9	10	12	13	14	15	17	18	19	20	22	23	24	25	27	28	29	♐0	1	3	4	5	6	8	9	10	11	13	♐14
♂	♓27	28	28	29	29	♈0	0	1	1	2	2	3	3	4	4	5	5	6	6	7	8	8	9	9	10	10	11	11	12	13	♈13

	1	6	12	18	24	30
♃	♍29	29	♎0	0	1	1
♄	♐6	6	7	8	8	9

	1	15	30
♅	♌7	7	6
♆	♏2	2	2
♇	♍0	0	0
☊	♏29	29	29

1957

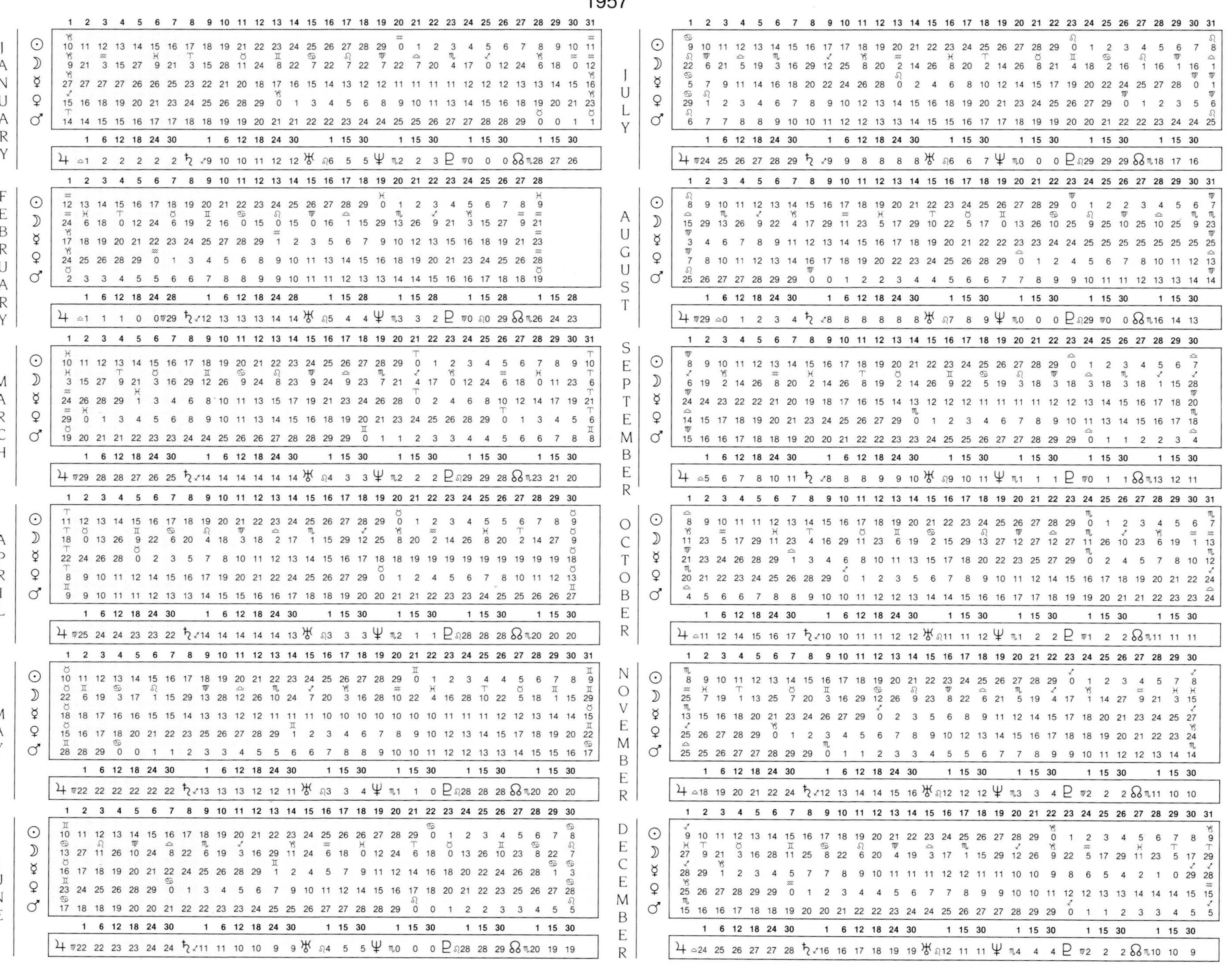

JANUARY

	1	2	3	4	5	6	7	8	9	10	11	12	13	14	15	16	17	18	19	20	21	22	23	24	25	26	27	28	29	30	31
☉	♑10	11	12	13	14	15	16	17	18	19	21	22	23	24	25	26	27	28	29	♒0	1	2	3	4	5	6	7	8	9	10	♒11
☽	♑9	21	♒3	15	27	♓9	21	♈3	15	28	♉11	24	♊8	22	♋7	22	♌7	22	♍7	22	♎7	20	♏4	17	♐0	12	24	♑6	18	♒0	♒12
☿	♑27	27	27	27	26	26	25	23	22	21	20	18	17	16	15	14	13	12	12	11	11	11	11	12	12	12	13	13	14	15	♑16
♀	♐15	16	18	19	20	21	23	24	25	26	28	29	♑0	1	3	4	5	6	8	9	10	11	13	14	15	16	18	19	20	21	♑23
♂	♈14	14	15	15	16	17	17	18	18	19	19	20	21	21	22	22	23	24	24	25	25	26	27	27	28	28	29	♉0	0	1	♉1

	1	6	12	18	24	30
♃	♎1	2	2	2	2	2
♄	♐9	10	10	11	12	12

	1	15	30
♅	♌6	5	5
♆	♏2	2	3
♇	♍0	0	0
☊	♏28	27	26

FEBRUARY

	1	2	3	4	5	6	7	8	9	10	11	12	13	14	15	16	17	18	19	20	21	22	23	24	25	26	27	28
☉	♒12	13	14	15	16	17	18	19	20	21	22	23	24	25	26	27	28	29	♓0	1	2	3	4	5	6	7	8	♓9
☽	♒24	♓6	18	♈0	12	24	♉6	19	♊2	16	♋0	15	♌0	15	♍0	16	♎1	15	29	♏13	26	♐9	21	♑3	15	27	♒9	♒21
☿	♑17	18	19	20	21	22	23	24	25	27	28	29	♒1	2	3	5	6	7	9	10	12	13	15	16	18	19	21	♒23
♀	♑24	25	26	28	29	♒0	1	3	4	5	6	8	9	10	11	13	14	15	16	18	19	20	21	23	24	25	26	♒28
♂	♉2	3	3	4	5	5	6	6	7	8	8	9	9	10	11	11	12	13	13	14	14	15	16	16	17	18	18	♉19

	1	6	12	18	24	28
♃	♎1	1	1	0	0	♍29
♄	♐12	13	13	13	14	14

	1	15	28
♅	♌5	4	4
♆	♏3	3	2
♇	♍0	♌0	29
☊	♏26	24	23

MARCH

	1	2	3	4	5	6	7	8	9	10	11	12	13	14	15	16	17	18	19	20	21	22	23	24	25	26	27	28	29	30	31
☉	♓10	11	12	13	14	15	16	17	18	19	20	21	22	23	24	25	26	27	28	29	♈0	1	2	3	4	5	6	7	8	9	♈10
☽	♓3	15	27	♈9	21	♉3	16	29	♊12	26	♋9	24	♌8	23	♍9	24	♎9	23	♏7	21	♐4	17	♑0	12	24	♒6	18	♓0	11	23	♈6
☿	♒24	26	28	29	♓1	3	4	6	8	10	11	13	15	17	19	21	23	24	26	28	♈0	2	4	6	8	10	12	14	17	19	♈21
♀	♒29	♓0	1	3	4	5	6	8	9	10	11	13	14	15	16	18	19	20	21	23	24	25	26	28	29	♈0	1	3	4	5	♈6
♂	♉19	20	21	21	22	23	23	24	24	25	26	26	27	28	28	29	29	♊0	1	1	2	3	3	4	4	5	6	6	7	8	♊8

	1	6	12	18	24	30
♃	♍29	28	28	27	26	25
♄	♐14	14	14	14	14	14

	1	15	30
♅	♌4	3	3
♆	♏2	2	2
♇	♌29	29	28
☊	♏23	21	20

APRIL

	1	2	3	4	5	6	7	8	9	10	11	12	13	14	15	16	17	18	19	20	21	22	23	24	25	26	27	28	29	30
☉	♈11	12	13	14	15	16	17	18	19	20	21	22	23	24	25	26	27	28	29	♉0	1	2	3	4	5	5	6	7	8	♉9
☽	♈18	♉0	13	26	♊9	22	♋6	20	♌4	18	♍3	18	♎2	17	♏1	15	29	♐12	25	♑8	20	♒2	14	26	♓8	20	♈2	14	27	♉9
☿	♈22	24	26	28	♉0	2	3	5	7	8	10	11	12	13	14	15	16	17	18	18	19	19	19	19	19	19	19	19	19	♉18
♀	♈8	9	10	11	12	14	15	16	17	19	20	21	22	24	25	26	27	29	♉0	1	2	4	5	6	7	8	10	11	12	♉13
♂	♊9	9	10	11	11	12	13	13	14	15	15	16	16	17	18	18	19	20	20	21	21	22	23	23	24	25	25	26	26	♊27

	1	6	12	18	24	30
♃	♍25	24	24	23	23	22
♄	♐14	14	14	14	14	13

	1	15	30
♅	♌3	3	3
♆	♏2	1	1
♇	♌28	28	28
☊	♏20	20	20

MAY

	1	2	3	4	5	6	7	8	9	10	11	12	13	14	15	16	17	18	19	20	21	22	23	24	25	26	27	28	29	30	31
☉	♉10	11	12	13	14	15	16	17	18	19	20	21	22	23	24	25	26	27	28	29	♊0	1	2	3	4	4	5	6	7	8	♊9
☽	♉22	♊6	19	♋3	17	♌1	15	29	♍13	28	♎12	26	♏10	24	♐7	20	♑3	16	28	♒10	22	♓4	16	28	♈10	22	♉5	18	♊1	15	♊29
☿	♉18	18	17	16	16	15	15	14	13	13	12	12	11	11	11	10	10	10	10	10	10	10	11	11	11	12	12	13	14	14	♉15
♀	♉15	16	17	18	20	21	22	23	25	26	27	28	29	♊1	2	3	4	6	7	8	9	10	12	13	14	15	17	18	19	20	♊22
♂	♊28	28	29	♋0	0	1	1	2	3	3	4	5	5	6	6	7	8	8	9	10	10	11	12	12	13	13	14	15	15	16	♋17

	1	6	12	18	24	30
♃	♍22	22	22	22	22	22
♄	♐13	13	13	12	12	11

	1	15	30
♅	♌3	3	4
♆	♏1	1	0
♇	♌28	28	28
☊	♏20	20	20

JUNE

	1	2	3	4	5	6	7	8	9	10	11	12	13	14	15	16	17	18	19	20	21	22	23	24	25	26	27	28	29	30
☉	♊10	11	12	13	14	15	16	17	18	19	20	21	22	23	24	25	26	26	27	28	29	♋0	1	2	3	4	5	6	7	♋8
☽	♋13	27	♌11	26	♍10	24	♎8	22	♏6	19	♐3	16	29	♑11	24	♒6	18	♓0	12	24	♈6	18	♉0	13	26	♊10	23	♋8	22	♌7
☿	♉16	17	18	19	20	21	22	24	25	26	28	29	♊1	2	4	5	7	9	11	12	14	16	18	20	22	24	26	28	♋1	♋3
♀	♊23	24	25	26	28	29	♋0	1	3	4	5	6	7	9	10	11	12	14	15	16	17	18	20	21	22	23	25	26	27	♋28
♂	♋17	18	18	19	20	20	21	22	22	23	23	24	25	25	26	27	27	28	28	29	♌0	0	1	2	2	3	3	4	5	♌5

	1	6	12	18	24	30
♃	♍22	22	23	23	24	24
♄	♐11	11	10	10	9	9

	1	15	30
♅	♌4	5	5
♆	♏0	0	0
♇	♌28	28	29
☊	♏20	19	19

JULY

	1	2	3	4	5	6	7	8	9	10	11	12	13	14	15	16	17	18	19	20	21	22	23	24	25	26	27	28	29	30	31
☉	♋9	10	11	12	13	14	15	16	17	17	18	19	20	21	22	23	24	25	26	27	28	29	♌0	1	2	3	4	5	6	7	♌8
☽	♌22	♍6	21	♎5	19	♏3	16	29	♐12	25	♑8	20	♒2	14	26	♓8	20	♈2	14	26	♉8	21	♊4	18	♋2	16	♌1	16	♍1	16	♎1
☿	♋5	7	9	11	14	16	18	20	22	24	26	28	♌0	2	4	6	8	10	12	14	15	17	19	20	22	24	25	27	28	♍0	♍1
♀	♋29	♌1	2	3	4	6	7	8	9	10	12	13	14	15	16	18	19	20	21	23	24	25	26	27	29	♍0	1	2	3	5	♍6
♂	♌6	7	7	8	8	9	10	10	11	12	12	13	13	14	15	15	16	17	17	18	19	19	20	20	21	22	22	23	24	24	♌25

	1	6	12	18	24	30
♃	♍24	25	26	27	28	29
♄	♐9	9	8	8	8	8

	1	15	30
♅	♌6	6	7
♆	♏0	0	0
♇	♌29	29	29
☊	♏18	17	16

AUGUST

	1	2	3	4	5	6	7	8	9	10	11	12	13	14	15	16	17	18	19	20	21	22	23	24	25	26	27	28	29	30	31
☉	♌8	9	10	11	12	13	14	15	16	17	18	19	20	21	22	23	24	25	26	27	28	29	♍0	1	2	2	3	4	5	6	♍7
☽	♎15	29	♏13	26	♐9	22	♑4	17	29	♒11	23	♓5	17	29	♈10	22	♉5	17	♊0	13	26	♋10	25	♌9	25	♍10	25	♎10	25	♏9	♏23
☿	♍3	4	6	7	8	9	11	12	13	14	15	16	17	18	19	20	21	22	22	23	23	24	24	25	25	25	25	25	25	25	♍25
♀	♍7	8	10	11	12	13	14	16	17	18	19	20	22	23	24	25	26	28	29	♎0	1	2	4	5	6	7	8	10	11	12	♎13
♂	♌25	26	27	27	28	29	29	♍0	0	1	2	2	3	4	4	5	6	6	7	7	8	9	9	10	11	11	12	13	13	14	♍14

	1	6	12	18	24	30
♃	♍29	♎0	1	2	3	4
♄	♐8	8	8	8	8	8

	1	15	30
♅	♌7	8	9
♆	♏0	0	0
♇	♌29	♍0	0
☊	♏16	14	13

SEPTEMBER

	1	2	3	4	5	6	7	8	9	10	11	12	13	14	15	16	17	18	19	20	21	22	23	24	25	26	27	28	29	30
☉	♍8	9	10	11	12	13	14	15	16	17	18	19	20	21	22	23	24	25	26	27	28	29	♎0	1	2	3	4	5	6	♎7
☽	♐6	19	♑2	14	26	♒8	20	♓2	14	26	♈8	19	♉2	14	26	♊9	22	♋5	19	♌3	18	♍3	18	♎3	18	♏3	18	♐1	15	♐28
☿	♍24	24	23	22	22	21	20	19	18	17	16	15	14	13	12	12	12	11	11	11	11	12	12	13	14	15	16	17	18	♍20
♀	♎14	15	17	18	19	20	21	23	24	25	26	27	29	♏0	1	2	3	4	6	7	8	9	10	11	13	14	15	16	17	♏18
♂	♍15	16	16	17	18	18	19	20	20	21	22	22	23	23	24	25	25	26	27	27	28	29	29	♎0	1	1	2	2	3	♎4

	1	6	12	18	24	30
♃	♎5	6	7	8	10	11
♄	♐8	8	8	9	9	10

	1	15	30
♅	♌9	10	11
♆	♏1	1	1
♇	♍0	1	1
☊	♏13	12	11

OCTOBER

	1	2	3	4	5	6	7	8	9	10	11	12	13	14	15	16	17	18	19	20	21	22	23	24	25	26	27	28	29	30	31
☉	♎8	9	10	11	11	12	13	14	15	16	17	18	19	20	21	22	23	24	25	26	27	28	29	♏0	1	2	3	4	5	6	♏7
☽	♑11	23	♒5	17	29	♓11	23	♈4	16	29	♉11	23	♊6	19	♋2	15	29	♌13	27	♍12	27	♎12	27	♏11	26	♐10	23	♑6	19	♒1	♒13
☿	♍21	23	24	26	28	29	♎1	3	4	6	8	10	11	13	15	17	18	20	22	23	25	27	29	♏0	2	4	5	7	8	10	♏12
♀	♏20	21	22	23	24	25	26	28	29	♐0	1	2	3	5	6	7	8	9	10	11	12	14	15	16	17	18	19	20	21	22	♐24
♂	♎4	5	6	6	7	8	8	9	10	10	11	12	12	13	14	14	15	16	16	17	17	18	19	19	20	21	21	22	23	23	♎24

	1	6	12	18	24	30
♃	♎11	12	14	15	16	17
♄	♐10	10	11	11	12	12

	1	15	30
♅	♌11	11	12
♆	♏1	2	2
♇	♍1	2	2
☊	♏11	11	11

NOVEMBER

	1	2	3	4	5	6	7	8	9	10	11	12	13	14	15	16	17	18	19	20	21	22	23	24	25	26	27	28	29	30
☉	♏8	9	10	11	12	13	14	15	16	17	18	19	20	21	22	23	24	25	26	27	28	29	♐0	1	2	3	4	5	7	♐8
☽	♒25	♓7	19	♈1	13	25	♉7	20	♊3	16	29	♋12	26	♌9	23	♍8	22	♎6	21	♏5	19	♐4	17	♑1	14	27	♒9	21	♓3	♓15
☿	♏13	15	16	18	20	21	23	24	26	27	29	♐0	2	3	5	6	8	9	11	12	14	15	17	18	20	21	23	24	25	♐27
♀	♐25	26	27	28	29	♑0	1	2	3	4	5	6	7	8	9	10	12	13	14	15	16	17	18	18	19	20	21	22	23	♑24
♂	♎25	25	26	27	27	28	29	29	♏0	1	1	2	3	3	4	5	5	6	7	7	8	9	9	10	11	12	12	13	14	♏14

	1	6	12	18	24	30
♃	♎18	19	20	21	22	24
♄	♐12	13	14	14	15	16

	1	15	30
♅	♌12	12	12
♆	♏3	3	4
♇	♍2	2	2
☊	♏11	10	10

DECEMBER

	1	2	3	4	5	6	7	8	9	10	11	12	13	14	15	16	17	18	19	20	21	22	23	24	25	26	27	28	29	30	31
☉	♐9	10	11	12	13	14	15	16	17	18	19	20	21	22	23	24	25	26	27	28	29	♑0	1	2	3	4	5	6	7	8	♑9
☽	♓27	♈9	21	♉3	16	28	♊11	25	♋8	22	♌6	20	♍4	19	♎3	17	♏1	15	29	♐12	26	♑9	22	♒5	17	29	♓11	23	♈5	17	♈29
☿	♐28	29	♑1	2	3	4	5	7	7	8	9	10	11	11	11	12	12	11	11	10	10	9	8	6	5	4	2	1	0	♐29	♐28
♀	♑25	26	27	28	29	29	♒0	1	2	3	4	4	5	6	7	7	8	9	9	10	10	11	12	12	13	13	14	14	14	15	♒15
♂	♏15	16	16	17	18	18	19	20	20	21	22	22	23	24	24	25	26	27	27	28	29	29	♐0	1	1	2	3	3	4	5	♐5

	1	6	12	18	24	30
♃	♎24	25	26	27	27	28
♄	♐16	16	17	18	19	19

	1	15	30
♅	♌12	11	11
♆	♏4	4	4
♇	♍2	2	2
☊	♏10	10	9

1958

JANUARY

	1	2	3	4	5	6	7	8	9	10	11	12	13	14	15	16	17	18	19	20	21	22	23	24	25	26	27	28	29	30	31
☉	♑10	11	12	13	14	15	16	17	18	19	20	21	22	23	24	25	26	27	28	29	♒0	1	2	3	5	6	7	8	9	10	♒11
☽	♉11	23	♊6	20	♋3	17	♌2	16	♍1	15	29	♎14	28	♏11	25	♐8	22	♑5	18	♒0	13	25	♓7	19	♈1	13	25	♉7	19	♊1	♊14
☿	♐27	26	26	25	25	25	25	26	26	27	27	28	29	♑0	1	2	3	4	5	6	7	8	10	11	12	13	15	16	17	19	♑20
♀	♒15	16	16	16	16	16	16	16	16	16	16	16	16	16	15	15	15	14	14	13	13	12	12	11	11	10	10	9	8	8	♒7
♂	♐6	7	8	8	9	10	10	11	12	12	13	14	15	15	16	17	17	18	19	20	20	21	22	22	23	24	24	25	26	27	♐27

	1	6	12	18	24	30		1	6	12	18	24	30		1	15	30		1	15	30		1	15	30		1	15	30
♃	♎29	29	♏0	0	1	1	♄	♐19	20	21	21	22	22	♅	♌11	10	10	♆	♏4	5	5	♇	♍2	2	2	☊	♏9	7	6

FEBRUARY

	1	2	3	4	5	6	7	8	9	10	11	12	13	14	15	16	17	18	19	20	21	22	23	24	25	26	27	28
☉	♒12	13	14	15	16	17	18	19	20	21	22	23	24	25	26	27	28	29	♓0	1	2	3	4	5	6	7	8	♓9
☽	♊27	♋11	25	♌10	25	♍10	25	♎10	24	♏8	22	♐5	19	♑2	14	27	♒9	22	♓4	16	28	♈9	21	♉3	15	27	♊9	♊22
☿	♑22	23	25	26	28	29	♒1	2	4	5	7	8	10	12	13	15	16	18	20	21	23	25	27	28	♓0	2	4	♓6
♀	♒6	6	5	5	4	4	3	3	2	2	2	1	1	1	1	1	1	1	1	1	1	1	1	1	2	2	2	♒2
♂	♐28	29	29	♑0	1	2	2	3	4	4	5	6	7	7	8	9	9	10	11	12	12	13	14	15	15	16	17	♑17

	1	6	12	18	24	28		1	6	12	18	24	28		1	15	28		1	15	28		1	15	28		1	15	28
♃	♏1	2	2	2	2	1	♄	♐23	23	24	24	24	25	♅	♌10	9	8	♆	♏5	5	5	♇	♍2	1	1	☊	♏5	4	3

MARCH

	1	2	3	4	5	6	7	8	9	10	11	12	13	14	15	16	17	18	19	20	21	22	23	24	25	26	27	28	29	30	31
☉	♓10	11	12	13	14	15	16	17	18	19	20	21	22	23	24	25	26	27	28	29	♈0	1	2	3	4	5	6	7	8	9	♈10
☽	♋5	19	♌3	18	♍3	18	♎3	19	♏3	18	♐2	15	29	♑11	24	♒6	19	♓1	13	24	♈6	18	♉0	12	24	♊6	18	♋1	14	28	♌12
☿	♓7	9	11	13	15	17	19	21	23	25	27	29	♈1	2	4	6	8	10	12	14	15	17	19	20	22	23	24	25	27	27	♈28
♀	♒3	3	4	4	5	5	6	6	7	7	8	9	9	10	11	11	12	13	14	14	15	16	17	18	18	19	20	21	22	23	♒24
♂	♑18	19	20	20	21	22	22	23	24	25	25	26	27	28	28	29	♒0	1	1	2	3	3	4	5	6	6	7	8	9	9	♒10

	1	6	12	18	24	30		1	6	12	18	24	30		1	15	30		1	15	30		1	15	30		1	15	30
♃	♏1	1	1	0	0	♎29	♄	♐25	25	25	25	26	26	♅	♌8	8	8	♆	♏5	4	4	♇	♍1	1	0	☊	♏3	2	1

APRIL

	1	2	3	4	5	6	7	8	9	10	11	12	13	14	15	16	17	18	19	20	21	22	23	24	25	26	27	28	29	30
☉	♈11	12	13	14	15	16	17	18	19	20	21	22	23	24	25	26	26	27	28	29	♉0	1	2	3	4	5	6	7	8	♉9
☽	♌26	♍11	26	♎11	27	♏12	26	♐11	24	♑8	21	♒3	16	28	♓10	21	♈3	15	27	♉9	21	♊3	15	28	♋11	24	♌8	21	♍6	♍20
☿	♈29	♉0	0	0	1	1	1	1	1	0	0	♈29	29	28	28	27	26	25	25	24	23	23	22	22	21	21	20	20	20	♈20
♀	♒25	26	27	27	28	29	♓0	1	2	3	4	5	6	7	8	9	10	11	12	13	14	16	17	18	19	20	21	22	23	♓24
♂	♒11	12	12	13	14	14	15	16	17	17	18	19	20	20	21	22	23	23	24	25	26	26	27	28	28	29	♓0	1	1	♓2

	1	6	12	18	24	30		1	6	12	18	24	30		1	15	30		1	15	30		1	15	30		1	15	30
♃	♎29	28	27	27	26	25	♄	♐26	26	26	26	25	25	♅	♌8	8	8	♆	♏4	4	3	♇	♍0	0	0	☊	♏1	1	1

MAY

	1	2	3	4	5	6	7	8	9	10	11	12	13	14	15	16	17	18	19	20	21	22	23	24	25	26	27	28	29	30	31
☉	♉10	11	12	13	14	15	16	17	18	19	20	21	22	23	24	25	26	27	28	28	29	♊0	1	2	3	4	5	6	7	8	♊9
☽	♎5	20	♏5	20	♐4	19	♑3	16	29	♒12	24	♓6	18	♈0	12	24	♉6	18	♊0	12	25	♋8	21	♌4	18	♍2	16	♎0	14	29	♏14
☿	♈20	20	20	21	21	21	22	22	23	24	24	25	26	27	28	29	♉0	1	2	3	5	6	7	9	10	12	13	15	16	18	♉19
♀	♓25	26	27	28	29	♈1	2	3	4	5	6	7	8	9	11	12	13	14	15	16	17	18	20	21	22	23	24	25	26	28	♈29
♂	♓3	4	4	5	6	7	7	8	9	9	10	11	12	12	13	14	15	15	16	17	18	18	19	20	20	21	22	23	23	24	♓25

	1	6	12	18	24	30		1	6	12	18	24	30		1	15	30		1	15	30		1	15	30		1	15	30
♃	♎25	24	24	23	23	22	♄	♐25	25	25	24	24	24	♅	♌8	8	8	♆	♏3	3	3	♇	♍0	0	0	☊	♏1	1	1

JUNE

	1	2	3	4	5	6	7	8	9	10	11	12	13	14	15	16	17	18	19	20	21	22	23	24	25	26	27	28	29	30
☉	♊10	11	12	13	14	15	16	17	18	19	20	21	21	22	23	24	25	26	27	28	29	♋0	1	2	3	4	5	6	7	♋8
☽	♏28	♐13	27	♑11	24	♒7	20	♓2	14	26	♈8	20	♉2	14	26	♊9	21	♋4	18	♌1	15	29	♍13	27	♎11	25	♏9	23	♐8	♐22
☿	♉21	23	25	26	28	♊0	2	4	6	8	10	12	15	17	19	21	23	25	28	♋0	2	4	6	8	11	13	15	17	19	♋21
♀	♉0	1	2	3	4	6	7	8	9	10	11	13	14	15	16	17	18	19	21	22	23	24	25	27	28	29	♊0	1	2	♊4
♂	♓26	26	27	28	28	29	♈0	1	1	2	3	3	4	5	6	6	7	8	8	9	10	10	11	12	12	13	14	15	15	♈16

	1	6	12	18	24	30		1	6	12	18	24	30		1	15	30		1	15	30		1	15	30		1	15	30
♃	♎22	22	22	22	22	22	♄	♐23	23	23	22	22	21	♅	♌8	9	10	♆	♏2	2	2	♇	♍0	0	0	☊	♏1	0	♎0

JULY

	1	2	3	4	5	6	7	8	9	10	11	12	13	14	15	16	17	18	19	20	21	22	23	24	25	26	27	28	29	30	31
☉	♋9	10	11	12	12	13	14	15	16	17	18	19	20	21	22	23	24	25	26	27	28	29	♌0	1	2	3	3	4	5	6	♌7
☽	♑5	19	♒2	15	28	♓10	22	♈4	16	28	♉10	22	♊4	17	♋0	13	27	♌11	25	♍9	23	♎8	22	♏6	20	♐4	18	♑1	15	28	♒11
☿	♋23	25	26	28	♌0	2	4	5	7	8	10	12	13	15	16	18	19	20	22	23	24	25	26	28	29	♍0	1	1	2	3	♍4
♀	♊5	6	7	8	9	11	12	13	14	15	17	18	19	20	21	23	24	25	26	27	29	♋0	1	2	3	5	6	7	8	9	♋11
♂	♈17	17	18	19	19	20	21	21	22	23	23	24	25	25	26	27	27	28	29	29	♉0	0	1	2	2	3	4	4	5	5	♉6

	1	6	12	18	24	30		1	6	12	18	24	30		1	15	30		1	15	30		1	15	30		1	15	30
♃	♎22	22	23	23	24	24	♄	♐21	21	20	20	20	20	♅	♌10	11	12	♆	♏2	2	2	♇	♍0	1	1	☊	♎29	27	26

AUGUST

	1	2	3	4	5	6	7	8	9	10	11	12	13	14	15	16	17	18	19	20	21	22	23	24	25	26	27	28	29	30	31
☉	♌8	9	10	11	12	13	14	15	16	17	18	19	20	21	22	23	24	25	26	26	27	28	29	♍0	1	2	3	4	5	6	♍7
☽	♒24	♓6	18	♈0	12	24	♉6	18	♊0	12	25	♋8	22	♌5	20	♍4	19	♎3	18	♏2	17	♐1	14	28	♑11	24	♒7	20	♓2	15	♓27
☿	♍5	5	6	6	7	7	7	8	8	8	8	7	7	7	6	6	5	5	4	3	2	1	1	0	♌29	28	27	27	26	25	♌25
♀	♋12	13	14	15	17	18	19	20	21	23	24	25	26	27	29	♌0	1	2	4	5	6	7	8	10	11	12	13	15	16	17	♌18
♂	♉7	7	8	8	9	10	10	11	11	12	12	13	13	14	15	15	16	16	17	17	18	18	19	19	20	20	21	21	22	22	♉22

	1	6	12	18	24	30		1	6	12	18	24	30		1	15	30		1	15	30		1	15	30		1	15	30
♃	♎24	25	26	27	28	29	♄	♐20	19	19	19	19	19	♅	♌12	13	14	♆	♏2	2	3	♇	♍1	2	2	☊	♎25	24	23

SEPTEMBER

	1	2	3	4	5	6	7	8	9	10	11	12	13	14	15	16	17	18	19	20	21	22	23	24	25	26	27	28	29	30
☉	♍8	9	10	11	12	13	14	15	16	17	18	19	20	21	22	23	24	25	26	27	28	28	29	♎0	1	2	3	4	5	♎6
☽	♈9	20	♉2	14	26	♊8	20	♋3	16	♌0	14	28	♍13	28	♎13	28	♏12	27	♐11	25	♑8	21	♒4	17	29	♓11	23	♈5	17	♈29
☿	♌25	25	25	25	25	26	26	27	28	29	♍0	1	2	4	5	7	9	10	12	14	15	17	19	21	23	25	26	28	♎0	♎2
♀	♌19	21	22	23	24	26	27	28	29	♍1	2	3	4	6	7	8	9	10	12	13	14	15	17	18	19	20	22	23	24	♍25
♂	♉23	23	24	24	25	25	25	26	26	27	27	27	28	28	28	29	29	29	29	♊0	0	0	0	1	1	1	1	1	2	♊2

	1	6	12	18	24	30		1	6	12	18	24	30		1	15	30		1	15	30		1	15	30		1	15	30
♃	♎29	♏0	1	2	3	4	♄	♐19	19	19	20	20	20	♅	♌14	14	15	♆	♏3	3	3	♇	♍2	3	3	☊	♎23	23	22

OCTOBER

	1	2	3	4	5	6	7	8	9	10	11	12	13	14	15	16	17	18	19	20	21	22	23	24	25	26	27	28	29	30	31
☉	♎7	8	9	10	11	12	13	14	15	16	17	18	19	20	21	22	23	24	25	26	27	28	29	♏0	1	2	3	4	5	6	♏7
☽	♉11	23	♊5	17	29	♋12	25	♌8	22	♍6	21	♎6	21	♏6	21	♐6	20	♑4	18	♒1	14	26	♓8	20	♈2	14	26	♉8	20	♊2	♊14
☿	♎4	6	7	9	11	13	14	16	18	19	21	23	24	26	28	29	♏1	3	4	6	7	9	10	12	14	15	17	18	20	21	♏23
♀	♍27	28	29	♎0	2	3	4	5	7	8	9	10	12	13	14	15	17	18	19	20	22	23	24	25	27	28	29	♏0	2	3	♏4
♂	♊2	2	2	2	2	2	2	2	3	3	3	3	2	2	2	2	2	2	2	2	2	2	1	1	1	1	1	0	0	0	♉29

	1	6	12	18	24	30		1	6	12	18	24	30		1	15	30		1	15	30		1	15	30		1	15	30
♃	♏5	6	7	8	9	11	♄	♐20	21	21	21	22	22	♅	♌15	16	16	♆	♏4	4	5	♇	♍3	4	4	☊	♎22	22	22

NOVEMBER

	1	2	3	4	5	6	7	8	9	10	11	12	13	14	15	16	17	18	19	20	21	22	23	24	25	26	27	28	29	30
☉	♏8	9	10	11	12	13	14	15	16	17	18	19	20	21	22	23	24	25	26	27	28	29	♐0	1	2	3	4	5	6	♐7
☽	♊26	♋8	21	♌4	17	♍1	15	29	♎14	29	♏14	29	♐14	29	♑13	27	♒10	23	♓5	17	29	♈11	23	♉5	17	28	♊11	23	♋5	♋18
☿	♏24	26	27	28	♐0	1	3	4	5	7	8	10	11	12	13	15	16	17	18	19	20	21	22	23	24	24	25	25	26	♐26
♀	♏5	7	8	9	10	12	13	14	15	17	18	19	20	22	23	24	25	27	28	29	♐1	2	3	4	6	7	8	9	11	♐12
♂	♉29	29	29	28	28	28	27	27	27	26	26	25	25	25	24	24	24	23	23	23	22	22	21	21	21	21	20	20	20	♉19

	1	6	12	18	24	30		1	6	12	18	24	30		1	15	30		1	15	30		1	15	30		1	15	30
♃	♏11	12	14	15	16	18	♄	♐23	23	24	24	25	26	♅	♌16	16	16	♆	♏5	5	6	♇	♍4	4	4	☊	♎22	22	21

DECEMBER

	1	2	3	4	5	6	7	8	9	10	11	12	13	14	15	16	17	18	19	20	21	22	23	24	25	26	27	28	29	30	31
☉	♐8	9	10	11	12	13	14	15	16	17	18	19	20	21	23	24	25	26	27	28	29	♑0	1	2	3	4	5	6	7	8	♑9
☽	♌1	14	27	♍11	24	♎9	23	♏8	23	♐7	22	♑7	21	♒5	18	♓1	13	26	♈8	19	♉1	13	25	♊7	19	♋2	15	28	♌11	24	♍8
☿	♐26	25	25	24	24	23	22	20	19	18	16	15	14	13	12	11	10	10	10	9	9	10	10	11	11	12	13	14	14	15	♐17
♀	♐13	14	16	17	18	19	21	22	23	24	26	27	28	29	♑1	2	3	4	6	7	8	9	11	12	13	15	16	17	18	20	♑21
♂	♉19	19	19	18	18	18	18	18	17	17	17	17	17	17	17	17	17	17	17	17	17	17	17	17	17	17	17	17	17	17	♉17

	1	6	12	18	24	30		1	6	12	18	24	30		1	15	30		1	15	30		1	15	30		1	15	30
♃	♏18	19	20	21	22	24	♄	♐26	26	27	28	29	29	♅	♌16	16	16	♆	♏6	6	7	♇	♍4	4	4	☊	♎21	20	18

1959

JANUARY

	1	2	3	4	5	6	7	8	9	10	11	12	13	14	15	16	17	18	19	20	21	22	23	24	25	26	27	28	29	30	31
☉	♑10	11	12	13	14	15	16	17	18	19	20	21	22	23	24	25	26	27	28	29	♒0	1	2	3	4	5	6	7	8	9	♒10
☽	♍21	♎5	19	♏3	17	♐2	16	♑1	15	29	♒13	26	♓9	21	♈3	15	27	♉9	21	♊3	15	27	♋10	23	♌7	20	♍4	18	♎2	16	♏0
☿	♐18	19	20	21	22	24	25	26	28	29	♑0	2	3	5	6	8	9	10	12	13	15	16	18	20	21	23	24	26	27	29	♒1
♀	♑22	23	25	26	27	28	♒0	1	2	3	5	6	7	8	10	11	12	13	15	16	17	18	20	21	22	23	25	26	27	28	♓0
♂	♉17	18	18	18	18	18	18	19	19	19	19	20	20	20	20	21	21	21	22	22	22	23	23	23	24	24	24	25	25	25	♉26

	1	6	12	18	24	30		1	6	12	18	24	30		1	15	30		1	15	30		1	15	30		1	15	30
♃	♏24	25	26	27	28	29	♄	♐29	♑0	1	1	2	3	♅	♌16	15	15	♆	♏7	7	7	♇	♍4	4	4	☊	♎18	17	15

FEBRUARY

	1	2	3	4	5	6	7	8	9	10	11	12	13	14	15	16	17	18	19	20	21	22	23	24	25	26	27	28
☉	♒11	12	13	14	15	16	17	18	19	21	22	23	24	25	26	27	28	29	♓0	1	2	3	4	5	6	7	8	♓9
☽	♏14	28	♐12	26	♑10	24	♒8	21	♓4	17	29	♈11	23	♉5	17	29	♊11	23	♋5	18	♌1	15	29	♍13	27	♎12	26	♏11
☿	♒2	4	5	7	9	10	12	14	16	17	19	21	23	24	26	28	♓0	2	4	5	7	9	11	13	15	17	18	♓20
♀	♓1	2	3	5	6	7	8	10	11	12	13	15	16	17	18	20	21	22	23	24	26	27	28	29	♈1	2	3	♈4
♂	♉26	26	27	27	28	28	28	29	29	♊0	0	1	1	1	2	2	3	3	4	4	5	5	6	6	7	7	8	♊8

	1	6	12	18	24	28		1	6	12	18	24	28		1	15	28		1	15	28		1	15	28		1	15	28
♃	♏29	29	♐0	1	1	1	♄	♑3	3	4	4	5	5	♅	♌14	14	13	♆	♏7	7	7	♇	♍4	3	3	☊	♎15	14	13

MARCH

	1	2	3	4	5	6	7	8	9	10	11	12	13	14	15	16	17	18	19	20	21	22	23	24	25	26	27	28	29	30	31
☉	♓10	11	12	13	14	15	16	17	18	19	20	21	22	23	24	25	26	27	28	29	♈0	1	2	3	4	5	6	7	8	9	♈10
☽	♏25	♐9	23	♑7	20	♒4	17	♓0	12	25	♈7	19	♉1	13	25	♊7	19	♋1	13	26	♌9	23	♍7	21	♎6	21	♏6	20	♐5	20	♑4
☿	♓22	24	26	27	29	♈1	2	4	5	7	8	9	10	11	11	12	12	13	13	13	13	13	12	12	11	11	10	9	8	7	♈7
♀	♈6	7	8	9	11	12	13	14	15	17	18	19	20	22	23	24	25	26	28	29	♉0	1	3	4	5	6	7	9	10	11	♉12
♂	♊9	9	10	10	11	11	12	12	13	13	14	14	15	15	16	16	17	17	18	18	19	19	20	20	21	22	22	23	23	24	♊24

	1	6	12	18	24	30		1	6	12	18	24	30		1	15	30		1	15	30		1	15	30		1	15	30
♃	♐1	2	2	2	2	2	♄	♑5	6	6	6	7	7	♅	♌13	13	12	♆	♏7	7	6	♇	♍3	2	2	☊	♎14	13	13

APRIL

	1	2	3	4	5	6	7	8	9	10	11	12	13	14	15	16	17	18	19	20	21	22	23	24	25	26	27	28	29	30
☉	♈11	12	12	13	14	15	16	17	18	19	20	21	22	23	24	25	26	27	28	29	♉0	1	2	3	4	5	6	7	8	♉9
☽	♑17	♒1	14	27	♓9	22	♈4	16	28	♉10	21	♊3	15	27	♋9	22	♌4	17	♍1	15	29	♎14	29	♏14	29	♐14	29	♑13	27	♒11
☿	♈6	5	4	4	3	2	2	1	1	1	1	1	1	1	1	1	2	2	3	3	4	5	5	6	7	8	9	10	11	♈12
♀	♉13	15	16	17	18	19	21	22	23	24	25	27	28	29	♊0	1	3	4	5	6	7	8	10	11	12	13	14	15	17	♊18
♂	♊25	25	26	26	27	28	28	29	29	♋0	0	1	1	2	3	3	4	4	5	5	6	7	7	8	8	9	9	10	11	♋11

	1	6	12	18	24	30		1	6	12	18	24	30		1	15	30		1	15	30		1	15	30		1	15	30
♃	♐2	1	1	1	0	♏29	♄	♑7	7	7	7	7	7	♅	♌12	12	12	♆	♏6	6	6	♇	♍2	2	2	☊	♎13	13	13

MAY

	1	2	3	4	5	6	7	8	9	10	11	12	13	14	15	16	17	18	19	20	21	22	23	24	25	26	27	28	29	30	31
☉	♉10	11	12	13	14	15	16	17	18	19	20	21	22	22	23	24	25	26	27	28	29	♊0	1	2	3	4	5	6	7	8	♊9
☽	♒24	♓6	19	♈1	13	25	♉7	18	♊0	12	24	♋6	18	♌1	13	26	♍10	23	♎8	22	♏7	22	♐8	23	♑8	22	♒6	20	♓3	15	♓28
☿	♈13	15	16	17	18	20	21	23	24	26	27	29	♉0	2	4	5	7	9	11	12	14	16	18	20	22	24	26	28	♊1	3	♊5
♀	♊19	20	21	22	24	25	26	27	28	29	♋0	2	3	4	5	6	7	8	9	11	12	13	14	15	16	17	18	19	20	22	♋23
♂	♋12	12	13	13	14	15	15	16	16	17	18	18	19	19	20	20	21	22	22	23	23	24	25	25	26	26	27	28	28	29	♋29

	1	6	12	18	24	30		1	6	12	18	24	30		1	15	30		1	15	30		1	15	30		1	15	30
♃	♏29	29	28	27	26	26	♄	♑7	7	7	6	6	6	♅	♌12	12	13	♆	♏5	5	5	♇	♍2	2	2	☊	♎13	12	11

JUNE

	1	2	3	4	5	6	7	8	9	10	11	12	13	14	15	16	17	18	19	20	21	22	23	24	25	26	27	28	29	30
☉	♊10	11	12	13	14	15	16	16	17	18	19	20	21	22	23	24	25	26	27	28	29	♋0	1	2	3	4	5	6	7	♋7
☽	♈10	22	♉4	15	27	♊9	21	♋3	15	28	♌10	23	♍6	19	♎3	17	♏1	16	♐1	16	♑1	16	♒1	15	28	♓11	24	♈6	18	♉0
☿	♊7	9	11	14	16	18	20	22	25	27	29	♋1	3	5	7	9	11	13	14	16	18	20	21	23	24	26	28	29	♌0	♌2
♀	♋24	25	26	27	28	29	♌0	1	2	3	4	5	6	7	8	9	10	11	12	13	14	15	16	17	18	19	20	21	22	♌23
♂	♌0	1	1	2	2	3	4	4	5	5	6	7	7	8	8	9	10	10	11	11	12	13	13	14	14	15	16	16	17	♌17

	1	6	12	18	24	30		1	6	12	18	24	30		1	15	30		1	15	30		1	15	30		1	15	30
♃	♏25	25	24	24	23	23	♄	♑6	5	5	4	4	3	♅	♌13	14	14	♆	♏5	4	4	♇	♍2	2	2	☊	♎12	10	9

JULY

	1	2	3	4	5	6	7	8	9	10	11	12	13	14	15	16	17	18	19	20	21	22	23	24	25	26	27	28	29	30	31
☉	♋8	9	10	11	12	13	14	15	16	17	18	19	20	21	22	23	24	25	26	27	28	28	29	♌0	1	2	3	4	5	6	♌7
☽	♉12	24	♊6	18	♋0	12	25	♌7	20	♍3	16	♎0	13	27	♏12	26	♐11	25	♑10	25	♒9	23	♓6	19	♈2	15	27	♉9	20	♊2	♊14
☿	♌3	4	6	7	8	9	10	11	12	13	14	15	16	16	17	18	18	18	19	19	19	19	19	19	19	19	19	18	18	17	♌17
♀	♌24	24	25	26	27	28	29	♍0	0	1	2	3	4	4	5	6	6	7	8	8	9	10	10	11	11	12	12	13	13	14	♍14
♂	♌18	19	19	20	20	21	22	22	23	24	24	25	25	26	27	27	28	28	29	♍0	0	1	2	2	3	3	4	5	5	6	♍7

	1	6	12	18	24	30		1	6	12	18	24	30		1	15	30		1	15	30		1	15	30		1	15	30
♃	♏23	22	22	22	22	22	♄	♑3	3	3	2	2	2	♅	♌14	15	16	♆	♏4	4	4	♇	♍2	3	3	☊	♎9	7	6

AUGUST

	1	2	3	4	5	6	7	8	9	10	11	12	13	14	15	16	17	18	19	20	21	22	23	24	25	26	27	28	29	30	31
☉	♌8	9	10	11	12	13	14	15	16	17	18	19	20	20	21	22	23	24	25	26	27	28	29	♍0	1	2	3	4	5	6	♍7
☽	♊26	♋8	21	♌4	17	♍0	13	27	♎10	24	♏8	22	♐7	21	♑5	19	♒4	17	♓1	14	27	♈10	22	♉5	16	28	♊10	22	♋4	17	♋29
☿	♌16	15	15	14	13	12	12	11	10	10	9	9	8	8	8	8	8	8	8	9	9	10	11	12	13	14	15	16	18	19	♌21
♀	♍14	15	15	15	15	16	16	16	16	16	16	16	16	16	16	16	15	15	15	15	14	14	13	13	12	12	11	11	10	9	♍9
♂	♍7	8	8	9	10	10	11	12	12	13	13	14	15	15	16	17	17	18	19	19	20	20	21	22	22	23	24	24	25	26	♍26

	1	6	12	18	24	30		1	6	12	18	24	30		1	15	30		1	15	30		1	15	30		1	15	30
♃	♏22	23	23	23	24	25	♄	♑1	1	1	1	1	0	♅	♌16	17	18	♆	♏4	4	5	♇	♍3	4	4	☊	♎6	5	4

SEPTEMBER

	1	2	3	4	5	6	7	8	9	10	11	12	13	14	15	16	17	18	19	20	21	22	23	24	25	26	27	28	29	30
☉	♍8	9	10	11	12	13	14	15	16	17	18	18	19	20	21	22	23	24	25	26	27	28	29	♎0	1	2	3	4	5	♎6
☽	♌12	25	♍9	22	♎6	21	♏5	19	♐3	18	♑2	16	♒0	13	27	♓10	23	♈6	18	♉0	12	24	♊6	18	♋0	12	24	♌7	20	♍3
☿	♌23	24	26	28	♍0	2	4	5	7	9	11	13	15	17	19	21	23	24	26	28	♎0	2	3	5	7	9	10	12	14	♎15
♀	♍8	8	7	6	6	5	5	4	4	3	3	2	2	1	1	1	1	0	0	0	0	0	0	0	0	0	0	0	1	♍1
♂	♍27	27	28	29	29	♎0	1	1	2	3	3	4	5	5	6	7	7	8	8	9	10	10	11	12	12	13	14	14	15	♎16

	1	6	12	18	24	30		1	6	12	18	24	30		1	15	30		1	15	30		1	15	30		1	15	30
♃	♏25	25	26	27	28	29	♄	♑0	0	0	1	1	1	♅	♌18	19	20	♆	♏5	5	6	♇	♍4	5	5	☊	♎4	4	4

OCTOBER

	1	2	3	4	5	6	7	8	9	10	11	12	13	14	15	16	17	18	19	20	21	22	23	24	25	26	27	28	29	30	31
☉	♎7	8	9	10	11	12	13	14	15	16	17	18	19	20	21	22	23	24	25	26	27	28	29	♏0	1	2	3	4	5	6	♏7
☽	♍17	♎1	15	♏0	15	29	♐14	28	♑13	26	♒10	23	♓6	19	♈2	14	27	♉9	21	♊3	14	26	♋8	20	♌3	15	28	♍11	25	♎9	♎24
☿	♎17	19	20	22	24	25	27	28	♏0	1	3	4	6	7	9	10	12	13	14	16	17	19	20	21	23	24	25	26	28	29	♐0
♀	♍1	1	2	2	3	3	4	4	5	5	6	6	7	7	8	9	9	10	11	12	12	13	14	15	16	16	17	18	19	20	♍21
♂	♎16	17	18	18	19	20	20	21	22	22	23	24	24	25	26	26	27	28	28	29	♏0	0	1	2	2	3	4	4	5	6	♏7

	1	6	12	18	24	30		1	6	12	18	24	30		1	15	30		1	15	30		1	15	30		1	15	30
♃	♏29	♐0	1	2	4	5	♄	♑1	1	2	2	2	3	♅	♌20	20	21	♆	♏6	6	7	♇	♍5	5	6	☊	♎4	4	4

NOVEMBER

	1	2	3	4	5	6	7	8	9	10	11	12	13	14	15	16	17	18	19	20	21	22	23	24	25	26	27	28	29	30
☉	♏8	9	10	11	12	13	14	15	16	17	18	19	20	21	22	23	24	25	26	27	28	29	♐0	1	2	3	4	5	6	♐7
☽	♏9	24	♐9	24	♑8	23	♒7	20	♓3	16	29	♈11	23	♉5	17	29	♊11	23	♋5	17	29	♌11	24	♍6	19	♎3	17	♏2	17	♐2
☿	♐1	2	3	4	5	6	7	8	8	9	9	10	10	10	10	10	9	9	8	7	6	5	3	2	1	♏29	28	27	26	♏25
♀	♍22	23	24	24	25	26	27	28	29	♎0	1	2	3	4	5	6	7	8	9	11	12	13	14	15	16	17	18	19	20	♎21
♂	♏7	8	9	9	10	11	11	12	13	13	14	15	15	16	17	18	18	19	20	20	21	22	22	23	24	25	25	26	27	♏27

	1	6	12	18	24	30		1	6	12	18	24	30		1	15	30		1	15	30		1	15	30		1	15	30
♃	♐5	6	8	9	10	12	♄	♑3	3	4	5	5	6	♅	♌21	21	21	♆	♏7	7	8	♇	♍6	6	6	☊	♎4	3	2

DECEMBER

	1	2	3	4	5	6	7	8	9	10	11	12	13	14	15	16	17	18	19	20	21	22	23	24	25	26	27	28	29	30	31
☉	♐8	9	10	11	12	13	14	15	16	17	18	19	20	21	22	23	24	25	26	27	28	29	♑0	1	2	3	4	5	7	8	♑9
☽	♐17	♑2	17	♒2	16	♓0	13	26	♈8	20	♉3	14	26	♊8	20	♋2	14	26	♌8	20	♍3	16	29	♎12	26	♏10	25	♐10	25	♑10	♑25
☿	♏24	24	24	24	24	24	24	25	26	26	27	28	29	♐0	2	3	4	5	6	8	9	11	12	13	15	16	18	19	21	22	♐23
♀	♎22	24	25	26	27	28	29	♏0	1	3	4	5	6	7	8	10	11	12	13	14	15	17	18	19	20	21	22	24	25	26	♏27
♂	♏28	29	29	♐0	1	2	2	3	4	4	5	6	7	7	8	9	9	10	11	12	12	13	14	14	15	16	17	17	18	19	♐20

	1	6	12	18	24	30		1	6	12	18	24	30		1	15	30		1	15	30		1	15	30		1	15	30
♃	♐12	13	14	16	17	18	♄	♑6	6	7	8	9	9	♅	♌21	21	21	♆	♏8	8	9	♇	♍6	6	6	☊	♎2	0	♍1

1960

JANUARY

	1	2	3	4	5	6	7	8	9	10	11	12	13	14	15	16	17	18	19	20	21	22	23	24	25	26	27	28	29	30	31
☉	♑10	11	12	13	14	15	16	17	18	19	20	21	22	23	24	25	26	27	28	29	♒0	1	2	3	4	5	6	7	8	9	♒10
☽	♒10	25	♓8	22	♈5	17	29	♉11	23	♊5	17	29	♋11	23	♌5	17	♍0	13	26	♎9	22	♏6	20	♐4	19	♑4	19	♒3	18	♓2	♓16
☿	♐25	26	28	29	♑1	3	4	6	7	9	10	12	13	15	17	18	20	21	23	25	26	28	♒0	1	3	5	6	8	10	11	♒13
♀	♏28	♐0	1	2	3	4	6	7	8	9	10	12	13	14	15	16	18	19	20	21	22	24	25	26	27	29	♑0	1	2	3	♑5
♂	♐20	21	22	22	23	24	25	25	26	27	28	28	29	♑0	1	1	2	3	4	4	5	6	7	7	8	9	10	10	11	12	♑12

	1	6	12	18	24	30		1	6	12	18	24	30		1	15	30		1	15	30		1	15	30		1	15	30
♃	♐19	20	21	22	24	25	♄	♑9	10	11	11	12	13	♅	♌21	20	19	♆	♏9	9	9	♇	♍6	6	6	☊	♍28	27	25

FEBRUARY

	1	2	3	4	5	6	7	8	9	10	11	12	13	14	15	16	17	18	19	20	21	22	23	24	25	26	27	28	29
☉	♒11	12	13	14	15	16	17	18	19	20	21	22	23	24	25	26	27	28	29	♓0	1	2	3	4	5	6	7	8	♓9
☽	♈0	13	25	♉8	20	♊1	13	25	♋7	19	♌1	14	27	♍9	22	♎6	19	♏3	16	♐0	15	29	♑13	28	♒12	26	♓10	24	♈7
☿	♒15	17	18	20	22	24	26	27	29	♓1	3	5	6	8	10	11	13	15	16	18	19	20	21	22	23	24	25	25	♓26
♀	♑6	7	8	10	11	12	13	14	16	17	18	19	21	22	23	24	25	27	28	29	♒0	2	3	4	5	7	8	9	♒10
♂	♑13	14	15	15	16	17	18	19	19	20	21	22	22	23	24	25	25	26	27	28	28	29	♒0	1	1	2	3	4	♒4

	1	6	12	18	24	29		1	6	12	18	24	29		1	15	29		1	15	29		1	15	29		1	15	29
♃	♐25	26	27	28	29	♑0	♄	♑13	14	14	15	15	16	♅	♌19	19	18	♆	♏9	9	9	♇	♍5	5	5	☊	♍25	25	25

MARCH

	1	2	3	4	5	6	7	8	9	10	11	12	13	14	15	16	17	18	19	20	21	22	23	24	25	26	27	28	29	30	31
☉	♓10	11	12	13	14	15	16	17	18	19	20	21	22	23	24	25	26	27	28	29	♈0	1	2	3	4	5	6	7	8	9	♈10
☽	♈20	♉3	15	27	♊9	21	♋3	15	27	♌10	22	♍5	18	♎2	15	29	♏13	27	♐11	26	♑10	24	♒8	22	♓6	19	♈2	16	28	♉11	♉23
☿	♓26	26	26	25	25	24	24	23	22	21	20	19	18	17	16	16	15	14	14	13	13	12	12	12	12	12	12	13	13	14	♓14
♀	♒11	13	14	15	16	18	19	20	21	23	24	25	26	27	29	♓0	1	2	4	5	6	7	9	10	11	12	13	15	16	17	♓18
♂	♒5	6	7	7	8	9	10	11	11	12	13	14	14	15	16	17	17	18	19	20	21	21	22	23	24	24	25	26	27	27	♒28

	1	6	12	18	24	30		1	6	12	18	24	30		1	15	30		1	15	30		1	15	30		1	15	30
♃	♑0	1	1	2	2	3	♄	♑16	16	17	17	17	18	♅	♌18	18	17	♆	♏9	9	9	♇	♍5	4	4	☊	♍25	25	25

APRIL

	1	2	3	4	5	6	7	8	9	10	11	12	13	14	15	16	17	18	19	20	21	22	23	24	25	26	27	28	29	30
☉	♈11	12	13	14	15	16	17	18	19	20	21	22	23	24	25	26	27	28	29	♉0	1	2	3	4	5	6	7	8	9	♉10
☽	♊5	17	29	♋11	23	♌5	17	♍0	13	26	♎10	24	♏8	23	♐8	22	♑7	21	♒5	19	♓2	16	29	♈12	24	♉7	19	♊1	13	♊25
☿	♓15	15	16	17	18	19	19	20	22	23	24	25	26	27	29	♈0	1	3	4	5	7	8	10	11	13	15	16	18	20	♈21
♀	♓20	21	22	23	25	26	27	28	29	♈1	2	3	4	6	7	8	9	11	12	13	14	15	17	18	19	20	22	23	24	♈25
♂	♒29	♓0	1	1	2	3	4	4	5	6	7	8	8	9	10	11	11	12	13	14	14	15	16	17	18	18	19	20	21	♓21

	1	6	12	18	24	30		1	6	12	18	24	30		1	15	30		1	15	30		1	15	30		1	15	30
♃	♑3	3	4	4	4	3	♄	♑18	18	18	18	18	18	♅	♌17	17	17	♆	♏8	8	8	♇	♍4	4	4	☊	♍25	24	24

MAY

	1	2	3	4	5	6	7	8	9	10	11	12	13	14	15	16	17	18	19	20	21	22	23	24	25	26	27	28	29	30	31
☉	♉11	12	13	14	15	15	16	17	18	19	20	21	22	23	24	25	26	27	28	29	♊0	1	2	3	4	5	6	7	8	9	♊10
☽	♋7	19	♌1	13	25	♍8	21	♎4	18	♏2	17	♐2	17	♑2	17	♒1	15	29	♓13	26	♈9	21	♉4	16	28	♊10	22	♋4	16	28	♌10
☿	♈23	25	27	29	♉1	2	4	6	8	10	12	15	17	19	21	23	25	27	♊0	2	4	6	8	11	13	15	17	19	21	23	♊25
♀	♈27	28	29	♉0	1	3	4	5	6	8	9	10	11	12	14	15	16	17	19	20	21	22	24	25	26	27	28	♊0	1	2	♊3
♂	♓22	23	24	24	25	26	27	27	28	29	♈0	1	1	2	3	4	4	5	6	7	7	8	9	10	10	11	12	13	13	14	♈15

	1	6	12	18	24	30		1	6	12	18	24	30		1	15	30		1	15	30		1	15	30		1	15	30
♃	♑3	3	3	2	2	1	♄	♑18	18	18	18	18	18	♅	♌17	17	17	♆	♏8	7	7	♇	♍4	4	4	☊	♍23	23	21

JUNE

	1	2	3	4	5	6	7	8	9	10	11	12	13	14	15	16	17	18	19	20	21	22	23	24	25	26	27	28	29	30
☉	♊10	11	12	13	14	15	16	17	18	19	20	21	22	23	24	25	26	27	28	29	♋0	1	2	2	3	4	5	6	7	♋8
☽	♌22	♍4	16	29	♎12	26	♏11	25	♐10	26	♑11	26	♒11	25	♓9	22	♈6	18	♉1	13	25	♊7	19	♋1	13	25	♌7	18	♍1	♍13
☿	♊27	28	♋0	2	4	5	7	9	10	12	13	14	16	17	18	19	20	22	23	24	24	25	26	27	27	28	29	29	29	♌0
♀	♊5	6	7	8	10	11	12	13	14	16	17	18	19	21	22	23	24	25	27	28	29	♋0	2	3	4	5	7	8	9	♋10
♂	♈16	16	17	18	19	19	20	21	22	22	23	24	25	25	26	27	28	28	29	♉0	0	1	2	3	3	4	5	6	6	♉7

	1	6	12	18	24	30		1	6	12	18	24	30		1	15	30		1	15	30		1	15	30		1	15	30
♃	♑1	0	0	♐29	28	27	♄	♑18	17	17	17	16	16	♅	♌18	18	19	♆	♏7	7	6	♇	♍4	4	4	☊	♍21	20	18

JULY

	1	2	3	4	5	6	7	8	9	10	11	12	13	14	15	16	17	18	19	20	21	22	23	24	25	26	27	28	29	30	31
☉	♋9	10	11	12	13	14	15	16	17	18	19	20	21	22	22	23	24	25	26	27	28	29	♌0	1	2	3	4	5	6	7	♌8
☽	♍25	♎8	21	♏5	19	♐4	19	♑4	19	♒5	19	♓4	18	♈2	15	27	♉10	22	♊4	16	28	♋10	22	♌4	16	28	♍10	22	♎5	18	♏1
☿	♌0	0	0	0	0	0	0	♋29	29	29	28	28	27	26	26	25	24	24	23	23	22	21	21	21	20	20	20	20	20	20	♋20
♀	♋11	13	14	15	16	18	19	20	21	23	24	25	26	27	29	♌0	1	2	4	5	6	7	9	10	11	12	13	15	16	17	♌18
♂	♉8	8	9	10	11	11	12	13	13	14	15	15	16	17	18	18	19	20	20	21	22	22	23	24	24	25	26	27	27	28	♉29

	1	6	12	18	24	30		1	6	12	18	24	30		1	15	30		1	15	30		1	15	30		1	15	30
♃	♐27	27	26	25	25	24	♄	♑16	15	15	14	14	14	♅	♌19	20	20	♆	♏6	6	6	♇	♍4	4	5	☊	♍18	17	16

AUGUST

	1	2	3	4	5	6	7	8	9	10	11	12	13	14	15	16	17	18	19	20	21	22	23	24	25	26	27	28	29	30	31
☉	♌9	10	11	12	13	14	14	15	16	17	18	19	20	21	22	23	24	25	26	27	28	29	♍0	1	2	3	4	5	6	7	♍8
☽	♏15	29	♐13	28	♑13	28	♒13	28	♓12	26	♈10	23	♉6	19	♊1	13	25	♋7	18	♌0	12	25	♍7	19	♎2	15	28	♏12	25	♐9	♐23
☿	♋21	21	22	23	23	24	25	26	28	29	♌0	2	3	5	7	8	10	12	14	16	18	20	22	24	26	28	♍0	2	4	6	♍8
♀	♌20	21	22	23	25	26	27	28	29	♍1	2	3	4	6	7	8	9	11	12	13	14	15	17	18	19	20	22	23	24	25	♍27
♂	♉29	♊0	1	1	2	3	3	4	4	5	6	6	7	8	8	9	10	10	11	11	12	13	13	14	15	15	16	16	17	18	♊18

	1	6	12	18	24	30		1	6	12	18	24	30		1	15	30		1	15	30		1	15	30		1	15	30
♃	♐24	24	24	24	24	24	♄	♑13	13	13	12	12	12	♅	♌21	21	22	♆	♏6	7	7	♇	♍5	5	6	☊	♍16	16	16

SEPTEMBER

	1	2	3	4	5	6	7	8	9	10	11	12	13	14	15	16	17	18	19	20	21	22	23	24	25	26	27	28	29	30
☉	♍9	10	10	11	12	13	14	15	16	17	18	19	20	21	22	23	24	25	26	27	28	29	♎0	1	2	3	4	5	6	♎7
☽	♑8	22	♒7	22	♓6	20	♈4	18	♉1	14	27	♊9	21	♋3	15	27	♌9	21	♍3	16	28	♎11	25	♏8	22	♐6	20	♑4	18	♒3
☿	♍10	11	13	15	17	19	21	23	24	26	28	♎0	1	3	5	6	8	9	11	13	14	16	17	19	20	22	23	25	26	♎28
♀	♍28	29	♎0	1	3	4	5	6	8	9	10	11	13	14	15	16	17	19	20	21	22	24	25	26	27	29	♏0	1	2	♏3
♂	♊19	19	20	21	21	22	22	23	23	24	25	25	26	26	27	27	28	28	29	29	♋0	0	1	1	2	2	3	3	4	♋4

	1	6	12	18	24	30		1	6	12	18	24	30		1	15	30		1	15	30		1	15	30		1	15	30
♃	♐24	24	25	25	26	26	♄	♑12	12	12	12	12	12	♅	♌23	23	24	♆	♏7	7	8	♇	♍6	6	7	☊	♍16	15	15

OCTOBER

	1	2	3	4	5	6	7	8	9	10	11	12	13	14	15	16	17	18	19	20	21	22	23	24	25	26	27	28	29	30	31
☉	♎8	9	10	11	12	13	14	15	16	17	18	19	20	21	22	23	24	25	26	27	28	29	♏0	1	2	3	4	5	6	7	♏8
☽	♒17	♓1	15	29	♈13	26	♉9	22	♊5	17	29	♋11	23	♌4	16	29	♍11	24	♎7	20	♏4	18	♐2	17	♑1	15	29	♒14	27	♓11	♓25
☿	♎29	♏0	2	3	4	6	7	8	10	11	12	13	14	15	16	17	18	19	20	21	22	22	23	23	24	24	24	24	24	24	♏23
♀	♏5	6	7	8	10	11	12	13	14	16	17	18	19	21	22	23	24	25	27	28	29	♐0	2	3	4	5	6	8	9	10	♐11
♂	♋5	5	6	6	7	7	8	8	8	9	9	10	10	10	11	11	12	12	12	13	13	13	14	14	14	15	15	15	15	16	♋16

	1	6	12	18	24	30		1	6	12	18	24	30		1	15	30		1	15	30		1	15	30		1	15	30
♃	♐26	27	28	29	♑0	1	♄	♑12	12	12	13	13	13	♅	♌24	25	25	♆	♏8	8	9	♇	♍7	7	8	☊	♍15	15	14

NOVEMBER

	1	2	3	4	5	6	7	8	9	10	11	12	13	14	15	16	17	18	19	20	21	22	23	24	25	26	27	28	29	30
☉	♏9	10	11	12	13	14	15	16	17	18	19	20	21	22	23	24	25	26	27	28	29	♐0	1	2	3	4	5	6	7	♐8
☽	♈8	22	♉5	17	♊0	13	25	♋7	19	♌0	12	24	♍6	19	♎2	15	28	♏12	27	♐11	26	♑11	26	♒10	24	♓8	22	♈5	18	♉1
☿	♏23	22	21	20	19	18	16	15	14	12	11	10	9	9	8	8	8	8	8	9	9	10	11	12	13	14	15	16	18	♏19
♀	♐13	14	15	16	17	19	20	21	22	23	25	26	27	28	♑0	1	2	3	4	6	7	8	9	10	12	13	14	15	16	♑18
♂	♋16	16	17	17	17	17	17	18	18	18	18	18	18	18	18	19	19	19	19	19	19	19	19	19	19	18	18	18	18	♋18

	1	6	12	18	24	30		1	6	12	18	24	30		1	15	30		1	15	30		1	15	30		1	15	30
♃	♑1	2	3	4	6	7	♄	♑14	14	14	15	15	16	♅	♌25	26	26	♆	♏9	9	10	♇	♍8	8	8	☊	♍14	13	12

DECEMBER

	1	2	3	4	5	6	7	8	9	10	11	12	13	14	15	16	17	18	19	20	21	22	23	24	25	26	27	28	29	30	31
☉	♐9	10	11	12	13	14	15	16	17	18	19	20	21	22	23	24	25	26	27	28	29	♑0	1	2	3	4	5	6	7	8	♑9
☽	♉14	26	♊9	21	♋3	15	27	♌9	20	♍2	14	27	♎9	23	♏6	20	♐5	20	♑5	20	♒5	20	♓4	18	♈2	15	28	♉11	23	♊6	♊18
☿	♏20	22	23	25	26	27	29	♐0	2	3	5	6	8	9	11	12	14	16	17	19	20	22	23	25	26	28	♑0	1	3	4	♑6
♀	♑19	20	21	22	24	25	26	27	28	♒0	1	2	3	4	5	7	8	9	10	11	13	14	15	16	17	18	20	21	22	23	♒24
♂	♋18	18	18	17	17	17	17	17	16	16	16	15	15	15	15	14	14	14	13	13	12	12	12	11	11	11	10	10	9	9	♋9

	1	6	12	18	24	30		1	6	12	18	24	30		1	15	30		1	15	30		1	15	30		1	15	30
♃	♑7	8	9	11	12	14	♄	♑16	17	17	18	19	19	♅	♌26	26	25	♆	♏10	10	11	♇	♍8	8	8	☊	♍11	10	8

1961

JANUARY

	1	2	3	4	5	6	7	8	9	10	11	12	13	14	15	16	17	18	19	20	21	22	23	24	25	26	27	28	29	30	31
☉	♑10	11	12	13	14	15	16	17	18	20	21	22	23	24	25	26	27	28	29	♒0	1	2	3	4	5	6	7	8	9	10	♒11
☽	♋0	12	24	♌5	17	29	♍11	23	♎5	18	♏1	14	28	♐13	28	♑13	28	♒13	28	♓13	27	♈11	25	♉8	20	♊3	15	27	♋9	21	♌2
☿	♑7	9	11	12	14	15	17	19	20	22	24	25	27	29	♒0	2	4	5	7	9	11	12	14	16	17	19	21	22	24	26	♒27
♀	♒25	26	28	29	♓0	1	2	3	4	5	7	8	9	10	11	12	13	14	15	16	17	19	20	21	22	23	24	25	26	27	♓28
♂	♋8	8	7	7	7	6	6	5	5	5	4	4	4	4	3	3	3	2	2	2	2	1	1	1	1	1	1	1	0	0	♋0

	1	6	12	18	24	30
♃	♑14	15	17	18	19	21
♄	♑20	20	21	22	22	23

	1	15	30
♅	♌25	25	24
♆	♏11	11	11
♇	♍8	8	8
☊	♍8	7	6

FEBRUARY

	1	2	3	4	5	6	7	8	9	10	11	12	13	14	15	16	17	18	19	20	21	22	23	24	25	26	27	28
☉	♒12	13	14	15	16	17	18	19	20	21	22	23	24	25	26	27	28	29	♓0	1	2	3	4	5	6	7	8	♓9
☽	♌14	26	♍8	20	♎2	15	27	♏10	24	♐7	22	♑6	21	♒6	21	♓6	21	♈6	20	♉3	16	29	♊11	24	♋6	17	29	♌11
☿	♒29	♓0	2	3	4	5	6	7	8	8	9	9	9	9	9	8	8	7	6	5	4	3	2	1	0	♒29	28	♒27
♀	♓29	♈0	1	2	3	4	5	6	6	7	8	9	10	11	12	13	14	14	15	16	17	17	18	19	20	20	21	♈22
♂	♋0	0	0	0	0	0	0	0	0	0	0	0	0	0	0	1	1	1	1	1	1	1	2	2	2	2	2	♋3

	1	6	12	18	24	28
♃	♑21	22	24	25	26	27
♄	♑23	24	24	25	26	26

	1	15	28
♅	♌24	24	23
♆	♏11	11	11
♇	♍7	7	7
☊	♍6	6	6

MARCH

	1	2	3	4	5	6	7	8	9	10	11	12	13	14	15	16	17	18	19	20	21	22	23	24	25	26	27	28	29	30	31
☉	♓10	11	12	13	14	15	16	17	18	19	20	21	22	23	24	25	26	27	28	29	♈0	1	2	3	4	5	6	7	8	9	♈10
☽	♌23	♍5	17	29	♎12	24	♏7	20	♐4	18	♑2	16	♒0	15	♓0	14	29	♈13	27	♉11	24	♊7	20	♋2	14	26	♌7	19	♍1	13	♍26
☿	♒26	26	25	25	25	24	24	24	25	25	25	26	26	27	27	28	29	♓0	1	1	2	3	5	6	7	8	9	10	12	13	♓14
♀	♈22	23	24	24	25	25	26	26	26	27	27	28	28	28	28	29	29	29	29	29	29	29	29	29	29	29	28	28	28	27	♈27
♂	♋3	3	3	4	4	4	4	5	5	5	6	6	6	7	7	7	8	8	8	9	9	9	10	10	11	11	11	12	12	13	♋13

	1	6	12	18	24	30
♃	♑27	28	29	♒0	1	2
♄	♑26	27	27	28	28	29

	1	15	30
♅	♌23	23	22
♆	♏11	11	11
♇	♍7	6	6
☊	♍6	6	6

APRIL

	1	2	3	4	5	6	7	8	9	10	11	12	13	14	15	16	17	18	19	20	21	22	23	24	25	26	27	28	29	30
☉	♈11	12	13	14	15	16	17	18	19	20	21	22	23	24	25	26	27	28	29	♉0	1	2	3	4	5	6	6	7	8	♉9
☽	♎8	21	♏4	17	♐1	14	28	♑12	26	♒11	25	♓9	24	♈8	22	♉6	19	♊2	15	28	♋10	22	♌4	15	27	♍9	21	♎4	17	♏0
☿	♓16	17	19	20	22	23	25	26	28	29	♈1	3	4	6	8	10	11	13	15	17	19	21	23	25	27	29	♉1	3	5	♉7
♀	♈27	26	26	25	25	24	23	23	22	21	21	20	20	19	18	18	17	17	16	16	15	15	14	14	14	14	13	13	13	♈13
♂	♋13	14	14	15	15	16	16	16	17	17	18	18	19	19	20	20	21	21	22	22	22	23	23	24	24	25	25	26	26	♋27

	1	6	12	18	24	30
♃	♒3	3	4	5	6	6
♄	♑29	29	29	29	♒0	0

	1	15	30
♅	♌22	22	22
♆	♏11	10	10
♇	♍6	6	6
☊	♍6	5	4

MAY

	1	2	3	4	5	6	7	8	9	10	11	12	13	14	15	16	17	18	19	20	21	22	23	24	25	26	27	28	29	30	31
☉	♉10	11	12	13	14	15	16	17	18	19	20	21	22	23	24	25	26	27	28	29	♊0	1	2	3	4	5	5	6	7	8	♊9
☽	♏13	27	♐11	25	♑9	23	♒7	22	♓6	20	♈3	17	♉1	14	28	♊10	23	♋6	18	♌0	11	23	♍5	17	29	♎12	25	♏8	22	♐6	♐20
☿	♉9	11	14	16	18	20	22	24	26	29	♊1	3	5	7	9	10	12	14	16	18	19	21	22	24	25	27	28	29	♋0	1	♋3
♀	♈13	13	13	13	13	13	13	13	14	14	14	15	15	15	16	16	17	17	18	18	19	19	20	21	21	22	23	23	24	25	♈25
♂	♋27	28	28	29	29	♌0	0	1	2	2	3	3	4	4	5	5	6	6	7	7	8	8	9	10	10	11	11	12	12	13	♌13

	1	6	12	18	24	30
♃	♒6	7	7	7	7	7
♄	♒0	0	0	0	0	0

	1	15	30
♅	♌22	22	22
♆	♏10	10	9
♇	♍6	6	6
☊	♍4	3	1

JUNE

	1	2	3	4	5	6	7	8	9	10	11	12	13	14	15	16	17	18	19	20	21	22	23	24	25	26	27	28	29	30
☉	♊10	11	12	13	14	15	16	17	18	19	20	21	22	23	24	25	26	27	27	28	29	♋0	1	2	3	4	5	6	7	♋8
☽	♑5	19	♒4	18	♓2	17	♈0	14	27	♉11	24	♊7	19	♋2	14	26	♌8	20	♍1	13	25	♎7	20	♏3	16	♐0	14	29	♑14	♑29
☿	♋4	4	5	6	7	8	8	9	9	10	10	10	10	10	10	10	10	10	10	9	9	9	8	8	7	6	6	5	5	♋4
♀	♈26	27	28	29	29	♉0	1	2	3	4	4	5	6	7	8	9	10	11	12	13	14	15	16	17	18	19	20	21	22	♉23
♂	♌14	15	15	16	16	17	17	18	18	19	20	20	21	21	22	22	23	24	24	25	25	26	26	27	28	28	29	29	♍0	♍1

	1	6	12	18	24	30
♃	♒7	7	7	6	6	5
♄	♑29	29	29	29	28	28

	1	15	30
♅	♌22	23	23
♆	♏9	9	9
♇	♍6	6	6
☊	♍1	♌0	28

JULY

	1	2	3	4	5	6	7	8	9	10	11	12	13	14	15	16	17	18	19	20	21	22	23	24	25	26	27	28	29	30	31
☉	♋9	10	11	12	13	14	15	16	17	17	18	19	20	21	22	23	24	25	26	27	28	29	♌0	1	2	3	4	5	6	7	♌8
☽	♒13	28	♓13	27	♈11	24	♉8	21	♊3	16	28	♋11	23	♌4	16	28	♍10	22	♎4	16	28	♏11	24	♐8	22	♑7	22	♒7	22	♓7	♓22
☿	♋4	3	3	2	2	2	1	1	1	1	2	2	2	3	3	4	4	5	6	7	8	9	10	11	13	14	16	17	19	21	♋22
♀	♉24	25	26	27	28	29	♊0	1	2	3	4	5	6	7	8	9	10	12	13	14	15	16	17	18	19	20	21	23	24	25	♊26
♂	♍1	2	2	3	4	4	5	5	6	7	7	8	8	9	10	10	11	11	12	13	13	14	14	15	16	16	17	17	18	19	♍19

	1	6	12	18	24	30
♃	♒5	5	4	3	2	2
♄	♑28	28	27	27	26	26

	1	15	30
♅	♌23	24	25
♆	♏9	9	9
♇	♍6	6	7
☊	♌28	27	27

AUGUST

	1	2	3	4	5	6	7	8	9	10	11	12	13	14	15	16	17	18	19	20	21	22	23	24	25	26	27	28	29	30	31
☉	♌9	9	10	11	12	13	14	15	16	17	18	19	20	21	22	23	24	25	26	27	28	29	♍0	1	2	3	3	4	5	6	♍7
☽	♈7	21	♉4	18	♊0	13	25	♋8	20	♌1	13	25	♍7	19	♎1	13	25	♏7	20	♐3	17	♑1	16	♒0	15	♓1	16	♈1	15	♉0	♉13
☿	♋24	26	28	♌0	2	4	6	8	10	12	14	16	18	20	22	24	26	28	♍0	2	4	6	8	10	12	13	15	17	19	20	♍22
♀	♊27	28	29	♋0	2	3	4	5	6	7	8	10	11	12	13	14	15	16	18	19	20	21	22	23	25	26	27	28	29	♌0	♌2
♂	♍20	21	21	22	22	23	24	24	25	26	26	27	27	28	29	29	♎0	1	1	2	3	3	4	4	5	6	6	7	8	8	♎9

	1	6	12	18	24	30
♃	♒1	1	0 ♑29	29	28	
♄	♑26	25	25	25	24	24

	1	15	30
♅	♌25	26	27
♆	♏9	9	9
♇	♍7	7	8
☊	♌27	27	27

SEPTEMBER

	1	2	3	4	5	6	7	8	9	10	11	12	13	14	15	16	17	18	19	20	21	22	23	24	25	26	27	28	29	30
☉	♍8	9	10	11	12	13	14	15	16	17	18	19	20	21	22	23	24	25	26	27	28	29	♎0	1	2	3	4	5	6	♎7
☽	♉27	♊10	22	♋5	17	29	♌10	22	♍4	16	28	♎10	22	♏4	17	♐0	13	27	♑11	25	♒9	24	♓9	24	♈9	24	♉8	22	♊5	♊18
☿	♍24	25	27	29	♎0	2	3	5	6	8	9	11	12	13	15	16	18	19	20	21	23	24	25	26	27	28	29	♏0	1	♏2
♀	♌3	4	5	6	8	9	10	11	12	14	15	16	17	18	20	21	22	23	24	26	27	28	29	♍0	2	3	4	5	7	♍8
♂	♎10	10	11	12	12	13	13	14	15	15	16	17	17	18	19	19	20	21	21	22	23	23	24	25	25	26	27	27	28	♎29

	1	6	12	18	24	30
♃	♑28	28	28	27	27	27
♄	♑24	24	23	23	23	23

	1	15	30
♅	♌27	28	29
♆	♏9	9	10
♇	♍8	8	9
☊	♌27	27	26

OCTOBER

	1	2	3	4	5	6	7	8	9	10	11	12	13	14	15	16	17	18	19	20	21	22	23	24	25	26	27	28	29	30	31
☉	♎8	9	10	11	12	12	13	14	15	16	17	18	19	20	21	22	23	24	25	26	27	28	29	♏0	1	2	3	4	5	6	♏7
☽	♋1	13	25	♌7	19	♍1	12	24	♎7	19	♏1	14	27	♐10	24	♑7	21	♒5	19	♓4	18	♈3	17	♉2	16	♊0	13	26	♋9	21	♌3
☿	♏3	4	5	6	6	7	7	8	8	8	8	8	8	7	7	6	6	5	4	3	1	0	♎29	28	26	25	24	24	23	23	♎22
♀	♍9	10	11	13	14	15	16	18	19	20	21	22	24	25	26	27	29	♎0	1	2	4	5	6	7	9	10	11	12	13	15	♎16
♂	♎29	♏0	1	1	2	3	4	4	5	6	6	7	8	8	9	10	10	11	12	12	13	14	15	15	16	17	17	18	19	19	♏20

	1	6	12	18	24	30
♃	♑27	28	28	28	29	29
♄	♑23	23	23	24	24	24

	1	15	30
♅	♌29	29	♍29
♆	♏10	10	11
♇	♍9	9	10
☊	♌26	25	24

NOVEMBER

	1	2	3	4	5	6	7	8	9	10	11	12	13	14	15	16	17	18	19	20	21	22	23	24	25	26	27	28	29	30
☉	♏8	9	10	11	12	13	14	15	16	17	18	19	20	21	22	23	24	25	26	27	28	29	♐0	1	2	3	5	6	7	♐8
☽	♌15	27	♍9	21	♎3	15	28	♏10	23	♐7	20	♑4	18	♒2	16	♓0	14	28	♈12	26	♉10	24	♊8	21	♋4	17	29	♌11	23	♍5
☿	♎22	22	23	23	24	25	26	27	28	29	♏0	1	3	4	5	7	8	10	11	13	14	16	18	19	21	22	24	25	27	♏29
♀	♎17	18	20	21	22	23	25	26	27	28	♏0	1	2	3	5	6	7	8	10	11	12	13	15	16	17	19	20	21	22	♏24
♂	♏21	22	22	23	24	24	25	26	26	27	28	29	29	♐0	1	1	2	3	4	4	5	6	7	7	8	9	9	10	11	♐12

	1	6	12	18	24	30
♃	♒0	0	1	2	3	4
♄	♑24	24	25	25	26	26

	1	15	30
♅	♍0	0	1
♆	♏11	11	12
♇	♍10	10	10
☊	♌24	23	21

DECEMBER

	1	2	3	4	5	6	7	8	9	10	11	12	13	14	15	16	17	18	19	20	21	22	23	24	25	26	27	28	29	30	31
☉	♐9	10	11	12	13	14	15	16	17	18	19	20	21	22	23	24	25	26	27	28	29	♑0	1	2	3	4	5	6	7	8	♑9
☽	♍17	28	♎11	23	♏6	19	♐2	16	♑0	14	28	♒12	27	♓11	25	♈9	23	♉6	20	♊3	17	♋0	12	25	♌7	19	♍1	13	24	♎6	♎18
☿	♐0	2	3	5	6	8	9	11	13	14	16	17	19	20	22	24	25	27	28	♑0	2	3	5	6	8	10	11	13	14	16	♑18
♀	♏25	26	27	29	♐0	1	2	4	5	6	7	9	10	11	12	14	15	16	17	19	20	21	22	24	25	26	27	29	♑0	1	♑3
♂	♐12	13	14	15	15	16	17	18	18	19	20	20	21	22	23	23	24	25	26	26	27	28	29	29	♑0	1	2	2	3	4	♑5

	1	6	12	18	24	30
♃	♒4	5	6	7	9	10
♄	♑26	27	28	28	29	29

	1	15	30
♅	♍1	1	0
♆	♏12	12	13
♇	♍10	10	10
☊	♌21	20	19

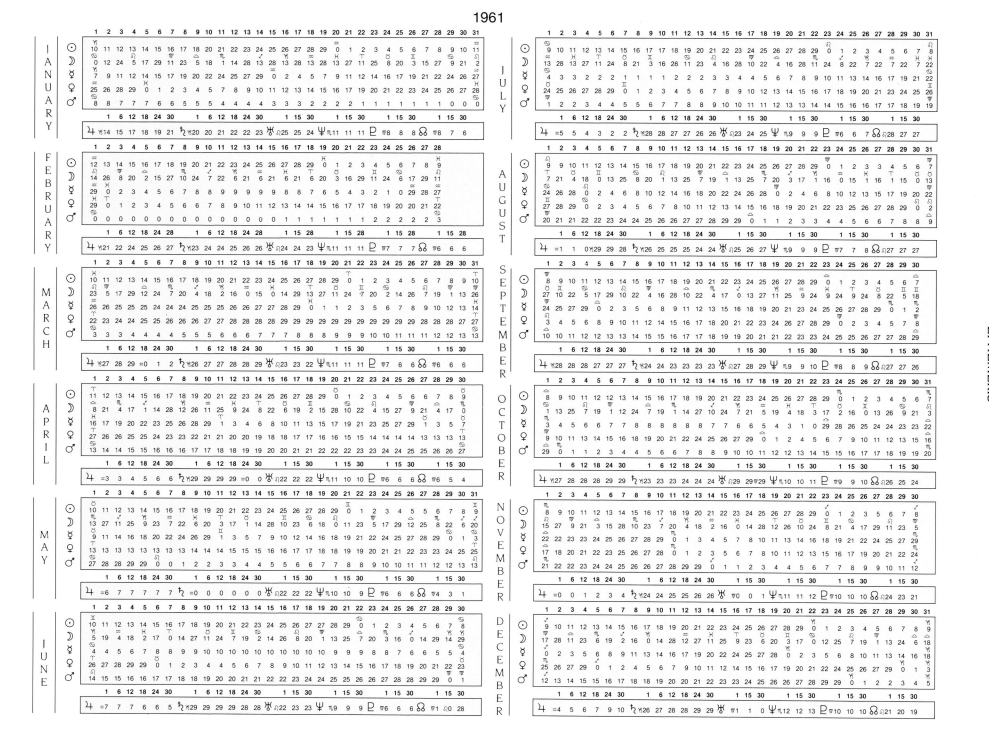

1962

JANUARY

	1	2	3	4	5	6	7	8	9	10	11	12	13	14	15	16	17	18	19	20	21	22	23	24	25	26	27	28	29	30	31
☉	♑10	11	12	13	14	15	16	17	18	19	20	21	22	23	24	25	26	27	28	29	♒0	1	3	4	5	6	7	8	9	10	♒11
☽	♏1	13	26	♐10	24	♑8	23	♒7	22	♓7	21	♈6	20	♉3	17	♊0	13	26	♋9	21	♌3	15	27	♍9	21	♎3	14	26	♏9	21	♐4
☿	♑19	21	22	24	26	27	29	♒1	2	4	5	7	8	10	11	13	14	16	17	18	19	20	21	22	22	23	23	23	23	22	♒22
♀	♑4	5	6	8	9	10	11	13	14	15	16	18	19	20	21	23	24	25	26	28	29	♒0	1	3	4	5	6	8	9	10	♒11
♂	♑5	6	7	8	9	9	10	11	12	12	13	14	15	15	16	17	18	18	19	20	21	22	22	23	24	25	25	26	27	28	♑28

♃ 1	6	12	18	24	30	♄ 1	6	12	18	24	30	♅ 1	15	30	♆ 1	15	30	♇ 1	15	30	☊ 1	15	30
♒10	12	13	14	16	17	♒0	0	1	2	2	3	♍0	0	♌0	♏13	13	13	♍10	10	10	♌19	18	18

FEBRUARY

	1	2	3	4	5	6	7	8	9	10	11	12	13	14	15	16	17	18	19	20	21	22	23	24	25	26	27	28
☉	♒12	13	14	15	16	17	18	19	20	21	22	23	24	25	26	27	28	29	♓0	1	2	3	4	5	6	7	8	♓9
☽	♐18	♑2	16	♒1	16	♓1	16	♈1	15	♉0	14	27	♊10	23	♋6	18	♌0	12	24	♍6	18	29	♎11	23	♏5	18	♐0	♐13
☿	♒21	20	19	18	17	16	15	13	12	11	10	9	9	8	8	7	7	7	7	7	8	8	9	9	10	10	11	♒12
♀	♒13	14	15	17	18	19	20	22	23	24	25	27	28	29	♓0	2	3	4	5	7	8	9	10	12	13	14	15	♓17
♂	♑29	♒0	1·	2	2	3	4	5	5	6	7	8	9	9	10	11	12	12	13	14	15	16	16	17	18	19	20	♒20

♃ 1	6	12	18	24	28	♄ 1	6	12	18	24	28	♅ 1	15	28	♆ 1	15	28	♇ 1	15	28	☊ 1	15	28
♒18	19	20	22	23	24	♒3	4	5	5	6	6	♌29	29	28	♏13	13	13	♍10	9	9	♌18	18	18

MARCH

	1	2	3	4	5	6	7	8	9	10	11	12	13	14	15	16	17	18	19	20	21	22	23	24	25	26	27	28	29	30	31
☉	♓10	11	12	13	14	15	16	17	18	19	20	21	22	23	24	25	26	27	28	29	♈0	1	2	3	4	5	6	7	8	9	♈10
☽	♐26	♑10	24	♒9	24	♓9	24	♈9	24	♉9	23	♊6	20	♋2	15	27	♌9	21	♍3	14	26	♎8	20	♏2	15	27	♐10	22	♑6	19	♒3
☿	♒13	14	15	16	17	18	19	20	21	23	24	25	27	28	29	♓1	2	4	5	7	8	10	11	13	14	16	18	19	21	23	♓24
♀	♓18	19	20	22	23	24	25	27	28	29	♈0	2	3	4	5	7	8	9	10	11	13	14	15	16	18	19	20	21	23	24	♈25
♂	♒21	22	23	23	24	25	26	27	27	28	29	♓0	1	1	2	3	4	4	5	6	7	8	8	9	10	11	12	12	13	14	♓15

♃ 1	6	12	18	24	30	♄ 1	6	12	18	24	30	♅ 1	15	30	♆ 1	15	30	♇ 1	15	30	☊ 1	15	30
♒24	26	27	28	♓0	1	♒7	7	8	8	9	9	♌28	27	27	♏13	13	13	♍9	8	8	♌18	18	17

APRIL

	1	2	3	4	5	6	7	8	9	10	11	12	13	14	15	16	17	18	19	20	21	22	23	24	25	26	27	28	29	30
☉	♈11	12	13	14	15	16	17	18	19	20	21	22	23	24	25	26	27	27	28	29	♉0	1	2	3	4	5	6	7	8	♉9
☽	♒17	♓2	17	♈2	17	♉2	17	♊1	15	28	♋11	24	♌6	18	♍0	11	23	♎5	17	29	♏11	24	♐7	19	♑3	16	29	♒13	27	♓12
☿	♓26	28	♈0	2	3	5	7	9	11	13	15	17	19	21	23	25	28	♉0	2	4	6	8	10	12	14	16	18	20	22	♉24
♀	♈26	28	29	♉0	1	3	4	5	6	7	9	10	11	12	14	15	16	17	19	20	21	22	23	25	26	27	28	♊0	1	♊2
♂	♓15	16	17	18	19	19	20	21	22	22	23	24	25	26	26	27	28	29	29	♈0	1	2	3	3	4	5	6	6	7	♈8

♃ 1	6	12	18	24	30	♄ 1	6	12	18	24	30	♅ 1	15	30	♆ 1	15	30	♇ 1	15	30	☊ 1	15	30
♓1	2	4	5	6	7	♒9	10	10	10	11	11	♌27	27	26	♏13	13	12	♍8	8	8	♌17	16	14

MAY

	1	2	3	4	5	6	7	8	9	10	11	12	13	14	15	16	17	18	19	20	21	22	23	24	25	26	27	28	29	30	31
☉	♉10	11	12	13	14	15	16	17	18	19	20	21	22	23	24	25	26	27	28	29	29	♊0	1	2	3	4	5	6	7	8	♊9
☽	♓26	♈11	26	♉11	25	♊9	23	♋6	19	♌2	14	26	♍8	20	♎1	13	26	♏8	20	♐3	16	29	♑13	26	♒10	24	♓8	22	♈6	21	♉5
☿	♉26	28	♊0	1	3	4	6	7	9	10	11	12	13	14	15	16	17	18	18	19	19	20	20	20	20	20	20	20	20	20	♊20
♀	♊3	4	6	7	8	9	10	12	13	14	15	17	18	19	20	21	23	24	25	26	27	29	♋0	1	2	3	5	6	7	8	♋9
♂	♈9	9	10	11	12	13	13	14	15	16	16	17	18	19	19	20	21	22	22	23	24	25	25	26	27	28	29	29	♉0	1	♉2

♃ 1	6	12	18	24	30	♄ 1	6	12	18	24	30	♅ 1	15	30	♆ 1	15	30	♇ 1	15	30	☊ 1	15	30
♓7	8	9	10	10	11	♒11	11	11	11	11	11	♌26	26	27	♏12	12	11	♍8	8	8	♌14	13	11

JUNE

	1	2	3	4	5	6	7	8	9	10	11	12	13	14	15	16	17	18	19	20	21	22	23	24	25	26	27	28	29	30
☉	♊10	11	12	13	14	15	16	17	18	19	20	21	22	22	23	24	25	26	27	28	29	♋0	1	2	3	4	5	6	7	♋8
☽	♉20	♊4	18	♋1	14	27	♌10	22	♍4	16	28	♎9	22	♏4	16	29	♐12	25	♑9	23	♒7	21	♓5	19	♈3	17	♉1	15	29	♊13
☿	♊19	19	18	18	17	17	16	16	15	15	14	14	13	13	13	12	12	12	12	12	12	12	12	13	13	14	14	15	15	♊16
♀	♋11	12	13	14	15	17	18	19	20	21	23	24	25	26	27	29	♌0	1	2	3	4	6	7	8	9	10	11	13	14	♌15
♂	♉2	3	4	4	5	6	7	7	8	9	10	10	11	12	13	13	14	15	16	16	17	18	18	19	20	21	21	22	23	♉23

♃ 1	6	12	18	24	30	♄ 1	6	12	18	24	30	♅ 1	15	30	♆ 1	15	30	♇ 1	15	30	☊ 1	15	30
♓11	12	12	12	13	13	♒11	11	11	11	11	10	♌27	27	28	♏11	11	11	♍8	8	8	♌11	10	9

JULY

	1	2	3	4	5	6	7	8	9	10	11	12	13	14	15	16	17	18	19	20	21	22	23	24	25	26	27	28	29	30	31
☉	♋9	10	11	12	13	13	14	15	16	17	18	19	20	21	22	23	24	25	26	27	28	29	♌0	1	2	3	3	4	5	6	♌7
☽	♊26	♋10	23	♌5	18	♍0	12	24	♎6	17	29	♏12	24	♐7	20	♑4	18	♒2	16	♓1	15	♈0	14	28	♉12	26	♊10	23	♋6	19	♌1
☿	♊17	18	19	20	21	22	24	25	26	28	29	♋1	3	4	6	8	10	12	14	16	18	20	22	24	26	28	♌0	3	5	7	♌9
♀	♌16	17	19	20	21	22	23	24	25	27	28	29	♍0	1	2	4	5	6	7	8	9	10	11	13	14	15	16	17	18	19	♍20
♂	♉24	25	26	26	27	28	28	29	♊0	1	1	2	3	3	4	5	5	6	7	8	8	9	10	10	11	12	12	13	14	14	♊15

♃ 1	6	12	18	24	30	♄ 1	6	12	18	24	30	♅ 1	15	30	♆ 1	15	30	♇ 1	15	30	☊ 1	15	30
♓13	13	13	12	12	11	♒10	10	9	9	9	8	♌28	28	29	♏11	11	11	♍8	8	9	♌9	9	9

AUGUST

	1	2	3	4	5	6	7	8	9	10	11	12	13	14	15	16	17	18	19	20	21	22	23	24	25	26	27	28	29	30	31
☉	♌8	9	10	11	12	13	14	15	16	17	18	19	20	21	22	23	24	25	26	26	27	28	29	♍0	1	2	3	4	5	6	♍7
☽	♌14	26	♍8	20	♎2	14	26	♏8	20	♐2	15	28	♑12	26	♒10	25	♓10	25	♈10	24	♉9	23	♊7	20	♋3	16	28	♌11	23	♍5	♍17
☿	♌11	13	15	17	19	21	23	25	27	29	♍0	2	4	6	7	9	11	12	14	16	17	19	20	22	23	25	26	28	29	♎0	♎2
♀	♍22	23	24	25	26	27	28	29	♎0	1	2	4	5	6	7	8	9	10	11	12	13	14	15	16	17	18	19	20	21	22	♎23
♂	♊16	16	17	18	18	19	20	21	21	22	22	23	24	24	25	26	26	27	28	28	29	♋0	0	1	2	2	3	4	4	5	♋5

♃ 1	6	12	18	24	30	♄ 1	6	12	18	24	30	♅ 1	15	30	♆ 1	15	30	♇ 1	15	30	☊ 1	15	30
♓11	11	10	9	9	8	♒8	8	7	7	6	6	♌29	♍0	1	♏11	11	11	♍9	9	10	♌9	9	9

SEPTEMBER

	1	2	3	4	5	6	7	8	9	10	11	12	13	14	15	16	17	18	19	20	21	22	23	24	25	26	27	28	29	30
☉	♍8	9	10	11	12	13	14	15	16	17	18	19	20	21	22	23	24	25	26	27	28	29	29	♎0	1	2	3	4	5	♎6
☽	♍29	♎10	22	♏4	16	28	♐11	23	♑6	20	♒4	18	♓3	18	♈3	19	♉4	18	♊3	16	♋0	13	25	♌8	20	♍2	14	25	♎7	♎19
☿	♎3	4	6	7	8	9	10	11	13	14	15	15	16	17	18	19	19	20	20	21	21	22	22	22	22	22	21	21	20	♎20
♀	♎24	25	26	27	28	29	♏0	1	2	3	4	5	5	6	7	8	9	10	11	11	12	13	14	15	15	16	17	18	18	♏19
♂	♋6	7	7	8	9	9	10	10	11	12	12	13	13	14	15	15	16	16	17	18	18	19	19	20	21	21	22	22	23	♋23

♃ 1	6	12	18	24	30	♄ 1	6	12	18	24	30	♅ 1	15	30	♆ 1	15	30	♇ 1	15	30	☊ 1	15	30
♓8	7	6	6	5	4	♒6	6	5	5	5	5	♍1	2	3	♏11	11	12	♍10	10	11	♌9	8	7

OCTOBER

	1	2	3	4	5	6	7	8	9	10	11	12	13	14	15	16	17	18	19	20	21	22	23	24	25	26	27	28	29	30	31
☉	♎7	8	9	10	11	12	13	14	15	16	17	18	19	20	21	22	23	24	25	26	27	28	29	♏0	1	2	3	4	5	6	♏7
☽	♏1	13	25	♐7	20	♑2	15	29	♒12	27	♓11	26	♈12	27	♉12	27	♊11	25	♋9	22	♌4	17	29	♍11	22	♎4	16	28	♏10	22	♐4
☿	♎19	18	17	16	15	14	13	11	10	9	8	8	7	7	7	7	7	7	8	8	9	10	11	12	13	15	16	17	19	20	♎22
♀	♏20	20	21	21	22	23	23	24	24	25	25	25	26	26	26	27	27	27	27	27	28	28	28	28	28	27	27	27	27	27	♏26
♂	♋24	25	25	26	26	27	27	28	28	29	29	♌0	1	1	2	2	3	3	4	4	5	5	6	6	7	7	8	8	9	9	♌9

♃ 1	6	12	18	24	30	♄ 1	6	12	18	24	30	♅ 1	15	30	♆ 1	15	30	♇ 1	15	30	☊ 1	15	30
♓4	4	3	3	3	3	♒5	5	5	5	5	5	♍3	4	4	♏12	12	13	♍11	11	12	♌7	6	4

NOVEMBER

	1	2	3	4	5	6	7	8	9	10	11	12	13	14	15	16	17	18	19	20	21	22	23	24	25	26	27	28	29	30
☉	♏8	9	10	11	12	13	14	15	16	17	18	19	20	21	22	23	24	25	26	27	28	29	♐0	1	2	3	4	5	6	♐7
☽	♐17	29	♑12	25	♒8	22	♓6	20	♈5	20	♉5	20	♊5	20	♋4	17	♌0	13	25	♍7	19	♎1	13	25	♏7	19	♐1	14	26	♑9
☿	♎23	25	27	28	♏0	1	3	5	6	8	10	11	13	14	16	18	19	21	22	24	26	27	29	♐0	2	4	5	7	8	♐10
♀	♏26	26	25	25	24	24	23	23	22	22	21	20	20	19	19	18	17	17	16	16	15	15	14	14	14	13	13	13	13	♏12
♂	♌10	10	11	11	12	12	13	13	13	14	14	15	15	15	16	16	17	17	17	18	18	18	19	19	19	20	20	20	21	♌21

♃ 1	6	12	18	24	30	♄ 1	6	12	18	24	30	♅ 1	15	30	♆ 1	15	30	♇ 1	15	30	☊ 1	15	30
♓3	3	3	3	4	4	♒5	5	6	6	6	7	♍5	5	5	♏13	14	14	♍12	12	12	♌4	2	1

DECEMBER

	1	2	3	4	5	6	7	8	9	10	11	12	13	14	15	16	17	18	19	20	21	22	23	24	25	26	27	28	29	30	31
☉	♐8	9	10	11	12	13	14	15	16	17	18	19	20	22	23	24	25	26	27	28	29	♑0	1	2	3	4	5	6	7	8	♑9
☽	♑22	♒5	19	♓2	16	♈0	15	29	♉14	29	♊13	27	♋11	25	♌8	21	♍3	15	27	♎9	21	♏3	15	27	♐10	22	♑5	18	♒2	15	♒29
☿	♐11	13	15	16	18	19	21	22	24	26	27	29	♑0	2	3	5	6	8	10	11	13	14	16	17	19	20	22	23	25	26	♑27
♀	♏12	12	12	12	12	12	12	13	13	13	13	14	14	14	15	15	16	16	17	17	18	18	19	20	20	21	22	22	23	24	♏24
♂	♌21	21	22	22	22	22	23	23	23	23	23	24	24	24	24	24	24	24	24	25	25	25	25	25	25	25	25	25	25	25	♌25

♃ 1	6	12	18	24	30	♄ 1	6	12	18	24	30	♅ 1	15	30	♆ 1	15	30	♇ 1	15	30	☊ 1	15	30
♓5	5	6	7	8	9	♒7	7	8	8	9	10	♍5	5	5	♏14	15	15	♍12	12	12	♌1	0	0

1963

JANUARY

	1	2	3	4	5	6	7	8	9	10	11	12	13	14	15	16	17	18	19	20	21	22	23	24	25	26	27	28	29	30	31
☉	♑10	11	12	13	14	15	16	17	18	19	20	21	22	23	24	25	26	27	28	29	♒0	1	2	3	4	5	6	7	8	9	♒10
☽	♓13	27	♈11	26	♉10	24	♊8	22	♋6	19	♌3	16	28	♍11	23	♎5	17	29	♏11	23	♐5	17	♑0	13	27	♒11	25	♓9	24	♈8	♈22
☿	♑29	♒0	1	2	3	4	5	6	6	6	7	7	6	6	6	5	4	3	2	0	♑29	28	26	25	24	23	22	22	21	21	♑21
♀	♏25	26	27	28	29	29	♐0	1	2	3	4	5	6	7	8	8	9	10	11	12	13	14	15	16	17	18	20	21	22	23	♐24
♂	♌25	24	24	24	24	24	24	24	24	23	23	23	23	22	22	22	22	21	21	21	20	20	20	19	19	19	18	18	18	17	♌17

♃	1	6	12	18	24	30	♄	1	6	12	18	24	30	♅	1	15	30	♆	1	15	30	♇	1	15	30	☊	1	15	30
	♓9	10	11	12	14	15		♒10	10	11	12	13	13		♍5	5	4		♏15	15	16		♍12	12	12		♌0	0	0

FEBRUARY

	1	2	3	4	5	6	7	8	9	10	11	12	13	14	15	16	17	18	19	20	21	22	23	24	25	26	27	28
☉	♒11	12	13	14	15	16	17	18	20	21	22	23	24	25	26	27	28	29	♓0	1	2	3	4	5	6	7	8	♓9
☽	♉7	21	♊5	18	♋2	15	28	♌11	24	♍6	19	♎1	13	25	♏7	19	♐1	13	25	♑8	21	♒5	19	♓3	18	♈3	18	♉3
☿	♑21	21	21	21	22	22	23	23	24	25	26	27	27	28	♒0	1	2	3	4	5	7	8	9	10	12	13	15	♒16
♀	♐25	26	27	28	29	♑0	1	2	3	5	6	7	8	9	10	11	12	13	15	16	17	18	19	20	21	23	24	♑25
♂	♌16	16	16	15	15	14	14	14	13	13	12	12	12	11	11	11	10	10	10	9	9	9	8	8	8	8	7	♌7

♃	1	6	12	18	24	28	♄	1	6	12	18	24	28	♅	1	15	28	♆	1	15	28	♇	1	15	28	☊	1	15	28
	♓15	16	18	19	21	22		♒14	14	15	16	16	17		♍4	4	3		♏16	16	16		♍12	11	11		♌0	♋0	29

MARCH

	1	2	3	4	5	6	7	8	9	10	11	12	13	14	15	16	17	18	19	20	21	22	23	24	25	26	27	28	29	30	31
☉	♓10	11	12	13	14	15	16	17	18	19	20	21	22	23	24	25	26	27	28	29	♈0	1	2	3	4	5	6	7	8	9	♈10
☽	♉17	♊1	15	29	♋12	25	♌8	20	♍3	15	27	♎9	21	♏3	15	27	♐9	21	♑3	16	29	♒13	27	♓12	26	♈12	27	♉12	27	♊11	♊25
☿	♒17	19	20	22	23	25	26	28	♓0	1	3	5	6	8	10	11	13	15	17	18	20	22	24	26	28	♈0	2	4	6	8	♈10
♀	♑26	27	28	29	♒1	2	3	4	5	6	8	9	10	11	12	13	15	16	17	18	19	20	22	23	24	25	26	28	29	♓0	♓1
♂	♌7	7	7	6	6	6	6	6	6	6	6	5	5	5	5	5	5	5	5	5	5	6	6	6	6	6	6	6	6	6	♌7

♃	1	6	12	18	24	30	♄	1	6	12	18	24	30	♅	1	15	30	♆	1	15	30	♇	1	15	30	☊	1	15	30
	♓22	23	24	26	27	29		♒17	17	18	19	19	20		♍3	2	2		♏16	15	15		♍11	11	10		♋29	28	27

APRIL

	1	2	3	4	5	6	7	8	9	10	11	12	13	14	15	16	17	18	19	20	21	22	23	24	25	26	27	28	29	30
☉	♈11	12	13	14	14	15	16	17	18	19	20	21	22	23	24	25	26	27	28	29	♉0	1	2	3	4	5	6	7	8	♉9
☽	♋9	22	♌5	17	♍0	12	24	♎6	18	♏0	12	24	♐6	18	♑0	12	25	♒8	21	♓5	20	♈5	20	♉5	20	♊6	20	♋4	18	♌1
☿	♈12	14	16	18	20	22	24	26	28	♉0	2	4	6	8	10	11	13	15	16	18	19	21	22	23	24	25	26	27	28	♉28
♀	♓2	4	5	6	7	8	9	11	12	13	14	15	17	18	19	20	21	23	24	25	26	27	29	♈0	1	2	3	5	6	♈7
♂	♌7	7	7	7	7	8	8	8	8	9	9	9	9	10	10	10	10	11	11	11	12	12	12	13	13	13	14	14	14	♌15

♃	1	6	12	18	24	30	♄	1	6	12	18	24	30	♅	1	15	30	♆	1	15	30	♇	1	15	30	☊	1	15	30
	♓29	♈0	2	3	5	6		♒20	20	21	21	22	22		♍2	1	1		♏15	15	14		♍10	10	10		♋27	25	24

MAY

	1	2	3	4	5	6	7	8	9	10	11	12	13	14	15	16	17	18	19	20	21	22	23	24	25	26	27	28	29	30	31
☉	♉10	11	12	13	14	15	16	17	18	19	20	21	22	22	23	24	25	26	27	28	29	♊0	1	2	3	4	5	6	7	8	♊9
☽	♌14	27	♍9	21	♎3	15	27	♏9	21	♐3	15	27	♑9	22	♒4	17	♓1	15	29	♈14	29	♉14	29	♊14	29	♋13	27	♌10	23	♍6	♍18
☿	♉29	♊0	0	0	0	1	1	1	0	0	0	0	♉29	29	28	28	27	27	26	25	25	24	24	23	23	23	22	22	22	22	♉22
♀	♈8	9	11	12	13	14	15	17	18	19	20	21	23	24	25	26	28	29	♉0	1	2	4	5	6	7	8	10	11	12	13	♉14
♂	♌15	16	16	16	17	17	18	18	18	19	19	20	20	20	21	21	22	22	23	23	24	24	25	25	25	26	26	27	27	28	♌28

♃	1	6	12	18	24	30	♄	1	6	12	18	24	30	♅	1	15	30	♆	1	15	30	♇	1	15	30	☊	1	15	30
	♈6	7	9	10	11	12		♒22	22	23	23	23	23		♍1	1	1		♏14	14	14		♍10	10	10		♋24	22	21

JUNE

	1	2	3	4	5	6	7	8	9	10	11	12	13	14	15	16	17	18	19	20	21	22	23	24	25	26	27	28	29	30
☉	♊10	11	12	13	14	15	16	17	17	18	19	20	21	22	23	24	25	26	27	28	29	♋0	1	2	3	4	5	6	7	♋8
☽	♎0	12	24	♏6	18	29	♐12	24	♑6	19	♒1	14	28	♓11	25	♈9	23	♉8	23	♊8	22	♋7	21	♌5	18	♍1	14	26	♎8	♎20
☿	♉22	22	22	22	23	23	24	24	25	26	26	27	28	29	♊0	1	2	3	5	6	7	9	10	12	13	15	17	18	20	♊22
♀	♉16	17	18	19	21	22	23	24	25	27	28	29	♊0	1	3	4	5	6	7	9	10	11	12	14	15	16	17	18	20	♊21
♂	♌29	29	♍0	0	1	1	2	2	3	3	4	4	5	6	6	7	7	8	8	9	9	10	10	11	11	12	13	13	14	♍14

♃	1	6	12	18	24	30	♄	1	6	12	18	24	30	♅	1	15	30	♆	1	15	30	♇	1	15	30	☊	1	15	30
	♈12	13	14	15	16	17		♒23	23	23	23	23	23		♍1	2	2		♏14	13	13		♍10	10	10		♋21	21	21

JULY

	1	2	3	4	5	6	7	8	9	10	11	12	13	14	15	16	17	18	19	20	21	22	23	24	25	26	27	28	29	30	31
☉	♋8	9	10	11	12	13	14	15	16	17	18	19	20	21	22	23	24	25	26	27	28	28	29	♌0	1	2	3	4	5	6	♌7
☽	♏2	14	26	♐8	20	♑3	15	28	♒11	24	♓8	22	♈6	20	♉4	18	♊3	17	♋1	15	29	♌13	26	♍9	22	♎4	16	28	♏10	22	♐4
☿	♊24	26	28	♋0	2	4	6	8	10	12	15	17	19	21	23	25	27	29	♌2	4	6	8	10	12	13	15	17	19	21	23	♌24
♀	♊22	23	25	26	27	28	29	♋1	2	3	4	6	7	8	9	10	12	13	14	15	17	18	19	20	21	23	24	25	26	28	♋29
♂	♍15	15	16	16	17	18	18	19	19	20	20	21	22	22	23	23	24	25	25	26	26	27	27	28	29	29	♎0	0	1	2	♎2

♃	1	6	12	18	24	30	♄	1	6	12	18	24	30	♅	1	15	30	♆	1	15	30	♇	1	15	30	☊	1	15	30
	♈17	18	18	19	19	19		♒23	22	22	22	21	21		♍2	3	4		♏13	13	13		♍10	10	11		♋21	20	20

AUGUST

	1	2	3	4	5	6	7	8	9	10	11	12	13	14	15	16	17	18	19	20	21	22	23	24	25	26	27	28	29	30	31
☉	♌8	9	10	11	12	13	14	15	16	17	18	19	20	20	21	22	23	24	25	26	27	28	29	♍0	1	2	3	4	5	6	♍7
☽	♐16	28	♑11	24	♒7	20	♓4	18	♈2	17	♉1	15	29	♊13	27	♋11	25	♌8	21	♍4	17	♎0	12	24	♏6	18	♐0	12	24	♑6	♑19
☿	♌26	28	29	♍1	3	4	6	7	9	10	12	13	14	16	17	18	20	21	22	23	24	25	26	27	28	29	♎0	1	2	2	♎3
♀	♌0	1	3	4	5	6	7	9	10	11	12	14	15	16	17	19	20	21	22	24	25	26	27	28	♍0	1	2	3	5	6	♍7
♂	♎3	4	4	5	5	6	7	7	8	8	9	10	10	11	12	12	13	13	14	15	15	16	17	17	18	19	19	20	21	21	♎22

♃	1	6	12	18	24	30	♄	1	6	12	18	24	30	♅	1	15	30	♆	1	15	30	♇	1	15	30	☊	1	15	30
	♈19	19	19	19	19	19		♒21	20	20	19	19	19		♍4	5	6		♏13	13	13		♍11	11	12		♋20	20	20

SEPTEMBER

	1	2	3	4	5	6	7	8	9	10	11	12	13	14	15	16	17	18	19	20	21	22	23	24	25	26	27	28	29	30
☉	♍8	9	10	11	12	13	14	15	16	17	18	19	19	20	21	22	23	24	25	26	27	28	29	♎0	1	2	3	4	5	♎6
☽	♒2	15	29	♓13	28	♈12	27	♉12	26	♊10	24	♋8	21	♌5	18	♍1	13	26	♎8	20	♏2	14	26	♐8	20	♑2	14	27	♒10	♒23
☿	♎4	4	4	5	5	5	5	5	5	5	4	4	3	2	2	1	0	♍29	28	27	26	25	24	23	22	21	21	21	21	♍21
♀	♍8	10	11	12	13	15	16	17	18	20	21	22	23	25	26	27	28	29	♎1	2	3	4	6	7	8	9	11	12	13	♎14
♂	♎23	23	24	24	25	26	26	27	28	28	29	♏0	0	1	2	2	3	4	4	5	6	6	7	8	9	9	10	11	11	♏12

♃	1	6	12	18	24	30	♄	1	6	12	18	24	30	♅	1	15	30	♆	1	15	30	♇	1	15	30	☊	1	15	30
	♈19	18	18	17	16	16		♒18	18	18	17	17	17		♍6	7	8		♏13	14	14		♍12	12	13		♋20	19	17

OCTOBER

	1	2	3	4	5	6	7	8	9	10	11	12	13	14	15	16	17	18	19	20	21	22	23	24	25	26	27	28	29	30	31
☉	♎7	8	9	10	11	12	13	14	15	16	17	18	19	20	21	22	23	24	25	26	27	28	29	♏0	1	2	3	4	5	6	♏7
☽	♓7	22	♈6	21	♉6	21	♊6	21	♋5	18	♌2	15	28	♍10	23	♎5	17	29	♏11	23	♐5	16	28	♑10	23	♒5	18	♓1	15	♈0	♈14
☿	♍21	21	22	22	23	24	25	26	28	29	♎0	2	3	5	7	8	10	12	13	15	17	18	20	22	24	25	27	29	♏0	2	♏4
♀	♎16	17	18	19	21	22	23	24	26	27	28	29	♏1	2	3	4	6	7	8	9	11	12	13	14	16	17	18	19	21	22	♏23
♂	♏13	13	14	15	15	16	17	17	18	19	20	20	21	22	22	23	24	24	25	26	27	27	28	29	29	♐0	1	2	2	3	♐4

♃	1	6	12	18	24	30	♄	1	6	12	18	24	30	♅	1	15	30	♆	1	15	30	♇	1	15	30	☊	1	15	30
	♈15	15	14	13	12	12		♒17	17	17	16	16	17		♍8	8	9		♏14	14	15		♍13	13	14		♋17	16	14

NOVEMBER

	1	2	3	4	5	6	7	8	9	10	11	12	13	14	15	16	17	18	19	20	21	22	23	24	25	26	27	28	29	30
☉	♏8	9	10	11	12	13	14	15	16	17	18	19	20	21	22	23	24	25	26	27	28	29	♐0	1	2	3	4	5	6	♐7
☽	♉0	15	♊0	15	♋0	14	28	♌11	25	♍7	20	♎2	14	26	♏8	20	♐2	13	25	♑7	19	♒2	14	27	♓10	24	♈8	23	♉8	♉23
☿	♏5	7	9	10	12	13	15	17	18	20	21	23	25	26	28	29	♐1	2	4	5	7	9	10	12	13	15	16	18	19	♐21
♀	♏24	26	27	28	29	♐1	2	3	4	6	7	8	9	11	12	13	14	16	17	18	19	20	22	23	24	25	27	28	29	♑0
♂	♐5	5	6	7	7	8	9	10	10	11	12	13	13	14	15	15	16	17	18	18	19	20	21	21	22	23	24	24	25	♐26

♃	1	6	12	18	24	30	♄	1	6	12	18	24	30	♅	1	15	30	♆	1	15	30	♇	1	15	30	☊	1	15	30
	♈11	11	10	10	10	10		♒17	17	17	17	17	18		♍9	10	10		♏15	16	16		♍14	14	14		♋14	12	12

DECEMBER

	1	2	3	4	5	6	7	8	9	10	11	12	13	14	15	16	17	18	19	20	21	22	23	24	25	26	27	28	29	30	31
☉	♐8	9	10	11	12	13	14	15	16	17	18	19	20	21	22	23	24	25	26	27	28	29	♑0	1	2	3	4	6	7	8	♑9
☽	♊8	23	♋8	23	♌7	20	♍4	16	29	♎11	23	♏5	17	29	♐10	22	♑4	16	29	♒11	24	♓7	20	♈4	18	♉2	16	♊1	16	♋1	♋16
☿	♐22	24	25	27	28	♑0	1	3	4	5	7	8	10	11	12	13	14	16	17	18	18	19	20	20	21	21	21	20	20	19	♑19
♀	♑2	3	4	5	7	8	9	10	12	13	14	15	17	18	19	20	22	23	24	25	27	28	29	♒0	2	3	4	5	6	8	♒9
♂	♐27	27	28	29	♑0	0	1	2	3	4	4	5	6	7	7	8	9	10	10	11	12	13	13	14	15	16	17	17	18	19	♑20

♃	1	6	12	18	24	30	♄	1	6	12	18	24	30	♅	1	15	30	♆	1	15	30	♇	1	15	30	☊	1	15	30
	♈10	10	10	10	10	11		♒18	18	19	19	20	20		♍10	10	10		♏16	17	17		♍14	14	14		♋12	11	11

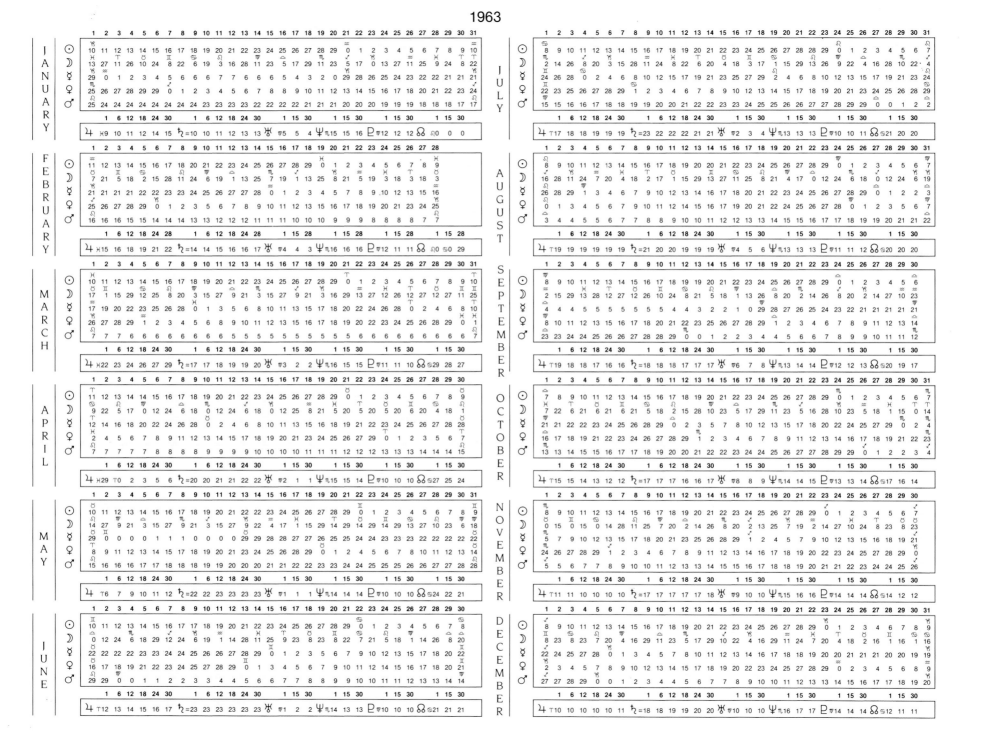

1964

JANUARY

	1	2	3	4	5	6	7	8	9	10	11	12	13	14	15	16	17	18	19	20	21	22	23	24	25	26	27	28	29	30	31
☉	♑10	11	12	13	14	15	16	17	18	19	20	21	22	23	24	25	26	27	28	29	♒0	1	2	3	4	5	6	7	8	9	♒10
☽	♌1	15	28	♍12	25	♎7	19	♏1	13	25	♐7	19	♑1	13	25	♒8	21	♓4	17	♈0	14	28	♉12	26	♊11	25	♋10	24	♌8	22	♍6
☿	♑18	17	15	14	13	11	10	9	8	7	6	5	5	5	5	5	5	5	5	6	6	7	8	9	9	10	11	12	13	15	♑16
♀	♒10	11	13	14	15	16	18	19	20	21	22	24	25	26	27	29	♓0	1	2	4	5	6	7	8	10	11	12	13	14	16	♓17
♂	♑20	21	22	23	24	24	25	26	27	27	28	29	♒0	1	1	2	3	4	5	5	6	7	8	8	9	10	11	12	12	13	♒14

	1	6	12	18	24	30
♃	♈11	11	12	13	13	14
♄	♒20	21	22	22	23	24

	1	15	30
♅	♍10	10	9
♆	♏17	17	18
♇	♍14	14	14
☊	♋11	11	11

FEBRUARY

	1	2	3	4	5	6	7	8	9	10	11	12	13	14	15	16	17	18	19	20	21	22	23	24	25	26	27	28	29
☉	♒11	12	13	14	15	16	17	18	19	20	21	22	23	24	25	26	27	28	29	♓0	1	2	3	4	5	6	7	8	♓9
☽	♍19	♎2	15	27	♏9	21	♐3	15	27	♑9	21	♒4	17	♓0	13	27	♈11	25	♉9	23	♊7	21	♋5	19	♌3	17	♍1	14	♍27
☿	♑17	18	19	21	22	23	25	26	27	29	♒0	2	3	4	6	7	9	11	12	14	15	17	18	20	22	23	25	27	♒28
♀	♓18	19	21	22	23	24	25	27	28	29	♈0	1	3	4	5	6	7	8	10	11	12	13	14	16	17	18	19	20	♈21
♂	♒15	16	16	17	18	19	19	20	21	22	23	23	24	25	26	27	27	28	29	♓0	1	1	2	3	4	4	5	6	♓7

	1	6	12	18	24	29
♃	♈15	16	17	18	19	20
♄	♒24	24	25	26	27	27

	1	15	29
♅	♍9	9	8
♆	♏18	18	18
♇	♍14	13	13
☊	♋11	10	9

MARCH

	1	2	3	4	5	6	7	8	9	10	11	12	13	14	15	16	17	18	19	20	21	22	23	24	25	26	27	28	29	30	31
☉	♓10	11	12	13	14	15	16	17	18	19	20	21	22	23	24	25	26	27	28	29	♈0	1	2	3	4	5	6	7	8	9	♈10
☽	♎10	23	♏5	17	29	♐11	23	♑5	17	29	♒12	25	♓8	22	♈6	21	♉5	20	♊4	18	♋2	16	♌0	13	27	♍10	23	♎6	19	♏1	♏13
☿	♓0	2	4	5	7	9	11	13	14	16	18	20	22	24	26	28	♈0	2	4	6	8	10	12	14	16	18	20	22	23	25	♈27
♀	♈23	24	25	26	27	28	29	♉1	2	3	4	5	6	7	8	10	11	12	13	14	15	16	17	18	19	20	22	23	24	25	♉26
♂	♓8	8	9	10	11	12	12	13	14	15	16	16	17	18	19	19	20	21	22	23	23	24	25	26	27	27	28	29	♈0	0	♈1

	1	6	12	18	24	30
♃	♈20	21	23	24	25	27
♄	♒27	28	29	29	♓0	1

	1	15	30
♅	♍8	7	7
♆	♏18	18	17
♇	♍13	13	12
☊	♋9	8	6

APRIL

	1	2	3	4	5	6	7	8	9	10	11	12	13	14	15	16	17	18	19	20	21	22	23	24	25	26	27	28	29	30
☉	♈11	12	13	14	15	16	17	18	19	20	21	22	23	24	25	26	27	28	29	♉0	1	2	3	4	5	6	7	8	9	♉10
☽	♏25	♐7	19	♑1	13	25	♒7	20	♓3	16	♈1	15	♉0	14	29	♊14	29	♋13	27	♌10	24	♍7	20	♎3	15	27	♏10	22	♐4	♐15
☿	♈28	♉0	1	3	4	5	6	7	8	9	10	10	11	11	11	11	12	11	11	11	11	10	10	9	9	8	7	7	6	♉5
♀	♉27	28	29	♊0	1	2	3	4	5	6	7	8	9	10	11	12	13	13	14	15	16	17	18	19	20	20	21	22	23	♊24
♂	♈2	3	4	4	5	6	7	7	8	9	10	10	11	12	13	14	14	15	16	17	17	18	19	20	20	21	22	23	23	♈24

	1	6	12	18	24	30
♃	♈27	28	♉0	1	3	4
♄	♓1	1	2	2	3	3

	1	15	30
♅	♍7	6	6
♆	♏17	17	17
♇	♍12	12	12
☊	♋6	5	3

MAY

	1	2	3	4	5	6	7	8	9	10	11	12	13	14	15	16	17	18	19	20	21	22	23	24	25	26	27	28	29	30	31
☉	♉11	12	13	14	15	15	16	17	18	19	20	21	22	23	24	25	26	27	28	29	♊0	1	2	3	4	5	6	7	8	9	♊10
☽	♐27	♑9	21	♒3	15	28	♓11	25	♈9	23	♉8	23	♊8	23	♋8	23	♌7	20	♍4	17	♎0	12	24	♏7	19	♐0	12	24	♑6	18	♒0
☿	♉5	4	4	3	3	2	2	2	2	2	2	2	2	2	2	3	3	4	4	5	5	6	7	8	9	10	11	12	13	14	♉16
♀	♊24	25	26	27	27	28	29	29	♋0	1	1	2	2	3	3	4	4	5	5	5	6	6	6	6	6	7	7	7	7	7	♋7
♂	♈25	26	27	27	28	29	♉0	0	1	2	3	3	4	5	6	6	7	8	9	9	10	11	11	12	13	14	14	15	16	17	♉17

	1	6	12	18	24	30
♃	♉4	6	7	9	10	11
♄	♓3	4	4	4	5	5

	1	15	30
♅	♍6	6	6
♆	♏17	16	16
♇	♍12	12	12
☊	♋3	3	2

JUNE

	1	2	3	4	5	6	7	8	9	10	11	12	13	14	15	16	17	18	19	20	21	22	23	24	25	26	27	28	29	30
☉	♊11	11	12	13	14	15	16	17	18	19	20	21	22	23	24	25	26	27	28	29	♋0	1	2	3	3	4	5	6	7	♋8
☽	♒12	24	♓7	20	♈3	17	♉2	16	♊1	17	♋2	17	♌1	16	♍0	13	26	♎9	21	♏4	16	28	♐9	21	♑3	15	27	♒9	21	♓4
☿	♉17	18	20	21	23	24	26	27	29	♊1	2	4	6	8	10	12	14	16	18	20	22	24	26	28	♋1	3	5	7	9	♋12
♀	♋7	7	6	6	6	6	5	5	5	4	4	3	3	2	2	1	0	0	♊29	29	28	27	27	26	26	25	24	24	23	♊23
♂	♉18	19	20	20	21	22	22	23	24	25	25	26	27	28	28	29	♊0	0	1	2	3	3	4	5	5	6	7	7	8	♊9

	1	6	12	18	24	30
♃	♉12	13	14	15	17	18
♄	♓5	5	5	5	5	5

	1	15	30
♅	♍6	6	7
♆	♏16	16	15
♇	♍12	12	12
☊	♋2	2	2

JULY

	1	2	3	4	5	6	7	8	9	10	11	12	13	14	15	16	17	18	19	20	21	22	23	24	25	26	27	28	29	30	31
☉	♋9	10	11	12	13	14	15	16	17	18	19	20	21	22	23	23	24	25	26	27	28	29	♌0	1	2	3	4	5	6	7	♌8
☽	♓16	♈0	13	27	♉11	25	♊10	25	♋10	25	♌10	24	♍8	22	♎5	18	♏0	12	24	♐6	18	♑0	12	24	♒6	18	♓1	13	26	♈10	♈23
☿	♋14	16	18	20	22	24	26	28	♌0	2	4	6	7	9	11	13	14	16	18	19	21	22	24	25	27	28	29	♍1	2	3	♍4
♀	♊23	22	22	21	21	21	21	21	20	20	20	20	20	20	21	21	21	21	21	22	22	22	23	23	24	24	24	25	25	26	♊27
♂	♊10	10	11	12	12	13	14	14	15	16	17	17	18	19	19	20	21	21	22	23	23	24	25	25	26	27	27	28	29	29	♋0

	1	6	12	18	24	30
♃	♉18	19	20	21	22	23
♄	♓5	5	4	4	4	4

	1	15	30
♅	♍7	8	8
♆	♏15	15	15
♇	♍12	12	13
☊	♋2	2	2

AUGUST

	1	2	3	4	5	6	7	8	9	10	11	12	13	14	15	16	17	18	19	20	21	22	23	24	25	26	27	28	29	30	31
☉	♌9	10	11	12	13	14	15	15	16	17	18	19	20	21	22	23	24	25	26	27	28	29	♍0	1	2	3	4	5	6	7	♍8
☽	♉7	21	♊5	20	♋4	19	♌4	18	♍2	16	♎0	13	26	♏9	21	♐3	14	26	♑8	20	♒2	15	27	♓10	23	♈7	20	♉4	18	♊2	♊16
☿	♍6	7	8	9	10	11	12	13	13	14	15	16	16	17	17	17	18	18	18	18	18	18	17	17	17	16	15	15	14	13	♍12
♀	♊27	28	28	29	♋0	0	1	2	3	3	4	5	6	6	7	8	9	10	11	12	12	13	14	15	16	17	18	19	20	21	♋22
♂	♋1	1	2	3	3	4	5	5	6	7	7	8	9	9	10	11	11	12	13	13	14	15	15	16	17	17	18	19	19	20	♋20

	1	6	12	18	24	30
♃	♉23	24	24	25	25	26
♄	♓3	3	3	2	2	1

	1	15	30
♅	♍8	9	10
♆	♏15	15	15
♇	♍13	13	14
☊	♋1	1	0

SEPTEMBER

	1	2	3	4	5	6	7	8	9	10	11	12	13	14	15	16	17	18	19	20	21	22	23	24	25	26	27	28	29	30
☉	♍9	10	11	11	12	13	14	15	16	17	18	19	20	21	22	23	24	25	26	27	28	29	♎0	1	2	3	4	5	6	♎7
☽	♋0	14	28	♌13	27	♍11	25	♎8	21	♏4	16	29	♐11	22	♑4	16	28	♒10	23	♓6	19	♈2	16	♉0	14	28	♊13	27	♋11	♋25
☿	♍11	10	9	8	7	7	6	5	5	5	4	4	4	5	5	6	6	7	8	9	11	12	13	15	16	18	20	21	23	♍25
♀	♋23	24	25	26	27	28	29	♌0	1	2	3	4	5	6	7	8	9	10	11	12	14	15	16	17	18	19	20	21	22	♌23
♂	♋21	22	22	23	24	24	25	26	26	27	27	28	29	29	♌0	0	1	2	2	3	4	4	5	5	6	7	7	8	8	♌9

	1	6	12	18	24	30
♃	♉26	26	26	26	26	26
♄	♓1	1	0	0	0	♒29

	1	15	30
♅	♍10	11	12
♆	♏15	16	16
♇	♍14	14	15
☊	♋0	♊29	27

OCTOBER

	1	2	3	4	5	6	7	8	9	10	11	12	13	14	15	16	17	18	19	20	21	22	23	24	25	26	27	28	29	30	31
☉	♎8	9	10	11	12	13	14	15	16	17	18	19	20	21	22	23	24	25	26	27	28	29	♏0	1	2	3	4	5	6	7	♏8
☽	♌9	23	♍6	20	♎3	17	29	♏12	24	♐7	18	♑0	12	24	♒6	18	♓1	14	27	♈11	25	♉9	24	♊8	23	♋7	22	♌6	20	♍3	♍17
☿	♍26	28	♎0	2	4	5	7	9	11	12	14	16	18	19	21	23	25	26	28	♏0	1	3	4	6	8	9	11	12	14	16	♏17
♀	♌25	26	27	28	29	♍0	1	3	4	5	6	7	8	9	11	12	13	14	15	16	18	19	20	21	22	24	25	26	27	28	♎0
♂	♌10	10	11	11	12	13	13	14	14	15	15	16	17	17	18	18	19	19	20	21	21	22	22	23	23	24	25	25	26	26	♌27

	1	6	12	18	24	30
♃	♉26	25	25	24	24	23
♄	♒29	29	29	29	28	28

	1	15	30
♅	♍12	13	14
♆	♏16	17	17
♇	♍15	15	16
☊	♊27	25	24

NOVEMBER

	1	2	3	4	5	6	7	8	9	10	11	12	13	14	15	16	17	18	19	20	21	22	23	24	25	26	27	28	29	30
☉	♏9	10	11	12	13	14	15	16	17	18	19	20	21	22	23	24	25	26	27	28	29	♐0	1	2	3	4	5	6	7	♐8
☽	♎0	13	26	♏8	20	♐3	15	27	♑8	20	♒2	14	26	♓9	22	♈5	19	♉3	18	♊2	17	♋2	17	♌2	16	♍0	14	27	♎10	♎22
☿	♏19	20	22	23	25	26	28	29	♐1	2	4	5	7	8	10	11	12	14	15	17	18	19	21	22	23	25	26	27	28	♐29
♀	♎1	2	3	4	6	7	8	9	10	12	13	14	15	16	18	19	20	21	23	24	25	26	27	29	♏0	1	2	4	5	♏6
♂	♌27	28	28	29	29	♍0	0	1	1	2	3	3	4	4	5	5	6	6	7	7	8	8	9	9	9	10	10	11	11	♍12

	1	6	12	18	24	30
♃	♉23	22	21	20	20	19
♄	♒28	28	28	29	29	29

	1	15	30
♅	♍14	14	15
♆	♏17	18	18
♇	♍16	16	16
☊	♊24	23	23

DECEMBER

	1	2	3	4	5	6	7	8	9	10	11	12	13	14	15	16	17	18	19	20	21	22	23	24	25	26	27	28	29	30	31
☉	♐9	10	11	12	13	14	15	16	17	18	19	20	21	22	23	24	25	26	27	28	29	♑0	1	2	3	4	5	6	7	8	♑9
☽	♏5	17	29	♐11	23	♑5	17	29	♒10	22	♓5	17	♈0	13	27	♉11	25	♊10	26	♋11	26	♌11	25	♍10	23	♎7	19	♏2	14	26	♐8
☿	♑0	1	2	3	3	4	4	5	5	5	5	4	4	3	2	1	♐29	28	27	25	24	23	22	21	20	19	19	19	19	19	♐19
♀	♏7	9	10	11	12	13	15	16	17	18	20	21	22	23	25	26	27	28	♐0	1	2	3	5	6	7	8	10	11	12	13	♐15
♂	♍12	13	13	14	14	14	15	15	16	16	17	17	17	18	18	18	19	19	20	20	20	21	21	21	22	22	22	23	23	23	♍24

	1	6	12	18	24	30
♃	♉19	18	18	17	17	16
♄	♒29	29	♓0	0	1	1

	1	15	30
♅	♍15	15	15
♆	♏18	19	19
♇	♍16	16	16
☊	♊23	23	23

1965

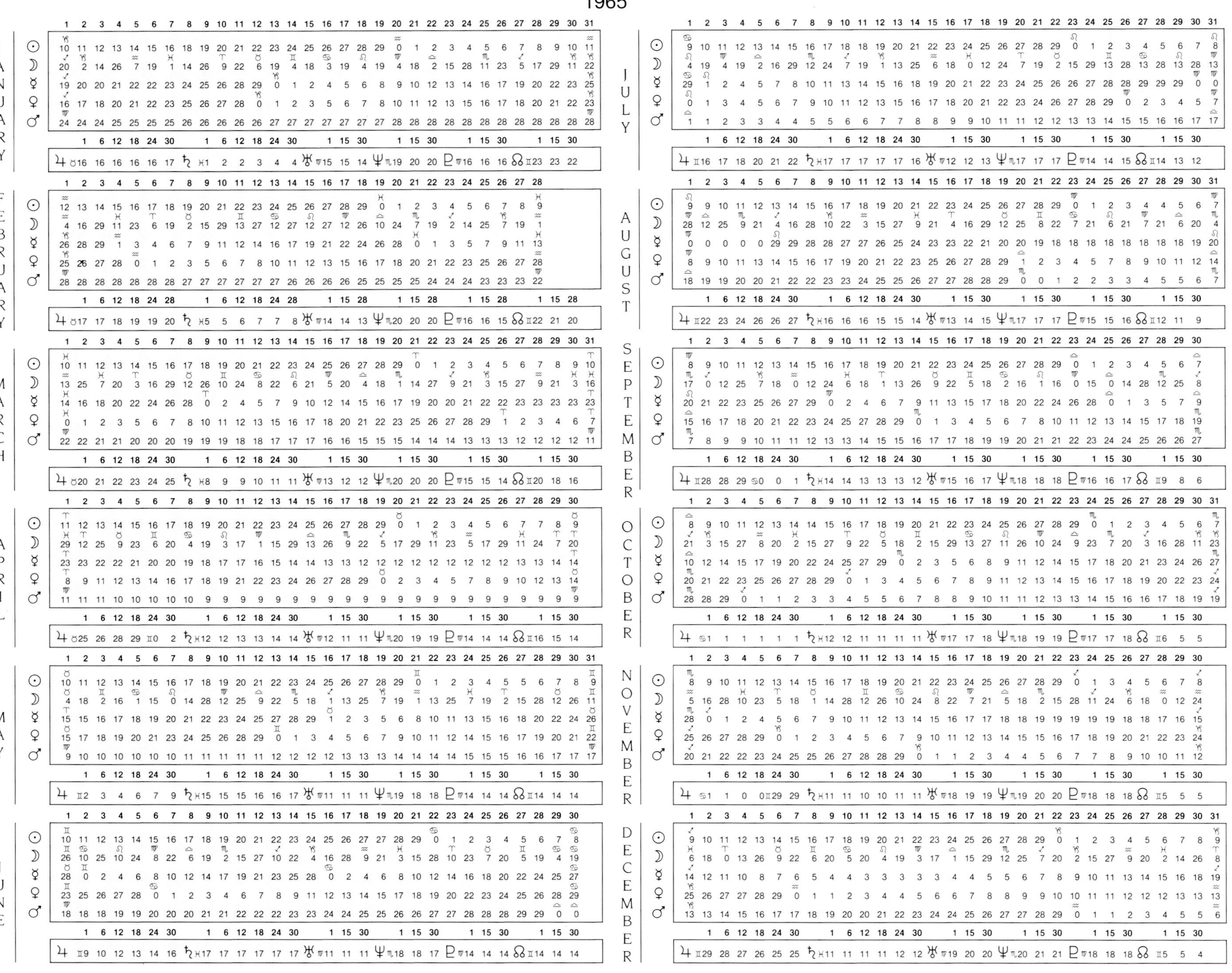

JANUARY

	1	2	3	4	5	6	7	8	9	10	11	12	13	14	15	16	17	18	19	20	21	22	23	24	25	26	27	28	29	30	31
☉	♑10	11	12	13	14	15	16	18	19	20	21	22	23	24	25	26	27	28	29	♒0	1	2	3	4	5	6	7	8	9	10	♒11
☽	♐20	♑2	14	26	♒7	19	♓1	14	26	♈9	22	♉6	19	♊4	18	♋3	19	♌4	19	♍4	18	♎2	15	28	♏11	23	♐5	17	29	♑11	♑22
☿	♐19	20	20	21	22	22	23	24	25	26	28	29	♑0	1	2	4	5	6	8	9	10	12	13	14	16	17	19	20	22	23	♑25
♀	♐16	17	18	20	21	22	23	25	26	27	28	♑0	1	2	3	5	6	7	8	10	11	12	13	15	16	17	18	20	21	22	♑23
♂	♍24	24	24	25	25	25	25	26	26	26	26	26	27	27	27	27	27	27	27	28	28	28	28	28	28	28	28	28	28	28	♍28

	1	6	12	18	24	30
♃	♉16	16	16	16	16	17
♄	♓1	2	2	3	4	4

	1	15	30
♅	♍15	15	14
♆	♏19	20	20
♇	♍16	16	16
☊	♊23	23	22

FEBRUARY

	1	2	3	4	5	6	7	8	9	10	11	12	13	14	15	16	17	18	19	20	21	22	23	24	25	26	27	28
☉	♒12	13	14	15	16	17	18	19	20	21	22	23	24	25	26	27	28	29	♓0	1	2	3	4	5	6	7	8	♓9
☽	♒4	16	29	♓11	23	♈6	19	♉2	15	29	♊13	27	♋12	27	♌12	27	♍12	26	♎10	24	♏7	19	♐2	14	25	♑7	19	♒1
☿	♑26	28	29	♒1	3	4	6	7	9	11	12	14	16	17	19	21	22	24	26	28	♓0	1	3	5	7	9	11	♓13
♀	♑25	26	27	28	♒0	1	2	3	5	6	7	8	10	11	12	13	15	16	17	18	20	21	22	23	25	26	27	♒28
♂	♍28	28	28	28	28	28	28	27	27	27	27	27	27	26	26	26	26	25	25	25	25	24	24	24	23	23	23	♍22

	1	6	12	18	24	28
♃	♉17	17	18	19	19	20
♄	♓5	5	6	7	7	8

	1	15	28
♅	♍14	14	13
♆	♏20	20	20
♇	♍16	16	15
☊	♊22	21	20

MARCH

	1	2	3	4	5	6	7	8	9	10	11	12	13	14	15	16	17	18	19	20	21	22	23	24	25	26	27	28	29	30	31
☉	♓10	11	12	13	14	15	16	17	18	19	20	21	22	23	24	25	26	27	28	29	♈0	1	2	3	4	5	6	7	8	9	♈10
☽	♒13	25	♓7	20	♈3	16	29	♉12	26	♊10	24	♋8	22	♌6	21	♍5	20	♎4	18	♏1	14	27	♐9	21	♑3	15	27	♒9	21	♓3	♓16
☿	♓14	16	18	20	22	24	26	28	♈0	2	4	5	7	9	10	12	14	15	16	17	19	20	20	21	22	22	23	23	23	23	♈23
♀	♓0	1	2	3	5	6	7	8	10	11	12	13	15	16	17	18	20	21	22	23	25	26	27	28	29	♈1	2	3	4	6	♈7
♂	♍22	22	21	21	20	20	20	19	19	19	18	18	17	17	17	16	16	15	15	15	14	14	14	13	13	13	12	12	12	12	♍11

	1	6	12	18	24	30
♃	♉20	21	22	23	24	25
♄	♓8	9	9	10	11	11

	1	15	30
♅	♍13	12	12
♆	♏20	20	20
♇	♍15	15	14
☊	♊20	18	16

APRIL

	1	2	3	4	5	6	7	8	9	10	11	12	13	14	15	16	17	18	19	20	21	22	23	24	25	26	27	28	29	30
☉	♈11	12	13	14	15	16	17	18	19	20	21	22	23	24	25	26	27	28	29	♉0	1	2	3	4	5	6	7	7	8	♉9
☽	♓29	♈12	25	♉9	23	♊6	20	♋4	19	♌3	17	♍1	15	29	♎13	26	♏9	22	♐5	17	29	♑11	23	♒5	17	29	♓11	24	♈7	♈20
☿	♈23	23	22	22	21	20	20	19	18	17	17	16	15	14	14	13	13	12	12	12	12	12	12	12	12	12	13	13	14	♈14
♀	♈8	9	11	12	13	14	16	17	18	19	21	22	23	24	26	27	28	29	♉0	2	3	4	5	7	8	9	10	12	13	♉14
♂	♍11	11	11	10	10	10	10	10	9	9	9	9	9	9	9	9	9	9	9	9	9	9	9	9	9	9	9	9	9	♍9

	1	6	12	18	24	30
♃	♉25	26	28	29	♊0	2
♄	♓12	12	13	13	14	14

	1	15	30
♅	♍12	11	11
♆	♏20	19	19
♇	♍14	14	14
☊	♊16	15	14

MAY

	1	2	3	4	5	6	7	8	9	10	11	12	13	14	15	16	17	18	19	20	21	22	23	24	25	26	27	28	29	30	31
☉	♉10	11	12	13	14	15	16	17	18	19	20	21	22	23	24	25	26	27	28	29	♊0	1	2	3	4	5	5	6	7	8	♊9
☽	♉4	18	♊2	16	♋1	15	♌0	14	28	♍12	25	♎9	22	♏5	18	♐1	13	25	♑7	19	♒1	13	25	♓7	19	♈2	15	28	♉12	26	♊11
☿	♈15	15	16	17	18	19	20	21	22	23	24	25	27	28	29	♉1	2	3	5	6	8	10	11	13	15	16	18	20	22	24	♉26
♀	♉15	17	18	19	20	21	23	24	25	26	28	29	♊0	1	3	4	5	6	7	9	10	11	12	14	15	16	17	19	20	21	♊22
♂	♍9	10	10	10	10	10	10	11	11	11	11	11	12	12	12	12	13	13	13	14	14	14	14	15	15	15	16	16	17	17	♍17

	1	6	12	18	24	30
♃	♊2	3	4	6	7	9
♄	♓15	15	15	16	16	17

	1	15	30
♅	♍11	11	11
♆	♏19	18	18
♇	♍14	14	14
☊	♊14	14	14

JUNE

	1	2	3	4	5	6	7	8	9	10	11	12	13	14	15	16	17	18	19	20	21	22	23	24	25	26	27	28	29	30
☉	♊10	11	12	13	14	15	16	17	18	19	20	21	22	23	24	25	26	27	27	28	29	♋0	1	2	3	4	5	6	7	♋8
☽	♊26	♋10	25	♌10	24	♍8	22	♎6	19	♏2	15	27	♐10	22	♑4	16	28	♒9	21	♓3	15	28	♈10	23	♉7	20	♊5	19	♋4	♋19
☿	♉28	♊0	2	4	6	8	10	12	14	17	19	21	23	25	28	♋0	2	4	6	8	10	12	14	16	18	20	22	24	25	♋27
♀	♊23	25	26	27	28	♋0	1	2	3	4	6	7	8	9	11	12	13	14	15	17	18	19	20	22	23	24	25	26	28	♋29
♂	♍18	18	18	19	19	20	20	20	21	21	22	22	22	23	23	24	24	25	25	26	26	27	27	28	28	28	29	29	♎0	♎0

	1	6	12	18	24	30
♃	♊9	10	12	13	14	16
♄	♓17	17	17	17	17	17

	1	15	30
♅	♍11	11	11
♆	♏18	18	17
♇	♍14	14	14
☊	♊14	14	14

JULY

	1	2	3	4	5	6	7	8	9	10	11	12	13	14	15	16	17	18	19	20	21	22	23	24	25	26	27	28	29	30	31
☉	♋9	10	11	12	13	14	15	16	17	18	18	19	20	21	22	23	24	25	26	27	28	29	♌0	1	2	3	4	5	6	7	♌8
☽	♌4	19	♍4	19	♎2	16	29	♏12	24	♐7	19	♑1	13	25	♒6	18	♓0	12	24	♈7	19	♉2	15	29	♊13	28	♋13	28	♌13	28	♍13
☿	♋29	♌1	2	4	5	7	8	10	11	13	14	15	16	18	19	20	21	22	23	24	25	26	26	27	28	28	29	29	29	♍0	♍0
♀	♌0	1	3	4	5	6	7	9	10	11	12	13	15	16	17	18	20	21	22	23	24	26	27	28	29	♍0	2	3	4	5	♍7
♂	♎1	1	2	3	3	4	4	5	5	6	6	7	7	8	8	9	9	10	11	11	12	12	13	13	14	15	15	16	16	17	♎17

	1	6	12	18	24	30
♃	♊16	17	18	20	21	22
♄	♓17	17	17	17	17	16

	1	15	30
♅	♍12	12	13
♆	♏17	17	17
♇	♍14	14	15
☊	♊14	13	12

AUGUST

	1	2	3	4	5	6	7	8	9	10	11	12	13	14	15	16	17	18	19	20	21	22	23	24	25	26	27	28	29	30	31
☉	♌9	9	10	11	12	13	14	15	16	17	18	19	20	21	22	23	24	25	26	27	28	29	♍0	1	2	3	4	4	5	6	♍7
☽	♍28	♎12	25	♏9	21	♐4	16	28	♑10	22	♒3	15	27	♓9	21	♈4	16	29	♉12	25	♊8	22	♋7	21	♌6	21	♍7	21	♎6	20	♏4
☿	♍0	0	0	0	0	♌29	29	28	28	27	27	26	25	24	23	23	22	21	20	20	19	18	18	18	18	18	18	18	18	19	♌20
♀	♍8	9	10	11	13	14	15	16	17	19	20	21	22	23	25	26	27	28	29	♎1	2	3	4	5	7	8	9	10	11	12	♎14
♂	♎18	19	19	20	20	21	22	22	23	23	24	25	25	26	27	27	28	28	29	♏0	0	1	2	2	3	3	4	5	5	6	♏7

	1	6	12	18	24	30
♃	♊22	23	24	26	26	27
♄	♓16	16	16	15	15	14

	1	15	30
♅	♍13	14	15
♆	♏17	17	17
♇	♍15	15	16
☊	♊12	11	9

SEPTEMBER

	1	2	3	4	5	6	7	8	9	10	11	12	13	14	15	16	17	18	19	20	21	22	23	24	25	26	27	28	29	30
☉	♍8	9	10	11	12	13	14	15	16	17	18	19	20	21	22	23	24	25	26	27	28	29	♎0	1	2	3	4	5	6	♎7
☽	♏17	♐0	12	25	♑7	18	♒0	12	24	♓6	18	♈1	13	26	♉9	22	♊5	18	♋2	16	♌1	16	♍0	15	♎0	14	28	♏12	25	♐8
☿	♌20	21	22	23	25	26	27	29	♍0	2	4	6	7	9	11	13	15	17	18	20	22	24	26	28	♎0	1	3	5	7	♎9
♀	♎15	16	17	18	20	21	22	23	24	25	27	28	29	♏0	1	3	4	5	6	7	8	10	11	12	13	14	15	17	18	♏19
♂	♏7	8	9	9	10	11	11	12	13	13	14	15	15	16	17	17	18	19	19	20	21	21	22	23	24	24	25	26	26	♏27

	1	6	12	18	24	30
♃	♊28	28	29	♋0	0	1
♄	♓14	14	13	13	13	12

	1	15	30
♅	♍15	16	17
♆	♏18	18	18
♇	♍16	16	17
☊	♊9	8	6

OCTOBER

	1	2	3	4	5	6	7	8	9	10	11	12	13	14	15	16	17	18	19	20	21	22	23	24	25	26	27	28	29	30	31
☉	♎8	9	10	11	12	13	14	14	15	16	17	18	19	20	21	22	23	24	25	26	27	28	29	♏0	1	2	3	4	5	6	♏7
☽	♐21	♑3	15	27	♒8	20	♓2	15	27	♈9	22	♉5	18	♊2	15	29	♋13	27	♌11	26	♍10	24	♎9	23	♏7	20	♐3	16	28	♑11	♑23
☿	♎10	12	14	15	17	19	20	22	24	25	27	29	♏0	2	3	5	6	8	9	11	12	14	15	17	18	20	21	23	24	26	♏27
♀	♏20	21	22	23	25	26	27	28	29	♐0	1	3	4	5	6	7	8	9	11	12	13	14	15	16	17	18	19	20	22	23	♐24
♂	♏28	28	29	♐0	1	1	2	3	3	4	5	5	6	7	8	8	9	10	11	11	12	13	13	14	15	16	16	17	18	19	♐19

	1	6	12	18	24	30
♃	♋1	1	1	1	1	1
♄	♓12	12	11	11	11	11

	1	15	30
♅	♍17	17	18
♆	♏18	19	19
♇	♍17	17	18
☊	♊6	5	5

NOVEMBER

	1	2	3	4	5	6	7	8	9	10	11	12	13	14	15	16	17	18	19	20	21	22	23	24	25	26	27	28	29	30
☉	♏8	9	10	11	12	13	14	15	16	17	18	19	20	21	22	23	24	25	26	27	28	29	♐0	1	3	4	5	6	7	♐8
☽	♒5	16	28	♓10	23	♈5	18	♉1	14	28	♊12	26	♋10	24	♌8	22	♍7	21	♎5	18	♏2	15	28	♐11	24	♑6	18	♒0	12	♒24
☿	♏28	♐0	1	2	4	5	6	7	9	10	11	12	13	14	15	16	17	17	18	18	19	19	19	19	19	18	18	17	16	♐15
♀	♐25	26	27	28	29	♑0	1	2	3	4	5	6	7	9	10	11	12	13	14	15	15	16	17	18	19	20	21	22	23	♑24
♂	♐20	21	22	22	23	24	25	25	26	27	28	28	29	♑0	1	1	2	3	4	4	5	6	7	7	8	9	10	10	11	♑12

	1	6	12	18	24	30
♃	♋1	1	0	0	♊29	29
♄	♓11	11	10	10	11	11

	1	15	30
♅	♍18	19	19
♆	♏19	20	20
♇	♍18	18	18
☊	♊5	5	5

DECEMBER

	1	2	3	4	5	6	7	8	9	10	11	12	13	14	15	16	17	18	19	20	21	22	23	24	25	26	27	28	29	30	31
☉	♐9	10	11	12	13	14	15	16	17	18	19	20	21	22	23	24	25	26	27	28	29	♑0	1	2	3	4	5	6	7	8	♑9
☽	♓6	18	♈0	13	26	♉9	22	♊6	20	♋5	20	♌4	19	♍3	17	♎1	15	29	♏12	25	♐7	20	♑2	15	27	♒9	20	♓2	14	26	♈8
☿	♐14	12	11	10	8	7	6	5	4	4	3	3	3	3	3	4	4	5	5	6	7	8	9	10	11	13	14	15	16	18	♐19
♀	♑25	26	27	27	28	29	♒0	1	1	2	3	4	4	5	6	6	7	8	8	9	9	10	10	11	11	12	12	12	13	13	♒13
♂	♑13	13	14	15	16	17	17	18	19	20	20	21	22	23	24	24	25	26	27	27	28	29	♒0	1	1	2	3	4	5	5	♒6

	1	6	12	18	24	30
♃	♊29	28	27	26	25	25
♄	♓11	11	11	11	12	12

	1	15	30
♅	♍19	20	20
♆	♏20	21	21
♇	♍18	18	18
☊	♊5	5	4

1966

JANUARY

	1	2	3	4	5	6	7	8	9	10	11	12	13	14	15	16	17	18	19	20	21	22	23	24	25	26	27	28	29	30	31
☉	♑10	11	12	13	14	15	16	17	18	19	20	21	22	23	24	25	26	27	28	29	♒0	2	3	4	5	6	7	8	9	10	♒11
☽	♈21	♉3	16	♊0	14	28	♋13	28	♌13	28	♍13	28	♎12	25	♏9	22	♐4	17	29	♑11	23	♒5	17	29	♓11	23	♈5	17	29	♉12	♉25
☿	♐20	22	23	25	26	27	29	♑0	2	3	5	6	8	9	11	12	14	15	17	19	20	22	23	25	26	28	♒0	1	3	5	♒6
♀	♒13	14	14	14	14	14	14	14	14	13	13	13	13	12	12	12	11	11	10	10	9	9	8	7	7	6	6	5	4	4	♒3
♂	♒7	8	8	9	10	11	12	12	13	14	15	16	16	17	18	19	19	20	21	22	23	23	24	25	26	27	27	28	29	♓0	♓1

	1	6	12	18	24	30
♃	♊24	24	23	23	22	22
♄	♓12	13	13	14	15	15

	1	15	30
♅	♍20	19	19
♆	♏21	22	22
♇	♍18	18	18
☊	♊4	3	2

FEBRUARY

	1	2	3	4	5	6	7	8	9	10	11	12	13	14	15	16	17	18	19	20	21	22	23	24	25	26	27	28
☉	♒12	13	14	15	16	17	18	19	20	21	22	23	24	25	26	27	28	29	♓0	1	2	3	4	5	6	7	8	♓9
☽	♊8	22	♋6	21	♌6	22	♍7	22	♎7	21	♏5	18	♐1	14	26	♑8	20	♒2	14	26	♓8	20	♈2	14	26	♉8	21	♊4
☿	♒8	10	11	13	15	17	18	20	22	24	26	27	29	♓1	3	5	7	8	10	12	14	16	17	19	21	23	24	♓26
♀	♒3	2	2	1	1	0	0	♑29	29	29	29	29	28	28	28	28	28	28	28	29	29	29	29	♒0	0	0	1	♒1
♂	♓1	2	3	4	5	5	6	7	8	8	9	10	11	12	12	13	14	15	16	16	17	18	19	19	20	21	22	♓23

	1	6	12	18	24	28
♃	♊22	21	21	21	21	22
♄	♓15	16	17	17	18	19

	1	15	28
♅	♍19	19	18
♆	♏22	22	22
♇	♍18	18	17
☊	♊2	1	♉1

MARCH

	1	2	3	4	5	6	7	8	9	10	11	12	13	14	15	16	17	18	19	20	21	22	23	24	25	26	27	28	29	30	31
☉	♓10	11	12	13	14	15	16	17	18	19	20	21	22	23	24	25	26	27	28	29	♈0	1	2	3	4	5	6	7	8	9	♈10
☽	♊17	♋1	15	29	♌14	♍0	15	♎0	15	♏0	14	27	♐10	23	♑5	17	29	♒11	23	♓5	17	29	♈11	23	♉5	18	♊1	14	27	♋11	♋25
☿	♓27	29	♈0	1	2	3	4	5	5	5	6	6	6	5	5	5	4	3	3	2	1	0	♓29	28	27	27	26	25	25	24	♓24
♀	♒1	2	2	3	3	4	5	5	6	6	7	8	9	9	10	11	12	12	13	14	15	16	16	17	18	19	20	21	22	23	♒24
♂	♓23	24	25	26	26	27	28	29	♈0	0	1	2	3	3	4	5	6	7	7	8	9	10	10	11	12	13	13	14	15	16	♈17

	1	6	12	18	24	30
♃	♊22	22	22	23	23	24
♄	♓19	19	20	21	21	22

	1	15	30
♅	♍18	17	17
♆	♏22	22	22
♇	♍17	17	17
☊	♉29	28	26

APRIL

	1	2	3	4	5	6	7	8	9	10	11	12	13	14	15	16	17	18	19	20	21	22	23	24	25	26	27	28	29	30
☉	♈11	12	13	14	15	16	17	18	19	20	21	22	23	24	25	26	27	28	28	29	♉0	1	2	3	4	5	6	7	8	♉9
☽	♌9	24	♍8	23	♎8	23	♏7	22	♐5	18	♑1	13	26	♒8	20	♓1	13	25	♈7	20	♉2	15	28	♊11	24	♋7	21	♌5	19	♍4
☿	♓23	23	23	23	23	23	23	23	24	24	25	25	26	27	27	28	29	♈0	1	2	3	4	5	7	8	9	11	12	13	♈15
♀	♒25	25	26	27	28	29	♓0	1	2	3	4	5	6	7	8	9	10	12	13	14	15	16	17	18	19	20	21	22	23	♓24
♂	♈17	18	19	20	20	21	22	23	23	24	25	26	26	27	28	29	29	♉0	1	2	2	3	4	5	5	6	7	8	8	♉9

	1	6	12	18	24	30
♃	♊24	25	26	27	28	29
♄	♓22	23	24	24	25	26

	1	15	30
♅	♍17	16	16
♆	♏22	22	21
♇	♍17	16	16
☊	♉26	26	25

MAY

	1	2	3	4	5	6	7	8	9	10	11	12	13	14	15	16	17	18	19	20	21	22	23	24	25	26	27	28	29	30	31
☉	♉10	11	12	13	14	15	16	17	18	19	20	21	22	23	24	25	26	27	28	29	29	♊0	1	2	3	4	5	6	7	8	♊9
☽	♍18	♎3	17	♏2	16	♐0	13	26	♑9	21	♒4	16	28	♓9	21	♈3	16	28	♉11	24	♊7	20	♋4	18	♌2	16	♍0	15	29	♎13	♎27
☿	♈16	18	19	21	22	24	26	27	29	♉1	2	4	6	8	10	12	14	16	18	20	22	24	26	28	♊1	3	5	7	9	12	♊14
♀	♓25	26	28	29	♈0	1	2	3	4	5	6	8	9	10	11	12	13	14	15	17	18	19	20	21	22	23	25	26	27	28	♈29
♂	♉10	10	11	12	13	13	14	15	16	16	17	18	19	19	20	21	21	22	23	24	24	25	26	26	27	28	29	29	♊0	1	♊1

	1	6	12	18	24	30
♃	♊29	♋0	1	2	4	5
♄	♓26	26	27	27	28	28

	1	15	30
♅	♍16	16	16
♆	♏21	21	20
♇	♍16	16	16
☊	♉25	25	25

JUNE

	1	2	3	4	5	6	7	8	9	10	11	12	13	14	15	16	17	18	19	20	21	22	23	24	25	26	27	28	29	30
☉	♊10	11	12	13	14	15	16	17	18	19	20	21	22	22	23	24	25	26	27	28	29	♋0	1	2	3	4	5	6	7	♋8
☽	♏11	25	♐8	21	♑4	17	29	♒12	24	♓5	17	29	♈11	24	♉6	19	♊2	15	29	♋14	28	♌12	27	♍11	26	♎10	24	♏7	21	♐4
☿	♊16	18	20	22	24	26	28	♋0	2	4	6	8	10	11	13	15	16	18	20	21	22	24	25	27	28	29	♌0	1	2	♌3
♀	♉0	1	3	4	5	6	7	8	10	11	12	13	14	15	17	18	19	20	21	22	24	25	26	27	28	29	♊1	2	3	♊4
♂	♊2	3	4	4	5	6	6	7	8	9	9	10	11	11	12	13	13	14	15	16	16	17	18	18	19	20	20	21	22	♊22

	1	6	12	18	24	30
♃	♋5	6	8	9	10	12
♄	♓28	29	29	29	29	♈0

	1	15	30
♅	♍16	16	16
♆	♏20	20	20
♇	♍16	16	16
☊	♉25	25	25

JULY

	1	2	3	4	5	6	7	8	9	10	11	12	13	14	15	16	17	18	19	20	21	22	23	24	25	26	27	28	29	30	31
☉	♋9	10	11	12	13	13	14	15	16	17	18	19	20	21	22	23	24	25	26	27	28	29	♌0	1	2	3	4	4	5	6	♌7
☽	♐17	♑0	13	25	♒8	20	♓2	14	25	♈7	19	♉2	14	27	♊10	24	♋8	22	♌7	22	♍7	22	♎6	20	♏4	18	♐1	14	27	♑9	♑22
☿	♌4	5	6	7	8	8	9	10	10	11	11	11	11	11	11	11	11	11	11	10	10	9	9	8	8	7	6	5	5	4	♌3
♀	♊5	7	8	9	10	11	12	14	15	16	17	18	20	21	22	23	24	26	27	28	29	♋0	2	3	4	5	6	8	9	10	♋11
♂	♊23	24	24	25	26	27	27	28	29	29	♋0	1	1	2	3	3	4	5	5	6	7	7	8	9	9	10	11	11	12	13	♋13

	1	6	12	18	24	30
♃	♋12	13	15	16	17	19
♄	♈0	0	0	0	0	♓29

	1	15	30
♅	♍16	17	17
♆	♏20	19	19
♇	♍16	16	17
☊	♉25	24	23

AUGUST

	1	2	3	4	5	6	7	8	9	10	11	12	13	14	15	16	17	18	19	20	21	22	23	24	25	26	27	28	29	30	31
☉	♌8	9	10	11	12	13	14	15	16	17	18	19	20	21	22	23	24	25	26	27	27	28	29	♍0	1	2	3	4	5	6	♍7
☽	♒4	16	28	♓10	22	♈4	16	28	♉10	22	♊5	18	♋2	16	♌1	16	♍1	16	♎1	16	♏0	14	28	♐11	24	♑6	19	♒1	13	25	♓7
☿	♌3	2	2	1	1	1	0	0	0	1	1	1	2	2	3	4	5	6	7	9	10	11	13	14	16	18	20	22	23	25	♌27
♀	♋12	14	15	16	17	18	20	21	22	23	24	26	27	28	29	♌1	2	3	4	5	7	8	9	10	12	13	14	15	16	18	♌19
♂	♋14	15	15	16	17	17	18	19	19	20	21	21	22	22	23	24	24	25	26	26	27	28	28	29	♌0	0	1	1	2	3	♌3

	1	6	12	18	24	30
♃	♋19	20	21	23	24	25
♄	♓29	29	29	29	28	28

	1	15	30
♅	♍17	18	19
♆	♏19	19	20
♇	♍17	17	18
☊	♉22	21	19

SEPTEMBER

	1	2	3	4	5	6	7	8	9	10	11	12	13	14	15	16	17	18	19	20	21	22	23	24	25	26	27	28	29	30
☉	♍8	9	10	11	12	13	14	15	16	17	18	19	20	21	22	23	24	25	26	27	28	29	♎0	1	1	2	3	4	5	♎6
☽	♓19	♈1	13	25	♉7	19	♊1	14	27	♋11	25	♌9	24	♍9	25	♎10	25	♏9	23	♐7	20	♑3	16	28	♒10	22	♓4	16	28	♈10
☿	♌29	♍1	3	5	7	9	11	13	15	17	18	20	22	24	26	28	29	♎1	3	5	6	8	10	11	13	15	16	18	19	♎21
♀	♌20	21	23	24	25	26	28	29	♍0	1	2	4	5	6	7	9	10	11	12	14	15	16	17	19	20	21	22	24	25	♍26
♂	♌4	5	5	6	7	7	8	8	9	10	10	11	12	12	13	14	14	15	15	16	17	17	18	19	19	20	20	21	22	♌22

	1	6	12	18	24	30
♃	♋25	26	27	28	29	♌0
♄	♓28	27	27	26	26	25

	1	15	30
♅	♍19	20	21
♆	♏20	20	20
♇	♍18	18	19
☊	♉19	18	17

OCTOBER

	1	2	3	4	5	6	7	8	9	10	11	12	13	14	15	16	17	18	19	20	21	22	23	24	25	26	27	28	29	30	31
☉	♎7	8	9	10	11	12	13	14	15	16	17	18	19	20	21	22	23	24	25	26	27	28	29	♏0	1	2	3	4	5	6	♏7
☽	♈22	♉4	16	28	♊11	23	♋6	20	♌4	18	♍3	18	♎3	18	♏3	18	♐2	16	29	♑12	24	♒7	19	♓1	13	25	♈6	18	♉0	13	♉25
☿	♎23	24	26	27	29	♏0	2	3	4	6	7	9	10	11	13	14	15	17	18	19	20	22	23	24	25	26	27	28	29	♐0	♐1
♀	♍27	29	♎0	1	2	4	5	6	7	9	10	11	12	14	15	16	17	19	20	21	22	24	25	26	27	29	♏0	1	2	4	♏5
♂	♌23	23	24	25	25	26	26	27	28	28	29	♍0	0	1	1	2	3	3	4	4	5	6	6	7	7	8	8	9	10	10	♍11

	1	6	12	18	24	30
♃	♌1	1	2	3	3	4
♄	♓25	25	25	24	24	24

	1	15	30
♅	♍21	22	23
♆	♏20	21	21
♇	♍19	19	20
☊	♉17	16	16

NOVEMBER

	1	2	3	4	5	6	7	8	9	10	11	12	13	14	15	16	17	18	19	20	21	22	23	24	25	26	27	28	29	30
☉	♏8	9	10	11	12	13	14	15	16	17	18	19	20	21	22	23	24	25	26	27	28	29	♐0	1	2	3	4	5	6	♐7
☽	♊8	20	♋3	17	♌0	14	28	♍12	27	♎12	26	♏11	25	♐10	23	♑7	20	♒3	15	27	♓9	21	♈3	15	27	♉9	21	♊4	17	♋0
☿	♐1	2	2	3	3	3	3	3	3	2	2	1	0	♏29	28	27	25	24	23	21	20	19	18	18	17	17	17	17	18	♏18
♀	♏6	7	9	10	11	12	14	15	16	17	19	20	21	22	24	25	26	27	29	♐0	1	2	4	5	6	7	9	10	11	♐13
♂	♍11	12	13	13	14	14	15	15	16	17	17	18	18	19	19	20	21	21	22	22	23	23	24	25	25	26	26	27	27	♍28

	1	6	12	18	24	30
♃	♌4	4	4	4	4	4
♄	♓23	23	23	23	23	23

	1	15	30
♅	♍23	23	24
♆	♏21	22	22
♇	♍20	20	20
☊	♉16	16	16

DECEMBER

	1	2	3	4	5	6	7	8	9	10	11	12	13	14	15	16	17	18	19	20	21	22	23	24	25	26	27	28	29	30	31
☉	♐8	9	10	11	12	13	14	15	16	17	18	20	21	22	23	24	25	26	27	28	29	♑0	1	2	3	4	5	6	7	8	♑9
☽	♋14	27	♌11	25	♍9	23	♎7	22	♏6	20	♐4	18	♑1	15	28	♒10	23	♓5	17	29	♈11	22	♉4	17	29	♊12	26	♋9	23	♌7	♌21
☿	♏19	19	20	21	22	23	24	25	27	28	29	♐0	2	3	5	6	7	9	10	12	13	15	16	18	19	21	22	24	25	27	♐28
♀	♐14	15	16	18	19	20	21	23	24	25	26	28	29	♑0	1	3	4	5	6	8	9	10	11	13	14	15	16	18	19	20	♑21
♂	♍28	29	29	♎0	1	1	2	2	3	3	4	4	5	5	6	6	7	7	8	8	9	9	10	10	11	11	12	12	13	13	♎14

	1	6	12	18	24	30
♃	♌4	4	4	3	3	2
♄	♓23	23	23	23	24	24

	1	15	30
♅	♍24	24	24
♆	♏23	23	23
♇	♍21	21	21
☊	♉16	16	15

1967

JANUARY

	1	2	3	4	5	6	7	8	9	10	11	12	13	14	15	16	17	18	19	20	21	22	23	24	25	26	27	28	29	30	31
☉	♑10	11	12	13	14	15	16	17	18	19	20	21	22	23	24	25	26	27	28	29	♒0	1	2	3	4	5	6	7	8	9	♒10
☽	♍6	20	♎4	18	♏2	16	♐0	13	27	♑10	23	♒6	18	♓1	13	25	♈6	18	♉0	12	24	♊7	20	♋3	17	♌2	16	♍1	16	♎0	♎15
☿	♑0	1	3	5	6	8	9	11	12	14	16	17	19	21	22	24	25	27	29	♒0	2	4	6	7	9	11	12	14	16	18	♒19
♀	♑23	24	25	26	28	29	♒0	1	3	4	5	6	8	9	10	12	13	14	15	17	18	19	20	22	23	24	25	27	28	29	♓0
♂	♎14	15	15	16	16	16	17	17	18	18	19	19	19	20	20	21	21	22	22	22	23	23	23	24	24	25	25	25	26	26	♎26

	1	6	12	18	24	30
♃	♌2	1	1	0	♋29	28
♄	♓24	24	25	25	26	26

	1	15	30
♅	♍24	24	24
♆	♏24	24	24
♇	♍21	21	20
☊	♉15	13	12

FEBRUARY

	1	2	3	4	5	6	7	8	9	10	11	12	13	14	15	16	17	18	19	20	21	22	23	24	25	26	27	28
☉	♒11	12	13	14	15	16	18	19	20	21	22	23	24	25	26	27	28	29	♓0	1	2	3	4	5	6	7	8	♓9
☽	♎29	♏13	27	♐10	23	♑6	19	♒2	14	27	♓9	21	♈3	15	26	♉8	20	♊2	15	28	♋11	25	♌10	24	♍9	24	♎10	♎24
☿	♒21	23	25	26	28	♓0	2	3	5	7	8	10	11	12	14	15	16	17	17	18	18	19	19	19	19	18	18	♓17
♀	♓2	3	4	5	6	8	9	10	11	13	14	15	16	18	19	20	21	23	24	25	26	28	29	♈0	1	3	4	♈5
♂	♎27	27	27	28	28	28	29	29	29	29	♏0	0	0	0	1	1	1	1	1	2	2	2	2	2	2	3	3	♏3

	1	6	12	18	24	28
♃	♋28	27	27	26	25	25
♄	♓27	27	28	28	29	♈0

	1	15	28
♅	♍24	23	23
♆	♏24	24	24
♇	♍20	20	20
☊	♉12	10	9

MARCH

	1	2	3	4	5	6	7	8	9	10	11	12	13	14	15	16	17	18	19	20	21	22	23	24	25	26	27	28	29	30	31
☉	♓10	11	12	13	14	15	16	17	18	19	20	21	22	23	24	25	26	27	28	29	♈0	1	2	3	4	5	6	7	8	9	♈10
☽	♏9	23	♐7	20	♑3	16	29	♒11	24	♓6	18	♈0	11	23	♉5	17	29	♊11	24	♋6	20	♌3	18	♍2	17	♎3	18	♏3	18	♐2	♐16
☿	♓16	15	14	13	12	11	10	9	8	8	7	6	6	5	5	5	5	5	5	5	5	5	6	6	7	8	8	9	10	11	♓12
♀	♈6	7	9	10	11	12	14	15	16	17	19	20	21	22	23	25	26	27	28	29	♉1	2	3	4	6	7	8	9	10	12	♉13
♂	♏3	3	3	3	3	3	3	3	3	3	3	3	3	3	3	3	3	3	3	2	2	2	2	2	2	1	1	1	1	0	♏0

	1	6	12	18	24	30
♃	♋25	25	25	24	24	25
♄	♈0	0	1	2	2	3

	1	15	30
♅	♍23	22	22
♆	♏24	24	24
♇	♍20	19	19
☊	♉9	8	7

APRIL

	1	2	3	4	5	6	7	8	9	10	11	12	13	14	15	16	17	18	19	20	21	22	23	24	25	26	27	28	29	30
☉	♈11	12	13	14	15	16	16	17	18	19	20	21	22	23	24	25	26	27	28	29	♉0	1	2	3	4	5	6	7	8	♉9
☽	♑0	13	26	♒8	21	♓3	15	27	♈8	20	♉2	14	26	♊8	20	♋3	16	29	♌13	27	♍11	26	♎11	26	♏11	26	♐11	25	♑9	♑22
☿	♓13	14	15	16	17	18	20	21	22	23	25	26	28	29	♈1	2	4	5	7	8	10	12	13	15	17	19	21	22	24	♈26
♀	♉14	15	16	18	19	20	21	22	24	25	26	27	28	♊0	1	2	3	4	5	7	8	9	10	11	12	14	15	16	17	♊18
♂	♏0	♎29	29	29	29	28	28	28	27	27	26	26	26	25	25	25	24	24	23	23	23	22	22	22	21	21	21	20	20	♎20

	1	6	12	18	24	30
♃	♋25	25	25	26	26	27
♄	♈3	4	5	6	6	7

	1	15	30
♅	♍22	21	21
♆	♏24	24	23
♇	♍19	18	18
☊	♉7	7	7

MAY

	1	2	3	4	5	6	7	8	9	10	11	12	13	14	15	16	17	18	19	20	21	22	23	24	25	26	27	28	29	30	31
☉	♉10	11	12	13	14	15	16	17	18	19	20	21	22	23	23	24	25	26	27	28	29	♊0	1	2	3	4	5	6	7	8	♊9
☽	♒5	17	♓0	12	24	♈5	17	29	♉11	23	♊5	17	♋0	13	26	♌9	23	♍6	21	♎5	20	♏5	19	♐4	19	♑3	17	♒0	13	26	♓8
☿	♈28	♉0	2	4	6	8	10	12	14	17	19	21	23	25	28	♊0	2	4	6	8	10	12	14	16	18	20	22	24	25	27	♊29
♀	♊19	21	22	23	24	25	26	27	29	♋0	1	2	3	4	5	6	8	9	10	11	12	13	14	15	16	18	19	20	21	22	♋23
♂	♎19	19	19	18	18	18	17	17	17	17	17	16	16	16	16	16	16	15	15	15	15	15	15	15	15	15	15	15	15	15	♎15

	1	6	12	18	24	30
♃	♋27	28	28	29	♌0	1
♄	♈7	8	8	9	9	10

	1	15	30
♅	♍21	20	20
♆	♏23	23	23
♇	♍18	18	18
☊	♉7	7	6

JUNE

	1	2	3	4	5	6	7	8	9	10	11	12	13	14	15	16	17	18	19	20	21	22	23	24	25	26	27	28	29	30
☉	♊10	11	12	13	14	15	16	17	17	18	19	20	21	22	23	24	25	26	27	28	29	♋0	1	2	3	4	5	6	7	♋8
☽	♓20	♈2	14	26	♉7	19	♊2	14	27	♋10	23	♌6	19	♍3	17	♎1	15	♏0	14	29	♐13	27	♑11	25	♒8	21	♓4	16	28	♈10
☿	♋0	2	3	5	6	8	9	10	11	12	14	15	16	16	17	18	19	19	20	20	21	21	22	22	22	22	22	22	22	♋21
♀	♋24	25	26	27	28	29	♌0	1	2	3	4	5	6	7	8	9	10	11	12	13	14	15	16	17	18	19	20	21	22	♌23
♂	♎15	15	15	15	16	16	16	16	16	16	16	17	17	17	17	18	18	18	18	19	19	19	19	20	20	20	21	21	21	♎22

	1	6	12	18	24	30
♃	♌1	2	3	5	6	7
♄	♈10	10	11	11	12	12

	1	15	30
♅	♍20	20	21
♆	♏23	22	22
♇	♍18	18	18
☊	♉6	6	5

JULY

	1	2	3	4	5	6	7	8	9	10	11	12	13	14	15	16	17	18	19	20	21	22	23	24	25	26	27	28	29	30	31
☉	♋8	9	10	11	12	13	14	15	16	17	18	19	20	21	22	23	24	25	26	27	28	29	29	♌0	1	2	3	4	5	6	♌7
☽	♈22	♉4	16	28	♊10	23	♋6	19	♌2	16	♍0	14	28	♎12	26	♏10	25	♐9	22	♑6	20	♒3	16	29	♓12	24	♈6	18	♉0	11	♉23
☿	♋21	21	20	20	19	19	18	18	17	16	16	15	15	14	14	13	13	13	12	12	12	12	13	13	13	14	14	15	16	17	♋18
♀	♌23	24	25	26	27	28	28	29	♍0	1	2	2	3	4	4	5	6	6	7	8	8	9	9	10	10	11	11	12	12	12	♍13
♂	♎22	22	23	23	24	24	24	25	25	26	26	26	27	27	28	28	29	29	♏0	0	0	1	1	2	2	3	3	4	4	5	♏6

	1	6	12	18	24	30
♃	♌7	8	9	11	12	13
♄	♈12	12	12	12	12	12

	1	15	30
♅	♍21	21	22
♆	♏22	22	22
♇	♍18	19	19
☊	♉5	4	2

AUGUST

	1	2	3	4	5	6	7	8	9	10	11	12	13	14	15	16	17	18	19	20	21	22	23	24	25	26	27	28	29	30	31
☉	♌8	9	10	11	12	13	14	15	16	17	18	19	20	21	21	22	23	24	25	26	27	28	29	♍0	1	2	3	4	5	6	♍7
☽	♊6	18	♋1	14	27	♌11	25	♍10	24	♎9	23	♏7	21	♐5	19	♑3	16	29	♒12	25	♓8	20	♈2	14	26	♉8	19	♊1	14	26	♋9
☿	♋19	20	21	22	24	25	27	28	♌0	2	4	6	7	9	11	13	15	17	19	21	23	25	27	29	♍1	3	5	7	9	11	♍13
♀	♍13	13	13	14	14	14	14	14	14	14	14	14	14	13	13	13	13	12	12	11	11	10	10	9	9	8	8	7	6	6	♍5
♂	♏6	7	7	8	8	9	9	10	10	11	12	12	13	13	14	14	15	16	16	17	17	18	19	19	20	20	21	22	22	23	♏24

	1	6	12	18	24	30
♃	♌14	15	16	18	19	20
♄	♈12	12	12	12	12	11

	1	15	30
♅	♍22	23	24
♆	♏22	22	22
♇	♍19	19	20
☊	♉2	1	♈1

SEPTEMBER

	1	2	3	4	5	6	7	8	9	10	11	12	13	14	15	16	17	18	19	20	21	22	23	24	25	26	27	28	29	30
☉	♍8	9	10	11	12	13	14	15	16	17	18	19	20	20	21	22	23	24	25	26	27	28	29	♎0	1	2	3	4	5	♎6
☽	♋22	♌6	20	♍4	19	♎4	18	♏3	18	♐2	16	♑0	13	26	♒9	22	♓4	16	29	♈11	22	♉4	16	28	♊10	22	♋4	17	♌0	♌14
☿	♍15	17	18	20	22	24	25	27	29	♎0	2	4	5	7	9	10	12	13	15	16	18	19	20	22	23	25	26	27	29	♏0
♀	♍5	4	3	3	2	2	1	1	0	0	♌29	29	29	28	28	28	28	28	28	28	28	28	28	28	28	28	28	29	29	♌29
♂	♏24	25	25	26	27	27	28	29	29	♐0	1	1	2	3	3	4	5	5	6	7	7	8	9	9	10	11	11	12	13	♐13

	1	6	12	18	24	30
♃	♌21	22	23	24	25	27
♄	♈11	11	11	10	10	9

	1	15	30
♅	♍24	25	26
♆	♏22	22	22
♇	♍20	20	21
☊	♈29	29	28

OCTOBER

	1	2	3	4	5	6	7	8	9	10	11	12	13	14	15	16	17	18	19	20	21	22	23	24	25	26	27	28	29	30	31
☉	♎7	8	9	10	11	12	13	14	15	16	17	18	19	20	21	22	23	24	25	26	27	28	29	♏0	1	2	3	4	5	6	♏7
☽	♌28	♍12	27	♎12	27	♏12	27	♐12	26	♑10	23	♒6	19	♓1	13	26	♈7	19	♉1	13	25	♊7	19	♋1	13	26	♌9	22	♍6	21	♎5
☿	♏1	2	4	5	6	7	8	9	10	11	12	13	14	15	15	16	16	17	17	17	17	17	17	17	16	16	15	14	13	12	♏11
♀	♍0	0	1	1	1	2	2	3	4	4	5	5	6	7	7	8	9	10	10	11	12	13	14	14	15	16	17	18	19	20	♍21
♂	♐14	15	16	16	17	18	18	19	20	21	21	22	23	23	24	25	26	26	27	28	28	29	♑0	1	1	2	3	4	4	5	♑6

	1	6	12	18	24	30
♃	♌27	28	29	♍0	1	2
♄	♈9	9	8	8	7	7

	1	15	30
♅	♍26	26	27
♆	♏22	23	23
♇	♍21	22	22
☊	♈28	28	28

NOVEMBER

	1	2	3	4	5	6	7	8	9	10	11	12	13	14	15	16	17	18	19	20	21	22	23	24	25	26	27	28	29	30
☉	♏8	9	10	11	12	13	14	15	16	17	18	19	20	21	22	23	24	25	26	27	28	29	♐0	1	2	3	4	5	6	♐7
☽	♎20	♏5	21	♐6	21	♑5	19	♒2	15	28	♓10	23	♈4	16	28	♉10	22	♊4	16	28	♋10	23	♌5	18	♍2	15	♎0	14	29	♏14
☿	♏9	8	7	6	4	4	3	2	2	1	1	2	2	2	3	4	5	6	7	8	9	10	12	13	14	16	17	19	20	♏22
♀	♍22	22	23	24	25	26	27	28	29	♎0	1	2	3	4	5	6	8	9	10	11	12	13	14	15	16	17	18	19	21	♎22
♂	♑7	7	8	9	10	10	11	12	13	13	14	15	16	16	17	18	19	19	20	21	22	22	23	24	25	26	26	27	28	♑29

	1	6	12	18	24	30
♃	♍2	3	3	4	5	5
♄	♈7	7	6	6	6	6

	1	15	30
♅	♍27	28	29
♆	♏23	24	25
♇	♍22	22	23
☊	♈28	28	27

DECEMBER

	1	2	3	4	5	6	7	8	9	10	11	12	13	14	15	16	17	18	19	20	21	22	23	24	25	26	27	28	29	30	31
☉	♐8	9	10	11	12	13	14	15	16	17	18	19	20	21	22	23	24	25	26	27	28	29	♑0	1	2	4	5	6	7	8	♑9
☽	♏29	♐14	29	♑13	27	♒11	24	♓7	19	♈1	13	25	♉7	18	♊0	12	25	♋7	20	♌2	15	29	♍12	26	♎10	24	♏8	23	♐7	22	♑7
☿	♏23	25	26	28	29	♐1	2	4	5	7	8	10	11	13	15	16	18	19	21	22	24	25	27	29	♑0	2	3	5	7	8	♑10
♀	♎23	24	25	26	27	28	♏0	1	2	3	4	5	6	8	9	10	11	12	13	15	16	17	18	19	21	22	23	24	25	26	♏28
♂	♑29	♒0	1	2	2	3	4	5	6	6	7	8	9	9	10	11	12	13	13	14	15	16	16	17	18	19	20	20	21	22	♒23

	1	6	12	18	24	30
♃	♍5	5	6	6	6	6
♄	♈6	6	6	6	6	6

	1	15	30
♅	♍29	29	29
♆	♏25	25	26
♇	♍23	23	23
☊	♈27	27	25

1968

JANUARY

	1	2	3	4	5	6	7	8	9	10	11	12	13	14	15	16	17	18	19	20	21	22	23	24	25	26	27	28	29	30	31
☉	♑10	11	12	13	14	15	16	17	18	19	20	21	22	23	24	25	26	27	28	29	♒0	1	2	3	4	5	6	7	8	9	♒10
☽	♑21	♒5	19	♓2	15	27	♈9	21	♉3	15	27	♊9	21	♋3	16	29	♌12	25	♍9	23	♎6	20	♏4	19	♐3	17	♑1	15	29	♒13	♒27
☿	♑11	13	15	16	18	20	21	23	24	26	28	29	♒1	3	5	6	8	10	11	13	14	16	18	19	21	22	24	25	26	27	♒29
♀	♏29	♐0	1	2	4	5	6	7	8	10	11	12	13	15	16	17	18	19	21	22	23	24	25	27	28	29	♑0	2	3	4	♑5
♂	♒23	24	25	26	27	27	28	29	♓0	0	1	2	3	4	4	5	6	7	7	8	9	10	11	11	12	13	14	14	15	16	♓17

	1	6	12	18	24	30
♃	♍6	5	5	5	4	4
♄	♈6	6	7	7	7	8

	1	15	30
♅	♍29	29	29
♆	♏26	26	26
♇	♍23	23	23
☊	♈25	23	22

FEBRUARY

	1	2	3	4	5	6	7	8	9	10	11	12	13	14	15	16	17	18	19	20	21	22	23	24	25	26	27	28	29
☉	♒11	12	13	14	15	16	17	18	19	20	21	22	23	24	25	26	27	28	29	♓0	1	2	3	4	5	6	7	8	♓9
☽	♓10	22	♈5	17	29	♉11	23	♊4	16	29	♋11	24	♌7	21	♍5	19	♎3	17	♏1	15	♐0	14	28	♑11	25	♒9	22	♓5	♓18
☿	♓0	0	1	2	2	2	2	2	2	1	1	0	♒29	28	27	26	24	23	22	21	20	19	19	18	18	17	17	17	♒17
♀	♑6	8	9	10	11	13	14	15	16	17	19	20	21	22	24	25	26	27	29	♒0	1	2	3	5	6	7	8	10	♒11
♂	♓18	18	19	20	21	21	22	23	24	25	25	26	27	28	28	29	♈0	1	1	2	3	4	4	5	6	7	8	8	♈9

	1	6	12	18	24	29
♃	♍3	3	2	1	0	0
♄	♈8	9	9	10	10	11

	1	15	29
♅	♍29	28	28
♆	♏26	26	27
♇	♍23	22	22
☊	♈21	20	19

MARCH

	1	2	3	4	5	6	7	8	9	10	11	12	13	14	15	16	17	18	19	20	21	22	23	24	25	26	27	28	29	30	31
☉	♓10	11	12	13	14	15	16	17	18	19	20	21	22	23	24	25	26	27	28	29	♈0	1	2	3	4	5	6	7	8	9	♈10
☽	♈0	13	25	♉7	19	♊0	12	24	♋6	19	♌2	15	29	♍13	27	♎12	27	♏11	26	♐10	24	♑8	22	♒5	19	♓1	14	27	♈9	21	♉3
☿	♒17	17	18	18	19	19	20	21	21	22	23	24	25	26	27	28	29	♓0	2	3	4	5	7	8	10	11	12	14	15	17	♓18
♀	♒12	13	15	16	17	18	19	21	22	23	24	26	27	28	29	♓1	2	3	4	5	7	8	9	10	12	13	14	15	17	18	♓19
♂	♈10	11	11	12	13	14	14	15	16	17	17	18	19	20	20	21	22	23	23	24	25	26	26	27	28	29	29	♉0	1	1	♉2

	1	6	12	18	24	30
♃	♍0	♌29	28	28	27	27
♄	♈11	12	12	13	14	15

	1	15	30
♅	♍28	27	27
♆	♏27	26	26
♇	♍22	21	21
☊	♈19	19	19

APRIL

	1	2	3	4	5	6	7	8	9	10	11	12	13	14	15	16	17	18	19	20	21	22	23	24	25	26	27	28	29	30
☉	♈11	12	13	14	15	16	17	18	19	20	21	22	23	24	25	26	27	28	29	♉0	1	2	3	4	5	6	7	8	9	♉10
☽	♉15	27	♊9	20	♋2	15	27	♌10	23	♍7	21	♎5	20	♏5	20	♐5	20	♑5	19	♒2	16	29	♓11	24	♈6	18	♉0	12	24	♊5
☿	♓20	22	23	25	27	28	♈0	2	3	5	7	9	11	13	15	16	18	20	22	24	26	29	♉1	3	5	7	9	11	13	♉16
♀	♓20	21	23	24	25	26	28	29	♈0	1	3	4	5	6	7	9	10	11	12	14	15	16	17	19	20	21	22	23	25	♈26
♂	♉3	4	4	5	6	7	7	8	9	10	10	11	12	12	13	14	15	15	16	17	17	18	19	20	20	21	22	22	23	♉24

	1	6	12	18	24	30
♃	♌27	26	26	26	26	26
♄	♈15	15	16	17	18	18

	1	15	30
♅	♍27	26	26
♆	♏26	26	26
♇	♍21	21	20
☊	♈19	19	19

MAY

	1	2	3	4	5	6	7	8	9	10	11	12	13	14	15	16	17	18	19	20	21	22	23	24	25	26	27	28	29	30	31
☉	♉11	12	13	14	15	16	16	17	18	19	20	21	22	23	24	25	26	27	28	29	♊0	1	2	3	4	5	6	7	8	9	♊10
☽	♊17	29	♋11	23	♌6	19	♍2	15	29	♎14	28	♏14	29	♐14	29	♑14	28	♒12	25	♓8	21	♈3	15	27	♉9	21	♊2	14	26	♋8	♋20
☿	♉18	20	22	24	26	28	♊0	2	4	6	8	9	11	13	14	16	17	18	20	21	22	23	24	25	26	27	28	29	29	♋0	♋1
♀	♈27	28	♉0	1	2	3	5	6	7	8	9	11	12	13	14	16	17	18	19	21	22	23	24	25	27	28	29	♊0	2	3	♊4
♂	♉25	25	26	27	27	28	29	♊0	0	1	2	2	3	4	4	5	6	7	7	8	9	9	10	11	11	12	13	14	14	15	♊16

	1	6	12	18	24	30
♃	♌26	26	26	27	27	28
♄	♈19	19	20	21	21	22

	1	15	30
♅	♍26	25	25
♆	♏26	25	25
♇	♍20	20	20
☊	♈19	18	17

JUNE

	1	2	3	4	5	6	7	8	9	10	11	12	13	14	15	16	17	18	19	20	21	22	23	24	25	26	27	28	29	30
☉	♊11	12	12	13	14	15	16	17	18	19	20	21	22	23	24	25	26	27	28	29	♋0	1	2	3	3	4	5	6	7	♋8
☽	♌3	15	28	♍11	24	♎8	22	♏7	22	♐7	22	♑7	22	♒7	21	♓4	17	♈0	12	24	♉6	18	29	♊11	23	♋5	17	♌0	12	♌25
☿	♋1	1	2	2	2	2	2	2	2	2	1	1	0	0	♊29	29	28	28	27	27	26	26	25	25	24	24	24	23	23	♊23
♀	♊5	6	8	9	10	11	13	14	15	16	18	19	20	21	22	24	25	26	27	29	♋0	1	2	4	5	6	7	8	10	♋11
♂	♊16	17	18	18	19	20	20	21	22	22	23	24	24	25	26	26	27	28	29	29	♋0	1	1	2	3	3	4	5	5	♋6

	1	6	12	18	24	30
♃	♌28	29	♍0	0	1	2
♄	♈22	22	23	23	24	24

	1	15	30
♅	♍25	25	25
♆	♏25	24	24
♇	♍20	20	20
☊	♈17	16	14

JULY

	1	2	3	4	5	6	7	8	9	10	11	12	13	14	15	16	17	18	19	20	21	22	23	24	25	26	27	28	29	30	31
☉	♋9	10	11	12	13	14	15	16	17	18	19	20	21	22	23	24	24	25	26	27	28	29	♌0	1	2	3	4	5	6	7	♌8
☽	♍8	21	♎4	18	♏2	17	♐1	16	♑1	16	♒1	15	29	♓12	25	♈8	20	♉2	14	26	♊8	20	♋2	14	26	♌9	22	♍5	18	♎1	♎15
☿	♊23	23	24	24	24	25	25	26	26	27	28	29	♋0	1	2	3	5	6	8	9	11	12	14	16	18	20	21	23	25	27	♋29
♀	♋12	13	15	16	17	18	19	21	22	23	24	26	27	28	29	♌1	2	3	4	5	7	8	9	10	12	13	14	15	17	18	♌19
♂	♋7	7	8	9	9	10	11	11	12	13	13	14	15	15	16	16	17	18	18	19	20	20	21	22	22	23	24	24	25	26	♋26

	1	6	12	18	24	30
♃	♍2	3	4	5	7	8
♄	♈24	25	25	25	25	25

	1	15	30
♅	♍25	26	26
♆	♏24	24	24
♇	♍20	21	21
☊	♈14	13	12

AUGUST

	1	2	3	4	5	6	7	8	9	10	11	12	13	14	15	16	17	18	19	20	21	22	23	24	25	26	27	28	29	30	31
☉	♌9	10	11	12	13	14	15	16	16	17	18	19	20	21	22	23	24	25	26	27	28	29	♍0	1	2	3	4	5	6	7	♍8
☽	♎29	♏13	27	♐11	26	♑10	25	♒9	23	♓7	20	♈3	16	28	♉10	22	♊4	16	28	♋10	22	♌5	18	♍1	14	28	♎12	26	♏10	24	♐8
☿	♌2	4	6	8	10	12	14	16	18	20	22	24	26	28	♍0	2	4	6	7	9	11	13	14	16	18	19	21	23	24	26	♍27
♀	♌20	21	23	24	25	26	28	29	♍0	1	3	4	5	6	7	9	10	11	12	14	15	16	17	19	20	21	22	24	25	26	♍27
♂	♋27	28	28	29	♌0	0	1	1	2	3	3	4	5	5	6	7	7	8	9	9	10	10	11	12	12	13	14	14	15	16	♌16

	1	6	12	18	24	30
♃	♍8	9	10	12	13	14
♄	♈26	26	26	25	25	25

	1	15	30
♅	♍27	27	28
♆	♏24	24	24
♇	♍21	22	22
☊	♈12	11	10

SEPTEMBER

	1	2	3	4	5	6	7	8	9	10	11	12	13	14	15	16	17	18	19	20	21	22	23	24	25	26	27	28	29	30
☉	♍9	10	11	12	12	13	14	15	16	17	18	19	20	21	22	23	24	25	26	27	28	29	♎0	1	2	3	4	5	6	♎7
☽	♐22	♑6	20	♒4	18	♓2	15	28	♈11	24	♉6	18	♊0	12	24	♋6	18	♌0	13	26	♍9	23	♎7	21	♏6	20	♐4	19	♑3	♑17
☿	♍29	♎0	2	3	5	6	8	9	10	12	13	14	16	17	18	19	20	21	22	23	24	25	26	27	28	28	29	♏0	0	♏1
♀	♍28	♎0	1	2	3	5	6	7	8	9	11	12	13	14	16	17	18	19	21	22	23	24	25	27	28	29	♏0	2	3	♏4
♂	♌17	18	18	19	19	20	21	21	22	23	23	24	24	25	26	26	27	28	28	29	♍0	0	1	1	2	3	3	4	5	♍5

	1	6	12	18	24	30
♃	♍15	16	17	18	20	21
♄	♈25	25	24	24	24	23

	1	15	30
♅	♍28	29	♎29
♆	♏24	24	25
♇	♍22	23	23
☊	♈10	10	10

OCTOBER

	1	2	3	4	5	6	7	8	9	10	11	12	13	14	15	16	17	18	19	20	21	22	23	24	25	26	27	28	29	30	31
☉	♎8	9	10	11	12	13	14	15	16	17	18	19	20	21	22	23	24	25	26	27	28	29	♏0	1	2	3	4	5	6	7	♏8
☽	♒1	15	28	♓11	24	♈7	20	♉2	14	26	♊8	20	♋2	14	26	♌8	21	♍4	17	♎1	15	♏0	15	♐0	15	29	♑14	28	♒12	25	♓8
☿	♏1	1	1	1	1	1	0	0	♎29	29	28	27	26	24	23	22	21	20	19	18	17	16	16	16	16	16	16	17	17	18	♎19
♀	♏5	6	8	9	10	11	13	14	15	16	18	19	20	21	22	24	25	26	27	29	♐0	1	2	3	5	6	7	8	9	11	♐12
♂	♍6	6	7	8	8	9	10	10	11	11	12	13	13	14	14	15	16	16	17	18	18	19	19	20	21	21	22	23	23	24	♍24

	1	6	12	18	24	30
♃	♍21	22	23	25	26	27
♄	♈23	23	22	22	21	21

	1	15	30
♅	♎0	1	2
♆	♏25	25	26
♇	♍23	24	24
☊	♈10	10	9

NOVEMBER

	1	2	3	4	5	6	7	8	9	10	11	12	13	14	15	16	17	18	19	20	21	22	23	24	25	26	27	28	29	30
☉	♏9	10	11	12	13	14	15	16	17	18	19	20	21	22	23	24	25	26	27	28	29	♐0	1	2	3	4	5	6	7	♐8
☽	♓21	♈4	16	28	♉11	23	♊5	16	28	♋10	22	♌4	16	29	♍12	25	♎9	23	♏8	23	♐8	23	♑9	23	♒8	22	♓5	18	♈1	♈13
☿	♎20	21	22	24	25	26	28	29	♏1	2	4	5	7	9	10	12	13	15	16	18	20	21	23	24	26	28	29	♐1	2	♐4
♀	♐13	14	16	17	18	19	20	22	23	24	25	26	28	29	♑0	1	3	4	5	6	7	9	10	11	12	13	15	16	17	♑18
♂	♍25	26	26	27	27	28	29	29	♎0	0	1	2	2	3	3	4	5	5	6	7	7	8	8	9	10	10	11	11	12	♎13

	1	6	12	18	24	30
♃	♍27	28	29	♎0	1	2
♄	♈21	20	20	20	19	19

	1	15	30
♅	♎2	3	3
♆	♏26	26	27
♇	♍24	25	25
☊	♈9	9	8

DECEMBER

	1	2	3	4	5	6	7	8	9	10	11	12	13	14	15	16	17	18	19	20	21	22	23	24	25	26	27	28	29	30	31
☉	♐9	10	11	12	13	14	15	16	17	18	19	20	21	22	23	24	25	26	27	28	29	♑0	1	2	3	4	5	6	7	8	♑9
☽	♈25	♉8	20	♊1	13	25	♋7	19	♌1	13	25	♍8	21	♎4	17	♏1	16	♐1	16	♑2	17	♒2	16	♓1	14	27	♈10	22	♉5	17	♉28
☿	♐5	7	9	10	12	13	15	16	18	20	21	23	24	26	27	29	♑1	2	4	5	7	9	10	12	13	15	17	18	20	21	♑23
♀	♑19	21	22	23	24	25	27	28	29	♒0	1	2	4	5	6	7	8	9	11	12	13	14	15	16	18	19	20	21	22	23	♒25
♂	♎13	14	14	15	15	16	17	17	18	18	19	20	20	21	21	22	23	23	24	24	25	25	26	27	27	28	28	29	29	♏0	♏1

	1	6	12	18	24	30
♃	♎2	3	4	4	5	5
♄	♈19	19	19	19	19	19

	1	15	30
♅	♎3	4	4
♆	♏27	27	28
♇	♍25	25	25
☊	♈8	6	5

1969

JANUARY

	1	2	3	4	5	6	7	8	9	10	11	12	13	14	15	16	17	18	19	20	21	22	23	24	25	26	27	28	29	30	31
☉	♑10	11	12	13	14	15	17	18	19	20	21	22	23	24	25	26	27	28	29	♒0	1	2	3	4	5	6	7	8	9	10	♒11
☽	♊10	22	♋4	16	28	♌10	22	♍5	17	♎0	13	27	♏11	25	♐10	25	♑10	25	♒10	24	♓9	22	♈6	18	♉1	13	25	♊7	19	♋1	♋13
☿	♑25	26	28	29	♒1	2	4	5	7	8	9	10	12	13	13	14	15	15	16	16	16	16	15	15	14	13	12	11	10	8	♒7
♀	♒26	27	28	29	♓0	1	2	4	5	6	7	8	9	10	11	12	13	14	16	17	18	19	20	21	22	23	24	25	26	27	♓28
♂	♏1	2	2	3	3	4	5	5	6	6	7	7	8	8	9	10	10	11	11	12	12	13	13	14	14	15	16	16	17	17	♏18

	1	6	12	18	24	30		1	6	12	18	24	30		1	15	30		1	15	30		1	15	30		1	15	30
♃	♎5	6	6	6	6	6	♄	♈19	19	19	19	20	20	♅	♎4	4	4	♆	♏28	28	28	♇	♍25	25	25	☊	♈5	3	2

FEBRUARY

	1	2	3	4	5	6	7	8	9	10	11	12	13	14	15	16	17	18	19	20	21	22	23	24	25	26	27	28
☉	♒12	13	14	15	16	17	18	19	20	21	22	23	24	25	26	27	28	29	♓0	1	2	3	4	5	6	7	8	♓9
☽	♋25	♌7	19	♍2	14	27	♎10	24	♏7	21	♐5	19	♑4	19	♒3	18	♓2	16	♈0	13	26	♉9	21	♊3	15	27	♋9	♋21
☿	♒6	5	4	3	2	2	1	1	0	0	0	0	1	1	1	2	3	3	4	5	6	7	7	8	10	11	12	♒13
♀	♓29	♈0	1	2	3	4	5	5	6	7	8	9	10	11	12	12	13	14	15	15	16	17	18	18	19	20	20	♈21
♂	♏18	19	19	20	20	21	21	22	22	23	23	24	24	25	25	26	26	27	27	28	28	29	29	29	♐0	0	1	♐1

	1	6	12	18	24	28		1	6	12	18	24	28		1	15	28		1	15	28		1	15	28		1	15	28
♃	♎6	6	5	5	4	4	♄	♈20	21	21	22	22	23	♅	♎4	3	3	♆	♏28	29	29	♇	♍25	24	24	☊	♈1	1	0

MARCH

	1	2	3	4	5	6	7	8	9	10	11	12	13	14	15	16	17	18	19	20	21	22	23	24	25	26	27	28	29	30	31
☉	♓10	11	12	13	14	15	16	17	18	19	20	21	22	23	24	25	26	27	28	29	♈0	1	2	3	4	5	6	7	8	9	♈10
☽	♌3	15	28	♍11	24	♎7	20	♏4	18	♐2	16	♑0	14	29	♒13	27	♓11	25	♈8	21	♉4	17	29	♊11	23	♋5	17	29	♌11	23	♍6
☿	♒14	15	17	18	19	21	22	23	25	26	28	29	♓1	2	4	5	7	8	10	12	13	15	17	18	20	22	24	26	27	29	♈1
♀	♈21	22	23	23	24	24	24	25	25	25	26	26	26	26	27	27	27	27	27	27	27	27	26	26	26	26	25	25	25	24	♈24
♂	♐2	2	3	3	3	4	4	5	5	5	6	6	7	7	7	8	8	9	9	9	10	10	10	11	11	11	12	12	12	12	♐13

	1	6	12	18	24	30		1	6	12	18	24	30		1	15	30		1	15	30		1	15	30		1	15	30
♃	♎4	3	2	2	1	0	♄	♈23	23	24	25	25	26	♅	♎3	2	2	♆	♏29	29	28	♇	♍24	24	23	☊	♈0	0	0

APRIL

	1	2	3	4	5	6	7	8	9	10	11	12	13	14	15	16	17	18	19	20	21	22	23	24	25	26	27	28	29	30
☉	♈11	12	13	14	15	16	17	18	19	20	21	22	23	24	25	26	27	28	29	♉0	1	2	3	4	5	6	7	8	9	♉9
☽	♍19	♎2	16	♏0	14	28	♐13	27	♑11	25	♒9	23	♓7	20	♈4	17	♉0	12	25	♊7	19	♋1	13	25	♌7	19	♍1	14	27	♎10
☿	♈3	5	7	9	11	13	15	17	19	21	23	25	27	29	♉2	4	6	8	10	12	14	16	18	19	21	23	25	26	28	♉29
♀	♈23	23	22	21	21	20	20	19	18	18	17	17	16	15	15	14	14	13	13	12	12	12	11	11	11	11	11	11	11	♈10
♂	♐13	13	13	14	14	14	14	15	15	15	15	15	16	16	16	16	16	16	16	16	17	17	17	17	17	17	17	17	17	♐17

	1	6	12	18	24	30		1	6	12	18	24	30		1	15	30		1	15	30		1	15	30		1	15	30
♃	♎0 ♍29	29	28	27	27		♄	♈26	27	28	28	29	♉0	♅	♎2	1	0	♆	♏28	28	28	♇	♍23	23	23	☊	♈0	0	0

MAY

	1	2	3	4	5	6	7	8	9	10	11	12	13	14	15	16	17	18	19	20	21	22	23	24	25	26	27	28	29	30	31
☉	♉10	11	12	13	14	15	16	17	18	19	20	21	22	23	24	25	26	27	28	29	♊0	1	2	3	4	5	6	6	7	8	♊9
☽	♎24	♏8	23	♐8	23	♑7	22	♒6	20	♓4	17	♈0	13	26	♉9	21	♊3	15	27	♋9	21	♌3	15	27	♍9	22	♎5	18	♏2	17	♐2
☿	♊0	2	3	4	5	6	7	8	9	10	10	11	11	11	12	12	12	12	12	12	12	11	11	11	10	10	9	9	8	8	♊7
♀	♈11	11	11	11	11	11	11	12	12	12	13	13	14	14	15	15	16	16	17	17	18	19	19	20	21	21	22	23	23	24	♈25
♂	♐17	17	17	16	16	16	16	16	16	16	16	15	15	15	15	15	14	14	14	14	13	13	13	12	12	12	12	11	11	11	♐10

	1	6	12	18	24	30		1	6	12	18	24	30		1	15	30		1	15	30		1	15	30		1	15	30
♃	♍27	27	26	26	26	26	♄	♉0	1	2	2	3	4	♅	♎0	0	0	♆	♏28	27	27	♇	♍23	22	22	☊	♈0 ♓29	28	

JUNE

	1	2	3	4	5	6	7	8	9	10	11	12	13	14	15	16	17	18	19	20	21	22	23	24	25	26	27	28	29	30
☉	♊10	11	12	13	14	15	16	17	18	19	20	21	22	23	24	25	26	27	28	28	29	♋0	1	2	3	4	5	6	7	♋8
☽	♐17	♑2	17	♒2	16	♓0	14	27	♈10	23	♉6	18	♊0	12	24	♋6	18	♌0	12	24	♍6	18	♎0	13	27	♏11	25	♐10	25	♑10
☿	♊6	6	5	5	5	4	4	4	4	3	3	3	4	4	4	5	5	5	6	7	7	8	9	10	11	12	13	14	16	♊17
♀	♈26	27	27	28	29	♉0	1	2	3	3	4	5	6	7	8	9	10	11	12	13	14	15	16	17	18	19	20	21	22	♉23
♂	♐10	10	9	9	9	8	8	8	7	7	7	6	6	6	5	5	5	4	4	4	4	4	3	3	3	3	3	2	2	♐2

	1	6	12	18	24	30		1	6	12	18	24	30		1	15	30		1	15	30		1	15	30		1	15	30
♃	♍26	26	27	27	28	28	♄	♉4	4	5	6	6	7	♅	♎0	0	0	♆	♏27	27	26	♇	♍22	22	23	☊	♓27	26	24

JULY

	1	2	3	4	5	6	7	8	9	10	11	12	13	14	15	16	17	18	19	20	21	22	23	24	25	26	27	28	29	30	31
☉	♋9	10	11	12	13	14	15	16	17	18	19	19	20	21	22	23	24	25	26	27	28	29	♌0	1	2	3	4	5	6	7	♌8
☽	♑26	♒11	26	♓10	24	♈7	20	♉3	15	27	♊9	21	♋3	15	27	♌9	21	♍3	15	27	♎10	23	♏6	20	♐4	19	♑4	19	♒4	19	♓4
☿	♊18	20	21	23	25	26	28	♋0	2	3	5	7	9	11	13	16	18	20	22	24	26	28	♌0	3	5	7	9	11	13	15	♌17
♀	♉24	25	26	27	28	29	♊0	1	2	3	4	5	6	8	9	10	11	12	13	14	15	16	17	19	20	21	22	23	24	25	♊26
♂	♐2	2	2	2	2	2	2	2	2	2	2	2	2	2	2	2	2	2	2	3	3	3	3	3	4	4	4	4	5	5	♐5

	1	6	12	18	24	30		1	6	12	18	24	30		1	15	30		1	15	30		1	15	30		1	15	30
♃	♍28	29	♎0	0	1	2	♄	♉7	7	8	8	8	9	♅	♎0	0	1	♆	♏26	26	26	♇	♍23	23	23	☊	♓24	23	22

AUGUST

	1	2	3	4	5	6	7	8	9	10	11	12	13	14	15	16	17	18	19	20	21	22	23	24	25	26	27	28	29	30	31
☉	♌9	10	10	11	12	13	14	15	16	17	18	19	20	21	22	23	24	25	26	27	28	29	♍0	1	2	3	4	5	5	6	♍7
☽	♓18	♈2	16	29	♉12	24	♊6	18	♋0	12	24	♌6	18	♍0	12	24	♎7	20	♏3	16	♐0	14	28	♑13	28	♒13	28	♓12	26	♈10	♈24
☿	♌19	21	22	24	26	28	♍0	1	3	5	7	8	10	11	13	14	16	17	19	20	22	23	25	26	27	28	♎0	1	2	3	♎4
♀	♊27	29	♋0	1	2	3	4	5	7	8	9	10	11	12	13	15	16	17	18	19	20	22	23	24	25	26	28	29	♌0	1	♌2
♂	♐5	6	6	6	7	7	7	8	8	8	9	9	10	10	10	11	11	12	12	13	13	13	14	14	15	15	16	16	17	17	♐18

	1	6	12	18	24	30		1	6	12	18	24	30		1	15	30		1	15	30		1	15	30		1	15	30
♃	♎2	3	4	5	7	8	♄	♉9	9	9	9	9	9	♅	♎1	2	3	♆	♏26	26	26	♇	♍23	24	24	☊	♓22	21	21

SEPTEMBER

	1	2	3	4	5	6	7	8	9	10	11	12	13	14	15	16	17	18	19	20	21	22	23	24	25	26	27	28	29	30
☉	♍8	9	10	11	12	13	14	15	16	17	18	19	20	21	22	23	24	25	26	27	28	29	♎0	1	2	3	4	5	6	♎7
☽	♉7	20	♊2	15	27	♋8	20	♌2	14	26	♍9	21	♎4	17	♏0	13	27	♐11	25	♑9	23	♒8	22	♓6	21	♈5	18	♉2	15	♉28
☿	♎5	6	7	8	9	10	11	12	12	13	13	14	14	15	15	15	15	15	15	14	14	13	12	12	11	10	9	8	7	♎5
♀	♌3	5	6	7	8	9	11	12	13	14	15	17	18	19	20	21	23	24	25	26	27	29	♍0	1	2	3	5	6	7	♍8
♂	♐18	19	19	20	21	21	22	22	23	23	24	24	25	26	26	27	27	28	29	29	♑0	0	1	2	2	3	4	4	5	♑5

	1	6	12	18	24	30		1	6	12	18	24	30		1	15	30		1	15	30		1	15	30		1	15	30
♃	♎8	9	10	12	13	14	♄	♉9	9	9	8	8	8	♅	♎3	4	5	♆	♏26	26	27	♇	♍24	25	25	☊	♓21	21	21

OCTOBER

	1	2	3	4	5	6	7	8	9	10	11	12	13	14	15	16	17	18	19	20	21	22	23	24	25	26	27	28	29	30	31
☉	♎8	9	10	11	12	13	14	15	16	17	18	18	19	20	21	22	23	24	25	26	27	28	29	♏0	1	2	3	4	5	6	♏7
☽	♊10	23	♋5	16	28	♌10	22	♍4	17	♎0	13	26	♏9	23	♐7	21	♑6	20	♒4	18	♓2	16	♈0	13	27	♉10	23	♊6	18	♋0	♋12
☿	♎4	3	2	2	1	0	0	0	0	0	0	1	2	2	3	4	6	7	8	10	11	13	14	16	17	19	21	22	24	26	♎27
♀	♍10	11	12	13	14	16	17	18	19	21	22	23	24	26	27	28	29	♎1	2	3	4	5	7	8	9	10	12	13	14	15	♎17
♂	♑6	7	7	8	9	9	10	11	11	12	13	13	14	15	15	16	17	17	18	19	20	20	21	22	22	23	24	24	25	26	♑27

	1	6	12	18	24	30		1	6	12	18	24	30		1	15	30		1	15	30		1	15	30		1	15	30
♃	♎14	16	17	18	19	21	♄	♉8	7	7	6	6	5	♅	♎5	5	6	♆	♏27	27	28	♇	♍25	26	26	☊	♓21	21	20

NOVEMBER

	1	2	3	4	5	6	7	8	9	10	11	12	13	14	15	16	17	18	19	20	21	22	23	24	25	26	27	28	29	30
☉	♏8	9	10	11	12	13	14	15	16	17	18	19	20	21	22	23	24	25	26	27	29	♐0	1	2	3	4	5	6	7	♐8
☽	♋24	♌6	18	♍0	12	25	♎8	21	♏4	18	♐3	17	♑2	16	♒1	15	29	♓13	26	♈10	23	♉6	19	♊2	14	26	♋8	20	♌2	♌14
☿	♎29	♏0	2	4	5	7	9	10	12	14	15	17	18	20	22	23	25	26	28	♐0	1	3	4	6	7	9	11	12	14	♐15
♀	♎18	19	20	22	23	24	25	27	28	29	♏0	2	3	4	5	7	8	9	10	12	13	14	15	17	18	19	20	22	23	♏24
♂	♑27	28	29	29	♒0	1	2	2	3	4	4	5	6	7	7	8	9	10	10	11	12	13	13	14	15	15	16	17	18	♒18

	1	6	12	18	24	30		1	6	12	18	24	30		1	15	30		1	15	30		1	15	30		1	15	30
♃	♎21	22	23	25	26	27	♄	♉5	5	4	4	4	3	♅	♎6	7	8	♆	♏28	28	29	♇	♍26	27	27	☊	♓20	19	17

DECEMBER

	1	2	3	4	5	6	7	8	9	10	11	12	13	14	15	16	17	18	19	20	21	22	23	24	25	26	27	28	29	30	31
☉	♐9	10	11	12	13	14	15	16	17	18	19	20	21	22	23	24	25	26	27	28	29	♑0	1	2	3	4	5	6	7	8	♑9
☽	♌26	♍8	20	♎2	15	29	♏12	27	♐11	26	♑11	26	♒11	25	♓9	23	♈7	20	♉3	16	28	♊11	23	♋5	17	29	♌11	22	♍4	16	♍28
☿	♐17	18	20	21	23	25	26	28	29	♑1	2	4	5	7	8	10	11	13	14	16	17	18	20	21	22	24	25	26	27	28	♑28
♀	♏25	27	28	29	♐0	2	3	4	6	7	8	9	11	12	13	14	16	17	18	19	21	22	23	24	26	27	28	29	♑1	2	♑3
♂	♒19	20	21	21	22	23	24	24	25	26	27	27	28	29	♓0	0	1	2	3	3	4	5	6	6	7	8	9	9	10	11	♓11

	1	6	12	18	24	30		1	6	12	18	24	30		1	15	30		1	15	30		1	15	30		1	15	30
♃	♎27	28	29	♏0	1	2	♄	♉3	3	3	2	2	2	♅	♎8	8	9	♆	♏29	29	♐29	♇	♍27	27	27	☊	♓17	16	14

1970

JANUARY

	1	2	3	4	5	6	7	8	9	10	11	12	13	14	15	16	17	18	19	20	21	22	23	24	25	26	27	28	29	30	31
☉	♑10	11	12	13	14	15	16	17	18	19	20	21	22	23	24	25	26	27	28	♒0	1	2	3	4	5	6	7	8	9	10	♒11
☽	♎11	23	♏7	20	♐4	19	♑4	19	♒5	20	♓5	19	♈3	17	♉0	13	25	♊8	20	♋2	14	26	♌8	19	♍1	13	25	♎7	20	♏2	♏15
☿	♑29	♒0	0	0	0	0	♑29	29	28	27	26	25	23	22	21	19	18	17	16	15	15	14	14	14	14	14	14	15	15	16	♑16
♀	♑4	6	7	8	9	11	12	13	15	16	17	18	20	21	22	23	25	26	27	28	♒0	1	2	3	5	6	7	8	10	11	♒12
♂	♓12	13	14	14	15	16	17	17	18	19	20	20	21	22	23	23	24	25	26	26	27	28	29	29	♈0	1	2	2	3	4	♈5

♃ 1	6	12	18	24	30	♄ 1	6	12	18	24	30	♅ 1	15	30	♆ 1	15	30	♇ 1	15	30	☊ 1	15	30
♏2	3	4	4	5	5	♉2	2	2	2	2	3	♎9	9	9	♐0	0	1	♍27	27	27	♓14	13	12

FEBRUARY

	1	2	3	4	5	6	7	8	9	10	11	12	13	14	15	16	17	18	19	20	21	22	23	24	25	26	27	28
☉	♒12	13	14	15	16	17	18	19	20	21	22	23	24	25	26	27	28	29	♓0	1	2	3	4	5	6	7	8	♓9
☽	♏29	♐13	27	♑12	27	♒12	28	♓13	27	♈12	26	♉9	22	♊4	17	29	♋11	23	♌4	16	28	♍10	22	♎4	17	29	♏12	♏25
☿	♑17	18	18	19	20	21	22	23	25	26	27	28	29	♒1	2	3	5	6	7	9	10	12	13	14	16	18	19	♒21
♀	♒13	15	16	17	18	20	21	22	23	25	26	27	28	♓0	1	2	3	5	6	7	8	10	11	12	13	15	16	♓17
♂	♈5	6	7	7	8	9	10	10	11	12	13	13	14	15	16	16	17	18	18	19	20	21	21	22	23	23	24	♈25

♃ 1	6	12	18	24	28	♄ 1	6	12	18	24	28	♅ 1	15	28	♆ 1	15	28	♇ 1	15	28	☊ 1	15	28
♏5	6	6	6	6	6	♉3	3	3	4	4	5	♎9	8	8	♐1	1	1	♍27	27	27	♓12	12	12

MARCH

	1	2	3	4	5	6	7	8	9	10	11	12	13	14	15	16	17	18	19	20	21	22	23	24	25	26	27	28	29	30	31
☉	♓10	11	12	13	14	15	16	17	18	19	20	21	22	23	24	25	26	27	28	29	♈0	1	2	3	4	5	6	7	8	9	♈10
☽	♐9	22	♑7	21	♒6	21	♓6	21	♈5	20	♉4	17	♊0	13	25	♋7	19	♌1	13	25	♍7	19	♎1	14	26	♏9	22	♐6	19	♑3	♑17
☿	♒22	24	25	27	29	♓0	2	4	5	7	9	11	12	14	16	18	20	22	24	25	27	29	♈1	3	5	7	9	11	13	16	♈18
♀	♓18	20	21	22	23	25	26	27	28	♈0	1	2	3	5	6	7	8	10	11	12	13	15	16	17	18	20	21	22	23	25	♈26
♂	♈26	26	27	28	29	29	♉0	1	1	2	3	4	4	5	6	6	7	8	9	9	10	11	11	12	13	13	14	15	16	16	♉17

♃ 1	6	12	18	24	30	♄ 1	6	12	18	24	30	♅ 1	15	30	♆ 1	15	30	♇ 1	15	30	☊ 1	15	30
♏6	6	5	5	4	4	♉5	5	6	7	7	8	♎8	7	7	♐1	1	1	♍26	26	26	♓12	12	12

APRIL

	1	2	3	4	5	6	7	8	9	10	11	12	13	14	15	16	17	18	19	20	21	22	23	24	25	26	27	28	29	30
☉	♈11	12	13	14	15	16	17	18	19	20	21	22	23	24	25	26	27	28	29	♉0	0	1	2	3	4	5	6	7	8	♉9
☽	♒1	15	♓0	15	29	♈13	28	♉12	25	♊8	21	♋3	15	27	♌9	21	♍3	15	27	♎10	22	♏5	19	♐2	16	♑0	14	28	♒12	♒26
☿	♈20	22	24	26	27	29	♉1	3	5	7	8	10	11	13	14	15	16	17	18	19	20	21	21	22	22	22	22	22	22	♉22
♀	♈27	28	29	♉1	2	3	4	6	7	8	9	11	12	13	14	15	17	18	19	20	22	23	24	25	27	28	29	♊0	1	♊3
♂	♉18	18	19	20	20	21	22	23	23	24	25	25	26	27	27	28	29	29	♊0	1	2	2	3	4	4	5	6	6	7	♊8

♃ 1	6	12	18	24	30	♄ 1	6	12	18	24	30	♅ 1	15	30	♆ 1	15	30	♇ 1	15	30	☊ 1	15	30
♏4	3	2	2	1	0	♉8	9	9	10	11	12	♎7	6	5	♐1	0	0	♍26	25	25	♓12	11	10

MAY

	1	2	3	4	5	6	7	8	9	10	11	12	13	14	15	16	17	18	19	20	21	22	23	24	25	26	27	28	29	30	31
☉	♉10	11	12	13	14	15	16	17	18	19	20	21	22	23	24	25	26	27	28	29	♊0	0	1	2	3	4	5	6	7	8	♊9
☽	♓10	24	♈8	22	♉6	20	♊3	16	29	♋11	23	♌5	17	29	♍11	23	♎5	18	♏1	14	28	♐12	26	♑10	24	♒9	23	♓7	21	♈5	♈19
☿	♉22	22	22	21	21	20	20	19	19	18	17	17	16	16	15	15	14	14	14	13	13	13	13	13	14	14	14	14	15	15	♉16
♀	♊4	5	6	7	9	10	11	12	14	15	16	17	18	20	21	22	23	24	26	27	28	29	♋0	2	3	4	5	6	8	9	♋10
♂	♊8	9	10	10	11	12	12	13	14	14	15	16	16	17	18	18	19	20	20	21	22	22	23	24	24	25	26	26	27	28	♊28

♃ 1	6	12	18	24	30	♄ 1	6	12	18	24	30	♅ 1	15	30	♆ 1	15	30	♇ 1	15	30	☊ 1	15	30
♏0	♎29	29	28	27	27	♉12	13	13	14	15	16	♎5	5	5	♐0	0	♏0	♍25	25	25	♓10	9	7

JUNE

	1	2	3	4	5	6	7	8	9	10	11	12	13	14	15	16	17	18	19	20	21	22	23	24	25	26	27	28	29	30
☉	♊10	11	12	13	14	15	16	17	18	19	20	21	22	23	23	24	25	26	27	28	29	♋0	1	2	3	4	5	6	7	♋8
☽	♉2	16	29	♊12	25	♋7	19	♌1	13	25	♍7	19	♎1	13	26	♏9	22	♐6	20	♑5	20	♒4	19	♓3	18	♈2	16	29	♉12	♉25
☿	♉17	17	18	19	20	21	22	23	24	25	27	28	29	♊1	2	4	5	7	8	10	12	14	15	17	19	21	23	25	27	♊29
♀	♋11	12	14	15	16	17	18	20	21	22	23	24	26	27	28	29	♌0	1	3	4	5	6	7	9	10	11	12	13	14	♌16
♂	♊29	♋0	0	1	2	2	3	4	4	5	6	6	7	8	8	9	10	10	11	12	12	13	14	14	15	16	16	17	18	♋18

♃ 1	6	12	18	24	30	♄ 1	6	12	18	24	30	♅ 1	15	30	♆ 1	15	30	♇ 1	15	30	☊ 1	15	30
♎27	27	26	26	26	26	♉16	16	17	18	18	19	♎5	5	5	♏29	29	29	♍25	25	25	♓7	6	5

JULY

	1	2	3	4	5	6	7	8	9	10	11	12	13	14	15	16	17	18	19	20	21	22	23	24	25	26	27	28	29	30	31
☉	♋9	10	11	12	13	14	14	15	16	17	18	19	20	21	22	23	24	25	26	27	28	29	♌0	1	2	3	4	5	5	6	♌7
☽	♊8	21	♋3	16	28	♌10	22	♍3	15	27	♎9	21	♏4	17	♐0	14	29	♑13	28	♒13	28	♓13	28	♈12	26	♉9	23	♊5	18	♋0	♋13
☿	♋2	4	6	8	10	12	15	17	19	21	23	25	27	29	♌1	3	5	7	9	11	13	15	16	18	20	22	23	25	27	28	♍0
♀	♌17	18	19	20	21	23	24	25	26	27	28	29	♍1	2	3	4	5	6	7	9	10	11	12	13	14	15	16	17	19	20	♍21
♂	♋19	19	20	21	21	22	23	23	24	25	25	26	27	27	28	29	29	♌0	0	1	2	2	3	4	4	5	6	6	7	8	♌8

♃ 1	6	12	18	24	30	♄ 1	6	12	18	24	30	♅ 1	15	30	♆ 1	15	30	♇ 1	15	30	☊ 1	15	30
♎26	26	27	27	27	28	♉19	20	20	21	21	21	♎5	5	6	♏29	28	28	♍25	25	25	♓4	4	3

AUGUST

	1	2	3	4	5	6	7	8	9	10	11	12	13	14	15	16	17	18	19	20	21	22	23	24	25	26	27	28	29	30	31
☉	♌8	9	10	11	12	13	14	15	16	17	18	19	20	21	22	23	24	25	26	27	28	28	29	♍0	1	2	3	4	5	6	♍7
☽	♋25	♌7	18	♍0	12	24	♎6	18	♏0	13	26	♐9	23	♑7	22	♒7	22	♓7	22	♈7	21	♉5	19	♊2	15	27	♋10	22	♌4	15	♌27
☿	♍1	3	4	6	7	8	10	11	12	13	15	16	17	18	19	20	21	22	23	24	24	25	26	26	27	27	28	28	28	28	♍28
♀	♍22	23	24	25	26	27	28	♎0	1	2	3	4	5	6	7	8	9	10	11	12	13	14	15	16	17	18	19	20	21	22	♎23
♂	♌9	9	10	11	11	12	13	13	14	15	15	16	16	17	18	18	19	20	20	21	22	22	23	24	24	25	25	26	27	27	♌28

♃ 1	6	12	18	24	30	♄ 1	6	12	18	24	30	♅ 1	15	30	♆ 1	15	30	♇ 1	15	30	☊ 1	15	30
♎28	29	29	♏0	1	2	♉22	22	22	22	23	23	♎6	6	7	♏28	28	28	♍26	26	26	♓3	3	3

SEPTEMBER

	1	2	3	4	5	6	7	8	9	10	11	12	13	14	15	16	17	18	19	20	21	22	23	24	25	26	27	28	29	30
☉	♍8	9	10	11	12	13	14	15	16	17	18	19	20	21	22	23	24	25	26	27	28	29	♎0	1	2	2	3	4	5	♎6
☽	♍9	21	♎3	15	27	♏9	22	♐5	18	♑2	16	♒0	15	♓0	15	♈0	15	♉0	14	28	♊11	24	♋6	19	♌1	12	24	♍6	18	♎0
☿	♍28	28	27	27	26	26	25	24	23	22	21	20	19	18	17	17	16	15	15	14	14	14	14	14	15	15	16	17	18	♍19
♀	♎24	25	26	27	28	29	♏0	1	2	3	4	4	5	6	7	8	9	9	10	11	12	13	13	14	15	15	16	17	17	♏18
♂	♌29	29	♍0	1	1	2	2	3	4	4	5	6	6	7	7	8	9	9	10	11	11	12	13	13	14	14	15	16	16	♍17

♃ 1	6	12	18	24	30	♄ 1	6	12	18	24	30	♅ 1	15	30	♆ 1	15	30	♇ 1	15	30	☊ 1	15	30
♏2	3	4	6	7	8	♉23	23	23	22	22	22	♎7	8	9	♏28	28	29	♍27	27	28	♓3	3	3

OCTOBER

	1	2	3	4	5	6	7	8	9	10	11	12	13	14	15	16	17	18	19	20	21	22	23	24	25	26	27	28	29	30	31
☉	♎7	8	9	10	11	12	13	14	15	16	17	18	19	20	21	22	23	24	25	26	27	28	29	♏0	1	2	3	4	5	6	♏7
☽	♎12	24	♏6	19	♐2	15	28	♑12	26	♒10	24	♓9	24	♈9	23	♉8	22	♊6	19	♋2	15	27	♌9	21	♍2	14	26	♎8	21	♏3	♏16
☿	♍20	21	23	24	26	27	29	♎0	2	4	6	7	9	11	12	14	16	18	19	21	23	25	26	28	♏0	1	3	5	6	8	♏9
♀	♏19	19	20	20	21	21	22	22	23	23	23	24	24	24	25	25	25	25	25	25	25	25	25	25	25	25	24	24	24	23	♏23
♂	♍18	18	19	20	20	21	21	22	23	23	24	25	25	26	27	27	28	28	29	♎0	0	1	2	2	3	4	4	5	5	6	♎7

♃ 1	6	12	18	24	30	♄ 1	6	12	18	24	30	♅ 1	15	30	♆ 1	15	30	♇ 1	15	30	☊ 1	15	30
♏8	9	10	12	13	14	♉22	22	21	21	21	20	♎9	10	11	♏29	29	♐29	♍28	28	29	♓3	2	1

NOVEMBER

	1	2	3	4	5	6	7	8	9	10	11	12	13	14	15	16	17	18	19	20	21	22	23	24	25	26	27	28	29	30
☉	♏8	9	10	11	12	13	14	15	16	17	18	19	20	21	22	23	24	25	26	27	28	29	♐0	1	2	3	4	5	6	♐7
☽	♏29	♐12	25	♑9	22	♒6	20	♓4	19	♈3	18	♉2	16	♊0	14	27	♋10	23	♌5	17	29	♍10	22	♎4	16	29	♏11	24	♐8	♐21
☿	♏11	13	14	16	17	19	21	22	24	25	27	28	♐0	1	3	5	6	8	9	11	12	14	15	17	18	19	21	22	24	♐25
♀	♏23	22	22	21	21	20	20	19	18	18	17	17	16	15	15	14	14	13	13	12	12	11	11	11	10	10	10	10	10	♏10
♂	♎7	8	9	9	10	11	11	12	13	13	14	15	15	16	16	17	17	18	19	19	20	21	21	22	23	23	24	24	25	♎26

♃ 1	6	12	18	24	30	♄ 1	6	12	18	24	30	♅ 1	15	30	♆ 1	15	30	♇ 1	15	30	☊ 1	15	30
♏15	16	17	18	20	21	♉20	20	19	19	18	18	♎11	12	12	♐0	0	1	♍29	29	29	♓0	♒0	27

DECEMBER

	1	2	3	4	5	6	7	8	9	10	11	12	13	14	15	16	17	18	19	20	21	22	23	24	25	26	27	28	29	30	31
☉	♐8	9	10	11	12	13	14	15	16	18	19	20	21	22	23	24	25	26	27	28	29	♑0	1	2	3	4	5	6	7	8	♑9
☽	♑5	19	♒3	17	♓1	15	29	♈13	27	♉11	25	♊9	22	♋5	18	♌0	13	25	♍6	18	♎0	12	24	♏7	19	♐3	16	♑0	14	29	♒13
☿	♐27	28	29	♑1	2	3	5	6	7	8	9	10	11	12	13	13	14	14	14	14	14	13	13	12	11	10	9	7	6	5	♑3
♀	♏10	10	10	10	10	10	10	11	11	11	12	12	12	13	13	14	14	15	16	16	17	17	18	19	19	20	21	22	22	23	♏24
♂	♎26	27	28	28	29	♏0	0	1	1	2	3	3	4	5	5	6	7	7	8	8	9	10	10	11	12	12	13	14	14	15	♏15

♃ 1	6	12	18	24	30	♄ 1	6	12	18	24	30	♅ 1	15	30	♆ 1	15	30	♇ 1	15	30	☊ 1	15	30
♏21	22	24	25	26	27	♉18	17	17	17	16	16	♎13	13	13	♐1	1	2	♍29	♎29	0	♒27	25	24

1971

JANUARY

	1	2	3	4	5	6	7	8	9	10	11	12	13	14	15	16	17	18	19	20	21	22	23	24	25	26	27	28	29	30	31
☉	♑10	11	12	13	14	15	16	17	18	19	20	21	22	23	24	25	26	27	28	29	♒0	1	2	3	4	5	6	7	8	9	♒10
☽	♒28	♓12	26	♈10	24	♉8	22	♊5	18	♋1	14	26	♌8	21	♍2	14	26	♎8	20	♏2	14	27	♐10	24	♑8	22	♒7	22	♓7	22	♈6
☿	♑2	1	0	♐29	29	28	28	28	28	28	28	29	29	♑0	1	1	2	3	4	5	6	7	9	10	11	12	13	15	16	17	♑19
♀	♏25	26	26	27	28	29	♐0	1	2	3	4	5	6	6	7	8	9	10	11	12	13	14	15	17	18	19	20	21	22	23	♐24
♂	♏16	17	17	18	19	19	20	20	21	22	22	23	24	24	25	26	26	27	27	28	29	29	♐0	1	1	2	2	3	4	4	♐5

	1	6	12	18	24	30
♃	♏28	29	♐0	1	2	2
♄	♉16	16	16	16	16	16

	1	15	30
♅	♎13	14	14
♆	♐2	2	3
♇	♎0	0	♍0
☊	♒24	24	24

FEBRUARY

	1	2	3	4	5	6	7	8	9	10	11	12	13	14	15	16	17	18	19	20	21	22	23	24	25	26	27	28
☉	♒11	12	14	15	16	17	18	19	20	21	22	23	24	25	26	27	28	29	♓0	1	2	3	4	5	6	7	8	♓9
☽	♈21	♉5	18	♊2	15	28	♋10	23	♌5	17	29	♍11	23	♎5	16	28	♏10	23	♐5	18	♑2	16	♒0	15	♓0	15	♈0	♈15
☿	♑20	22	23	24	26	27	29	♒0	2	3	5	6	8	9	11	13	14	16	17	19	21	22	24	26	28	29	♓1	♓3
♀	♐25	26	27	28	29	♑0	2	3	4	5	6	7	8	9	10	12	13	14	15	16	17	18	20	21	22	23	24	♑25
♂	♐6	6	7	7	8	9	9	10	11	11	12	12	13	14	14	15	16	16	17	17	18	19	19	20	21	21	22	♐22

	1	6	12	18	24	28
♃	♐3	3	4	5	5	6
♄	♉16	16	16	17	17	17

	1	15	28
♅	♎13	13	13
♆	♐3	3	3
♇	♍29	29	29
☊	♒24	24	24

MARCH

	1	2	3	4	5	6	7	8	9	10	11	12	13	14	15	16	17	18	19	20	21	22	23	24	25	26	27	28	29	30	31
☉	♓10	11	12	13	14	15	16	17	18	19	20	21	22	23	24	25	26	27	28	29	♈0	1	2	3	4	5	6	7	8	9	♈10
☽	♉0	14	28	♊12	25	♋7	20	♌2	14	26	♍8	20	♎1	13	25	♏7	19	♐2	15	27	♑11	24	♒9	23	♓8	23	♈8	24	♉9	23	♊7
☿	♓5	7	8	10	12	14	16	18	20	22	24	26	28	♈0	2	4	6	7	9	11	13	15	17	18	20	22	23	25	26	27	♈28
♀	♑26	28	29	♒0	1	2	3	5	6	7	8	9	10	12	13	14	15	16	17	19	20	21	22	23	25	26	27	28	29	♓0	♓2
♂	♐23	24	24	25	25	26	27	27	28	29	29	♑0	0	1	2	2	3	3	4	5	5	6	6	7	8	8	9	9	10	11	♑11

	1	6	12	18	24	30
♃	♐6	6	6	6	6	6
♄	♉17	18	18	19	19	20

	1	15	30
♅	♎13	12	12
♆	♐3	3	3
♇	♍29	28	28
☊	♒24	23	23

APRIL

	1	2	3	4	5	6	7	8	9	10	11	12	13	14	15	16	17	18	19	20	21	22	23	24	25	26	27	28	29	30
☉	♈11	12	13	14	15	16	17	18	18	19	20	21	22	23	24	25	26	27	28	29	♉0	1	2	3	4	5	6	7	8	♉9
☽	♊21	♋4	17	29	♌11	23	♍5	17	28	♎10	22	♏4	17	29	♐11	24	♑7	21	♒4	18	♓2	17	♈2	17	♉2	17	♊1	15	29	♋12
☿	♈29	♉0	1	2	3	3	3	4	4	4	4	3	3	3	2	2	1	1	0	♈29	29	28	27	26	26	25	25	24	24	♈24
♀	♓3	4	5	6	8	9	10	11	12	14	15	16	17	18	20	21	22	23	24	26	27	28	29	♈0	2	3	4	5	6	♈8
♂	♑12	12	13	13	14	15	15	16	16	17	17	18	19	19	20	20	21	21	22	23	23	24	24	25	25	26	26	27	27	♑28

	1	6	12	18	24	30
♃	♐6	6	6	5	5	4
♄	♉20	21	21	22	23	24

	1	15	30
♅	♎12	11	10
♆	♐3	3	2
♇	♍28	28	27
☊	♒22	21	20

MAY

	1	2	3	4	5	6	7	8	9	10	11	12	13	14	15	16	17	18	19	20	21	22	23	24	25	26	27	28	29	30	31
☉	♉10	11	12	13	14	15	16	17	18	19	20	21	22	23	24	24	25	26	27	28	29	♊0	1	2	3	4	5	6	7	8	♊9
☽	♋25	♌7	20	♍1	13	25	♎7	19	♏1	13	26	♐8	21	♑4	18	♒1	15	28	♓13	27	♈11	26	♉11	25	♊9	23	♋7	20	♌3	15	♌28
☿	♈23	23	23	23	23	23	24	24	24	25	25	26	27	27	28	29	♉0	1	2	3	4	5	6	8	9	10	12	13	14	16	♉18
♀	♈9	10	11	12	14	15	16	17	18	20	21	22	23	25	26	27	28	29	♉1	2	3	4	5	7	8	9	10	11	13	14	♉15
♂	♑28	29	♒0	0	1	1	2	2	3	3	4	4	5	5	6	6	7	7	7	8	8	9	9	10	10	11	11	11	12	12	♒13

	1	6	12	18	24	30
♃	♐4	4	3	2	2	1
♄	♉24	24	25	26	27	28

	1	15	30
♅	♎10	10	10
♆	♐2	2	2
♇	♍27	27	27
☊	♒20	18	17

JUNE

	1	2	3	4	5	6	7	8	9	10	11	12	13	14	15	16	17	18	19	20	21	22	23	24	25	26	27	28	29	30
☉	♊10	11	12	13	14	15	16	17	18	18	19	20	21	22	23	24	25	26	27	28	29	♋0	1	2	3	4	5	6	7	♋8
☽	♍10	21	♎3	15	27	♏9	22	♐5	17	♑1	14	28	♒11	25	♓9	23	♈8	22	♉6	20	♊4	18	♋2	15	28	♌11	23	♍5	17	♍29
☿	♉19	21	22	24	26	28	29	♊1	3	5	7	9	11	13	15	18	20	22	24	26	28	♋1	3	5	7	9	11	14	16	♋18
♀	♉16	18	19	20	21	22	24	25	26	27	28	♊0	1	2	3	5	6	7	8	9	11	12	13	14	15	17	18	19	20	♊22
♂	♒13	13	14	14	15	15	15	16	16	16	17	17	17	18	18	18	18	19	19	19	19	20	20	20	20	21	21	21	21	♒21

	1	6	12	18	24	30
♃	♐1	0	♏29	29	28	28
♄	♉28	28	29	♊0	1	1

	1	15	30
♅	♎10	9	10
♆	♐1	1	1
♇	♍27	27	27
☊	♒17	16	15

JULY

	1	2	3	4	5	6	7	8	9	10	11	12	13	14	15	16	17	18	19	20	21	22	23	24	25	26	27	28	29	30	31
☉	♋9	9	10	11	12	13	14	15	16	17	18	19	20	21	22	23	24	25	26	27	28	29	♌0	0	1	2	3	4	5	6	♌7
☽	♎11	23	♏5	17	♐0	13	26	♑10	23	♒7	22	♓6	20	♈4	19	♉3	17	♊1	14	28	♋11	24	♌7	19	♍1	14	25	♎7	19	♏1	♏13
☿	♋20	22	24	26	27	29	♌1	3	5	6	8	10	11	13	14	16	17	19	20	22	23	24	26	27	28	29	♍0	1	2	3	♍4
♀	♊23	24	25	26	28	29	♋0	1	3	4	5	6	7	9	10	11	12	14	15	16	17	18	20	21	22	23	25	26	27	28	♌0
♂	♒21	21	22	22	22	22	22	22	22	22	22	22	22	22	22	22	22	22	22	21	21	21	21	21	21	21	20	20	20	20	♒20

	1	6	12	18	24	30
♃	♏27	27	27	27	27	27
♄	♊1	2	3	3	4	4

	1	15	30
♅	♎10	10	10
♆	♐1	1	0
♇	♍27	27	28
☊	♒15	15	15

AUGUST

	1	2	3	4	5	6	7	8	9	10	11	12	13	14	15	16	17	18	19	20	21	22	23	24	25	26	27	28	29	30	31
☉	♌8	9	10	11	12	13	14	15	16	17	18	19	20	21	22	22	23	24	25	26	27	28	29	♍0	1	2	3	4	5	6	♍7
☽	♏25	♐8	21	♑4	18	♒2	16	♓1	16	♈0	15	29	♉14	28	♊11	25	♋8	21	♌3	16	28	♍10	22	♎4	16	27	♏9	21	♐4	16	♐29
☿	♍5	6	7	7	8	9	9	10	10	10	10	11	11	10	10	10	10	9	9	8	8	7	6	5	4	3	2	2	1	0	♌29
♀	♌1	2	3	4	6	7	8	9	11	12	13	14	16	17	18	19	20	22	23	24	25	27	28	29	♍0	2	3	4	5	7	♍8
♂	♒19	19	19	19	18	18	18	18	17	17	17	17	16	16	16	16	15	15	15	15	14	14	14	14	13	13	13	13	13	13	♒12

	1	6	12	18	24	30
♃	♏27	27	27	27	28	29
♄	♊4	5	5	6	6	6

	1	15	30
♅	♎10	11	12
♆	♐0	0	0
♇	♍28	28	29
☊	♒15	15	14

SEPTEMBER

	1	2	3	4	5	6	7	8	9	10	11	12	13	14	15	16	17	18	19	20	21	22	23	24	25	26	27	28	29	30
☉	♍8	9	10	11	12	13	14	15	16	17	18	19	20	21	22	22	23	24	25	26	27	28	29	♎0	1	2	3	4	5	♎6
☽	♑12	26	♒10	25	♓9	24	♈10	25	♉9	24	♊8	21	♋5	18	♌0	13	25	♍7	19	♎1	12	24	♏6	18	♐0	12	25	♑8	21	♒4
☿	♌29	28	28	27	27	27	28	28	28	29	♍0	1	2	3	4	5	7	8	10	11	13	15	17	18	20	22	24	26	27	♍29
♀	♍9	10	12	13	14	15	17	18	19	20	21	23	24	25	26	28	29	♎0	1	3	4	5	6	8	9	10	11	13	14	♎15
♂	♒12	12	12	12	12	12	12	12	12	12	12	12	12	12	12	12	12	12	12	13	13	13	13	13	13	14	14	14	14	♒15

	1	6	12	18	24	30
♃	♏29	29	♐0	1	2	3
♄	♊6	6	6	7	7	6

	1	15	30
♅	♎12	13	13
♆	♐0	1	1
♇	♍29	29	♎29
☊	♒14	14	13

OCTOBER

	1	2	3	4	5	6	7	8	9	10	11	12	13	14	15	16	17	18	19	20	21	22	23	24	25	26	27	28	29	30	31
☉	♎7	8	9	10	11	12	13	14	15	16	17	18	19	20	21	22	23	24	25	26	27	28	29	♏0	1	2	3	4	5	6	♏7
☽	♒18	♓3	18	♈3	18	♉3	18	♊3	17	♋1	14	27	♌10	22	♍4	16	28	♎9	21	♏3	15	27	♐9	22	♑4	17	♒0	13	27	♓11	♓26
☿	♎1	3	5	7	8	10	12	14	15	17	19	20	22	24	25	27	29	♏0	2	4	5	7	8	10	12	13	15	16	18	19	♏21
♀	♎16	18	19	20	21	23	24	25	26	28	29	♏0	1	3	4	5	6	8	9	10	11	13	14	15	16	18	19	20	21	22	♏24
♂	♒15	15	15	16	16	16	17	17	17	18	18	18	19	19	20	20	20	21	21	22	22	22	23	23	24	24	25	25	26	26	♒27

	1	6	12	18	24	30
♃	♐3	4	5	6	7	8
♄	♊6	6	6	6	5	5

	1	15	30
♅	♎14	14	15
♆	♐1	1	2
♇	♎0	0	1
☊	♒13	12	10

NOVEMBER

	1	2	3	4	5	6	7	8	9	10	11	12	13	14	15	16	17	18	19	20	21	22	23	24	25	26	27	28	29	30
☉	♏8	9	10	11	12	13	14	15	16	17	18	19	20	21	22	23	24	25	26	27	28	29	♐0	1	2	3	4	5	6	♐7
☽	♈11	26	♉11	27	♊11	26	♋10	23	♌6	18	♍1	13	25	♎6	18	♏0	12	24	♐6	19	♑1	14	27	♒10	23	♓7	21	♈5	20	♉5
☿	♏22	24	25	27	28	♐0	1	2	4	5	7	8	9	11	12	13	15	16	17	19	20	21	22	23	24	25	26	26	27	♐28
♀	♏25	26	27	29	♐0	1	2	4	5	6	7	9	10	11	12	14	15	16	17	19	20	21	22	24	25	26	27	29	♑0	♑1
♂	♒27	28	28	29	29	♓0	0	1	1	2	2	3	3	4	5	5	6	6	7	7	8	9	9	10	10	11	12	12	13	♓13

	1	6	12	18	24	30
♃	♐9	10	11	12	14	15
♄	♊5	5	4	4	3	3

	1	15	30
♅	♎15	16	17
♆	♐2	2	3
♇	♎1	1	2
☊	♒10	9	7

DECEMBER

	1	2	3	4	5	6	7	8	9	10	11	12	13	14	15	16	17	18	19	20	21	22	23	24	25	26	27	28	29	30	31
☉	♐8	9	10	11	12	13	14	15	16	17	18	19	20	21	22	23	24	25	26	27	28	29	♑0	2	3	4	5	6	7	8	♑9
☽	♉20	♊5	19	♋4	18	♌1	14	27	♍9	21	♎3	15	27	♏8	21	♐3	15	28	♑11	24	♒7	20	♓4	18	♈2	16	♉0	15	29	♊13	♊28
☿	♐28	28	28	28	28	28	27	26	25	24	23	21	20	19	17	16	15	14	13	13	12	12	12	12	12	13	13	14	15	15	♐16
♀	♑2	4	5	6	7	9	10	11	12	14	15	16	17	19	20	21	22	23	25	26	27	28	♒0	1	2	3	5	6	7	8	♒10
♂	♓14	15	15	16	16	17	18	18	19	19	20	21	21	22	23	23	24	24	25	26	26	27	28	28	29	♈0	0	1	1	2	♈3

	1	6	12	18	24	30
♃	♐15	16	18	19	21	22
♄	♊3	2	2	1	1	1

	1	15	30
♅	♎17	18	18
♆	♐3	4	4
♇	♎2	2	2
☊	♒7	6	5

1972

JANUARY

	1	2	3	4	5	6	7	8	9	10	11	12	13	14	15	16	17	18	19	20	21	22	23	24	25	26	27	28	29	30	31
☉	♑10	11	12	13	14	15	16	17	18	19	20	21	22	23	24	25	26	27	28	29	♒0	1	2	3	4	5	6	7	8	9	♒10
☽	♋12	25	♌9	22	♍4	17	29	♎11	23	♏4	16	28	♐11	23	♑6	19	♒3	16	♓0	14	28	♈13	27	♉11	25	♊9	23	♋7	20	♌4	♌17
☿	♐17	18	19	20	21	23	24	25	26	28	29	♑0	2	3	4	6	7	9	10	12	13	15	16	18	19	21	22	24	25	27	♑28
♀	♒11	12	13	14	16	17	18	19	21	22	23	24	26	27	28	29	♓0	2	3	4	5	7	8	9	10	11	13	14	15	16	♓17
♂	♈3	4	5	5	6	7	7	8	9	9	10	11	11	12	12	13	14	14	15	16	16	17	18	18	19	20	20	21	22	22	♈23

	1	6	12	18	24	30
♃	♐22	23	25	26	27	28
♄	♊0	0	0	0	0	0

	1	15	30
♅	♎18	18	18
♆	♐4	5	5
♇	♎2	2	2
☊	♒5	5	5

FEBRUARY

	1	2	3	4	5	6	7	8	9	10	11	12	13	14	15	16	17	18	19	20	21	22	23	24	25	26	27	28	29
☉	♒11	12	13	14	15	16	17	18	19	20	21	22	23	24	25	26	27	28	29	♓0	1	2	3	4	5	6	7	9	♓10
☽	♍0	12	24	♎6	18	♏0	12	24	♐6	19	♑1	14	27	♒11	25	♓9	24	♈9	23	♉8	22	♊6	20	♋3	17	♌0	13	25	♍8
☿	♒0	2	3	5	7	8	10	11	13	15	17	18	20	22	24	25	27	29	♓1	3	5	6	8	10	12	14	16	18	♓20
♀	♓19	20	21	22	24	25	26	27	28	29	♈1	2	3	4	5	7	8	9	10	11	13	14	15	16	17	18	20	21	♈22
♂	♈24	24	25	26	26	27	28	28	29	♉0	0	1	2	2	3	4	4	5	6	6	7	8	8	9	10	10	11	11	♉12

	1	6	12	18	24	29
♃	♐29	♑0	1	2	3	4
♄	♊0	0	0	0	0	0

	1	15	29
♅	♎18	18	18
♆	♐5	5	5
♇	♎2	2	1
☊	♒5	5	5

MARCH

	1	2	3	4	5	6	7	8	9	10	11	12	13	14	15	16	17	18	19	20	21	22	23	24	25	26	27	28	29	30	31
☉	♓11	12	13	14	15	16	17	18	19	20	21	22	23	24	25	26	27	27	28	29	♈0	1	2	3	4	5	6	7	8	9	♈10
☽	♍20	♎3	15	27	♏8	20	♐2	14	26	♑9	22	♒5	19	♓3	18	♈3	18	♉3	18	♊2	16	♋0	14	27	♌10	22	♍5	17	29	♎11	♎23
☿	♓21	23	25	27	29	♈1	2	4	5	7	8	10	11	12	13	14	14	15	15	16	16	16	16	16	15	15	14	14	13	12	♈11
♀	♈23	24	25	26	28	29	♉0	1	2	3	4	5	7	8	9	10	11	12	13	14	15	16	18	19	20	21	22	23	24	25	♉26
♂	♉13	13	14	15	15	16	17	17	18	19	19	20	21	21	22	23	23	24	25	25	26	27	27	28	29	29	♊0	1	1	2	♊2

	1	6	12	18	24	30
♃	♑4	5	5	6	7	7
♄	♊0	1	1	2	2	3

	1	15	30
♅	♎18	17	17
♆	♐5	5	5
♇	♎1	1	0
☊	♒5	4	3

APRIL

	1	2	3	4	5	6	7	8	9	10	11	12	13	14	15	16	17	18	19	20	21	22	23	24	25	26	27	28	29	30
☉	♈11	12	13	14	15	16	17	18	19	20	21	22	23	24	25	26	27	28	29	♉0	1	2	3	4	5	6	7	8	9	♉10
☽	♏5	17	29	♐11	23	♑5	17	♒0	13	27	♓11	26	♈11	26	♉12	27	♊12	26	♋10	24	♌7	19	♍2	14	26	♎8	20	♏2	14	♏26
☿	♈10	10	9	8	7	7	6	5	5	4	4	4	4	4	4	4	4	4	5	5	6	6	7	8	8	9	10	11	12	♈13
♀	♉27	28	29	♊0	1	2	3	4	5	6	7	8	9	10	11	12	13	13	14	15	16	17	18	19	19	20	21	22	23	♊23
♂	♊3	4	4	5	6	6	7	8	8	9	10	10	11	12	12	13	14	14	15	15	16	17	17	18	19	19	20	21	21	♊22

	1	6	12	18	24	30
♃	♑7	8	8	8	8	8
♄	♊3	3	4	5	5	6

	1	15	30
♅	♎17	16	15
♆	♐5	5	5
♇	♎0	0	0
☊	♒3	1	♑2

MAY

	1	2	3	4	5	6	7	8	9	10	11	12	13	14	15	16	17	18	19	20	21	22	23	24	25	26	27	28	29	30	31
☉	♉11	12	13	14	15	16	17	17	18	19	20	21	22	23	24	25	26	27	28	29	♊0	1	2	3	4	5	6	7	8	9	♊10
☽	♐8	20	♑2	14	27	♒9	22	♓6	20	♈5	19	♉5	20	♊5	20	♋5	19	♌2	16	28	♍11	23	♎5	17	29	♏11	23	♐5	17	29	♑11
☿	♈14	15	16	17	19	20	21	23	24	25	27	28	♉0	2	3	5	7	8	10	12	14	15	17	19	21	23	25	27	29	♊2	♊4
♀	♊24	25	25	26	27	27	28	29	29	♋0	0	1	1	2	2	2	3	3	4	4	4	4	4	5	5	5	5	5	5	5	♋4
♂	♊23	23	24	25	25	26	26	27	28	28	29	♋0	0	1	2	2	3	3	4	5	5	6	7	7	8	9	9	10	11	11	♋12

	1	6	12	18	24	30
♃	♑8	8	8	8	7	6
♄	♊6	7	7	8	9	10

	1	15	30
♅	♎15	15	14
♆	♐5	4	4
♇	♎0	♍0	29
☊	♑29	28	27

JUNE

	1	2	3	4	5	6	7	8	9	10	11	12	13	14	15	16	17	18	19	20	21	22	23	24	25	26	27	28	29	30
☉	♊11	12	13	13	14	15	16	17	18	19	20	21	22	23	24	25	26	27	28	29	♋0	1	2	3	4	4	5	6	7	♋8
☽	♑24	♒6	19	♓2	16	♈0	14	29	♉13	28	♊13	28	♋13	27	♌11	24	♍7	19	♎2	14	26	♏8	19	♐1	13	26	♑8	20	♒3	♒16
☿	♊6	8	10	12	15	17	19	21	23	25	28	♋0	2	4	6	8	10	12	14	16	17	19	21	23	24	26	27	29	♌0	♌2
♀	♋4	4	4	4	3	3	2	2	1	1	0	0	♊29	29	28	28	27	26	26	25	24	24	23	23	22	22	21	21	20	♊20
♂	♋12	13	14	14	15	16	16	17	18	18	19	19	20	21	21	22	23	23	24	25	25	26	26	27	28	28	29	♌0	0	♌1

	1	6	12	18	24	30
♃	♑6	6	5	4	4	3
♄	♊10	11	11	12	13	14

	1	15	30
♅	♎14	14	14
♆	♐4	3	3
♇	♍29	29	29
☊	♑27	26	26

JULY

	1	2	3	4	5	6	7	8	9	10	11	12	13	14	15	16	17	18	19	20	21	22	23	24	25	26	27	28	29	30	31
☉	♋9	10	11	12	13	14	15	16	17	18	19	20	21	22	23	24	25	25	26	27	28	29	♌0	1	2	3	4	5	6	7	♌8
☽	♒29	♓13	26	♈10	24	♉9	23	♊8	22	♋7	21	♌5	19	♍2	15	28	♎10	22	♏4	16	28	♐10	22	♑4	17	29	♒12	26	♓9	23	♈7
☿	♌3	5	6	7	9	10	11	12	13	14	15	16	17	18	19	19	20	20	21	21	22	22	22	22	22	22	22	22	22	21	♌21
♀	♊20	19	19	19	19	18	18	18	18	18	18	18	18	19	19	19	19	20	20	20	21	21	22	22	22	23	24	24	25	25	♊26
♂	♌1	2	3	3	4	5	5	6	7	7	8	8	9	10	10	11	12	12	13	14	14	15	15	16	17	17	18	19	19	20	♌20

	1	6	12	18	24	30
♃	♑3	2	1	1	0	0
♄	♊14	14	15	16	16	17

	1	15	30
♅	♎14	14	15
♆	♐3	3	3
♇	♍29	♎0	0
☊	♑26	26	26

AUGUST

	1	2	3	4	5	6	7	8	9	10	11	12	13	14	15	16	17	18	19	20	21	22	23	24	25	26	27	28	29	30	31
☉	♌9	10	11	12	13	14	15	16	16	17	18	19	20	21	22	23	24	25	26	27	28	29	♍0	1	2	3	4	5	6	7	♍8
☽	♈21	♉5	20	♊4	18	♋2	16	♌0	14	27	♍10	23	♎5	18	♏0	12	24	♐6	18	♑0	12	25	♒8	21	♓5	19	♈3	18	♉2	16	♊1
☿	♌20	20	19	18	18	17	16	15	14	14	13	12	12	11	11	11	11	10	11	11	11	11	12	13	14	15	16	17	18	19	♌21
♀	♊26	27	28	29	29	♋0	1	1	2	3	4	5	5	6	7	8	9	10	11	11	12	13	14	15	16	17	18	19	20	21	♋22
♂	♌21	22	22	23	24	24	25	26	26	27	27	28	29	29	♍0	1	1	2	3	3	4	4	5	6	6	7	8	8	9	10	♍10

	1	6	12	18	24	30
♃	♐29	29	29	29	28	29
♄	♊17	18	18	19	19	20

	1	15	30
♅	♎15	15	16
♆	♐3	2	3
♇	♎0	0	1
☊	♑26	26	25

SEPTEMBER

	1	2	3	4	5	6	7	8	9	10	11	12	13	14	15	16	17	18	19	20	21	22	23	24	25	26	27	28	29	30
☉	♍9	10	11	12	13	13	14	15	16	17	18	19	20	21	22	23	24	25	26	27	28	29	♎0	1	2	3	4	5	6	♎7
☽	♊15	29	♋13	26	♌10	23	♍6	19	♎1	14	26	♏8	20	♐2	13	25	♑8	20	♒3	16	29	♓13	28	♈12	27	♉12	27	♊11	26	♋9
☿	♌22	24	26	27	29	♍1	3	5	7	8	10	12	14	16	18	20	22	24	25	27	29	♎1	3	4	6	8	10	11	13	♎15
♀	♋23	24	25	26	27	28	29	♌0	1	2	3	4	5	6	7	8	10	11	12	13	14	15	16	17	18	19	21	22	23	♌24
♂	♍11	11	12	13	13	14	15	15	16	17	17	18	18	19	20	20	21	22	22	23	24	24	25	26	26	27	27	28	29	♍29

	1	6	12	18	24	30
♃	♐29	29	29	29	♑0	0
♄	♊20	20	20	20	21	21

	1	15	30
♅	♎16	17	18
♆	♐3	3	3
♇	♎1	2	2
☊	♑25	24	23

OCTOBER

	1	2	3	4	5	6	7	8	9	10	11	12	13	14	15	16	17	18	19	20	21	22	23	24	25	26	27	28	29	30	31
☉	♎8	9	10	11	12	13	14	15	16	17	18	19	20	21	22	23	24	25	26	27	28	29	♏0	1	2	3	4	5	6	7	♏8
☽	♋23	♌6	20	♍2	15	28	♎10	22	♏4	16	28	♐10	22	♑4	16	28	♒11	24	♓7	21	♈6	21	♉6	21	♊6	21	♋6	20	♌3	17	♌29
☿	♎16	18	20	21	23	25	26	28	29	♏1	2	4	5	7	8	10	11	13	14	16	17	18	20	21	23	24	25	26	28	29	♐0
♀	♌25	26	27	28	♍0	1	2	3	4	5	6	8	9	10	11	12	13	15	16	17	18	19	21	22	23	24	25	27	28	29	♎0
♂	♎0	1	1	2	3	3	4	5	5	6	6	7	8	8	9	10	10	11	12	12	13	14	14	15	16	16	17	18	18	19	♎20

	1	6	12	18	24	30
♃	♑1	1	2	3	4	5
♄	♊21	21	21	20	20	20

	1	15	30
♅	♎18	19	20
♆	♐3	3	4
♇	♎2	3	3
☊	♑23	21	20

NOVEMBER

	1	2	3	4	5	6	7	8	9	10	11	12	13	14	15	16	17	18	19	20	21	22	23	24	25	26	27	28	29	30
☉	♏9	10	11	12	13	14	15	16	17	18	19	20	21	22	23	24	25	26	27	28	29	♐0	1	2	3	4	5	6	7	♐8
☽	♍12	25	♎7	19	♏1	13	25	♐7	19	♑0	12	24	♒7	19	♓2	16	♈0	14	29	♉14	29	♊15	♋0	14	29	♌13	26	♍9	22	♎4
☿	♐1	3	4	5	6	7	8	9	9	10	11	11	12	12	12	12	12	12	12	11	10	9	8	7	6	4	3	2	0	♏29
♀	♎1	3	4	5	6	7	9	10	11	12	13	15	16	17	18	20	21	22	23	24	26	27	28	29	♏1	2	3	4	5	♏7
♂	♎20	21	21	22	23	23	24	25	25	26	27	27	28	29	29	♏0	1	1	2	3	3	4	5	5	6	7	7	8	9	♏9

	1	6	12	18	24	30
♃	♑5	6	7	8	9	11
♄	♊20	20	19	19	18	18

	1	15	30
♅	♎20	21	22
♆	♐4	5	5
♇	♎3	4	4
☊	♑20	18	18

DECEMBER

	1	2	3	4	5	6	7	8	9	10	11	12	13	14	15	16	17	18	19	20	21	22	23	24	25	26	27	28	29	30	31
☉	♐9	10	11	12	13	14	15	16	17	18	19	20	21	22	23	24	25	26	27	28	29	♑0	1	2	3	4	5	6	7	8	♑9
☽	♎16	28	♏10	22	♐4	16	27	♑9	21	♒4	16	29	♓12	25	♈9	23	♉7	22	♊7	22	♋8	22	♌7	21	♍4	18	♎0	13	25	♏7	♏19
☿	♏28	27	27	26	26	26	26	27	27	28	28	29	♐0	1	2	3	4	5	7	8	9	10	12	13	15	16	17	19	20	22	♐23
♀	♏8	9	10	12	13	14	15	17	18	19	20	22	23	24	25	27	28	29	♐0	2	3	4	5	7	8	9	10	12	13	14	♐15
♂	♏10	11	11	12	13	13	14	15	15	16	17	17	18	19	19	20	21	21	22	23	23	24	25	25	26	27	28	28	29	♐0	♐0

	1	6	12	18	24	30
♃	♑11	12	13	15	16	17
♄	♊18	17	17	16	16	15

	1	15	30
♅	♎22	22	23
♆	♐5	6	6
♇	♎4	4	4
☊	♑18	17	17

1973

JANUARY

	1	2	3	4	5	6	7	8	9	10	11	12	13	14	15	16	17	18	19	20	21	22	23	24	25	26	27	28	29	30	31
☉	♑10	11	12	13	15	16	17	18	19	20	21	22	23	24	25	26	27	28	29	♒0	1	2	3	4	5	6	7	8	9	10	♒11
☽	♐1	12	24	♑6	18	♒1	13	26	♓9	22	♈5	19	♉3	17	♊1	16	♋1	16	♌0	15	29	♍12	26	♎8	21	♏3	15	27	♐9	21	♑3
☿	♐25	26	28	29	♑1	2	4	5	7	8	10	11	13	14	16	18	19	21	22	24	26	27	29	♒1	2	4	6	7	9	11	♒13
♀	♐16	18	19	20	21	23	24	25	26	28	29	♑0	1	3	4	5	7	8	9	10	12	13	14	15	17	18	19	20	22	23	♑24
♂	♐1	2	2	3	4	4	5	6	6	7	8	8	9	10	10	11	12	13	13	14	15	15	16	17	17	18	19	19	20	21	♐21

	1	6	12	18	24	30
♃	♑18	19	20	22	23	25
♄	♊15	15	15	14	14	14

	1	15	30
♅	♎23	23	23
♆	♐6	7	7
♇	♎4	4	4
☊	♑17	17	17

FEBRUARY

	1	2	3	4	5	6	7	8	9	10	11	12	13	14	15	16	17	18	19	20	21	22	23	24	25	26	27	28
☉	♒12	13	14	15	16	17	18	19	20	21	22	23	24	25	26	27	28	29	♓0	1	2	3	4	5	6	7	8	♓9
☽	♑15	27	♒9	22	♓5	19	♈2	16	29	♉13	28	♊12	26	♋10	25	♌9	23	♍7	20	♎3	16	29	♏11	23	♐5	17	28	♑10
☿	♒14	16	18	20	21	23	25	27	29	♓0	2	4	6	8	9	11	13	14	16	18	19	21	22	23	24	25	26	♓27
♀	♑25	27	28	29	♒0	2	3	4	5	7	8	9	10	12	13	14	15	17	18	19	20	22	23	24	25	27	28	♒29
♂	♐22	23	24	24	25	26	26	27	28	28	29	♑0	1	1	2	3	3	4	5	5	6	7	8	8	9	10	10	♑11

	1	6	12	18	24	28
♃	♑25	26	28	29	♒0	1
♄	♊14	14	14	14	14	14

	1	15	28
♅	♎23	23	23
♆	♐7	7	7
♇	♎4	4	4
☊	♑17	16	15

MARCH

	1	2	3	4	5	6	7	8	9	10	11	12	13	14	15	16	17	18	19	20	21	22	23	24	25	26	27	28	29	30	31
☉	♓10	11	12	13	14	15	16	17	18	19	20	21	22	23	24	25	26	27	28	29	♈0	1	2	3	4	5	6	7	8	9	♈10
☽	♑23	♒5	18	♓1	14	28	♈12	26	♉10	24	♊9	23	♋7	21	♌5	18	♍2	15	28	♎11	24	♏7	19	♐1	13	24	♑6	18	♒0	13	♒26
☿	♓28	28	28	29	29	28	28	28	27	26	26	25	24	23	22	21	20	19	18	18	17	16	16	16	15	15	15	15	15	15	♓16
♀	♓0	2	3	4	5	7	8	9	10	12	13	14	15	16	18	19	20	21	23	24	25	26	28	29	♈0	1	3	4	5	6	♈8
♂	♑12	12	13	14	15	15	16	17	17	18	19	19	20	21	22	22	23	24	24	25	26	27	27	28	29	29	♒0	1	2	2	♒3

	1	6	12	18	24	30
♃	♒1	2	3	5	6	7
♄	♊14	14	14	15	15	15

	1	15	30
♅	♎23	22	22
♆	♐7	7	7
♇	♎4	3	3
☊	♑15	14	13

APRIL

	1	2	3	4	5	6	7	8	9	10	11	12	13	14	15	16	17	18	19	20	21	22	23	24	25	26	27	28	29	30
☉	♈11	12	13	14	15	16	17	18	19	20	21	22	23	24	25	26	27	28	29	♉0	1	2	3	4	5	6	7	8	9	♉10
☽	♓9	23	♈7	21	♉5	20	♊5	19	♋4	18	♌1	15	28	♍12	25	♎8	20	♏3	15	27	♐9	21	♑3	14	26	♒8	21	♓4	17	♈1
☿	♓16	16	17	18	18	19	20	21	21	22	23	24	25	27	28	29	♈0	1	3	4	5	7	8	10	11	13	14	16	18	♈19
♀	♈9	10	11	13	14	15	16	18	19	20	21	23	24	25	26	27	29	♉0	1	2	4	5	6	7	9	10	11	12	14	♉15
♂	♒4	4	5	6	6	7	8	9	9	10	11	11	12	13	14	14	15	16	16	17	18	19	19	20	21	21	22	23	24	♒24

	1	6	12	18	24	30
♃	♒7	8	9	9	10	11
♄	♊16	16	17	17	18	18

	1	15	30
♅	♎21	21	20
♆	♐7	7	7
♇	♎3	2	2
☊	♑13	11	10

MAY

	1	2	3	4	5	6	7	8	9	10	11	12	13	14	15	16	17	18	19	20	21	22	23	24	25	26	27	28	29	30	31
☉	♉10	11	12	13	14	15	16	17	18	19	20	21	22	23	24	25	26	27	28	29	♊0	1	2	3	4	5	6	7	7	8	♊9
☽	♈15	29	♉14	29	♊14	29	♋14	28	♌12	25	♍9	22	♎4	17	29	♏12	24	♐6	17	29	♑11	23	♒5	17	29	♓12	25	♈9	23	♉8	♉23
☿	♈21	23	24	26	28	♉0	2	4	5	7	9	11	13	16	18	20	22	24	26	28	♊1	3	5	7	9	12	14	16	18	20	♊22
♀	♉16	17	18	20	21	22	23	25	26	27	28	♊0	1	2	3	4	6	7	8	9	11	12	13	14	16	17	18	19	20	22	♊23
♂	♒25	26	26	27	28	28	29	♓0	1	1	2	3	3	4	5	6	6	7	8	8	9	10	10	11	12	12	13	14	15	15	♓16

	1	6	12	18	24	30
♃	♒11	11	12	12	12	12
♄	♊18	19	20	20	21	22

	1	15	30
♅	♎20	20	19
♆	♐7	6	6
♇	♎2	2	2
☊	♑9	9	8

JUNE

	1	2	3	4	5	6	7	8	9	10	11	12	13	14	15	16	17	18	19	20	21	22	23	24	25	26	27	28	29	30
☉	♊10	11	12	13	14	15	16	17	18	19	20	21	22	23	24	25	26	27	28	29	29	♋0	1	2	3	4	5	6	7	♋8
☽	♊8	23	♋8	23	♌7	21	♍5	18	♎1	14	26	♏9	21	♐3	14	26	♑8	20	♒2	14	26	♓9	21	♈5	18	♉2	16	♊1	16	♋1
☿	♊24	26	28	♋0	1	3	5	7	8	10	12	13	14	16	17	19	20	21	22	23	25	26	27	27	28	29	♌0	0	1	♌2
♀	♊24	25	27	28	29	♋0	1	3	4	5	6	8	9	10	11	12	14	15	16	17	19	20	21	22	23	25	26	27	28	♌0
♂	♓17	17	18	19	19	20	21	21	22	23	23	24	25	25	26	27	27	28	29	29	♈0	1	1	2	3	3	4	5	5	♈6

	1	6	12	18	24	30
♃	♒12	12	12	12	11	11
♄	♊22	23	24	24	25	26

	1	15	30
♅	♎19	19	19
♆	♐6	6	5
♇	♎2	2	2
☊	♑8	8	8

JULY

	1	2	3	4	5	6	7	8	9	10	11	12	13	14	15	16	17	18	19	20	21	22	23	24	25	26	27	28	29	30	31
☉	♋9	10	11	12	13	14	15	16	17	18	19	20	20	21	22	23	24	25	26	27	28	29	♌0	1	2	3	4	5	6	7	♌8
☽	♋16	♌1	16	♍0	14	28	♎11	23	♏6	18	♐0	11	23	♑5	17	29	♒11	23	♓6	18	♈1	14	28	♉12	26	♊10	25	♋10	25	♌10	♌24
☿	♌2	2	3	3	3	3	3	3	3	3	3	2	2	1	1	0	0	♋29	28	28	27	26	26	25	24	24	24	23	23	23	♋23
♀	♌1	2	3	4	6	7	8	9	10	12	13	14	15	17	18	19	20	21	23	24	25	26	27	29	♍0	1	2	4	5	6	♍7
♂	♈7	7	8	8	9	10	10	11	12	12	13	13	14	15	15	16	16	17	17	18	19	19	20	20	21	21	22	22	23	23	♈24

	1	6	12	18	24	30
♃	♒11	10	10	9	8	7
♄	♊26	27	28	28	29	♋0

	1	15	30
♅	♎19	19	19
♆	♐5	5	5
♇	♎2	2	2
☊	♑8	8	7

AUGUST

	1	2	3	4	5	6	7	8	9	10	11	12	13	14	15	16	17	18	19	20	21	22	23	24	25	26	27	28	29	30	31
☉	♌9	10	11	11	12	13	14	15	16	17	18	19	20	21	22	23	24	25	26	27	28	29	♍0	1	2	3	4	5	6	6	♍7
☽	♍9	23	♎6	19	♏2	14	26	♐8	20	♑2	14	26	♒8	20	♓3	15	28	♈11	25	♉8	22	♊6	20	♋5	19	♌4	18	♍3	17	♎1	♎14
☿	♋23	23	23	24	24	25	26	26	27	28	29	♌1	2	3	5	6	8	10	11	13	15	17	19	21	23	25	27	29	♍1	3	♍5
♀	♍8	10	11	12	13	14	16	17	18	19	20	22	23	24	25	26	28	29	♎0	1	2	4	5	6	7	8	9	11	12	13	♎14
♂	♈24	25	26	26	26	27	27	28	28	29	29	♉0	0	1	1	1	2	2	3	3	3	4	4	4	5	5	5	6	6	6	♉7

	1	6	12	18	24	30
♃	♒7	6	6	5	4	4
♄	♋0	0	1	2	2	3

	1	15	30
♅	♎19	20	21
♆	♐5	5	5
♇	♎2	3	3
☊	♑7	7	6

SEPTEMBER

	1	2	3	4	5	6	7	8	9	10	11	12	13	14	15	16	17	18	19	20	21	22	23	24	25	26	27	28	29	30
☉	♍8	9	10	11	12	13	14	15	16	17	18	19	20	21	22	23	24	25	26	27	28	29	♎0	1	2	3	4	5	6	♎7
☽	♎27	♏10	22	♐4	16	28	♑10	22	♒4	16	29	♓11	24	♈8	21	♉5	19	♊3	17	♋1	15	29	♌14	28	♍12	25	♎9	22	♏5	♏18
☿	♍7	9	10	12	14	16	18	20	22	24	25	27	29	♎1	2	4	6	7	9	11	12	14	15	17	18	20	21	23	24	♎26
♀	♎15	17	18	19	20	21	22	24	25	26	27	28	♏0	1	2	3	4	5	7	8	9	10	11	12	14	15	16	17	18	♏19
♂	♉7	7	7	7	8	8	8	8	8	9	9	9	9	9	9	9	9	9	9	9	9	9	9	9	9	9	9	9	9	♉9

	1	6	12	18	24	30
♃	♒3	3	3	2	2	2
♄	♋3	3	4	4	4	4

	1	15	30
♅	♎21	21	22
♆	♐5	5	5
♇	♎3	4	4
☊	♑5	4	3

OCTOBER

	1	2	3	4	5	6	7	8	9	10	11	12	13	14	15	16	17	18	19	20	21	22	23	24	25	26	27	28	29	30	31
☉	♎8	9	10	11	12	13	14	15	16	17	18	19	20	21	21	22	23	24	25	26	27	28	29	♏0	1	2	3	4	5	6	♏7
☽	♐0	12	24	♑6	18	♒0	12	24	♓7	20	♈3	17	♉1	15	29	♊14	28	♋12	26	♌10	24	♍8	21	♎5	18	♏1	13	26	♐8	20	♑2
☿	♎27	29	♏0	2	3	4	6	7	8	10	11	12	13	15	16	17	18	19	20	21	22	23	23	24	25	25	26	26	26	27	♏27
♀	♏20	22	23	24	25	26	27	28	♐0	1	2	3	4	5	6	8	9	10	11	12	13	14	15	16	17	19	20	21	22	23	♐24
♂	♉8	8	8	8	8	7	7	7	7	6	6	6	6	5	5	5	4	4	4	3	3	3	2	2	2	1	1	1	0	0	♉0

	1	6	12	18	24	30
♃	♒2	2	3	3	3	4
♄	♋5	5	5	5	5	5

	1	15	30
♅	♎22	23	24
♆	♐5	6	6
♇	♎4	5	5
☊	♑2	1	0

NOVEMBER

	1	2	3	4	5	6	7	8	9	10	11	12	13	14	15	16	17	18	19	20	21	22	23	24	25	26	27	28	29	30
☉	♏8	9	10	11	12	13	14	15	16	17	18	19	20	21	22	23	24	26	27	28	29	♐0	1	2	3	4	5	6	7	♐8
☽	♑14	26	♒7	20	♓2	15	28	♈11	25	♉9	24	♊9	23	♋8	23	♌7	21	♍5	18	♎1	15	27	♏10	22	♐4	17	28	♑10	22	♒4
☿	♏26	26	26	25	24	23	22	21	20	18	17	16	15	14	13	12	11	11	11	11	11	11	12	12	13	14	15	16	17	♏18
♀	♐25	26	27	28	29	♑0	1	2	3	5	6	7	8	9	10	11	12	13	14	14	15	16	17	18	19	20	21	22	23	♑24
♂	♈29	29	29	28	28	28	28	27	27	27	27	27	26	26	26	26	26	26	26	26	25	25	25	25	25	25	25	25	25	♈25

	1	6	12	18	24	30
♃	♒4	5	5	6	7	8
♄	♋5	4	4	4	3	3

	1	15	30
♅	♎24	25	26
♆	♐6	7	7
♇	♎6	6	6
☊	♑0	♐0	29

DECEMBER

	1	2	3	4	5	6	7	8	9	10	11	12	13	14	15	16	17	18	19	20	21	22	23	24	25	26	27	28	29	30	31
☉	♐9	10	11	12	13	14	15	16	17	18	19	20	21	22	23	24	25	26	27	28	29	♑0	1	2	3	4	5	6	7	8	♑9
☽	♒16	28	♓10	23	♈6	19	♉3	17	♊2	17	♋2	17	♌2	17	♍1	15	28	♎12	24	♏7	19	♐1	13	25	♑7	19	♒1	12	24	♓6	♓19
☿	♏19	20	22	23	24	26	27	29	♐0	2	3	5	6	8	9	11	12	14	15	17	18	20	21	23	24	26	27	29	♑1	2	♑4
♀	♑24	25	26	27	28	29	29	♒0	1	2	2	3	4	4	5	5	6	7	7	8	8	9	9	9	10	10	10	11	11	11	♒11
♂	♈25	26	26	26	26	26	26	26	26	27	27	27	27	27	28	28	28	28	28	29	29	29	♉0	0	0	1	1	1	1	2	♉2

	1	6	12	18	24	30
♃	♒8	9	10	11	13	14
♄	♋3	3	2	2	1	1

	1	15	30
♅	♎26	27	27
♆	♐7	8	8
♇	♎6	7	7
☊	♐29	29	29

1974

JANUARY

	1	2	3	4	5	6	7	8	9	10	11	12	13	14	15	16	17	18	19	20	21	22	23	24	25	26	27	28	29	30	31
☉	♑10	11	12	13	14	15	16	17	18	19	20	21	22	23	24	25	26	28	29	♒0	1	2	3	4	5	6	7	8	9	10	♒11
☽	♈1	14	27	♉11	25	♊10	25	♋10	25	♌10	25	♍10	24	♎8	21	♏4	16	28	♐10	22	♑4	16	28	♒9	21	♓4	16	28	♈11	24	♉7
☿	♑5	7	8	10	12	13	15	16	18	20	21	23	25	26	28	♒0	1	3	5	7	8	10	12	13	15	17	19	20	22	24	♒25
♀	♒11	11	11	11	11	11	11	11	11	10	10	10	9	9	9	8	8	7	6	6	5	5	4	3	3	2	2	1	0	0	♑29
♂	♉3	3	3	4	4	4	5	5	6	6	6	7	7	8	8	9	9	9	10	10	11	11	12	12	13	13	14	14	15	15	♉16

	1	6	12	18	24	30
♃	♒14	16	17	18	20	21
♄	♋1	0	0	♊29	29	29

	1	15	30
♅	♎27	28	28
♆	♐8	9	9
♇	♎7	7	7
☊	♐28	28	28

FEBRUARY

	1	2	3	4	5	6	7	8	9	10	11	12	13	14	15	16	17	18	19	20	21	22	23	24	25	26	27	28
☉	♒12	13	14	15	16	17	18	19	20	21	22	23	24	25	26	27	28	29	♓0	1	2	3	4	5	6	7	8	♓9
☽	♉20	♊4	18	♋3	18	♌3	18	♍3	18	♎2	16	29	♏12	25	♐7	19	♑1	13	24	♒6	18	♓0	13	25	♈8	21	♉4	♉17
☿	♒27	29	♓0	2	3	4	6	7	8	9	10	11	11	12	12	12	12	11	11	10	10	9	8	7	6	5	4	♓3
♀	♑29	28	28	28	27	27	27	26	26	26	26	26	26	26	26	26	26	26	26	27	27	27	28	28	28	29	29	♒0
♂	♉16	17	17	18	18	19	19	20	20	21	21	22	22	23	23	24	24	25	25	26	26	27	28	28	29	29	♊0	♊0

	1	6	12	18	24	28
♃	♒22	23	24	26	27	28
♄	♊28	28	28	28	28	28

	1	15	28
♅	♎28	28	27
♆	♐9	9	10
♇	♎7	6	6
☊	♐28	27	25

MARCH

	1	2	3	4	5	6	7	8	9	10	11	12	13	14	15	16	17	18	19	20	21	22	23	24	25	26	27	28	29	30	31
☉	♓10	11	12	13	14	15	16	17	18	19	20	21	22	23	24	25	26	27	28	29	♈0	1	2	3	4	5	6	7	8	9	♈10
☽	♊0	14	28	♋13	27	♌12	27	♍11	26	♎10	24	♏7	20	♐3	15	27	♑9	21	♒3	15	27	♓9	21	♈4	17	♉0	14	27	♊11	25	♋9
☿	♓2	1	0	♒29	28	28	28	27	27	27	27	27	28	28	28	29	29	♓0	1	2	2	3	4	5	6	7	8	10	11	12	♓13
♀	♒0	1	1	2	2	3	4	4	5	6	6	7	8	9	10	10	11	12	13	14	14	15	16	17	18	19	20	21	22	23	♒24
♂	♊1	1	2	3	3	4	4	5	5	6	6	7	8	8	9	9	10	10	11	12	12	13	13	14	15	15	16	16	17	17	♊18

	1	6	12	18	24	30
♃	♒28	29	♓1	2	4	5
♄	♊28	28	28	28	28	29

	1	15	30
♅	♎27	27	26
♆	♐10	10	10
♇	♎6	6	5
☊	♐25	24	22

APRIL

	1	2	3	4	5	6	7	8	9	10	11	12	13	14	15	16	17	18	19	20	21	22	23	24	25	26	27	28	29	30
☉	♈11	12	13	14	15	16	17	18	19	20	21	22	23	24	25	26	27	28	29	♉0	1	1	2	3	4	5	6	7	8	♉9
☽	♋23	♌7	22	♍6	20	♎4	18	♏2	15	28	♐11	23	♑5	17	29	♒11	23	♓5	17	♈0	13	26	♉10	24	♊7	22	♋6	20	♌4	♌18
☿	♓15	16	17	19	20	21	23	24	26	27	29	♈1	2	4	6	7	9	11	12	14	16	18	20	22	24	26	28	♉0	2	♉4
♀	♒25	25	26	27	28	29	♓0	1	2	3	4	5	7	8	9	10	11	12	13	14	15	16	17	18	19	20	21	22	24	♓25
♂	♊19	19	20	20	21	22	22	23	23	24	24	25	26	26	27	27	28	29	29	♋0	0	1	2	2	3	3	4	5	5	♋6

	1	6	12	18	24	30
♃	♓5	6	8	9	10	11
♄	♊29	29	29	♋0	0	1

	1	15	30
♅	♎26	26	25
♆	♐10	9	9
♇	♎5	5	5
☊	♐22	21	20

MAY

	1	2	3	4	5	6	7	8	9	10	11	12	13	14	15	16	17	18	19	20	21	22	23	24	25	26	27	28	29	30	31
☉	♉10	11	12	13	14	15	16	17	18	19	20	21	22	23	24	25	26	27	28	29	♊0	1	1	2	3	4	5	6	7	8	♊9
☽	♍2	16	♎0	14	27	♏11	24	♐6	19	♑1	13	25	♒7	18	♓0	13	25	♈8	21	♉4	18	♊2	17	♋1	16	♌0	15	29	♍13	27	♎11
☿	♉6	8	10	12	14	17	19	21	23	25	27	♊0	2	4	6	8	10	12	14	15	17	19	21	22	24	25	27	28	♋0	1	♋2
♀	♓26	27	28	29	♈0	1	2	4	5	6	7	8	9	10	11	12	14	15	16	17	18	19	20	22	23	24	25	26	27	28	♉0
♂	♋6	7	8	8	9	9	10	11	11	12	12	13	14	14	15	15	16	17	17	18	18	19	20	20	21	21	22	23	23	24	♋24

	1	6	12	18	24	30
♃	♓11	12	13	14	15	16
♄	♋1	2	2	3	4	4

	1	15	30
♅	♎25	25	24
♆	♐9	9	8
♇	♎5	4	4
☊	♐20	20	19

JUNE

	1	2	3	4	5	6	7	8	9	10	11	12	13	14	15	16	17	18	19	20	21	22	23	24	25	26	27	28	29	30
☉	♊10	11	12	13	14	15	16	17	18	19	20	21	22	23	24	24	25	26	27	28	29	♋0	1	2	3	4	5	6	7	♋8
☽	♎24	♏7	20	♐2	15	27	♑9	21	♒3	15	27	♓9	21	♈3	16	29	♉13	26	♊11	25	♋10	25	♌10	25	♍10	24	♎7	21	♏4	♏17
☿	♋3	4	6	7	7	8	9	10	11	11	12	12	13	13	13	14	14	14	14	13	13	13	13	12	12	11	11	10	10	♋9
♀	♉1	2	3	4	5	7	8	9	10	11	12	14	15	16	17	18	19	21	22	23	24	25	26	28	29	♊0	1	2	4	♊5
♂	♋25	26	26	27	28	28	29	29	♌0	1	1	2	2	3	4	4	5	5	6	7	7	8	9	9	10	10	11	12	12	♌13

	1	6	12	18	24	30
♃	♓16	16	17	17	18	18
♄	♋5	5	6	7	7	8

	1	15	30
♅	♎24	24	24
♆	♐8	8	7
♇	♎4	4	4
☊	♐19	19	19

JULY

	1	2	3	4	5	6	7	8	9	10	11	12	13	14	15	16	17	18	19	20	21	22	23	24	25	26	27	28	29	30	31
☉	♋9	10	11	12	13	14	15	15	16	17	18	19	20	21	22	23	24	25	26	27	28	29	♌0	1	2	3	4	5	6	6	♌7
☽	♏29	♐12	24	♑6	18	♒0	11	23	♓5	17	29	♈12	24	♉7	21	♊5	19	♋4	19	♌4	19	♍4	19	♎3	17	♏1	14	26	♐9	21	♑3
☿	♋9	8	7	7	6	6	5	5	5	5	4	4	4	5	5	5	5	6	7	7	8	9	10	11	12	13	14	16	17	19	♋20
♀	♊6	7	8	9	11	12	13	14	15	17	18	19	20	21	23	24	25	26	27	29	♋0	1	2	3	5	6	7	8	9	11	♋12
♂	♌13	14	15	15	16	17	17	18	18	19	20	20	21	22	22	23	23	24	25	25	26	27	27	28	28	29	♍0	0	1	2	♍2

	1	6	12	18	24	30
♃	♓18	18	18	18	17	17
♄	♋8	9	10	11	11	12

	1	15	30
♅	♎24	24	24
♆	♐7	7	7
♇	♎4	4	5
☊	♐19	19	19

AUGUST

	1	2	3	4	5	6	7	8	9	10	11	12	13	14	15	16	17	18	19	20	21	22	23	24	25	26	27	28	29	30	31
☉	♌8	9	10	11	12	13	14	15	16	17	18	19	20	21	22	23	24	25	26	27	28	29	29	♍0	1	2	3	4	5	6	♍7
☽	♑15	27	♒8	20	♓2	14	26	♈9	21	♉4	17	♊0	14	28	♋12	27	♌12	28	♍13	28	♎12	26	♏10	23	♐5	18	♑0	12	24	♒5	♒17
☿	♋22	24	25	27	29	♌1	3	5	7	9	11	13	15	17	19	21	23	25	27	29	♍1	3	5	7	9	11	13	14	16	18	♍20
♀	♋13	14	15	17	18	19	20	21	23	24	25	26	28	29	♌0	1	2	4	5	6	7	9	10	11	12	13	15	16	17	18	♌20
♂	♍3	3	4	5	5	6	7	7	8	8	9	10	10	11	12	12	13	13	14	15	15	16	17	17	18	19	19	20	20	21	♍22

	1	6	12	18	24	30
♃	♓17	17	16	15	15	14
♄	♋12	13	14	14	15	16

	1	15	30
♅	♎24	24	25
♆	♐7	7	7
♇	♎5	5	6
☊	♐19	17	16

SEPTEMBER

	1	2	3	4	5	6	7	8	9	10	11	12	13	14	15	16	17	18	19	20	21	22	23	24	25	26	27	28	29	30
☉	♍8	9	10	11	12	13	14	15	16	17	18	19	20	21	22	23	24	25	26	27	28	29	♎0	1	2	3	4	4	5	♎6
☽	♒29	♓11	23	♈6	18	♉1	13	26	♊10	23	♋7	22	♌6	21	♍6	21	♎6	20	♏4	18	♐1	14	26	♑8	20	♒2	14	26	♓8	♓20
☿	♍21	23	25	26	28	♎0	1	3	4	6	7	9	10	12	13	15	16	17	19	20	22	23	24	25	27	28	29	♏0	1	♏2
♀	♌21	22	23	25	26	27	28	29	♍1	2	3	4	6	7	8	9	11	12	13	14	16	17	18	19	21	22	23	24	26	♍27
♂	♍22	23	24	24	25	26	26	27	28	28	29	29	♎0	1	1	2	3	3	4	5	5	6	7	7	8	9	9	10	11	♎11

	1	6	12	18	24	30
♃	♓14	13	12	11	11	10
♄	♋16	16	17	17	18	18

	1	15	30
♅	♎25	26	27
♆	♐7	7	7
♇	♎6	6	7
☊	♐16	14	13

OCTOBER

	1	2	3	4	5	6	7	8	9	10	11	12	13	14	15	16	17	18	19	20	21	22	23	24	25	26	27	28	29	30	31
☉	♎7	8	9	10	11	12	13	14	15	16	17	18	19	20	21	22	23	24	25	26	27	28	29	♏0	1	2	3	4	5	6	♏7
☽	♈2	15	28	♉10	23	♊7	20	♋4	18	♌2	16	♍1	15	♎0	14	29	♏12	26	♐9	22	♑4	16	28	♒10	22	♓4	16	28	♈11	24	♉7
☿	♏3	4	5	6	7	7	8	9	9	10	10	10	11	11	11	10	10	9	9	8	7	6	5	4	2	1	0	♎29	28	27	♎26
♀	♍28	29	♎0	2	3	4	5	7	8	9	10	12	13	14	15	17	18	19	20	22	23	24	25	27	28	29	♏1	2	3	4	♏6
♂	♎12	13	13	14	14	15	16	16	17	18	18	19	20	20	21	22	22	23	24	24	25	26	26	27	28	28	29	♏0	0	1	♏2

	1	6	12	18	24	30
♃	♓10	9	9	8	8	8
♄	♋18	18	19	19	19	19

	1	15	30
♅	♎27	28	29
♆	♐7	8	8
♇	♎7	7	8
☊	♐12	11	11

NOVEMBER

	1	2	3	4	5	6	7	8	9	10	11	12	13	14	15	16	17	18	19	20	21	22	23	24	25	26	27	28	29	30
☉	♏8	9	10	11	12	13	14	15	16	17	18	19	20	21	22	23	24	25	26	27	28	29	♐0	1	2	3	4	5	6	♐7
☽	♉20	♊3	17	♋1	14	29	♌13	27	♍11	25	♎9	23	♏7	21	♐4	17	♑0	12	24	♒6	18	♓0	12	24	♈6	19	♉2	15	28	♊12
☿	♎25	25	25	25	25	25	26	27	27	28	29	♏0	2	3	4	5	7	8	10	11	13	14	16	17	19	20	22	23	25	♏26
♀	♏7	8	9	11	12	13	14	16	17	18	19	21	22	23	24	26	27	28	29	♐1	2	3	4	6	7	8	9	11	12	♐13
♂	♏2	3	4	5	5	6	7	7	8	9	9	10	11	11	12	13	13	14	15	15	16	17	18	18	19	20	20	21	22	♏22

	1	6	12	18	24	30
♃	♓8	8	8	8	9	9
♄	♋19	19	19	19	18	18

	1	15	30
♅	♎29	♏29	0
♆	♐8	9	9
♇	♎8	8	9
☊	♐10	10	10

DECEMBER

	1	2	3	4	5	6	7	8	9	10	11	12	13	14	15	16	17	18	19	20	21	22	23	24	25	26	27	28	29	30	31
☉	♐8	9	10	11	12	13	14	16	17	18	19	20	21	22	23	24	25	26	27	28	29	♑0	1	2	3	4	5	6	7	8	♑9
☽	♊26	♋10	25	♌9	24	♍8	22	♎6	20	♏3	17	♐0	13	25	♑8	20	♒2	14	26	♓8	20	♈2	14	26	♉9	22	♊6	20	♋5	19	♌4
☿	♏28	♐0	1	3	4	6	7	9	11	12	14	15	17	18	20	21	23	25	26	28	29	♑1	3	4	6	7	9	11	12	14	♑15
♀	♐14	16	17	18	19	21	22	23	24	26	27	28	♑0	1	2	3	5	6	7	8	10	11	12	13	15	16	17	18	20	21	♑22
♂	♏23	24	24	25	26	27	27	28	29	29	♐0	1	1	2	3	4	4	5	6	6	7	8	9	9	10	11	11	12	13	14	♐14

	1	6	12	18	24	30
♃	♓9	10	10	11	12	13
♄	♋18	18	17	17	17	16

	1	15	30
♅	♏1	1	2
♆	♐9	10	10
♇	♎9	9	9
☊	♐10	10	10

1975

JANUARY

	1	2	3	4	5	6	7	8	9	10	11	12	13	14	15	16	17	18	19	20	21	22	23	24	25	26	27	28	29	30	31
☉	♑10	11	12	13	14	15	16	17	18	19	20	21	22	23	24	25	26	27	28	29	♒0	1	2	3	4	5	6	7	8	9	♒10
☽	♌19	♍4	18	♎3	17	♏0	13	26	♐9	22	♑4	16	28	♒10	22	♓4	16	28	♈10	22	♉4	17	♊0	14	28	♋13	27	♌13	28	♍13	♍28
☿	♑17	19	20	22	24	25	27	28	♒0	2	3	5	7	8	10	11	13	14	16	17	18	20	21	22	23	24	24	25	25	25	♒25
♀	♑23	25	26	27	28	♒0	1	2	3	5	6	7	8	10	11	12	13	15	16	17	18	20	21	22	23	25	26	27	28	♓0	♓1
♂	♐15	16	16	17	18	19	19	20	21	21	22	23	24	24	25	26	27	27	28	29	29	♑0	1	2	2	3	4	5	5	6	♑7

	1	6	12	18	24	30
♃	♓13	14	15	16	18	19
♄	♋16	15	15	14	14	14
	1	15	30			
♅	♏2	2	2			
♆	♐10	11	11			
♇	♎9	9	9			
☊	♐10	9	8			

FEBRUARY

	1	2	3	4	5	6	7	8	9	10	11	12	13	14	15	16	17	18	19	20	21	22	23	24	25	26	27	28
☉	♒11	13	14	15	16	17	18	19	20	21	22	23	24	25	26	27	28	29	♓0	1	2	3	4	5	6	7	8	♓9
☽	♎13	27	♏10	23	♐6	19	♑1	13	25	♒7	19	♓1	13	25	♈7	19	♉1	13	26	♊9	22	♋6	21	♌5	21	♍6	21	♎6
☿	♒25	25	24	24	23	22	21	19	18	17	16	15	14	13	12	11	11	10	10	10	10	10	10	11	11	11	12	♒13
♀	♓2	3	5	6	7	8	10	11	12	13	15	16	17	18	20	21	22	23	25	26	27	28	29	♈1	2	3	4	♈6
♂	♑7	8	9	10	10	11	12	13	13	14	15	16	16	17	18	19	19	20	21	22	22	23	24	25	25	26	27	♑28

	1	6	12	18	24	28
♃	♓19	20	22	23	25	26
♄	♋13	13	13	12	12	12
	1	15	28			
♅	♏2	2	2			
♆	♐11	12	12			
♇	♎9	9	9			
☊	♐8	6	5			

MARCH

	1	2	3	4	5	6	7	8	9	10	11	12	13	14	15	16	17	18	19	20	21	22	23	24	25	26	27	28	29	30	31
☉	♓10	11	12	13	14	15	16	17	18	19	20	21	22	23	24	25	26	27	28	29	♈0	1	2	3	4	5	6	7	8	9	♈10
☽	♎21	♏6	19	♐3	16	28	♑10	22	♒4	16	28	♓10	22	♈4	16	28	♉10	23	♊5	18	♋2	16	♌0	14	29	♍14	29	♎15	29	♏14	♏28
☿	♒13	14	15	16	17	18	19	20	21	22	23	24	25	27	28	29	♓1	2	3	5	6	8	9	11	12	14	16	17	19	20	♓22
♀	♈7	8	9	11	12	13	14	15	17	18	19	20	22	23	24	25	26	28	29	♉0	1	3	4	5	6	7	9	10	11	12	♉13
♂	♑28	29	♒0	1	1	2	3	4	4	5	6	7	7	8	9	10	10	11	12	13	13	14	15	16	16	17	18	19	19	20	♒21

	1	6	12	18	24	30
♃	♓26	27	28	♈0	1	3
♄	♋12	12	12	12	12	12
	1	15	30			
♅	♏2	2	1			
♆	♐12	12	12			
♇	♎9	8	8			
☊	♐5	3	2			

APRIL

	1	2	3	4	5	6	7	8	9	10	11	12	13	14	15	16	17	18	19	20	21	22	23	24	25	26	27	28	29	30
☉	♈11	12	13	14	15	16	17	18	19	20	20	21	22	23	24	25	26	27	28	29	♉0	1	2	3	4	5	6	7	8	♉9
☽	♐11	24	♑7	19	♒1	13	25	♓7	19	♈1	13	25	♉7	20	♊3	15	29	♋12	26	♌10	24	♍9	23	♎8	23	♏7	22	♐6	19	♑2
☿	♓24	26	27	29	♈1	3	5	6	8	10	12	14	16	18	20	22	24	26	28	♉1	3	5	7	9	11	13	15	17	20	♉22
♀	♉15	16	17	18	19	21	22	23	24	25	27	28	29	♊0	1	2	4	5	6	7	8	9	11	12	13	14	15	16	18	♊19
♂	♒22	23	23	24	25	26	26	27	28	29	29	♓0	1	2	2	3	4	5	5	6	7	8	9	9	10	11	12	12	13	♓14

	1	6	12	18	24	30
♃	♈3	4	6	7	9	10
♄	♋12	12	13	13	13	14
	1	15	30			
♅	♏1	1	0			
♆	♐12	12	11			
♇	♎8	7	7			
☊	♐2	1	1			

MAY

	1	2	3	4	5	6	7	8	9	10	11	12	13	14	15	16	17	18	19	20	21	22	23	24	25	26	27	28	29	30	31
☉	♉10	11	12	13	14	15	16	17	18	19	20	21	22	23	24	25	25	26	27	28	29	♊0	1	2	3	4	5	6	7	8	♊9
☽	♑15	27	♒9	21	♓3	15	27	♈9	21	♉4	16	29	♊12	25	♋9	23	♌7	21	♍5	19	♎4	18	♏2	16	♐0	14	27	♑10	23	♒5	♒17
☿	♉23	25	27	29	♊1	3	4	6	7	9	10	12	13	14	15	16	17	18	19	20	21	21	22	22	23	23	23	23	24	24	♊24
♀	♊20	21	22	23	24	26	27	28	29	♋0	1	2	4	5	6	7	8	9	10	11	12	14	15	16	17	18	19	20	21	22	♋23
♂	♓15	15	16	17	18	18	19	20	21	21	22	23	24	24	25	26	27	27	28	29	♈0	0	1	2	3	3	4	5	6	6	♈7

	1	6	12	18	24	30
♃	♈10	11	13	14	15	16
♄	♋14	14	15	15	16	17
	1	15	30			
♅	♏0	♎0	29			
♆	♐11	11	10			
♇	♎7	7	7			
☊	♐1	1	1			

JUNE

	1	2	3	4	5	6	7	8	9	10	11	12	13	14	15	16	17	18	19	20	21	22	23	24	25	26	27	28	29	30
☉	♊10	11	12	13	14	15	16	17	18	19	19	20	21	22	23	24	25	26	27	28	29	♋0	1	2	3	4	5	6	7	♋8
☽	♒29	♓11	23	♈5	17	29	♉12	25	♊8	21	♋5	19	♌3	17	♍2	16	♎0	14	28	♏12	26	♐9	22	♑5	18	♒1	13	25	♓7	♓19
☿	♊23	23	23	23	22	22	21	21	20	20	19	19	18	17	17	17	16	16	16	15	15	15	15	15	15	15	16	16	17	♊17
♀	♋24	25	26	27	28	♌0	1	2	3	4	5	6	7	8	9	10	11	12	12	13	14	15	16	17	18	19	20	21	22	♌22
♂	♈8	9	9	10	11	12	12	13	14	15	15	16	17	18	18	19	20	21	21	22	23	23	24	25	26	26	27	28	28	♈29

	1	6	12	18	24	30
♃	♈17	18	19	20	21	21
♄	♋17	18	18	19	20	20
	1	15	30			
♅	♎29	29	28			
♆	♐10	10	10			
♇	♎7	6	7			
☊	♐1	1	0			

JULY

	1	2	3	4	5	6	7	8	9	10	11	12	13	14	15	16	17	18	19	20	21	22	23	24	25	26	27	28	29	30	31
☉	♋9	10	10	11	12	13	14	15	16	17	18	19	20	21	22	23	24	25	26	27	28	29	♌0	1	1	2	3	4	5	6	♌7
☽	♈1	13	25	♉7	20	♊3	16	♋0	14	28	♌13	28	♍12	27	♎11	25	♏9	22	♐6	19	♑2	14	27	♒9	21	♓4	15	27	♈9	21	♉3
☿	♊18	18	19	20	21	22	23	24	25	27	28	29	♋1	2	4	6	7	9	11	13	15	17	19	21	23	25	27	29	♌1	4	♌6
♀	♌23	24	25	26	27	27	28	29	♍0	0	1	2	2	3	4	4	5	6	6	7	7	8	8	9	9	9	10	10	10	11	♍11
♂	♉0	1	1	2	3	3	4	5	6	6	7	8	8	9	10	10	11	12	12	13	14	14	15	16	17	17	18	19	19	20	♉21

	1	6	12	18	24	30
♃	♈22	22	23	23	24	24
♄	♋21	21	22	23	24	24
	1	15	30			
♅	♎28	28	29			
♆	♐10	9	9			
♇	♎7	7	7			
☊	♐0	0	♏0			

AUGUST

	1	2	3	4	5	6	7	8	9	10	11	12	13	14	15	16	17	18	19	20	21	22	23	24	25	26	27	28	29	30	31
☉	♌8	9	10	11	12	13	14	15	16	17	18	19	20	21	22	23	23	24	25	26	27	28	29	♍0	1	2	3	4	5	6	♍7
☽	♉15	28	♊11	24	♋8	22	♌7	22	♍7	22	♎7	21	♏6	19	♐3	16	29	♑11	24	♒6	18	♓0	12	24	♈6	18	♉0	12	24	♊6	♊19
☿	♌8	10	12	14	16	18	20	22	24	26	28	♍0	1	3	5	7	8	10	12	14	15	17	18	20	22	23	25	26	28	29	♎0
♀	♍11	11	12	12	12	12	12	12	12	11	11	11	11	11	10	10	9	9	9	8	8	7	6	6	5	5	4	3	3	2	♍2
♂	♉21	22	22	23	24	24	25	26	26	27	28	28	29	29	♊0	1	1	2	3	3	4	4	5	6	6	7	7	8	8	9	♊10

	1	6	12	18	24	30
♃	♈24	25	25	25	25	24
♄	♋25	25	26	27	27	28
	1	15	30			
♅	♎29	29	♏29			
♆	♐9	9	9			
♇	♎7	7	8			
☊	♏28	27	25			

SEPTEMBER

	1	2	3	4	5	6	7	8	9	10	11	12	13	14	15	16	17	18	19	20	21	22	23	24	25	26	27	28	29	30
☉	♍8	9	10	11	12	13	14	15	16	17	18	19	20	21	22	23	23	24	25	26	27	28	29	♎0	1	2	3	4	5	♎6
☽	♋2	16	♌1	15	♍0	16	♎1	16	♏1	15	29	♐13	26	♑8	21	♒3	15	27	♓9	21	♈3	15	27	♉9	21	♊3	15	28	♋12	♋25
☿	♎2	3	4	6	7	8	10	11	12	13	14	15	16	17	18	19	20	21	21	22	23	23	24	24	24	24	24	24	24	♎24
♀	♍1	0	0	♌29	29	28	28	27	27	27	26	26	26	26	26	26	25	25	25	26	26	26	26	26	26	27	27	27	28	♌28
♂	♊10	11	11	12	12	13	13	14	14	15	15	16	17	17	18	18	18	19	19	20	20	21	21	22	22	23	23	23	24	♊24

	1	6	12	18	24	30
♃	♈24	24	23	23	22	21
♄	♋28	29	29	♌0	1	1
	1	15	30			
♅	♏0	0	1			
♆	♐9	9	9			
♇	♎8	8	9			
☊	♏25	24	23			

OCTOBER

	1	2	3	4	5	6	7	8	9	10	11	12	13	14	15	16	17	18	19	20	21	22	23	24	25	26	27	28	29	30	31
☉	♎7	8	9	10	11	12	13	14	15	16	17	18	19	20	21	22	23	24	25	26	27	28	29	♏0	1	2	3	4	5	6	♏7
☽	♌9	24	♍9	24	♎9	24	♏9	24	♐8	21	♑5	17	♒0	12	24	♓6	18	♈0	12	24	♉6	18	♊0	13	25	♋8	21	♌5	19	♍3	♍18
☿	♎23	23	22	21	21	20	18	17	16	15	14	13	12	11	10	10	9	9	9	9	10	10	11	12	13	14	15	16	17	19	♎20
♀	♌28	29	29	♍0	0	1	2	2	3	3	4	5	5	6	7	8	8	9	10	11	12	12	13	14	15	16	17	18	19	20	♍21
♂	♊25	25	25	26	26	27	27	27	28	28	28	29	29	29	29	♋0	0	0	0	1	1	1	1	1	2	2	2	2	2	2	♋2

	1	6	12	18	24	30
♃	♈21	21	20	19	18	18
♄	♌1	2	2	2	3	3
	1	15	30			
♅	♏1	2	3			
♆	♐9	10	10			
♇	♎9	10	10			
☊	♏23	22	22			

NOVEMBER

	1	2	3	4	5	6	7	8	9	10	11	12	13	14	15	16	17	18	19	20	21	22	23	24	25	26	27	28	29	30
☉	♏8	9	10	11	12	13	14	15	16	17	18	19	20	21	22	23	24	25	26	27	28	29	♐0	1	2	3	4	5	6	♐7
☽	♎3	17	♏2	17	♐2	16	♑0	13	26	♒8	21	♓3	15	26	♈8	20	♉2	14	27	♊9	22	♋5	18	♌2	15	29	♍13	28	♎12	♎27
☿	♎22	23	25	26	28	29	♏1	3	4	6	7	9	11	12	14	16	17	19	20	22	24	25	27	28	♐0	1	3	5	6	♐8
♀	♍22	22	23	24	25	26	27	28	29	♎0	1	2	4	5	6	7	8	9	10	11	12	13	14	15	16	18	19	20	21	♎22
♂	♋2	3	3	3	3	3	3	3	3	3	3	2	2	2	2	2	2	2	2	1	1	1	1	0	0	0	0	♊29	29	♊29

	1	6	12	18	24	30
♃	♈17	17	16	16	15	15
♄	♌3	3	3	3	3	3
	1	15	30			
♅	♏3	4	5			
♆	♐10	11	11			
♇	♎10	11	11			
☊	♏22	22	22			

DECEMBER

	1	2	3	4	5	6	7	8	9	10	11	12	13	14	15	16	17	18	19	20	21	22	23	24	25	26	27	28	29	30	31
☉	♐8	9	10	11	12	13	14	15	16	17	18	19	20	21	22	23	24	25	26	27	28	♑0	1	2	3	4	5	6	7	8	♑9
☽	♏11	25	♐10	24	♑7	21	♒4	16	29	♓11	23	♈4	16	28	♉10	23	♊5	18	♋1	15	28	♌12	26	♍10	24	♎9	23	♏7	21	♐5	♐18
☿	♐9	11	12	14	16	17	19	20	22	23	25	27	28	♑0	1	3	4	6	8	9	11	12	14	15	17	19	20	22	23	25	♑26
♀	♎23	24	25	27	28	29	♏0	1	2	3	5	6	7	8	9	10	12	13	14	15	16	17	19	20	21	22	23	25	26	27	♏28
♂	♊28	28	28	27	27	27	26	26	26	25	25	24	24	24	23	23	22	22	22	21	21	21	20	20	19	19	19	19	18	18	♊18

	1	6	12	18	24	30
♃	♈15	15	15	15	15	15
♄	♌3	3	2	2	2	1
	1	15	30			
♅	♏5	6	6			
♆	♐11	12	12			
♇	♎11	11	12			
☊	♏22	22	21			

1976

JANUARY

	1	2	3	4	5	6	7	8	9	10	11	12	13	14	15	16	17	18	19	20	21	22	23	24	25	26	27	28	29	30	31
☉	♑10	11	12	13	14	15	16	17	18	19	20	21	22	23	24	25	26	27	28	29	♒0	1	2	3	4	5	6	7	8	9	♒10
☽	♑2	15	29	♒11	24	♓6	18	♈0	12	24	♉6	18	♊0	13	26	♋10	23	♌8	22	♍6	21	♎5	20	♏4	18	♐1	15	28	♑11	24	♒7
☿	♑27	29	♒0	2	3	4	5	6	7	8	8	9	9	9	9	9	9	8	7	6	5	4	3	1	0	♑29	28	27	26	25	♑24
♀	♏29	♐1	2	3	4	5	7	8	9	10	11	13	14	15	16	18	19	20	21	22	24	25	26	27	28	♑0	1	2	3	5	♑6
♂	♊17	17	17	17	16	16	16	16	16	16	15	15	15	15	15	15	15	15	15	15	15	15	15	15	15	15	15	15	15	15	♊15

	1	6	12	18	24	30		1	6	12	18	24	30		1	15	30		1	15	30		1	15	30		1	15	30
♃	♈16	16	17	17	18	19	♄	♌1	1	0	0	♋29	29	♅	♏6	7	7	♆	♐13	13	13	♇	♎12	12	12	☊	♏21	20	18

FEBRUARY

	1	2	3	4	5	6	7	8	9	10	11	12	13	14	15	16	17	18	19	20	21	22	23	24	25	26	27	28	29
☉	♒11	12	13	14	15	16	17	18	19	20	21	22	23	24	25	26	27	28	29	♓0	1	2	3	5	6	7	8	9	♓10
☽	♒20	♓2	14	26	♈8	20	♉2	14	26	♊8	21	♋4	17	♌1	16	♍1	16	♎0	15	♏0	14	28	♐12	25	♑8	21	♒4	16	♒29
☿	♑24	24	23	23	23	24	24	24	25	25	26	27	27	28	29	♒0	1	2	3	4	6	7	8	9	11	12	13	15	♒16
♀	♑7	8	9	11	12	13	14	16	17	18	19	21	22	23	24	25	27	28	29	♒0	2	3	4	5	7	8	9	10	♒11
♂	♊15	16	16	16	16	16	16	17	17	17	17	18	18	18	18	19	19	19	19	20	20	20	21	21	21	22	22	22	♊23

	1	6	12	18	24	29		1	6	12	18	24	29		1	15	29		1	15	29		1	15	29		1	15	29
♃	♈19	20	21	22	23	24	♄	♋29	28	28	27	27	27	♅	♏7	7	7	♆	♐13	14	14	♇	♎12	11	11	☊	♏18	16	15

MARCH

	1	2	3	4	5	6	7	8	9	10	11	12	13	14	15	16	17	18	19	20	21	22	23	24	25	26	27	28	29	30	31
☉	♓11	12	13	14	15	16	17	18	19	20	21	22	23	24	25	26	27	28	29	♈0	1	1	2	3	4	5	6	7	8	9	♈10
☽	♓11	23	♈5	17	28	♉10	22	♊4	16	29	♋12	25	♌9	24	♍9	24	♎9	24	♏9	24	♐8	22	♑5	18	♒1	13	26	♓8	20	♈2	♈13
☿	♒17	19	20	22	23	25	26	28	29	♓1	2	4	6	7	9	11	12	14	16	18	19	21	23	25	27	29	♈1	3	5	7	♈9
♀	♒13	14	15	16	18	19	20	21	23	24	25	26	27	29	♓0	1	2	4	5	6	7	9	10	11	12	14	15	16	17	18	♓20
♂	♊23	23	24	24	24	25	25	26	26	26	27	27	28	28	28	29	29	♋0	0	1	1	2	2	2	3	3	4	4	5	5	♋6

	1	6	12	18	24	30		1	6	12	18	24	30		1	15	30		1	15	30		1	15	30		1	15	30
♃	♈24	25	27	28	29	♉1	♄	♋27	26	26	26	26	26	♅	♏7	7	6	♆	♐14	14	14	♇	♎11	11	10	☊	♏15	14	13

APRIL

	1	2	3	4	5	6	7	8	9	10	11	12	13	14	15	16	17	18	19	20	21	22	23	24	25	26	27	28	29	30
☉	♈11	12	13	14	15	16	17	18	19	20	21	22	23	24	25	26	27	28	29	♉0	1	2	3	4	5	6	7	8	9	♉10
☽	♈25	♉7	19	♊1	13	25	♋8	21	♌4	18	♍2	17	♎2	17	♏2	17	♐2	17	♑1	14	27	♒10	23	♓5	17	29	♈11	22	♉4	♉16
☿	♈11	13	15	17	19	21	23	25	27	29	♉1	3	5	7	9	11	13	15	16	18	19	21	22	24	25	26	27	28	29	♊0
♀	♓21	22	23	25	26	27	28	♈0	1	2	3	4	6	7	8	9	11	12	13	14	16	17	18	19	20	22	23	24	25	♈27
♂	♋6	7	7	8	8	9	9	10	10	11	11	12	12	13	13	14	14	15	15	16	16	17	17	18	18	19	19	20	20	♋21

	1	6	12	18	24	30		1	6	12	18	24	30		1	15	30		1	15	30		1	15	30		1	15	30
♃	♉1	2	4	5	7	8	♄	♋26	26	26	26	27	27	♅	♏6	6	5	♆	♐14	14	13	♇	♎10	10	10	☊	♏13	13	13

MAY

	1	2	3	4	5	6	7	8	9	10	11	12	13	14	15	16	17	18	19	20	21	22	23	24	25	26	27	28	29	30	31
☉	♉11	12	13	14	15	16	17	18	18	19	20	21	22	23	24	25	26	27	28	29	♊0	1	2	3	4	5	6	7	8	9	♊10
☽	♉28	♊10	22	♋5	17	♌0	14	27	♍12	26	♎11	26	♏11	26	♐10	25	♑9	23	♒6	19	♓1	14	25	♈7	19	♉1	13	25	♊7	19	♋2
☿	♊1	1	2	3	3	3	4	4	4	4	4	3	3	3	2	2	2	1	0	0	♉29	29	28	28	27	27	26	26	26	25	♉25
♀	♈28	29	♉0	2	3	4	5	6	8	9	10	11	13	14	15	16	18	19	20	21	22	24	25	26	27	29	♊0	1	2	3	♊5
♂	♋22	22	23	23	24	24	25	25	26	26	27	28	28	29	29	♌0	0	1	1	2	3	3	4	4	5	5	6	7	7	8	♌8

	1	6	12	18	24	30		1	6	12	18	24	30		1	15	30		1	15	30		1	15	30		1	15	30
♃	♉8	10	11	12	14	15	♄	♋27	27	28	28	29	29	♅	♏5	4	4	♆	♐13	13	13	♇	♎10	9	9	☊	♏13	13	12

JUNE

	1	2	3	4	5	6	7	8	9	10	11	12	13	14	15	16	17	18	19	20	21	22	23	24	25	26	27	28	29	30
☉	♊11	12	13	14	14	15	16	17	18	19	20	21	22	23	24	25	26	27	28	29	♋0	1	2	3	4	5	5	6	7	♋8
☽	♋14	27	♌11	24	♍8	22	♎6	20	♏5	20	♐4	19	♑3	17	♒1	14	27	♓9	22	♈4	16	27	♉9	21	♊3	16	28	♋11	24	♌7
☿	♉25	25	25	25	25	26	26	26	27	27	28	29	29	♊0	1	2	3	4	5	6	8	9	10	12	13	15	16	18	20	♊21
♀	♊6	7	8	10	11	12	13	15	16	17	18	19	21	22	23	24	26	27	28	29	♋1	2	3	4	5	7	8	9	10	♋12
♂	♌9	9	10	11	11	12	12	13	13	14	15	15	16	16	17	18	18	19	19	20	20	21	22	22	23	23	24	25	25	♌26

	1	6	12	18	24	30		1	6	12	18	24	30		1	15	30		1	15	30		1	15	30		1	15	30
♃	♉16	17	18	19	21	22	♄	♌0	0	1	1	2	3	♅	♏4	3	3	♆	♐13	12	12	♇	♎9	9	9	☊	♏12	12	11

JULY

	1	2	3	4	5	6	7	8	9	10	11	12	13	14	15	16	17	18	19	20	21	22	23	24	25	26	27	28	29	30	31
☉	♋9	10	11	12	13	14	15	16	17	18	19	20	21	22	23	24	25	25	26	27	28	29	♌0	1	2	3	4	5	6	7	♌8
☽	♌21	♍5	19	♎3	17	♏1	15	29	♐14	28	♑12	26	♒9	22	♓5	17	♈0	12	24	♉5	17	29	♊11	24	♋7	20	♌3	17	♍1	15	♍29
☿	♊23	25	27	29	♋1	3	5	7	9	11	13	15	18	20	22	24	26	28	♌0	2	5	7	9	11	12	14	16	18	20	22	♌24
♀	♋13	14	15	16	18	19	20	21	23	24	25	26	28	29	♌0	1	2	4	5	6	7	9	10	11	12	14	15	16	17	18	♌20
♂	♌26	27	28	28	29	29	♍0	1	1	2	2	3	4	4	5	5	6	7	7	8	9	9	10	10	11	12	12	13	13	14	♍15

	1	6	12	18	24	30		1	6	12	18	24	30		1	15	30		1	15	30		1	15	30		1	15	30
♃	♉22	23	24	25	26	27	♄	♌3	4	4	5	6	7	♅	♏3	3	3	♆	♐12	12	11	♇	♎9	9	9	☊	♏11	9	8

AUGUST

	1	2	3	4	5	6	7	8	9	10	11	12	13	14	15	16	17	18	19	20	21	22	23	24	25	26	27	28	29	30	31
☉	♌9	10	11	12	13	14	15	16	17	17	18	19	20	21	22	23	24	25	26	27	28	29	♍0	1	2	3	4	5	6	7	♍8
☽	♎13	28	♏12	26	♐10	24	♑7	21	♒4	18	♓1	13	26	♈8	20	♉1	13	25	♊7	19	♋2	15	28	♌12	26	♍10	25	♎9	24	♏8	♏23
☿	♌25	27	29	♍1	2	4	5	7	8	10	11	13	14	16	17	18	20	21	22	24	25	26	27	28	29	♎0	1	2	3	4	♎4
♀	♌21	22	23	25	26	27	28	♍0	1	2	3	4	6	7	8	9	11	12	13	14	16	17	18	19	20	22	23	24	25	27	♍28
♂	♍15	16	17	17	18	18	19	20	20	21	22	22	23	23	24	25	25	26	27	27	28	29	29	♎0	0	1	2	2	3	4	♎4

	1	6	12	18	24	30		1	6	12	18	24	30		1	15	30		1	15	30		1	15	30		1	15	30
♃	♉27	28	29	29	♊0	1	♄	♌7	8	8	9	10	11	♅	♏3	4	4	♆	♐11	11	11	♇	♎9	10	10	☊	♏8	6	5

SEPTEMBER

	1	2	3	4	5	6	7	8	9	10	11	12	13	14	15	16	17	18	19	20	21	22	23	24	25	26	27	28	29	30
☉	♍9	10	11	12	13	14	14	15	16	17	18	19	20	21	22	23	24	25	26	27	28	29	♎0	1	2	3	4	5	6	♎7
☽	♐7	21	♑4	18	♒1	14	27	♓9	22	♈4	16	28	♉10	21	♊3	15	27	♋10	23	♌6	20	♍4	19	♎3	18	♏3	18	♐3	17	♑1
☿	♎5	6	6	7	7	7	8	8	8	8	8	7	7	6	6	5	4	3	2	1	0	♍29	28	27	26	25	25	24	24	♍23
♀	♍29	♎0	2	3	4	5	6	8	9	10	11	13	14	15	16	18	19	20	21	22	24	25	26	27	29	♏0	1	2	3	♏5
♂	♎5	6	6	7	8	8	9	10	10	11	11	12	13	13	14	15	15	16	17	17	18	19	19	20	21	21	22	23	23	♎24

	1	6	12	18	24	30		1	6	12	18	24	30		1	15	30		1	15	30		1	15	30		1	15	30
♃	♊1	1	1	1	1	1	♄	♌11	11	12	13	13	14	♅	♏4	5	6	♆	♐11	11	12	♇	♎10	11	11	☊	♏5	4	4

OCTOBER

	1	2	3	4	5	6	7	8	9	10	11	12	13	14	15	16	17	18	19	20	21	22	23	24	25	26	27	28	29	30	31
☉	♎8	9	10	11	12	13	14	15	16	17	18	19	20	21	22	23	24	25	26	27	28	29	♏0	1	2	3	4	5	6	7	♏8
☽	♑15	28	♒11	24	♓6	18	♈1	13	24	♉6	18	♊0	12	24	♋6	18	♌1	14	28	♍12	27	♎12	27	♏12	27	♐12	26	♑11	24	♒8	♒21
☿	♍23	23	23	24	24	25	26	27	28	29	♎1	2	3	5	6	8	10	11	13	14	16	18	20	21	23	25	26	28	♏0	1	♏3
♀	♏6	7	8	10	11	12	13	14	16	17	18	19	21	22	23	24	25	27	28	29	♐0	2	3	4	5	6	8	9	10	11	♐13
♂	♎25	25	26	27	27	28	29	29	♏0	1	1	2	3	3	4	5	6	6	7	8	8	9	10	10	11	12	12	13	14	15	♏15

	1	6	12	18	24	30		1	6	12	18	24	30		1	15	30		1	15	30		1	15	30		1	15	30
♃	♊1	1	0	0	♉29	29	♄	♌14	14	15	15	16	16	♅	♏6	6	7	♆	♐12	12	12	♇	♎11	12	13	☊	♏4	4	4

NOVEMBER

	1	2	3	4	5	6	7	8	9	10	11	12	13	14	15	16	17	18	19	20	21	22	23	24	25	26	27	28	29	30
☉	♏9	10	11	12	13	14	15	16	17	18	19	20	21	22	23	24	25	26	27	28	29	♐0	1	2	3	4	5	6	7	♐8
☽	♓3	15	28	♈10	21	♉3	15	27	♊9	21	♋3	15	28	♌10	23	♍7	21	♎5	20	♏5	20	♐5	20	♑5	19	♒3	17	♓0	12	♓24
☿	♏5	6	8	10	11	13	14	16	18	19	21	22	24	26	27	29	♐0	2	3	5	7	8	10	11	13	14	16	17	19	♐20
♀	♐14	15	16	17	19	20	21	22	23	25	26	27	28	29	♑1	2	3	4	5	7	8	9	10	11	13	14	15	16	17	♑19
♂	♏16	17	17	18	19	19	20	21	21	22	23	24	24	25	26	26	27	28	29	29	♐0	1	1	2	3	4	4	5	6	♐6

	1	6	12	18	24	30		1	6	12	18	24	30		1	15	30		1	15	30		1	15	30		1	15	30
♃	♉28	28	27	26	25	25	♄	♌16	16	17	17	17	17	♅	♏8	8	9	♆	♐12	13	13	♇	♎13	13	14	☊	♏4	3	3

DECEMBER

	1	2	3	4	5	6	7	8	9	10	11	12	13	14	15	16	17	18	19	20	21	22	23	24	25	26	27	28	29	30	31
☉	♐9	10	11	12	13	14	15	16	17	18	19	20	21	22	23	24	25	26	27	28	29	♑0	1	2	3	4	5	6	7	8	♑9
☽	♈6	18	♉0	12	24	♊6	18	♋0	12	25	♌7	20	♍3	17	♎0	14	29	♏13	28	♐13	28	♑13	27	♒11	25	♓8	20	♈3	15	27	♉8
☿	♐22	23	25	26	28	29	♑1	2	4	5	7	8	10	11	12	14	15	16	17	18	19	20	21	22	22	23	23	23	23	23	♑23
♀	♑20	21	22	23	25	26	27	28	29	♒1	2	3	4	5	6	8	9	10	11	12	13	15	16	17	18	19	20	21	23	24	♒25
♂	♐7	8	9	9	10	11	12	12	13	14	14	15	16	17	17	18	19	20	20	21	22	23	23	24	25	26	26	27	28	28	♐29

	1	6	12	18	24	30		1	6	12	18	24	30		1	15	30		1	15	30		1	15	30		1	15	30
♃	♉24	24	23	23	22	22	♄	♌17	17	17	17	16	16	♅	♏9	10	11	♆	♐14	14	15	♇	♎14	14	14	☊	♏3	2	1

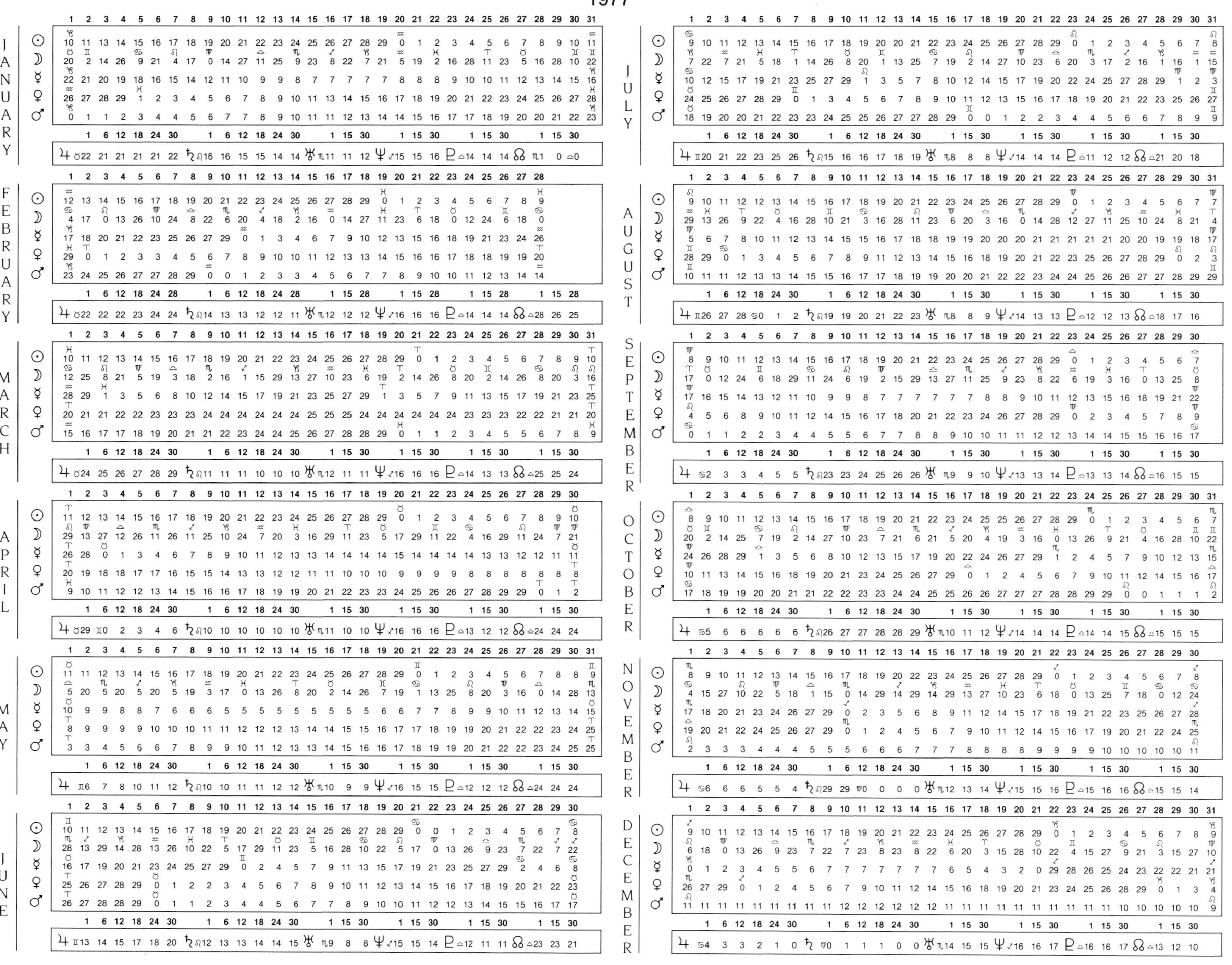

1977

JANUARY

	1	2	3	4	5	6	7	8	9	10	11	12	13	14	15	16	17	18	19	20	21	22	23	24	25	26	27	28	29	30	31
☉	♑10	11	13	14	15	16	17	18	19	20	21	22	23	24	25	26	27	28	29	♒0	1	2	3	4	5	6	7	8	9	10	♒11
☽	♉20	♊2	14	26	♋9	21	♌4	17	♍0	14	27	♎11	25	♏9	23	♐8	22	♑7	21	♒5	19	♓2	16	28	♈11	23	♉5	16	28	♊10	♊22
☿	♑22	21	20	19	18	16	15	14	12	11	10	9	9	8	7	7	7	7	7	8	8	8	9	10	10	11	12	13	14	15	♑16
♀	♒26	27	28	29	♓1	2	3	4	5	6	7	8	9	10	11	13	14	15	16	17	18	19	20	21	22	23	24	25	26	27	♓28
♂	♑0	1	1	2	3	4	4	5	6	7	7	8	9	10	11	11	12	13	14	14	15	16	17	17	18	19	20	20	21	22	♑23

	1	6	12	18	24	30
♃	♉22	21	21	21	21	22
♄	♌16	16	15	15	14	14

	1	15	30
♅	♏11	11	12
♆	♐15	15	16
♇	♎14	14	14
☊	♏1	0	♎0

FEBRUARY

	1	2	3	4	5	6	7	8	9	10	11	12	13	14	15	16	17	18	19	20	21	22	23	24	25	26	27	28
☉	♒12	13	14	15	16	17	18	19	20	21	22	23	24	25	26	27	28	29	♓0	1	2	3	4	5	6	7	8	♓9
☽	♋4	17	♌0	13	26	♍10	24	♎8	22	♏6	20	♐4	18	♑2	16	♒0	14	27	♓11	23	♈6	18	♉0	12	24	♊6	18	♋0
☿	♑17	18	20	21	22	23	25	26	27	29	♒0	1	3	4	6	7	9	10	12	13	15	16	18	19	21	23	24	♒26
♀	♓29	♈0	1	2	3	3	4	5	6	7	8	9	10	10	11	12	13	13	14	15	16	16	17	18	18	19	19	♈20
♂	♑23	24	25	26	27	27	28	29	♒0	0	1	2	3	3	4	5	6	7	7	8	9	10	10	11	12	13	14	♒14

	1	6	12	18	24	28
♃	♉22	22	22	23	24	24
♄	♌14	13	13	12	12	11

	1	15	28
♅	♏12	12	12
♆	♐16	16	16
♇	♎14	14	14
☊	♎28	26	25

MARCH

	1	2	3	4	5	6	7	8	9	10	11	12	13	14	15	16	17	18	19	20	21	22	23	24	25	26	27	28	29	30	31
☉	♓10	11	12	13	14	15	16	17	18	19	20	21	22	23	24	25	26	27	28	29	♈0	1	2	3	4	5	6	7	8	9	♈10
☽	♋12	25	♌8	21	♍5	19	♎3	18	♏2	16	♐1	15	29	♑13	27	♒10	23	♓6	19	♈2	14	26	♉8	20	♊2	14	26	♋8	20	♌3	♌16
☿	♒28	29	♓1	3	5	6	8	10	12	14	15	17	19	21	23	25	27	29	♈1	3	5	7	9	11	13	15	17	19	21	23	♈25
♀	♈20	21	21	22	22	23	23	23	24	24	24	24	24	24	25	25	25	24	24	24	24	24	24	23	23	23	22	22	21	21	♈20
♂	♒15	16	17	17	18	19	20	21	21	22	23	24	24	25	26	27	28	28	29	♓0	1	1	2	3	4	5	5	6	7	8	♓9

	1	6	12	18	24	30
♃	♉24	25	26	27	28	29
♄	♌11	11	11	10	10	10

	1	15	30
♅	♏12	11	11
♆	♐16	16	16
♇	♎14	13	13
☊	♎25	25	24

APRIL

	1	2	3	4	5	6	7	8	9	10	11	12	13	14	15	16	17	18	19	20	21	22	23	24	25	26	27	28	29	30
☉	♈11	12	13	14	15	16	17	18	19	20	21	22	23	24	25	26	27	28	29	♉0	1	2	3	4	5	6	7	8	9	♉10
☽	♌29	♍13	27	♎12	26	♏11	26	♐11	25	♑10	24	♒7	20	♓3	16	29	♈11	23	♉5	17	29	♊11	22	♋4	16	29	♌11	24	♍7	♍21
☿	♈26	28	♉0	1	3	4	6	7	8	9	10	11	12	13	13	14	14	14	14	15	14	14	14	14	13	13	12	12	11	♉11
♀	♈20	19	18	18	17	17	16	15	15	14	13	13	12	12	11	11	10	10	10	9	9	9	9	8	8	8	8	8	8	♈8
♂	♓9	10	11	12	12	13	14	15	16	16	17	18	19	19	20	21	22	23	23	24	25	26	26	27	28	29	29	♈0	1	♈2

	1	6	12	18	24	30
♃	♉29	♊0	2	3	4	6
♄	♌10	10	10	10	10	10

	1	15	30
♅	♏11	10	10
♆	♐16	16	16
♇	♎13	12	12
☊	♎24	24	24

MAY

	1	2	3	4	5	6	7	8	9	10	11	12	13	14	15	16	17	18	19	20	21	22	23	24	25	26	27	28	29	30	31
☉	♉11	11	12	13	14	15	16	17	18	19	20	21	22	23	24	25	26	27	28	29	♊0	1	2	3	4	5	6	7	8	8	♊9
☽	♎5	20	♏5	20	♐5	20	♑5	19	♒3	17	♓0	13	26	♈8	20	♉2	14	26	♊7	19	♋1	13	25	♌8	20	♍3	16	♎0	14	28	♏13
☿	♉10	9	9	8	8	7	6	6	6	5	5	5	5	5	5	5	5	5	6	6	7	7	8	9	9	10	11	12	13	14	♉15
♀	♈8	9	9	9	9	10	10	10	11	11	12	12	12	13	14	14	15	15	16	17	17	18	19	19	20	21	22	22	23	24	♈25
♂	♈3	3	4	5	6	6	7	8	9	9	10	11	12	13	13	14	15	16	16	17	18	19	19	20	21	22	22	23	24	25	♈25

	1	6	12	18	24	30
♃	♊6	7	8	10	11	12
♄	♌10	10	11	11	12	12

	1	15	30
♅	♏10	9	9
♆	♐16	15	15
♇	♎12	12	12
☊	♎24	24	24

JUNE

	1	2	3	4	5	6	7	8	9	10	11	12	13	14	15	16	17	18	19	20	21	22	23	24	25	26	27	28	29	30
☉	♊10	11	12	13	14	15	16	17	18	19	20	21	22	23	24	25	26	27	28	29	♋0	0	1	2	3	4	5	6	7	♋8
☽	♏28	♐13	29	♑14	28	♒13	26	♓10	22	♈5	17	29	♉11	23	♊5	16	28	♋10	22	♌5	17	♍0	13	26	♎9	23	♏7	22	♐7	♐22
☿	♉16	17	19	20	21	23	24	25	27	29	♊0	2	4	5	7	9	11	13	15	17	19	21	23	25	27	29	♋2	4	6	♋8
♀	♈25	26	27	28	29	♉0	1	2	2	3	4	5	6	7	8	9	10	11	12	13	14	15	16	17	18	19	20	21	22	♉23
♂	♈26	27	28	28	29	♉0	1	1	2	3	4	4	5	6	7	7	8	9	10	10	11	12	12	13	14	15	15	16	17	♉17

	1	6	12	18	24	30
♃	♊13	14	15	17	18	20
♄	♌12	13	13	14	14	15

	1	15	30
♅	♏9	8	8
♆	♐15	15	14
♇	♎12	11	11
☊	♎23	23	21

JULY

	1	2	3	4	5	6	7	8	9	10	11	12	13	14	15	16	17	18	19	20	21	22	23	24	25	26	27	28	29	30	31
☉	♋9	10	11	12	13	14	15	16	17	18	19	20	20	21	22	23	24	25	26	27	28	29	♌0	1	2	3	4	5	6	7	♌8
☽	♑7	22	♒7	21	♓5	18	♈1	14	26	♉8	20	♊1	13	25	♋7	19	♌2	14	27	♍10	23	♎6	20	♏3	17	♐2	16	♑1	16	♒1	♒15
☿	♋10	12	15	17	19	21	23	25	27	29	♌1	3	5	7	8	10	12	14	15	17	19	20	22	24	25	27	28	29	♍1	2	♍3
♀	♉24	25	26	27	28	29	♊0	1	3	4	5	6	7	8	9	10	11	12	13	15	16	17	18	19	20	21	22	23	25	26	♊27
♂	♉18	19	20	20	21	22	23	23	24	25	25	26	27	27	28	29	♊0	0	1	2	2	3	4	4	5	6	6	7	8	9	♊9

	1	6	12	18	24	30
♃	♊20	21	22	23	25	26
♄	♌15	16	16	17	18	19

	1	15	30
♅	♏8	8	8
♆	♐14	14	14
♇	♎11	12	12
☊	♎21	20	18

AUGUST

	1	2	3	4	5	6	7	8	9	10	11	12	13	14	15	16	17	18	19	20	21	22	23	24	25	26	27	28	29	30	31
☉	♌9	10	11	12	12	13	14	15	16	17	18	19	20	21	22	23	24	25	26	27	28	29	♍0	1	2	3	4	5	6	7	♍7
☽	♒29	♓13	26	♈9	22	♉4	16	28	♊10	21	♋3	16	28	♌11	23	♍6	20	♎3	16	♏0	14	28	♐12	27	♑11	25	♒10	24	♓8	21	♈4
☿	♍5	6	7	8	10	11	12	13	14	15	15	16	17	18	18	19	19	20	20	20	21	21	21	21	21	20	20	19	19	18	♍17
♀	♊28	29	♋0	1	3	4	5	6	7	8	9	11	12	13	14	15	16	18	19	20	21	22	23	25	26	27	28	29	♌0	2	♌3
♂	♊10	11	11	12	13	13	14	15	15	16	17	17	18	19	19	20	20	21	22	22	23	24	24	25	26	26	27	27	28	29	♊29

	1	6	12	18	24	30
♃	♊26	27	28	♋0	1	2
♄	♌19	19	20	21	22	23

	1	15	30
♅	♏8	8	9
♆	♐14	13	13
♇	♎12	12	13
☊	♎18	17	16

SEPTEMBER

	1	2	3	4	5	6	7	8	9	10	11	12	13	14	15	16	17	18	19	20	21	22	23	24	25	26	27	28	29	30
☉	♍8	9	10	11	12	13	14	15	16	17	18	19	20	21	22	23	24	25	26	27	28	29	♎0	1	2	3	4	5	6	♎7
☽	♈17	♉0	12	24	♊6	18	29	♋11	24	♌6	19	♍2	15	29	♎13	27	♏11	25	♐9	23	♑8	22	♒6	19	♓3	16	♈0	13	25	♉8
☿	♍17	16	15	14	13	12	11	10	9	9	8	7	7	7	7	7	7	8	8	9	10	11	12	13	15	16	18	19	21	♍22
♀	♌4	5	6	8	9	10	11	12	14	15	16	17	18	20	21	22	23	24	26	27	28	29	♍0	2	3	4	5	7	8	♍9
♂	♋0	1	1	2	2	3	4	4	5	5	6	7	7	8	8	9	10	10	11	11	12	12	13	14	14	15	15	16	16	♋17

	1	6	12	18	24	30
♃	♋2	3	3	4	5	5
♄	♌23	23	24	25	26	26

	1	15	30
♅	♏9	9	10
♆	♐13	13	14
♇	♎13	13	14
☊	♎16	15	15

OCTOBER

	1	2	3	4	5	6	7	8	9	10	11	12	13	14	15	16	17	18	19	20	21	22	23	24	25	26	27	28	29	30	31
☉	♎8	9	10	11	12	13	14	15	16	17	18	19	20	21	22	23	24	25	25	26	27	28	29	♏0	1	2	3	4	5	6	♏7
☽	♉20	♊2	14	25	♋7	19	♌2	14	27	♍10	23	♎7	21	♏6	21	♐5	20	♑4	19	♒3	16	♓0	13	26	♈9	21	♉4	16	28	♊10	♊22
☿	♍24	26	28	29	♎1	3	5	6	8	10	12	13	15	17	19	20	22	24	26	27	29	♏1	2	4	5	7	9	10	12	13	♏15
♀	♍10	11	13	14	15	16	18	19	20	21	23	24	25	26	27	29	♎0	1	2	4	5	6	7	9	10	11	12	14	15	16	♎17
♂	♋17	18	19	19	20	20	21	21	22	22	23	23	24	24	25	25	26	26	27	27	27	28	28	29	29	♌0	0	1	1	1	♌2

	1	6	12	18	24	30
♃	♋5	6	6	6	6	6
♄	♌26	27	27	28	28	29

	1	15	30
♅	♏10	11	12
♆	♐14	14	14
♇	♎14	14	15
☊	♎15	15	15

NOVEMBER

	1	2	3	4	5	6	7	8	9	10	11	12	13	14	15	16	17	18	19	20	21	22	23	24	25	26	27	28	29	30
☉	♏8	9	10	11	12	13	14	15	16	17	18	19	20	22	23	24	25	26	27	28	29	♐0	1	2	3	4	5	6	7	♐8
☽	♋4	15	27	♌10	22	♍5	18	♎1	15	♏0	14	29	♐14	29	♑14	29	♒13	27	♓10	23	♈6	18	♉0	13	25	♊7	18	♋0	12	♋24
☿	♏17	18	20	21	23	24	26	27	29	♐0	2	3	5	6	8	9	11	12	14	15	17	18	19	21	22	23	25	26	27	♐28
♀	♎19	20	21	22	24	25	26	27	29	♏0	1	2	4	5	6	7	9	10	11	12	14	15	16	17	19	20	21	22	24	♏25
♂	♌2	3	3	3	4	4	4	5	5	5	6	6	6	7	7	7	8	8	8	8	9	9	9	9	10	10	10	10	10	♌11

	1	6	12	18	24	30
♃	♋6	6	6	5	5	4
♄	♌29	29	♍0	0	0	0

	1	15	30
♅	♏12	13	14
♆	♐15	15	16
♇	♎15	16	16
☊	♎15	15	14

DECEMBER

	1	2	3	4	5	6	7	8	9	10	11	12	13	14	15	16	17	18	19	20	21	22	23	24	25	26	27	28	29	30	31
☉	♐9	10	11	12	13	14	15	16	17	18	19	20	21	22	23	24	25	26	27	28	29	♑0	1	2	3	4	5	6	7	8	♑9
☽	♌6	18	♍0	13	26	♎9	23	♏7	22	♐7	23	♑8	23	♒8	22	♓6	20	♈3	15	28	♉10	22	♊4	15	27	♋9	21	♌3	15	27	♍10
☿	♑0	1	2	3	4	5	5	6	7	7	7	7	7	7	7	6	5	4	3	2	0	♐29	28	26	25	24	23	22	22	21	♐21
♀	♏26	27	29	♐0	1	2	4	5	6	7	9	10	11	12	14	15	16	18	19	20	21	23	24	25	26	28	29	♑0	1	3	♑4
♂	♌11	11	11	11	11	11	11	11	11	12	12	12	12	12	12	11	11	11	11	11	11	11	11	11	11	10	10	10	10	10	♌9

	1	6	12	18	24	30
♃	♋4	3	3	2	1	0
♄	♍0	1	1	1	0	0

	1	15	30
♅	♏14	15	15
♆	♐16	16	17
♇	♎16	16	17
☊	♎13	12	10

1978

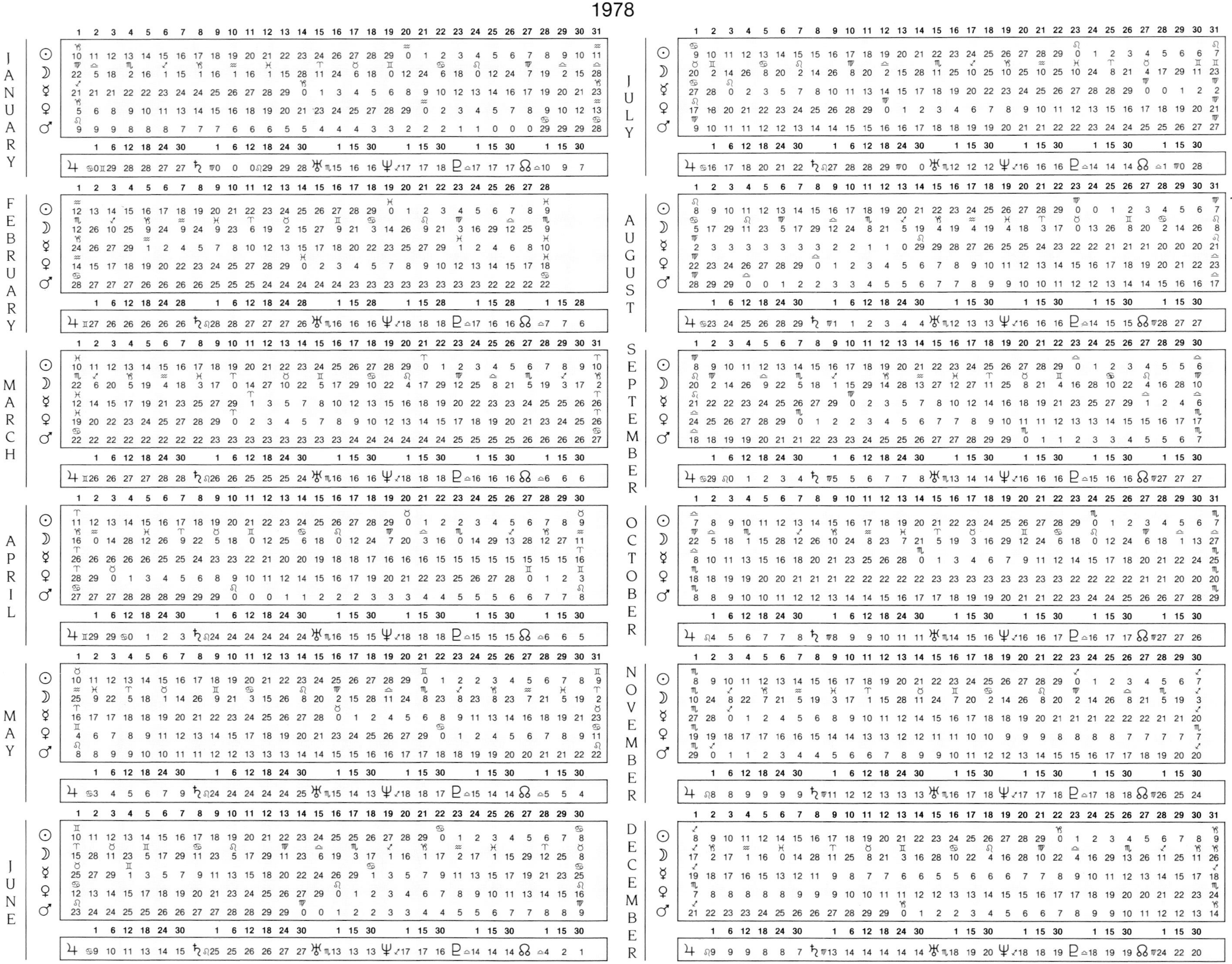

JANUARY

	1	2	3	4	5	6	7	8	9	10	11	12	13	14	15	16	17	18	19	20	21	22	23	24	25	26	27	28	29	30	31
☉	♑10	11	12	13	14	15	16	17	18	19	20	21	22	23	24	26	27	28	29	♒0	1	2	3	4	5	6	7	8	9	10	♒11
☽	♍22	♎5	18	♏2	16	♐1	15	♑1	16	♒1	16	♓1	15	28	♈11	24	♉6	18	♊0	12	24	♋6	18	♌0	12	24	♍7	19	♎2	15	♎28
☿	♐21	21	21	22	22	23	24	24	25	26	27	28	29	♑0	1	3	4	5	6	8	9	10	12	13	14	16	17	19	20	21	♑23
♀	♑5	6	8	9	10	11	13	14	15	16	18	19	20	21	23	24	25	27	28	29	♒0	2	3	4	5	7	8	9	10	12	♒13
♂	♌9	9	9	8	8	8	7	7	7	6	6	6	5	5	4	4	4	3	3	2	2	2	1	1	0	0	0	♋29	29	29	♋28

	1	6	12	18	24	30
♃	♋0	♊29	28	28	27	27
♄	♍0	0	0	♌29	29	28

	1	15	30
♅	♏15	16	16
♆	♐17	17	18
♇	♎17	17	17
☊	♎10	9	7

FEBRUARY

	1	2	3	4	5	6	7	8	9	10	11	12	13	14	15	16	17	18	19	20	21	22	23	24	25	26	27	28
☉	♒12	13	14	15	16	17	18	19	20	21	22	23	24	25	26	27	28	29	♓0	1	2	3	4	5	6	7	8	♓9
☽	♏12	26	♐10	25	♑9	24	♒9	24	♓9	23	♈6	19	♉2	15	27	♊9	21	♋3	14	26	♌9	21	♍3	16	29	♎12	25	♏9
☿	♑24	26	27	29	♒1	2	4	5	7	8	10	12	13	15	17	18	20	22	23	25	27	29	♓1	2	4	6	8	♓10
♀	♒14	15	17	18	19	20	22	23	24	25	27	28	29	♓0	2	3	4	5	7	8	9	10	12	13	14	15	17	♓18
♂	♋28	27	27	27	26	26	26	26	25	25	25	24	24	24	24	24	23	23	23	23	23	23	23	23	22	22	22	♋22

	1	6	12	18	24	28
♃	♊27	26	26	26	26	26
♄	♌28	28	27	27	27	26

	1	15	28
♅	♏16	16	16
♆	♐18	18	18
♇	♎17	16	16
☊	♎7	7	6

MARCH

	1	2	3	4	5	6	7	8	9	10	11	12	13	14	15	16	17	18	19	20	21	22	23	24	25	26	27	28	29	30	31
☉	♓10	11	12	13	14	15	16	17	18	19	20	21	22	23	24	25	26	27	28	29	♈0	1	2	3	4	5	6	7	8	9	♈10
☽	♏22	♐6	20	♑5	19	♒4	18	♓3	17	♈0	14	27	♉10	22	♊5	17	29	♋10	22	♌4	17	29	♍12	25	♎8	21	♏5	19	♐3	17	♑2
☿	♓12	14	15	17	19	21	23	25	27	29	♈1	3	5	7	8	10	12	13	15	16	18	19	20	22	23	23	24	25	25	26	♈26
♀	♓19	20	22	23	24	25	27	28	29	♈0	2	3	4	5	7	8	9	10	12	13	14	15	17	18	19	20	21	23	24	25	♈26
♂	♋22	22	22	22	22	22	22	22	23	23	23	23	23	23	23	23	24	24	24	24	24	24	25	25	25	25	26	26	26	26	♋27

	1	6	12	18	24	30
♃	♊26	26	27	27	28	28
♄	♌26	26	25	25	25	24

	1	15	30
♅	♏16	16	16
♆	♐18	18	18
♇	♎16	16	16
☊	♎6	6	6

APRIL

	1	2	3	4	5	6	7	8	9	10	11	12	13	14	15	16	17	18	19	20	21	22	23	24	25	26	27	28	29	30
☉	♈11	12	13	14	15	16	17	18	19	20	21	22	23	24	25	26	27	28	29	♉0	1	2	2	3	4	5	6	7	8	♉9
☽	♑16	♒0	14	28	♓12	26	♈9	22	♉5	18	♊0	12	25	♋6	18	♌0	12	24	♍7	20	♎3	16	♏0	14	29	♐13	28	♑12	27	♒11
☿	♈26	26	26	26	26	25	25	24	23	23	22	21	20	20	19	18	18	17	16	16	16	15	15	15	15	15	15	15	15	♈16
♀	♈28	29	♉0	1	3	4	5	6	8	9	10	11	12	14	15	16	17	19	20	21	22	23	25	26	27	28	♊0	1	2	♊3
♂	♋27	27	27	28	28	28	29	29	29	♌0	0	0	1	1	2	2	2	3	3	3	4	4	5	5	5	6	6	7	7	♌8

	1	6	12	18	24	30
♃	♊29	29	♋0	1	2	3
♄	♌24	24	24	24	24	24

	1	15	30
♅	♏16	15	15
♆	♐18	18	18
♇	♎15	15	15
☊	♎6	6	5

MAY

	1	2	3	4	5	6	7	8	9	10	11	12	13	14	15	16	17	18	19	20	21	22	23	24	25	26	27	28	29	30	31
☉	♉10	11	12	13	14	15	16	17	18	19	20	21	22	23	24	25	26	27	28	29	♊0	1	2	2	3	4	5	6	7	8	♊9
☽	♒25	♓9	22	♈5	18	♉1	14	26	♊9	21	♋3	15	26	♌8	20	♍2	15	28	♎11	24	♏8	23	♐8	23	♑8	23	♒7	21	♓5	19	♈2
☿	♈16	17	17	18	18	19	20	21	22	23	24	25	26	27	28	♉0	1	2	4	5	6	8	9	11	13	14	16	18	19	21	♉23
♀	♊4	6	7	8	9	11	12	13	14	15	17	18	19	20	21	23	24	25	26	27	29	♋0	1	2	4	5	6	7	8	9	♋11
♂	♌8	8	9	9	10	10	11	11	12	12	13	13	13	14	14	15	15	16	16	17	17	18	18	19	19	20	20	21	21	22	♌22

	1	6	12	18	24	30
♃	♋3	4	5	6	7	9
♄	♌24	24	24	24	24	25

	1	15	30
♅	♏15	14	13
♆	♐18	18	17
♇	♎15	14	14
☊	♎5	5	4

JUNE

	1	2	3	4	5	6	7	8	9	10	11	12	13	14	15	16	17	18	19	20	21	22	23	24	25	26	27	28	29	30
☉	♊10	11	12	13	14	15	16	17	18	19	20	21	22	23	24	25	25	26	27	28	29	♋0	1	2	3	4	5	6	7	♋8
☽	♈15	28	♉11	23	♊5	17	29	♋11	23	♌5	17	29	♍11	23	♎6	19	♏3	17	♐1	16	♑1	17	♒2	17	♓1	15	29	♈12	25	♉8
☿	♉25	27	29	♊1	3	5	7	9	11	13	15	18	20	22	24	26	29	♋1	3	5	7	9	11	13	15	17	19	21	23	♋25
♀	♋12	13	14	15	17	18	19	20	21	23	24	25	26	27	29	♌0	1	2	3	4	6	7	8	9	10	11	13	14	15	♌16
♂	♌23	24	24	25	25	26	26	27	27	28	28	29	29	♍0	0	1	2	2	3	3	4	4	5	5	6	7	7	8	8	♍9

	1	6	12	18	24	30
♃	♋9	10	11	13	14	15
♄	♌25	25	26	26	27	27

	1	15	30
♅	♏13	13	13
♆	♐17	17	16
♇	♎14	14	14
☊	♎4	2	1

JULY

	1	2	3	4	5	6	7	8	9	10	11	12	13	14	15	16	17	18	19	20	21	22	23	24	25	26	27	28	29	30	31
☉	♋9	10	11	12	13	14	15	15	16	17	18	19	20	21	22	23	24	25	26	27	28	29	♌0	1	2	3	4	5	6	6	♌7
☽	♉20	♊2	14	26	♋8	20	♌2	14	26	♍8	20	♎2	15	28	♏11	25	♐10	25	♑10	25	♒10	25	♓10	24	♈8	21	♉4	17	29	♊11	♊23
☿	♋27	28	♌0	2	3	5	7	8	10	11	13	14	15	17	18	19	20	22	23	24	25	26	27	28	28	29	♍0	0	1	2	♍2
♀	♌17	18	20	21	22	23	24	25	26	28	29	♍0	1	2	3	4	6	7	8	9	10	11	12	13	15	16	17	18	19	20	♍21
♂	♍9	10	11	11	12	12	13	14	14	15	15	16	16	17	18	18	19	19	20	21	21	22	22	23	24	24	25	25	26	27	♍27

	1	6	12	18	24	30
♃	♋16	17	18	20	21	22
♄	♌27	28	28	29	♍0	0

	1	15	30
♅	♏12	12	12
♆	♐16	16	16
♇	♎14	14	14
☊	♎1	♍0	28

AUGUST

	1	2	3	4	5	6	7	8	9	10	11	12	13	14	15	16	17	18	19	20	21	22	23	24	25	26	27	28	29	30	31
☉	♌8	9	10	11	12	13	14	15	16	17	18	19	20	21	22	23	24	25	26	27	28	29	♍0	0	1	2	3	4	5	6	♍7
☽	♋5	17	29	♌11	23	♍5	17	29	♎12	24	♏8	21	♐5	19	♑4	19	♒4	19	♓4	18	♈3	17	♉0	13	26	♊8	20	♋2	14	26	♌8
☿	♍2	3	3	3	3	3	3	3	2	2	1	1	0	♌29	29	28	27	26	25	25	24	23	22	22	21	21	21	20	20	20	♌21
♀	♍22	23	24	26	27	28	29	♎0	1	2	3	4	5	6	7	8	9	10	11	12	13	14	15	16	17	18	19	20	21	22	♎23
♂	♍28	29	29	♎0	0	1	2	2	3	3	4	5	5	6	7	7	8	9	9	10	10	11	12	12	13	14	14	15	16	16	♎17

	1	6	12	18	24	30
♃	♋23	24	25	26	28	29
♄	♍1	1	2	3	4	4

	1	15	30
♅	♏12	13	13
♆	♐16	16	16
♇	♎14	15	15
☊	♍28	27	27

SEPTEMBER

	1	2	3	4	5	6	7	8	9	10	11	12	13	14	15	16	17	18	19	20	21	22	23	24	25	26	27	28	29	30
☉	♍8	9	10	11	12	13	14	15	16	17	18	19	20	21	22	23	24	25	26	27	28	29	♎0	1	2	3	4	5	5	♎6
☽	♌20	♍2	14	26	♎9	22	♏5	18	♐1	15	29	♑14	28	♒13	27	♓12	27	♈11	25	♉8	21	♊4	16	28	♋10	22	♌4	16	28	♍10
☿	♌21	22	22	23	24	25	26	27	29	♍0	2	3	5	7	8	10	12	14	16	18	19	21	23	25	27	29	♎1	2	4	♎6
♀	♎24	25	26	27	28	29	♏0	1	2	2	3	4	5	6	7	7	8	9	10	11	11	12	13	13	14	15	15	16	17	♏17
♂	♎18	18	19	19	20	21	21	22	23	23	24	25	25	26	27	27	28	29	29	♏0	1	1	2	3	3	4	5	5	6	♏7

	1	6	12	18	24	30
♃	♋29	♌0	1	2	3	4
♄	♍5	5	6	7	7	8

	1	15	30
♅	♏13	14	14
♆	♐16	16	16
♇	♎15	16	16
☊	♍27	27	27

OCTOBER

	1	2	3	4	5	6	7	8	9	10	11	12	13	14	15	16	17	18	19	20	21	22	23	24	25	26	27	28	29	30	31
☉	♎7	8	9	10	11	12	13	14	15	16	17	18	19	20	21	22	23	24	25	26	27	28	29	♏0	1	2	3	4	5	6	♏7
☽	♍22	♎5	18	♏1	15	28	♐12	26	♑10	24	♒8	23	♓7	21	♈5	19	♉3	16	29	♊12	24	♋6	18	♌0	12	24	♍6	18	♎1	13	♎27
☿	♎8	10	11	13	15	16	18	20	21	23	25	26	28	♏0	1	3	4	6	7	9	11	12	14	15	17	18	20	21	22	24	♏25
♀	♏18	18	19	19	20	20	21	21	21	22	22	22	22	22	23	23	23	23	23	23	23	23	22	22	22	22	21	21	20	20	♏20
♂	♏8	8	9	10	10	11	12	12	13	14	14	15	16	17	17	18	19	19	20	21	21	22	23	24	24	25	26	26	27	28	♏29

	1	6	12	18	24	30
♃	♌4	5	6	7	7	8
♄	♍8	9	9	10	11	11

	1	15	30
♅	♏14	15	16
♆	♐16	16	17
♇	♎16	17	17
☊	♍27	27	26

NOVEMBER

	1	2	3	4	5	6	7	8	9	10	11	12	13	14	15	16	17	18	19	20	21	22	23	24	25	26	27	28	29	30
☉	♏8	9	10	11	12	13	14	15	16	17	18	19	20	21	22	23	24	25	26	27	28	29	♐0	1	2	3	4	5	6	♐7
☽	♏10	24	♐8	22	♑7	21	♒5	19	♓3	17	♈1	15	28	♉11	24	♊7	20	♋2	14	26	♌8	20	♍2	14	26	♎8	21	♏5	19	♐3
☿	♏27	28	♐0	1	2	4	5	6	8	9	10	11	12	14	15	16	17	18	18	19	20	21	21	21	22	22	22	21	21	♐20
♀	♏19	19	18	17	17	16	16	15	14	14	13	13	12	12	11	11	10	10	9	9	9	8	8	8	8	7	7	7	7	♏7
♂	♏29	♐0	1	1	2	3	4	4	5	6	6	7	8	9	9	10	11	12	12	13	14	15	15	16	17	17	18	19	20	♐20

	1	6	12	18	24	30
♃	♌8	8	9	9	9	9
♄	♍11	12	12	13	13	13

	1	15	30
♅	♏16	17	18
♆	♐17	17	18
♇	♎17	18	18
☊	♍26	25	24

DECEMBER

	1	2	3	4	5	6	7	8	9	10	11	12	13	14	15	16	17	18	19	20	21	22	23	24	25	26	27	28	29	30	31
☉	♐8	9	10	11	12	14	15	16	17	18	19	20	21	22	23	24	25	26	27	28	29	♑0	1	2	3	4	5	6	7	8	♑9
☽	♐17	♑2	17	♒1	16	♓0	14	28	♈11	25	♉8	21	♊3	16	28	♋10	22	♌4	16	28	♍10	22	♎4	16	29	♏13	26	♐11	25	♑11	♑26
☿	♐19	18	17	16	15	13	12	11	9	8	7	7	6	6	5	5	6	6	6	7	7	8	9	10	11	12	13	14	15	17	♐18
♀	♏7	8	8	8	8	8	9	9	9	10	10	11	11	12	12	13	13	14	15	15	16	17	17	18	19	20	20	21	22	23	♏24
♂	♐21	22	23	23	24	25	26	26	27	28	29	29	♑0	1	2	2	3	4	5	6	6	7	8	9	9	10	11	12	12	13	♑14

	1	6	12	18	24	30
♃	♌9	9	9	8	8	7
♄	♍13	14	14	14	14	14

	1	15	30
♅	♏18	19	20
♆	♐18	18	19
♇	♎18	19	19
☊	♍24	22	20

1979

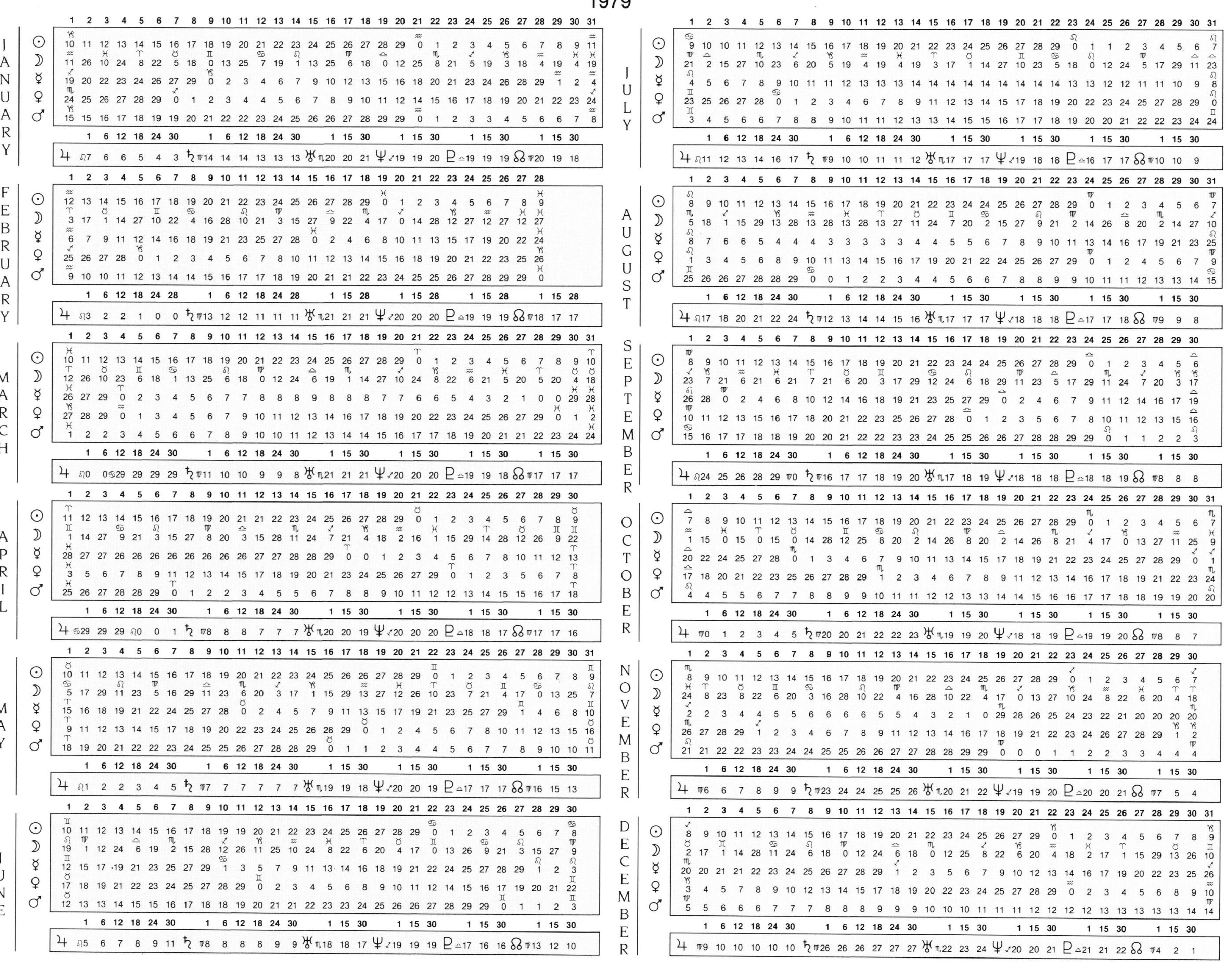

JANUARY

	1	2	3	4	5	6	7	8	9	10	11	12	13	14	15	16	17	18	19	20	21	22	23	24	25	26	27	28	29	30	31
☉	♑10	11	12	13	14	15	16	17	18	19	20	21	22	23	24	25	26	27	28	29	♒0	1	2	3	4	5	6	7	8	9	♒11
☽	♒11	26	♓10	24	♈8	22	♉5	18	♊0	13	25	♋7	19	♌1	13	25	♍6	18	♎0	12	25	♏8	21	♐5	19	♑3	18	♒4	19	♓4	♓19
☿	♐19	20	22	23	24	26	27	29	♑0	2	3	4	6	7	9	10	12	13	15	16	18	20	21	23	24	26	28	29	♒1	2	♒4
♀	♏24	25	26	27	28	29	♐0	1	2	3	4	4	5	6	7	8	9	10	11	12	14	15	16	17	18	19	20	21	22	23	♐24
♂	♑15	15	16	17	18	19	19	20	21	22	22	23	24	25	26	26	27	28	29	29	♒0	1	2	3	3	4	5	6	6	7	♒8

	1	6	12	18	24	30
♃	♌7	6	6	5	4	3
♄	♍14	14	14	13	13	13

	1	15	30
♅	♏20	20	21
♆	♐19	19	20
♇	♎19	19	19
☊	♍20	19	18

FEBRUARY

	1	2	3	4	5	6	7	8	9	10	11	12	13	14	15	16	17	18	19	20	21	22	23	24	25	26	27	28
☉	♒12	13	14	15	16	17	18	19	20	21	22	23	24	25	26	27	28	29	♓0	1	2	3	4	5	6	7	8	♓9
☽	♈3	17	♉1	14	27	♊10	22	♋4	16	28	♌10	21	♍3	15	27	♎9	22	♏4	17	♐0	14	28	♑12	27	♒12	27	♓12	♓27
☿	♒6	7	9	11	12	14	16	18	19	21	23	25	27	28	♓0	2	4	6	8	10	11	13	15	17	19	20	22	♓24
♀	♐25	26	27	28	♑0	1	2	3	4	5	6	7	8	10	11	12	13	14	15	16	18	19	20	21	22	23	25	♑26
♂	♒9	10	10	11	12	13	14	14	15	16	17	17	18	19	20	21	21	22	23	24	25	25	26	27	28	29	29	♓0

	1	6	12	18	24	28
♃	♌3	2	2	1	0	0
♄	♍13	12	12	11	11	11

	1	15	28
♅	♏21	21	21
♆	♐20	20	20
♇	♎19	19	19
☊	♍18	17	17

MARCH

	1	2	3	4	5	6	7	8	9	10	11	12	13	14	15	16	17	18	19	20	21	22	23	24	25	26	27	28	29	30	31
☉	♓10	11	12	13	14	15	16	17	18	19	20	21	22	23	24	25	26	27	28	29	♈0	1	2	3	4	5	6	7	8	9	♈10
☽	♈12	26	♉10	23	♊6	18	♋1	13	25	♌6	18	♍0	12	24	♎6	19	♏1	14	27	♐10	24	♑8	22	♒6	21	♓5	20	♈5	20	♉4	♉18
☿	♓26	27	29	♈0	2	3	4	5	6	7	7	8	8	8	9	8	8	8	7	7	6	6	5	4	3	2	1	0	0	♓29	♓28
♀	♑27	28	29	♒0	1	3	4	5	6	7	9	10	11	12	13	14	16	17	18	19	20	22	23	24	25	26	27	29	♓0	1	♓2
♂	♓1	2	2	3	4	5	6	6	7	8	9	10	10	11	12	13	14	14	15	16	17	17	18	19	20	21	21	22	23	24	♓24

	1	6	12	18	24	30
♃	♌0	0	♋29	29	29	29
♄	♍11	10	10	9	9	8

	1	15	30
♅	♏21	21	21
♆	♐20	20	20
♇	♎19	19	18
☊	♍17	17	17

APRIL

	1	2	3	4	5	6	7	8	9	10	11	12	13	14	15	16	17	18	19	20	21	22	23	24	25	26	27	28	29	30
☉	♈11	12	13	14	15	16	17	18	19	20	21	21	22	23	24	25	26	27	28	29	♉0	1	2	3	4	5	6	7	8	♉9
☽	♊1	14	27	♋9	21	♌3	15	27	♍8	20	♎3	15	28	♏11	24	♐7	21	♑4	18	♒2	16	♓1	15	29	♈14	28	♉12	26	♊9	♊22
☿	♓28	27	27	26	26	26	26	26	26	26	26	27	27	28	28	29	♈0	0	1	2	3	4	5	6	7	8	10	11	12	♈13
♀	♓3	5	6	7	8	9	11	12	13	14	15	17	18	19	20	21	23	24	25	26	27	29	♈0	1	2	3	5	6	7	♈8
♂	♓25	26	27	28	28	29	♈0	1	2	2	3	4	5	5	6	7	8	8	9	10	11	12	12	13	14	15	15	16	17	♈18

	1	6	12	18	24	30
♃	♋29	29	29	♌0	0	1
♄	♍8	8	8	7	7	7

	1	15	30
♅	♏20	20	19
♆	♐20	20	20
♇	♎18	18	17
☊	♍17	17	16

MAY

	1	2	3	4	5	6	7	8	9	10	11	12	13	14	15	16	17	18	19	20	21	22	23	24	25	26	27	28	29	30	31
☉	♉10	11	12	13	14	15	16	17	18	19	20	21	22	23	24	25	26	26	27	28	29	♊0	1	2	3	4	5	6	7	8	♊9
☽	♋5	17	29	♌11	23	♍5	16	29	♎11	23	♏6	20	♐3	17	♑1	15	29	♒13	27	♓12	26	♈10	23	♉7	21	♊4	17	♋0	13	25	♌7
☿	♈15	16	18	19	21	22	24	25	27	28	♉0	2	4	5	7	9	11	13	15	17	19	21	23	25	27	29	♊1	4	6	8	♊10
♀	♈9	11	12	13	14	15	17	18	19	20	22	23	24	25	26	28	29	♉0	1	2	4	5	6	7	8	10	11	12	13	15	♉16
♂	♈18	19	20	21	22	22	23	24	25	25	26	27	28	28	29	♉0	1	1	2	3	4	4	5	6	7	7	8	9	10	10	♉11

	1	6	12	18	24	30
♃	♌1	2	2	3	4	5
♄	♍7	7	7	7	7	7

	1	15	30
♅	♏19	19	18
♆	♐20	20	19
♇	♎17	17	17
☊	♍16	15	13

JUNE

	1	2	3	4	5	6	7	8	9	10	11	12	13	14	15	16	17	18	19	20	21	22	23	24	25	26	27	28	29	30
☉	♊10	11	12	13	14	15	16	17	18	19	19	20	21	22	23	24	25	26	27	28	29	♋0	1	2	3	4	5	6	7	♋8
☽	♌19	♍1	12	24	♎6	19	♏2	15	28	♐12	26	♑11	25	♒10	24	♓8	22	♈6	20	♉4	17	♊0	13	26	♋9	21	♌3	15	27	♍9
☿	♊12	15	17	19	21	23	25	27	29	♋1	3	5	7	9	11	13	14	16	18	19	21	22	24	25	27	28	29	♌1	2	♌3
♀	♉17	18	19	21	22	23	24	25	27	28	29	♊0	2	3	4	5	6	8	9	10	11	12	14	15	16	17	19	20	21	♊22
♂	♉12	13	13	14	15	15	16	17	18	18	19	20	21	21	22	23	23	24	25	26	26	27	28	29	29	♊0	1	1	2	♊3

	1	6	12	18	24	30
♃	♌5	6	7	8	9	11
♄	♍8	8	8	8	9	9

	1	15	30
♅	♏18	18	17
♆	♐19	19	19
♇	♎17	16	16
☊	♍13	12	10

JULY

	1	2	3	4	5	6	7	8	9	10	11	12	13	14	15	16	17	18	19	20	21	22	23	24	25	26	27	28	29	30	31
☉	♋9	10	10	11	12	13	14	15	16	17	18	19	20	21	22	23	24	25	26	27	28	29	♌0	1	1	2	3	4	5	6	♌7
☽	♍21	♎2	15	27	♏10	23	♐6	20	♑5	19	♒4	19	♓4	19	♈3	17	♉1	14	27	♊10	23	♋5	18	♌0	12	24	♍5	17	29	♎11	♎23
☿	♌4	5	6	7	8	9	10	11	11	12	13	13	13	14	14	14	14	14	14	14	14	14	13	13	12	12	11	11	10	9	♌8
♀	♊23	25	26	27	28	♋0	1	2	3	4	6	7	8	9	11	12	13	14	15	17	18	19	20	22	23	24	25	27	28	29	♌0
♂	♊3	4	5	6	6	7	8	8	9	10	11	11	12	13	13	14	15	15	16	17	17	18	19	20	20	21	22	22	23	24	♊24

	1	6	12	18	24	30
♃	♌11	12	13	14	16	17
♄	♍9	10	10	11	11	12

	1	15	30
♅	♏17	17	17
♆	♐19	18	18
♇	♎16	17	17
☊	♍10	10	9

AUGUST

	1	2	3	4	5	6	7	8	9	10	11	12	13	14	15	16	17	18	19	20	21	22	23	24	25	26	27	28	29	30	31
☉	♌8	9	10	11	12	13	14	15	16	17	18	19	20	21	22	23	24	24	25	26	27	28	29	♍0	1	2	3	4	5	6	♍7
☽	♏5	18	♐1	15	29	♑13	28	♒13	28	♓13	28	♈13	27	♉11	24	♊7	20	♋2	15	27	♌9	21	♍2	14	26	♎8	20	♏2	14	27	♐10
☿	♌8	7	6	6	5	4	4	4	3	3	3	3	3	4	4	5	5	6	7	8	9	10	11	13	14	16	17	19	21	23	♌25
♀	♌1	3	4	5	6	8	9	10	11	13	14	15	16	17	19	20	21	22	24	25	26	27	29	♍0	1	2	4	5	6	7	♍9
♂	♊25	26	26	27	28	28	29	♋0	0	1	2	2	3	4	4	5	6	6	7	8	8	9	9	10	11	11	12	13	13	14	♋15

	1	6	12	18	24	30
♃	♌17	18	20	21	22	24
♄	♍12	13	14	14	15	16

	1	15	30
♅	♏17	17	17
♆	♐18	18	18
♇	♎17	17	18
☊	♍9	9	8

SEPTEMBER

	1	2	3	4	5	6	7	8	9	10	11	12	13	14	15	16	17	18	19	20	21	22	23	24	25	26	27	28	29	30
☉	♍8	9	10	11	12	13	14	15	16	17	18	19	20	21	22	23	24	24	25	26	27	28	29	♎0	1	2	3	4	5	♎6
☽	♐23	♑7	21	♒6	21	♓6	21	♈7	21	♉6	20	♊3	17	29	♋12	24	♌6	18	29	♍11	23	♎5	17	29	♏11	24	♐7	20	♑3	♑17
☿	♌26	28	♍0	2	4	6	8	10	12	14	16	18	19	21	23	25	27	29	♎0	2	4	6	7	9	11	12	14	16	17	♎19
♀	♍10	11	12	13	15	16	17	18	20	21	22	23	25	26	27	28	♎0	1	2	3	5	6	7	8	10	11	12	13	15	♎16
♂	♋15	16	17	17	18	18	19	20	20	21	22	22	23	23	24	25	25	26	26	27	28	28	29	29	♌0	1	1	2	2	♌3

	1	6	12	18	24	30
♃	♌24	25	26	28	29	♍0
♄	♍16	17	17	18	19	20

	1	15	30
♅	♏17	18	19
♆	♐18	18	18
♇	♎18	18	19
☊	♍8	8	8

OCTOBER

	1	2	3	4	5	6	7	8	9	10	11	12	13	14	15	16	17	18	19	20	21	22	23	24	25	26	27	28	29	30	31
☉	♎7	8	9	10	11	12	13	14	15	16	17	18	19	20	21	22	23	24	25	26	27	28	29	♏0	1	2	3	4	5	6	♏7
☽	♒1	15	♓0	15	♈0	15	♉0	14	28	♊12	25	♋8	20	♌2	14	26	♍8	20	♎2	14	26	♏8	21	♐4	17	♑0	13	27	♒11	25	♓9
☿	♎20	22	24	25	27	28	♏0	1	3	4	6	7	9	10	11	13	14	15	17	18	19	21	22	23	24	25	27	28	29	♐0	♐1
♀	♎17	18	20	21	22	23	25	26	27	28	29	♏1	2	3	4	6	7	8	9	11	12	13	14	16	17	18	19	21	22	23	♏24
♂	♌4	4	5	5	6	7	7	8	8	9	9	10	11	11	12	12	13	13	14	14	15	16	16	17	17	18	18	19	19	20	♌20

	1	6	12	18	24	30
♃	♍0	1	2	3	4	5
♄	♍20	20	21	22	22	23

	1	15	30
♅	♏19	19	20
♆	♐18	18	19
♇	♎19	19	20
☊	♍8	8	7

NOVEMBER

	1	2	3	4	5	6	7	8	9	10	11	12	13	14	15	16	17	18	19	20	21	22	23	24	25	26	27	28	29	30
☉	♏8	9	10	11	12	13	14	15	16	17	18	19	20	21	22	23	24	25	26	27	28	29	♐0	1	2	3	4	5	6	♐7
☽	♓24	♈8	23	♉8	22	♊6	20	♋3	16	28	♌10	22	♍4	16	28	♎10	22	♏4	17	♐0	13	27	♑10	24	♒8	22	♓6	20	♈4	♈18
☿	♐2	2	3	4	4	5	5	6	6	6	6	5	5	4	3	2	1	0	♏29	28	26	25	24	23	22	21	20	20	20	♏20
♀	♏26	27	28	29	♐1	2	3	4	6	7	8	9	11	12	13	14	16	17	18	19	21	22	23	24	26	27	28	29	♑1	♑2
♂	♌21	21	22	22	23	23	24	24	25	25	26	26	27	27	28	28	29	29	♍0	0	0	1	1	2	2	3	3	4	4	♍4

	1	6	12	18	24	30
♃	♍6	6	7	8	9	9
♄	♍23	24	24	25	25	26

	1	15	30
♅	♏20	21	22
♆	♐19	19	20
♇	♎20	20	21
☊	♍7	5	4

DECEMBER

	1	2	3	4	5	6	7	8	9	10	11	12	13	14	15	16	17	18	19	20	21	22	23	24	25	26	27	28	29	30	31
☉	♐8	9	10	11	12	13	14	15	16	17	18	19	20	21	22	23	24	25	26	27	29	♑0	1	2	3	4	5	6	7	8	♑9
☽	♉2	17	♊1	14	28	♋11	24	♌6	18	♍0	12	24	♎6	18	♏0	12	25	♐8	22	♑6	20	♒4	18	♓2	17	♈1	15	29	♉13	26	♊10
☿	♏20	20	21	21	22	23	24	25	26	27	28	29	♐1	2	3	5	6	7	9	10	12	13	14	16	17	19	20	22	23	25	♐26
♀	♑3	4	5	7	8	9	10	12	13	14	15	17	18	19	20	22	23	24	25	27	28	29	♒0	2	3	4	5	6	8	9	♒10
♂	♍5	5	6	6	6	7	7	7	8	8	8	9	9	9	10	10	10	11	11	11	12	12	12	12	13	13	13	13	13	14	♍14

	1	6	12	18	24	30
♃	♍9	10	10	10	10	10
♄	♍26	26	26	27	27	27

	1	15	30
♅	♏22	23	24
♆	♐20	20	21
♇	♎21	21	22
☊	♍4	2	1

1980

JANUARY

	1	2	3	4	5	6	7	8	9	10	11	12	13	14	15	16	17	18	19	20	21	22	23	24	25	26	27	28	29	30	31
☉	♑10	11	12	13	14	15	16	17	18	19	20	21	22	23	24	25	26	27	28	29	♒0	1	2	3	4	5	6	7	8	9	♒10
☽	♊23	♋6	19	♌2	14	26	♍8	20	♎2	13	25	♏8	20	♐3	16	♑0	14	29	♒13	28	♓12	27	♈11	26	♉10	23	♊7	20	♋3	15	♋28
☿	♐28	29	♑1	3	4	6	7	9	10	12	14	15	17	18	20	22	23	25	27	28	♒0	2	3	5	7	8	10	12	14	15	♒17
♀	♒11	13	14	15	16	18	19	20	21	22	24	25	26	27	29	♓0	1	2	3	5	6	7	8	10	11	12	13	14	16	17	♓18
♂	♍14	14	14	14	15	15	15	15	15	15	15	15	15	15	15	15	15	15	15	15	15	15	15	15	15	15	15	14	14	14	♍14

	1	6	12	18	24	30
♃	♍10	10	10	9	9	8
♄	♍27	27	27	27	27	27

	1	15	30
♅	♏24	25	25
♆	♐21	21	22
♇	♎22	22	22
☊	♍0	0	♌0

FEBRUARY

	1	2	3	4	5	6	7	8	9	10	11	12	13	14	15	16	17	18	19	20	21	22	23	24	25	26	27	28	29
☉	♒11	12	13	14	15	16	17	18	19	20	21	22	23	24	25	26	27	28	29	♓1	2	3	4	5	6	7	8	9	♓10
☽	♌10	22	♍4	16	28	♎10	22	♏4	16	28	♐11	24	♑8	22	♒6	21	♓6	21	♈6	21	♉6	20	♊3	17	♋0	12	25	♌7	♌19
☿	♒19	21	22	24	26	28	29	♓1	3	5	6	8	9	11	13	14	15	16	18	19	19	20	21	21	21	22	21	21	♓21
♀	♓19	20	22	23	24	25	26	28	29	♈0	1	2	4	5	6	7	8	9	11	12	13	14	15	16	18	19	20	21	♈22
♂	♍14	14	13	13	13	13	12	12	12	11	11	11	10	10	10	9	9	9	8	8	7	7	7	6	6	5	5	5	♍4

	1	6	12	18	24	29
♃	♍8	8	7	6	5	5
♄	♍26	26	26	26	25	25

	1	15	29
♅	♏25	25	26
♆	♐22	22	23
♇	♎22	22	21
☊	♌29	29	29

MARCH

	1	2	3	4	5	6	7	8	9	10	11	12	13	14	15	16	17	18	19	20	21	22	23	24	25	26	27	28	29	30	31
☉	♓11	12	13	14	15	16	17	18	19	20	21	22	23	24	25	26	27	28	29	♈0	1	2	3	4	4	5	6	7	8	9	♈10
☽	♍1	13	25	♎7	18	♏0	12	25	♐7	20	♑3	16	♒0	15	29	♓14	♈0	15	♉0	15	29	♊13	26	♋9	22	♌4	16	28	♍10	22	♎4
☿	♓20	20	19	18	17	16	15	14	13	12	11	10	10	9	8	8	8	8	7	7	8	8	8	8	9	9	10	10	11	12	♓13
♀	♈23	25	26	27	28	29	♉0	1	2	4	5	6	7	8	9	10	11	12	14	15	16	17	18	19	20	21	22	23	24	25	♉26
♂	♍4	4	3	3	2	2	2	1	1	1	0	0	0	♌29	29	29	29	28	28	28	28	27	27	27	27	27	27	26	26	26	♌26

	1	6	12	18	24	30
♃	♍5	4	3	3	2	1
♄	♍25	24	24	23	23	22

	1	15	30
♅	♏26	25	25
♆	♐23	23	23
♇	♎21	21	21
☊	♌29	29	29

APRIL

	1	2	3	4	5	6	7	8	9	10	11	12	13	14	15	16	17	18	19	20	21	22	23	24	25	26	27	28	29	30
☉	♈11	12	13	14	15	16	17	18	19	20	21	22	23	24	25	26	27	28	29	♉0	1	2	3	4	5	6	7	8	9	♉10
☽	♎15	27	♏9	22	♐4	16	29	♑12	25	♒9	23	♓8	23	♈8	23	♉8	23	♊7	21	♋5	18	♌1	13	25	♍7	19	♎0	12	24	♏6
☿	♓14	15	16	17	18	19	20	21	22	24	25	26	28	29	♈0	2	3	5	6	8	10	11	13	15	16	18	20	22	23	♈25
♀	♉27	28	29	♊0	1	2	3	4	5	6	7	8	9	10	11	12	12	13	14	15	16	17	17	18	19	20	21	21	22	♊23
♂	♌26	26	26	26	26	26	26	26	26	26	26	26	26	26	26	26	27	27	27	27	27	27	27	28	28	28	28	28	29	♌29

	1	6	12	18	24	30
♃	♍1	1	1	0	0	0
♄	♍22	22	22	21	21	21

	1	15	30
♅	♏25	25	24
♆	♐23	23	22
♇	♎21	20	20
☊	♌29	28	26

MAY

	1	2	3	4	5	6	7	8	9	10	11	12	13	14	15	16	17	18	19	20	21	22	23	24	25	26	27	28	29	30	31
☉	♉11	12	13	14	15	16	17	18	19	19	20	21	22	23	24	25	26	27	28	29	♊0	1	2	3	4	5	6	7	8	9	♊10
☽	♏18	♐1	13	26	♑9	22	♒6	19	♓3	17	♈2	17	♉2	16	♊1	16	29	♋13	26	♌9	21	♍3	15	27	♎9	21	♏3	15	27	♐10	♐23
☿	♈27	29	♉1	3	5	7	9	11	13	15	18	20	22	24	26	28	♊1	3	5	7	9	11	13	15	17	19	21	23	25	27	♊28
♀	♊23	24	25	25	26	27	27	28	28	29	29	♋0	0	0	1	1	1	2	2	2	2	2	3	3	3	3	2	2	2	2	♋2
♂	♌29	29	♍0	0	0	1	1	1	1	2	2	2	3	3	3	4	4	4	5	5	6	6	6	7	7	8	8	8	9	9	♍10

	1	6	12	18	24	30
♃	♍0	0	1	1	1	2
♄	♍21	20	20	20	20	20

	1	15	30
♅	♏24	24	23
♆	♐22	22	22
♇	♎20	19	19
☊	♌26	25	23

JUNE

	1	2	3	4	5	6	7	8	9	10	11	12	13	14	15	16	17	18	19	20	21	22	23	24	25	26	27	28	29	30
☉	♊11	12	13	14	14	15	16	17	18	19	20	21	22	23	24	25	26	27	28	29	♋0	1	2	3	4	5	5	6	7	♋8
☽	♑6	19	♒3	16	♓0	14	28	♈12	27	♉11	26	♊10	24	♋8	21	♌4	17	29	♍11	23	♎5	17	29	♏11	23	♐6	19	♑2	15	♑29
☿	♋0	2	3	5	6	8	9	11	12	13	14	15	17	18	19	19	20	21	22	22	23	24	24	24	25	25	25	25	25	♋25
♀	♋2	1	1	1	0	0	♊29	29	28	28	27	26	26	25	25	24	23	23	22	21	21	20	20	19	19	18	18	18	17	♊17
♂	♍10	11	11	11	12	12	13	13	14	14	15	15	16	16	17	17	17	18	18	19	19	20	21	21	22	22	23	23	24	♍24

	1	6	12	18	24	30
♃	♍2	3	3	4	5	6
♄	♍20	20	21	21	21	21

	1	15	30
♅	♏23	22	22
♆	♐22	21	21
♇	♎19	19	19
☊	♌23	22	21

JULY

	1	2	3	4	5	6	7	8	9	10	11	12	13	14	15	16	17	18	19	20	21	22	23	24	25	26	27	28	29	30	31
☉	♋9	10	11	12	13	14	15	16	17	18	19	20	21	22	23	24	25	26	26	27	28	29	♌0	1	2	3	4	5	6	7	♌8
☽	♒13	27	♓11	25	♈9	23	♉7	21	♊5	19	♋3	16	29	♌12	25	♍7	19	♎1	13	25	♏7	19	♐1	14	27	♑10	24	♒8	22	♓7	♓21
☿	♋25	25	24	24	24	23	23	22	21	21	20	19	19	18	18	17	17	16	16	16	15	15	15	15	15	16	16	17	17	18	♋19
♀	♊17	17	16	16	16	16	16	16	16	16	16	17	17	17	17	18	18	18	19	19	20	20	20	21	22	22	23	23	24	25	♊25
♂	♍25	25	26	26	27	27	28	28	29	♎0	0	1	1	2	2	3	4	4	5	5	6	6	7	8	8	9	9	10	11	11	♎12

	1	6	12	18	24	30
♃	♍6	7	8	9	10	11
♄	♍21	22	22	23	23	24

	1	15	30
♅	♏22	22	21
♆	♐21	20	20
♇	♎19	19	19
☊	♌21	20	20

AUGUST

	1	2	3	4	5	6	7	8	9	10	11	12	13	14	15	16	17	18	19	20	21	22	23	24	25	26	27	28	29	30	31
☉	♌9	10	11	12	13	14	15	16	17	18	18	19	20	21	22	23	24	25	26	27	28	29	♍0	1	2	3	4	5	6	7	♍8
☽	♈5	20	♉4	18	♊2	16	29	♋13	26	♌8	21	♍3	15	27	♎9	21	♏3	15	27	♐9	22	♑5	18	♒2	16	♓1	16	♈1	15	♉0	♉15
☿	♋19	20	22	23	24	25	27	28	♌0	1	3	5	7	9	10	12	14	16	18	20	22	24	26	28	♍0	2	4	6	8	10	♍12
♀	♊26	27	27	28	29	♋0	0	1	2	3	4	4	5	6	7	8	9	10	11	11	12	13	14	15	16	17	18	19	20	21	♋22
♂	♎12	13	14	14	15	15	16	17	17	18	18	19	20	20	21	22	22	23	23	24	25	25	26	27	27	28	29	29	♏0	0	♏1

	1	6	12	18	24	30
♃	♍12	13	14	15	16	18
♄	♍24	25	25	26	27	27

	1	15	30
♅	♏22	22	22
♆	♐20	20	20
♇	♎19	20	20
☊	♌20	20	20

SEPTEMBER

	1	2	3	4	5	6	7	8	9	10	11	12	13	14	15	16	17	18	19	20	21	22	23	24	25	26	27	28	29	30
☉	♍9	10	11	12	13	14	15	15	16	17	18	19	20	21	22	23	24	25	26	27	28	29	♎0	1	2	3	4	5	6	♎7
☽	♉29	♊13	26	♋9	22	♌5	17	♍0	12	24	♎6	18	29	♏11	23	♐5	18	♑0	13	26	♒10	24	♓9	24	♈9	24	♉9	24	♊9	♊23
☿	♍14	16	18	19	21	23	25	26	28	♎0	2	3	5	6	8	10	11	13	14	16	17	19	20	22	23	24	26	27	29	♏0
♀	♋23	24	25	26	27	28	29	♌0	1	2	3	4	6	7	8	9	10	11	12	13	14	15	16	18	19	20	21	22	23	♌24
♂	♏2	2	3	4	4	5	6	6	7	8	8	9	10	10	11	12	12	13	14	14	15	16	17	17	18	19	19	20	21	♏21

	1	6	12	18	24	30
♃	♍18	19	20	22	23	24
♄	♍27	28	29	♎0	0	1

	1	15	30
♅	♏22	22	23
♆	♐20	20	20
♇	♎20	21	21
☊	♌20	20	19

OCTOBER

	1	2	3	4	5	6	7	8	9	10	11	12	13	14	15	16	17	18	19	20	21	22	23	24	25	26	27	28	29	30	31
☉	♎8	9	10	11	12	13	14	15	16	17	18	19	20	21	22	23	24	25	26	27	28	29	♏0	1	2	3	4	5	6	7	♏8
☽	♋6	19	♌2	15	27	♍9	21	♎3	15	26	♏8	20	♐2	14	27	♑9	22	♒5	19	♓3	17	♈2	17	♉3	18	♊3	18	♋2	15	29	♌11
☿	♏1	3	4	5	6	7	9	10	11	12	13	14	15	16	16	17	18	18	19	19	20	20	20	20	20	19	19	18	17	16	♏15
♀	♌25	27	28	29	♍0	1	2	3	5	6	7	8	9	10	12	13	14	15	16	18	19	20	21	22	23	25	26	27	28	29	♎1
♂	♏22	23	23	24	25	26	26	27	28	28	29	♐0	1	1	2	3	3	4	5	6	6	7	8	8	9	10	11	11	12	13	♐14

	1	6	12	18	24	30
♃	♍25	26	27	28	29	♎1
♄	♎1	2	3	3	4	5

	1	15	30
♅	♏23	24	25
♆	♐20	20	21
♇	♎21	22	22
☊	♌19	18	17

NOVEMBER

	1	2	3	4	5	6	7	8	9	10	11	12	13	14	15	16	17	18	19	20	21	22	23	24	25	26	27	28	29	30
☉	♏9	10	11	12	13	14	15	16	17	18	19	20	21	22	23	24	25	26	27	28	29	♐0	1	2	3	4	5	6	7	♐8
☽	♌24	♍6	18	♎0	12	23	♏5	17	29	♐11	24	♑6	19	♒2	15	28	♓12	26	♈11	26	♉11	26	♊11	26	♋10	24	♌7	20	♍2	♍14
☿	♏14	13	12	10	9	8	7	6	5	5	4	4	4	4	5	5	6	6	7	8	9	11	12	13	14	16	17	18	20	♏21
♀	♎2	3	4	5	7	8	9	10	12	13	14	15	16	18	19	20	21	23	24	25	26	27	29	♏0	1	2	4	5	6	♏7
♂	♐14	15	16	16	17	18	19	19	20	21	22	22	23	24	25	25	26	27	28	28	29	♑0	1	1	2	3	4	5	5	♑6

	1	6	12	18	24	30
♃	♎1	2	3	4	5	6
♄	♎5	5	6	7	7	8

	1	15	30
♅	♏25	26	27
♆	♐21	21	22
♇	♎22	23	23
☊	♌17	15	13

DECEMBER

	1	2	3	4	5	6	7	8	9	10	11	12	13	14	15	16	17	18	19	20	21	22	23	24	25	26	27	28	29	30	31
☉	♐9	10	11	12	13	14	15	16	17	18	19	20	21	22	23	24	25	26	27	28	29	♑0	1	2	3	4	5	6	7	8	♑9
☽	♍26	♎8	20	♏2	14	26	♐8	21	♑3	16	29	♒12	25	♓8	22	♈6	21	♉5	20	♊4	19	♋4	18	♌1	15	28	♍10	22	♎4	16	♎28
☿	♏23	24	26	27	29	♐0	2	3	5	6	8	9	11	13	14	16	17	19	20	22	23	25	27	28	♑0	1	3	4	6	8	♑9
♀	♏9	10	11	12	14	15	16	17	18	20	21	22	23	25	26	27	28	♐0	1	2	3	5	6	7	8	10	11	12	13	15	♐16
♂	♑7	8	8	9	10	11	11	12	13	14	14	15	16	17	18	18	19	20	21	21	22	23	24	25	25	26	27	28	28	29	♒0

	1	6	12	18	24	30
♃	♎6	7	8	8	9	9
♄	♎8	8	9	9	9	9

	1	15	30
♅	♏27	27	28
♆	♐22	22	23
♇	♎23	24	24
☊	♌13	12	11

1981

JANUARY

	1	2	3	4	5	6	7	8	9	10	11	12	13	14	15	16	17	18	19	20	21	22	23	24	25	26	27	28	29	30	31
☉	♑10	12	13	14	15	16	17	18	19	20	21	22	23	24	25	26	27	28	29	♒0	1	2	3	4	5	6	7	8	9	10	♒11
☽	♏10	22	♐4	17	29	♑12	25	♒8	22	♓5	19	♈3	17	♉1	16	♊0	14	28	♋12	26	♌9	22	♍5	18	♎0	12	24	♏6	18	♐0	♐12
☿	♑11	12	14	16	17	19	21	22	24	26	27	29	♒1	2	4	6	7	9	11	12	14	16	17	19	21	22	24	25	27	28	♒29
♀	♐17	18	20	21	22	23	25	26	27	28	♑0	1	2	3	5	6	7	8	10	11	12	13	15	16	17	18	20	21	22	23	♑25
♂	♒1	2	2	3	4	5	6	6	7	8	9	9	10	11	12	13	13	14	15	16	17	17	18	19	20	21	21	22	23	24	♒24

	1	6	12	18	24	30
♃	♎10	10	10	10	10	10
♄	♎10	10	10	10	10	10

	1	15	30
♅	♏28	29	♐29
♆	♐23	24	24
♇	♎24	24	24
☊	♌11	11	11

FEBRUARY

	1	2	3	4	5	6	7	8	9	10	11	12	13	14	15	16	17	18	19	20	21	22	23	24	25	26	27	28
☉	♒12	13	14	15	16	17	18	19	20	21	22	23	24	25	26	27	28	29	♓0	1	2	3	4	5	6	7	8	♓9
☽	♐24	♑7	20	♒3	17	♓1	15	29	♈14	28	♉12	27	♊11	24	♋8	22	♌5	18	♍1	13	26	♎8	20	♏2	14	26	♐8	♐20
☿	♓0	1	2	3	4	4	5	5	5	5	4	4	3	2	1	0	♒29	28	27	26	25	24	23	22	21	21	20	♒20
♀	♑26	27	28	♒0	1	2	3	5	6	7	8	10	11	12	13	15	16	17	18	20	21	22	23	25	26	27	28	♓0
♂	♒25	26	27	28	28	29	♓0	1	2	2	3	4	5	6	6	7	8	9	10	10	11	12	13	13	14	15	16	♓17

	1	6	12	18	24	28
♃	♎10	10	10	9	9	9
♄	♎10	9	9	9	9	8

	1	15	28
♅	♐0	0	0
♆	♐24	24	25
♇	♎24	24	24
☊	♌11	11	11

MARCH

	1	2	3	4	5	6	7	8	9	10	11	12	13	14	15	16	17	18	19	20	21	22	23	24	25	26	27	28	29	30	31
☉	♓10	11	12	13	14	15	16	17	18	19	20	21	22	23	24	25	26	27	28	29	♈0	1	2	3	4	5	6	7	8	9	♈10
☽	♑2	15	28	♒11	25	♓9	24	♈9	24	♉8	23	♊7	21	♋5	18	♌2	15	27	♍10	22	♎4	16	28	♏10	22	♐4	16	28	♑10	23	♒6
☿	♒20	20	20	20	20	21	21	21	22	23	23	24	25	26	27	28	29	♓0	1	2	3	4	6	7	8	10	11	12	14	15	♓17
♀	♓1	2	3	5	6	7	8	10	11	12	13	15	16	17	18	20	21	22	23	25	26	27	28	♈0	1	2	3	5	6	7	♈8
♂	♓17	18	19	20	21	21	22	23	24	24	25	26	27	28	28	29	♈0	1	1	2	3	4	5	5	6	7	8	8	9	10	♈11

	1	6	12	18	24	30
♃	♎9	8	7	7	6	5
♄	♎8	8	8	7	7	6

	1	15	30
♅	♐0	0	0
♆	♐25	25	25
♇	♎24	24	23
☊	♌11	10	9

APRIL

	1	2	3	4	5	6	7	8	9	10	11	12	13	14	15	16	17	18	19	20	21	22	23	24	25	26	27	28	29	30
☉	♈11	12	13	14	15	16	17	18	19	20	21	22	23	24	25	26	27	28	29	♉0	1	2	3	4	5	6	7	8	9	♉10
☽	♒19	♓3	17	♈2	17	♉2	18	♊3	17	♋1	15	29	♌12	24	♍7	19	♎1	13	25	♏7	19	♐1	13	25	♑7	19	♒2	14	28	♓12
☿	♓18	20	21	23	24	26	28	29	♈1	3	5	6	8	10	12	14	16	17	19	21	23	25	27	♉0	2	4	6	8	10	♉12
♀	♈10	11	12	13	15	16	17	18	19	21	22	23	24	26	27	28	29	♉1	2	3	4	6	7	8	9	10	12	13	14	♉15
♂	♈12	12	13	14	15	15	16	17	18	18	19	20	21	21	22	23	24	24	25	26	27	28	28	29	♉0	1	1	2	3	♉4

	1	6	12	18	24	30
♃	♎5	4	3	3	2	2
♄	♎6	6	5	5	4	4

	1	15	30
♅	♐0	♏0	29
♆	♐25	25	25
♇	♎23	23	22
☊	♌9	8	6

MAY

	1	2	3	4	5	6	7	8	9	10	11	12	13	14	15	16	17	18	19	20	21	22	23	24	25	26	27	28	29	30	31
☉	♉11	12	12	13	14	15	16	17	18	19	20	21	22	23	24	25	26	27	28	29	♊0	1	2	3	4	5	6	7	8	8	♊9
☽	♓26	♈10	26	♉11	26	♊11	26	♋11	25	♌8	21	♍4	16	28	♎10	22	♏4	16	28	♐10	22	♑4	16	28	♒11	24	♓7	21	♈5	19	♉4
☿	♉14	17	19	21	23	25	27	29	♊1	3	5	7	9	11	12	14	16	17	19	20	21	23	24	25	26	27	28	29	♋0	1	♋2
♀	♉17	18	19	20	22	23	24	25	27	28	29	♊0	1	3	4	5	6	8	9	10	11	13	14	15	16	17	19	20	21	22	♊24
♂	♉4	5	6	6	7	8	9	9	10	11	12	12	13	14	15	15	16	17	18	18	19	20	20	21	22	23	23	24	25	26	♉26

	1	6	12	18	24	30
♃	♎2	1	1	1	0	0
♄	♎4	4	3	3	3	3

	1	15	30
♅	♏29	28	28
♆	♐25	24	24
♇	♎22	22	22
☊	♌6	5	3

JUNE

	1	2	3	4	5	6	7	8	9	10	11	12	13	14	15	16	17	18	19	20	21	22	23	24	25	26	27	28	29	30
☉	♊10	11	12	13	14	15	16	17	18	19	20	21	22	23	24	25	26	27	28	29	♋0	0	1	2	3	4	5	6	7	♋8
☽	♉19	♊5	20	♋5	19	♌3	17	♍0	13	25	♎7	19	♏1	13	25	♐7	19	♑1	13	26	♒8	21	♓4	17	♈1	15	29	♉14	29	♊13
☿	♋2	3	4	4	4	5	5	5	5	5	5	5	5	4	4	4	3	3	2	2	1	1	0	♊29	29	28	28	27	27	♊27
♀	♊25	26	27	28	♋0	1	2	3	5	6	7	8	9	11	12	13	14	16	17	18	19	20	22	23	24	25	27	28	29	♌0
♂	♉27	28	28	29	♊0	1	1	2	3	3	4	5	6	6	7	8	8	9	10	10	11	12	13	13	14	15	15	16	17	♊17

	1	6	12	18	24	30
♃	♎0	1	1	1	2	2
♄	♎3	3	3	3	3	4

	1	15	30
♅	♏28	27	27
♆	♐24	23	23
♇	♎22	22	22
☊	♌3	2	2

JULY

	1	2	3	4	5	6	7	8	9	10	11	12	13	14	15	16	17	18	19	20	21	22	23	24	25	26	27	28	29	30	31
☉	♋9	10	11	12	13	14	15	16	17	18	19	20	21	21	22	23	24	25	26	27	28	29	♌0	1	2	3	4	5	6	7	♌8
☽	♊28	♋13	27	♌11	25	♍8	21	♎3	15	27	♏9	21	♐3	15	27	♑10	22	♒5	18	♓1	14	28	♈12	26	♉10	24	♊9	23	♋7	22	♌6
☿	♊27	26	26	26	26	27	27	27	28	28	29	29	♋0	1	2	3	4	5	6	8	9	11	12	14	15	17	19	21	23	24	♋26
♀	♌1	3	4	5	6	7	9	10	11	12	14	15	16	17	18	20	21	22	23	24	26	27	28	29	♍0	2	3	4	5	7	♍8
♂	♊18	19	20	20	21	22	22	23	24	24	25	26	26	27	28	28	29	♋0	0	1	2	2	3	4	4	5	6	6	7	8	♋8

	1	6	12	18	24	30
♃	♎2	3	3	4	5	6
♄	♎4	4	4	4	5	5

	1	15	30
♅	♏27	26	26
♆	♐23	23	22
♇	♎22	22	22
☊	♌2	2	2

AUGUST

	1	2	3	4	5	6	7	8	9	10	11	12	13	14	15	16	17	18	19	20	21	22	23	24	25	26	27	28	29	30	31
☉	♌9	10	11	12	12	13	14	15	16	17	18	19	20	21	22	23	24	25	26	27	28	29	♍0	1	2	3	4	5	6	7	♍7
☽	♌19	♍3	16	29	♎11	23	♏6	17	29	♐11	23	♑5	18	♒1	14	27	♓10	24	♈8	22	♉7	21	♊5	19	♋3	17	♌1	15	28	♍11	♍24
☿	♋28	♌0	3	5	7	9	11	13	15	17	19	21	23	25	27	29	♍1	3	5	7	8	10	12	14	15	17	19	21	22	24	♍25
♀	♍9	10	11	13	14	15	16	17	19	20	21	22	23	25	26	27	28	29	♎1	2	3	4	5	6	8	9	10	11	12	14	♎15
♂	♋9	10	10	11	12	12	13	14	14	15	16	16	17	18	18	19	20	20	21	22	22	23	24	24	25	25	26	27	27	28	♋29

	1	6	12	18	24	30
♃	♎6	7	8	9	10	11
♄	♎6	6	7	7	8	8

	1	15	30
♅	♏26	26	26
♆	♐22	22	22
♇	♎22	22	22
☊	♌2	2	1

SEPTEMBER

	1	2	3	4	5	6	7	8	9	10	11	12	13	14	15	16	17	18	19	20	21	22	23	24	25	26	27	28	29	30
☉	♍8	9	10	11	12	13	14	15	16	17	18	19	20	21	22	23	24	25	26	27	28	29	♎0	1	2	3	4	5	6	♎7
☽	♎7	19	♏1	13	25	♐7	19	♑1	13	26	♒9	22	♓5	19	♈4	18	♉3	17	♊2	16	♋0	14	28	♌11	24	♍7	20	♎3	15	♎28
☿	♍27	29	♎0	2	3	5	6	7	9	10	12	13	14	16	17	18	19	21	22	23	24	25	26	27	28	29	♏0	0	1	♏2
♀	♎16	17	18	19	21	22	23	24	25	27	28	29	♏0	1	2	4	5	6	7	8	9	11	12	13	14	15	16	17	19	♏20
♂	♋29	♌0	1	1	2	2	3	4	4	5	6	6	7	8	8	9	9	10	11	11	12	12	13	14	14	15	16	16	17	♌17

	1	6	12	18	24	30
♃	♎12	13	14	15	16	18
♄	♎9	9	10	11	11	12

	1	15	30
♅	♏26	27	27
♆	♐22	22	22
♇	♎23	23	24
☊	♌1	1	♋1

OCTOBER

	1	2	3	4	5	6	7	8	9	10	11	12	13	14	15	16	17	18	19	20	21	22	23	24	25	26	27	28	29	30	31
☉	♎8	9	10	11	12	13	14	15	16	17	18	19	20	21	22	23	24	25	26	27	28	28	29	♏0	1	2	3	4	5	6	♏7
☽	♏10	22	♐3	15	27	♑9	21	♒4	16	♓0	13	28	♈12	27	♉12	27	♊12	26	♋11	25	♌8	21	♍4	17	♎0	12	24	♏6	18	♐0	♐12
☿	♏2	3	3	4	4	4	4	4	3	3	2	2	1	0	♎29	28	27	25	24	23	22	21	20	19	19	18	18	18	18	19	♎19
♀	♏21	22	23	24	25	27	28	29	♐0	1	2	3	4	6	7	8	9	10	11	12	13	14	16	17	18	19	20	21	22	23	♐24
♂	♌18	19	19	20	20	21	22	22	23	23	24	25	25	26	26	27	28	28	29	29	♍0	1	1	2	2	3	3	4	5	5	♍6

	1	6	12	18	24	30
♃	♎18	19	20	22	23	24
♄	♎12	13	14	14	15	16

	1	15	30
♅	♏27	28	29
♆	♐22	23	23
♇	♎24	24	25
☊	♋29	28	26

NOVEMBER

	1	2	3	4	5	6	7	8	9	10	11	12	13	14	15	16	17	18	19	20	21	22	23	24	25	26	27	28	29	30
☉	♏8	9	10	11	12	13	14	15	16	18	19	20	21	22	23	24	25	26	27	28	29	♐0	1	2	3	4	5	6	7	♐8
☽	♐24	♑6	17	♒0	12	25	♓8	21	♈6	20	♉5	20	♊6	21	♋6	20	♌4	18	♍1	14	27	♎9	21	♏3	15	27	♐9	21	♑3	♑14
☿	♎20	21	22	23	24	25	27	28	29	♏1	2	4	5	7	8	10	11	13	14	16	18	19	21	22	24	25	27	29	♐0	♐2
♀	♐25	26	27	28	29	♑0	2	3	4	5	6	7	8	9	10	11	12	12	13	14	15	16	17	18	19	20	21	22	22	♑23
♂	♍6	7	7	8	9	9	10	10	11	11	12	12	13	14	14	15	15	16	16	17	17	18	18	19	19	20	21	21	22	♍22

	1	6	12	18	24	30
♃	♎25	26	27	28	29	♏1
♄	♎16	17	17	18	18	19

	1	15	30
♅	♏29	♐29	1
♆	♐23	23	24
♇	♎25	25	26
☊	♋26	24	23

DECEMBER

	1	2	3	4	5	6	7	8	9	10	11	12	13	14	15	16	17	18	19	20	21	22	23	24	25	26	27	28	29	30	31
☉	♐9	10	11	12	13	14	15	16	17	18	19	20	21	22	23	24	25	26	27	28	29	♑0	1	2	3	4	5	6	7	8	♑9
☽	♑26	♒9	21	♓4	17	♈0	14	28	♉13	28	♊14	29	♋14	29	♌13	27	♍10	23	♎6	18	♏0	12	24	♐6	18	♑0	11	23	♒6	18	♓1
☿	♐3	5	7	8	10	11	13	14	16	17	19	21	22	24	25	27	29	♑0	2	3	5	6	8	10	11	13	14	16	18	19	♑21
♀	♑24	25	26	26	27	28	29	29	♒0	1	1	2	3	3	4	4	5	5	6	6	7	7	7	8	8	8	8	9	9	9	♒9
♂	♍23	23	24	24	25	25	26	26	27	27	28	28	29	29	♎0	0	0	1	1	2	2	3	3	4	4	5	5	5	6	6	♎7

	1	6	12	18	24	30
♃	♏1	2	3	4	5	6
♄	♎19	20	20	21	21	21

	1	15	30
♅	♐1	2	3
♆	♐24	25	25
♇	♎26	26	27
☊	♋23	23	22

1982

JANUARY

	1	2	3	4	5	6	7	8	9	10	11	12	13	14	15	16	17	18	19	20	21	22	23	24	25	26	27	28	29	30	31
☉	♑10	11	12	13	14	15	16	17	18	19	20	21	22	23	25	26	27	28	29	♒0	1	2	3	4	5	6	7	8	9	10	♒11
☽	♓13	26	♈10	24	♉8	22	♊7	22	♋7	22	♌6	21	♍5	18	♎1	14	27	♏9	21	♐2	14	26	♑8	20	♒2	15	27	♓10	23	♈7	♈20
☿	♑23	24	26	27	29	♒0	2	4	5	7	8	9	11	12	13	14	15	16	17	18	18	18	19	19	18	18	17	17	16	15	♒13
♀	♒9	9	9	9	9	8	8	8	8	7	7	6	6	5	5	4	4	3	3	2	1	1	0	♑29	29	28	28	27	27	26	♑26
♂	♎7	7	8	8	9	9	9	10	10	11	11	11	12	12	12	13	13	13	14	14	14	14	15	15	15	16	16	16	16	17	♎17

	1	6	12	18	24	30		1	6	12	18	24	30		1	15	30		1	15	30		1	15	30		1	15	30
♃	♏6	7	8	8	9	9	♄	♎21	22	22	22	22	22	♅	♐3	3	4	♆	♐25	26	26	♇	♎27	27	27	☊	♋22	22	22

FEBRUARY

	1	2	3	4	5	6	7	8	9	10	11	12	13	14	15	16	17	18	19	20	21	22	23	24	25	26	27	28
☉	♒12	13	14	15	16	17	18	19	20	21	22	23	24	25	26	27	28	29	♓0	1	2	3	4	5	6	7	8	♓9
☽	♉4	18	♊2	17	♋1	16	♌0	14	29	♍13	26	♎9	22	♏4	17	29	♐10	22	♑4	16	28	♒11	23	♓6	20	♈3	17	♉1
☿	♒12	11	10	9	7	6	6	5	4	4	3	3	3	3	3	3	4	4	5	5	6	7	7	8	9	10	11	♒12
♀	♑25	25	25	24	24	24	24	24	23	23	23	23	23	24	24	24	24	24	25	25	25	26	26	27	27	27	28	♑29
♂	♎17	17	17	18	18	18	18	18	18	18	19	19	19	19	19	19	19	19	19	19	19	19	19	19	19	19	19	♎19

	1	6	12	18	24	28		1	6	12	18	24	28		1	15	28		1	15	28		1	15	28		1	15	28
♃	♏9	10	10	10	10	10	♄	♎22	22	22	22	22	22	♅	♐4	4	5	♆	♐26	27	27	♇	♎27	27	27	☊	♋22	22	21

MARCH

	1	2	3	4	5	6	7	8	9	10	11	12	13	14	15	16	17	18	19	20	21	22	23	24	25	26	27	28	29	30	31
☉	♓10	11	12	13	14	15	16	17	18	19	20	21	22	23	24	25	26	27	28	29	♈0	1	2	3	4	5	6	7	8	9	♈10
☽	♉15	29	♊13	27	♋11	25	♌9	23	♍7	21	♎4	17	♏0	12	24	♐6	18	♑0	12	24	♒6	19	♓2	15	28	♈12	27	♉11	25	♊10	♊24
☿	♒13	14	16	17	18	19	21	22	23	25	26	27	29	♓0	2	3	5	6	8	9	11	13	14	16	18	19	21	23	25	27	♓28
♀	♑29	♒0	0	1	2	2	3	4	4	5	6	7	7	8	9	10	11	12	12	13	14	15	16	17	18	19	20	21	22	23	♒24
♂	♎19	19	19	18	18	18	18	18	18	17	17	17	17	16	16	16	15	15	15	15	14	14	14	13	13	12	12	12	11	11	♎11

	1	6	12	18	24	30		1	6	12	18	24	30		1	15	30		1	15	30		1	15	30		1	15	30
♃	♏10	10	10	10	9	9	♄	♎22	21	21	21	20	20	♅	♐5	5	4	♆	♐27	27	27	♇	♎27	26	26	☊	♋21	20	19

APRIL

	1	2	3	4	5	6	7	8	9	10	11	12	13	14	15	16	17	18	19	20	21	22	23	24	25	26	27	28	29	30
☉	♈11	12	13	14	15	16	17	18	19	20	21	22	23	24	25	26	27	28	29	♉0	1	2	3	3	4	5	6	7	8	♉9
☽	♋8	22	♌6	20	♍3	17	♎0	13	26	♏8	20	♐2	14	26	♑8	20	♒2	14	27	♓10	23	♈7	21	♉5	20	♊5	20	♋4	19	♌3
☿	♈0	2	4	6	8	10	12	14	16	18	20	22	24	26	28	♉0	3	5	7	9	11	13	15	17	19	21	22	24	26	♉28
♀	♒25	25	26	27	28	29	♓0	2	3	4	5	6	7	8	9	10	11	12	13	14	15	16	17	18	20	21	22	23	24	♓25
♂	♎10	10	9	9	9	8	8	7	7	7	6	6	6	5	5	5	4	4	4	3	3	3	3	2	2	2	2	2	1	♎1

	1	6	12	18	24	30		1	6	12	18	24	30		1	15	30		1	15	30		1	15	30		1	15	30
♃	♏8	8	7	6	6	5	♄	♎20	19	19	18	18	17	♅	♐4	4	4	♆	♐27	27	27	♇	♎26	26	25	☊	♋19	17	16

MAY

	1	2	3	4	5	6	7	8	9	10	11	12	13	14	15	16	17	18	19	20	21	22	23	24	25	26	27	28	29	30	31
☉	♉10	11	12	13	14	15	16	17	18	19	20	21	22	23	24	25	26	27	28	29	♊0	1	2	3	3	4	5	6	7	8	♊9
☽	♌17	♍0	13	26	♎9	22	♏4	17	29	♐11	23	♑4	16	28	♒10	22	♓5	18	♈1	15	29	♉14	29	♊14	29	♋14	29	♌13	27	♍10	♍23
☿	♉29	♊1	2	3	5	6	7	8	9	10	11	12	13	13	14	14	15	15	15	15	15	15	15	15	15	14	14	13	13	13	♊12
♀	♓26	27	28	29	♈1	2	3	4	5	6	7	8	10	11	12	13	14	15	16	17	19	20	21	22	23	24	26	27	28	29	♉0
♂	♎1	1	1	1	1	1	1	0	0	0	0	0	0	0	0	0	1	1	1	1	1	1	1	1	1	2	2	2	2	2	♎3

	1	6	12	18	24	30		1	6	12	18	24	30		1	15	30		1	15	30		1	15	30		1	15	30
♃	♏5	4	3	3	2	2	♄	♎17	17	17	16	16	16	♅	♐4	3	2	♆	♐27	27	26	♇	♎25	25	24	☊	♋16	15	14

JUNE

	1	2	3	4	5	6	7	8	9	10	11	12	13	14	15	16	17	18	19	20	21	22	23	24	25	26	27	28	29	30
☉	♊10	11	12	13	14	15	16	17	18	19	20	21	22	23	24	25	25	26	27	28	29	♋0	1	2	3	4	5	6	7	♋8
☽	♎6	19	♏1	14	26	♐8	20	♑1	13	25	♒7	19	♓1	14	27	♈10	23	♉8	22	♊7	22	♋7	23	♌7	22	♍6	20	♎3	16	♎28
☿	♊11	11	10	10	9	9	8	8	7	7	7	7	7	7	7	7	7	7	8	8	8	9	10	10	11	12	13	14	15	♊16
♀	♉1	2	4	5	6	7	8	9	11	12	13	14	15	16	18	19	20	21	22	23	25	26	27	28	29	♊1	2	3	4	♊5
♂	♎3	3	3	3	4	4	4	5	5	5	5	6	6	6	7	7	7	8	8	9	9	9	10	10	10	11	11	12	12	♎13

	1	6	12	18	24	30		1	6	12	18	24	30		1	15	30		1	15	30		1	15	30		1	15	30
♃	♏1	1	1	1	0	0	♄	♎16	16	16	15	16	16	♅	♐2	2	1	♆	♐26	26	25	♇	♎24	24	24	☊	♋14	13	13

JULY

	1	2	3	4	5	6	7	8	9	10	11	12	13	14	15	16	17	18	19	20	21	22	23	24	25	26	27	28	29	30	31
☉	♋9	10	11	12	13	14	15	16	16	17	18	19	20	21	22	23	24	25	26	27	28	29	♌0	1	2	3	4	5	6	7	♌7
☽	♏11	23	♐5	17	28	♑10	22	♒4	16	28	♓11	23	♈6	19	♉3	17	♊1	16	♋1	16	♌1	16	♍0	15	28	♎12	25	♏7	20	♐2	♐13
☿	♊17	19	20	21	23	24	26	27	29	♋1	3	5	6	8	10	12	14	16	19	21	23	25	27	29	♌1	3	6	8	10	12	♌14
♀	♊7	8	9	10	11	12	14	15	16	17	18	20	21	22	23	24	26	27	28	29	♋0	2	3	4	5	6	8	9	10	11	♋12
♂	♎13	13	14	14	15	15	16	16	17	17	18	18	19	19	20	20	21	21	22	22	23	23	24	24	25	25	26	26	27	27	♎28

	1	6	12	18	24	30		1	6	12	18	24	30		1	15	30		1	15	30		1	15	30		1	15	30
♃	♏0	1	1	1	1	2	♄	♎16	16	16	16	17	17	♅	♐1	1	1	♆	♐25	25	25	♇	♎24	24	24	☊	♋13	13	13

AUGUST

	1	2	3	4	5	6	7	8	9	10	11	12	13	14	15	16	17	18	19	20	21	22	23	24	25	26	27	28	29	30	31
☉	♌8	9	10	11	12	13	14	15	16	17	18	19	20	21	22	23	24	25	26	27	28	29	♍0	1	1	2	3	4	5	6	♍7
☽	♐25	♑7	19	♒1	13	25	♓8	20	♈3	16	29	♉13	27	♊11	25	♋10	25	♌9	24	♍9	23	♎7	20	♏3	16	28	♐10	22	♑4	15	♑27
☿	♌16	18	20	22	23	25	27	29	♍1	2	4	6	8	9	11	13	14	16	17	19	20	22	23	24	26	27	29	♎0	1	2	♎4
♀	♋14	15	16	17	18	20	21	22	23	25	26	27	28	29	♌1	2	3	4	6	7	8	9	10	12	13	14	15	17	18	19	♌20
♂	♎29	29	♏0	0	1	1	2	3	3	4	4	5	6	6	7	7	8	9	9	10	10	11	12	12	13	14	14	15	15	16	♏17

	1	6	12	18	24	30		1	6	12	18	24	30		1	15	30		1	15	30		1	15	30		1	15	30
♃	♏2	3	3	4	5	6	♄	♎17	17	18	18	19	19	♅	♐1	1	1	♆	♐25	24	24	♇	♎24	25	25	☊	♋13	13	12

SEPTEMBER

	1	2	3	4	5	6	7	8	9	10	11	12	13	14	15	16	17	18	19	20	21	22	23	24	25	26	27	28	29	30
☉	♍8	9	10	11	12	13	14	15	16	17	18	19	20	21	22	23	24	25	26	27	28	29	♎0	1	2	3	4	5	6	♎7
☽	♒9	22	♓4	17	♈0	13	26	♉10	24	♊8	22	♋6	20	♌4	19	♍3	17	♎1	15	28	♏11	24	♐6	18	♑0	12	23	♒5	17	♓0
☿	♎5	6	7	8	9	10	11	12	13	14	14	15	16	16	17	17	17	17	18	18	17	17	17	16	16	15	14	13	12	♎11
♀	♌21	23	24	25	26	28	29	♍0	1	3	4	5	6	8	9	10	11	13	14	15	16	17	19	20	21	22	24	25	26	♍27
♂	♏17	18	19	19	20	21	21	22	23	23	24	25	25	26	27	27	28	29	29	♐0	1	1	2	3	3	4	5	5	6	♐7

	1	6	12	18	24	30		1	6	12	18	24	30		1	15	30		1	15	30		1	15	30		1	15	30
♃	♏6	7	8	9	10	11	♄	♎20	20	21	21	22	23	♅	♐1	1	2	♆	♐24	24	24	♇	♎25	25	26	☊	♋12	11	9

OCTOBER

	1	2	3	4	5	6	7	8	9	10	11	12	13	14	15	16	17	18	19	20	21	22	23	24	25	26	27	28	29	30	31
☉	♎7	8	9	10	11	12	13	14	15	16	17	18	19	20	21	22	23	24	25	26	27	28	29	♏0	1	2	3	4	5	6	♏7
☽	♓13	26	♈9	22	♉6	20	♊4	18	♋3	17	♌1	15	29	♍13	26	♎10	23	♏6	19	♐2	14	26	♑8	19	♒1	13	25	♓8	20	♈4	♈17
☿	♎10	9	8	7	6	5	4	3	3	3	2	2	3	3	4	4	5	6	7	8	10	11	12	14	15	17	19	20	22	23	♎25
♀	♍29	♎0	1	2	4	5	6	7	9	10	11	12	14	15	16	17	19	20	21	22	24	25	26	27	29	♏0	1	2	4	5	♏6
♂	♐8	8	9	10	10	11	12	13	13	14	15	15	16	17	18	18	19	20	20	21	22	23	23	24	25	26	26	27	28	29	♐29

	1	6	12	18	24	30		1	6	12	18	24	30		1	15	30		1	15	30		1	15	30		1	15	30
♃	♏12	13	14	15	16	18	♄	♎23	24	24	25	26	27	♅	♐2	2	3	♆	♐24	25	25	♇	♎26	27	27	☊	♋9	8	6

NOVEMBER

	1	2	3	4	5	6	7	8	9	10	11	12	13	14	15	16	17	18	19	20	21	22	23	24	25	26	27	28	29	30
☉	♏8	9	10	11	12	13	14	15	16	17	18	19	20	21	22	23	24	25	26	27	28	29	♐0	1	2	3	4	5	6	♐7
☽	♉1	15	♊0	14	29	♋13	28	♌12	26	♍9	23	♎6	19	♏2	15	27	♐10	22	♑4	16	27	♒9	21	♓3	16	28	♈11	25	♉9	♉24
☿	♎27	28	♏0	2	3	5	7	8	10	11	13	15	16	18	19	21	23	24	26	27	29	♐1	2	4	5	7	8	10	12	♐13
♀	♏7	9	10	11	12	14	15	16	17	19	20	21	23	24	25	26	28	29	♐0	1	3	4	5	6	8	9	10	11	13	♐14
♂	♑0	1	2	2	3	4	5	5	6	7	8	8	9	10	11	11	12	13	14	14	15	16	17	17	18	19	20	21	21	♑22

	1	6	12	18	24	30		1	6	12	18	24	30		1	15	30		1	15	30		1	15	30		1	15	30
♃	♏18	19	21	22	23	24	♄	♎27	27	28	29	29	♏0	♅	♐3	4	5	♆	♐25	26	26	♇	♎27	28	28	☊	♋6	5	4

DECEMBER

	1	2	3	4	5	6	7	8	9	10	11	12	13	14	15	16	17	18	19	20	21	22	23	24	25	26	27	28	29	30	31
☉	♐8	9	10	11	13	14	15	16	17	18	19	20	21	22	23	24	25	26	27	28	29	♑0	1	2	3	4	5	6	7	8	♑9
☽	♊8	23	♋8	23	♌8	22	♍6	20	♎3	16	29	♏12	24	♐6	18	♑0	12	24	♒6	18	♓0	12	24	♈7	20	♉3	17	♊1	16	♋1	♋16
☿	♐15	16	18	19	21	22	24	26	27	29	♑0	2	3	5	6	8	9	11	13	14	15	17	18	20	21	23	24	25	26	27	♑29
♀	♐15	16	18	19	20	21	23	24	25	26	28	29	♑0	1	3	4	5	6	8	9	10	11	13	14	15	17	18	19	20	22	♑23
♂	♑23	24	24	25	26	27	27	28	29	♒0	1	1	2	3	4	4	5	6	7	8	8	9	10	11	12	12	13	14	15	15	♒16

	1	6	12	18	24	30		1	6	12	18	24	30		1	15	30		1	15	30		1	15	30		1	15	30
♃	♏25	26	27	28	♐0	1	♄	♏0	1	1	2	2	3	♅	♐5	6	7	♆	♐26	27	27	♇	♎28	29	29	☊	♋4	4	4

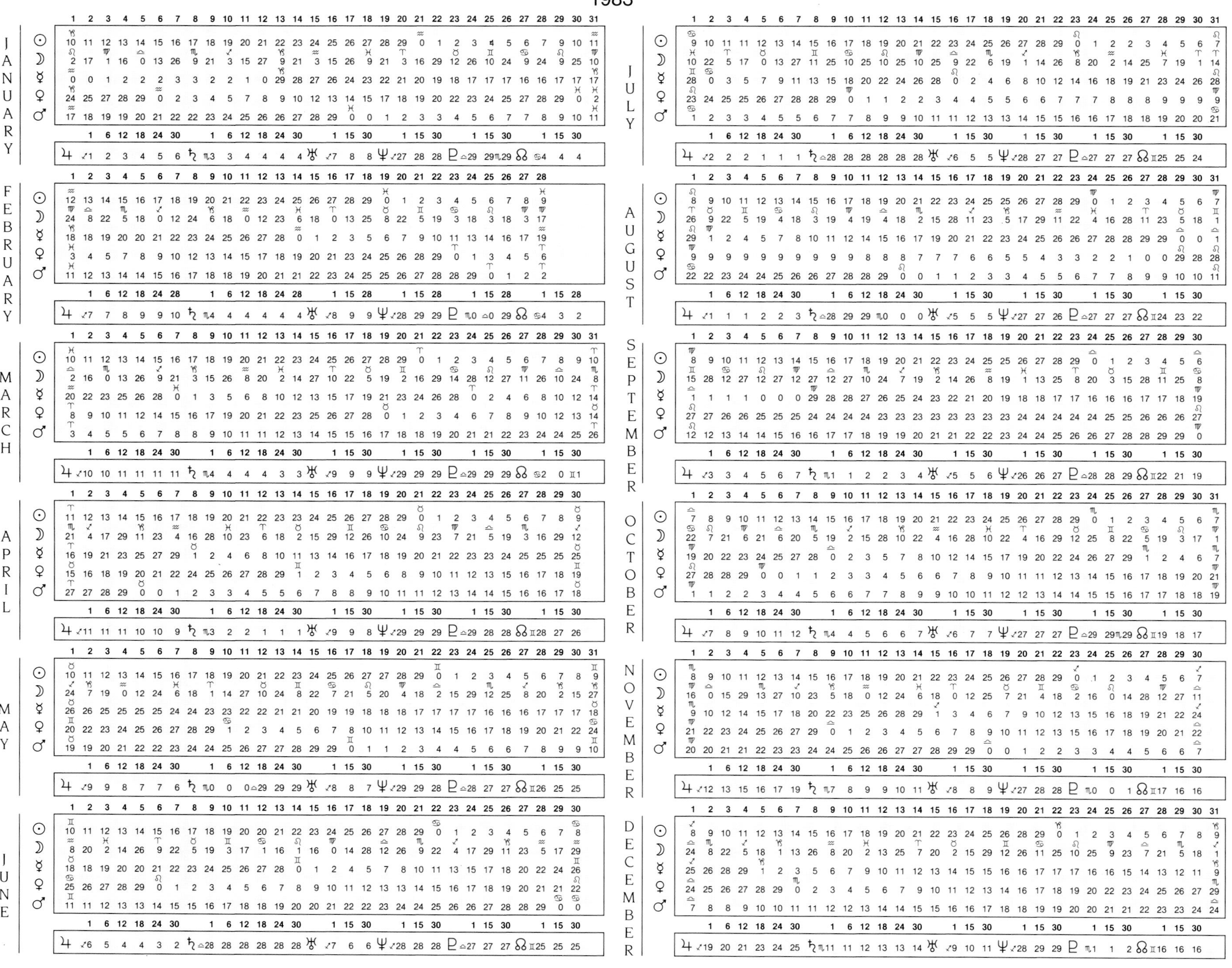

1983

JANUARY

	1	2	3	4	5	6	7	8	9	10	11	12	13	14	15	16	17	18	19	20	21	22	23	24	25	26	27	28	29	30	31
☉	10	11	12	13	14	15	16	17	18	19	20	21	22	23	24	25	26	27	28	29	0	1	2	3	4	5	6	7	9	10	11
☽	2	17	1	16	0	13	26	9	21	3	15	27	9	21	3	15	26	9	21	3	16	29	12	26	10	24	9	24	9	25	10
☿	0	0	1	2	2	2	3	3	2	2	1	0	29	28	27	26	24	23	22	21	20	19	18	17	17	17	16	16	17	17	17
♀	24	25	27	28	29	0	2	3	4	5	7	8	9	10	12	13	14	15	17	18	19	20	22	23	24	25	27	28	29	0	2
♂	17	18	19	19	20	21	22	22	23	24	25	26	26	27	28	29	0	0	1	2	3	3	4	5	6	7	7	8	9	10	11

♃	1	6	12	18	24	30	♄	1	6	12	18	24	30	♅	1	15	30	♆	1	15	30	♇	1	15	30	☊	1	15	30
	♐1	2	3	4	5	6		♏3	3	4	4	4	4		♐7	8	8		♐27	28	28		♎29	29	♏29		♋4	4	4

FEBRUARY

	1	2	3	4	5	6	7	8	9	10	11	12	13	14	15	16	17	18	19	20	21	22	23	24	25	26	27	28
☉	12	13	14	15	16	17	18	19	20	21	22	23	24	25	26	27	28	29	0	1	2	3	4	5	6	7	8	9
☽	24	8	22	5	18	0	12	24	6	18	0	12	23	6	18	0	13	25	8	22	5	19	3	18	3	18	3	17
☿	18	18	19	20	20	21	22	23	24	25	26	27	28	0	1	2	3	5	6	7	9	10	11	13	14	16	17	19
♀	3	4	5	7	8	9	10	12	13	14	15	17	18	19	20	21	23	24	25	26	28	29	0	1	3	4	5	6
♂	11	12	13	14	14	15	16	17	18	18	19	20	21	21	22	23	24	25	25	26	27	28	28	29	0	1	2	2

♃	1	6	12	18	24	28	♄	1	6	12	18	24	28	♅	1	15	28	♆	1	15	28	♇	1	15	28	☊	1	15	28
	♐7	7	8	9	9	10		♏4	4	4	4	4	4		♐8	9	9		♐28	29	29		♏0	♎0	29		♋4	3	2

MARCH

	1	2	3	4	5	6	7	8	9	10	11	12	13	14	15	16	17	18	19	20	21	22	23	24	25	26	27	28	29	30	31
☉	10	11	12	13	14	15	16	17	18	19	20	21	22	23	24	25	26	27	28	29	0	1	2	3	4	5	6	7	8	9	10
☽	2	16	0	13	26	9	21	3	15	26	8	20	2	14	27	10	22	5	19	2	16	29	14	28	12	27	11	26	10	24	8
☿	20	22	23	25	26	28	0	1	3	5	6	8	10	12	13	15	17	19	21	23	24	26	28	0	2	4	6	8	10	12	14
♀	8	9	10	11	12	14	15	16	17	19	20	21	22	23	25	26	27	28	0	1	2	3	4	6	7	8	9	10	12	13	14
♂	3	4	5	5	6	7	8	8	9	10	11	11	12	13	14	15	15	16	17	18	18	19	20	21	21	22	23	24	24	25	26

♃	1	6	12	18	24	30	♄	1	6	12	18	24	30	♅	1	15	30	♆	1	15	30	♇	1	15	30	☊	1	15	30
	♐10	10	11	11	11	11		♏4	4	4	4	3	3		♐9	9	9		♐29	29	29		♎29	29	29		♋2	0	♊1

APRIL

	1	2	3	4	5	6	7	8	9	10	11	12	13	14	15	16	17	18	19	20	21	22	23	24	25	26	27	28	29	30
☉	11	12	13	14	15	16	17	18	19	20	21	22	23	23	24	25	26	27	28	29	0	1	2	3	4	5	6	7	8	9
☽	21	4	17	29	11	23	4	16	28	10	23	6	18	2	15	29	12	26	10	24	9	23	7	21	5	19	3	16	29	12
☿	16	19	21	23	25	27	29	1	2	4	6	8	10	11	13	14	16	17	18	19	20	21	22	23	23	24	25	25	25	25
♀	15	16	18	19	20	21	22	24	25	26	27	28	29	1	2	3	4	5	6	8	9	10	11	12	13	15	16	17	18	19
♂	27	27	28	29	0	0	1	2	3	3	4	5	5	6	7	8	8	9	10	11	11	12	13	14	14	15	16	16	17	18

♃	1	6	12	18	24	30	♄	1	6	12	18	24	30	♅	1	15	30	♆	1	15	30	♇	1	15	30	☊	1	15	30
	♐11	11	11	10	10	9		♏3	2	2	1	1	1		♐9	9	8		♐29	29	29		♎29	28	28		♊28	27	26

MAY

	1	2	3	4	5	6	7	8	9	10	11	12	13	14	15	16	17	18	19	20	21	22	23	24	25	26	27	28	29	30	31
☉	10	11	12	13	14	15	16	17	18	19	20	21	22	23	24	25	26	27	27	28	29	0	1	2	3	4	5	6	7	8	9
☽	24	7	19	0	12	24	6	18	1	14	27	10	24	8	22	7	21	5	20	4	18	2	15	29	12	25	8	20	2	15	27
☿	26	26	25	25	25	25	24	24	23	23	22	22	21	21	20	19	19	18	18	18	17	17	17	17	16	16	16	17	17	17	18
♀	20	22	23	24	25	26	27	28	29	1	2	3	4	5	6	7	8	10	11	12	13	14	15	16	17	18	19	20	21	22	24
♂	19	19	20	21	22	22	23	24	24	25	26	27	27	28	29	29	0	1	1	2	3	4	4	5	6	6	7	8	9	9	10

♃	1	6	12	18	24	30	♄	1	6	12	18	24	30	♅	1	15	30	♆	1	15	30	♇	1	15	30	☊	1	15	30
	♐9	9	8	7	7	6		♏0	0	0	♎29	29	29		♐8	8	7		♐29	29	28		♎28	27	27		♊26	25	25

JUNE

	1	2	3	4	5	6	7	8	9	10	11	12	13	14	15	16	17	18	19	20	21	22	23	24	25	26	27	28	29	30
☉	10	11	12	13	14	15	16	17	18	19	20	20	21	22	23	24	25	26	27	28	29	0	1	2	3	4	5	6	7	8
☽	8	20	2	14	26	9	22	5	19	3	17	1	16	1	16	0	14	28	12	26	9	22	4	17	29	11	23	5	17	29
☿	18	18	19	20	20	21	22	23	24	25	26	27	28	0	1	2	4	5	7	8	10	11	13	15	17	18	20	22	24	26
♀	25	26	27	28	29	0	1	2	3	4	5	6	7	8	9	10	11	12	13	13	14	15	16	17	18	19	20	21	21	22
♂	11	11	12	13	13	14	15	15	16	17	18	18	19	20	20	21	22	22	23	24	24	25	26	26	27	28	28	29	0	0

♃	1	6	12	18	24	30	♄	1	6	12	18	24	30	♅	1	15	30	♆	1	15	30	♇	1	15	30	☊	1	15	30
	♐6	5	4	4	3	2		♎28	28	28	28	28	28		♐7	6	6		♐28	28	28		♎27	27	27		♊25	25	25

JULY

	1	2	3	4	5	6	7	8	9	10	11	12	13	14	15	16	17	18	19	20	21	22	23	24	25	26	27	28	29	30	31
☉	9	10	11	11	12	13	14	15	16	17	18	19	20	21	22	23	24	25	26	27	28	29	0	1	2	2	3	4	5	6	7
☽	10	22	5	17	0	13	27	11	25	10	25	10	25	10	25	9	22	6	19	1	14	26	8	20	2	14	25	7	19	1	14
☿	28	0	3	5	7	9	11	13	15	18	20	22	24	26	28	0	2	4	6	8	10	12	14	16	18	19	21	23	24	26	28
♀	23	24	25	25	26	27	28	28	29	0	1	1	2	2	3	4	4	5	5	6	6	7	7	7	8	8	8	9	9	9	9
♂	1	2	3	3	4	5	5	6	7	7	8	9	9	10	11	11	12	13	13	14	15	15	16	16	17	18	18	19	20	20	21

♃	1	6	12	18	24	30	♄	1	6	12	18	24	30	♅	1	15	30	♆	1	15	30	♇	1	15	30	☊	1	15	30
	♐2	2	2	1	1	1		♎28	28	28	28	28	28		♐6	5	5		♐28	27	27		♎27	27	27		♊25	25	24

AUGUST

	1	2	3	4	5	6	7	8	9	10	11	12	13	14	15	16	17	18	19	20	21	22	23	24	25	26	27	28	29	30	31
☉	8	9	10	11	12	13	14	15	16	17	18	19	20	21	22	23	24	25	25	26	27	28	29	0	1	2	3	4	5	6	7
☽	26	9	22	5	19	4	18	3	19	4	19	4	18	2	15	28	11	23	5	17	29	11	22	4	16	28	11	23	5	18	1
☿	29	1	2	4	5	7	8	10	11	12	14	15	16	17	19	20	21	22	23	24	25	26	26	27	28	28	29	29	0	0	1
♀	9	9	9	9	9	9	9	9	9	9	8	8	8	7	7	7	6	6	5	5	4	3	3	2	2	1	0	0	29	28	28
♂	22	22	23	24	24	25	26	26	27	28	28	29	0	0	1	1	2	3	3	4	5	5	6	7	7	8	9	9	10	10	11

♃	1	6	12	18	24	30	♄	1	6	12	18	24	30	♅	1	15	30	♆	1	15	30	♇	1	15	30	☊	1	15	30
	♐1	1	1	2	2	3		♎28	29	29	♏0	0	0		♐5	5	5		♐27	27	26		♎27	27	27		♊24	23	22

SEPTEMBER

	1	2	3	4	5	6	7	8	9	10	11	12	13	14	15	16	17	18	19	20	21	22	23	24	25	26	27	28	29	30
☉	8	9	10	11	12	13	14	15	16	17	18	19	20	21	22	23	24	25	25	26	27	28	29	0	1	2	3	4	5	6
☽	15	28	12	27	12	27	12	27	12	27	10	24	7	19	2	14	26	8	19	1	13	25	8	20	3	15	28	11	25	8
☿	1	1	1	1	0	0	0	29	28	28	27	26	25	24	23	22	21	20	19	18	18	17	17	16	16	16	17	17	18	19
♀	27	27	26	26	25	25	25	24	24	24	24	23	23	23	23	23	23	23	23	24	24	24	24	24	25	25	26	26	26	27
♂	12	12	13	14	14	15	16	16	17	17	18	19	19	20	21	21	22	22	23	24	24	25	26	26	27	28	28	29	29	0

♃	1	6	12	18	24	30	♄	1	6	12	18	24	30	♅	1	15	30	♆	1	15	30	♇	1	15	30	☊	1	15	30
	♐3	3	4	5	6	7		♏1	1	2	2	3	4		♐5	5	6		♐26	26	27		♎28	28	29		♊22	21	19

OCTOBER

	1	2	3	4	5	6	7	8	9	10	11	12	13	14	15	16	17	18	19	20	21	22	23	24	25	26	27	28	29	30	31
☉	7	8	9	10	11	12	13	14	15	16	17	18	19	20	21	22	23	24	25	26	27	28	29	0	1	2	3	4	5	6	7
☽	22	7	21	6	21	6	20	5	19	2	15	28	10	22	4	16	28	10	22	4	16	29	12	25	8	22	5	19	3	17	1
☿	19	20	22	23	24	25	27	28	0	2	3	5	7	8	10	12	14	15	17	19	20	22	24	26	27	29	1	2	4	6	7
♀	27	28	28	29	0	0	1	1	2	3	3	4	5	6	6	7	8	9	10	11	11	12	13	14	15	16	17	18	19	20	21
♂	1	1	2	2	3	4	4	5	6	6	7	7	8	9	9	10	10	11	12	12	13	14	14	15	15	16	17	17	18	18	19

♃	1	6	12	18	24	30	♄	1	6	12	18	24	30	♅	1	15	30	♆	1	15	30	♇	1	15	30	☊	1	15	30
	♐7	8	9	10	11	12		♏4	4	5	6	6	7		♐6	7	7		♐27	27	27		♎29	29	♏29		♊19	18	17

NOVEMBER

	1	2	3	4	5	6	7	8	9	10	11	12	13	14	15	16	17	18	19	20	21	22	23	24	25	26	27	28	29	30
☉	8	9	10	11	12	13	14	15	16	17	18	19	20	21	22	23	24	25	26	27	28	29	0	1	2	3	4	5	6	7
☽	16	0	15	29	13	27	10	23	5	18	0	12	24	6	18	0	12	25	7	21	4	18	2	16	0	14	28	12	27	11
☿	9	10	12	14	15	17	18	20	22	23	25	26	28	29	1	3	4	6	7	9	10	12	13	15	16	18	19	21	22	24
♀	21	22	23	24	25	26	27	29	0	1	2	3	4	5	6	7	8	9	10	11	12	13	15	16	17	18	19	20	21	22
♂	20	20	21	21	22	23	23	24	24	25	26	26	27	27	28	29	29	0	0	1	2	2	3	3	4	4	5	6	6	7

♃	1	6	12	18	24	30	♄	1	6	12	18	24	30	♅	1	15	30	♆	1	15	30	♇	1	15	30	☊	1	15	30
	♐12	13	15	16	17	19		♏7	8	9	9	10	11		♐8	8	9		♐27	28	28		♏0	0	1		♊17	16	16

DECEMBER

	1	2	3	4	5	6	7	8	9	10	11	12	13	14	15	16	17	18	19	20	21	22	23	24	25	26	27	28	29	30	31
☉	8	9	10	11	12	13	14	15	16	17	18	19	20	21	22	23	24	25	26	28	29	0	1	2	3	4	5	6	7	8	9
☽	24	8	22	5	18	1	13	26	8	20	2	13	25	7	20	2	15	29	12	26	11	25	10	25	9	23	7	21	5	18	1
☿	25	26	28	29	1	2	3	5	6	7	9	10	11	12	13	14	15	15	16	16	17	17	17	16	16	15	14	13	12	11	9
♀	24	25	26	27	28	29	0	2	3	4	5	6	7	9	10	11	12	13	14	16	17	18	19	20	22	23	24	25	26	27	29
♂	7	8	8	9	10	10	11	11	12	12	13	14	14	15	15	16	16	17	18	18	19	19	20	20	21	21	22	23	23	24	24

♃	1	6	12	18	24	30	♄	1	6	12	18	24	30	♅	1	15	30	♆	1	15	30	♇	1	15	30	☊	1	15	30
	♐19	20	21	23	24	25		♏11	11	12	13	13	14		♐9	10	11		♐28	29	29		♏1	1	2		♊16	16	16

1984

JANUARY

	1	2	3	4	5	6	7	8	9	10	11	12	13	14	15	16	17	18	19	20	21	22	23	24	25	26	27	28	29	30	31
☉	♑10	11	12	13	14	15	16	17	18	19	20	21	22	23	24	25	26	27	28	29	♒0	1	2	3	4	5	6	7	8	9	♒10
☽	♐14	27	♑9	22	♒4	16	28	♓10	21	♈3	15	28	♉10	23	♊6	20	♋4	19	♌4	19	♍4	19	♎4	18	♏2	15	28	♐11	24	♑6	♑18
☿	♑8	7	6	4	3	2	2	1	1	0	0	0	1	1	1	2	3	3	4	5	6	7	8	9	10	11	12	14	15	16	♑17
♀	♐0	1	2	4	5	6	7	8	10	11	12	13	14	16	17	18	19	20	22	23	24	25	27	28	29	♑0	1	3	4	5	♑6
♂	♎25	25	26	26	27	27	28	28	29	29	♏0	0	1	1	2	2	3	3	4	4	5	5	6	6	7	7	8	8	9	9	♏10

	1	6	12	18	24	30
♃	♐26	27	28	♑0	1	2
♄	♏14	14	15	15	16	16

	1	15	30
♅	♐11	12	13
♆	♐29	♑0	0
♇	♏2	2	2
☊	♊16	15	15

FEBRUARY

	1	2	3	4	5	6	7	8	9	10	11	12	13	14	15	16	17	18	19	20	21	22	23	24	25	26	27	28	29
☉	♒11	12	13	14	15	16	17	18	19	20	21	22	23	24	25	26	28	29	♓0	1	2	3	4	5	6	7	8	9	♓10
☽	♒0	12	24	♓6	18	♈0	12	24	♉6	18	♊1	14	28	♋12	27	♌12	27	♍12	28	♎13	27	♏11	25	♐8	21	♑3	15	27	♒9
☿	♑19	20	21	23	24	26	27	28	♒0	1	3	4	6	7	9	11	12	14	15	17	19	20	22	24	25	27	29	♓0	♓2
♀	♑8	9	10	11	13	14	15	16	17	19	20	21	22	24	25	26	27	29	♒0	1	2	3	5	6	7	8	10	11	♒12
♂	♏10	11	11	12	12	12	13	13	14	14	15	15	16	16	16	17	17	18	18	18	19	19	19	20	20	21	21	21	♏22

	1	6	12	18	24	29
♃	♑3	4	5	6	7	8
♄	♏16	16	16	16	16	16

	1	15	29
♅	♐13	13	13
♆	♑0	1	1
♇	♏2	2	2
☊	♊14	13	12

MARCH

	1	2	3	4	5	6	7	8	9	10	11	12	13	14	15	16	17	18	19	20	21	22	23	24	25	26	27	28	29	30	31
☉	♓11	12	13	14	15	16	17	18	19	20	21	22	23	24	25	26	27	28	29	♈0	1	2	3	4	5	6	7	7	8	9	♈10
☽	♒21	♓3	15	27	♈9	21	♉3	15	28	♊10	23	♋7	21	♌5	20	♍5	21	♎6	21	♏6	20	♐4	17	♑0	12	24	♒6	18	♓0	12	♓24
☿	♓4	6	8	9	11	13	15	17	19	21	23	25	27	29	♈1	3	5	7	9	10	12	14	16	18	20	21	23	25	26	28	♈29
♀	♒13	15	16	17	18	19	21	22	23	24	26	27	28	29	♓1	2	3	4	6	7	8	9	10	12	13	14	15	17	18	19	♓20
♂	♏22	22	23	23	23	23	24	24	24	25	25	25	25	26	26	26	26	26	27	27	27	27	27	27	28	28	28	28	28	28	♏28

	1	6	12	18	24	30
♃	♑8	9	9	10	11	12
♄	♏16	16	16	16	16	15

	1	15	30
♅	♐13	14	14
♆	♑1	1	1
♇	♏2	2	1
☊	♊12	10	8

APRIL

	1	2	3	4	5	6	7	8	9	10	11	12	13	14	15	16	17	18	19	20	21	22	23	24	25	26	27	28	29	30
☉	♈11	12	13	14	15	16	17	18	19	20	21	22	23	24	25	26	27	28	29	♉0	1	2	3	4	5	6	7	8	9	♉10
☽	♈6	18	♉0	12	25	♊7	20	♋3	17	♌1	15	29	♍14	29	♎14	29	♏14	28	♐12	25	♑8	21	♒3	15	27	♓9	21	♈2	14	♈27
☿	♉0	1	2	3	4	5	5	6	6	7	7	7	7	6	6	6	5	5	4	4	3	2	2	1	0	0	♈29	28	28	♈28
♀	♓22	23	24	25	26	28	29	♈0	1	3	4	5	6	8	9	10	11	13	14	15	16	17	19	20	21	22	24	25	26	♈27
♂	♏28	28	28	28	28	28	28	28	28	28	28	28	28	28	28	28	28	27	27	27	27	27	26	26	26	26	25	25	25	♏25

	1	6	12	18	24	30
♃	♑12	12	12	13	13	13
♄	♏15	15	15	14	14	13

	1	15	30
♅	♐13	13	13
♆	♑1	1	1
♇	♏1	1	0
☊	♊8	7	7

MAY

	1	2	3	4	5	6	7	8	9	10	11	12	13	14	15	16	17	18	19	20	21	22	23	24	25	26	27	28	29	30	31
☉	♉11	12	13	14	15	16	17	18	19	20	20	21	22	23	24	25	26	27	28	29	♊0	1	2	3	4	5	6	7	8	9	♊10
☽	♉9	22	♊4	17	♋0	14	27	♌11	25	♍10	24	♎9	23	♏8	22	♐6	20	♑3	16	28	♒11	23	♓5	17	29	♈11	23	♉5	18	♊0	♊13
☿	♈27	27	27	26	26	26	26	27	27	27	27	28	28	29	♉0	0	1	2	3	4	5	6	7	8	9	11	12	13	15	16	♉17
♀	♈29	♉0	1	2	3	5	6	7	8	10	11	12	13	15	16	17	18	19	21	22	23	24	26	27	28	29	♊0	2	3	4	♊5
♂	♏24	24	24	23	23	23	22	22	22	21	21	21	20	20	20	19	19	18	18	18	17	17	17	16	16	16	15	15	15	15	♏14

	1	6	12	18	24	30
♃	♑13	13	13	12	12	12
♄	♏13	13	12	12	12	11

	1	15	30
♅	♐13	12	12
♆	♑1	1	1
♇	♏0	0	0
☊	♊7	7	7

JUNE

	1	2	3	4	5	6	7	8	9	10	11	12	13	14	15	16	17	18	19	20	21	22	23	24	25	26	27	28	29	30
☉	♊11	12	13	14	15	15	16	17	18	19	20	21	22	23	24	25	26	27	28	29	♋0	1	2	3	4	5	6	6	7	♋8
☽	♊27	♋10	24	♌8	22	♍6	20	♎5	19	♏3	17	♐1	15	28	♑11	24	♒6	19	♓1	13	25	♈7	19	♉1	13	26	♊9	22	♋6	♋20
☿	♉19	20	22	24	25	27	29	♊1	2	4	6	8	10	12	14	16	19	21	23	25	27	29	♋2	4	6	8	10	12	15	♋17
♀	♊7	8	9	10	12	13	14	15	16	18	19	20	21	23	24	25	26	28	29	♋0	1	2	4	5	6	7	9	10	11	♋12
♂	♏14	14	14	13	13	13	13	13	12	12	12	12	12	12	12	12	12	12	12	12	12	12	12	12	12	12	12	12	12	♏12

	1	6	12	18	24	30
♃	♑11	11	10	10	9	8
♄	♏11	11	10	10	10	10

	1	15	30
♅	♐12	11	10
♆	♑1	0	0
♇	♏0	♎0	29
☊	♊7	7	6

JULY

	1	2	3	4	5	6	7	8	9	10	11	12	13	14	15	16	17	18	19	20	21	22	23	24	25	26	27	28	29	30	31
☉	♋9	10	11	12	13	14	15	16	17	18	19	20	21	22	23	24	25	26	27	27	28	29	♌0	1	2	3	4	5	6	7	♌8
☽	♌4	18	♍3	17	♎2	16	♏0	14	27	♐11	24	♑7	20	♒2	15	27	♓9	21	♈3	15	27	♉9	21	♊4	17	♋0	14	28	♌13	28	♍13
☿	♋19	21	23	25	27	29	♌0	2	4	6	8	9	11	13	14	16	17	19	20	22	23	25	26	27	28	♍0	1	2	3	4	♍5
♀	♋13	15	16	17	18	20	21	22	23	25	26	27	28	29	♌1	2	3	4	6	7	8	9	11	12	13	14	15	17	18	19	♌20
♂	♏13	13	13	13	13	13	14	14	14	14	15	15	15	15	16	16	16	17	17	17	18	18	18	19	19	19	20	20	21	21	♏21

	1	6	12	18	24	30
♃	♑8	7	7	6	5	5
♄	♏10	10	10	10	10	10

	1	15	30
♅	♐10	10	10
♆	♑0	♐0	29
♇	♎29	29	29
☊	♊6	6	5

AUGUST

	1	2	3	4	5	6	7	8	9	10	11	12	13	14	15	16	17	18	19	20	21	22	23	24	25	26	27	28	29	30	31
☉	♌9	10	11	12	13	14	15	16	17	18	19	19	20	21	22	23	24	25	26	27	28	29	♍0	1	2	3	4	5	6	7	♍8
☽	♍28	♎12	26	♏10	24	♐7	21	♑4	16	29	♒11	23	♓5	17	29	♈11	23	♉5	17	29	♊12	25	♋8	22	♌7	21	♍7	22	♎7	22	♏6
☿	♍6	7	8	9	10	10	11	11	12	12	13	13	13	13	13	13	13	13	13	12	12	11	10	10	9	8	7	6	5	4	♍3
♀	♌22	23	24	25	27	28	29	♍0	1	3	4	5	6	8	9	10	11	13	14	15	16	17	19	20	21	22	24	25	26	27	♍29
♂	♏22	22	23	23	24	24	25	25	26	26	27	27	28	28	29	29	♐0	0	1	1	2	2	3	3	4	4	5	6	6	7	♐7

	1	6	12	18	24	30
♃	♑4	4	4	3	3	3
♄	♏10	10	10	11	11	11

	1	15	30
♅	♐10	10	10
♆	♐29	29	29
♇	♎29	♏0	0
☊	♊4	3	1

SEPTEMBER

	1	2	3	4	5	6	7	8	9	10	11	12	13	14	15	16	17	18	19	20	21	22	23	24	25	26	27	28	29	30
☉	♍9	10	11	12	13	14	15	16	16	17	18	19	20	21	22	23	24	25	26	27	28	29	♎0	1	2	3	4	5	6	♎7
☽	♏21	♐4	18	♑1	13	26	♒8	20	♓2	14	26	♈8	20	♉2	14	26	♊8	21	♋3	17	♌1	15	♍0	15	♎0	15	♏1	15	♐0	♐14
☿	♍3	2	1	1	0	0	0	0	0	1	1	2	3	3	4	6	7	8	10	11	13	14	16	18	20	21	23	25	27	♍29
♀	♎0	1	2	3	5	6	7	8	10	11	12	13	14	16	17	18	19	21	22	23	24	26	27	28	29	♏0	2	3	4	♏5
♂	♐8	9	9	10	10	11	12	12	13	13	14	15	15	16	17	17	18	18	19	20	20	21	22	22	23	24	24	25	26	♐26

	1	6	12	18	24	30
♃	♑3	3	3	4	4	5
♄	♏12	12	13	13	14	14

	1	15	30
♅	♐10	10	10
♆	♐29	29	29
♇	♏0	1	1
☊	♊1	0	♉0

OCTOBER

	1	2	3	4	5	6	7	8	9	10	11	12	13	14	15	16	17	18	19	20	21	22	23	24	25	26	27	28	29	30	31
☉	♎8	9	10	11	12	13	14	15	16	17	18	19	20	21	22	23	24	25	26	27	28	29	♏0	1	2	3	4	5	6	7	♏8
☽	♐27	♑10	23	♒5	17	29	♓11	23	♈5	17	29	♉11	23	♊5	17	♋0	13	26	♌10	24	♍9	23	♎8	24	♏9	23	♐8	22	♑6	19	♒1
☿	♎0	2	4	6	8	9	11	13	15	16	18	20	21	23	25	26	28	♏0	1	3	5	6	8	9	11	13	14	16	17	19	♏20
♀	♏7	8	9	10	11	13	14	15	16	18	19	20	21	22	24	25	26	27	28	♐0	1	2	3	5	6	7	8	9	11	12	♐13
♂	♐27	28	28	29	♑0	1	1	2	3	3	4	5	5	6	7	8	8	9	10	10	11	12	13	13	14	15	15	16	17	18	♑18

	1	6	12	18	24	30
♃	♑5	5	6	7	8	9
♄	♏14	15	16	16	17	18

	1	15	30
♅	♐10	11	12
♆	♐29	29	29
♇	♏1	2	2
☊	♉29	28	28

NOVEMBER

	1	2	3	4	5	6	7	8	9	10	11	12	13	14	15	16	17	18	19	20	21	22	23	24	25	26	27	28	29	30
☉	♏9	10	11	12	13	14	15	16	17	18	19	20	21	22	23	24	25	26	27	28	29	♐0	1	2	3	4	5	6	7	♐8
☽	♒14	26	♓8	20	♈2	14	26	♉8	20	♊2	14	27	♋10	23	♌6	20	♍4	18	♎3	17	♏2	17	♐1	16	♑0	13	27	♒10	22	♓4
☿	♏22	23	25	26	28	29	♐1	2	4	5	7	8	9	11	12	13	15	16	17	19	20	21	22	23	25	26	27	27	28	♐29
♀	♐14	16	17	18	19	20	22	23	24	25	26	28	29	♑0	1	2	4	5	6	7	8	10	11	12	13	14	16	17	18	♑19
♂	♑19	20	21	21	22	23	23	24	25	26	26	27	28	29	29	♒0	1	2	2	3	4	5	5	6	7	8	8	9	10	♒11

	1	6	12	18	24	30
♃	♑9	10	11	12	13	14
♄	♏18	18	19	20	21	21

	1	15	30
♅	♐12	13	13
♆	♐29	♑0	0
♇	♏2	3	3
☊	♉28	27	27

DECEMBER

	1	2	3	4	5	6	7	8	9	10	11	12	13	14	15	16	17	18	19	20	21	22	23	24	25	26	27	28	29	30	31
☉	♐9	10	11	12	13	14	15	16	17	18	19	20	21	22	23	24	25	26	27	28	29	♑0	1	2	3	4	5	6	7	8	♑9
☽	♓16	28	♈10	22	♉4	16	28	♊11	24	♋7	20	♌3	17	♍1	15	29	♎13	27	♏12	26	♐10	24	♑8	21	♒4	17	♓0	12	24	♈6	♈18
☿	♑0	0	1	1	1	1	0	0	♐29	28	27	26	25	24	22	21	20	18	17	16	16	15	15	15	15	15	15	15	16	16	♐17
♀	♑20	22	23	24	25	26	27	29	♒0	1	2	3	5	6	7	8	9	10	12	13	14	15	16	17	18	20	21	22	23	24	♒25
♂	♒11	12	13	14	15	15	16	17	18	18	19	20	21	21	22	23	24	24	25	26	27	27	28	29	♓0	1	1	2	3	4	♓4

	1	6	12	18	24	30
♃	♑15	16	17	18	20	21
♄	♏21	22	23	23	24	25

	1	15	30
♅	♐14	14	15
♆	♑0	1	1
♇	♏3	4	4
☊	♉27	27	27

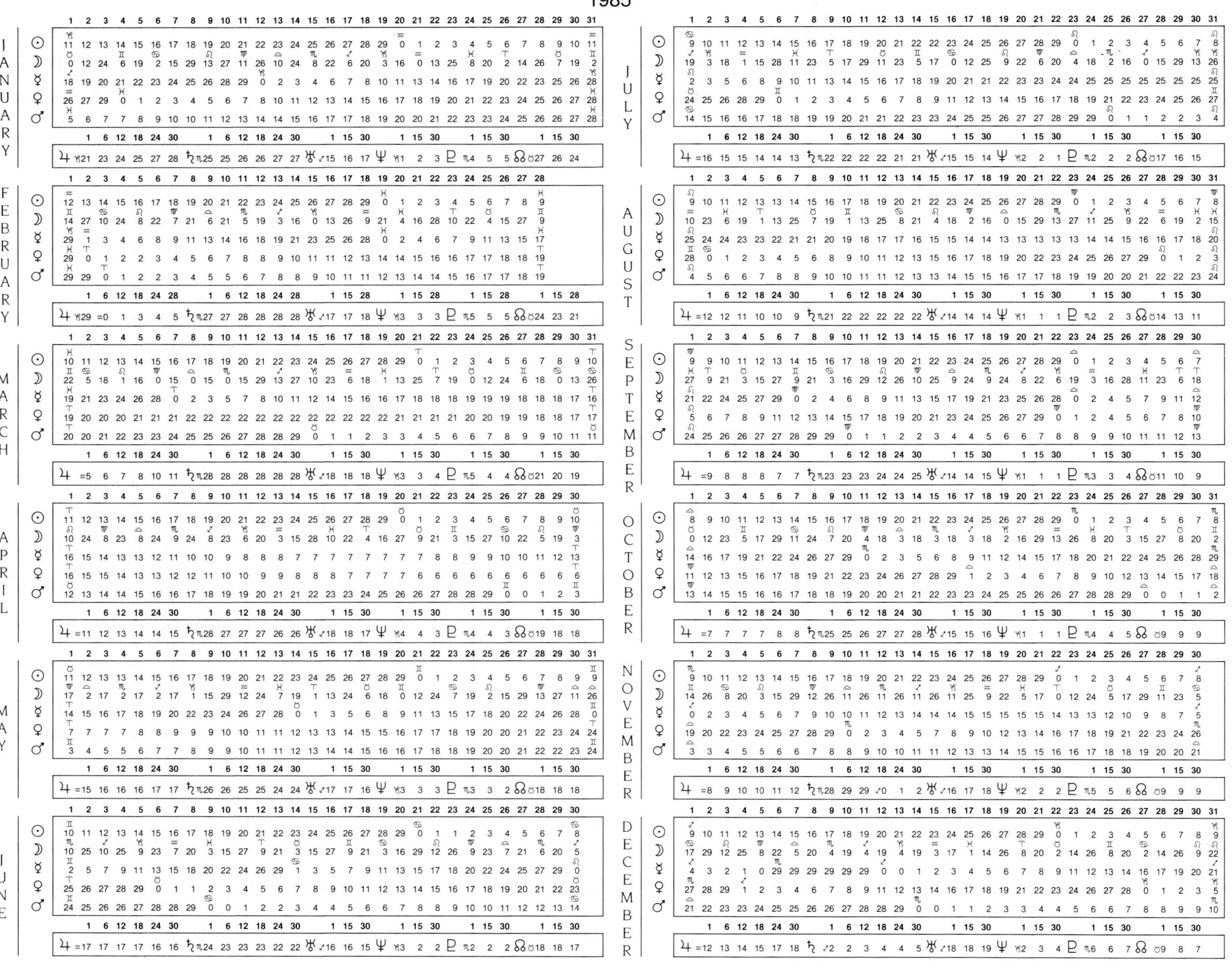

1985

JANUARY

	1	2	3	4	5	6	7	8	9	10	11	12	13	14	15	16	17	18	19	20	21	22	23	24	25	26	27	28	29	30	31
☉	♑11	12	13	14	15	16	17	18	19	20	21	22	23	24	25	26	27	28	29	♒0	1	2	3	4	5	6	7	8	9	10	♒11
☽	♉0	12	24	♊6	19	♋2	15	29	♌13	27	♍11	26	♎10	24	♏8	22	♐6	20	♑3	16	♒0	13	25	♓8	20	♈2	14	26	♉7	19	♊2
☿	♐18	19	20	21	22	23	24	25	26	28	29	♑0	2	3	4	6	7	8	10	11	13	14	16	17	19	20	22	23	25	26	♑28
♀	♒26	27	29	♓0	1	2	3	4	5	6	7	8	10	11	12	13	14	15	16	17	18	19	20	21	22	23	24	25	26	27	♓28
♂	♓5	6	7	7	8	9	10	10	11	12	13	14	14	15	16	17	17	18	19	20	20	21	22	23	23	24	25	26	26	27	♓28

	1	6	12	18	24	30
♃	♑21	23	24	25	27	28
♄	♏25	25	26	26	27	27

	1	15	30
♅	♐15	16	17
♆	♑1	2	3
♇	♏4	5	5
☊	♉27	26	24

FEBRUARY

	1	2	3	4	5	6	7	8	9	10	11	12	13	14	15	16	17	18	19	20	21	22	23	24	25	26	27	28
☉	♒12	13	14	15	16	17	18	19	20	21	22	23	24	25	26	27	28	29	♓0	1	2	3	4	5	6	7	8	♓9
☽	♊14	27	♋10	24	♌8	22	♍7	21	♎6	21	♏5	19	♐3	16	♑0	13	26	♒9	21	♓4	16	28	♈10	22	♉4	15	27	♊9
☿	♑29	♒1	3	4	6	8	9	11	13	14	16	18	19	21	23	25	26	28	♓0	2	4	6	7	9	11	13	15	♓17
♀	♓29	♈0	1	2	2	3	4	5	6	7	8	8	9	10	11	11	12	13	14	14	15	16	16	17	17	18	18	♈19
♂	♓29	29	♈0	1	2	2	3	4	5	5	6	7	8	8	9	10	11	11	12	13	14	14	15	16	17	17	18	♈19

	1	6	12	18	24	28
♃	♑29	♒0	1	3	4	5
♄	♏27	27	28	28	28	28

	1	15	28
♅	♐17	17	18
♆	♑3	3	3
♇	♏5	5	5
☊	♉24	23	21

MARCH

	1	2	3	4	5	6	7	8	9	10	11	12	13	14	15	16	17	18	19	20	21	22	23	24	25	26	27	28	29	30	31
☉	♓10	11	12	13	14	15	16	17	18	19	20	21	22	23	24	25	26	27	28	29	♈0	1	2	3	4	5	6	7	8	9	♈10
☽	♊22	♋5	18	♌1	16	♍0	15	♎0	15	♏0	15	29	♐13	27	♑10	23	♒6	18	♓1	13	25	♈7	19	♉0	12	24	♊6	18	♋0	13	♋26
☿	♓19	21	23	24	26	28	♈0	2	3	5	7	8	10	11	12	14	15	16	16	17	18	18	18	19	19	19	18	18	18	17	♈16
♀	♈19	20	20	20	21	21	21	22	22	22	22	22	22	22	22	22	22	22	22	21	21	21	21	20	20	19	19	18	18	17	♈17
♂	♈20	20	21	22	23	23	24	25	25	26	27	28	28	29	♉0	1	1	2	3	3	4	5	6	6	7	8	9	9	10	11	♉11

	1	6	12	18	24	30
♃	♒5	6	7	8	10	11
♄	♏28	28	28	28	28	28

	1	15	30
♅	♐18	18	18
♆	♑3	3	4
♇	♏5	4	4
☊	♉21	20	19

APRIL

	1	2	3	4	5	6	7	8	9	10	11	12	13	14	15	16	17	18	19	20	21	22	23	24	25	26	27	28	29	30
☉	♈11	12	13	14	15	16	17	18	19	20	21	22	23	24	25	26	27	28	29	♉0	1	2	3	4	5	6	7	8	9	♉10
☽	♌10	24	♍8	23	♎8	24	♏9	24	♐8	23	♑6	20	♒3	15	28	♓10	22	♈4	16	27	♉9	21	♊3	15	27	♋10	22	♌5	19	♍3
☿	♈16	15	14	13	13	12	11	10	10	9	8	8	8	7	7	7	7	7	7	7	7	8	8	9	9	10	10	11	12	♈13
♀	♈16	15	15	14	13	13	12	12	11	10	10	9	9	8	8	8	7	7	7	7	6	6	6	6	6	6	6	6	6	♈6
♂	♉12	13	14	14	15	16	16	17	18	19	19	20	21	21	22	23	23	24	25	26	26	27	28	28	29	♊0	0	1	2	♊3

	1	6	12	18	24	30
♃	♒11	12	13	14	14	15
♄	♏28	27	27	27	26	26

	1	15	30
♅	♐18	18	17
♆	♑4	4	3
♇	♏4	4	3
☊	♉19	18	18

MAY

	1	2	3	4	5	6	7	8	9	10	11	12	13	14	15	16	17	18	19	20	21	22	23	24	25	26	27	28	29	30	31
☉	♉11	12	13	13	14	15	16	17	18	19	20	21	22	23	24	25	26	27	28	29	♊0	1	2	3	4	5	6	7	8	9	♊9
☽	♍17	♎2	17	♏2	17	♐2	17	♑1	15	29	♒12	24	♓7	19	♈1	13	24	♉6	18	♊0	12	24	♋7	19	♌2	15	29	♍13	27	♎11	♎26
☿	♈14	15	16	17	18	19	20	22	23	24	26	27	28	♉0	1	3	5	6	8	9	11	13	15	17	18	20	22	24	26	28	♊0
♀	♈7	7	7	7	8	8	9	9	9	10	10	11	11	12	13	13	14	15	15	16	17	17	18	19	20	20	21	22	23	24	♈24
♂	♊3	4	5	5	6	7	7	8	9	9	10	11	11	12	13	14	14	15	16	16	17	18	18	19	20	20	21	22	22	23	♊24

	1	6	12	18	24	30
♃	♒15	16	16	16	17	17
♄	♏26	26	25	25	24	24

	1	15	30
♅	♐17	17	16
♆	♑3	3	3
♇	♏3	3	2
☊	♉18	18	18

JUNE

	1	2	3	4	5	6	7	8	9	10	11	12	13	14	15	16	17	18	19	20	21	22	23	24	25	26	27	28	29	30
☉	♊10	11	12	13	14	15	16	17	18	19	20	21	22	23	24	25	26	27	28	29	♋0	1	1	2	3	4	5	6	7	♋8
☽	♏10	25	♐10	25	♑9	23	♒7	20	♓3	15	27	♈9	21	♉3	15	27	♊9	21	♋3	16	29	♌12	26	♍9	23	♎7	21	♏6	20	♐5
☿	♊2	5	7	9	11	13	15	18	20	22	24	26	29	♋1	3	5	7	9	11	13	15	17	18	20	22	24	25	27	29	♌0
♀	♈25	26	27	28	29	♉0	1	1	2	3	4	5	6	7	8	9	10	11	12	13	14	15	16	17	18	19	20	21	22	♉23
♂	♊24	25	26	26	27	28	28	29	♋0	0	1	2	2	3	4	4	5	6	6	7	8	8	9	10	10	11	12	12	13	♋14

	1	6	12	18	24	30
♃	♒17	17	17	17	16	16
♄	♏24	23	23	23	22	22

	1	15	30
♅	♐16	16	15
♆	♑3	2	2
♇	♏2	2	2
☊	♉18	18	17

JULY

	1	2	3	4	5	6	7	8	9	10	11	12	13	14	15	16	17	18	19	20	21	22	23	24	25	26	27	28	29	30	31
☉	♋9	10	11	12	13	14	15	16	17	18	19	20	21	22	22	23	24	25	26	27	28	29	♌0	1	2	3	4	5	6	7	♌8
☽	♐19	♑3	18	♒1	15	28	♓11	23	♈5	17	29	♉11	23	♊5	17	♋0	12	25	♌9	22	♍6	20	♎4	18	♏2	16	♐0	15	29	♑13	♑26
☿	♌2	3	5	6	8	9	10	11	13	14	15	16	17	18	19	20	21	21	22	23	23	24	24	25	25	25	25	25	25	25	♌25
♀	♉24	25	26	28	29	♊0	1	2	3	4	5	6	7	8	9	11	12	13	14	15	16	17	18	19	21	22	23	24	25	26	♊27
♂	♋14	15	16	16	17	18	18	19	19	20	21	21	22	23	23	24	25	25	26	27	27	28	29	29	♌0	1	1	2	2	3	♌4

	1	6	12	18	24	30
♃	♒16	15	15	14	14	13
♄	♏22	22	22	22	21	21

	1	15	30
♅	♐15	15	14
♆	♑2	2	1
♇	♏2	2	2
☊	♉17	16	15

AUGUST

	1	2	3	4	5	6	7	8	9	10	11	12	13	14	15	16	17	18	19	20	21	22	23	24	25	26	27	28	29	30	31
☉	♌9	10	11	12	13	13	14	15	16	17	18	19	20	21	22	23	24	25	26	27	28	29	♍0	1	2	3	4	5	6	7	♍8
☽	♒10	23	♓6	19	♈1	13	25	♉7	19	♊1	13	25	♋8	21	♌4	18	♍2	16	♎0	15	29	♏13	27	♐11	25	♑9	22	♒6	19	♓2	♓15
☿	♌25	24	24	23	23	22	21	21	20	19	18	17	17	16	15	15	14	14	13	13	13	13	13	14	14	15	16	16	17	18	♌20
♀	♊28	♋0	1	2	3	4	5	6	8	9	10	11	12	13	15	16	17	18	19	20	22	23	24	25	26	27	29	♌0	1	2	♌3
♂	♌4	5	6	6	7	8	8	9	10	10	11	11	12	13	13	14	15	15	16	17	17	18	19	19	20	20	21	22	22	23	♌24

	1	6	12	18	24	30
♃	♒12	12	11	10	10	9
♄	♏21	22	22	22	22	22

	1	15	30
♅	♐14	14	14
♆	♑1	1	1
♇	♏2	2	3
☊	♉14	13	11

SEPTEMBER

	1	2	3	4	5	6	7	8	9	10	11	12	13	14	15	16	17	18	19	20	21	22	23	24	25	26	27	28	29	30
☉	♍9	9	10	11	12	13	14	15	16	17	18	19	20	21	22	23	24	25	26	27	28	29	♎0	1	2	3	4	5	6	♎7
☽	♓27	♈9	21	♉3	15	27	♊9	21	♋3	16	29	♌12	26	♍10	25	♎9	24	♏9	24	♐8	22	♑6	19	♒3	16	28	♓11	23	♈6	♈18
☿	♌21	22	24	25	27	29	♍0	2	4	6	8	9	11	13	15	17	19	21	23	25	26	28	♎0	2	4	5	7	9	11	♎12
♀	♌5	6	7	8	9	11	12	13	14	15	17	18	19	20	21	23	24	25	26	27	29	♍0	1	2	4	5	6	7	8	♍10
♂	♌24	25	26	26	27	27	28	29	29	♍0	1	1	2	2	3	4	4	5	6	6	7	8	8	9	9	10	11	11	12	♍13

	1	6	12	18	24	30
♃	♒9	8	8	8	7	7
♄	♏23	23	23	24	24	25

	1	15	30
♅	♐14	14	15
♆	♑1	1	1
♇	♏3	3	4
☊	♉11	10	9

OCTOBER

	1	2	3	4	5	6	7	8	9	10	11	12	13	14	15	16	17	18	19	20	21	22	23	24	25	26	27	28	29	30	31
☉	♎8	9	10	11	12	13	14	15	16	17	18	19	20	21	22	23	24	25	26	27	28	29	♏0	1	2	3	4	5	6	7	♏8
☽	♉0	12	23	♊5	17	29	♋11	24	♌7	20	♍4	18	♎3	18	♏3	18	♐3	18	♑2	16	29	♒13	26	♓8	20	♈3	15	27	♉8	20	♊2
☿	♎14	16	17	19	21	22	24	26	27	29	♏0	2	3	5	6	8	9	11	12	14	15	17	18	20	21	22	24	25	26	28	♏29
♀	♍11	12	13	15	16	17	18	19	21	22	23	24	26	27	28	29	♎1	2	3	4	6	7	8	9	10	12	13	14	15	17	♎18
♂	♍13	14	15	15	16	16	17	18	18	19	20	20	21	21	22	23	23	24	25	25	26	26	27	28	28	29	♎0	0	1	1	♎2

	1	6	12	18	24	30
♃	♒7	7	7	7	8	8
♄	♏25	25	26	27	27	28

	1	15	30
♅	♐15	15	16
♆	♑1	1	1
♇	♏4	4	5
☊	♉9	9	9

NOVEMBER

	1	2	3	4	5	6	7	8	9	10	11	12	13	14	15	16	17	18	19	20	21	22	23	24	25	26	27	28	29	30
☉	♏9	10	11	12	13	14	15	16	17	18	19	20	21	22	23	24	25	26	27	28	29	♐0	1	2	3	4	5	6	7	♐8
☽	♊14	26	♋8	20	♌3	15	29	♍12	26	♎11	26	♏11	26	♐11	26	♑11	25	♒9	22	♓5	17	♈0	12	24	♉5	17	29	♊11	23	♋5
☿	♐0	2	3	4	5	6	7	9	10	10	11	12	13	14	14	14	15	15	15	15	15	14	13	13	12	10	9	8	7	♐5
♀	♎19	20	22	23	24	25	27	28	29	♏0	2	3	4	5	7	8	9	10	12	13	14	16	17	18	19	21	22	23	24	♏26
♂	♎3	3	4	5	5	6	6	7	8	8	9	10	10	11	11	12	13	13	14	15	15	16	16	17	18	18	19	20	20	♎21

	1	6	12	18	24	30
♃	♒8	9	10	10	11	12
♄	♏28	29	29	♐0	1	2

	1	15	30
♅	♐16	17	18
♆	♑2	2	2
♇	♏5	5	6
☊	♉9	9	9

DECEMBER

	1	2	3	4	5	6	7	8	9	10	11	12	13	14	15	16	17	18	19	20	21	22	23	24	25	26	27	28	29	30	31
☉	♐9	10	11	12	13	14	15	16	17	18	19	20	21	22	23	24	25	26	27	28	29	♑0	1	2	3	4	5	6	7	8	♑9
☽	♋17	29	♌12	25	♍8	22	♎5	20	♏4	19	♐4	19	♑4	19	♒3	17	♓1	14	26	♈8	20	♉2	14	26	♊8	20	♋2	14	26	♌9	♌22
☿	♐4	3	2	1	0	♏29	29	29	29	29	29	♐0	0	1	2	3	4	5	6	7	8	9	11	12	13	14	16	17	19	20	♐21
♀	♏27	28	29	♐1	2	3	4	6	7	8	9	11	12	13	14	16	17	18	19	21	22	23	24	26	27	28	♑0	1	2	3	♑5
♂	♎21	22	23	23	24	25	25	26	26	27	28	28	29	♏0	0	1	1	2	3	3	4	4	5	6	6	7	8	8	9	9	♏10

	1	6	12	18	24	30
♃	♒12	13	14	15	17	18
♄	♐2	2	3	4	4	5

	1	15	30
♅	♐18	18	19
♆	♑2	3	4
♇	♏6	6	7
☊	♉9	8	7

1986

JANUARY

	1	2	3	4	5	6	7	8	9	10	11	12	13	14	15	16	17	18	19	20	21	22	23	24	25	26	27	28	29	30	31
☉	♑10	11	12	13	14	15	16	17	18	19	20	21	22	24	25	26	27	28	29	♒0	1	2	3	4	5	6	7	8	9	10	♒11
☽	♍5	18	♎2	16	♏0	14	28	♐13	28	♑12	27	♒11	25	♓9	22	♈4	16	28	♉10	22	♊4	16	28	♋10	23	♌5	18	♍2	15	29	♎12
☿	♐23	24	26	27	29	♑0	2	3	5	6	8	9	11	12	14	15	17	19	20	22	23	25	27	28	♒0	2	3	5	7	8	♒10
♀	♑6	7	8	10	11	12	13	15	16	17	18	20	21	22	23	25	26	27	28	♒0	1	2	3	5	6	7	9	10	11	12	♒14
♂	♏11	11	12	12	13	14	14	15	15	16	17	17	18	18	19	20	20	21	21	22	23	23	24	24	25	26	26	27	27	28	♏29

	1	6	12	18	24	30
♃	♒18	19	21	22	23	25
♄	♐5	6	6	7	7	8

	1	15	30
♅	♐19	20	21
♆	♑4	4	5
♇	♏7	7	7
☊	♉7	5	4

FEBRUARY

	1	2	3	4	5	6	7	8	9	10	11	12	13	14	15	16	17	18	19	20	21	22	23	24	25	26	27	28
☉	♒12	13	14	15	16	17	18	19	20	21	22	23	24	25	26	27	28	29	♓0	1	2	3	4	5	6	7	8	♓9
☽	♎26	♏10	24	♐9	23	♑7	21	♒6	19	♓3	16	29	♈12	24	♉6	18	♊0	12	24	♋6	18	♌1	14	27	♍11	25	♎9	♎23
☿	♒12	14	15	17	19	21	22	24	26	28	♓0	1	3	5	7	9	10	12	14	16	17	19	21	22	23	25	26	♓27
♀	♒15	16	17	19	20	21	22	24	25	26	27	29	♓0	1	2	4	5	6	7	9	10	11	12	14	15	16	17	♓19
♂	♏29	♐0	0	1	2	2	3	3	4	5	5	6	6	7	7	8	9	9	10	10	11	11	12	13	13	14	14	♐15

	1	6	12	18	24	28
♃	♒25	26	28	29	♓1	2
♄	♐8	8	9	9	9	9

	1	15	28
♅	♐21	22	22
♆	♑5	5	5
♇	♏7	7	7
☊	♉4	2	1

MARCH

	1	2	3	4	5	6	7	8	9	10	11	12	13	14	15	16	17	18	19	20	21	22	23	24	25	26	27	28	29	30	31
☉	♓10	11	12	13	14	15	16	17	18	19	20	21	22	23	24	25	26	27	28	29	♈0	1	2	3	4	5	6	7	8	9	♈10
☽	♏7	21	♐5	19	♑4	17	♒1	15	28	♓12	25	♈7	20	♉2	14	26	♊8	20	♋1	14	26	♌9	22	♍5	19	♎3	18	♏2	17	♐2	♐16
☿	♓28	29	♈0	0	1	1	1	1	1	1	0	0	♓29	28	28	27	26	25	24	23	22	21	21	20	19	19	18	18	18	18	♓18
♀	♓20	21	22	24	25	26	27	29	♈0	1	2	4	5	6	7	9	10	11	12	13	15	16	17	18	20	21	22	23	25	26	♈27
♂	♐15	16	17	17	18	18	19	19	20	20	21	22	22	23	23	24	24	25	25	26	26	27	27	28	28	29	29	♑0	0	1	♑1

	1	6	12	18	24	30
♃	♓2	3	5	6	7	9
♄	♐9	10	10	10	10	10

	1	15	30
♅	♐22	22	22
♆	♑5	6	6
♇	♏7	7	7
☊	♉1	0	0

APRIL

	1	2	3	4	5	6	7	8	9	10	11	12	13	14	15	16	17	18	19	20	21	22	23	24	25	26	27	28	29	30
☉	♈11	12	13	14	15	16	17	18	19	20	21	22	23	24	25	26	27	28	29	♉0	1	2	3	4	4	5	6	7	8	♉9
☽	♑0	14	28	♒12	25	♓8	21	♈4	16	28	♉10	22	♊4	16	28	♋10	22	♌4	17	♍0	13	27	♎11	26	♏11	26	♐11	26	♑10	♑25
☿	♓18	18	19	19	19	20	20	21	22	23	23	24	25	26	27	28	29	♈1	2	3	4	6	7	8	10	11	13	14	16	♈17
♀	♈28	♉0	1	2	3	5	6	7	8	9	11	12	13	14	16	17	18	19	20	22	23	24	25	27	28	29	♊0	1	3	♊4
♂	♑2	2	3	3	4	4	5	5	6	6	7	7	8	8	9	9	9	10	10	11	11	12	12	12	13	13	14	14	14	♑15

	1	6	12	18	24	30
♃	♓9	10	12	13	14	15
♄	♐10	9	9	9	9	8

	1	15	30
♅	♐22	22	22
♆	♑6	6	6
♇	♏7	6	6
☊	♉0	0	0

MAY

	1	2	3	4	5	6	7	8	9	10	11	12	13	14	15	16	17	18	19	20	21	22	23	24	25	26	27	28	29	30	31
☉	♉10	11	12	13	14	15	16	17	18	19	20	21	22	23	24	25	26	27	28	29	♊0	1	2	3	4	4	5	6	7	8	♊9
☽	♒9	22	♓5	18	♈1	13	25	♉7	19	♊1	13	24	♋6	18	♌0	13	25	♍8	22	♎5	20	♏4	19	♐4	20	♑5	20	♒4	18	♓2	♓15
☿	♈19	20	22	24	26	27	29	♉1	3	5	7	8	10	12	14	17	19	21	23	25	27	29	♊2	4	6	8	10	12	15	17	♊19
♀	♊5	6	8	9	10	11	12	14	15	16	17	18	20	21	22	23	24	26	27	28	29	♋1	2	3	4	5	7	8	9	10	♋11
♂	♑15	15	16	16	17	17	17	17	18	18	18	19	19	19	20	20	20	20	21	21	21	21	21	22	22	22	22	22	22	23	♑23

	1	6	12	18	24	30
♃	♓15	16	17	18	19	20
♄	♐8	8	8	7	7	6

	1	15	30
♅	♐22	21	21
♆	♑6	5	5
♇	♏6	5	5
☊	♉0	0	♈0

JUNE

	1	2	3	4	5	6	7	8	9	10	11	12	13	14	15	16	17	18	19	20	21	22	23	24	25	26	27	28	29	30
☉	♊10	11	12	13	14	15	16	17	18	19	20	21	22	23	24	25	26	26	27	28	29	♋0	1	2	3	4	5	6	7	♋8
☽	♓28	♈10	22	♉4	16	28	♊10	21	♋3	15	27	♌10	22	♍5	18	♎1	14	28	♏13	28	♐13	28	♑13	28	♒13	27	♓11	24	♈7	♈19
☿	♊21	23	25	27	29	♋1	3	4	6	8	10	11	13	14	16	17	19	20	22	23	24	25	26	27	28	29	♌0	1	2	♌3
♀	♋12	14	15	16	17	18	20	21	22	23	24	26	27	28	29	♌0	1	3	4	5	6	7	8	10	11	12	13	14	15	♌17
♂	♑23	23	23	23	23	23	23	23	23	23	23	23	23	23	23	23	23	23	22	22	22	22	22	22	22	21	21	21	21	♑20

	1	6	12	18	24	30
♃	♓20	21	21	22	22	23
♄	♐6	6	5	5	5	4

	1	15	30
♅	♐21	20	20
♆	♑5	5	4
♇	♏5	5	5
☊	♈29	28	27

JULY

	1	2	3	4	5	6	7	8	9	10	11	12	13	14	15	16	17	18	19	20	21	22	23	24	25	26	27	28	29	30	31
☉	♋9	10	11	12	13	14	15	16	17	17	18	19	20	21	22	23	24	25	26	27	28	29	♌0	1	2	3	4	5	6	7	♌8
☽	♉1	13	25	♊7	18	♋0	12	24	♌7	19	♍2	14	27	♎11	24	♏8	22	♐7	22	♑7	22	♒7	21	♓5	19	♈2	15	27	♉9	21	♊3
☿	♌3	4	5	5	6	6	6	6	6	6	6	6	6	6	5	5	4	4	3	3	2	1	1	0	♋29	29	28	27	27	27	♋26
♀	♌18	19	20	21	22	24	25	26	27	28	29	♍0	1	3	4	5	6	7	8	9	11	12	13	14	15	16	17	18	19	20	♍22
♂	♑20	20	20	19	19	19	19	18	18	18	17	17	17	17	16	16	16	15	15	15	15	14	14	14	14	13	13	13	13	13	♑12

	1	6	12	18	24	30
♃	♓23	23	23	23	23	22
♄	♐4	4	4	3	3	3

	1	15	30
♅	♐20	19	19
♆	♑4	4	4
♇	♏5	5	5
☊	♈27	26	24

AUGUST

	1	2	3	4	5	6	7	8	9	10	11	12	13	14	15	16	17	18	19	20	21	22	23	24	25	26	27	28	29	30	31
☉	♌8	9	10	11	12	13	14	15	16	17	18	19	20	21	22	23	24	25	26	27	28	29	♍0	1	2	2	3	4	5	6	♍7
☽	♊15	27	♋9	21	♌3	16	29	♍11	24	♎8	21	♏5	19	♐3	17	♑2	16	♒1	15	29	♓13	27	♈10	23	♉5	18	29	♊11	23	♋5	♋17
☿	♋26	26	26	26	26	26	27	27	28	28	29	♌0	1	2	3	5	6	8	9	11	13	14	16	18	20	22	24	26	28	♍0	♍2
♀	♍23	24	25	26	27	28	29	♎0	1	2	3	4	5	6	7	9	10	11	12	13	14	15	16	17	18	19	19	20	21	22	♎23
♂	♑12	12	12	12	12	12	12	12	11	11	11	11	11	11	11	12	12	12	12	12	12	12	12	12	13	13	13	13	13	14	♑14

	1	6	12	18	24	30
♃	♓22	22	21	21	20	19
♄	♐3	3	3	3	3	3

	1	15	30
♅	♐19	18	18
♆	♑4	3	3
♇	♏5	5	5
☊	♈24	23	22

SEPTEMBER

	1	2	3	4	5	6	7	8	9	10	11	12	13	14	15	16	17	18	19	20	21	22	23	24	25	26	27	28	29	30
☉	♍8	9	10	11	12	13	14	15	16	17	18	19	20	21	22	23	24	25	26	27	28	29	♎0	1	2	3	4	5	6	♎7
☽	♋29	♌12	25	♍8	21	♎4	18	♏2	16	♐0	14	28	♑12	26	♒11	25	♓8	22	♈5	18	♉1	13	25	♊7	19	♋1	13	25	♌7	♌20
☿	♍4	6	8	10	11	13	15	17	19	21	23	25	26	28	♎0	2	3	5	7	8	10	12	13	15	16	18	20	21	23	♎24
♀	♎24	25	26	27	28	29	♏0	0	1	2	3	4	5	5	6	7	8	9	9	10	11	11	12	13	13	14	14	15	16	♏16
♂	♑14	14	15	15	15	15	16	16	16	17	17	17	18	18	19	19	19	20	20	21	21	21	22	22	23	23	24	24	25	♑25

	1	6	12	18	24	30
♃	♓19	19	18	17	16	15
♄	♐4	4	4	4	5	5

	1	15	30
♅	♐18	18	19
♆	♑3	3	3
♇	♏5	6	6
☊	♈22	21	21

OCTOBER

	1	2	3	4	5	6	7	8	9	10	11	12	13	14	15	16	17	18	19	20	21	22	23	24	25	26	27	28	29	30	31
☉	♎8	9	9	10	11	12	13	14	15	16	17	18	19	20	21	22	23	24	25	26	27	28	29	♏0	1	2	3	4	5	6	♏7
☽	♍3	16	29	♎13	27	♏12	26	♐10	25	♑9	23	♒7	21	♓4	18	♈1	14	27	♉9	21	♊3	15	27	♋9	21	♌3	15	28	♍11	24	♎7
☿	♎26	27	29	♏0	1	3	4	6	7	8	10	11	12	14	15	16	17	18	19	21	22	23	24	24	25	26	27	27	28	28	♏29
♀	♏17	17	18	18	18	19	19	19	20	20	20	20	20	20	20	20	20	20	20	20	20	20	19	19	19	18	18	17	17	16	♏16
♂	♑26	26	27	27	28	28	29	29	♒0	1	1	2	2	3	3	4	4	5	6	6	7	7	8	9	9	10	10	11	12	12	♒13

	1	6	12	18	24	30
♃	♓15	15	14	14	13	13
♄	♐5	6	6	7	7	8

	1	15	30
♅	♐19	19	20
♆	♑3	3	4
♇	♏6	7	7
☊	♈21	21	21

NOVEMBER

	1	2	3	4	5	6	7	8	9	10	11	12	13	14	15	16	17	18	19	20	21	22	23	24	25	26	27	28	29	30
☉	♏8	9	10	11	12	13	14	15	16	17	18	19	20	21	22	23	24	25	26	27	28	29	♐0	1	2	3	4	5	6	♐7
☽	♎21	♏6	21	♐5	20	♑5	20	♒4	18	♓1	15	28	♈10	23	♉5	18	♊0	12	24	♋6	17	29	♌11	23	♍6	19	♎2	15	29	♏14
☿	♏29	29	29	29	29	28	27	27	26	25	23	22	21	19	18	17	16	15	14	14	13	13	13	13	14	14	15	16	16	♏17
♀	♏15	15	14	14	13	12	12	11	11	10	9	9	8	8	7	7	7	6	6	6	5	5	5	5	5	5	5	5	5	♏5
♂	♒14	14	15	15	16	17	17	18	19	19	20	21	21	22	23	23	24	25	25	26	27	27	28	29	29	♓0	1	1	2	♓3

	1	6	12	18	24	30
♃	♓13	13	13	13	13	14
♄	♐8	9	10	10	11	12

	1	15	30
♅	♐20	21	22
♆	♑4	4	5
♇	♏7	8	8
☊	♈21	21	20

DECEMBER

	1	2	3	4	5	6	7	8	9	10	11	12	13	14	15	16	17	18	19	20	21	22	23	24	25	26	27	28	29	30	31
☉	♐8	10	11	12	13	14	15	16	17	18	19	20	21	22	23	24	25	26	27	28	29	♑0	1	2	3	4	5	6	7	8	♑9
☽	♏29	♐14	29	♑14	29	♒14	28	♓11	25	♈8	20	♉2	15	27	♊9	21	♋2	14	26	♌8	20	♍2	15	27	♎10	24	♏7	22	♐7	22	♑7
☿	♏18	20	21	22	23	24	26	27	29	♐0	1	3	4	6	7	9	10	12	13	15	16	18	19	21	22	24	25	27	28	♑0	♑2
♀	♏5	6	6	6	6	7	7	8	8	8	9	9	10	11	11	12	12	13	14	14	15	16	17	17	18	19	20	21	21	22	♏23
♂	♓3	4	5	5	6	7	7	8	9	9	10	11	12	12	13	14	14	15	16	16	17	18	18	19	20	21	21	22	23	23	♓24

	1	6	12	18	24	30
♃	♓14	14	15	16	16	17
♄	♐12	12	13	14	14	15

	1	15	30
♅	♐22	23	23
♆	♑5	5	6
♇	♏9	9	9
☊	♈20	19	17

1987

1988

JANUARY

	1	2	3	4	5	6	7	8	9	10	11	12	13	14	15	16	17	18	19	20	21	22	23	24	25	26	27	28	29	30	31
☉	♑10	11	12	13	14	15	16	17	18	19	20	21	22	23	24	25	26	27	28	29	♒0	1	2	3	4	5	6	7	8	9	♒10
☽	♊5	18	♋0	12	24	♌6	18	♍0	12	23	♎5	18	♏0	13	27	♐11	25	♑10	25	♒10	25	♓10	25	♈9	23	♉6	19	♊2	15	27	♋9
☿	♑15	16	18	20	21	23	25	26	28	♒0	1	3	5	6	8	9	11	13	14	16	17	19	20	21	23	24	25	26	26	27	♒28
♀	♒12	13	14	16	17	18	19	21	22	23	24	26	27	28	29	♓0	2	3	4	5	6	8	9	10	11	13	14	15	16	17	♓19
♂	♏25	26	26	27	28	28	29	♐0	0	1	2	2	3	4	4	5	6	6	7	8	8	9	10	10	11	12	12	13	14	14	♐15

	1	6	12	18	24	30
♃	♈20	21	21	22	22	23
♄	♐25	26	27	27	28	29

	1	15	30
♅	♐28	28	29
♆	♑8	8	9
♇	♏12	12	13
☊	♓27	25	24

FEBRUARY

	1	2	3	4	5	6	7	8	9	10	11	12	13	14	15	16	17	18	19	20	21	22	23	24	25	26	27	28	29
☉	♒11	12	13	14	15	16	17	18	19	20	21	22	23	25	26	27	28	29	♓0	1	2	3	4	5	6	7	8	9	♓10
☽	♋21	♌3	15	27	♍8	20	♎2	14	27	♏9	22	♐5	19	♑3	18	♒3	18	♓3	18	♈3	18	♉2	15	29	♊11	24	♋6	18	♌0
☿	♒28	28	28	28	27	27	26	25	24	23	22	21	20	18	17	16	15	15	14	14	13	13	13	13	13	13	13	14	♒14
♀	♓20	21	22	23	25	26	27	28	29	♈1	2	3	4	5	6	8	9	10	11	12	13	15	16	17	18	19	20	22	♈23
♂	♐16	16	17	18	18	19	20	20	21	22	22	23	24	24	25	26	26	27	28	28	29	♑0	0	1	2	2	3	4	♑4

	1	6	12	18	24	29
♃	♈23	24	25	26	27	28
♄	♐29	29	♑0	0	1	1

	1	15	29
♅	♐29	♑0	0
♆	♑9	9	10
♇	♏13	13	13
☊	♓24	23	23

MARCH

	1	2	3	4	5	6	7	8	9	10	11	12	13	14	15	16	17	18	19	20	21	22	23	24	25	26	27	28	29	30	31
☉	♓11	12	13	14	15	16	17	18	19	20	21	22	23	24	25	26	27	28	29	♈0	1	2	3	4	5	6	7	8	9	10	♈10
☽	♌12	24	♍5	17	29	♎11	24	♏6	19	♐2	15	29	♑13	27	♒12	26	♓11	26	♈11	26	♉10	24	♊7	20	♋2	15	27	♌8	20	♍2	♍14
☿	♒15	15	16	17	18	18	19	20	21	22	23	25	26	27	28	29	♓1	2	3	5	6	8	9	11	12	14	15	17	18	20	♓22
♀	♈24	25	26	27	28	♉0	1	2	3	4	5	6	7	8	9	11	12	13	14	15	16	17	18	19	20	21	22	23	24	25	♉26
♂	♑5	6	6	7	8	8	9	10	11	11	12	13	13	14	15	15	16	17	17	18	19	19	20	21	21	22	23	23	24	25	♑25

	1	6	12	18	24	30
♃	♈28	29	♉1	2	3	5
♄	♑1	1	2	2	2	2

	1	15	30
♅	♑1	1	1
♆	♑10	10	10
♇	♏13	12	12
☊	♓23	23	23

APRIL

	1	2	3	4	5	6	7	8	9	10	11	12	13	14	15	16	17	18	19	20	21	22	23	24	25	26	27	28	29	30
☉	♈11	12	13	14	15	16	17	18	19	20	21	22	23	24	25	26	27	28	29	♉0	1	2	3	4	5	6	7	8	9	♉10
☽	♍26	♎8	20	♏3	16	29	♐12	25	♑9	23	♒7	21	♓6	20	♈5	20	♉4	18	♊2	15	28	♋10	23	♌5	17	28	♍10	22	♎4	♎17
☿	♓23	25	27	28	♈0	2	4	6	7	9	11	13	15	17	19	21	23	25	27	29	♉2	4	6	8	10	12	14	16	19	♉21
♀	♉27	28	29	♊0	1	2	3	4	5	6	7	8	9	10	11	11	12	13	14	15	16	16	17	18	19	19	20	21	21	♊22
♂	♑26	27	27	28	29	29	♒0	1	1	2	3	3	4	5	5	6	7	7	8	9	9	10	11	11	12	13	13	14	15	♒15

	1	6	12	18	24	30
♃	♉5	6	8	9	11	12
♄	♑2	3	3	3	2	2

	1	15	30
♅	♑1	1	1
♆	♑10	10	10
♇	♏12	12	11
☊	♓23	23	22

MAY

	1	2	3	4	5	6	7	8	9	10	11	12	13	14	15	16	17	18	19	20	21	22	23	24	25	26	27	28	29	30	31
☉	♉11	12	13	14	15	16	17	18	19	20	21	21	22	23	24	25	26	27	28	29	♊0	1	2	3	4	5	6	7	8	9	♊10
☽	♎29	♏12	25	♐8	22	♑6	20	♒4	18	♓2	16	♈0	15	29	♉13	26	♊10	23	♋6	18	♌1	13	24	♍6	18	♎0	12	25	♏7	21	♐4
☿	♉23	25	27	28	♊0	2	4	6	7	9	10	12	13	15	16	17	18	19	20	21	22	23	24	24	25	25	26	26	26	27	♊27
♀	♊23	23	24	25	25	26	26	27	27	28	28	28	29	29	29	♋0	0	0	0	0	0	0	0	0	0	0	0	0	0	♊29	♊29
♂	♒16	17	17	18	19	19	20	21	21	22	23	23	24	25	25	26	27	27	28	29	29	♓0	0	1	2	2	3	4	4	5	♓5

	1	6	12	18	24	30
♃	♉12	13	15	16	18	19
♄	♑2	2	2	1	1	1

	1	15	30
♅	♑1	0	0
♆	♑10	10	10
♇	♏11	11	10
☊	♓22	21	20

JUNE

	1	2	3	4	5	6	7	8	9	10	11	12	13	14	15	16	17	18	19	20	21	22	23	24	25	26	27	28	29	30
☉	♊11	12	13	14	15	16	16	17	18	19	20	21	22	23	24	25	26	27	28	29	♋0	1	2	3	4	5	6	7	7	♋8
☽	♐18	♑2	16	♒0	15	29	♓13	27	♈11	25	♉9	22	♊5	19	♋1	14	26	♌9	21	♍2	14	26	♎8	20	♏3	15	29	♐12	26	♑11
☿	♊27	27	27	26	26	26	25	25	25	24	24	23	22	22	21	21	20	20	19	19	19	18	18	18	18	18	18	19	19	♊19
♀	♊29	28	28	27	27	26	26	25	25	24	23	23	22	22	21	20	20	19	19	18	18	17	17	16	16	15	15	15	15	♊14
♂	♓6	7	7	8	9	9	10	10	11	12	12	13	13	14	15	15	16	16	17	18	18	19	19	20	20	21	21	22	23	♓23

	1	6	12	18	24	30
♃	♉20	21	22	23	25	26
♄	♑1	0	0	♐29	29	29

	1	15	30
♅	♑0	♐0	29
♆	♑10	9	9
♇	♏10	10	10
☊	♓19	18	16

JULY

	1	2	3	4	5	6	7	8	9	10	11	12	13	14	15	16	17	18	19	20	21	22	23	24	25	26	27	28	29	30	31
☉	♋9	10	11	12	13	14	15	16	17	18	19	20	21	22	23	24	25	26	27	27	28	29	♌0	1	2	3	4	5	6	7	♌8
☽	♑25	♒10	25	♓9	24	♈8	22	♉5	19	♊2	15	28	♋10	23	♌5	17	29	♍11	22	♎4	16	28	♏11	24	♐7	21	♑5	19	♒4	19	♓4
☿	♊20	20	21	21	22	23	24	25	26	27	28	♋0	1	2	4	5	7	9	10	12	14	16	18	20	22	24	26	28	♌0	2	♌4
♀	♊14	14	14	14	14	14	14	14	14	14	15	15	15	16	16	16	17	17	18	18	19	19	20	20	21	21	22	23	23	24	♊25
♂	♓24	24	25	25	26	26	27	27	28	28	29	29	♈0	0	1	1	1	2	2	3	3	4	4	4	5	5	5	6	6	7	♈7

	1	6	12	18	24	30
♃	♉26	27	28	29	♊0	1
♄	♐28	28	28	27	27	27

	1	15	30
♅	♐29	28	28
♆	♑9	8	8
♇	♏10	10	10
☊	♓16	15	15

AUGUST

	1	2	3	4	5	6	7	8	9	10	11	12	13	14	15	16	17	18	19	20	21	22	23	24	25	26	27	28	29	30	31
☉	♌9	10	11	12	13	14	15	16	17	18	19	20	20	21	22	23	24	25	26	27	28	29	♍0	1	2	3	4	5	6	7	♍8
☽	♓19	♈4	18	♉2	16	29	♊12	25	♋7	20	♌2	14	26	♍7	19	♎1	13	25	♏7	19	♐2	15	29	♑13	27	♒12	27	♓13	28	♈13	♈27
☿	♌7	9	11	13	15	17	19	21	23	25	27	29	♍1	2	4	6	8	10	11	13	15	16	18	20	21	23	24	26	27	29	♎0
♀	♊25	26	27	28	28	29	♋0	1	2	3	3	4	5	6	7	8	9	10	11	11	12	13	14	15	16	17	18	19	20	21	♋22
♂	♈7	7	8	8	8	9	9	9	9	10	10	10	10	10	11	11	11	11	11	11	11	11	11	11	11	11	11	11	11	11	♈11

	1	6	12	18	24	30
♃	♊2	2	3	4	5	5
♄	♐27	26	26	26	26	26

	1	15	30
♅	♐28	27	27
♆	♑8	8	8
♇	♏10	10	10
☊	♓14	14	14

SEPTEMBER

	1	2	3	4	5	6	7	8	9	10	11	12	13	14	15	16	17	18	19	20	21	22	23	24	25	26	27	28	29	30
☉	♍9	10	11	12	13	14	15	16	17	18	18	19	20	21	22	23	24	25	26	27	28	29	♎0	1	2	3	4	5	6	♎7
☽	♉12	25	♊9	22	♋4	17	29	♌11	23	♍5	16	28	♎10	22	♏4	16	29	♐11	25	♑8	22	♒6	21	♓6	21	♈6	21	♉6	20	♊4
☿	♎2	3	4	6	7	8	10	11	12	13	15	16	17	18	19	20	21	22	23	23	24	25	25	26	26	27	27	27	27	♎27
♀	♋23	24	25	26	27	28	29	♌1	2	3	4	5	6	7	8	9	10	11	12	14	15	16	17	18	19	20	21	23	24	♌25
♂	♈11	11	11	11	11	11	11	10	10	10	10	10	9	9	9	9	8	8	8	8	7	7	7	6	6	6	6	5	5	♈5

	1	6	12	18	24	30
♃	♊5	6	6	6	6	6
♄	♐26	26	26	26	26	27

	1	15	30
♅	♐27	27	27
♆	♑8	7	7
♇	♏10	11	11
☊	♓14	14	14

OCTOBER

	1	2	3	4	5	6	7	8	9	10	11	12	13	14	15	16	17	18	19	20	21	22	23	24	25	26	27	28	29	30	31
☉	♎8	9	10	11	12	13	14	15	16	17	18	19	20	21	22	23	24	25	26	27	28	29	♏0	1	2	3	4	5	6	7	♏8
☽	♊18	♋1	13	26	♌8	20	♍1	13	25	♎7	19	♏1	13	26	♐8	21	♑5	18	♒2	16	♓0	15	29	♈14	29	♉14	28	♊12	26	♋9	♋22
☿	♎27	26	26	25	25	24	23	22	21	20	18	17	16	15	14	13	13	12	12	12	12	12	12	13	14	14	15	16	18	19	♎20
♀	♌26	27	28	29	♍1	2	3	4	5	6	7	9	10	11	12	13	15	16	17	18	19	20	22	23	24	25	26	28	29	♎0	♎1
♂	♈4	4	4	4	3	3	3	3	2	2	2	2	1	1	1	1	1	1	0	0	0	0	0	0	0	0	0	0	0	0	♈0

	1	6	12	18	24	30
♃	♊6	6	6	5	5	4
♄	♐27	27	27	28	28	29

	1	15	30
♅	♐27	28	28
♆	♑7	8	8
♇	♏11	12	12
☊	♓14	13	12

NOVEMBER

	1	2	3	4	5	6	7	8	9	10	11	12	13	14	15	16	17	18	19	20	21	22	23	24	25	26	27	28	29	30
☉	♏9	10	11	12	13	14	15	16	17	18	19	20	21	22	23	24	25	26	27	28	29	♐0	1	2	3	4	5	6	7	♐8
☽	♌4	16	28	♍10	22	♎3	15	28	♏10	22	♐5	18	♑2	15	29	♒12	26	♓10	24	♈9	23	♉8	22	♊6	20	♋4	17	♌0	12	♌24
☿	♎22	23	24	26	27	29	♏1	2	4	5	7	9	10	12	13	15	17	18	20	21	23	25	26	28	29	♐1	2	4	6	♐7
♀	♎2	4	5	6	7	8	10	11	12	13	15	16	17	18	19	21	22	23	24	26	27	28	29	♏1	2	3	4	5	7	♏8
♂	♈0	0	0	0	0	0	0	1	1	1	1	1	1	2	2	2	2	3	3	3	3	4	4	4	4	5	5	5	6	♈6

	1	6	12	18	24	30
♃	♊4	3	3	2	1	0
♄	♐29	29	♑0	1	1	2

	1	15	30
♅	♐28	29	♑29
♆	♑8	8	9
♇	♏12	13	14
☊	♓12	11	10

DECEMBER

	1	2	3	4	5	6	7	8	9	10	11	12	13	14	15	16	17	18	19	20	21	22	23	24	25	26	27	28	29	30	31
☉	♐9	10	11	12	13	14	15	16	17	18	19	20	21	22	23	24	25	26	27	28	29	♑0	1	2	3	4	5	6	7	9	♑10
☽	♍6	18	♎0	11	23	♏6	18	♐1	14	28	♑11	25	♒9	23	♓7	21	♈5	19	♉3	17	♊1	15	29	♋12	25	♌7	20	♍2	14	25	♎7
☿	♐9	10	12	14	15	17	18	20	21	23	24	26	28	29	♑1	2	4	6	7	9	10	12	13	15	17	18	20	21	23	24	♑26
♀	♏9	10	12	13	14	15	17	18	19	20	22	23	24	25	27	28	29	♐0	2	3	4	5	7	8	9	10	12	13	14	15	♐17
♂	♈6	7	7	8	8	8	9	9	10	10	10	11	11	12	12	13	13	13	14	14	15	15	16	16	17	17	18	18	19	19	♈20

	1	6	12	18	24	30
♃	♊0	♉29	29	28	27	27
♄	♑2	3	3	4	5	5

	1	15	30
♅	♑0	1	2
♆	♑9	9	10
♇	♏14	14	15
☊	♓10	8	7

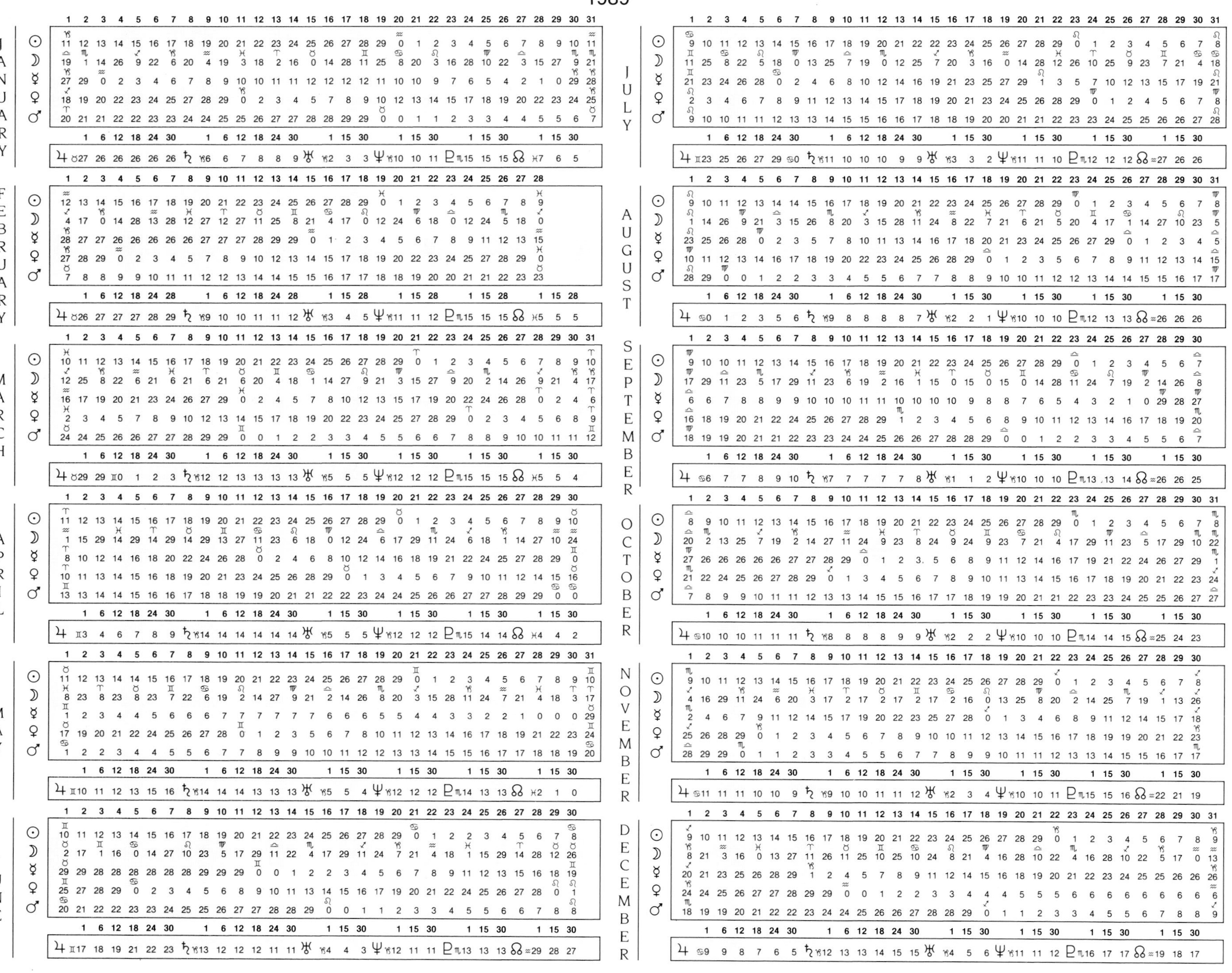

1989

JANUARY

	1	2	3	4	5	6	7	8	9	10	11	12	13	14	15	16	17	18	19	20	21	22	23	24	25	26	27	28	29	30	31
☉	♑11	12	13	14	15	16	17	18	19	20	21	22	23	24	25	26	27	28	29	♒0	1	2	3	4	5	6	7	8	9	10	♒11
☽	♎19	♏1	14	26	♐9	22	♑6	20	♒4	19	♓3	18	♈2	16	♉0	14	28	♊11	25	♋8	20	♌3	16	28	♍10	22	♎3	15	27	♏9	♏21
☿	♑27	29	♒0	2	3	4	6	7	8	9	10	10	11	11	12	12	12	12	11	10	10	9	7	6	5	4	2	1	0	♑29	♑28
♀	♐18	19	20	22	23	24	25	27	28	29	♑0	2	3	4	5	7	8	9	10	12	13	14	15	17	18	19	20	22	23	24	♑25
♂	♈20	21	21	22	22	23	23	24	24	25	25	26	27	27	28	28	29	29	♉0	0	1	1	2	3	3	4	4	5	5	6	♉7

	1	6	12	18	24	30
♃	♉27	26	26	26	26	26
♄	♑6	6	7	8	8	9

	1	15	30
♅	♑2	3	3
♆	♑10	10	11
♇	♏15	15	15
☊	♓7	6	5

FEBRUARY

	1	2	3	4	5	6	7	8	9	10	11	12	13	14	15	16	17	18	19	20	21	22	23	24	25	26	27	28
☉	♒12	13	14	15	16	17	18	19	20	21	22	23	24	25	26	27	28	29	♓0	1	2	3	4	5	6	7	8	♓9
☽	♐4	17	♑0	14	28	♒13	28	♓12	27	♈12	27	♉11	25	♊8	21	♋4	17	♌0	12	24	♍6	18	♎0	12	24	♏5	18	♐0
☿	♑28	27	27	26	26	26	26	26	27	27	27	28	29	29	♒0	1	2	3	4	5	6	7	8	9	11	12	13	♒15
♀	♑27	28	29	♒0	2	3	4	5	7	8	9	10	12	13	14	15	17	18	19	20	22	23	24	25	27	28	29	♓0
♂	♉7	8	8	9	9	10	11	11	12	12	13	14	14	15	15	16	17	17	18	18	19	20	20	21	21	22	23	♉23

	1	6	12	18	24	28
♃	♉26	27	27	27	28	29
♄	♑9	10	10	11	11	12

	1	15	28
♅	♑3	4	5
♆	♑11	11	12
♇	♏15	15	15
☊	♓5	5	5

MARCH

	1	2	3	4	5	6	7	8	9	10	11	12	13	14	15	16	17	18	19	20	21	22	23	24	25	26	27	28	29	30	31
☉	♓10	11	12	13	14	15	16	17	18	19	20	21	22	23	24	25	26	27	28	29	♈0	1	2	3	4	5	6	7	8	9	♈10
☽	♐12	25	♑8	22	♒6	21	♓6	21	♈6	21	♉6	20	♊4	18	♋1	14	27	♌9	21	♍3	15	27	♎9	20	♏2	14	26	♐9	21	♑4	♑17
☿	♒16	17	19	20	21	23	24	26	27	29	♓0	2	4	5	7	8	10	12	13	15	17	19	20	22	24	26	28	♈0	2	4	♈6
♀	♓2	3	4	5	7	8	9	10	12	13	14	15	17	18	19	20	22	23	24	25	27	28	29	♈0	2	3	4	5	6	8	♈9
♂	♉24	24	25	26	26	27	27	28	29	29	♊0	0	1	2	2	3	3	4	5	5	6	6	7	8	8	9	10	10	11	11	♊12

	1	6	12	18	24	30
♃	♉29	29	♊0	1	2	3
♄	♑12	12	13	13	13	13

	1	15	30
♅	♑5	5	5
♆	♑12	12	12
♇	♏15	15	15
☊	♓5	5	4

APRIL

	1	2	3	4	5	6	7	8	9	10	11	12	13	14	15	16	17	18	19	20	21	22	23	24	25	26	27	28	29	30
☉	♈11	12	13	14	15	16	17	18	19	20	21	22	23	24	25	26	27	28	29	♉0	1	2	3	4	5	6	7	8	9	♉10
☽	♒1	15	29	♓14	29	♈14	29	♉14	29	♊13	27	♋11	23	♌6	18	♍0	12	24	♎6	17	29	♏11	24	♐6	18	♑1	14	27	♒10	♒24
☿	♈8	10	12	14	16	18	20	22	24	26	28	♉0	2	4	6	8	10	12	14	16	18	19	21	22	24	25	27	28	29	♊0
♀	♈10	11	13	14	15	16	18	19	20	21	23	24	25	26	28	29	♉0	1	3	4	5	6	7	9	10	11	12	14	15	♉16
♂	♊13	13	14	14	15	16	16	17	18	18	19	19	20	21	21	22	22	23	24	24	25	26	26	27	27	28	29	29	♋0	♋0

	1	6	12	18	24	30
♃	♊3	4	6	7	8	9
♄	♑14	14	14	14	14	14

	1	15	30
♅	♑5	5	5
♆	♑12	12	12
♇	♏15	14	14
☊	♓4	4	2

MAY

	1	2	3	4	5	6	7	8	9	10	11	12	13	14	15	16	17	18	19	20	21	22	23	24	25	26	27	28	29	30	31
☉	♉11	12	13	14	14	15	16	17	18	19	20	21	22	23	24	25	26	27	28	29	♊0	1	2	3	4	5	6	7	8	9	♊10
☽	♓8	23	♈8	23	♉8	23	♊7	22	♋6	19	♌2	14	27	♍9	21	♎2	14	26	♏8	20	♐3	15	28	♑11	24	♒7	21	♓4	18	♈3	♈17
☿	♊1	2	3	4	4	5	6	6	6	7	7	7	7	7	7	6	6	6	5	5	4	4	3	3	2	2	1	0	0	0	♉29
♀	♉17	19	20	21	22	24	25	26	27	28	♊0	1	2	3	5	6	7	8	10	11	12	13	14	16	17	18	19	21	22	23	♊24
♂	♋1	2	2	3	4	4	5	5	6	7	7	8	9	9	10	10	11	12	12	13	13	14	15	15	16	17	17	18	18	19	♋20

	1	6	12	18	24	30
♃	♊10	11	12	13	15	16
♄	♑14	14	14	13	13	13

	1	15	30
♅	♑5	5	4
♆	♑12	12	12
♇	♏14	13	13
☊	♓2	1	0

JUNE

	1	2	3	4	5	6	7	8	9	10	11	12	13	14	15	16	17	18	19	20	21	22	23	24	25	26	27	28	29	30
☉	♊10	11	12	13	14	15	16	17	18	19	20	21	22	23	24	25	26	27	28	29	♋0	1	2	2	3	4	5	6	7	♋8
☽	♉2	17	♊1	16	♋0	14	27	♌10	23	♍5	17	29	♎11	22	♏4	17	29	♐11	24	♑7	21	♒4	18	♓1	15	29	♈14	28	♉12	♉26
☿	♉29	29	28	28	28	28	28	28	29	29	29	♊0	0	1	2	2	3	4	5	6	7	8	9	11	12	13	15	16	18	♊19
♀	♊25	27	28	29	♋0	2	3	4	5	6	8	9	10	11	13	14	15	16	17	19	20	21	22	24	25	26	27	28	♌0	♌1
♂	♋20	21	22	22	23	23	24	25	25	26	27	27	28	28	29	♌0	0	1	1	2	3	3	4	5	5	6	6	7	8	♌8

	1	6	12	18	24	30
♃	♊17	18	19	21	22	23
♄	♑13	12	12	12	11	11

	1	15	30
♅	♑4	4	3
♆	♑12	11	11
♇	♏13	13	13
☊	♒29	28	27

JULY

	1	2	3	4	5	6	7	8	9	10	11	12	13	14	15	16	17	18	19	20	21	22	23	24	25	26	27	28	29	30	31
☉	♋9	10	11	12	13	14	15	16	17	18	19	20	21	22	22	23	24	25	26	27	28	29	♌0	1	2	3	4	5	6	7	♌8
☽	♊11	25	♋8	22	♌5	18	♍0	13	25	♎7	19	♏0	12	25	♐7	20	♑3	16	♒0	14	28	♓12	26	♈10	25	♉9	23	♊7	21	♋4	♋18
☿	♊21	23	24	26	28	♋0	2	4	6	8	10	12	14	16	19	21	23	25	27	29	♌1	3	5	7	10	12	13	15	17	19	♌21
♀	♌2	3	4	6	7	8	9	11	12	13	14	15	17	18	19	20	21	23	24	25	26	28	29	♍0	1	2	4	5	6	7	♍8
♂	♌9	10	10	11	11	12	13	13	14	15	15	16	16	17	18	18	19	20	20	21	21	22	23	23	24	25	25	26	26	27	♌28

	1	6	12	18	24	30
♃	♊23	25	26	27	29	♋0
♄	♑11	10	10	10	9	9

	1	15	30
♅	♑3	3	2
♆	♑11	11	10
♇	♏12	12	12
☊	♒27	26	26

AUGUST

	1	2	3	4	5	6	7	8	9	10	11	12	13	14	15	16	17	18	19	20	21	22	23	24	25	26	27	28	29	30	31
☉	♌9	10	11	12	13	14	14	15	16	17	18	19	20	21	22	23	24	25	26	27	28	29	♍0	1	2	3	4	5	6	7	♍8
☽	♌1	14	26	♍9	21	♎3	15	26	♏8	20	♐3	15	28	♑11	24	♒8	22	♓7	21	♈6	21	♉5	20	♊4	17	♋1	14	27	♌10	23	♍5
☿	♌23	25	26	28	♍0	2	3	5	7	8	10	11	13	14	16	17	18	20	21	23	24	25	26	27	29	♎0	1	2	3	4	♎5
♀	♍10	11	12	13	14	16	17	18	19	20	22	23	24	25	26	28	29	♎0	1	2	3	5	6	7	8	9	11	12	13	14	♎15
♂	♌28	29	♍0	0	1	2	2	3	3	4	5	5	6	7	7	8	8	9	10	10	11	12	12	13	14	14	15	15	16	17	♍17

	1	6	12	18	24	30
♃	♋0	1	2	3	5	6
♄	♑9	8	8	8	8	7

	1	15	30
♅	♑2	2	1
♆	♑10	10	10
♇	♏12	13	13
☊	♒26	26	26

SEPTEMBER

	1	2	3	4	5	6	7	8	9	10	11	12	13	14	15	16	17	18	19	20	21	22	23	24	25	26	27	28	29	30
☉	♍9	10	10	11	12	13	14	15	16	17	18	19	20	21	22	23	24	25	26	27	28	29	♎0	1	2	3	4	5	6	♎7
☽	♍17	29	♎11	23	♏5	17	29	♐11	23	♑6	19	♒2	16	♓1	15	♈0	15	♉0	15	♊0	14	28	♋11	24	♌7	19	♍2	14	26	♎8
☿	♎6	6	7	8	8	9	9	10	10	10	11	11	10	10	10	10	9	8	8	7	6	5	4	3	2	1	0	♍29	28	♍27
♀	♎16	18	19	20	21	22	24	25	26	27	28	29	♏1	2	3	4	5	6	8	9	10	11	12	13	14	16	17	18	19	♏20
♂	♍18	19	19	20	21	21	22	23	23	24	24	25	26	26	27	28	28	29	♎0	0	1	2	2	3	3	4	5	5	6	♎7

	1	6	12	18	24	30
♃	♋6	7	7	8	9	10
♄	♑7	7	7	7	7	8

	1	15	30
♅	♑1	1	2
♆	♑10	10	10
♇	♏13	13	14
☊	♒26	26	25

OCTOBER

	1	2	3	4	5	6	7	8	9	10	11	12	13	14	15	16	17	18	19	20	21	22	23	24	25	26	27	28	29	30	31
☉	♎8	9	10	11	12	13	14	15	16	17	18	19	20	21	22	23	24	25	26	27	28	29	♏0	1	2	3	4	5	6	7	♏8
☽	♎20	♏2	13	25	♐7	19	♑2	14	27	♒11	24	♓9	23	♈8	24	♉9	24	♊9	23	♋7	21	♌4	17	29	♍11	23	♎5	17	29	♏10	♏22
☿	♍27	26	26	26	26	26	27	27	28	29	♎0	1	2	3	5	6	8	9	11	12	14	16	17	19	21	22	24	26	27	29	♏1
♀	♏21	22	24	25	26	27	28	29	♐0	1	3	4	5	6	7	8	9	10	11	13	14	15	16	17	18	19	20	21	22	23	♐24
♂	♎7	8	9	9	10	11	11	12	13	13	14	15	15	16	17	17	18	19	19	20	21	21	22	23	23	24	25	25	26	27	♎27

	1	6	12	18	24	30
♃	♋10	10	10	11	11	11
♄	♑8	8	8	8	9	9

	1	15	30
♅	♑2	2	2
♆	♑10	10	10
♇	♏14	14	15
☊	♒25	24	23

NOVEMBER

	1	2	3	4	5	6	7	8	9	10	11	12	13	14	15	16	17	18	19	20	21	22	23	24	25	26	27	28	29	30
☉	♏9	10	11	12	13	14	15	16	17	18	19	20	21	22	23	24	25	26	27	28	29	♐0	1	2	3	4	5	6	7	♐8
☽	♐4	16	29	♑11	24	♒6	20	♓3	17	♈2	17	♉2	17	♊2	17	♋2	16	♌0	13	25	♍8	20	♎2	14	25	♏7	19	♐1	13	♐26
☿	♏2	4	6	7	9	11	12	14	15	17	19	20	22	23	25	27	28	♐0	1	3	4	6	8	9	11	12	14	15	17	♐18
♀	♐25	26	28	29	♑0	1	2	3	4	5	6	7	8	9	10	10	11	12	13	14	15	16	17	18	19	19	20	21	22	♑23
♂	♎28	29	29	♏0	1	1	2	3	3	4	5	5	6	7	7	8	9	9	10	11	11	12	13	13	14	15	15	16	17	♏17

	1	6	12	18	24	30
♃	♋11	11	11	10	10	9
♄	♑9	10	10	11	11	12

	1	15	30
♅	♑2	3	4
♆	♑10	10	11
♇	♏15	15	16
☊	♒22	21	19

DECEMBER

	1	2	3	4	5	6	7	8	9	10	11	12	13	14	15	16	17	18	19	20	21	22	23	24	25	26	27	28	29	30	31
☉	♐9	10	11	12	13	14	15	16	17	18	19	20	21	22	23	24	25	26	27	28	29	♑0	1	2	3	4	5	6	7	8	♑9
☽	♑8	21	♒3	16	♓0	13	27	♈11	26	♉11	25	♊10	25	♋10	24	♌8	21	♍4	16	28	♎10	22	♏4	16	28	♐10	22	♑5	17	♒0	♒13
☿	♐20	21	23	25	26	28	29	♑1	2	4	5	7	8	9	11	12	14	15	16	18	19	20	21	22	23	24	25	25	26	26	♑26
♀	♑24	24	25	26	27	27	28	29	29	♒0	0	1	2	2	3	3	4	4	4	5	5	5	6	6	6	6	6	6	6	6	♒6
♂	♏18	19	19	20	21	22	22	23	24	24	25	26	26	27	28	28	29	♐0	1	1	2	3	3	4	5	5	6	7	8	8	♐9

	1	6	12	18	24	30
♃	♋9	9	8	7	6	5
♄	♑12	13	13	14	15	15

	1	15	30
♅	♑4	5	6
♆	♑11	11	12
♇	♏16	17	17
☊	♒19	18	17

1990

JANUARY

	1	2	3	4	5	6	7	8	9	10	11	12	13	14	15	16	17	18	19	20	21	22	23	24	25	26	27	28	29	30	31
☉	♑10	11	12	13	14	15	16	17	18	19	20	22	23	24	25	26	27	28	29	♒0	1	2	3	4	5	6	7	8	9	10	♒11
☽	♒27	♓10	24	♈8	22	♉6	20	♊5	19	♋4	18	♌2	15	28	♍11	24	♎6	18	♏0	12	24	♐6	18	♑0	13	26	♒9	23	♓6	20	♈4
☿	♑26	26	25	24	23	22	21	20	19	17	16	15	14	13	12	11	10	10	10	10	10	10	10	11	11	12	12	13	14	15	♑16
♀	♒6	6	6	6	6	5	5	5	4	4	3	3	2	2	1	0	0	♑29	29	28	27	27	26	26	25	25	24	24	23	23	♑22
♂	♐10	10	11	12	12	13	14	15	15	16	17	17	18	19	20	20	21	22	22	23	24	25	25	26	27	27	28	29	♑0	0	♑1

	1	6	12	18	24	30
♃	♋5	5	4	3	2	2
♄	♑16	16	17	18	18	19

	1	15	30
♅	♑6	7	7
♆	♑12	13	13
♇	♏17	17	18
☊	♒17	17	16

FEBRUARY

	1	2	3	4	5	6	7	8	9	10	11	12	13	14	15	16	17	18	19	20	21	22	23	24	25	26	27	28
☉	♒12	13	14	15	16	17	18	19	20	21	22	23	24	25	26	27	28	29	♓0	1	2	3	4	5	6	7	8	♓9
☽	♈18	♉3	17	♊1	15	29	♋13	27	♌10	23	♍6	19	♎1	14	26	♏8	20	♐1	13	26	♑8	21	♒4	17	♓1	15	♈0	♈14
☿	♑17	18	19	20	21	22	23	25	26	27	29	♒0	1	3	4	5	7	8	10	11	13	14	16	17	19	21	22	♒24
♀	♑22	22	22	21	21	21	21	21	21	21	21	21	21	22	22	22	22	23	23	23	24	24	25	25	26	26	27	♑28
♂	♑2	2	3	4	5	5	6	7	8	8	9	10	10	11	12	13	13	14	15	16	16	17	18	18	19	20	21	♑21

	1	6	12	18	24	28
♃	♋2	1	1	1	1	1
♄	♑19	20	20	21	22	22

	1	15	28
♅	♑8	8	9
♆	♑13	14	14
♇	♏18	18	18
☊	♒16	16	16

MARCH

	1	2	3	4	5	6	7	8	9	10	11	12	13	14	15	16	17	18	19	20	21	22	23	24	25	26	27	28	29	30	31
☉	♓10	11	12	13	14	15	16	17	18	19	20	21	22	23	24	25	26	27	28	29	♈0	1	2	3	4	5	6	7	8	9	♈10
☽	♈29	♉13	28	♊12	26	♋10	23	♌6	19	♍2	15	27	♎10	22	♏4	16	28	♐9	21	♑4	16	29	♒12	25	♓9	24	♈8	23	♉8	23	♊8
☿	♒25	27	29	♓0	2	4	6	7	9	11	13	15	16	18	20	22	24	26	28	♈0	2	4	6	8	10	12	14	16	18	20	♈22
♀	♑28	29	29	♒0	1	2	2	3	4	5	5	6	7	8	9	10	10	11	12	13	14	15	16	17	18	19	20	21	22	23	♒24
♂	♑22	23	24	24	25	26	27	27	28	29	♒0	0	1	2	2	3	4	5	5	6	7	8	8	9	10	11	11	12	13	14	♒14

	1	6	12	18	24	30
♃	♋1	1	1	2	2	3
♄	♑22	23	23	24	24	24

	1	15	30
♅	♑9	9	9
♆	♑14	14	14
♇	♏18	18	17
☊	♒16	16	15

APRIL

	1	2	3	4	5	6	7	8	9	10	11	12	13	14	15	16	17	18	19	20	21	22	23	24	25	26	27	28	29	30
☉	♈11	12	13	14	15	16	17	18	19	20	21	22	23	24	25	26	27	28	29	♉0	1	2	3	4	5	6	6	7	8	♉9
☽	♊22	♋6	20	♌3	16	29	♍12	24	♎6	18	♏0	12	24	♐6	18	♑0	12	24	♒7	20	♓3	17	♈2	17	♉2	17	♊2	17	♋2	♋16
☿	♈24	26	28	29	♉1	3	4	6	7	9	10	11	12	13	14	15	16	16	17	17	17	17	18	18	17	17	17	17	16	♉16
♀	♒25	26	27	28	29	♓0	1	2	3	4	5	6	7	8	9	10	11	12	13	14	15	17	18	19	20	21	22	23	24	♓25
♂	♒15	16	17	17	18	19	20	20	21	22	23	23	24	25	26	26	27	28	29	29	♓0	1	2	2	3	4	5	5	6	♓7

	1	6	12	18	24	30
♃	♋3	3	4	5	6	7
♄	♑24	25	25	25	25	25

	1	15	30
♅	♑10	10	9
♆	♑15	15	15
♇	♏17	17	17
☊	♒15	13	12

MAY

	1	2	3	4	5	6	7	8	9	10	11	12	13	14	15	16	17	18	19	20	21	22	23	24	25	26	27	28	29	30	31
☉	♉10	11	12	13	14	15	16	17	18	19	20	21	22	23	24	25	26	27	28	29	♊0	1	2	3	4	5	5	6	7	8	♊9
☽	♌0	13	26	♍9	21	♎3	15	27	♏9	21	♐3	15	27	♑9	21	♒3	16	29	♓12	26	♈10	25	♉10	26	♊11	26	♋11	25	♌9	22	♍5
☿	♉15	15	14	13	13	12	11	11	10	10	9	9	9	8	8	8	8	8	8	8	9	9	9	10	10	11	12	12	13	14	♉15
♀	♓26	28	29	♈0	1	2	3	4	5	7	8	9	10	11	12	13	15	16	17	18	19	20	21	23	24	25	26	27	28	♉0	♉1
♂	♓8	8	9	10	11	11	12	13	13	14	15	16	16	17	18	19	19	20	21	22	22	23	24	25	25	26	27	28	28	29	♈0

	1	6	12	18	24	30
♃	♋7	8	9	10	11	12
♄	♑25	25	25	25	25	25

	1	15	30
♅	♑9	9	9
♆	♑15	14	14
♇	♏17	16	16
☊	♒12	10	9

JUNE

	1	2	3	4	5	6	7	8	9	10	11	12	13	14	15	16	17	18	19	20	21	22	23	24	25	26	27	28	29	30
☉	♊10	11	12	13	14	15	16	17	18	19	20	21	22	23	24	25	26	27	27	28	29	♋0	1	2	3	4	5	6	7	♋8
☽	♍18	♎0	12	24	♏6	18	♐0	12	24	♑6	18	♒0	13	26	♓9	22	♈6	20	♉4	19	♊4	19	♋4	19	♌3	17	♍1	14	26	♎9
☿	♉16	17	18	19	20	22	23	24	26	27	28	♊0	2	3	5	7	8	10	12	14	16	18	20	22	24	26	28	♋0	2	♋5
♀	♉2	3	4	5	6	8	9	10	11	12	13	15	16	17	18	19	21	22	23	24	25	26	28	29	♊0	1	2	4	5	♊6
♂	♈1	1	2	3	3	4	5	6	6	7	8	9	9	10	11	11	12	13	14	14	15	16	16	17	18	19	19	20	21	♈21

	1	6	12	18	24	30
♃	♋13	14	15	16	18	19
♄	♑25	25	24	24	23	23

	1	15	30
♅	♑9	8	8
♆	♑14	14	13
♇	♏16	15	15
☊	♒9	8	8

JULY

	1	2	3	4	5	6	7	8	9	10	11	12	13	14	15	16	17	18	19	20	21	22	23	24	25	26	27	28	29	30	31
☉	♋9	10	11	12	13	14	15	16	17	18	18	19	20	21	22	23	24	25	26	27	28	29	♌0	1	2	3	4	5	6	7	♌8
☽	♎21	♏3	15	27	♐9	21	♑3	15	27	♒10	23	♓6	19	♈2	16	♉0	15	29	♊14	28	♋13	27	♌11	25	♍9	22	♎5	17	29	♏11	♏23
☿	♋7	9	11	13	15	18	20	22	24	26	28	♌0	2	4	6	8	10	11	13	15	17	18	20	22	23	25	26	28	29	♍1	♍2
♀	♊7	8	9	11	12	13	14	15	17	18	19	20	21	23	24	25	26	27	29	♋0	1	2	3	5	6	7	8	9	11	12	♋13
♂	♈22	23	23	24	25	25	26	27	28	28	29	♉0	0	1	2	2	3	4	4	5	6	6	7	8	8	9	9	10	11	11	♉12

	1	6	12	18	24	30
♃	♋19	20	22	23	24	26
♄	♑23	23	22	22	21	21

	1	15	30
♅	♑8	7	6
♆	♑13	13	13
♇	♏15	15	15
☊	♒8	7	7

AUGUST

	1	2	3	4	5	6	7	8	9	10	11	12	13	14	15	16	17	18	19	20	21	22	23	24	25	26	27	28	29	30	31
☉	♌9	9	10	11	12	13	14	15	16	17	18	19	20	21	22	23	24	25	26	27	28	29	♍0	1	2	3	3	4	5	6	♍7
☽	♐5	17	29	♑11	24	♒6	19	♓2	16	29	♈13	27	♉11	25	♊10	24	♋8	22	♌6	20	♍4	17	♎0	13	25	♏7	19	♐1	13	25	♑7
☿	♍4	5	6	8	9	10	11	12	13	14	15	16	17	18	19	20	20	21	22	22	23	23	23	23	24	24	23	23	23	23	♍22
♀	♋14	16	17	18	19	20	22	23	24	25	26	28	29	♌0	1	3	4	5	6	7	9	10	11	12	14	15	16	17	18	20	♌21
♂	♉13	13	14	15	15	16	16	17	18	18	19	19	20	21	21	22	22	23	23	24	24	25	26	26	27	27	28	28	29	29	♊0

	1	6	12	18	24	30
♃	♋26	27	29	♌0	1	2
♄	♑21	20	20	20	19	19

	1	15	30
♅	♑6	6	6
♆	♑13	12	12
♇	♏15	15	15
☊	♒7	7	7

SEPTEMBER

	1	2	3	4	5	6	7	8	9	10	11	12	13	14	15	16	17	18	19	20	21	22	23	24	25	26	27	28	29	30
☉	♍8	9	10	11	12	13	14	15	16	17	18	19	20	21	22	23	24	25	26	27	28	29	♎0	1	2	3	4	5	6	♎7
☽	♑19	♒2	15	28	♓11	25	♈9	23	♉8	22	♊6	21	♋5	19	♌2	16	29	♍12	25	♎8	21	♏3	15	27	♐9	21	♑3	15	27	♒9
☿	♍22	21	20	19	18	17	16	15	14	14	13	12	11	11	10	10	10	10	10	10	11	11	12	13	14	15	16	18	19	♍21
♀	♌22	23	25	26	27	28	♍0	1	2	3	5	6	7	8	9	11	12	13	14	16	17	18	19	21	22	23	24	26	27	♍28
♂	♊0	1	1	2	2	3	3	4	4	4	5	5	6	6	7	7	7	8	8	8	9	9	10	10	10	10	11	11	11	♊12

	1	6	12	18	24	30
♃	♌3	4	5	6	7	8
♄	♑19	19	19	19	19	19

	1	15	30
♅	♑6	6	6
♆	♑12	12	12
♇	♏15	16	16
☊	♒7	7	5

OCTOBER

	1	2	3	4	5	6	7	8	9	10	11	12	13	14	15	16	17	18	19	20	21	22	23	24	25	26	27	28	29	30	31
☉	♎8	9	10	11	11	12	13	14	15	16	17	18	19	20	21	22	23	24	25	26	27	28	29	♏0	1	2	3	4	5	6	♏7
☽	♒22	♓6	20	♈4	18	♉3	18	♊3	17	♋1	16	29	♌13	26	♍9	22	♎4	17	29	♏11	23	♐5	17	29	♑11	23	♒5	17	♓0	14	♓27
☿	♍22	24	25	27	29	♎0	2	4	6	7	9	11	13	15	16	18	20	21	23	25	27	28	♏0	2	3	5	6	8	10	11	♏13
♀	♍29	♎1	2	3	4	6	7	8	9	11	12	13	14	16	17	18	19	21	22	23	24	26	27	28	29	♏1	2	3	4	6	♏7
♂	♊12	12	12	13	13	13	13	13	14	14	14	14	14	14	14	14	14	15	15	15	15	15	15	14	14	14	14	14	14	14	♊14

	1	6	12	18	24	30
♃	♌8	9	10	11	11	12
♄	♑19	19	19	19	19	20

	1	15	30
♅	♑6	6	6
♆	♑12	12	12
♇	♏16	17	17
☊	♒5	4	2

NOVEMBER

	1	2	3	4	5	6	7	8	9	10	11	12	13	14	15	16	17	18	19	20	21	22	23	24	25	26	27	28	29	30
☉	♏8	9	10	11	12	13	14	15	16	17	18	19	20	21	22	23	24	25	26	27	28	29	♐0	1	2	3	4	5	6	♐8
☽	♈12	27	♉12	27	♊12	27	♋11	26	♌10	23	♍6	19	♎1	14	26	♏8	20	♐2	14	26	♑8	19	♒1	14	26	♓9	22	♈6	20	♉5
☿	♏14	16	18	19	21	22	24	25	27	28	♐0	2	3	5	6	8	9	10	12	13	15	16	18	19	21	22	23	25	26	♐27
♀	♏8	9	11	12	13	14	16	17	18	19	21	22	23	24	26	27	28	29	♐1	2	3	5	6	7	8	10	11	12	13	♐15
♂	♊14	13	13	13	13	13	12	12	12	12	11	11	11	10	10	10	9	9	9	8	8	8	7	7	6	6	6	5	5	♊5

	1	6	12	18	24	30
♃	♌12	13	13	13	14	14
♄	♑20	20	21	21	22	22

	1	15	30
♅	♑7	7	8
♆	♑12	13	13
♇	♏17	18	18
☊	♒2	1	♑1

DECEMBER

	1	2	3	4	5	6	7	8	9	10	11	12	13	14	15	16	17	18	19	20	21	22	23	24	25	26	27	28	29	30	31
☉	♐9	10	11	12	13	14	15	16	17	18	19	20	21	22	23	24	25	26	27	28	29	♑0	1	2	3	4	5	6	7	8	♑9
☽	♉20	♊5	20	♋5	20	♌5	19	♍2	16	28	♎11	23	♏5	17	29	♐11	23	♑5	17	28	♒11	23	♓5	18	♈1	15	29	♉13	28	♊13	♊28
☿	♐29	♑0	1	2	4	5	6	7	7	8	9	9	10	10	10	10	10	9	8	8	6	5	4	3	1	0	♐29	27	26	26	♐25
♀	♐16	17	18	20	21	22	23	25	26	27	28	♑0	1	2	3	5	6	7	8	10	11	12	13	15	16	17	18	20	21	22	♑23
♂	♊4	4	3	3	3	2	2	2	1	1	1	1	0	0	0	0	♉29	29	29	29	29	28	28	28	28	28	28	28	28	28	♉28

	1	6	12	18	24	30
♃	♌14	14	13	13	13	12
♄	♑22	23	23	24	25	25

	1	15	30
♅	♑8	9	10
♆	♑13	13	14
♇	♏19	19	20
☊	♑29	29	28

1991

JANUARY

	1	2	3	4	5	6	7	8	9	10	11	12	13	14	15	16	17	18	19	20	21	22	23	24	25	26	27	28	29	30	31
☉	♑10	11	12	13	14	15	16	17	18	19	20	21	22	23	24	25	26	27	28	29	♒0	1	2	3	5	6	7	8	9	10	♒11
☽	♋13	28	♌13	27	♍11	24	♎7	20	♏2	14	26	♐8	20	♑1	13	25	♒8	20	♓2	15	28	♈11	25	♉9	23	♊7	22	♋7	21	♌6	♌21
☿	♐24	24	24	24	24	24	24	25	26	26	27	28	29	♑0	1	2	3	4	5	6	8	9	10	11	13	14	16	17	18	20	♑21
♀	♑25	26	27	28	♒0	1	2	3	5	6	7	9	10	11	12	14	15	16	17	19	20	21	22	24	25	26	27	29	♓0	1	♓2
♂	♉28	28	28	28	28	28	28	28	28	28	28	28	29	29	29	29	29	29	♊0	0	0	0	0	1	1	1	1	2	2	2	♊3

	1	6	12	18	24	30
♃	♌12	11	11	10	9	8
♄	♑26	26	27	28	28	29

	1	15	30
♅	♑10	11	11
♆	♑14	15	15
♇	♏20	20	20
☊	♑28	28	28

FEBRUARY

	1	2	3	4	5	6	7	8	9	10	11	12	13	14	15	16	17	18	19	20	21	22	23	24	25	26	27	28
☉	♒12	13	14	15	16	17	18	19	20	21	22	23	24	25	26	27	28	29	♓0	1	2	3	4	5	6	7	8	♓9
☽	♍5	19	♎2	15	28	♏10	22	♐4	16	28	♑10	22	♒4	16	29	♓12	25	♈8	22	♉5	19	♊3	18	♋2	16	♌0	15	♌29
☿	♑23	24	26	27	29	♒0	2	3	5	6	8	9	11	13	14	16	18	19	21	23	25	26	28	♓0	2	3	5	♓7
♀	♓3	5	6	7	8	10	11	12	13	15	16	17	18	20	21	22	23	25	26	27	28	♈0	1	2	3	4	6	♈7
♂	♊3	3	4	4	4	5	5	5	6	6	6	7	7	7	8	8	9	9	9	10	10	11	11	11	12	12	13	♊13

	1	6	12	18	24	28
♃	♌8	8	7	6	5	5
♄	♑29	♒0	1	1	2	2

	1	15	28
♅	♑12	12	13
♆	♑15	16	16
♇	♏20	20	20
☊	♑28	28	27

MARCH

	1	2	3	4	5	6	7	8	9	10	11	12	13	14	15	16	17	18	19	20	21	22	23	24	25	26	27	28	29	30	31
☉	♓10	11	12	13	14	15	16	17	18	19	20	21	22	23	24	25	26	27	28	29	♈0	1	2	3	4	5	6	7	8	9	♈10
☽	♍13	27	♎10	23	♏6	18	♐0	12	24	♑6	18	♒0	12	25	♓7	21	♈4	18	♉2	16	♊0	14	29	♋13	27	♌11	24	♍8	22	♎5	♎18
☿	♓9	11	13	15	17	18	20	22	24	26	28	♈0	2	4	6	8	10	11	13	15	16	18	19	21	22	23	24	25	26	27	♈28
♀	♈8	9	11	12	13	14	16	17	18	19	20	22	23	24	25	26	28	29	♉0	1	3	4	5	6	7	9	10	11	12	13	♉15
♂	♊14	14	15	15	16	16	16	17	17	18	18	19	19	20	20	21	21	22	22	23	23	24	24	25	25	26	26	27	27	28	♊28

	1	6	12	18	24	30
♃	♌5	5	4	4	4	4
♄	♒2	3	4	4	5	5

	1	15	30
♅	♑13	13	14
♆	♑16	16	17
♇	♏20	20	20
☊	♑27	27	25

APRIL

	1	2	3	4	5	6	7	8	9	10	11	12	13	14	15	16	17	18	19	20	21	22	23	24	25	26	27	28	29	30
☉	♈11	12	13	14	15	16	17	18	19	20	21	22	23	24	25	26	26	27	28	29	♉0	1	2	3	4	5	6	7	8	♉9
☽	♏1	14	26	♐8	20	♑2	14	25	♒8	20	♓2	16	29	♈13	27	♉11	26	♊11	25	♋9	24	♌7	21	♍5	18	♎1	14	27	♏10	♏22
☿	♈28	29	29	29	29	29	29	28	28	28	27	26	26	25	24	24	23	22	21	21	20	20	19	19	18	18	18	18	18	♈18
♀	♉16	17	18	19	21	22	23	24	25	26	28	29	♊0	1	2	4	5	6	7	8	9	11	12	13	14	15	16	17	19	♊20
♂	♊29	29	♋0	1	1	2	2	3	3	4	4	5	5	6	6	7	8	8	9	9	10	10	11	11	12	13	13	14	14	♋15

	1	6	12	18	24	30
♃	♌4	4	4	4	4	5
♄	♒5	5	6	6	6	7

	1	15	30
♅	♑14	14	14
♆	♑17	17	17
♇	♏20	20	19
☊	♑25	23	22

MAY

	1	2	3	4	5	6	7	8	9	10	11	12	13	14	15	16	17	18	19	20	21	22	23	24	25	26	27	28	29	30	31
☉	♉10	11	12	13	14	15	16	17	18	19	20	21	22	23	24	25	26	27	28	29	29	♊0	1	2	3	4	5	6	7	8	♊9
☽	♐4	16	28	♑10	22	♒4	16	28	♓11	24	♈7	21	♉5	20	♊5	20	♋5	19	♌4	18	♍2	15	28	♎11	24	♏6	19	♐1	13	25	♑7
☿	♈18	19	19	19	20	20	21	22	22	23	24	25	26	27	28	29	♉0	1	2	4	5	6	8	9	11	12	14	16	17	19	♉21
♀	♊21	22	23	24	25	27	28	29	♋0	1	2	3	4	6	7	8	9	10	11	12	13	14	15	16	17	19	20	21	22	23	♋24
♂	♋15	16	16	17	18	18	19	19	20	20	21	22	22	23	23	24	24	25	26	26	27	27	28	29	29	♌0	0	1	1	2	♌3

	1	6	12	18	24	30
♃	♌5	6	6	7	8	9
♄	♒7	7	7	7	7	7

	1	15	30
♅	♑14	14	13
♆	♑17	17	16
♇	♏19	19	18
☊	♑21	20	19

JUNE

	1	2	3	4	5	6	7	8	9	10	11	12	13	14	15	16	17	18	19	20	21	22	23	24	25	26	27	28	29	30
☉	♊10	11	12	13	14	15	16	17	18	19	20	21	22	22	23	24	25	26	27	28	29	♋0	1	2	3	4	5	6	7	♋8
☽	♑18	♒0	12	24	♓6	19	♈2	15	29	♉14	28	♊13	29	♋14	29	♌13	28	♍12	25	♎8	21	♏3	16	28	♐10	22	♑4	15	27	♒9
☿	♉22	24	26	28	♊0	2	4	6	8	10	12	14	16	19	21	23	25	27	29	♋2	4	6	8	10	12	14	16	18	20	♋22
♀	♋25	26	27	28	29	♌0	1	2	3	4	5	6	7	8	9	10	11	12	13	13	14	15	16	17	18	19	20	20	21	♌22
♂	♌3	4	4	5	6	6	7	7	8	9	9	10	10	11	12	12	13	13	14	15	15	16	16	17	18	18	19	19	20	♌21

	1	6	12	18	24	30
♃	♌9	10	11	12	13	14
♄	♒7	7	6	6	6	5

	1	15	30
♅	♑13	13	12
♆	♑16	16	16
♇	♏18	18	18
☊	♑19	19	19

JULY

	1	2	3	4	5	6	7	8	9	10	11	12	13	14	15	16	17	18	19	20	21	22	23	24	25	26	27	28	29	30	31
☉	♋9	10	11	12	13	13	14	15	16	17	18	19	20	21	22	23	24	25	26	27	28	29	♌0	1	2	3	3	4	5	6	♌7
☽	♒21	♓3	15	28	♈11	24	♉8	22	♊7	22	♋7	22	♌7	22	♍6	21	♎4	17	♏0	13	25	♐7	19	♑1	12	24	♒6	18	♓0	13	♓25
☿	♋24	26	28	♌0	1	3	5	6	8	10	11	13	14	15	17	18	20	21	22	23	24	26	27	28	29	♍0	0	1	2	3	♍3
♀	♌23	24	24	25	26	27	27	28	29	29	♍0	0	1	2	2	3	3	4	4	5	5	5	6	6	6	7	7	7	7	7	♍7
♂	♌21	22	22	23	24	24	25	25	26	27	27	28	28	29	♍0	0	1	2	2	3	3	4	5	5	6	6	7	8	8	9	♍10

	1	6	12	18	24	30
♃	♌14	15	17	18	19	20
♄	♒5	5	5	4	4	3

	1	15	30
♅	♑12	11	11
♆	♑16	15	15
♇	♏18	18	18
☊	♑19	19	19

AUGUST

	1	2	3	4	5	6	7	8	9	10	11	12	13	14	15	16	17	18	19	20	21	22	23	24	25	26	27	28	29	30	31
☉	♌8	9	10	11	12	13	14	15	16	17	18	19	20	21	22	23	24	25	26	27	27	28	29	♍0	1	2	3	4	5	6	♍7
☽	♈8	21	♉4	18	♊2	16	♋1	16	♌1	15	♍0	15	29	♎13	26	♏9	21	♐3	15	27	♑9	21	♒3	15	27	♓9	22	♈5	18	♉1	♉15
☿	♍4	4	5	5	6	6	6	6	6	6	6	5	5	4	4	3	2	2	1	0	♌29	28	27	27	26	25	24	24	24	23	♌23
♀	♍7	7	7	7	7	7	7	6	6	6	6	5	5	4	4	3	3	2	2	1	0	0	♌29	29	28	27	27	26	26	25	♌24
♂	♍10	11	11	12	13	13	14	15	15	16	16	17	18	18	19	20	20	21	22	22	23	23	24	25	25	26	27	27	28	29	♍29

	1	6	12	18	24	30
♃	♌21	22	23	25	26	27
♄	♒3	3	2	2	2	1

	1	15	30
♅	♑11	10	10
♆	♑15	14	14
♇	♏18	18	18
☊	♑19	18	18

SEPTEMBER

	1	2	3	4	5	6	7	8	9	10	11	12	13	14	15	16	17	18	19	20	21	22	23	24	25	26	27	28	29	30
☉	♍8	9	10	11	12	13	14	15	16	17	18	19	20	21	22	23	24	25	26	27	28	28	29	♎0	1	2	3	4	5	♎6
☽	♉28	♊12	26	♋11	25	♌10	24	♍9	23	♎7	21	♏4	17	29	♐12	24	♑5	17	29	♒11	23	♓6	18	♈1	14	28	♉11	25	♊9	♊23
☿	♌23	23	23	24	24	25	26	27	28	29	♍0	2	3	5	6	8	10	11	13	15	17	19	21	22	24	26	28	♎0	2	♎3
♀	♌24	24	23	23	22	22	22	22	21	21	21	21	21	21	21	21	21	21	22	22	22	22	23	23	23	24	24	25	25	♌26
♂	♎0	0	1	2	2	3	4	4	5	6	6	7	8	8	9	10	10	11	12	12	13	13	14	15	15	16	17	17	18	♎19

	1	6	12	18	24	30
♃	♌28	29	♍0	1	2	4
♄	♒1	1	1	0	0	0

	1	15	30
♅	♑10	10	10
♆	♑14	14	14
♇	♏18	18	19
☊	♑18	17	15

OCTOBER

	1	2	3	4	5	6	7	8	9	10	11	12	13	14	15	16	17	18	19	20	21	22	23	24	25	26	27	28	29	30	31
☉	♎7	8	9	10	11	12	13	14	15	16	17	18	19	20	21	22	23	24	25	26	27	28	29	♏0	1	2	3	4	5	6	♏7
☽	♋7	21	♌5	20	♍4	18	♎2	15	29	♏12	25	♐7	19	♑1	13	25	♒7	19	♓1	14	26	♈10	23	♉7	21	♊5	20	♋4	18	♌2	♌16
☿	♎5	7	9	11	12	14	16	17	19	21	22	24	26	27	29	♏1	2	4	5	7	9	10	12	13	15	16	18	19	21	22	♏24
♀	♌26	27	28	28	29	29	♍0	1	1	2	3	4	4	5	6	7	8	9	9	10	11	12	13	14	15	16	17	18	19	20	♍21
♂	♎19	20	21	21	22	23	23	24	25	25	26	27	27	28	29	29	♏0	1	1	2	3	4	4	5	6	6	7	8	8	9	♏10

	1	6	12	18	24	30
♃	♍4	5	6	7	8	9
♄	♒0	0	0	0	0	1

	1	15	30
♅	♑10	10	11
♆	♑14	14	14
♇	♏19	19	20
☊	♑15	14	12

NOVEMBER

	1	2	3	4	5	6	7	8	9	10	11	12	13	14	15	16	17	18	19	20	21	22	23	24	25	26	27	28	29	30
☉	♏8	9	10	11	12	13	14	15	16	17	18	19	20	21	22	23	24	25	26	27	28	29	♐0	1	2	3	4	5	6	♐7
☽	♍0	14	28	♎11	24	♏8	20	♐3	15	27	♑9	21	♒3	15	27	♓9	21	♈4	18	♉1	15	♊0	14	29	♋14	28	♌13	27	♍11	♍25
☿	♏25	27	28	29	♐1	2	4	5	6	8	9	10	11	13	14	15	16	17	18	19	20	21	22	23	23	24	24	24	24	♐24
♀	♍22	23	24	25	26	27	28	29	♎0	1	2	3	4	5	6	7	8	9	10	12	13	14	15	16	17	18	19	20	22	♎23
♂	♏10	11	12	12	13	14	15	15	16	17	17	18	19	19	20	21	21	22	23	24	24	25	26	26	27	28	29	29	♐0	♐1

	1	6	12	18	24	30
♃	♍9	10	11	12	13	13
♄	♒1	1	1	2	2	3

	1	15	30
♅	♑11	11	12
♆	♑14	15	15
♇	♏20	20	21
☊	♑12	11	10

DECEMBER

	1	2	3	4	5	6	7	8	9	10	11	12	13	14	15	16	17	18	19	20	21	22	23	24	25	26	27	28	29	30	31
☉	♐8	9	10	11	12	13	14	15	16	17	18	19	20	21	22	24	25	26	27	28	29	♑0	1	2	3	4	5	6	7	8	♑9
☽	♎8	21	♏4	17	29	♐12	24	♑6	17	29	♒11	23	♓5	17	29	♈12	25	♉9	23	♊8	23	♋8	23	♌8	22	♍7	21	♎5	18	♏1	♏14
☿	♐24	23	23	22	21	20	18	17	15	14	13	12	11	10	9	8	8	8	8	8	8	9	9	10	11	12	13	14	15	16	♐17
♀	♎24	25	26	27	28	♏0	1	2	3	4	5	7	8	9	10	11	13	14	15	16	17	18	20	21	22	23	24	26	27	28	♏29
♂	♐1	2	3	3	4	5	6	6	7	8	9	9	10	11	11	12	13	14	14	15	16	16	17	18	19	19	20	21	22	22	♐23

	1	6	12	18	24	30
♃	♍13	14	14	14	15	15
♄	♒3	3	4	4	5	6

	1	15	30
♅	♑12	13	14
♆	♑15	16	16
♇	♏21	22	22
☊	♑10	10	10

1992

JANUARY

	1	2	3	4	5	6	7	8	9	10	11	12	13	14	15	16	17	18	19	20	21	22	23	24	25	26	27	28	29	30	31
☉	♑10	11	12	13	14	15	16	17	18	19	20	21	22	23	24	25	26	27	28	29	♒0	1	2	3	4	5	6	7	8	9	♒10
☽	♏26	♐8	20	♑2	14	26	♒8	20	♓2	14	26	♈8	21	♉4	17	♊1	16	♋0	15	♌1	16	♍1	16	♎0	14	28	♏11	23	♐5	18	♐29
☿	♐18	19	21	22	23	24	26	27	29	♑0	1	3	4	6	7	9	10	12	13	15	16	18	19	21	22	24	25	27	29	♒0	♒2
♀	♐0	2	3	4	5	6	8	9	10	11	13	14	15	16	17	19	20	21	22	24	25	26	27	28	♑0	1	2	3	5	6	♑7
♂	♐24	25	25	26	27	27	28	29	♑0	0	1	2	3	3	4	5	6	6	7	8	9	9	10	11	12	12	13	14	15	15	♑16

	1	6	12	18	24	30		1	6	12	18	24	30		1	15	30		1	15	30		1	15	30		1	15	30
♃	♍15	15	14	14	14	13	♄	♒6	6	7	8	9	9	♅	♑14	15	15	♆	♑16	17	17	♇	♏22	22	23	☊	♑10	10	10

FEBRUARY

	1	2	3	4	5	6	7	8	9	10	11	12	13	14	15	16	17	18	19	20	21	22	23	24	25	26	27	28	29
☉	♒11	12	13	14	15	16	17	18	19	20	22	23	24	25	26	27	28	29	♓0	1	2	3	4	5	6	7	8	9	♓10
☽	♑11	23	♒5	17	29	♓11	23	♈5	17	♉0	13	27	♊10	24	♋9	24	♌9	24	♍9	24	♎8	22	♏6	19	♐2	14	26	♑8	♑20
☿	♒3	5	7	8	10	12	14	15	17	19	20	22	24	26	28	29	♓1	3	5	7	9	11	12	14	16	18	20	22	♓23
♀	♑8	9	11	12	13	14	16	17	18	19	21	22	23	24	25	27	28	29	♒0	2	3	4	5	7	8	9	10	11	♒13
♂	♑17	18	18	19	20	21	21	22	23	24	25	25	26	27	28	28	29	♒0	1	1	2	3	4	4	5	6	7	8	♒8

	1	6	12	18	24	29		1	6	12	18	24	29		1	15	29		1	15	29		1	15	29		1	15	29
♃	♍13	13	12	11	10	10	♄	♒9	10	11	11	12	13	♅	♑15	16	17	♆	♑17	18	18	♇	♏23	23	23	☊	♑10	9	8

MARCH

	1	2	3	4	5	6	7	8	9	10	11	12	13	14	15	16	17	18	19	20	21	22	23	24	25	26	27	28	29	30	31
☉	♓11	12	13	14	15	16	17	18	19	20	21	22	23	24	25	26	27	28	29	♈0	1	2	3	4	5	6	7	8	9	10	♈11
☽	♒2	13	25	♓7	20	♈2	15	27	♉10	23	♊7	20	♋4	18	♌3	18	♍2	17	♎2	16	♏0	14	27	♐10	22	♑4	16	28	♒10	22	♓4
☿	♓25	27	29	♈0	2	3	4	6	7	8	9	10	10	11	11	11	11	11	11	11	10	10	9	8	8	7	6	5	4	3	♈3
♀	♒14	15	16	18	19	20	21	23	24	25	26	28	29	♓0	1	2	4	5	6	7	9	10	11	12	14	15	16	17	19	20	♓21
♂	♒9	10	11	11	12	13	14	14	15	16	17	18	18	19	20	21	21	22	23	24	25	25	26	27	28	28	29	♓0	1	1	♓2

	1	6	12	18	24	30		1	6	12	18	24	30		1	15	30		1	15	30		1	15	30		1	15	30
♃	♍10	9	8	7	7	6	♄	♒13	13	14	15	15	16	♅	♑17	17	18	♆	♑18	19	19	♇	♏23	23	23	☊	♑8	7	5

APRIL

	1	2	3	4	5	6	7	8	9	10	11	12	13	14	15	16	17	18	19	20	21	22	23	24	25	26	27	28	29	30
☉	♈12	13	13	14	15	16	17	18	19	20	21	22	23	24	25	26	27	28	29	♉0	1	2	3	4	5	6	7	8	9	♉10
☽	♓16	28	♈11	24	♉7	20	♊4	17	♋1	15	29	♌13	28	♍12	26	♎11	25	♏8	22	♐5	18	♑0	12	24	♒6	18	♓0	12	24	♈7
☿	♈2	1	1	0	0	♓29	29	29	29	29	29	29	29	♈0	0	1	1	2	3	3	4	5	6	7	8	9	10	11	12	♈14
♀	♓22	23	25	26	27	28	♈0	1	2	3	5	6	7	8	9	11	12	13	14	16	17	18	19	21	22	23	24	26	27	♈28
♂	♓3	4	5	5	6	7	8	8	9	10	11	12	12	13	14	15	15	16	17	18	19	19	20	21	22	22	23	24	25	♓25

	1	6	12	18	24	30		1	6	12	18	24	30		1	15	30		1	15	30		1	15	30		1	15	30
♃	♍6	6	5	5	5	5	♄	♒16	16	17	17	18	18	♅	♑18	18	18	♆	♑19	19	19	♇	♏23	22	22	☊	♑5	3	2

MAY

	1	2	3	4	5	6	7	8	9	10	11	12	13	14	15	16	17	18	19	20	21	22	23	24	25	26	27	28	29	30	31
☉	♉11	12	13	14	15	16	17	18	19	20	21	22	22	23	24	25	26	27	28	29	♊0	1	2	3	4	5	6	7	8	9	♊10
☽	♈20	♉3	16	♊0	14	28	♋12	26	♌10	24	♍8	22	♎6	20	♏4	17	♐0	13	26	♑8	20	♒2	14	26	♓8	20	♈2	15	28	♉11	♉25
☿	♈15	16	18	19	20	22	23	25	26	28	♉0	1	3	5	7	8	10	12	14	16	18	20	22	24	26	28	♊0	2	5	7	♊9
♀	♈29	♉0	2	3	4	5	7	8	9	10	11	13	14	15	16	18	19	20	21	23	24	25	26	27	29	♊0	1	2	4	5	♊6
♂	♓26	27	28	29	29	♈0	1	2	2	3	4	5	5	6	7	8	8	9	10	11	12	12	13	14	15	15	16	17	18	18	♈19

	1	6	12	18	24	30		1	6	12	18	24	30		1	15	30		1	15	30		1	15	30		1	15	30
♃	♍5	5	5	5	5	6	♄	♒18	18	18	18	18	18	♅	♑18	18	17	♆	♑19	19	19	♇	♏22	21	21	☊	♑2	1	1

JUNE

	1	2	3	4	5	6	7	8	9	10	11	12	13	14	15	16	17	18	19	20	21	22	23	24	25	26	27	28	29	30
☉	♊11	12	13	14	15	16	16	17	18	19	20	21	22	23	24	25	26	27	28	29	♋0	1	2	3	4	5	6	7	8	♋8
☽	♊9	23	♋7	22	♌6	21	♍5	19	♎3	17	♏0	14	27	♐9	22	♑4	16	28	♒10	22	♓4	16	28	♈10	23	♉6	19	♊3	17	♋1
☿	♊11	13	16	18	20	22	24	26	28	♋0	2	4	6	8	10	12	14	16	17	19	21	22	24	25	27	28	♌0	1	2	♌4
♀	♊7	9	10	11	12	13	15	16	17	18	20	21	22	23	25	26	27	28	29	♋1	2	3	4	6	7	8	9	10	12	♋13
♂	♈20	21	21	22	23	24	24	25	26	27	27	28	29	♉0	0	1	2	2	3	4	5	5	6	7	8	8	9	10	10	♉11

	1	6	12	18	24	30		1	6	12	18	24	30		1	15	30		1	15	30		1	15	30		1	15	30
♃	♍6	7	7	8	9	10	♄	♒18	18	18	18	18	18	♅	♑17	17	16	♆	♑19	18	18	♇	♏21	21	20	☊	♑1	1	1

JULY

	1	2	3	4	5	6	7	8	9	10	11	12	13	14	15	16	17	18	19	20	21	22	23	24	25	26	27	28	29	30	31
☉	♋9	10	11	12	13	14	15	16	17	18	19	20	21	22	23	24	25	26	27	28	28	29	♌0	1	2	3	4	5	6	7	♌8
☽	♋16	♌1	16	♍1	15	♎0	14	27	♏11	23	♐6	19	♑1	13	25	♒7	19	♓1	12	24	♈6	19	♉1	14	27	♊11	25	♋10	25	♌10	♌25
☿	♌5	6	7	8	9	10	11	12	13	14	14	15	16	16	16	17	17	17	17	17	17	17	17	17	16	16	16	15	14	14	♌13
♀	♋14	15	17	18	19	20	22	23	24	25	26	28	29	♌0	1	3	4	5	6	8	9	10	11	12	14	15	16	17	19	20	♌21
♂	♉12	13	13	14	15	15	16	17	18	18	19	20	20	21	22	23	23	24	25	25	26	27	27	28	29	29	♊0	1	2	2	♊3

	1	6	12	18	24	30		1	6	12	18	24	30		1	15	30		1	15	30		1	15	30		1	15	30
♃	♍10	11	12	13	14	15	♄	♒18	17	17	17	16	16	♅	♑16	16	15	♆	♑18	17	17	♇	♏20	20	20	☊	♑1	1	0

AUGUST

	1	2	3	4	5	6	7	8	9	10	11	12	13	14	15	16	17	18	19	20	21	22	23	24	25	26	27	28	29	30	31
☉	♌9	10	11	12	13	14	15	16	17	18	19	20	20	21	22	23	24	25	26	27	28	29	♍0	1	2	3	4	5	6	7	♍8
☽	♍10	25	♎9	24	♏7	20	♐3	16	28	♑10	22	♒4	16	28	♓9	21	♈3	16	28	♉10	23	♊6	20	♋4	18	♌3	18	♍3	19	♎4	♎18
☿	♌12	11	11	10	9	9	8	7	7	7	6	6	6	6	6	6	7	7	8	9	10	11	12	13	14	16	17	19	20	22	♌24
♀	♌22	24	25	26	27	28	♍0	1	2	3	5	6	7	8	10	11	12	13	14	16	17	18	19	21	22	23	24	25	27	28	♍29
♂	♊4	4	5	6	6	7	8	8	9	10	10	11	11	12	13	13	14	15	15	16	17	17	18	18	19	20	20	21	22	22	♊23

	1	6	12	18	24	30		1	6	12	18	24	30		1	15	30		1	15	30		1	15	30		1	15	30
♃	♍15	16	17	19	20	21	♄	♒16	15	15	14	14	14	♅	♑15	15	14	♆	♑17	17	16	♇	♏20	20	20	☊	♑0	♐0	28

SEPTEMBER

	1	2	3	4	5	6	7	8	9	10	11	12	13	14	15	16	17	18	19	20	21	22	23	24	25	26	27	28	29	30
☉	♍9	10	11	12	13	14	15	16	17	18	19	19	20	21	22	23	24	25	26	27	28	29	♎0	1	2	3	4	5	6	♎7
☽	♏3	16	♐0	12	25	♑7	19	♒1	13	25	♓6	18	♈0	13	25	♉7	20	♊3	16	29	♋13	27	♌12	27	♍12	27	♎12	27	♏11	♏25
☿	♌26	28	29	♍1	3	5	7	9	11	13	15	17	19	20	22	24	26	28	♎0	1	3	5	7	8	10	12	13	15	17	♎18
♀	♎0	2	3	4	5	7	8	9	10	11	13	14	15	16	18	19	20	21	22	24	25	26	27	29	♏0	1	2	3	5	♏6
♂	♊23	24	25	25	26	26	27	28	28	29	29	♋0	0	1	2	2	3	3	4	4	5	5	6	6	7	8	8	9	9	♋10

	1	6	12	18	24	30		1	6	12	18	24	30		1	15	30		1	15	30		1	15	30		1	15	30
♃	♍21	23	24	25	26	28	♄	♒13	13	13	12	12	12	♅	♑14	14	14	♆	♑16	16	16	♇	♏20	21	21	☊	♐28	26	25

OCTOBER

	1	2	3	4	5	6	7	8	9	10	11	12	13	14	15	16	17	18	19	20	21	22	23	24	25	26	27	28	29	30	31
☉	♎8	9	10	11	12	13	14	15	16	17	18	19	20	21	22	23	24	25	26	27	28	29	♏0	1	2	3	4	5	6	7	♏8
☽	♐8	21	♑3	16	28	♒9	21	♓3	15	27	♈9	22	♉4	17	♊0	13	26	♋10	24	♌8	22	♍6	21	♎6	20	♏5	19	♐3	16	29	♑11
☿	♎20	22	23	25	26	28	29	♏1	2	4	5	7	8	10	11	13	14	15	17	18	19	21	22	23	25	26	27	28	29	♐0	♐1
♀	♏7	8	10	11	12	13	14	16	17	18	19	21	22	23	24	25	27	28	29	♐0	2	3	4	5	6	8	9	10	11	12	♐14
♂	♋10	11	11	12	12	13	13	13	14	14	15	15	16	16	17	17	17	18	18	19	19	19	20	20	21	21	21	22	22	22	♋23

	1	6	12	18	24	30		1	6	12	18	24	30		1	15	30		1	15	30		1	15	30		1	15	30
♃	♍28	29	♎0	2	3	4	♄	♒12	12	12	12	12	12	♅	♑14	14	15	♆	♑16	16	16	♇	♏21	22	22	☊	♐25	23	22

NOVEMBER

	1	2	3	4	5	6	7	8	9	10	11	12	13	14	15	16	17	18	19	20	21	22	23	24	25	26	27	28	29	30
☉	♏9	10	11	12	13	14	15	16	17	18	19	20	21	22	23	24	25	26	27	28	29	♐0	1	2	3	4	5	6	7	♐8
☽	♑24	♒6	18	29	♓11	23	♈5	18	♉0	13	26	♊10	23	♋7	20	♌4	19	♍3	17	♎1	15	29	♏13	27	♐11	24	♑7	19	♒1	♒13
☿	♐2	3	4	5	6	7	7	8	8	8	8	8	8	8	7	7	6	5	4	2	1	0	♏28	27	26	25	24	23	23	♏22
♀	♐15	16	17	19	20	21	22	23	25	26	27	28	29	♑1	2	3	4	5	7	8	9	10	11	13	14	15	16	17	18	♑20
♂	♋23	23	24	24	24	24	25	25	25	25	26	26	26	26	26	27	27	27	27	27	27	27	27	27	28	28	28	28	28	♋28

	1	6	12	18	24	30		1	6	12	18	24	30		1	15	30		1	15	30		1	15	30		1	15	30
♃	♎4	5	6	8	9	10	♄	♒12	12	12	13	13	13	♅	♑15	15	16	♆	♑17	17	17	♇	♏22	23	23	☊	♐22	22	22

DECEMBER

	1	2	3	4	5	6	7	8	9	10	11	12	13	14	15	16	17	18	19	20	21	22	23	24	25	26	27	28	29	30	31
☉	♐9	10	11	12	13	14	15	16	17	18	19	20	21	22	23	24	25	26	27	28	29	♑0	1	2	3	4	5	7	8	9	♑10
☽	♒25	♓7	19	♈1	13	26	♉8	21	♊5	18	♋2	16	♌1	15	29	♍14	28	♎12	26	♏9	23	♐6	19	♑2	15	27	♒9	21	♓3	15	♓27
☿	♏22	22	22	23	23	24	25	25	26	27	28	♐0	1	2	3	5	6	7	9	10	11	13	14	16	17	19	20	22	23	25	♐26
♀	♑21	22	23	24	26	27	28	29	♒0	1	3	4	5	6	7	8	10	11	12	13	14	15	17	18	19	20	21	22	23	24	♒26
♂	♋28	28	28	27	27	27	27	27	27	27	27	26	26	26	26	26	25	25	25	25	24	24	24	23	23	23	22	22	22	21	♋21

	1	6	12	18	24	30		1	6	12	18	24	30		1	15	30		1	15	30		1	15	30		1	15	30
♃	♎10	10	11	12	13	13	♄	♒14	14	14	15	16	16	♅	♑16	17	18	♆	♑17	18	18	♇	♏24	24	25	☊	♐22	21	21

1993

JANUARY

	1	2	3	4	5	6	7	8	9	10	11	12	13	14	15	16	17	18	19	20	21	22	23	24	25	26	27	28	29	30	31
☉	♑11	12	13	14	15	16	17	18	19	20	21	22	23	24	25	26	27	28	29	♒0	1	2	3	4	5	6	7	8	9	10	♒11
☽	♈9	21	♉3	16	29	♊12	26	♋11	25	♌10	25	♍10	24	♎9	23	♏6	20	♐3	16	29	♑11	23	♒6	18	♓0	11	23	♈5	17	29	♉11
☿	♐28	29	♑1	2	4	5	7	8	10	11	13	15	16	18	19	21	23	24	26	28	29	♒1	3	4	6	8	9	11	13	15	♒16
♀	♒27	28	29	♓0	1	2	3	4	5	7	8	9	10	11	12	13	14	15	16	17	18	19	20	21	22	23	24	25	26	27	♓28
♂	♋20	20	20	19	19	18	18	18	17	17	16	16	16	15	15	15	14	14	14	13	13	13	12	12	12	11	11	11	11	10	♋10

	1	6	12	18	24	30		1	6	12	18	24	30		1	15	30		1	15	30		1	15	30		1	15	30
♃	♎13	14	14	15	15	15	♄	♒16	17	18	18	19	20	♅	♑18	19	19	♆	♑18	19	19	♇	♏25	25	25	☊	♐21	21	20

FEBRUARY

	1	2	3	4	5	6	7	8	9	10	11	12	13	14	15	16	17	18	19	20	21	22	23	24	25	26	27	28
☉	♒12	13	14	15	16	17	18	19	20	21	22	23	24	25	26	27	28	29	♓0	1	2	3	4	5	6	7	8	♓9
☽	♉24	♊7	20	♋4	18	♌3	18	♍3	19	♎4	18	♏3	17	♐0	13	26	♑8	20	♒2	14	26	♓8	20	♈2	14	26	♉8	♉20
☿	♒18	20	22	23	25	27	29	♓1	2	4	6	8	9	11	12	14	15	17	18	19	20	21	22	23	24	24	24	♓24
♀	♓29	♈0	0	1	2	3	4	5	6	6	7	8	9	9	10	11	12	12	13	13	14	15	15	16	16	17	17	♈18
♂	♋10	10	10	10	9	9	9	9	9	9	9	9	9	9	9	9	9	9	9	9	9	9	9	9	9	9	9	♋10

	1	6	12	18	24	28		1	6	12	18	24	28		1	15	28		1	15	28		1	15	28		1	15	28
♃	♎15	15	14	14	14	13	♄	♒20	20	21	22	23	23	♅	♑19	20	21	♆	♑20	20	20	♇	♏25	25	26	☊	♐20	19	17

MARCH

	1	2	3	4	5	6	7	8	9	10	11	12	13	14	15	16	17	18	19	20	21	22	23	24	25	26	27	28	29	30	31
☉	♓10	11	12	13	14	15	16	17	18	19	20	21	22	23	24	25	26	27	28	29	♈0	1	2	3	4	5	6	7	8	9	♈10
☽	♊3	16	29	♋12	27	♌11	26	♍12	27	♎12	27	♏12	26	♐9	22	♑5	17	♒0	12	23	♓5	17	29	♈11	23	♉5	17	♊0	12	25	♋8
☿	♓24	24	23	23	22	22	21	20	19	18	17	16	15	14	13	12	12	11	11	11	10	10	10	10	11	11	11	12	12	13	♓13
♀	♈18	18	19	19	19	19	20	20	20	20	20	20	20	20	20	20	19	19	19	19	18	18	17	17	16	16	15	15	14	13	♈13
♂	♋10	10	10	10	10	11	11	11	11	12	12	12	12	13	13	13	13	14	14	14	15	15	15	16	16	16	17	17	17	18	♋18

	1	6	12	18	24	30		1	6	12	18	24	30		1	15	30		1	15	30		1	15	30		1	15	30
♃	♎13	13	12	11	11	10	♄	♒23	24	24	25	26	26	♅	♑21	21	22	♆	♑20	21	21	♇	♏26	25	25	☊	♐17	16	14

APRIL

	1	2	3	4	5	6	7	8	9	10	11	12	13	14	15	16	17	18	19	20	21	22	23	24	25	26	27	28	29	30
☉	♈11	12	13	14	15	16	17	18	19	20	21	22	23	24	25	26	27	28	29	♉0	1	2	3	4	5	6	7	8	9	♉10
☽	♋22	♌6	20	♍5	20	♎5	20	♏5	20	♐4	18	♑1	14	26	♒8	20	♓2	14	26	♈8	20	♉2	14	27	♊9	22	♋5	18	♌2	♌16
☿	♓14	15	16	17	17	18	19	21	22	23	24	25	27	28	29	♈0	2	3	5	6	8	9	11	13	14	16	18	19	21	♈23
♀	♈12	12	11	10	10	9	8	8	7	7	6	6	6	5	5	5	4	4	4	4	4	4	4	4	4	4	4	4	5	♈5
♂	♋18	19	19	20	20	20	21	21	22	22	22	23	23	24	24	25	25	25	26	26	27	27	28	28	29	29	♌0	0	0	♌1

	1	6	12	18	24	30		1	6	12	18	24	30		1	15	30		1	15	30		1	15	30		1	15	30
♃	♎10	9	8	8	7	6	♄	♒27	27	28	28	29	29	♅	♑22	22	22	♆	♑21	21	21	♇	♏25	25	25	☊	♐14	13	13

MAY

	1	2	3	4	5	6	7	8	9	10	11	12	13	14	15	16	17	18	19	20	21	22	23	24	25	26	27	28	29	30	31
☉	♉11	12	13	14	15	15	16	17	18	19	20	21	22	23	24	25	26	27	28	29	♊0	1	2	3	4	5	6	7	8	9	♊10
☽	♍0	14	29	♎14	29	♏13	28	♐12	26	♑9	22	♒4	17	29	♓10	22	♈4	16	28	♉11	23	♊6	19	♋2	15	29	♌13	27	♍11	25	♎9
☿	♈25	26	28	♉0	2	4	6	8	10	12	14	16	18	21	23	25	27	29	♊2	4	6	8	10	12	14	16	18	20	22	24	♊26
♀	♈5	5	6	6	6	7	7	8	8	9	9	10	11	11	12	13	13	14	15	15	16	17	18	18	19	20	21	22	23	23	♈24
♂	♌1	2	2	3	3	4	4	5	5	6	6	7	7	8	8	9	9	10	11	11	12	12	13	13	14	14	15	15	16	16	♌17

	1	6	12	18	24	30		1	6	12	18	24	30		1	15	30		1	15	30		1	15	30		1	15	30
♃	♎6	6	5	5	5	5	♄	♒29	29	♓0	0	0	0	♅	♑22	22	22	♆	♑21	21	21	♇	♏25	24	24	☊	♐13	12	12

JUNE

	1	2	3	4	5	6	7	8	9	10	11	12	13	14	15	16	17	18	19	20	21	22	23	24	25	26	27	28	29	30
☉	♊11	11	12	13	14	15	16	17	18	19	20	21	22	23	24	25	26	27	28	29	♋0	1	2	3	3	4	5	6	7	♋8
☽	♎24	♏8	22	♐6	20	♑4	17	♒0	12	24	♓7	18	♈0	12	24	♉6	19	♊1	14	28	♋11	25	♌9	23	♍8	22	♎6	20	♏4	♏18
☿	♊28	♋0	1	3	5	6	8	9	11	12	14	15	16	17	18	19	21	21	22	23	24	25	25	26	27	27	27	28	28	♋28
♀	♈25	26	27	28	29	♉0	1	1	2	3	4	5	6	7	8	9	10	11	12	13	14	15	16	17	18	19	20	21	23	♉24
♂	♌17	18	19	19	20	20	21	21	22	22	23	24	24	25	25	26	26	27	28	28	29	29	♍0	0	1	2	2	3	3	♍4

	1	6	12	18	24	30		1	6	12	18	24	30		1	15	30		1	15	30		1	15	30		1	15	30
♃	♎5	5	5	5	6	6	♄	♓0	0	0	0	0	0	♅	♑22	21	21	♆	♑21	20	20	♇	♏24	23	23	☊	♐12	12	12

JULY

	1	2	3	4	5	6	7	8	9	10	11	12	13	14	15	16	17	18	19	20	21	22	23	24	25	26	27	28	29	30	31
☉	♋9	10	11	12	13	14	15	16	17	18	19	20	21	22	23	23	24	25	26	27	28	29	♌0	1	2	3	4	5	6	7	♌8
☽	♐2	16	29	♑12	25	♒8	20	♓2	15	26	♈8	20	♉2	14	27	♊10	23	♋6	20	♌4	19	♍3	18	♎3	17	♏1	15	29	♐12	25	♑8
☿	♋28	28	28	28	28	28	27	27	26	26	25	25	24	23	23	22	21	21	20	20	19	19	19	18	18	18	18	18	19	19	♋19
♀	♉25	26	27	28	29	♊0	1	2	3	4	5	7	8	9	10	11	12	13	14	15	16	18	19	20	21	22	23	24	26	27	♊28
♂	♍4	5	6	6	7	7	8	9	9	10	10	11	12	12	13	13	14	15	15	16	16	17	18	18	19	19	20	21	21	22	♍22

	1	6	12	18	24	30		1	6	12	18	24	30		1	15	30		1	15	30		1	15	30		1	15	30
♃	♎6	7	7	8	9	9	♄	♓0	0	0	♒29	29	28	♅	♑21	20	20	♆	♑20	20	19	♇	♏23	23	23	☊	♐12	12	11

AUGUST

	1	2	3	4	5	6	7	8	9	10	11	12	13	14	15	16	17	18	19	20	21	22	23	24	25	26	27	28	29	30	31
☉	♌9	10	11	12	13	14	15	15	16	17	18	19	20	21	22	23	24	25	26	27	28	29	♍0	1	2	3	4	5	6	7	♍8
☽	♑21	♒4	16	29	♓11	23	♈5	16	28	♉10	22	♊5	18	♋1	14	28	♌13	28	♍13	28	♎13	27	♏12	26	♐9	22	♑5	18	♒1	13	♒25
☿	♋20	21	21	22	23	24	26	27	28	♌0	1	3	4	6	8	10	12	14	15	17	19	21	23	25	27	29	♍1	3	5	7	♍9
♀	♊29	♋0	1	2	4	5	6	7	8	9	10	12	13	14	15	16	17	19	20	21	22	23	24	26	27	28	29	♌0	2	3	♌4
♂	♍23	24	24	25	26	26	27	27	28	29	29	♎0	1	1	2	2	3	4	4	5	6	6	7	8	8	9	10	10	11	11	♎12

	1	6	12	18	24	30		1	6	12	18	24	30		1	15	30		1	15	30		1	15	30		1	15	30
♃	♎10	11	12	13	14	15	♄	♒28	28	28	27	27	26	♅	♑19	19	19	♆	♑19	19	19	♇	♏23	23	23	☊	♐11	9	8

SEPTEMBER

	1	2	3	4	5	6	7	8	9	10	11	12	13	14	15	16	17	18	19	20	21	22	23	24	25	26	27	28	29	30
☉	♍9	10	11	11	12	13	14	15	16	17	18	19	20	21	22	23	24	25	26	27	28	29	♎0	1	2	3	4	5	6	♎7
☽	♓7	19	♈1	13	25	♉7	19	♊1	13	26	♋9	23	♌7	21	♍6	21	♎7	22	♏7	21	♐5	19	♑2	15	28	♒10	22	♓4	16	♓28
☿	♍11	13	15	17	19	20	22	24	26	27	29	♎1	3	4	6	8	9	11	12	14	15	17	18	20	21	23	24	26	27	♎29
♀	♌5	6	8	9	10	11	12	14	15	16	17	18	20	21	22	23	24	26	27	28	29	♍0	2	3	4	5	7	8	9	♍10
♂	♎13	13	14	15	15	16	17	17	18	19	19	20	21	21	22	23	23	24	25	25	26	27	27	28	29	29	♏0	1	1	♏2

	1	6	12	18	24	30		1	6	12	18	24	30		1	15	30		1	15	30		1	15	30		1	15	30
♃	♎15	16	17	19	20	21	♄	♒26	26	25	25	25	24	♅	♑19	18	18	♆	♑19	18	18	♇	♏23	23	24	☊	♐8	6	5

OCTOBER

	1	2	3	4	5	6	7	8	9	10	11	12	13	14	15	16	17	18	19	20	21	22	23	24	25	26	27	28	29	30	31
☉	♎8	9	10	11	12	13	14	15	16	17	18	19	20	21	22	23	24	25	26	27	28	29	♏0	1	2	3	4	5	6	7	♏8
☽	♈10	22	♉4	16	28	♊10	22	♋5	18	♌1	15	♍0	14	29	♎15	♏0	15	♐0	14	28	♑11	24	♒7	19	♓1	13	25	♈7	19	♉1	♉13
☿	♏0	1	3	4	5	6	8	9	10	11	12	13	14	16	16	17	18	19	20	20	21	22	22	22	22	23	22	22	22	21	♏21
♀	♍11	13	14	15	16	18	19	20	21	23	24	25	26	28	29	♎0	1	2	4	5	6	7	9	10	11	12	14	15	16	17	♎19
♂	♏3	3	4	5	5	6	7	7	8	9	9	10	11	12	12	13	14	14	15	16	16	17	18	18	19	20	21	21	22	23	♏23

	1	6	12	18	24	30		1	6	12	18	24	30		1	15	30		1	15	30		1	15	30		1	15	30
♃	♎21	22	24	25	26	28	♄	♒24	24	24	24	24	24	♅	♑18	18	19	♆	♑18	18	19	♇	♏24	24	25	☊	♐4	4	3

NOVEMBER

	1	2	3	4	5	6	7	8	9	10	11	12	13	14	15	16	17	18	19	20	21	22	23	24	25	26	27	28	29	30
☉	♏9	10	11	12	13	14	15	16	17	18	19	20	21	22	23	24	25	26	27	28	29	♐0	1	2	3	4	5	6	7	♐8
☽	♉25	♊7	19	♋2	15	28	♌11	25	♍9	23	♎8	23	♏8	23	♐8	22	♑6	20	♒3	15	28	♓10	22	♈4	16	27	♉9	21	♊4	♊16
☿	♏20	19	18	17	15	14	13	11	10	9	8	8	7	7	7	7	7	7	8	8	9	10	11	12	13	15	16	17	18	♏20
♀	♎20	21	22	24	25	26	27	29	♏0	1	2	4	5	6	7	9	10	11	12	14	15	16	17	19	20	21	22	24	25	♏26
♂	♏24	25	26	26	27	28	28	29	♐0	1	1	2	3	3	4	5	6	6	7	8	9	9	10	11	11	12	13	14	14	♐15

	1	6	12	18	24	30		1	6	12	18	24	30		1	15	30		1	15	30		1	15	30		1	15	30
♃	♎28	29	♏0	2	3	4	♄	♒24	24	24	24	24	25	♅	♑19	19	20	♆	♑19	19	19	♇	♏25	25	26	☊	♐3	3	3

DECEMBER

	1	2	3	4	5	6	7	8	9	10	11	12	13	14	15	16	17	18	19	20	21	22	23	24	25	26	27	28	29	30	31
☉	♐9	10	11	12	13	14	15	16	17	18	19	20	21	22	23	24	25	26	27	28	29	♑0	1	2	3	4	5	6	7	8	♑9
☽	♊29	♋12	25	♌8	22	♍5	19	♎4	18	♏2	17	♐1	16	♑0	14	27	♒10	23	♓6	18	♈0	12	24	♉5	17	♊0	12	25	♋8	21	♌5
☿	♏21	23	24	25	27	28	♐0	1	3	4	6	7	9	11	12	14	15	17	18	20	21	23	24	26	28	29	♑1	2	4	5	♑7
♀	♏27	29	♐0	1	3	4	5	6	8	9	10	11	13	14	15	16	18	19	20	21	23	24	25	26	28	29	♑0	1	3	4	♑5
♂	♐16	17	17	18	19	20	20	21	22	22	23	24	25	25	26	27	28	28	29	♑0	1	1	2	3	4	5	5	6	7	8	♑8

	1	6	12	18	24	30		1	6	12	18	24	30		1	15	30		1	15	30		1	15	30		1	15	30
♃	♏4	5	6	7	8	9	♄	♒25	25	25	26	26	27	♅	♑20	21	21	♆	♑19	20	20	♇	♏26	26	27	☊	♐3	3	3

YEAR		JAN	FEB	MAR	APR	MAY	JUN	JUL	SEP	AUG	OCT	NOV	DEC
1930	1	18 41 39	20 43 52	22 34 16	0 36 29	2 34 45	4 36 59	6 35 16	8 37 29	10 39 42	12 37 59	14 40 12	16 38 29
	2	18 45 35	20 47 49	22 38 12	0 40 25	2 38 42	4 40 55	6 39 12	8 41 25	10 43 39	12 41 55	14 44 8	16 42 25
	3	18 49 32	20 51 45	22 42 9	0 44 22	2 42 39	4 44 52	6 43 9	8 45 22	10 47 35	12 45 52	14 48 5	16 46 22
	4	18 53 29	20 55 42	22 46 5	0 48 19	2 46 35	4 48 48	6 47 5	8 49 18	10 51 32	12 49 48	14 52 1	16 50 18
	5	18 57 25	20 59 38	22 50 2	0 52 15	2 50 32	4 52 45	6 51 2	8 53 15	10 55 28	12 53 45	14 55 58	16 54 15
	6	19 1 22	21 3 35	22 53 58	0 56 12	2 54 28	4 56 42	6 54 58	8 57 12	10 59 25	12 57 41	14 59 55	16 58 11
	7	19 5 18	21 7 31	22 57 55	1 0 8	2 58 25	5 0 38	6 58 55	9 1 8	11 3 21	13 1 38	15 3 51	17 2 8
	8	19 9 15	21 11 28	23 1 52	1 4 5	3 2 21	5 4 35	7 2 51	9 5 5	11 7 18	13 5 35	15 7 48	17 6 4
	9	19 13 11	21 15 25	23 5 48	1 8 1	3 6 18	5 8 31	7 6 48	9 9 1	11 11 14	13 9 31	15 11 44	17 10 1
	10	19 17 8	21 19 21	23 9 45	1 11 58	3 10 15	5 12 28	7 10 45	9 12 58	11 15 11	13 13 28	15 15 41	17 13 58
	11	19 21 4	21 23 18	23 13 41	1 15 54	3 14 11	5 16 24	7 14 41	9 16 54	11 19 8	13 17 24	15 19 37	17 17 54
	12	19 25 1	21 27 14	23 17 38	1 19 51	3 18 8	5 20 21	7 18 38	9 20 51	11 23 4	13 21 21	15 23 34	17 21 51
	13	19 28 58	21 31 11	23 21 34	1 23 48	3 22 4	5 24 17	7 22 34	9 24 47	11 27 1	13 25 17	15 27 31	17 25 47
	14	19 32 54	21 35 7	23 25 31	1 27 44	3 26 1	5 28 14	7 26 31	9 28 44	11 30 57	13 29 14	15 31 27	17 29 44
	15	19 36 51	21 39 4	23 29 27	1 31 41	3 29 57	5 32 11	7 30 27	9 32 41	11 34 54	13 33 10	15 35 24	17 33 40
	16	19 40 47	21 43 0	23 33 24	1 35 37	3 33 54	5 36 7	7 34 24	9 36 37	11 38 50	13 37 7	15 39 20	17 37 37
	17	19 44 44	21 46 57	23 37 21	1 39 34	3 37 50	5 40 4	7 38 20	9 40 34	11 42 47	13 41 4	15 43 17	17 41 33
	18	19 48 40	21 50 54	23 41 17	1 43 30	3 41 47	5 44 0	7 42 17	9 44 30	11 46 43	13 45 0	15 47 13	17 45 30
	19	19 52 37	21 54 50	23 45 14	1 47 27	3 45 44	5 47 57	7 46 14	9 48 27	11 50 40	13 48 57	15 51 10	17 49 27
	20	19 56 33	21 58 47	23 49 10	1 51 23	3 49 40	5 51 53	7 50 10	9 52 23	11 54 37	13 52 53	15 55 6	17 53 23
	21	20 0 30	22 2 43	23 53 7	1 55 20	3 53 37	5 55 50	7 54 7	9 56 20	11 58 33	13 56 50	15 59 3	17 57 20
	22	20 4 27	22 6 40	23 57 3	1 59 17	3 57 33	5 59 46	7 58 3	10 0 16	12 2 30	14 0 46	16 3 0	18 1 16
	23	20 8 23	22 10 36	0 1 0	2 3 13	4 1 30	6 3 43	8 2 0	10 4 13	12 6 26	14 4 43	16 6 56	18 5 13
	24	20 12 20	22 14 33	0 4 56	2 7 10	4 5 26	6 7 40	8 5 56	10 8 10	12 10 23	14 8 39	16 10 53	18 9 9
	25	20 16 16	22 18 29	0 8 53	2 11 6	4 9 23	6 11 36	8 9 53	10 12 6	12 14 19	14 12 36	16 14 49	18 13 6
	26	20 20 13	22 22 26	0 12 50	2 15 3	4 13 19	6 15 33	8 13 49	10 16 3	12 18 16	14 16 33	16 18 46	18 17 3
	27	20 24 9	22 26 23	0 16 46	2 18 59	4 17 16	6 19 29	8 17 46	10 19 59	12 22 12	14 20 29	16 22 42	18 20 59
	28	20 28 6	22 30 19	0 20 43	2 22 56	4 21 13	6 23 26	8 21 43	10 23 56	12 26 9	14 24 26	16 26 39	18 24 56
	29	20 32 2		0 24 39	2 26 52	4 25 9	6 27 22	8 25 39	10 27 52	12 30 6	14 28 22	16 30 35	18 28 52
	30	20 35 59		0 28 36	2 30 49	4 29 6	6 31 19	8 29 36	10 31 49	12 34 2	14 32 19	16 34 32	18 32 49
	31	20 39 56		0 32 32		4 33 2		8 33 32	10 35 45		14 36 15		18 36 45
1931	1	18 40 42	20 42 55	22 33 19	0 35 32	2 33 49	4 36 2	6 34 19	8 36 32	10 38 45	12 37 2	14 39 15	16 37 32
	2	18 44 38	20 46 52	22 37 15	0 39 28	2 37 45	4 39 58	6 38 15	8 40 28	10 42 42	12 40 58	14 43 11	16 41 28
	3	18 48 35	20 50 48	22 41 12	0 43 25	2 41 42	4 43 55	6 42 12	8 44 25	10 46 38	12 44 55	14 47 8	16 45 25
	4	18 52 32	20 54 45	22 45 8	0 47 22	2 45 38	4 47 51	6 46 8	8 48 22	10 50 35	12 48 51	14 51 5	16 49 21
	5	18 56 28	20 58 41	22 49 5	0 51 18	2 49 35	4 51 48	6 50 5	8 52 18	10 54 31	12 52 48	14 55 1	16 53 18
	6	19 0 25	21 2 38	22 53 1	0 55 15	2 53 31	4 55 45	6 54 1	8 56 15	10 58 28	12 56 44	14 58 58	16 57 14
	7	19 4 21	21 6 35	22 56 58	0 59 11	2 57 28	4 59 41	6 57 58	9 0 11	11 2 24	13 0 41	15 2 54	17 1 11
	8	19 8 18	21 10 31	23 0 55	1 3 8	3 1 24	5 3 38	7 1 54	9 4 8	11 6 21	13 4 38	15 6 51	17 5 7
	9	19 12 14	21 14 28	23 4 51	1 7 4	3 5 21	5 7 34	7 5 51	9 8 4	11 10 18	13 8 34	15 10 47	17 9 4
	10	19 16 11	21 18 24	23 8 48	1 11 1	3 9 18	5 11 31	7 9 48	9 12 1	11 14 14	13 12 31	15 14 44	17 13 1
	11	19 20 7	21 22 21	23 12 44	1 14 57	3 13 14	5 15 27	7 13 44	9 15 57	11 18 11	13 16 27	15 18 40	17 16 57
	12	19 24 4	21 26 17	23 16 41	1 18 54	3 17 11	5 19 24	7 17 41	9 19 54	11 22 7	13 20 24	15 22 37	17 20 54
	13	19 28 1	21 30 14	23 20 37	1 22 51	3 21 7	5 23 20	7 21 37	9 23 51	11 26 4	13 24 20	15 26 34	17 24 50
	14	19 31 57	21 34 10	23 24 34	1 26 47	3 25 4	5 27 17	7 25 34	9 27 47	11 30 0	13 28 17	15 30 30	17 28 47
	15	19 35 54	21 38 7	23 28 30	1 30 44	3 29 0	5 31 14	7 29 30	9 31 44	11 33 57	13 32 13	15 34 27	17 32 43
	16	19 39 50	21 42 4	23 32 27	1 34 40	3 32 57	5 35 10	7 33 27	9 35 40	11 37 53	13 36 10	15 38 23	17 36 40
	17	19 43 47	21 46 0	23 36 24	1 38 37	3 36 53	5 39 7	7 37 24	9 39 37	11 41 50	13 40 7	15 42 20	17 40 37
	18	19 47 43	21 49 57	23 40 20	1 42 33	3 40 50	5 43 3	7 41 20	9 43 33	11 45 46	13 44 3	15 46 16	17 44 33
	19	19 51 40	21 53 53	23 44 17	1 46 30	3 44 47	5 47 0	7 45 17	9 47 30	11 49 43	13 48 0	15 50 13	17 48 30
	20	19 55 36	21 57 50	23 48 13	1 50 26	3 48 43	5 50 56	7 49 13	9 51 26	11 53 40	13 51 56	15 54 9	17 52 26
	21	19 59 33	22 1 46	23 52 10	1 54 23	3 52 40	5 54 53	7 53 10	9 55 23	11 57 36	13 55 53	15 58 6	17 56 23
	22	20 3 30	22 5 43	23 56 6	1 58 20	3 56 36	5 58 50	7 57 6	9 59 20	12 1 33	13 59 49	16 2 3	18 0 19
	23	20 7 26	22 9 39	0 0 3	2 2 16	4 0 33	6 2 46	8 1 3	10 3 16	12 5 29	14 3 46	16 5 59	18 4 16
	24	20 11 23	22 13 36	0 3 59	2 6 13	4 4 29	6 6 43	8 4 59	10 7 13	12 9 26	14 7 42	16 9 56	18 8 12
	25	20 15 19	22 17 32	0 7 56	2 10 9	4 8 26	6 10 39	8 8 56	10 11 9	12 13 22	14 11 39	16 13 52	18 12 9
	26	20 19 16	22 21 29	0 11 53	2 14 6	4 12 22	6 14 36	8 12 53	10 15 6	12 17 19	14 15 36	16 17 49	18 16 6
	27	20 23 12	22 25 26	0 15 49	2 18 2	4 16 19	6 18 32	8 16 49	10 19 2	12 21 15	14 19 32	16 21 45	18 20 2
	28	20 27 9	22 29 22	0 19 46	2 21 59	4 20 16	6 22 29	8 20 46	10 22 59	12 25 12	14 23 29	16 25 42	18 23 59
	29	20 31 5		0 23 42	2 25 55	4 24 12	6 26 25	8 24 42	10 26 55	12 29 9	14 27 25	16 29 38	18 27 55
	30	20 35 2		0 27 39	2 29 52	4 28 9	6 30 22	8 28 39	10 30 52	12 33 5	14 31 22	16 33 35	18 31 52
	31	20 38 59		0 31 35		4 32 5		8 32 35	10 34 49		14 35 18		18 35 48
1932	1	18 39 45	20 41 58	22 36 18	0 38 32	2 36 48	4 39 1	6 37 18	8 39 31	10 41 45	12 40 1	14 42 14	16 40 31
	2	18 43 41	20 45 55	22 40 15	0 42 28	2 40 45	4 42 58	6 41 15	8 43 28	10 45 41	12 43 58	14 46 11	16 44 28
	3	18 47 38	20 49 51	22 44 11	0 46 25	2 44 41	4 46 55	6 45 11	8 47 25	10 49 38	12 47 54	14 50 8	16 48 24
	4	18 51 35	20 53 48	22 48 8	0 50 21	2 48 38	4 50 51	6 49 8	8 51 21	10 53 34	12 51 51	14 54 4	16 52 21
	5	18 55 31	20 57 44	22 52 5	0 54 18	2 52 34	4 54 48	6 53 4	8 55 18	10 57 31	12 55 48	14 58 1	16 56 17
	6	18 59 28	21 1 41	22 56 1	0 58 14	2 56 31	4 58 44	6 57 1	8 59 14	11 1 27	12 59 44	15 1 57	17 0 14
	7	19 3 24	21 5 38	22 59 58	1 2 11	3 0 27	5 2 41	7 0 58	9 3 11	11 5 24	13 3 41	15 5 54	17 4 11
	8	19 7 21	21 9 34	23 3 54	1 6 7	3 4 24	5 6 37	7 4 54	9 7 7	11 9 21	13 7 37	15 9 50	17 8 7
	9	19 11 17	21 13 31	23 7 51	1 10 4	3 8 21	5 10 34	7 8 51	9 11 4	11 13 17	13 11 34	15 13 47	17 12 4
	10	19 15 14	21 17 27	23 11 47	1 14 0	3 12 17	5 14 30	7 12 47	9 15 0	11 17 14	13 15 30	15 17 43	17 16 0
	11	19 19 11	21 21 24	23 15 44	1 17 57	3 16 14	5 18 27	7 16 44	9 18 57	11 21 10	13 19 27	15 21 40	17 19 57
	12	19 23 7	21 25 20	23 19 40	1 21 54	3 20 10	5 22 24	7 20 40	9 22 54	11 25 7	13 23 23	15 25 37	17 23 53
	13	19 27 4	21 29 17	23 23 37	1 25 50	3 24 7	5 26 20	7 24 37	9 26 50	11 29 3	13 27 20	15 29 33	17 27 50
	14	19 31 0	21 33 13	23 27 34	1 29 47	3 28 3	5 30 17	7 28 33	9 30 47	11 33 0	13 31 16	15 33 30	17 31 46
	15	19 34 57	21 37 10	23 31 30	1 33 43	3 32 0	5 34 13	7 32 30	9 34 43	11 36 56	13 35 13	15 37 26	17 35 43
	16	19 38 53	21 41 7	23 35 27	1 37 40	3 35 56	5 38 10	7 36 27	9 38 40	11 40 53	13 39 10	15 41 23	17 39 40
	17	19 42 50	21 45 3	23 39 23	1 41 36	3 39 53	5 42 6	7 40 23	9 42 36	11 44 50	13 43 6	15 45 19	17 43 36
	18	19 46 46	21 49 0	23 43 20	1 45 33	3 43 50	5 46 3	7 44 20	9 46 33	11 48 46	13 47 3	15 49 16	17 47 33
	19	19 50 43	21 52 56	23 47 16	1 49 29	3 47 46	5 49 59	7 48 16	9 50 29	11 52 43	13 50 59	15 53 13	17 51 29
	20	19 54 40	21 56 53	23 51 13	1 53 26	3 51 43	5 53 56	7 52 13	9 54 26	11 56 39	13 54 56	15 57 9	17 55 26
	21	19 58 36	22 0 49	23 55 9	1 57 23	3 55 39	5 57 53	7 56 9	9 58 23	12 0 36	13 58 52	16 1 6	17 59 22
	22	20 2 33	22 4 46	23 59 6	2 1 19	3 59 36	6 1 49	8 0 6	10 2 19	12 4 32	14 2 49	16 5 2	18 3 19
	23	20 6 29	22 8 42	0 3 3	2 5 16	4 3 32	6 5 46	8 4 2	10 6 16	12 8 29	14 6 45	16 8 59	18 7 15
	24	20 10 26	22 12 39	0 6 59	2 9 12	4 7 29	6 9 42	8 7 59	10 10 12	12 12 25	14 10 42	16 12 55	18 11 12
	25	20 14 22	22 16 36	0 10 56	2 13 9	4 11 26	6 13 39	8 11 56	10 14 9	12 16 22	14 14 39	16 16 52	18 15 9
	26	20 18 19	22 20 32	0 14 52	2 17 5	4 15 22	6 17 35	8 15 52	10 18 5	12 20 19	14 18 35	16 20 48	18 19 5
	27	20 22 15	22 24 29	0 18 49	2 21 2	4 19 19	6 21 32	8 19 49	10 22 2	12 24 15	14 22 32	16 24 45	18 23 2
	28	20 26 12	22 28 25	0 22 45	2 24 58	4 23 15	6 25 28	8 23 45	10 25 58	12 28 12	14 26 28	16 28 42	18 26 58
	29	20 30 9	22 32 22	0 26 42	2 28 55	4 27 12	6 29 25	8 27 42	10 29 55	12 32 8	14 30 25	16 32 38	18 30 55
	30	20 34 5		0 30 38	2 32 52	4 31 8	6 33 22	8 31 38	10 33 52	12 36 5	14 34 21	16 36 35	18 34 51
	31	20 38 2		0 34 35		4 35 5		8 35 35	10 37 48		14 38 18		18 38 48
1933	1	18 42 45	20 44 58	22 35 21	0 37 35	2 35 51	4 38 4	6 36 21	8 38 34	10 40 48	12 39 4	14 41 17	16 39 34
	2	18 46 41	20 48 54	22 39 18	0 41 31	2 39 48	4 42 1	6 40 18	8 42 31	10 44 44	12 43 1	14 45 14	16 43 31
	3	18 50 38	20 52 51	22 43 14	0 45 28	2 43 44	4 45 58	6 44 14	8 46 28	10 48 41	12 46 57	14 49 11	16 47 27
	4	18 54 34	20 56 47	22 47 11	0 49 24	2 47 41	4 49 54	6 48 11	8 50 24	10 52 37	12 50 54	14 53 7	16 51 24
	5	18 58 31	21 0 44	22 51 8	0 53 21	2 51 37	4 53 51	6 52 7	8 54 21	10 56 34	12 54 51	14 57 4	16 55 20
	6	19 2 27	21 4 41	22 55 4	0 57 17	2 55 34	4 57 47	6 56 4	8 58 17	11 0 30	12 58 47	15 1 0	16 59 17
	7	19 6 24	21 8 37	22 59 1	1 1 14	2 59 31	5 1 44	7 0 1	9 2 14	11 4 27	13 2 44	15 4 57	17 3 14
	8	19 10 20	21 12 34	23 2 57	1 5 10	3 3 27	5 5 40	7 3 57	9 6 10	11 8 24	13 6 40	15 8 53	17 7 10
	9	19 14 17	21 16 30	23 6 54	1 9 7	3 7 24	5 9 37	7 7 54	9 10 7	11 12 20	13 10 37	15 12 50	17 11 7
	10	19 18 14	21 20 27	23 10 50	1 13 4	3 11 20	5 13 33	7 11 50	9 14 3	11 16 17	13 14 33	15 16 47	17 15 3
	11	19 22 10	21 24 23	23 14 47	1 17 0	3 15 17	5 17 30	7 15 47	9 18 0	11 20 13	13 18 30	15 20 43	17 19 0
	12	19 26 7	21 28 20	23 18 43	1 20 57	3 19 13	5 21 27	7 19 43	9 21 57	11 24 10	13 22 26	15 24 40	17 22 56
	13	19 30 3	21 32 16	23 22 40	1 24 53	3 23 10	5 25 23	7 23 40	9 25 53	11 28 6	13 26 23	15 28 36	17 26 53
	14	19 34 0	21 36 13	23 26 37	1 28 50	3 27 6	5 29 20	7 27 36	9 29 50	11 32 3	13 30 20	15 32 33	17 30 49
	15	19 37 56	21 40 10	23 30 33	1 32 46	3 31 3	5 33 16	7 31 33	9 33 46	11 35 59	13 34 16	15 36 29	17 34 46
	16	19 41 53	21 44 6	23 34 30	1 36 43	3 35 0	5 37 13	7 35 30	9 37 43	11 39 56	13 38 13	15 40 26	17 38 43
	17	19 45 49	21 48 3	23 38 26	1 40 39	3 38 56	5 41 9	7 39 26	9 41 39	11 43 53	13 42 9	15 44 22	17 42 39
	18	19 49 46	21 51 59	23 42 23	1 44 36	3 42 53	5 45 6	7 43 23	9 45 36	11 47 49	13 46 6	15 48 19	17 46 36
	19	19 53 43	21 55 56	23 46 19	1 48 33	3 46 49	5 49 2	7 47 19	9 49 33	11 51 46	13 50 2	15 52 16	17 50 32
	20	19 57 39	21 59 52	23 50 16	1 52 29	3 50 46	5 52 59	7 51 16	9 53 29	11 55 42	13 53 59	15 56 12	17 54 29
	21	20 1 36	22 3 49	23 54 12	1 56 26	3 54 42	5 56 56	7 55 12	9 57 26	11 59 39	13 57 55	16 0 9	17 58 25
	22	20 5 32	22 7 46	23 58 9	2 0 22	3 58 39	6 0 52	7 59 9	10 1 22	12 3 35	14 1 52	16 4 5	18 2 22
	23	20 9 29	22 11 42	0 2 6	2 4 19	4 2 35	6 4 49	8 3 5	10 5 19	12 7 32	14 5 49	16 8 2	18 6 19
	24	20 13 25	22 15 39	0 6 2	2 8 15	4 6 32	6 8 45	8 7 2	10 9 15	12 11 28	14 9 45	16 11 58	18 10 15
	25	20 17 22	22 19 35	0 9 59	2 12 12	4 10 29	6 12 42	8 10 59	10 13 12	12 15 25	14 13 42	16 15 55	18 14 12
	26	20 21 19	22 23 32	0 13 55	2 16 8	4 14 25	6 16 38	8 14 55	10 17 8	12 19 22	14 17 38	16 19 51	18 18 8
	27	20 25 15	22 27 28	0 17 52	2 20 5	4 18 22	6 20 35	8 18 52	10 21 5	12 23 18	14 21 35	16 23 48	18 22 5
	28	20 29 12	22 31 25	0 21 48	2 24 2	4 22 18	6 24 32	8 22 48	10 25 1	12 27 15	14 25 31	16 27 45	18 26 1
	29	20 33 8		0 25 45	2 27 58	4 26 15	6 28 28	8 26 45	10 28 58	12 31 11	14 29 28	16 31 41	18 29 58
	30	20 37 5		0 29 41	2 31 55	4 30 11	6 32 25	8 30 41	10 32 55	12 35 8	14 33 24	16 35 38	18 33 54
	31	20 41 1		0 33 38		4 34 8		8 34 38	10 36 51		14 37 21		18 37 51

YEAR		JAN	FEB	MAR	APR	MAY	JUN	JUL	AUG	SEP	OCT	NOV	DEC
1934	1	18 41 48	20 44 1	22 34 24	0 36 38	2 34 54	4 37 7	6 35 24	8 37 37	10 39 51	12 38 7	14 40 20	16 38 37
	2	18 45 44	20 47 57	22 38 21	0 40 34	2 38 51	4 41 4	6 39 21	8 41 34	10 43 47	12 42 4	14 44 17	16 42 34
	3	18 49 41	20 51 54	22 42 17	0 44 31	2 42 47	4 45 1	6 43 17	8 45 31	10 47 44	12 46 0	14 48 14	16 46 30
	4	18 53 37	20 55 50	22 46 14	0 48 27	2 46 44	4 48 57	6 47 14	8 49 27	10 51 40	12 49 57	14 52 10	16 50 27
	5	18 57 34	20 59 47	22 50 11	0 52 24	2 50 40	4 52 54	6 51 10	8 53 24	10 55 37	12 53 54	14 56 7	16 54 23
	6	19 1 30	21 3 44	22 54 7	0 56 20	2 54 37	4 56 50	6 55 7	8 57 20	10 59 33	12 57 50	15 0 3	16 58 20
	7	19 5 27	21 7 40	22 58 4	1 0 17	2 58 34	5 0 47	6 59 4	9 1 17	11 3 30	13 1 47	15 4 0	17 2 17
	8	19 9 23	21 11 37	23 2 0	1 4 13	3 2 30	5 4 43	7 3 0	9 5 13	11 7 27	13 5 43	15 7 56	17 6 13
	9	19 13 20	21 15 33	23 5 57	1 8 10	3 6 27	5 8 40	7 6 57	9 9 10	11 11 23	13 9 40	15 11 53	17 10 10
	10	19 17 17	21 19 30	23 9 53	1 12 7	3 10 23	5 12 36	7 10 53	9 13 6	11 15 20	13 13 36	15 15 49	17 14 6
	11	19 21 13	21 23 26	23 13 50	1 16 3	3 14 20	5 16 33	7 14 50	9 17 3	11 19 16	13 17 33	15 19 46	17 18 3
	12	19 25 10	21 27 23	23 17 46	1 20 0	3 18 16	5 20 30	7 18 46	9 21 0	11 23 13	13 21 29	15 23 43	17 21 59
	13	19 29 6	21 31 20	23 21 43	1 23 56	3 22 13	5 24 26	7 22 43	9 24 56	11 27 9	13 25 26	15 27 39	17 25 56
	14	19 33 3	21 35 16	23 25 40	1 27 53	3 26 9	5 28 23	7 26 39	9 28 53	11 31 6	13 29 22	15 31 36	17 29 52
	15	19 36 59	21 39 13	23 29 36	1 31 49	3 30 6	5 32 19	7 30 36	9 32 49	11 35 2	13 33 19	15 35 32	17 33 49
	16	19 40 56	21 43 9	23 33 33	1 35 46	3 34 3	5 36 16	7 34 33	9 36 46	11 38 59	13 37 16	15 39 29	17 37 46
	17	19 44 52	21 47 6	23 37 29	1 39 42	3 37 59	5 40 12	7 38 29	9 40 42	11 42 56	13 41 12	15 43 25	17 41 42
	18	19 48 49	21 51 2	23 41 26	1 43 39	3 41 56	5 44 9	7 42 26	9 44 39	11 46 52	13 45 9	15 47 22	17 45 39
	19	19 52 46	21 54 59	23 45 22	1 47 36	3 45 52	5 48 5	7 46 22	9 48 35	11 50 49	13 49 5	15 51 18	17 49 35
	20	19 56 42	21 58 55	23 49 19	1 51 32	3 49 49	5 52 2	7 50 19	9 52 32	11 54 45	13 53 2	15 55 15	17 53 32
	21	20 0 39	22 2 52	23 53 15	1 55 29	3 53 45	5 55 59	7 54 15	9 56 29	11 58 42	13 56 58	15 59 12	17 57 28
	22	20 4 35	22 6 48	23 57 12	1 59 25	3 57 42	5 59 55	7 58 12	10 0 25	12 2 38	14 0 55	16 3 8	18 1 25
	23	20 8 32	22 10 45	0 1 9	2 3 22	4 1 38	6 3 52	8 2 8	10 4 22	12 6 35	14 4 51	16 7 5	18 5 21
	24	20 12 28	22 14 42	0 5 5	2 7 18	4 5 35	6 7 48	8 6 5	10 8 18	12 10 31	14 8 48	16 11 1	18 9 18
	25	20 16 25	22 18 38	0 9 2	2 11 15	4 9 32	6 11 45	8 10 2	10 12 15	12 14 28	14 12 45	16 14 58	18 13 15
	26	20 20 21	22 22 35	0 12 58	2 15 11	4 13 28	6 15 41	8 13 58	10 16 11	12 18 25	14 16 41	16 18 54	18 17 11
	27	20 24 18	22 26 31	0 16 55	2 19 8	4 17 25	6 19 38	8 17 55	10 20 8	12 22 21	14 20 38	16 22 51	18 21 8
	28	20 28 15	22 30 28	0 20 51	2 23 4	4 21 21	6 23 35	8 21 51	10 24 4	12 26 18	14 24 34	16 26 48	18 25 4
	29	20 32 11		0 24 48	2 27 1	4 25 18	6 27 31	8 25 48	10 28 1	12 30 14	14 28 31	16 30 44	18 29 1
	30	20 36 8		0 28 44	2 30 58	4 29 14	6 31 28	8 29 44	10 31 58	12 34 11	14 32 27	16 34 41	18 32 57
	31	20 40 4		0 32 41		4 33 11		8 33 41	10 35 54		14 36 24		18 36 54
1935	1	18 40 50	20 43 4	22 33 27	0 35 40	2 33 57	4 36 10	6 34 27	8 36 40	10 38 54	12 37 10	14 39 23	16 37 40
	2	18 44 47	20 47 0	22 37 24	0 39 37	2 37 54	4 40 7	6 38 24	8 40 37	10 42 50	12 41 7	14 43 20	16 41 37
	3	18 48 44	20 50 57	22 41 20	0 43 34	2 41 50	4 44 3	6 42 20	8 44 33	10 46 47	12 45 3	14 47 16	16 45 33
	4	18 52 40	20 54 53	22 45 17	0 47 30	2 45 47	4 48 0	6 46 17	8 48 30	10 50 43	12 49 0	14 51 13	16 49 30
	5	18 56 37	20 58 50	22 49 14	0 51 27	2 49 43	4 51 57	6 50 13	8 52 27	10 54 40	12 52 56	14 55 10	16 53 26
	6	19 0 33	21 2 47	22 53 10	0 55 23	2 53 40	4 55 53	6 54 10	8 56 23	10 58 36	12 56 53	14 59 6	16 57 23
	7	19 4 30	21 6 43	22 57 7	0 59 20	2 57 36	4 59 50	6 58 6	9 0 20	11 2 33	13 0 49	15 3 3	17 1 19
	8	19 8 26	21 10 40	23 1 3	1 3 16	3 1 33	5 3 46	7 2 3	9 4 16	11 6 29	13 4 46	15 6 59	17 5 16
	9	19 12 23	21 14 36	23 5 0	1 7 13	3 5 30	5 7 43	7 6 0	9 8 13	11 10 26	13 8 43	15 10 56	17 9 12
	10	19 16 20	21 18 33	23 8 56	1 11 9	3 9 26	5 11 39	7 9 56	9 12 9	11 14 23	13 12 39	15 14 52	17 13 9
	11	19 20 16	21 22 29	23 12 53	1 15 6	3 13 23	5 15 36	7 13 53	9 16 6	11 18 19	13 16 36	15 18 49	17 17 6
	12	19 24 13	21 26 26	23 16 49	1 19 3	3 17 19	5 19 32	7 17 49	9 20 2	11 22 16	13 20 32	15 22 45	17 21 2
	13	19 28 9	21 30 22	23 20 46	1 22 59	3 21 16	5 23 29	7 21 46	9 23 59	11 26 12	13 24 29	15 26 42	17 24 59
	14	19 32 6	21 34 19	23 24 43	1 26 56	3 25 12	5 27 26	7 25 42	9 27 56	11 30 9	13 28 25	15 30 39	17 28 55
	15	19 36 2	21 38 16	23 28 39	1 30 52	3 29 9	5 31 22	7 29 39	9 31 52	11 34 5	13 32 22	15 34 35	17 32 52
	16	19 39 59	21 42 12	23 32 36	1 34 49	3 33 5	5 35 19	7 33 35	9 35 49	11 38 2	13 36 18	15 38 32	17 36 48
	17	19 43 55	21 46 9	23 36 32	1 38 45	3 37 2	5 39 15	7 37 32	9 39 45	11 41 58	13 40 15	15 42 28	17 40 45
	18	19 47 52	21 50 5	23 40 29	1 42 42	3 40 59	5 43 12	7 41 29	9 43 42	11 45 55	13 44 12	15 46 25	17 44 42
	19	19 51 49	21 54 2	23 44 25	1 46 38	3 44 55	5 47 8	7 45 25	9 47 38	11 49 52	13 48 8	15 50 21	17 48 38
	20	19 55 45	21 57 58	23 48 22	1 50 35	3 48 52	5 51 5	7 49 22	9 51 35	11 53 48	13 52 5	15 54 18	17 52 35
	21	19 59 42	22 1 55	23 52 18	1 54 32	3 52 48	5 55 2	7 53 18	9 55 31	11 57 45	13 56 1	15 58 14	17 56 31
	22	20 3 38	22 5 51	23 56 15	1 58 28	3 56 45	5 58 58	7 57 15	9 59 28	12 1 41	13 59 58	16 2 11	18 0 28
	23	20 7 35	22 9 48	0 0 11	2 2 25	4 0 41	6 2 55	8 1 11	10 3 25	12 5 38	14 3 54	16 6 8	18 4 24
	24	20 11 31	22 13 45	0 4 8	2 6 21	4 4 38	6 6 51	8 5 8	10 7 21	12 9 34	14 7 51	16 10 4	18 8 21
	25	20 15 28	22 17 41	0 8 5	2 10 18	4 8 34	6 10 48	8 9 4	10 11 18	12 13 31	14 11 47	16 14 1	18 12 17
	26	20 19 24	22 21 38	0 12 1	2 14 14	4 12 31	6 14 44	8 13 1	10 15 14	12 17 27	14 15 44	16 17 57	18 16 14
	27	20 23 21	22 25 34	0 15 58	2 18 11	4 16 28	6 18 41	8 16 58	10 19 11	12 21 24	14 19 41	16 21 54	18 20 11
	28	20 27 18	22 29 31	0 19 54	2 22 7	4 20 24	6 22 37	8 20 54	10 23 7	12 25 20	14 23 37	16 25 50	18 24 7
	29	20 31 14		0 23 51	2 26 4	4 24 21	6 26 34	8 24 51	10 27 4	12 29 17	14 27 34	16 29 47	18 28 4
	30	20 35 11		0 27 47	2 30 1	4 28 17	6 30 31	8 28 47	10 31 0	12 33 14	14 31 30	16 33 43	18 32 0
	31	20 39 7		0 31 44		4 32 14		8 32 44	10 34 57		14 35 27		18 35 57
1936	1	18 39 53	20 42 7	22 36 27	0 38 40	2 36 56	4 39 10	6 37 26	8 39 40	10 41 53	12 40 9	14 42 23	16 40 39
	2	18 43 50	20 46 3	22 40 23	0 42 36	2 40 53	4 43 6	6 41 23	8 43 36	10 45 49	12 44 6	14 46 19	16 44 36
	3	18 47 46	20 50 0	22 44 20	0 46 33	2 44 50	4 47 3	6 45 20	8 47 33	10 49 46	12 48 3	14 50 16	16 48 32
	4	18 51 43	20 53 56	22 48 16	0 50 30	2 48 46	4 50 59	6 49 16	8 51 29	10 53 43	12 51 59	14 54 12	16 52 29
	5	18 55 40	20 57 53	22 52 13	0 54 26	2 52 43	4 54 56	6 53 13	8 55 26	10 57 39	12 55 56	14 58 9	16 56 26
	6	18 59 36	21 1 49	22 56 9	0 58 23	2 56 39	4 58 52	6 57 9	8 59 22	11 1 36	12 59 52	15 2 5	17 0 22
	7	19 3 33	21 5 46	23 0 6	1 2 19	3 0 36	5 2 49	7 1 6	9 3 19	11 5 32	13 3 49	15 6 2	17 4 19
	8	19 7 29	21 9 43	23 4 3	1 6 16	3 4 32	5 6 46	7 5 2	9 7 16	11 9 29	13 7 45	15 9 59	17 8 15
	9	19 11 26	21 13 39	23 7 59	1 10 12	3 8 29	5 10 42	7 8 59	9 11 12	11 13 25	13 11 42	15 13 55	17 12 12
	10	19 15 22	21 17 36	23 11 56	1 14 9	3 12 25	5 14 39	7 12 55	9 15 9	11 17 22	13 15 38	15 17 52	17 16 8
	11	19 19 19	21 21 32	23 15 52	1 18 5	3 16 22	5 18 35	7 16 52	9 19 5	11 21 18	13 19 35	15 21 48	17 20 5
	12	19 23 15	21 25 29	23 19 49	1 22 2	3 20 19	5 22 32	7 20 49	9 23 2	11 25 15	13 23 32	15 25 45	17 24 1
	13	19 27 12	21 29 25	23 23 45	1 25 58	3 24 15	5 26 28	7 24 45	9 26 58	11 29 12	13 27 28	15 29 41	17 27 58
	14	19 31 9	21 33 22	23 27 42	1 29 55	3 28 12	5 30 25	7 28 42	9 30 55	11 33 8	13 31 25	15 33 38	17 31 55
	15	19 35 5	21 37 18	23 31 38	1 33 52	3 32 8	5 34 21	7 32 38	9 34 51	11 37 5	13 35 21	15 37 34	17 35 51
	16	19 39 2	21 41 15	23 35 35	1 37 48	3 36 5	5 38 18	7 36 35	9 38 48	11 41 1	13 39 18	15 41 31	17 39 48
	17	19 42 58	21 45 11	23 39 32	1 41 45	3 40 1	5 42 15	7 40 31	9 42 45	11 44 58	13 43 14	15 45 28	17 43 44
	18	19 46 55	21 49 8	23 43 28	1 45 41	3 43 58	5 46 11	7 44 28	9 46 41	11 48 54	13 47 11	15 49 24	17 47 41
	19	19 50 51	21 53 5	23 47 25	1 49 38	3 47 54	5 50 8	7 48 24	9 50 38	11 52 51	13 51 7	15 53 21	17 51 37
	20	19 54 48	21 57 1	23 51 21	1 53 34	3 51 51	5 54 4	7 52 21	9 54 34	11 56 47	13 55 4	15 57 17	17 55 34
	21	19 58 44	22 0 58	23 55 18	1 57 31	3 55 48	5 58 1	7 56 18	9 58 31	12 0 44	13 59 1	16 1 14	17 59 30
	22	20 2 41	22 4 54	23 59 14	2 1 27	3 59 44	6 1 57	8 0 14	10 2 27	12 4 40	14 2 57	16 5 10	18 3 27
	23	20 6 38	22 8 51	0 3 11	2 5 24	4 3 41	6 5 54	8 4 11	10 6 24	12 8 37	14 6 54	16 9 7	18 7 24
	24	20 10 34	22 12 47	0 7 7	2 9 21	4 7 37	6 9 51	8 8 7	10 10 20	12 12 34	14 10 50	16 13 3	18 11 20
	25	20 14 31	22 16 44	0 11 4	2 13 17	4 11 34	6 13 47	8 12 4	10 14 17	12 16 30	14 14 47	16 17 0	18 15 17
	26	20 18 27	22 20 40	0 15 1	2 17 14	4 15 30	6 17 44	8 16 0	10 18 14	12 20 27	14 18 43	16 20 57	18 19 13
	27	20 22 24	22 24 37	0 18 57	2 21 10	4 19 27	6 21 40	8 19 57	10 22 10	12 24 23	14 22 40	16 24 53	18 23 10
	28	20 26 20	22 28 34	0 22 54	2 25 7	4 23 23	6 25 37	8 23 53	10 26 7	12 28 20	14 26 36	16 28 50	18 27 6
	29	20 30 17	22 32 30	0 26 50	2 29 3	4 27 20	6 29 33	8 27 50	10 30 3	12 32 16	14 30 33	16 32 46	18 31 3
	30	20 34 13		0 30 47	2 33 0	4 31 17	6 33 30	8 31 47	10 34 0	12 36 13	14 34 30	16 36 43	18 35 0
	31	20 38 10		0 34 43		4 35 13		8 35 43	10 37 56		14 38 26		18 38 56
1937	1	18 42 53	20 45 6	22 35 29	0 37 43	2 35 59	4 38 12	6 36 29	8 38 42	10 40 56	12 39 12	14 41 25	16 39 42
	2	18 46 49	20 49 2	22 39 26	0 41 39	2 39 56	4 42 9	6 40 26	8 42 39	10 44 52	12 43 9	14 45 22	16 43 38
	3	18 50 46	20 52 59	22 43 23	0 45 36	2 43 52	4 46 5	6 44 22	8 46 35	10 48 49	12 47 5	14 49 18	16 47 35
	4	18 54 42	20 56 56	22 47 19	0 49 32	2 47 49	4 50 2	6 48 19	8 50 32	10 52 45	12 51 2	14 53 15	16 51 32
	5	18 58 39	21 0 52	22 51 16	0 53 29	2 51 45	4 53 59	6 52 15	8 54 29	10 56 42	12 54 58	14 57 11	16 55 28
	6	19 2 35	21 4 49	22 55 12	0 57 25	2 55 42	4 57 55	6 56 12	8 58 25	11 0 38	12 58 55	15 1 8	16 59 25
	7	19 6 32	21 8 45	22 59 9	1 1 22	2 59 38	5 1 52	7 0 8	9 2 22	11 4 35	13 2 51	15 5 5	17 3 21
	8	19 10 29	21 12 42	23 3 5	1 5 18	3 3 35	5 5 48	7 4 5	9 6 18	11 8 31	13 6 48	15 9 1	17 7 18
	9	19 14 25	21 16 38	23 7 2	1 9 15	3 7 32	5 9 45	7 8 2	9 10 15	11 12 28	13 10 45	15 12 58	17 11 14
	10	19 18 22	21 20 35	23 10 58	1 13 12	3 11 28	5 13 41	7 11 58	9 14 11	11 16 25	13 14 41	15 16 54	17 15 11
	11	19 22 18	21 24 31	23 14 55	1 17 8	3 15 25	5 17 38	7 15 55	9 18 8	11 20 21	13 18 38	15 20 51	17 19 8
	12	19 26 15	21 28 28	23 18 51	1 21 5	3 19 21	5 21 35	7 19 51	9 22 4	11 24 18	13 22 34	15 24 47	17 23 4
	13	19 30 11	21 32 25	23 22 48	1 25 1	3 23 18	5 25 31	7 23 48	9 26 1	11 28 14	13 26 31	15 28 44	17 27 1
	14	19 34 8	21 36 21	23 26 45	1 28 58	3 27 14	5 29 28	7 27 44	9 29 58	11 32 11	13 30 27	15 32 40	17 30 57
	15	19 38 4	21 40 18	23 30 41	1 32 54	3 31 11	5 33 24	7 31 41	9 33 54	11 36 7	13 34 24	15 36 37	17 34 54
	16	19 42 1	21 44 14	23 34 38	1 36 51	3 35 8	5 37 21	7 35 37	9 37 51	11 40 4	13 38 20	15 40 34	17 38 50
	17	19 45 58	21 48 11	23 38 34	1 40 47	3 39 4	5 41 17	7 39 34	9 41 47	11 44 0	13 42 17	15 44 30	17 42 47
	18	19 49 54	21 52 7	23 42 31	1 44 44	3 43 1	5 45 14	7 43 31	9 45 44	11 47 57	13 46 14	15 48 27	17 46 43
	19	19 53 51	21 56 4	23 46 27	1 48 41	3 46 57	5 49 10	7 47 27	9 49 40	11 51 54	13 50 10	15 52 23	17 50 40
	20	19 57 47	22 0 0	23 50 24	1 52 37	3 50 54	5 53 7	7 51 24	9 53 37	11 55 50	13 54 7	15 56 20	17 54 37
	21	20 1 44	22 3 57	23 54 20	1 56 34	3 54 50	5 57 4	7 55 20	9 57 33	11 59 47	13 58 3	16 0 16	17 58 33
	22	20 5 40	22 7 54	23 58 17	2 0 30	3 58 47	6 1 0	7 59 17	10 1 30	12 3 43	14 2 0	16 4 13	18 2 30
	23	20 9 37	22 11 50	0 2 14	2 4 27	4 2 43	6 4 57	8 3 13	10 5 27	12 7 40	14 5 56	16 8 10	18 6 26
	24	20 13 33	22 15 47	0 6 10	2 8 23	4 6 40	6 8 53	8 7 10	10 9 23	12 11 36	14 9 53	16 12 6	18 10 23
	25	20 17 30	22 19 43	0 10 7	2 12 20	4 10 36	6 12 50	8 11 6	10 13 20	12 15 33	14 13 49	16 16 3	18 14 19
	26	20 21 27	22 23 40	0 14 3	2 16 16	4 14 33	6 16 46	8 15 3	10 17 16	12 19 29	14 17 46	16 19 59	18 18 16
	27	20 25 23	22 27 36	0 18 0	2 20 13	4 18 30	6 20 43	8 19 0	10 21 13	12 23 26	14 21 43	16 23 56	18 22 12
	28	20 29 20	22 31 33	0 21 56	2 24 9	4 22 26	6 24 39	8 22 56	10 25 9	12 27 22	14 25 39	16 27 52	18 26 9
	29	20 33 16		0 25 53	2 28 6	4 26 23	6 28 36	8 26 53	10 29 6	12 31 19	14 29 36	16 31 49	18 30 6
	30	20 37 13		0 29 49	2 32 3	4 30 19	6 32 33	8 30 49	10 33 2	12 35 16	14 33 32	16 35 45	18 34 2
	31	20 41 9		0 33 46		4 34 16		8 34 46	10 36 59		14 37 29		18 37 59

YEAR		JAN	FEB	MAR	APR	MAY	JUN	JUL	AUG	SEP	OCT	NOV	DEC
1938	1	18 41 55	20 44 9	22 34 32	0 36 45	2 35 2	4 37 15	6 35 32	8 37 45	10 39 58	12 38 15	14 40 28	16 38 44
	2	18 45 52	20 48 5	22 38 29	0 40 42	2 38 58	4 41 12	6 39 28	8 41 41	10 43 55	12 42 11	14 44 24	16 42 41
	3	18 49 48	20 52 2	22 42 25	0 44 38	2 42 55	4 45 8	6 43 25	8 45 38	10 47 51	12 46 8	14 48 21	16 46 38
	4	18 53 45	20 55 58	22 46 22	0 48 35	2 46 51	4 49 5	6 47 21	8 49 35	10 51 48	12 50 4	14 52 17	16 50 34
	5	18 57 41	20 59 55	22 50 18	0 52 31	2 50 48	4 53 1	6 51 18	8 53 31	10 55 44	12 54 1	14 56 14	16 54 31
	6	19 1 38	21 3 51	22 54 15	0 56 28	2 54 45	4 56 58	6 55 14	8 57 28	10 59 41	12 57 57	15 0 11	16 58 27
	7	19 5 35	21 7 48	22 58 11	1 0 24	2 58 41	5 0 54	6 59 11	9 1 24	11 3 37	13 1 54	15 4 7	17 2 24
	8	19 9 31	21 11 44	23 2 8	1 4 21	3 2 38	5 4 51	7 3 8	9 5 21	11 7 34	13 5 51	15 8 4	17 6 20
	9	19 13 28	21 15 41	23 6 4	1 8 18	3 6 34	5 8 47	7 7 4	9 9 17	11 11 31	13 9 47	15 12 0	17 10 17
	10	19 17 24	21 19 37	23 10 1	1 12 14	3 10 31	5 12 44	7 11 1	9 13 14	11 15 27	13 13 44	15 15 57	17 14 13
	11	19 21 21	21 23 34	23 13 58	1 16 11	3 14 27	5 16 41	7 14 57	9 17 10	11 19 24	13 17 40	15 19 53	17 18 10
	12	19 25 17	21 27 31	23 17 54	1 20 7	3 18 24	5 20 37	7 18 54	9 21 7	11 23 20	13 21 37	15 23 50	17 22 7
	13	19 29 14	21 31 27	23 21 51	1 24 4	3 22 20	5 24 34	7 22 50	9 25 4	11 27 17	13 25 33	15 27 46	17 26 3
	14	19 33 10	21 35 24	23 25 47	1 28 0	3 26 17	5 28 30	7 26 47	9 29 0	11 31 13	13 29 30	15 31 43	17 30 0
	15	19 37 7	21 39 20	23 29 44	1 31 57	3 30 13	5 32 27	7 30 43	9 32 57	11 35 10	13 33 26	15 35 40	17 33 56
	16	19 41 4	21 43 17	23 33 40	1 35 53	3 34 10	5 36 23	7 34 40	9 36 53	11 39 6	13 37 23	15 39 36	17 37 53
	17	19 45 0	21 47 13	23 37 37	1 39 50	3 38 7	5 40 20	7 38 37	9 40 50	11 43 3	13 41 20	15 43 33	17 41 49
	18	19 48 57	21 51 10	23 41 33	1 43 47	3 42 3	5 44 16	7 42 33	9 44 46	11 46 59	13 45 16	15 47 29	17 45 46
	19	19 52 53	21 55 6	23 45 30	1 47 43	3 46 0	5 48 13	7 46 30	9 48 43	11 50 56	13 49 13	15 51 26	17 49 42
	20	19 56 50	21 59 3	23 49 26	1 51 40	3 49 56	5 52 10	7 50 26	9 52 39	11 54 53	13 53 9	15 55 22	17 53 39
	21	20 0 46	22 3 0	23 53 23	1 55 36	3 53 53	5 56 6	7 54 23	9 56 36	11 58 49	13 57 6	15 59 19	17 57 36
	22	20 4 43	22 6 56	23 57 20	1 59 33	3 57 49	6 0 3	7 58 19	10 0 33	12 2 46	14 1 2	16 3 15	18 1 32
	23	20 8 39	22 10 53	0 1 16	2 3 29	4 1 46	6 3 59	8 2 16	10 4 29	12 6 42	14 4 59	16 7 12	18 5 29
	24	20 12 36	22 14 49	0 5 13	2 7 26	4 5 43	6 7 56	8 6 12	10 8 26	12 10 39	14 8 55	16 11 9	18 9 25
	25	20 16 33	22 18 46	0 9 9	2 11 22	4 9 39	6 11 52	8 10 9	10 12 22	12 14 35	14 12 52	16 15 5	18 13 22
	26	20 20 29	22 22 42	0 13 6	2 15 19	4 13 36	6 15 49	8 14 6	10 16 19	12 18 32	14 16 48	16 19 2	18 17 18
	27	20 24 26	22 26 39	0 17 2	2 19 16	4 17 32	6 19 45	8 18 2	10 20 15	12 22 28	14 20 45	16 22 58	18 21 15
	28	20 28 22	22 30 35	0 20 59	2 23 12	4 21 29	6 23 42	8 21 59	10 24 12	12 26 25	14 24 42	16 26 55	18 25 12
	29	20 32 19		0 24 55	2 27 9	4 25 25	6 27 39	8 25 55	10 28 8	12 30 22	14 28 38	16 30 51	18 29 8
	30	20 36 15		0 28 52	2 31 5	4 29 22	6 31 35	8 29 52	10 32 5	12 34 18	14 32 35	16 34 48	18 33 5
	31	20 40 12		0 32 49		4 33 18		8 33 48	10 36 2		14 36 31		18 37 1
1939	1	18 40 58	20 43 11	22 33 35	0 35 48	2 34 4	4 36 17	6 34 34	8 36 47	10 39 1	12 37 17	14 39 30	16 37 47
	2	18 44 54	20 47 8	22 37 31	0 39 44	2 38 1	4 40 14	6 38 31	8 40 44	10 42 57	12 41 14	14 43 27	16 41 43
	3	18 48 51	20 51 4	22 41 28	0 43 41	2 41 57	4 44 11	6 42 27	8 44 40	10 46 54	12 45 10	14 47 23	16 45 40
	4	18 52 47	20 55 1	22 45 24	0 47 37	2 45 54	4 48 7	6 46 24	8 48 37	10 50 50	12 49 7	14 51 20	16 49 37
	5	18 56 44	20 58 57	22 49 21	0 51 34	2 49 50	4 52 4	6 50 20	8 52 34	10 54 47	12 53 3	14 55 16	16 53 33
	6	19 0 41	21 2 54	22 53 17	0 55 30	2 53 47	4 56 0	6 54 17	8 56 30	10 58 43	12 57 0	14 59 13	16 57 30
	7	19 4 37	21 6 50	22 57 14	0 59 27	2 57 44	4 59 57	6 58 13	9 0 27	11 2 40	13 0 56	15 3 10	17 1 26
	8	19 8 34	21 10 47	23 1 10	1 3 23	3 1 40	5 3 53	7 2 10	9 4 23	11 6 36	13 4 53	15 7 6	17 5 23
	9	19 12 30	21 14 43	23 5 7	1 7 20	3 5 37	5 7 50	7 6 7	9 8 20	11 10 33	13 8 50	15 11 3	17 9 19
	10	19 16 27	21 18 40	23 9 3	1 11 17	3 9 33	5 11 46	7 10 3	9 12 16	11 14 30	13 12 46	15 14 59	17 13 16
	11	19 20 23	21 22 37	23 13 0	1 15 13	3 13 30	5 15 43	7 14 0	9 16 13	11 18 26	13 16 43	15 18 56	17 17 12
	12	19 24 20	21 26 33	23 16 57	1 19 10	3 17 26	5 19 40	7 17 56	9 20 9	11 22 23	13 20 39	15 22 52	17 21 9
	13	19 28 16	21 30 30	23 20 53	1 23 6	3 21 23	5 23 36	7 21 53	9 24 6	11 26 19	13 24 36	15 26 49	17 25 6
	14	19 32 13	21 34 26	23 24 50	1 27 3	3 25 19	5 27 33	7 25 49	9 28 3	11 30 16	13 28 32	15 30 45	17 29 2
	15	19 36 10	21 38 23	23 28 46	1 30 59	3 29 16	5 31 29	7 29 46	9 31 59	11 34 12	13 32 29	15 34 42	17 32 59
	16	19 40 6	21 42 19	23 32 43	1 34 56	3 33 13	5 35 26	7 33 42	9 35 56	11 38 9	13 36 25	15 38 39	17 36 55
	17	19 44 3	21 46 16	23 36 39	1 38 52	3 37 9	5 39 22	7 37 39	9 39 52	11 42 5	13 40 22	15 42 35	17 40 52
	18	19 47 59	21 50 12	23 40 36	1 42 49	3 41 6	5 43 19	7 41 36	9 43 49	11 46 2	13 44 18	15 46 32	17 44 48
	19	19 51 56	21 54 9	23 44 32	1 46 46	3 45 2	5 47 15	7 45 32	9 47 45	11 49 58	13 48 15	15 50 28	17 48 45
	20	19 55 52	21 58 6	23 48 29	1 50 42	3 48 59	5 51 12	7 49 29	9 51 42	11 53 55	13 52 12	15 54 25	17 52 41
	21	19 59 49	22 2 2	23 52 26	1 54 39	3 52 55	5 55 9	7 53 25	9 55 38	11 57 52	13 56 8	15 58 21	17 56 38
	22	20 3 45	22 5 59	23 56 22	1 58 35	3 56 52	5 59 5	7 57 22	9 59 35	12 1 48	14 0 5	16 2 18	18 0 35
	23	20 7 42	22 9 55	0 0 19	2 2 32	4 0 48	6 3 2	8 1 18	10 3 32	12 5 45	14 4 1	16 6 14	18 4 31
	24	20 11 39	22 13 52	0 4 15	2 6 28	4 4 45	6 6 58	8 5 15	10 7 28	12 9 41	14 7 58	16 10 11	18 8 28
	25	20 15 35	22 17 48	0 8 12	2 10 25	4 8 42	6 10 55	8 9 11	10 11 25	12 13 38	14 11 54	16 14 8	18 12 24
	26	20 19 32	22 21 45	0 12 8	2 14 21	4 12 38	6 14 51	8 13 8	10 15 21	12 17 34	14 15 51	16 18 4	18 16 21
	27	20 23 28	22 25 41	0 16 5	2 18 18	4 16 35	6 18 48	8 17 5	10 19 18	12 21 31	14 19 47	16 22 1	18 20 17
	28	20 27 25	22 29 38	0 20 1	2 22 15	4 20 31	6 22 44	8 21 1	10 23 14	12 25 27	14 23 44	16 25 57	18 24 14
	29	20 31 21		0 23 58	2 26 11	4 24 28	6 26 41	8 24 58	10 27 11	12 29 24	14 27 41	16 29 54	18 28 10
	30	20 35 18		0 27 55	2 30 8	4 28 24	6 30 38	8 28 54	10 31 7	12 33 21	14 31 37	16 33 50	18 32 7
	31	20 39 14		0 31 51		4 32 21		8 32 51	10 35 4		14 35 34		18 36 4
1940	1	18 40 0	20 42 13	22 36 33	0 38 47	2 37 3	4 39 16	6 37 33	8 39 46	10 41 59	12 40 16	14 42 29	16 40 46
	2	18 43 57	20 46 10	22 40 30	0 42 43	2 41 0	4 43 13	6 41 30	8 43 43	10 45 56	12 44 13	14 46 26	16 44 42
	3	18 47 53	20 50 7	22 44 27	0 46 40	2 44 56	4 47 9	6 45 26	8 47 39	10 49 53	12 48 9	14 50 22	16 48 39
	4	18 51 50	20 54 3	22 48 23	0 50 36	2 48 53	4 51 6	6 49 23	8 51 36	10 53 49	12 52 6	14 54 19	16 52 35
	5	18 55 46	20 58 0	22 52 20	0 54 33	2 52 49	4 55 3	6 53 19	8 55 33	10 57 46	12 56 2	14 58 15	16 56 32
	6	18 59 43	21 1 56	22 56 16	0 58 29	2 56 46	4 58 59	6 57 16	8 59 29	11 1 42	12 59 59	15 2 12	17 0 29
	7	19 3 39	21 5 53	23 0 13	1 2 26	3 0 42	5 2 56	7 1 12	9 3 26	11 5 39	13 3 55	15 6 8	17 4 25
	8	19 7 36	21 9 49	23 4 9	1 6 22	3 4 39	5 6 52	7 5 9	9 7 22	11 9 35	13 7 52	15 10 5	17 8 22
	9	19 11 33	21 13 46	23 8 6	1 10 19	3 8 36	5 10 49	7 9 6	9 11 19	11 13 32	13 11 48	15 14 2	17 12 18
	10	19 15 29	21 17 42	23 12 2	1 14 16	3 12 32	5 14 45	7 13 2	9 15 15	11 17 28	13 15 45	15 17 58	17 16 15
	11	19 19 26	21 21 39	23 15 59	1 18 12	3 16 29	5 18 42	7 16 59	9 19 12	11 21 25	13 19 42	15 21 55	17 20 11
	12	19 23 22	21 25 35	23 19 56	1 22 9	3 20 25	5 22 38	7 20 55	9 23 8	11 25 22	13 23 38	15 25 51	17 24 8
	13	19 27 19	21 29 32	23 23 52	1 26 5	3 24 22	5 26 35	7 24 52	9 27 5	11 29 18	13 27 35	15 29 48	17 28 4
	14	19 31 15	21 33 29	23 27 49	1 30 2	3 28 18	5 30 32	7 28 48	9 31 2	11 33 15	13 31 31	15 33 44	17 32 1
	15	19 35 12	21 37 25	23 31 45	1 33 58	3 32 15	5 34 28	7 32 45	9 34 58	11 37 11	13 35 28	15 37 41	17 35 58
	16	19 39 9	21 41 22	23 35 42	1 37 55	3 36 11	5 38 25	7 36 41	9 38 55	11 41 8	13 39 24	15 41 37	17 39 54
	17	19 43 5	21 45 18	23 39 38	1 41 51	3 40 8	5 42 21	7 40 38	9 42 51	11 45 4	13 43 21	15 45 34	17 43 51
	18	19 47 2	21 49 15	23 43 35	1 45 48	3 44 5	5 46 18	7 44 35	9 46 48	11 49 1	13 47 17	15 49 31	17 47 47
	19	19 50 58	21 53 11	23 47 31	1 49 45	3 48 1	5 50 14	7 48 31	9 50 44	11 52 57	13 51 14	15 53 27	17 51 44
	20	19 54 55	21 57 8	23 51 28	1 53 41	3 51 58	5 54 11	7 52 28	9 54 41	11 56 54	13 55 10	15 57 24	17 55 40
	21	19 58 51	22 1 4	23 55 25	1 57 38	3 55 54	5 58 8	7 56 24	9 58 37	12 0 50	13 59 7	16 1 20	17 59 37
	22	20 2 48	22 5 1	23 59 21	2 1 34	3 59 51	6 2 4	8 0 21	10 2 34	12 4 47	14 3 4	16 5 17	18 3 34
	23	20 6 44	22 8 58	0 3 18	2 5 31	4 3 47	6 6 1	8 4 17	10 6 30	12 8 44	14 7 0	16 9 13	18 7 30
	24	20 10 41	22 12 54	0 7 14	2 9 27	4 7 44	6 9 57	8 8 14	10 10 27	12 12 40	14 10 57	16 13 10	18 11 27
	25	20 14 38	22 16 51	0 11 11	2 13 24	4 11 40	6 13 54	8 12 10	10 14 24	12 16 37	14 14 53	16 17 6	18 15 23
	26	20 18 34	22 20 47	0 15 7	2 17 20	4 15 37	6 17 50	8 16 7	10 18 20	12 20 33	14 18 50	16 21 3	18 19 20
	27	20 22 31	22 24 44	0 19 4	2 21 17	4 19 34	6 21 47	8 20 4	10 22 17	12 24 30	14 22 46	16 25 0	18 23 16
	28	20 26 27	22 28 40	0 23 0	2 25 14	4 23 30	6 25 43	8 24 0	10 26 13	12 28 26	14 26 43	16 28 56	18 27 13
	29	20 30 24	22 32 37	0 26 57	2 29 10	4 27 27	6 29 40	8 27 57	10 30 10	12 32 23	14 30 39	16 32 53	18 31 9
	30	20 34 20		0 30 53	2 33 7	4 31 23	6 33 36	8 31 53	10 34 6	12 36 19	14 34 36	16 36 49	18 35 6
	31	20 38 17		0 34 50		4 35 20		8 35 50	10 38 3		14 38 33		18 39 3
1941	1	18 42 59	20 45 12	22 35 36	0 37 49	2 36 5	4 38 19	6 36 35	8 38 49	10 41 2	12 39 18	14 41 31	16 39 48
	2	18 46 56	20 49 9	22 39 32	0 41 45	2 40 2	4 42 15	6 40 32	8 42 45	10 44 58	12 43 15	14 45 28	16 43 45
	3	18 50 52	20 53 5	22 43 29	0 45 42	2 43 59	4 46 12	6 44 29	8 46 42	10 48 55	12 47 11	14 49 25	16 47 41
	4	18 54 49	20 57 2	22 47 25	0 49 39	2 47 55	4 50 8	6 48 25	8 50 38	10 52 51	12 51 8	14 53 21	16 51 38
	5	18 58 45	21 0 59	22 51 22	0 53 35	2 51 52	4 54 5	6 52 22	8 54 35	10 56 48	12 55 5	14 57 18	16 55 34
	6	19 2 42	21 4 55	22 55 19	0 57 32	2 55 48	4 58 1	6 56 18	8 58 31	11 0 45	12 59 1	15 1 14	16 59 31
	7	19 6 38	21 8 52	22 59 15	1 1 28	2 59 45	5 1 58	7 0 15	9 2 28	11 4 41	13 2 58	15 5 11	17 3 27
	8	19 10 35	21 12 48	23 3 12	1 5 25	3 3 41	5 5 55	7 4 11	9 6 25	11 8 38	13 6 54	15 9 7	17 7 24
	9	19 14 32	21 16 45	23 7 8	1 9 21	3 7 38	5 9 51	7 8 8	9 10 21	11 12 34	13 10 51	15 13 4	17 11 21
	10	19 18 28	21 20 41	23 11 5	1 13 18	3 11 34	5 13 48	7 12 4	9 14 18	11 16 31	13 14 47	15 17 0	17 15 17
	11	19 22 25	21 24 38	23 15 1	1 17 14	3 15 31	5 17 44	7 16 1	9 18 14	11 20 27	13 18 44	15 20 57	17 19 14
	12	19 26 21	21 28 34	23 18 58	1 21 11	3 19 28	5 21 41	7 19 58	9 22 11	11 24 24	13 22 40	15 24 54	17 23 10
	13	19 30 18	21 32 31	23 22 54	1 25 8	3 23 24	5 25 37	7 23 54	9 26 7	11 28 20	13 26 37	15 28 50	17 27 7
	14	19 34 14	21 36 28	23 26 51	1 29 4	3 27 21	5 29 34	7 27 51	9 30 4	11 32 17	13 30 34	15 32 47	17 31 3
	15	19 38 11	21 40 24	23 30 48	1 33 1	3 31 17	5 33 31	7 31 47	9 34 0	11 36 14	13 34 30	15 36 43	17 35 0
	16	19 42 7	21 44 21	23 34 44	1 36 57	3 35 14	5 37 27	7 35 44	9 37 57	11 40 10	13 38 27	15 40 40	17 38 56
	17	19 46 4	21 48 17	23 38 41	1 40 54	3 39 10	5 41 24	7 39 40	9 41 54	11 44 7	13 42 23	15 44 36	17 42 53
	18	19 50 1	21 52 14	23 42 37	1 44 50	3 43 7	5 45 20	7 43 37	9 45 50	11 48 3	13 46 20	15 48 33	17 46 50
	19	19 53 57	21 56 10	23 46 34	1 48 47	3 47 3	5 49 17	7 47 33	9 49 47	11 52 0	13 50 16	15 52 29	17 50 46
	20	19 57 54	22 0 7	23 50 30	1 52 43	3 51 0	5 53 13	7 51 30	9 53 43	11 55 56	13 54 13	15 56 26	17 54 43
	21	20 1 50	22 4 3	23 54 27	1 56 40	3 54 57	5 57 10	7 55 27	9 57 40	11 59 53	13 58 9	16 0 23	17 58 39
	22	20 5 47	22 8 0	23 58 23	2 0 37	3 58 53	6 1 6	7 59 23	10 1 36	12 3 49	14 2 6	16 4 19	18 2 36
	23	20 9 43	22 11 57	0 2 20	2 4 33	4 2 50	6 5 3	8 3 20	10 5 33	12 7 46	14 6 3	16 8 16	18 6 32
	24	20 13 40	22 15 53	0 6 17	2 8 30	4 6 46	6 9 0	8 7 16	10 9 29	12 11 42	14 9 59	16 12 12	18 10 29
	25	20 17 36	22 19 50	0 10 13	2 12 26	4 10 43	6 12 56	8 11 13	10 13 26	12 15 39	14 13 56	16 16 9	18 14 26
	26	20 21 33	22 23 46	0 14 10	2 16 23	4 14 39	6 16 53	8 15 9	10 17 22	12 19 36	14 17 52	16 20 5	18 18 22
	27	20 25 30	22 27 43	0 18 6	2 20 19	4 18 36	6 20 49	8 19 6	10 21 19	12 23 32	14 21 49	16 24 2	18 22 19
	28	20 29 26	22 31 39	0 22 3	2 24 16	4 22 32	6 24 46	8 23 2	10 25 16	12 27 29	14 25 45	16 27 58	18 26 15
	29	20 33 23		0 25 59	2 28 12	4 26 29	6 28 42	8 26 59	10 29 12	12 31 25	14 29 42	16 31 55	18 30 12
	30	20 37 19		0 29 56	2 32 9	4 30 26	6 32 39	8 30 56	10 33 9	12 35 22	14 33 38	16 35 52	18 34 8
	31	20 41 16		0 33 52		4 34 22		8 34 52	10 37 5		14 37 35		18 38 5

YEAR		JAN	FEB	MAR	APR	MAY	JUN	JUL	AUG	SEP	OCT	NOV	DEC
1942	1	18 42 1	20 44 15	22 34 38	0 36 51	2 35 8	4 37 21	6 35 38	8 37 51	10 40 4	12 38 21	14 40 34	16 38 51
	2	18 45 58	20 48 11	22 38 35	0 40 48	2 39 4	4 41 18	6 39 34	8 41 48	10 44 1	12 42 17	14 44 30	16 42 47
	3	18 49 55	20 52 8	22 42 31	0 44 44	2 43 1	4 45 14	6 43 31	8 45 44	10 47 57	12 46 14	14 48 27	16 46 44
	4	18 53 51	20 56 4	22 46 28	0 48 41	2 46 58	4 49 11	6 47 27	8 49 41	10 51 54	12 50 10	14 52 24	16 50 40
	5	18 57 48	21 0 1	22 50 24	0 52 37	2 50 54	4 53 7	6 51 24	8 53 37	10 55 50	12 54 7	14 56 20	16 54 37
	6	19 1 44	21 3 57	22 54 21	0 56 34	2 54 51	4 57 4	6 55 21	8 57 34	10 59 47	12 58 3	15 0 17	16 58 33
	7	19 5 41	21 7 54	22 58 17	1 0 31	2 58 47	5 1 0	6 59 17	9 1 30	11 3 43	13 2 0	15 4 13	17 2 30
	8	19 9 37	21 11 51	23 2 14	1 4 27	3 2 44	5 4 57	7 3 14	9 5 27	11 7 40	13 5 57	15 8 10	17 6 26
	9	19 13 34	21 15 47	23 6 11	1 8 24	3 6 40	5 8 54	7 7 10	9 9 23	11 11 37	13 9 53	15 12 6	17 10 23
	10	19 17 30	21 19 44	23 10 7	1 12 20	3 10 37	5 12 50	7 11 7	9 13 20	11 15 33	13 13 50	15 16 3	17 14 20
	11	19 21 27	21 23 40	23 14 4	1 16 17	3 14 33	5 16 47	7 15 3	9 17 17	11 19 30	13 17 46	15 19 59	17 18 16
	12	19 25 24	21 27 37	23 18 0	1 20 13	3 18 30	5 20 43	7 19 0	9 21 13	11 23 26	13 21 43	15 23 56	17 22 13
	13	19 29 20	21 31 33	23 21 57	1 24 10	3 22 26	5 24 40	7 22 56	9 25 10	11 27 23	13 25 39	15 27 53	17 26 9
	14	19 33 17	21 35 30	23 25 53	1 28 6	3 26 23	5 28 36	7 26 53	9 29 6	11 31 19	13 29 36	15 31 49	17 30 6
	15	19 37 13	21 39 26	23 29 50	1 32 3	3 30 20	5 32 33	7 30 50	9 33 3	11 35 16	13 33 32	15 35 46	17 34 2
	16	19 41 10	21 43 23	23 33 46	1 36 0	3 34 16	5 36 29	7 34 46	9 36 59	11 39 12	13 37 29	15 39 42	17 37 59
	17	19 45 6	21 47 20	23 37 43	1 39 56	3 38 13	5 40 26	7 38 43	9 40 56	11 43 9	13 41 26	15 43 39	17 41 55
	18	19 49 3	21 51 16	23 41 40	1 43 53	3 42 9	5 44 23	7 42 39	9 44 52	11 47 6	13 45 22	15 47 35	17 45 52
	19	19 52 59	21 55 13	23 45 36	1 47 49	3 46 6	5 48 19	7 46 36	9 48 49	11 51 2	13 49 19	15 51 32	17 49 49
	20	19 56 56	21 59 9	23 49 33	1 51 46	3 50 2	5 52 16	7 50 32	9 52 46	11 54 59	13 53 15	15 55 28	17 53 45
	21	20 0 53	22 3 6	23 53 29	1 55 42	3 53 59	5 56 12	7 54 29	9 56 42	11 58 55	13 57 12	15 59 25	17 57 42
	22	20 4 49	22 7 2	23 57 26	1 59 39	3 57 56	6 0 9	7 58 25	10 0 39	12 2 52	14 1 8	16 3 22	18 1 38
	23	20 8 46	22 10 59	0 1 22	2 3 35	4 1 52	6 4 5	8 2 22	10 4 35	12 6 48	14 5 5	16 7 18	18 5 35
	24	20 12 42	22 14 55	0 5 19	2 7 32	4 5 49	6 8 2	8 6 19	10 8 32	12 10 45	14 9 1	16 11 15	18 9 31
	25	20 16 39	22 18 52	0 9 15	2 11 29	4 9 45	6 11 58	8 10 15	10 12 28	12 14 41	14 12 58	16 15 11	18 13 28
	26	20 20 35	22 22 49	0 13 12	2 15 25	4 13 42	6 15 55	8 14 12	10 16 25	12 18 38	14 16 55	16 19 8	18 17 24
	27	20 24 32	22 26 45	0 17 9	2 19 22	4 17 38	6 19 52	8 18 8	10 20 21	12 22 35	14 20 51	16 23 4	18 21 21
	28	20 28 28	22 30 42	0 21 5	2 23 18	4 21 35	6 23 48	8 22 5	10 24 18	12 26 31	14 24 48	16 27 1	18 25 18
	29	20 32 25		0 25 2	2 27 15	4 25 31	6 27 45	8 26 1	10 28 15	12 30 28	14 28 44	16 30 57	18 29 14
	30	20 36 22		0 28 58	2 31 11	4 29 28	6 31 41	8 29 58	10 32 11	12 34 24	14 32 41	16 34 54	18 33 11
	31	20 40 18		0 32 55		4 33 25		8 33 54	10 36 8		14 36 37		18 37 7
1943	1	18 41 4	20 43 17	22 33 41	0 35 54	2 34 10	4 36 23	6 34 40	8 36 53	10 39 7	12 37 23	14 39 36	16 37 53
	2	18 45 0	20 47 14	22 37 37	0 39 50	2 38 7	4 40 20	6 38 37	8 40 50	10 43 3	12 41 20	14 43 33	16 41 50
	3	18 48 57	20 51 10	22 41 34	0 43 47	2 42 3	4 44 17	6 42 33	8 44 47	10 47 0	12 45 16	14 47 29	16 45 46
	4	18 52 53	20 55 7	22 45 30	0 47 43	2 46 0	4 48 13	6 46 30	8 48 43	10 50 56	12 49 13	14 51 26	16 49 43
	5	18 56 50	20 59 3	22 49 27	0 51 40	2 49 56	4 52 10	6 50 26	8 52 40	10 54 53	12 53 9	14 55 23	16 53 39
	6	19 0 47	21 3 0	22 53 23	0 55 36	2 53 53	4 56 6	6 54 23	8 56 36	10 58 49	12 57 6	14 59 19	16 57 36
	7	19 4 43	21 6 56	22 57 20	0 59 33	2 57 50	5 0 3	6 58 20	9 0 33	11 2 46	13 1 2	15 3 16	17 1 32
	8	19 8 40	21 10 53	23 1 16	1 3 30	3 1 46	5 3 59	7 2 16	9 4 29	11 6 42	13 4 59	15 7 12	17 5 29
	9	19 12 36	21 14 49	23 5 13	1 7 26	3 5 43	5 7 56	7 6 13	9 8 26	11 10 39	13 8 56	15 11 9	17 9 25
	10	19 16 33	21 18 46	23 9 10	1 11 23	3 9 39	5 11 52	7 10 9	9 12 22	11 14 36	13 12 52	15 15 5	17 13 22
	11	19 20 29	21 22 43	23 13 6	1 15 19	3 13 36	5 15 49	7 14 6	9 16 19	11 18 32	13 16 49	15 19 2	17 17 19
	12	19 24 26	21 26 39	23 17 3	1 19 16	3 17 32	5 19 46	7 18 2	9 20 16	11 22 29	13 20 45	15 22 58	17 21 15
	13	19 28 22	21 30 36	23 20 59	1 23 12	3 21 29	5 23 42	7 21 59	9 24 12	11 26 25	13 24 42	15 26 55	17 25 12
	14	19 32 19	21 34 32	23 24 56	1 27 9	3 25 25	5 27 39	7 25 55	9 28 9	11 30 22	13 28 38	15 30 51	17 29 8
	15	19 36 16	21 38 29	23 28 52	1 31 5	3 29 22	5 31 35	7 29 52	9 32 5	11 34 18	13 32 35	15 34 48	17 33 5
	16	19 40 12	21 42 25	23 32 49	1 35 2	3 33 19	5 35 32	7 33 49	9 36 2	11 38 15	13 36 31	15 38 45	17 37 1
	17	19 44 9	21 46 22	23 36 45	1 38 59	3 37 15	5 39 28	7 37 45	9 39 58	11 42 11	13 40 28	15 42 41	17 40 58
	18	19 48 5	21 50 18	23 40 42	1 42 55	3 41 12	5 43 25	7 41 42	9 43 55	11 46 8	13 44 25	15 46 38	17 44 54
	19	19 52 2	21 54 15	23 44 38	1 46 52	3 45 8	5 47 21	7 45 38	9 47 51	11 50 5	13 48 21	15 50 34	17 48 51
	20	19 55 58	21 58 12	23 48 35	1 50 48	3 49 5	5 51 18	7 49 35	9 51 48	11 54 1	13 52 18	15 54 31	17 52 48
	21	19 59 55	22 2 8	23 52 32	1 54 45	3 53 1	5 55 15	7 53 31	9 55 44	11 57 58	13 56 14	15 58 27	17 56 44
	22	20 3 51	22 6 5	23 56 28	1 58 41	3 56 58	5 59 11	7 57 28	9 59 41	12 1 54	14 0 11	16 2 24	18 0 41
	23	20 7 48	22 10 1	0 0 25	2 2 38	4 0 54	6 3 8	8 1 24	10 3 38	12 5 51	14 4 7	16 6 21	18 4 37
	24	20 11 45	22 13 58	0 4 21	2 6 34	4 4 51	6 7 4	8 5 21	10 7 34	12 9 47	14 8 4	16 10 17	18 8 34
	25	20 15 41	22 17 54	0 8 18	2 10 31	4 8 48	6 11 1	8 9 18	10 11 31	12 13 44	14 12 0	16 14 14	18 12 30
	26	20 19 38	22 21 51	0 12 14	2 14 27	4 12 44	6 14 57	8 13 14	10 15 27	12 17 40	14 15 57	16 18 10	18 16 27
	27	20 23 34	22 25 47	0 16 11	2 18 24	4 16 41	6 18 54	8 17 11	10 19 24	12 21 37	14 19 54	16 22 7	18 20 23
	28	20 27 31	22 29 44	0 20 7	2 22 21	4 20 37	6 22 50	8 21 7	10 23 20	12 25 33	14 23 50	16 26 3	18 24 20
	29	20 31 27		0 24 4	2 26 17	4 24 34	6 26 47	8 25 4	10 27 17	12 29 30	14 27 47	16 30 0	18 28 17
	30	20 35 24		0 28 1	2 30 14	4 28 30	6 30 44	8 29 0	10 31 13	12 33 27	14 31 43	16 33 56	18 32 13
	31	20 39 20		0 31 57		4 32 27		8 32 57	10 35 10		14 35 40		18 36 10
1944	1	18 40 6	20 42 19	22 36 40	0 38 53	2 37 9	4 39 23	6 37 39	8 39 52	10 42 6	12 40 22	14 42 35	16 40 52
	2	18 44 3	20 46 16	22 40 36	0 42 49	2 41 6	4 43 19	6 41 36	8 43 49	10 46 2	12 44 19	14 46 32	16 44 49
	3	18 47 59	20 50 13	22 44 33	0 46 46	2 45 2	4 47 16	6 45 32	8 47 46	10 49 59	12 48 15	14 50 28	16 48 45
	4	18 51 56	20 54 9	22 48 29	0 50 42	2 48 59	4 51 12	6 49 29	8 51 42	10 53 55	12 52 12	14 54 25	16 52 42
	5	18 55 52	20 58 6	22 52 26	0 54 39	2 52 55	4 55 9	6 53 25	8 55 39	10 57 52	12 56 8	14 58 22	16 56 38
	6	18 59 49	21 2 2	22 56 22	0 58 35	2 56 52	4 59 5	6 57 22	8 59 35	11 1 48	13 0 5	15 2 18	17 0 35
	7	19 3 46	21 5 59	23 0 19	1 2 32	3 0 49	5 3 2	7 1 19	9 3 32	11 5 45	13 4 2	15 6 15	17 4 31
	8	19 7 42	21 9 55	23 4 15	1 6 29	3 4 45	5 6 58	7 5 15	9 7 28	11 9 42	13 7 58	15 10 11	17 8 28
	9	19 11 39	21 13 52	23 8 12	1 10 25	3 8 42	5 10 55	7 9 12	9 11 25	11 13 38	13 11 55	15 14 8	17 12 25
	10	19 15 35	21 17 48	23 12 9	1 14 22	3 12 38	5 14 52	7 13 8	9 15 21	11 17 35	13 15 51	15 18 4	17 16 21
	11	19 19 32	21 21 45	23 16 5	1 18 18	3 16 35	5 18 48	7 17 5	9 19 18	11 21 31	13 19 48	15 22 1	17 20 18
	12	19 23 28	21 25 42	23 20 2	1 22 15	3 20 31	5 22 45	7 21 1	9 23 15	11 25 28	13 23 44	15 25 57	17 24 14
	13	19 27 25	21 29 38	23 23 58	1 26 11	3 24 28	5 26 41	7 24 58	9 27 11	11 29 24	13 27 41	15 29 54	17 28 11
	14	19 31 21	21 33 35	23 27 55	1 30 8	3 28 24	5 30 38	7 28 54	9 31 8	11 33 21	13 31 37	15 33 51	17 32 7
	15	19 35 18	21 37 31	23 31 51	1 34 4	3 32 21	5 34 34	7 32 51	9 35 4	11 37 17	13 35 34	15 37 47	17 36 4
	16	19 39 15	21 41 28	23 35 48	1 38 1	3 36 18	5 38 31	7 36 48	9 39 1	11 41 14	13 39 31	15 41 44	17 40 0
	17	19 43 11	21 45 24	23 39 44	1 41 58	3 40 14	5 42 27	7 40 44	9 42 57	11 45 10	13 43 27	15 45 40	17 43 57
	18	19 47 8	21 49 21	23 43 41	1 45 54	3 44 11	5 46 24	7 44 41	9 46 54	11 49 7	13 47 24	15 49 37	17 47 54
	19	19 51 4	21 53 17	23 47 37	1 49 51	3 48 7	5 50 21	7 48 37	9 50 50	11 53 4	13 51 20	15 53 33	17 51 50
	20	19 55 1	21 57 14	23 51 34	1 53 47	3 52 4	5 54 17	7 52 34	9 54 47	11 57 0	13 55 17	15 57 30	17 55 47
	21	19 58 57	22 1 11	23 55 31	1 57 44	3 56 0	5 58 14	7 56 30	9 58 44	12 0 57	13 59 13	16 1 26	17 59 43
	22	20 2 54	22 5 7	23 59 27	2 1 40	3 59 57	6 2 10	8 0 27	10 2 40	12 4 53	14 3 10	16 5 23	18 3 40
	23	20 6 50	22 9 4	0 3 24	2 5 37	4 3 53	6 6 7	8 4 23	10 6 37	12 8 50	14 7 6	16 9 20	18 7 36
	24	20 10 47	22 13 0	0 7 20	2 9 33	4 7 50	6 10 3	8 8 20	10 10 33	12 12 46	14 11 3	16 13 16	18 11 33
	25	20 14 44	22 16 57	0 11 17	2 13 30	4 11 47	6 14 0	8 12 17	10 14 30	12 16 43	14 14 59	16 17 13	18 15 29
	26	20 18 40	22 20 53	0 15 13	2 17 27	4 15 43	6 17 56	8 16 13	10 18 26	12 20 39	14 18 56	16 21 9	18 19 26
	27	20 22 37	22 24 50	0 19 10	2 21 23	4 19 40	6 21 53	8 20 10	10 22 23	12 24 36	14 22 53	16 25 6	18 23 23
	28	20 26 33	22 28 46	0 23 6	2 25 20	4 23 36	6 25 50	8 24 6	10 26 19	12 28 33	14 26 49	16 29 2	18 27 19
	29	20 30 30	22 32 43	0 27 3	2 29 16	4 27 33	6 29 46	8 28 3	10 30 16	12 32 29	14 30 46	16 32 59	18 31 16
	30	20 34 26		0 31 0	2 33 13	4 31 29	6 33 43	8 31 59	10 34 13	12 36 26	14 34 42	16 36 55	18 35 12
	31	20 38 23		0 34 56		4 35 26		8 35 56	10 38 9		14 38 39		18 39 9
1945	1	18 43 5	20 45 19	22 35 42	0 37 55	2 36 12	4 38 25	6 36 42	8 38 55	10 41 8	12 39 25	14 41 38	16 39 55
	2	18 47 2	20 49 15	22 39 39	0 41 52	2 40 8	4 42 22	6 40 38	8 42 52	10 45 5	12 43 21	14 45 35	16 43 51
	3	18 50 58	20 53 12	22 43 35	0 45 48	2 44 5	4 46 18	6 44 35	8 46 48	10 49 1	12 47 18	14 49 31	16 47 48
	4	18 54 55	20 57 8	22 47 32	0 49 45	2 48 2	4 50 15	6 48 31	8 50 45	10 52 58	12 51 15	14 53 28	16 51 44
	5	18 58 52	21 1 5	22 51 28	0 53 41	2 51 58	4 54 11	6 52 28	8 54 41	10 56 54	12 55 11	14 57 24	16 55 41
	6	19 2 48	21 5 1	22 55 25	0 57 38	2 55 55	4 58 8	6 56 25	8 58 38	11 0 51	12 59 8	15 1 21	16 59 37
	7	19 6 45	21 8 58	22 59 21	1 1 35	2 59 51	5 2 4	7 0 21	9 2 34	11 4 48	13 3 4	15 5 17	17 3 34
	8	19 10 41	21 12 54	23 3 18	1 5 31	3 3 48	5 6 1	7 4 18	9 6 31	11 8 44	13 7 1	15 9 14	17 7 31
	9	19 14 38	21 16 51	23 7 15	1 9 28	3 7 44	5 9 58	7 8 14	9 10 28	11 12 41	13 10 57	15 13 10	17 11 27
	10	19 18 34	21 20 48	23 11 11	1 13 24	3 11 41	5 13 54	7 12 11	9 14 24	11 16 37	13 14 54	15 17 7	17 15 24
	11	19 22 31	21 24 44	23 15 8	1 17 21	3 15 37	5 17 51	7 16 7	9 18 21	11 20 34	13 18 50	15 21 4	17 19 20
	12	19 26 27	21 28 41	23 19 4	1 21 17	3 19 34	5 21 47	7 20 4	9 22 17	11 24 30	13 22 47	15 25 0	17 23 17
	13	19 30 24	21 32 37	23 23 1	1 25 14	3 23 31	5 25 44	7 24 1	9 26 14	11 28 27	13 26 43	15 28 57	17 27 13
	14	19 34 21	21 36 34	23 26 57	1 29 10	3 27 27	5 29 40	7 27 57	9 30 10	11 32 23	13 30 40	15 32 53	17 31 10
	15	19 38 17	21 40 30	23 30 54	1 33 7	3 31 24	5 33 37	7 31 54	9 34 7	11 36 20	13 34 37	15 36 50	17 35 6
	16	19 42 14	21 44 27	23 34 50	1 37 4	3 35 20	5 37 33	7 35 50	9 38 3	11 40 17	13 38 33	15 40 46	17 39 3
	17	19 46 10	21 48 23	23 38 47	1 41 0	3 39 17	5 41 30	7 39 47	9 42 0	11 44 13	13 42 30	15 44 43	17 43 0
	18	19 50 7	21 52 20	23 42 44	1 44 57	3 43 13	5 45 27	7 43 43	9 45 57	11 48 10	13 46 26	15 48 39	17 46 56
	19	19 54 3	21 56 17	23 46 40	1 48 53	3 47 10	5 49 23	7 47 40	9 49 53	11 52 6	13 50 23	15 52 36	17 50 53
	20	19 58 0	22 0 13	23 50 37	1 52 50	3 51 6	5 53 20	7 51 36	9 53 50	11 56 3	13 54 19	15 56 33	17 54 49
	21	20 1 56	22 4 10	23 54 33	1 56 46	3 55 3	5 57 16	7 55 33	9 57 46	11 59 59	13 58 16	16 0 29	17 58 46
	22	20 5 53	22 8 6	23 58 30	2 0 43	3 59 0	6 1 13	7 59 30	10 1 43	12 3 56	14 2 12	16 4 26	18 2 42
	23	20 9 50	22 12 3	0 2 26	2 4 39	4 2 56	6 5 9	8 3 26	10 5 39	12 7 52	14 6 9	16 8 22	18 6 39
	24	20 13 46	22 15 59	0 6 23	2 8 36	4 6 53	6 9 6	8 7 23	10 9 36	12 11 49	14 10 6	16 12 19	18 10 36
	25	20 17 43	22 19 56	0 10 19	2 12 33	4 10 49	6 13 2	8 11 19	10 13 32	12 15 46	14 14 2	16 16 15	18 14 32
	26	20 21 39	22 23 52	0 14 16	2 16 29	4 14 46	6 16 59	8 15 16	10 17 29	12 19 42	14 17 59	16 20 12	18 18 29
	27	20 25 36	22 27 49	0 18 12	2 20 26	4 18 42	6 20 56	8 19 12	10 21 25	12 23 39	14 21 55	16 24 8	18 22 25
	28	20 29 32	22 31 46	0 22 9	2 24 22	4 22 39	6 24 52	8 23 9	10 25 22	12 27 35	14 25 52	16 28 5	18 26 22
	29	20 33 29		0 26 6	2 28 19	4 26 35	6 28 49	8 27 5	10 29 19	12 31 32	14 29 48	16 32 2	18 30 18
	30	20 37 26		0 30 2	2 32 15	4 30 32	6 32 45	8 31 2	10 33 15	12 35 28	14 33 45	16 35 58	18 34 15
	31	20 41 22		0 33 59		4 34 29		8 34 59	10 37 12		14 37 41		18 38 11

YEAR	JAN	FEB	MAR	APR	MAY	JUN	JUL	SEP	AUG	OCT	NOV	DEC
1946 1	18 42 8	20 44 21	22 34 45	0 36 58	2 35 15	4 37 28	6 35 45	8 37 58	10 40 11	12 38 28	14 40 41	16 38 57
2	18 46 5	20 48 18	22 38 41	0 40 54	2 39 11	4 41 24	6 39 41	8 41 54	10 44 8	12 42 24	14 44 37	16 42 54
3	18 50 1	20 52 14	22 42 38	0 44 51	2 43 8	4 45 21	6 43 38	8 45 51	10 48 4	12 46 21	14 48 34	16 46 51
4	18 53 58	20 56 11	22 46 34	0 48 48	2 47 4	4 49 17	6 47 34	8 49 47	10 52 1	12 50 17	14 52 30	16 50 47
5	18 57 54	21 0 7	22 50 31	0 52 44	2 51 1	4 53 14	6 51 31	8 53 44	10 55 57	12 54 14	14 56 27	16 54 44
6	19 1 51	21 4 4	22 54 28	0 56 41	2 54 57	4 57 11	6 55 27	8 57 41	10 59 54	12 58 10	15 0 24	16 58 40
7	19 5 47	21 8 1	22 58 24	1 0 37	2 58 54	5 1 7	6 59 24	9 1 37	11 3 50	13 2 7	15 4 20	17 2 37
8	19 9 44	21 11 57	23 2 21	1 4 34	3 2 50	5 5 4	7 3 20	9 5 34	11 7 47	13 6 3	15 8 17	17 6 33
9	19 13 40	21 15 54	23 6 17	1 8 30	3 6 47	5 9 0	7 7 17	9 9 30	11 11 43	13 10 0	15 12 13	17 10 30
10	19 17 37	21 19 50	23 10 14	1 12 27	3 10 44	5 12 57	7 11 14	9 13 27	11 15 40	13 13 57	15 16 10	17 14 26
11	19 21 34	21 23 47	23 14 10	1 16 23	3 14 40	5 16 53	7 15 10	9 17 23	11 19 37	13 17 53	15 20 6	17 18 23
12	19 25 30	21 27 43	23 18 7	1 20 20	3 18 37	5 20 50	7 19 7	9 21 20	11 23 33	13 21 50	15 24 3	17 22 20
13	19 29 27	21 31 40	23 22 3	1 24 17	3 22 33	5 24 46	7 23 3	9 25 16	11 27 30	13 25 46	15 27 59	17 26 16
14	19 33 23	21 35 36	23 26 0	1 28 13	3 26 30	5 28 43	7 27 0	9 29 13	11 31 26	13 29 43	15 31 56	17 30 13
15	19 37 20	21 39 33	23 29 57	1 32 10	3 30 26	5 32 40	7 30 56	9 33 10	11 35 23	13 33 39	15 35 53	17 34 9
16	19 41 16	21 43 30	23 33 53	1 36 6	3 34 23	5 36 36	7 34 53	9 37 6	11 39 19	13 37 36	15 39 49	17 38 6
17	19 45 13	21 47 26	23 37 50	1 40 3	3 38 19	5 40 33	7 38 49	9 41 3	11 43 16	13 41 32	15 43 46	17 42 2
18	19 49 9	21 51 23	23 41 46	1 43 59	3 42 16	5 44 29	7 42 46	9 44 59	11 47 12	13 45 29	15 47 42	17 45 59
19	19 53 6	21 55 19	23 45 43	1 47 56	3 46 13	5 48 26	7 46 43	9 48 56	11 51 9	13 49 26	15 51 39	17 49 56
20	19 57 3	21 59 16	23 49 39	1 51 52	3 50 9	5 52 22	7 50 39	9 52 52	11 55 6	13 53 22	15 55 35	17 53 52
21	20 0 59	22 3 12	23 53 36	1 55 49	3 54 6	5 56 19	7 54 36	9 56 49	11 59 2	13 57 19	15 59 32	17 57 49
22	20 4 56	22 7 9	23 57 32	1 59 46	3 58 2	6 0 16	7 58 32	10 0 45	12 2 59	14 1 15	16 3 28	18 1 45
23	20 8 52	22 11 5	0 1 29	2 3 42	4 1 59	6 4 12	8 2 29	10 4 42	12 6 55	14 5 12	16 7 25	18 5 42
24	20 12 49	22 15 2	0 5 26	2 7 39	4 5 55	6 8 9	8 6 25	10 8 39	12 10 52	14 9 8	16 11 22	18 9 38
25	20 16 45	22 18 59	0 9 22	2 11 35	4 9 52	6 12 5	8 10 22	10 12 35	12 14 48	14 13 5	16 15 18	18 13 35
26	20 20 42	22 22 55	0 13 19	2 15 32	4 13 48	6 16 2	8 14 18	10 16 32	12 18 45	14 17 1	16 19 15	18 17 31
27	20 24 38	22 26 52	0 17 15	2 19 28	4 17 45	6 19 58	8 18 15	10 20 28	12 22 41	14 20 58	16 23 11	18 21 28
28	20 28 35	22 30 48	0 21 12	2 23 25	4 21 42	6 23 55	8 22 12	10 24 25	12 26 38	14 24 55	16 27 8	18 25 25
29	20 32 32		0 25 8	2 27 21	4 25 38	6 27 51	8 26 8	10 28 21	12 30 34	14 28 51	16 31 4	18 29 21
30	20 36 28		0 29 5	2 31 18	4 29 35	6 31 48	8 30 5	10 32 18	12 34 31	14 32 48	16 35 1	18 33 18
31	20 40 25		0 33 1		4 33 31		8 34 1	10 36 14		14 36 44		18 37 14
1947 1	18 41 11	20 43 24	22 33 48	0 36 1	2 34 17	4 36 31	6 34 47	8 37 1	10 39 14	12 37 30	14 39 44	16 38 0
2	18 45 7	20 47 21	22 37 44	0 39 57	2 38 14	4 40 27	6 38 44	8 40 57	10 43 10	12 41 27	14 43 40	16 41 57
3	18 49 4	20 51 17	22 41 41	0 43 54	2 42 10	4 44 24	6 42 40	8 44 54	10 47 7	12 45 24	14 47 37	16 45 53
4	18 53 0	20 55 14	22 45 37	0 47 50	2 46 7	4 48 20	6 46 37	8 48 50	10 51 4	12 49 20	14 51 33	16 49 50
5	18 56 57	20 59 10	22 49 34	0 51 47	2 50 4	4 52 17	6 50 34	8 52 47	10 55 0	12 53 17	14 55 30	16 53 47
6	19 0 54	21 3 7	22 53 30	0 55 44	2 54 0	4 56 13	6 54 30	8 56 43	10 58 57	12 57 13	14 59 26	16 57 43
7	19 4 50	21 7 3	22 57 27	0 59 40	2 57 57	5 0 10	6 58 27	9 0 40	11 2 53	13 1 10	15 3 23	17 1 40
8	19 8 47	21 11 0	23 1 23	1 3 37	3 1 53	5 4 7	7 2 23	9 4 37	11 6 50	13 5 6	15 7 20	17 5 36
9	19 12 43	21 14 57	23 5 20	1 7 33	3 5 50	5 8 3	7 6 20	9 8 33	11 10 46	13 9 3	15 11 16	17 9 33
10	19 16 40	21 18 53	23 9 17	1 11 30	3 9 46	5 12 0	7 10 16	9 12 30	11 14 43	13 12 59	15 15 13	17 13 29
11	19 20 36	21 22 50	23 13 13	1 15 26	3 13 43	5 15 56	7 14 13	9 16 26	11 18 39	13 16 56	15 19 9	17 17 26
12	19 24 33	21 26 46	23 17 10	1 19 23	3 17 39	5 19 53	7 18 9	9 20 23	11 22 36	13 20 53	15 23 6	17 21 22
13	19 28 29	21 30 43	23 21 6	1 23 19	3 21 36	5 23 49	7 22 6	9 24 19	11 26 33	13 24 49	15 27 2	17 25 19
14	19 32 26	21 34 39	23 25 3	1 27 16	3 25 33	5 27 46	7 26 3	9 28 16	11 30 29	13 28 46	15 30 59	17 29 16
15	19 36 23	21 38 36	23 28 59	1 31 13	3 29 29	5 31 42	7 29 59	9 32 12	11 34 26	13 32 42	15 34 55	17 33 12
16	19 40 19	21 42 32	23 32 56	1 35 9	3 33 26	5 35 39	7 33 56	9 36 9	11 38 22	13 36 39	15 38 52	17 37 9
17	19 44 16	21 46 29	23 36 52	1 39 6	3 37 22	5 39 36	7 37 52	9 40 6	11 42 19	13 40 35	15 42 49	17 41 5
18	19 48 12	21 50 26	23 40 49	1 43 2	3 41 19	5 43 32	7 41 49	9 44 2	11 46 15	13 44 32	15 46 45	17 45 2
19	19 52 9	21 54 22	23 44 46	1 46 59	3 45 15	5 47 29	7 45 45	9 47 59	11 50 12	13 48 28	15 50 42	17 48 58
20	19 56 5	21 58 19	23 48 42	1 50 55	3 49 12	5 51 25	7 49 42	9 51 55	11 54 8	13 52 25	15 54 38	17 52 55
21	20 0 2	22 2 15	23 52 39	1 54 52	3 53 8	5 55 22	7 53 39	9 55 52	11 58 5	13 56 22	15 58 35	17 56 52
22	20 3 58	22 6 12	23 56 35	1 58 48	3 57 5	5 59 18	7 57 35	9 59 48	12 2 1	14 0 18	16 2 31	18 0 48
23	20 7 55	22 10 8	0 0 32	2 2 45	4 1 2	6 3 15	8 1 32	10 3 45	12 5 58	14 4 15	16 6 28	18 4 45
24	20 11 52	22 14 5	0 4 28	2 6 41	4 4 58	6 7 11	8 5 28	10 7 41	12 9 55	14 8 11	16 10 24	18 8 41
25	20 15 48	22 18 1	0 8 25	2 10 38	4 8 55	6 11 8	8 9 25	10 11 38	12 13 51	14 12 8	16 14 21	18 12 38
26	20 19 45	22 21 58	0 12 21	2 14 35	4 12 51	6 15 5	8 13 21	10 15 35	12 17 48	14 16 4	16 18 18	18 16 34
27	20 23 41	22 25 54	0 16 18	2 18 31	4 16 48	6 19 1	8 17 18	10 19 31	12 21 44	14 20 1	16 22 14	18 20 31
28	20 27 38	22 29 51	0 20 15	2 22 28	4 20 44	6 22 58	8 21 14	10 23 28	12 25 41	14 23 57	16 26 11	18 24 27
29	20 31 34		0 24 11	2 26 24	4 24 41	6 26 54	8 25 11	10 27 24	12 29 37	14 27 54	16 30 7	18 28 24
30	20 35 31		0 28 8	2 30 21	4 28 38	6 30 51	8 29 8	10 31 21	12 33 34	14 31 51	16 34 4	18 32 21
31	20 39 27		0 32 4		4 32 34		8 33 4	10 35 17		14 35 47		18 36 17
1948 1	18 40 14	20 42 27	22 36 47	0 39 0	2 37 17	4 39 30	6 37 47	8 40 0	10 42 13	12 40 30	14 42 43	16 41 0
2	18 44 10	20 46 23	22 40 44	0 42 57	2 41 13	4 43 27	6 41 43	8 43 57	10 46 10	12 44 27	14 46 40	16 44 56
3	18 48 7	20 50 20	22 44 40	0 46 53	2 45 10	4 47 23	6 45 40	8 47 53	10 50 6	12 48 23	14 50 36	16 48 53
4	18 52 3	20 54 17	22 48 37	0 50 50	2 49 7	4 51 20	6 49 37	8 51 50	10 54 3	12 52 20	14 54 33	16 52 50
5	18 56 0	20 58 13	22 52 33	0 54 46	2 53 3	4 55 16	6 53 33	8 55 46	10 58 0	12 56 16	14 58 29	16 56 46
6	18 59 56	21 2 10	22 56 30	0 58 43	2 57 0	4 59 13	6 57 30	8 59 43	11 1 56	13 0 13	15 2 26	17 0 43
7	19 3 53	21 6 6	23 0 26	1 2 40	3 0 56	5 3 9	7 1 26	9 3 39	11 5 53	13 4 9	15 6 23	17 4 39
8	19 7 50	21 10 3	23 4 23	1 6 36	3 4 53	5 7 6	7 5 23	9 7 36	11 9 49	13 8 6	15 10 19	17 8 36
9	19 11 46	21 13 59	23 8 19	1 10 33	3 8 49	5 11 3	7 9 19	9 11 33	11 13 46	13 12 2	15 14 16	17 12 32
10	19 15 43	21 17 56	23 12 16	1 14 29	3 12 46	5 14 59	7 13 16	9 15 29	11 17 42	13 15 59	15 18 12	17 16 29
11	19 19 39	21 21 53	23 16 13	1 18 26	3 16 42	5 18 56	7 17 12	9 19 26	11 21 39	13 19 56	15 22 9	17 20 25
12	19 23 36	21 25 49	23 20 9	1 22 22	3 20 39	5 22 52	7 21 9	9 23 22	11 25 35	13 23 52	15 26 5	17 24 22
13	19 27 32	21 29 46	23 24 6	1 26 19	3 24 36	5 26 49	7 25 6	9 27 19	11 29 32	13 27 49	15 30 2	17 28 19
14	19 31 29	21 33 42	23 28 2	1 30 15	3 28 32	5 30 45	7 29 2	9 31 15	11 33 29	13 31 45	15 33 58	17 32 15
15	19 35 25	21 37 39	23 31 59	1 34 12	3 32 29	5 34 42	7 32 59	9 35 12	11 37 25	13 35 42	15 37 55	17 36 12
16	19 39 22	21 41 35	23 35 55	1 38 9	3 36 25	5 38 38	7 36 55	9 39 8	11 41 22	13 39 38	15 41 51	17 40 8
17	19 43 19	21 45 32	23 39 52	1 42 5	3 40 22	5 42 35	7 40 52	9 43 5	11 45 18	13 43 35	15 45 48	17 44 5
18	19 47 15	21 49 28	23 43 48	1 46 2	3 44 18	5 46 32	7 44 48	9 47 2	11 49 15	13 47 31	15 49 45	17 48 1
19	19 51 12	21 53 25	23 47 45	1 49 58	3 48 15	5 50 28	7 48 45	9 50 58	11 53 11	13 51 28	15 53 41	17 51 58
20	19 55 8	21 57 21	23 51 42	1 53 55	3 52 11	5 54 25	7 52 41	9 54 55	11 57 8	13 55 24	15 57 38	17 55 54
21	19 59 5	22 1 18	23 55 38	1 57 51	3 56 8	5 58 21	7 56 38	9 58 51	12 1 4	13 59 21	16 1 34	17 59 51
22	20 3 1	22 5 15	23 59 35	2 1 48	4 0 5	6 2 18	8 0 35	10 2 48	12 5 1	14 3 18	16 5 31	18 3 48
23	20 6 58	22 9 11	0 3 31	2 5 44	4 4 1	6 6 14	8 4 31	10 6 44	12 8 58	14 7 14	16 9 27	18 7 44
24	20 10 54	22 13 8	0 7 28	2 9 41	4 7 58	6 10 11	8 8 28	10 10 41	12 12 54	14 11 11	16 13 24	18 11 41
25	20 14 51	22 17 4	0 11 24	2 13 38	4 11 54	6 14 8	8 12 24	10 14 37	12 16 51	14 15 7	16 17 21	18 15 37
26	20 18 48	22 21 1	0 15 21	2 17 34	4 15 51	6 18 4	8 16 21	10 18 34	12 20 47	14 19 4	16 21 17	18 19 34
27	20 22 44	22 24 57	0 19 17	2 21 31	4 19 47	6 22 1	8 20 17	10 22 31	12 24 44	14 23 0	16 25 14	18 23 30
28	20 26 41	22 28 54	0 23 14	2 25 27	4 23 44	6 25 57	8 24 14	10 26 27	12 28 40	14 26 57	16 29 10	18 27 27
29	20 30 37	22 32 50	0 27 11	2 29 24	4 27 40	6 29 54	8 28 10	10 30 24	12 32 37	14 30 53	16 33 7	18 31 24
30	20 34 34		0 31 7	2 33 20	4 31 37	6 33 50	8 32 7	10 34 20	12 36 33	14 34 50	16 37 3	18 35 20
31	20 38 30		0 35 4		4 35 34		8 36 4	10 38 17		14 38 47		18 39 17
1949 1	18 43 13	20 45 26	22 35 50	0 38 3	2 36 20	4 38 33	6 36 50	8 39 3	10 41 16	12 39 33	14 41 46	16 40 3
2	18 47 10	20 49 23	22 39 47	0 42 0	2 40 16	4 42 30	6 40 46	8 43 0	10 45 13	12 43 30	14 45 43	16 43 59
3	18 51 6	20 53 20	22 43 43	0 45 56	2 44 13	4 46 26	6 44 43	8 46 56	10 49 9	12 47 26	14 49 39	16 47 56
4	18 55 3	20 57 16	22 47 40	0 49 53	2 48 10	4 50 23	6 48 40	8 50 53	10 53 6	12 51 23	14 53 36	16 51 53
5	18 58 59	21 1 13	22 51 36	0 53 49	2 52 6	4 54 19	6 52 36	8 54 49	10 57 3	12 55 19	14 57 32	16 55 49
6	19 2 56	21 5 9	22 55 33	0 57 46	2 56 3	4 58 16	6 56 33	8 58 46	11 0 59	12 59 16	15 1 29	16 59 46
7	19 6 53	21 9 6	22 59 29	1 1 43	2 59 59	5 2 12	7 0 29	9 2 43	11 4 56	13 3 12	15 5 25	17 3 42
8	19 10 49	21 13 2	23 3 26	1 5 39	3 3 56	5 6 9	7 4 26	9 6 39	11 8 52	13 7 9	15 9 22	17 7 39
9	19 14 46	21 16 59	23 7 22	1 9 36	3 7 52	5 10 6	7 8 22	9 10 36	11 12 49	13 11 5	15 13 19	17 11 35
10	19 18 42	21 20 55	23 11 19	1 13 32	3 11 49	5 14 2	7 12 19	9 14 32	11 16 45	13 15 2	15 17 15	17 15 32
11	19 22 39	21 24 52	23 15 16	1 17 29	3 15 45	5 17 59	7 16 15	9 18 29	11 20 42	13 18 59	15 21 12	17 19 28
12	19 26 35	21 28 49	23 19 12	1 21 25	3 19 42	5 21 55	7 20 12	9 22 25	11 24 38	13 22 55	15 25 8	17 23 25
13	19 30 32	21 32 45	23 23 9	1 25 22	3 23 39	5 25 52	7 24 9	9 26 22	11 28 35	13 26 52	15 29 5	17 27 22
14	19 34 28	21 36 42	23 27 5	1 29 18	3 27 35	5 29 48	7 28 5	9 30 18	11 32 32	13 30 48	15 33 1	17 31 18
15	19 38 25	21 40 38	23 31 2	1 33 15	3 31 32	5 33 45	7 32 2	9 34 15	11 36 28	13 34 45	15 36 58	17 35 15
16	19 42 22	21 44 35	23 34 58	1 37 12	3 35 28	5 37 41	7 35 58	9 38 11	11 40 25	13 38 41	15 40 55	17 39 11
17	19 46 18	21 48 31	23 38 55	1 41 8	3 39 25	5 41 38	7 39 55	9 42 8	11 44 21	13 42 38	15 44 51	17 43 8
18	19 50 15	21 52 28	23 42 51	1 45 5	3 43 21	5 45 35	7 43 51	9 46 5	11 48 18	13 46 34	15 48 48	17 47 4
19	19 54 11	21 56 24	23 46 48	1 49 1	3 47 18	5 49 31	7 47 48	9 50 1	11 52 14	13 50 31	15 52 44	17 51 1
20	19 58 8	22 0 21	23 50 45	1 52 58	3 51 14	5 53 28	7 51 44	9 53 58	11 56 11	13 54 28	15 56 41	17 54 58
21	20 2 4	22 4 18	23 54 41	1 56 54	3 55 11	5 57 24	7 55 41	9 57 54	12 0 7	13 58 24	16 0 37	17 58 54
22	20 6 1	22 8 14	23 58 38	2 0 51	3 59 8	6 1 21	7 59 38	10 1 51	12 4 4	14 2 21	16 4 34	18 2 51
23	20 9 57	22 12 11	0 2 34	2 4 47	4 3 4	6 5 17	8 3 34	10 5 47	12 8 1	14 6 17	16 8 30	18 6 47
24	20 13 54	22 16 7	0 6 31	2 8 44	4 7 1	6 9 14	8 7 31	10 9 44	12 11 57	14 10 14	16 12 27	18 10 44
25	20 17 51	22 20 4	0 10 27	2 12 41	4 10 57	6 13 10	8 11 27	10 13 40	12 15 54	14 14 10	16 16 24	18 14 40
26	20 21 47	22 24 0	0 14 24	2 16 37	4 14 54	6 17 7	8 15 24	10 17 37	12 19 50	14 18 7	16 20 20	18 18 37
27	20 25 44	22 27 57	0 18 20	2 20 34	4 18 50	6 21 4	8 19 20	10 21 34	12 23 47	14 22 3	16 24 17	18 22 33
28	20 29 40	22 31 53	0 22 17	2 24 30	4 22 47	6 25 0	8 23 17	10 25 30	12 27 43	14 26 0	16 28 13	18 26 30
29	20 33 37		0 26 14	2 28 27	4 26 43	6 28 57	8 27 13	10 29 27	12 31 40	14 29 57	16 32 10	18 30 27
30	20 37 33		0 30 10	2 32 23	4 30 40	6 32 53	8 31 10	10 33 23	12 35 36	14 33 53	16 36 6	18 34 23
31	20 41 30		0 34 7		4 34 37		8 35 7	10 37 20		14 37 50		18 38 20

YEAR	JAN	FEB	MAR	APR	MAY	JUN	JUL	AUG	SEP	OCT	NOV	DEC
1950 1	18 42 16	20 44 30	22 34 53	0 37 6	2 35 23	4 37 36	6 35 53	8 38 6	10 40 19	12 38 36	14 40 49	16 39 6
2	18 46 13	20 48 26	22 38 50	0 41 3	2 39 19	4 41 33	6 39 49	8 42 3	10 44 16	12 42 33	14 44 46	16 43 3
3	18 50 9	20 52 23	22 42 46	0 44 59	2 43 16	4 45 29	6 43 46	8 45 59	10 48 13	12 46 29	14 48 42	16 46 59
4	18 54 6	20 56 19	22 46 43	0 48 56	2 47 13	4 49 26	6 47 43	8 49 56	10 52 9	12 50 26	14 52 39	16 50 56
5	18 58 2	21 0 16	22 50 39	0 52 52	2 51 9	4 53 22	6 51 39	8 53 52	10 56 6	12 54 22	14 56 35	16 54 52
6	19 1 59	21 4 12	22 54 36	0 56 49	2 55 6	4 57 19	6 55 36	8 57 49	11 0 2	12 58 19	15 0 32	16 58 49
7	19 5 56	21 8 9	22 58 32	1 0 46	2 59 2	5 1 16	6 59 32	9 1 46	11 3 59	13 2 15	15 4 29	17 2 45
8	19 9 52	21 12 5	23 2 29	1 4 42	3 2 59	5 5 12	7 3 29	9 5 42	11 7 55	13 6 12	15 8 25	17 6 42
9	19 13 49	21 16 2	23 6 25	1 8 39	3 6 55	5 9 9	7 7 25	9 9 39	11 11 52	13 10 8	15 12 22	17 10 38
10	19 17 45	21 19 59	23 10 22	1 12 35	3 10 52	5 13 5	7 11 22	9 13 35	11 15 48	13 14 5	15 16 18	17 14 35
11	19 21 42	21 23 55	23 14 19	1 16 32	3 14 48	5 17 2	7 15 18	9 17 32	11 19 45	13 18 2	15 20 15	17 18 32
12	19 25 38	21 27 52	23 18 15	1 20 28	3 18 45	5 20 58	7 19 15	9 21 28	11 23 42	13 21 58	15 24 11	17 22 28
13	19 29 35	21 31 48	23 22 12	1 24 25	3 22 42	5 24 55	7 23 12	9 25 25	11 27 38	13 25 55	15 28 8	17 26 25
14	19 33 31	21 35 45	23 26 8	1 28 21	3 26 38	5 28 51	7 27 8	9 29 21	11 31 35	13 29 51	15 32 4	17 30 21
15	19 37 28	21 39 41	23 30 5	1 32 18	3 30 35	5 32 48	7 31 5	9 33 18	11 35 31	13 33 48	15 36 1	17 34 18
16	19 41 25	21 43 38	23 34 1	1 36 15	3 34 31	5 36 45	7 35 1	9 37 15	11 39 28	13 37 44	15 39 58	17 38 14
17	19 45 21	21 47 34	23 37 58	1 40 11	3 38 28	5 40 41	7 38 58	9 41 11	11 43 24	13 41 41	15 43 54	17 42 11
18	19 49 18	21 51 31	23 41 54	1 44 8	3 42 24	5 44 38	7 42 54	9 45 8	11 47 21	13 45 37	15 47 51	17 46 7
19	19 53 14	21 55 28	23 45 51	1 48 4	3 46 21	5 48 34	7 46 51	9 49 4	11 51 17	13 49 34	15 51 47	17 50 4
20	19 57 11	21 59 24	23 49 48	1 52 1	3 50 17	5 52 31	7 50 48	9 53 1	11 55 14	13 53 31	15 55 44	17 54 1
21	20 1 7	22 3 21	23 53 44	1 55 57	3 54 14	5 56 27	7 54 44	9 56 57	11 59 11	13 57 27	15 59 40	17 57 57
22	20 5 4	22 7 17	23 57 41	1 59 54	3 58 11	6 0 24	7 58 41	10 0 54	12 3 7	14 1 24	16 3 37	18 1 54
23	20 9 1	22 11 14	0 1 37	2 3 50	4 2 7	6 4 20	8 2 37	10 4 50	12 7 4	14 5 20	16 7 33	18 5 50
24	20 12 57	22 15 10	0 5 34	2 7 47	4 6 4	6 8 17	8 6 34	10 8 47	12 11 0	14 9 17	16 11 30	18 9 47
25	20 16 54	22 19 7	0 9 30	2 11 44	4 10 0	6 12 14	8 10 30	10 12 44	12 14 57	14 13 13	16 15 27	18 13 43
26	20 20 50	22 23 3	0 13 27	2 15 40	4 13 57	6 16 10	8 14 27	10 16 40	12 18 53	14 17 10	16 19 23	18 17 40
27	20 24 47	22 27 0	0 17 23	2 19 37	4 17 53	6 20 7	8 18 23	10 20 37	12 22 50	14 21 6	16 23 20	18 21 36
28	20 28 43	22 30 57	0 21 20	2 23 33	4 21 50	6 24 3	8 22 20	10 24 33	12 26 46	14 25 3	16 27 16	18 25 33
29	20 32 40		0 25 17	2 27 30	4 25 46	6 28 0	8 26 17	10 28 30	12 30 43	14 29 0	16 31 13	18 29 30
30	20 36 36		0 29 13	2 31 26	4 29 43	6 31 56	8 30 13	10 32 26	12 34 39	14 32 56	16 35 9	18 33 26
31	20 40 33		0 33 10		4 33 40		8 34 10	10 36 23		14 36 53		18 37 23
1951 1	18 41 19	20 43 33	22 33 56	0 36 9	2 34 26	4 36 39	6 34 56	8 37 9	10 39 22	12 37 39	14 39 52	16 38 9
2	18 45 16	20 47 29	22 37 53	0 40 6	2 38 22	4 40 36	6 38 53	8 41 6	10 43 19	12 41 36	14 43 49	16 42 6
3	18 49 12	20 51 26	22 41 49	0 44 2	2 42 19	4 44 32	6 42 49	8 45 2	10 47 16	12 45 32	14 47 45	16 46 2
4	18 53 9	20 55 22	22 45 46	0 47 59	2 46 16	4 48 29	6 46 46	8 48 59	10 51 12	12 49 29	14 51 42	16 49 59
5	18 57 5	20 59 19	22 49 42	0 51 56	2 50 12	4 52 25	6 50 42	8 52 55	10 55 9	12 53 25	14 55 39	16 53 55
6	19 1 2	21 3 15	22 53 39	0 55 52	2 54 9	4 56 22	6 54 39	8 56 52	10 59 5	12 57 22	14 59 35	16 57 52
7	19 4 59	21 7 12	22 57 35	0 59 49	2 58 5	5 0 19	6 58 35	9 0 49	11 3 2	13 1 18	15 3 32	17 1 48
8	19 8 55	21 11 8	23 1 32	1 3 45	3 2 2	5 4 15	7 2 32	9 4 45	11 6 58	13 5 15	15 7 28	17 5 45
9	19 12 52	21 15 5	23 5 29	1 7 42	3 5 58	5 8 12	7 6 28	9 8 42	11 10 55	13 9 12	15 11 25	17 9 41
10	19 16 48	21 19 2	23 9 25	1 11 38	3 9 55	5 12 8	7 10 25	9 12 38	11 14 51	13 13 8	15 15 21	17 13 38
11	19 20 45	21 22 58	23 13 22	1 15 35	3 13 51	5 16 5	7 14 22	9 16 35	11 18 48	13 17 5	15 19 18	17 17 35
12	19 24 41	21 26 55	23 17 18	1 19 31	3 17 48	5 20 1	7 18 18	9 20 31	11 22 45	13 21 1	15 23 14	17 21 31
13	19 28 38	21 30 51	23 21 15	1 23 28	3 21 45	5 23 58	7 22 15	9 24 28	11 26 41	13 24 58	15 27 11	17 25 28
14	19 32 35	21 34 48	23 25 11	1 27 25	3 25 41	5 27 54	7 26 11	9 28 24	11 30 38	13 28 54	15 31 7	17 29 24
15	19 36 31	21 38 44	23 29 8	1 31 21	3 29 38	5 31 51	7 30 8	9 32 21	11 34 34	13 32 51	15 35 4	17 33 21
16	19 40 28	21 42 41	23 33 4	1 35 18	3 33 34	5 35 48	7 34 4	9 36 18	11 38 31	13 36 47	15 39 1	17 37 17
17	19 44 24	21 46 37	23 37 1	1 39 14	3 37 31	5 39 44	7 38 1	9 40 14	11 42 27	13 40 44	15 42 57	17 41 14
18	19 48 21	21 50 34	23 40 58	1 43 11	3 41 27	5 43 41	7 41 57	9 44 11	11 46 24	13 44 40	15 46 54	17 45 10
19	19 52 17	21 54 31	23 44 54	1 47 7	3 45 24	5 47 37	7 45 54	9 48 7	11 50 20	13 48 37	15 50 50	17 49 7
20	19 56 14	21 58 27	23 48 51	1 51 4	3 49 20	5 51 34	7 49 51	9 52 4	11 54 17	13 52 34	15 54 47	17 53 4
21	20 0 10	22 2 24	23 52 47	1 55 0	3 53 17	5 55 30	7 53 47	9 56 0	11 58 14	13 56 30	15 58 43	17 57 0
22	20 4 7	22 6 20	23 56 44	1 58 57	3 57 14	5 59 27	7 57 44	9 59 57	12 2 10	14 0 27	16 2 40	18 0 57
23	20 8 4	22 10 17	0 0 40	2 2 53	4 1 10	6 3 24	8 1 40	10 3 53	12 6 7	14 4 23	16 6 37	18 4 53
24	20 12 0	22 14 13	0 4 37	2 6 50	4 5 7	6 7 20	8 5 37	10 7 50	12 10 3	14 8 20	16 10 33	18 8 50
25	20 15 57	22 18 10	0 8 33	2 10 47	4 9 3	6 11 17	8 9 33	10 11 47	12 14 0	14 12 16	16 14 30	18 12 46
26	20 19 53	22 22 6	0 12 30	2 14 43	4 13 0	6 15 13	8 13 30	10 15 43	12 17 56	14 16 13	16 18 26	18 16 43
27	20 23 50	22 26 3	0 16 27	2 18 40	4 16 56	6 19 10	8 17 26	10 19 40	12 21 53	14 20 9	16 22 23	18 20 40
28	20 27 46	22 30 0	0 20 23	2 22 36	4 20 53	6 23 6	8 21 23	10 23 36	12 25 49	14 24 6	16 26 19	18 24 36
29	20 31 43		0 24 20	2 26 33	4 24 50	6 27 3	8 25 20	10 27 33	12 29 46	14 28 3	16 30 16	18 28 33
30	20 35 39		0 28 16	2 30 29	4 28 46	6 30 59	8 29 16	10 31 29	12 33 43	14 31 59	16 34 12	18 32 29
31	20 39 36		0 32 13		4 32 43		8 33 13	10 35 26		14 35 56		18 36 26
1952 1	18 40 22	20 42 36	22 36 56	0 39 9	2 37 26	4 39 39	6 37 56	8 40 9	10 42 22	12 40 39	14 42 52	16 41 9
2	18 44 19	20 46 32	22 40 52	0 43 5	2 41 22	4 43 35	6 41 52	8 44 5	10 46 19	12 44 35	14 46 48	16 45 5
3	18 48 15	20 50 29	22 44 49	0 47 2	2 45 19	4 47 32	6 45 49	8 48 2	10 50 15	12 48 32	14 50 45	16 49 2
4	18 52 12	20 54 25	22 48 45	0 50 59	2 49 15	4 51 28	6 49 45	8 51 58	10 54 12	12 52 28	14 54 41	16 52 58
5	18 56 9	20 58 22	22 52 42	0 54 55	2 53 12	4 55 25	6 53 42	8 55 55	10 58 8	12 56 25	14 58 38	16 56 55
6	19 0 5	21 2 18	22 56 38	0 58 52	2 57 8	4 59 22	6 57 38	8 59 52	11 2 5	13 0 21	15 2 35	17 0 51
7	19 4 2	21 6 15	23 0 35	1 2 48	3 1 5	5 3 18	7 1 35	9 3 48	11 6 1	13 4 18	15 6 31	17 4 48
8	19 7 58	21 10 12	23 4 32	1 6 45	3 5 1	5 7 15	7 5 31	9 7 45	11 9 58	13 8 15	15 10 28	17 8 44
9	19 11 55	21 14 8	23 8 28	1 10 41	3 8 58	5 11 11	7 9 28	9 11 41	11 13 54	13 12 11	15 14 24	17 12 41
10	19 15 51	21 18 5	23 12 25	1 14 38	3 12 55	5 15 8	7 13 25	9 15 38	11 17 51	13 16 8	15 18 21	17 16 38
11	19 19 48	21 22 1	23 16 21	1 18 34	3 16 51	5 19 4	7 17 21	9 19 34	11 21 48	13 20 4	15 22 17	17 20 34
12	19 23 44	21 25 58	23 20 18	1 22 31	3 20 48	5 23 1	7 21 18	9 23 31	11 25 44	13 24 1	15 26 14	17 24 31
13	19 27 41	21 29 54	23 24 14	1 26 28	3 24 44	5 26 57	7 25 14	9 27 27	11 29 41	13 27 57	15 30 10	17 28 27
14	19 31 38	21 33 51	23 28 11	1 30 24	3 28 41	5 30 54	7 29 11	9 31 24	11 33 37	13 31 54	15 34 7	17 32 24
15	19 35 34	21 37 47	23 32 7	1 34 21	3 32 37	5 34 51	7 33 7	9 35 21	11 37 34	13 35 50	15 38 4	17 36 20
16	19 39 31	21 41 44	23 36 4	1 38 17	3 36 34	5 38 47	7 37 4	9 39 17	11 41 30	13 39 47	15 42 0	17 40 17
17	19 43 27	21 45 40	23 40 1	1 42 14	3 40 30	5 42 44	7 41 0	9 43 14	11 45 27	13 43 44	15 45 57	17 44 13
18	19 47 24	21 49 37	23 43 57	1 46 10	3 44 27	5 46 40	7 44 57	9 47 10	11 49 23	13 47 40	15 49 53	17 48 10
19	19 51 20	21 53 34	23 47 54	1 50 7	3 48 24	5 50 37	7 48 54	9 51 7	11 53 20	13 51 37	15 53 50	17 52 7
20	19 55 17	21 57 30	23 51 50	1 54 3	3 52 20	5 54 33	7 52 50	9 55 3	11 57 17	13 55 33	15 57 46	17 56 3
21	19 59 13	22 1 27	23 55 47	1 58 0	3 56 17	5 58 30	7 56 47	9 59 0	12 1 13	13 59 30	16 1 43	18 0 0
22	20 3 10	22 5 23	23 59 43	2 1 57	4 0 13	6 2 27	8 0 43	10 2 56	12 5 10	14 3 26	16 5 40	18 3 56
23	20 7 7	22 9 20	0 3 40	2 5 53	4 4 10	6 6 23	8 4 40	10 6 53	12 9 6	14 7 23	16 9 36	18 7 53
24	20 11 3	22 13 16	0 7 36	2 9 50	4 8 6	6 10 20	8 8 36	10 10 50	12 13 3	14 11 19	16 13 33	18 11 49
25	20 15 0	22 17 13	0 11 33	2 13 46	4 12 3	6 14 16	8 12 33	10 14 46	12 16 59	14 15 16	16 17 29	18 15 46
26	20 18 56	22 21 10	0 15 30	2 17 43	4 15 59	6 18 13	8 16 29	10 18 43	12 20 56	14 19 13	16 21 26	18 19 42
27	20 22 53	22 25 6	0 19 26	2 21 39	4 19 56	6 22 9	8 20 26	10 22 39	12 24 52	14 23 9	16 25 22	18 23 39
28	20 26 49	22 29 3	0 23 23	2 25 36	4 23 53	6 26 6	8 24 23	10 26 36	12 28 49	14 27 6	16 29 19	18 27 36
29	20 30 46	22 32 59	0 27 19	2 29 32	4 27 49	6 30 2	8 28 19	10 30 32	12 32 46	14 31 2	16 33 15	18 31 32
30	20 34 43		0 31 16	2 33 29	4 31 46	6 33 59	8 32 16	10 34 29	12 36 42	14 34 59	16 37 12	18 35 29
31	20 38 39		0 35 12		4 35 42		8 36 12	10 38 25		14 38 55		18 39 25
1953 1	18 43 22	20 45 35	22 35 59	0 38 12	2 36 28	4 38 42	6 36 58	8 39 12	10 41 25	12 39 42	14 41 55	16 40 11
2	18 47 18	20 49 32	22 39 55	0 42 8	2 40 25	4 42 38	6 40 55	8 43 8	10 45 22	12 43 38	14 45 51	16 44 8
3	18 51 15	20 53 28	22 43 52	0 46 5	2 44 22	4 46 35	6 44 52	8 47 5	10 49 18	12 47 35	14 49 48	16 48 5
4	18 55 12	20 57 25	22 47 48	0 50 1	2 48 18	4 50 31	6 48 48	8 51 1	10 53 15	12 51 31	14 53 44	16 52 1
5	18 59 8	21 1 21	22 51 45	0 53 58	2 52 15	4 54 28	6 52 45	8 54 58	10 57 11	12 55 28	14 57 41	16 55 58
6	19 3 5	21 5 18	22 55 41	0 57 55	2 56 11	4 58 25	6 56 41	8 58 55	11 1 8	12 59 24	15 1 38	16 59 54
7	19 7 1	21 9 14	22 59 38	1 1 51	3 0 8	5 2 21	7 0 38	9 2 51	11 5 4	13 3 21	15 5 34	17 3 51
8	19 10 58	21 13 11	23 3 35	1 5 48	3 4 4	5 6 18	7 4 34	9 6 48	11 9 1	13 7 17	15 9 31	17 7 47
9	19 14 54	21 17 8	23 7 31	1 9 44	3 8 1	5 10 14	7 8 31	9 10 44	11 12 57	13 11 14	15 13 27	17 11 44
10	19 18 51	21 21 4	23 11 28	1 13 41	3 11 57	5 14 11	7 12 28	9 14 41	11 16 54	13 15 11	15 17 24	17 15 40
11	19 22 47	21 25 1	23 15 24	1 17 37	3 15 54	5 18 7	7 16 24	9 18 37	11 20 51	13 19 7	15 21 20	17 19 37
12	19 26 44	21 28 57	23 19 21	1 21 34	3 19 51	5 22 4	7 20 21	9 22 34	11 24 47	13 23 4	15 25 17	17 23 34
13	19 30 41	21 32 54	23 23 17	1 25 30	3 23 47	5 26 0	7 24 17	9 26 30	11 28 44	13 27 0	15 29 13	17 27 30
14	19 34 37	21 36 50	23 27 14	1 29 27	3 27 44	5 29 57	7 28 14	9 30 27	11 32 40	13 30 57	15 33 10	17 31 27
15	19 38 34	21 40 47	23 31 10	1 33 24	3 31 40	5 33 54	7 32 10	9 34 24	11 36 37	13 34 53	15 37 7	17 35 23
16	19 42 30	21 44 43	23 35 7	1 37 20	3 35 37	5 37 50	7 36 7	9 38 20	11 40 33	13 38 50	15 41 3	17 39 20
17	19 46 27	21 48 40	23 39 4	1 41 17	3 39 33	5 41 47	7 40 3	9 42 17	11 44 30	13 42 46	15 45 0	17 43 16
18	19 50 23	21 52 37	23 43 0	1 45 13	3 43 30	5 45 43	7 44 0	9 46 13	11 48 26	13 46 43	15 48 56	17 47 13
19	19 54 20	21 56 33	23 46 57	1 49 10	3 47 27	5 49 40	7 47 57	9 50 10	11 52 23	13 50 40	15 52 53	17 51 9
20	19 58 16	22 0 30	23 50 53	1 53 6	3 51 23	5 53 36	7 51 53	9 54 6	11 56 20	13 54 36	15 56 49	17 55 6
21	20 2 13	22 4 26	23 54 50	1 57 3	3 55 20	5 57 33	7 55 50	9 58 3	12 0 16	13 58 33	16 0 46	17 59 3
22	20 6 10	22 8 23	23 58 46	2 1 0	3 59 16	6 1 29	7 59 46	10 1 59	12 4 13	14 2 29	16 4 42	18 2 59
23	20 10 6	22 12 19	0 2 43	2 4 56	4 3 13	6 5 26	8 3 43	10 5 56	12 8 9	14 6 26	16 8 39	18 6 56
24	20 14 3	22 16 16	0 6 39	2 8 53	4 7 9	6 9 23	8 7 39	10 9 53	12 12 6	14 10 22	16 12 36	18 10 52
25	20 17 59	22 20 12	0 10 36	2 12 49	4 11 6	6 13 19	8 11 36	10 13 49	12 16 2	14 14 19	16 16 32	18 14 49
26	20 21 56	22 24 9	0 14 33	2 16 46	4 15 2	6 17 16	8 15 32	10 17 46	12 19 59	14 18 15	16 20 29	18 18 45
27	20 25 52	22 28 6	0 18 29	2 20 42	4 18 59	6 21 12	8 19 29	10 21 42	12 23 55	14 22 12	16 24 25	18 22 42
28	20 29 49	22 32 2	0 22 26	2 24 39	4 22 55	6 25 9	8 23 26	10 25 39	12 27 52	14 26 9	16 28 22	18 26 39
29	20 33 45		0 26 22	2 28 35	4 26 52	6 29 5	8 27 22	10 29 35	12 31 48	14 30 5	16 32 18	18 30 35
30	20 37 42		0 30 19	2 32 32	4 30 49	6 33 2	8 31 19	10 33 32	12 35 45	14 34 2	16 36 15	18 34 32
31	20 41 39		0 34 15		4 34 45		8 35 15	10 37 28		14 37 58		18 38 28

YEAR		JAN	FEB	MAR	APR	MAY	JUN	JUL	AUG	SEP	OCT	NOV	DEC
1954	1	18 42 25	20 44 38	22 35 2	0 37 15	2 35 31	4 37 45	6 36 1	8 38 15	10 40 28	12 38 44	14 40 58	16 39 14
	2	18 46 21	20 48 35	22 38 58	0 41 11	2 39 28	4 41 41	6 39 58	8 42 11	10 44 24	12 42 41	14 44 54	16 43 11
	3	18 50 18	20 52 31	22 42 55	0 45 8	2 43 24	4 45 38	6 43 54	8 46 8	10 48 21	12 46 38	14 48 51	16 47 7
	4	18 54 14	20 56 28	22 46 51	0 49 4	2 47 21	4 49 34	6 47 51	8 50 4	10 52 17	12 50 34	14 52 47	16 51 4
	5	18 58 11	21 0 24	22 50 48	0 53 1	2 51 18	4 53 31	6 51 48	8 54 1	10 56 14	12 54 31	14 56 44	16 55 0
	6	19 2 8	21 4 21	22 54 44	0 56 57	2 55 14	4 57 27	6 55 44	8 57 57	11 0 11	12 58 27	15 0 40	16 58 57
	7	19 6 4	21 8 17	22 58 41	1 0 54	2 59 11	5 1 24	6 59 41	9 1 54	11 4 7	13 2 24	15 4 37	17 2 54
	8	19 10 1	21 12 14	23 2 37	1 4 51	3 3 7	5 5 21	7 3 37	9 5 50	11 8 4	13 6 20	15 8 33	17 6 50
	9	19 13 57	21 16 10	23 6 34	1 8 47	3 7 4	5 9 17	7 7 34	9 9 47	11 12 0	13 10 17	15 12 30	17 10 47
	10	19 17 54	21 20 7	23 10 31	1 12 44	3 11 0	5 13 14	7 11 30	9 13 44	11 15 57	13 14 13	15 16 27	17 14 43
	11	19 21 50	21 24 4	23 14 27	1 16 40	3 14 57	5 17 10	7 15 27	9 17 40	11 19 53	13 18 10	15 20 23	17 18 40
	12	19 25 47	21 28 0	23 18 24	1 20 37	3 18 53	5 21 7	7 19 23	9 21 37	11 23 50	13 22 6	15 24 20	17 22 36
	13	19 29 43	21 31 57	23 22 20	1 24 33	3 22 50	5 25 3	7 23 20	9 25 33	11 27 46	13 26 3	15 28 16	17 26 33
	14	19 33 40	21 35 53	23 26 17	1 28 30	3 26 47	5 29 0	7 27 17	9 29 30	11 31 43	13 30 0	15 32 13	17 30 30
	15	19 37 37	21 39 50	23 30 13	1 32 26	3 30 43	5 32 56	7 31 13	9 33 26	11 35 40	13 33 56	15 36 9	17 34 26
	16	19 41 33	21 43 46	23 34 10	1 36 23	3 34 40	5 36 53	7 35 10	9 37 23	11 39 36	13 37 53	15 40 6	17 38 23
	17	19 45 30	21 47 43	23 38 6	1 40 20	3 38 36	5 40 50	7 39 6	9 41 20	11 43 33	13 41 49	15 44 2	17 42 19
	18	19 49 26	21 51 40	23 42 3	1 44 16	3 42 33	5 44 46	7 43 3	9 45 16	11 47 29	13 45 46	15 47 59	17 46 16
	19	19 53 23	21 55 36	23 46 0	1 48 13	3 46 29	5 48 43	7 46 59	9 49 13	11 51 26	13 49 42	15 51 56	17 50 12
	20	19 57 19	21 59 33	23 49 56	1 52 9	3 50 26	5 52 39	7 50 56	9 53 9	11 55 22	13 53 39	15 55 52	17 54 9
	21	20 1 16	22 3 29	23 53 53	1 56 6	3 54 22	5 56 36	7 54 52	9 57 6	11 59 19	13 57 35	15 59 49	17 58 5
	22	20 5 12	22 7 26	23 57 49	2 0 2	3 58 19	6 0 32	7 58 49	10 1 2	12 3 15	14 1 32	16 3 45	18 2 2
	23	20 9 9	22 11 22	0 1 46	2 3 59	4 2 16	6 4 29	8 2 46	10 4 59	12 7 12	14 5 29	16 7 42	18 5 59
	24	20 13 6	22 15 19	0 5 42	2 7 55	4 6 12	6 8 25	8 6 42	10 8 55	12 11 9	14 9 25	16 11 38	18 9 55
	25	20 17 2	22 19 15	0 9 39	2 11 52	4 10 9	6 12 22	8 10 39	10 12 52	12 15 5	14 13 22	16 15 35	18 13 52
	26	20 20 59	22 23 12	0 13 35	2 15 49	4 14 5	6 16 19	8 14 35	10 16 49	12 19 2	14 17 18	16 19 31	18 17 48
	27	20 24 55	22 27 8	0 17 32	2 19 45	4 18 2	6 20 15	8 18 32	10 20 45	12 22 58	14 21 15	16 23 28	18 21 45
	28	20 28 52	22 31 5	0 21 29	2 23 42	4 21 58	6 24 12	8 22 28	10 24 42	12 26 55	14 25 11	16 27 25	18 25 41
	29	20 32 48		0 25 25	2 27 38	4 25 55	6 28 8	8 26 25	10 28 38	12 30 51	14 29 8	16 31 21	18 29 38
	30	20 36 45		0 29 22	2 31 35	4 29 51	6 32 5	8 30 22	10 32 35	12 34 48	14 33 4	16 35 18	18 33 34
	31	20 40 41		0 33 18		4 33 48		8 34 18	10 36 31		14 37 1		18 37 31
1955	1	18 41 28	20 43 41	22 34 4	0 36 18	2 34 34	4 36 47	6 35 4	8 37 17	10 39 31	12 37 47	14 40 0	16 38 17
	2	18 45 24	20 47 37	22 38 1	0 40 14	2 38 31	4 40 44	6 39 1	8 41 14	10 43 27	12 41 44	14 43 57	16 42 14
	3	18 49 21	20 51 34	22 41 57	0 44 11	2 42 27	4 44 40	6 42 57	8 45 10	10 47 24	12 45 40	14 47 53	16 46 10
	4	18 53 17	20 55 31	22 45 54	0 48 7	2 46 24	4 48 37	6 46 54	8 49 7	10 51 20	12 49 37	14 51 50	16 50 7
	5	18 57 14	20 59 27	22 49 51	0 52 4	2 50 20	4 52 34	6 50 50	8 53 4	10 55 17	12 53 33	14 55 47	16 54 3
	6	19 1 10	21 3 24	22 53 47	0 56 0	2 54 17	4 56 30	6 54 47	8 57 0	10 59 13	12 57 30	14 59 43	16 58 0
	7	19 5 7	21 7 20	22 57 44	0 59 57	2 58 13	5 0 27	6 58 43	9 0 57	11 3 10	13 1 26	15 3 40	17 1 56
	8	19 9 3	21 11 17	23 1 40	1 3 53	3 2 10	5 4 23	7 2 40	9 4 53	11 7 6	13 5 23	15 7 36	17 5 53
	9	19 13 0	21 15 13	23 5 37	1 7 50	3 6 7	5 8 20	7 6 37	9 8 50	11 11 3	13 9 20	15 11 33	17 9 49
	10	19 16 57	21 19 10	23 9 33	1 11 46	3 10 3	5 12 16	7 10 33	9 12 46	11 15 0	13 13 16	15 15 29	17 13 46
	11	19 20 53	21 23 6	23 13 30	1 15 43	3 14 0	5 16 13	7 14 30	9 16 43	11 18 56	13 17 13	15 19 26	17 17 43
	12	19 24 50	21 27 3	23 17 26	1 19 40	3 17 56	5 20 10	7 18 26	9 20 39	11 22 53	13 21 9	15 23 22	17 21 39
	13	19 28 46	21 31 0	23 21 23	1 23 36	3 21 53	5 24 6	7 22 23	9 24 36	11 26 49	13 25 6	15 27 19	17 25 36
	14	19 32 43	21 34 56	23 25 20	1 27 33	3 25 49	5 28 3	7 26 19	9 28 33	11 30 46	13 29 2	15 31 15	17 29 32
	15	19 36 39	21 38 53	23 29 16	1 31 29	3 29 46	5 31 59	7 30 16	9 32 29	11 34 42	13 32 59	15 35 12	17 33 29
	16	19 40 36	21 42 49	23 33 13	1 35 26	3 33 42	5 35 56	7 34 12	9 36 26	11 38 39	13 36 55	15 39 9	17 37 25
	17	19 44 32	21 46 46	23 37 9	1 39 22	3 37 39	5 39 52	7 38 9	9 40 22	11 42 35	13 40 52	15 43 5	17 41 22
	18	19 48 29	21 50 42	23 41 6	1 43 19	3 41 36	5 43 49	7 42 6	9 44 19	11 46 32	13 44 49	15 47 2	17 45 18
	19	19 52 26	21 54 39	23 45 2	1 47 15	3 45 32	5 47 45	7 46 2	9 48 15	11 50 28	13 48 45	15 50 58	17 49 15
	20	19 56 22	21 58 35	23 48 59	1 51 12	3 49 29	5 51 42	7 49 59	9 52 12	11 54 25	13 52 42	15 54 55	17 53 12
	21	20 0 19	22 2 32	23 52 55	1 55 9	3 53 25	5 55 39	7 53 55	9 56 8	11 58 22	13 56 38	15 58 51	17 57 8
	22	20 4 15	22 6 29	23 56 52	1 59 5	3 57 22	5 59 35	7 57 52	10 0 5	12 2 18	14 0 35	16 2 48	18 1 5
	23	20 8 12	22 10 25	0 0 49	2 3 2	4 1 18	6 3 32	8 1 48	10 4 2	12 6 15	14 4 31	16 6 45	18 5 1
	24	20 12 8	22 14 22	0 4 45	2 6 58	4 5 15	6 7 28	8 5 45	10 7 58	12 10 11	14 8 28	16 10 41	18 8 58
	25	20 16 5	22 18 18	0 8 42	2 10 55	4 9 11	6 11 25	8 9 41	10 11 55	12 14 8	14 12 24	16 14 38	18 12 54
	26	20 20 2	22 22 15	0 12 38	2 14 51	4 13 8	6 15 21	8 13 38	10 15 51	12 18 4	14 16 21	16 18 34	18 16 51
	27	20 23 58	22 26 11	0 16 35	2 18 48	4 17 5	6 19 18	8 17 35	10 19 48	12 22 1	14 20 18	16 22 31	18 20 47
	28	20 27 55	22 30 8	0 20 31	2 22 44	4 21 1	6 23 14	8 21 31	10 23 44	12 25 57	14 24 14	16 26 27	18 24 44
	29	20 31 51		0 24 28	2 26 41	4 24 58	6 27 11	8 25 28	10 27 41	12 29 54	14 28 11	16 30 24	18 28 41
	30	20 35 48		0 28 24	2 30 38	4 28 54	6 31 8	8 29 24	10 31 37	12 33 51	14 32 7	16 34 20	18 32 37
	31	20 39 44		0 32 21		4 32 51		8 33 21	10 35 34		14 36 4		18 36 34
1956	1	18 40 30	20 42 44	22 37 4	0 39 17	2 37 33	4 39 47	6 38 3	8 40 17	10 42 30	12 40 46	14 42 59	16 41 16
	2	18 44 27	20 46 40	22 41 0	0 43 13	2 41 30	4 43 43	6 42 0	8 44 13	10 46 26	12 44 43	14 46 56	16 45 13
	3	18 48 23	20 50 37	22 44 57	0 47 10	2 45 26	4 47 40	6 45 56	8 48 10	10 50 23	12 48 39	14 50 53	16 49 9
	4	18 52 20	20 54 33	22 48 53	0 51 6	2 49 23	4 51 36	6 49 53	8 52 6	10 54 19	12 52 36	14 54 49	16 53 6
	5	18 56 16	20 58 30	22 52 50	0 55 3	2 53 20	4 55 33	6 53 49	8 56 3	10 58 16	12 56 32	14 58 46	16 57 2
	6	19 0 13	21 2 26	22 56 46	0 59 0	2 57 16	4 59 29	6 57 46	8 59 59	11 2 12	13 0 29	15 2 42	17 0 59
	7	19 4 10	21 6 23	23 0 43	1 2 56	3 1 13	5 3 26	7 1 43	9 3 56	11 6 9	13 4 26	15 6 39	17 4 55
	8	19 8 6	21 10 19	23 4 39	1 6 53	3 5 9	5 7 22	7 5 39	9 7 52	11 10 6	13 8 22	15 10 35	17 8 52
	9	19 12 3	21 14 16	23 8 36	1 10 49	3 9 6	5 11 19	7 9 36	9 11 49	11 14 2	13 12 19	15 14 32	17 12 49
	10	19 15 59	21 18 13	23 12 33	1 14 46	3 13 2	5 15 16	7 13 32	9 15 46	11 17 59	13 16 15	15 18 28	17 16 45
	11	19 19 56	21 22 9	23 16 29	1 18 42	3 16 59	5 19 12	7 17 29	9 19 42	11 21 55	13 20 12	15 22 25	17 20 42
	12	19 23 52	21 26 6	23 20 26	1 22 39	3 20 55	5 23 9	7 21 25	9 23 39	11 25 52	13 24 8	15 26 22	17 24 38
	13	19 27 49	21 30 2	23 24 22	1 26 35	3 24 52	5 27 5	7 25 22	9 27 35	11 29 48	13 28 5	15 30 18	17 28 35
	14	19 31 46	21 33 59	23 28 19	1 30 32	3 28 49	5 31 2	7 29 19	9 31 32	11 33 45	13 32 1	15 34 15	17 32 31
	15	19 35 42	21 37 55	23 32 15	1 34 28	3 32 45	5 34 58	7 33 15	9 35 28	11 37 41	13 35 58	15 38 11	17 36 28
	16	19 39 39	21 41 52	23 36 12	1 38 25	3 36 42	5 38 55	7 37 12	9 39 25	11 41 38	13 39 55	15 42 8	17 40 24
	17	19 43 35	21 45 48	23 40 8	1 42 22	3 40 38	5 42 51	7 41 8	9 43 21	11 45 35	13 43 51	15 46 4	17 44 21
	18	19 47 32	21 49 45	23 44 5	1 46 18	3 44 35	5 46 48	7 45 5	9 47 18	11 49 31	13 47 48	15 50 1	17 48 18
	19	19 51 28	21 53 42	23 48 2	1 50 15	3 48 31	5 50 45	7 49 1	9 51 15	11 53 28	13 51 44	15 53 57	17 52 14
	20	19 55 25	21 57 38	23 51 58	1 54 11	3 52 28	5 54 41	7 52 58	9 55 11	11 57 24	13 55 41	15 57 54	17 56 11
	21	19 59 21	22 1 35	23 55 55	1 58 8	3 56 24	5 58 38	7 56 54	9 59 8	12 1 21	13 59 37	16 1 51	18 0 7
	22	20 3 18	22 5 31	23 59 51	2 2 4	4 0 21	6 2 34	8 0 51	10 3 4	12 5 17	14 3 34	16 5 47	18 4 4
	23	20 7 15	22 9 28	0 3 48	2 6 1	4 4 18	6 6 31	8 4 48	10 7 1	12 9 14	14 7 30	16 9 44	18 8 0
	24	20 11 11	22 13 24	0 7 44	2 9 57	4 8 14	6 10 27	8 8 44	10 10 57	12 13 10	14 11 27	16 13 40	18 11 57
	25	20 15 8	22 17 21	0 11 41	2 13 54	4 12 11	6 14 24	8 12 41	10 14 54	12 17 7	14 15 24	16 17 37	18 15 53
	26	20 19 4	22 21 17	0 15 37	2 17 51	4 16 7	6 18 21	8 16 37	10 18 50	12 21 4	14 19 20	16 21 33	18 19 50
	27	20 23 1	22 25 14	0 19 34	2 21 47	4 20 4	6 22 17	8 20 34	10 22 47	12 25 0	14 23 17	16 25 30	18 23 47
	28	20 26 57	22 29 10	0 23 31	2 25 44	4 24 0	6 26 14	8 24 30	10 26 43	12 28 57	14 27 13	16 29 26	18 27 43
	29	20 30 54	22 33 7	0 27 27	2 29 40	4 27 57	6 30 10	8 28 27	10 30 40	12 32 53	14 31 10	16 33 23	18 31 40
	30	20 34 50		0 31 24	2 33 37	4 31 53	6 34 7	8 32 23	10 34 37	12 36 50	14 35 6	16 37 20	18 35 36
	31	20 38 47		0 35 20		4 35 50		8 36 20	10 38 33		14 39 3		18 39 33
1957	1	18 43 29	20 45 43	22 36 6	0 38 19	2 36 36	4 38 49	6 37 6	8 39 19	10 41 32	12 39 49	14 42 2	16 40 19
	2	18 47 26	20 49 39	22 40 3	0 42 16	2 40 32	4 42 46	6 41 2	8 43 16	10 45 29	12 43 45	14 45 58	16 44 15
	3	18 51 23	20 53 36	22 43 59	0 46 12	2 44 29	4 46 42	6 44 59	8 47 12	10 49 25	12 47 42	14 49 55	16 48 12
	4	18 55 19	20 57 32	22 47 56	0 50 9	2 48 26	4 50 39	6 48 55	8 51 9	10 53 22	12 51 38	14 53 52	16 52 8
	5	18 59 16	21 1 29	22 51 52	0 54 5	2 52 22	4 54 35	6 52 52	8 55 5	10 57 18	12 55 35	14 57 48	16 56 5
	6	19 3 12	21 5 25	22 55 49	0 58 2	2 56 19	4 58 32	6 56 49	8 59 2	11 1 15	12 59 32	15 1 45	17 0 1
	7	19 7 9	21 9 22	22 59 45	1 1 59	3 0 15	5 2 28	7 0 45	9 2 58	11 5 12	13 3 28	15 5 41	17 3 58
	8	19 11 5	21 13 19	23 3 42	1 5 55	3 4 12	5 6 25	7 4 42	9 6 55	11 9 8	13 7 25	15 9 38	17 7 54
	9	19 15 2	21 17 15	23 7 39	1 9 52	3 8 8	5 10 22	7 8 38	9 10 51	11 13 5	13 11 21	15 13 34	17 11 51
	10	19 18 58	21 21 12	23 11 35	1 13 48	3 12 5	5 14 18	7 12 35	9 14 48	11 17 1	13 15 18	15 17 31	17 15 48
	11	19 22 55	21 25 8	23 15 32	1 17 45	3 16 1	5 18 15	7 16 31	9 18 45	11 20 58	13 19 14	15 21 27	17 19 44
	12	19 26 52	21 29 5	23 19 28	1 21 41	3 19 58	5 22 11	7 20 28	9 22 41	11 24 54	13 23 11	15 25 24	17 23 41
	13	19 30 48	21 33 1	23 23 25	1 25 38	3 23 55	5 26 8	7 24 24	9 26 38	11 28 51	13 27 7	15 29 21	17 27 37
	14	19 34 45	21 36 58	23 27 21	1 29 34	3 27 51	5 30 4	7 28 21	9 30 34	11 32 47	13 31 4	15 33 17	17 31 34
	15	19 38 41	21 40 54	23 31 18	1 33 31	3 31 48	5 34 1	7 32 18	9 34 31	11 36 44	13 35 1	15 37 14	17 35 30
	16	19 42 38	21 44 51	23 35 14	1 37 28	3 35 44	5 37 57	7 36 14	9 38 27	11 40 40	13 38 57	15 41 10	17 39 27
	17	19 46 34	21 48 48	23 39 11	1 41 24	3 39 41	5 41 54	7 40 11	9 42 24	11 44 37	13 42 54	15 45 7	17 43 23
	18	19 50 31	21 52 44	23 43 8	1 45 21	3 43 37	5 45 51	7 44 7	9 46 20	11 48 34	13 46 50	15 49 3	17 47 20
	19	19 54 27	21 56 41	23 47 4	1 49 17	3 47 34	5 49 47	7 48 4	9 50 17	11 52 30	13 50 47	15 53 0	17 51 17
	20	19 58 24	22 0 37	23 51 1	1 53 14	3 51 30	5 53 44	7 52 0	9 54 14	11 56 27	13 54 43	15 56 56	17 55 13
	21	20 2 21	22 4 34	23 54 57	1 57 10	3 55 27	5 57 40	7 55 57	9 58 10	12 0 23	13 58 40	16 0 53	17 59 10
	22	20 6 17	22 8 30	23 58 54	2 1 7	3 59 24	6 1 37	7 59 53	10 2 7	12 4 20	14 2 36	16 4 50	18 3 6
	23	20 10 14	22 12 27	0 2 50	2 5 3	4 3 20	6 5 33	8 3 50	10 6 3	12 8 16	14 6 33	16 8 46	18 7 3
	24	20 14 10	22 16 23	0 6 47	2 9 0	4 7 17	6 9 30	8 7 47	10 10 0	12 12 13	14 10 29	16 12 43	18 10 59
	25	20 18 7	22 20 20	0 10 43	2 12 57	4 11 13	6 13 26	8 11 43	10 13 56	12 16 9	14 14 26	16 16 39	18 14 56
	26	20 22 3	22 24 17	0 14 40	2 16 53	4 15 10	6 17 23	8 15 40	10 17 53	12 20 6	14 18 23	16 20 36	18 18 53
	27	20 26 0	22 28 13	0 18 37	2 20 50	4 19 6	6 21 20	8 19 36	10 21 49	12 24 3	14 22 19	16 24 32	18 22 49
	28	20 29 56	22 32 10	0 22 33	2 24 46	4 23 3	6 25 16	8 23 33	10 25 46	12 27 59	14 26 16	16 28 29	18 26 46
	29	20 33 53		0 26 30	2 28 43	4 26 59	6 29 13	8 27 29	10 29 43	12 31 56	14 30 12	16 32 25	18 30 42
	30	20 37 50		0 30 26	2 32 39	4 30 56	6 33 9	8 31 26	10 33 39	12 35 52	14 34 9	16 36 22	18 34 39
	31	20 41 46		0 34 23		4 34 53		8 35 22	10 37 36		14 38 5		18 38 35

YEAR		JAN	FEB	MAR	APR	MAY	JUN	JUL	AUG	SEP	OCT	NOV	DEC
1958	1	18 42 32	20 44 45	22 35 9	0 37 22	2 35 38	4 37 52	6 36 8	8 38 21	10 40 35	12 38 51	14 41 4	16 39 21
	2	18 46 28	20 48 42	22 39 5	0 41 18	2 39 35	4 41 48	6 40 5	8 42 18	10 44 31	12 42 48	14 45 1	16 43 18
	3	18 50 25	20 52 38	22 43 2	0 45 15	2 43 31	4 45 45	6 44 1	8 46 15	10 48 28	12 46 44	14 48 57	16 47 14
	4	18 54 22	20 56 35	22 46 58	0 49 11	2 47 28	4 49 41	6 47 58	8 50 11	10 52 24	12 50 41	14 52 54	16 51 11
	5	18 58 18	21 0 31	22 50 55	0 53 8	2 51 25	4 53 38	6 51 54	8 54 8	10 56 21	12 54 37	14 56 51	16 55 7
	6	19 2 15	21 4 28	22 54 51	0 57 4	2 55 21	4 57 34	6 55 51	8 58 4	11 0 17	12 58 34	15 0 47	16 59 4
	7	19 6 11	21 8 24	22 58 48	1 1 1	2 59 18	5 1 31	6 59 48	9 2 1	11 4 14	13 2 31	15 4 44	17 3 0
	8	19 10 8	21 12 21	23 2 44	1 4 58	3 3 14	5 5 27	7 3 44	9 5 57	11 8 10	13 6 27	15 8 40	17 6 57
	9	19 14 4	21 16 18	23 6 41	1 8 54	3 7 11	5 9 24	7 7 41	9 9 54	11 12 7	13 10 24	15 12 37	17 10 53
	10	19 18 1	21 20 14	23 10 38	1 12 51	3 11 7	5 13 21	7 11 37	9 13 50	11 16 4	13 14 20	15 16 33	17 14 50
	11	19 21 57	21 24 11	23 14 34	1 16 47	3 15 4	5 17 17	7 15 34	9 17 47	11 20 0	13 18 17	15 20 30	17 18 47
	12	19 25 54	21 28 7	23 18 31	1 20 44	3 19 0	5 21 14	7 19 30	9 21 44	11 23 57	13 22 13	15 24 26	17 22 43
	13	19 29 51	21 32 4	23 22 27	1 24 40	3 22 57	5 25 10	7 23 27	9 25 40	11 27 53	13 26 10	15 28 23	17 26 40
	14	19 33 47	21 36 0	23 26 24	1 28 37	3 26 54	5 29 7	7 27 23	9 29 37	11 31 50	13 30 6	15 32 20	17 30 36
	15	19 37 44	21 39 57	23 30 20	1 32 33	3 30 50	5 33 3	7 31 20	9 33 33	11 35 46	13 34 3	15 36 16	17 34 33
	16	19 41 40	21 43 53	23 34 17	1 36 30	3 34 47	5 37 0	7 35 17	9 37 30	11 39 43	13 37 59	15 40 13	17 38 29
	17	19 45 37	21 47 50	23 38 13	1 40 27	3 38 43	5 40 56	7 39 13	9 41 26	11 43 39	13 41 56	15 44 9	17 42 26
	18	19 49 33	21 51 47	23 42 10	1 44 23	3 42 40	5 44 53	7 43 10	9 45 23	11 47 36	13 45 53	15 48 6	17 46 22
	19	19 53 30	21 55 43	23 46 7	1 48 20	3 46 36	5 48 50	7 47 6	9 49 19	11 51 33	13 49 49	15 52 2	17 50 19
	20	19 57 26	21 59 40	23 50 3	1 52 16	3 50 33	5 52 46	7 51 3	9 53 16	11 55 29	13 53 46	15 55 59	17 54 16
	21	20 1 23	22 3 36	23 54 0	1 56 13	3 54 29	5 56 43	7 54 59	9 57 13	11 59 26	13 57 42	15 59 55	17 58 12
	22	20 5 20	22 7 33	23 57 56	2 0 9	3 58 26	6 0 39	7 58 56	10 1 9	12 3 22	14 1 39	16 3 52	18 2 9
	23	20 9 16	22 11 29	0 1 53	2 4 6	4 2 23	6 4 36	8 2 52	10 5 6	12 7 19	14 5 35	16 7 49	18 6 5
	24	20 13 13	22 15 26	0 5 49	2 8 2	4 6 19	6 8 32	8 6 49	10 9 2	12 11 15	14 9 32	16 11 45	18 10 2
	25	20 17 9	22 19 22	0 9 46	2 11 59	4 10 16	6 12 29	8 10 46	10 12 59	12 15 12	14 13 28	16 15 42	18 13 58
	26	20 21 6	22 23 19	0 13 42	2 15 56	4 14 12	6 16 25	8 14 42	10 16 55	12 19 8	14 17 25	16 19 38	18 17 55
	27	20 25 2	22 27 15	0 17 39	2 19 52	4 18 9	6 20 22	8 18 39	10 20 52	12 23 5	14 21 22	16 23 35	18 21 51
	28	20 28 59	22 31 12	0 21 36	2 23 49	4 22 5	6 24 19	8 22 35	10 24 48	12 27 2	14 25 18	16 27 31	18 25 48
	29	20 32 55		0 25 32	2 27 45	4 26 2	6 28 15	8 26 32	10 28 45	12 30 58	14 29 15	16 31 28	18 29 45
	30	20 36 52		0 29 29	2 31 42	4 29 58	6 32 12	8 30 28	10 32 42	12 34 55	14 33 11	16 35 24	18 33 41
	31	20 40 49		0 33 25		4 33 55		8 34 25	10 36 38		14 37 8		18 37 38
1959	1	18 41 34	20 43 47	22 34 11	0 36 24	2 34 41	4 36 54	6 35 11	8 37 24	10 39 37	12 37 54	14 40 7	16 38 23
	2	18 45 31	20 47 44	22 38 8	0 40 21	2 38 37	4 40 50	6 39 7	8 41 20	10 43 34	12 41 50	14 44 3	16 42 20
	3	18 49 27	20 51 41	22 42 4	0 44 17	2 42 34	4 44 47	6 43 4	8 45 17	10 47 30	12 45 47	14 48 0	16 46 16
	4	18 53 24	20 55 37	22 46 1	0 48 14	2 46 30	4 48 44	6 47 0	8 49 13	10 51 27	12 49 43	14 51 56	16 50 13
	5	18 57 20	20 59 34	22 49 57	0 52 10	2 50 27	4 52 40	6 50 57	8 53 10	10 55 23	12 53 40	14 55 53	16 54 10
	6	19 1 17	21 3 30	22 53 54	0 56 7	2 54 23	4 56 37	6 54 53	8 57 7	10 59 20	12 57 36	14 59 49	16 58 6
	7	19 5 14	21 7 27	22 57 50	1 0 3	2 58 20	5 0 33	6 58 50	9 1 3	11 3 16	13 1 33	15 3 46	17 2 3
	8	19 9 10	21 11 23	23 1 47	1 4 0	3 2 17	5 4 30	7 2 46	9 5 0	11 7 13	13 5 29	15 7 43	17 5 59
	9	19 13 7	21 15 20	23 5 43	1 7 57	3 6 13	5 8 26	7 6 43	9 8 56	11 11 9	13 9 26	15 11 39	17 9 56
	10	19 17 3	21 19 16	23 9 40	1 11 53	3 10 10	5 12 23	7 10 40	9 12 53	11 15 6	13 13 23	15 15 36	17 13 52
	11	19 21 0	21 23 13	23 13 37	1 15 50	3 14 6	5 16 19	7 14 36	9 16 49	11 19 3	13 17 19	15 19 32	17 17 49
	12	19 24 56	21 27 10	23 17 33	1 19 46	3 18 3	5 20 16	7 18 33	9 20 46	11 22 59	13 21 16	15 23 29	17 21 45
	13	19 28 53	21 31 6	23 21 30	1 23 43	3 21 59	5 24 13	7 22 29	9 24 42	11 26 56	13 25 12	15 27 25	17 25 42
	14	19 32 49	21 35 3	23 25 26	1 27 39	3 25 56	5 28 9	7 26 26	9 28 39	11 30 52	13 29 9	15 31 22	17 29 39
	15	19 36 46	21 38 59	23 29 23	1 31 36	3 29 52	5 32 6	7 30 22	9 32 36	11 34 49	13 33 5	15 35 18	17 33 35
	16	19 40 43	21 42 56	23 33 19	1 35 32	3 33 49	5 36 2	7 34 19	9 36 32	11 38 45	13 37 2	15 39 15	17 37 32
	17	19 44 39	21 46 52	23 37 16	1 39 29	3 37 46	5 39 59	7 38 15	9 40 29	11 42 42	13 40 58	15 43 12	17 41 28
	18	19 48 36	21 50 49	23 41 12	1 43 25	3 41 42	5 43 55	7 42 12	9 44 25	11 46 38	13 44 55	15 47 8	17 45 25
	19	19 52 32	21 54 45	23 45 9	1 47 22	3 45 39	5 47 52	7 46 9	9 48 22	11 50 35	13 48 51	15 51 5	17 49 21
	20	19 56 29	21 58 42	23 49 5	1 51 19	3 49 35	5 51 48	7 50 5	9 52 18	11 54 31	13 52 48	15 55 1	17 53 18
	21	20 0 25	22 2 39	23 53 2	1 55 15	3 53 32	5 55 45	7 54 2	9 56 15	11 58 28	13 56 45	15 58 58	17 57 14
	22	20 4 22	22 6 35	23 56 59	1 59 12	3 57 28	5 59 42	7 57 58	10 0 11	12 2 25	14 0 41	16 2 54	18 1 11
	23	20 8 18	22 10 32	0 0 55	2 3 8	4 1 25	6 3 38	8 1 55	10 4 8	12 6 21	14 4 38	16 6 51	18 5 8
	24	20 12 15	22 14 28	0 4 52	2 7 5	4 5 21	6 7 35	8 5 51	10 8 5	12 10 18	14 8 34	16 10 47	18 9 4
	25	20 16 12	22 18 25	0 8 48	2 11 1	4 9 18	6 11 31	8 9 48	10 12 1	12 14 14	14 12 31	16 14 44	18 13 1
	26	20 20 8	22 22 21	0 12 45	2 14 58	4 13 15	6 15 28	8 13 44	10 15 58	12 18 11	14 16 27	16 18 41	18 16 57
	27	20 24 5	22 26 18	0 16 41	2 18 54	4 17 11	6 19 24	8 17 41	10 19 54	12 22 7	14 20 24	16 22 37	18 20 54
	28	20 28 1	22 30 14	0 20 38	2 22 51	4 21 8	6 23 21	8 21 38	10 23 51	12 26 4	14 24 20	16 26 34	18 24 50
	29	20 31 58		0 24 34	2 26 48	4 25 4	6 27 17	8 25 34	10 27 47	12 30 0	14 28 17	16 30 30	18 28 47
	30	20 35 54		0 28 31	2 30 44	4 29 1	6 31 14	8 29 31	10 31 44	12 33 57	14 32 14	16 34 27	18 32 43
	31	20 39 51		0 32 28		4 32 57		8 33 27	10 35 40		14 36 10		18 36 40
1960	1	18 40 37	20 42 50	22 37 10	0 39 23	2 37 40	4 39 53	6 38 9	8 40 23	10 42 36	12 40 52	14 43 6	16 41 22
	2	18 44 33	20 46 46	22 41 6	0 43 20	2 41 36	4 43 49	6 42 6	8 44 19	10 46 32	12 44 49	14 47 2	16 45 19
	3	18 48 30	20 50 43	22 45 3	0 47 16	2 45 33	4 47 46	6 46 3	8 48 16	10 50 29	12 48 46	14 50 59	16 49 15
	4	18 52 26	20 54 39	22 49 0	0 51 13	2 49 29	4 51 42	6 49 59	8 52 12	10 54 26	12 52 42	14 54 55	16 53 12
	5	18 56 23	20 58 36	22 52 56	0 55 9	2 53 26	4 55 39	6 53 56	8 56 9	10 58 22	12 56 39	14 58 52	16 57 8
	6	19 0 19	21 2 33	22 56 53	0 59 6	2 57 22	4 59 36	6 57 52	9 0 6	11 2 19	13 0 35	15 2 48	17 1 5
	7	19 4 16	21 6 29	23 0 49	1 3 2	3 1 19	5 3 32	7 1 49	9 4 2	11 6 15	13 4 32	15 6 45	17 5 2
	8	19 8 12	21 10 26	23 4 46	1 6 59	3 5 15	5 7 29	7 5 45	9 7 59	11 10 12	13 8 28	15 10 41	17 8 58
	9	19 12 9	21 14 22	23 8 42	1 10 55	3 9 12	5 11 25	7 9 42	9 11 55	11 14 8	13 12 25	15 14 38	17 12 55
	10	19 16 6	21 18 19	23 12 39	1 14 52	3 13 9	5 15 22	7 13 39	9 15 52	11 18 5	13 16 21	15 18 35	17 16 51
	11	19 20 2	21 22 15	23 16 35	1 18 49	3 17 5	5 19 18	7 17 35	9 19 48	11 22 1	13 20 18	15 22 31	17 20 48
	12	19 23 59	21 26 12	23 20 32	1 22 45	3 21 2	5 23 15	7 21 32	9 23 45	11 25 58	13 24 15	15 26 28	17 24 44
	13	19 27 55	21 30 8	23 24 29	1 26 42	3 24 58	5 27 11	7 25 28	9 27 41	11 29 55	13 28 11	15 30 24	17 28 41
	14	19 31 52	21 34 5	23 28 25	1 30 38	3 28 55	5 31 8	7 29 25	9 31 38	11 33 51	13 32 8	15 34 21	17 32 37
	15	19 35 48	21 38 2	23 32 22	1 34 35	3 32 51	5 35 5	7 33 21	9 35 34	11 37 48	13 36 4	15 38 17	17 36 34
	16	19 39 45	21 41 58	23 36 18	1 38 31	3 36 48	5 39 1	7 37 18	9 39 31	11 41 44	13 40 1	15 42 14	17 40 31
	17	19 43 42	21 45 55	23 40 15	1 42 28	3 40 44	5 42 58	7 41 14	9 43 28	11 45 41	13 43 57	15 46 10	17 44 27
	18	19 47 38	21 49 51	23 44 11	1 46 24	3 44 41	5 46 54	7 45 11	9 47 24	11 49 37	13 47 54	15 50 7	17 48 24
	19	19 51 35	21 53 48	23 48 8	1 50 21	3 48 38	5 50 51	7 49 7	9 51 21	11 53 34	13 51 50	15 54 4	17 52 20
	20	19 55 31	21 57 44	23 52 4	1 54 18	3 52 34	5 54 47	7 53 4	9 55 17	11 57 30	13 55 47	15 58 0	17 56 17
	21	19 59 28	22 1 41	23 56 1	1 58 14	3 56 31	5 58 44	7 57 1	9 59 14	12 1 27	13 59 43	16 1 57	18 0 13
	22	20 3 24	22 5 37	23 59 57	2 2 11	4 0 27	6 2 40	8 0 57	10 3 10	12 5 23	14 3 40	16 5 53	18 4 10
	23	20 7 21	22 9 34	0 3 54	2 6 7	4 4 24	6 6 37	8 4 54	10 7 7	12 9 20	14 7 37	16 9 50	18 8 7
	24	20 11 17	22 13 31	0 7 51	2 10 4	4 8 20	6 10 34	8 8 50	10 11 3	12 13 17	14 11 33	16 13 46	18 12 3
	25	20 15 14	22 17 27	0 11 47	2 14 0	4 12 17	6 14 30	8 12 47	10 15 0	12 17 13	14 15 30	16 17 43	18 16 0
	26	20 19 11	22 21 24	0 15 44	2 17 57	4 16 13	6 18 27	8 16 43	10 18 57	12 21 10	14 19 26	16 21 39	18 19 56
	27	20 23 7	22 25 20	0 19 40	2 21 53	4 20 10	6 22 23	8 20 40	10 22 53	12 25 6	14 23 23	16 25 36	18 23 53
	28	20 27 4	22 29 17	0 23 37	2 25 50	4 24 7	6 26 20	8 24 37	10 26 50	12 29 3	14 27 19	16 29 33	18 27 49
	29	20 31 0	22 33 13	0 27 33	2 29 46	4 28 3	6 30 16	8 28 33	10 30 46	12 32 59	14 31 16	16 33 29	18 31 46
	30	20 34 57		0 31 30	2 33 43	4 32 0	6 34 13	8 32 30	10 34 43	12 36 56	14 35 12	16 37 26	18 35 42
	31	20 38 53		0 35 26		4 35 56		8 36 26	10 38 39		14 39 9		18 39 39
1961	1	18 43 36	20 45 49	22 36 12	0 38 25	2 36 42	4 38 55	6 37 12	8 39 25	10 41 38	12 39 55	14 42 8	16 40 25
	2	18 47 32	20 49 45	22 40 9	0 42 22	2 40 38	4 42 52	6 41 8	8 43 22	10 45 35	12 43 51	14 46 5	16 44 21
	3	18 51 29	20 53 42	22 44 5	0 46 18	2 44 35	4 46 48	6 45 5	8 47 18	10 49 31	12 47 48	14 50 1	16 48 18
	4	18 55 25	20 57 38	22 48 2	0 50 15	2 48 32	4 50 45	6 49 2	8 51 15	10 53 28	12 51 44	14 53 58	16 52 14
	5	18 59 22	21 1 35	22 51 58	0 54 12	2 52 28	4 54 41	6 52 58	8 55 11	10 57 24	12 55 41	14 57 54	16 56 11
	6	19 3 18	21 5 32	22 55 55	0 58 8	2 56 25	4 58 38	6 56 55	8 59 8	11 1 21	12 59 38	15 1 51	17 0 7
	7	19 7 15	21 9 28	22 59 52	1 2 5	3 0 21	5 2 34	7 0 51	9 3 4	11 5 18	13 3 34	15 5 47	17 4 4
	8	19 11 11	21 13 25	23 3 48	1 6 1	3 4 18	5 6 31	7 4 48	9 7 1	11 9 14	13 7 31	15 9 44	17 8 1
	9	19 15 8	21 17 21	23 7 45	1 9 58	3 8 14	5 10 28	7 8 44	9 10 58	11 13 11	13 11 27	15 13 40	17 11 57
	10	19 19 5	21 21 18	23 11 41	1 13 54	3 12 11	5 14 24	7 12 41	9 14 54	11 17 7	13 15 24	15 17 37	17 15 54
	11	19 23 1	21 25 14	23 15 38	1 17 51	3 16 7	5 18 21	7 16 37	9 18 51	11 21 4	13 19 20	15 21 33	17 19 50
	12	19 26 58	21 29 11	23 19 34	1 21 47	3 20 4	5 22 17	7 20 34	9 22 47	11 25 0	13 23 17	15 25 30	17 23 47
	13	19 30 54	21 33 7	23 23 31	1 25 44	3 24 1	5 26 14	7 24 31	9 26 44	11 28 57	13 27 13	15 29 27	17 27 43
	14	19 34 51	21 37 4	23 27 27	1 29 41	3 27 57	5 30 10	7 28 27	9 30 40	11 32 53	13 31 10	15 33 23	17 31 40
	15	19 38 47	21 41 1	23 31 24	1 33 37	3 31 54	5 34 7	7 32 24	9 34 37	11 36 50	13 35 7	15 37 20	17 35 36
	16	19 42 44	21 44 57	23 35 21	1 37 34	3 35 50	5 38 4	7 36 20	9 38 33	11 40 47	13 39 3	15 41 16	17 39 33
	17	19 46 40	21 48 54	23 39 17	1 41 30	3 39 47	5 42 0	7 40 17	9 42 30	11 44 43	13 43 0	15 45 13	17 43 30
	18	19 50 37	21 52 50	23 43 14	1 45 27	3 43 43	5 45 57	7 44 13	9 46 27	11 48 40	13 46 56	15 49 9	17 47 26
	19	19 54 34	21 56 47	23 47 10	1 49 23	3 47 40	5 49 53	7 48 10	9 50 23	11 52 36	13 50 53	15 53 6	17 51 23
	20	19 58 30	22 0 43	23 51 7	1 53 20	3 51 36	5 53 50	7 52 6	9 54 20	11 56 33	13 54 49	15 57 2	17 55 19
	21	20 2 27	22 4 40	23 55 3	1 57 16	3 55 33	5 57 46	7 56 3	9 58 16	12 0 29	13 58 46	16 0 59	17 59 16
	22	20 6 23	22 8 36	23 59 0	2 1 13	3 59 30	6 1 43	8 0 0	10 2 13	12 4 26	14 2 42	16 4 56	18 3 12
	23	20 10 20	22 12 33	0 2 56	2 5 10	4 3 26	6 5 39	8 3 56	10 6 9	12 8 22	14 6 39	16 8 52	18 7 9
	24	20 14 16	22 16 29	0 6 53	2 9 6	4 7 23	6 9 36	8 7 53	10 10 6	12 12 19	14 10 36	16 12 49	18 11 5
	25	20 18 13	22 20 26	0 10 50	2 13 3	4 11 19	6 13 33	8 11 49	10 14 2	12 16 16	14 14 32	16 16 45	18 15 2
	26	20 22 9	22 24 23	0 14 46	2 16 59	4 15 16	6 17 29	8 15 46	10 17 59	12 20 12	14 18 29	16 20 42	18 18 59
	27	20 26 6	22 28 19	0 18 43	2 20 56	4 19 12	6 21 26	8 19 42	10 21 56	12 24 9	14 22 25	16 24 38	18 22 55
	28	20 30 3	22 32 16	0 22 39	2 24 52	4 23 9	6 25 22	8 23 39	10 25 52	12 28 5	14 26 22	16 28 35	18 26 52
	29	20 33 59		0 26 36	2 28 49	4 27 5	6 29 19	8 27 35	10 29 49	12 32 2	14 30 18	16 32 32	18 30 48
	30	20 37 56		0 30 32	2 32 45	4 31 2	6 33 15	8 31 32	10 33 45	12 35 58	14 34 15	16 36 28	18 34 45
	31	20 41 52		0 34 29		4 34 59		8 35 29	10 37 42		14 38 11		18 38 41

YEAR		JAN	FEB	MAR	APR	MAY	JUN	JUL	SEP	AUG	OCT	NOV	DEC
1962	1	18 42 38	20 44 51	22 35 15	0 37 28	2 35 44	4 37 58	6 36 14	8 38 28	10 40 41	12 38 57	14 41 10	16 39 27
	2	18 46 34	20 48 48	22 39 11	0 41 24	2 39 41	4 41 54	6 40 11	8 42 24	10 44 37	12 42 54	14 45 7	16 43 24
	3	18 50 31	20 52 44	22 43 8	0 45 21	2 43 37	4 45 51	6 44 7	8 46 21	10 48 34	12 46 50	14 49 4	16 47 20
	4	18 54 28	20 56 41	22 47 4	0 49 17	2 47 34	4 49 47	6 48 4	8 50 17	10 52 30	12 50 47	14 53 0	16 51 17
	5	18 58 24	21 0 37	22 51 1	0 53 14	2 51 31	4 53 44	6 52 1	8 54 14	10 56 27	12 54 43	14 56 57	16 55 13
	6	19 2 21	21 4 34	22 54 57	0 57 11	2 55 27	4 57 40	6 55 57	8 58 10	11 0 23	12 58 40	15 0 53	16 59 10
	7	19 6 17	21 8 30	22 58 54	1 1 7	2 59 24	5 1 37	6 59 54	9 2 7	11 4 20	13 2 37	15 4 50	17 3 6
	8	19 10 14	21 12 27	23 2 51	1 5 4	3 3 20	5 5 33	7 3 50	9 6 3	11 8 17	13 6 33	15 8 46	17 7 3
	9	19 14 10	21 16 24	23 6 47	1 9 0	3 7 17	5 9 30	7 7 47	9 10 0	11 12 13	13 10 30	15 12 43	17 11 0
	10	19 18 7	21 20 20	23 10 44	1 12 57	3 11 13	5 13 27	7 11 43	9 13 57	11 16 10	13 14 26	15 16 39	17 14 56
	11	19 22 3	21 24 17	23 14 40	1 16 53	3 15 10	5 17 23	7 15 40	9 17 53	11 20 6	13 18 23	15 20 36	17 18 53
	12	19 26 0	21 28 13	23 18 37	1 20 50	3 19 6	5 21 20	7 19 36	9 21 50	11 24 3	13 22 19	15 24 33	17 22 49
	13	19 29 57	21 32 10	23 22 33	1 24 46	3 23 3	5 25 16	7 23 33	9 25 46	11 27 59	13 26 16	15 28 29	17 26 46
	14	19 33 53	21 36 6	23 26 30	1 28 43	3 27 0	5 29 13	7 27 30	9 29 43	11 31 56	13 30 12	15 32 26	17 30 42
	15	19 37 50	21 40 3	23 30 26	1 32 40	3 30 56	5 33 9	7 31 26	9 33 39	11 35 52	13 34 9	15 36 22	17 34 39
	16	19 41 46	21 43 59	23 34 23	1 36 36	3 34 53	5 37 6	7 35 23	9 37 36	11 39 49	13 38 6	15 40 19	17 38 35
	17	19 45 43	21 47 56	23 38 20	1 40 33	3 38 49	5 41 2	7 39 19	9 41 32	11 43 46	13 42 2	15 44 15	17 42 32
	18	19 49 39	21 51 53	23 42 16	1 44 29	3 42 46	5 44 59	7 43 16	9 45 29	11 47 42	13 45 59	15 48 12	17 46 29
	19	19 53 36	21 55 49	23 46 13	1 48 26	3 46 42	5 48 56	7 47 12	9 49 26	11 51 39	13 49 55	15 52 8	17 50 25
	20	19 57 32	21 59 46	23 50 9	1 52 22	3 50 39	5 52 52	7 51 9	9 53 22	11 55 35	13 53 52	15 56 5	17 54 22
	21	20 1 29	22 3 42	23 54 6	1 56 19	3 54 35	5 56 49	7 55 5	9 57 19	11 59 32	13 57 48	16 0 2	17 58 18
	22	20 5 26	22 7 39	23 58 2	2 0 15	3 58 32	6 0 45	7 59 2	10 1 15	12 3 28	14 1 45	16 3 58	18 2 15
	23	20 9 22	22 11 35	0 1 59	2 4 12	4 2 29	6 4 42	8 2 59	10 5 12	12 7 25	14 5 41	16 7 55	18 6 11
	24	20 13 19	22 15 32	0 5 55	2 8 8	4 6 25	6 8 38	8 6 55	10 9 8	12 11 21	14 9 38	16 11 51	18 10 8
	25	20 17 15	22 19 28	0 9 52	2 12 5	4 10 22	6 12 35	8 10 52	10 13 5	12 15 18	14 13 35	16 15 48	18 14 4
	26	20 21 12	22 23 25	0 13 48	2 16 2	4 14 18	6 16 32	8 14 48	10 17 1	12 19 15	14 17 31	16 19 44	18 18 1
	27	20 25 8	22 27 22	0 17 45	2 19 58	4 18 15	6 20 28	8 18 45	10 20 58	12 23 11	14 21 28	16 23 41	18 21 58
	28	20 29 5	22 31 18	0 21 42	2 23 55	4 22 11	6 24 25	8 22 41	10 24 55	12 27 8	14 25 24	16 27 37	18 25 54
	29	20 33 1		0 25 38	2 27 51	4 26 8	6 28 21	8 26 38	10 28 51	12 31 4	14 29 21	16 31 34	18 29 51
	30	20 36 58		0 29 35	2 31 48	4 30 4	6 32 18	8 30 34	10 32 48	12 35 1	14 33 17	16 35 31	18 33 47
	31	20 40 55		0 33 31		4 34 1		8 34 31	10 36 44		14 37 14		18 37 44
1963	1	18 41 40	20 43 54	22 34 17	0 36 30	2 34 47	4 37 0	6 35 17	8 37 30	10 39 43	12 38 0	14 40 13	16 38 30
	2	18 45 37	20 47 50	22 38 14	0 40 27	2 38 43	4 40 57	6 39 13	8 41 27	10 43 40	12 41 56	14 44 10	16 42 26
	3	18 49 33	20 51 47	22 42 10	0 44 23	2 42 40	4 44 53	6 43 10	8 45 23	10 47 36	12 45 53	14 48 6	16 46 23
	4	18 53 30	20 55 43	22 46 7	0 48 20	2 46 37	4 48 50	6 47 6	8 49 20	10 51 33	12 49 49	14 52 3	16 50 19
	5	18 57 27	20 59 40	22 50 3	0 52 17	2 50 33	4 52 46	6 51 3	8 53 16	10 55 29	12 53 46	14 55 59	16 54 16
	6	19 1 23	21 3 36	22 54 0	0 56 13	2 54 30	4 56 43	6 55 0	8 57 13	10 59 26	12 57 43	14 59 56	16 58 12
	7	19 5 20	21 7 33	22 57 56	1 0 10	2 58 26	5 0 39	6 58 56	9 1 9	11 3 23	13 1 39	15 3 52	17 2 9
	8	19 9 16	21 11 30	23 1 53	1 4 6	3 2 23	5 4 36	7 2 53	9 5 6	11 7 19	13 5 36	15 7 49	17 6 6
	9	19 13 13	21 15 26	23 5 50	1 8 3	3 6 19	5 8 33	7 6 49	9 9 3	11 11 16	13 9 32	15 11 45	17 10 2
	10	19 17 9	21 19 23	23 9 46	1 11 59	3 10 16	5 12 29	7 10 46	9 12 59	11 15 12	13 13 29	15 15 42	17 13 59
	11	19 21 6	21 23 19	23 13 43	1 15 56	3 14 12	5 16 26	7 14 42	9 16 56	11 19 9	13 17 25	15 19 39	17 17 55
	12	19 25 3	21 27 16	23 17 39	1 19 52	3 18 9	5 20 22	7 18 39	9 20 52	11 23 5	13 21 22	15 23 35	17 21 52
	13	19 28 59	21 31 12	23 21 36	1 23 49	3 22 6	5 24 19	7 22 36	9 24 49	11 27 2	13 25 18	15 27 32	17 25 48
	14	19 32 56	21 35 9	23 25 32	1 27 45	3 26 2	5 28 15	7 26 32	9 28 45	11 30 58	13 29 15	15 31 28	17 29 45
	15	19 36 52	21 39 5	23 29 29	1 31 42	3 29 59	5 32 12	7 30 29	9 32 42	11 34 55	13 33 12	15 35 25	17 33 41
	16	19 40 49	21 43 2	23 33 25	1 35 39	3 33 55	5 36 8	7 34 25	9 36 38	11 38 52	13 37 8	15 39 21	17 37 38
	17	19 44 45	21 46 59	23 37 22	1 39 35	3 37 52	5 40 5	7 38 22	9 40 35	11 42 48	13 41 5	15 43 18	17 41 35
	18	19 48 42	21 50 55	23 41 19	1 43 32	3 41 48	5 44 2	7 42 18	9 44 32	11 46 45	13 45 1	15 47 14	17 45 31
	19	19 52 38	21 54 52	23 45 15	1 47 28	3 45 45	5 47 58	7 46 15	9 48 28	11 50 41	13 48 58	15 51 11	17 49 28
	20	19 56 35	21 58 48	23 49 12	1 51 25	3 49 41	5 51 55	7 50 11	9 52 25	11 54 38	13 52 54	15 55 8	17 53 24
	21	20 0 32	22 2 45	23 53 8	1 55 21	3 53 38	5 55 51	7 54 8	9 56 21	11 58 34	13 56 51	15 59 4	17 57 21
	22	20 4 28	22 6 41	23 57 5	1 59 18	3 57 35	5 59 48	7 58 5	10 0 18	12 2 31	14 0 47	16 3 1	18 1 17
	23	20 8 25	22 10 38	0 1 1	2 3 14	4 1 31	6 3 44	8 2 1	10 4 14	12 6 27	14 4 44	16 6 57	18 5 14
	24	20 12 21	22 14 34	0 4 58	2 7 11	4 5 28	6 7 41	8 5 58	10 8 11	12 10 24	14 8 41	16 10 54	18 9 11
	25	20 16 18	22 18 31	0 8 54	2 11 8	4 9 24	6 11 37	8 9 54	10 12 7	12 14 21	14 12 37	16 14 50	18 13 7
	26	20 20 14	22 22 27	0 12 51	2 15 4	4 13 21	6 15 34	8 13 51	10 16 4	12 18 17	14 16 34	16 18 47	18 17 4
	27	20 24 11	22 26 24	0 16 48	2 19 1	4 17 17	6 19 31	8 17 47	10 20 0	12 22 14	14 20 30	16 22 43	18 21 0
	28	20 28 7	22 30 21	0 20 44	2 22 57	4 21 14	6 23 27	8 21 44	10 23 57	12 26 10	14 24 27	16 26 40	18 24 57
	29	20 32 4		0 24 41	2 26 54	4 25 10	6 27 24	8 25 40	10 27 54	12 30 7	14 28 23	16 30 37	18 28 53
	30	20 36 1		0 28 37	2 30 50	4 29 7	6 31 20	8 29 37	10 31 50	12 34 3	14 32 20	16 34 33	18 32 50
	31	20 39 57		0 32 34		4 33 4		8 33 34	10 35 47		14 36 16		18 36 46
1964	1	18 40 43	20 42 56	22 37 16	0 39 29	2 37 46	4 39 59	6 38 16	8 40 29	10 42 42	12 40 59	14 43 12	16 41 29
	2	18 44 40	20 46 53	22 41 13	0 43 26	2 41 43	4 43 56	6 42 13	8 44 26	10 46 39	12 44 56	14 47 9	16 45 25
	3	18 48 36	20 50 49	22 45 9	0 47 23	2 45 39	4 47 52	6 46 9	8 48 22	10 50 36	12 48 52	14 51 5	16 49 22
	4	18 52 33	20 54 46	22 49 6	0 51 19	2 49 36	4 51 49	6 50 6	8 52 19	10 54 32	12 52 49	14 55 2	16 53 19
	5	18 56 29	20 58 42	22 53 3	0 55 16	2 53 32	4 55 46	6 54 2	8 56 16	10 58 29	12 56 45	14 58 58	16 57 15
	6	19 0 26	21 2 39	22 56 59	0 59 12	2 57 29	4 59 42	6 57 59	9 0 12	11 2 25	13 0 42	15 2 55	17 1 12
	7	19 4 22	21 6 36	23 0 56	1 3 9	3 1 25	5 3 39	7 1 55	9 4 9	11 6 22	13 4 38	15 6 52	17 5 8
	8	19 8 19	21 10 32	23 4 52	1 7 5	3 5 22	5 7 35	7 5 52	9 8 5	11 10 18	13 8 35	15 10 48	17 9 5
	9	19 12 15	21 14 29	23 8 49	1 11 2	3 9 18	5 11 32	7 9 48	9 12 2	11 14 15	13 12 31	15 14 45	17 13 1
	10	19 16 12	21 18 25	23 12 45	1 14 58	3 13 15	5 15 28	7 13 45	9 15 58	11 18 11	13 16 28	15 18 41	17 16 58
	11	19 20 9	21 22 22	23 16 42	1 18 55	3 17 12	5 19 25	7 17 42	9 19 55	11 22 8	13 20 25	15 22 38	17 20 55
	12	19 24 5	21 26 18	23 20 38	1 22 52	3 21 8	5 23 21	7 21 38	9 23 51	11 26 5	13 24 21	15 26 34	17 24 51
	13	19 28 2	21 30 15	23 24 35	1 26 48	3 25 5	5 27 18	7 25 35	9 27 48	11 30 1	13 28 18	15 30 31	17 28 48
	14	19 31 58	21 34 11	23 28 32	1 30 45	3 29 1	5 31 15	7 29 31	9 31 45	11 33 58	13 32 14	15 34 27	17 32 44
	15	19 35 55	21 38 8	23 32 28	1 34 41	3 32 58	5 35 11	7 33 28	9 35 41	11 37 54	13 36 11	15 38 24	17 36 41
	16	19 39 51	21 42 5	23 36 25	1 38 38	3 36 54	5 39 8	7 37 24	9 39 38	11 41 51	13 40 7	15 42 21	17 40 37
	17	19 43 48	21 46 1	23 40 21	1 42 34	3 40 51	5 43 4	7 41 21	9 43 34	11 45 47	13 44 4	15 46 17	17 44 34
	18	19 47 44	21 49 58	23 44 18	1 46 31	3 44 48	5 47 1	7 45 17	9 47 31	11 49 44	13 48 0	15 50 14	17 48 30
	19	19 51 41	21 53 54	23 48 14	1 50 27	3 48 44	5 50 57	7 49 14	9 51 27	11 53 40	13 51 57	15 54 10	17 52 27
	20	19 55 38	21 57 51	23 52 11	1 54 24	3 52 41	5 54 54	7 53 11	9 55 24	11 57 37	13 55 54	15 58 7	17 56 24
	21	19 59 34	22 1 47	23 56 7	1 58 21	3 56 37	5 58 50	7 57 7	9 59 20	12 1 34	13 59 50	16 2 3	18 0 20
	22	20 3 31	22 5 44	0 0 4	2 2 17	4 0 34	6 2 47	8 1 4	10 3 17	12 5 30	14 3 47	16 6 0	18 4 17
	23	20 7 27	22 9 40	0 4 0	2 6 14	4 4 30	6 6 44	8 5 0	10 7 14	12 9 27	14 7 43	16 9 56	18 8 13
	24	20 11 24	22 13 37	0 7 57	2 10 10	4 8 27	6 10 40	8 8 57	10 11 10	12 13 23	14 11 40	16 13 53	18 12 10
	25	20 15 20	22 17 34	0 11 54	2 14 7	4 12 23	6 14 37	8 12 53	10 15 7	12 17 20	14 15 36	16 17 50	18 16 6
	26	20 19 17	22 21 30	0 15 50	2 18 3	4 16 20	6 18 33	8 16 50	10 19 3	12 21 16	14 19 33	16 21 46	18 20 3
	27	20 23 13	22 25 27	0 19 47	2 22 0	4 20 17	6 22 30	8 20 47	10 23 0	12 25 13	14 23 29	16 25 43	18 23 59
	28	20 27 10	22 29 23	0 23 43	2 25 56	4 24 13	6 26 26	8 24 43	10 26 56	12 29 9	14 27 26	16 29 39	18 27 56
	29	20 31 7	22 33 20	0 27 40	2 29 53	4 28 10	6 30 23	8 28 40	10 30 53	12 33 6	14 31 23	16 33 36	18 31 53
	30	20 35 3		0 31 36	2 33 49	4 32 6	6 34 19	8 32 36	10 34 49	12 37 3	14 35 19	16 37 32	18 35 49
	31	20 39 0		0 35 33		4 36 3		8 36 33	10 38 46		14 39 16		18 39 46
1965	1	18 43 42	20 45 56	22 36 19	0 38 32	2 36 49	4 39 2	6 37 19	8 39 32	10 41 45	12 40 2	14 42 15	16 40 32
	2	18 47 39	20 49 52	22 40 16	0 42 29	2 40 45	4 42 59	6 41 15	8 43 29	10 45 42	12 43 58	14 46 12	16 44 28
	3	18 51 35	20 53 49	22 44 12	0 46 25	2 44 42	4 46 55	6 45 12	8 47 25	10 49 38	12 47 55	14 50 8	16 48 25
	4	18 55 32	20 57 45	22 48 9	0 50 22	2 48 38	4 50 52	6 49 8	8 51 22	10 53 35	12 51 52	14 54 5	16 52 21
	5	18 59 28	21 1 42	22 52 5	0 54 18	2 52 35	4 54 48	6 53 5	8 55 18	10 57 31	12 55 48	14 58 1	16 56 18
	6	19 3 25	21 5 38	22 56 2	0 58 15	2 56 32	4 58 45	6 57 2	8 59 15	11 1 28	12 59 45	15 1 58	17 0 15
	7	19 7 22	21 9 35	22 59 58	1 2 11	3 0 28	5 2 41	7 0 58	9 3 11	11 5 25	13 3 41	15 5 54	17 4 11
	8	19 11 18	21 13 31	23 3 55	1 6 8	3 4 25	5 6 38	7 4 55	9 7 8	11 9 21	13 7 38	15 9 51	17 8 8
	9	19 15 15	21 17 28	23 7 51	1 10 5	3 8 21	5 10 35	7 8 51	9 11 5	11 13 18	13 11 34	15 13 47	17 12 4
	10	19 19 11	21 21 24	23 11 48	1 14 1	3 12 18	5 14 31	7 12 48	9 15 1	11 17 14	13 15 31	15 17 44	17 16 1
	11	19 23 8	21 25 21	23 15 45	1 17 58	3 16 14	5 18 28	7 16 44	9 18 58	11 21 11	13 19 27	15 21 41	17 19 57
	12	19 27 4	21 29 18	23 19 41	1 21 54	3 20 11	5 22 24	7 20 41	9 22 54	11 25 7	13 23 24	15 25 37	17 23 54
	13	19 31 1	21 33 14	23 23 38	1 25 51	3 24 7	5 26 21	7 24 37	9 26 51	11 29 4	13 27 20	15 29 34	17 27 50
	14	19 34 57	21 37 11	23 27 34	1 29 47	3 28 4	5 30 17	7 28 34	9 30 47	11 33 0	13 31 17	15 33 30	17 31 47
	15	19 38 54	21 41 7	23 31 31	1 33 44	3 32 1	5 34 14	7 32 31	9 34 44	11 36 57	13 35 14	15 37 27	17 35 44
	16	19 42 51	21 45 4	23 35 27	1 37 40	3 35 57	5 38 10	7 36 27	9 38 40	11 40 54	13 39 10	15 41 23	17 39 40
	17	19 46 47	21 49 0	23 39 24	1 41 37	3 39 54	5 42 7	7 40 24	9 42 37	11 44 50	13 43 7	15 45 20	17 43 37
	18	19 50 44	21 52 57	23 43 21	1 45 34	3 43 50	5 46 4	7 44 20	9 46 33	11 48 47	13 47 3	15 49 17	17 47 33
	19	19 54 40	21 56 54	23 47 17	1 49 30	3 47 47	5 50 0	7 48 17	9 50 30	11 52 43	13 51 0	15 53 13	17 51 30
	20	19 58 37	22 0 50	23 51 14	1 53 27	3 51 43	5 53 57	7 52 13	9 54 27	11 56 40	13 54 56	15 57 10	17 55 26
	21	20 2 33	22 4 47	23 55 10	1 57 23	3 55 40	5 57 53	7 56 10	9 58 23	12 0 36	13 58 53	16 1 6	17 59 23
	22	20 6 30	22 8 43	23 59 7	2 1 20	3 59 36	6 1 50	8 0 6	10 2 20	12 4 33	14 2 49	16 5 3	18 3 19
	23	20 10 27	22 12 40	0 3 3	2 5 16	4 3 33	6 5 46	8 4 3	10 6 16	12 8 29	14 6 46	16 8 59	18 7 16
	24	20 14 23	22 16 36	0 7 0	2 9 13	4 7 30	6 9 43	8 8 0	10 10 13	12 12 26	14 10 43	16 12 56	18 11 13
	25	20 18 20	22 20 33	0 10 56	2 13 9	4 11 26	6 13 39	8 11 56	10 14 9	12 16 22	14 14 39	16 16 52	18 15 9
	26	20 22 16	22 24 29	0 14 53	2 17 6	4 15 23	6 17 36	8 15 53	10 18 6	12 20 19	14 18 36	16 20 49	18 19 6
	27	20 26 13	22 28 26	0 18 49	2 21 3	4 19 19	6 21 33	8 19 49	10 22 3	12 24 16	14 22 32	16 24 46	18 23 2
	28	20 30 9	22 32 22	0 22 46	2 24 59	4 23 16	6 25 29	8 23 46	10 25 59	12 28 12	14 26 29	16 28 42	18 26 59
	29	20 34 6		0 26 43	2 28 56	4 27 12	6 29 26	8 27 42	10 29 56	12 32 9	14 30 25	16 32 39	18 30 55
	30	20 38 2		0 30 39	2 32 52	4 31 9	6 33 22	8 31 39	10 33 52	12 36 5	14 34 22	16 36 35	18 34 52
	31	20 41 59		0 34 36		4 35 5		8 35 36	10 37 49		14 38 18		18 38 48

YEAR		JAN	FEB	MAR	APR	MAY	JUN	JUL	AUG	SEP	OCT	NOV	DEC
1966	1	18 42 45	20 44 58	22 35 22	0 37 35	2 35 52	4 38 5	6 36 22	8 38 35	10 40 48	12 39 5	14 41 18	16 39 35
	2	18 46 42	20 48 55	22 39 18	0 41 32	2 39 48	4 42 1	6 40 18	8 42 32	10 44 45	12 43 1	14 45 14	16 43 31
	3	18 50 38	20 52 51	22 43 15	0 45 28	2 43 45	4 45 58	6 44 15	8 46 28	10 48 41	12 46 58	14 49 11	16 47 28
	4	18 54 35	20 56 48	22 47 12	0 49 25	2 47 41	4 49 55	6 48 11	8 50 25	10 52 38	12 50 54	14 53 8	16 51 24
	5	18 58 31	21 0 45	22 51 8	0 53 21	2 51 38	4 53 51	6 52 8	8 54 21	10 56 34	12 54 51	14 57 4	16 55 21
	6	19 2 28	21 4 41	22 55 5	0 57 18	2 55 34	4 57 48	6 56 4	8 58 18	11 0 31	12 58 48	15 1 1	16 59 17
	7	19 6 24	21 8 38	22 59 1	1 1 14	2 59 31	5 1 44	7 0 1	9 2 14	11 4 27	13 2 44	15 4 57	17 3 14
	8	19 10 21	21 12 34	23 2 58	1 5 11	3 3 28	5 5 41	7 3 58	9 6 11	11 8 24	13 6 41	15 8 54	17 7 11
	9	19 14 18	21 16 31	23 6 54	1 9 7	3 7 24	5 9 37	7 7 54	9 10 7	11 12 21	13 10 37	15 12 50	17 11 7
	10	19 18 14	21 20 27	23 10 51	1 13 4	3 11 21	5 13 34	7 11 51	9 14 4	11 16 17	13 14 34	15 16 47	17 15 4
	11	19 22 11	21 24 24	23 14 47	1 17 1	3 15 17	5 17 31	7 15 47	9 18 0	11 20 14	13 18 30	15 20 43	17 19 0
	12	19 26 7	21 28 20	23 18 44	1 20 57	3 19 14	5 21 27	7 19 44	9 21 57	11 24 10	13 22 27	15 24 40	17 22 57
	13	19 30 4	21 32 17	23 22 41	1 24 54	3 23 10	5 25 24	7 23 40	9 25 54	11 28 7	13 26 23	15 28 37	17 26 53
	14	19 34 0	21 36 14	23 26 37	1 28 50	3 27 7	5 29 20	7 27 37	9 29 50	11 32 3	13 30 20	15 32 33	17 30 50
	15	19 37 57	21 40 10	23 30 34	1 32 47	3 31 3	5 33 17	7 31 33	9 33 47	11 36 0	13 34 17	15 36 30	17 34 46
	16	19 41 53	21 44 7	23 34 30	1 36 43	3 35 0	5 37 13	7 35 30	9 37 43	11 39 56	13 38 13	15 40 26	17 38 43
	17	19 45 50	21 48 3	23 38 27	1 40 40	3 38 57	5 41 10	7 39 27	9 41 40	11 43 53	13 42 10	15 44 23	17 42 40
	18	19 49 47	21 52 0	23 42 23	1 44 36	3 42 53	5 45 6	7 43 23	9 45 36	11 47 50	13 46 6	15 48 19	17 46 36
	19	19 53 43	21 55 56	23 46 20	1 48 33	3 46 50	5 49 3	7 47 20	9 49 33	11 51 46	13 50 3	15 52 16	17 50 33
	20	19 57 40	21 59 53	23 50 16	1 52 30	3 50 46	5 53 0	7 51 16	9 53 30	11 55 43	13 53 59	15 56 13	17 54 29
	21	20 1 36	22 3 49	23 54 13	1 56 26	3 54 43	5 56 56	7 55 13	9 57 26	11 59 39	13 57 56	16 0 9	17 58 26
	22	20 5 33	22 7 46	23 58 10	2 0 23	3 58 39	6 0 53	7 59 9	10 1 23	12 3 36	14 1 52	16 4 6	18 2 22
	23	20 9 29	22 11 43	0 2 6	2 4 19	4 2 36	6 4 49	8 3 6	10 5 19	12 7 32	14 5 49	16 8 2	18 6 19
	24	20 13 26	22 15 39	0 6 3	2 8 16	4 6 32	6 8 46	8 7 2	10 9 16	12 11 29	14 9 46	16 11 59	18 10 15
	25	20 17 22	22 19 36	0 9 59	2 12 12	4 10 29	6 12 42	8 10 59	10 13 12	12 15 25	14 13 42	16 15 55	18 14 12
	26	20 21 19	22 23 32	0 13 56	2 16 9	4 14 26	6 16 39	8 14 56	10 17 9	12 19 22	14 17 39	16 19 52	18 18 9
	27	20 25 16	22 27 29	0 17 52	2 20 5	4 18 22	6 20 35	8 18 52	10 21 5	12 23 19	14 21 35	16 23 48	18 22 5
	28	20 29 12	22 31 25	0 21 49	2 24 2	4 22 19	6 24 32	8 22 49	10 25 2	12 27 15	14 25 32	16 27 45	18 26 2
	29	20 33 9		0 25 45	2 27 59	4 26 15	6 28 29	8 26 45	10 28 59	12 31 12	14 29 28	16 31 42	18 29 58
	30	20 37 5		0 29 42	2 31 55	4 30 12	6 32 25	8 30 42	10 32 55	12 35 8	14 33 25	16 35 38	18 33 55
	31	20 41 2		0 33 38		4 34 8		8 34 38	10 36 52		14 37 21		18 37 51
1967	1	18 41 48	20 44 1	22 34 25	0 36 38	2 34 55	4 37 8	6 35 25	8 37 38	10 39 51	12 38 8	14 40 21	16 38 38
	2	18 45 45	20 47 58	22 38 21	0 40 35	2 38 51	4 41 4	6 39 21	8 41 34	10 43 48	12 42 4	14 44 17	16 42 34
	3	18 49 41	20 51 54	22 42 18	0 44 31	2 42 48	4 45 1	6 43 18	8 45 31	10 47 44	12 46 1	14 48 14	16 46 31
	4	18 53 38	20 55 51	22 46 14	0 48 28	2 46 44	4 48 58	6 47 14	8 49 28	10 51 41	12 49 57	14 52 11	16 50 27
	5	18 57 34	20 59 47	22 50 11	0 52 24	2 50 41	4 52 54	6 51 11	8 53 24	10 55 37	12 53 54	14 56 7	16 54 24
	6	19 1 31	21 3 44	22 54 8	0 56 21	2 54 37	4 56 51	6 55 7	8 57 21	10 59 34	12 57 51	15 0 4	16 58 20
	7	19 5 27	21 7 41	22 58 4	1 0 17	2 58 34	5 0 47	6 59 4	9 1 17	11 3 30	13 1 47	15 4 0	17 2 17
	8	19 9 24	21 11 37	23 2 1	1 4 14	3 2 30	5 4 44	7 3 1	9 5 14	11 7 27	13 5 44	15 7 57	17 6 14
	9	19 13 20	21 15 34	23 5 57	1 8 10	3 6 27	5 8 40	7 6 57	9 9 10	11 11 24	13 9 40	15 11 53	17 10 10
	10	19 17 17	21 19 30	23 9 54	1 12 7	3 10 24	5 12 37	7 10 54	9 13 7	11 15 20	13 13 37	15 15 50	17 14 7
	11	19 21 14	21 23 27	23 13 50	1 16 4	3 14 20	5 16 33	7 14 50	9 17 3	11 19 17	13 17 33	15 19 47	17 18 3
	12	19 25 10	21 27 23	23 17 47	1 20 0	3 18 17	5 20 30	7 18 47	9 21 0	11 23 13	13 21 30	15 23 43	17 22 0
	13	19 29 7	21 31 20	23 21 43	1 23 57	3 22 13	5 24 27	7 22 43	9 24 57	11 27 10	13 25 26	15 27 40	17 25 56
	14	19 33 3	21 35 16	23 25 40	1 27 53	3 26 10	5 28 23	7 26 40	9 28 53	11 31 6	13 29 23	15 31 36	17 29 53
	15	19 37 0	21 39 13	23 29 37	1 31 50	3 30 6	5 32 20	7 30 36	9 32 50	11 35 3	13 33 20	15 35 33	17 33 49
	16	19 40 56	21 43 10	23 33 33	1 35 46	3 34 3	5 36 16	7 34 33	9 36 46	11 38 59	13 37 16	15 39 29	17 37 46
	17	19 44 53	21 47 6	23 37 30	1 39 43	3 38 0	5 40 13	7 38 30	9 40 43	11 42 56	13 41 13	15 43 26	17 41 43
	18	19 48 49	21 51 3	23 41 26	1 43 39	3 41 56	5 44 9	7 42 26	9 44 39	11 46 53	13 45 9	15 47 22	17 45 39
	19	19 52 46	21 54 59	23 45 23	1 47 36	3 45 53	5 48 6	7 46 23	9 48 36	11 50 49	13 49 6	15 51 19	17 49 36
	20	19 56 43	21 58 56	23 49 19	1 51 33	3 49 49	5 52 2	7 50 19	9 52 32	11 54 46	13 53 2	15 55 16	17 53 32
	21	20 0 39	22 2 52	23 53 16	1 55 29	3 53 46	5 55 59	7 54 16	9 56 29	11 58 42	13 56 59	15 59 12	17 57 29
	22	20 4 36	22 6 49	23 57 12	1 59 26	3 57 42	5 59 56	7 58 12	10 0 26	12 2 39	14 0 55	16 3 9	18 1 25
	23	20 8 32	22 10 46	0 1 9	2 3 22	4 1 39	6 3 52	8 2 9	10 4 22	12 6 35	14 4 52	16 7 5	18 5 22
	24	20 12 29	22 14 42	0 5 6	2 7 19	4 5 35	6 7 49	8 6 5	10 8 19	12 10 32	14 8 48	16 11 2	18 9 19
	25	20 16 25	22 18 39	0 9 2	2 11 15	4 9 32	6 11 45	8 10 2	10 12 15	12 14 28	14 12 45	16 14 58	18 13 15
	26	20 20 22	22 22 35	0 12 59	2 15 12	4 13 29	6 15 42	8 13 59	10 16 12	12 18 25	14 16 42	16 18 55	18 17 12
	27	20 24 18	22 26 32	0 16 55	2 19 8	4 17 25	6 19 38	8 17 55	10 20 8	12 22 22	14 20 38	16 22 51	18 21 8
	28	20 28 15	22 30 28	0 20 52	2 23 5	4 21 22	6 23 35	8 21 52	10 24 5	12 26 18	14 24 35	16 26 48	18 25 5
	29	20 32 12		0 24 48	2 27 2	4 25 18	6 27 32	8 25 48	10 28 1	12 30 15	14 28 31	16 30 45	18 29 1
	30	20 36 8		0 28 45	2 30 58	4 29 15	6 31 28	8 29 45	10 31 58	12 34 11	14 32 28	16 34 41	18 32 58
	31	20 40 5		0 32 41		4 33 11		8 33 41	10 35 55		14 36 24		18 36 54
1968	1	18 40 51	20 43 4	22 37 24	0 39 38	2 37 54	4 40 7	6 38 24	8 40 37	10 42 51	12 41 7	14 43 21	16 41 37
	2	18 44 48	20 47 1	22 41 21	0 43 34	2 41 51	4 44 4	6 42 21	8 44 34	10 46 47	12 45 4	14 47 17	16 45 34
	3	18 48 44	20 50 57	22 45 17	0 47 31	2 45 47	4 48 1	6 46 17	8 48 31	10 50 44	12 49 0	14 51 14	16 49 30
	4	18 52 41	20 54 54	22 49 14	0 51 27	2 49 44	4 51 57	6 50 14	8 52 27	10 54 40	12 52 57	14 55 10	16 53 27
	5	18 56 37	20 58 50	22 53 11	0 55 24	2 53 40	4 55 54	6 54 10	8 56 24	10 58 37	12 56 54	14 59 7	16 57 23
	6	19 0 34	21 2 47	22 57 7	0 59 20	2 57 37	4 59 50	6 58 7	9 0 20	11 2 34	13 0 50	15 3 3	17 1 20
	7	19 4 30	21 6 44	23 1 4	1 3 17	3 1 34	5 3 47	7 2 4	9 4 17	11 6 30	13 4 47	15 7 0	17 5 17
	8	19 8 27	21 10 40	23 5 0	1 7 13	3 5 30	5 7 43	7 6 0	9 8 13	11 10 27	13 8 43	15 10 56	17 9 13
	9	19 12 23	21 14 37	23 8 57	1 11 10	3 9 27	5 11 40	7 9 57	9 12 10	11 14 23	13 12 40	15 14 53	17 13 10
	10	19 16 20	21 18 33	23 12 53	1 15 7	3 13 23	5 15 36	7 13 53	9 16 7	11 18 20	13 16 36	15 18 50	17 17 6
	11	19 20 17	21 22 30	23 16 50	1 19 3	3 17 20	5 19 33	7 17 50	9 20 3	11 22 16	13 20 33	15 22 46	17 21 3
	12	19 24 13	21 26 26	23 20 46	1 23 0	3 21 16	5 23 30	7 21 46	9 24 0	11 26 13	13 24 29	15 26 43	17 24 59
	13	19 28 10	21 30 23	23 24 43	1 26 56	3 25 13	5 27 26	7 25 43	9 27 56	11 30 9	13 28 26	15 30 39	17 28 56
	14	19 32 6	21 34 20	23 28 40	1 30 53	3 29 9	5 31 23	7 29 39	9 31 53	11 34 6	13 32 22	15 34 36	17 32 53
	15	19 36 3	21 38 16	23 32 36	1 34 49	3 33 6	5 35 19	7 33 36	9 35 49	11 38 2	13 36 19	15 38 32	17 36 49
	16	19 39 59	21 42 13	23 36 33	1 38 46	3 37 3	5 39 16	7 37 33	9 39 46	11 41 59	13 40 16	15 42 29	17 40 46
	17	19 43 56	21 46 9	23 40 29	1 42 42	3 40 59	5 43 12	7 41 29	9 43 42	11 45 56	13 44 12	15 46 25	17 44 42
	18	19 47 52	21 50 6	23 44 26	1 46 39	3 44 56	5 47 9	7 45 26	9 47 39	11 49 52	13 48 9	15 50 22	17 48 39
	19	19 51 49	21 54 2	23 48 22	1 50 36	3 48 52	5 51 6	7 49 22	9 51 36	11 53 49	13 52 5	15 54 19	17 52 35
	20	19 55 46	21 57 59	23 52 19	1 54 32	3 52 49	5 55 2	7 53 19	9 55 32	11 57 45	13 56 2	15 58 15	17 56 32
	21	19 59 42	22 1 55	23 56 15	1 58 29	3 56 45	5 58 59	7 57 15	9 59 29	12 1 42	13 59 58	16 2 12	18 0 28
	22	20 3 39	22 5 52	0 0 12	2 2 25	4 0 42	6 2 55	8 1 12	10 3 25	12 5 38	14 3 55	16 6 8	18 4 25
	23	20 7 35	22 9 48	0 4 9	2 6 22	4 4 38	6 6 52	8 5 8	10 7 22	12 9 35	14 7 52	16 10 5	18 8 22
	24	20 11 32	22 13 45	0 8 5	2 10 18	4 8 35	6 10 48	8 9 5	10 11 18	12 13 31	14 11 48	16 14 1	18 12 18
	25	20 15 28	22 17 42	0 12 2	2 14 15	4 12 32	6 14 45	8 13 2	10 15 15	12 17 28	14 15 45	16 17 58	18 16 15
	26	20 19 25	22 21 38	0 15 58	2 18 11	4 16 28	6 18 41	8 16 58	10 19 11	12 21 25	14 19 41	16 21 54	18 20 11
	27	20 23 21	22 25 35	0 19 55	2 22 8	4 20 25	6 22 38	8 20 55	10 23 8	12 25 21	14 23 38	16 25 51	18 24 8
	28	20 27 18	22 29 31	0 23 51	2 26 5	4 24 21	6 26 35	8 24 51	10 27 4	12 29 18	14 27 34	16 29 48	18 28 4
	29	20 31 15	22 33 28	0 27 48	2 30 1	4 28 18	6 30 31	8 28 48	10 31 1	12 33 14	14 31 31	16 33 44	18 32 1
	30	20 35 11		0 31 44	2 33 58	4 32 14	6 34 28	8 32 44	10 34 58	12 37 11	14 35 27	16 37 41	18 35 57
	31	20 39 8		0 35 41		4 36 11		8 36 41	10 38 54		14 39 24		18 39 54
1969	1	18 43 51	20 46 4	22 36 27	0 38 41	2 36 57	4 39 10	6 37 27	8 39 41	10 41 54	12 40 10	14 42 24	16 40 40
	2	18 47 47	20 50 0	22 40 24	0 42 37	2 40 54	4 43 7	6 41 24	8 43 37	10 45 50	12 44 7	14 46 20	16 44 37
	3	18 51 44	20 53 57	22 44 21	0 46 34	2 44 50	4 47 4	6 45 20	8 47 34	10 49 47	12 48 4	14 50 17	16 48 33
	4	18 55 40	20 57 54	22 48 17	0 50 30	2 48 47	4 51 0	6 49 17	8 51 30	10 53 43	12 52 0	14 54 13	16 52 30
	5	18 59 37	21 1 50	22 52 14	0 54 27	2 52 43	4 54 57	6 53 14	8 55 27	10 57 40	12 55 57	14 58 10	16 56 27
	6	19 3 33	21 5 47	22 56 10	0 58 23	2 56 40	4 58 53	6 57 10	8 59 23	11 1 37	12 59 53	15 2 6	17 0 23
	7	19 7 30	21 9 43	23 0 7	1 2 20	3 0 37	5 2 50	7 1 7	9 3 20	11 5 33	13 3 50	15 6 3	17 4 20
	8	19 11 26	21 13 40	23 4 3	1 6 16	3 4 33	5 6 46	7 5 3	9 7 16	11 9 30	13 7 46	15 9 59	17 8 16
	9	19 15 23	21 17 36	23 8 0	1 10 13	3 8 30	5 10 43	7 9 0	9 11 13	11 13 26	13 11 43	15 13 56	17 12 13
	10	19 19 20	21 21 33	23 11 56	1 14 10	3 12 26	5 14 40	7 12 56	9 15 10	11 17 23	13 15 39	15 17 53	17 16 9
	11	19 23 16	21 25 29	23 15 53	1 18 6	3 16 23	5 18 36	7 16 53	9 19 6	11 21 19	13 19 36	15 21 49	17 20 6
	12	19 27 13	21 29 26	23 19 50	1 22 3	3 20 19	5 22 33	7 20 49	9 23 3	11 25 16	13 23 32	15 25 46	17 24 2
	13	19 31 9	21 33 23	23 23 46	1 25 59	3 24 16	5 26 29	7 24 46	9 26 59	11 29 12	13 27 29	15 29 42	17 27 59
	14	19 35 6	21 37 19	23 27 43	1 29 56	3 28 12	5 30 26	7 28 43	9 30 56	11 33 9	13 31 26	15 33 39	17 31 56
	15	19 39 2	21 41 16	23 31 39	1 33 52	3 32 9	5 34 22	7 32 39	9 34 52	11 37 6	13 35 22	15 37 35	17 35 52
	16	19 42 59	21 45 12	23 35 36	1 37 49	3 36 6	5 38 19	7 36 36	9 38 49	11 41 2	13 39 19	15 41 32	17 39 49
	17	19 46 56	21 49 9	23 39 32	1 41 45	3 40 2	5 42 15	7 40 32	9 42 45	11 44 59	13 43 15	15 45 29	17 43 45
	18	19 50 52	21 53 5	23 43 29	1 45 42	3 43 59	5 46 12	7 44 29	9 46 42	11 48 55	13 47 12	15 49 25	17 47 42
	19	19 54 49	21 57 2	23 47 25	1 49 39	3 47 55	5 50 9	7 48 25	9 50 39	11 52 52	13 51 8	15 53 22	17 51 38
	20	19 58 45	22 0 58	23 51 22	1 53 35	3 51 52	5 54 5	7 52 22	9 54 35	11 56 48	13 55 5	15 57 18	17 55 35
	21	20 2 42	22 4 55	23 55 18	1 57 32	3 55 48	5 58 2	7 56 18	9 58 32	12 0 45	13 59 1	16 1 15	17 59 31
	22	20 6 38	22 8 52	23 59 15	2 1 28	3 59 45	6 1 58	8 0 15	10 2 28	12 4 41	14 2 58	16 5 11	18 3 28
	23	20 10 35	22 12 48	0 3 12	2 5 25	4 3 41	6 5 55	8 4 12	10 6 25	12 8 38	14 6 55	16 9 8	18 7 25
	24	20 14 31	22 16 45	0 7 8	2 9 21	4 7 38	6 9 51	8 8 8	10 10 21	12 12 35	14 10 51	16 13 4	18 11 21
	25	20 18 28	22 20 41	0 11 5	2 13 18	4 11 35	6 13 48	8 12 5	10 14 18	12 16 31	14 14 48	16 17 1	18 15 18
	26	20 22 25	22 24 38	0 15 1	2 17 14	4 15 31	6 17 44	8 16 1	10 18 14	12 20 28	14 18 44	16 20 58	18 19 14
	27	20 26 21	22 28 34	0 18 58	2 21 11	4 19 28	6 21 41	8 19 58	10 22 11	12 24 24	14 22 41	16 24 54	18 23 11
	28	20 30 18	22 32 31	0 22 54	2 25 8	4 23 24	6 25 38	8 23 54	10 26 8	12 28 21	14 26 37	16 28 51	18 27 7
	29	20 34 14		0 26 51	2 29 4	4 27 21	6 29 34	8 27 51	10 30 4	12 32 17	14 30 34	16 32 47	18 31 4
	30	20 38 11		0 30 47	2 33 1	4 31 17	6 33 31	8 31 47	10 34 1	12 36 14	14 34 30	16 36 44	18 35 1
	31	20 42 7		0 34 44		4 35 14		8 35 44	10 37 57		14 38 27		18 38 57

YEAR		JAN	FEB	MAR	APR	MAY	JUN	JUL	AUG	SEP	OCT	NOV	DEC
1970	1	18 42 54	20 45 7	22 35 30	0 37 44	2 36 0	4 38 14	6 36 30	8 38 44	10 40 57	12 39 13	14 41 27	16 39 43
	2	18 46 50	20 49 3	22 39 27	0 41 40	2 39 57	4 42 10	6 40 27	8 42 40	10 44 53	12 43 10	14 45 23	16 43 40
	3	18 50 47	20 53 0	22 43 24	0 45 37	2 43 53	4 46 7	6 44 23	8 46 37	10 48 50	12 47 7	14 49 20	16 47 36
	4	18 54 43	20 56 57	22 47 20	0 49 33	2 47 50	4 50 3	6 48 20	8 50 33	10 52 46	12 51 3	14 53 16	16 51 33
	5	18 58 40	21 0 53	22 51 17	0 53 30	2 51 46	4 54 0	6 52 17	8 54 30	10 56 43	12 55 0	14 57 13	16 55 30
	6	19 2 36	21 4 50	22 55 13	0 57 26	2 55 43	4 57 56	6 56 13	8 58 26	11 0 40	12 58 56	15 1 9	16 59 26
	7	19 6 33	21 8 46	22 59 10	1 1 23	2 59 40	5 1 53	7 0 10	9 2 23	11 4 36	13 2 53	15 5 6	17 3 23
	8	19 10 30	21 12 43	23 3 6	1 5 20	3 3 36	5 5 49	7 4 6	9 6 19	11 8 33	13 6 49	15 9 3	17 7 19
	9	19 14 26	21 16 39	23 7 3	1 9 16	3 7 33	5 9 46	7 8 3	9 10 16	11 12 29	13 10 46	15 12 59	17 11 16
	10	19 18 23	21 20 36	23 10 59	1 13 13	3 11 29	5 13 43	7 11 59	9 14 13	11 16 26	13 14 42	15 16 56	17 15 12
	11	19 22 19	21 24 32	23 14 56	1 17 9	3 15 26	5 17 39	7 15 56	9 18 9	11 20 22	13 18 39	15 20 52	17 19 9
	12	19 26 16	21 28 29	23 18 53	1 21 6	3 19 22	5 21 36	7 19 52	9 22 6	11 24 19	13 22 36	15 24 49	17 23 5
	13	19 30 12	21 32 26	23 22 49	1 25 2	3 23 19	5 25 32	7 23 49	9 26 2	11 28 15	13 26 32	15 28 45	17 27 2
	14	19 34 9	21 36 22	23 26 46	1 28 59	3 27 16	5 29 29	7 27 46	9 29 59	11 32 12	13 30 29	15 32 42	17 30 59
	15	19 38 5	21 40 19	23 30 42	1 32 55	3 31 12	5 33 25	7 31 42	9 33 55	11 36 9	13 34 25	15 36 38	17 34 55
	16	19 42 2	21 44 15	23 34 39	1 36 52	3 35 9	5 37 22	7 35 39	9 37 52	11 40 5	13 38 22	15 40 35	17 38 52
	17	19 45 59	21 48 12	23 38 35	1 40 49	3 39 5	5 41 18	7 39 35	9 41 49	11 44 2	13 42 18	15 44 32	17 42 48
	18	19 49 55	21 52 8	23 42 32	1 44 45	3 43 2	5 45 15	7 43 32	9 45 45	11 47 58	13 46 15	15 48 28	17 46 45
	19	19 53 52	21 56 5	23 46 28	1 48 42	3 46 58	5 49 12	7 47 28	9 49 42	11 51 55	13 50 11	15 52 25	17 50 41
	20	19 57 48	22 0 2	23 50 25	1 52 38	3 50 55	5 53 8	7 51 25	9 53 38	11 55 51	13 54 8	15 56 21	17 54 38
	21	20 1 45	22 3 58	23 54 22	1 56 35	3 54 51	5 57 5	7 55 21	9 57 35	11 59 48	13 58 5	16 0 18	17 58 34
	22	20 5 41	22 7 55	23 58 18	2 0 31	3 58 48	6 1 1	7 59 18	10 1 31	12 3 44	14 2 1	16 4 14	18 2 31
	23	20 9 38	22 11 51	0 2 15	2 4 28	4 2 45	6 4 58	8 3 15	10 5 28	12 7 41	14 5 58	16 8 11	18 6 28
	24	20 13 34	22 15 48	0 6 11	2 8 24	4 6 41	6 8 54	8 7 11	10 9 24	12 11 38	14 9 54	16 12 7	18 10 24
	25	20 17 31	22 19 44	0 10 8	2 12 21	4 10 38	6 12 51	8 11 8	10 13 21	12 15 34	14 13 51	16 16 4	18 14 21
	26	20 21 28	22 23 41	0 14 4	2 16 18	4 14 34	6 16 48	8 15 4	10 17 17	12 19 31	14 17 47	16 20 1	18 18 17
	27	20 25 24	22 27 37	0 18 1	2 20 14	4 18 31	6 20 44	8 19 1	10 21 14	12 23 27	14 21 44	16 23 57	18 22 14
	28	20 29 21	22 31 34	0 21 57	2 24 11	4 22 27	6 24 41	8 22 57	10 25 11	12 27 24	14 25 40	16 27 54	18 26 10
	29	20 33 17		0 25 54	2 28 7	4 26 24	6 28 37	8 26 54	10 29 7	12 31 20	14 29 37	16 31 50	18 30 7
	30	20 37 14		0 29 51	2 32 4	4 30 20	6 32 34	8 30 50	10 33 4	12 35 17	14 33 33	16 35 47	18 34 4
	31	20 41 10		0 33 47		4 34 17		8 34 47	10 37 0		14 37 30		18 38 0
1971	1	18 41 57	20 44 10	22 34 33	0 36 47	2 35 3	4 37 17	6 35 33	8 37 47	10 40 0	12 38 16	14 40 30	16 38 46
	2	18 45 53	20 48 6	22 38 30	0 40 43	2 39 0	4 41 13	6 39 30	8 41 43	10 43 56	12 42 13	14 44 26	16 42 43
	3	18 49 50	20 52 3	22 42 27	0 44 40	2 42 56	4 45 10	6 43 26	8 45 40	10 47 53	12 46 10	14 48 23	16 46 39
	4	18 53 46	20 56 0	22 46 23	0 48 36	2 46 53	4 49 6	6 47 23	8 49 36	10 51 49	12 50 6	14 52 19	16 50 36
	5	18 57 43	20 59 56	22 50 20	0 52 33	2 50 50	4 53 3	6 51 20	8 53 33	10 55 46	12 54 3	14 56 16	16 54 33
	6	19 1 39	21 3 53	22 54 16	0 56 29	2 54 46	4 56 59	6 55 16	8 57 29	10 59 43	12 57 59	15 0 12	16 58 29
	7	19 5 36	21 7 49	22 58 13	1 0 26	2 58 43	5 0 56	6 59 13	9 1 26	11 3 39	13 1 56	15 4 9	17 2 26
	8	19 9 33	21 11 46	23 2 9	1 4 23	3 2 39	5 4 52	7 3 9	9 5 22	11 7 36	13 5 52	15 8 5	17 6 22
	9	19 13 29	21 15 42	23 6 6	1 8 19	3 6 36	5 8 49	7 7 6	9 9 19	11 11 32	13 9 49	15 12 2	17 10 19
	10	19 17 26	21 19 39	23 10 2	1 12 16	3 10 32	5 12 46	7 11 2	9 13 16	11 15 29	13 13 45	15 15 59	17 14 15
	11	19 21 22	21 23 36	23 13 59	1 16 12	3 14 29	5 16 42	7 14 59	9 17 12	11 19 25	13 17 42	15 19 55	17 18 12
	12	19 25 19	21 27 32	23 17 56	1 20 9	3 18 25	5 20 39	7 18 55	9 21 9	11 23 22	13 21 39	15 23 52	17 22 8
	13	19 29 15	21 31 29	23 21 52	1 24 5	3 22 22	5 24 35	7 22 52	9 25 5	11 27 18	13 25 35	15 27 48	17 26 5
	14	19 33 12	21 35 25	23 25 49	1 28 2	3 26 19	5 28 32	7 26 49	9 29 2	11 31 15	13 29 32	15 31 45	17 30 2
	15	19 37 8	21 39 22	23 29 45	1 31 58	3 30 15	5 32 28	7 30 45	9 32 58	11 35 12	13 33 28	15 35 41	17 33 58
	16	19 41 5	21 43 18	23 33 42	1 35 55	3 34 12	5 36 25	7 34 42	9 36 55	11 39 8	13 37 25	15 39 38	17 37 55
	17	19 45 2	21 47 15	23 37 38	1 39 52	3 38 8	5 40 21	7 38 38	9 40 51	11 43 5	13 41 21	15 43 34	17 41 51
	18	19 48 58	21 51 11	23 41 35	1 43 48	3 42 5	5 44 18	7 42 35	9 44 48	11 47 1	13 45 18	15 47 31	17 45 48
	19	19 52 55	21 55 8	23 45 31	1 47 45	3 46 1	5 48 15	7 46 31	9 48 45	11 50 58	13 49 14	15 51 28	17 49 44
	20	19 56 51	21 59 4	23 49 28	1 51 41	3 49 58	5 52 11	7 50 28	9 52 41	11 54 54	13 53 11	15 55 24	17 53 41
	21	20 0 48	22 3 1	23 53 25	1 55 38	3 53 54	5 56 8	7 54 24	9 56 38	11 58 51	13 57 7	15 59 21	17 57 37
	22	20 4 44	22 6 58	23 57 21	1 59 34	3 57 51	6 0 4	7 58 21	10 0 34	12 2 47	14 1 4	16 3 17	18 1 34
	23	20 8 41	22 10 54	0 1 18	2 3 31	4 1 48	6 4 1	8 2 18	10 4 31	12 6 44	14 5 1	16 7 14	18 5 31
	24	20 12 37	22 14 51	0 5 14	2 7 27	4 5 44	6 7 57	8 6 14	10 8 27	12 10 41	14 8 57	16 11 10	18 9 27
	25	20 16 34	22 18 47	0 9 11	2 11 24	4 9 41	6 11 54	8 10 11	10 12 24	12 14 37	14 12 54	16 15 7	18 13 24
	26	20 20 31	22 22 44	0 13 7	2 15 21	4 13 37	6 15 51	8 14 7	10 16 20	12 18 34	14 16 50	16 19 4	18 17 20
	27	20 24 27	22 26 40	0 17 4	2 19 17	4 17 34	6 19 47	8 18 4	10 20 17	12 22 30	14 20 47	16 23 0	18 21 17
	28	20 28 24	22 30 37	0 21 0	2 23 14	4 21 30	6 23 44	8 22 0	10 24 14	12 26 27	14 24 43	16 26 57	18 25 13
	29	20 32 20		0 24 57	2 27 10	4 25 27	6 27 40	8 25 57	10 28 10	12 30 23	14 28 40	16 30 53	18 29 10
	30	20 36 17		0 28 54	2 31 7	4 29 23	6 31 37	8 29 53	10 32 7	12 34 20	14 32 36	16 34 50	18 33 6
	31	20 40 13		0 32 50		4 33 20		8 33 50	10 36 3		14 36 33		18 37 3
1972	1	18 41 0	20 43 13	22 37 33	0 39 46	2 38 3	4 40 16	6 38 33	8 40 46	10 42 59	12 41 16	14 43 29	16 41 46
	2	18 44 56	20 47 9	22 41 30	0 43 43	2 41 59	4 44 13	6 42 29	8 44 43	10 46 56	12 45 12	14 47 26	16 45 42
	3	18 48 53	20 51 6	22 45 26	0 47 39	2 45 56	4 48 9	6 46 26	8 48 39	10 50 52	12 49 9	14 51 22	16 49 39
	4	18 52 49	20 55 3	22 49 23	0 51 36	2 49 52	4 52 6	6 50 22	8 52 36	10 54 49	12 53 6	14 55 19	16 53 35
	5	18 56 46	20 58 59	22 53 19	0 55 32	2 53 49	4 56 2	6 54 19	8 56 32	10 58 45	12 57 2	14 59 15	16 57 32
	6	19 0 42	21 2 56	22 57 16	0 59 29	2 57 46	4 59 59	6 58 16	9 0 29	11 2 42	13 0 59	15 3 12	17 1 29
	7	19 4 39	21 6 52	23 1 12	1 3 25	3 1 42	5 3 55	7 2 12	9 4 25	11 6 39	13 4 55	15 7 8	17 5 25
	8	19 8 36	21 10 49	23 5 9	1 7 22	3 5 39	5 7 52	7 6 9	9 8 22	11 10 35	13 8 52	15 11 5	17 9 22
	9	19 12 32	21 14 45	23 9 5	1 11 19	3 9 35	5 11 48	7 10 5	9 12 19	11 14 32	13 12 48	15 15 1	17 13 18
	10	19 16 29	21 18 42	23 13 2	1 15 15	3 13 32	5 15 45	7 14 2	9 16 15	11 18 28	13 16 45	15 18 58	17 17 15
	11	19 20 25	21 22 38	23 16 59	1 19 12	3 17 28	5 19 42	7 17 58	9 20 12	11 22 25	13 20 41	15 22 55	17 21 11
	12	19 24 22	21 26 35	23 20 55	1 23 8	3 21 25	5 23 38	7 21 55	9 24 8	11 26 21	13 24 38	15 26 51	17 25 8
	13	19 28 18	21 30 32	23 24 52	1 27 5	3 25 21	5 27 35	7 25 51	9 28 5	11 30 18	13 28 34	15 30 48	17 29 4
	14	19 32 15	21 34 28	23 28 48	1 31 1	3 29 18	5 31 31	7 29 48	9 32 1	11 34 14	13 32 31	15 34 44	17 33 1
	15	19 36 11	21 38 25	23 32 45	1 34 58	3 33 15	5 35 28	7 33 45	9 35 58	11 38 11	13 36 28	15 38 41	17 36 58
	16	19 40 8	21 42 21	23 36 41	1 38 54	3 37 11	5 39 24	7 37 41	9 39 54	11 42 8	13 40 24	15 42 37	17 40 54
	17	19 44 5	21 46 18	23 40 38	1 42 51	3 41 8	5 43 21	7 41 38	9 43 51	11 46 4	13 44 21	15 46 34	17 44 51
	18	19 48 1	21 50 14	23 44 34	1 46 48	3 45 4	5 47 18	7 45 34	9 47 47	11 50 1	13 48 17	15 50 30	17 48 47
	19	19 51 58	21 54 11	23 48 31	1 50 44	3 49 1	5 51 14	7 49 31	9 51 44	11 53 57	13 52 14	15 54 27	17 52 44
	20	19 55 54	21 58 7	23 52 28	1 54 41	3 52 57	5 55 11	7 53 27	9 55 41	11 57 54	13 56 10	15 58 24	17 56 40
	21	19 59 51	22 2 4	23 56 24	1 58 37	3 56 54	5 59 7	7 57 24	9 59 37	12 1 50	14 0 7	16 2 20	18 0 37
	22	20 3 47	22 6 1	0 0 21	2 2 34	4 0 50	6 3 4	8 1 20	10 3 34	12 5 47	14 4 3	16 6 17	18 4 33
	23	20 7 44	22 9 57	0 4 17	2 6 30	4 4 47	6 7 0	8 5 17	10 7 30	12 9 43	14 8 0	16 10 13	18 8 30
	24	20 11 40	22 13 54	0 8 14	2 10 27	4 8 44	6 10 57	8 9 14	10 11 27	12 13 40	14 11 57	16 14 10	18 12 27
	25	20 15 37	22 17 50	0 12 10	2 14 23	4 12 40	6 14 53	8 13 10	10 15 23	12 17 37	14 15 53	16 18 6	18 16 23
	26	20 19 34	22 21 47	0 16 7	2 18 20	4 16 37	6 18 50	8 17 7	10 19 20	12 21 33	14 19 50	16 22 3	18 20 20
	27	20 23 30	22 25 43	0 20 3	2 22 17	4 20 33	6 22 47	8 21 3	10 23 16	12 25 30	14 23 46	16 26 0	18 24 16
	28	20 27 27	22 29 40	0 24 0	2 26 13	4 24 30	6 26 43	8 25 0	10 27 13	12 29 26	14 27 43	16 29 56	18 28 13
	29	20 31 23	22 33 36	0 27 56	2 30 10	4 28 26	6 30 40	8 28 56	10 31 10	12 33 23	14 31 39	16 33 53	18 32 9
	30	20 35 20		0 31 53	2 34 6	4 32 23	6 34 36	8 32 53	10 35 6	12 37 19	14 35 36	16 37 49	18 36 6
	31	20 39 16		0 35 50		4 36 19		8 36 49	10 39 3		14 39 32		18 40 2
1973	1	18 43 59	20 46 12	22 36 36	0 38 49	2 37 6	4 39 19	6 37 36	8 39 49	10 42 2	12 40 19	14 42 32	16 40 49
	2	18 47 56	20 50 9	22 40 32	0 42 46	2 41 2	4 43 15	6 41 32	8 43 45	10 45 59	12 44 15	14 46 28	16 44 45
	3	18 51 52	20 54 5	22 44 29	0 46 42	2 44 59	4 47 12	6 45 29	8 47 42	10 49 55	12 48 12	14 50 25	16 48 42
	4	18 55 49	20 58 2	22 48 26	0 50 39	2 48 55	4 51 9	6 49 25	8 51 39	10 53 52	12 52 8	14 54 21	16 52 38
	5	18 59 45	21 1 59	22 52 22	0 54 35	2 52 52	4 55 5	6 53 22	8 55 35	10 57 48	12 56 5	14 58 18	16 56 35
	6	19 3 42	21 5 55	22 56 19	0 58 32	2 56 48	4 59 2	6 57 18	8 59 32	11 1 45	13 0 1	15 2 15	17 0 31
	7	19 7 38	21 9 52	23 0 15	1 2 28	3 0 45	5 2 58	7 1 15	9 3 28	11 5 41	13 3 58	15 6 11	17 4 28
	8	19 11 35	21 13 48	23 4 12	1 6 25	3 4 42	5 6 55	7 5 12	9 7 25	11 9 38	13 7 55	15 10 8	17 8 24
	9	19 15 32	21 17 45	23 8 8	1 10 21	3 8 38	5 10 51	7 9 8	9 11 21	11 13 35	13 11 51	15 14 4	17 12 21
	10	19 19 28	21 21 41	23 12 5	1 14 18	3 12 35	5 14 48	7 13 5	9 15 18	11 17 31	13 15 48	15 18 1	17 16 18
	11	19 23 25	21 25 38	23 16 1	1 18 15	3 16 31	5 18 44	7 17 1	9 19 14	11 21 28	13 19 44	15 21 57	17 20 14
	12	19 27 21	21 29 34	23 19 58	1 22 11	3 20 28	5 22 41	7 20 58	9 23 11	11 25 24	13 23 41	15 25 54	17 24 11
	13	19 31 18	21 33 31	23 23 55	1 26 8	3 24 24	5 26 38	7 24 54	9 27 8	11 29 21	13 27 37	15 29 50	17 28 7
	14	19 35 14	21 37 28	23 27 51	1 30 4	3 28 21	5 30 34	7 28 51	9 31 4	11 33 17	13 31 34	15 33 47	17 32 4
	15	19 39 11	21 41 24	23 31 48	1 34 1	3 32 17	5 34 31	7 32 47	9 35 1	11 37 14	13 35 30	15 37 44	17 36 0
	16	19 43 7	21 45 21	23 35 44	1 37 57	3 36 14	5 38 27	7 36 44	9 38 57	11 41 10	13 39 27	15 41 40	17 39 57
	17	19 47 4	21 49 17	23 39 41	1 41 54	3 40 11	5 42 24	7 40 41	9 42 54	11 45 7	13 43 24	15 45 37	17 43 53
	18	19 51 1	21 53 14	23 43 37	1 45 50	3 44 7	5 46 20	7 44 37	9 46 50	11 49 3	13 47 20	15 49 33	17 47 50
	19	19 54 57	21 57 10	23 47 34	1 49 47	3 48 4	5 50 17	7 48 34	9 50 47	11 53 0	13 51 17	15 53 30	17 51 47
	20	19 58 54	22 1 7	23 51 30	1 53 44	3 52 0	5 54 13	7 52 30	9 54 43	11 56 57	13 55 13	15 57 26	17 55 43
	21	20 2 50	22 5 3	23 55 27	1 57 40	3 55 57	5 58 10	7 56 27	9 58 40	12 0 53	13 59 10	16 1 23	17 59 40
	22	20 6 47	22 9 0	23 59 23	2 1 37	3 59 53	6 2 7	8 0 23	10 2 37	12 4 50	14 3 6	16 5 19	18 3 36
	23	20 10 43	22 12 57	0 3 20	2 5 33	4 3 50	6 6 3	8 4 20	10 6 33	12 8 46	14 7 3	16 9 16	18 7 33
	24	20 14 40	22 16 53	0 7 17	2 9 30	4 7 46	6 10 0	8 8 16	10 10 30	12 12 43	14 10 59	16 13 13	18 11 29
	25	20 18 36	22 20 50	0 11 13	2 13 26	4 11 43	6 13 56	8 12 13	10 14 26	12 16 39	14 14 56	16 17 9	18 15 26
	26	20 22 33	22 24 46	0 15 10	2 17 23	4 15 40	6 17 53	8 16 10	10 18 23	12 20 36	14 18 52	16 21 6	18 19 22
	27	20 26 30	22 28 43	0 19 6	2 21 19	4 19 36	6 21 49	8 20 6	10 22 19	12 24 33	14 22 49	16 25 2	18 23 19
	28	20 30 26	22 32 39	0 23 3	2 25 16	4 23 33	6 25 46	8 24 3	10 26 16	12 28 29	14 26 46	16 28 59	18 27 16
	29	20 34 23		0 26 59	2 29 13	4 27 29	6 29 42	8 27 59	10 30 12	12 32 26	14 30 42	16 32 55	18 31 12
	30	20 38 19		0 30 56	2 33 9	4 31 26	6 33 39	8 31 56	10 34 9	12 36 22	14 34 39	16 36 52	18 35 9
	31	20 42 16		0 34 52		4 35 22		8 35 52	10 38 6		14 38 35		18 39 5

YEAR		JAN	FEB	MAR	APR	MAY	JUN	JUL	AUG	SEP	OCT	NOV	DEC
1974	1	18 43 2	20 45 15	22 35 39	0 37 52	2 36 8	4 38 22	6 36 38	8 38 52	10 41 5	12 39 21	14 41 34	16 39 51
	2	18 46 58	20 49 12	22 39 35	0 41 48	2 40 5	4 42 18	6 40 35	8 42 48	10 45 1	12 43 18	14 45 31	16 43 48
	3	18 50 55	20 53 8	22 43 32	0 45 45	2 44 1	4 46 15	6 44 31	8 46 45	10 48 58	12 47 14	14 49 28	16 47 44
	4	18 54 51	20 57 5	22 47 28	0 49 41	2 47 58	4 50 11	6 48 28	8 50 41	10 52 54	12 51 11	14 53 24	16 51 41
	5	18 58 48	21 1 1	22 51 25	0 53 38	2 51 55	4 54 8	6 52 25	8 54 38	10 56 51	12 55 8	14 57 21	16 55 37
	6	19 2 45	21 4 58	22 55 21	0 57 35	2 55 51	4 58 4	6 56 21	8 58 34	11 0 48	12 59 4	15 1 17	16 59 34
	7	19 6 41	21 8 54	22 59 18	1 1 31	2 59 48	5 2 1	7 0 18	9 2 31	11 4 44	13 3 1	15 5 14	17 3 31
	8	19 10 38	21 12 51	23 3 14	1 5 28	3 3 44	5 5 57	7 4 14	9 6 27	11 8 41	13 6 57	15 9 10	17 7 27
	9	19 14 34	21 16 48	23 7 11	1 9 24	3 7 41	5 9 54	7 8 11	9 10 24	11 12 37	13 10 54	15 13 7	17 11 24
	10	19 18 31	21 20 44	23 11 8	1 13 21	3 11 37	5 13 51	7 12 7	9 14 21	11 16 34	13 14 50	15 17 3	17 15 20
	11	19 22 27	21 24 41	23 15 4	1 17 17	3 15 34	5 17 47	7 16 4	9 18 17	11 20 30	13 18 47	15 21 0	17 19 17
	12	19 26 24	21 28 37	23 19 1	1 21 14	3 19 30	5 21 44	7 20 0	9 22 14	11 24 27	13 22 43	15 24 57	17 23 13
	13	19 30 21	21 32 34	23 22 57	1 25 10	3 23 27	5 25 40	7 23 57	9 26 10	11 28 23	13 26 40	15 28 53	17 27 10
	14	19 34 17	21 36 30	23 26 54	1 29 7	3 27 24	5 29 37	7 27 54	9 30 7	11 32 20	13 30 37	15 32 50	17 31 6
	15	19 38 14	21 40 27	23 30 50	1 33 3	3 31 20	5 33 33	7 31 50	9 34 3	11 36 16	13 34 33	15 36 46	17 35 3
	16	19 42 10	21 44 23	23 34 47	1 37 0	3 35 17	5 37 30	7 35 47	9 38 0	11 40 13	13 38 30	15 40 43	17 39 0
	17	19 46 7	21 48 20	23 38 43	1 40 57	3 39 13	5 41 26	7 39 43	9 41 56	11 44 10	13 42 26	15 44 39	17 42 56
	18	19 50 3	21 52 17	23 42 40	1 44 53	3 43 10	5 45 23	7 43 40	9 45 53	11 48 6	13 46 23	15 48 36	17 46 53
	19	19 54 0	21 56 13	23 46 37	1 48 50	3 47 6	5 49 20	7 47 36	9 49 50	11 52 3	13 50 19	15 52 32	17 50 49
	20	19 57 56	22 0 10	23 50 33	1 52 46	3 51 3	5 53 16	7 51 33	9 53 46	11 55 59	13 54 16	15 56 29	17 54 46
	21	20 1 53	22 4 6	23 54 30	1 56 43	3 54 59	5 57 13	7 55 29	9 57 43	11 59 56	13 58 12	16 0 26	17 58 42
	22	20 5 50	22 8 3	23 58 26	2 0 39	3 58 56	6 1 9	7 59 26	10 1 39	12 3 52	14 2 9	16 4 22	18 2 39
	23	20 9 46	22 11 59	0 2 23	2 4 36	4 2 53	6 5 6	8 3 23	10 5 36	12 7 49	14 6 6	16 8 19	18 6 35
	24	20 13 43	22 15 56	0 6 19	2 8 32	4 6 49	6 9 2	8 7 19	10 9 32	12 11 45	14 10 2	16 12 15	18 10 32
	25	20 17 39	22 19 52	0 10 16	2 12 29	4 10 46	6 12 59	8 11 16	10 13 29	12 15 42	14 13 59	16 16 12	18 14 29
	26	20 21 36	22 23 49	0 14 12	2 16 26	4 14 42	6 16 56	8 15 12	10 17 25	12 19 39	14 17 55	16 20 8	18 18 25
	27	20 25 32	22 27 45	0 18 9	2 20 22	4 18 39	6 20 52	8 19 9	10 21 22	12 23 35	14 21 52	16 24 5	18 22 22
	28	20 29 29	22 31 42	0 22 6	2 24 19	4 22 35	6 24 49	8 23 5	10 25 19	12 27 32	14 25 48	16 28 1	18 26 18
	29	20 33 25		0 26 2	2 28 15	4 26 32	6 28 45	8 27 2	10 29 15	12 31 28	14 29 45	16 31 58	18 30 15
	30	20 37 22		0 29 59	2 32 12	4 30 28	6 32 42	8 30 58	10 33 12	12 35 25	14 33 41	16 35 55	18 34 11
	31	20 41 19		0 33 55		4 34 25		8 34 55	10 37 8		14 37 38		18 38 8
1975	1	18 42 4	20 44 18	22 34 41	0 36 54	2 35 11	4 37 24	6 35 41	8 37 54	10 40 7	12 38 24	14 40 37	16 38 54
	2	18 46 1	20 48 14	22 38 38	0 40 51	2 39 8	4 41 21	6 39 37	8 41 51	10 44 4	12 42 20	14 44 34	16 42 50
	3	18 49 58	20 52 11	22 42 34	0 44 47	2 43 4	4 45 17	6 43 34	8 45 47	10 48 0	12 46 17	14 48 30	16 46 47
	4	18 53 54	20 56 7	22 46 31	0 48 44	2 47 1	4 49 14	6 47 31	8 49 44	10 51 57	12 50 14	14 52 27	16 50 43
	5	18 57 51	21 0 4	22 50 27	0 52 41	2 50 57	4 53 10	6 51 27	8 53 40	10 55 54	12 54 10	14 56 23	16 54 40
	6	19 1 47	21 4 0	22 54 24	0 56 37	2 54 54	4 57 7	6 55 24	8 57 37	10 59 50	12 58 7	15 0 20	16 58 36
	7	19 5 44	21 7 57	22 58 21	1 0 34	2 58 50	5 1 4	6 59 20	9 1 33	11 3 47	13 2 3	15 4 16	17 2 33
	8	19 9 40	21 11 54	23 2 17	1 4 30	3 2 47	5 5 0	7 3 17	9 5 30	11 7 43	13 6 0	15 8 13	17 6 30
	9	19 13 37	21 15 50	23 6 14	1 8 27	3 6 43	5 8 57	7 7 13	9 9 27	11 11 40	13 9 56	15 12 9	17 10 26
	10	19 17 33	21 19 47	23 10 10	1 12 23	3 10 40	5 12 53	7 11 10	9 13 23	11 15 36	13 13 53	15 16 6	17 14 23
	11	19 21 30	21 23 43	23 14 7	1 16 20	3 14 36	5 16 50	7 15 6	9 17 20	11 19 33	13 17 49	15 20 3	17 18 19
	12	19 25 27	21 27 40	23 18 3	1 20 16	3 18 33	5 20 46	7 19 3	9 21 16	11 23 29	13 21 46	15 23 59	17 22 16
	13	19 29 23	21 31 36	23 22 0	1 24 13	3 22 30	5 24 43	7 23 0	9 25 13	11 27 26	13 25 43	15 27 56	17 26 12
	14	19 33 20	21 35 33	23 25 56	1 28 10	3 26 26	5 28 39	7 26 56	9 29 9	11 31 23	13 29 39	15 31 52	17 30 9
	15	19 37 16	21 39 29	23 29 53	1 32 6	3 30 23	5 32 36	7 30 53	9 33 6	11 35 19	13 33 36	15 35 49	17 34 5
	16	19 41 13	21 43 26	23 33 50	1 36 3	3 34 19	5 36 33	7 34 49	9 37 2	11 39 16	13 37 32	15 39 45	17 38 2
	17	19 45 9	21 47 23	23 37 46	1 39 59	3 38 16	5 40 29	7 38 46	9 40 59	11 43 12	13 41 29	15 43 42	17 41 59
	18	19 49 6	21 51 19	23 41 43	1 43 56	3 42 12	5 44 26	7 42 42	9 44 56	11 47 9	13 45 25	15 47 38	17 45 55
	19	19 53 2	21 55 16	23 45 39	1 47 52	3 46 9	5 48 22	7 46 39	9 48 52	11 51 5	13 49 22	15 51 35	17 49 52
	20	19 56 59	21 59 12	23 49 36	1 51 49	3 50 6	5 52 19	7 50 35	9 52 49	11 55 2	13 53 18	15 55 32	17 53 48
	21	20 0 56	22 3 9	23 53 32	1 55 45	3 54 2	5 56 15	7 54 32	9 56 45	11 58 58	13 57 15	15 59 28	17 57 45
	22	20 4 52	22 7 5	23 57 29	1 59 42	3 57 59	6 0 12	7 58 29	10 0 42	12 2 55	14 1 11	16 3 25	18 1 41
	23	20 8 49	22 11 2	0 1 25	2 3 39	4 1 55	6 4 8	8 2 25	10 4 38	12 6 51	14 5 8	16 7 21	18 5 38
	24	20 12 45	22 14 58	0 5 22	2 7 35	4 5 52	6 8 5	8 6 22	10 8 35	12 10 48	14 9 5	16 11 18	18 9 35
	25	20 16 42	22 18 55	0 9 18	2 11 32	4 9 48	6 12 2	8 10 18	10 12 31	12 14 45	14 13 1	16 15 14	18 13 31
	26	20 20 38	22 22 52	0 13 15	2 15 28	4 13 45	6 15 58	8 14 15	10 16 28	12 18 41	14 16 58	16 19 11	18 17 28
	27	20 24 35	22 26 48	0 17 12	2 19 25	4 17 41	6 19 55	8 18 11	10 20 25	12 22 38	14 20 54	16 23 7	18 21 24
	28	20 28 32	22 30 45	0 21 8	2 23 21	4 21 38	6 23 51	8 22 8	10 24 21	12 26 34	14 24 51	16 27 4	18 25 21
	29	20 32 28		0 25 5	2 27 18	4 25 35	6 27 48	8 26 4	10 28 18	12 30 31	14 28 47	16 31 1	18 29 17
	30	20 36 25		0 29 1	2 31 14	4 29 31	6 31 44	8 30 1	10 32 14	12 34 27	14 32 44	16 34 57	18 33 14
	31	20 40 21		0 32 58		4 33 28		8 33 58	10 36 11		14 36 40		18 37 10
1976	1	18 41 7	20 43 20	22 37 40	0 39 53	2 38 10	4 40 23	6 38 40	8 40 53	10 43 6	12 41 23	14 43 36	16 41 53
	2	18 45 4	20 47 17	22 41 37	0 43 50	2 42 7	4 44 20	6 42 36	8 44 50	10 47 3	12 45 19	14 47 33	16 45 49
	3	18 49 0	20 51 13	22 45 33	0 47 47	2 46 3	4 48 16	6 46 33	8 48 46	10 50 59	12 49 16	14 51 29	16 49 46
	4	18 52 57	20 55 10	22 49 30	0 51 43	2 50 0	4 52 13	6 50 30	8 52 43	10 54 56	12 53 13	14 55 26	16 53 42
	5	18 56 53	20 59 6	22 53 26	0 55 40	2 53 56	4 56 9	6 54 26	8 56 39	10 58 53	12 57 9	14 59 22	16 57 39
	6	19 0 50	21 3 3	22 57 23	0 59 36	2 57 53	5 0 6	6 58 23	9 0 36	11 2 49	13 1 6	15 3 19	17 1 35
	7	19 4 46	21 7 0	23 1 20	1 3 33	3 1 49	5 4 3	7 2 19	9 4 33	11 6 46	13 5 2	15 7 15	17 5 32
	8	19 8 43	21 10 56	23 5 16	1 7 29	3 5 46	5 7 59	7 6 16	9 8 29	11 10 42	13 8 59	15 11 12	17 9 29
	9	19 12 39	21 14 53	23 9 13	1 11 26	3 9 42	5 11 56	7 10 12	9 12 26	11 14 39	13 12 55	15 15 8	17 13 25
	10	19 16 36	21 18 49	23 13 9	1 15 22	3 13 39	5 15 52	7 14 9	9 16 22	11 18 35	13 16 52	15 19 5	17 17 22
	11	19 20 33	21 22 46	23 17 6	1 19 19	3 17 36	5 19 49	7 18 6	9 20 19	11 22 32	13 20 48	15 23 2	17 21 18
	12	19 24 29	21 26 42	23 21 2	1 23 15	3 21 32	5 23 45	7 22 2	9 24 15	11 26 28	13 24 45	15 26 58	17 25 15
	13	19 28 26	21 30 39	23 24 59	1 27 12	3 25 29	5 27 42	7 25 59	9 28 12	11 30 25	13 28 42	15 30 55	17 29 11
	14	19 32 22	21 34 35	23 28 55	1 31 9	3 29 25	5 31 38	7 29 55	9 32 8	11 34 22	13 32 38	15 34 51	17 33 8
	15	19 36 19	21 38 32	23 32 52	1 35 5	3 33 22	5 35 35	7 33 52	9 36 5	11 38 18	13 36 35	15 38 48	17 37 4
	16	19 40 15	21 42 29	23 36 49	1 39 2	3 37 18	5 39 32	7 37 48	9 40 1	11 42 15	13 40 31	15 42 44	17 41 1
	17	19 44 12	21 46 25	23 40 45	1 42 58	3 41 15	5 43 28	7 41 45	9 43 58	11 46 11	13 44 28	15 46 41	17 44 58
	18	19 48 8	21 50 22	23 44 42	1 46 55	3 45 11	5 47 25	7 45 41	9 47 55	11 50 8	13 48 24	15 50 37	17 48 54
	19	19 52 5	21 54 18	23 48 38	1 50 51	3 49 8	5 51 21	7 49 38	9 51 51	11 54 4	13 52 21	15 54 34	17 52 51
	20	19 56 2	21 58 15	23 52 35	1 54 48	3 53 5	5 55 18	7 53 34	9 55 48	11 58 1	13 56 17	15 58 31	17 56 47
	21	19 59 58	22 2 11	23 56 31	1 58 44	3 57 1	5 59 14	7 57 31	9 59 44	12 1 57	14 0 14	16 2 27	18 0 44
	22	20 3 55	22 6 8	0 0 28	2 2 41	4 0 58	6 3 11	8 1 28	10 3 41	12 5 54	14 4 10	16 6 24	18 4 40
	23	20 7 51	22 10 4	0 4 24	2 6 38	4 4 54	6 7 7	8 5 24	10 7 37	12 9 50	14 8 7	16 10 20	18 8 37
	24	20 11 48	22 14 1	0 8 21	2 10 34	4 8 51	6 11 4	8 9 21	10 11 34	12 13 47	14 12 4	16 14 17	18 12 34
	25	20 15 44	22 17 58	0 12 18	2 14 31	4 12 47	6 15 1	8 13 17	10 15 30	12 17 44	14 16 0	16 18 13	18 16 30
	26	20 19 41	22 21 54	0 16 14	2 18 27	4 16 44	6 18 57	8 17 14	10 19 27	12 21 40	14 19 57	16 22 10	18 20 27
	27	20 23 37	22 25 51	0 20 11	2 22 24	4 20 40	6 22 54	8 21 10	10 23 24	12 25 37	14 23 53	16 26 6	18 24 23
	28	20 27 34	22 29 47	0 24 7	2 26 20	4 24 37	6 26 50	8 25 7	10 27 20	12 29 33	14 27 50	16 30 3	18 28 20
	29	20 31 31	22 33 44	0 28 4	2 30 17	4 28 34	6 30 47	8 29 4	10 31 17	12 33 30	14 31 46	16 34 0	18 32 16
	30	20 35 27		0 32 0	2 34 13	4 32 30	6 34 43	8 33 0	10 35 13	12 37 26	14 35 43	16 37 56	18 36 13
	31	20 39 24		0 35 57		4 36 27		8 36 57	10 39 10		14 39 39		18 40 9
1977	1	18 44 6	20 46 19	22 36 43	0 38 56	2 37 12	4 39 26	6 37 42	8 39 56	10 42 9	12 40 25	14 42 38	16 40 55
	2	18 48 3	20 50 16	22 40 39	0 42 52	2 41 9	4 43 22	6 41 39	8 43 52	10 46 5	12 44 22	14 46 35	16 44 52
	3	18 51 59	20 54 12	22 44 36	0 46 49	2 45 6	4 47 19	6 45 35	8 47 49	10 50 2	12 48 18	14 50 32	16 48 48
	4	18 55 56	20 58 9	22 48 32	0 50 45	2 49 2	4 51 15	6 49 32	8 51 45	10 53 58	12 52 15	14 54 28	16 52 45
	5	18 59 52	21 2 5	22 52 29	0 54 42	2 52 59	4 55 12	6 53 29	8 55 42	10 57 55	12 56 11	14 58 25	16 56 41
	6	19 3 49	21 6 2	22 56 25	0 58 39	2 56 55	4 59 8	6 57 25	8 59 38	11 1 51	13 0 8	15 2 21	17 0 38
	7	19 7 45	21 9 59	23 0 22	1 2 35	3 0 52	5 3 5	7 1 22	9 3 35	11 5 48	13 4 5	15 6 18	17 4 34
	8	19 11 42	21 13 55	23 4 19	1 6 32	3 4 48	5 7 2	7 5 18	9 7 31	11 9 45	13 8 1	15 10 14	17 8 31
	9	19 15 38	21 17 52	23 8 15	1 10 28	3 8 45	5 10 58	7 9 15	9 11 28	11 13 41	13 11 58	15 14 11	17 12 28
	10	19 19 35	21 21 48	23 12 12	1 14 25	3 12 41	5 14 55	7 13 11	9 15 25	11 17 38	13 15 54	15 18 7	17 16 24
	11	19 23 32	21 25 45	23 16 8	1 18 21	3 16 38	5 18 51	7 17 8	9 19 21	11 21 34	13 19 51	15 22 4	17 20 21
	12	19 27 28	21 29 41	23 20 5	1 22 18	3 20 35	5 22 48	7 21 4	9 23 18	11 25 31	13 23 47	15 26 0	17 24 17
	13	19 31 25	21 33 38	23 24 1	1 26 14	3 24 31	5 26 44	7 25 1	9 27 14	11 29 27	13 27 44	15 29 57	17 28 14
	14	19 35 21	21 37 34	23 27 58	1 30 11	3 28 28	5 30 41	7 28 58	9 31 11	11 33 24	13 31 40	15 33 54	17 32 10
	15	19 39 18	21 41 31	23 31 54	1 34 8	3 32 24	5 34 37	7 32 54	9 35 7	11 37 20	13 35 37	15 37 50	17 36 7
	16	19 43 14	21 45 28	23 35 51	1 38 4	3 36 21	5 38 34	7 36 51	9 39 4	11 41 17	13 39 34	15 41 47	17 40 3
	17	19 47 11	21 49 24	23 39 48	1 42 1	3 40 17	5 42 31	7 40 47	9 43 0	11 45 14	13 43 30	15 45 43	17 44 0
	18	19 51 7	21 53 21	23 43 44	1 45 57	3 44 14	5 46 27	7 44 44	9 46 57	11 49 10	13 47 27	15 49 40	17 47 57
	19	19 55 4	21 57 17	23 47 41	1 49 54	3 48 10	5 50 24	7 48 40	9 50 54	11 53 7	13 51 23	15 53 36	17 51 53
	20	19 59 1	22 1 14	23 51 37	1 53 50	3 52 7	5 54 20	7 52 37	9 54 50	11 57 3	13 55 20	15 57 33	17 55 50
	21	20 2 57	22 5 10	23 55 34	1 57 47	3 56 4	5 58 17	7 56 33	9 58 47	12 1 0	13 59 16	16 1 30	17 59 46
	22	20 6 54	22 9 7	23 59 30	2 1 43	4 0 0	6 2 13	8 0 30	10 2 43	12 4 56	14 3 13	16 5 26	18 3 43
	23	20 10 50	22 13 3	0 3 27	2 5 40	4 3 57	6 6 10	8 4 27	10 6 40	12 8 53	14 7 9	16 9 23	18 7 39
	24	20 14 47	22 17 0	0 7 23	2 9 37	4 7 53	6 10 6	8 8 23	10 10 36	12 12 49	14 11 6	16 13 19	18 11 36
	25	20 18 43	22 20 56	0 11 20	2 13 33	4 11 50	6 14 3	8 12 20	10 14 33	12 16 46	14 15 3	16 17 16	18 15 32
	26	20 22 40	22 24 53	0 15 17	2 17 30	4 15 46	6 18 0	8 16 16	10 18 29	12 20 43	14 18 59	16 21 12	18 19 29
	27	20 26 36	22 28 50	0 19 13	2 21 26	4 19 43	6 21 56	8 20 13	10 22 26	12 24 39	14 22 56	16 25 9	18 23 26
	28	20 30 33	22 32 46	0 23 10	2 25 23	4 23 39	6 25 53	8 24 9	10 26 23	12 28 36	14 26 52	16 29 5	18 27 22
	29	20 34 30		0 27 6	2 29 19	4 27 36	6 29 49	8 28 6	10 30 19	12 32 32	14 30 49	16 33 2	18 31 19
	30	20 38 26		0 31 3	2 33 16	4 31 32	6 33 46	8 32 2	10 34 16	12 36 29	14 34 45	16 36 59	18 35 15
	31	20 42 23		0 34 59		4 35 29		8 35 59	10 38 12		14 38 42		18 39 12

YEAR	JAN	FEB	MAR	APR	MAY	JUN	JUL	SEP	AUG	OCT	NOV	DEC
1978 1	18 43 8	20 45 22	22 35 45	0 37 58	2 36 15	4 38 28	6 36 45	8 38 58	10 41 11	12 39 28	14 41 41	16 39 57
2	18 47 5	20 49 18	22 39 42	0 41 55	2 40 11	4 42 25	6 40 41	8 42 54	10 45 8	12 43 24	14 45 37	16 43 54
3	18 51 1	20 53 15	22 43 38	0 45 51	2 44 8	4 46 21	6 44 38	8 46 51	10 49 4	12 47 21	14 49 34	16 47 51
4	18 54 58	20 57 11	22 47 35	0 49 48	2 48 4	4 50 18	6 48 34	8 50 48	10 53 1	12 51 17	14 53 30	16 51 47
5	18 58 55	21 1 8	22 51 31	0 53 44	2 52 1	4 54 14	6 52 31	8 54 44	10 56 57	12 55 14	14 57 27	16 55 44
6	19 2 51	21 5 4	22 55 28	0 57 41	2 55 58	4 58 11	6 56 27	8 58 41	11 0 54	12 59 10	15 1 24	16 59 40
7	19 6 48	21 9 1	22 59 24	1 1 37	2 59 54	5 2 7	7 0 24	9 2 37	11 4 50	13 3 7	15 5 20	17 3 37
8	19 10 44	21 12 57	23 3 21	1 5 34	3 3 51	5 6 4	7 4 21	9 6 34	11 8 47	13 7 3	15 9 17	17 7 33
9	19 14 41	21 16 54	23 7 18	1 9 31	3 7 47	5 10 0	7 8 17	9 10 30	11 12 43	13 11 0	15 13 13	17 11 30
10	19 18 37	21 20 51	23 11 14	1 13 27	3 11 44	5 13 57	7 12 14	9 14 27	11 16 40	13 14 57	15 17 10	17 15 26
11	19 22 34	21 24 47	23 15 11	1 17 24	3 15 40	5 17 54	7 16 10	9 18 23	11 20 37	13 18 53	15 21 6	17 19 23
12	19 26 30	21 28 44	23 19 7	1 21 20	3 19 37	5 21 50	7 20 7	9 22 20	11 24 33	13 22 50	15 25 3	17 23 20
13	19 30 27	21 32 40	23 23 4	1 25 17	3 23 33	5 25 47	7 24 3	9 26 17	11 28 30	13 26 46	15 28 59	17 27 16
14	19 34 24	21 36 37	23 27 0	1 29 13	3 27 30	5 29 43	7 28 0	9 30 13	11 32 26	13 30 43	15 32 56	17 31 13
15	19 38 20	21 40 33	23 30 57	1 33 10	3 31 27	5 33 40	7 31 56	9 34 10	11 36 23	13 34 39	15 36 53	17 35 9
16	19 42 17	21 44 30	23 34 53	1 37 6	3 35 23	5 37 36	7 35 53	9 38 6	11 40 19	13 38 36	15 40 49	17 39 6
17	19 46 13	21 48 26	23 38 50	1 41 3	3 39 20	5 41 33	7 39 50	9 42 3	11 44 16	13 42 32	15 44 46	17 43 2
18	19 50 10	21 52 23	23 42 46	1 45 0	3 43 16	5 45 29	7 43 46	9 45 59	11 48 12	13 46 29	15 48 42	17 46 59
19	19 54 6	21 56 20	23 46 43	1 48 56	3 47 13	5 49 26	7 47 43	9 49 56	11 52 9	13 50 26	15 52 39	17 50 55
20	19 58 3	22 0 16	23 50 40	1 52 53	3 51 9	5 53 23	7 51 39	9 53 52	11 56 6	13 54 22	15 56 35	17 54 52
21	20 1 59	22 4 13	23 54 36	1 56 49	3 55 6	5 57 19	7 55 36	9 57 49	12 0 2	13 58 19	16 0 32	17 58 49
22	20 5 56	22 8 9	23 58 33	2 0 46	3 59 2	6 1 16	7 59 32	10 1 46	12 3 59	14 2 15	16 4 28	18 2 45
23	20 9 53	22 12 6	0 2 29	2 4 42	4 2 59	6 5 12	8 3 29	10 5 42	12 7 55	14 6 12	16 8 25	18 6 42
24	20 13 49	22 16 2	0 6 26	2 8 39	4 6 56	6 9 9	8 7 25	10 9 39	12 11 52	14 10 8	16 12 22	18 10 38
25	20 17 46	22 19 59	0 10 22	2 12 35	4 10 52	6 13 5	8 11 22	10 13 35	12 15 48	14 14 5	16 16 18	18 14 35
26	20 21 42	22 23 55	0 14 19	2 16 32	4 14 49	6 17 2	8 15 19	10 17 32	12 19 45	14 18 1	16 20 15	18 18 31
27	20 25 39	22 27 52	0 18 15	2 20 29	4 18 45	6 20 58	8 19 15	10 21 28	12 23 41	14 21 58	16 24 11	18 22 28
28	20 29 35	22 31 49	0 22 12	2 24 25	4 22 42	6 24 55	8 23 12	10 25 25	12 27 38	14 25 55	16 28 8	18 26 24
29	20 33 32		0 26 9	2 28 22	4 26 38	6 28 52	8 27 8	10 29 21	12 31 35	14 29 51	16 32 4	18 30 21
30	20 37 28		0 30 5	2 32 18	4 30 35	6 32 48	8 31 5	10 33 18	12 35 31	14 33 48	16 36 1	18 34 18
31	20 41 25		0 34 2		4 34 31		8 35 1	10 37 15		14 37 44		18 38 14
1979 1	18 42 11	20 44 24	22 34 47	0 37 1	2 35 17	4 37 30	6 35 47	8 38 0	10 40 13	12 38 30	14 40 43	16 39 0
2	18 46 7	20 48 20	22 38 44	0 40 57	2 39 14	4 41 27	6 39 44	8 41 57	10 44 10	12 42 27	14 44 40	16 42 56
3	18 50 4	20 52 17	22 42 41	0 44 54	2 43 10	4 45 23	6 43 40	8 45 53	10 48 7	12 46 23	14 48 36	16 46 53
4	18 54 0	20 56 14	22 46 37	0 48 50	2 47 7	4 49 20	6 47 37	8 49 50	10 52 3	12 50 20	14 52 33	16 50 49
5	18 57 57	21 0 10	22 50 34	0 52 47	2 51 3	4 53 17	6 51 33	8 53 46	10 56 0	12 54 16	14 56 29	16 54 46
6	19 1 53	21 4 7	22 54 30	0 56 43	2 55 0	4 57 13	6 55 30	8 57 43	10 59 56	12 58 13	15 0 26	16 58 43
7	19 5 50	21 8 3	22 58 27	1 0 40	2 58 56	5 1 10	6 59 26	9 1 40	11 3 53	13 2 9	15 4 22	17 2 39
8	19 9 47	21 12 0	23 2 23	1 4 36	3 2 53	5 5 6	7 3 23	9 5 36	11 7 49	13 6 6	15 8 19	17 6 36
9	19 13 43	21 15 56	23 6 20	1 8 33	3 6 50	5 9 3	7 7 19	9 9 33	11 11 46	13 10 2	15 12 16	17 10 32
10	19 17 40	21 19 53	23 10 16	1 12 30	3 10 46	5 12 59	7 11 16	9 13 29	11 15 42	13 13 59	15 16 12	17 14 29
11	19 21 36	21 23 49	23 14 13	1 16 26	3 14 43	5 16 56	7 15 13	9 17 26	11 19 39	13 17 56	15 20 9	17 18 25
12	19 25 33	21 27 46	23 18 10	1 20 23	3 18 39	5 20 52	7 19 9	9 21 22	11 23 35	13 21 52	15 24 5	17 22 22
13	19 29 29	21 31 43	23 22 6	1 24 19	3 22 36	5 24 49	7 23 6	9 25 19	11 27 32	13 25 49	15 28 2	17 26 18
14	19 33 26	21 35 39	23 26 3	1 28 16	3 26 32	5 28 46	7 27 2	9 29 15	11 31 29	13 29 45	15 31 58	17 30 15
15	19 37 22	21 39 36	23 29 59	1 32 12	3 30 29	5 32 42	7 30 59	9 33 12	11 35 25	13 33 42	15 35 55	17 34 12
16	19 41 19	21 43 32	23 33 56	1 36 9	3 34 25	5 36 39	7 34 55	9 37 9	11 39 22	13 37 38	15 39 51	17 38 8
17	19 45 16	21 47 29	23 37 52	1 40 5	3 38 22	5 40 35	7 38 52	9 41 5	11 43 18	13 41 35	15 43 48	17 42 5
18	19 49 12	21 51 25	23 41 49	1 44 2	3 42 19	5 44 32	7 42 48	9 45 2	11 47 15	13 45 31	15 47 45	17 46 1
19	19 53 9	21 55 22	23 45 45	1 47 58	3 46 15	5 48 28	7 46 45	9 48 58	11 51 11	13 49 28	15 51 41	17 49 58
20	19 57 5	21 59 18	23 49 42	1 51 55	3 50 12	5 52 25	7 50 42	9 52 55	11 55 8	13 53 24	15 55 38	17 53 54
21	20 1 2	22 3 15	23 53 38	1 55 52	3 54 8	5 56 21	7 54 38	9 56 51	11 59 4	13 57 21	15 59 34	17 57 51
22	20 4 58	22 7 12	23 57 35	1 59 48	3 58 5	6 0 18	7 58 35	10 0 48	12 3 1	14 1 18	16 3 31	18 1 47
23	20 8 55	22 11 8	0 1 32	2 3 45	4 2 1	6 4 15	8 2 31	10 4 44	12 6 58	14 5 14	16 7 27	18 5 44
24	20 12 51	22 15 5	0 5 28	2 7 41	4 5 58	6 8 11	8 6 28	10 8 41	12 10 54	14 9 11	16 11 24	18 9 41
25	20 16 48	22 19 1	0 9 25	2 11 38	4 9 54	6 12 8	8 10 24	10 12 38	12 14 51	14 13 7	16 15 20	18 13 37
26	20 20 45	22 22 58	0 13 21	2 15 34	4 13 51	6 16 4	8 14 21	10 16 34	12 18 47	14 17 4	16 19 17	18 17 34
27	20 24 41	22 26 54	0 17 18	2 19 31	4 17 48	6 20 1	8 18 17	10 20 31	12 22 44	14 21 0	16 23 14	18 21 30
28	20 28 38	22 30 51	0 21 14	2 23 27	4 21 44	6 23 57	8 22 14	10 24 27	12 26 40	14 24 57	16 27 10	18 25 27
29	20 32 34		0 25 11	2 27 24	4 25 41	6 27 54	8 26 11	10 28 24	12 30 37	14 28 53	16 31 7	18 29 23
30	20 36 31		0 29 7	2 31 21	4 29 37	6 31 50	8 30 7	10 32 20	12 34 33	14 32 50	16 35 3	18 33 20
31	20 40 27		0 33 4		4 33 34		8 34 4	10 36 17		14 36 47		18 37 16
1980 1	18 41 13	20 43 26	22 37 46	0 39 59	2 38 16	4 40 29	6 38 46	8 40 59	10 43 12	12 41 29	14 43 42	16 41 59
2	18 45 10	20 47 23	22 41 43	0 43 56	2 42 13	4 44 26	6 42 43	8 44 56	10 47 9	12 45 26	14 47 39	16 45 55
3	18 49 6	20 51 19	22 45 39	0 47 53	2 46 9	4 48 22	6 46 39	8 48 52	10 51 5	12 49 22	14 51 35	16 49 52
4	18 53 3	20 55 16	22 49 36	0 51 49	2 50 6	4 52 19	6 50 36	8 52 49	10 55 2	12 53 19	14 55 32	16 53 48
5	18 56 59	20 59 13	22 53 33	0 55 46	2 54 2	4 56 16	6 54 32	8 56 45	10 58 59	12 57 15	14 59 28	16 57 45
6	19 0 56	21 3 9	22 57 29	0 59 42	2 57 59	5 0 12	6 58 29	9 0 42	11 2 55	13 1 12	15 3 25	17 1 42
7	19 4 52	21 7 6	23 1 26	1 3 39	3 1 55	5 4 9	7 2 25	9 4 39	11 6 52	13 5 8	15 7 21	17 5 38
8	19 8 49	21 11 2	23 5 22	1 7 35	3 5 52	5 8 5	7 6 22	9 8 35	11 10 48	13 9 5	15 11 18	17 9 35
9	19 12 46	21 14 59	23 9 19	1 11 32	3 9 48	5 12 2	7 10 18	9 12 32	11 14 45	13 13 1	15 15 15	17 13 31
10	19 16 42	21 18 55	23 13 15	1 15 28	3 13 45	5 15 58	7 14 15	9 16 28	11 18 41	13 16 58	15 19 11	17 17 28
11	19 20 39	21 22 52	23 17 12	1 19 25	3 17 42	5 19 55	7 18 12	9 20 25	11 22 38	13 20 54	15 23 8	17 21 24
12	19 24 35	21 26 48	23 21 8	1 23 22	3 21 38	5 23 51	7 22 8	9 24 21	11 26 34	13 24 51	15 27 4	17 25 21
13	19 28 32	21 30 45	23 25 5	1 27 18	3 25 35	5 27 48	7 26 5	9 28 18	11 30 31	13 28 48	15 31 1	17 29 17
14	19 32 28	21 34 42	23 29 2	1 31 15	3 29 31	5 31 45	7 30 1	9 32 14	11 34 28	13 32 44	15 34 57	17 33 14
15	19 36 25	21 38 38	23 32 58	1 35 11	3 33 28	5 35 41	7 33 58	9 36 11	11 38 24	13 36 41	15 38 54	17 37 11
16	19 40 21	21 42 35	23 36 55	1 39 8	3 37 24	5 39 38	7 37 54	9 40 8	11 42 21	13 40 37	15 42 50	17 41 7
17	19 44 18	21 46 31	23 40 51	1 43 4	3 41 21	5 43 34	7 41 51	9 44 4	11 46 17	13 44 34	15 46 47	17 45 4
18	19 48 15	21 50 28	23 44 48	1 47 1	3 45 17	5 47 31	7 45 47	9 48 1	11 50 14	13 48 30	15 50 44	17 49 0
19	19 52 11	21 54 24	23 48 44	1 50 57	3 49 14	5 51 27	7 49 44	9 51 57	11 54 10	13 52 27	15 54 40	17 52 57
20	19 56 8	21 58 21	23 52 41	1 54 54	3 53 11	5 55 24	7 53 41	9 55 54	11 58 7	13 56 23	15 58 37	17 56 53
21	20 0 4	22 2 17	23 56 37	1 58 51	3 57 7	5 59 20	7 57 37	9 59 50	12 2 3	14 0 20	16 2 33	18 0 50
22	20 4 1	22 6 14	0 0 34	2 2 47	4 1 4	6 3 17	8 1 34	10 3 47	12 6 0	14 4 17	16 6 30	18 4 46
23	20 7 57	22 10 10	0 4 30	2 6 44	4 5 0	6 7 14	8 5 30	10 7 43	12 9 57	14 8 13	16 10 26	18 8 43
24	20 11 54	22 14 7	0 8 27	2 10 40	4 8 57	6 11 10	8 9 27	10 11 40	12 13 53	14 12 10	16 14 23	18 12 40
25	20 15 50	22 18 4	0 12 24	2 14 37	4 12 53	6 15 7	8 13 23	10 15 37	12 17 50	14 16 6	16 18 19	18 16 36
26	20 19 47	22 22 0	0 16 20	2 18 33	4 16 50	6 19 3	8 17 20	10 19 33	12 21 46	14 20 3	16 22 16	18 20 33
27	20 23 44	22 25 57	0 20 17	2 22 30	4 20 46	6 23 0	8 21 16	10 23 30	12 25 43	14 23 59	16 26 13	18 24 29
28	20 27 40	22 29 53	0 24 13	2 26 26	4 24 43	6 26 56	8 25 13	10 27 26	12 29 39	14 27 56	16 30 9	18 28 26
29	20 31 37	22 33 50	0 28 10	2 30 23	4 28 40	6 30 53	8 29 10	10 31 23	12 33 36	14 31 52	16 34 6	18 32 22
30	20 35 33		0 32 6	2 34 19	4 32 36	6 34 49	8 33 6	10 35 19	12 37 32	14 35 49	16 38 2	18 36 19
31	20 39 30		0 36 3		4 36 33		8 37 3	10 39 16		14 39 46		18 40 15
1981 1	18 44 12	20 46 25	22 36 49	0 39 2	2 37 19	4 39 32	6 37 48	8 40 2	10 42 15	12 40 31	14 42 45	16 41 1
2	18 48 9	20 50 22	22 40 45	0 42 58	2 41 15	4 43 28	6 41 45	8 43 58	10 46 11	12 44 28	14 46 41	16 44 58
3	18 52 5	20 54 18	22 44 42	0 46 55	2 45 12	4 47 25	6 45 42	8 47 55	10 50 8	12 48 25	14 50 38	16 48 54
4	18 56 2	20 58 15	22 48 38	0 50 52	2 49 8	4 51 21	6 49 38	8 51 51	10 54 5	12 52 21	14 54 34	16 52 51
5	18 59 58	21 2 12	22 52 35	0 54 48	2 53 5	4 55 18	6 53 35	8 55 48	10 58 1	12 56 18	14 58 31	16 56 47
6	19 3 55	21 6 8	22 56 32	0 58 45	2 57 1	4 59 15	6 57 31	8 59 44	11 1 58	13 0 14	15 2 27	17 0 44
7	19 7 51	21 10 5	23 0 28	1 2 41	3 0 58	5 3 11	7 1 28	9 3 41	11 5 54	13 4 11	15 6 24	17 4 41
8	19 11 48	21 14 1	23 4 25	1 6 38	3 4 54	5 7 8	7 5 24	9 7 38	11 9 51	13 8 7	15 10 20	17 8 37
9	19 15 44	21 17 58	23 8 21	1 10 34	3 8 51	5 11 4	7 9 21	9 11 34	11 13 47	13 12 4	15 14 17	17 12 34
10	19 19 41	21 21 54	23 12 18	1 14 31	3 12 48	5 15 1	7 13 17	9 15 31	11 17 44	13 16 0	15 18 14	17 16 30
11	19 23 38	21 25 51	23 16 14	1 18 27	3 16 44	5 18 57	7 17 14	9 19 27	11 21 40	13 19 57	15 22 10	17 20 27
12	19 27 34	21 29 47	23 20 11	1 22 24	3 20 41	5 22 54	7 21 11	9 23 24	11 25 37	13 23 54	15 26 7	17 24 23
13	19 31 31	21 33 44	23 24 7	1 26 21	3 24 37	5 26 50	7 25 7	9 27 20	11 29 34	13 27 50	15 30 3	17 28 20
14	19 35 27	21 37 40	23 28 4	1 30 17	3 28 34	5 30 47	7 29 4	9 31 17	11 33 30	13 31 47	15 34 0	17 32 17
15	19 39 24	21 41 37	23 32 1	1 34 14	3 32 30	5 34 44	7 33 0	9 35 13	11 37 27	13 35 43	15 37 56	17 36 13
16	19 43 20	21 45 34	23 35 57	1 38 10	3 36 27	5 38 40	7 36 57	9 39 10	11 41 23	13 39 40	15 41 53	17 40 10
17	19 47 17	21 49 30	23 39 54	1 42 7	3 40 23	5 42 37	7 40 53	9 43 7	11 45 20	13 43 36	15 45 49	17 44 6
18	19 51 14	21 53 27	23 43 50	1 46 3	3 44 20	5 46 33	7 44 50	9 47 3	11 49 16	13 47 33	15 49 46	17 48 3
19	19 55 10	21 57 23	23 47 47	1 50 0	3 48 16	5 50 30	7 48 46	9 51 0	11 53 13	13 51 29	15 53 43	17 51 59
20	19 59 7	22 1 20	23 51 43	1 53 56	3 52 13	5 54 26	7 52 43	9 54 56	11 57 9	13 55 26	15 57 39	17 55 56
21	20 3 3	22 5 16	23 55 40	1 57 53	3 56 10	5 58 23	7 56 40	9 58 53	12 1 6	13 59 23	16 1 36	17 59 52
22	20 7 0	22 9 13	23 59 36	2 1 50	4 0 6	6 2 19	8 0 36	10 2 49	12 5 2	14 3 19	16 5 32	18 3 49
23	20 10 56	22 13 9	0 3 33	2 5 46	4 4 3	6 6 16	8 4 33	10 6 46	12 8 59	14 7 16	16 9 29	18 7 46
24	20 14 53	22 17 6	0 7 29	2 9 43	4 7 59	6 10 13	8 8 29	10 10 42	12 12 56	14 11 12	16 13 25	18 11 42
25	20 18 49	22 21 3	0 11 26	2 13 39	4 11 56	6 14 9	8 12 26	10 14 39	12 16 52	14 15 9	16 17 22	18 15 39
26	20 22 46	22 24 59	0 15 23	2 17 36	4 15 52	6 18 6	8 16 22	10 18 36	12 20 49	14 19 5	16 21 18	18 19 35
27	20 26 42	22 28 56	0 19 19	2 21 32	4 19 49	6 22 2	8 20 19	10 22 32	12 24 45	14 23 2	16 25 15	18 23 32
28	20 30 39	22 32 52	0 23 16	2 25 29	4 23 46	6 25 59	8 24 15	10 26 29	12 28 42	14 26 58	16 29 12	18 27 28
29	20 34 36		0 27 12	2 29 25	4 27 42	6 29 55	8 28 12	10 30 25	12 32 38	14 30 55	16 33 8	18 31 25
30	20 38 32		0 31 9	2 33 22	4 31 39	6 33 52	8 32 9	10 34 22	12 36 35	14 34 51	16 37 5	18 35 21
31	20 42 29		0 35 5		4 35 35		8 36 5	10 38 18		14 38 48		18 39 18

YEAR	JAN	FEB	MAR	APR	MAY	JUN	JUL	AUG	SEP	OCT	NOV	DEC
1982 1	18 43 15	20 45 28	22 35 51	0 38 4	2 36 21	4 38 34	6 36 51	8 39 4	10 41 17	12 39 34	14 41 47	16 40 4
2	18 47 11	20 49 24	22 39 48	0 42 1	2 40 18	4 42 31	6 40 48	8 43 1	10 45 14	12 43 31	14 45 44	16 44 0
3	18 51 8	20 53 21	22 43 44	0 45 58	2 44 14	4 46 27	6 44 44	8 46 57	10 49 11	12 47 27	14 49 40	16 47 57
4	18 55 4	20 57 17	22 47 41	0 49 54	2 48 11	4 50 24	6 48 41	8 50 54	10 53 7	12 51 24	14 53 37	16 51 54
5	18 59 1	21 1 14	22 51 38	0 53 51	2 52 7	4 54 21	6 52 37	8 54 51	10 57 4	12 55 20	14 57 33	16 55 50
6	19 2 57	21 5 11	22 55 34	0 57 47	2 56 4	4 58 17	6 56 34	8 58 47	11 1 0	12 59 17	15 1 30	16 59 47
7	19 6 54	21 9 7	22 59 31	1 1 44	3 0 0	5 2 14	7 0 30	9 2 44	11 4 57	13 3 13	15 5 27	17 3 43
8	19 10 50	21 13 4	23 3 27	1 5 40	3 3 57	5 6 10	7 4 27	9 6 40	11 8 53	13 7 10	15 9 23	17 7 40
9	19 14 47	21 17 0	23 7 24	1 9 37	3 7 53	5 10 7	7 8 23	9 10 37	11 12 50	13 11 6	15 13 20	17 11 36
10	19 18 44	21 20 57	23 11 20	1 13 33	3 11 50	5 14 3	7 12 20	9 14 33	11 16 46	13 15 3	15 17 16	17 15 33
11	19 22 40	21 24 53	23 15 17	1 17 30	3 15 47	5 18 0	7 16 17	9 18 30	11 20 43	13 19 0	15 21 13	17 19 29
12	19 26 37	21 28 50	23 19 13	1 21 27	3 19 43	5 21 56	7 20 13	9 22 26	11 24 40	13 22 56	15 25 9	17 23 26
13	19 30 33	21 32 46	23 23 10	1 25 23	3 23 40	5 25 53	7 24 10	9 26 23	11 28 36	13 26 53	15 29 6	17 27 23
14	19 34 30	21 36 43	23 27 7	1 29 20	3 27 36	5 29 50	7 28 6	9 30 19	11 32 33	13 30 49	15 33 2	17 31 19
15	19 38 26	21 40 40	23 31 3	1 33 16	3 31 33	5 33 46	7 32 3	9 34 16	11 36 29	13 34 46	15 36 59	17 35 16
16	19 42 23	21 44 36	23 35 0	1 37 13	3 35 29	5 37 43	7 35 59	9 38 13	11 40 26	13 38 42	15 40 56	17 39 12
17	19 46 19	21 48 33	23 38 56	1 41 9	3 39 26	5 41 39	7 39 56	9 42 9	11 44 22	13 42 39	15 44 52	17 43 9
18	19 50 16	21 52 29	23 42 53	1 45 6	3 43 23	5 45 36	7 43 52	9 46 6	11 48 19	13 46 35	15 48 49	17 47 5
19	19 54 13	21 56 26	23 46 49	1 49 2	3 47 19	5 49 32	7 47 49	9 50 2	11 52 15	13 50 32	15 52 45	17 51 2
20	19 58 9	22 0 22	23 50 46	1 52 59	3 51 16	5 53 29	7 51 46	9 53 59	11 56 12	13 54 29	15 56 42	17 54 58
21	20 2 6	22 4 19	23 54 42	1 56 56	3 55 12	5 57 25	7 55 42	9 57 55	12 0 9	13 58 25	16 0 38	17 58 55
22	20 6 2	22 8 15	23 58 39	2 0 52	3 59 9	6 1 22	7 59 39	10 1 52	12 4 5	14 2 22	16 4 35	18 2 52
23	20 9 59	22 12 12	0 2 35	2 4 49	4 3 5	6 5 19	8 3 35	10 5 48	12 8 2	14 6 18	16 8 31	18 6 48
24	20 13 55	22 16 9	0 6 32	2 8 45	4 7 2	6 9 15	8 7 32	10 9 45	12 11 58	14 10 15	16 12 28	18 10 45
25	20 17 52	22 20 5	0 10 29	2 12 42	4 10 58	6 13 12	8 11 28	10 13 42	12 15 55	14 14 11	16 16 25	18 14 41
26	20 21 48	22 24 2	0 14 25	2 16 38	4 14 55	6 17 8	8 15 25	10 17 38	12 19 51	14 18 8	16 20 21	18 18 38
27	20 25 45	22 27 58	0 18 22	2 20 35	4 18 52	6 21 5	8 19 21	10 21 35	12 23 48	14 22 4	16 24 18	18 22 34
28	20 29 42	22 31 55	0 22 18	2 24 31	4 22 48	6 25 1	8 23 18	10 25 31	12 27 44	14 26 1	16 28 14	18 26 31
29	20 33 38		0 26 15	2 28 28	4 26 45	6 28 58	8 27 15	10 29 28	12 31 41	14 29 58	16 32 11	18 30 27
30	20 37 35		0 30 11	2 32 25	4 30 41	6 32 54	8 31 11	10 33 24	12 35 37	14 33 54	16 36 7	18 34 24
31	20 41 31		0 34 8		4 34 38		8 35 8	10 37 21		14 37 51		18 38 21
1983 1	18 42 17	20 44 30	22 34 54	0 37 7	2 35 24	4 37 37	6 35 54	8 38 7	10 40 20	12 38 37	14 40 50	16 39 7
2	18 46 14	20 48 27	22 38 51	0 41 4	2 39 20	4 41 34	6 39 50	8 42 4	10 44 17	12 42 33	14 44 46	16 43 3
3	18 50 10	20 52 24	22 42 47	0 45 0	2 43 17	4 45 30	6 43 47	8 46 0	10 48 13	12 46 30	14 48 43	16 47 0
4	18 54 7	20 56 20	22 46 44	0 48 57	2 47 13	4 49 27	6 47 43	8 49 57	10 52 10	12 50 26	14 52 40	16 50 56
5	18 58 3	21 0 17	22 50 40	0 52 53	2 51 10	4 53 23	6 51 40	8 53 53	10 56 6	12 54 23	14 56 36	16 54 53
6	19 2 0	21 4 13	22 54 37	0 56 50	2 55 7	4 57 20	6 55 36	8 57 50	11 0 3	12 58 20	15 0 33	16 58 49
7	19 5 57	21 8 10	22 58 33	1 0 46	2 59 3	5 1 16	6 59 33	9 1 46	11 4 0	13 2 16	15 4 29	17 2 46
8	19 9 53	21 12 6	23 2 30	1 4 43	3 3 0	5 5 13	7 3 30	9 5 43	11 7 56	13 6 13	15 8 26	17 6 43
9	19 13 50	21 16 3	23 6 26	1 8 40	3 6 56	5 9 9	7 7 26	9 9 39	11 11 53	13 10 9	15 12 22	17 10 39
10	19 17 46	21 19 59	23 10 23	1 12 36	3 10 53	5 13 6	7 11 23	9 13 36	11 15 49	13 14 6	15 16 19	17 14 36
11	19 21 43	21 23 56	23 14 20	1 16 33	3 14 49	5 17 3	7 15 19	9 17 33	11 19 46	13 18 2	15 20 15	17 18 32
12	19 25 39	21 27 53	23 18 16	1 20 29	3 18 46	5 20 59	7 19 16	9 21 29	11 23 42	13 21 59	15 24 12	17 22 29
13	19 29 36	21 31 49	23 22 13	1 24 26	3 22 42	5 24 56	7 23 12	9 25 26	11 27 39	13 25 55	15 28 9	17 26 25
14	19 33 32	21 35 46	23 26 9	1 28 22	3 26 39	5 28 52	7 27 9	9 29 22	11 31 35	13 29 52	15 32 5	17 30 22
15	19 37 29	21 39 42	23 30 6	1 32 19	3 30 36	5 32 49	7 31 6	9 33 19	11 35 32	13 33 49	15 36 2	17 34 18
16	19 41 26	21 43 39	23 34 2	1 36 15	3 34 32	5 36 45	7 35 2	9 37 15	11 39 28	13 37 45	15 39 58	17 38 15
17	19 45 22	21 47 35	23 37 59	1 40 12	3 38 29	5 40 42	7 38 59	9 41 12	11 43 25	13 41 42	15 43 55	17 42 12
18	19 49 19	21 51 32	23 41 55	1 44 9	3 42 25	5 44 38	7 42 55	9 45 8	11 47 22	13 45 38	15 47 51	17 46 8
19	19 53 15	21 55 28	23 45 52	1 48 5	3 46 22	5 48 35	7 46 52	9 49 5	11 51 18	13 49 35	15 51 48	17 50 5
20	19 57 12	21 59 25	23 49 48	1 52 2	3 50 18	5 52 32	7 50 48	9 53 2	11 55 15	13 53 31	15 55 44	17 54 1
21	20 1 8	22 3 22	23 53 45	1 55 58	3 54 15	5 56 28	7 54 45	9 56 58	11 59 11	13 57 28	15 59 41	17 57 58
22	20 5 5	22 7 18	23 57 42	1 59 55	3 58 11	6 0 25	7 58 41	10 0 55	12 3 8	14 1 24	16 3 38	18 1 54
23	20 9 1	22 11 15	0 1 38	2 3 51	4 2 8	6 4 21	8 2 38	10 4 51	12 7 4	14 5 21	16 7 34	18 5 51
24	20 12 58	22 15 11	0 5 35	2 7 48	4 6 5	6 8 18	8 6 35	10 8 48	12 11 1	14 9 17	16 11 31	18 9 47
25	20 16 55	22 19 8	0 9 31	2 11 44	4 10 1	6 12 14	8 10 31	10 12 44	12 14 57	14 13 14	16 15 27	18 13 44
26	20 20 51	22 23 4	0 13 28	2 15 41	4 13 58	6 16 11	8 14 28	10 16 41	12 18 54	14 17 11	16 19 24	18 17 41
27	20 24 48	22 27 1	0 17 24	2 19 38	4 17 54	6 20 7	8 18 24	10 20 37	12 22 51	14 21 7	16 23 20	18 21 37
28	20 28 44	22 30 57	0 21 21	2 23 34	4 21 51	6 24 4	8 22 21	10 24 34	12 26 47	14 25 4	16 27 17	18 25 34
29	20 32 41		0 25 17	2 27 31	4 25 47	6 28 1	8 26 17	10 28 30	12 30 44	14 29 0	16 31 14	18 29 30
30	20 36 37		0 29 14	2 31 27	4 29 44	6 31 57	8 30 14	10 32 27	12 34 40	14 32 57	16 35 10	18 33 27
31	20 40 34		0 33 11		4 33 40		8 34 10	10 36 24		14 36 53		18 37 23
1984 1	18 41 20	20 43 33	22 37 53	0 40 6	2 38 23	4 40 36	6 38 53	8 41 6	10 43 20	12 41 36	14 43 49	16 42 6
2	18 45 16	20 47 30	22 41 50	0 44 3	2 42 20	4 44 33	6 42 50	8 45 3	10 47 16	12 45 33	14 47 46	16 46 3
3	18 49 13	20 51 26	22 45 46	0 48 0	2 46 16	4 48 29	6 46 46	8 48 59	10 51 13	12 49 29	14 51 42	16 49 59
4	18 53 10	20 55 23	22 49 43	0 51 56	2 50 13	4 52 26	6 50 43	8 52 56	10 55 9	12 53 26	14 55 39	16 53 56
5	18 57 6	20 59 19	22 53 40	0 55 53	2 54 9	4 56 23	6 54 39	8 56 53	10 59 6	12 57 22	14 59 36	16 57 52
6	19 1 3	21 3 16	22 57 36	0 59 49	2 58 6	5 0 19	6 58 36	9 0 49	11 3 2	13 1 19	15 3 32	17 1 49
7	19 4 59	21 7 13	23 1 33	1 3 46	3 2 2	5 4 16	7 2 32	9 4 46	11 6 59	13 5 15	15 7 29	17 5 45
8	19 8 56	21 11 9	23 5 29	1 7 42	3 5 59	5 8 12	7 6 29	9 8 42	11 10 55	13 9 12	15 11 25	17 9 42
9	19 12 52	21 15 6	23 9 26	1 11 39	3 9 56	5 12 9	7 10 26	9 12 39	11 14 52	13 13 9	15 15 22	17 13 38
10	19 16 49	21 19 2	23 13 22	1 15 35	3 13 52	5 16 5	7 14 22	9 16 35	11 18 49	13 17 5	15 19 18	17 17 35
11	19 20 46	21 22 59	23 17 19	1 19 32	3 17 49	5 20 2	7 18 19	9 20 32	11 22 45	13 21 2	15 23 15	17 21 32
12	19 24 42	21 26 55	23 21 15	1 23 29	3 21 45	5 23 58	7 22 15	9 24 28	11 26 42	13 24 58	15 27 11	17 25 28
13	19 28 39	21 30 52	23 25 12	1 27 25	3 25 42	5 27 55	7 26 12	9 28 25	11 30 38	13 28 55	15 31 8	17 29 25
14	19 32 35	21 34 48	23 29 9	1 31 22	3 29 38	5 31 52	7 30 8	9 32 22	11 34 35	13 32 51	15 35 5	17 33 21
15	19 36 32	21 38 45	23 33 5	1 35 18	3 33 35	5 35 48	7 34 5	9 36 18	11 38 31	13 36 48	15 39 1	17 37 18
16	19 40 28	21 42 42	23 37 2	1 39 15	3 37 31	5 39 45	7 38 1	9 40 15	11 42 28	13 40 44	15 42 58	17 41 14
17	19 44 25	21 46 38	23 40 58	1 43 11	3 41 28	5 43 41	7 41 58	9 44 11	11 46 24	13 44 41	15 46 54	17 45 11
18	19 48 21	21 50 35	23 44 55	1 47 8	3 45 25	5 47 38	7 45 55	9 48 8	11 50 21	13 48 38	15 50 51	17 49 8
19	19 52 18	21 54 31	23 48 51	1 51 4	3 49 21	5 51 34	7 49 51	9 52 4	11 54 18	13 52 34	15 54 47	17 53 4
20	19 56 15	21 58 28	23 52 48	1 55 1	3 53 18	5 55 31	7 53 48	9 56 1	11 58 14	13 56 31	15 58 44	17 57 1
21	20 0 11	22 2 24	23 56 44	1 58 58	3 57 14	5 59 27	7 57 44	9 59 57	12 2 11	14 0 27	16 2 40	18 0 57
22	20 4 8	22 6 21	0 0 41	2 2 54	4 1 11	6 3 24	8 1 41	10 3 54	12 6 7	14 4 24	16 6 37	18 4 54
23	20 8 4	22 10 17	0 4 37	2 6 51	4 5 7	6 7 21	8 5 37	10 7 51	12 10 4	14 8 20	16 10 34	18 8 50
24	20 12 1	22 14 14	0 8 34	2 10 47	4 9 4	6 11 17	8 9 34	10 11 47	12 14 0	14 12 17	16 14 30	18 12 47
25	20 15 57	22 18 11	0 12 31	2 14 44	4 13 0	6 15 14	8 13 30	10 15 44	12 17 57	14 16 13	16 18 27	18 16 43
26	20 19 54	22 22 7	0 16 27	2 18 40	4 16 57	6 19 10	8 17 27	10 19 40	12 21 53	14 20 10	16 22 23	18 20 40
27	20 23 50	22 26 4	0 20 24	2 22 37	4 20 54	6 23 7	8 21 24	10 23 37	12 25 50	14 24 7	16 26 20	18 24 37
28	20 27 47	22 30 0	0 24 20	2 26 33	4 24 50	6 27 3	8 25 20	10 27 33	12 29 46	14 28 3	16 30 16	18 28 33
29	20 31 44	22 33 57	0 28 17	2 30 30	4 28 47	6 31 0	8 29 17	10 31 30	12 33 43	14 32 0	16 34 13	18 32 30
30	20 35 40		0 32 13	2 34 27	4 32 43	6 34 57	8 33 13	10 35 26	12 37 40	14 35 56	16 38 9	18 36 26
31	20 39 37		0 36 10		4 36 40		8 37 10	10 39 23		14 39 53		18 40 23
1985 1	18 44 19	20 46 33	22 36 56	0 39 9	2 37 26	4 39 39	6 37 56	8 40 9	10 42 22	12 40 39	14 42 52	16 41 9
2	18 48 16	20 50 29	22 40 53	0 43 6	2 41 23	4 43 36	6 41 53	8 44 6	10 46 19	12 44 36	14 46 49	16 45 6
3	18 52 12	20 54 26	22 44 49	0 47 2	2 45 19	4 47 32	6 45 49	8 48 2	10 50 16	12 48 32	14 50 45	16 49 2
4	18 56 9	20 58 22	22 48 46	0 50 59	2 49 16	4 51 29	6 49 46	8 51 59	10 54 12	12 52 29	14 54 42	16 52 59
5	19 0 6	21 2 19	22 52 42	0 54 56	2 53 12	4 55 25	6 53 42	8 55 55	10 58 9	12 56 25	14 58 39	16 56 55
6	19 4 2	21 6 15	22 56 39	0 58 52	2 57 9	4 59 22	6 57 39	8 59 52	11 2 5	13 0 22	15 2 35	17 0 52
7	19 7 59	21 10 12	23 0 36	1 2 49	3 1 5	5 3 19	7 1 35	9 3 49	11 6 2	13 4 18	15 6 32	17 4 48
8	19 11 55	21 14 9	23 4 32	1 6 45	3 5 2	5 7 15	7 5 32	9 7 45	11 9 58	13 8 15	15 10 28	17 8 45
9	19 15 52	21 18 5	23 8 29	1 10 42	3 8 58	5 11 12	7 9 28	9 11 42	11 13 55	13 12 12	15 14 25	17 12 41
10	19 19 48	21 22 2	23 12 25	1 14 38	3 12 55	5 15 8	7 13 25	9 15 38	11 17 51	13 16 8	15 18 21	17 16 38
11	19 23 45	21 25 58	23 16 22	1 18 35	3 16 52	5 19 5	7 17 22	9 19 35	11 21 48	13 20 5	15 22 18	17 20 35
12	19 27 42	21 29 55	23 20 18	1 22 31	3 20 48	5 23 1	7 21 18	9 23 31	11 25 45	13 24 1	15 26 14	17 24 31
13	19 31 38	21 33 51	23 24 15	1 26 28	3 24 45	5 26 58	7 25 15	9 27 28	11 29 41	13 27 58	15 30 11	17 28 28
14	19 35 35	21 37 48	23 28 11	1 30 25	3 28 41	5 30 54	7 29 11	9 31 25	11 33 38	13 31 54	15 34 7	17 32 24
15	19 39 31	21 41 44	23 32 8	1 34 21	3 32 38	5 34 51	7 33 8	9 35 21	11 37 34	13 35 51	15 38 4	17 36 21
16	19 43 28	21 45 41	23 36 5	1 38 18	3 36 34	5 38 48	7 37 4	9 39 18	11 41 31	13 39 47	15 42 1	17 40 17
17	19 47 24	21 49 38	23 40 1	1 42 14	3 40 31	5 42 44	7 41 1	9 43 14	11 45 27	13 43 44	15 45 57	17 44 14
18	19 51 21	21 53 34	23 43 58	1 46 11	3 44 27	5 46 41	7 44 57	9 47 11	11 49 24	13 47 41	15 49 54	17 48 11
19	19 55 17	21 57 31	23 47 54	1 50 7	3 48 24	5 50 37	7 48 54	9 51 7	11 53 20	13 51 37	15 53 50	17 52 7
20	19 59 14	22 1 27	23 51 51	1 54 4	3 52 21	5 54 34	7 52 51	9 55 4	11 57 17	13 55 34	15 57 47	17 56 4
21	20 3 11	22 5 24	23 55 47	1 58 0	3 56 17	5 58 30	7 56 47	9 59 0	12 1 14	13 59 30	16 1 43	18 0 0
22	20 7 7	22 9 20	23 59 44	2 1 57	4 0 14	6 2 27	8 0 44	10 2 57	12 5 10	14 3 27	16 5 40	18 3 57
23	20 11 4	22 13 17	0 3 40	2 5 54	4 4 10	6 6 24	8 4 40	10 6 53	12 9 7	14 7 23	16 9 37	18 7 53
24	20 15 0	22 17 13	0 7 37	2 9 50	4 8 7	6 10 20	8 8 37	10 10 50	12 13 3	14 11 20	16 13 33	18 11 50
25	20 18 57	22 21 10	0 11 33	2 13 47	4 12 3	6 14 17	8 12 33	10 14 47	12 17 0	14 15 16	16 17 30	18 15 46
26	20 22 53	22 25 7	0 15 30	2 17 43	4 16 0	6 18 13	8 16 30	10 18 43	12 20 56	14 19 13	16 21 26	18 19 43
27	20 26 50	22 29 3	0 19 27	2 21 40	4 19 56	6 22 10	8 20 26	10 22 40	12 24 53	14 23 9	16 25 23	18 23 40
28	20 30 46	22 33 0	0 23 23	2 25 36	4 23 53	6 26 6	8 24 23	10 26 36	12 28 49	14 27 6	16 29 19	18 27 36
29	20 34 43		0 27 20	2 29 33	4 27 50	6 30 3	8 28 20	10 30 33	12 32 46	14 31 3	16 33 16	18 31 33
30	20 38 40		0 31 16	2 33 29	4 31 46	6 33 59	8 32 16	10 34 29	12 36 43	14 34 59	16 37 12	18 35 29
31	20 42 36		0 35 13		4 35 43		8 36 13	10 38 26		14 38 56		18 39 26

SIDEREAL TIMES

YEAR	JAN	FEB	MAR	APR	MAY	JUN	JUL	AUG	SEP	OCT	NOV	DEC
1986 1	18 43 22	20 45 36	22 35 59	0 38 12	2 36 29	4 38 42	6 36 59	8 39 12	10 41 25	12 39 42	14 41 55	16 40 12
2	18 47 19	20 49 32	22 39 56	0 42 9	2 40 26	4 42 39	6 40 56	8 43 9	10 45 22	12 43 39	14 45 52	16 44 9
3	18 51 15	20 53 29	22 43 52	0 46 5	2 44 22	4 46 35	6 44 52	8 47 5	10 49 19	12 47 35	14 49 48	16 48 5
4	18 55 12	20 57 25	22 47 49	0 50 2	2 48 19	4 50 32	6 48 49	8 51 2	10 53 15	12 51 32	14 53 45	16 52 2
5	18 59 9	21 1 22	22 51 45	0 53 59	2 52 15	4 54 28	6 52 45	8 54 59	10 57 12	12 55 28	14 57 42	16 55 58
6	19 3 5	21 5 18	22 55 42	0 57 55	2 56 12	4 58 25	6 56 42	8 58 55	11 1 8	12 59 25	15 1 38	16 59 55
7	19 7 2	21 9 15	22 59 38	1 1 52	3 0 8	5 2 22	7 0 38	9 2 52	11 5 5	13 3 21	15 5 35	17 3 51
8	19 10 58	21 13 12	23 3 35	1 5 48	3 4 5	5 6 18	7 4 35	9 6 48	11 9 1	13 7 18	15 9 31	17 7 48
9	19 14 55	21 17 8	23 7 32	1 9 45	3 8 1	5 10 15	7 8 31	9 10 45	11 12 58	13 11 15	15 13 28	17 11 44
10	19 18 51	21 21 5	23 11 28	1 13 41	3 11 58	5 14 11	7 12 28	9 14 41	11 16 54	13 15 11	15 17 24	17 15 41
11	19 22 48	21 25 1	23 15 25	1 17 38	3 15 55	5 18 8	7 16 25	9 18 38	11 20 51	13 19 8	15 21 21	17 19 38
12	19 26 44	21 28 58	23 19 21	1 21 34	3 19 51	5 22 4	7 20 21	9 22 34	11 24 48	13 23 4	15 25 17	17 23 34
13	19 30 41	21 32 54	23 23 18	1 25 31	3 23 48	5 26 1	7 24 18	9 26 31	11 28 44	13 27 1	15 29 14	17 27 31
14	19 34 38	21 36 51	23 27 14	1 29 28	3 27 44	5 29 57	7 28 14	9 30 27	11 32 41	13 30 57	15 33 11	17 31 27
15	19 38 34	21 40 47	23 31 11	1 33 24	3 31 41	5 33 54	7 32 11	9 34 24	11 36 37	13 34 54	15 37 7	17 35 24
16	19 42 31	21 44 44	23 35 7	1 37 21	3 35 37	5 37 51	7 36 7	9 38 21	11 40 34	13 38 50	15 41 4	17 39 20
17	19 46 27	21 48 40	23 39 4	1 41 17	3 39 34	5 41 47	7 40 4	9 42 17	11 44 30	13 42 47	15 45 0	17 43 17
18	19 50 24	21 52 37	23 43 1	1 45 14	3 43 30	5 45 44	7 44 0	9 46 14	11 48 27	13 46 44	15 48 57	17 47 14
19	19 54 20	21 56 34	23 46 57	1 49 10	3 47 27	5 49 40	7 47 57	9 50 10	11 52 23	13 50 40	15 52 53	17 51 10
20	19 58 17	22 0 30	23 50 54	1 53 7	3 51 24	5 53 37	7 51 54	9 54 7	11 56 20	13 54 37	15 56 50	17 55 7
21	20 2 13	22 4 27	23 54 50	1 57 3	3 55 20	5 57 33	7 55 50	9 58 3	12 0 17	13 58 33	16 0 46	17 59 3
22	20 6 10	22 8 23	23 58 47	2 1 0	3 59 17	6 1 30	7 59 47	10 2 0	12 4 13	14 2 30	16 4 43	18 3 0
23	20 10 7	22 12 20	0 2 43	2 4 57	4 3 13	6 5 27	8 3 43	10 5 56	12 8 10	14 6 26	16 8 40	18 6 56
24	20 14 3	22 16 16	0 6 40	2 8 53	4 7 10	6 9 23	8 7 40	10 9 53	12 12 6	14 10 23	16 12 36	18 10 53
25	20 18 0	22 20 13	0 10 36	2 12 50	4 11 6	6 13 20	8 11 36	10 13 50	12 16 3	14 14 19	16 16 33	18 14 49
26	20 21 56	22 24 9	0 14 33	2 16 46	4 15 3	6 17 16	8 15 33	10 17 46	12 19 59	14 18 16	16 20 29	18 18 46
27	20 25 53	22 28 6	0 18 30	2 20 43	4 18 59	6 21 13	8 19 29	10 21 43	12 23 56	14 22 13	16 24 26	18 22 43
28	20 29 49	22 32 3	0 22 26	2 24 39	4 22 56	6 25 9	8 23 26	10 25 39	12 27 52	14 26 9	16 28 22	18 26 39
29	20 33 46		0 26 23	2 28 36	4 26 53	6 29 6	8 27 23	10 29 36	12 31 49	14 30 6	16 32 19	18 30 36
30	20 37 42		0 30 19	2 32 32	4 30 49	6 33 2	8 31 19	10 33 32	12 35 46	14 34 2	16 36 15	18 34 32
31	20 41 39		0 34 16		4 34 46		8 35 16	10 37 29		14 37 59		18 38 29
1987 1	18 42 25	20 44 39	22 35 2	0 37 15	2 35 32	4 37 45	6 36 2	8 38 15	10 40 29	12 38 45	14 40 58	16 39 15
2	18 46 22	20 48 35	22 38 59	0 41 12	2 39 29	4 41 42	6 39 59	8 42 12	10 44 25	12 42 42	14 44 55	16 43 12
3	18 50 18	20 52 32	22 42 55	0 45 8	2 43 25	4 45 38	6 43 55	8 46 8	10 48 22	12 46 38	14 48 51	16 47 8
4	18 54 15	20 56 28	22 46 52	0 49 5	2 47 22	4 49 35	6 47 52	8 50 5	10 52 18	12 50 35	14 52 48	16 51 5
5	18 58 12	21 0 25	22 50 48	0 53 2	2 51 18	4 53 31	6 51 48	8 54 2	10 56 15	12 54 31	14 56 45	16 55 1
6	19 2 8	21 4 21	22 54 45	0 56 58	2 55 15	4 57 28	6 55 45	8 57 58	11 0 11	12 58 28	15 0 41	16 58 58
7	19 6 5	21 8 18	22 58 42	1 0 55	2 59 11	5 1 25	6 59 41	9 1 55	11 4 8	13 2 24	15 4 38	17 2 54
8	19 10 1	21 12 15	23 2 38	1 4 51	3 3 8	5 5 21	7 3 38	9 5 51	11 8 4	13 6 21	15 8 34	17 6 51
9	19 13 58	21 16 11	23 6 35	1 8 48	3 7 4	5 9 18	7 7 34	9 9 48	11 12 1	13 10 18	15 12 31	17 10 48
10	19 17 54	21 20 8	23 10 31	1 12 44	3 11 1	5 13 14	7 11 31	9 13 44	11 15 58	13 14 14	15 16 27	17 14 44
11	19 21 51	21 24 4	23 14 28	1 16 41	3 14 58	5 17 11	7 15 28	9 17 41	11 19 54	13 18 11	15 20 24	17 18 41
12	19 25 47	21 28 1	23 18 24	1 20 37	3 18 54	5 21 7	7 19 24	9 21 37	11 23 51	13 22 7	15 24 20	17 22 37
13	19 29 44	21 31 57	23 22 21	1 24 34	3 22 51	5 25 4	7 23 21	9 25 34	11 27 47	13 26 4	15 28 17	17 26 34
14	19 33 41	21 35 54	23 26 17	1 28 31	3 26 47	5 29 1	7 27 17	9 29 31	11 31 44	13 30 0	15 32 14	17 30 30
15	19 37 37	21 39 50	23 30 14	1 32 27	3 30 44	5 32 57	7 31 14	9 33 27	11 35 40	13 33 57	15 36 10	17 34 27
16	19 41 34	21 43 47	23 34 10	1 36 24	3 34 40	5 36 54	7 35 10	9 37 24	11 39 37	13 37 53	15 40 7	17 38 23
17	19 45 30	21 47 44	23 38 7	1 40 20	3 38 37	5 40 50	7 39 7	9 41 20	11 43 33	13 41 50	15 44 3	17 42 20
18	19 49 27	21 51 40	23 42 4	1 44 17	3 42 33	5 44 47	7 43 4	9 45 17	11 47 30	13 45 47	15 48 0	17 46 17
19	19 53 23	21 55 37	23 46 0	1 48 13	3 46 30	5 48 43	7 47 0	9 49 13	11 51 27	13 49 43	15 51 56	17 50 13
20	19 57 20	21 59 33	23 49 57	1 52 10	3 50 27	5 52 40	7 50 57	9 53 10	11 55 23	13 53 40	15 55 53	17 54 10
21	20 1 16	22 3 30	23 53 53	1 56 6	3 54 23	5 56 36	7 54 53	9 57 6	11 59 20	13 57 36	15 59 49	17 58 6
22	20 5 13	22 7 26	23 57 50	2 0 3	3 58 20	6 0 33	7 58 50	10 1 3	12 3 16	14 1 33	16 3 46	18 2 3
23	20 9 10	22 11 23	0 1 46	2 4 0	4 2 16	6 4 30	8 2 46	10 5 0	12 7 13	14 5 29	16 7 43	18 5 59
24	20 13 6	22 15 19	0 5 43	2 7 56	4 6 13	6 8 26	8 6 43	10 8 56	12 11 9	14 9 26	16 11 39	18 9 56
25	20 17 3	22 19 16	0 9 39	2 11 53	4 10 9	6 12 23	8 10 39	10 12 53	12 15 6	14 13 22	16 15 36	18 13 52
26	20 20 59	22 23 13	0 13 36	2 15 49	4 14 6	6 16 19	8 14 36	10 16 49	12 19 2	14 17 19	16 19 32	18 17 49
27	20 24 56	22 27 9	0 17 33	2 19 46	4 18 2	6 20 16	8 18 33	10 20 46	12 22 59	14 21 16	16 23 29	18 21 46
28	20 28 52	22 31 6	0 21 29	2 23 42	4 21 59	6 24 12	8 22 29	10 24 42	12 26 55	14 25 12	16 27 25	18 25 42
29	20 32 49		0 25 26	2 27 39	4 25 56	6 28 9	8 26 26	10 28 39	12 30 52	14 29 9	16 31 22	18 29 39
30	20 36 46		0 29 22	2 31 35	4 29 52	6 32 5	8 30 22	10 32 35	12 34 49	14 33 5	16 35 18	18 33 35
31	20 40 42		0 33 19		4 33 49		8 34 19	10 36 32		14 37 2		18 37 32
1988 1	18 41 28	20 43 42	22 38 2	0 40 15	2 38 32	4 40 45	6 39 2	8 41 15	10 43 28	12 41 45	14 43 58	16 42 15
2	18 45 25	20 47 38	22 41 58	0 44 12	2 42 28	4 44 41	6 42 58	8 45 11	10 47 25	12 45 41	14 47 55	16 46 11
3	18 49 22	20 51 35	22 45 55	0 48 8	2 46 25	4 48 38	6 46 55	8 49 8	10 51 21	12 49 38	14 51 51	16 50 8
4	18 53 18	20 55 31	22 49 51	0 52 5	2 50 21	4 52 35	6 50 51	8 53 5	10 55 18	12 53 34	14 55 48	16 54 4
5	18 57 15	20 59 28	22 53 48	0 56 1	2 54 18	4 56 31	6 54 48	8 57 1	10 59 14	12 57 31	14 59 44	16 58 1
6	19 1 11	21 3 24	22 57 45	0 59 58	2 58 14	5 0 28	6 58 44	9 0 58	11 3 11	13 1 28	15 3 41	17 1 57
7	19 5 8	21 7 21	23 1 41	1 3 54	3 2 11	5 4 24	7 2 41	9 4 54	11 7 7	13 5 24	15 7 37	17 5 54
8	19 9 4	21 11 18	23 5 38	1 7 51	3 6 8	5 8 21	7 6 38	9 8 51	11 11 4	13 9 21	15 11 34	17 9 51
9	19 13 1	21 15 14	23 9 34	1 11 47	3 10 4	5 12 17	7 10 34	9 12 47	11 15 1	13 13 17	15 15 30	17 13 47
10	19 16 57	21 19 11	23 13 31	1 15 44	3 14 1	5 16 14	7 14 31	9 16 44	11 18 57	13 17 14	15 19 27	17 17 44
11	19 20 54	21 23 7	23 17 27	1 19 41	3 17 57	5 20 10	7 18 27	9 20 40	11 22 54	13 21 10	15 23 23	17 21 40
12	19 24 51	21 27 4	23 21 24	1 23 37	3 21 54	5 24 7	7 22 24	9 24 37	11 26 50	13 25 7	15 27 20	17 25 37
13	19 28 47	21 31 0	23 25 20	1 27 34	3 25 50	5 28 4	7 26 20	9 28 34	11 30 47	13 29 3	15 31 17	17 29 33
14	19 32 44	21 34 57	23 29 17	1 31 30	3 29 47	5 32 0	7 30 17	9 32 30	11 34 43	13 33 0	15 35 13	17 33 30
15	19 36 40	21 38 53	23 33 14	1 35 27	3 33 43	5 35 57	7 34 13	9 36 27	11 38 40	13 36 56	15 39 10	17 37 26
16	19 40 37	21 42 50	23 37 10	1 39 23	3 37 40	5 39 53	7 38 10	9 40 23	11 42 36	13 40 53	15 43 6	17 41 23
17	19 44 33	21 46 47	23 41 7	1 43 20	3 41 37	5 43 50	7 42 7	9 44 20	11 46 33	13 44 50	15 47 3	17 45 20
18	19 48 30	21 50 43	23 45 3	1 47 16	3 45 33	5 47 46	7 46 3	9 48 16	11 50 30	13 48 46	15 50 59	17 49 16
19	19 52 26	21 54 40	23 49 0	1 51 13	3 49 30	5 51 43	7 50 0	9 52 13	11 54 26	13 52 43	15 54 56	17 53 13
20	19 56 23	21 58 36	23 52 56	1 55 9	3 53 26	5 55 39	7 53 56	9 56 9	11 58 23	13 56 39	15 58 53	17 57 9
21	20 0 20	22 2 33	23 56 53	1 59 6	3 57 23	5 59 36	7 57 53	10 0 6	12 2 19	14 0 36	16 2 49	18 1 6
22	20 4 16	22 6 29	0 0 49	2 3 3	4 1 19	6 3 33	8 1 49	10 4 3	12 6 16	14 4 32	16 6 46	18 5 2
23	20 8 13	22 10 26	0 4 46	2 6 59	4 5 16	6 7 29	8 5 46	10 7 59	12 10 12	14 8 29	16 10 42	18 8 59
24	20 12 9	22 14 22	0 8 43	2 10 56	4 9 12	6 11 26	8 9 42	10 11 56	12 14 9	14 12 25	16 14 39	18 12 56
25	20 16 6	22 18 19	0 12 39	2 14 52	4 13 9	6 15 22	8 13 39	10 15 52	12 18 5	14 16 22	16 18 35	18 16 52
26	20 20 2	22 22 16	0 16 36	2 18 49	4 17 6	6 19 19	8 17 36	10 19 49	12 22 2	14 20 19	16 22 32	18 20 49
27	20 23 59	22 26 12	0 20 32	2 22 45	4 21 2	6 23 15	8 21 32	10 23 45	12 25 59	14 24 15	16 26 28	18 24 45
28	20 27 55	22 30 9	0 24 29	2 26 42	4 24 59	6 27 12	8 25 29	10 27 42	12 29 55	14 28 12	16 30 25	18 28 42
29	20 31 52	22 34 5	0 28 25	2 30 38	4 28 55	6 31 9	8 29 25	10 31 38	12 33 52	14 32 8	16 34 22	18 32 38
30	20 35 49		0 32 22	2 34 35	4 32 52	6 35 5	8 33 22	10 35 35	12 37 48	14 36 5	16 38 18	18 36 35
31	20 39 45		0 36 18		4 36 48		8 37 18	10 39 32		14 40 1		18 40 31
1989 1	18 44 28	20 46 41	22 37 5	0 39 18	2 37 35	4 39 48	6 38 5	8 40 18	10 42 31	12 40 48	14 43 1	16 41 18
2	18 48 25	20 50 38	22 41 1	0 43 15	2 41 31	4 43 44	6 42 1	8 44 15	10 46 28	12 44 44	14 46 58	16 45 14
3	18 52 21	20 54 34	22 44 58	0 47 11	2 45 28	4 47 41	6 45 58	8 48 11	10 50 24	12 48 41	14 50 54	16 49 11
4	18 56 18	20 58 31	22 48 55	0 51 8	2 49 24	4 51 38	6 49 54	8 52 8	10 54 21	12 52 37	14 54 51	16 53 7
5	19 0 14	21 2 28	22 52 51	0 55 4	2 53 21	4 55 34	6 53 51	8 56 4	10 58 17	12 56 34	14 58 47	16 57 4
6	19 4 11	21 6 24	22 56 48	0 59 1	2 57 17	4 59 31	6 57 47	9 0 1	11 2 14	13 0 31	15 2 44	17 1 0
7	19 8 7	21 10 21	23 0 44	1 2 57	3 1 14	5 3 27	7 1 44	9 3 57	11 6 10	13 4 27	15 6 40	17 4 57
8	19 12 4	21 14 17	23 4 41	1 6 54	3 5 11	5 7 24	7 5 41	9 7 54	11 10 7	13 8 24	15 10 37	17 8 54
9	19 16 0	21 18 14	23 8 37	1 10 50	3 9 7	5 11 20	7 9 37	9 11 50	11 14 4	13 12 20	15 14 33	17 12 50
10	19 19 57	21 22 10	23 12 34	1 14 47	3 13 4	5 15 17	7 13 34	9 15 47	11 18 0	13 16 17	15 18 30	17 16 47
11	19 23 54	21 26 7	23 16 30	1 18 44	3 17 0	5 19 13	7 17 30	9 19 43	11 21 57	13 20 13	15 22 27	17 20 43
12	19 27 50	21 30 3	23 20 27	1 22 40	3 20 57	5 23 10	7 21 27	9 23 40	11 25 53	13 24 10	15 26 23	17 24 40
13	19 31 47	21 34 0	23 24 23	1 26 37	3 24 53	5 27 7	7 25 23	9 27 37	11 29 50	13 28 6	15 30 20	17 28 36
14	19 35 43	21 37 57	23 28 20	1 30 33	3 28 50	5 31 3	7 29 20	9 31 33	11 33 46	13 32 3	15 34 16	17 32 33
15	19 39 40	21 41 53	23 32 17	1 34 30	3 32 46	5 35 0	7 33 16	9 35 30	11 37 43	13 36 0	15 38 13	17 36 30
16	19 43 36	21 45 50	23 36 13	1 38 26	3 36 43	5 38 56	7 37 13	9 39 26	11 41 39	13 39 56	15 42 9	17 40 26
17	19 47 33	21 49 46	23 40 10	1 42 23	3 40 40	5 42 53	7 41 10	9 43 23	11 45 36	13 43 53	15 46 6	17 44 23
18	19 51 29	21 53 43	23 44 6	1 46 19	3 44 36	5 46 49	7 45 6	9 47 19	11 49 33	13 47 49	15 50 2	17 48 19
19	19 55 26	21 57 39	23 48 3	1 50 16	3 48 33	5 50 46	7 49 3	9 51 16	11 53 29	13 51 46	15 53 59	17 52 16
20	19 59 23	22 1 36	23 51 59	1 54 13	3 52 29	5 54 43	7 52 59	9 55 13	11 57 26	13 55 42	15 57 56	17 56 12
21	20 3 19	22 5 32	23 55 56	1 58 9	3 56 26	5 58 39	7 56 56	9 59 9	12 1 22	13 59 39	16 1 52	18 0 9
22	20 7 16	22 9 29	23 59 52	2 2 6	4 0 22	6 2 36	8 0 52	10 3 6	12 5 19	14 3 35	16 5 49	18 4 5
23	20 11 12	22 13 26	0 3 49	2 6 2	4 4 19	6 6 32	8 4 49	10 7 2	12 9 15	14 7 32	16 9 45	18 8 2
24	20 15 9	22 17 22	0 7 46	2 9 59	4 8 15	6 10 29	8 8 45	10 10 59	12 13 12	14 11 29	16 13 42	18 11 59
25	20 19 5	22 21 19	0 11 42	2 13 55	4 12 12	6 14 25	8 12 42	10 14 55	12 17 8	14 15 25	16 17 38	18 15 55
26	20 23 2	22 25 15	0 15 39	2 17 52	4 16 9	6 18 22	8 16 39	10 18 52	12 21 5	14 19 22	16 21 35	18 19 52
27	20 26 58	22 29 12	0 19 35	2 21 48	4 20 5	6 22 18	8 20 35	10 22 48	12 25 2	14 23 18	16 25 31	18 23 48
28	20 30 55	22 33 8	0 23 32	2 25 45	4 24 2	6 26 15	8 24 32	10 26 45	12 28 58	14 27 15	16 29 28	18 27 45
29	20 34 52		0 27 28	2 29 42	4 27 58	6 30 12	8 28 28	10 30 42	12 32 55	14 31 11	16 33 25	18 31 41
30	20 38 48		0 31 25	2 33 38	4 31 55	6 34 8	8 32 25	10 34 38	12 36 51	14 35 8	16 37 21	18 35 38
31	20 42 45		0 35 21		4 35 51		8 36 21	10 38 35		14 39 4		18 39 34

YEAR	JAN	FEB	MAR	APR	MAY	JUN	JUL	AUG	SEP	OCT	NOV	DEC
1990 1	18 43 31	20 45 44	22 36 8	0 38 21	2 36 38	4 38 51	6 37 8	8 39 21	10 41 34	12 39 51	14 42 4	16 40 21
2	18 47 28	20 49 41	22 40 4	0 42 18	2 40 34	4 42 47	6 41 4	8 43 17	10 45 31	12 43 47	14 46 0	16 44 17
3	18 51 24	20 53 37	22 44 1	0 46 14	2 44 31	4 46 44	6 45 1	8 47 14	10 49 27	12 47 44	14 49 57	16 48 14
4	18 55 21	20 57 34	22 47 57	0 50 11	2 48 27	4 50 41	6 48 57	8 51 11	10 53 24	12 51 40	14 53 54	16 52 10
5	18 59 17	21 1 31	22 51 54	0 54 7	2 52 24	4 54 37	6 52 54	8 55 7	10 57 20	12 55 37	14 57 50	16 56 7
6	19 3 14	21 5 27	22 55 51	0 58 4	2 56 20	4 58 34	6 56 50	8 59 4	11 1 17	12 59 33	15 1 47	17 0 3
7	19 7 10	21 9 24	22 59 47	1 2 0	3 0 17	5 2 30	7 0 47	9 3 0	11 5 13	13 3 30	15 5 43	17 4 0
8	19 11 7	21 13 20	23 3 44	1 5 57	3 4 14	5 6 27	7 4 44	9 6 57	11 9 10	13 7 27	15 9 40	17 7 57
9	19 15 3	21 17 17	23 7 40	1 9 53	3 8 10	5 10 23	7 8 40	9 10 53	11 13 7	13 11 23	15 13 36	17 11 53
10	19 19 0	21 21 13	23 11 37	1 13 50	3 12 7	5 14 20	7 12 37	9 14 50	11 17 3	13 15 20	15 17 33	17 15 50
11	19 22 57	21 25 10	23 15 33	1 17 47	3 16 3	5 18 16	7 16 33	9 18 46	11 21 0	13 19 16	15 21 29	17 19 46
12	19 26 53	21 29 6	23 19 30	1 21 43	3 20 0	5 22 13	7 20 30	9 22 43	11 24 56	13 23 13	15 25 26	17 23 43
13	19 30 50	21 33 3	23 23 26	1 25 40	3 23 56	5 26 10	7 24 26	9 26 40	11 28 53	13 27 9	15 29 23	17 27 39
14	19 34 46	21 37 0	23 27 23	1 29 36	3 27 53	5 30 6	7 28 23	9 30 36	11 32 49	13 31 6	15 33 19	17 31 36
15	19 38 43	21 40 56	23 31 20	1 33 33	3 31 49	5 34 3	7 32 19	9 34 33	11 36 46	13 35 2	15 37 16	17 35 32
16	19 42 39	21 44 53	23 35 16	1 37 29	3 35 46	5 37 59	7 36 16	9 38 29	11 40 42	13 38 59	15 41 12	17 39 29
17	19 46 36	21 48 49	23 39 13	1 41 26	3 39 43	5 41 56	7 40 13	9 42 26	11 44 39	13 42 56	15 45 9	17 43 26
18	19 50 32	21 52 46	23 43 9	1 45 22	3 43 39	5 45 52	7 44 9	9 46 22	11 48 36	13 46 52	15 49 5	17 47 22
19	19 54 29	21 56 42	23 47 6	1 49 19	3 47 36	5 49 49	7 48 6	9 50 19	11 52 32	13 50 49	15 53 2	17 51 19
20	19 58 26	22 0 39	23 51 2	1 53 16	3 51 32	5 53 45	7 52 2	9 54 15	11 56 29	13 54 45	15 56 58	17 55 15
21	20 2 22	22 4 35	23 54 59	1 57 12	3 55 29	5 57 42	7 55 59	9 58 12	12 0 25	13 58 42	16 0 55	17 59 12
22	20 6 19	22 8 32	23 58 55	2 1 9	3 59 25	6 1 39	7 59 55	10 2 9	12 4 22	14 2 38	16 4 52	18 3 8
23	20 10 15	22 12 29	0 2 52	2 5 5	4 3 22	6 5 35	8 3 52	10 6 5	12 8 18	14 6 35	16 8 48	18 7 5
24	20 14 12	22 16 25	0 6 49	2 9 2	4 7 18	6 9 32	8 7 48	10 10 2	12 12 15	14 10 31	16 12 45	18 11 1
25	20 18 8	22 20 22	0 10 45	2 12 58	4 11 15	6 13 28	8 11 45	10 13 58	12 16 11	14 14 28	16 16 41	18 14 58
26	20 22 5	22 24 18	0 14 42	2 16 55	4 15 12	6 17 25	8 15 42	10 17 55	12 20 8	14 18 25	16 20 38	18 18 55
27	20 26 2	22 28 15	0 18 38	2 20 51	4 19 8	6 21 21	8 19 38	10 21 51	12 24 5	14 22 21	16 24 34	18 22 51
28	20 29 58	22 32 11	0 22 35	2 24 48	4 23 5	6 25 18	8 23 35	10 25 48	12 28 1	14 26 18	16 28 31	18 26 48
29	20 33 55		0 26 31	2 28 45	4 27 1	6 29 15	8 27 31	10 29 44	12 31 58	14 30 14	16 32 27	18 30 44
30	20 37 51		0 30 28	2 32 41	4 30 58	6 33 11	8 31 28	10 33 41	12 35 54	14 34 11	16 36 24	18 34 41
31	20 41 48		0 34 24		4 34 54		8 35 24	10 37 38		14 38 7		18 38 37
1991 1	18 42 34	20 44 47	22 35 11	0 37 24	2 35 41	4 37 54	6 36 11	8 38 24	10 40 37	12 38 54	14 41 7	16 39 23
2	18 46 30	20 48 44	22 39 7	0 41 20	2 39 37	4 41 50	6 40 7	8 42 20	10 44 34	12 42 50	14 45 3	16 43 20
3	18 50 27	20 52 40	22 43 4	0 45 17	2 43 34	4 45 47	6 44 4	8 46 17	10 48 30	12 46 47	14 49 0	16 47 17
4	18 54 24	20 56 37	22 47 0	0 49 14	2 47 30	4 49 43	6 48 0	8 50 13	10 52 27	12 50 43	14 52 56	16 51 13
5	18 58 20	21 0 33	22 50 57	0 53 10	2 51 27	4 53 40	6 51 57	8 54 10	10 56 23	12 54 40	14 56 53	16 55 10
6	19 2 17	21 4 30	22 54 54	0 57 7	2 55 23	4 57 37	6 55 53	8 58 7	11 0 20	12 58 36	15 0 50	16 59 6
7	19 6 13	21 8 27	22 58 50	1 1 3	2 59 20	5 1 33	6 59 50	9 2 3	11 4 16	13 2 33	15 4 46	17 3 3
8	19 10 10	21 12 23	23 2 47	1 5 0	3 3 16	5 5 30	7 3 46	9 6 0	11 8 13	13 6 29	15 8 43	17 6 59
9	19 14 6	21 16 20	23 6 43	1 8 56	3 7 13	5 9 26	7 7 43	9 9 56	11 12 9	13 10 26	15 12 39	17 10 56
10	19 18 3	21 20 16	23 10 40	1 12 53	3 11 10	5 13 23	7 11 40	9 13 53	11 16 6	13 14 23	15 16 36	17 14 52
11	19 21 59	21 24 13	23 14 36	1 16 49	3 15 6	5 17 19	7 15 36	9 17 49	11 20 3	13 18 19	15 20 32	17 18 49
12	19 25 56	21 28 9	23 18 33	1 20 46	3 19 3	5 21 16	7 19 33	9 21 46	11 23 59	13 22 16	15 24 29	17 22 46
13	19 29 53	21 32 6	23 22 29	1 24 43	3 22 59	5 25 12	7 23 29	9 25 42	11 27 56	13 26 12	15 28 25	17 26 42
14	19 33 49	21 36 2	23 26 26	1 28 39	3 26 56	5 29 9	7 27 26	9 29 39	11 31 52	13 30 9	15 32 22	17 30 39
15	19 37 46	21 39 59	23 30 22	1 32 36	3 30 52	5 33 6	7 31 22	9 33 36	11 35 49	13 34 5	15 36 19	17 34 35
16	19 41 42	21 43 56	23 34 19	1 36 32	3 34 49	5 37 2	7 35 19	9 37 32	11 39 45	13 38 2	15 40 15	17 38 32
17	19 45 39	21 47 52	23 38 16	1 40 29	3 38 45	5 40 59	7 39 15	9 41 29	11 43 42	13 41 58	15 44 12	17 42 28
18	19 49 35	21 51 49	23 42 12	1 44 25	3 42 42	5 44 55	7 43 12	9 45 25	11 47 38	13 45 55	15 48 8	17 46 25
19	19 53 32	21 55 45	23 46 9	1 48 22	3 46 39	5 48 52	7 47 9	9 49 22	11 51 35	13 49 52	15 52 5	17 50 21
20	19 57 29	21 59 42	23 50 5	1 52 18	3 50 35	5 52 48	7 51 5	9 53 18	11 55 32	13 53 48	15 56 1	17 54 18
21	20 1 25	22 3 38	23 54 2	1 56 15	3 54 32	5 56 45	7 55 2	9 57 15	11 59 28	13 57 45	15 59 58	17 58 15
22	20 5 22	22 7 35	23 57 58	2 0 12	3 58 28	6 0 41	7 58 58	10 1 11	12 3 25	14 1 41	16 3 54	18 2 11
23	20 9 18	22 11 31	0 1 55	2 4 8	4 2 25	6 4 38	8 2 55	10 5 8	12 7 21	14 5 38	16 7 51	18 6 8
24	20 13 15	22 15 28	0 5 51	2 8 5	4 6 21	6 8 35	8 6 51	10 9 5	12 11 18	14 9 34	16 11 48	18 10 4
25	20 17 11	22 19 25	0 9 48	2 12 1	4 10 18	6 12 31	8 10 48	10 13 1	12 15 14	14 13 31	16 15 44	18 14 1
26	20 21 8	22 23 21	0 13 45	2 15 58	4 14 14	6 16 28	8 14 44	10 16 58	12 19 11	14 17 27	16 19 41	18 17 57
27	20 25 4	22 27 18	0 17 41	2 19 54	4 18 11	6 20 24	8 18 41	10 20 54	12 23 7	14 21 24	16 23 37	18 21 54
28	20 29 1	22 31 14	0 21 38	2 23 51	4 22 8	6 24 21	8 22 38	10 24 51	12 27 4	14 25 21	16 27 34	18 25 51
29	20 32 58		0 25 34	2 27 47	4 26 4	6 28 17	8 26 34	10 28 47	12 31 0	14 29 17	16 31 30	18 29 47
30	20 36 54		0 29 31	2 31 44	4 30 1	6 32 14	8 30 31	10 32 44	12 34 57	14 33 14	16 35 27	18 33 44
31	20 40 51		0 33 27		4 33 57		8 34 27	10 36 40		14 37 10		18 37 40
1992 1	18 41 37	20 43 50	22 38 10	0 40 23	2 38 40	4 40 53	6 39 10	8 41 23	10 43 36	12 41 53	14 44 6	16 42 23
2	18 45 33	20 47 47	22 42 7	0 44 20	2 42 36	4 44 50	6 43 6	8 45 20	10 47 33	12 45 49	14 48 3	16 46 19
3	18 49 30	20 51 43	22 46 3	0 48 16	2 46 33	4 48 46	6 47 3	8 49 16	10 51 29	12 49 46	14 51 59	16 50 16
4	18 53 26	20 55 40	22 50 0	0 52 13	2 50 30	4 52 43	6 51 0	8 53 13	10 55 26	12 53 43	14 55 56	16 54 12
5	18 57 23	20 59 36	22 53 56	0 56 9	2 54 26	4 56 39	6 54 56	8 57 9	10 59 23	12 57 39	14 59 52	16 58 9
6	19 1 20	21 3 33	22 57 53	1 0 6	2 58 23	5 0 36	6 58 53	9 1 6	11 3 19	13 1 36	15 3 49	17 2 6
7	19 5 16	21 7 29	23 1 49	1 4 3	3 2 19	5 4 32	7 2 49	9 5 2	11 7 16	13 5 32	15 7 45	17 6 2
8	19 9 13	21 11 26	23 5 46	1 7 59	3 6 16	5 8 29	7 6 46	9 8 59	11 11 12	13 9 29	15 11 42	17 9 59
9	19 13 9	21 15 22	23 9 43	1 11 56	3 10 12	5 12 26	7 10 42	9 12 56	11 15 9	13 13 25	15 15 38	17 13 55
10	19 17 6	21 19 19	23 13 39	1 15 52	3 14 9	5 16 22	7 14 39	9 16 52	11 19 5	13 17 22	15 19 35	17 17 52
11	19 21 2	21 23 16	23 17 36	1 19 49	3 18 5	5 20 19	7 18 35	9 20 49	11 23 2	13 21 18	15 23 32	17 21 48
12	19 24 59	21 27 12	23 21 32	1 23 45	3 22 2	5 24 15	7 22 32	9 24 45	11 26 58	13 25 15	15 27 28	17 25 45
13	19 28 55	21 31 9	23 25 29	1 27 42	3 25 59	5 28 12	7 26 29	9 28 42	11 30 55	13 29 12	15 31 25	17 29 41
14	19 32 52	21 35 5	23 29 25	1 31 38	3 29 55	5 32 8	7 30 25	9 32 38	11 34 51	13 33 8	15 35 21	17 33 38
15	19 36 49	21 39 2	23 33 22	1 35 35	3 33 52	5 36 5	7 34 22	9 36 35	11 38 48	13 37 5	15 39 18	17 37 35
16	19 40 45	21 42 58	23 37 18	1 39 32	3 37 48	5 40 1	7 38 18	9 40 31	11 42 45	13 41 1	15 43 14	17 41 31
17	19 44 42	21 46 55	23 41 15	1 43 28	3 41 45	5 43 58	7 42 15	9 44 28	11 46 41	13 44 58	15 47 11	17 45 28
18	19 48 38	21 50 51	23 45 12	1 47 25	3 45 41	5 47 55	7 46 11	9 48 25	11 50 38	13 48 54	15 51 7	17 49 24
19	19 52 35	21 54 48	23 49 8	1 51 21	3 49 38	5 51 51	7 50 8	9 52 21	11 54 34	13 52 51	15 55 4	17 53 21
20	19 56 31	21 58 45	23 53 5	1 55 18	3 53 34	5 55 48	7 54 4	9 56 18	11 58 31	13 56 47	15 59 1	17 57 17
21	20 0 28	22 2 41	23 57 1	1 59 14	3 57 31	5 59 44	7 58 1	10 0 14	12 2 27	14 0 44	16 2 57	18 1 14
22	20 4 24	22 6 38	0 0 58	2 3 11	4 1 28	6 3 41	8 1 58	10 4 11	12 6 24	14 4 41	16 6 54	18 5 10
23	20 8 21	22 10 34	0 4 54	2 7 7	4 5 24	6 7 37	8 5 54	10 8 7	12 10 20	14 8 37	16 10 50	18 9 7
24	20 12 18	22 14 31	0 8 51	2 11 4	4 9 21	6 11 34	8 9 51	10 12 4	12 14 17	14 12 34	16 14 47	18 13 4
25	20 16 14	22 18 27	0 12 47	2 15 1	4 13 17	6 15 30	8 13 47	10 16 0	12 18 14	14 16 30	16 18 43	18 17 0
26	20 20 11	22 22 24	0 16 44	2 18 57	4 17 14	6 19 27	8 17 44	10 19 57	12 22 10	14 20 27	16 22 40	18 20 57
27	20 24 7	22 26 20	0 20 41	2 22 54	4 21 10	6 23 24	8 21 40	10 23 54	12 26 7	14 24 23	16 26 37	18 24 53
28	20 28 4	22 30 17	0 24 37	2 26 50	4 25 7	6 27 20	8 25 37	10 27 50	12 30 3	14 28 20	16 30 33	18 28 50
29	20 32 0	22 34 14	0 28 34	2 30 47	4 29 3	6 31 17	8 29 33	10 31 47	12 34 0	14 32 16	16 34 30	18 32 46
30	20 35 57		0 32 30	2 34 43	4 33 0	6 35 13	8 33 30	10 35 43	12 37 56	14 36 13	16 38 26	18 36 43
31	20 39 53		0 36 27		4 36 57		8 37 27	10 39 40		14 40 10		18 40 39
1993 1	18 44 36	20 46 49	22 37 13	0 39 26	2 37 43	4 39 56	6 38 12	8 40 26	10 42 39	12 40 56	14 43 9	16 41 25
2	18 48 33	20 50 46	22 41 9	0 43 23	2 41 39	4 43 52	6 42 9	8 44 22	10 46 35	12 44 52	14 47 5	16 45 22
3	18 52 29	20 54 42	22 45 6	0 47 19	2 45 36	4 47 49	6 46 6	8 48 19	10 50 32	12 48 49	14 51 2	16 49 18
4	18 56 26	20 58 39	22 49 2	0 51 16	2 49 32	4 51 45	6 50 2	8 52 15	10 54 29	12 52 45	14 54 58	16 53 15
5	19 0 22	21 2 36	22 52 59	0 55 12	2 53 29	4 55 42	6 53 59	8 56 12	10 58 25	12 56 42	14 58 55	16 57 12
6	19 4 19	21 6 32	22 56 56	0 59 9	2 57 25	4 59 39	6 57 55	9 0 9	11 2 22	13 0 38	15 2 51	17 1 8
7	19 8 15	21 10 29	23 0 52	1 3 5	3 1 22	5 3 35	7 1 52	9 4 5	11 6 18	13 4 35	15 6 48	17 5 5
8	19 12 12	21 14 25	23 4 49	1 7 2	3 5 18	5 7 32	7 5 48	9 8 2	11 10 15	13 8 31	15 10 45	17 9 1
9	19 16 9	21 18 22	23 8 45	1 10 58	3 9 15	5 11 28	7 9 45	9 11 58	11 14 11	13 12 28	15 14 41	17 12 58
10	19 20 5	21 22 18	23 12 42	1 14 55	3 13 12	5 15 25	7 13 42	9 15 55	11 18 8	13 16 24	15 18 38	17 16 54
11	19 24 2	21 26 15	23 16 38	1 18 51	3 17 8	5 19 21	7 17 38	9 19 51	11 22 4	13 20 21	15 22 34	17 20 51
12	19 27 58	21 30 11	23 20 35	1 22 48	3 21 5	5 23 18	7 21 35	9 23 48	11 26 1	13 24 18	15 26 31	17 24 47
13	19 31 55	21 34 8	23 24 31	1 26 45	3 25 1	5 27 14	7 25 31	9 27 44	11 29 58	13 28 14	15 30 27	17 28 44
14	19 35 51	21 38 5	23 28 28	1 30 41	3 28 58	5 31 11	7 29 28	9 31 41	11 33 54	13 32 11	15 34 24	17 32 41
15	19 39 48	21 42 1	23 32 25	1 34 38	3 32 54	5 35 8	7 33 24	9 35 38	11 37 51	13 36 7	15 38 20	17 36 37
16	19 43 44	21 45 58	23 36 21	1 38 34	3 36 51	5 39 4	7 37 21	9 39 34	11 41 47	13 40 4	15 42 17	17 40 34
17	19 47 41	21 49 54	23 40 18	1 42 31	3 40 47	5 43 1	7 41 17	9 43 31	11 45 44	13 44 0	15 46 14	17 44 30
18	19 51 38	21 53 51	23 44 14	1 46 27	3 44 44	5 46 57	7 45 14	9 47 27	11 49 40	13 47 57	15 50 10	17 48 27
19	19 55 34	21 57 47	23 48 11	1 50 24	3 48 41	5 50 54	7 49 11	9 51 24	11 53 37	13 51 53	15 54 7	17 52 23
20	19 59 31	22 1 44	23 52 7	1 54 20	3 52 37	5 54 50	7 53 7	9 55 20	11 57 33	13 55 50	15 58 3	17 56 20
21	20 3 27	22 5 40	23 56 4	1 58 17	3 56 34	5 58 47	7 57 4	9 59 17	12 1 30	13 59 47	16 2 0	18 0 16
22	20 7 24	22 9 37	0 0 0	2 2 14	4 0 30	6 2 43	8 1 0	10 3 13	12 5 27	14 3 43	16 5 56	18 4 13
23	20 11 20	22 13 33	0 3 57	2 6 10	4 4 27	6 6 40	8 4 57	10 7 10	12 9 23	14 7 40	16 9 53	18 8 10
24	20 15 17	22 17 30	0 7 54	2 10 7	4 8 23	6 10 37	8 8 53	10 11 7	12 13 20	14 11 36	16 13 49	18 12 6
25	20 19 13	22 21 27	0 11 50	2 14 3	4 12 20	6 14 33	8 12 50	10 15 3	12 17 16	14 15 33	16 17 46	18 16 3
26	20 23 10	22 25 23	0 15 47	2 18 0	4 16 16	6 18 30	8 16 46	10 19 0	12 21 13	14 19 29	16 21 43	18 19 59
27	20 27 7	22 29 20	0 19 43	2 21 56	4 20 13	6 22 26	8 20 43	10 22 56	12 25 9	14 23 26	16 25 39	18 23 56
28	20 31 3	22 33 16	0 23 40	2 25 53	4 24 10	6 26 23	8 24 40	10 26 53	12 29 6	14 27 22	16 29 36	18 27 52
29	20 35 0		0 27 36	2 29 49	4 28 6	6 30 19	8 28 36	10 30 49	12 33 2	14 31 19	16 33 32	18 31 49
30	20 38 56		0 31 33	2 33 46	4 32 3	6 34 16	8 32 33	10 34 46	12 36 59	14 35 16	16 37 29	18 35 46
31	20 42 53		0 35 29		4 35 59		8 36 29	10 38 42		14 39 12		18 39 42

NORTHERN LATITUDE

		0°N	4°N	8°N	12°N	16°N	20°N	22°N	24°N	26°N	28°N	30°N	32°N	34°N	36°N	38°N	40°N	42°N	44°N	46°N	48°N	50°N	52°N	54°N	56°N	58°N	60°N
ST	MC	ASC	ASC	ASC	ASC	ASC	ASC	ASC	ASC	ASC	ASC	ASC	ASC	ASC	ASC	ASC	ASC	ASC	ASC	ASC	ASC	ASC	ASC	ASC	ASC	ASC	ASC
0 0 0	0 ♈	0 ♋ 0	1 ♋36	3 ♋12	4 ♋50	6 ♋31	8 ♋14	9 ♋ 8	10 ♋ 3	10 ♋59	11 ♋57	12 ♋56	13 ♋58	15 ♋ 1	16 ♋ 7	17 ♋16	18 ♋28	19 ♋43	21 ♋ 1	22 ♋24	23 ♋51	25 ♋22	26 ♋59	28 ♋43	0 ♌32	2 ♌29	4 ♌35
0 3 40	1	0 51	2 26	4 2	5 40	7 20	9 4	9 57	10 52	11 48	12 45	13 44	14 45	15 48	16 54	18 2	19 13	20 27	21 45	23 7	24 33	26 3	27 39	29 21	1 10	3 5	5 9
0 7 20	2	1 41	3 17	4 53	6 30	8 10	9 53	10 46	11 41	12 36	13 33	14 32	15 33	16 35	17 40	18 48	19 58	21 12	22 29	23 50	25 15	26 44	28 19	0 ♌ 0	1 47	3 41	5 43
0 11 1	3	2 32	4 7	5 43	7 20	9 0	10 43	11 35	12 29	13 25	14 21	15 20	16 20	17 22	18 27	19 34	20 44	21 56	23 13	24 33	25 57	27 25	28 59	0 39	2 24	4 17	6 17
0 14 41	4	3 22	4 57	6 33	8 10	9 50	11 32	12 24	13 18	14 13	15 9	16 7	17 7	18 9	19 13	20 19	21 29	22 41	23 56	25 15	26 39	28 6	29 39	1 17	3 1	4 53	6 51
0 18 21	5	4 13	5 48	7 24	9 0	10 39	12 21	13 13	14 7	15 1	15 57	16 55	17 54	18 56	19 59	21 5	22 14	23 25	24 40	25 58	27 20	28 47	0 ♌19	1 56	3 39	5 28	7 25
0 22 2	6	5 3	6 38	8 14	9 50	11 29	13 10	14 2	14 55	15 49	16 45	17 42	18 41	19 42	20 45	21 50	22 58	24 9	25 23	26 41	28 2	29 28	0 58	2 34	4 16	6 4	7 59
0 25 42	7	5 54	7 29	9 4	10 40	12 18	13 59	14 51	15 44	16 38	17 33	18 30	19 28	20 29	21 31	22 36	23 43	24 53	26 6	27 23	28 44	0 ♌ 8	1 38	3 12	4 53	6 39	8 33
0 29 23	8	6 45	8 20	9 54	11 30	13 8	14 48	15 40	16 32	17 26	18 21	19 17	20 15	21 15	22 17	23 21	24 28	25 37	26 50	28 5	29 25	0 49	2 17	3 51	5 30	7 15	9 7
0 33 4	9	7 36	9 10	10 45	12 20	13 58	15 37	16 29	17 21	18 14	19 9	20 5	21 2	22 1	23 3	24 6	25 12	26 21	27 33	28 48	0 ♌ 7	1 29	2 57	4 29	6 7	7 50	9 41
0 36 45	10	8 26	10 1	11 35	13 10	14 47	16 27	17 17	18 9	19 2	19 56	20 52	21 49	22 48	23 49	24 52	25 57	27 5	28 16	29 30	0 48	2 10	3 36	5 7	6 43	8 26	10 15
0 40 27	11	9 17	10 52	12 26	14 1	15 37	17 16	18 6	18 58	19 50	20 44	21 39	22 36	23 34	24 34	25 37	26 41	27 49	28 59	0 ♌12	1 29	2 50	4 15	5 45	7 20	9 1	10 49
0 44 8	12	10 9	11 43	13 16	14 51	16 27	18 5	18 55	19 46	20 38	21 32	22 26	23 23	24 20	25 20	26 22	27 26	28 33	29 42	0 55	2 11	3 30	4 54	6 23	7 57	9 37	11 23
0 47 50	13	11 0	12 33	14 7	15 41	17 16	18 54	19 44	20 35	21 26	22 19	23 14	24 9	25 7	26 6	27 7	28 10	29 16	0 ♌25	1 37	2 52	4 11	5 34	7 1	8 34	10 12	11 57
0 51 32	14	11 51	13 25	14 58	16 31	18 6	19 43	20 33	21 23	22 14	23 7	24 1	24 56	25 53	26 52	27 52	28 55	0 ♌ 0	1 8	2 19	3 33	4 51	6 13	7 39	9 11	10 48	12 31
0 55 15	15	12 43	14 16	15 48	17 22	18 56	20 32	21 22	22 12	23 3	23 55	24 48	25 43	26 39	27 37	28 37	29 39	0 44	1 51	3 1	4 14	5 31	6 52	8 17	9 48	11 23	13 5
0 58 57	16	13 34	15 7	16 39	18 12	19 46	21 22	22 10	23 0	23 51	24 42	25 35	26 30	27 25	28 23	29 22	0 ♌24	1 28	2 34	3 43	4 56	6 12	7 31	8 56	10 25	11 59	13 39
1 2 40	17	14 26	15 58	17 30	19 3	20 36	22 11	22 59	23 49	24 39	25 30	26 23	27 16	28 12	29 9	0 ♌ 7	1 8	2 11	3 17	4 25	5 37	6 52	8 11	9 34	11 1	12 34	14 13
1 6 24	18	15 18	16 50	18 21	19 53	21 26	23 0	23 49	24 37	25 27	26 18	27 10	28 3	28 58	29 54	0 52	1 53	2 55	4 0	5 7	6 18	7 32	8 50	10 12	11 38	13 10	14 47
1 10 7	19	16 10	17 42	19 13	20 44	22 16	23 50	24 38	25 26	26 16	27 6	27 57	28 50	29 44	0 ♌40	1 38	2 37	3 39	4 43	5 50	6 59	8 12	9 29	10 50	12 15	13 46	15 22
1 13 52	20	17 2	18 33	20 4	21 35	23 6	24 39	25 27	26 15	27 4	27 54	28 45	29 37	0 ♌31	1 26	2 23	3 22	4 22	5 26	6 32	7 41	8 53	10 8	11 28	12 52	14 21	15 56
1 17 36	21	17 54	19 25	20 56	22 26	23 57	25 29	26 16	27 4	27 52	28 42	29 32	0 ♌24	1 17	2 12	3 8	4 6	5 6	6 9	7 14	8 22	9 33	10 48	12 6	13 29	14 57	16 30
1 21 21	22	18 47	20 17	21 47	23 17	24 47	26 19	27 5	27 53	28 41	29 30	0 ♌20	1 11	2 4	2 58	3 53	4 51	5 50	6 52	7 56	9 3	10 13	11 27	12 45	14 6	15 33	17 4
1 25 6	23	19 40	21 10	22 39	24 8	25 38	27 9	27 55	28 42	29 29	0 ♌18	1 7	1 58	2 50	3 43	4 38	5 35	6 34	7 35	8 38	9 45	10 54	12 6	13 23	14 43	16 8	17 39
1 28 52	24	20 33	22 2	23 31	24 59	26 28	27 59	28 44	29 31	0 ♌18	1 6	1 55	2 45	3 37	4 29	5 24	6 20	7 18	8 18	9 21	10 26	11 34	12 46	14 1	15 20	16 44	18 13
1 32 39	25	21 26	22 55	24 23	25 51	27 19	28 49	29 34	0 ♌20	1 7	1 54	2 43	3 32	4 23	5 15	6 9	7 5	8 2	9 1	10 3	11 8	12 15	13 25	14 40	15 58	17 20	18 48
1 36 26	26	22 19	23 48	25 15	26 43	28 10	29 39	0 ♌24	1 9	1 56	2 43	3 31	4 20	5 10	6 2	6 55	7 49	8 46	9 45	10 46	11 49	12 55	14 5	15 18	16 35	17 56	19 22
1 40 13	27	23 13	24 41	26 8	27 34	29 1	0 ♌29	1 14	1 59	2 45	3 31	4 19	5 7	5 57	6 48	7 40	8 34	9 30	10 28	11 28	12 31	13 36	14 45	15 56	17 12	18 32	19 57
1 44 1	28	24 7	25 34	27 1	28 26	29 53	1 20	2 4	2 48	3 34	4 20	5 7	5 55	6 44	7 34	8 26	9 19	10 14	11 11	12 11	13 12	14 17	15 24	16 35	17 50	19 8	20 32
1 47 49	29	25 1	26 28	27 53	29 19	0 ♌44	2 10	2 54	3 38	4 23	5 9	5 55	6 42	7 31	8 20	9 11	10 4	10 58	11 55	12 53	13 54	14 58	16 4	17 14	18 27	19 45	21 7
1 51 38	30	25 55	27 21	28 47	0 ♌11	1 36	3 1	3 44	4 28	5 12	5 57	6 43	7 30	8 18	9 7	9 57	10 49	11 43	12 38	13 36	14 36	15 38	16 44	17 52	19 5	20 21	21 42

		0°N	4°N	8°N	12°N	16°N	20°N	22°N	24°N	26°N	28°N	30°N	32°N	34°N	36°N	38°N	40°N	42°N	44°N	46°N	48°N	50°N	52°N	54°N	56°N	58°N	60°N
ST	MC	ASC	ASC	ASC	ASC	ASC	ASC	ASC	ASC	ASC	ASC	ASC	ASC	ASC	ASC	ASC	ASC	ASC	ASC	ASC	ASC	ASC	ASC	ASC	ASC	ASC	ASC
1 51 38	0 ♉	25 ♋55	27 ♋21	28 ♋47	0 ♌11	1 ♌36	3 ♌ 1	3 ♌44	4 ♌28	5 ♌12	5 ♌57	6 ♌43	7 ♌30	8 ♌18	9 ♌ 7	9 ♌57	10 ♌49	11 ♌43	12 ♌38	13 ♌36	14 ♌36	15 ♌38	16 ♌44	17 ♌52	19 ♌ 5	20 ♌21	21 ♌42
1 55 28	1	26 50	28 15	29 40	1 4	2 27	3 52	4 35	5 18	6 2	6 46	7 32	8 18	9 5	9 53	10 43	11 34	12 27	13 22	14 19	15 18	16 19	17 24	18 31	19 42	20 57	22 17
1 59 18	2	27 44	29 10	0 ♌33	1 56	3 19	4 43	5 25	6 8	6 51	7 35	8 20	9 6	9 52	10 40	11 29	12 20	13 12	14 6	15 2	16 0	17 0	18 4	19 10	20 20	21 34	22 52
2 3 9	3	28 40	0 ♌ 4	1 27	2 49	4 12	5 34	6 16	6 58	7 41	8 25	9 9	9 54	10 40	11 27	12 15	13 5	13 56	14 49	15 44	16 42	17 41	18 44	19 49	20 58	22 10	23 27
2 7 0	4	29 35	0 59	2 21	3 43	5 4	6 26	7 7	7 49	8 31	9 14	9 58	10 42	11 27	12 14	13 1	13 50	14 41	15 33	16 28	17 24	18 23	19 24	20 28	21 36	22 47	24 2
2 10 52	5	0 ♌31	1 54	3 15	4 36	5 56	7 17	7 58	8 39	9 21	10 3	10 46	11 30	12 15	13 1	13 48	14 36	15 26	16 17	17 11	18 6	19 4	20 4	21 7	22 14	23 24	24 38
2 14 44	6	1 27	2 49	4 10	5 30	6 49	8 9	8 49	9 30	10 11	10 53	11 36	12 19	13 3	13 48	14 34	15 22	16 11	17 1	17 54	18 48	19 45	20 45	21 47	22 52	24 0	25 13
2 18 38	7	2 23	3 45	5 5	6 24	7 42	9 1	9 41	10 21	11 2	11 43	12 25	13 7	13 51	14 35	15 21	16 8	16 56	17 46	18 37	19 31	20 27	21 25	22 26	23 30	24 37	25 49
2 22 32	8	3 20	4 41	6 0	7 18	8 35	9 53	10 33	11 12	11 52	12 33	13 14	13 56	14 39	15 23	16 8	16 54	17 41	18 30	19 21	20 14	21 8	22 6	23 5	24 8	25 15	26 24
2 26 26	9	4 17	5 37	6 55	8 12	9 29	10 46	11 24	12 4	12 43	13 23	14 4	14 45	15 27	16 10	16 54	17 40	18 26	19 15	20 4	20 56	21 50	22 46	23 45	24 47	25 52	27 0
2 30 21	10	5 14	6 33	7 50	9 7	10 22	11 38	12 16	12 55	13 34	14 13	14 53	15 34	16 16	16 58	17 41	18 26	19 12	19 59	20 48	21 39	22 32	23 27	24 25	25 25	26 29	27 36
2 34 17	11	6 11	7 30	8 46	10 1	11 16	12 31	13 9	13 47	14 25	15 4	15 43	16 23	17 4	17 46	18 28	19 12	19 57	20 44	21 32	22 22	23 14	24 8	25 5	26 4	27 6	28 12
2 38 14	12	7 9	8 27	9 42	10 57	12 10	13 24	14 1	14 39	15 16	15 55	16 33	17 13	17 53	18 34	19 16	19 59	20 43	21 29	22 16	23 5	23 56	24 49	25 44	26 43	27 44	28 49
2 42 11	13	8 8	9 24	10 39	11 52	13 5	14 17	14 54	15 31	16 8	16 45	17 24	18 2	18 42	19 22	20 3	20 45	21 29	22 14	23 0	23 48	24 38	25 30	26 25	27 22	28 22	29 25
2 46 9	14	9 6	10 22	11 35	12 48	13 59	15 11	15 47	16 23	17 0	17 36	18 14	18 52	19 31	20 10	20 51	21 32	22 15	22 59	23 44	24 31	25 20	26 11	27 5	28 1	28 59	0 ♍ 1
2 50 8	15	10 5	11 20	12 32	13 43	14 54	16 4	16 40	17 15	17 51	18 28	19 5	19 42	20 20	20 59	21 38	22 19	23 1	23 44	24 29	25 15	26 3	26 53	27 45	28 40	29 37	0 38
2 54 8	16	11 4	12 18	13 30	14 40	15 49	16 58	17 33	18 8	18 43	19 19	19 55	20 32	21 9	21 47	22 26	23 6	23 47	24 30	25 13	25 58	26 45	27 34	28 25	29 19	0 ♍15	1 15
2 58 8	17	12 4	13 17	14 27	15 36	16 44	17 52	18 27	19 1	19 36	20 11	20 46	21 22	21 59	22 36	23 14	23 54	24 34	25 15	25 58	26 42	27 28	28 16	29 6	29 58	0 53	1 51
3 2 9	18	13 4	14 16	15 25	16 33	17 40	18 47	19 20	19 54	20 28	21 3	21 37	22 13	22 49	23 25	24 3	24 41	25 20	26 1	26 43	27 26	28 11	28 58	29 47	0 ♍38	1 32	2 28
3 6 10	19	14 4	15 15	16 23	17 30	18 36	19 41	20 14	20 48	21 21	21 55	22 29	23 3	23 39	24 14	24 51	25 29	26 7	26 47	27 28	28 10	28 54	29 40	0 ♍28	1 18	2 10	3 5
3 10 13	20	15 5	16 14	17 22	18 27	19 32	20 36	21 9	21 41	22 14	22 47	23 20	23 54	24 29	25 4	25 40	26 16	26 54	27 33	28 13	28 54	29 37	0 ♍22	1 8	1 57	2 49	3 43
3 14 16	21	16 6	17 14	18 20	19 25	20 28	21 31	22 3	22 35	23 7	23 39	24 12	24 45	25 19	25 53	26 28	27 4	27 41	28 19	28 58	29 38	0 ♍20	1 4	1 50	2 37	3 27	4 20
3 18 20	22	17 8	18 15	19 19	20 23	21 25	22 27	22 58	23 29	24 0	24 32	25 4	25 36	26 9	26 43	27 17	27 52	28 28	29 5	29 43	0 ♍23	1 4	1 46	2 31	3 17	4 6	4 57
3 22 24	23	18 10	19 15	20 19	21 21	22 22	23 22	23 53	24 23	24 54	25 25	25 56	26 28	27 0	27 33	28 6	28 40	29 15	29 52	0 ♍29	1 7	1 47	2 29	3 12	3 57	4 45	5 35
3 26 29	24	19 12	20 16	21 18	22 19	23 19	24 18	24 48	25 18	25 48	26 18	26 48	27 19	27 51	28 23	28 55	29 29	0 ♍ 3	0 ♍38	1 15	1 52	2 31	3 11	3 54	4 38	5 24	6 13
3 30 35	25	20 15	21 18	22 18	23 18	24 16	25 14	25 43	26 12	26 42	27 11	27 41	28 11	28 42	29 13	29 45	0 ♍17	0 51	1 25	2 0	2 37	3 15	3 54	4 35	5 18	6 3	6 51
3 34 42	26	21 17	22 19	23 19	24 17	25 14	26 10	26 39	27 7	27 36	28 4	28 34	29 3	29 33	0 ♍ 3	0 ♍34	1 6	1 38	2 12	2 46	3 22	3 59	4 37	5 17	5 59	6 42	7 29
3 38 50	27	22 21	23 21	24 19	25 16	26 12	27 7	27 35	28 2	28 30	28 58	29 26	29 55	0 ♍24	0 54	1 24	1 55	2 26	2 59	3 32	4 7	4 43	5 20	5 59	6 39	7 22	8 7
3 42 58	28	23 25	24 24	25 20	26 16	27 10	28 4	28 31	28 58	29 25	29 52	0 ♍20	0 ♍47	1 16	1 45	2 14	2 44	3 15	3 46	4 19	4 52	5 27	6 3	6 41	7 20	8 1	8 45
3 47 7	29	24 29	25 26	26 22	27 15	28 8	29 1	29 27	29 53	0 ♍20	0 ♍46	1 13	1 40	2 7	2 35	3 4	3 33	4 3	4 34	5 5	5 38	6 11	6 46	7 23	8 1	8 41	9 23
3 51 16	30	25 33	26 29	27 23	28 16	29 7	29 58	0 ♍23	0 ♍49	1 15	1 40	2 6	2 33	2 59	3 27	3 54	4 22	4 51	5 21	5 52	6 23	6 56	7 30	8 5	8 42	9 21	10 2

		0°N	4°N	8°N	12°N	16°N	20°N	22°N	24°N	26°N	28°N	30°N	32°N	34°N	36°N	38°N	40°N	42°N	44°N	46°N	48°N	50°N	52°N	54°N	56°N	58°N	60°N
ST	MC	ASC	ASC	ASC	ASC	ASC	ASC	ASC	ASC	ASC	ASC	ASC	ASC	ASC	ASC	ASC	ASC	ASC	ASC	ASC	ASC	ASC	ASC	ASC	ASC	ASC	ASC
3 51 16	0 ♊	25 ♌33	26 ♌29	27 ♌23	28 ♌16	29 ♌ 7	29 ♌58	0 ♍23	0 ♍49	1 ♍15	1 ♍40	2 ♍ 6	2 ♍33	2 ♍59	3 ♍27	3 ♍54	4 ♍22	4 ♍51	5 ♍21	5 ♍52	6 ♍23	6 ♍56	7 ♍30	8 ♍ 5	8 ♍42	9 ♍21	10 ♍ 2
3 55 26	1	26 38	27 32	28 25	29 16	0 ♍ 6	0 ♍55	1 20	1 45	2 10	2 35	3 0	3 26	3 51	4 18	4 45	5 12	5 40	6 9	6 38	7 9	7 41	8 13	8 48	9 23	10 1	10 40
3 59 37	2	27 43	28 36	29 27	0 ♍17	1 5	1 53	2 17	2 41	3 5	3 29	3 54	4 19	4 44	5 9	5 35	6 2	6 29	6 57	7 25	7 55	8 25	8 57	9 30	10 5	10 41	11 19
4 3 49	3	28 49	29 40	0 ♍30	1 18	2 5	2 51	3 14	3 38	4 1	4 24	4 48	5 12	5 36	6 1	6 26	6 51	7 18	7 44	8 12	8 41	9 10	9 41	10 13	10 46	11 21	11 58
4 8 1	4	29 54	0 ♍44	1 32	2 19	3 4	3 49	4 12	4 34	4 57	5 19	5 42	6 5	6 29	6 52	7 17	7 41	8 7	8 33	8 59	9 27	9 55	10 25	10 56	11 28	12 1	12 37
4 12 14	5	1 ♍ 1	1 49	2 35	3 20	4 4	4 48	5 9	5 31	5 53	6 15	6 37	6 59	7 21	7 44	8 8	8 31	8 56	9 21	9 47	10 13	10 40	11 9	11 39	12 10	12 42	13 16
4 16 27	6	2 7	2 54	3 39	4 22	5 4	5 46	6 7	6 28	6 49	7 10	7 31	7 53	8 14	8 36	8 59	9 22	9 45	10 9	10 34	10 59	11 26	11 53	12 22	12 51	13 22	13 55
4 20 41	7	3 14	3 59	4 42	5 24	6 5	6 45	7 5	7 25	7 45	8 6	8 26	8 47	9 7	9 29	9 50	10 12	10 35	10 58	11 21	11 46	12 11	12 37	13 5	13 33	14 3	14 34
4 24 56	8	4 21	5 5	5 46	6 26	7 5	7 44	8 3	8 23	8 42	9 1	9 21	9 41	10 1	10 21	10 42	11 3	11 24	11 46	12 9	12 33	12 57	13 22	13 48	14 15	14 44	15 14
4 29 11	9	5 29	6 11	6 50	7 29	8 6	8 43	9 2	9 20	9 39	9 57	10 16	10 35	10 54	11 13	11 33	11 53	12 14	12 35	12 57	13 19	13 42	14 6	14 31	14 57	15 25	15 53
4 33 26	10	6 37	7 17	7 55	8 31	9 7	9 43	10 0	10 18	10 36	10 53	11 11	11 29	11 48	12 6	12 25	12 44	13 4	13 24	13 45	14 6	14 28	14 51	15 15	15 40	16 6	16 33
4 37 43	11	7 45	8 23	8 59	9 34	10 9	10 42	10 59	11 16	11 33	11 50	12 7	12 24	12 41	12 59	13 17	13 35	13 54	14 13	14 33	14 53	15 14	15 36	15 58	16 22	16 47	17 13
4 41 59	12	8 53	9 30	10 4	10 38	11 10	11 42	11 58	12 14	12 30	12 46	13 2	13 19	13 35	13 52	14 9	14 26	14 44	15 2	15 21	15 40	16 0	16 21	16 42	17 4	17 28	17 53
4 46 17	13	10 2	10 36	11 9	11 41	12 12	12 42	12 57	13 12	13 27	13 43	13 58	14 13	14 29	14 45	15 1	15 17	15 34	15 51	16 9	16 27	16 46	17 6	17 26	17 47	18 9	18 32
4 50 34	14	11 11	11 44	12 15	12 44	13 14	13 42	13 57	14 11	14 25	14 39	14 54	15 8	15 23	15 38	15 53	16 9	16 25	16 41	16 57	17 15	17 32	17 51	18 10	18 30	18 51	19 12
4 54 52	15	12 20	12 51	13 20	13 48	14 16	14 43	14 56	15 9	15 23	15 36	15 50	16 3	16 17	16 31	16 46	17 0	17 15	17 30	17 46	18 2	18 19	18 36	18 54	19 12	19 32	19 52
4 59 11	16	13 30	13 59	14 26	14 52	15 18	15 43	15 56	16 8	16 21	16 33	16 46	16 59	17 12	17 25	17 38	17 52	18 5	18 20	18 34	18 49	19 5	19 21	19 38	19 55	20 13	20 33
5 3 30	17	14 40	15 6	15 32	15 56	16 20	16 44	16 55	17 7	17 19	17 30	17 42	17 54	18 6	18 18	18 31	18 43	18 56	19 9	19 23	19 37	19 51	20 6	20 22	20 38	20 55	21 13
5 7 49	18	15 50	16 14	16 38	17 1	17 23	17 44	17 55	18 6	18 17	18 28	18 38	18 49	19 1	19 12	19 23	19 35	19 47	19 59	20 12	20 25	20 38	20 52	21 6	21 21	21 37	21 53
5 12 9	19	17 0	17 22	17 44	18 5	18 25	18 45	18 55	19 5	19 15	19 25	19 35	19 45	19 55	20 5	20 16	20 27	20 38	20 49	21 0	21 12	21 24	21 37	21 50	22 4	22 18	22 33
5 16 29	20	18 10	18 31	18 50	19 9	19 28	19 46	19 55	20 4	20 13	20 22	20 31	20 41	20 50	20 59	21 9	21 19	21 29	21 39	21 49	22 0	22 11	22 23	22 35	22 47	23 0	23 14
5 20 49	21	19 21	19 39	19 57	20 14	20 31	20 47	20 55	21 3	21 12	21 20	21 28	21 36	21 45	21 53	22 2	22 11	22 19	22 29	22 38	22 48	22 58	23 8	23 19	23 30	23 42	23 54
5 25 10	22	20 31	20 48	21 4	21 19	21 34	21 48	21 56	22 3	22 10	22 17	22 25	22 32	22 39	22 47	22 55	23 3	23 10	23 19	23 27	23 36	23 45	23 54	24 3	24 13	24 24	24 35
5 29 30	23	21 42	21 57	22 10	22 24	22 37	22 50	22 56	23 2	23 9	23 15	23 21	23 28	23 34	23 41	23 48	23 55	24 2	24 9	24 16	24 24	24 31	24 39	24 48	24 57	25 6	25 15
5 33 51	24	22 53	23 5	23 17	23 29	23 40	23 51	23 56	24 2	24 7	24 13	24 18	24 24	24 29	24 35	24 41	24 47	24 53	24 59	25 5	25 12	25 18	25 25	25 32	25 40	25 48	25 56
5 38 13	25	24 4	24 14	24 24	24 34	24 43	24 52	24 57	25 1	25 6	25 11	25 15	25 20	25 24	25 29	25 34	25 39	25 44	25 49	25 54	26 0	26 5	26 11	26 17	26 23	26 30	26 37
5 42 34	26	25 15	25 23	25 31	25 39	25 47	25 54	25 57	26 1	26 5	26 8	26 12	26 16	26 19	26 23	26 27	26 31	26 35	26 39	26 43	26 48	26 52	26 57	27 2	27 7	27 12	27 17
5 46 55	27	26 26	26 33	26 38	26 44	26 50	26 55	26 58	27 1	27 4	27 6	27 9	27 12	27 15	27 17	27 20	27 23	27 26	27 29	27 32	27 36	27 39	27 43	27 46	27 50	27 54	27 58
5 51 17	28	27 37	27 42	27 46	27 49	27 53	27 57	27 59	28 1	28 2	28 4	28 6	28 8	28 10	28 12	28 14	28 15	28 17	28 20	28 22	28 24	28 26	28 28	28 31	28 33	28 36	28 39
5 55 38	29	28 49	28 51	28 53	28 55	28 57	28 58	28 59	29 0	29 1	29 2	29 3	29 4	29 5	29 6	29 7	29 8	29 9	29 10	29 11	29 12	29 13	29 14	29 15	29 17	29 18	29 19
6 0 0	30	0 ♎ 0	0 ♎ 0	0 ♎ 0	0 ♎ 0	0 ♎ 0	0 ♎ 0	0 ♎ 0	0 ♎ 0	0 ♎ 0	0 ♎ 0	0 ♎ 0	0 ♎ 0	0 ♎ 0	0 ♎ 0	0 ♎ 0	0 ♎ 0	0 ♎ 0	0 ♎ 0	0 ♎ 0	0 ♎ 0	0 ♎ 0	0 ♎ 0	0 ♎ 0	0 ♎ 0	0 ♎ 0	0 ♎ 0

KEY: N: NORTHERN LATITUDE ST: SIDEREAL TIME MC: MIDHEAVEN ASC: ASCENDANT

NORTHERN LATITUDE

ST	MC	0°N ASC	4°N ASC	8°N ASC	12°N ASC	16°N ASC	20°N ASC	22°N ASC	24°N ASC	26°N ASC	28°N ASC	30°N ASC	32°N ASC	34°N ASC	36°N ASC	38°N ASC	40°N ASC	42°N ASC	44°N ASC	46°N ASC	48°N ASC	50°N ASC	52°N ASC	54°N ASC	56°N ASC	58°N ASC	60°N ASC
6 0 0	0 ♋	0 ♎ 0	0 ♎ 0	0 ♎ 0	0 ♎ 0	0 ♎ 0	0 ♎ 0	0 ♎ 0	0 ♎ 0	0 ♎ 0	0 ♎ 0	0 ♎ 0	0 ♎ 0	0 ♎ 0	0 ♎ 0	0 ♎ 0	0 ♎ 0	0 ♎ 0	0 ♎ 0	0 ♎ 0	0 ♎ 0	0 ♎ 0	0 ♎ 0	0 ♎ 0	0 ♎ 0	0 ♎ 0	0 ♎ 0
6 4 22	1	1 11	1 9	1 7	1 5	1 3	1 2	1 1	1 0	0 59	0 58	0 57	0 56	0 55	0 54	0 53	0 52	0 51	0 50	0 49	0 48	0 47	0 46	0 45	0 43	0 42	0 41
6 8 43	2	2 23	2 18	2 14	2 11	2 7	2 3	2 1	1 59	1 58	1 56	1 54	1 52	1 50	1 48	1 46	1 45	1 43	1 40	1 38	1 36	1 34	1 32	1 29	1 27	1 24	1 21
6 13 5	3	3 34	3 27	3 22	3 16	3 10	3 5	3 2	2 59	2 56	2 54	2 51	2 48	2 45	2 43	2 40	2 37	2 34	2 31	2 28	2 24	2 21	2 17	2 14	2 10	2 6	2 2
6 17 26	4	4 45	4 37	4 29	4 21	4 13	4 6	4 3	3 59	3 55	3 52	3 48	3 44	3 41	3 37	3 33	3 29	3 25	3 21	3 17	3 12	3 8	3 3	2 58	2 53	2 48	2 43
6 21 47	5	5 56	5 46	5 36	5 26	5 17	5 8	5 3	4 59	4 54	4 49	4 45	4 40	4 36	4 31	4 26	4 21	4 16	4 11	4 6	4 0	3 55	3 49	3 43	3 37	3 30	3 23
6 26 9	6	7 7	6 55	6 43	6 31	6 20	6 9	6 4	5 58	5 53	5 47	5 42	5 36	5 31	5 25	5 19	5 13	5 7	5 1	4 55	4 48	4 42	4 35	4 28	4 20	4 12	4 4
6 30 30	7	8 18	8 3	7 50	7 36	7 23	7 10	7 4	6 58	6 51	6 45	6 39	6 32	6 26	6 19	6 12	6 5	5 58	5 51	5 44	5 36	5 29	5 21	5 12	5 3	4 54	4 45
6 34 50	8	9 29	9 12	8 56	8 41	8 26	8 12	8 4	7 57	7 50	7 43	7 35	7 28	7 21	7 13	7 5	6 57	6 50	6 41	6 33	6 24	6 15	6 6	5 57	5 47	5 36	5 25
6 39 11	9	10 39	10 21	10 3	9 46	9 29	9 13	9 5	8 57	8 48	8 40	8 32	8 24	8 15	8 7	7 58	7 49	7 41	7 31	7 22	7 12	7 2	6 52	6 41	6 30	6 18	6 6
6 43 31	10	11 50	11 29	11 10	10 51	10 32	10 14	10 5	9 56	9 47	9 38	9 29	9 19	9 10	9 1	8 51	8 41	8 31	8 21	8 11	8 0	7 49	7 37	7 25	7 13	7 0	6 46
6 47 51	11	13 0	12 38	12 16	11 55	11 35	11 15	11 5	10 55	10 45	10 35	10 25	10 15	10 5	9 55	9 44	9 33	9 22	9 11	9 0	8 48	8 36	8 23	8 10	7 56	7 42	7 27
6 52 11	12	14 10	13 46	13 22	12 59	12 37	12 16	12 5	11 54	11 43	11 32	11 22	11 11	10 59	10 48	10 37	10 25	10 13	10 1	9 48	9 35	9 22	9 8	8 54	8 39	8 23	8 7
6 56 30	13	15 20	14 54	14 28	14 4	13 40	13 16	13 5	12 53	12 41	12 30	12 18	12 6	11 54	11 42	11 29	11 17	11 4	10 51	10 37	10 23	10 9	9 54	9 38	9 22	9 5	8 47
7 0 49	14	16 30	16 1	15 34	15 8	14 42	14 17	14 4	13 52	13 39	13 27	13 14	13 1	12 48	12 35	12 22	12 8	11 55	11 40	11 26	11 11	10 55	10 39	10 22	10 5	9 47	9 27
7 5 8	15	17 40	17 9	16 40	16 12	15 44	15 17	15 4	14 51	14 37	14 24	14 10	13 57	13 43	13 29	13 14	13 0	12 45	12 30	12 14	11 58	11 41	11 24	11 6	10 48	10 28	10 8
7 9 26	16	18 49	18 16	17 45	17 16	16 46	16 18	16 3	15 49	15 35	15 21	15 6	14 52	14 37	14 22	14 7	13 51	13 35	13 19	13 3	12 45	12 28	12 9	11 50	11 30	11 9	10 48
7 13 43	17	19 58	19 24	18 51	18 19	17 48	17 18	17 3	16 48	16 33	16 17	16 2	15 47	15 31	15 15	14 59	14 43	14 26	14 9	13 51	13 33	13 14	12 54	12 34	12 13	11 51	11 28
7 18 1	18	21 7	20 30	19 56	19 22	18 50	18 18	18 2	17 46	17 30	17 14	16 58	16 41	16 25	16 8	15 51	15 34	15 16	14 58	14 39	14 20	14 0	13 39	13 18	12 56	12 32	12 7
7 22 17	19	22 15	21 37	21 1	20 26	19 51	19 18	19 1	18 44	18 27	18 10	17 53	17 36	17 19	17 1	16 43	16 25	16 6	15 47	15 27	15 7	14 46	14 24	14 2	13 38	13 13	12 47
7 26 34	20	23 23	22 43	22 5	21 29	20 53	20 17	20 0	19 42	19 24	19 7	18 49	18 31	18 12	17 54	17 35	17 16	16 56	16 36	16 15	15 54	15 32	15 9	14 45	14 20	13 54	13 27
7 30 49	21	24 31	23 49	23 10	22 31	21 54	21 17	20 58	20 40	20 21	20 3	19 44	19 25	19 6	18 47	18 27	18 7	17 46	17 25	17 3	16 41	16 18	15 54	15 29	15 3	14 35	14 7
7 35 4	22	25 39	24 55	24 14	23 34	22 55	22 16	21 57	21 37	21 18	20 59	20 39	20 19	19 59	19 39	19 18	18 57	18 36	18 14	17 51	17 27	17 3	16 38	16 12	15 45	15 16	14 46
7 39 19	23	26 46	26 1	25 18	24 36	23 55	23 15	22 55	22 35	22 15	21 54	21 34	21 13	20 53	20 31	20 10	19 48	19 25	19 2	18 39	18 14	17 49	17 23	16 55	16 27	15 57	15 26
7 43 33	24	27 53	27 6	26 21	25 38	24 56	24 14	23 53	23 32	23 11	22 50	22 29	22 7	21 46	21 24	21 1	20 38	20 15	19 51	19 26	19 1	18 34	18 7	17 38	17 9	16 38	16 5
7 47 46	25	28 59	28 11	27 25	26 40	25 56	25 12	24 51	24 29	24 7	23 45	23 23	23 1	22 39	22 16	21 52	21 29	21 4	20 39	20 13	19 47	19 20	18 51	18 21	17 50	17 18	16 44
7 51 59	26	0 ♏ 6	29 16	28 28	27 41	26 56	26 11	25 48	25 26	25 3	24 41	24 18	23 55	23 31	23 8	22 43	22 19	21 53	21 27	21 1	20 33	20 5	19 35	19 4	18 32	17 59	17 23
7 56 11	27	1 11	0 ♏20	29 30	28 42	27 55	27 9	26 46	26 22	25 59	25 36	25 12	24 48	24 24	23 59	23 34	23 9	22 42	22 16	21 48	21 19	20 50	20 19	19 47	19 14	18 39	18 2
8 0 23	28	2 17	1 24	0 ♏33	29 43	28 55	28 7	27 43	27 19	26 55	26 31	26 6	25 41	25 16	24 51	24 25	23 58	23 31	23 3	22 35	22 5	21 35	21 3	20 30	19 55	19 19	18 41
8 4 34	29	3 22	2 28	1 35	0 ♏44	29 54	29 5	28 40	28 15	27 50	27 25	27 0	26 34	26 9	25 42	25 15	24 48	24 20	23 51	23 22	22 51	22 19	21 47	21 12	20 37	19 59	19 20
8 8 44	30	4 27	3 31	2 37	1 44	0 ♏53	0 ♏ 2	29 37	29 11	28 45	28 20	27 54	27 27	27 1	26 33	26 6	25 38	25 9	24 39	24 8	23 37	23 4	22 30	21 55	21 18	20 39	19 58

ST	MC	0°N ASC	4°N ASC	8°N ASC	12°N ASC	16°N ASC	20°N ASC	22°N ASC	24°N ASC	26°N ASC	28°N ASC	30°N ASC	32°N ASC	34°N ASC	36°N ASC	38°N ASC	40°N ASC	42°N ASC	44°N ASC	46°N ASC	48°N ASC	50°N ASC	52°N ASC	54°N ASC	56°N ASC	58°N ASC	60°N ASC
8 8 44	0 ♌	4 ♏27	3 ♏31	2 ♏37	1 ♏44	0 ♏53	0 ♏ 2	29 ♎37	29 ♎11	28 ♎45	28 ♎20	27 ♎54	27 ♎27	27 ♎ 1	26 ♎33	26 ♎ 6	25 ♎38	25 ♎ 9	24 ♎39	24 ♎ 8	23 ♎37	23 ♎ 4	22 ♎30	21 ♎55	21 ♎18	20 ♎39	19 ♎58
8 12 53	1	5 31	4 34	3 38	2 45	1 52	0 59	0 ♏33	0 ♏ 7	29 40	29 14	28 47	28 20	27 53	27 25	26 56	26 27	25 57	25 26	24 55	24 22	23 49	23 14	22 37	21 59	21 19	20 37
8 17 2	2	6 35	5 36	4 40	3 44	2 50	1 56	1 29	1 2	0 ♏35	0 ♏ 8	29 40	29 13	28 44	28 15	27 46	27 16	26 45	26 14	25 41	25 8	24 33	23 57	23 19	22 40	21 59	21 15
8 21 10	3	7 39	6 39	5 41	4 44	3 48	2 53	2 25	1 58	1 30	1 2	0 ♏34	0 ♏ 5	29 36	29 6	28 36	28 5	27 34	27 1	26 28	25 53	25 17	24 40	24 1	23 21	22 38	21 53
8 25 18	4	8 43	7 41	6 41	5 43	4 46	3 50	3 21	2 53	2 24	1 56	1 26	0 57	0 ♏27	29 57	29 26	28 54	28 22	27 48	27 14	26 38	26 1	25 23	24 43	24 1	23 18	22 31
8 29 25	5	9 45	8 42	7 42	6 42	5 44	4 46	4 17	3 48	3 18	2 49	2 19	1 49	1 18	0 ♏47	0 ♏15	29 43	29 9	28 35	28 0	27 23	26 45	26 6	25 25	24 42	23 57	23 9
8 33 31	6	10 48	9 44	8 42	7 41	6 41	5 42	5 12	4 42	4 12	3 42	3 12	2 41	2 9	1 37	1 5	0 ♏31	29 57	29 22	28 45	28 8	27 29	26 49	26 6	25 22	24 36	23 47
8 37 36	7	11 50	10 45	9 41	8 39	7 38	6 38	6 7	5 37	5 6	4 35	4 4	3 32	3 0	2 27	1 54	1 20	0 ♏45	0 ♏ 8	29 31	28 53	28 13	27 31	26 48	26 3	25 15	24 25
8 41 40	8	12 52	11 45	10 41	9 37	8 35	7 33	7 2	6 31	6 0	5 28	4 56	4 24	3 51	3 17	2 43	2 8	1 32	0 55	0 ♏17	29 37	28 56	28 14	27 29	26 43	25 54	25 3
8 45 44	9	13 54	12 46	11 40	10 35	9 32	8 29	7 57	7 25	6 53	6 21	5 48	5 15	4 41	4 7	3 32	2 56	2 19	1 41	1 2	0 ♏22	29 40	28 56	28 10	27 23	26 33	25 40
8 49 47	10	14 55	13 46	12 38	11 33	10 28	9 24	8 51	8 19	7 46	7 13	6 40	6 6	5 31	4 56	4 20	3 44	3 6	2 27	1 47	1 6	0 ♏23	29 38	28 52	28 3	27 11	26 17
8 53 50	11	15 56	14 45	13 37	12 30	11 24	10 19	9 46	9 12	8 39	8 5	7 31	6 57	6 21	5 46	5 9	4 31	3 53	3 13	2 32	1 50	1 6	0 ♏20	29 32	28 42	27 50	26 55
8 57 51	12	16 56	15 44	14 35	13 27	12 20	11 13	10 40	10 6	9 32	8 57	8 23	7 47	7 11	6 35	5 57	5 19	4 40	3 59	3 17	2 34	1 49	1 2	0 ♏13	29 22	28 28	27 32
9 1 52	13	17 56	16 43	15 33	14 24	13 16	12 8	11 33	10 59	10 24	9 49	9 14	8 38	8 1	7 24	6 46	6 6	5 26	4 45	4 2	3 18	2 32	1 44	0 54	0 ♏ 2	29 7	28 9
9 5 52	14	18 56	17 42	16 30	15 20	14 11	13 2	12 27	11 52	11 17	10 41	10 5	9 28	8 51	8 13	7 34	6 54	6 13	5 30	4 47	4 2	3 15	2 26	1 35	0 41	29 45	28 45
9 9 52	15	19 55	18 40	17 28	16 17	15 6	13 56	13 20	12 45	12 9	11 32	10 55	10 18	9 40	9 1	8 22	7 41	6 59	6 16	5 31	4 45	3 57	3 7	2 15	1 20	0 ♏23	29 22
9 13 51	16	20 54	19 38	18 25	17 12	16 1	14 49	14 13	13 37	13 0	12 24	11 46	11 8	10 29	9 50	9 9	8 28	7 45	7 1	6 16	5 29	4 40	3 49	2 55	1 59	1 1	29 59
9 17 49	17	21 52	20 36	19 21	18 8	16 55	15 43	15 6	14 29	13 52	13 15	12 36	11 58	11 18	10 38	9 57	9 15	8 31	7 46	7 0	6 12	5 22	4 30	3 35	2 38	1 38	0 ♏35
9 21 46	18	22 51	21 33	20 18	19 3	17 50	16 36	15 59	15 21	14 44	14 5	13 27	12 47	12 7	11 26	10 44	10 1	9 17	8 31	7 44	6 55	6 4	5 11	4 16	3 17	2 16	1 11
9 25 43	19	23 49	22 30	21 14	19 59	18 44	17 29	16 51	16 13	15 35	14 56	14 17	13 37	12 56	12 14	11 32	10 48	10 3	9 16	8 28	7 38	6 46	5 52	4 55	3 56	2 54	1 48
9 29 39	20	24 46	23 27	22 10	20 53	19 38	18 22	17 44	17 5	16 26	15 47	15 7	14 26	13 44	13 2	12 19	11 34	10 48	10 1	9 12	8 21	7 28	6 33	5 35	4 35	3 31	2 24
9 33 34	21	25 43	24 23	23 5	21 48	20 31	19 14	18 36	17 56	17 17	16 37	15 56	15 15	14 33	13 50	13 6	12 20	11 34	10 45	9 56	9 4	8 10	7 14	6 15	5 13	4 8	3 0
9 37 28	22	26 40	25 19	24 0	22 42	21 25	20 7	19 27	18 48	18 8	17 27	16 46	16 4	15 21	14 37	13 52	13 6	12 19	11 30	10 39	9 46	8 52	7 54	6 55	5 52	4 45	3 36
9 41 22	23	27 37	26 15	24 55	23 36	22 18	20 59	20 19	19 39	18 58	18 17	17 35	16 53	16 9	15 25	14 39	13 52	13 4	12 14	11 23	10 29	9 33	8 35	7 34	6 30	5 23	4 11
9 45 16	24	28 33	27 11	25 50	24 30	23 11	21 51	21 11	20 30	19 49	19 7	18 24	17 41	16 57	16 12	15 26	14 38	13 49	12 59	12 6	11 12	10 15	9 15	8 13	7 8	6 0	4 47
9 49 8	25	29 29	28 6	26 45	25 24	24 4	22 43	22 2	21 21	20 39	19 57	19 14	18 30	17 45	16 59	16 12	15 24	14 34	13 43	12 49	11 54	10 56	9 56	8 53	7 46	6 36	5 22
9 53 0	26	0 ♐25	29 1	27 39	26 17	24 56	23 34	22 53	22 11	21 29	20 46	20 2	19 18	18 33	17 46	16 59	16 10	15 19	14 27	13 32	12 36	11 37	10 36	9 32	8 24	7 13	5 58
9 56 51	27	1 20	29 56	28 33	27 11	25 48	24 26	23 44	23 2	22 19	21 35	20 51	20 6	19 20	18 33	17 45	16 55	16 4	15 11	14 16	13 18	12 19	11 16	10 11	9 2	7 50	6 33
10 0 42	28	2 16	0 ♐50	29 27	28 4	26 41	25 17	24 35	23 52	23 9	22 25	21 40	20 54	20 8	19 20	18 31	17 40	16 48	15 54	14 58	14 0	13 0	11 56	10 50	9 40	8 26	7 8
10 4 32	29	3 10	1 45	0 ♐20	28 56	27 33	26 8	25 25	24 42	23 58	23 14	22 28	21 42	20 55	20 7	19 17	18 26	17 33	16 38	15 41	14 42	13 41	12 36	11 29	10 18	9 3	7 43
10 8 22	30	4 5	2 39	1 13	29 49	28 24	26 59	26 16	25 32	24 48	24 3	23 17	22 30	21 42	20 53	20 3	19 11	18 17	17 22	16 24	15 24	14 22	13 16	12 8	10 55	9 39	8 18

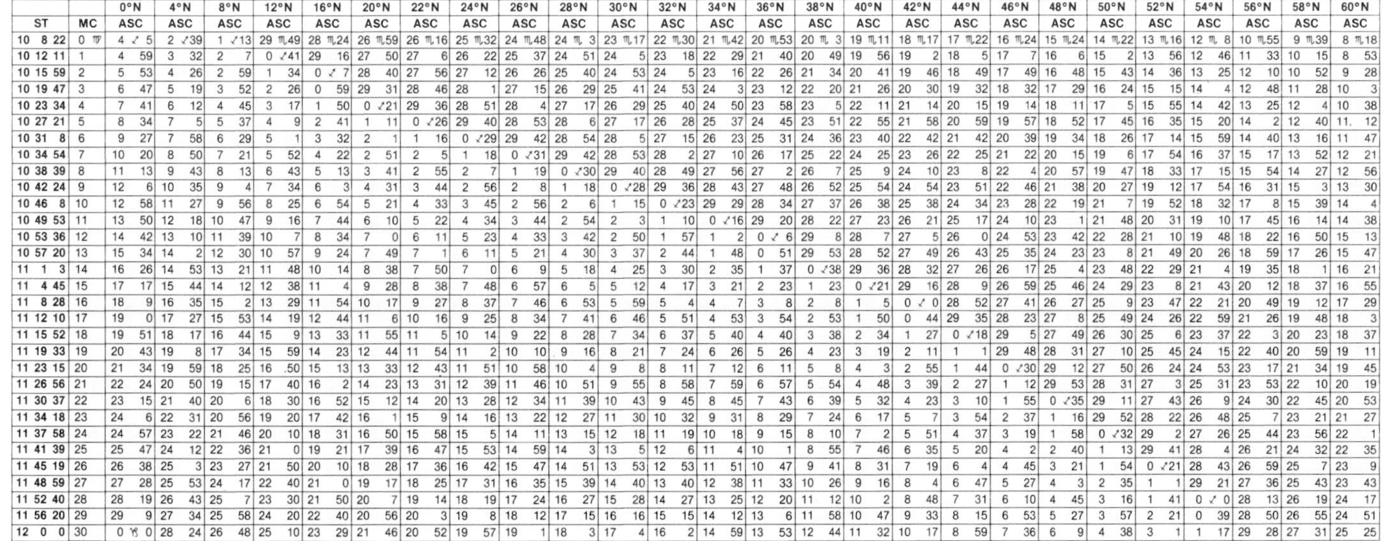

ST	MC	0°N ASC	4°N ASC	8°N ASC	12°N ASC	16°N ASC	20°N ASC	22°N ASC	24°N ASC	26°N ASC	28°N ASC	30°N ASC	32°N ASC	34°N ASC	36°N ASC	38°N ASC	40°N ASC	42°N ASC	44°N ASC	46°N ASC	48°N ASC	50°N ASC	52°N ASC	54°N ASC	56°N ASC	58°N ASC	60°N ASC
10 8 22	0 ♍	4 ♐ 5	2 ♐39	1 ♐13	29 ♏49	28 ♏24	26 ♏59	26 ♏16	25 ♏32	24 ♏48	24 ♏ 3	23 ♏17	22 ♏30	21 ♏42	20 ♏53	20 ♏ 3	19 ♏11	18 ♏17	17 ♏22	16 ♏24	15 ♏24	14 ♏22	13 ♏16	12 ♏ 8	10 ♏55	9 ♏39	8 ♏18
10 12 11	1	4 59	3 32	2 7	0 ♐41	29 16	27 50	27 6	26 22	25 37	24 51	24 5	23 18	22 29	21 40	20 49	19 56	19 2	18 5	17 7	16 6	15 2	13 56	12 46	11 33	10 15	8 53
10 15 59	2	5 53	4 26	2 59	1 34	0 ♐ 7	28 40	27 56	27 12	26 26	25 40	24 53	24 5	23 16	22 26	21 34	20 41	19 46	18 49	17 49	16 48	15 43	14 36	13 25	12 10	10 52	9 28
10 19 47	3	6 47	5 19	3 52	2 26	0 59	29 31	28 46	28 1	27 15	26 29	25 41	24 53	24 3	23 12	22 20	21 26	20 30	19 32	18 32	17 29	16 24	15 15	14 4	12 48	11 28	10 3
10 23 34	4	7 41	6 12	4 45	3 17	1 50	0 ♐21	29 36	28 51	28 4	27 17	26 29	25 40	24 50	23 58	23 5	22 11	21 14	20 15	19 14	18 11	17 5	15 55	14 42	13 25	12 4	10 38
10 27 21	5	8 34	7 5	5 37	4 9	2 41	1 11	0 ♐26	29 40	28 53	28 6	27 17	26 28	25 37	24 45	23 51	22 55	21 58	20 59	19 57	18 52	17 45	16 35	15 20	14 2	12 40	11. 12
10 31 8	6	9 27	7 58	6 29	5 1	3 32	2 1	1 16	0 ♐29	29 42	28 54	28 5	27 15	26 23	25 31	24 36	23 40	22 42	21 42	20 39	19 34	18 26	17 14	15 59	14 40	13 16	11 47
10 34 54	7	10 20	8 50	7 21	5 52	4 22	2 51	2 5	1 18	0 ♐31	29 42	28 53	28 2	27 10	26 17	25 22	24 25	23 26	22 25	21 22	20 15	19 6	17 54	16 37	15 17	13 52	12 21
10 38 39	8	11 13	9 43	8 13	6 43	5 13	3 41	2 55	2 7	1 19	0 ♐30	29 40	28 49	27 56	27 2	26 7	25 9	24 10	23 8	22 4	20 57	19 47	18 33	17 15	15 54	14 27	12 56
10 42 24	9	12 6	10 35	9 4	7 34	6 3	4 31	3 44	2 56	2 8	1 18	0 ♐28	29 36	28 43	27 48	26 52	25 54	24 54	23 51	22 46	21 38	20 27	19 12	17 54	16 31	15 3	13 30
10 46 8	10	12 58	11 27	9 56	8 25	6 54	5 21	4 33	3 45	2 56	2 6	1 15	0 ♐23	29 29	28 34	27 37	26 38	25 38	24 34	23 28	22 19	21 7	19 52	18 32	17 8	15 39	14 4
10 49 53	11	13 50	12 18	10 47	9 16	7 44	6 10	5 22	4 34	3 44	2 54	2 3	1 10	0 ♐16	29 20	28 22	27 23	26 21	25 17	24 10	23 1	21 48	20 31	19 10	17 45	16 14	14 38
10 53 36	12	14 42	13 10	11 39	10 7	8 34	7 0	6 11	5 23	4 33	3 42	2 50	1 57	1 2	0 ♐ 6	29 8	28 7	27 5	26 0	24 53	23 42	22 28	21 10	19 48	18 22	16 50	15 13
10 57 20	13	15 34	14 2	12 30	10 57	9 24	7 49	7 1	6 11	5 21	4 30	3 37	2 44	1 48	0 51	29 53	28 52	27 49	26 43	25 35	24 23	23 8	21 49	20 26	18 59	17 26	15 47
11 1 3	14	16 26	14 53	13 21	11 48	10 14	8 38	7 50	7 0	6 9	5 18	4 25	3 30	2 35	1 37	0 ♐38	29 36	28 32	27 26	26 17	25 4	23 48	22 29	21 4	19 35	18 1	16 21
11 4 45	15	17 17	15 44	14 12	12 38	11 4	9 28	8 38	7 48	6 57	6 5	5 12	4 17	3 21	2 23	1 23	0 ♐21	29 16	28 9	26 59	25 46	24 29	23 8	21 43	20 12	18 37	16 55
11 8 28	16	18 9	16 35	15 2	13 29	11 54	10 17	9 27	8 37	7 46	6 53	5 59	5 4	4 7	3 8	2 8	1 5	0 ♐ 0	28 52	27 41	26 27	25 9	23 47	22 21	20 49	19 12	17 29
11 12 10	17	19 0	17 27	15 53	14 19	12 44	11 6	10 16	9 25	8 34	7 41	6 46	5 51	4 53	3 54	2 53	1 50	0 44	29 35	28 23	27 8	25 49	24 26	22 59	21 26	19 48	18 3
11 15 52	18	19 51	18 17	16 44	15 9	13 33	11 55	11 5	10 14	9 22	8 28	7 34	6 37	5 40	4 40	3 38	2 34	1 27	0 ♐18	29 5	27 49	26 30	25 6	23 37	22 3	20 23	18 37
11 19 33	19	20 43	19 8	17 34	15 59	14 23	12 44	11 54	11 2	10 10	9 16	8 21	7 24	6 26	5 26	4 23	3 19	2 11	1 1	29 48	28 31	27 10	25 45	24 15	22 40	20 59	19 11
11 23 15	20	21 34	19 59	18 25	16 .50	15 13	13 33	12 43	11 51	10 58	10 4	9 8	8 11	7 12	6 11	5 8	4 3	2 55	1 44	0 ♐30	29 12	27 50	26 24	24 53	23 17	21 34	19 45
11 26 56	21	22 24	20 50	19 15	17 40	16 2	14 23	13 31	12 39	11 46	10 51	9 55	8 58	7 59	6 57	5 54	4 48	3 39	2 27	1 12	29 53	28 31	27 3	25 31	23 53	22 10	20 19
11 30 37	22	23 15	21 40	20 6	18 30	16 52	15 12	14 20	13 28	12 34	11 39	10 43	9 45	8 45	7 43	6 39	5 32	4 23	3 10	1 55	0 ♐35	29 11	27 43	26 9	24 30	22 45	20 53
11 34 18	23	24 6	22 31	20 56	19 20	17 42	16 1	15 9	14 16	13 22	12 27	11 30	10 32	9 31	8 29	7 24	6 17	5 7	3 54	2 37	1 16	29 52	28 22	26 48	25 7	23 21	21 27
11 37 58	24	24 57	23 22	21 46	20 10	18 31	16 50	15 58	15 5	14 11	13 15	12 18	11 19	10 18	9 15	8 10	7 2	5 51	4 37	3 19	1 58	0 ♐32	29 2	27 26	25 44	23 56	22 1
11 41 39	25	25 47	24 12	22 36	21 0	19 21	17 39	16 47	15 53	14 59	14 3	13 5	12 6	11 4	10 1	8 55	7 46	6 35	5 20	4 2	2 40	1 13	29 41	28 4	26 21	24 32	22 35
11 45 19	26	26 38	25 3	23 27	21 50	20 10	18 28	17 36	16 42	15 47	14 51	13 53	12 53	11 51	10 47	9 41	8 31	7 19	6 4	4 45	3 21	1 54	0 ♐21	28 43	26 59	25 7	23 9
11 48 59	27	27 28	25 53	24 17	22 40	21 0	19 17	18 25	17 31	16 35	15 39	14 40	13 40	12 38	11 33	10 26	9 16	8 4	6 47	5 27	4 3	2 35	1 1	29 21	27 36	25 43	23 43
11 52 40	28	28 19	26 43	25 7	23 30	21 50	20 7	19 14	18 19	17 24	16 27	15 28	14 27	13 25	12 20	11 12	10 2	8 48	7 31	6 10	4 45	3 16	1 41	0 ♐ 0	28 13	26 19	24 17
11 56 20	29	29 9	27 34	25 58	24 20	22 40	20 56	20 3	19 8	18 12	17 15	16 16	15 15	14 12	13 6	11 58	10 47	9 33	8 15	6 53	5 27	3 57	2 21	0 39	28 50	26 55	24 51
12 0 0	30	0 ♑ 0	28 24	26 48	25 10	23 29	21 46	20 52	19 57	19 1	18 3	17 4	16 2	14 59	13 53	12 44	11 32	10 17	8 59	7 36	6 9	4 38	3 1	1 17	29 28	27 31	25 25

KEY: N: NORTHERN LATITUDE ST: SIDEREAL TIME MC: MIDHEAVEN ASC: ASCENDANT

NORTHERN LATITUDE

		0°N	4°N	8°N	12°N	16°N	20°N	22°N	24°N	26°N	28°N	30°N	32°N	34°N	36°N	38°N	40°N	42°N	44°N	46°N	48°N	50°N	52°N	54°N	56°N	58°N	60°N
ST	MC	ASC	ASC	ASC	ASC	ASC	ASC	ASC	ASC	ASC	ASC	ASC	ASC	ASC	ASC	ASC	ASC	ASC	ASC	ASC	ASC	ASC	ASC	ASC	ASC	ASC	ASC
12 0 0	0 ♎	0 ♑ 0	28 ♐ 24	26 ♐ 48	25 ♐ 10	23 ♐ 29	21 ♐ 46	20 ♐ 52	19 ♐ 57	19 ♐ 1	18 ♐ 3	17 ♐ 4	16 ♐ 2	14 ♐ 59	13 ♐ 53	12 ♐ 44	11 ♐ 32	10 ♐ 17	8 ♐ 59	7 ♐ 36	6 ♐ 9	4 ♐ 38	3 ♐ 1	1 ♐ 17	29 ♏ 28	27 ♏ 31	25 ♏ 25
12 3 40	1	0 51	29 15	27 38	26 0	24 19	22 35	21 41	20 46	19 50	18 52	17 52	16 50	15 46	14 39	13 30	12 18	11 2	9 43	8 20	6 52	5 19	3 41	1 56	0 ♐ 5	28 7	26 0
12 7 20	2	1 41	0 ♑ 5	28 29	26 50	25 9	23 25	22 31	21 35	20 39	19 40	18 40	17 38	16 33	15 26	14 16	13 3	11 47	10 27	9 3	7 34	6 0	4 21	2 35	0 43	28 43	26 34
12 11 1	3	2 32	0 56	29 19	27 41	25 59	24 14	23 20	22 25	21 28	20 29	19 28	18 25	17 20	16 13	15 3	13 49	12 32	11 11	9 47	8 17	6 42	5 1	3 15	1 21	29 19	27 8
12 14 41	4	3 22	1 46	0 ♑ 10	28 31	26 49	25 4	24 10	23 14	22 17	21 18	20 17	19 14	18 8	17 0	15 49	14 35	13 18	11 56	10 30	9 0	7 24	5 42	3 54	1 58	29 55	27 43
12 18 21	5	4 13	2 37	1 0	29 21	27 40	25 54	24 59	24 3	23 6	22 6	21 5	20 2	18 56	17 47	16 36	15 21	14 3	12 41	11 14	9 43	8 6	6 23	4 33	2 36	0 ♐ 31	28 18
12 22 2	6	5 3	3 28	1 51	0 ♑ 12	28 30	26 44	25 49	24 53	23 55	22 56	21 54	20 50	19 44	18 35	17 23	16 8	14 49	13 26	11 58	10 26	8 48	7 4	5 13	3 15	1 8	28 52
12 25 42	7	5 54	4 19	2 42	1 3	29 21	27 34	26 39	25 43	24 45	23 45	22 43	21 39	20 32	19 23	18 10	16 54	15 35	14 11	12 42	11 9	9 30	7 45	5 53	3 53	1 45	29 27
12 29 23	8	6 45	5 9	3 33	1 53	0 ♑ 11	28 25	27 29	26 33	25 34	24 34	23 32	22 27	21 20	20 10	18 57	17 41	16 21	14 56	13 27	11 53	10 12	8 26	6 33	4 31	2 21	0 ♐ 2
12 33 4	9	7 36	6 0	4 23	2 44	1 2	29 15	28 20	27 23	26 24	25 24	24 21	23 16	22 9	20 58	19 45	18 28	17 7	15 42	14 12	12 36	10 55	9 8	7 13	5 10	2 58	0 37
12 36 45	10	8 26	6 51	5 15	3 35	1 53	0 ♑ 6	29 10	28 13	27 14	26 14	25 11	24 6	22 58	21 47	20 33	19 15	17 53	16 27	14 57	13 20	11 38	9 49	7 53	5 49	3 35	1 12
12 40 27	11	9 17	7 42	6 6	4 27	2 44	0 57	0 ♑ 1	29 4	28 5	27 4	26 1	24 55	23 47	22 35	21 21	20 3	18 40	17 14	15 42	14 5	12 21	10 31	8 34	6 28	4 12	1 47
12 44 8	12	10 9	8 34	6 57	5 18	3 35	1 48	0 52	29 54	28 55	27 54	26 51	25 45	24 36	23 24	22 9	20 50	19 27	18 0	16 27	14 49	13 5	11 13	9 14	7 7	4 50	2 23
12 47 50	13	11 0	9 25	7 49	6 9	4 27	2 39	1 43	0 ♑ 45	29 46	28 45	27 41	26 34	25 25	24 13	22 58	21 38	20 15	18 46	17 13	15 34	13 48	11 56	9 55	7 46	5 27	2 58
12 51 32	14	11 51	10 17	8 40	7 1	5 18	3 30	2 34	1 37	0 ♑ 37	29 35	28 31	27 25	26 15	25 3	23 47	22 27	21 2	19 33	17 59	16 19	14 32	12 38	10 37	8 26	6 5	3 34
12 55 15	15	12 43	11 8	9 32	7 53	6 10	4 22	3 26	2 28	1 28	0 ♑ 26	29 22	28 15	27 5	25 52	24 36	23 15	21 50	20 21	18 45	17 4	15 16	13 21	11 18	9 6	6 43	4 10
12 58 57	16	13 34	12 0	10 24	8 45	7 2	5 14	4 18	3 20	2 20	1 18	0 ♑ 13	29 6	27 56	26 42	25 25	24 4	22 39	21 8	19 32	17 50	16 1	14 5	12 0	9 46	7 21	4 46
13 2 40	17	14 26	12 52	11 16	9 37	7 54	6 6	5 10	4 12	3 11	2 9	1 4	29 57	28 46	27 32	26 15	24 53	23 27	21 56	20 19	18 36	16 46	14 48	12 42	10 26	8 0	5 22
13 6 24	18	15 18	13 44	12 8	10 30	8 47	6 59	6 2	5 4	4 4	3 1	1 56	0 ♑ 48	29 37	28 23	27 5	25 43	24 16	22 44	21 6	19 22	17 31	15 32	13 24	11 7	8 39	5 59
13 10 7	19	16 10	14 36	13 1	11 22	9 39	7 51	6 55	5 56	4 56	3 53	2 48	1 40	0 ♑ 29	29 14	27 56	26 33	25 5	23 33	21 54	20 9	18 17	16 16	14 7	11 48	9 18	6 35
13 13 52	20	17 2	15 29	13 54	12 15	10 32	8 44	7 48	6 49	5 49	4 46	3 40	2 32	1 20	0 ♑ 5	28 46	27 23	25 55	24 22	22 42	20 56	19 3	17 1	14 50	12 29	9 57	7 12
13 17 36	21	17 54	16 22	14 47	13 8	11 26	9 37	8 41	7 42	6 41	5 38	4 33	3 24	2 12	0 57	29 38	28 14	26 45	25 11	23 31	21 43	19 49	17 46	15 33	13 11	10 36	7 49
13 21 21	22	18 47	17 15	15 40	14 2	12 19	10 31	9 34	8 36	7 35	6 32	5 26	4 17	3 5	1 49	0 ♑ 29	29 5	27 36	26 1	24 19	22 31	20 36	18 31	16 17	13 53	11 16	8 27
13 25 6	23	19 40	18 8	16 33	14 55	13 13	11 25	10 28	9 29	8 28	7 25	6 19	5 10	3 58	2 41	1 21	29 56	28 26	26 51	25 9	23 20	21 23	19 17	17 1	14 35	11 56	9 4
13 28 52	24	20 33	19 1	17 27	15 49	14 7	12 19	11 22	10 23	9 22	8 19	7 13	6 4	4 51	3 34	2 14	0 ♑ 48	29 18	27 41	25 58	24 8	22 10	20 3	17 46	15 17	12 37	9 42
13 32 39	25	21 26	19 55	18 21	16 43	15 1	13 13	12 17	11 18	10 17	9 13	8 7	6 57	5 44	4 28	3 7	1 41	0 ♑ 10	28 32	26 49	24 58	22 58	20 50	18 31	16 0	13 18	10 21
13 36 26	26	22 19	20 48	19 15	17 38	15 56	14 8	13 11	12 13	11 12	10 8	9 1	7 52	6 39	5 21	4 0	2 34	1 2	29 24	27 39	25 47	23 47	21 37	19 16	16 44	13 59	10 59
13 40 13	27	23 13	21 43	20 10	18 33	16 51	15 3	14 7	13 8	12 7	11 3	9 56	8 47	7 33	6 16	4 54	3 27	1 55	0 ♑ 16	28 31	26 37	24 36	22 24	20 2	17 28	14 40	11 38
13 44 1	28	24 7	22 37	21 4	19 28	17 46	15 59	15 2	14 3	13 2	11 59	10 52	9 42	8 28	7 10	5 48	4 21	2 48	1 9	29 22	27 28	25 25	23 12	20 48	18 12	15 22	12 17
13 47 49	29	25 1	23 31	21 59	20 23	18 42	16 55	15 58	14 59	13 58	12 54	11 48	10 37	9 24	8 6	6 43	5 15	3 42	2 2	0 ♑ 15	28 19	26 15	24 1	21 35	18 57	16 5	12 57
13 51 38	30	25 55	24 26	22 55	21 19	19 38	17 51	16 55	15 56	14 55	13 51	12 44	11 34	10 20	9 1	7 38	6 10	4 36	2 55	1 8	29 11	27 6	24 50	22 23	19 42	16 48	13 37

		0°N	4°N	8°N	12°N	16°N	20°N	22°N	24°N	26°N	28°N	30°N	32°N	34°N	36°N	38°N	40°N	42°N	44°N	46°N	48°N	50°N	52°N	54°N	56°N	58°N	60°N
ST	MC	ASC	ASC	ASC	ASC	ASC	ASC	ASC	ASC	ASC	ASC	ASC	ASC	ASC	ASC	ASC	ASC	ASC	ASC	ASC	ASC	ASC	ASC	ASC	ASC	ASC	ASC
13 51 38	0 ♏	25 ♑ 55	24 ♑ 26	22 ♑ 55	21 ♑ 19	19 ♑ 38	17 ♑ 51	16 ♑ 55	15 ♑ 56	14 ♑ 55	13 ♑ 51	12 ♑ 44	11 ♑ 34	10 ♑ 20	9 ♑ 1	7 ♑ 38	6 ♑ 10	4 ♑ 36	2 ♑ 55	1 ♑ 8	29 ♐ 11	27 ♐ 6	24 ♐ 50	22 ♐ 23	19 ♐ 42	16 ♐ 48	13 ♐ 37
13 55 28	1	26 50	25 22	23 50	22 15	20 35	18 48	17 51	16 53	15 52	14 48	13 41	12 30	11 16	9 58	8 34	7 6	5 31	3 50	2 1	0 ♑ 4	27 57	25 40	23 11	20 28	17 31	14 17
13 59 18	2	27 44	26 17	24 46	23 12	21 31	19 45	18 49	17 50	16 49	15 45	14 38	13 28	12 13	10 54	9 31	8 2	6 27	4 45	2 55	0 57	28 49	26 30	23 59	21 14	18 15	14 58
14 3 9	3	28 40	27 13	25 43	24 8	22 29	20 42	19 46	18 48	17 47	16 43	15 36	14 25	13 11	11 52	10 28	8 58	7 23	5 40	3 50	1 51	29 41	27 21	24 48	22 1	18 59	15 39
14 7 0	4	29 35	28 9	26 39	25 5	23 26	21 40	20 44	19 46	18 45	17 41	16 34	15 24	14 9	12 50	11 26	9 56	8 20	6 36	4 45	2 45	0 ♑ 34	28 13	25 38	22 49	19 44	16 21
14 10 52	5	0 ♒ 31	29 5	27 36	26 3	24 24	22 39	21 43	20 45	19 44	18 40	17 33	16 22	15 8	13 48	12 24	10 54	9 17	7 33	5 41	3 40	1 28	29 5	26 28	23 37	20 29	17 3
14 14 44	6	1 27	0 ♒ 2	28 34	27 1	25 23	23 38	22 42	21 44	20 43	19 40	18 33	17 22	16 7	14 48	13 23	11 52	10 15	8 31	6 38	4 36	2 23	29 58	27 20	24 26	21 15	17 46
14 18 38	7	2 23	0 59	29 31	27 59	26 22	24 37	23 41	22 44	21 43	20 39	19 33	18 22	17 7	15 47	14 22	12 52	11 14	9 29	7 36	5 32	3 18	0 ♑ 52	28 11	25 15	22 2	18 29
14 22 32	8	3 20	1 56	0 ♒ 29	28 58	27 21	25 37	24 42	23 44	22 43	21 40	20 33	19 22	18 8	16 48	15 23	13 52	12 14	10 28	8 34	6 30	4 14	1 46	29 4	26 6	22 49	19 13
14 26 26	9	4 17	2 54	1 28	29 57	28 21	26 37	25 42	24 45	23 44	22 41	21 34	20 24	19 9	17 49	16 24	14 53	13 14	11 28	9 33	7 28	5 11	2 42	29 58	26 57	23 37	19 58
14 30 21	10	5 14	3 52	2 27	0 ♒ 57	29 21	27 38	26 43	25 46	24 46	23 43	22 36	21 26	20 11	18 51	17 26	15 54	14 15	12 29	10 33	8 27	6 9	3 38	0 ♑ 52	27 49	24 26	20 43
14 34 17	11	6 11	4 50	3 26	1 57	0 ♒ 21	28 39	27 45	26 48	25 48	24 45	23 39	22 28	21 13	19 54	18 28	16 56	15 17	13 30	11 34	9 27	7 8	4 35	1 47	28 41	25 16	21 28
14 38 14	12	7 9	5 49	4 25	2 57	1 23	29 41	28 47	27 50	26 51	25 48	24 42	23 31	22 17	20 57	19 31	17 59	16 20	14 33	12 36	10 28	8 7	5 33	2 43	29 35	26 6	22 15
14 42 11	13	8 8	6 48	5 25	3 58	2 24	0 ♒ 43	29 50	28 53	27 54	26 52	25 46	24 35	23 21	22 1	20 36	19 3	17 24	15 36	13 38	11 29	9 8	6 32	3 40	0 ♑ 29	26 57	23 2
14 46 9	14	9 6	7 48	6 26	4 59	3 26	1 46	0 ♒ 53	29 57	28 58	27 56	26 50	25 40	24 26	23 6	21 40	20 8	18 29	16 40	14 42	12 32	10 10	7 32	4 38	1 25	27 49	23 50
14 50 8	15	10 5	8 48	7 27	6 1	4 29	2 50	1 57	1 ♒ 1	0 ♒ 2	29 1	27 55	26 46	25 31	24 12	22 46	21 14	19 34	17 45	15 46	13 36	11 12	8 33	5 37	2 21	28 43	24 39
14 54 8	16	11 4	9 48	8 28	7 3	5 32	3 54	3 1	2 6	1 8	0 ♒ 6	29 1	27 52	26 38	25 18	23 53	22 21	20 41	18 51	16 52	14 41	12 16	9 36	6 37	3 19	29 37	25 29
14 58 8	17	12 4	10 49	9 30	8 6	6 36	4 58	4 6	3 11	2 13	1 12	0 ♒ 8	28 59	27 45	26 26	25 0	23 28	21 48	19 59	17 59	15 47	13 21	10 39	7 39	4 17	0 ♑ 32	26 19
15 2 9	18	13 4	11 50	10 32	9 9	7 40	6 3	5 12	4 17	3 20	2 19	1 15	0 ♒ 6	28 53	27 34	26 9	24 37	22 56	21 7	19 7	16 54	14 27	11 44	8 41	5 17	1 28	27 11
15 6 10	19	14 4	12 51	11 34	10 12	8 44	7 9	6 18	5 24	4 27	3 27	2 23	1 15	0 ♒ 2	28 43	27 18	25 46	24 6	22 16	20 16	18 2	15 35	12 50	9 45	6 18	2 26	28 4
15 10 13	20	15 5	13 53	12 37	11 16	9 50	8 15	7 25	6 31	5 35	4 35	3 32	2 24	1 11	29 53	28 29	26 57	25 17	23 27	21 26	19 12	16 43	13 57	10 51	7 21	3 24	28 58
15 14 16	21	16 6	14 55	13 41	12 21	10 55	9 22	8 32	7 39	6 44	5 44	4 41	3 34	2 22	1 ♒ 4	29 40	28 8	26 28	24 38	22 37	20 23	17 53	15 6	11 57	8 25	4 24	29 53
15 18 20	22	17 8	15 58	14 44	13 26	12 2	10 30	9 40	8 48	7 53	6 54	5 52	4 45	3 33	2 16	0 ♒ 52	29 21	27 41	25 51	23 50	21 35	19 5	16 16	13 5	9 30	5 26	0 ♑ 49
15 22 24	23	18 10	17 1	15 49	14 32	13 9	11 38	10 49	9 57	9 3	8 5	7 3	5 57	4 46	3 29	2 6	0 ♒ 35	28 55	27 5	25 4	22 49	20 18	17 28	14 15	10 37	6 29	1 47
15 26 29	24	19 12	18 5	16 54	15 38	14 16	12 46	11 58	11 7	10 14	9 16	8 15	7 10	5 59	4 43	3 20	1 50	0 ♒ 10	28 21	26 19	24 4	21 32	18 41	15 27	11 46	7 34	2 46
15 30 35	25	20 15	19 9	17 59	16 44	15 24	13 56	13 8	12 18	11 25	10 28	9 28	8 23	7 13	5 58	4 35	3 5	1 27	29 38	27 36	25 21	22 48	19 56	16 40	12 56	8 40	3 47
15 34 42	26	21 17	20 13	19 4	17 51	16 32	15 6	14 19	13 30	12 37	11 41	10 42	9 38	8 28	7 14	5 52	4 23	2 44	0 ♒ 56	28 54	26 39	24 6	21 12	17 55	14 8	9 48	4 49
15 38 50	27	22 21	21 18	20 11	18 59	17 41	16 16	15 30	14 42	13 50	12 55	11 56	10 53	9 45	8 30	7 10	5 41	4 3	2 15	0 ♒ 14	27 58	25 25	22 31	19 12	15 22	10 58	5 53
15 42 58	28	23 25	22 23	21 17	20 7	18 51	17 27	16 42	15 55	15 4	14 10	13 12	12 9	11 2	9 48	8 28	7 1	5 24	3 36	1 35	29 20	26 46	23 51	20 30	16 39	12 10	6 59
15 47 7	29	24 29	23 28	22 24	21 16	20 1	18 39	17 55	17 8	16 18	15 25	14 28	13 26	12 20	11 7	9 48	8 21	6 45	4 58	2 58	0 ♒ 43	28 9	25 14	21 51	17 57	13 25	8 8
15 51 16	30	25 33	24 34	23 32	22 25	21 12	19 52	19 8	18 22	17 33	16 41	15 45	14 44	13 39	12 28	11 9	9 43	8 8	6 22	4 23	2 8	29 34	26 38	23 15	19 18	14 42	9 18

		0°N	4°N	8°N	12°N	16°N	20°N	22°N	24°N	26°N	28°N	30°N	32°N	34°N	36°N	38°N	40°N	42°N	44°N	46°N	48°N	50°N	52°N	54°N	56°N	58°N	60°N
ST	MC	ASC	ASC	ASC	ASC	ASC	ASC	ASC	ASC	ASC	ASC	ASC	ASC	ASC	ASC	ASC	ASC	ASC	ASC	ASC	ASC	ASC	ASC	ASC	ASC	ASC	ASC
15 51 16	0 ♐	25 ♒ 33	24 ♒ 34	23 ♒ 32	22 ♒ 25	21 ♒ 12	19 ♒ 52	19 ♒ 8	18 ♒ 22	17 ♒ 33	16 ♒ 41	15 ♒ 45	14 ♒ 44	13 ♒ 39	12 ♒ 28	11 ♒ 9	9 ♒ 43	8 ♒ 8	6 ♒ 22	4 ♒ 23	2 ♒ 8	29 ♑ 34	26 ♑ 38	23 ♑ 15	19 ♑ 18	14 ♑ 42	9 ♑ 18
15 55 26	1	26 38	25 41	24 40	23 34	22 23	21 5	20 22	19 37	18 49	17 58	17 3	16 3	14 59	13 49	12 32	11 7	9 33	7 47	5 49	3 35	1 ♒ 1	28 5	24 40	20 41	16 1	10 31
15 59 37	2	27 43	26 47	25 48	24 44	23 35	22 18	21 37	20 53	20 6	19 16	18 22	17 23	16 20	15 11	13 55	12 31	10 58	9 14	7 17	5 3	2 30	29 34	26 8	22 7	17 23	11 47
16 3 49	3	28 49	27 54	26 57	25 55	24 47	23 33	22 52	22 9	21 23	20 34	19 41	18 44	17 42	16 34	15 20	13 57	12 25	10 43	8 46	6 34	4 2	1 ♒ 5	27 39	23 36	18 48	13 5
16 8 1	4	29 54	29 2	28 6	27 6	26 0	24 47	24 8	23 26	22 41	21 53	21 2	20 6	19 5	17 59	16 46	15 25	13 54	12 13	10 18	8 6	5 35	2 39	29 12	25 7	20 16	14 26
16 12 14	5	1 ♓ 1	0 ♓ 10	29 16	28 17	27 13	26 3	25 25	24 44	24 0	23 14	22 23	21 29	20 29	19 24	18 13	16 53	15 24	13 44	11 51	9 41	7 11	4 15	0 ♒ 48	26 42	21 47	15 51
16 16 27	6	2 7	1 18	0 ♓ 26	29 29	28 27	27 19	26 42	26 2	25 20	24 34	23 45	22 52	21 54	20 51	19 41	18 23	16 56	15 18	13 26	11 17	8 48	5 54	2 27	28 20	23 21	17 19
16 20 41	7	3 14	2 27	1 36	0 ♓ 42	29 42	28 36	28 0	27 21	26 40	25 56	25 9	24 17	23 21	22 19	21 10	19 54	18 29	16 53	15 3	12 56	10 29	7 36	4 10	0 ♒ 1	25 0	18 51
16 24 56	8	4 21	3 36	2 47	1 54	0 ♓ 57	29 53	29 18	28 41	28 1	27 19	26 32	25 42	24 48	23 47	22 41	21 27	20 4	18 29	16 41	14 37	12 12	9 20	5 55	1 47	26 43	20 28
16 29 11	9	5 29	4 45	3 58	3 8	2 12	1 ♓ 11	0 ♓ 37	0 ♓ 1	29 23	28 42	27 57	27 9	26 16	25 17	24 13	23 1	21 40	20 8	18 22	16 20	13 57	11 7	7 44	3 36	28 30	22 9
16 33 26	10	6 37	5 55	5 10	4 21	3 28	2 29	1 57	1 22	0 ♓ 45	0 ♓ 6	29 23	28 36	27 45	26 48	25 46	24 36	23 17	21 48	20 5	18 5	15 45	12 58	9 36	5 29	0 ♒ 21	23 55
16 37 43	11	7 45	7 5	6 22	5 36	4 45	3 48	3 17	2 44	2 9	1 30	0 ♓ 49	0 ♓ 4	29 15	28 20	27 20	26 12	24 56	23 29	21 49	19 53	17 35	14 51	11 32	7 26	2 18	25 47
16 41 59	12	8 53	8 15	7 34	6 50	6 1	5 7	4 38	4 6	3 32	2 56	2 16	1 33	0 ♓ 46	29 53	28 55	27 50	26 37	25 13	23 36	21 43	19 29	16 48	13 32	9 28	4 20	27 44
16 46 17	13	10 2	9 26	8 47	8 5	7 19	6 27	5 59	5 29	4 57	4 22	3 44	3 3	2 17	1 ♓ 27	0 ♓ 32	29 29	28 19	26 58	25 24	23 34	21 24	18 48	15 35	11 34	6 27	29 49
16 50 34	14	11 11	10 37	10 0	9 20	8 36	7 48	7 21	6 52	6 22	5 49	5 13	4 33	3 50	3 2	2 9	1 ♓ 10	0 ♓ 2	28 44	27 14	25 29	23 23	20 51	17 43	13 46	8 41	2 ♒ 0
16 54 52	15	12 20	11 48	11 13	10 36	9 55	9 9	8 43	8 16	7 47	7 16	6 42	6 5	5 24	4 38	3 48	2 51	1 47	0 ♓ 32	29 6	27 25	25 24	22 57	19 54	16 2	11 1	4 19
16 59 11	16	13 30	13 0	12 27	11 52	11 13	10 30	10 6	9 41	9 13	8 44	8 12	7 37	6 58	6 15	5 28	4 34	3 33	2 22	1 ♓ 0	29 24	27 28	25 6	22 10	18 24	13 27	6 47
17 3 30	17	14 40	14 11	13 41	13 8	12 32	11 52	11 29	11 6	10 40	10 12	9 42	9 9	8 33	7 53	7 8	6 18	5 20	4 14	2 56	1 ♓ 24	29 34	27 19	24 29	20 51	16 1	9 24
17 7 49	18	15 50	15 23	14 55	14 25	13 51	13 14	12 53	12 31	12 7	11 42	11 14	10 43	10 9	9 32	8 50	8 3	7 9	6 6	4 54	3 27	1 ♓ 43	29 35	26 53	23 23	18 42	12 11
17 12 9	19	17 0	16 36	16 10	15 42	15 11	14 36	14 17	13 57	13 35	13 11	12 45	12 17	11 46	11 11	10 32	9 48	8 58	8 0	6 53	5 32	3 55	1 ♓ 54	29 21	26 1	21 31	15 8
17 16 29	20	18 10	17 48	17 25	16 59	16 31	15 59	15 42	15 23	15 3	14 41	14 18	13 52	13 23	12 51	12 16	11 35	10 49	9 56	8 53	7 39	6 8	4 16	1 ♓ 53	28 45	24 27	18 17
17 20 49	21	19 21	19 1	18 39	18 16	17 51	17 22	17 6	16 50	16 31	16 12	15 50	15 27	15 1	14 32	14 0	13 23	12 41	11 53	10 56	9 47	8 24	6 41	4 29	1 ♓ 34	27 31	21 37
17 25 10	22	20 31	20 14	19 55	19 34	19 11	18 46	18 32	18 17	18 0	17 43	17 24	17 3	16 39	16 14	15 45	15 12	14 34	13 50	12 59	11 58	10 43	9 9	7 8	4 28	0 ♓ 43	25 10
17 29 30	23	21 42	21 27	21 10	20 52	20 32	20 9	19 57	19 44	19 30	19 14	18 57	18 39	18 18	17 56	17 30	17 1	16 28	15 49	15 4	14 9	13 3	11 39	9 51	7 27	4 3	28 55
17 33 51	24	22 53	22 40	22 25	22 10	21 53	21 33	21 23	21 11	20 59	20 46	20 31	20 15	19 58	19 38	19 16	18 51	18 22	17 49	17 10	16 22	15 25	14 12	12 38	10 30	7 29	2 ♓ 53
17 38 13	25	24 4	23 53	23 41	23 28	23 14	22 57	22 49	22 39	22 29	22 18	22 6	21 52	21 38	21 21	21 3	20 42	20 18	19 50	19 17	18 37	17 48	16 47	15 27	13 38	11 3	7 2
17 42 34	26	25 15	25 6	24 57	24 46	24 35	24 22	24 15	24 7	23 59	23 50	23 40	23 29	23 18	23 4	22 50	22 33	22 13	21 51	21 24	20 52	20 13	19 23	18 18	16 50	14 42	11 23
17 46 55	27	26 26	26 20	26 12	26 5	25 56	25 46	25 41	25 35	25 29	25 22	25 15	25 7	24 58	24 48	24 37	24 24	24 10	23 53	23 33	23 8	22 39	22 1	21 12	20 5	18 27	15 53
17 51 17	28	27 37	27 33	27 28	27 23	27 17	27 11	27 7	27 3	26 59	26 55	26 50	26 44	26 39	26 32	26 24	26 16	26 6	25 55	25 41	25 25	25 5	24 40	24 7	23 22	22 16	20 31
17 55 38	29	28 49	28 46	28 44	28 41	28 39	28 35	28 34	28 32	28 30	28 27	28 25	28 22	28 19	28 16	28 12	28 8	28 3	27 57	27 51	27 42	27 32	27 20	27 3	26 40	26 7	25 14
18 0 0	30	0 ♈ 0	0 ♈ 0	0 ♈ 0	0 ♈ 0	0 ♈ 0	0 ♈ 0	0 ♈ 0	0 ♈ 0	0 ♈ 0	0 ♈ 0	0 ♈ 0	0 ♈ 0	0 ♈ 0	0 ♈ 0	0 ♈ 0	0 ♈ 0	0 ♈ 0	0 ♈ 0	0 ♈ 0	0 ♈ 0	0 ♈ 0	0 ♈ 0	0 ♈ 0	0 ♈ 0	0 ♈ 0	0 ♈ 0

KEY: N: NORTHERN LATITUDE ST: SIDEREAL TIME MC: MIDHEAVEN ASC: ASCENDANT

NORTHERN LATITUDE

		0°N	4°N	8°N	12°N	16°N	20°N	22°N	24°N	26°N	28°N	30°N	32°N	34°N	36°N	38°N	40°N	42°N	44°N	46°N	48°N	50°N	52°N	54°N	56°N	58°N	60°N
ST	MC	ASC	ASC	ASC	ASC	ASC	ASC	ASC	ASC	ASC	ASC	ASC	ASC	ASC	ASC	ASC	ASC	ASC	ASC	ASC	ASC	ASC	ASC	ASC	ASC	ASC	ASC
18 0 0	0 ♑	0 ♈ 0	0 ♈ 0	0 ♈ 0	0 ♈ 0	0 ♈ 0	0 ♈ 0	0 ♈ 0	0 ♈ 0	0 ♈ 0	0 ♈ 0	0 ♈ 0	0 ♈ 0	0 ♈ 0	0 ♈ 0	0 ♈ 0	0 ♈ 0	0 ♈ 0	0 ♈ 0	0 ♈ 0	0 ♈ 0	0 ♈ 0	0 ♈ 0	0 ♈ 0	0 ♈ 0	0 ♈ 0	0 ♈ 0
18 4 22	1	1 11	1 14	1 16	1 19	1 21	1 25	1 26	1 28	1 30	1 33	1 35	1 38	1 41	1 44	1 48	1 52	1 57	2 3	2 9	2 18	2 28	2 40	2 57	3 20	3 53	4 46
18 8 43	2	2 23	2 27	2 32	2 37	2 43	2 49	2 53	2 57	3 1	3 5	3 10	3 16	3 21	3 28	3 36	3 44	3 54	4 5	4 19	4 35	4 55	5 20	5 53	6 38	7 44	9 29
18 13 5	3	3 34	3 40	3 48	3 55	4 4	4 14	4 19	4 25	4 31	4 38	4 45	4 53	5 2	5 12	5 23	5 36	5 50	6 7	6 27	6 52	7 21	7 59	8 48	9 55	11 33	14 7
18 17 26	4	4 45	4 54	5 3	5 14	5 25	5 38	5 45	5 53	6 1	6 10	6 20	6 31	6 42	6 56	7 10	7 27	7 47	8 9	8 36	9 8	9 47	10 37	11 42	13 10	15 18	18 37
18 21 47	5	5 56	6 7	6 19	6 32	6 46	7 3	7 11	7 21	7 31	7 42	7 54	8 8	8 22	8 39	8 57	9 18	9 42	10 10	10 43	11 23	12 12	13 13	14 33	16 22	18 57	22 58
18 26 9	6	7 7	7 20	7 35	7 50	8 7	8 27	8 37	8 49	9 1	9 14	9 29	9 45	10 2	10 22	10 44	11 9	11 38	12 11	12 50	13 38	14 35	15 48	17 22	19 30	22 31	27 7
18 30 30	7	8 18	8 33	8 50	9 8	9 28	9 51	10 3	10 16	10 30	10 46	11 3	11 21	11 42	12 4	12 30	12 59	13 32	14 11	14 56	15 51	16 57	18 21	20 9	22 33	25 57	1 ♉ 5
18 34 50	8	9 29	9 46	10 5	10 26	10 49	11 14	11 28	11 43	12 0	12 17	12 36	12 57	13 21	13 46	14 15	14 48	15 26	16 10	17 1	18 2	19 17	20 51	22 52	25 32	29 17	4 50
18 39 11	9	10 39	10 59	11 21	11 44	12 9	12 38	12 54	13 10	13 29	13 48	14 10	14 33	14 59	15 28	16 0	16 37	17 19	18 7	19 4	20 13	21 36	23 19	25 31	28 26	2 ♉ 29	8 23
18 43 31	10	11 50	12 12	12 35	13 1	13 29	14 1	14 18	14 37	14 57	15 19	15 42	16 8	16 37	17 9	17 44	18 25	19 11	20 4	21 7	22 21	23 52	25 44	28 7	1 ♉ 15	5 33	11 43
18 47 51	11	13 0	13 24	13 50	14 18	14 49	15 24	15 43	16 3	16 25	16 49	17 15	17 43	18 14	18 49	19 28	20 12	21 2	22 0	23 7	24 28	26 5	28 6	0 ♉ 39	3 59	8 29	14 52
18 52 11	12	14 10	14 37	15 5	15 35	16 9	16 46	17 7	17 29	17 53	18 18	18 46	19 17	19 51	20 28	21 10	21 57	22 51	23 54	25 6	26 33	28 17	0 ♉ 25	3 7	6 37	11 18	17 49
18 56 30	13	15 20	15 49	16 19	16 52	17 28	18 8	18 31	18 54	19 20	19 48	20 18	20 51	21 27	22 7	22 52	23 42	24 40	25 46	27 4	28 36	0 ♉ 26	2 41	5 31	9 9	13 59	20 36
19 0 49	14	16 30	17 0	17 33	18 8	18 47	19 30	19 54	20 19	20 47	21 16	21 48	22 23	23 2	23 45	24 32	25 26	26 27	27 38	29 0	0 ♉ 36	2 32	4 54	7 50	11 36	16 33	23 13
19 5 8	15	17 40	18 12	18 47	19 24	20 5	20 51	21 17	21 44	22 13	22 44	23 18	23 55	24 36	25 22	26 12	27 9	28 13	29 28	0 ♉ 54	2 35	4 36	7 3	10 6	13 58	18 59	25 41
19 9 26	16	18 49	19 23	20 0	20 40	21 24	22 12	22 39	23 8	23 38	24 11	24 47	25 27	26 10	26 58	27 51	28 50	29 58	1 ♉ 16	2 46	4 31	6 37	9 9	12 17	16 14	21 19	28 0
19 13 43	17	19 58	20 34	21 13	21 55	22 41	23 33	24 1	24 31	25 3	25 38	26 16	26 57	27 43	28 33	29 28	0 ♉ 31	1 ♉ 41	3 2	4 36	6 26	8 36	11 12	14 25	18 26	23 33	0 ♊ 11
19 18 1	18	21 7	21 45	22 26	23 10	23 59	24 53	25 22	25 54	26 28	27 4	27 44	28 27	29 14	0 ♉ 7	1 ♉ 5	2 10	3 23	4 47	6 24	8 17	10 31	13 12	16 28	20 32	25 40	2 16
19 22 17	19	22 15	22 55	23 38	24 24	25 15	26 12	26 43	27 16	27 51	28 30	29 11	29 56	0 ♉ 45	1 40	2 40	3 48	5 4	6 31	8 11	10 7	12 25	15 9	18 28	22 34	27 42	4 13
19 26 34	20	23 23	24 5	24 50	25 39	26 32	27 31	28 3	28 38	29 15	29 54	0 ♉ 37	1 ♉ 24	2 15	3 12	4 14	5 24	6 43	8 12	9 55	11 55	14 15	17 2	20 24	24 31	29 39	6 5
19 30 49	21	24 31	25 15	26 2	26 52	27 48	28 49	29 23	29 59	0 ♉ 37	1 ♉ 18	2 3	2 51	3 44	4 43	5 47	6 59	8 20	9 52	11 38	13 40	16 3	18 53	22 16	26 24	1 ♊ 30	7 51
19 35 4	22	25 39	26 24	27 13	28 6	29 3	0 ♉ 7	0 ♉ 42	1 ♉ 19	1 59	2 41	3 28	4 18	5 12	6 13	7 19	8 33	9 56	11 31	13 19	15 23	17 48	20 40	24 5	28 13	3 17	9 32
19 39 19	23	26 46	27 33	28 24	29 18	0 ♉ 18	1 24	2 0	2 39	3 20	4 4	4 51	5 43	6 39	7 41	8 50	10 6	11 31	13 7	14 57	17 4	19 31	22 24	25 50	29 59	5 0	11 9
19 43 33	24	27 53	28 42	29 34	0 ♉ 31	1 33	2 41	3 18	3 58	4 40	5 26	6 15	7 8	8 6	9 9	10 19	11 37	13 4	14 42	16 34	18 43	21 12	24 6	27 33	1 ♊ 40	6 39	12 41
19 47 46	25	28 59	29 50	0 ♉ 44	1 43	2 47	3 57	4 35	5 16	6 0	6 46	7 37	8 31	9 31	10 36	11 47	13 7	14 36	16 16	18 9	20 19	22 49	25 45	29 12	3 18	8 13	14 9
19 51 59	26	0 ♉ 6	0 ♉ 58	1 54	2 54	4 0	5 13	5 52	6 34	7 19	8 7	8 58	9 54	10 55	12 1	13 14	14 35	16 6	17 47	19 42	21 54	24 25	27 21	0 ♊ 48	4 53	9 44	15 34
19 56 11	27	1 11	2 6	3 3	4 5	5 13	6 27	7 8	7 51	8 37	9 26	10 19	11 16	12 18	13 26	14 40	16 3	17 35	19 17	21 14	23 26	25 58	28 55	2 21	6 24	11 12	16 55
20 0 23	28	2 17	3 13	4 12	5 16	6 25	7 42	8 23	9 7	9 54	10 44	11 38	12 37	13 40	14 49	16 5	17 29	19 2	20 46	22 43	24 57	27 30	0 ♊ 26	3 52	7 53	12 37	18 13
20 4 34	29	3 22	4 19	5 20	6 26	7 37	8 55	9 38	10 23	11 11	12 2	12 57	13 57	15 1	16 11	17 28	18 53	20 27	22 13	24 11	26 25	28 59	1 55	5 20	9 19	13 59	19 29
20 8 44	30	4 27	5 26	6 28	7 35	8 48	10 8	10 52	11 38	12 27	13 19	14 15	15 16	16 21	17 32	18 51	20 17	21 52	23 38	25 37	27 52	0 ♊ 26	3 22	6 45	10 42	15 18	20 42

		0°N	4°N	8°N	12°N	16°N	20°N	22°N	24°N	26°N	28°N	30°N	32°N	34°N	36°N	38°N	40°N	42°N	44°N	46°N	48°N	50°N	52°N	54°N	56°N	58°N	60°N
ST	MC	ASC	ASC	ASC	ASC	ASC	ASC	ASC	ASC	ASC	ASC	ASC	ASC	ASC	ASC	ASC	ASC	ASC	ASC	ASC	ASC	ASC	ASC	ASC	ASC	ASC	ASC
20 8 44	0 ♒	4 ♉ 27	5 ♉ 26	6 ♉ 28	7 ♉ 35	8 ♉ 48	10 ♉ 8	10 ♉ 52	11 ♉ 38	12 ♉ 27	13 ♉ 19	14 ♉ 15	15 ♉ 16	16 ♉ 21	17 ♉ 32	18 ♉ 51	20 ♉ 17	21 ♉ 52	23 ♉ 38	25 ♉ 37	27 ♉ 52	0 ♊ 26	3 ♊ 22	6 ♊ 45	10 ♊ 42	15 ♊ 18	20 ♊ 42
20 12 53	1	5 31	6 32	7 36	8 44	9 59	11 21	12 5	12 52	13 42	14 35	15 32	16 34	17 40	18 53	20 12	21 39	23 15	25 2	27 2	29 17	1 51	4 46	8 9	12 3	16 35	21 52
20 17 2	2	6 35	7 37	8 43	9 53	11 9	12 33	13 18	14 5	14 56	15 50	16 48	17 51	18 58	20 12	21 32	22 59	24 36	26 24	28 25	0 ♊ 40	3 14	6 9	9 30	13 21	17 50	23 1
20 21 10	3	7 39	8 42	9 49	11 1	12 19	13 44	14 30	15 18	16 10	17 5	18 4	19 7	20 15	21 30	22 50	24 19	25 57	27 45	29 46	2 2	4 35	7 29	10 48	14 38	19 2	24 7
20 25 18	4	8 43	9 47	10 56	12 9	13 28	14 54	15 41	16 30	17 23	18 19	19 18	20 22	21 32	22 46	24 8	25 37	27 16	29 4	1 ♊ 6	3 21	5 54	8 48	12 5	15 52	20 12	25 11
20 29 25	5	9 45	10 51	12 1	13 16	14 36	16 4	16 52	17 42	18 35	19 32	20 32	21 37	22 47	24 2	25 25	26 55	28 33	0 ♊ 22	2 24	4 39	7 12	10 4	13 20	17 4	21 20	26 13
20 33 31	6	10 48	11 55	13 6	14 22	15 44	17 14	18 2	18 53	19 46	20 44	21 45	22 50	24 1	25 17	26 40	28 10	29 50	1 39	3 41	5 56	8 28	11 19	14 33	18 14	22 26	27 14
20 37 36	7	11 50	12 59	14 11	15 28	16 51	18 22	19 11	20 3	20 57	21 55	22 57	24 3	25 14	26 31	27 54	29 25	1 ♊ 5	2 55	4 56	7 11	9 42	12 32	15 45	19 23	23 31	28 13
20 41 40	8	12 52	14 2	15 16	16 34	17 58	19 30	20 20	21 12	22 7	23 6	24 8	25 15	26 27	27 44	29 8	0 ♊ 39	2 19	4 9	6 10	8 25	10 55	13 44	16 55	20 30	24 34	29 11
20 45 44	9	13 54	15 5	16 19	17 39	19 5	20 38	21 28	22 21	23 16	24 16	25 19	26 26	27 38	28 56	0 ♊ 20	1 52	3 32	5 22	7 23	9 37	12 7	14 54	18 3	21 35	25 36	0 ♋ 7
20 49 47	10	14 55	16 7	17 23	18 44	20 10	21 45	22 35	23 29	24 25	25 25	26 28	27 36	28 49	0 ♊ 7	1 31	3 3	4 43	6 33	8 34	10 48	13 17	16 3	19 9	22 39	26 36	1 2
20 53 50	11	15 56	17 9	18 26	19 48	21 16	22 51	23 42	24 36	25 33	26 33	27 37	28 45	29 58	1 17	2 42	4 14	5 54	7 44	9 44	11 58	14 25	17 10	20 15	23 42	27 34	1 56
20 57 51	12	16 56	18 10	19 28	20 51	22 20	23 57	24 48	25 43	26 40	27 41	28 45	29 54	1 ♊ 7	2 26	3 51	5 23	7 4	8 53	10 53	13 6	15 33	18 16	21 19	24 43	28 32	2 49
21 1 52	13	17 56	19 11	20 30	21 54	23 24	25 2	25 54	26 49	27 47	28 48	29 52	1 ♊ 1	2 15	3 34	5 0	6 32	8 12	10 1	12 1	14 13	16 39	19 21	22 21	25 43	29 28	3 41
21 5 52	14	18 56	20 12	21 32	22 57	24 28	26 6	26 59	27 54	28 52	29 54	0 ♊ 59	2 8	3 22	4 42	6 7	7 39	9 19	11 9	13 8	15 19	17 44	20 24	23 23	26 41	0 ♋ 23	4 31
21 9 52	15	19 55	21 12	22 33	23 59	25 31	27 10	28 3	28 59	29 58	0 ♊ 59	2 5	3 14	4 29	5 48	7 14	8 46	10 26	12 15	14 14	16 24	18 48	21 27	24 23	27 39	1 17	5 21
21 13 51	16	20 54	22 12	23 34	25 1	26 34	28 14	29 7	0 ♊ 3	1 ♊ 2	2 4	3 10	4 20	5 34	6 54	8 20	9 52	11 31	13 20	15 18	17 28	19 50	22 28	25 22	28 35	2 11	6 10
21 17 49	17	21 52	23 12	24 35	26 2	27 36	29 17	0 ♊ 10	1 7	2 6	3 8	4 14	5 25	6 39	7 59	9 24	10 57	12 36	14 24	16 22	18 31	20 52	23 28	26 20	29 31	3 3	6 58
21 21 46	18	22 51	24 11	25 35	27 3	28 37	0 ♊ 19	1 13	2 10	3 9	4 12	5 18	6 29	7 43	9 3	10 29	12 1	13 40	15 27	17 24	19 32	21 53	24 27	27 17	0 ♋ 25	3 54	7 45
21 25 43	19	23 49	25 10	26 34	28 3	29 39	1 21	2 15	3 12	4 12	5 15	6 21	7 32	8 47	10 6	11 32	13 4	14 43	16 30	18 26	20 33	22 52	25 25	28 13	1 19	4 44	8 32
21 29 39	20	24 46	26 8	27 33	29 3	0 ♊ 39	2 22	3 17	4 14	5 14	6 17	7 24	8 34	9 49	11 9	12 34	14 6	15 45	17 31	19 27	21 33	23 51	26 22	29 8	2 11	5 34	9 17
21 33 34	21	25 43	27 6	28 32	0 ♊ 3	1 39	3 23	4 18	5 15	6 16	7 19	8 26	9 36	10 51	12 11	13 36	15 7	16 46	18 32	20 27	22 32	24 49	27 18	0 ♋ 2	3 3	6 23	10 2
21 37 28	22	26 40	28 4	29 31	1 2	2 39	4 23	5 18	6 16	7 17	8 20	9 27	10 38	11 52	13 12	14 37	16 8	17 46	19 32	21 26	23 30	25 46	28 14	0 56	3 54	7 11	10 47
21 41 22	23	27 37	29 1	0 ♊ 29	2 1	3 38	5 23	6 19	7 16	8 17	9 21	10 27	11 38	12 53	14 13	15 38	17 8	18 46	20 31	22 24	24 28	26 42	29 8	1 49	4 45	7 58	11 31
21 45 16	24	28 33	29 58	1 26	2 59	4 37	6 22	7 18	8 16	9 17	10 20	11 27	12 38	13 53	15 12	16 37	18 8	19 45	21 29	23 22	25 24	27 37	0 ♋ 2	2 40	5 34	8 45	12 14
21 49 8	25	29 29	0 ♊ 55	2 24	3 57	5 36	7 21	8 17	9 15	10 16	11 20	12 27	13 38	14 52	16 12	17 36	19 6	20 43	22 27	24 19	26 20	28 32	0 55	3 32	6 23	9 31	12 57
21 53 0	26	0 ♊ 25	1 51	3 21	4 55	6 34	8 20	9 16	10 14	11 15	12 19	13 26	14 36	15 51	17 10	18 34	20 4	21 40	23 24	25 15	27 15	29 26	1 47	4 22	7 11	10 16	13 39
21 56 51	27	1 20	2 47	4 17	5 52	7 31	9 18	10 14	11 12	12 13	13 17	14 24	15 35	16 49	18 8	19 32	21 2	22 37	24 20	26 10	28 9	0 ♋ 19	2 39	5 12	7 59	11 1	14 21
22 0 42	28	2 16	3 43	5 14	6 48	8 29	10 15	11 11	12 10	13 11	14 15	15 22	16 32	17 47	19 6	20 29	21 58	23 33	25 15	27 5	29 3	1 11	3 30	6 1	8 46	11 45	15 2
22 4 32	29	3 10	4 38	6 10	7 45	9 25	11 12	12 9	13 7	14 8	15 12	16 19	17 30	18 44	20 2	21 26	22 54	24 29	26 10	27 59	29 56	2 3	4 20	6 49	9 32	12 29	15 43
22 8 22	30	4 5	5 34	7 5	8 41	10 22	12 9	13 5	14 4	15 5	16 9	17 16	18 26	19 40	20 59	22 22	23 50	25 24	27 5	28 52	0 ♋ 49	2 54	5 10	7 37	10 18	13 12	16 23

		0°N	4°N	8°N	12°N	16°N	20°N	22°N	24°N	26°N	28°N	30°N	32°N	34°N	36°N	38°N	40°N	42°N	44°N	46°N	48°N	50°N	52°N	54°N	56°N	58°N	60°N
ST	MC	ASC	ASC	ASC	ASC	ASC	ASC	ASC	ASC	ASC	ASC	ASC	ASC	ASC	ASC	ASC	ASC	ASC	ASC	ASC	ASC	ASC	ASC	ASC	ASC	ASC	ASC
22 8 22	0 ♓	4 ♊ 5	5 ♊ 34	7 ♊ 5	8 ♊ 41	10 ♊ 22	12 ♊ 9	13 ♊ 5	14 ♊ 4	15 ♊ 5	16 ♊ 9	17 ♊ 16	18 ♊ 26	19 ♊ 40	20 ♊ 59	22 ♊ 22	23 ♊ 50	25 ♊ 24	27 ♊ 5	28 ♊ 52	0 ♋ 49	2 ♋ 54	5 ♋ 10	7 ♋ 37	10 ♋ 18	13 ♋ 12	16 ♋ 23
22 12 11	1	4 59	6 29	8 1	9 37	11 18	13 5	14 2	15 1	16 2	17 6	18 12	19 23	20 36	21 54	23 17	24 45	26 18	27 58	29 45	1 41	3 45	5 59	8 25	11 3	13 55	17 3
22 15 59	2	5 53	7 23	8 56	10 32	12 14	14 1	14 58	15 57	16 58	18 1	19 8	20 18	21 32	22 50	24 12	25 39	27 12	28 51	0 ♋ 38	2 32	4 35	6 48	9 12	11 48	14 38	17 43
22 19 47	3	6 47	8 17	9 50	11 27	13 9	14 57	15 53	16 52	17 53	18 57	20 4	21 13	22 27	23 44	25 6	26 33	28 5	29 44	1 29	3 23	5 24	7 36	9 58	12 32	15 20	18 22
22 23 34	4	7 41	9 12	10 45	12 22	14 4	15 52	16 49	17 47	18 48	19 52	20 59	22 8	23 21	24 39	26 0	27 26	28 58	0 ♋ 36	2 21	4 13	6 13	8 23	10 44	13 16	16 1	19 1
22 27 21	5	8 34	10 5	11 39	13 17	14 59	16 47	17 43	18 42	19 43	20 47	21 53	23 3	24 16	25 32	26 53	28 19	29 50	1 28	3 11	5 2	7 2	9 10	11 29	14 0	16 42	19 39
22 31 8	6	9 27	10 59	12 33	14 11	15 53	17 41	18 38	19 37	20 38	21 41	22 47	23 56	25 9	26 26	27 46	29 12	0 ♋ 42	2 19	4 2	5 52	7 50	9 57	12 14	14 43	17 23	20 18
22 34 54	7	10 20	11 52	13 27	15 5	16 47	18 35	19 32	20 31	21 32	22 35	23 41	24 50	26 2	27 19	28 39	0 ♋ 4	1 34	3 9	4 51	6 40	8 37	10 43	12 59	15 25	18 4	20 56
22 38 39	8	11 13	12 45	14 20	15 58	17 41	19 29	20 26	21 24	22 25	23 28	24 34	25 43	26 55	28 11	29 31	0 55	2 24	3 59	5 41	7 29	9 24	11 29	13 43	16 7	18 44	21 33
22 42 24	9	12 6	13 38	15 13	16 52	18 34	20 23	21 19	22 18	23 19	24 22	25 27	26 36	27 48	29 3	0 ♋ 22	1 46	3 15	4 49	6 29	8 17	10 11	12 14	14 27	16 49	19 24	22 11
22 46 8	10	12 58	14 31	16 6	17 45	19 28	21 16	22 12	23 11	24 11	25 14	26 20	27 28	28 40	29 55	1 14	2 37	4 5	5 38	7 18	9 4	10 57	12 59	15 10	17 31	20 3	22 48
22 49 53	11	13 50	15 24	16 59	18 38	20 21	22 9	23 5	24 4	25 4	26 7	27 12	28 20	29 31	0 ♋ 46	2 4	3 27	4 55	6 27	8 6	9 51	11 43	13 44	15 53	18 12	20 42	23 25
22 53 36	12	14 42	16 16	17 52	19 30	21 13	23 1	23 58	24 56	25 56	26 59	28 4	29 12	0 ♋ 23	1 37	2 55	4 17	5 44	7 16	8 54	10 38	12 29	14 28	16 36	18 53	21 21	24 1
22 57 20	13	15 34	17 8	18 44	20 23	22 6	23 54	24 50	25 48	26 49	27 51	28 56	0 ♋ 3	1 14	2 28	3 45	5 7	6 33	8 4	9 41	11 24	13 14	15 12	17 18	19 34	22 0	24 38
23 1 3	14	16 26	18 0	19 36	21 15	22 58	24 46	25 42	26 40	27 40	28 42	29 47	0 54	2 4	3 18	4 35	5 56	7 21	8 52	10 28	12 10	13 59	15 55	18 0	20 14	22 39	25 14
23 4 45	15	17 17	18 52	20 28	22 7	23 50	25 38	26 34	27 32	28 32	29 34	0 ♋ 38	1 45	2 55	4 8	5 24	6 45	8 10	9 39	11 15	12 56	14 44	16 39	18 42	20 54	23 17	25 50
23 8 28	16	18 9	19 43	21 20	22 59	24 42	26 30	27 26	28 23	29 23	0 ♋ 25	1 29	2 35	3 45	4 57	6 13	7 33	8 58	10 27	12 1	13 41	15 28	17 22	19 23	21 34	23 55	26 26
23 12 10	17	19 0	20 35	22 11	23 51	25 33	27 21	28 17	29 15	0 ♋ 14	1 15	2 19	3 26	4 35	5 47	7 2	8 22	9 45	11 14	12 47	14 26	16 12	18 4	20 5	22 14	24 33	27 2
23 15 52	18	19 51	21 26	23 3	24 42	26 25	28 12	29 8	0 ♋ 6	1 5	2 6	3 9	4 15	5 24	6 36	7 51	9 10	10 33	12 0	13 33	15 11	16 55	18 47	20 46	22 53	25 10	27 37
23 19 33	19	20 43	22 18	23 54	25 33	27 16	29 3	29 59	0 56	1 55	2 56	3 59	5 5	6 13	7 25	8 39	9 57	11 20	12 46	14 18	15 55	17 39	19 29	21 26	23 32	25 48	28 13
23 23 15	20	21 34	23 9	24 45	26 25	28 7	29 54	0 ♋ 50	1 47	2 46	3 46	4 49	5 54	7 2	8 13	9 27	10 45	12 7	13 33	15 3	16 40	18 22	20 11	22 7	24 11	26 25	28 48
23 26 56	21	22 24	24 0	25 37	27 16	28 58	0 ♋ 45	1 40	2 37	3 36	4 36	5 39	6 44	7 51	9 2	10 15	11 32	12 53	14 18	15 48	17 24	19 5	20 52	22 47	24 50	27 2	29 23
23 30 37	22	23 15	24 51	26 27	28 7	29 49	1 35	2 31	3 27	4 26	5 26	6 28	7 33	8 40	9 50	11 3	12 19	13 39	15 4	16 33	18 7	19 48	21 34	23 27	25 29	27 39	29 58
23 34 18	23	24 6	25 41	27 18	28 57	0 ♋ 39	2 26	3 21	4 17	5 15	6 15	7 17	8 21	9 28	10 37	11 50	13 6	14 25	15 49	17 18	18 51	20 30	22 15	24 7	26 7	28 15	0 ♌ 33
23 37 58	24	24 57	26 32	28 9	29 48	1 30	3 16	4 11	5 7	6 5	7 4	8 6	9 10	10 16	11 25	12 37	13 52	15 11	16 34	18 2	19 34	21 12	22 56	24 47	26 45	28 52	1 8
23 41 39	25	25 47	27 23	29 0	0 ♋ 39	2 20	4 6	5 1	5 57	6 54	7 54	8 55	9 58	11 4	12 13	13 24	14 39	15 57	17 19	18 46	20 17	21 54	23 37	25 27	27 24	29 29	1 42
23 45 19	26	26 38	28 14	29 50	1 29	3 11	4 56	5 50	6 46	7 43	8 42	9 43	10 46	11 52	13 0	14 11	15 25	16 42	18 4	19 30	21 0	22 36	24 18	26 6	28 2	0 ♌ 5	2 17
23 48 59	27	27 28	29 4	0 ♋ 41	2 19	4 1	5 46	6 40	7 35	8 32	9 31	10 32	11 35	12 40	13 47	14 57	16 11	17 28	18 49	20 13	21 43	23 18	24 59	26 45	28 39	0 41	2 52
23 52 40	28	28 19	29 55	1 31	3 10	4 51	6 35	7 29	8 25	9 21	10 20	11 20	12 22	13 27	14 34	15 44	16 57	18 13	19 33	20 57	22 26	24 0	25 39	27 25	29 17	1 17	3 26
23 56 20	29	29 9	0 ♋ 45	2 22	4 0	5 41	7 25	8 19	9 14	10 10	11 8	12 8	13 10	14 14	15 21	16 30	17 42	18 58	20 17	21 40	23 8	24 41	26 19	28 4	29 55	1 53	4 0
0 0 0	30	0 ♋ 0	1 36	3 12	4 50	6 31	8 14	9 8	10 3	10 59	11 57	12 56	13 58	15 1	16 7	17 16	18 28	19 43	21 1	22 24	23 51	25 22	26 59	28 43	0 ♌ 32	2 29	4 35

KEY: N: NORTHERN LATITUDE ST: SIDEREAL TIME MC: MIDHEAVEN ASC: ASCENDANT

YEAR	JAN	FEB	MAR	APR	MAY	JUN	JUL	AUG	SEP	OCT	NOV	DEC
1930	20 ♒ 18:33	19 ♓ 9:00	21 ♈ 8:30	20 ♉ 20:06	21 ♊ 19:42	22 ♋ 3:53	23 ♌ 14:42	23 ♍ 21:26	23 ♎ 18:36	24 ♏ 3:26	23 ♐ 0:34	22 ♑ 13:39
1931	21 ♒ 0:17	19 ♓ 14:40	21 ♈ 14:06	21 ♉ 1:40	22 ♊ 1:15	22 ♋ 9:28	23 ♌ 20:21	24 ♍ 3:10	24 ♎ 0:23	24 ♏ 9:15	23 ♐ 6:25	22 ♑ 19:30
1932	21 ♒ 6:07	19 ♓ 20:28	20 ♈ 19:54	20 ♉ 7:28	21 ♊ 7:07	21 ♋ 15:23	23 ♌ 2:18	23 ♍ 9:06	23 ♎ 6:16	23 ♏ 15:04	22 ♐ 12:10	22 ♑ 1:14
1933	20 ♒ 11:53	19 ♓ 2:16	21 ♈ 1:43	20 ♉ 13:18	21 ♊ 12:57	21 ♋ 21:12	23 ♌ 8:05	23 ♍ 14:52	23 ♎ 12:01	23 ♏ 20:48	22 ♐ 17:53	22 ♑ 6:57
1934	20 ♒ 17:37	19 ♓ 8:02	21 ♈ 7:28	20 ♉ 19:00	21 ♊ 18:35	22 ♋ 2:48	23 ♌ 13:42	23 ♍ 20:32	23 ♎ 17:45	24 ♏ 2:36	22 ♐ 23:44	22 ♑ 12:49
1935	20 ♒ 23:28	19 ♓ 13:52	21 ♈ 13:18	21 ♉ 0:50	22 ♊ 0:25	22 ♋ 8:38	23 ♌ 19:33	24 ♍ 2:24	23 ♎ 23:38	24 ♏ 8:29	23 ♐ 5:35	22 ♑ 18:37
1936	21 ♒ 5:12	19 ♓ 19:33	20 ♈ 18:58	20 ♉ 6:31	21 ♊ 6:07	21 ♋ 14:22	23 ♌ 1:18	23 ♍ 8:10	23 ♎ 5:26	23 ♏ 14:18	22 ♐ 11:25	22 ♑ 0:27
1937	20 ♒ 11:01	19 ♓ 1:21	21 ♈ 0:45	20 ♉ 12:19	21 ♊ 11:57	21 ♋ 20:12	23 ♌ 7:07	23 ♍ 13:58	23 ♎ 11:13	23 ♏ 20:06	22 ♐ 17:16	22 ♑ 6:22
1938	20 ♒ 16:59	19 ♓ 7:20	21 ♈ 6:43	20 ♉ 18:15	21 ♊ 17:50	22 ♋ 2:04	23 ♌ 12:57	23 ♍ 19:46	23 ♎ 16:59	24 ♏ 1:54	22 ♐ 23:06	22 ♑ 12:13
1939	20 ♒ 22:51	19 ♓ 13:09	21 ♈ 12:28	20 ♉ 23:55	21 ♊ 23:27	22 ♋ 7:39	23 ♌ 18:37	24 ♍ 1:31	23 ♎ 22:49	24 ♏ 7:46	23 ♐ 4:58	22 ♑ 18:06
1940	21 ♒ 4:44	19 ♓ 19:04	20 ♈ 18:24	20 ♉ 5:51	21 ♊ 5:23	21 ♋ 13:36	23 ♌ 0:34	23 ♍ 7:28	23 ♎ 4:46	23 ♏ 13:39	22 ♐ 10:49	21 ♑ 23:55
1941	20 ♒ 10:34	19 ♓ 0:56	21 ♈ 0:20	20 ♉ 11:50	21 ♊ 11:23	21 ♋ 19:33	23 ♌ 6:26	23 ♍ 13:17	23 ♎ 10:33	23 ♏ 19:27	22 ♐ 16:38	22 ♑ 5:44
1942	20 ♒ 16:23	19 ♓ 6:47	21 ♈ 6:11	20 ♉ 17:39	21 ♊ 17:09	22 ♋ 1:16	23 ♌ 12:07	23 ♍ 18:58	23 ♎ 16:16	24 ♏ 1:15	22 ♐ 22:30	22 ♑ 11:40
1943	20 ♒ 22:19	19 ♓ 12:40	21 ♈ 12:03	20 ♉ 23:31	21 ♊ 23:03	22 ♋ 7:12	23 ♌ 18:04	24 ♍ 0:55	23 ♎ 22:12	24 ♏ 7:08	23 ♐ 4:21	22 ♑ 17:29
1944	21 ♒ 4:07	19 ♓ 18:27	20 ♈ 17:49	20 ♉ 5:18	21 ♊ 4:51	21 ♋ 13:02	22 ♌ 23:56	23 ♍ 6:46	23 ♎ 4:02	23 ♏ 12:56	22 ♐ 10:08	21 ♑ 23:15
1945	20 ♒ 9:54	19 ♓ 0:15	20 ♈ 23:37	20 ♉ 11:07	21 ♊ 10:40	21 ♋ 18:52	23 ♌ 5:45	23 ♍ 12:35	23 ♎ 9:50	23 ♏ 18:44	22 ♐ 15:55	22 ♑ 5:04
1946	20 ♒ 15:45	19 ♓ 6:09	21 ♈ 5:33	20 ♉ 17:02	21 ♊ 16:34	22 ♋ 0:44	23 ♌ 11:37	23 ♍ 18:26	23 ♎ 15:41	24 ♏ 0:35	22 ♐ 21:46	22 ♑ 10:53
1947	20 ♒ 21:32	19 ♓ 11:52	21 ♈ 11:13	20 ♉ 22:39	21 ♊ 22:09	22 ♋ 6:19	23 ♌ 17:14	24 ♍ 0:09	23 ♎ 21:29	24 ♏ 6:26	23 ♐ 3:38	22 ♑ 16:43
1948	21 ♒ 3:18	19 ♓ 17:37	20 ♈ 16:57	20 ♉ 4:25	21 ♊ 3:58	21 ♋ 12:11	22 ♌ 23:08	23 ♍ 6:03	23 ♎ 3:22	23 ♏ 12:18	22 ♐ 9:29	21 ♑ 22:33
1949	20 ♒ 9:09	18 ♓ 23:27	20 ♈ 22:48	20 ♉ 10:17	21 ♊ 9:51	21 ♋ 18:03	23 ♌ 4:57	23 ♍ 11:48	23 ♎ 9:06	23 ♏ 18:03	22 ♐ 15:16	22 ♑ 4:23
1950	20 ♒ 15:00	19 ♓ 5:18	21 ♈ 4:35	20 ♉ 15:59	21 ♊ 15:27	21 ♋ 23:36	23 ♌ 10:30	23 ♍ 17:23	23 ♎ 14:44	23 ♏ 23:45	22 ♐ 21:03	22 ♑ 10:13
1951	20 ♒ 20:52	19 ♓ 11:10	21 ♈ 10:26	20 ♉ 21:48	21 ♊ 21:15	22 ♋ 5:25	23 ♌ 16:21	23 ♍ 23:16	23 ♎ 20:37	24 ♏ 5:36	23 ♐ 2:51	22 ♑ 16:00
1952	21 ♒ 2:38	19 ♓ 16:57	20 ♈ 16:14	20 ♉ 3:37	21 ♊ 3:04	21 ♋ 11:13	22 ♌ 22:07	23 ♍ 5:03	23 ♎ 2:24	23 ♏ 11:22	22 ♐ 8:36	21 ♑ 21:43
1953	20 ♒ 8:21	18 ♓ 22:41	20 ♈ 22:01	20 ♉ 9:25	21 ♊ 8:53	21 ♋ 17:00	23 ♌ 3:52	23 ♍ 10:45	23 ♎ 8:06	23 ♏ 17:06	22 ♐ 14:22	22 ♑ 3:31
1954	20 ♒ 14:11	19 ♓ 4:32	21 ♈ 3:53	20 ♉ 15:20	21 ♊ 14:47	21 ♋ 22:54	23 ♌ 9:45	23 ♍ 16:36	23 ♎ 13:55	23 ♏ 22:56	22 ♐ 20:14	22 ♑ 9:24
1955	20 ♒ 20:02	19 ♓ 10:19	21 ♈ 9:35	20 ♉ 20:58	21 ♊ 20:24	22 ♋ 4:31	23 ♌ 15:25	23 ♍ 22:19	23 ♎ 19:41	24 ♏ 4:43	23 ♐ 2:01	22 ♑ 15:11
1956	21 ♒ 1:48	19 ♓ 16:05	20 ♈ 15:20	20 ♉ 2:43	21 ♊ 2:13	21 ♋ 10:24	22 ♌ 21:20	23 ♍ 4:15	23 ♎ 1:35	23 ♏ 10:34	22 ♐ 7:50	21 ♑ 21:00
1957	20 ♒ 7:39	18 ♓ 21:58	20 ♈ 21:17	20 ♉ 8:41	21 ♊ 8:10	21 ♋ 16:21	23 ♌ 3:15	23 ♍ 10:08	23 ♎ 7:26	23 ♏ 16:24	22 ♐ 13:39	22 ♑ 2:49
1958	20 ♒ 13:29	19 ♓ 3:49	21 ♈ 3:06	20 ♉ 14:27	21 ♊ 13:51	21 ♋ 21:57	23 ♌ 8:51	23 ♍ 15:46	23 ♎ 13:09	23 ♏ 22:11	22 ♐ 19:29	22 ♑ 8:40
1959	20 ♒ 19:19	19 ♓ 9:38	21 ♈ 8:55	20 ♉ 20:17	21 ♊ 19:42	22 ♋ 3:50	23 ♌ 14:46	23 ♍ 21:44	23 ♎ 19:09	24 ♏ 4:11	23 ♐ 1:27	22 ♑ 14:34
1960	21 ♒ 1:10	19 ♓ 15:26	20 ♈ 14:43	20 ♉ 2:06	21 ♊ 1:34	21 ♋ 9:42	22 ♌ 20:38	23 ♍ 3:34	23 ♎ 0:59	23 ♏ 10:02	22 ♐ 7:18	21 ♑ 20:26
1961	20 ♒ 7:01	18 ♓ 21:17	20 ♈ 20:32	20 ♉ 7:55	21 ♊ 7:22	21 ♋ 15:30	23 ♌ 2:24	23 ♍ 9:19	23 ♎ 6:43	23 ♏ 15:47	22 ♐ 13:08	22 ♑ 2:20
1962	20 ♒ 12:58	19 ♓ 3:15	21 ♈ 2:30	20 ♉ 13:51	21 ♊ 13:17	21 ♋ 21:24	23 ♌ 8:18	23 ♍ 15:13	23 ♎ 12:35	23 ♏ 21:40	22 ♐ 19:02	22 ♑ 8:15
1963	20 ♒ 18:54	19 ♓ 9:09	21 ♈ 8:20	20 ♉ 19:36	21 ♊ 18:58	22 ♋ 3:04	23 ♌ 13:59	23 ♍ 20:58	23 ♎ 18:24	24 ♏ 3:29	23 ♐ 0:49	22 ♑ 14:02
1964	21 ♒ 0:41	19 ♓ 14:57	20 ♈ 14:10	20 ♉ 1:27	21 ♊ 0:50	21 ♋ 8:57	22 ♌ 19:53	23 ♍ 2:51	23 ♎ 0:17	23 ♏ 9:21	22 ♐ 6:39	21 ♑ 19:50
1965	20 ♒ 6:29	18 ♓ 20:48	20 ♈ 20:05	20 ♉ 7:26	21 ♊ 6:50	21 ♋ 14:56	23 ♌ 1:48	23 ♍ 8:43	23 ♎ 6:06	23 ♏ 15:10	22 ♐ 12:29	22 ♑ 1:41
1966	20 ♒ 12:20	19 ♓ 2:38	21 ♈ 1:53	20 ♉ 13:12	21 ♊ 12:32	21 ♋ 20:34	23 ♌ 7:23	23 ♍ 14:18	23 ♎ 11:43	23 ♏ 20:51	22 ♐ 18:14	22 ♑ 7:28
1967	20 ♒ 18:08	19 ♓ 8:24	21 ♈ 7:37	20 ♉ 18:55	21 ♊ 18:18	22 ♋ 2:23	23 ♌ 13:16	23 ♍ 20:13	23 ♎ 17:38	24 ♏ 2:44	23 ♐ 0:05	22 ♑ 13:16
1968	20 ♒ 23:54	19 ♓ 14:09	20 ♈ 13:22	20 ♉ 0:41	21 ♊ 0:06	21 ♋ 8:13	22 ♌ 19:08	23 ♍ 2:03	22 ♎ 23:26	23 ♏ 8:30	22 ♐ 5:49	21 ♑ 19:00
1969	20 ♒ 5:38	18 ♓ 19:55	20 ♈ 19:08	20 ♉ 6:27	21 ♊ 5:50	21 ♋ 13:55	23 ♌ 0:48	23 ♍ 7:44	23 ♎ 5:07	23 ♏ 14:11	22 ♐ 11:31	22 ♑ 0:44
1970	20 ♒ 11:24	19 ♓ 1:42	21 ♈ 0:57	20 ♉ 12:15	21 ♊ 11:38	21 ♋ 19:43	23 ♌ 6:37	23 ♍ 13:34	23 ♎ 10:59	23 ♏ 20:04	22 ♐ 17:25	22 ♑ 6:36
1971	20 ♒ 17:13	19 ♓ 7:27	21 ♈ 6:38	20 ♉ 17:54	21 ♊ 17:15	22 ♋ 1:20	23 ♌ 12:15	23 ♍ 19:15	23 ♎ 16:45	24 ♏ 1:53	22 ♐ 23:14	22 ♑ 12:24
1972	20 ♒ 22:59	19 ♓ 13:12	20 ♈ 12:22	19 ♉ 23:38	20 ♊ 23:00	21 ♋ 7:06	22 ♌ 18:03	23 ♍ 1:03	22 ♎ 22:33	23 ♏ 7:42	22 ♐ 5:03	21 ♑ 18:13
1973	20 ♒ 4:48	18 ♓ 19:01	20 ♈ 18:13	20 ♉ 5:31	21 ♊ 4:54	21 ♋ 13:01	22 ♌ 23:56	23 ♍ 6:54	23 ♎ 4:21	23 ♏ 13:30	22 ♐ 10:54	22 ♑ 0:08
1974	20 ♒ 10:46	19 ♓ 0:59	21 ♈ 0:07	20 ♉ 11:19	21 ♊ 10:36	21 ♋ 18:38	23 ♌ 5:30	23 ♍ 12:29	23 ♎ 9:59	23 ♏ 19:11	22 ♐ 16:39	22 ♑ 5:56
1975	20 ♒ 16:37	19 ♓ 6:50	21 ♈ 5:57	20 ♉ 17:08	21 ♊ 16:24	22 ♋ 0:27	23 ♌ 11:22	23 ♍ 18:24	23 ♎ 15:55	24 ♏ 1:06	22 ♐ 22:31	22 ♑ 11:46
1976	20 ♒ 22:25	19 ♓ 12:40	20 ♈ 11:50	19 ♉ 23:03	20 ♊ 22:21	21 ♋ 6:25	22 ♌ 17:19	23 ♍ 0:19	22 ♎ 21:48	23 ♏ 6:58	22 ♐ 4:22	21 ♑ 17:35
1977	20 ♒ 4:15	18 ♓ 18:31	20 ♈ 17:43	20 ♉ 4:58	21 ♊ 4:15	21 ♋ 12:14	22 ♌ 23:04	23 ♍ 6:01	23 ♎ 3:30	23 ♏ 12:41	22 ♐ 10:07	21 ♑ 23:23
1978	20 ♒ 10:04	19 ♓ 0:21	20 ♈ 23:34	20 ♉ 10:50	21 ♊ 10:09	21 ♋ 18:10	23 ♌ 5:01	23 ♍ 11:57	23 ♎ 9:26	23 ♏ 18:37	22 ♐ 16:05	22 ♑ 5:21
1979	20 ♒ 16:00	19 ♓ 6:14	21 ♈ 5:22	20 ♉ 16:36	21 ♊ 15:54	21 ♋ 23:57	23 ♌ 10:49	23 ♍ 17:47	23 ♎ 15:17	24 ♏ 0:28	22 ♐ 21:54	22 ♑ 11:10
1980	20 ♒ 21:49	19 ♓ 12:02	20 ♈ 11:10	19 ♉ 22:23	20 ♊ 21:42	21 ♋ 5:47	22 ♌ 16:42	22 ♍ 23:41	22 ♎ 21:09	23 ♏ 6:18	22 ♐ 3:42	21 ♑ 16:56
1981	20 ♒ 3:36	18 ♓ 17:52	20 ♈ 17:03	20 ♉ 4:19	21 ♊ 3:40	21 ♋ 11:45	22 ♌ 22:40	23 ♍ 5:39	23 ♎ 3:06	23 ♏ 12:13	22 ♐ 9:36	21 ♑ 22:51
1982	20 ♒ 9:31	18 ♓ 23:47	20 ♈ 22:56	20 ♉ 10:08	21 ♊ 9:23	21 ♋ 17:23	23 ♌ 4:16	23 ♍ 11:16	23 ♎ 8:47	23 ♏ 17:58	22 ♐ 15:24	22 ♑ 4:39
1983	20 ♒ 15:17	19 ♓ 5:31	21 ♈ 4:39	20 ♉ 15:51	21 ♊ 15:07	21 ♋ 23:09	23 ♌ 10:05	23 ♍ 17:08	23 ♎ 14:42	23 ♏ 23:55	22 ♐ 21:19	22 ♑ 10:30
1984	20 ♒ 21:05	19 ♓ 11:17	20 ♈ 10:25	19 ♉ 21:39	20 ♊ 20:58	21 ♋ 5:03	22 ♌ 15:59	22 ♍ 23:01	22 ♎ 20:33	23 ♏ 5:46	22 ♐ 3:11	21 ♑ 16:23
1985	20 ♒ 2:58	18 ♓ 17:08	20 ♈ 16:14	20 ♉ 3:26	21 ♊ 2:43	21 ♋ 10:45	22 ♌ 21:37	23 ♍ 4:36	23 ♎ 2:08	23 ♏ 11:22	22 ♐ 8:51	21 ♑ 22:08
1986	20 ♒ 8:47	18 ♓ 22:58	20 ♈ 22:03	20 ♉ 9:13	21 ♊ 8:28	21 ♋ 16:30	23 ♌ 3:25	23 ♍ 10:26	23 ♎ 7:59	23 ♏ 17:15	22 ♐ 14:45	22 ♑ 4:03
1987	20 ♒ 14:41	19 ♓ 4:50	21 ♈ 3:52	20 ♉ 14:58	21 ♊ 14:10	21 ♋ 22:11	23 ♌ 9:06	23 ♍ 16:10	23 ♎ 13:46	23 ♏ 23:01	22 ♐ 20:30	22 ♑ 9:46
1988	20 ♒ 20:25	19 ♓ 10:36	20 ♈ 9:39	19 ♉ 20:45	20 ♊ 19:57	21 ♋ 3:57	22 ♌ 14:52	22 ♍ 21:54	22 ♎ 19:29	23 ♏ 4:45	22 ♐ 2:12	21 ♑ 15:28
1989	20 ♒ 2:07	18 ♓ 16:21	20 ♈ 15:29	20 ♉ 2:39	21 ♊ 1:54	21 ♋ 9:53	22 ♌ 20:46	23 ♍ 3:47	23 ♎ 1:20	23 ♏ 10:36	22 ♐ 8:05	21 ♑ 21:22
1990	20 ♒ 8:02	18 ♓ 22:14	20 ♈ 21:20	20 ♉ 8:27	21 ♊ 7:38	21 ♋ 15:33	23 ♌ 2:22	23 ♍ 9:21	23 ♎ 6:56	23 ♏ 16:14	22 ♐ 13:47	22 ♑ 3:07
1991	20 ♒ 13:48	19 ♓ 3:59	21 ♈ 3:02	20 ♉ 14:09	21 ♊ 13:21	21 ♋ 21:19	23 ♌ 8:12	23 ♍ 15:13	23 ♎ 12:49	23 ♏ 22:06	22 ♐ 19:36	22 ♑ 8:54
1992	20 ♒ 19:33	19 ♓ 9:44	20 ♈ 8:49	19 ♉ 19:57	20 ♊ 19:13	21 ♋ 3:15	22 ♌ 14:09	22 ♍ 21:11	22 ♎ 18:43	23 ♏ 3:58	22 ♐ 1:26	21 ♑ 14:44
1993	20 ♒ 1:23	18 ♓ 15:36	20 ♈ 14:41	20 ♉ 1:50	21 ♊ 1:02	21 ♋ 9:00	22 ♌ 19:51	23 ♍ 2:51	23 ♎ 0:23	23 ♏ 9:38	22 ♐ 7:07	21 ♑ 20:26

Sun-sign changes.
This table shows the time and day in each month when the Sun changes signs. The year is given in the left hand column, and the months are written across the top. For each month the day is given on the left, the glyph for the sign that the Sun is entering in the centre, and the time on the right. The time is given in GMT. For example: in January 1960 the Sun entered Aquarius on the twenty-first day of the month at 1.10 hours (1.10 am).

THE LONGITUDE EQUIVALENT IN TIME

The longitude equivalent in time is based upon the Sun's movement through 1° of longitude in 4 minutes of time and 1° of longitude in 4 seconds of time.
The table below can be used simultaneously for converting degrees of longitude into hours and minutes of time, and minutes of longitude into minutes and seconds of time.

Example for Chigago 87 39 W. 87 = 5hr 48min
39 = 0hr 2min 36sec

5hr 50min 36sec

H M	°	H M	°	H M	°	H M	°	H M	°	H M	°
M S	'	M S	'	M S	'	M S	'	M S	'	M S	'
4	**1**	2 4	**31**	4 4	**61**	6 4	**91**	8 4	**121**	10 4	**151**
8	**2**	2 8	**32**	4 8	**62**	6 8	**92**	8 8	**122**	10 8	**152**
12	**3**	2 12	**33**	4 12	**63**	6 12	**93**	8 12	**123**	10 12	**153**
16	**4**	2 16	**34**	4 16	**64**	6 16	**94**	8 16	**124**	10 16	**154**
0 20	**5**	2 20	**35**	4 20	**65**	6 20	**95**	8 20	**125**	10 20	**155**
24	**6**	2 24	**36**	4 24	**66**	6 24	**96**	8 24	**126**	10 24	**156**
28	**7**	2 28	**37**	4 28	**67**	6 28	**97**	8 28	**127**	10 28	**157**
32	**8**	2 32	**38**	4 32	**68**	6 32	**98**	8 32	**128**	10 32	**158**
36	**9**	2 36	**39**	4 36	**69**	6 36	**99**	8 36	**129**	10 36	**159**
0 40	**10**	2 40	**40**	4 40	**70**	6 40	**100**	8 40	**130**	10 40	**160**
44	**11**	2 44	**41**	4 44	**71**	6 44	**101**	8 44	**131**	10 44	**161**
48	**12**	2 48	**42**	4 48	**72**	6 48	**102**	8 48	**132**	10 48	**162**
52	**13**	2 52	**43**	4 52	**73**	6 52	**103**	8 52	**133**	10 52	**163**
56	**14**	2 56	**44**	4 56	**74**	6 56	**104**	8 56	**134**	10 56	**164**
1 0	**15**	3 0	**45**	5 0	**75**	7 0	**105**	9 0	**135**	11 0	**165**
1 4	**16**	3 4	**46**	5 4	**76**	7 4	**106**	9 4	**136**	11 4	**166**
1 8	**17**	3 8	**47**	5 8	**77**	7 8	**107**	9 8	**137**	11 8	**167**
1 12	**18**	3 12	**48**	5 12	**78**	7 12	**108**	9 12	**138**	11 12	**168**
1 16	**19**	3 16	**49**	5 16	**79**	7 16	**109**	9 16	**139**	11 16	**169**
1 20	**20**	3 20	**50**	5 20	**80**	7 20	**110**	9 20	**140**	11 20	**170**
1 24	**21**	3 24	**51**	5 24	**81**	7 24	**111**	9 24	**141**	11 24	**171**
1 28	**22**	3 28	**52**	5 28	**82**	7 28	**112**	9 28	**142**	11 28	**172**
1 32	**23**	3 32	**53**	5 32	**83**	7 32	**113**	9 32	**143**	11 32	**173**
1 36	**24**	3 36	**54**	5 36	**84**	7 36	**114**	9 36	**144**	11 36	**174**
1 40	**25**	3 40	**55**	5 40	**85**	7 40	**115**	9 40	**145**	11 40	**175**
1 44	**26**	3 44	**56**	5 44	**86**	7 44	**116**	9 44	**146**	11 44	**176**
1 48	**27**	3 48	**57**	5 48	**87**	7 48	**117**	9 48	**147**	11 48	**177**
1 52	**28**	3 52	**58**	5 52	**88**	7 52	**118**	9 52	**148**	11 52	**178**
1 56	**29**	3 56	**59**	5 56	**89**	7 56	**119**	9 56	**149**	11 56	**179**
2 0	**30**	4 0	**60**	6 0	**90**	8 0	**120**	10 0	**150**	12 0	**180**

*Adapted from Brown's Nautical Almanac, by permission.

THE ACCELERATION ON THE INTERVAL

The acceleration on the interval is a minor adjustment necessary to convert the interval into sidereal time.
This table provides a handy guide for calculating the acceleration. Hours of interval are listed in the top column and minutes down the left hand side. The resulting acceleration will be found in the vertical columns in minutes and seconds.

Example: Acceleration on 5hr 36mins = 0min 55·2secs
Acceleration on 22hr 4mins = 3min 37·5secs

m.	0 h.	1 h.	2 h.	3 h.	4 h.	5 h.	6 h.	7 h.	8 h.	9 h.	10 h.	11 h.
	m. s.	m. s.	m. s.	m. s.	m. s.	m. s.	m. s.	m. s.	m. s.	m. s.	m. s.	m. s.
0	0 0·0	0 9·9	0 19·7	0 29·6	0 39·4	0 49·3	0 59·1	1 9·0	1 18·9	1 28·7	1 38·6	1 48·4
4	0 0·7	0 10·5	0 20·4	0 30·2	0 40·1	0 49·9	0 59·8	1 9·7	1 19·5	1 29·4	1 39·2	1 49·1
8	0 1·3	0 11·2	0 21·0	0 30·9	0 40·7	0 50·6	1 0·5	1 10·3	1 20·2	1 30·0	1 39·9	1 49·7
12	0 2·0	0 11·8	0 21·7	0 31·5	0 41·1	0 51·3	1 1·1	1 11·0	1 20·8	1 30·7	1 40·5	1 50·4
16	0 02·6	0 12·5	0 22·3	0 32·2	0 42·1	0 51·9	1 1·8	1 11·6	1 21·5	1 31·3	1 41·2	1 51·0
20	0 3·3	0 13·1	0 23·0	0 32·9	0 42·7	0 52·6	1 2·4	1 12·3	1 22·1	1 32·0	1 41·9	1 51·7
24	0 3·9	0 13·8	0 23·7	0 33·5	0 43·4	0 53·2	1 3·1	1 12·9	1 22·8	1 32·7	1 42·5	1 52·4
28	0 4·6	0 14·5	0 24·3	0 34·2	0 44·0	0 53·9	1 3·7	1 13·6	1 23·5	1 33·3	1 43·2	1 53·0
32	0 5·3	0 15·1	0 25·0	0 34·8	0 44·7	0 54·5	1 4·4	1 14·3	1 24·1	1 34·0	1 43·8	1 53·7
36	0 5·9	0 15·8	0 25·6	0 35·5	0 45·3	0 55·2	1 5·1	1 14·9	1 24·8	1 34·6	1 44·5	1 54·3
40	0 6·6	0 16·4	0 26·3	0 36·1	0 46·0	0 55·9	1 5·7	1 15·6	1 25·4	1 35·3	1 45·1	1 55·0
44	0 7·2	0 17·1	0 26·9	0 36·8	0 46·7	0 56·5	1 6·4	1 16·2	1 26·1	1 35·9	1 45·8	1 55·6
48	0 7·9	0 17·7	0 27·6	0 37·5	0 47·3	0 57·2	1 7·0	1 16·9	1 26·7	1 36·6	1 46·4	1 56·3
52	0 8·5	0 18·4	0 28·3	0 38·1	0 48·0	0 57·8	1 7·7	1 17·6	1 27·4	1 37·3	1 47·1	1 57·0
56	0 9·2	0 19·1	0 28·9	0 38·8	0 48·6	0 58·5	1 8·3	1 18·2	1 28·1	1 37·9	1 47·8	1 57·6

m.	12 h.	13 h.	14 h.	15 h.	16 h.	17 h.	18 h.	19 h.	20 h.	21 h.	22 h.	23 h.
	m. s.	m. s.	m. s.	m. s.	m. s.	m. s.	m. s.	m. s.	m. s.	m. s.	m. s.	m. s.
0	1 58·3	2 8·1	2 18·0	2 27·8	2 37·7	2 47·6	2 57·4	3 7·3	3 17·1	3 27·0	3 36·8	3 46·7
4	1 58·9	2 8·8	2 18·6	2 28·5	2 38·4	2 48·2	2 58·2	3 7·9	3 17·8	3 27·6	3 37·5	3 47·4
8	1 59·6	2 9·4	2 19·3	2 29·2	1 39·0	2 48·9	2 58·7	3 8·6	3 18·4	3 28·3	3 38·2	3 48·0
12	2 0·2	2 10·1	2 20·0	2 29·8	2 39·7	2 49·5	2 59·4	3 9·2	3 19·1	3 28·9	3 38·8	3 48·7
16	2 0·9	2 10·8	2 20·6	2 30·5	2 40·3	2 50·2	3 0·0	3 9·9	3 19·8	3 29·6	3 39·5	3 49·3
20	2 1·6	2 11·4	2 21·3	2 31·1	2 41·0	2 50·8	3 0·7	3 10·6	3 20·4	3 30·3	3 40·1	3 50·0
24	2 2·2	2 12·1	2 21·9	2 31·8	2 41·6	2 51·5	3 1·4	3 11·2	3 21·1	3 30·9	3 40·8	3 50·6
28	2 2·9	2 12·7	2 22·6	2 32·4	2 42·3	2 52·2	3 2·0	3 11·9	3 21·7	3 31·6	3 41·4	3 51·3
32	2 3·5	2 13·4	2 23·2	2 33·1	2 43·0	2 52·8	3 2·7	3 12·5	3 22·2	3 32·2	3 42·1	3 52·0
36	2 4·2	2 14·0	2 23·9	2 33·8	2 43·6	2 53·5	3 3·3	3 13·2	3 23·0	3 32·9	3 42·8	3 52·6
40	2 4·8	2 14·7	2 24·6	2 34·4	2 44·3	2 54·1	3 4·0	3 13·8	3 23·7	3 33·6	3 43·4	3 53·3
44	2 5·5	2 15·4	2 25·2	2 35·1	2 44·9	2 54·8	3 4·6	3 14·5	3 24·4	3 34·2	3 44·1	3 53·9
48	2 6·2	2 16·0	2 25·9	2 35·7	2 45·6	2 55·4	3 5·3	3 15·2	3 25·0	2 34·9	3 44·7	3 54·6
52	2 6·8	2 16·7	2 26·5	2 36·4	2 46·2	2 56·1	3 6·0	3 15·8	3 25·7	3 35·5	3 45·4	3 55·2
56	2 7·5	2 17·3	2 27·2	2 37·0	2 46·9	2 56·8	3 6·6	3 16·5	3 26·3	3 36·2	3 46·0	3 55·9

*Adapted from Brown's Nautical Almanac, by permission.

DAYLIGHT SAVING TIME (SUMMER TIME) IN THE UNITED KINGDOM

For those born in the United Kingdom between any of these dates subtract one hour from the birth time to get the Greenwich Mean Time (GMT) equivalent. The change to summer time takes place at 1.00am GMT, and the change back to GMT takes place at 2.00am summer time.

1916 21 May : 1 Oct	1941 1 Jan : 4 May	1960 10 Apr : 2 Oct
1917 8 Apr : 17 Sep	1941 10 Aug : 31 Dec	1961 26 Apr : 29 Oct
1918 24 Mar : 30 Sep	1942 1 Jan : 5 Apr	1962 25 Mar : 28 Oct
1919 30 Mar : 29 Sep	1942 9 Aug : 31 Dec	1963 31 Mar : 27 Oct
1920 28 Mar : 25 Oct	1943 1 Jan : 4 Arn	1964 22 Mar : 25 Oct
1921 3 Apr : 3 Oct	1943 15 Aug : 31 Dec	1965 21 Mar : 24 Oct
1922 26 Mar : 8 Apr	1944 1 Jan : 2 Apr	1966 20 Mar : 23 Oct
1923 22 Mar : 16 Sep	1944 17 Sep : 31 Dec	1967 19 Mar : 29 Oct
1924 13 Mar : 21 Sep	1945 1 Jan : 2 Apr	1968 18 Feb : 31 Dec
1925 19 Mar : 4 Oct	1945 15 Jul : 7 Oct	1969 1 Jan : 31 Dec
1926 18 Mar : 3 Oct	1946 14 Apr : 6 Oct	1970 1 Jan : 31 Dec
1927 10 Mar : 2 Oct	1947 16 Mar : 13 Apr	1971 1 Jan : 31 Dec
1928 22 Mar : 7 Oct	1947 10 Aug : 2 Nov	1972 19 Mar : 29 Oct
1929 21 Mar : 6 Oct	1948 14 Mar : 31 Oct	1973 18 Mar : 28 Oct
1930 13 Mar : 5 Oct	1949 3 Apr : 30 Oct	1974 17 Mar : 27 Oct
1931 19 Mar : 4 Oct	1950 16 Apr : 22 Oct	1975 16 Mar : 26 Oct
1932 17 Mar : 2 Oct	1951 15 Apr : 21 Oct	1976 21 Mar : 24 Oct
1933 9 Mar : 8 Oct	1952 20 Apr : 26 Oct	1977 20 Mar : 23 Oct
1934 22 Mar : 7 Oct	1953 19 Apr : 4 Oct	1978 19 Mar : 29 Oct
1935 14 Mar : 6 Oct	1954 11 Apr : 3 Oct	1979 18 Mar : 28 Oct
1936 19 Mar : 4 Oct	1955 17 Apr : 2 Oct	1980 16 Mar : 26 Oct
1937 18 Mar : 3 Oct	1956 22 Apr : 7 Oct	1981 29 Mar : 25 Oct
1938 10 Mar : 2 Oct	1957 14 Apr : 6 Oct	1982 28 Mar : 24 Oct
1939 16 Mar : 19 Nov	1958 20 Apr : 5 Oct	1983 27 Mar : 23 Oct
1940 25 Feb : 31 Dec	1959 19 Apr : 4 Oct	1984 25 Mar : 28 Oct
		1985 31 Mar 27 Oct

In future years summer time will be in force in the United Kingdom between 1.00 am on the last Sunday in March and 2.00 am on the last Sunday in October.

DOUBLE SUMMER TIME For those born between any of the dates listed below subtract two hours from the time of birth to find the GMT of birth.

1941 4 May : 10 Aug	1943 4 Apr : 15 Aug	1945 2 Apr : 15 Jul
1942 5 Apr : 9 Aug	1944 2 Apr : 17 Sep	1947 13 Apr : 10 Aug

DAYLIGHT SAVING TIME (SUMMER TIME) IN THE UNITED STATES

For those born in the United States it may be difficult to find out when daylight saving time was used in some areas. However, since 1966 daylight saving time has been in force throughout the United States. To draw a birth chart after this date subtract one hour from the birth time as a first step to calculating the GMT. The change from standard time to daylight saving time and back again always occurs at 2.00am.

1966 24 Apr : 30 Oct	1975 27 Apr : 26 Oct	1984 29 Apr : 28 Oct
1967 30 Apr : 29 Oct	1976 25 Apr : 31 Oct	1985 28 Apr : 27 Oct
1968 28 Apr : 27 Oct	1977 24 Apr : 30 Oct	1986 27 Apr : 26 Oct
1969 27 Apr : 26 Oct	1978 30 Apr : 29 Oct	1987 26 Apr : 25 Oct
1970 26 Apr : 25 Oct	1979 29 Apr : 28 Oct	1988 24 Apr : 30 Oct
1971 25 Apr : 24 Oct	1980 27 Apr : 26 Oct	1989 30 Apr : 29 Oct
1972 30 Apr : 29 Oct	1981 26 Apr : 25 Oct	1990 29 Apr : 28 Oct
1973 29 Apr : 27 Oct	1982 25 Apr : 31 Oct	
1974 28 Apr : 27 Oct	1983 24 Apr : 30 Oct	

After 1990, the time changes will occur on the last Sunday in April and on the last Sunday in October.

For those born in California before 1966 daylight saving time was observed between the following dates:

1918 31 Mar : 27 Oct	1951 29 Apr : 30 Sep	1959 26 Apr : 27 Sep
1919 30 Mar : 26 Oct	1952 27 Apr : 28 Sep	1960 24 Apr : 25 Sep
1942 9 Feb : 31 Dec	1953 26 Apr : 27 Sep	1961 30 Apr : 24 Sep
1943 1 Jan : 31 Dec	1954 25 Apr : 26 Sep	1962 29 Sep : 28 Oct
1944 1 Jan : 31 Dec	1955 24 Apr : 25 Sep	1963 28 Apr : 27 Oct
1945 1 Jan : 30 Sep	1956 29 Apr : 30 Sep	1964 26 Apr : 25 Oct
1948 14 Mar : 1 Jan	1957 27 Apr : 29 Sep	1965 25 Apr : 31 Oct
1950 30 Apr : 24 Sep	1958 27 Apr : 28 Sep	

FURTHER READING AND INFORMATION

The best guide to astronomy for astrologers is *The Astrologer's Astronomical Handbook* by Jeff Mayo, published by L. N. Fowler & Co. Ltd, 1970. The most detailed ephemeris is *Raphael's Ephemeris*, published annually by W. Foulsham & Co. Ltd, but for longer periods the best buy is the *American Ephemeris*, published by Astro Computing Services.

The Astrology of Personality by Dane Rudhyar, first published in 1936 by Lucis Publishing, provides a spiritual dimension to psychological astrology, and *Relating*, by Liz Greene, published by Coventure, 1977, is the modern classic on this subject. Also central to contemporary natal astrology are the books of Alan Leo and Charles Carter. Ronald Davison's *The Technique of Prediction* published by L. N. Fowler & Co. Ltd, 1955, is the most intelligent account of progressions, and Robert Hand's *Planets in Transit*, published by Para Research, 1980, is the most thorough work on the interpretation of transits.

For beginners the clearest introduction to horary astrology is given in *Horary Astrology* by Derek Appleby, published by the Aquarian Press, 1985. *Mundane Astrology* by Michael Baigent, Nicholas Campion and Charles Harvey, also published by Aquarian Press, 1984, is the classic book on all aspects of political astrology. *Electional Astrology* by Vivian Robson, published by Samuel Weiser, 1979, is the essential guide to planning the future by using astrology. *Planting by the Moon* by Nick Kollerstrom and Simon Best, published by Astro Computing Services, 1984, is an invaluable guide to astrological gardening, containing fascinating material on the connections between the planets and plant growth.

The scientific implications of astrology, and the physical correlations between cosmic and terrestial cycles are covered in the books of Michel Gauquelin. A good starting point is *The Cosmic Clocks*, published by Astro Computing Services, 1982.

There is no published work on Astro-Cartography, but maps and booklets can be obtained from Astro*Carto*Graphy, Box 959, El Cerrito, CA 94530, USA, or Freepost, 51 Christchurch Street East, Frome, Somerset BA11 1YE, U.K. Astrological computer programmes can be obtained through Astrocalc, 67 Peascroft Road, Hemel Hempstead, Herts HP3 8ER, U.K., or Matrix Software, 315 Marion Avenue, Big Rapids, MI 49307, USA.

Computer calculated horoscopes are available from Astro Computing Services, PO Box 16430, San Diego, CA 92116, USA.

Information about courses on astrology may be obtained from the Faculty of Astrological Studies, BCM 7470, London WC1N 3XX, who offer correspondence courses throughout the world. In the USA information about astrology classes may be obtained by writing to the National Council for Geocosmic Research (NCGR), 78 Hubbard Avenue, Stamford, CT 06905.

ACKNOWLEDGEMENT

The author would like to thank A. T. Mann for the use of his solar system illustration on p.10 and Michel Gauquelin for the information included in the illustration of lunar rhythms on p. 157.

GLOSSARY

ASCENDANT The degree of the zodiac rising over the eastern horizon.

ASPECT A precise distance between two planets in the zodiac. There are five main aspects — conjunction, sextile, square, trine and opposition.

ASTROLOGY The use of celestial phenomena, especially the movements of the planets, to attribute meaning to life on Earth, to analyse events and predict the future.

ASTRONOMY The physical study of celestial phenomena.

CHART A diagram of the heavens drawn for the time of a particular event, see horoscope.

CUSP The dividing point between any two signs or houses.

DEGREE The basic unit used to measure a circle. The zodiac is divided into 360 degrees.

DESCENDANT The exact opposite of the Ascendant, i.e. the degree of the zodiac descending over the western horizon.

DIRECT The forward movement of planets through the zodiac.

ECLIPTIC The apparent path of the Sun around the Earth.

ELECTION The use of astrology to plan the future.

ELEMENT Four different types of sign — Fire, Air, Earth and Water.

EPHEMERIS Table of planetary positions.

EQUINOX Marks the points when the Sun is overhead at the Equator, usually on 21 March and 21 September.

HORARY The use of astrology to answer precise questions.

HOROSCOPE A diagram of the heavens drawn for the time of a particular event. Also known as a chart. When drawn for the moment of birth it is usually known as a birth chart.

HOUSE One of 12 sections of the horoscope ruling different circumstances and activities.

IC The Imum Coeli, the nadir, or lowest point of the horoscope.

MIDHEAVEN The Medium Coeli, usually known as MC, this is the zenith, or highest point in the horoscope.

MIDPOINT The halfway point between two planets.

MINUTE One sixtieth of a degree.

MOON'S NODES The points at which the Moon's apparent path around the Earth crosses the Sun's apparent path.

MUNDANE The use of astrology in politics, history and general world affairs.

NATAL The use of astrology to analyse personality and make predictions for individuals.

PLANET One of the 10 bodies that appear to orbit the Earth. The planets are the Sun, the Moon, Mercury, Venus, Mars, Jupiter, Saturn, Uranus, Neptune and Pluto. In 1977 an eleventh, Chiron, was discovered.

POLARITY The division of the signs of the zodiac into two groups described either as male or female or positive and negative.

PROGRESSION The symbolic movement of the planets around the horoscope, used for prediction.

QUALITY Three different types of sign — Cardinal, Fixed and Mutable.

QUERENT A person who asks an astrologer a question.

QUESITED The subject of any question which an astrologer is asked.

RETROGRADE The apparent backwards movement of planets in the zodiac.

RISING SIGN The sign of the zodiac rising over the eastern horizon.

SIGN One of 12 divisions of the zodiac. The signs are Aries, Taurus, Gemini, Cancer, Leo, Virgo, Libra, Scorpio, Sagittarius, Capricorn, Aquarius, Pisces.

SOLSTICE Marks the points when the Sun reaches its furthest extent north and south, usually on 21 June and 21 December.

STAR Any physical body in the sky used in astrology. The 'fixed' stars are distinguished from the 'wandering' stars, or planets.

SYNASTRY The use of astrology to analyse human relationships through the comparison of horoscopes.

TRANSIT The movement of planets through the zodiac, used in prediction.

ZODIAC A band of sky extending on either side of the ecliptic.